Frommer's

Spain 2004

POSTCARDS FROM

P9-CNH-838

On a hiking tour, you might discover a forgotten village nestled into the valleys of the Pyrenees. See chapters 1 and 3. © Ric Ergenbright Photography.

Antoni Gaudí's unfinished Sagrada Familia cathedral is one of Barcelona's best examples of modernismo architecture. See chapter 11. © Jon Bradley/Tony Stone Images.

Street entertainers, flower vendors, cafe patrons, and strollers congregate on Barcelona's Les Rambles, the most famous promenade in Spain. See chapter 11. © Robert Frerck/Odyssey/Chicago.

MARQUES DEL MÉRITO

VINOS Y COÑAC

JEREZ DE LA FRONTERA

Drink in Madrid's vibrant nightlife surrounded by the elaborately tiled walls of historic Los Gabrieles. See chapter 4. © Robert Frerck/Odyssey/Chicago.

Follow the sounds of castanets to Seville's Club Los Gallos for an evening of flamenco dancing. See chapter 8. © Kelly/Mooney Photography.

At Seville's landmark square, the Plaza de España, you can rent rowboats for excursions. See chapter 8. © P. & G. Bowater/ The Image Bank.

If you visit only a few Spanish cities in your lifetime, make beautiful, romantic Toledo one of them. © P. & G. Bowater/The Image Bank.

The Mezquita (mosque) in
Córdoba is a fantastic
labyrinth of red-and-white
peppermint-striped pillars.
See chapter 8.
© Bill Wassman/The Stock Market.

The Alhambra, a lavish palace
in Granada, is one of the most
exotic settings in Europe.
See chapter 8.
© Nik Wheeler Photography.

The arid plains of New Castile are visible from Toledo's lofty hilltop position. See chapter 5. © Nik Wheeler Photography.

The controversial Guggenheim Museum, Bilbao's newest attraction. See chapter 16. © F. Ontanon Núñez/The Image Bank.

A visit to Segovia's Alcázar, where Isabella first met Ferdinand, makes a great side trip from Madrid. See chapter 5. © Superstock, Inc.

Frommer's®

Spain
2004
with Majorca & Ibiza

by Darwin Porter & Danforth Prince

Here's what the critics say about Frommer's:

"Amazingly easy to use. Very portable, very complete."
—*Booklist*

"Detailed, accurate, and easy-to-read information for all price ranges."
—*Glamour Magazine*

"Hotel information is close to encyclopedic."
—*Des Moines Sunday Register*

"Frommer's Guides have a way of giving you a real feel for a place."
—*Knight Ridder Newspapers*

WILEY

Wiley Publishing, Inc.

About the Authors

Veteran travel writers **Darwin Porter** and **Danforth Prince** have written numerous bestselling Frommer's guides, notably to France, Italy, England, Germany, and Spain. Porter, who was bureau chief for the *Miami Herald* when he was 21, wrote the first-ever Frommer's guide to Spain while still a student. Prince, who began writing with Porter in 1982, worked for the Paris bureau of the *New York Times*.

Published by:

Wiley Publishing, Inc.

111 River St.
Hoboken, NJ 07030

ISBN 0-7645-3817-9
ISSN 1093-1910

Editor: John Vorwald
Production Editor: Suzanna R. Thompson
Cartographer: Elizabeth Puhl
Photo Editor: Richard Fox
Production by Wiley Indianapolis Composition Services
Chapter 2 illustrations by Rashell Smith, Brent Savage, and Karl Brandt.

Front cover photo: The Mezquita-Catedral, Córdoba
Back cover photo: A sheepherder with his flock in the Spanish countryside

For information on our other products and services or to obtain technical support, please contact our Customer Care Department within the U.S. at 800-762-2974, outside the U.S. at 317-572-3993 or fax 317-572-4002.

Wiley also publishes its books in a variety of electronic formats. Some content that appears in print may not be available in electronic formats.

Manufactured in the United States of America

5 4 3 2 1

Contents

List of Maps

An Invitation to the Reader

In researching this book, we discovered many wonderful places—hotels, restaurants, shops, and more. We're sure you'll find others. Please tell us about them, so we can share the information with your fellow travelers in upcoming editions. If you were disappointed with a recommendation, we'd love to know that, too. Please write to:

Frommer's Spain 2004
Wiley Publishing, Inc. • 111 River St. • Hoboken, NJ 07030

An Additional Note

Please be advised that travel information is subject to change at any time—and this is especially true of prices. We therefore suggest that you write or call ahead for confirmation when making your travel plans. The authors, editors, and publisher cannot be held responsible for the experiences of readers while traveling. Your safety is important to us, however, so we encourage you to stay alert and be aware of your surroundings. Keep a close eye on cameras, purses, and wallets, all favorite targets of thieves and pickpockets.

Other Great Guides for Your Trip:

Spain For Dummies
Frommer's Barcelona, Madrid & Seville
Frommer's Spain's Best-Loved Driving Tours
Frommer's Europe
Frommer's Road Atlas Europe

Frommer's Star Ratings, Icons & Abbreviations

Every hotel, restaurant, and attraction listing in this guide has been ranked for quality, value, service, amenities, and special features using a **star-rating system.** In country, state, and regional guides, we also rate towns and regions to help you narrow down your choices and budget your time accordingly. Hotels and restaurants are rated on a scale of zero (recommended) to three stars (exceptional). Attractions, shopping, nightlife, towns, and regions are rated according to the following scale: zero stars (recommended), one star (highly recommended), two stars (very highly recommended), and three stars (must-see).

In addition to the star-rating system, we also use **seven feature icons** that point you to the great deals, in-the-know advice, and unique experiences that separate travelers from tourists. Throughout the book, look for:

Finds	Special finds—those places only insiders know about
Fun Fact	Fun facts—details that make travelers more informed and their trips more fun
Kids	Best bets for kids, and advice for the whole family
Moments	Special moments—those experiences that memories are made of
Overrated	Places or experiences not worth your time or money
Tips	Insider tips—great ways to save time and money
Value	Great values—where to get the best deals

The following **abbreviations** are used for credit cards:

AE	American Express	DISC	Discover	V	Visa
DC	Diners Club	MC	MasterCard		

Frommers.com

Now that you have the guidebook to a great trip, visit our website at **www.frommers.com** for travel information on more than 3,000 destinations. With features updated regularly, we give you instant access to the most current trip-planning information available. At Frommers.com, you'll also find the best prices on airfares, accommodations, and car rentals—and you can even book travel online through our travel booking partners. At Frommers.com, you'll also find the following:

- Online updates to our most popular guidebooks
- Vacation sweepstakes and contest giveaways
- Newsletter highlighting the hottest travel trends
- Online travel message boards with featured travel discussions

What's New in Spain

As Spain—along with France and the United States—moves into the forefront of world tourism, here is a roundup of some late-breaking developments.

MADRID ACCOMMODATIONS

Right across from the Prado, **Hotel Mora,** Paseo del Prado (℗ **91-420-15-69**) is being discovered by art lovers all over the world. A modestly priced choice, it offers bright, tastefully furnished accommodations in one of the best locations in town. See chapter 4 more details.

MADRID DINING

Grand dining is to be had at **Santceloni,** in the hotel Hespera, Paseo de la Castellana 57 (℗ **91-210-88-40**), currently the rage among serious Madrid foodies. Santi Santamaria, ranked as among the top three chefs in Spain, made his fame in a restaurant outside Barcelona but today also dazzles Madrileños with his succulent Mediterranean cuisine. See chapter 4 for more details.

SEGOVIA DINING

El Molino de la Lasa, Bajada de la Losa 12 (℗ **92-021-11-01**), is a mill dating from the 15th century that stands near the Adaja River. Today it's been turned into one of the finest restaurants in this highly competitive city. The roast lamb is among the best in Castile. See chapter 5 for more details.

SALAMANCA ACCOMMODATIONS

In this ancient university city, **AC Palacio de San Esteban,** Arroyo de Santonio de Salamanca (℗ **92-326-22-96**), is a former 17th-century convent that has been successfully converted into a government-rated four-star hotel in the heart of monumental Salamanca. It's been totally restored in a traditional style and furnished with luxuries. See chapter 6 for more details.

TRUJILLO ACCOMMODATIONS

In the walled town of Trujillo, deep in Extremedura, **Meliá Trujillo,** Plaza del Campillo 1 (℗ **92-745-89-00**), has opened to acclaim. The Meliá hotel chain took a former monastery from the 17th century and restored it and its adjoining cloisters, turning it into a hotel of charm and grace in this hot, arid climate. Its swimming pool is the greatest place to be in the area on an August afternoon. See chapter 7 for more details.

SEVILLE DINING

In the heart of Seville in the romantic Barrio de Santa Cruz, **La Albahaca,** Plaza Santa Cruz 12 (℗ **95-422-07-14**), has opened to acclaim with its savory blend of Andalusian and Basque cuisine. The house itself was constructed by Juan Talavera, a celebrated architect of his day, and many visiting celebs come to call here and to partake of a first-rate cuisine. See chapter 8 for more details.

COSTA DEL SOL ACCOMMODATIONS

In the western resort of Estepona, **Kempinski Resort Hotel,** Carretera de Cádiz, Km 159 (© **95-280-95-00**), since its opening, has been hailed as one of the most spectacular resorts along this sunny coast. This member of "The Leading Hotels of the World" is set in palm-studded gardens fronting the ocean, and is a monument to *La Dolce Vita* with its grand comfort. See chapter 9 for more details.

VALENCIA ACCOMMODATIONS

Monte Picayo, Urbanización Monte Picayo (© **96-142-01-00**), is a luxurious government-rated five-star retreat that has opened 18km (11 miles) north of Valencia. For those who want to enjoy this city of the Levante, but from a landscaped hillside location, this is an idyllic summer resort, each accommodation with a private terrace opening onto a view. Good sandy beaches are within driving distance. See chapter 10 for more details.

BARCELONA ACCOMMODATIONS

Freshly remodeled and more inviting than ever, **Gallery Hotel,** Calle Rosello 249 (© **93-415-99-11**), lies in the upper district of the Eixample, a moderately priced choice gaining more and more fans every month. See chapter 11 for more details.

BARCELONA DINING

Food critics in Barcelona are hailing the Catalán cuisine of Carles Abellan, who holds forth at **Comerç 24,** Comerç 24, La Ribera (© **93-319-21-02**). A culinary artist of the first rank, he uses some of the freshest and best of seasonal ingredients to concoct combinations often called "outrageous," but which are a delight to the taste buds. See chapter 11 for more details.

SANTIAGO DE COMPOSTELA ACCOMMODATIONS

In this ancient cathedral city in Galicia, more and more visitors are discovering **Casa Hotel as Artes,** Traversía de Dos Puertas 2 (© **98-157-25-90**). It's an especially rewarding choice for those who can't afford the town's landmark hotel, Hostel de los Reyes Católicos. Rooms honor various artists—from Rodin to Dante, from Gaudí to Picasso. See chapter 18 for more details.

MAJORCA ACCOMMODATIONS

One of the most charming boutique hotels to open in this Balearic island in many a day, **Palau Sa Font,** Carrer Apuntadores (© **97-171-22-77**), has been installed in a former 16th-century palace. It's been successfully converted to this somewhat funky hotel with its jelly bean colors. Filled with atmosphere, it's also become one of the hippest hotel addresses in town. See chapter 19 for more details.

The Best of Spain

Spain is one of the most diverse and visually stunning nations of Europe. As you begin to plan your trip, you may find yourself overwhelmed with so many fascinating sights, beautiful landscapes, and charming towns to fit into your limited time. So let us give you a hand. We've scoured the country in search of the best places and experiences, and we've chosen our very favorites below, admittedly very personal and opinionated choices.

1 The Best Travel Experiences

- **Sitting in *Sol* or *Sombra* at the Bullfights:** With origins as old as pagan Spain, the art of bullfighting is the expression of Iberian temperament and passions. Detractors object to the sport as cruel, bloody, and savage. Fans, however, view bullfighting as a microcosm of death, catharsis, and rebirth. If you strive to understand the bullfight, it can be one of the most evocative and memorable events in Spain. Head for the *plaza de toros* (bullring) in any major city, but particularly in Madrid, Seville, or Granada. Tickets are either *sol* (sunny side) or *sombra* (in the shade); you'll pay more to get out of the sun.

- **Feasting on Tapas in the *Tascas*:** Tapas, those bite-size portions washed down with wine, beer, or sherry, are reason enough to go to Spain! Tapas bars, called *tascas*, are a quintessential Spanish experience. Originally tapas were cured ham or *chorizo* (spicy sausage). Today they are likely to be anything—*gambas* (deep-fried shrimp), anchovies marinated in vinegar, stuffed peppers, a cool, spicy gazpacho, or hake salad.

- **Getting Caught Up in the Passions of Flamenco:** It's best heard in some old tavern, in a neighborhood like the Barrio de Triana in Seville. From the lowliest *taberna* to the poshest nightclub, you can hear the staccato foot stomping, castanet rattling, hand clapping, and sultry guitar sound. Some say its origins lie deep in Asia, but the Spanish gypsy has given the art form, which dramatizes inner conflict and pain, an original style. Performed by a great artist, flamenco can tear your heart out with its soulful, throaty singing.

- **Seeing the Masterpieces at the Prado:** One of the world's premier art museums, it's home to some 4,000 masterpieces, many of them acquired by Spanish kings. The wealth of Spanish art is staggering—everything from Goya's *Naked Maja* to the celebrated *Las Meninas (The Maids of Honor)* by Velázquez (our favorite). Masterpiece after masterpiece unfolds before your eyes, including works by Hieronymus Bosch, Goya, Caravaggio, Fra Angelico, and Botticelli. See p. 134.

Spain

- **Sipping Sherry in Jerez de la Frontera:** In Spain, sherry is called *jerez,* and it's a major industry and subculture in its own right. Hispanophiles compare its complexities to the finest wines produced in France and make pilgrimages to the bodegas in Andalusia that ferment this amber-colored liquid. More than 100 bodegas are available for visits, tours, and tastings, and most open their gates to visitors interested in a process that dates from the country's Roman occupation. See chapter 8.

- **Wandering the Crooked Streets of Barcelona's Gothic Quarter:** Long before Madrid was founded, the kingdom of Catalonia was a bastion of art and architecture. Whether the Barri Gòtic, as it's called in Catalán, is truly Gothic is the subject of endless debate, but the Ciutat Vella, or old city, of Barcelona is one of the most evocative neighborhoods in Spain. Its richly textured streets, with their gurgling fountains, vintage stores, and ancient fortifications, inspired such artists as Pablo Picasso and Joan Miró (who was born in this neighborhood). See chapter 11.

- **Going Gaga Over Gaudí:** No architect in Europe was as fantastical as Antoni Gaudí y Cornet, the foremost proponent of Catalán modernisme (aka modernismo). Barcelona is studded with the works of this extraordinary artist, all of which UNESCO now lists as World Trust Properties. A recluse and a celibate bachelor, as well as a fervent Catalán nationalist, he lived out his own fantasy in his work. Nothing is more stunning than his Sagrada

Família, Barcelona's best-known landmark, a cathedral on which Gaudí labored for the last 43 years of his life. The landmark cathedral was never completed, but they're still working on it. If it's ever finished, "The Sacred Family" will be Europe's largest cathedral. See chapter 11.

- **Running with the Bulls in Pamplona:** Okay, maybe it's smarter to watch, rather than run with, the bulls. The Fiesta de San Fermín in July is the most dangerous ritual in Spain, made even worse by copious amounts of wine consumed by participants and observers. Broadcast live on TV throughout Spain and the rest of Europe, the festival features herds of furious bulls that charge down medieval streets, sometimes trampling and goring some of the hundreds of people who run beside them. Few other rituals in Spain are as breathtaking and foolhardy. And few others as memorable. See chapter 15.

- **Following the Ancient Pilgrim Route to Santiago de Compostela:** Tourism as we know it began during the Middle Ages, as thousands of European pilgrims journeyed to the shrine of Santiago (St. James) in Galicia in northwestern Spain. Even if you're not motivated by faith, you should come to see some of the most dramatic landscapes and the grandest scenery in Spain by crossing the northern tier of the country—all the way from the Pyrenees to Santiago de Compostela. Some of the country's most stunning architecture can be viewed along the way, including gems in Roncevalles, Burgos, and León. See chapter 18.

Impressions
Three Spaniards, four opinions.

—Old Spanish proverb

2 The Best Small Towns

- **Cuenca:** Set amid a landscape of rugged limestone outcroppings at the junction of two rivers, Cuenca is a fascinating combination of medieval masonry and cantilevered balconies that seem to float above the steep gorges below. The angularity of the architecture here is said to have inspired early versions of cubism, a fact commemorated in Cuenca's Museo de Arte Abstracto Español. This museum is considered to be one of the finest modern art museums in Spain. See chapter 5.

- **Zafra:** Zafra's 15th-century castle is the largest and best preserved in the region. It is set within the angular, stark white architecture of Zafra, which is also said to have inspired the cubists. See chapter 7.

- **Baeza:** After it was wrenched away from the Moors in 1227, Baeza became a frontier town between the Christian and Moorish worlds, and a diehard symbol of the Catholic ambition to occupy all of Iberia. Today, a wealth of architecture survives as evidence of the splendor of Iberian history. See chapter 8.

- **Carmona:** Pint-size, sleepy Carmona packs a historical wallop, evoking the Roman occupation of Iberia. The town claims an architectural legacy from every occupying force dating from 206 B.C., when the Romans defeated the resident Carthaginian army. See chapter 8.

- **Ronda:** The site appears inhospitable—a gorge slices through the town center and its twin halves are interconnected with bridges that are antiques in their own right. But the winding streets of this old Moorish town are perfect for wandering, and the views of the surrounding Andalusian countryside are stupendous. Ronda is also revered by bullfighting fans, both for its bullring (the oldest and most beautiful in Spain) and the region's skill in breeding the fiercest bulls in the country. See chapter 8.

- **Mijas:** Wander through streets and alleys once trod by the Phoenicians, the Celts, and the Moors. Today, the town offers a welcome dose of medieval flair on the Costa del Sol, a region otherwise filled with modern, anonymous, and often ugly resort hotels. See chapter 9.

- **Nerja:** On the Costa del Sol at the Balcón de Europa (Balcony of Europe) lies this Mediterranean gem, with a palm-shaded promenade jutting out into the sea. Lined with antique iron lampposts, the village overlooks a pretty beach and fishing fleet. The resort town is on a sloping site at the foot of a wall of jagged coastal mountains. You can snuggle up in the parador or lodge in one of the little inns on the narrow streets. See chapter 9.

- **Elche:** Although famed as a charming medieval village, Elche is best known as the excavation site of one of the premier sculptures of the Roman Empire in

Iberia, La Dama de Elche, now exhibited in Madrid's archaeological museum. These days, you can still see date palms planted originally by the Phoenicians and a mystery play celebrating the Assumption of the Virgin, which has been performed in the village church every year since the 1300s. See chapter 10.

- **Sitges:** South of Barcelona is Spain's most romantic Mediterranean beach town, with a 2.5km (1½-mile) long sandy beach and a promenade studded with flowers and palm trees. Sitges is a town with a rich connection to art; Picasso and Dalí both spent time here. Wander its little lanes and inspect the old villas of its Casco Antiguo, the old quarter. When not at the beach, you can view three good art museums. Nowadays, thousands of gay men and lesbians flock to Sitges, but there's a wide spectrum of visitors of all persuasions. See chapter 12.

- **Cadaqués:** The 16th-century church that dominates this town from a nearby hilltop isn't particularly noteworthy, but Cadaqués—on the Costa Brava near the French border—still charms with whitewashed, fishing-village simplicity. The azure waters of the Mediterranean appealed to surrealist master Salvador Dalí, who built a suitably bizarre villa in the adjoining hamlet of Lligat. See chapter 13.

- **Santillana del Mar:** Jean-Paul Sartre called it "the prettiest village in Spain." Only 6 blocks long and just 5km (3 miles) from the sea, Santillana del Mar perfectly captures the spirit of Cantabria. It's also near the Cuevas de Altamira, often called "the Sistine Chapel of prehistoric art." Romanesque houses and mansions line the ironstone streets. People still sell fresh milk from their stable doors, as if the Middle Ages had never ended, but you can live in comfort at one of Spain's grandest paradors, Parador de Santillana, a converted 17th-century mansion. See chapter 17.

- **Deià:** On the island of Majorca, you'll find this lovely old village (also spelled Deyá), where the poet Robert Graves lived until his death in 1985. Following in his footsteps, artists and writers flock to this haven of natural beauty, 27km (17 miles) northwest of Palma. The views of the sea and mountains are panoramic. Gnarled and ancient olive trees dot the landscape. You can book into cozy nests of luxury like La Residencia or Es Molí. See chapter 19.

3 The Best Beaches

Spain may be flanked to the east by France and the Pyrenees and to the west by Portugal, but most of the country is ringed with sand, rock, and seawater. That, coupled with almost year-round sunshine, has attracted many millions of beachgoers.

- **Costa de la Luz:** This stretch of coastline in southwestern Andalusia boasts long stretches of sand and almost-constant sunshine. The blue, sometimes rough, Atlantic waters are enticement enough for a visit, as is the region's proximity to several historic cities, including Cádiz and Seville. This area is less developed than the more popular Costa del Sol. See chapter 8.

- **Costa del Sol:** Stretching east from Gibraltar along the southernmost coast of Spain, the Costa del Sol is the most famous, party-hearty, and overdeveloped string of beaches in Iberia. The beaches feature superb sand, and the Mediterranean waters are calm and warm throughout most of the year. But these charms have brought throngs of visitors, making this the most congested string of coastal resorts in Europe. The most important resorts here are Marbella, Torremolinos, Málaga, and Nerja. Look for soaring skyscrapers; eye-popping bikinis; sophisticated resorts and restaurants; lots of sunshine; and interminable traffic jams. See chapter 9.

- **Costa Blanca:** This southeastern coast embraces the industrial city of Valencia, but its best-known resorts, Benidorm and Alicante, are packed with northern-European sun-seekers every year. The surrounding scenery isn't particularly dramatic, but the water is turquoise, the sand is white, and a low annual rainfall virtually guarantees a sunny vacation. See chapter 10.

- **Costa Brava:** Rockier, more serpentine, and without the long stretches of sand that mark the Costa Blanca, the cliff-edged Costa Brava stretches from Barcelona to the French border. Look for the charming, sandy-bottomed coves that dot the coast. Although there are fewer undiscovered beaches here than along Spain's Atlantic coast, the Costa Brava still retains a sense of rocky wilderness. One of the more eccentric-looking villas along this coast belonged to the late Salvador Dalí, the region's most famous modern son who lived much of his life near Cadaqués. See chapter 13.

- **Costa Verde:** Radically different from the dry and sunbaked coastline of Andalusia, the rocky Costa Verde (Green Coast) resembles a sunny version of Ireland's western shore. It's temperate in summer, when the rest of Spain can be unbearably hot. Much of the coast is within the ancient province of Asturias, a region rife with Romanesque architecture and medieval pilgrimage sites—and one that has not yet been overwhelmed with tourism. Premier resorts include some districts of Santander, Gijón, and, a short distance inland, Oviedo. See chapter 17.

- **The Balearic Islands:** Just off the coast of Catalonia and a 45-minute flight from Barcelona, this rocky, sand-fringed archipelago attracts urban refugees seeking the sun, jet-set glitterati, and exhibitionists in scanty beachwear. The Mediterranean climate is warmer here than on the mainland. The city of Palma de Majorca has the greatest number of high-rises and the most crowded shorelines. Much of Ibiza is party central for young people and gay visitors during the summer. Sleepy Minorca offers more isolation. See chapter 19.

4 The Best Castles & Palaces

- **Palacio Real** (Madrid): No longer occupied by royalty, but still used for state occasions, the Royal Palace sits on the bank of the Manzanares River. It was built in the mid–18th century over the site of a former palace. It's not Versailles, but it's still mighty impressive, with around 2,000 rooms. No one has lived here since 1931, but the chandeliers, marble columns, gilded borders, paintings, and objets d'art, including Flemish tapestries and Tiepolo ceiling frescoes, are still well pre-served. The empty thrones of King Juan Carlos and Queen Sofía are among the highlights of the tour. See chapter 4.

- **El Alcázar** (Segovia): Once the most impregnable castle in Spain, it rises dramatically from a rock spur near the ancient heart of town. Isabella married Ferdinand at this foreboding site, creating a union that eventually led to the unification of Spain. Today, it's the single most photographed and dramatic castle in Iberia. See chapter 5.

- **Palacio Real** (Aranjuez): Built at enormous expense by the Bour-bon cousins of the rulers of France, it was designed to emulate the glories of Versailles in its 18th-century neoclassicism. The gar-dens are even more fascinating than the palace. The gem of the complex is the Casita del Labrador, an annex as rich and ornate as its model—Marie Antoinette's Petit Trianon at Ver-sailles. See chapter 5.

- **Alhambra** (Granada): One of Spain's grandest sights, the Alhambra was originally con-ceived by the Muslims as a forti-fied pleasure pavilion. Its allure was instantly recognized by Catholic monarchs after the Reconquest. Despite the presence of a decidedly European palace in its center, the setting remains one of the most exotic (and Moorish) in all of Europe. See chapter 8.

- **Alcázar** (Seville): The oldest royal residence in Europe still in use was built by Peter the Cruel (1350–69) in 1364, 78 years after the Moors left Seville. Ferdinand and Isabella once lived here. One of the purest examples of the Mudé-jar, or Moorish, style, its decora-tion is based on that of the Alhambra in Granada. A multi-tude of Christian and Islamic motifs are combined architec-turally in this labyrinth of gar-dens, halls, and courts, none more notable than the Patio de las Doncellas (Court of the Maidens). See chapter 8.

5 The Best Museums

The spectacular Prado in Madrid is no mere museum, but a travel experience. It's worth a journey to Spain just to visit it (see "The Best Travel Experi-ences," earlier in this chapter).

- **Museo Lázaro Galdiano** (Madrid): This rare collection demonstrates the evolution of enamel and ivory crafts from the Byzantine era to 19th-century Limoges. Of almost equal impor-tance are displays of superb medieval gold and silver work along with Italian Renaissance jewelry. The museum also con-tains galleries with rare paintings, everything from Flemish primi-tives to works by Spanish masters of the golden age, including El Greco, Murillo, and Zurbarán. There are also paintings from Goya's "Black Period" and from the English and Italian masters Constable and Tiepolo. See p. 138.

- **Thyssen-Bornemisza Museum** (Madrid): Madrid's acquisition of this treasure trove of art in the 1980s was one of the greatest coups in European art history. Amassed by a central European collector beginning around 1920, and formerly displayed in Lugano, Switzerland, its 700 canvasses, with works by artists ranging from El Greco to Picasso, are arranged in chronological order. The collec-tion rivals the legendary holdings of the queen of England herself. See p. 139.

- **Museo de Arte Abstracto Español** (Cuenca): The angular medieval architecture of the town that contains it is an appropriate foil for a startling collection of modern masters. A group of some of Spain's most celebrated artists settled in Cuenca in the 1950s and 1960s, and their works are displayed here. They included Fernando Zobel, Antoni Tàpies, Eduardo Chillida, Luis Feito, and Antonio Saura. See p. 197.

- **Museo de Santa Cruz** (Toledo): Built by the archbishop of Toledo as a hospital for the poor, this is the most important museum in New Castile. It's known for its Plateresque architecture, notably its intricate facade, and for the wealth of art inside. Among its noteworthy collection of 16th- and 17th-century paintings are 18 works by El Greco, including his Altarpiece of the Assumption, completed in 1613 during his final period. The gallery also contains a collection of primitive paintings. See p. 168.

- **Museo Nacional de Escultura** (Valladolid): The greatest collection of gilded polychrome sculpture—an art form that reached its pinnacle in Valladolid—is on display here in the 15th-century San Gregorio College. Figures are first carved in wood, then painted with great artistry to achieve a lifelike appearance. The most remarkable exhibit is an altarpiece designed by Alonso Berruguete for the Church of San Benito. Be sure to see his Martyrdom of St. Sebastian. See p. 217.

- **Museo Nacional de Arte Romano** (Mérida): A museum that makes most archaeologists salivate, this modern building contains hundreds of pieces of ancient Roman sculpture discovered in and around Mérida. The Roman treasures included theaters, amphitheaters, racecourses, and hundreds of tombs full of art objects, many of which are on display here. In 1986, the well-known and award-winning architect Rafael Moneo designed this ambitious and innovative brick building. Designing the building on a grand scale, he freely borrowed from Roman motifs and daringly incorporated an ancient Roman road that was discovered when the foundations were dug. See p. 238.

- **Museo Provincial de Bellas Artes de Sevilla** (Seville): The Prado doesn't own all the great Spanish art in the country. Located in the early-17th-century convent of La Merced, this museum is famous for its works by such Spanish masters as Valdés Leal, Zurbarán, and Murillo. Spain's golden age is best exemplified by Murillo's monumental Immaculate Conception and Zurbarán's Apotheosis of St. Thomas Aquinas. See p. 265.

- **Museu Picasso** (Barcelona): Picasso, who spent many of his formative years in Barcelona, donated some 2,500 of his paintings, drawings, and engravings to launch this museum in 1970. It's second only to the Picasso Museum in Paris. Seek out his notebooks, which contain many sketches of Barcelona scenes. The pieces are arranged in rough chronological order, so you'll discover that he completely mastered traditional representational painting before tiring of it and beginning to experiment. Watch for numerous portraits of his family, as well as examples from both his Blue Period and his Rose Period. His obsessive Las Meninas series—painted in 1959—offers exaggerated variations of the theme of the famous picture by Velázquez hanging in Madrid's Prado Museum. See p. 417.

- **Teatre Museu Dalí** (Figueres): The eccentric Salvador Dalí is showcased here as nowhere else. The surrealist artist—known for everything from lobster telephones to *Rotting Mannequin in a Taxicab*—conceived of his art partly as theater. But be warned: As Dalí's final joke, he wanted the museum to spew forth "false information." See p. 471.

6 The Best Cathedrals & Churches

- **Catedral de Avila:** One of the earliest Gothic cathedrals in Castile, this rugged and plain edifice was called "a soldier's church." A brooding, granite monolith, which in some ways resembles a fortress, it is the centerpiece of a city that produced St. Teresa, the most famous mystic of the Middle Ages. The interior of the cathedral, with its High Gothic nave, is filled with notable works of art, including many Plateresque statues. See p. 191.

- **Catedral de Toledo:** Ranked among the greatest of all Gothic structures, this cathedral was built on the site of an old Arab mosque. A vast pile from the 13th to the 15th centuries, it has an interior filled with masterpieces—notably an immense polychrome retable carved in flamboyant style and magnificent 15th- and 16th-century choir stalls. In the treasury is a splendid 16th-century silver and gilt monstrance, weighing about 500 pounds. See p. 167.

- **Real Monasterio de San Lorenzo de El Escorial** (near Madrid): Philip II, who commissioned this monastery in the 1530s, envisioned it as a monastic fortress against the distractions of the secular world. More awesome than beautiful, it's the world's best example of the religious devotion of Renaissance Spain. This huge granite fortress, the burial place for Spanish kings, houses a wealth of paintings and tapestries—works by everyone from Titian to Velázquez. See p. 180.

- **Catedral de León:** Filled with more sunlight than any other cathedral in Spain, it was begun in 1250 with a design pierced by 125 stained-glass windows and 57 oculi, the oldest of which date from the 13th century. This architectural achievement is stunning but also dangerous. Architects fear that an urgent restoration is needed to strengthen the walls to prevent collapse. The well-preserved cloisters are also worth a visit. See p. 213.

- **Catedral de Santa María** (Burgos): After its cornerstone was laid in 1221, this cathedral became the beneficiary of creative talent imported from England, Germany, and France. It is the third-largest cathedral in Spain, after Seville and Toledo. Art historians claim that among medieval religious buildings, it has the most diverse spectrum of sculpture in Gothic Spain—so diverse that a special name has been conjured up to describe it: the School of Burgos. El Cid is buried here. See p. 221.

- **Catedral de Sevilla:** The Christians are not the only occupants of Seville who considered this site holy; an enormous mosque stood here before the Reconquista. To quote the Christians who built the cathedral, they planned one "so immense that everyone, on beholding it, will take us for madmen." They succeeded. After St. Peter's in Rome and St. Paul's in London, the cathedral of this Andalusian capital is the largest in Europe. Among its most important features are the tomb of Columbus, the Patio de los Naranjos (Courtyard of the Orange Trees), the Giralda Tower, and the Capilla Real (Royal Chapel). See p. 264.

- **Mezquita-Catedral de Córdoba:** In the 1500s, the Christian rulers of Spain tried to convert one of the largest and most elaborate mosques in the Muslim world, the Mezquita, into a Catholic cathedral. The result, a bizarre amalgam of Gothic and Muslim architecture, is an awesomely proportioned cultural compromise that defies categorization. In its 8th-century heyday, the Mezquita was the crowning Muslim architectural achievement in the West. See p. 252.

- **Catedral de Barcelona:** Completed in 1450, this cathedral grew to represent the spiritual power of the Catalán empire. With its 81m (270-ft.) facade and flying buttresses and gargoyles, it is the Gothic Quarter's most stunning monument. The interior is in the Catalán Gothic style with slender pillars. See p. 416.

- **Montserrat** (near Barcelona): Since its inauguration in the 9th

century by Benedictine monks, Montserrat has been the preeminent religious shrine of Catalonia and the site of the legendary statue of La Moreneta (the Black Madonna). Its glory years ended in 1812, when it was sacked by the armies of Napoléon. Today, sitting atop a 1,200m (4,000-ft.) mountain, 11km (7 miles) long and 5.5km (3½ miles) wide, it is one of the three most important pilgrimage sites in Spain. See chapter 12.

- **Catedral de Santiago de Compostela:** During the Middle Ages, this verdant city on the northwestern tip of Iberia attracted thousands of religious pilgrims who walked from as far away as Italy to seek salvation at the tomb of St. James. The cathedral itself shows the architectural influences of nearly 800 years of religious conviction, much of it financed by donations from exhausted pilgrims. Its two most stunning features are its Obradoiro facade, a baroque masterpiece, and its carved Doorway of Glory behind the facade. An enormous silver censor called the Botafumeiro swings from the transept during major liturgical ceremonies. See p. 566.

7 The Best Vineyards & Wineries

Spanish wines are some of the best in the world and are remarkably affordable here. Here's a list of bodegas that receive visitors. For more information about the 10 wine regions—and the 39 officially recognized wine-producing Denominaciones de Origen scattered across those regions—contact **Wines from Spain,** c/o the Commercial Office of Spain, 405 Lexington Ave., 44th Floor, New York, NY 10174-0331 (© **212/661-4959**).

RIBERA DEL DUERO

Halfway between Madrid and Santander, this region near Burgos is the fastest developing wine district in the country and the beneficiary of massive investments in the past few years. Cold nights, sunny days, the highest altitudes of any wine-producing region in Spain, and a fertile alkaline soil produce flavorful, award-winning wines. Among the noteworthy individual vineyards is:

- **Bodegas Señorío de Nava** (Nava de Roa; © **98-720-97-12**): This is one of the region's best examples of a once-sleepy and now-booming vintner. Merlot and cabernet sauvignon grapes are cultivated, as are more obscure local varieties such as Tinta del País (also known as Tempranillo) and Garnacha (or Grenache, as it's called across the border in France). Some of the wines bottled here are distributed under the brand name Vega Cubillas.

JEREZ DE LA FRONTERA

This town of 200,000 (most of whom work in the wine trade) is surrounded by a sea of vineyards, which thrive in the hot, chalky soil. Ninety-five percent of the region is planted with the hardy and flavorful Palomino Fino to produce sherry, one of the most beloved products of Spain. Few other regions contain so many bodegas, any of which can be visited. See chapter 8 for more information, but some of the outstanding choices include:

- **Allied Domeck** (Jerez de la Frontera; © **95-615-15-00**): Established in 1795, its products have been judged among the finest in the region since the 1980s. Connoisseurs consider this sherry a perfect accompaniment for tapas, for which the town of Jerez is also well known.
- **Emilio Lustao** (Jerez de la Frontera; © **95-634-15-97**): This bodega was established in 1896 by a local lawyer, and ever since, it has produced exotic forms of sherry snapped up as collectors' items by aficionados everywhere.
- **Antonio Barbadillo** (Sanlúcar de Barrameda; © **95-638-55-00**): This firm controls 70% of the sherry produced in the region around Sanlúcar, a town just 24km (15 miles) north of Jerez. Venerable and respected, it boasts

impressive headquarters—a palace originally conceived as a residence for a local bishop. Although established in 1821, it remained a small-time player until the 1960s, when production and quality zoomed upward. Some of its wine is distributed in Britain as Harvey's of Bristol.

- **González Byass** (Jerez de la Frontera; © **95-635-70-00**): Flourishing since 1835, this bodega has gained enormous recognition from one of the most famous brand names and the world's best-selling sherry, Tío Pepe. It isn't as picturesque as you might have hoped, since modernization has added some rather bulky concrete buildings to its historic core. Nonetheless, it's one of the most visible names in the industry.
- **Pedro Domecq** (Jerez de la Frontera; © **95-615-15-00**): The oldest of all the large sherry houses was established in 1730 by Patrick Murphy, an Irishman. Its bodega contains casks whose contents were once destined for such sherry lovers as William Pitt, Lord Nelson, and the duke of Wellington. If you visit this sprawling compound, look for La Mezquita bodega, whose many-columned interior somewhat resembles the famous mosque in Córdoba.

PENEDES

In ancient times, thousands of vessels of wine were shipped from this region of Catalonia to fuel the orgies of the Roman Empire. Much of the inspiration for the present industry was developed in the 19th century by French vintners, who found the climate and soil similar to those of Bordeaux. The region produces still wines, as well as 98% of Spain's sparkling wine *(cava),* which stands an excellent chance of supplanting French champagne in the minds of celebrants throughout the world. In fact, Freixenet is the largest selling sparkling wine in the world.

- **Cordoníu** (Sant Sadurní d'Anoia; ✆ **93-818-32-32**): With a history dating from the mid-1500s, this vineyard became famous after its owner, Josep Raventós, produced Spain's first version of sparkling wine. During the harvest, more than 2.2 million pounds of grapes, collected from about 1,000 growers, are pressed daily. The company's headquarters, designed around the turn of the 20th century by Puig i Cadafalch, a contemporary of Gaudí, sits above the 31km (19 miles) of underground tunnels where the product is aged.
- **Freixenet** (Sant Sadurní d'Anoia; ✆ **93-891-70-00**): Cordoníu's largest and most innovative competitor began in 1889 as a family-run wine business that quickly changed its production process to incorporate the radical developments in sparkling cava. Today, although still family owned, it's an awesomely efficient factory pressing vast numbers of grapes, with at least a million cases sold to the United States every year. Award-winning brand names include Cordon Negro Brut and Carta Nevada Brut. The company now operates a vineyard in California, which produces the sparkling wine Gloria Ferrer, which has won awards in the United States.
- **Miguel Torres** (Vilafranca del Penedés; ✆ **93-817-74-27**): This winery was established in 1870 by a local son (Jaime Torres), who returned to his native town after making a fortune trading petroleum and oil in Cuba. Today, you can see what was once the world's largest wine vat (132,000 gal.); its interior was used as the site of a banquet held in honor of the Spanish king. Thanks to

generations of management by French-trained specialists, it is now one of the most sophisticated and advanced vineyards in the region. Like the others, it's also close enough to Barcelona, the beach resort of Sitges, and the ancient monastery of Montserrat to permit a side trip.

LA RIOJA

Set in the foothills of the Pyrenees close to the French border, La Rioja turns out what most people have in mind when they think of Spanish wines. The region produced millions of gallons during the regime of the ancient Romans, and it boasts quality-control laws promulgated by a local bishop in the 9th century. Here are some of the best vineyards for a visit:

- **Herederos de Marqués de Riscal** (Elciego; ✆ **94-560-60-00**): This vineyard was founded around 1850 by a local entrepreneur who learned wine-growing techniques in France. The modern-day enterprise still bases most of its income on the 199 hectares (492 acres) acquired by the organization's founding father. Despite several disappointing years between 1975 and 1985, it is still one of the most respected in the region.
- **Bodegas Riojanas** (Cenicero; ✆ **94-145-40-50**): Set on the main street of the wine-growing hamlet of Cenicero, this century-old bodega expanded massively in the 1980s, and upgraded its visitor information program. You'll be received in a mock-feudal tower where you can learn the nuances of the wine industry.
- **Bodegas Muga** (Haro; ✆ **94-131-04-98**): This bodega adheres more to the 19th-century old-world craftsmanship than any of its competitors. The winery contains an assortment of old-fashioned casks made from

American or French oak. Production is small, eclectic, and choice.

• **La Rioja Alta** (Haro; ℂ **94-131-03-46**): Another bodega in the wine-growing community of Haro, La Rioja Alta is set near the railway station. Founded in 1890, it has the dank and atmospheric cellars you'd expect and was graced in 1984 by a visit from Spain's royal family. About 85% of the production at this small but quality outfit is bottled as reservas (aged at least 3 years) and gran reservas (aged at least 5 years).

GALICIA

This Celtic outpost in the northwestern corner of Spain produces white wines that connoisseurs praise as the perfect accompaniment to local seafood. The marketing name for the product, appropriately, is "El Vino del Mar" ("Sea Wine"), although the Denominación de Origen includes the appellations "Rías Baixas" and "Ribeiro." Per capita wine consumption in Galicia is the highest in Spain, and formerly, a majority of the wine produced here was consumed locally. Massive investments during the 1980s changed all that.

• **Bodega Morgadio** (Albeos-Crecente; ℂ **98-666-61-50**): This vineyard, near Pontevedra, launched the Denominación de Origen "Rias Baixas" in 1984. Four friends whom locals referred to as "madmen" bought 28 hectares (70 acres) of land that, with the Albariño grape, they transformed into one of the most respected and award-winning vineyards in the district. Fertilizers for each year's crop comes from the bodega's own flock of sheep. The success of old-fashioned farming methods coupled with state-of-the-art fermentation tanks is a model of entrepreneurial courage in an otherwise economically depressed outpost of Spain.

8 The Best Festivals

• **The Autumn Festival** (Madrid; ℂ **91-580-25-75**): Held in October and November, the **Festival de Otoño** is the best music festival in Spain, with a lineup that attracts the cream of the European and South American musical communities. The usual roster of chamber music, symphonic pieces, and orchestral works is supplemented by a program of zarzuela (musical comedy), as well as Arabic and Sephardic pieces composed during the Middle Ages. See p. 51.

• **Feria del Caballo** (Jerez de la Frontera; ℂ **95-633-11-50**): Few events show off Spain's equestrian traditions in such flattering light. Costumes are appropriately ornate; riders demonstrate the stern, carefully controlled movements developed during medieval battles; and the entire city of Jerez becomes one enormous riding ring for the presentation of dressage and jumping events. Horse buying and trading is commonplace at this May event. See p. 48.

• **Las Hogueras de San Juan** (Alicante; ℂ **96-520-00-00**): Bonfires blaze through the night on June 20 as a celebration of a festival revered by the Celtic pagans and Romans alike—the summer solstice. Stacks of flammable objects, including discarded finery and cardboard replicas of sinners and witches, are set ablaze. The bonfire signals the beginning of 5 days of nightly fireworks and daily parades during which normal business comes virtually to a standstill. See p. 49.

- **Moros y Cristianos** (Alcoy, near Alicante; ✆ **96-520-00-00**): The agonizing, century-long process of evicting the Moors from Iberia is re-created during 2 days of simulated, vaudeville-style fighting between "Moors" and "Christians" every April (dates vary). Circus-style costumes worn by the Moors are as absurdly anachronistic as possible. When the Christians win, a statue of the Virgin is carried proudly through the city as proof of Alcoy's staunchly passionate defense of its role as a bastion of Christianity. See p. 48.
- **La Tomatina** (Buñol, Valencia; ✆ **96-351-49-07**): Held every year on the last Wednesday in August, nearly everyone in the town along with thousands from neighboring towns and villages join this 2-hour-long tomato war (11am–1pm). The local government sponsors the festival, bringing in truckloads of tomatoes totaling more than 88,000 pounds of vegetable artillery. Local bands provide the music for dancing and singing and plenty of drinking. Portable showers are installed for the participants. See p. 50.
- **La Rapa das Bestas** (The Capture of the Beasts, San Lorenzo de Sabuceno, Galicia; ✆ **98-685-08-14**): In the verdant hills of northwestern Spain, horses graze at will. On the first weekend of July, they are rounded up and herded into a corral. Here, each is branded and then released back into the wild after a few days of medical observation. For information, contact the Office of Tourism in Pontevedra. See p. 49 and p. 578.
- **Misteri d'Elx** or "The Mystery Play of Elche" (Elche; ✆ **96-545-38-31**): Based on the reputed mystical powers of an ancient, black-faced statue of the Virgin, the citizens of Elche have staged a mystery play in the local church every year for more than 6 centuries. The chanting and songs that accompany the plot line are in an archaic dialect that even the Castilians can barely understand. Competition is fierce for seats during the August event, and celebrations precede and follow the play. See p. 366.

9 The Best Paradors

Funded and maintained by the government, Spain's paradors (*paradores* in Spanish) are hostelries that showcase a building or setting of important cultural and historic interest. Some are much older and grander than others. Here are the country's most interesting and unusual.

- **Parador de Avila** (Avila; ✆ **92-021-13-40**): Built as an enlargement of a 15th-century palace (Palacio de Piedras Albas, also known as the Palacio de Benavides), this parador features gardens that flank the northern fortifications of this well-preserved 11th-century walled city. While only some of the comfortable, airy bedrooms are in the original palace, it's still the region's most intriguing hotel. In the parador restaurant, try the roast suckling pig, a regional specialty. See p. 193.
- **Parador de Cuenca** (Cuenca; ✆ **96-923-23-20**): This 16th-century building, once a Dominican convent, is one of the newer paradors in Spain. Like the medieval houses for which Cuenca is famous, the balconies here jut out over rocky cliffs, overlooking swift-moving rivers below. The

sight of the *casas colgadas,* or "suspended houses," is unforgettable. An adjoining restaurant specializes in seasonal wild game. See p. 197.

- **Parador de Toledo** (Toledo; © **92-522-18-50**): Although this is a relatively modern building, the architecture subtly evokes much older models. Views from the windows, boasting a faraway glimpse of the city's historic core, evoke the scenes El Greco painted in his View of Toledo. A swimming pool comes as a welcome relief in blistering Toledo. Such regional dishes as stewed partridge are featured in the hotel restaurant. See p. 171.

- **Parador San Marcos** (León; © **98-723-73-00**): Originally home to the Order of Santiago— a group of knights charged with protecting journeying pilgrims— the building was expanded and embellished into a monastery some 400 years later. These days, set beside the Bernesga River and with a lavishly decorated church on the grounds, it's one of Spain's most deluxe paradors. The public areas are pure medieval grandeur: a dramatic lobby, huge cast-iron chandelier, and stone staircases. See p. 214.

- **Parador de Zamora** (Zamora; © **98-051-44-97**): This one-time Moorish fortress-turned-Renaissance palace is among the most beautiful and richly decorated paradors in Spain. A medieval aura is reflected in the details: armor, coats-of-arms, tapestries, and attractive four-poster beds. A swimming pool enhances the tranquil back garden. Castilian fare such as stuffed roast veal typifies the restaurant's offerings. See p. 211.

- **Parador de Cáceres** (Cáceres; © **92-721-17-59**): Live like royalty at this palace, built in the 1400s on the site of Arab fortifications. The parador is in the city's old quarter, recently declared a World Heritage Site. The spacious public areas are decorated with soft cream shades and rough-hewn ceiling beams. Venison with goat cheese and roast kid with rosemary are typical of the varied Extremaduran cuisine served in the parador restaurant. See p. 235.

- **Parador de Trujillo** (Trujillo; © **92-732-13-50**): A parador set in the inviting 16th-century convent of Santa Clara, this was originally built in a combination of medieval and Renaissance styles. The building was transformed into a hotel in 1984 and the bedrooms are considerably more lavish than they were during their stint as nuns' cells. The cuisine is the best in town. See p. 232.

- **Parador de Mérida** (Mérida; © **92-431-38-00**): A 16th-century building that was at various times a convent and a prison, this parador once hosted a meeting between the much-hated dictators of Spain (Franco) and Portugal (Salazar) in the 1960s. Mudéjar, Roman, and Visigothic elements adorn the interior in unusual but stunning juxtaposition. The inner courtyard and Mozarabic gardens add a graceful note. The kitchen serves the best of the area, including gazpacho, *calderetas extremeñas* (stews), and the famous Almoharin figs. See p. 239.

- **Parador Castillo de Santa Catalina** (Jaén; © **95-323-00-00**): In the 10th century, Muslims built this fortress on a cliff high above town. Later, Christians added Gothic vaulting and touches of luxury, which remain in place thanks to a renovation by the government. Bedrooms provide sweeping views over Andalusia. A swimming pool is a welcome retreat from the burning sun. Sample such dishes as cold garlic soup and partridge salad in the panoramic restaurant. See p. 245.

- **Parador de Santillana Gil Blas** (Santillana del Mar; © 94-281-80-00): This bucolic parador recalls the manor houses that dotted northern Spain's verdant hillsides more than 400 years ago. Composed of thick stone walls and heavy timbers, it's pleasantly isolated and elegantly countrified. An added bonus is its proximity to what has been called "the Sistine Chapel of prehistoric art"—the Caves of Altamira. See p. 544.
- **Parador del Molino Viejo (Parador de Gijón)** (Gijón; © 98-537-05-11): As the name implies, this hotel grew up around the decrepit remains of a molino, or cider mill (and the antique presses are still on hand). Close to San Lorenzo Beach, it's the only parador in the northern province of Asturias. The dining room serves up typical Asturian cuisine, including the famous fabada, a rich white bean and pork stew. See p. 554.

- **Parador de Pontevedra** (Pontevedra; © 98-685-58-00): The building is a 16th-century Renaissance palace built on foundations that are at least 200 years older than that. It's famous as one of Spain's first paradors. Inaugurated in 1955, its success led to the amplification of the parador program. The hotel is still alluring today, with its delightful terrace garden and stately dining room, which serves the fresh fish and seafood for which Galicia is known. See p. 578.
- **Hostal de Los Reyes Católicos** (Santiago de Compostela; © 98-158-22-00): We saved the best for last—this is one of the most spectacular hotels in Europe. Originally a hospice for wayfaring pilgrims, it boasts a lavish 16th-century facade, four open-air courtyards, and a bedchamber once occupied by Franco. Today, the hotel is a virtual museum, with Gothic, Renaissance, and baroque architectural elements. There are four beautiful cloisters, elegant public areas, and spectacular bedrooms. See p. 568.

10 The Best Luxury Hotels

- **Park Hyatt Villa Magna** (Madrid; © 91-587-12-34): Although it looks like a House of Parliament, this elegant hotel is regal and sedate, giving off the aura of a country estate. Fine furnishings, beautiful linen, and such designer toiletries as fragrant Maja soaps are part of the exquisite guest rooms. The hotel is surrounded by beautiful gardens. See p. 103.
- **The Ritz** (Madrid; © 91-701-67-67): Flawless service is the hallmark of Madrid's most distinguished hotel. Bedrooms contain antiques, gracious marble bathrooms, and elegant detailing. This Edwardian grand hotel is

more relaxed than it once was, the old haughtiness of former management gone with the wind—it long ago rescinded its policy of not allowing movie stars as guests. You still may have to wear a coat and tie, however. See p. 104.
- **Hotel Alfonso XIII** (Seville; © 95-491-70-00): This is where the royal family stayed when the Infanta Elena, daughter of Juan Carlos, married in Seville in 1995. Built to house visitors for the Iberoamerican Exposition of 1929, this grand hotel features Moorish-style rooms, with doors opening onto little balconies overlooking

a Spanish courtyard with a bubbling fountain and potted palms. Set in front of the city's fabled Alcázar, the Alfonso XIII is one of the most legendary hotels of Spain. See p. 268.

- **La Bobadilla** (Loja; © **95-832-18-61**): The most luxurious retreat in the south of Spain, this secluded oasis lies in the foothills of the Sierra Nevada, an hour's drive northeast of Málaga. Whitewashed casas (small individual villas) cluster around a tower and a church. Each individually designed casa is complete with a roof terrace and balcony overlooking olive groves. Guests live in luxury within the private compound of 708 hectares (1,750 acres). See p. 337.

- **Marbella Club** (Marbella; © **95-282-22-11**): Built during the golden age of the Costa del Sol (the 1950s), this bastion of chic is composed of ecologically conscious clusters of garden pavilions, bungalows, and small-scale annexes. The luxurious rooms are modeled after pages of a European design magazine. It has many competitors but remains an elite retreat. See p. 319.

- **Puente Romano** (Marbella; © **95-282-09-00**): On manicured and landscaped grounds facing the beach, Puente Romano evokes a highly stylized Andalusian village. Exotic bird life flutters through lush gardens planted with banana trees and other vegetation. Villas are spacious and beautifully furnished, with marble floors and bathrooms, big mirrors, and tasteful wood furnishings. In the summer, flamenco dancers entertain here. See p. 320.

- **Hotel Ritz** (Barcelona; © **93-318-52-00**): A 1919 grand luxe hotel formerly known as the Palace, this is one of the finest hotels in Spain, if not all of Europe. Guests are enveloped in dazzling elegance, with all the gilt, marble, and fresh flowers they would ever want. Classic Belle Epoque detailing extends to the plush guest quarters, many of which have high, ornate ceilings and gold bathroom fixtures. See p. 390.

- **Hotel María Cristina** (San Sebastián; © **94-343-76-00**): One of the country's great Belle Epoque treasures, this old-world seafront hotel has sheltered discriminating guests since 1912. Oriental rugs, antiques, potted palms, high ceilings, formal lounges, marble pillars, and marble floors show off a turn-of-the-20th-century glamour. The bedrooms are traditional with wood furnishings and tasteful pastel fabrics. Nothing else in the Basque country quite measures up to this old charmer. See p. 510.

- **La Residencia** (Deià, Majorca; © **97-163-90-11**): Set amid 12 hectares (30 acres) of citrus and olive groves, this tranquil hotel was converted from two Renaissance-era manor houses. Jasmine-scented terraces open onto panoramic views of the surrounding villages and mountains. Pampered guests are served a creative cuisine that features local produce. Leisure facilities include a swimming pool fed by mountain spring water. Many of the bedrooms have regal four-poster beds. It's a haven from the rest of overcrowded Majorca. See p. 606.

11 The Best Hotel Bargains

- **Hostal del Cardenal** (Toledo; © **92-522-49-00**): The summer residence of Toledo's 18th-century Cardinal Lorenzano, built right into the walls of the old city next to the Bisagra Gate, this just happens to be Toledo's best restaurant. But the setting—rose gardens, cascading vines, and Moorish fountains—makes it an ideal place to stay as well. Spanish furniture and a scattering of antiques recapture the aura of old Castile. See p. 171.

- **Posada de San José** (Cuenca; ☎ 96-921-13-00): This hotel, located in the oldest part of medieval Cuenca, is a remarkable bargain. In the 17th century it was a convent, but the rooms have been converted to receive guests and are now decorated in rustic style. The posada sits atop a cliff, overlooking the forbidding depths of a gorge and the river below; views are superb. See p. 198.

- **Hostería Real de Zamora** (Zamora; ☎ 98-053-45-45): Once the dreaded headquarters of the local Spanish Inquisition, today this hotel offers a far friendlier welcome. Guests enjoy coffee on the patio and the pleasure of a garden planted along the city's medieval fortifications. Imagine if these 15th-century walls could talk. See p. 211.

- **Hotel Doña María** (Seville; ☎ 95-422-49-90): Near the fabled cathedral, this hotel boasts a rooftop terrace with unmatched views of the Andalusian capital. A private villa that dates from the 1840s, the Doña María has a swimming pool ringed with garden-style lattices and antique wrought-iron railings. Bedrooms are uniquely designed with tasteful Iberian antiques. See p. 270.

- **Hotel Reina Victoria** (Ronda; ☎ 95-287-12-40): This country-style hotel is best known as the place where the German poet Rainer Maria Rilke wrote *The Spanish Trilogy*. Its terrace, perched on a dramatic precipice, offers commanding views of the countryside. An Englishman built this Victorian charmer in 1906 to honor his recently deceased monarch, Queen Victoria. See p. 292.

- **Hotel América** (Granada; ☎ 95-822-74-71): This one-time private villa, within the walls of the Alhambra, is one of the most popular small hotels in Granada. Its cozy bedrooms are filled with reproductions of Andalusian antiques. Plants cascade down the white plaster walls and the ornate grillwork onto the shady patio. Good-tasting, inexpensive meals are served in the hotel restaurant. See p. 302.

- **Hotel Mijas** (Mijas; ☎ 95-248-58-00): This is the most charming of affordable hotels along the Costa del Sol. It's designed in typical Andalusian style, with flowering terraces, wrought-iron accents, and sun-flooded bedrooms. Although built in the 1970s, it blends in perfectly with the region's gleaming white buildings. See p. 328.

- **Huerto del Cura** (Elche; ☎ 96-661-00-11): From your bedroom you'll have a panoramic view of Priest's Grove, a formidable date-palm forest. Between Alicante and Murcia, this is one of the choice addresses in the south of Spain. Bedrooms are handsomely maintained and beautifully furnished, and a swimming pool separates the palm grove from the rooms. The regional cuisine in the hotel's restaurant is excellent. See p. 367.

- **Mesón Castilla** (Barcelona; ☎ 93-318-21-82): This two-star charmer with an Art Nouveau facade is right in the heart of Barcelona. It is well maintained and well managed, with prices that are blessedly easy on the wallet. Comfortable rooms often come with large terraces. Only breakfast is served, but there are many nearby taverns with excellent food. See p. 389.

- **Hotel Pampinot** (Fuenterrabía; ℂ **94-364-06-00**): The Infanta María Teresa stayed at this 16th-century aristocratic mansion on a journey to France for her eventual marriage to the Sun King, Louis XIV. Now a stately hotel, it's on a quiet side street in this Basque seaside resort near the French border. Behind a richly textured stone facade and Renaissance detailing are bedrooms furnished with both antiques and reproductions. See p. 519.

12 The Best Restaurants

- **El Amparo** (Madrid; ℂ **91-431-64-56**): In the old days of Franco, gastronomes flocked to Jockey or Horcher. Today their savvy sons and daughters head to El Amparo, the trendiest of Madrid's gourmet restaurants. It serves haute Basque cuisine against a backdrop of cosmopolitan glamour. Patrons sample everything from cold marinated salmon with a tomato sorbet to ravioli stuffed with seafood. See p. 120.

- **Sobrino de Botín** (Madrid; ℂ **91-366-42-17**): Since 1725, this restaurant has been celebrated for its roast suckling pig, prepared in a 200-year-old tile oven. Hemingway even mentioned it in *The Sun Also Rises.* The roast Segovian lamb is equally delectable. There is little subtlety of flavor here—only food prepared by time-tested recipes that have appealed to kings as well as Castilian peasants. The aromas waft clear across Madrid's old town. See p. 130.

- **Mesón de Cándido** (Segovia; ℂ **92-142-59-11**): Foodies from around the country flock to this 19th-century Spanish inn, "The House of Cándido," for one dish: roast suckling pig, acclaimed the best in Spain (even by Hemingway, who might otherwise be seen at Botín in Madrid). In Spanish it's called cochinillo asado, and it's delectable—prepared according to a century-old recipe. The cordero asado, or roast baby lamb, is not as well known, but it's equally flavorful. See p. 186.

- **Mesón Casa Colgadas** (Cuenca; ℂ **96-922-35-09**): Without a doubt, this is the most spectacularly situated restaurant in Spain— a "hanging house" suspended over a precarious precipice. The food is Spanish and international, with an emphasis on regional ingredients. The dishes can be ingenious, but the culinary repertoire usually reflects proven classics that might have pleased your grandparents. See p. 198.

- **Chez Víctor** (Salamanca; ℂ **92-321-31-23**): In the historic center of this university town, this is the most glamorous Continental restaurant around. Chef Victoriano Salvador gives customers terrific value for their pesetas with his imaginative, oft-renewed menus. The freshly prepared fish and his traditional version of roast lamb are especially tempting. Regionally rooted but modern in outlook, Salvador has a finely honed technique and isn't afraid to be inventive on occasion. See p. 208.

- **El Caballo Rojo** (Córdoba; ℂ **95-747-53-75**): Begin your evening with a sherry in the popular bar, followed by a visit to the traditional dining room. Not only Andalusian dishes are served here;

some classics are based on ancient Sephardic and Mozarabic specialties. Most guests begin with a soothing gazpacho and wash everything down with sangria. Finish off the meal with one of the homemade ice creams—we recommend pistachio. See p. 259.

- **Jaume de Provença** (Barcelona; ✆ **93-430-00-29**): The Catalán capital has more great restaurants than even Madrid. At the western end of the Eixample district, this Catalán/French restaurant is the domain of one of the city's most talented chefs, Jaume Bargués. He serves modern interpretations of traditional Catalán and southern French cuisine—such dishes as pigs' trotters with plums and truffles or crabmeat lasagna. His personal cooking repertoire is distinctive, and he has been known to create new taste sensations when he's feeling experimental. See p. 401.

- **Botafumeiro** (Barcelona; ✆ **93-218-42-30**): The city's finest seafood is prepared here, in a glistening, modern kitchen visible from the dining room. The king of Spain is a frequent patron, enjoying paellas, zarzuelas, or any of the 100 or so ultrafresh seafood dishes. The chef's treatment of fish is the most intelligent and subtle in town—but don't expect such quality to come cheap. See p. 404.

- **La Dama** (Barcelona; ✆ **93-202-06-86**): One of the most acclaimed restaurants in Spain, this "dame" serves one of the most refined Catalán and international cuisines along the east coast of the country.

Stylish and well managed, it turns out masterpieces based on the best in food shopping in any season. See p. 402.

- **Empordá** (Figueres; ✆ **97-250-05-62**): Although ordinary on the outside, this hotel restaurant is one of the finest on the Costa Brava. It was a favorite of Salvador Dalí, who once wrote his own cookbook. Haute Catalán cuisine is the specialty—everything from duck foie gras with Armagnac to suprême of sea bass with flan. The flavors are refined yet definite. See p. 472.

- **Akelare** (San Sebastián; ✆ **94-321-20-52**): The Basques are renowned for their cooking, and the owner-chef of this San Sebastián restaurant, Pedro Sabijana, pioneered the school of *nueva cocina vasca* (modern Basque cuisine). His restaurant has attracted gourmets from around Europe. Sabijana transforms such seemingly simple dishes as fish cooked on a griddle with garlic and parsley into something magical. No other eatery in northern Spain comes close to equaling the superb viands dispensed here. There are those (and we are among them) who consider Subijana the best chef in Spain. See p. 512.

- **Oscar Torrijos** (Valencia; ✆ **96-373-29-49**): The Costa Levante's best restaurant, in the city that's said to have "invented" paella, this stellar restaurant serves a Mediterranean and international cuisine, and does so superbly well. Expect a flavor-filled cuisine based on the freshest of ingredients. See p. 356.

2

A Traveler's Guide to Spanish Art & Architecture

by Reid Bramblett

Spain's art ranges from Romanesque frescoes and El Greco's warped mannerism to Velázquez's royal portraits and Picasso's *Guernica,* its architecture from Moorish palaces and Gothic cathedrals to Gaudí's Art Nouveau creations and Frank Gehry's metallic flower of Bilbao's Guggenheim Museum. This brief overview should help you make sense of it all.

1 Art 101

ROMANESQUE (10TH–13TH C.)

From the 8th century, most of Spain was under **Moorish** rule. The Muslims took the biblical injunction against graven images so seriously that they produced no art in a traditional Western sense—though the remarkably intricate **geometric designs** and swooping, exaggerated letters of **Kufic inscriptions** played out in woodcarving, painted tiles, and plasterwork on Moorish palaces are decorations of the highest aesthetic order (see "Architecture 101," later in this chapter).

Starting with the late-10th-century Reconquest, **Christian** Spaniards began producing art in the northern and eastern provinces. **Painting** and **mosaics** in Catalonia show the Byzantine influence of northern Italy, while **sculptures** along the northerly pilgrimage route to Compostela are related to French models, though they are often more symbolic (and primitive looking) than realistic.

Significant examples include:

- *Códex del Beatus.* A Mozarab (a Christian living under Moorish rule), the monk Beatus de Liébana illuminated this 10th-century "Commentary on the Apocalypse" manuscript in an influential hybrid style, which includes many Arabic devices. Its pages are now dispersed internationally; the best remaining chunk is in Girona's Catedral.
- **Barcelona's Museu Nacional d'Art de Catalunya.** Most of Catalonia's great Romanesque paintings were detached from their village churches in the early 20th century and are now housed in this museum.
- **Santiago de Compostela's Cathedral.** The Pórtico de la Gloria is a 12th-century masterpiece of Romanesque sculpture.

GOTHIC (13TH–16TH C.)

The influence of Catalonia and France continued to dominate in the **Gothic** era—though, in painting especially, a dollop of Italian style and a dash of Flemish attention to detail were added, often set against a solid gold-leaf background. In the art of this period, colors became more varied and vivid, compositions more complex, lines more fluid and with a sense of motion, and features more expressive.

Significant artists and examples include:

- **Jaime Huguet** (1415–92). The primary artist in the Catalán School, Huguet mixed Flemish and Italian influences with true local Catalán Romanesque conventions. He left works in his native Barcelona's Palau Reial and Museu Nacional d'Art de Catalunya.
- **Bartolomé Bermejo** (active 1474–98). Though Andalusian by birth, Bermejo was the lead painter in the Italianate Valencian School, and the first Spanish painter to use oils. Some of his best early paintings are in Madrid's Museo del Prado; one of his last is *La Pietat* (1498) in the Catedral de Barcelona.
- **Fernando Gallego** (1466–1507). Leader of the Gothic Castilian School, Gallego worked in a strong Flemish style melded to Spanish traditions, most evident in his masterpiece triptych in Salamanca's Catedral Vieja.

RENAISSANCE (16TH C.)

Renaissance means "rebirth," in this case of classical ideals originating in ancient Greece and Rome. Artists strove for greater naturalism, using recently developed techniques such as linear perspective to achieve new heights of realism. The style started in Italy, and only slowly displaced Spain's Gothic tendencies. When it finally got rolling in Spain, the style had already mutated into the baroque.

Renaissance art flowered in Castille, where its greatest artists strove for court appointments at Toledo (though sculpture really flowered in Valladolid).

Significant artists include:

- **Pedro Berruguete** (1450–1504). The court painter to Ferdinand and Isabella, Berruguete worked for a time in Italy's Urbino, where he picked up an Italian softness, ethereality, and *chiaroscuro* (dramatically playing areas of harsh lighting off dark shadows) to add to his Flemish-influenced obsession with details and Spanish-style gold backgrounds. You can see his works in the Catedral de Avila and Jaén's Museo Provincial.
- **Alonso Berruguete** (1488–1561). Pedro's talented son was not only court painter to Charles V, but also the greatest native sculptor in Spain, having traveled to Italy to study painting under Filippino Lippi and sculpture with Michelangelo himself. The latter studies lent him a powerful, natural style intent on expressing the psychology of his figures in such masterworks as the *San Sebastián* (1526–32) in Valladolid's Museo Nacional de Escultura and a *reredos* (a floor piece with Biblical scenes in relief, 1539–43) in the Catedral de Toledo.
- **Juan de Juni** (1507–77). A Frenchman who also took up Michelangelo's sensibilities, sculptor Juni developed a Catalán Renaissance style that predicted the baroque in its expressiveness and drama. His greatest works are in Valladolid, including the *Entombments* (1544) in the Museo Nacional de Escultura and an altarpiece (1551) in the Cathedral, and a *Deposition* (1571) reredos in the Cabildo Catedral de Segovia.
- **El Greco** (1540–1614). Spain's most significant Renaissance artist was actually from Crete. Domenikos Thetocopoulos (his real name) traveled first to Italy, where he picked up Tintoretto's color palette in Venice and the twisting figures of late Renaissance mannerism in Rome before heading to Toledo (then Spain's capital) to seek his fortune with a combination of weirdly lit scenes, broodingly dark colors, crowded compositions, eerily elongated figures, and a mystical touch. He never became court painter, though plenty of

religious commissions and lesser nobility portraits came his way. Toledo's churches and Casa y Museo de El Greco retain many of his works, as does Madrid's Museo del Prado; other works are scattered across Spain in collections at Sitges, Bilbao, Valencia, Seville, Cuenca, El Escorial, and Madrid's Thyssen-Bornemisza and Fine Arts museums.

BAROQUE (17TH–18TH C.)

The **baroque** was Spain's greatest artistic era, producing several painters who rank among Europe's greatest. A more theatrical and decorative take on the Renaissance, the baroque had a rich exuberance that dovetailed nicely with Spain's Counter-Reformation fervor. The style mixes a kind of super-realism based on the use of peasant models and the *chiaroscuro,* or tenebrism (dramatically playing areas of harsh lighting off dark shadows), of Italy's Caravaggio with compositional complexity and explosions of dynamic fury, movement, color, and figures.

Many baroque commissions were officially sanctioned religious subjects or noble and royal portraits, but middle class merchants, flush with wealth from the American colonies, were also ravenous for smaller genre scenes.

Significant artists include:

- **José de Ribera** (1591–1652). The greatest master of *chiaroscuro* and *tenebrism* after Caravaggio, Ribera cranked out numerous, pale, wrinkle-faced, flaccid-armed *St. Jeromes.* He worked mostly in Italy, but largely at the Spanish court in Naples, then under Spanish rule, so many of his earthily realistic works found their way back home, including *Archimedes* (1630) in Madrid's Museo del Prado.

- **Diego Velázquez** (1599–1660). Spain's greatest painter, a prodigy who became Philip IV's court painter at 24, Velázquez studied in Italy where he polished his unflinchingly naturalistic technique. Though his position meant the bulk of his work was portraiture (and he did this better than anyone), he was a master of all painting genres. The collection of Madrid's Museo del Prado spans his career, from the early *Adoration of the Magi* (1619) to the *Surrender of Breda* (1634) to his masterpiece *Las Meninas* (1656).

- **Francisco de Zubarán** (1598–1664). Seville's master of *chiaroscuro,* Zubarán had a unique style that used the orangey glow of candles to light his clay figures, rather than the out-of-frame white light of Ribera and Caravaggio. Seville's Museo Provincial has several of his works. The *Defense of Cadiz* (1634) in Madrid's Museo del Prado shows how he was adapting and lightening his formerly dark style to align more with prevailing tastes.

- **Bartolomé Esteban Murillo** (1617–82). Zubarán's Seville competitor, Murillo created work with a distinctly brighter, more saccharine and sentimental quality. His approach was well suited to Counter-Reformation devotional images, which were used as models throughout Spain and Europe for the next few centuries. He eventually developed an *estilo vaporoso* (vaporous style) of loose brushwork, rich colors, and soft contours that loosely parallels the French rococo. His native Seville's Museo Provincial preserves several devout paintings, and the best of his patented (and oft-copied) *Immaculate Conceptions* are in Madrid's Museo del Prado.

BOURBON ROCOCO & NEOCLASSICAL (18TH–19TH C.)

Spain's turbulent late 18th and early 19th centuries are best seen in the progression of work by the unique master Goya. His works started in the prevailing

rococo style (a chaotic, frothy version of the baroque) but soon went of on its own track. Spanish **neoclassicism** was dry, academic, and rather uninteresting. Significant artists include:

- **Francisco Goya** (1746–1828). Goya started as a painter of frothy, pastel-colored rococo works often of silly, joyful scenes (*Parasol,* 1777). He then became a courtly portraitist in the position of principal painter to Charles IV (*Family of Charles IV,* 1800), but his republican tendencies and encroaching deafness left him angry and prone to paint and engrave satirical attacks on the social system (*Los Caprichos,* 1796–98). He turned increasingly to more harshly, realistically painted works with the French Invasion (*Clothed Maja* and *Naked Maja,* 1800–03; the *Third of May,* 1808; *Execution,* 1814), but after the Restoration was turned away by the new court. He retreated to his house, a deaf embittered old man, where he painted the deeply disturbing mythological/psychological *Black Paintings* (1821–22). He spent his final 4 years in Bordeaux, apparently happier, and returned to the brighter color and simpler, happier themes of his youth. All of these works, along with 108 more, are in Madrid's Museo del Prado.
- **Madrid's Palacio Real.** The Bourbons imported many artists, including **Anton Mengs** (1728–79) from Bohemia and **Tiepolo** (1696–1770) from Italy, to decorate their palace in the high baroque/emergent rococo style.

20TH CENTURY

Spain became an artistic hotbed again at the turn of the 20th century—even if Barcelona's own Picasso moved to Paris. Though both movements were born in France, Spanish artists were key in developing cubism and surrealism. **Cubists,** including Spaniards Picasso and Gris, accepted that the canvas is flat and painted objects from all points of view at once, rather than using optical tricks like perspective to fool viewers into seeing three dimensions; the effect is a fractured, imploded look. **Surrealists** such as Dalí and Miró tried to express the inner working of their minds in paint, plumbing their ids for imagery.

Significant artists include:

- **Joan Miró** (1893–1983). Greatest of the true surrealists in Spain, Miró created largely appealing work with a whimsical and childlike quality (save the dark works he did during the Spanish Civil War). The Catalán tended toward bright colors, especially blue, and was an accomplished sculptor as well (the assemblages often look like three-dimensional versions of his paintings). Barcelona's Fundació Joan Miró is the best place to get an overview of his work.
- **Pablo Picasso** (1881–1973). The most important artist of the last century, Picasso dipped his brush into several of the important early-20th-century movements, helping establish cubism and redefine surrealism in the process. Though he lived in France after 1904, Spain has always hungrily acquired his works to serve as stars of modern art museums from Bilbao's Guggenheim Museum to Madrid's Centro de Arte Reina Sofía, which houses his masterpiece *Guernica* (1937), a bleak, confusing polemic against the horrors of war. Many of his early works are housed in Barcelona's Museu Picasso, where you find surprising examples of his teenage talent for realism.
- **Juan Gris** (1887–1927). The truest of the cubists, Gris had a palette more colorful than that of Picasso or France's Braque. He worked mostly in France, but Madrid's Centro de Arte Reina Sofía and the contemporary art museum in Palma de Majorca hang some of his paintings.

- **Salvador Dalí** (1904–89). The most famous surrealist was only briefly a member of that group (his anti-Marxist and pro-Franco position got him kicked out). Dalí's art used an intensely realistic technique to explore the very unreal worlds of dreams (nightmares, really) and paranoia in an attempt to plumb the Freudian depths of his own psyche. Some of his better works in Spain are at Madrid's Centro de Arte Reina Sofía and Cadaqués's Perrot-Moore Museum, but make sure to visit the quirky Teatre Museu Dalí, which he founded in his native Figueres.
- **Antoni Tàpies** (b. 1923). This abstract surrealist has been Spain's only significant artist since the Civil War. He founded his own museum for his art, the Fundació Antoni Tàpies, in Barcelona.

2 Architecture 101

There are a few points to keep in mind when considering a building's style, particularly for structures built before the 20th century. Very few buildings (especially churches) were actually built in only one style. Massive, expensive structures often took centuries to complete, during which time tastes would change and plans would be altered. While each architectural era has its own distinctive features, some elements, general floor plans, and terms are common to many, or may appear near the end of one era and continue through several later ones.

From the **Christian** Romanesque period on, most churches consist either of a single wide **aisle,** or a wide central **nave** flanked by two narrow aisles. The aisles are separated from the nave by a row of **columns,** or by square stacks of masonry called **piers,** usually connected by **arches.**

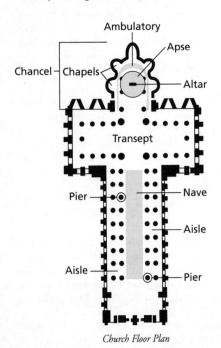

Church Floor Plan

This main nave/aisle assemblage is usually crossed by a perpendicular corridor called a **transept** near the far, east end of the church so that the floor plan looks like a **Latin cross** (shaped like a crucifix). The shorter, east arm of the nave is the holiest area, called the **chancel;** it often houses the stalls of the **choir** and the **altar.** If the far end of the chancel is rounded off, we call it an **apse.** An **ambulatory** is a curving corridor outside the altar and choir area, separating it from the ring of smaller chapels radiating off the chancel and apse.

MOORISH & MUDEJAR (8TH–15TH C.)

The Moors brought with them an Arabic architectural style that changed over the centuries but kept many features that give their remaining buildings, especially in Andalusia, a distinctly Eastern flair.

The early **Caliphate** style of Córdoba lasted from the 8th to the 11th century, replaced when the Caliphate fell by the simpler, more austerely religious **Almohad** style in Seville in the 12th and 13th centuries. As the Moors were being driven from most of Spain, in the Arabs' last stronghold of Granada, they constructed the Alhambra in the most sophisticated and ornately decorated style called **Nasrid** (13th–14th c.). After the Reconquest, Arab builders living under Christian rule developed the **Mudéjar** style, embellishing churches and palaces with Moorish elements.

The Moors built three major structures: mosques, alcázares, and alcazabas. **Mosques,** Islamic religious buildings, were connected to minarets, tall towers from which the muezzin would call the people to prayer. *Alcázares* were palaces built with many small courtyards and gardens with fountains and greenery (the Arabs started as a desert people, so their version of paradise has an abundance of water). *Alcazabas* were fortresses built high atop hills and fortified as any defensive structure.

Identifiable Moorish features, and with the name of the period when the feature first appeared, include:

- **Horseshoe arch (Caliphate).** This arch describes more than 180° of the circle's arc.
- **Ornamental brickwork in relief alternating with stone (Caliphate).**
- **Cupolas (Caliphate).** These domes rest on arches, often dripping with coffered stuccoed decorations.
- **Geometric and plant-motif decorations (Caliphate).** The Koran forbids images of men or beasts, so the Moors had to find other ways to decorate their mosques and palaces.
- **Kufic script (Caliphate).** Using another ingenious technique to get around the injunctions against imagery in art, artists turned religious passages from the Koran into an elaborately swooping calligraphy.

Alhambra, Granada

- **Doors and arches surmounted by blind arcades (all periods).**
- **Pointed arch (Almohad).** Although horseshoe arches were still used during the Almohad period, they were often replaced by narrow pointy ones.
- **Artesonado ceilings (Almohad).** These paneled wood ceilings were often painted and carved.
- **Azulejos (Almohad).** Patterns were created with these painted tiles.

Mezquita-Catedral de Córdoba is the best-preserved building in the Caliphate style. Of the Almohad period, the best remaining example is **Seville**'s **Giralda Tower,** a minaret but little altered when its accompanying mosque was converted into a cathedral; the mosque and tower at **Zaragosa**'s **Palacio de la Aljafería** have survived from the era as well. The crowning achievement of the Nasrid—of all Spanish Moorish architecture—is **Granada**'s **Alhambra** palace and the adjacent **Generalife** gardens.

ROMANESQUE (8TH–13TH C.)

As the Reconquest freed the north of Spain, a pilgrimage route sprang up along the coast to Santiago de Compostela. French and Italian pilgrims and Cistercian monks traveling the route brought the European Romanesque with them, sprinkling the way with many small churches and leaving a mighty cathedral at the trail's end.

The Romanesque took its inspiration and rounded arches from ancient Rome (hence the name). Romanesque architects concentrated on building large churches with wide aisles to accommodate the pilgrims. But to support the weight of all that masonry, the walls had to be thick and solid (meaning they could be pierced only by few and rather small windows) resting on huge piers, giving Romanesque churches a dark, somber, mysterious, and often oppressive feeling.

Identifiable features of the Romanesque include:

- **Rounded arches.** These load-bearing architectural devices allowed architects to open up wide naves and spaces, channeling all the weight of the stone walls and ceiling across the curve of the arch and down into the ground via the columns or pilasters.
- **Thick walls.**

Catedral de Santiago de Compostela

- **Infrequent and small windows.**
- **Huge piers.**

Although the great **Catedral de Santiago de Compostela,** the undisputed masterpiece of the style, has many baroque accretions, the floor plan is solidly Romanesque. Other good examples include **Sanguesa's Iglesia de Santa María** and **Iglesia de Santiago.**

GOTHIC (13TH–16TH C.)

By the late 12th century, engineering developments freed church architecture from the heavy, thick walls of Romanesque structures and allowed ceilings to soar, walls to thin, and windows to proliferate. Spain imported the style (and often the masons and architects) from its birthplace in France.

Instead of dark, somber, relatively unadorned Romanesque interiors that forced the eyes of the faithful toward the altar, where the priest stood droning on in unintelligible Latin, the Gothic interior enticed the churchgoers' gaze upward to high ceilings filled with light. The priests still conducted Mass in Latin, but now peasants could "read" the Gothic comic books of stained-glass windows.

The French style eventually developed into a genuine Spanish idiom, the elaborate, late-15th-century **Isabelline style,** named after the Catholic queen.

Identifiable features of the Gothic include:

- **Pointed arches.** The most significant development of the Gothic era was the discovery that pointed arches could carry far more weight than rounded ones.
- **Cross vaults.** Instead of being flat, the square patch of ceiling between four columns arches up to a point in the center, creating four sail shapes, sort of like the underside of a pyramid. The X separating these four sails is often reinforced with ridges called **ribbing.** As the Gothic progressed, four-sided cross vaults became six- or eight-sided as architects played with the angles.
- **Tracery.** These lacy spider webs of carved stone grace the pointy ends of windows and sometimes the spans of ceiling vaults.

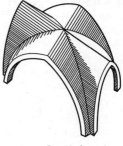

Cross Vault

- **Flying buttresses.** These free-standing exterior pillars connected by graceful, thin arms of stone help channel the weight of the building and its roof out and down into the ground. To help counter the cross forces involved in this engineering sleight of hand, the piers of buttresses were often topped by heavy pinnacles or statues.
- **Stained glass.** Because pointy arches can carry more weight than

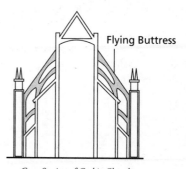

Cross Section of Gothic Church

rounded ones, windows could be larger and more numerous. They were often filled with Bible stories and symbolism written in the colorful patterns of stained glass.

The French style of Gothic was energetically pursued in Spain in the early to mid–13th century, first in adapting the Romanesque **Catedral de Santa María** in **Burgos,** then in **Catedral de Toledo** and **Catedral de León,** the most ornate. Fourteenth- and 15th-century Gothic cathedrals include those at **Avila, Segovia, Pamplona, Barcelona,** and **Girona** (the last a peculiar aisle-less Catalán plan, although the interior is now baroque). The best of the **Isabelline style** can be seen in **Valladolid** in the facades of **Iglesia de San Pablo** and the **Colegio San Gregorio.**

Catedral de Barcelona

RENAISSANCE (16TH C.)

As in painting, the rules of Renaissance architecture stressed proportion, order, classical inspiration, and mathematical precision to create unified, balanced structures based on Italian models. The earliest—and most Spanish—Renaissance style (really a transitional form from Gothic) was marked by facades done in an almost Moorish intricacy and was called **Plateresque,** for it was said to resemble the work of silversmiths *(plateros).*

Some identifiable Renaissance features include:

• **A sense of proportion.**
• **A reliance on symmetry.**

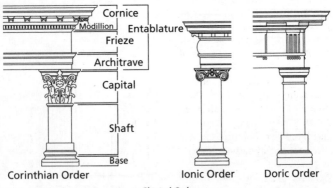

Classical Orders

- **The use of classical orders,** which specifies three different column capitals: Doric, Ionic, and Corinthian.

The best of the **Plateresque** decorates the facades of **Salamanca**'s **Convento de San Esteban** and **Universidad.** Charles V's **Summer Palace** built in the middle of **Granada**'s Moorish **Alhambra** is the greatest High Renaissance building in Spain. The most monumentally classical of Renaissance structures was Phillip II's **El Escorial** monastery outside Madrid, designed by Juan de Herrera

Real Monasterio de San Lorenzo de El Escorial

(1530–97), who also started **Valladolid**'s **Cathedral** in 1580, although the exterior was later finished in flamboyant baroque style.

BAROQUE (17TH–18TH C.)

The overall effect of the baroque is to lighten the appearance of structures and add movement of line and vibrancy to the static look of the classical Renaissance. At the beginning of this period, however, the classicism of Juan de Herrera continued to dominate, making the Spanish baroque more austere and simple than contemporary European versions. But soon the Churriguera family of architects and their contemporaries gave rise to the overly ornate, sumptuously decorated **Churriguesque** style.

Identifiable features include:

- **Classical architecture rewritten with curves.** The baroque is similar to Renaissance, but many of the right angles and ruler-straight lines are exchanged for curves of complex geometry and an interplay of concave and convex surfaces.
- **Multiplying forms.** To create a rich, busy effect, the baroque loved to pile up its elements, such as columns, *pediments* (a low-pitched, triangular feature above a window, door, or pavilion), or *porticoes* (a projecting pavilion).
- **Churriguesque decorations.** The style was characterized by a proliferation of statues, curves, carvings, and twisty columns stacked into pyramids.

Madrid's **Plaza Mayor** is the classic example of the restrained Herrera-style early baroque. Churriguesque masterpieces include **Granada**'s **Monasterio Cartuja** and **Salamanca**'s **Plaza Mayor.** The baroque was largely used to embellish existing buildings, such as the fine, ornate facade on **Santiago de Compostela**'s **Cathedral.**

NEOCLASSICAL (18TH–19TH C.)

As a backlash against the excesses of the baroque, by the middle of the 18th century, Bourbon architects began turning to the austere simplicity and grandeur of the Classical Age and inaugurated the **neoclassical** style. Their work was inspired by the rediscovery of Italy's Pompeii and other ancient sites.

Identifiable neoclassical features include:

- **Mathematical proportion and symmetry.** These classical ideals first rediscovered during the Renaissance are the hallmark of every classically styled era.
- **Reinterpreting ancient architecture.** Features of temples and other buildings of ancient Greece and Rome, such as classical orders, colonnaded porticoes, and pediments, were adapted to new structures.
- **Monumental.** The neoclassical never did anything small.

The primary neoclassical architect, **Ventura Rodríguez** (1717–85), designed the facade of **Pamplona**'s **Cathedral** and **Madrid**'s grand boulevard of the **Paseo del Prado.** On that boulevard is one of Spain's best neoclassical buildings, the **Museo del Prado.**

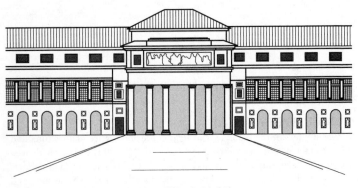

Museo del Prado, Madrid

MODERNISME & MODERN (20TH C.)

In Barcelona, architects such as **Lluis Doménech i Montaner** (1850–1923) and the great master **Antoni Gaudí** (1852–1926) developed one of the most appealing, idiosyncratic forms of Art Nouveau, called **modernisme.** This Catalán variant took a playful stab at building with undulating lines and colorful, broken tile mosaics.

Guggenheim Museum, Bilbao

During the long Franco years, architecture languished as utilitarian and bland, but in the late 1990s American Frank Gehry (b. 1929) gave a wake-up call to Spanish architecture with his curvaceous, gleaming silver **Guggenheim Museum** in **Bilbao.**

Identifiable features of modernisme include:

- **An emphasis on the uniqueness of craft.** Like Art Nouveau practitioners in other countries, Spanish artists and architects rebelled against the era of mass production.
- **A use of organic motifs.** Asymmetrical, curvaceous designs were often based on plants and flowers.
- **A variety of mediums.** Wrought iron, stained glass, tile, and hand-painted wallpaper were some of the most-popular materials.

The best of modernisme is in **Barcelona,** including **Gaudí's apartment buildings** along Passeig de Gràcia and his massive unfinished cathedral, **La Sagrada Família.**

3

Planning Your Trip to Spain

In this chapter, you'll find everything you need to plan your trip, from a sketch of Spain's various regions to tips on when to go and how to get the best airfare.

1 The Regions in Brief

Three times the size of Illinois, with a population of approximately 40 million, Spain faces the Atlantic Ocean and the Bay of Biscay to the north and the Mediterranean Sea to the south and east. Portugal borders on the west, with the Pyrenees separating Spain from France and the rest of Europe. The southern coastline is only a few sea miles from the north coast of Africa. It's difficult to generalize about Spain because it is composed of so many regions—50 provinces in all—each with its own geography, history, and culture. The country's topography divides it into many regions: the Cantabrian mountains in the north, those of Cuenca in the east, and the Sierra Morena in the south, which mark off a high central tableland that is itself cut by hills.

MADRID & ENVIRONS

Set on a high, arid plateau near the geographic center of Iberia, Madrid was created by royal decree in the 1600s, long after the much older kingdoms of León, Navarre, Aragón, and Catalonia, and long after the final Moor was ousted by Catholic armies. Since its birth, all roads within Spain have radiated outward from its precincts, and as the country's most important airline and railway hub, it's likely to be your point of arrival (although many international flights and European trains now arrive in Barcelona as well).

Despite the city's increasingly unpleasant urban sprawl, its paralyzing traffic jams, and skyrocketing prices, Madrid remains one of Europe's great cities. Take in the Prado, the Thyssen-Bornemisza Museum, and perhaps the Royal Palace. Walk through historic neighborhoods around the Plaza Mayor (but beware of muggers). Devote time to one of the city's greatest pastimes, a round of tapas tasting.

Plan on at least 2 days to explore the city and another 3 for trips to the attractions beyond the capital. Perhaps as important as a visit to Madrid is a day trip to the imperial city of **Toledo,** which brims with monuments and paintings by El Greco and is home to one of Spain's greatest cathedrals. Other worthy excursions include a view of the Roman aqueduct at **Segovia,** tours through such monuments as **El Escorial,** and a visit to the "hanging village" of **Cuenca,** site of a world-class museum of modern art.

OLD CASTILE & LEON

The proud kingdoms of Castile and León in north-central Iberia are part of the core from which modern Spain developed. Some of their greatest cathedrals and monuments were erected when each was staunchly independent. But León's annexation by Queen Isabella of Castile in 1474 (5 years after her politically advantageous but unhappy marriage to

Ferdinand of Aragón) irrevocably linked the two regions.

Even Spaniards are sometimes confused about the terms *Old Castile* (see chapter 6) and *New Castile,* a modern linguistic and governmental concept that includes a territory much larger than the medieval entity known by Isabella and her subjects. Although it's easy to take a train to and from Madrid, we don't recommend you try to see the regions' highlights as day trips from Madrid; it's better to treat them as overnight destinations in their own right.

Highlights include **Burgos** (the ancient cradle of Castile), **Salamanca** (a medieval Castilian university town), and **León** (capital on the northern plains of the district bearing its name and site of one of the most unusual cathedrals in Iberia). If time remains, consider an overnight stay at the extraordinary parador (a government-owned inn) in **Ciudad Rodrigo,** as well as trips to **Zamora,** known for its stunning Romanesque churches, and **Valladolid.**

EXTREMADURA

Far from the mainstream of urbanized Spain, fascinating Extremadura lives in a time warp where hints of the Middle Ages and ancient Rome crop up unexpectedly beside sun-baked highways. Many of the conquistadors who pillaged native civilizations in the New World came from this hard, granite land.

Be prepared for hot, arid landscapes and smoking diesel trucks carrying heavy loads through this corridor between Madrid and Lisbon. You can see a lot in about 2 days, stopping off at such sites as **Guadalupe,** whose Mudéjar monastery revolves around the medieval cult of the Dark (or Black) Virgin, and **Trujillo,** where many of the monuments were built with gold sent home by native sons like Pizarro, Peru's conqueror. **Cáceres**

is a beautiful, fortified city with one foot planted firmly in the Middle Ages, while **Zafra** displays greater evidence of the Moorish occupation than anywhere in Spain outside of Andalusia.

ANDALUSIA

In A.D. 711 Muslim armies swept into Iberia from strongholds in what is now Morocco. Since then, Spain's southernmost district has been enmeshed in the mores, art, and architecture of the Muslim world.

During the 900s, *Andalucía* blossomed into a sophisticated society—advanced in philosophy, mathematics, and trading—that far surpassed a feudal Europe still trapped in the Dark Ages. Moorish domination ended completely in 1492, when Granada was captured by the armies of Isabella and Ferdinand, but even today the region offers echoes of this Muslim occupation. Andalusia is a dry district that isn't highly prosperous, despite such economically rejuvenating events as Seville's Expo.

The major cities of Andalusia deserve at least a week, with overnights in **Seville** (hometown of Carmen, Don Giovanni, and the barber); **Córdoba,** site of the Mezquita, one of history's most versatile religious edifices; and **Cádiz,** the seaport where thousands of ships embarked on their colonization of the New World. Perhaps greatest of all is **Granada,** a town of such impressive artistry that it inspired many of the works by the 20th-century romantic poet Federico García Lorca.

THE COSTA DEL SOL

The Costa del Sol sprawls across the southernmost edge of Spain between Algeciras to the west—a few miles from the rocky heights of British-controlled Gibraltar—and Almería to the east. Think traffic jams, suntan oil, sun-bleached high-rises, and near-naked flesh. The beaches here are some of the best in Europe, but this can also be an overly crowded, crime-filled region.

Unless you travel by car or rail from Madrid, chances are you'll arrive by plane via **Málaga,** the district's most historic city. The coast's largest resort town is distinctive, Renaissance-era **Marbella,** the centerpiece of 28km (17 miles) of beaches. Today it's a chic hangout for the tanned and wealthy. **Nerja** is just one of the booming resorts that has kept its out-of-the-way, fishing-village feel. The most overcrowded and action-packed resort is **Torremolinos.** One modern development that has managed to remain distinctive is **Puerto Banús,** a neo-Moorish village curving around a sheltered marina where the wintering rich dock their yachts.

VALENCIA & THE COSTA BLANCA

Valencia, the third-largest city in Spain, is rarely visited by foreign tourists because of the heavy industry that surrounds its inner core. More alluring are such resorts as **Alicante** and **Benidorm** or the medieval town of **Elche** (where some of the world's most famous ancient Roman statues were discovered). Unless you opt to skip Valencia completely, plan to see the city's cathedral, the exterior of its Palacio de la Generalidad, and as many of its three important museums as you can fit into a 1-day trip. For the Costa Blanca, allow as much or as little time as you want to spend on the beach.

BARCELONA & CATALONIA

Barcelona's history is older than that of its rival, Madrid, and its streets are filled with Gothic and medieval buildings that Spain's relatively newer capital lacks. During the 1200s it rivaled the trading prowess of such cities as Genoa and Pisa, and it became the Spanish city that most resembled

other great cities of Europe. Allow yourself at least 3 days to explore the city, with stops at the Picasso Museum, the Joan Miró foundation, the Gothic quarter, and a crowning triumph of early *modernista* (or modernisme) architecture, the Eixample District, where you'll find many of Antoni Gaudí's signature works. Make time for a stroll along Les Rambles, one of the most delightful outdoor promenades in Spain.

Don't overlook Catalonia's other attractions, all within easy reach of Barcelona. A short drive to the south is **Sitges,** a stylish beach resort that caters to a diverse clientele ranging from freewheeling nudists and gay party crowds to fun-seeking families. Other destinations are **Tarragona,** one of ancient Rome's district capitals, and **Montserrat,** the "Serrated Mountain," site of one of Europe's best-preserved medieval monasteries.

THE COSTA BRAVA

It's Spain's other Riviera, a region with a deep sense of medieval history and a topography that's rockier and more interesting than that of the Costa del Sol. The "Wild Coast" stretches from the resort of Blanes, just north of Barcelona, along 153km (95 miles) of dangerously winding cliff-top roads that bypass peninsulas and sheltered coves on their way to the French border. Despite hordes of Spanish and Northern European midsummer visitors, the Costa Brava resorts still manage to feel less congested and less spoiled than those along the Costa del Sol.

Sun worshippers usually head for the twin beachfront resorts of **Lloret de Mar** and **Tossa de Mar.** Travelers interested in the history of 20th-century painting go to **Figueres;** Salvador Dalí was born here in 1904, and a controversial and bizarre museum of his design is devoted exclusively to his surrealist works.

ARAGON

Except for Aragón's association with Ferdinand, the unsavory, often unethical husband of Queen Isabella, few foreign visitors ever thought much about this northeastern quadrant of Iberia. A land of noteworthy Mudéjar architecture and high altitudes that guarantee cool midsummer temperatures, it's also one of the foremost bull-breeding regions of Spain.

Aragón is best visited as a stopover between Barcelona and Madrid. Stay overnight in **Zaragoza,** the district capital, and take a series of day trips to **Tarazona** ("The Toledo of Aragón"), **Calatayud,** and **Daroca,** all important Moorish and Roman military outposts, and **Nuévalos/Piedra,** the site of an extraordinary riverside hotel built in 1194 as a Cistercian monastery. Also worth a trip is **Sos del Rey Católico,** the rocky, relatively unspoiled village where Ferdinand was born.

NAVARRE & LA RIOJA

This strategic province, one of the four original Christian kingdoms in Iberia, shares a border, and numerous historical references, with France. One of France's Renaissance kings, Henri IV "de Navarre," was linked to the province's royal family. Many Navarre customs, and some of its local dialect, reflect the influence of its passionately politicized neighbors, the Basques. Celtic pagans, Romans, Christians, and Arabs have all left architectural reminders of their presence. The province contains nine points where traffic is funneled into and out of Spain, so if you're driving or riding the train, say, from Paris to Madrid, chances are you'll get a fast overview of Navarre. The province's best-known destination is **Pamplona,** the district capital and annual host for the bull-running Fiesta de San Fermín.

One small corner of Navarre is composed of **La Rioja,** the smallest *autonomía* (semiautonomous province) of Spain. Irrigated by the Ebro River, it produces some of the country's finest wines. If wine tasting appeals to you, head for the town of **Haro** and drop in on several bodegas to sample local vintages.

THE BASQUE COUNTRY

This is the native land of Europe's oldest traceable ethnic group. The Basque people have been more heavily persecuted than any other group within Spain, by Madrid regimes determined to shoehorn their unusual language and culture into that of mainstream Spain. The region of rolling peaks and fertile, sunny valleys hugs the Atlantic coast adjacent to the French border. It also boasts the best regional cuisine in Spain.

Unless you want to spend more time relaxing on the beach, allow 3 leisurely days for this unusual district. Visit **San Sebastián** (Donostia) for its international glamour, **Fuenterrabía** (Hondarribía) for its medieval history, **Guernica** for a sobering reminder of the Spanish Civil War, and **Lekeitio** for its simple fishing-village charm.

CANTABRIA & ASTURIAS

Positioned on Iberia's north-central coastline, these are the most verdant regions of Spain. In the Middle Ages, pilgrims passed through here on their way to **Santiago de Compostela**—a legacy evident from the wealth of Romanesque churches and abbeys in the vicinity. Come for beaches that are rainier, but much less crowded, than those along Spain's southern coasts.

Enjoy such beach resorts as **El Sardinero** and **Laredo,** as well as the rugged beauty of **Los Picos de Europa,** a dramatic mountain range that is home to rich colonies of wildlife. Sites of interest include the **Caves of Altamira** (called "the Sistine Chapel of prehistoric art," although admission is strictly regulated), the pre-Romanesque town of **Oviedo,** and the architecturally important old quarter of **Gijón.** The region's largest city, **Santander,** lies amid a maze of peninsulas and estuaries favored by boaters. In summer it becomes a major beach resort, although **San Sebastián** is more fashionable.

GALICIA

A true Celtic outpost in northwestern Iberia, Galicia's landscape is often compared to rainy, windswept Ireland. Known for a spectacularly dramatic coastline, the region is wild and relatively underpopulated. Spend at least 2 days here enjoying some of the most scenic drives in Iberia. Stop at historic and religious sites like **Santiago de Compostela** or the ancient Roman outpost of **Lugo.** Perhaps the region's greatest city is **La Coruña,** the point of embarkation for Spain's tragic Armada, sunk by the English army on its way to invade Britain in the late l6th century.

THE BALEARIC ISLANDS

"Discovered" by English Romantics in the early 19th century, and long known as a strategic naval outpost in the western Mediterranean, these islands are sunny, subtropical, mountainous, and more verdant than the Costa del Sol. They have their pockets of style and posh, although Majorca and Ibiza are overrun in summer, especially by British and German travelers on package tours. Ibiza also attracts a large gay crowd. Minorca is more fashionable, although more inconvenient to get to.

2 Visitor Information

VISITOR INFORMATION

TOURIST OFFICES The Tourist Office of Spain's official page can be found on the Net at **www.okspain. org.**

In the U.S. 666 Fifth Ave., 35th Floor, New York, NY 10103 (*©* **212/ 265-8822;** fax 212/265-8864); 845 N. Michigan Ave., Suite 915E, Chicago, IL 60611 (*©* **312/642- 1992;** fax 312/642-9817); 8383 Wilshire Blvd., Suite 956, Beverly Hills, CA 90211 (*©* **323/658-7188;** fax 323/658-1061); 1221 Brickell Ave., Suite 1850, Miami, FL 33131 (*©* **305/358-1992;** fax 305/358- 8223).

In Canada 2 Bloor St. W., Suite 3402, Toronto, ON M5S 1M9 (*©* **416/961-3131;** fax 416/961- 1992).

In the U.K. 22–23 Manchester Sq., London W1M 5AP (*©* **00891/66- 99-20** or 020/7486-8077; fax 020/ 7486-8034).

WEBSITES For general info on the Net, check out **www.okspain.org,** the official page of the Tourist Office of Spain; **www.red2000.com;** or **www. cyberspain.com.** You'll find more details at **www.softguides.com.** If you're interested in the Prado's treasures, go to **www.mcu.es.** The highly personalized **www.madridman.com** has a home page that sounds frivolous but provides a surprising amount of info.

3 Entry Requirements & Customs

ENTRY REQUIREMENTS

Visas are not needed by U.S., Canadian, Irish, Australian, New Zealand, or British citizens for visits of less than 3 months. You do need a valid passport unless you're a citizen of another E.U. country (in which case you need only an identity card, although we always recommend you carry a passport anyway).

Safeguard your passport in an inconspicuous, inaccessible place like a money belt. If you lose it, visit the nearest consulate of your native country as soon as possible for a replacement.

For information on how to get a passport, go to the Fast Facts section of this chapter—the websites listed provide downloadable passport applications as well as the current fees for processing passport applications. For an up-to-date country-by-country listing of passport requirements around the world, go the "Foreign Entry Requirement" Web page of the U.S. State Department at **http://travel. state.gov/foreignentryreqs.html**.

CUSTOMS
WHAT YOU CAN BRING INTO SPAIN

You can take into Spain most personal effects and the following items duty free: a portable typewriter, one video camera or two still cameras with 10 rolls of film each. A portable radio, a tape recorder, and a laptop PC per person are admitted free of duty provided they show signs of use; 200 cigarettes, or 50 cigars, or 250 grams of tobacco; and 2 liters of wine or 1 liter of liquor per person over 17 years of age. Sports equipment: fishing gear, one bicycle, skis, tennis or squash racquets, and golf clubs.

WHAT YOU CAN TAKE HOME FROM SPAIN

Returning **U.S. citizens** who have been away for at least 48 hours are allowed to bring back, once every 30 days, $800 worth of merchandise duty-free. You'll be charged a flat rate of 4% duty on the next $1,000 worth of purchases. Be sure to have your receipts handy. On mailed gifts, the duty-free limit is $200. With some

Destination Spain: Red Alert Checklist

- If you purchased traveler's checks, have you recorded the check numbers, and stored the documentation separately from the checks?
- Did you stop the newspaper and mail delivery, and leave a set of keys with someone reliable?
- Did you pack your camera and an extra set of camera batteries, and purchase enough film? If you packed film in your checked baggage, did you invest in protective pouches to shield film from airport X-rays?
- Do you have a safe, accessible place to store money?
- Did you bring your ID cards that could entitle you to discounts such as AAA and AARP cards, student IDs, and so on?
- Did you bring emergency drug prescriptions and extra glasses and/or contact lenses?
- Did you find out your daily ATM withdrawal limit?
- Do you have your credit card PINs? Is there a daily withdrawal limit on credit card cash advances?
- If you have an E-ticket, do you have documentation?
- Did you leave a copy of your itinerary with someone at home?
- Do you have the measurements for those people you plan to buy clothes for on your trip?
- Do you have the address and phone number of your country's embassy with you?

Tips   Passport Savvy

Allow plenty of time before your trip to apply for a passport; processing normally takes 6 weeks (3 weeks expedited) but can take longer during busy periods, especially spring. And keep in mind that if you need a passport in a hurry, you'll pay a higher processing fee. When traveling, safeguard your passport in an inconspicuous, inaccessible place like a money belt and keep a copy of the critical pages with your passport number in a separate place. If you lose your passport, visit the nearest consulate of your native country as soon as possible for a replacement.

---

exceptions, you cannot bring fresh fruits and vegetables into the United States. For specifics on what you can bring back, download the invaluable free pamphlet *Know Before You Go* online at **www.customs.gov**. (Click on "Travel," then "Know Before You Go Online Brochure.") Or contact the **U.S. Customs Service,** 1300 Pennsylvania Ave. NW, Washington, DC 20229 (© **877/287-8667**), and request the pamphlet.

For a clear summary of **Canadian** rules, write for the booklet *I Declare,* issued by the **Canada Customs and Revenue Agency** (© **800/461-9999** in Canada, or 204/983-3500; www.ccra-adrc.gc.ca). Canada allows its citizens a C$750 exemption, and you're allowed to bring back duty-free one carton of cigarettes, 1 can of tobacco, 40 imperial ounces of liquor, and 50 cigars. In addition, you're allowed to mail gifts to Canada valued at less than C$60 a day, provided they're unsolicited and don't contain alcohol or tobacco (write on the package "Unsolicited gift, under $60 value"). All valuables should be declared on the Y-38 form before departure from Canada, including serial numbers of valuables you already own, such as expensive foreign cameras. *Note:* The $750 exemption can only be used once a year and only after an absence of 7 days.

Citizens of the U.K. who are **returning from a European Union** **(E.U.) country** will go through a separate Customs Exit (called the "Blue Exit") especially for E.U. travelers. In essence, there is no limit on what you can bring back from an E.U. country, as long as the items are for personal use (this includes gifts), and you have already paid the necessary duty and tax. However, customs law sets out guidance levels. If you bring in more than these levels, you may be asked to prove that the goods are for your own use. Guidance levels on goods bought in the E.U. for your own use are 3,200 cigarettes, 200 cigars, 400 cigarillos, 3 kilograms of smoking tobacco, 10 liters of spirits, 90 liters of wine, 20 liters of fortified wine (such as port or sherry), and 110 liters of beer.

The duty-free allowance in **Australia** is A$400 or, for those under 18, A$200. Citizens can bring in 250 cigarettes or 250 grams of loose tobacco, and 1,125 milliliters of alcohol. If you're returning with valuables you already own, such as foreign-made cameras, you should file form B263. A helpful brochure available from Australian consulates or Customs offices is *Know Before You Go.* For more information, call the **Australian Customs Service** at © **1300/363-263,** or log on to www.customs.gov.au.

The duty-free allowance for **New Zealand** is NZ$700. Citizens over 17 can bring in 200 cigarettes, 50 cigars, or 250 grams of tobacco (or a mixture of all 3 if their combined weight doesn't exceed 250g); plus 4.5 liters of wine and beer, or 1,125 milliliters of liquor. New Zealand currency does not carry import or export restrictions. Fill out a certificate of export, listing the valuables you are taking out of the country; that way, you can bring them back without paying duty. Most questions are answered in a free pamphlet available at New Zealand consulates and Customs offices: *New Zealand Customs Guide for Travellers, Notice no. 4.* For more information, contact **New Zealand Customs,** The Customhouse, 17–21 Whitmore St., Box 2218, Wellington (*C* **04/473-6099,** or 0800/428-786 in New Zealand; www.customs.govt.nz).

4 Money

If there is one thing old Spaniards wax nostalgically over, it's not the police state they experienced under the dictatorship of Franco, but the prices paid back then. How they miss the days when you could go into a restaurant and order a meal with wine for 50 U.S. cents.

Regrettably Spain is no longer a budget destination. In such major cities as Barcelona or Madrid, you can often find hotels charging the same prices as in London or Paris. Once you move beyond Spain's tourist meccas into regional towns, provincial capitals, and especially the countryside, the prices drop considerably. For example, it's possible to enjoy a 6-week vacation in rural Spain for about the same price that 10 days to 2 weeks could cost in Madrid.

Taken as a whole, though, Spain remains slightly below the cost-of-living index of such countries as England, Italy, Germany, and France. Unless the current monetary situation is drastically altered, there is a very favorable exchange rate in Spain when you pay in U.S. dollars.

Prices in Spain are generally high, but you get good value for your money. Hotels are usually clean and comfortable, and restaurants generally offer good cuisine and ample portions made with quality ingredients. Trains are fast and on time, and most service personnel treat you with respect.

In Spain, many prices for children—generally defined as ages 6 to 17—are lower than for adults. Fees for children under 6 are generally waived.

CURRENCY

The **euro (€),** the new single European currency, became the official currency of Spain and 11 other participating countries on January 1, 1999. However, the euro didn't go into general circulation until early in 2002. The old currency, the Spanish peseta, disappeared into history on March 1, 2002, replaced by the euro, whose official abbreviation is "EUR." Exchange rates of participating countries are locked into a common currency fluctuating against the dollar.

For more details on the euro, check out **www.europa.eu.int/euro**.

Regarding the Euro

Since the euro's inception, the U.S. dollar and the euro have traded almost on par (i.e., $1 equals approximately 1€); therefore, all prices in this book are given in euros. But as this book went to press, 1€ was worth approximately $1.15 and gaining in strength, so your dollars might not go as far as you'd expect. For up-to-the minute exchange rates between the euro and the dollar, check the currency converter website www.xe.com/ucc.

It's a good idea to exchange at least some money—just enough to cover airport incidentals and transportation to your hotel—before you leave home, so you can avoid lines at airport ATMs (automated teller machines). You can exchange money at your local American Express or Thomas Cook office or your bank. If you're far away from a bank with currency-exchange services, American Express offers traveler's checks and foreign currency, though with a $15 order fee and additional shipping costs, at www.american express.com or **800/807-6233.**

ATMS

The easiest and best way to get cash away from home is from an ATM (automated teller machine). The **Cirrus** (✆ **800/424-7787;** www.master card.com) and **PLUS** (✆ **800/843-7587;** www.visa.com) networks span the globe; look at the back of your bank card to see which network you're on, then call or check online for ATM locations at your destination. Be sure you know your personal identification number (PIN) before you leave home and be sure to find out your daily withdrawal limit before you depart. Also keep in mind that many banks impose a fee every time a card is used at a different bank's ATM, and that fee can be higher for international transactions (up to $5 or more) than for domestic ones (where they're rarely more than $1.50). On top of this, the bank from which you withdraw cash may charge its own fee. To compare banks' ATM fees within the U.S., use www.bankrate.com. For international withdrawal fees, ask your bank.

You can also get cash advances on your credit card at an ATM. Keep in mind that credit card companies try to protect themselves from theft by limiting the funds someone can withdraw outside their home country, so call your credit card company before you leave home.

TRAVELER'S CHECKS

Traveler's checks are something of an anachronism from the days before the ATM made cash accessible at any time. Traveler's checks used to be the only sound alternative to traveling with dangerously large amounts of cash. They were as reliable as currency, but, unlike cash, could be replaced if lost or stolen.

These days, traveler's checks are less necessary because most cities have 24-hour ATMs that allow you to withdraw small amounts of cash as needed. However, keep in mind that you will likely be charged an ATM withdrawal fee if the bank is not your own, so if you're withdrawing money every day, you might be better off with traveler's checks—provided that you don't mind showing identification every time you want to cash one.

You can get traveler's checks at almost any bank. **American Express** offers denominations of $20, $50, $100, $500, and (for cardholders only) $1,000. You'll pay a service charge ranging from 1% to 4%. You can also get American Express traveler's checks over the phone by calling ✆ **800/221-7282;** Amex gold and platinum cardholders who use this number are exempt from the 1% fee.

> *Tips* **Small Change**
>
> When you change money, ask for some small bills or loose change. Petty cash will come in handy for tipping and public transportation. Consider keeping the change separate from your larger bills, so that it's readily accessible and you'll be less of a target for theft.

Visa offers traveler's checks at Citibank locations nationwide, as well as at several other banks. The service charge ranges between 1.5% and 2%; checks come in denominations of $20, $50, $100, $500, and $1,000. Call ✆ **800/732-1322** for information. AAA members can obtain checks without a fee at most AAA offices. **MasterCard** also offers traveler's checks. Call ✆ **800/223-9920** for a location near you.

Foreign currency traveler's checks are useful if you're traveling to one country, or to the euro zone; they're accepted at locations such as bed & breakfasts where dollar checks may not be, and they minimize the amount of math you have to do at your destination. **American Express** offers checks in Australian dollars, Canadian dollars, British pounds, euros, and Japanese yen. **Visa** checks come in Australian, Canadian, British, and euro versions; **MasterCard** offers those four plus yen and South African rands.

If you choose to carry traveler's checks, be sure to keep a record of their serial numbers separate from your checks in the event that they are stolen or lost. You'll get a refund faster if you know the numbers.

CREDIT CARDS

Credit cards are a safe way to carry money, they provide a convenient record of all your expenses, and they generally offer good exchange rates. You can also withdraw cash advances from your credit cards at banks or ATMs, provided you know your PIN. If you've forgotten yours, or didn't even know you had one, call the number on the back of your credit card and ask the bank to send it to you. It usually takes 5 to 7 business days, though some banks will provide the number over the phone if you tell them your mother's maiden name or some other personal information. Your credit card company will likely charge a commission (1% or 2%) on every foreign purchase you make, but don't sweat this small stuff; for most purchases, you'll still get the best deal with credit cards when you factor in things like ATM fees and higher traveler's check exchange rates.

In Spain, American Express, Diners Club, MasterCard, and Visa are commonly accepted, with the latter two cards predominating. For tips and telephone numbers to call if your wallet is stolen or lost, go to "Police" in "Fast Facts," later in this chapter.

5 When to Go

Spring and fall are ideal times to visit nearly all of Spain, with the possible exception of the Atlantic coast, which experiences heavy rains in October and November. May and October are the best months, in terms of both weather and crowds.

In summer it's hot, hot, and hotter still, with the cities in Castile (Madrid) and Andalusia (Seville and Córdoba) heating up the most. Madrid has dry heat; the average temperature can hover around 84°F (29°C) in July and 75°F (24°C) in September. Seville has the dubious reputation of being about the hottest part of Spain in July and August, often baking under average temperatures of 93°F (34°C).

Barcelona, cooler in temperature, is often quite humid. Midsummer temperatures in Majorca often reach 91°F (33°C). The overcrowded Costa Brava has temperatures around 81°F (27°C) in July and August. The Costa del Sol has an average of 77°F (25°C) in summer. The coolest spot in Spain is the Atlantic coast from San Sebastián to La Coruña, with temperatures in the 70s in July and August.

August remains the major vacation month in Europe. The traffic from France, the Netherlands, and Germany to Spain becomes a veritable migration, and low-cost hotels along the coastal areas are virtually impossible to find. To compound the problem, many restaurants and shops also decide it's time for a vacation, thereby limiting the visitors' selections for both dining and shopping.

In winter, the coast from Algeciras to Málaga is the most popular, with temperatures reaching a warm 60°F to 63°F (16°C–17°C). Madrid gets cold, as low as 34°F (1°C). Majorca is warmer, usually in the 50s, but it often dips into the 40s. Some mountain resorts can experience extreme cold.

Weather Chart for Spain

Barcelona

	Jan	Feb	Mar	Apr	May	June	July	Aug	Sept	Oct	Nov	Dec
Temp. (°F)	48	49	52	55	61	68	73	73	70	63	55	50
Temp. (°C)	9	9	11	13	16	20	23	23	21	17	13	10
Rainfall (in.)	1.70	1.40	1.90	2.00	2.20	1.50	.90	1.60	3.10	3.70	2.90	2.00

Basque Coast (N. Coast)

	Jan	Feb	Mar	Apr	May	June	July	Aug	Sept	Oct	Nov	Dec
Temp. (°F)	45	48	51	52	55	65	67	67	61	53	52	48
Temp. (°C)	7	9	11	11	13	18	19	19	16	12	11	9
Rainfall (in.)	.91	.83	.91	1.30	1.50	1.22	.59	.67	1.02	1.18	1.42	.83

Madrid

	Jan	Feb	Mar	Apr	May	June	July	Aug	Sept	Oct	Nov	Dec
Temp. (°F)	42	45	49	53	60	69	76	75	69	58	48	43
Temp. (°C)	6	7	9	12	16	21	24	24	21	14	9	6
Rainfall (in.)	1.60	1.80	1.20	1.80	1.50	1.00	.30	.40	1.10	1.50	2.30	1.70

Málaga (S. Coast)

	Jan	Feb	Mar	Apr	May	June	July	Aug	Sept	Oct	Nov	Dec
Temp. (°F)	54	54	64	70	73	81	84	86	81	73	68	63
Temp. (°C)	12	12	18	21	23	27	29	30	27	23	20	17
Rainfall (in.)	2.40	2.01	2.44	1.81	1.02	.20	.04	.12	1.14	2.52	2.52	2.44

Seville

	Jan	Feb	Mar	Apr	May	June	July	Aug	Sept	Oct	Nov	Dec
Temp. (°F)	59	63	68	75	81	90	97	97	90	79	68	61
Temp. (°C)	15	17	20	24	27	32	36	36	32	26	20	16
Rainfall (in.)	2.60	2.40	3.60	2.30	1.60	.30	0	.20	.80	2.80	2.70	3.20

HOLIDAYS

Holidays include January 1 (New Year's Day), January 6 (Feast of the Epiphany), March 19 (Feast of St. Joseph), Good Friday, Easter Monday, May 1 (May Day), June 10 (Corpus Christi), June 29 (Feast of St. Peter and St. Paul), July 25 (Feast of St. James), August 15 (Feast of the Assumption), October 12 (Spain's National Day), November 1 (All Saints' Day), December 8 (Immaculate Conception), and December 25 (Christmas).

Tips **On Time in Spain**

In Spain a time change occurs the first weekend of spring. Check your watch. Many unsuspecting visitors have arrived at the airport too late and missed their planes.

No matter how large or small, every city or town in Spain also celebrates its local saint's day. In Madrid it's May 15 (St. Isidro). You'll rarely know what the local holidays are in your next destination in Spain. Try to keep money on hand, because you may arrive in town only to find banks and stores closed. In some cases, intercity bus services are suspended on holidays.

SPAIN CALENDAR OF EVENTS

The dates given below may not be precise. Sometimes the exact days are not announced until 6 weeks before the actual festival. Check with the National Tourist Office of Spain (see "Visitor Information," earlier in this chapter) if you're planning to attend a specific event.

January

Granada Reconquest Festival, Granada. The whole city celebrates the Christians' victory over the Moors in 1492. The highest tower at the Alhambra is open to the public on January 2. For information, contact the Tourist Office of Granada (*©* **95-824-71-28**). January 2.

Día de los Reyes (Three Kings Day), throughout Spain. Parades are held around the country on the eve of the Festival of the Epiphany. Various "kings" dispense candy to all the kids. January 6.

Día de San Antonio (St. Anthony's Day), La Puebla, Majorca. Bonfires, dancing, revelers dressed as devils, and other riotous events honor St. Anthony on the eve of his day. January 17.

February

Bocairente Festival of Christians and Moors, Bocairente (Valencia). Fireworks, colorful costumes, parades, and a reenactment of the struggle between Christians and Moors mark this exuberant festival. A stuffed effigy of Mohammed is blown to bits. Call *©* **96-290-50-62** for more information. First week of February.

ARCO (Madrid's International Contemporary Art Fair), Madrid. One of the biggest draws on Spain's cultural calendar, this exhibit showcases the best in contemporary art from Europe and America. At the Nuevo Recinto Ferial Juan Carlos I, the exhibition draws galleries from throughout Europe, the Americas, Australia, and Asia, who bring with them the works of regional and internationally known artists. To buy tickets contact Parque Ferial Juan Carlos I at *©* **91-722-50-00.** The cost is between 19€ and 23€. You can get schedules from the tourist office closer to the event. Dates vary, but usually mid-February. For more information, call *©* **90-240-02-22.**

Madrid Carnaval. The carnival kicks off with a big parade along the Paseo de la Castellana, culminating in a masked ball at the Círculo de Bellas Artes on the following night. Fancy-dress competitions last until February 28, when the festivities end with a tear-jerking "burial of a sardine" at the Fuente de los Pajaritos in the Casa de Campo. This is followed that evening by a concert in the Plaza Mayor. Call ✆ **91-429-31-77** for more information. Dates vary. Normally 40 days before Easter.

Carnavales de Cádiz, Cádiz. The oldest and best-attended carnival in Spain is a freewheeling event full of costumes, parades, strolling troubadours, and drum beating. Call ✆ **95-622-71-11** or go to www.carnavaldecadiz.com for more information. Late February or early March.

March

Fallas de Valencia, Valencia. Dating from the 1400s, this fiesta centers around the burning of papier-mâché effigies of winter demons. Burnings are preceded by bullfights, fireworks, and parades. Call ✆ **96-351-04-17** for more information. March 12 to March 19.

April

Semana Santa (Holy Week), Seville. Although many of the country's smaller towns stage similar celebrations (especially notable in Zamora), the festivities in Seville are by far the most elaborate. From Palm Sunday until Easter Sunday a series of processions with hooded penitents moves to the piercing wail of the *saeta,* a love song to the Virgin or Christ. *Pasos* (heavy floats) bear images of the Virgin or Christ. Again, make hotel reservations way in advance. Call the Seville Office of Tourism for details (✆ **95-422-14-04**). The week before Easter (Apr 4–10, 2004).

Feria de Sevilla (Seville Fair). This is the most celebrated week of revelry in all of Spain, with all-night flamenco dancing, entertainment booths, bullfights, horseback riding, flower-decked coaches, and dancing in the streets. You'll need to reserve a hotel early for this one. For general information and exact festival dates, contact the Office of Tourism in Seville (✆ **95-422-1404**). Second week after Easter.

May

Moros y Cristianos (Moors and Christians), Alcoy, near Alicante. During 3 days every April, the centuries-old battle between the Moors and the Christians is restaged with soldiers in period costumes. Naturally, the Christians who drove the Moors from Spain always win. The simulated fighting takes on almost a circuslike flair, and the costumes worn by the Moors are always absurd and anachronistic. Call ✆ **96-520-00-00** for more information. May 2 to May 5, 2004.

Feria del Caballo, Jerez de la Frontera. The major wine festival in Andalusia honors the famous sherry of Jerez, with 5 days of processions, flamenco dancing, livestock on parade, and, of course, sherry drinking. For information, call ✆ **95-633-11-50.** May 11 to May 18, 2004.

Festival de los Patios, Córdoba. At this famous fair residents decorate their patios with cascades of flowers. Visitors wander from patio to patio. Call ✆ **95-747-12-35** for more information. May 6 to May 18, 2004.

Fiesta de San Isidro, Madrid. Madrileños run wild with a 10-day celebration honoring their city's patron saint. Food fairs, Castilian folkloric events, street parades, parties, music, dances, bullfights, and other festivities mark the occasion. Make hotel reservations early. Expect crowds and traffic (and beware of pickpockets). For information, write to Oficina Municipal de Información y Turismo, Plaza Mayor 3, 28014 Madrid, or call ✆ **91-588-16-36.** Second week of May.

Romería del Rocío (Pilgrimage of the Virgin of the Dew), El Rocío (Huelva). The most famous pilgrimage in Andalusia attracts a million people. Fifty men carry the statue of the Virgin 14.5km (9 miles) to Almonte for consecration. May 14 to May 24.

June

Corpus Christi, all over Spain. A major holiday on the Spanish calendar, this event is marked by big processions, especially in Toledo, Málaga, Seville, and Granada. June 2, 2004.

Veranos de la Villa, Madrid. This program presents folkloric dancing, pop music, classical music, zarzuelas, and flamenco at various venues throughout the city. Open-air cinema is a feature in the Parque del Retiro. Ask at the tourist office for complete details (the program changes every summer). Sometimes admission is charged, but often these events are free. Mid-June until the end of August.

International Music and Dance Festival, Granada. Celebrating its 54th year in 2004, Granada's prestigious program of dance and music attracts international artists who perform at the Alhambra and other venues. It's a major event on the cultural calendar of Europe. Reserve well in advance. For a complete schedule and tickets, contact El Festival Internacional de Música y Danza de Granada (© **95-822-18-44**). June 20 to July 6, 2004.

Las Hogueras de San Juan (St. John's Bonfires), Alicante. On June 20 to 24 during the summer solstice, bonfires blaze through the night to honor the event, just as they did in Celtic and Roman times. The bonfire signals the launching of 5 days of gala celebrations with fireworks and parades.

Business in Alicante comes to a standstill. Call © **96-520-00-00** for more information. June 20 to June 24, 2004.

Verbena de Sant Joan, Barcelona. This traditional festival occupies all Cataláns. Barcelona literally lights up—with fireworks, bonfires, and dances until dawn. The highlight of the festival is the fireworks show at Montjuïc. June 23 and June 24, 2004.

July

La Rapa das Bestas (The Capture of the Beasts), San Lorenzo de Sabucedo, Galicia. Spain's greatest horse roundup attracts equestrian lovers from throughout Europe. Horses in the verdant hills of northwestern Spain are rounded up, branded, and medically checked before their release into the wild again. For more information, phone © **98-685-08-14.** First Sunday in July.

Festival of St. James, Santiago de Compostela. Pomp and ceremony mark this annual pilgrimage to the tomb of St. James the Apostle in Galicia. Galician folklore shows, concerts, parades, and the swinging of the *botafumeiro* (a mammoth incense burner) mark the event. July 15 to July 30, 2004.

Fiesta de San Fermín, Pamplona. Vividly described in Ernest Hemingway's novel *The Sun Also Rises,* the running of the bulls through the streets of Pamplona is the most popular celebration in Spain. It also includes wine tasting, fireworks, and, of course, bullfights. Reserve many months in advance. For more information, such as a list of accommodations, contact the Office of Tourism, Calle Eslava 1, 31002 Pamplona (© **94-0820-65-40**). July 6 to July 14, 2004.

San Sebastián Jazz Festival, San Sebastián. Having celebrated its 35th year in 2000, this festival brings together the jazz greats of the world at the pavilion of the Anoeta Sport Complex. Other programs take place alfresco at the Plaza de Trinidad in the old quarter. The Office of the San Sebastián Jazz Festival (© **94-344-00-34**) can provide schedules and tickets. July 24 to July 29, 2004.

August

Santander International Festival of Music and Dance, Santander. The repertoire includes classical music, ballet, contemporary dance, chamber music, and recitals. Most performances are staged at the Plaza de la Porticada. For further information, contact Festival Internacional de Santander (© **94-221-05-08**). Throughout August.

Fiestas of Lavapiés and La Paloma, Madrid. These two fiestas begin with the Lavapiés on August 1 and continue through the hectic La Paloma celebration on August 15, the day of the Virgen de la Paloma. During the fiestas, thousands of people race through the narrow streets. Apartment dwellers hurl buckets of cold water onto the crowds below to cool them off. There are children's games, floats, music, flamenco, and zarzuelas, along with street fairs. For more information, call © **91-429-31-77.** August 1 to August 15, 2004.

The Mystery Play of Elche. This sacred drama is reenacted in the 17th-century Basilica of Santa María in Elche (near Alicante). It represents the Assumption and the Crowning of the Virgin. For tickets, call the Office of Tourism in Elche (© **96-545-38-31**). August 11 to August 15, 2004.

Feria de Málaga (Málaga Fair). One of the longest summer fairs in southern Europe (generally lasting 10 days), this celebration kicks off with fireworks displays and is highlighted by a parade of Arabian horses pulling brightly decorated carriages. Participants are dressed in colorful Andalusian garb. Plazas rattle with castanets, and wine is dispensed by the gallon. For information, call © **95-221-34-45.** Always the weekend before August 19.

La Tomatina (Battle of the Tomatoes), Buñol (Valencia). This is one of the most photographed festivals in Spain, growing in popularity every year. Truckloads of tomatoes are shipped into Buñol, where they become vegetable missiles between warring towns and villages. Portable showers are brought in for the cleanup, followed by music for dancing and singing. For information, call © **96-398-64-22.** Last Wednesday in August.

September

Diada de Catalunya, Barcelona. This is the most significant festival in Catalonia. It celebrates the region's autonomy from the rest of Spain, following years of repression under the dictator Franco. Demonstrations and other flag-waving events take place. The *senyera,* the flag of Catalonia, is everywhere. Not your typical tourist fare, but interesting. September 11, 2004.

International Film Festival, San Sebastián. The premier film festival of Spain takes place in the Basque capital, often at the Victoria Eugenia Theater, a Belle Epoque masterpiece. Retrospectives are often featured, and weeklong screenings are held. For more information, call © **94-348-12-12.** Second week in September.

Fiestas de la Merced, Barcelona. This celebration honors Nostra Senyora de la Merced, the city's patron saint, known for her compassion for animals. Beginning after dark, and after a Mass in the Iglesia de la Merced, a procession of as many as 50 "animals" (humans dressed like tigers, lions, and horses) proceeds with lots of firecrackers and sparklers to the Cathedral of Santa Eulalia, then on to the Plaza de Sant Jaume, and eventually into Les Rambles, Plaza de Catalunya, and the harbor front. For more information, call © 93-478-47-04. September 24, 2004.

October

St. Teresa Week, Avila. Verbenas (carnivals), parades, singing, and dancing honor the patron saint of this walled city. October 8 to October 15, 2004.

Autumn Festival, Madrid. Both Spanish and international artists participate in this cultural program, with a series of operatic, ballet, dance, music, and theatrical performances from Strasbourg to Tokyo. This event is a premier attraction, yet tickets are reasonable. Make hotel reservations early. For tickets, contact Festival de Otoño, Plaza de España 8, 28008 Madrid (© **91-580-25-75**). Late October to late November.

November

All Saints' Day, all over Spain. This public holiday is reverently celebrated, as relatives and friends lay flowers on the graves of the dead. November 1, 2004.

December

Día de los Santos Inocentes, all over Spain. This equivalent of April Fools' Day is an excuse for people to do loco things. December 28, 2004.

6 Travel Insurance

Since Spain for most of us is far from home, and a number of things could go wrong—lost luggage, trip cancellation, a medical emergency—consider the following types of insurance.

Check your existing insurance policies and credit-card coverage before you buy travel insurance. You may already be covered for lost luggage, canceled tickets, or medical expenses. The cost of travel insurance varies widely, depending on the cost and length of your trip, your age, health, and the type of trip you're taking.

TRIP-CANCELLATION INSURANCE Trip-cancellation insurance helps you get your money back if you have to back out of a trip, if you have to go home early, or if your travel supplier goes bankrupt. Allowed reasons for cancellation can range from sickness to natural disasters to the State Department declaring your destination unsafe for travel. (Insurers usually won't cover vague fears, though, as many travelers discovered who tried to cancel their trips in Oct 2001 because they were wary of flying.) In this unstable world, trip-cancellation insurance is a good buy if you're getting tickets well in advance—who knows what the state of the world, or of your airline, will be in 9 months? Insurance policy details vary, so read the fine print—and especially make sure that your airline or cruise line is on the list of carriers covered in case of bankruptcy. For information, contact one of the following insurers: **Access America** (© 866/807-3982; www.accessamerica.com); **Travel Guard International** (© 800/826-4919; www.travelguard.com); **Travel Insured International** (© 800/243-3174; www.travelinsured.com); and **Travelex Insurance Services** (© 888/457-4602; www.travelex-insurance.com).

MEDICAL INSURANCE Most health insurance policies cover you if you get sick away from home—but check, particularly if you're insured by an HMO. With the exception of certain HMOs and Medicare/Medicaid, your medical insurance should cover medical treatment—even hospital care—overseas. However, most out-of-country hospitals make you pay your bills up front, and send you a refund after you've returned home and filed the necessary paperwork. And in a worst-case scenario, there's the high cost of emergency evacuation. If you require additional medical insurance, try **MEDEX International** (© 888/MEDEX-00 or 410/453-6300; www.medexassist.com) or **Travel Assistance International** (© 800/821-2828; www.travelassistance.com; for general information on services, call the company's Worldwide Assistance Services, Inc., at © 800/777-8710).

LOST-LUGGAGE INSURANCE
On international flights (including U.S. portions of international trips), coverage on baggage is limited to approximately $9.05 per pound, up to approximately $635 per checked bag. If you plan to check items more valuable than the standard liability, see if your valuables are covered by your homeowner's policy, get baggage insurance as part of your comprehensive travel-insurance package, or buy Travel Guard's "BagTrak" product. Don't buy insurance at the airport, as it's usually overpriced. Be sure to take any valuables or irreplaceable items with you in your carry-on luggage, as many valuables (including books, money, and electronics) aren't covered by airline policies.

If your luggage is lost, immediately file a lost-luggage claim at the airport, detailing the luggage contents. For most airlines, you must report delayed, damaged, or lost baggage within 4 hours of arrival. The airlines are required to deliver luggage, once found, directly to your house or destination free of charge.

7 Health & Safety

STAYING HEALTHY

Spain should not pose any major health hazards. The rich cuisine—garlic, olive oil, and wine—may give some travelers mild diarrhea, so take along some antidiarrhea medicine, moderate your eating habits, and even though the water is generally safe, drink mineral water only. Fish and shellfish from the horrendously polluted Mediterranean should only be eaten if cooked.

If you are traveling around Spain (particularly southern Spain) over the summer, limit your exposure to the sun, especially during the first few days of your trip and, thereafter, from 11am to 2pm. Use a sunscreen with a high protection factor and apply it liberally. Remember that children need more protection than adults do.

The water is safe to drink throughout Spain; however, do not drink the water in mountain streams, regardless of how clear and pure it looks.

WHAT TO DO IF YOU GET SICK AWAY FROM HOME

Spanish medical facilities are among the best in the world. If a medical emergency arises, your hotel staff can usually put you in touch with a reliable doctor. If not, contact the American embassy or a consulate; each one maintains a list of English-speaking doctors. Medical and hospital services aren't free, so be sure that you have appropriate insurance coverage before you travel.

If you worry about getting sick away from home, consider purchasing **medical travel insurance** and carry your ID card in your purse or wallet. In most cases, your existing health plan will provide the coverage you need. See the section on insurance earlier in this chapter for more information.

Tips Quick ID

Tie a colorful ribbon or piece of yarn around your luggage handle, or slap a distinctive sticker on the side of your bag. This makes it less likely that someone will mistakenly appropriate it. And if your luggage gets lost, it will be easier to find.

If you suffer from a chronic illness, consult your doctor before your departure. For conditions like epilepsy, diabetes, or heart problems, wear a **Medic Alert Identification Tag** (✆ 800/825-3785; www.medic alert.org), which will immediately alert doctors to your condition and give them access to your records through Medic Alert's 24-hour hot line.

Pack **prescription medications** in your carry-on luggage, and carry prescription medications in their original containers, with pharmacy labels—otherwise they won't make it through airport security. Also bring along copies of your prescriptions in case you lose your pills or run out. Don't forget an extra pair of contact lenses or prescription glasses. Carry the generic name of prescription medicines, in case a local pharmacist is unfamiliar with the brand name.

Contact the **International Association for Medical Assistance to Travelers (IAMAT)** (✆ 716/754-4883 or 416/652-0137; www.iamat.org) for tips on travel and health concerns in the countries you're visiting, and lists of local, English-speaking doctors. The United States **Centers for Disease Control and Prevention** (✆ 800/311-3435; www.cdc.gov) provides up-to-date information on necessary vaccines and health hazards by region or country. Any foreign consulate can provide a list of area doctors who speak English. If you get sick, consider asking your hotel concierge to recommend a local doctor—even his or her own. You can also try the emergency room at a local hospital; many have walk-in clinics for emergency cases that are not life threatening. You may not get immediate attention, but you won't pay the high price of an emergency room visit.

STAYING SAFE

The ETA terrorist organization remains active in Spain. Although ETA efforts have historically been directed against police, military, and other Spanish government targets, in March 2001, ETA issued a communiqué announcing its intention to target Spanish tourist areas. Americans have not been the specific targets of ETA activities. The Spanish government is vigorously engaged in combating terrorism at home and abroad and has been able to avert many terrorist activities. Over the years, ETA has conducted many successful attacks, many of which have resulted in deaths and injuries. In 2002, ETA attacks included a number of car bomb incidents, which occurred in areas frequented by tourists, including the Madrid and Málaga airports. While there were no tourist fatalities from any of these incidents, a number of innocent bystanders suffered injuries. A smaller Marxist group, GRAPO, has also mounted several attacks since 1999 and killed three people. U.S. tourists traveling to Spain should exercise caution and refer to the guidance offered in the Worldwide Caution Public Announcements issued in the wake of the September 11, 2001, terrorist attacks.

While most of Spain has a moderate rate of crime, and most of the estimated one million American tourists have trouble-free visits to Spain each

Dealing with Discrimination

A fierce sense of national pride might lead many Spaniards to bristle at the suggestion that racism is a problem in their country, but certain events and a report by Amnesty International have brought to the fore concerns over racism and racial profiling in Spain. In January 2002, Rodney Mack, an African American and the principal trumpet player with the Barcelona Symphony Orchestra, was attacked and beaten in Madrid by four police officers who later said they mistook the musician for a car thief. The thief had been described as a black man of roughly Mr. Mack's height, and a police official later admitted that Mack was singled out because of "the color of his skin and his height." In April 2002, Amnesty International cited the Mack case in an exhaustive report accusing Spain of "frequent and widespread" mistreatment of foreigners and ethnic minorities. The report investigated more than 320 cases of abuse from 1995 to 2002, including deaths and rapes while in police custody, as well as beatings, verbal abuse, and the use of racial profiling by police. The report claims that an increase in racist attacks in Spain has coincided with a dramatic growth in the country's immigrant population over the last 20 years. Spanish officials, however, rejected the report, and Congressman Ingacio Gil-Lázaro of Spain's ruling Popular Party said, "The police and Civil Guard confront immigration in a deeply humanitarian way."

While Amnesty's report may rightfully dispel the notion that Spain is exempt from the problems of racism, it does not suggest that the country is Europe's only offender. In recent years, Amnesty has pointed up race-based abuses in numerous European nations, including Austria, Greece, and Italy, as well as the United States. Travelers of color may have a perfectly enjoyable trip in Spain, but visitors to the area should travel with the knowledge that racism and xenophobia may well be as serious a problem in Spain as anywhere in Europe or the United States. If you encounter discrimination or mistreatment while traveling in Spain, please report it to your embassy immediately or contact **S.O.S. Racismo,** an independent antidiscrimination organization based in Madrid, Calle Campomanes 13, 2° Izq. (ⓒ **91-559-29-06;** www.nodo50.org/sosracismo.madrid).

—John Vorwald

year, the principal tourist areas have been experiencing an increase in violent crime. Madrid and Barcelona, in particular, have reported growing incidents of muggings and violent attacks, and older tourists and Asian-Americans seem to be particularly at risk. Criminals frequent tourist areas and major attractions such as museums, monuments, restaurants, hotels, beach resorts, trains, train stations, airports, subways, and ATMs. In Barcelona, violent attacks have occurred near the Picasso Museum and in the Gothic Quarter, Parc Guell, Plaza Real, and Mont Juic. In Madrid, reported incidents occur in key tourist areas, including the area near the Prado Museum and Atocha train station, and areas of old Madrid like Sol,

El Rastro flea market, and Plaza Mayor. Travelers should exercise caution, carry limited cash and credit cards, and leave extra cash, credit cards, passports, and personal documents in a safe location. Crimes have occurred at all times of day and night.

Thieves often work in teams or pairs. In most cases, one person distracts a victim while the accomplice performs the robbery. For example, a stranger might wave a map in your face and ask for directions or "inadvertently" spill something on you. While your attention is diverted, an accomplice makes off with the valuables. Attacks can also be initiated from behind, with the victim being grabbed around the neck and choked by one assailant while others rifle through the belongings. A group of assailants may surround the victim, maybe in a crowded popular tourist area or on public transportation, and only after the group has departed does the person discover he/she has been robbed. Some attacks have been so violent that victims have needed to seek medical attention after the attack.

Theft from parked cars is also common. Small items like luggage, cameras, or briefcases are often stolen from parked cars. Travelers are advised not to leave valuables in parked cars and to keep doors locked, windows rolled up, and valuables out of sight when driving. "Good Samaritan" scams are unfortunately common. A passing car will attempt to divert the driver's attention by indicating there is a mechanical problem. If the driver stops to check the vehicle, accomplices steal from the car while the driver is looking elsewhere. Drivers should be cautious about accepting help from anyone other than a uniformed Spanish police officer or Civil Guard.

The loss or theft abroad of a U.S. passport should be reported immediately to the local police and the nearest U.S. embassy or consulate. U.S. citizens may refer to the Department of State's pamphlet, *A Safe Trip Abroad,* for ways to promote a more trouble-free journey. The pamphlet is available by mail from the Superintendent of Documents, U.S. Government Printing Office, Washington, DC 20402, via the Internet at www. access.gpo.gov/su_docs, or via the Bureau of Consular Affairs home page at http://travel.state.gov.

8 Specialized Travel Resources

TRAVELERS WITH DISABILITIES

Most disabilities shouldn't stop anyone from traveling. There are more options and resources out there than ever before.

Because of Spain's many hills and endless flights of stairs, visitors with disabilities may have difficulty getting around the country, but conditions are slowly improving. Newer hotels are more sensitive to the needs of those with disabilities, and the more expensive restaurants, in general, are wheelchair-accessible. However, since most places have limited, if any, facilities for people with disabilities, you might consider taking an organized tour specifically designed to accommodate travelers with disabilities.

Organizations that offer assistance to travelers with disabilities include the **Moss Rehab Hospital** www. mossresourcenet.org), which provides a library of accessible-travel resources online; the **Society for Accessible Travel and Hospitality** (© 212/447-7284; www.sath.org; annual membership fees: $45 adults, $30 seniors and students), which offers a wealth of travel resources for all types of disabilities and informed recommendations on destinations, access guides, travel agents, tour operators, vehicle rentals, and companion services; and the **American Foundation for the Blind** (© 800/232-5463; www.afb.org), which provides information on traveling with Seeing Eye dogs.

For more information specifically targeted to travelers with disabilities, the community website **iCan** (www.icanonline.net/channels/travel/index.cfm) has destination guides and several regular columns on accessible travel. Also check out the quarterly magazine **Emerging Horizons** ($15 per year, $20 outside the U.S.; www.emerginghorizons.com); **Twin Peaks Press** (© 360/694-2462; http://disabilitybookshop.virtualave.net/blist 84.htm), offering travel-related books for travelers with special needs; and *Open World Magazine,* published by the Society for Accessible Travel and Hospitality (see above; subscription: $18 per year, $35 outside the U.S.).

GAY & LESBIAN TRAVELERS

In 1978, Spain legalized homosexuality among consenting adults. In April 1995, the parliament of Spain banned discrimination based on sexual orientation. Madrid and Barcelona are the major centers of gay life in Spain, and the most popular resorts for gay travelers are Sitges (south of Barcelona), Torremolinos, and Ibiza.

Before you go, consider picking up a copy of *Frommer's Gay & Lesbian Europe,* which contains chapters on Madrid, Barcelona, Sitges, and Ibiza.

The **International Gay & Lesbian Travel Association** (IGLTA) (© 800/448-8550 or 954/776-2626; www.iglta.org) is the trade association for the gay and lesbian travel industry, and offers an online directory of gay and lesbian-friendly travel businesses; go to their website and click on "Members."

Many agencies offer tours and travel itineraries specifically for gay and lesbian travelers. **Above and Beyond Tours** (© 800/397-2681; www.abovebeyondtours.com) is the exclusive gay and lesbian tour operator for United Airlines. **Now, Voyager** (© 800/255-6951; www.nowvoyager.com) is a well-known San Francisco–based gay-owned and -operated travel service. **Olivia Cruises & Resorts** (© 800/631-6277 or 510/655-0364; www.olivia.com) charters entire resorts and ships for exclusive lesbian vacations and offers smaller group experiences for both gay and lesbian travelers.

The following travel guides are available at most travel bookstores and gay and lesbian bookstores, or you can order them from **Giovanni's Room** bookstore, 1145 Pine St., Philadelphia, PA 19107 (© 215/923-2960; www.giovannisroom.com): *Frommer's Gay & Lesbian Europe,* an excellent travel resource; *Out and About* (© 800/929-2268 or 415-644-8044; www.outandabout.com), which offers guidebooks and a newsletter 10 times a year packed with solid information on the global gay and lesbian scene; *Spartacus International Gay Guide* and *Odysseus,* both good, annual English-language guidebooks focused on gay men; the *Damron* guides, with separate, annual books for gay men and lesbians; and *Gay Travel A to Z: The World of Gay & Lesbian Travel Options at Your Fingertips,* by Marianne Ferrari (Ferrari Publications; Box 35575, Phoenix, AZ 85069), a very good gay and lesbian guidebook series.

SENIOR TRAVEL

Mention the fact that you're a senior when you make your travel reservations. Although all of the major U.S. airlines except America West have canceled their senior discount and coupon book programs, many hotels still offer discounts for seniors. In most cities, people over the age of 60 qualify for reduced admission to theaters, museums, and other attractions, as well as discounted fares on public transportation.

Members of **AARP** (formerly known as the American Association of Retired Persons), 601 E St. NW, Washington, DC 20049 (© **800/ 424-3410** or 202/434-2277; www. aarp.org), get discounts on hotels, airfares, and car rentals. AARP offers members a wide range of benefits, including *AARP The Magazine* and a monthly newsletter. Anyone over 50 can join.

Many reliable agencies and organizations target the 50-plus market. **Elderhostel** (© **877/426-8056;** www.elderhostel.org) arranges study programs for those 55 and over (and a spouse or companion of any age) in the U.S. and in more than 80 countries around the world. Most courses last 5 to 7 days in the U.S. (2–4 weeks abroad), and many include airfare, accommodations in university dormitories or modest inns, meals, and tuition. **ElderTreks** (© **800/741-7956;** www.eldertreks.com) offers small-group tours to off-the-beaten-path or adventure-travel locations, restricted to travelers 50 and older.

Recommended publications offering travel resources and discounts for seniors include: the quarterly magazine *Travel 50 & Beyond* (www.travel 50andbeyond.com); *Travel Unlimited: Uncommon Adventures for the Mature Traveler* (Avalon); *101 Tips for Mature Travelers,* available from Grand Circle Travel (© **800/221-2610** or 617/350-7500; www.gct. com); *The 50+ Traveler's Guidebook* (St. Martin's Press); and *Unbelievably Good Deals and Great Adventures That You Absolutely Can't Get Unless You're Over 50* (McGraw-Hill).

FOR BLACK TRAVELERS

Agencies and organizations that provide resources for black travelers include **Rodgers Travel** (© **215/ 473-1775;** www.rodgerstravel.com), a Philadelphia-based travel agency with an extensive menu of tours in destinations worldwide, including heritage and private group tours.

The Internet offers a number of helpful travel sites for the black traveler. **Black Travel Online** (www.black travelonline.com) posts news on upcoming events and includes links to articles and travel-booking sites. **Soul of America** (www.soulofamerica.com) is a more comprehensive website, with travel tips, event and family reunion postings, and sections on historically black beach resorts and active vacations.

For more information, check out the following collections and guides: *Go Girl: The Black Woman's Guide to Travel & Adventure* (Eighth Mountain Press), a compilation of travel essays by writers including Jill Nelson and Audre Lorde, with some practical information and trip-planning advice; *Travel and Enjoy Magazine* (© 866/266-6211; www. travelandenjoy.com; subscription: $24 per year), which focuses on discounts and destination reviews; and the more narrative *Pathfinders Magazine* (© 877/977-**PATH**; www.pathfinders travel.com; subscription: $15 per year), which includes articles on everything from Rio de Janeiro to Ghana.

9 Planning Your Trip Online

SURFING FOR AIRFARES

The "big three" online travel agencies, **Expedia.com, Travelocity.com,** and **Orbitz.com** sell most of the air tickets bought on the Internet. (Canadian travelers should try expedia.ca and Travelocity.ca; U.K. residents can go for expedia.co.uk and opodo.co.uk.) Each has different business deals with the airlines and may offer different fares on the same flights, so it's wise to shop around. Expedia and Travelocity will also send you **e-mail notification** when a cheap fare becomes available to your favorite destination. Of the smaller travel agency websites, **Side-Step** (www.sidestep.com) has gotten the best reviews from Frommer's authors. It's a browser add-on that purports to "search 140 sites at once," but in reality only beats competitors' fares as often as other sites do.

Also remember to check **airline websites,** especially those for low-fare carriers whose fares are often misreported or simply missing from travel agency websites. Even with major airlines, you can often shave a few bucks from a fare by booking directly through the airline and avoiding a travel agency's transaction fee. But you'll get these discounts only by **booking online:** Most airlines now offer online-only fares that even their phone agents know nothing about. For the websites of airlines that fly to and from your destination, go to "Getting There," later in this chapter.

Great **last-minute deals** are available through free weekly e-mail services provided directly by the airlines.

Most of these are announced on Tuesday or Wednesday and must be purchased online. Most are only valid for travel that weekend, but some can be booked weeks or months in advance. Sign up for weekly e-mail alerts at airline websites or check megasites that compile comprehensive lists of last-minute specials, such as **Smarter Living** (smarterliving.com). For last-minute trips, **site59.com** in the U.S. and **lastminute.com** in Europe often have better deals than the major-label sites.

If you're willing to give up some control over your flight details, use an **opaque fare service** like **Priceline** (www.priceline.com; www.priceline. co.uk for Europeans) or **Hotwire** (www.hotwire.com). Both offer rock-bottom prices in exchange for travel on a "mystery airline" at a mysterious time of day, often with a mysterious change of planes en route. The mystery airlines are all major, well-known carriers. Priceline usually has better deals than Hotwire, but you have to play their "name our price" game. If you're new at this, the helpful folks at **BiddingForTravel** (www.bidding fortravel.com) do a good job of

 Frommers.com: The Complete Travel Resource

For an excellent travel-planning resource, we highly recommend Frommers.com (www.frommers.com). We're a little biased, of course, but we guarantee that you'll find the travel tips, reviews, monthly vacation giveaways, and online-booking capabilities thoroughly indispensable. Among the special features are our popular **Message Boards,** where Frommer's readers post queries and share advice (sometimes even our authors show up to answer questions); **Frommers.com Newsletter,** for the latest travel bargains and insider travel secrets; and **Frommer's Destinations Section,** where you'll get expert travel tips, hotel and dining recommendations, and advice on the sights to see for more than 3,000 destinations around the globe. When your research is done, the **Online Reservations System** (www.frommers.com/book_a_trip) takes you to Frommer's preferred online partners for booking your vacation at affordable prices.

demystifying Priceline's prices. Priceline and Hotwire are great for flights within North America and between the U.S. and Europe.

For much more about airfares and savvy air-travel tips and advice, pick up a copy of *Frommer's Fly Safe, Fly Smart* (Wiley Publishing, Inc.).

SURFING FOR HOTELS

Shopping online for hotels is much easier in the U.S., Canada, and certain parts of Europe, including Spain, than it is in the rest of the world. Of the "big three" sites, **Expedia** may be the best choice, thanks to its long list of special deals. **Travelocity** runs a close second. Hotel specialist sites **hotels.com** and **hoteldiscounts.com** are also reliable. An excellent free program, **TravelAxe** (www.travelaxe.net), can help you search multiple hotel sites at once, even ones you may never have heard of.

Priceline and Hotwire are even better for hotels than for airfares; with both, you're allowed to pick the neighborhood and quality level of your hotel before offering up your money. Priceline's hotel product even covers Europe and Asia, though it's much better at getting five-star lodging for three-star prices than at finding anything at the bottom of the scale. *Note:* Hotwire overrates its hotels by one star—what Hotwire calls a four-star is a three-star anywhere else.

SURFING FOR RENTAL CARS

For booking rental cars online, the best deals are usually found at rental-car company websites, although all the major online travel agencies also offer rental-car reservations services. Priceline and Hotwire work well for rental cars, too; the only "mystery" is which major rental company you get, and for most travelers the difference between Hertz, Avis, and Budget is negligible.

10 The 21st-Century Traveler

INTERNET ACCESS AWAY FROM HOME

Travelers have any number of ways to check their e-mail and access the Internet on the road. Of course, using your own laptop—or even a PDA (personal desk assistant) or electronic organizer with a modem—gives you the most flexibility. But even if you don't have a computer, you can still access your e-mail and even your office computer from cybercafes.

WITHOUT YOUR OWN COMPUTER

It's hard nowadays to find a city that *doesn't* have a few cybercafes. Although there's no definitive directory for cybercafes—these are independent businesses, after all—three places to start looking are at **www.cybercaptive. com**, **www.netcafeguide.com**, and **www.cybercafe.com**.

Most major airports now have **Internet kiosks** scattered throughout their gates. These kiosks, which you'll also see in shopping malls, hotel lobbies, and tourist information offices around the world, give you basic Web access for a per-minute fee that's usually higher than cybercafe prices. The kiosks' clunkiness and high price means they should be avoided whenever possible.

To retrieve your e-mail, ask your **Internet service provider (ISP)** if it has a Web-based interface tied to your existing e-mail account. If your ISP doesn't have such an interface, you can use the free **mail2web** service (www.mail2web.com) to view (but not reply to) your home e-mail. For more flexibility, you may want to open a free, Web-based e-mail account with **Yahoo! Mail** (mail.yahoo.com).

(Microsoft's Hotmail is another popular option, but Hotmail has severe spam problems.) Your home ISP may be able to forward your e-mail to the Web-based account automatically.

If you need to access files on your office computer, look into a service called **GoToMyPC** (www.gotomypc. com). The service provides a Web-based interface for you to access and manipulate a distant PC from anywhere—even a cybercafe—provided your "target" PC is on and has an always-on connection to the Internet (such as with Road Runner cable). The service offers top-quality security, but if you're worried about hackers, use your own laptop rather than a cybercafe to access the GoToMyPC system.

WITH YOUR OWN COMPUTER

Major Internet service providers have **local access numbers** around the world, allowing you to go online by simply placing a local call. Check your ISP's website or call its toll-free number and ask how you can use your current account away from home, and how much it will cost.

If you're traveling outside the reach of your ISP, the **iPass** network has dial-up numbers in most of the world's countries. You'll have to sign up with an iPass provider, who will then tell you how to set up your computer for your destination(s). For a list of iPass providers, go to www.ipass. com and click on "Individuals." One solid provider is **i2roam** (© **866/811-6209** or 920/235-0475; www.i2roam. com).

Wherever you go, bring a **connection kit** of the right power and phone adapters, a spare phone cord, and a spare Ethernet network cable.

Most business-class hotels throughout the world offer dataports for laptop modems, and a few hundred hotels in Spain now offer high-speed

Internet access using an Ethernet network cable. You'll have to bring your own cables either way, so **call your hotel in advance** to find out what the options are.

OUTSIDE THE U.S.

The three letters that define much of the world's **wireless capabilities** are GSM (Global System for Mobiles), a big, seamless network that makes for easy cross-border cellphone use throughout Europe and dozens of other countries worldwide. In the U.S., T-Mobile, AT&T Wireless, and Cingular use this quasi-universal system; in Canada, Microcell and some Rogers customers are GSM, and all Europeans and most Australians use GSM.

If your cellphone is on a GSM system, and you have a world-capable phone such as many (but not all) Sony Ericsson, Motorola, or Samsung models, you can make and receive calls across civilized areas on much of the globe, from Andorra to Uganda. Just call your wireless operator and ask for "international roaming" to be activated on your account. Unfortunately, per-minute charges can be high—usually $1 to $1.50 in Spain.

World-phone owners can bring down their per-minute charges with a bit of trickery. Call up your cellular operator and say you'll be going abroad for several months and want to "unlock" your phone to use it with a local provider. Usually, they'll oblige. Then, in your destination country, pick up a cheap, prepaid phone chip at a mobile phone store and slip it into your phone. (Show your phone to the salesperson, as not all phones work on all networks.) You'll get a local phone number in your destination country—and much, much lower calling rates.

Otherwise, **renting** a phone is a good idea. While you can rent a phone from any number of overseas sites, including kiosks at airports and at

Online Traveler's Toolbox

Veteran travelers usually carry some essential items to make their trips easier. Following is a selection of online tools to bookmark and use.

- **Visa ATM Locator** (www.visa.com), for locations of Plus ATMs worldwide, or **MasterCard ATM Locator** (www.mastercard.com), for locations of Cirrus ATMs worldwide.
- **Foreign Languages for Travelers** (www.travlang.com). Learn basic terms in more than 70 languages and click on any underlined phrase to hear what it sounds like.
- **Intellicast** (www.intellicast.com) and **Weather.com** (www.weather.com). Gives weather forecasts for all 50 states and for cities around the world, including Madrid, Seville, and Barcelona.
- **Mapquest** (www.mapquest.com). This best of the mapping sites lets you choose a specific address or destination, and in seconds, it will return a map and detailed directions.
- **Universal Currency Converter** (www.xe.com/ucc). See what your dollar or pound is worth in more than 100 other countries.

car-rental agencies, we suggest renting the phone before you leave home. That way you can give loved ones your new number, make sure the phone works, and take the phone wherever you go—especially helpful when you rent overseas, where phone-rental agencies bill in local currency and may not let you take the phone to another country.

Phone rental isn't cheap. You'll usually pay $40 to $50 per week, plus airtime fees of at least a dollar a minute. If you're traveling to Europe, though, local rental companies often offer free incoming calls within their home country, which can save you big bucks. The bottom line: Shop around.

Two good wireless rental companies are **InTouch USA** (© 800/872-7626; www.intouchglobal.com) and **RoadPost** (© 888/290-1606 or 905/272-5665; www.roadpost.com). Give them your itinerary, and they'll tell you what wireless products you need. InTouch will also, for free, advise you on whether your existing phone will work overseas; simply call © **703/222-7161** between 9am and 4pm ET, or go to http://intouchglobal.com/travel.htm.

11 Getting There

BY PLANE
FROM NORTH AMERICA Flights from the U.S. east coast to Spain take 6 to 7 hours. The national carrier of Spain, **Iberia Airlines** (© **800/772-4642**; www.iberia.com), has more routes into and within Spain than any other airline. It offers daily nonstop service to Madrid from New York, Chicago, and Miami. Also available are attractive rates on fly/drive packages within Iberia and Europe; they can substantially reduce the cost of both the air ticket and the car rental.

A good money-saver to consider is **Iberia**'s **EuroPass.** Available only to passengers who simultaneously arrange for transatlantic passage on Iberia and a minimum of two additional flights, it allows passage on any flight within Iberia's European or

Mediterranean dominion for $139 per person one-way for each additional flight. This is especially attractive for passengers wishing to combine trips to Spain with, for example, visits to such far-flung destinations as Cairo, Tel Aviv, Istanbul, Moscow, and Munich. For details, ask Iberia's phone representative. The EuroPass can be purchased as a part of an Iberian Air itinerary from your home country only.

Iberia's main Spain-based competitor is **Air Europa** (© **888/238-7672**; www.air-europa.com), which offers nonstop service from Newark Airport to Madrid, with continuing service to major cities within Spain. Fares are usually lower than Iberia's.

American Airlines (© **800/433-7300**; www.aa.com) offers daily nonstop service to Madrid from its massive hub in Miami.

Delta (© **800/241-4141**; www.delta.com) runs daily nonstop service from Atlanta (its worldwide hub) and New York (JFK) to both Madrid and Barcelona. Delta's Dream Vacation department offers independent fly/drive packages, land packages, and escorted bus tours.

United Airlines (© **800/241-6522**; www.ual.com) does not fly into Spain directly. It does, however, offer airfares from the United States to Spain with United flying as far as Zurich, and then using another carrier to complete the journey. United also offers fly/drive packages and escorted motor coach tours.

Continental Airlines (© **800/231-0856**; www.continental.com) offers daily nonstop flights, depending on the season, to Madrid from Newark, New Jersey.

US Airways (© **800/428-4322**; www.usairways.com) offers daily nonstop service between Philadelphia and Madrid. The carrier also has connecting flights to Philadelphia from more than 50 cities throughout the United States, Canada, and the Bahamas.

FROM THE U.K.   **British Airways (BA;** © **0845/773-3377)** and **Iberia** (© **020/7830-0011** in London) are the two major carriers flying between England and Spain. More than a dozen daily flights, on either BA or Iberia, depart from London's Heathrow and Gatwick airports. The Midlands is served by flights from Manchester and Birmingham, two major airports that can also be used by Scottish travelers flying to Spain. There are about seven flights a day from London to Madrid and back and at least six to Barcelona (trip time: 2–2½ hr.). From either the Madrid airport or the Barcelona airport, you can tap into Iberia's domestic network—flying, for example, to Seville or the Costa del Sol. The best air deals on scheduled flights from England are those requiring a Saturday night stopover.

British newspapers are always full of classified advertisements touting "slashed" fares to Spain. A good source is *Time Out*. London's *Evening Standard* has a daily travel section, and the Sunday editions of most papers are full of charter deals. A travel agent can always advise what the best values are at the time of your intended departure.

Charter flights to specific destinations leave from most British regional airports (for example, Málaga), bypassing the congestion at the Barcelona and Madrid airports. Figure on saving approximately 10% to 15% on regularly scheduled flight tickets. But check carefully into the restrictions and terms; read the fine print, especially in regard to cancellation penalties. One recommended company is **Trailfinders** (© **020/7937-5400** in London; www.trailfinder.com), which operates charters.

In London, there are many bucket shops around Victoria Station and Earls Court that offer cheap fares. Make sure the company you deal with is a member of the IATA, ABTA, or ATOL. These umbrella organizations will help you out if anything goes wrong.

CEEFAX, the British television information service, runs details of package holidays and flights to Europe and beyond. Just switch to your CEEFAX channel and you'll find travel information.

FROM AUSTRALIA From Australia, there are a number of options to fly to Spain. The most popular is Qantas/British Airways (© **612/13-13-13**), which flies daily via Asia and London. Other popular and cheaper options are Qantas/Lufthansa via Asia and Frankfurt, Qantas/Air France via Asia and Paris, and Alitalia via Bangkok and Rome. The most direct option is on Singapore Airlines, with just one stop in Singapore. Alternatively, there are flights on Thai Airways via Bangkok and Rome, but the connections are not always good.

GETTING THROUGH THE AIRPORT

With the federalization of airport security, security procedures at U.S. airports are more stable and consistent than ever. Generally, you'll be fine if you arrive at the airport **1 hour** before a domestic flight and **2 hours** before an international flight; if you show up late, tell an airline employee and he or she will probably whisk you to the front of the line.

Bring a **current, government-issued photo ID** such as a driver's license or passport, and if you've got an E-ticket, print out the **official confirmation page;** you'll need to show your confirmation at the security checkpoint, and your ID at the ticket counter or the gate. (Children under 18 do not need photo IDs for domestic flights, but the adults checking in with them do.)

Security lines are getting shorter than they were during 2001 and 2002, but some doozies remain. If you have trouble standing for long periods of time, tell an airline employee; the airline will provide a wheelchair. Speed up security by **not wearing metal objects** such as big belt buckles or clanky earrings. If you've got metallic body parts, a note from your doctor can prevent a long chat with the security screeners. Keep in mind that only **ticketed passengers** are allowed past security, except for folks escorting passengers with disabilities or children.

Federalization has stabilized **what you can carry on** and **what you can't.** The general rule is that sharp things are out, nail clippers are okay, and

---

Tips Don't Stow It—Ship It

If ease of travel is your main concern and money is no object, you can ship your luggage with one of the growing number of luggage-service companies that pick up, track, and deliver your luggage (often through couriers such as Federal Express) with minimum hassle for you. Traveling luggage-free may be ultraconvenient, but it's not cheap: One-way overnight shipping can cost from $100 to $200, depending on what you're sending. Still, for some people, especially the elderly or the infirm, it's a sensible solution to lugging heavy baggage. Specialists in door-to-door luggage delivery are **Virtual Bellhop** (www.virtualbellhop.com), **SkyCap International** (wwww.skycapinternational.com), and **Luggage Express** (www.usxpluggageexpress.com).

food and beverages must be passed through the X-ray machine—but that security screeners can't make you drink from your coffee cup. Bring food in your carry-on rather than checking it, as explosive-detection machines used on checked luggage have been known to mistake food (especially chocolate, for some reason) for bombs. Travelers in the U.S. are allowed one carry-on bag, plus a "personal item" such as a purse, briefcase, or laptop bag. Carry-on hoarders can stuff all sorts of things into a laptop bag; as long as it has a laptop in it, it's still considered a personal item. The Transportation Security Administration (TSA) has issued a list of restricted items; check its website (www.tsa.gov/public/index.jsp) for details.

In 2003 the TSA was phasing out **gate check-in** at all U.S. airports. Passengers with E-tickets and without checked bags can still beat the ticket-counter lines by using **electronic kiosks** or even **online check-in.** Ask your airline which alternatives are available, and if you're using a kiosk, bring the credit card you used to book the ticket. If you're checking bags, you will still be able to use most airlines' kiosks; again call your airline for up-to-date information. **Curbside check-in** is also a good way to avoid lines, although a few airlines still ban curbside check-in entirely; call before you go.

At press time, the TSA is also recommending that you **not lock your checked luggage** so screeners can search it by hand if necessary. The agency says to use plastic "zip ties" instead, which can be bought at hardware stores and can be easily cut off.

FLYING FOR LESS: TIPS FOR GETTING THE BEST AIRFARE

Passengers sharing the same airplane cabin rarely pay the same fare. Travelers who need to purchase tickets at the last minute, change their itinerary at a moment's notice, or fly one-way often get stuck paying the premium rate. Here are some ways to keep your airfare costs down.

- Passengers who can book their ticket **long in advance,** who can **stay over Saturday night,** or who **fly midweek** or **at less-trafficked hours** will pay a fraction of the full fare. If your schedule is flexible, say so, and ask if you can secure a cheaper fare by changing your flight plans.

- You can also save on airfares by keeping an eye out in local newspapers for **promotional specials** or **fare wars,** when airlines lower prices on their most popular routes. You rarely see fare wars offered for peak travel times, but if you can travel in the off-months, you may snag a bargain.

- Search **the Internet** for cheap fares (see "Planning Your Trip Online," earlier in this chapter).

- **Consolidators,** also known as bucket shops, are great sources for international tickets, although they usually can't beat the Internet on fares within North America. Start by looking in Sunday newspaper travel sections; U.S. travelers should focus on the *New York Times,* the *Los Angeles Times,* and the *Miami Herald.* For less-developed destinations, small travel agents who cater to immigrant communities in large cities often have the best deals. *Beware:* Bucket shop tickets are usually nonrefundable or rigged with stiff cancellation penalties, often as high as 50% to 75% of the ticket price, and some put you on charter airlines with questionable safety records. Several reliable consolidators are worldwide and available on the Net. **STA Travel** (**www. statravel.com**) is now the world's leader in student travel, thanks to its purchase of Council Travel. It also offers good fares for travelers of all ages. **Flights.com** (© **800/ TRAV-800;** www.flights.com) started in Europe and has excellent fares worldwide, but particularly to that continent. It also has "local" websites in 12 countries. **FlyCheap** (© **800/FLY-CHEAP;** www.1800 flycheap.com) is owned by package-holiday megalith MyTravel and so has especially good access to fares for sunny destinations. **Air Tickets Direct** (© **800/778- 3447;** www.airticketsdirect.com) is based in Montreal and leverages the currently weak Canadian dollar for low fares; it'll also book trips to places that U.S. travel agents won't touch, such as Cuba.

- Join **frequent-flier clubs.** Accrue enough miles, and you'll be rewarded with free flights and elite status. It's free and you'll get the best choice of seats, faster response to phone inquiries, and prompter service if your luggage is stolen, your flight is canceled or delayed, or if you want to change your seat. You don't need to fly to build frequent-flier miles—**frequent-flier credit cards** can provide thousands of miles for doing your everyday shopping.

GETTING THERE BY CAR

If you're touring the rest of Europe in a rented car, you might, for an added cost, be allowed to drop off your vehicle in a major city such as Madrid or Barcelona.

Highway approaches to Spain are across France on expressways. The most popular border crossing is near Biarritz, but there are 17 other border stations between Spain and France. If you're planning to visit the north or west of Spain (Galicia), the Hendaye-Irún

border is the most convenient frontier crossing. If you're going to Barcelona or Catalonia and along the Levante coast (Valencia), take the expressway in France to Toulouse, then the A-61 to Narbonne, and then the A-9 toward the border crossing at La Junquera. You can also take the RN-20, with a border station at Puigcerdà.

If you're driving from Britain, make sure you have a cross-Channel reservation, as traffic tends to be very heavy, especially in summer.

The major ferry crossings connect Dover and Folkestone with Dunkirk. Newhaven is connected with Dieppe, and the British city of Portsmouth with Roscoff. To take a car on the ferry from Dover to Calais on P & O Ferries (© **800/677-85-85** or 08705/ 20-20-20; www.posl.com) costs £116 ($186) and takes 1 hour, 15 minutes. This cost includes the car and two passengers.

One of the fastest crossings is by hovercraft from Dover to Boulogne or Calais. It costs more than the ferry, but it takes only about half an hour. For reservations and information, call **Hoverspeed** (© **800/677-8585** for reservations in North America, or 0870/524-0241 in England; www. hoverspeed.com). The hovercraft takes 35 minutes and costs £160 to £225 ($256–$360) for the car and two passengers. The drive from Calais to the border would take about 15 hours.

You can take the Chunnel, the underwater Channel Tunnel linking Britain (Folkestone) and France (Calais) by road and rail. **Eurostar** tickets, for train service between London and Paris or Brussels, are available through Rail Europe (© **800/ EUROSTAR;** www.eurostar.com for information). In London, make reservations for Eurostar at © **0870/ 530-00-03;** in Paris at © 01-44-51- 06-02; and in the United States at © 800/EUROSTAR. The tunnel also accommodates passenger cars, charter buses, taxis, and motorcycles, transporting them under the English Channel from Folkestone, England, to Calais, France. It operates 24 hours a day, 365 days a year, running every 15 minutes during peak travel times, and at least once an hour at night. Tickets may be purchased at the tollbooth at the tunnel's entrance. With "Le Shuttle," gone are the days of weather-related delays, seasickness, and advance reservations.

Once you land, you'll have about a 15-hour drive to Spain.

If you plan to transport a rental car between England and France, check in advance with the rental company about license and insurance requirements and additional drop-off charges. And be aware that many car-rental companies, for insurance reasons, forbid transport of one of their vehicles over the water between England and France.

GETTING THERE BY TRAIN

If you're already in Europe, you might want to go to Spain by train, especially if you have a EurailPass. Even without a pass, you'll find that the cost of a train ticket is relatively moderate. Rail passengers who visit from Britain or France should make couchette and sleeper reservations as far in advance as possible, especially during the peak summer season.

Since Spain's rail tracks are of a wider gauge than those used for French trains (except for the TALGO and Trans-Europe-Express trains), you'll probably have to change trains at the border unless you're on an express train (see below). For long journeys on Spanish rails, seat and sleeper reservations are mandatory.

The most comfortable and the fastest trains in Spain are the TER, TALGO, and Electrotren. However, you pay a supplement to ride on these fast trains. Both first- and second-class fares are sold on Spanish trains. Tickets can be purchased in the United States or Canada at the nearest office of Rail Europe or from any reputable travel agent. Confirmation of your reservation takes about a week.

If you want your car carried aboard the train, you must travel Auto-Expreso in Spain. This type of auto transport can be booked only through travel agents or rail offices once you arrive in Europe.

To go from London to Spain by rail, you'll need to change not only the train but also the rail terminus in Paris. In Paris it's worth the extra bucks to purchase a TALGO express or a "Puerta del Sol" express—that way, you can avoid having to change trains once again at the Spanish border. Trip time from London to Paris is about 6 hours; from Paris to Madrid, about 15 hours or so, which includes 2 hours spent in Paris just changing trains and stations. Many different rail passes are available in the United Kingdom for travel in Europe.

BY BUS

Bus travel to Spain is possible but not popular—it's quite slow (service from London will take 24 hr. or more). But coach services do operate regularly from major capitals of Western Europe, and once in Spain, usually head for Madrid or Barcelona. The major bus line running from London to Spain is **Eurolines Limited,** 52 Grosvenor Gardens, London SW1W 0AU, UK (© **0870/514-32-19** or 020/7730-8235).

12 Packages for the Independent Traveler

Before you start your search for the lowest airfare, you may want to consider booking your flight as part of a travel package. Package tours are not the same thing as escorted tours. Package tours are simply a way to buy the airfare, accommodations, and other elements of your trip (such as car rentals, airport transfers, and sometimes even activities) at the same time and often at discounted prices—kind of like one-stop shopping. Packages are sold in bulk to tour operators—who resell them to the public at a cost that usually undercuts standard rates.

One good source of package deals is the airlines themselves. Most major airlines offer air/land packages, including **American Airlines Vacations** (© 800/321-2121; www.aavacations.com), **Delta Vacations** (© 800/221-6666; www.deltavacations.com), **Continental Airlines Vacations** (© 800/301-3800; www.coolvacations.com), and **United Vacations** (© 888/854-3899; www.unitedvacations.com). Among the airline packagers, **Iberia Airlines** (© **800/772-4642,** or 90-240-05-00 in Spain; www.iberia.com) leads the way.

Several big **online travel agencies**—Expedia, Travelocity, Orbitz, Site59, and Lastminute.com—also do a brisk business in packages. If you're unsure about the pedigree of a smaller packager, check with the Better Business Bureau in the city where the company is based, or go online at www.bbb.org. If a packager won't tell you where it's based, don't fly with them.

Solar Tours (© **800/388-7652;** www.solartours.com) is a wholesaler that offers a number of package tours to Madrid, Barcelona, and Seville, as well as to major beach resorts. Self-drive packages through Andalusia and other areas are also featured. A 9-day "Moorish Escapade" tour of Andalusia is its most popular jaunt. **Spanish Heritage Tours** (© **800/456-5050;** www.shtours.com) is known for searching for low-cost airfare deals to Spain—round-trips to Madrid for $399 or to Málaga for $523. The tour agent also features both air and land packages to Barcelona and Madrid. **Homeric Tours** (© **800/223-5570** or 212/753-1000; www.homerictours.com/contact.asp), the marketing arm of Iberia, is the most reliable tour operator and the agency used for air and land packages to some of the highlights of Spain, including Madrid, Córdoba, Seville, Granada, and the Costa del Sol. Naturally, round-trip airfares on Iberia are included in the deal. Several fly/drive packages are also offered.

13 Escorted General-Interest Tours

Escorted tours are structured group tours, with a group leader. The price usually includes everything from airfare to hotels, meals, tours, admission costs, and local transportation.

There are many escorted tour companies to choose from, each offering transportation to and within Spain, prearranged hotel space, and such extras as bilingual tour guides and lectures. Many of these tours to Spain include excursions to Morocco or Portugal.

Some of the most expensive and luxurious tours are run by **Abercrombie & Kent International** (© **800/323-7308** or 630/954-2944; www.abercrombiekent.com), including deluxe 13- or 19-day tours of the Iberian Peninsula by train. Guests stay in fine hotels, ranging from a late medieval palace to the exquisite Alfonso XIII in Seville.

American Express Travel (© **800/941-2639** in the U.S. and Canada; www.travelimpressions.com) is one of the biggest tour operators in the world. Its offerings are comprehensive, and unescorted customized package tours are available, too.

Trafalgar Tours (© **800/854-0103** or 212/689-8977; www.trafalgartours.com) is cheaper, offering a number of tours of Spain. One of the most popular offerings is a 16-day trip called "The Best of Spain." This land-only package is $1,499.

Alternative Travel Group Ltd. (© 01865/310-399; www.atg-oxford.co.uk) is a British firm that organizes walking and cycling vacations, plus wine tours in Spain, Italy, and France. Tours explore the scenic countryside and medieval towns of each country. If you'd like a brochure outlining the tours, call © 01865/315-663.

Petrabax Tours (© 800/634-1188; www.petrabax.com) attracts those who prefer to see Spain by bus, although fly/drive packages are also offered, featuring stays in paradors. A number of city packages are also available, plus an 8- or 9-day trip that tries to capture the essence of Spain, with stops in places ranging from Madrid to Granada.

Isramworld (© 800/223-7460; www.isram.com) sells both escorted and package tours to Spain. It can book you on bus tours as well as land and air packages. Its grandest offering is "Ultimate Spain" with a private driver and guides. Naturally, only Spain's best hotels are used by this upmarket outfitter.

More and more special-interest tours to Spain are being offered, including tours by **Archetours, Inc.** (© 800/770-3051; www.archetours.com), which features tours devoted to Spanish architecture. **Bravo Adventures** (© 800/938-9311) will take you across the country on foot or by bike. Walking tours cross the Pyrenees and the Picos de Europa, and biking tours go through the south of Spain or La Rioja wine country. Tours are limited to groups of 6 to 20 people.

Many people derive a certain ease and security from escorted trips. Escorted tours—whether by bus, motor coach, train, or boat—let travelers sit back and enjoy their trip without having to spend lots of time behind the wheel. All the little details are taken care of; you know your costs

up front; and there are few surprises. Escorted tours can take you to the maximum number of sights in the minimum amount of time with the least amount of hassle—you don't have to sweat over the plotting and planning of a vacation schedule. Escorted tours are particularly convenient for people with limited mobility.

On the downside, an escorted tour often requires a big deposit up front, and lodging and dining choices are predetermined. As part of a cloud of tourists, you'll get little opportunity for serendipitous interactions with locals. The tours can be jam-packed with activities, leaving little room for individual sightseeing, whim, or adventure—plus they also often focus only on the heavily touristed sites, so you miss out on the lesser-known gems.

Before you invest in an escorted tour, ask about the **cancellation policy:** Is a deposit required? Can they cancel the trip if they don't get enough people? Do you get a refund if they cancel? If *you* cancel? How late can you cancel if you are unable to go? When do you pay in full? *Note:* If you choose an escorted tour, think strongly about purchasing trip-cancellation insurance, especially if the tour operator asks you to pay up front. See the section on "Travel Insurance," earlier in this chapter.

You'll also want to get a complete **schedule** of the trip to find out how much sightseeing is planned each day and whether enough time has been allotted for relaxing or wandering solo.

The **size** of the group is also important to know up front. Generally, the smaller the group, the more flexible the itinerary, and the less time you'll spend waiting for people to get on and off the bus. Find out the **demographics** of the group as well. What is the age range? What is the gender breakdown? Is this mostly a trip for couples or singles?

Discuss what is included in the **price.** You may have to pay for transportation to and from the airport. A box lunch may be included in an excursion, but drinks might cost extra. Tips may not be included. Find out if you will be charged if you decide to opt out of certain activities or meals.

Before you invest in a package tour, get some answers. Ask about the **accommodations choices** and prices for each. Then look up the hotels' reviews in a Frommer's guide and check their rates for your specific dates of travel online. You'll also want to find out what **type of room** you get. If you need a certain type of room, ask for it; don't take whatever is thrown your way. Request a nonsmoking room, a quiet room, a room with a view, or whatever you fancy.

Finally, if you plan to travel alone, you'll need to know if a **single supplement** will be charged and if the company can match you up with a roommate.

14 Special-Interest Trips

Spain is one of the best destinations in Europe for enjoying the outdoors. Lounging on the beach leads the list of activities for most travelers, but there's a lot more to do. Spain's mountains lure thousands of mountaineers and hikers, and fishing and hunting are long-standing Iberian obsessions. The Pyrenees of Catalonia and Aragón, plus the Guadarramas outside Madrid, attract devoted skiers in the winter. Watersports ranging from sailing to windsurfing are prime summer attractions.

In addition to sports and adventures, we've also detailed some of the best educational and cultural programs below.

Note: The inclusion of an organization in this section is in no way to be interpreted as a guarantee. This information is presented only as a preview, to be followed by your own investigation.

BIKING

The leading U.S.-based outfitter is **Easy Rider Tours,** P.O. Box 228, Newburyport, MA 01950 (© **800/488-8332** or 978/463-6955; www.easyridertours.com). Their tours average between 48km and 81km (30–50 miles) a day; and the most appealing follows the route trod by medieval pilgrims on their way to Santiago. The bike tours offered by **Backroads,** 801 Cedar St., Berkeley, CA 94710 (© **800/GO-ACTIVE** or 510/527-1555; www.backroads.com), take you through the verdant countryside of Galicia and into Portugal's Minho region. Companies that specialize in bike tours of Camino de Santiago include **Bravo Adventures,** Seattle, WA 98115 (© **800/938-9311** or 206/523-1764), and **Saranjan Tours,** P.O. Box 292, Kirkland, WA 98033 (© **800/858-9594** or 425/869-8636; www.saranjan.com).

Bravo Bike, c/ Montera 25-27, E-28013, Madrid (© **91-640-12-98;** www.bravobike.com), is a travel agency featuring organized cycling tours around Madrid. They have branched out to include other parts of Spain as well, notably the route between Salamanca to Santiago de Compostela and the route of the conquerors in Extremadura. One of the most intriguing bike tours is the *ruta de vino* (the wine route) in La Rioja country.

In England, the **Cyclists' Touring Club,** 69 Meadrow, Godalming, Surrey GU7 3HS, UK (© **0870/873-0060;** www.ctc.org.uk), charges £27 ($43) a year for membership; part of the fee provides for information and suggested cycling routes through Spain and dozens of other countries.

GOLF

In recent decades, thousands of British retirees have settled in Spain, and their presence has sparked the development of dozens of new golf courses. Although the Costa Blanca has become an increasingly popular setting for golf, more than a third of the country's approximately 160 courses lie within its southern tier, within a short drive of the Costa del Sol.

Packages that include guaranteed playing time on some of the country's finest courses, as well as airfare and accommodations, can be arranged through such firms as **Golf International** (© **800/833-1389** or 212/986-9176 in the U.S.; www.golf international.com), **Spanish Golf Adventures** (© **800/772-6465** in the U.S. and Canada; www.spanishgolf.com), **Central Holidays** (© **800/935-5000** in the U.S. and Canada; www.centralholidays.com), **PGA Travel** (© **800/283-4653** in the U.S., or 770/455-8019; www.pgatravel.com), and **Comtours** (© **800/248-1331** in the U.S.; www.comtours.com).

What are the two most talked-about golf courses in Spain? The well-established **Valderrama** on the Costa del Sol, a Robert Trent Jones–designed course carved out of an oak plantation in the 1980s, and Hyatt's new **La Manga Club** on the Costa Blanca near Murcia. It's the site of three golf courses, one of which was recently remodeled by Arnold Palmer. The Ryder Cup between Spain and the United States was held in 1997 at Valderrama, Av. Los Cortijos, 11310 Sotogrande (© **95-6791-200;** www.valderrama.com), on the western tip of the Costa del Sol, near Gibraltar.

HIKING & WALKING

If you're drawn to the idea of combining hiking with stopovers at local inns, contact **Winetrails,** Greenways, Vann Lake, Ockley, Dorking RH5 5NT, UK (© **01306/712-111;** www.winetrails.co.uk). This U.K.-based company conducts 10-day treks through northern Spain's wine districts.

To venture into the more rugged countryside of Catalonia, Andalusia's valley of the Guadalquivir, or the arid, beautiful Extremaduran plains, contact **Ramblers Holidays,** P.O. Box 43, Welwyn Garden AL8 6PQ, UK (© **01707/331-133;** www.ramblers holidays.co.uk). Walking tours through the Pyrenees, the region around Alicante, and across the eerie volcanic expanses of the Canary Islands are conducted by **Waymark Holidays,** 44 Windsor Rd., Slough SL1 2EJ, UK (© **01753/516-477;** www.waymark holidays.co.uk).

An outfit known for its luxurious and pricey tours is **Abercrombie & Kent International,** 1520 Kensington Rd., Oak Brook, IL 60521 (© **800/323-7308** or 630/954-2944; www.abercrombiekent.com). They conduct a 9-day "Walking the Pyrenees" tour on the Spanish side of the mountainous border with France. Special emphasis is placed on the medieval churches that provided rest and hope to 10th-century pilgrims on their way to Santiago.

HORSEBACK RIDING

You can take a tour that winds across Asturia and Galicia on your way to the medieval religious shrine at Santiago de Compostela. Lodging, the use of a horse, and all necessary equipment are included in the price. For information and reservations, contact the **Centro Hípico "O Castelo,"** Calle Urzáiz 91, no. 5-A Vigo, Spain (© **98-642-59-37;** www.galicianet.com/castelo).

A well-known equestrian center that conducts tours of the Alpujarras highlands is **Cabalgar,** Rutas Alternativas, Bubión, Granada (© **95-876-31-35**). The farm is best known for its weekend treks through the scrub-covered hills of southern and central Spain, although longer tours are available.

SAILING

Alventus, an agency based in Seville, offers weeklong cruises along the coast of Andalusia and the Algarve. Its three-masted, 12.5m (42-ft.) sailing yacht departs from the Andalusian port of Huelva. For reservations and information, contact Alventus at Calle Huelva 6, 41004 Sevilla (© **95-421-00-62;** www.alventus.com).

In northern Spain, consider a journey with **Voyages Jules Verne,** 21 Dorset Sq., London NW1 6QG, UK (© **020/7616-1000;** www.vjv.co.uk). Its guided vacations take in Galicia, its Portuguese neighbors, Trás-os-Montes and the Minho district, and Porto, the second-largest city in Portugal. The trips end with a boat ride up the Douro River back into Spain.

LEARNING VACATIONS

See "Specialized Travel Resources," earlier in this chapter, for details on Interhostel and Elderhostel programs for seniors.

STUDYING SPANISH Salminter, Calle Toro 25, 37002 Salamanca (© **92-321-18-08;** fax 92-326-02-63; www.salminter.helcom.es), conducts courses in conversational Spanish, with optional courses in business Spanish, translation techniques, and Spanish culture. Classes contain no more than 10 persons. There are courses of 2 weeks, 1 month, and 3 months at seven progressive levels. The school can arrange housing with Spanish families or in furnished apartments shared with other students.

Another good source of information about courses in Spain is the **American Institute for Foreign Study (AIFS),** River Plaza, 9 W. Broad St., Stamford, CT 06902

(© **800/727-2437** or 203/399-5000; www.aifs.com). This organization can set up transportation and arrange for summer courses, with bed and board included.

The biggest organization dealing with higher education in Europe is the **Institute of International Education (IIE),** 809 United Nations Plaza, New York, NY 10017 (© **800/445-0443** or 212/883-8200; www.iie.org). A few of its booklets are free, but for $47, plus $6 for postage, you can purchase the more definitive *Vacation Study Abroad.* To order the book, call © **800/445-0443.**

One well-recommended clearinghouse for academic programs throughout the world is the **National Registration Center for Study Abroad (NRCSA),** 823 N. 2nd St., Milwaukee, WI 53203 (© **414/278-0631;** fax 414/224-3466; www.nrcsa.com). The organization maintains language-study programs throughout Europe, including at about 10 cities throughout Spain. Most popular are the organization's programs in Seville, Salamanca, and Málaga, where language courses last between 4 and 6 hours a day. With lodgings in private homes included as part of the price and part of the experience, tuition begins at around $768 for an intensive 2-week language course. Courses accept participants ages 17 to 80.

A clearinghouse for information on at least nine different Spain-based language schools is **Lingua Service Worldwide,** 75 Prospect St., Suite 4, Huntington, NY 11743 (© **800/394-LEARN** or 631/424-0777; fax 631/271-3441; www.linguaserviceworldwide.com). Maintaining information about learning programs in 10 languages in 17 countries outside the United States, it represents organizations devoted to the teaching of Spanish and culture in 11 cities of Spain, including one in the Canary Islands.

One well-recommended language school that manages to combine a resort setting with intensive linguistic immersion is the **Escuela de Idiomas Nerja,** Calle Almirante Ferrándiz 73, 29780 Nerja, Málaga (© **95-252-16-87;** www.idnerja.es). It offers a 2-week Spanish course for 318€ and a 4-week course for 528€. Also offered are one-on-one courses, refresher courses for teachers, and Spanish for business. Classes are limited to a maximum of 10 students each.

For more information about study abroad, contact the **Council on International Educational Exchange (CIEE),** 205 E. 42nd St., New York, NY 10017 (© **020/7478-2000** or 212/822-2700; www.ciee.org).

"EARTHWATCHING" Earthwatch, 3 Clock Tower Place, Suite 100, Box 75, Maynard, MA 01754 (© **800/776-0188** or 978/461-0081; www.earthwatch.org), is a nonprofit organization that recruits ordinary people to work as paying volunteers for university professors on field expeditions throughout the world. Volunteers are almost never specialists in any particular field but interested intergenerational participants. Note that only 10% of volunteers are students; many are senior citizens. Ongoing projects in Spain include monitoring the S'Albufera wetlands on the island of Majorca, excavating a prehistoric cluster of Copper Age villages on Majorca, researching the remains of a Bronze Age Iberian village near Borja in Aragón, and participating in the Spanish dolphin project off the southern coast.

Participation in Earthwatch's 2-week Spanish projects involves a tax-deductible contribution of between $700 and $3,000, depending on the project, plus airfare to Spain. Living arrangements, as well as all meals and drinks at the organization's Saturday-night beer parties, are provided.

BIRDING The Iberian Peninsula lies directly across migration routes of species that travel with the seasons between Africa and Europe. Some of the most comprehensive studies on these migratory patterns are conducted by Spain's **Centro de Migración de Aves,** SEO/BirdLife, Calle Melquiades Biencinto 34, 28053 Madrid (© **91-434-09-10;** www.seo.org). Based at a rustic outpost near Gibraltar, their summer work camps and field projects appeal to participants who want to identify, catalog, and "ring" (mark with an identifying leg band) some of the millions of birds that nest on Spanish soil every year. Participants are expected to pay for their "tuition," room, and board, but can often use the experience toward university credit, especially in such fields as zoology and ecology.

BOTANICAL TOURS Travel specialist **Cox & Kings Travel,** Gordon House, 10 GreenCoat Place, London SW1P 1PH, UK (© **020/7873-5000;** www.coxandkings.co.uk), leads 2-week treks in search of wild orchids, unusual ferns, and samples of the varied flora that grow in the damp but sunny foothills of the Pyrenees in Aragón. The firm also conducts other organized tours through Spain.

15 Getting Around

BY CAR

A car offers the greatest flexibility while you're touring, even if you're just doing day trips from Madrid. Don't, however, plan to drive in Madrid or Barcelona for city sightseeing; it's too

congested. Theoretically, rush hour is Monday through Saturday from 8 to 10am, 1 to 2pm, and 4 to 6pm. In reality, it's always busy.

CAR RENTALS Many of North America's biggest car-rental companies, including Avis, Budget, and Hertz, maintain offices throughout Spain. Although several Spanish car-rental companies exist, we've gotten lots of letters from readers of previous editions telling us they've had a hard time resolving billing irregularities and insurance claims, so you might want to stick with the U.S.-based rental firms.

Note that tax on car rentals is a whopping 15%, so don't forget to factor that into your travel budget. Usually, prepaid rates do not include taxes, which will be collected at the rental kiosk itself. Be sure to ask explicitly what's included when you're quoted a rate.

Avis (© 800/331-1084; www.avis. com) maintains about 100 branches throughout Spain, including about a dozen in Madrid, eight in Barcelona, a half dozen in Seville, and four in Murcia. If you reserve and pay your rental by telephone at least 2 weeks before your departure from North America, you'll qualify for the company's best rate, with unlimited kilometers included. You can usually get competitive rates from **Hertz** (© 800/ 654-3001; www.hertz.com) and **Budget** (© 800/472-3325; www.budget. com); it always pays to comparison shop. Budget doesn't have a drop-off charge if you pick up in one Spanish city and return to another. All three companies require that drivers be at least 21 years of age and, in some cases, not older than 72. To be able to rent a car, you must have a passport and a valid driver's license; you must also have a valid credit card or a prepaid voucher. An international driver's license is not essential, but you might want to present it if you have one; it's available from any North American office of the American Automobile Association (AAA).

Two other agencies of note include **Kemwel Holiday auto** (© 800/678- 0678; www.kemwel.com) and **Auto Europe** (© 800/223-5555; www. autoeurope.com).

Many packages include airfare, accommodations, and a rental car with unlimited mileage. Compare these prices with the cost of booking airline tickets and renting a car separately to see if these offers are good deals. Internet resources can make comparison shopping easier. **Microsoft Expedia** (www.expedia. com) and **Travelocity** (www.travelo city.com) help you compare prices and locate car-rental bargains from various companies nationwide. They will even make your reservation for you once you've found the best deal. See "Planning Your Trip Online," earlier in this chapter, for tips.

DRIVING RULES   Spaniards drive on the right side of the road. Drivers should pass on the left; local drivers sound their horns when passing another car and flash their lights at you if you're driving slowly (slowly for high-speed Spain) in the left lane. Autos coming from the right have the right-of-way.

Spain's express highways are known as *autopistas,* which charge a toll, and *autovías,* which don't. To exit in Spain, follow the *salida* (exit) sign, except in Catalonia, where the word to exit is *sortida.* On most express highways, the speed limit is 120kmph (75 mph). On other roads, speed limits range from 90kmph (56 mph) to 100kmph (62 mph). You will see many drivers far exceeding these limits.

The greatest number of accidents in Spain is recorded along the notorious Costa del Sol highway, the Carretera de Cádiz.

If you must drive through a Spanish city, try to avoid morning and evening rush hours. Never park your car facing oncoming traffic, as that is against the law. If you are fined by the highway patrol *(Guardia Civil de Tráfico),* you must pay on the spot. Penalties for drinking and driving are very stiff.

MAPS   For one of the best overviews of the Iberian Peninsula (Spain and Portugal), get a copy of Michelin map number 990 (for a folding version) or number 460 for the same map in a spiral-bound version. For more detailed looks at Spain, Michelin has a series of six maps (nos. 441–446), showing specific regions, complete with many minor roads.

For extensive touring, purchase *Mapas de Carreteras-España y Portugal,* published by Almax Editores and available at most leading bookstores in Spain. This cartographic compendium of Spain provides an overview of the country and includes road and street maps of some of its major cities as well.

The American Automobile Association (© **800/222-4357**; fax 407/444-4300; www.aaa.com) publishes a regional map of Spain that's available free to members at most AAA offices in the United States. Also available free to members is a guide of approximately 60 pages, *Motoring in Europe,* that gives helpful information about road signs and speed limits, as well as insurance regulations and other relevant matters. Incidentally, the AAA is associated with the **Real Automóvil Club de España,** José Abascal 10, Madrid 28003 (© **91-594-74-00**). This organization can supply helpful information about road conditions in Spain, including tourist and travel data. It will also provide limited road service, in an emergency, if your car breaks down.

BREAKDOWNS   These can be a serious problem. If you're driving a Spanish-made vehicle, you'll probably be able to find spare parts, if needed. But if you have a foreign-made vehicle, you may be stranded. Have the car checked out before setting out on a long trek through Spain. On a major motorway you'll find strategically placed emergency phone boxes. On secondary roads, call for help by asking the operator to locate the nearest Guardia Civil, which will put you in touch with a garage that can tow you to a repair shop.

As noted above, the Spanish affiliate of AAA can provide limited assistance in the event of a breakdown.

BY PLANE

Two affiliated airlines operate within Spain: Iberia and its smaller cousin, Aviaco. (For reservations on either of these airlines, call © **800/772-4642.**) By European standards, domestic flights within Spain are relatively inexpensive, and considering the vast distances within the country, flying between distant points sometimes makes sense.

If you plan to travel to a number of cities and regions, Iberia's "Visit Spain" ticket can be a good deal. Sold only in conjunction with a transatlantic ticket and valid for any airport within Spain and the Canary or Balearic Islands, it requires that you choose up to four different cities in advance, in the order you'll visit them. Restrictions forbid flying immediately back to the city of departure, instead encouraging far-flung visits to widely scattered regions of the peninsula. Only one change within the preset itinerary is permitted once the ticket is issued. The dates and departure times of the actual flights, however, can be determined or changed without penalty once you arrive in Spain. Three coupons, allowing stopovers in three different cities, sell for 228€, going up to 292€ for four cities. For either the Canary Islands or the Balearics, the tickets are more expensive, three coupons (or stopovers) costing 396€ going up to 463€ for four coupons. Children under 2 travel for 10% of the adult fare, and children 2 to 11 travel for 50% of the adult fare. The ticket is valid for up to 60 days after your initial transatlantic arrival in Spain.

BY TRAIN

Spain is crisscrossed with a comprehensive network of rail lines. Hundreds of trains depart every day for points around the country, including the fast TALGO and the newer, faster AVE trains, which reduced rail time between Madrid and Seville to only 2½ hours.

If you plan to travel a great deal on the European railroads, it's worth buying a copy of the *Thomas Cook Timetable of European Passenger Railroads.* It's available exclusively in North America from **Forsyth Travel Library,** 44 S. Broadway, White Plains, NY 10601 (© **800/ FORSYTH;** www.forsyth.com), at a cost of $28, plus $4.95 postage priority airmail in the United States plus $2 for shipments to Canada.

The most economical way to travel in Spain is on the Spanish State Railways (RENFE), the national railway of Spain. Most main long-distance connections are served with night express trains having first- and second-class seats as well as beds and bunks. There are also comfortable high-speed daytime trains of the TALGO, TER, and Electrotren types. There is a general fare for these trains; bunks, beds, and certain superior-quality trains cost extra. Nevertheless, the Spanish railway is one of the most economical in Europe; in most cases, this is the best way to go.

SPANISH RAIL PASSES   RENFE, the national railway of Spain, offers several discounted rail passes. You must buy these passes in the United States prior to your departure. For more information, consult a travel agent or **Rail Europe** (© **800/4-EURAIL;** www.raileurope.com).

The **Iberic Railpass,** good for both Spain and Portugal, offers any 3 days of unlimited first-class train travel in a 2-month period for $205 (children 4–11 pay ½ fare on any of these discount passes). An **Iberic Saverpass,** again including both Spain and Portugal, offers any 3 to 10 days unlimited, first-class train travel in a 2-month period for $200, or any 4 days in 2 months for $240. A **Spain Flexipass** offers any 3 to 10 days unlimited train travel in a 2-month period. Three days in 2 months costs $215 in first class or $165 in second class. The pass can be extended to as much as any 10 days in 2 months, this latter discount selling for $460 in first class or $410 in second class.

EURAILPASSES   The Eurailpass is one of Europe's greatest bargains, permitting unlimited first-class rail travel through 17 countries in Europe, including Spain. Passes are for periods as short as 15 days or as long as 3 months and are strictly nontransferable.

Your best bet is to buy a **Eurailpass** outside Europe (it's available in Europe but will cost more). It costs $588 for 15 days, $762 for 21 days, $946 for 1 month, $1,338 for 2 months, and $1,654 for 3 months. Children 3 and under travel free providing they don't occupy a seat (otherwise they're charged ½ fare); children 4 to 11 are charged half fare. If you're under 26, you can purchase a **Eurail Youthpass,** entitling you to unlimited second-class travel for $414 for 15 days, $534 for 21 days, $664 for 1 month, $938 for 2 months, and $1,160 for 3 months.

Seat reservations are required on some trains. Many of the trains have *couchettes* (sleeping cars), which cost extra. Obviously, the 2- or 3-month traveler gets the greatest economic advantages; the Eurailpass is ideal for such extensive trips. With the pass you can visit all of Spain's major sights, from Barcelona to Seville. Eurailpass holders are entitled to considerable

Riding the Rails in Style

Al Andalús Expreso (or simply Al Andalús) is a restored vintage train that travels through some of the most historic destinations in Andalusia. The train retains an atmosphere and level of service you just don't see very often these days. The passenger and dining cars boast panels of inlaid marquetry, hardwoods, brass fittings, and etched glass that could well be found in the Edwardian parlor of a private mansion; beneath the antique veneers, state-of-the-art engineering maintains comfortably high speeds. The train offers fine dining and such amenities as individual showers on wheels.

Al Andalús consists of 13 carriages manufactured in Britain, Spain, or France between 1929 and 1930. These carriages were collected and restored by railway historians at RENFE. Included are two restaurant cars, a games and lounge car, a bar car where live piano music and evening flamenco dances are presented, five sleeping carriages, and two shower cars. All carriages (except the shower cars) are air-conditioned and heated.

For reservations, contact your travel agent. For additional brochures and information, contact **Marketing Ahead,** 381 Park Ave. S., Suite 718, New York, NY 10016 (© **800/223-1356** or 212/686-9213; www.marketing ahead.com).

reductions on certain buses and ferries as well.

If you'll be traveling for 2 weeks or a month, think carefully before you buy a pass. To get full advantage of a pass for 15 days or a month, you'll have to spend a great deal of time on the train. The **Eurail Flexipass** allows you to travel through Europe with more flexibility. It's valid in first class and offers the same privileges as the Eurailpass. However, it provides a number of individual travel days that you can use over a much longer period of consecutive days. That makes it possible to stay in one city and yet not lose a single day of travel. There are two passes: 10 days of travel in 2 months for $694, and 15 days of travel in 2 months for $914. The **Eurail Youth Flexipass** is identical except that it's sold only to travelers under 26, and costs less: $592 for 10 days of travel within 2 months, and $778 for 15 days of travel within 2 months.

A **Eurail Selectpass** allows travelers to select three countries linked by rail or ferry out of the 17 countries covered by Eurailpass. This is a flexipass, meaning that travel days need not be consecutive; passes are offered for 5, 6, 8, or 10 days within a 2-month period. Prices for a Eurail Selectpass begin at $356 per person for 5 days.

WHERE TO BUY RAIL PASSES Travel agents in all towns and railway agents in major North American cities sell all these tickets, but the biggest supplier is **Rail Europe** (© **800/ 848-7245;** www.raileurope.com), which can also give you informational brochures.

Many different rail passes are available in the United Kingdom for travel in Britain and continental Europe. Stop in at the **International Rail Centre,** Victoria Station, London SWIV 1JY (© **0870/5848-848** in the U.K.). Some of the most popular passes, including Inter-Rail and Euro

Youth, are offered only to travelers under 26 years of age; these allow unlimited second-class travel through most European countries.

You can reduce costs with this means of transport by sharing your trip with another adult, who will receive a 50% discount on each of the above-mentioned fares.

Note: You can add what Europass refers to as an "associate country" (Austria, Benelux, Greece, or Portugal) to the reach of your Europass by paying a surcharge.

BY BUS

Bus service in Spain is extensive, low priced, and comfortable enough for short distances. You'll rarely encounter a bus terminal in Spain. The station might be a cafe, a bar, the street in front of a hotel, or simply a spot at an intersection.

A bus may be the cheapest mode of transportation, but it's not really the best option for distances of more than 161km (100 miles). On long hauls, buses are often uncomfortable. Another major drawback might be a lack of toilet facilities, although rest stops are frequent. It's best for 1-day excursions outside a major tourist center such as Madrid. In the rural areas of the country, bus networks are more extensive than the railway system; they go virtually everywhere, connecting every village. In general, a bus ride between two major cities in Spain, such as from Córdoba to Seville or Madrid to Barcelona, is about two-thirds the price of a train ride and a few hours faster.

16 Tips on Accommodations

From castles converted into hotels to modern high-rise resorts overlooking the Mediterranean, Spain has some of the most varied hotel accommodations in the world—with equally varied price ranges. Accommodations are broadly classified as follows:

ONE- TO FIVE-STAR HOTELS

The Spanish government rates hotels by according them stars. A five-star hotel is truly deluxe, with deluxe prices; a one-star hotel is the most modest accommodation officially recognized as a hotel by the government. A four-star hotel offers first-class accommodations; a three-star hotel is moderately priced; and a one- or two-star hotel is inexpensively priced. The government grants stars based on such amenities as elevators, private bathrooms, and air-conditioning. If a hotel is classified as a *residencia,* it means that it serves breakfast (usually) but no other meals.

HOSTALS

Not to be confused with a hostel for students, an *hostal* is a modest hotel without services, where you can save money by carrying your own bags and the like. You'll know it's an *hostal* if a small S follows the capital letter H on the blue plaque by the door. An *hostal* with three stars is about the equivalent of a hotel with two stars.

PENSIONS

These boardinghouses are among the least expensive accommodations, but you're required to take either full board (3 meals) or half board, which is breakfast plus lunch or dinner.

CASAS HUESPEDES & FONDAS

These are the cheapest places in Spain and can be recognized by the light-blue plaques at the door displaying CH and F, respectively. They are invariably basic but respectable establishments.

YOUTH HOSTELS

Spain has about 140 hostels (*albergues de juventud*). In theory, those 25 or under have the first chance at securing a bed for the night, but these places are certainly not limited to young people. Some of them are equipped for persons with disabilities. Most hostels impose an 11pm curfew. For information, contact **Red Española de Alberques Juveniles,** Calle José Ortega y Gasset 71, 28006 Madrid (© **91-543-74-12;** www.reaj.com).

PARADORS

The Spanish government runs a series of unique state-owned inns called paradors (*paradores* in Spanish), which now blanket the country. Deserted castles, monasteries, palaces, and other buildings have been taken over and converted into hotels. Today there are 86 paradors in all, and they're documented in a booklet called *Visiting the Paradors,* available at Spanish tourist offices (see "Visitor Information," earlier in this chapter).

At great expense, modern bathrooms, steam heat, and the like have been added to these buildings, yet classic Spanish architecture, where it existed, has been retained. Establishments are often furnished with antiques or at least good reproductions and decorative objects typical of the country.

Meals are also served in these government-owned inns. Usually, typical dishes of the region are featured. Paradors are likely to be overcrowded in the summer months, so advance reservations, arranged through any travel agent, are wise.

The government also operates a type of accommodation known as *albergues:* These are comparable to motels, standing along the roadside and usually built in hotel-scarce sections for the convenience of passing motorists. A client is not allowed to stay in an *albergue* for more than 48 hours, and the management doesn't accept reservations.

In addition, the government runs *refugios* (refuges), mostly in remote areas, attracting hunters, fishers, and mountain climbers. Another state-sponsored establishment is the *hostería,* or specialty restaurant, such as the one at Alcalá de Henares, near Madrid. *Hosterías* don't offer rooms; decorated in the style of a particular province, they serve regional dishes at reasonable prices.

The central office of paradors is **Paradores de España,** Requeña 3, 28013 Madrid (© **91-516-66-66;** www.parador.es). The U.S. representative for the Paradores of Spain is **Marketing Ahead,** 381 Park Ave. S., New York, NY 10016 (© **800/223-1356** or 212/686/9213). Travel agents can also arrange reservations.

RENTING A HOUSE OR APARTMENT

If you rent a home or an apartment, you can save money on accommodations and dining and still take daily trips to see the surrounding area.

Apartments in Spain generally fall into two different categories: hotel *apartamentos* and *residencia apartamentos.* The hotel apartments have full facilities, with chamber service, equipped kitchenettes, and often restaurants and bars. The residencia apartments, also called *apartamentos turísticos,* are fully furnished with kitchenettes but lack the facilities of the hotel complexes. They are cheaper, however.

One rental company to try is **Hometours International** (© **866/ 367-4668** or 865/690-8484), which mainly handles properties in Andalusia. Call them and they'll send you a 40-page color catalog with descriptions and pictures for $5 to cover postage and handling. Units are rented for a minimum of 7 days.

Another agency is **ILC (International Lodging Corp.;** © **800/ SPAIN-44** or 212/228-5900; www. ilcweb.com), which rents privately owned apartments, houses, and villas, for a week or more. It also offers access to suites in well-known hotels for stays of a week or longer, sometimes at bargain rates. Rental units, regardless of their size, usually contain a kitchen.

The company's listings cover accommodations in Madrid, Barcelona, Seville, Granada, and Majorca.

17 Recommended Books

ECONOMIC, POLITICAL & SOCIAL HISTORY

Historically, Spain's golden age lasted from the late 15th to the early 17th century, a period when the country reached the height of its prestige and influence. This era is well surveyed in J. H. Elliot's *Imperial Spain 1469–1716* (New American Library).

Most accounts of the Spanish Armada's defeat are written from the English point of view. For a change of perspective, try David Howarth's *The Voyage of the Armada* (Penguin).

The nightmarish story of the Spanish Inquisition is told by Edward Peters in his *Inquisition* (University of California Press).

One of the best accounts of Spain's earlier history is found in Joseph F. O'Callaghan's *History of Medieval Spain* (Cornell University).

In the 20th century the focus shifts to the Spanish Civil War, recounted in Hugh Thomas's classic, *The Spanish Civil War* (Harper & Row). For a personal account of the war, read George Orwell's *Homage to Catalonia* (Harcourt Brace Jovanovich). The poet García Lorca was killed during the Civil War; the best account of his death is found in Ian Gibson's *The Assassination of Federico García Lorca* (Penguin).

If you like more contemporary history, read John Hooper's *The Spaniards* (Penguin). Hooper provides insight into the events of the post-Franco era, when the country came to grips with democracy after years of fascism.

THE ARTS

The Moors contributed much to Spanish culture, leaving Spain with a distinct legacy that is documented in Titus Burckhardt's *Moorish Culture in Spain* (McGraw-Hill).

Antoni Gaudí is the Spanish architect who most excites visitors' curiosity. The latest study is *Gaudí*, by Gijs van Hensbergen, published in 2001. The author claims Gaudí was "drunk on form," and that the architect still has not lost his power to astonish with his idiosyncratic and innovative designs.

Spain's most famous artist was Pablo Picasso. The most controversial book about the late painter is *Picasso, Creator and Destroyer* by Arianna Stassinopoulos Huffington (Simon & Schuster).

Spain's other headline-grabbing artist was Salvador Dalí. In *Salvador Dalí: A Biography* (Dutton), author Meryle Secrest asks: Was he a mad genius or a cunning manipulator?

Andrés Segovia: An Autobiography of the Years 1893–1920 (Macmillan), with a translation by W. F. O'Brien, is worth seeking out.

For the most intimate glimpse into the world of a Spanish film director, read *Mi Ultimo Suspiro (My Last Sigh)*, the autobiography of Luis Buñuel, whose films mirrored the social, political, and religious conflicts that have torn Spain apart in the 20th century.

Residents of Catalonia truthfully maintain that their unique language, culture, and history have been overshadowed (and squelched) by the richer and better-publicized accomplishments of Castile. Robert Hughes, a former art critic at *Time* magazine, has written an elegant testament to the glories of the capital of this region: *Barcelona* (Knopf); this book offers a well-versed and often witty articulation of the city's architectural and cultural legacy. According to the *New York Times,* the book is probably destined to become "a classic in the genre of urban history."

FICTION & BIOGRAPHY

Denounced by some as superficial, James A. Michener's *Iberia* (Random House) remains the classic travelog on Spain. The *Houston Post* claimed that this book "will make you fall in love with Spain."

The latest biography on one of the 20th century's most durable dictators is *Franco: A Concise Biography,* which was released in the spring of 2002. Gabrielle Ashford Hodges documents with great flair the Orwellian repression and widespread corruption that marked the notorious regime of this "deeply flawed" politician.

The most famous Spanish novel is *Don Quixote* by Miguel de Cervantes. Readily available everywhere, it deals with the conflict between the ideal and the real in human nature. Despite the unparalleled fame of Miguel de Cervantes within Spanish literature, very little is known about his life. One of the most searching biographies of the literary master is Jean Canavaggio's *Cervantes,* translated from the Spanish by J. R. Jones (Norton).

Although the work of Cervantes has attained an almost mystical significance in the minds of many Spaniards, in the words of Somerset Maugham, "It would be hard to find a work so great that has so many defects." Nicholas Wollaston's *Tilting at Don Quixote* (André Deutsch Publishers)

punctures any illusions that the half-crazed Don is only a matter of good and rollicking fun.

The major works of pre–Civil War playwright, Federico García Lorca, can be enjoyed in *Five Plays: Comedies and Tragicomedies* (New Directions).

Ernest Hemingway completed many works on Spain, none more notable than his novels of 1926 and 1940, respectively: *The Sun Also Rises* (Macmillan) and *For Whom the Bell Tolls* (Macmillan), the latter based on his experiences in the Spanish Civil War. Don Ernesto's *Death in the Afternoon* (various editions) remains the English-language classic on bullfighting.

For a very different, but dated, view of Spain, read W. Somerset Maugham's *Don Fernando* (Ayer), with the famed English author's comments on everything from the Spanish diet to *Don Quixote.*

For travelers to Granada and the Alhambra, the classic is *Tales of the Alhambra* (Sleepy Hollow Press) by Washington Irving. If you're visiting Majorca, read George Sand's *A Winter in Majorca* (Academy Chicago Publications), detailing the troubled time she spent with Chopin at Valldemossa. Many translations (the best one is by Robert Graves) are for sale on Majorca.

The Life of Saint Teresa of Avila by Herself (Penguin), translated by J. M. Cohen, is reputedly the third most widely read book in Spain, after the Bible and *Don Quixote.* Some parts are heavy going, but the remainder is lively.

 FAST FACTS: Spain

Business Hours Banks are open Monday through Friday from 9:30am to 2pm and Saturday from 9:30am to 1pm. Most offices are open Monday through Friday from 9am to 5 or 5:30pm; the longtime practice of early closings in summer seems to be dying out. In restaurants, lunch is usually from 1 to 4pm and dinner from 9 to 11:30pm or midnight. There are no set rules for the opening of bars and taverns, many opening at 8am, others at noon; most stay open until 1:30am or later. Major stores are open Monday through Saturday from 9:30am to 8pm; smaller establishments, however, often take a siesta, doing business from 9:30am to 1:30pm and 4:30 to 8pm. Hours can vary from store to store.

Climate See "When to Go," earlier in this chapter.

Currency See "Money," earlier in this chapter.

Customs See "Visitor Information," earlier in this chapter.

Driving Rules See "Getting Around," earlier in this chapter.

Drugstores To find an open pharmacy outside normal business hours, check the list of stores posted on the door of any drugstore. The law requires drugstores to operate on a rotating system of hours so that there's always a drugstore open somewhere, even Sunday at midnight.

Electricity Most hotels have 220 volts AC (50 cycles). Some older places have 110 or 125 volts AC. Carry your adapter with you, and always check at your hotel desk before plugging in any electrical appliance. It's best to travel with battery-operated equipment or just buy a new hair dryer in Spain.

Embassies/Consulates If you lose your passport, fall seriously ill, get into legal trouble, or have some other serious problem, your embassy or consulate can help. These are the Madrid addresses and hours: The **United States Embassy,** Calle Serrano 75 (© **91-587-22-00;** metro: Núñez de Balboa), is open Monday through Friday from 9am to 6pm. The **Canadian Embassy,** Núñez de Balboa 35 (© **91-423-32-50;** metro: Velázquez), is open Monday through Friday from 8:30am to 5:30pm. The **United Kingdom Embassy,** Calle Fernando el Santo 16 (© **91-917-00-82;** metro: Colón), is open Monday through Friday from 9am to 1:30pm and 3 to 6pm. The **Republic of Ireland** has an embassy at Paseo Castellana 46 (© **91-436-40-93;** metro: Serrano); it's open Monday through Friday from 9am to 2pm. The **Australian Embassy,** Plaza Diego de Ordas 3, Edificio Santa Engracia 120 (© **91-441-60-25;** metro: Ríos Rosas), is open Monday though Thursday from 8:30am to 5pm and Friday from 8:30am to 2:15pm. Citizens of **New Zealand** have an embassy at Plaza de la Lealtad 2 (© **91-523-02-26;** metro: Banco de España); it's open Monday through Friday from 9am to 1:30pm and 2:30 to 5:30pm.

Emergencies The national emergency number for Spain (except the Basque country) is © **006;** in the Basque country it is © **088.**

Etiquette In Franco's day, many visitors would be arrested for the skimpy, revealing wear worn around the city streets of Spain today. Nonetheless, it is considered extremely rude for many to go bare-chested except at the beach or at poolside. Spaniards and church officials do object to your visiting churches and cathedrals if scantily clad even on the hottest day of summer. Casual dress is acceptable, but one should "cover up" as much skin as possible.

In spite of what you've heard in days of yore, when Spaniards showed up for appointments 2 or 3 hours late, most nationals now show up on time as they do in the rest of the E.U. countries. It's always wise for men to wear a suit for business meetings. Spanish speakers should address strangers with the formal *usted* instead of the more familiar *tú*.

Language The official language in Spain is Castilian (or *Castellano*). Although Spanish is spoken in every province of Spain, local tongues reasserted themselves with the restoration of democracy in 1975. After years of being outlawed during the Franco dictatorship, Catalán has returned to Barcelona and Catalonia, even appearing on street signs; this language and its derivatives are also spoken in the Valencia area and in the Balearic Islands, including Majorca (even though natives there will tell you they speak *Mallorquín*). The Basque language is widely spoken in the Basque region (the northeast, near France), which is seeking independence from Spain. Likewise, the Gallego language, which sounds and looks very much like Portuguese, has enjoyed a renaissance in Galicia (the northwest). Of course, English is spoken in most hotels, restaurants, and shops.

The best phrase book is *Spanish for Travellers* by Berlitz; it has a menu supplement and a 12,500-word glossary of both English and Spanish.

Liquor Laws The legal drinking age is 18. Bars, taverns, and cafeterias usually open at 8am, and many serve alcohol to 1:30am or later. Generally, you can purchase alcoholic beverages in almost any market.

Mail Airmail letters to the United States and Canada cost .75€ up to 15 grams, and letters to Britain or other E.U. countries cost .50€ up to 20 grams; letters within Spain cost .25€. Postcards have the same rates as letters. Allow about 8 days for delivery to North America, generally less to the United Kingdom; in some cases, letters take 2 weeks to reach North America. Rates change frequently, so check at your local hotel before mailing anything. As for surface mail to North America, forget it. Chances are you'll be home long before your letter arrives.

Passports **For Residents of the United States:** Whether you're applying in person or by mail, you can download passport applications from the U.S. State Department website at **http://travel.state.gov**. For general information, call the **National Passport Agency** (℡ 202/647-0518). To find your regional passport office, either check the U.S. State Department website or call the **National Passport Information Center** (℡ 900/225-5674); the fee is 55¢ per minute for automated information and $1.50 per minute for operator-assisted calls.

For Residents of Canada: Passport applications are available at travel agencies throughout Canada or from the central **Passport Office,** Department of Foreign Affairs and International Trade, Ottawa, ON K1A 0G3 (℡ 800/567-6868; www.dfait-maeci.gc.ca/passport).

For Residents of the United Kingdom: To pick up an application for a standard 10-year passport (5-year passport for children under 16), visit your nearest passport office, major post office, or travel agency or contact the **United Kingdom Passport Service** at ℡ 0870/521-0410 or search its website at www.ukpa.gov.uk.

For Residents of Ireland: You can apply for a 10-year passport at the **Passport Office,** Setanta Centre, Molesworth Street, Dublin 2 (℡ 01/671-1633;

www.irlgov.ie/iveagh). Those under age 18 and over 65 must apply for a 12€ 3-year passport. You can also apply at 1A South Mall, Cork (© 021/ 272-525) or at most main post offices.

For Residents of Australia: You can pick up an application from your local post office or any branch of Passports Australia, but you must schedule an interview at the passport office to present your application materials. Call the **Australian Passport Information Service** at © **131-232,** or visit the government website at www.passports.gov.au.

For Residents of New Zealand: You can pick up a passport application at any New Zealand Passports Office or download it from their website. Contact the **Passports Office** at © **0800/225-050** in New Zealand, or 04/474-8100, or log on to www.passports.govt.nz.

Police The national emergency number is © **006** throughout Spain, except in the Basque country, where it is © **088.**

Restrooms In Spain they're called *aseos* and *servicios* or simply *lavabos* and labeled *caballeros* for men and *damas* or *señoras* for women. If you can't find any, go into a bar, but you should order something.

Safety See "Health & Safety," earlier in this chapter.

Taxes The internal sales tax (known in Spain as *IVA*) ranges between 7% and 33%, depending on the commodity being sold. Food, wine, and basic necessities are taxed at 7%; most goods and services (including car rentals) at 13%; luxury items (jewelry, all tobacco, imported liquors) at 33%; and hotels at 7%.

If you are not a European Union resident and make purchases in Spain worth more than 90€, you can get a tax refund. To get this refund, you must complete three copies of a form that the store will give you, detailing the nature of your purchase and its value. Citizens of non-E.U. countries show the purchase and the form to the Spanish Customs Office. The shop is supposed to refund the amount due you. Inquire at the time of purchase how they will do so and discuss in what currency your refund will arrive.

Telephones If you don't speak Spanish, you'll find it easier to telephone from your hotel, but remember that this is often very expensive because hotels impose a surcharge on every operator-assisted call. In some cases it can be as high as 40% or more. On the street, phone booths (known as *cabinas*) have dialing instructions in English; you can make local calls by inserting a .25€ coin for 3 minutes. For example, if you wanted to call the British Embassy in Washington, D.C., you would dial 00-1-202-588-7800.

For directory assistance: Dial © **1003** in Spain.

For operator assistance: If you need operator assistance in making an international call, dial © **025.**

Toll-free numbers: Numbers beginning with **900** in Spain are toll-free, but calling a 1-800 number in the States from Spain is not toll-free. In fact, it costs the same as an overseas call.

In Spain many smaller establishments, especially bars, discos, and a few informal restaurants, don't have phones. Further, many summer-only bars and discos secure a phone for the season only, then get a new number the next season. Many attractions, such as small churches or even minor museums, have no staff to receive inquiries from the public.

In 1998, all telephone numbers in Spain changed to a nine-digit system instead of the six- or seven-digit method used previously. Each number is now preceded by its provincial code for local, national, and international calls. For example, when calling to Madrid from Madrid or another province within Spain, telephone customers must dial 91-123-4567. Similarly, when calling Valladolid from within or outside the province, dial 979-123-4567.

When in Spain, the access number for an **AT&T** calling card is © **800/ CALL-ATT.** The access number for **Sprint** is © **800/888-0013.**

More information is also available on the Telefónica website at www.telefonica.es.

To call Spain: If you're calling Spain from the United States:

1. Dial the international access code: **011.**
2. Dial the country code for Spain: **34.**
3. Dial the city code for Spain and then the number. So the whole number you'd dial would be 011-34-93-000-0000.

To make international calls: To make international calls from Spain, first dial 00 and then the country code (U.S. and Canada 1, U.K. 44, Ireland 353, Australia 61, New Zealand 64). Next you dial the area code and number.

Time Spain is 6 hours ahead of Eastern Standard Time in the United States. Daylight saving time is in effect from the last Sunday in March to the last Sunday in September.

Tipping Don't overtip. The government requires restaurants and hotels to include their service charges—usually 15% of the bill. However, that doesn't mean you should skip out of a place without dispensing an extra euro or two. The following are some guidelines:

Your hotel porter should get .60€ per bag. Maids should be given .85€ per day, more if you're generous. Tip doormen .75€ for assisting with baggage and .50€ for calling a cab. In top-ranking hotels the concierge will often submit a separate bill, showing charges for newspapers and other services; if he or she has been particularly helpful, tip extra. For cab drivers, add about 10% to the fare as shown on the meter. At airports, such as Barajas in Madrid and major terminals, the porter who handles your luggage will present you with a fixed-charge bill.

In both restaurants and nightclubs, a 15% service charge is added to the bill. To that, add another 3% to 5% tip, depending on the quality of the service. Waiters in deluxe restaurants and nightclubs are accustomed to the extra 5%, which means you'll end up tipping 20%. If that seems excessive, you must remember that the initial service charge reflected in the fixed price is distributed among all the help.

Barbers and hairdressers expect a 10% to 15% tip. Tour guides expect 2€, although a tip is not mandatory. Theater and bullfight ushers get from .30€ to .45€.

Madrid

Madrid was conceived, planned, and built when Spain was at the peak of its confidence and power, and the city became the solid and dignified seat of a great empire stretching around the world. Monumental Madrid glitters almost as much as Paris, Rome, or London—and parties more than any other city on the continent. Although it lacks the spectacular Romanesque and Gothic monuments of older Spanish cities, Madrid never fails to convey its own sense of grandeur.

Madrid has the highest altitude of any European capital, and its climate is blisteringly hot in summer but often quite cold in winter. Traffic roars down wide boulevards that stretch from the narrow streets of the city's 17th-century core to the ugly concrete suburbs that have spread in recent years.

Don't come to Madrid expecting a city that looks classically Iberian. True, many of the older buildings in the historic core look as Spanish as those you might encounter in rural towns across the plains of La Mancha. However, a great number of the monuments and palaces mirror the architecture of France—an oddity that reflects the link between the royal families of Spain and France.

Most striking is how the city has blossomed since Franco's demise. During the 1980s Madrid was the epicenter of *la movida* (the movement), a resuscitation of the arts after years of dictatorial creative repression. Today, despite stiff competition from such smaller cities as Barcelona and Seville,

Madrid still reigns as the country's artistic and creative centerpiece.

More world-class art is on view in the central neighborhood around the stellar Prado Museum than within virtually any concentrated area in the world. You can see Caravaggios and Rembrandts at the Thyssen-Bornemisza; El Grecos and Velázquezes at the Prado itself; and Dalís and Mirós—not to mention Picasso's wrenching *Guernica*—at the Reina Sofía. Much of the city's art was collected by 18th-century Spanish monarchs, whose artistic sense was frequently more astute than their political savvy.

Regrettably, within the city limits you'll also find sprawling expanses of concrete towers, sometimes paralyzing traffic, growing street crime, and entire districts that, as in every other Metropolis, bear virtually no historic or cultural interest for a temporary visitor. Many long-time visitors to the city find that its quintessential Spanish feel has subsided somewhat in the face of a Brussels-like "Europeanization" that has occurred since Spain's 1986 induction into the European Union. The city's gems remain the opulence of the Palacio Real, the bustle of El Rastro's flea market, and the sultry fever of late-night flamenco. When urban commotion starts to overwhelm, seek respite in the Parque del Retiro, a vast, verdant oasis in the heart of the city just a stone's throw from the Prado.

If your time in Spain is limited, a stopover in Madrid coupled with day trips to its environs can provide a primer in virtually every major period and school of Spanish art and architecture dating from the Roman occupation. No fewer than nine world-class destinations are within 161km (100 miles). They include Toledo, one of the most successful blends of medieval Arab, Jewish, and Christian cultures in the world; Segovia, site of a well-preserved ancient Roman aqueduct and monuments commemorating Queen Isabella's coronation in 1474; and Avila, the most perfectly preserved medieval fortified city in Iberia, with its 11th-century battlements and endless references to Catholicism's most

down-to-earth mystic, St. Teresa. El Escorial, El Pardo (Franco's favorite hangout), and the palace and monuments at Aranjuez reveal the tastes and manias that inspired rulers of Spain throughout history. The neofascist monument at El Valle de los Caídos (the Valley of the Fallen) is a powerful testament to those who died in the Spanish Civil War. To see rural Iberia at its most charming, head for Chinchón or, better yet, the cliff-top village of Cuenca, where a lavish homage to modern art and music has recently been installed. For more information on these day trips, see chapter 5, "Side Trips from Madrid."

1 Orientation

ARRIVING

BY PLANE   Madrid's international airport, **Barajas,** lies 15km (9 miles) east of the center and has two terminals—one for international traffic, the other for domestic—connected by a moving sidewalk. For Barajas Airport information, call © **91-305-83-43.**

Air-conditioned airport buses can take you from the arrival terminal to a bus depot beneath the central Plaza de Colón. You can get off at stops along the way, provided that your baggage isn't stored in the hold. The fare is 2.40€; buses leave every 15 minutes, either to or from the airport.

By taxi, expect to pay 24€ and up, plus surcharges, for the trip to the airport and for baggage handling. If you take an unmetered limousine, make sure you negotiate the price in advance.

A subway connecting Barajas Airport and central Madrid was completed in 1999, allowing additional ground transportation options. However, the ride involves a change: Take line 8 to Mar de Cristal and switch to line 4; the one-way trip costs 1.10€.

BY TRAIN   Madrid has three major railway stations: **Atocha** (Av. Ciudad de Barcelona; Metro: Atocha RENFE), for trains to and from Lisbon, Toledo, Andalusia, and Extremadura; **Chamartín** (in the northern suburbs at Augustín de Foxá; Metro: Chamartín), for trains to and from Barcelona, Asturias, Cantabria, Castilla-León, the Basque country, Aragón, Catalonia, Levante (Valencia), Murcia, and the French frontier; and **Estación Príncipe Pío** or Norte (Paseo del Rey 30; Metro: Norte), for trains to and from northwest Spain (Salamanca and Galicia). For information about connections from any of these stations, call RENFE (Spanish Railways) at © **90-224-02-02,** daily 5:30am to 11:50pm.

For tickets, go to the principal office of **RENFE,** Alcalá 44 (© **91-506-63-29;** Metro: Banco de España). The office is open Monday through Friday from 9:30am to 8pm.

BY BUS   Madrid has at least eight major bus terminals, including the large **Estación Sur de Autobuses,** Calle Méndez Alvaro 83 (© **91-468-42-00;** Metro: Mendez Alvaro). Most buses pass through this station.

BY CAR   All highways within Spain radiate outward from Madrid. The following are the major highways into Madrid, with information on driving distances to the city:

Highways to Madrid

Route	From	Distance to Madrid
N-I	Irún	507km (315 miles)
N-II	Barcelona	626km (389 miles)
N-III	Valencia	349km (217 miles)
N-IV	Cádiz	625km (388 miles)
N-V	Badajoz	409km (254 miles)
N-VI	Galicia	602km (374 miles)

VISITOR INFORMATION

The most convenient **tourist office,** www.munimadrid.es, is near the American Express office, on Duque de Medinaceli 2, Banco de España (© **91-429-31-77;** Metro: Plaza de España; www.comadrid.org); it's open Monday through Friday from 9am to 7pm and Saturday from 9:30am to 1pm. Ask for a street map of the next town on your itinerary, especially if you're driving. The staff here can give you a list of hotels and *hostales* but cannot recommend any particular lodging.

CITY LAYOUT

All roads lead to Madrid, which has outgrown its previous boundaries and is branching out in all directions.

MAIN ARTERIES & SQUARES   Every new arrival must find the **Gran Vía,** which cuts a winding pathway across the city beginning at the **Plaza de España,** where you'll find one of Europe's tallest skyscrapers, the Edificio España. This avenue is home to the largest concentration of shops, hotels, restaurants, and movie houses in the city, with **Calle de Serrano** a close runner-up.

South of the Gran Vía lies the **Puerta del Sol,** the starting point for all road distances within Spain. However, its tourism significance has declined, and today it is a prime hunting ground for pickpockets and purse snatchers. **Calle de Alcalá** begins here at Sol and runs for 4km (2½ miles).

The **Plaza Mayor** lies at the heart of Old Madrid and is an attraction in itself with its mix of French and Georgian architecture. (Again, be wary of thieves here, especially late at night.) Pedestrians pass under the arches of the huge square onto the narrow streets of the old town, where you can find some of the capital's most intriguing restaurants and *tascas,* serving tasty tapas and drinks. The colonnaded ground level of the plaza is filled with shops, many selling souvenir hats of turn-of-the-20th-century Spanish sailors or army officers.

The area south of the Plaza Mayor—known as *barrios bajos*—is made up of narrow cobblestone streets lined with 16th- and 17th-century architecture. From the Plaza, take **Arco de Cuchilleros,** a street packed with markets, restaurants, flamenco clubs, and taverns, to explore this district.

Gran Vía ends at Calle de Alcalá, and at this juncture lies the grand **Plaza de la Cibeles,** with its fountain to Cybele, "the mother of the gods," and the main post office (known as "the cathedral of post offices"). From Cibeles, the wide **Paseo de Recoletos** begins a short run north to Plaza de Colón. From this latter square rolls the serpentine central artery of Madrid: **Paseo de la Castellana,** flanked by expensive shops, apartment buildings, luxury hotels, and foreign embassies.

Tips **Finding an Address**

Madrid is a city of both grand boulevards and cramped meandering streets. Finding an address can sometimes be a problem, primarily because of the way buildings are numbered. On most streets, the numbering begins on one side and runs consecutively until the end, resuming on the other side and going in the opposite direction. Thus, number 50 could be opposite number 250. But there are many exceptions to this system. That's why it's important to know the cross street as well as the number of the address you're looking for. To complicate matters, some addresses don't have a number at all. What they have is the designation *s/n,* meaning *sin número* (without number). For example, the address of the Panteón de Goya (Goya's Tomb) is Glorieta de San Antonio de la Florida s/n. Note that in Spain, as in many other European countries, the building number comes after the street name.

Heading south from Cibeles is **Paseo del Prado,** where you'll find Spain's major attraction, the Museo del Prado, as well as the Jardín Botánico (Botanical Garden). The *paseo* leads to the Atocha Railway Station. To the west of the garden lies **Parque del Retiro,** a magnificent park once reserved for royalty, with restaurants, nightclubs, a rose garden, and two lakes.

STREET MAPS   Arm yourself with a good map before setting out. Falk publishes the best, and it's available at most newsstands and kiosks in Madrid. The free maps given away by tourist offices and hotels aren't really adequate for more than general orientation, as they don't list the maze of little streets that is Old Madrid.

NEIGHBORHOODS IN BRIEF

Madrid can be divided into three principal districts—Old Madrid, which holds the most tourist interest; Ensanche, the new district, often with the best shops and hotels; and the periphery, which is of little interest to visitors.

Plaza Mayor/Puerta del Sol   This is the heart of Old Madrid, often called the tourist zone. Filled with taverns and bars, it is bounded by Carrera de San Jerónimo, Calle Mayor, Cava de San Miguel, Cava Baja, and Calle de la Cruz. From the Plaza Mayor, the Arco de Cuchilleros is filled with Castilian restaurants and taverns; more of these traditional spots, called *cuevas,* line the Cava de San Miguel, Cava Alta, and Cava Baja. To the west of this old district is the Manzanares River. Also in this area, Muslim Madrid is centered on the Palacio de Oriente and Las Vistillas. What is now the Plaza de la Paja was actually the heart of the city and its main marketplace during the medieval and Christian period. In 1617, the Plaza Mayor became the hub of Madrid, and it remains to this day the nighttime center of tourist activity, more so than the Puerta del Sol.

The Salamanca Quarter Ever since Madrid's city walls came tumbling down in the 1860s, the district of Salamanca to the north has been the fashionable address. Calle de Serrano cuts through this neighborhood and is lined with stores and boutiques. Calle de Serrano is also home to the U.S. Embassy.

Gran Vía/Plaza de España Gran Vía is the city's main street, lined with cinemas, department stores, and the headquarters of banks and corporations. It begins at the Plaza de España, with its bronze figures of Don Quixote and his faithful squire, Sancho Panza.

Argüelles/Moncloa The university area is bounded by Pintor Rosales, Cea Bermúdez, Bravo Murillo, San Bernardo, and Conde Duque. Students haunt its famous alehouses.

Chueca This old, decaying area north of the Gran Vía includes the main streets of Hortaleza, Infantas, Barquillo, and San Lucas. It is the center of gay nightlife, with dozens of clubs and cheap restaurants. It can be dangerous at night, although police presence is usually notable.

Castellana/Recoletos/Paseo del Prado Not a real city district, this is Madrid's north-south axis, its name changing along the way. The Museo del Prado and some of the city's more expensive hotels are found here. Many restaurants and other hotels are located along its side streets. In summer its large medians serve as home to open-air terraces filled with animated crowds. The most famous cafe is the Gran Café de Gijón (see "Where to Dine," later in this chapter).

2 Getting Around

Getting around Madrid is not easy, because everything is spread out. Even many Madrileño taxi drivers, often new arrivals themselves, are unfamiliar with their own city once they're off the main boulevards.

BY SUBWAY

The Metro system is quite easy to learn and use. The fare is 1.10€ for a one-way trip, and the central converging point is the Puerta del Sol. The Metro operates from 6am to 1:30am, and you should try to avoid rush hours. For information, call ✆ 91-429-31-77. You can save money on public transportation by purchasing a 10-trip ticket known as a *bonos*—it costs 5.20€.

BY BUS

A bus network also services the city and suburbs, with routes clearly shown at each stop on a schematic diagram. Buses are fast and efficient because they travel along special lanes. Both red and blue buses charge 1.10€ per ride. For 5.20€ you can purchase a 10-trip *bonos* ticket (but without transfers) for Madrid's bus system. It's sold at Empresa Municipal de Transportes, Alcántara 24-26 (✆ 91-406-88-00), where you can buy a guide to the bus routes. The office is open daily from 8am to 2pm.

BY TAXI

Cab fares are pretty reasonable. When you flag down a taxi, the meter should register 1.50€; for every kilometer thereafter, the fare increases by .95€. A supplement is charged for trips to the railway station or the bullring, as well as on Sundays and holidays. The ride to Barajas Airport carries a 4€ surcharge, and there is a 2€ supplement from railway stations. In addition, there is a 1.50€ supplement on Sundays and holidays, plus a .95€ supplement at night. It's customary to tip at least 10% of the fare.

Warning: Make sure the meter is turned on when you get into a taxi. Otherwise, some drivers assess the cost of the ride, and their assessment, you can be sure, will involve higher mathematics.

Madrid Metro

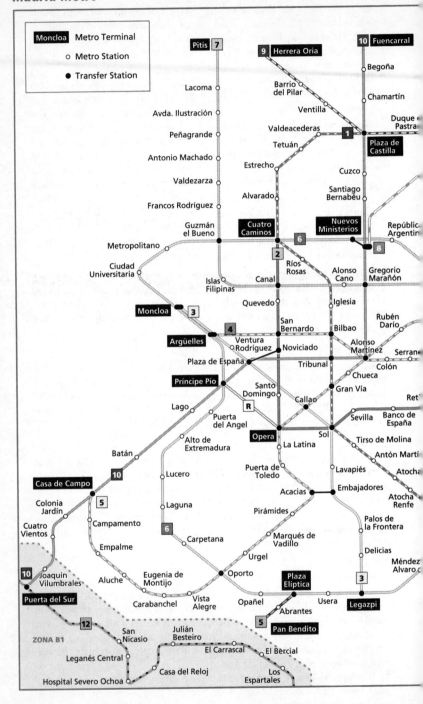

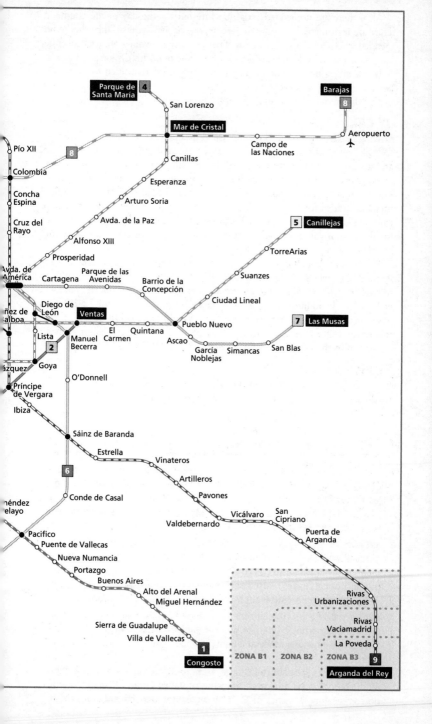

Also, there are unmetered taxis that hire out for the day or the afternoon. They are legitimate, but some drivers operate as gypsy cabs. Since they're not metered, they can charge high rates. They are easy to avoid—always take either a black taxi with horizontal red bands or a white one with diagonal red bands.

If you take a taxi outside the city limits, the driver is entitled to charge you twice the rate shown on the meter.

To call a taxi, dial © **91-447-51-80.**

BY CAR

Driving in congested Madrid is a nightmare and potentially dangerous. It always feels like rush hour, although theoretically, these are from 8 to 10am, 1 to 2pm, and 4 to 6pm Monday through Saturday. Parking is next to impossible except in expensive garages. About the only time you can drive around Madrid with a minimum of hassle is in August, when thousands of Madrileños have taken their cars and headed for Spain's vacation oases. Save your car rentals for excursions from the capital. If you drive into Madrid from another city, ask at your hotel for the nearest garage or parking possibility and leave your vehicle there until you're ready to leave.

For more information on renting a car before you leave home, see "Getting Around" in chapter 3, "Planning Your Trip To Spain." If you decide you want to rent one while in Madrid to explore its environs or to move on, you have several choices. In addition to its office at Barajas Airport (© **91-393-72-22**), Avis has a main office in the city center at Gran Vía 60 (© **91-548-42-04**). Hertz, too, has an office at Barajas Airport (© **91-393-72-28**) and another in the heart of Madrid in the Edificio España, Gran Vía 88 (© **91-542-58-03**).

BY BICYCLE

Ever wonder why you see so few people riding bicycles in Madrid? Those who tried were overcome by the traffic pollution. It's better to walk.

 FAST FACTS: **Madrid**

American Express For your mail or banking needs, you can go to the American Express office at the corner of Marqués de Cubas and Plaza de las Cortes 2, across the street from the Palace Hotel (© **91-322-55-00** or 91-322-54-45; Metro: Gran Vía). Open Monday through Friday from 9am to 7:30pm and Saturday from 9am to 2pm.

Babysitters Most major hotels can arrange for babysitters, called *canguros* (literally, kangaroos) or *niñeras.* Usually the concierge keeps a list of reliable nursemaids and will contact them for you, provided you give adequate notice. Rates vary considerably but are usually reasonable. Although many babysitters in Madrid speak English, don't count on it.

Currency Exchange The currency exchange at Chamartín railway station (Metro: Chamartín) is open 24 hours and gives the best rates in the capital. If you exchange money at a bank, ask about the minimum commission charged.

Many banks in Spain still charge a 1% to 3% commission with a minimum charge of 3€. However, branches of **Banco Central Hispano** charge no commission. Branches of **El Corte Inglés,** the department store chain, offer currency exchange facilities at various rates. You get the worst rates at street kiosks such as Chequepoint, Exact Change, and Cambios-Uno. Although they're handy and charge no commission, their rates are very low. Naturally, **American Express** offices offer the best rates on their own checks. ATMs are plentiful in Madrid.

Dentist For an English-speaking dentist, contact the **U.S. Embassy,** Serrano 75 (© **91-587-22-00**); it maintains a list of dentists who have offered their services to Americans abroad. For dental services, also consult **Unidad Médica Anglo-Americana,** Conde de Arandá 1 (© **91-435-18-23**). Office hours are Monday through Friday from 9am to 8pm, and there is a 24-hour answering service.

Doctor For an English-speaking doctor, contact the **U.S. Embassy,** Serrano 75 (© **91-587-22-00**).

Drugstores For a late-night pharmacy, look in the daily newspaper under *Farmacias de Guardia* to learn which drugstores are open after 8pm. Another way to find one is to go to any pharmacy, which, even if closed, always posts a list of nearby pharmacies that are open late that day. Madrid has hundreds of pharmacies, but one of the most central is **Farmacia Gayoso,** Arenal 2 (© **91-521-28-60**; Metro: Puerta del Sol). It is open Monday through Saturday from 9:30am to 9:30pm.

Embassies/Consulates See "Fast Facts: Spain" in chapter 3.

Emergencies A centralized number for fire, police, or ambulance is © **112**.

Hospitals/Clinics **Unidad Médica Anglo-Americana,** Conde de Arandá 1 (© **91-435-18-23**; Metro: Retiro), is not a hospital but a private outpatient clinic offering the services of various specialists. This is not an emergency clinic, although someone on the staff is always available. The daily hours are from 9am to 8pm. For a real medical emergency, call © **112** for an ambulance.

Internet Access To check your e-mail, head for **Conéctate,** Calle Hilarión Eslava 27 (© **91-544-54-65**), which is open 24 hours daily. It costs 1.50 to 2€ per hour. Metro: Moncloa. Another choice is **La Casa de Internet,** Calle Luchana 20 (© **91-594-42-00**). It costs 1.50€ per hour, and is open daily from 10am to 3 am.

Newspapers & Magazines The Paris-based *International Herald Tribune* is sold at most newsstands in the tourist districts, as is *USA Today,* plus the European editions of *Time* and *Newsweek. Guía del Ocio,* a small magazine sold in newsstands, has entertainment listings and addresses, but in Spanish only.

Police Dial © **112**.

Post Office Madrid's central office is in the Palacio de Comunicaciones at Plaza de la Cibeles (© **91-396-20-00**).

Restrooms Some public restrooms are available, including those in the Parque del Retiro and on Plaza de Oriente across from the Palacio Real. Otherwise, you can go into a bar or *tasca,* but you should always order something. All the major department stores, such as Galerías Preciados and El Corte Inglés, have good, clean restrooms.

Safety Because of an increasing crime rate in Madrid, the U.S. Embassy has warned visitors to leave valuables in a hotel safe or another secure place when going out. Your passport may be needed, however, as the police often stop foreigners for identification checks. See "Safety" under "Fast Facts: Spain" in chapter 3 for more details about this requirement. The embassy advises against carrying purses and suggests that you keep valuables in front pockets and carry only enough cash for the day's needs. Be aware of those around you and keep a separate record of your passport number, traveler's check numbers, and credit-card numbers.

Purse snatching is common, and criminals often work in pairs, grabbing purses from pedestrians, cyclists, and even cars. A popular scam involves one robber smearing the back of the victim's clothing, perhaps with mustard, ice cream, or something worse. An accomplice then pretends to help clean up the mess, all the while picking the victim's pockets.

Every car can be a target, parked or just stopped at a light, so don't leave anything in sight in your car. If a vehicle is standing still, a thief may open the door or break a window to snatch a purse or package, even from under the seat. Place valuables in the trunk when you park and always assume that someone is watching to see whether you're putting something away for safekeeping. Keep the car locked while driving.

Taxes There are no special city taxes for tourists, except for the value-added tax (VAT, known as *IVA* in Spain) levied nationwide on all goods and services, ranging from 7% to 33%.

Telephone To make calls in Madrid, follow the instructions in "Fast Facts: Spain" in chapter 3. However, for long-distance calls, especially transatlantic ones, it may be best to go to the main telephone exchange, **Locutorio Gran Vía**, Gran Vía 30, or **Locutorio Recoletos**, Paseo de Recoletos 37–41. You may not be lucky enough to find an English-speaking operator, but you can fill out a simple form that will facilitate the placement of a call.

Transit Information For Metro information, call ✆ **91-552-69-09**; www.ctm.madrid.es.

3 Where to Stay

Although expensive, Madrid's hotels are among the finest in the world. More than 50,000 hotel rooms blanket the city—from *grand luxe* bedchambers fit for a prince to bunker-style beds in the hundreds of neighborhood *hostales* and *pensiones* (low-cost boardinghouses). Three-quarters of our recommendations are modern, yet many guests prefer the landmarks of yesteryear, including those grand old establishments, the Ritz and the Westin Palace (ca. 1910–12). *Beware:* Many older hotels in Madrid haven't kept up with the times and a handful haven't added improvements or overhauled bedrooms substantially since the 1970s.

Traditionally, hotels are clustered around the Atocha Railway Station and the Gran Vía. In our search for the most outstanding hotels, we've downplayed these two popular but noisy districts. The newer hotels have been built away from the center, especially on residential streets jutting off from Paseo de la Castellana.

Bargain seekers, however, will still find great pickings along the Gran Vía and in the Atocha district.

Note: In inexpensive hotels, be warned that you'll have to carry your bags to and from your room. Don't expect bellboys or doormen in cheaper hotels.

PARKING   This is a serious problem, as so few hotels have garages; many buildings turned into hotels were constructed before the invention of the auto- mobile. Street parking is rarely avail- able, and even if it is, you run the risk of having your car broken into. If you're driving into Madrid, most hotels (and most police) will allow you to park in front of the hotel long enough to unload your luggage. Some- one on the staff can usually pinpoint the location of the nearest garage in the neighborhood, often giving you a map showing the way. Be prepared to

> **Telephone Tip**
> The telephone area code for Madrid is **91** if you're calling from within Spain. If you're call- ing from the United States, dial **011**, the country code (34), Madrid's city code (91), and then the local number.

walk a few blocks to your car. Parking charges given in most hotel listings are the prices these neighborhood garages charge for an average-size vehicle. Don't plan on renting a car for your time in Madrid. If you're moving on to explore the countryside, just pick up your rental when you're ready to set out.

NEAR THE PLAZA DE LAS CORTES
VERY EXPENSIVE

Hotel Villa Real 🏨🏨🏨   It's not on the same level as the Ritz, but it is the first major hotel nearby to give the Westin Palace serious competition. Until 1989, the Villa Real was little more than a run-down 19th-century apartment house across a three-sided park from the Spanish parliament (Congreso de los Diputa- dos) between Puerta del Sol and Paseo del Prado. Since then, developers have poured billions of pesetas into renovations to produce this stylish hotel patron- ized by the cognoscenti of Spain. The facade combines an odd mix of neoclassi- cal and Aztec motifs and is guarded by footmen and doormen. Rooms at the Villa Real are more consistent in quality than those offered by its neighbor, the Palace (see below), but lack the latter's mellow charm and patina. The interior contains a scattering of modern paintings amid neoclassical detailing.

Each of the accommodations offers soundproofing, a sunken salon with leather-upholstered furniture, and built-in furniture accented with burl-wood inlays. Although rooms aren't imaginative, they're mostly large, with separate sit- ting areas and big, bright, well-equipped bathrooms with tub/shower combos.

Plaza de las Cortes 10, 28014 Madrid. ⓒ **91-420-37-67.** Fax 91-420-25-47. www.derbyhotels.es. 115 units. 321€ double; from 451€ suite. AE, DC, MC, V. Parking 18€. Metro: Sevilla, Banco de España. **Amenities:** 2 restaurants; 2 bars; pool; gym; sauna; room service; babysitting; laundry service; dry cleaning. *In room:* A/C, TV, kitchenette, minibar, hair dryer, coffeemaker, iron, safe.

Westin Palace 🏨🏨🏨   The Palace is an ornate Victorian wedding cake known as the *gran dueña* of Spanish hotels. It had an auspicious beginning, inaugurated personally by King Alfonso XIII in 1912, and covers an entire city block in the historical and artistic area. It faces the Prado and Neptune Fountain and lies within walking distance of the main shopping center and best antiques shops. Some of the city's most intriguing *tascas* and restaurants are a short stroll away.

Architecturally, the Palace captures the grand pre–World War I style, with an emphasis on space and comfort. Although it doesn't achieve the snob appeal of

Accommodations in Central Madrid

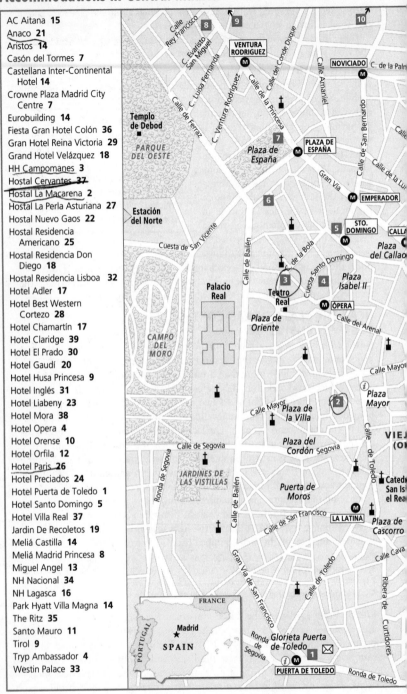

Calle de la Palma
Calle de Fuencarral
Calle de Genova
Paseo de la Castellana

■ Wax Museum

Plaza de la Villa

Plaza de Colón

Calle de Goya

SERRANO Ⓜ 17

C. de El Escorial

Calle Fernando VI

COLÓN Ⓜ

JARDINES DEL DESCUBRIMIENTO

Pez

Corredera Baja de San Pablo

Calle de Valverde

Calle de Fuencarral

Hortaleza

Calle de Augusto

Gravina

Ⓜ CHUECA

Figueroa

Calle Bárbara de Braganza

Calle de Serrano

Claudio Coello

18 →

San Marcos

Calle de Prim

Paseo de Recoletos

BARRIO DE SALAMANCA

19

Infantas

22

Ⓜ GRAN VÍA

Red. de San Luis

23

21

Gran Vía

C. del Carmen

Calle de Preciados

4

5

Puerta del Sol

Ⓜ SOL

26

Carrera de San

Calle de Alcalá

Calle de Barquillo

Plaza de la Cibeles

Calle de Alcalá

Plaza de la Independencia

BANCO DE ESPAÑA

Ⓜ

20

Ⓜ SEVILLA

Palacio de Villahermosa

Calle de Montalbán

■ Naval Museum

Paseo del Prado

Plaza de la Lealtad

Calle A. Maura

Calle de Alfonso XII

36 →

Jerónimo

Thyssen-Bornemisza Museum

34

35

27

Plaza Jacinto Benavente

(ADRID) (ADRID)

31

32

31

29 30

ⓘ

Calle del Prado

Calle de la Cruz

Plaza de las Cortes

Plaza C. del Castillo

37

■ Army Museum

PARQUE DEL BUEN RETIRO

28

Ⓜ TIRSO DE MOLINA

Calle de Cervantes

Calle Atocha

Calle de las Huertas

Museo del Prado

Calle de la Magdalena

⊠ Calle de la Cabeza

Ⓜ ANTÓN MARTÍN

Calle de Gobernador

Calle de Espalter

Calle Jesús y María Levapiés

Calle del Amparo

Calle Mesón de Paredes

Calle de Santa Isabel

Calle Atocha

38

REAL JARDÍN BOTÁNICO

Plaza Lavapiés

Ⓜ LAVAPIES

Reina Sofía

⊠

Ⓜ ATOCHA

Calle de Alfonso XII

39 →

C. Miguel Servet

C. de Embajadores

Sta. María de la Cabeza

Estación de Atocha

Paseo de la Infanta Isabel

Ronda de Atocha

0		1/5 mi
0	0.2 km	

N

✝ Church
ⓘ Information
Ⓜ Metro
⊠ Post Office
----- Railway

97

Tips **If You Have an Early Flight**

Unless absolutely necessary, it's worth making the journey into Madrid rather than staying at rather bleak Barajas, where the airport is located. If you find that you have to stay here, the least expensive option is the **Best Western Villa de Barajas,** Av. De Logroño 331 (✆ **91-329-28-18;** fax 91-329-27-04), where double rooms go for 93€. Each room has TV and telephone, and offers room service. There is also a restaurant offering traditional Spanish food. The hotel runs a free shuttle bus to and from the airport. The trip takes about 5 minutes.

---

its nearby siblings, the Ritz and the Villa Real, it's one of the largest hotels in Madrid and offers first-class service. The air-conditioned hotel has conservative, traditional rooms, boasting plenty of space, large bathrooms, and lots of extras. Accommodations vary widely, with the best rooms found on the fourth, fifth, and sixth floors. Rooms on the side are noisy and lack views. Many rooms appear not to have been renovated for some time. All units contain immaculate bathrooms with tub/shower combos.

Plaza de las Cortes 7, 28014 Madrid. ✆ **800/325-3535** in the U.S., 800/325-3589 in Canada, or 91-360-80-00. Fax 91-360-81-00. www.palacemadrid.com. 465 units. 239€–439€ double; from 306€ suite. AE, DC, MC, V. Parking 20€. Metro: Banco de España. **Amenities:** Restaurant; bar; lounge; gym; sauna; room service; babysitting; laundry service. *In room:* A/C, TV, kitchenette, minibar, hair dryer, iron, safe.

INEXPENSIVE

Hostal Cervantes *(Value* One of Madrid's most pleasant family-run hotels, the Cervantes is much appreciated by our readers and has been for years. You'll take a tiny birdcage-style elevator to the immaculately maintained second floor of this stone-and-brick building. Each room contains a comfortable bed, spartan furniture, and a tiny bathroom with a tub/shower combination. No breakfast is served, but the owners, the Alfonsos, will direct you to a nearby cafe. The establishment is convenient to the Prado, Retiro Park, and the older sections of Madrid.

Cervantes 34, 28014 Madrid. ✆ **91-429-83-65.** Fax 91-429-27-45. 14 units. 55€ double. MC, V. Metro: Banco de España. **Amenities:** Laundry/dry cleaning. *In room:* TV, safe.

Hotel Mora   This hotel could be recommended for location alone, as it lies across from the Paseo del Prado and the Botanical Gardens. It is a fine and decent choice, especially if you want to make several visits to the Prado. The reception is bright and airy, with *trompe l'oeil* marble columns and carpets. Most of the bedrooms range from midsize to spacious, and each is comfortably and tastefully furnished, though far from lavish. About half the accommodations come with bathtubs, the rest with showers. Opt for a bedroom opening onto the street as those have the best views of the gardens and the magnificent Prado itself. Double glazing keeps down some of the noise level. There is an adjoining cafe-restaurant serving routine Spanish fare.

Paseo del Prado, Madrid 28014. ✆ **91-420-15-69.** Fax 91-420-05-65. 60 units. 69€ double; 87€ triple. AE, DC, MC, V. Metro: Atocha or Cibeles. **Amenities:** Cafe; bar. *In room:* A/C, TV, minibar, safe.

NEAR PLAZA ESPAÑA
EXPENSIVE

Crowne Plaza Madrid City Centre *(Kids* Built in 1953 atop a city garage, the Crowne Plaza could be called the Waldorf-Astoria of Spain. A massive rose-and-white structure soaring upward to a central tower 26 stories high, it's one of the tallest skyscrapers in Europe. Once one of the best hotels in Spain, the Crowne Plaza has long since ceased to be a market leader. Its accommodations include conventional doubles as well as luxurious suites, each containing a sitting room and abundant extras, such as bedside controls and even in some cases alcoves for sitting. Many families are drawn to this hotel because of its spacious accommodations, great location, and special welcome provided by the staff. Each room, regardless of its size, has a marble bathroom with a tub/shower combo. Furniture is usually of a standardized modern style, in harmonized colors. The upper floor rooms are quieter.

Plaza de España, 28013 Madrid. ☎ 800/465-4329 in the U.S., or 91-547-12-00. Fax 91-548-23-89. http://madrid-citycentre.crownplaza.com. 306 units. 145€–295€ double; from 190€–405€ suite. AE, DC, MC, V. Parking 10€. Metro: Plaza de España. **Amenities:** Restaurant; bar; health club; sauna; whirlpool; salon; room service; laundry service. *In room:* A/C, TV, kitchenette, minibar, coffeemaker, hair dryer, iron, trouser press, safe.

MODERATE

Casón del Tormes   This attractive hotel is around the corner from the Royal Palace and Plaza de España. Behind a four-story red-brick facade with stone-trimmed windows, it overlooks a quiet one-way street. A long, narrow lobby contains a marble floor opening into a separate room. Guest rooms are generally roomy and comfortable with color-coordinated fabrics and dark wood, including mahogany headboards. Bathrooms are very small but with adequate shelf space and tub/shower combinations. Motorists appreciate the public parking lot near the hotel.

Calle del Río 7, 28013 Madrid. ☎ 91-541-97-46. Fax 91-541-18-52. www.bestwestern.com/es/hotelcason deltormes. 63 units. 93€–103€ double; 119€–129€ triple. AE, DC, MC, V. Parking 14€. Metro: Plaza de España. **Amenities:** Laundry service; dry cleaning. *In room:* A/C, TV, hair dryer, safe.

Hotel Santo Domingo 🌟   This stylish, carefully decorated hotel rises from a position adjacent to the Gran Vía, a 2-minute walk from the Plaza de España. It was inaugurated in 1994, after an older building was gutted and reconfigured into the comfortable modern structure you'll see today. Rooms are decorated individually, each in a style a wee bit different from that of its neighbor, in pastel-derived shades. Some contain gold damask wall coverings, faux tortoiseshell desks, and striped satin bedspreads. Bathrooms are generally spacious and outfitted with ceramics, marble slabs, and tub/shower combos. The best units are the fifth-floor doubles, especially those with furnished balconies and views over the tile roofs of Old Madrid. Each is soundproofed to guard against noise from the street and from its neighbors.

Plaza Santo Domingo 13, 28013 Madrid. ☎ 91-547-98-00. Fax 91-547-59-95. www.hotelsantodomingo. com. 120 units. 153€–184€ double. Breakfast free Sat–Mon mornings; otherwise, 11€ extra. AE, DC, MC, V. Parking 16€. Metro: Santo Domingo. **Amenities:** Restaurant; bar; room service; babysitting; laundry service; dry cleaning. *In room:* A/C, TV, minibar, hair dryer, iron, safe.

ON OR NEAR THE GRAN VIA
EXPENSIVE

Hotel Gaudí 🌟   In a turn-of-the-20th-century building in the heart of Madrid, this hotel is located in a beautifully restored landmark Modernist building. It was constructed in 1898 by Emilio Salas y Cortés, one of the teachers of the great Barcelona architect Gaudí, and was overhauled in 1998. Some of the most important attractions of Madrid are within an easy walk, including the Prado, the Thyssen Museum, and the Plaza Mayor with its rustic taverns. The bedrooms come in a number of sizes, but each is comfortably furnished and beautifully maintained with bathrooms containing tub/shower combos.

Gran Vía 9, 28013 Madrid. ℂ **91-531-22-22.** Fax 91-531-54-69. www.hoteles-catalonia.es. 184 units. 118€–186€ double; 300€ suite. AE, DC, MC, V. Metro: Gran Vía. **Amenities:** Restaurant; bar; whirlpool; sauna; room service; laundry. *In room:* A/C, TV, minibar, hair dryer, safe.

MODERATE

Hotel Liabeny   The Liabeny, behind an austere stone facade, is in a prime location midway between the Gran Vía and Puerta del Sol. It has seven floors of comfortable, contemporary rooms, which are newly redecorated but a bit pristine. They are of a good size and functionally furnished with comfortable beds and neatly organized bathrooms, mainly with shower stalls.

Salud 3, 28013 Madrid. ℂ **91-531-90-00.** Fax 91-532-74-21. www.liabeny.es. 222 units. 125€–186€ double; from 245€ suite. AE, MC, V. Parking 10€. Metro: Puerta del Sol or Gran Vía. **Amenities:** Restaurant; bar; room service; babysitting; laundry service; dry cleaning. *In room:* A/C, TV, minibar, hair dryer, iron, safe.

INEXPENSIVE

Anaco   Modest yet modern, the Anaco is just off the Gran Vía but opens onto a tree-shaded plaza. It's for those who want a clean resting place for a good price, and don't expect much more. The rooms are compact and contemporary, with built-in headboards, reading lamps, and lounge chairs. Each has a compact tiled bathroom with a shower stall. Ask for one of the five terraced rooms on the top floor, which rent at no extra charge. English is spoken here. There's a municipally operated garage nearby.

Tres Cruces 3, 28013 Madrid. ℂ **91-522-46-04.** Fax 91-531-64-84. www.anacohotel.com. 39 units. 88€–93€ double; 119€–125€ triple. AE, DC, MC, V. Parking 12€. Metro: Gran Vía, Callao, or Puerta del Sol. **Amenities:** Restaurant; bar; room service; babysitting; laundry service; dry cleaning. *In room:* A/C, TV, hair dryer, safe.

Hotel El Prado   You might get the feeling this hotel is both overbooked and understaffed. But it has comfortable rooms, relatively reasonable rates, and a well-scrubbed interior less than a decade old. You'll register in a somewhat claustrophobic lobby, then head upstairs to a room that's cozy and sleekly outfitted with contemporary-looking, full-grained walls and partitions. Each unit comes with a small tiled bathroom with shower. Other than breakfast, no meals are served.

Calle Prado 11, 28014 Madrid. ℂ **91-369-02-34.** Fax 91-429-28-29. www.pradohotel.com. 50 units. 108€–144€ double. AE, MC, V. Metro: Antón Martín. **Amenities:** Restaurant (closed on weekends); cafe; bar; limited room service; babysitting; laundry service; dry cleaning. *In room:* A/C, TV, minibar, hair dryer.

NEAR THE PUERTA DEL SOL
EXPENSIVE

Gran Hotel Reina Victoria ✮   This hotel is as legendary as the famous bullfighter Manolete who used to stay here, giving lavish parties and attracting mobs in the square below. Since the recent renovation and upgrading of this property by Spain's Tryp Hotel Group, it's less staid and more impressive than ever.

Built in 1923, the hotel sits behind an ornate stone facade, which the Spanish government protects as a historic monument. Although it's located in a congested and noisy neighborhood in the center of town, the Reina Victoria opens onto one of Madrid's landmark plazas. Activity on this square begins about 8:30 in the morning and goes on until well past midnight, so this is not the place for the "noise-sensitive."

The accommodations are midsize and fairly standard, with tub/shower combos, plus tidily organized bathrooms with hair dryers and marble vanities.

Plaza Santa Ana 14, 28012 Madrid. ℂ **91-531-45-00.** Fax 91-522-03-07. www.solmelia.com. 201 units. 218€ double; from 287€ suite. AE, DC, MC, V. Metro: Tirso de Molina or Puerta del Sol or Sevilla. **Amenities:** Restaurant; bar; room service; babysitting; laundry service; dry cleaning. *In room:* A/C, TV, minibar, hair dryer, safe.

Hotel Preciados 🛈 *Kids*　One of Madrid's newest hotels has been created from a historic 1861 structure. The original facade, entryway, grand staircase, and other architectural details have been retained, but everything else has been reconstructed from scratch for modern comfort. The five-floor hotel, which opened in 2001, is close to such landmarks as the royal palace, the opera house, and the Puerta del Sol (the very center of Madrid). Children are especially welcome here, and there are special facilities for them such as extra beds, which can be added to the standard rooms and even a special kiddies menu in the restaurant. Bedrooms are midsize to spacious, and the bathrooms have all new plumbing, including large sinks and tub/shower combinations. The on-site restaurant, serving a savory Mediterranean cuisine, used to be the famous Café Varela, a favorite of Madrid's literati.

Preciados 37, 28013 Madrid. ℂ **91-454-44-00.** Fax 91-454-44-01. www.precisadoshotel.com. 73 units. 110€–138€ double; 180€–204€ suite. MC, V. Parking: 18€. Metro: Puerta del Sol or Santo Domingo/Callao. **Amenities:** Restaurant; bar; room service; babysitting; laundry service; dry cleaning; dance club. *In room:* A/C, TV, minibar, hair dryer, iron, safe.

Tryp Ambassador 🛈　In the 19th century the dukes of Granada made their town house home in Madrid, but from the early 1990s on it's been the property of the Tryp hotel chain. The result is a lavishly restored, four-story historic hotel with grand public areas that's interconnected via a sunny lobby to a six-story annex containing about 60% of the establishment's rooms. All rooms are conservatively modern, and outfitted in white and salmon accented with mahogany. Most are large and soundproofed and come with twin beds. Bathrooms contain marble tub/shower combos, robes, and deluxe toiletries.

Cuesta Santo Domingo 5 and 7, 28013 Madrid. ℂ **91-541-67-00.** Fax 91-559-10-40. 183 units. 232€ double; from 315€ suite. AE, DC, MC, V. Metro: Opera or Santo Domingo. **Amenities:** Restaurant; bar; room service; babysitting; laundry service; dry cleaning. *In room:* A/C, TV, minibar, coffeemaker, hair dryer, safe.

MODERATE

Hotel Opera 🛈🛈 *Finds*　Don't judge this little discovery by its dreary facade or its narrow windows; it livens up considerably once you enter. Set close to the royal palace and the opera house, this hotel isn't regal but offers first-rate comfort and a warm welcome from its English-speaking staff. Guest rooms range from medium to surprisingly spacious, each with first-rate furnishings. Bathrooms are excellent, clad in marble with dual basins and tub/shower combos. It's adorned with fabric-covered walls and horsey art. The Opera remains one of Madrid's relatively undiscovered boutique hotels.

Cuesta de Santo Domingo 2, 28013 Madrid. ℂ **91-541-28-00.** Fax 91-541-69-23. 79 units. 120€ double; 156€ triple. AE, DC, MC, V. Parking 18€. Metro: Opera. **Amenities:** Restaurant; bar; laundry service; dry cleaning. *In room:* A/C, TV, minibar, hair dryer, safe.

INEXPENSIVE

Hostal Campomanes *Value*　Near the opera house and the Palacio Real, this is one of the most affordable choices in the area in spite of its heartbeat central location. The hotel doesn't have a lot of extras, but if you're seeking a clean, decent, and cheap choice in the area, consider this for a night or two. The bedrooms, though small, have modern Philippe Stark furnishings along with well-maintained private bathrooms with shower units. The hotel was once a youth hostel, and a bit of that aura still remains even though it was converted into a hotel. The best room is no. 201, which is also the most requested. It is more spacious than the rest. If you don't want to spend a lot of time in your room, but want to be out on the streets, dining out and experiencing the city's throbbing nightlife, consider booking here. The folks at the reception desk are very helpful, especially when it comes to recommending local restaurants and decoding rail timetables.

Calle Campomanes 34, 28013 Madrid. (C) **91-548-85-48** or 91-559-12-98. www.hhcampomanes.com. 30 units. 97€–110€ double; 122€–144€ suite. Rates include continental breakfast. AE, DC, MC, V. Metro: Opera. **Amenities:** Room service, laundry/dry cleaning. *In room:* A/C, TV, minibar, hair dryer.

Hostal la Macarena ★ (Value)

Known for its reasonable prices and praised by readers for its warm hospitality, this unpretentious hostel is run by the Ricardo González family. A 19th-century facade with Belle Epoque patterns stands in ornate contrast to the chiseled simplicity of the ancient buildings facing it. The location is one of the hostel's assets: it's on a street (a noisy one) immediately behind Plaza Mayor near one of the best clusters of *tascas* in Madrid. Rooms range from small to medium and are all well kept, with modest furnishings and comfortable beds. Windows facing the street have double panes. Bathrooms are tiny and contain stall showers.

Cava de San Miguel 8, 28005 Madrid. (C) **91-365-92-21.** Fax 91-364-27-57. 25 units. 65€ double; 84€ triple; 96€ quad. MC, V. Metro: Puerta del Sol, Opera, or La Latina. **Amenities:** Bar; lounge, room service. *In room:* TV, hair dryer.

Hostal la Perla Asturiana

Ideal for those who want to stay in the heart of old Madrid (1 block off Plaza Mayor and 2 blocks from Puerta del Sol), this small family-run place welcomes you with a courteous staff at the desk 24 hours a day for security and convenience. You can socialize in the small, comfortable lobby adjacent to the reception area but stay here for the cheap prices and location, not grand comfort. Each of the small rooms comes with a comfortable bed plus a simple and adequate bathroom with a shower unit. Many inexpensive restaurants and tapas bars are nearby. No breakfast is served.

Plaza de Santa Cruz 3, 28012 Madrid. (C) **91-366-46-00.** Fax 91-366-46-08. www.perlaasturiana.com. 33 units. 45€ double; 58€ triple. MC, V. Metro: Puerta del Sol. **Amenities:** Laundry service; dry cleaning. *In room:* TV, safe.

Hotel Inglés ★

You'll find this little hotel (where Virginia Woolf used to stay) on a central street lined with *tascas*. Behind the red-brick facade is a modern, impersonal hotel with contemporary, well-maintained rooms. The lobby is air-conditioned, but guest rooms are not; guests who open their windows at night are likely to hear noise from the enclosed courtyard, so light sleepers beware. Rooms come in a variety of shapes, most of them small, and some in the back are quite dark. Tiled bathrooms are cramped but tidily maintained, with shower stalls.

Calle Echegaray 8, 28014 Madrid. (C) **91-429-65-51.** Fax 91-420-24-23. 58 units. 90€ double; 112€ suite. AE, DC, MC, V. Parking 10€. Metro: Puerta del Sol or Sevilla. **Amenities:** Cafeteria; bar; room service; laundry service; dry cleaning. *In room:* TV, hair dryer, safe.

Hotel París

Originally built in grandiose style in the 1870s when it was undoubtedly more chic than it is today, this hotel occupies a prime location adjacent to the hysterical traffic of the Puerta del Sol. It contains five floors of simple but clean and comfortable rooms, each with parquet floors, white walls, and views that extend either over the surrounding neighborhood or over a quiet courtyard. Rooms are generally small. Bathrooms are also small, with shower stalls. Something about the dark-paneled lobby might remind you of the old-fashioned, hot, and somnolent Spain of long ago. This hotel is a good bargain if your tastes aren't too demanding, if you're not a budding decorator, or if you just want a central location.

Alcalá 2, 28014 Madrid. (C) **91-521-64-96.** Fax 91-531-01-88. 121 units. 84€ double. Rates include break-fast. AE, DC, MC, V. Metro: Puerta del Sol. **Amenities:** Bar; room service, laundry service; dry cleaning. *In room:* A/C, TV, safe.

NEAR ATOCHA STATION
EXPENSIVE

NH Nacional ✦ This stately hotel was built around 1900 to house the hundreds of passengers flooding into Madrid through the nearby Atocha railway station. In 1997, a well-respected nationwide chain, NH Hotels, ripped out much of the building's dowdy interior, reconstructing the public areas and bedrooms into a smooth, seamless decor that takes maximum advantage of the building's tall ceilings and large spaces. In the bedrooms, the Belle Epoque trappings of another day have been replaced with modern designer decor, even avant-garde art, giving the units a welcoming ambience. Rooms also come equipped with immaculately kept bathrooms containing tub/shower combos. Today, the Nacional is a destination for dozens of corporate conventions.

Paseo del Prado 48, 28014 Madrid. (C) **91-429-66-29.** Fax 91-369-15-64. www.nh-hotels.com. 214 units. 199€–154€ double; 345€–440€ suite. AE, DC, MC, V. Metro: Atocha. **Amenities:** Restaurant; bar; room service; babysitting; laundry service; dry cleaning. *In room:* A/C, TV, minibar, hair dryer, safe.

INEXPENSIVE

Hotel Best Western Cortezo Just off Calle de Atocha, which leads to the railroad station of the same name, the Cortezo is a short walk from Plaza Mayor and Puerta del Sol. The accommodations are comfortable but simply furnished, with contemporary bathrooms containing tub/shower combos. Beds are springy and the furniture is pleasantly modern; many rooms have sitting areas with a desk and armchair. The public rooms match the guest rooms in freshness. The hotel was built in 1959 and last renovated in 1997.

Doctor Cortezo 3, 28012 Madrid. (C) **91-369-01-01.** Fax 91-369-37-74. 88 units. 120€–125€ double; 150€–170€ suite. AE, DC, MC, V. Parking 15€. Metro: Tirso de Molina. **Amenities:** Restaurant; bar; room service; babysitting; laundry service; dry cleaning. *In room:* A/C, TV, minibar, hair dryer, safe.

NEAR RETIRO/SALAMANCA
VERY EXPENSIVE

Park Hyatt Villa Magna ✦✦✦ One of the finest hotels in Europe, the nine-story Park Hyatt is faced with slabs of rose-colored granite set behind a bank of pines and laurels on the city's most fashionable boulevard. It's an even finer choice than the Palace or Villa Real and is matched in luxury, ambience, and service only by the Ritz, which has a greater patina since it's much older.

Separated from the busy boulevard by a parklike garden, the hotel has contemporary lines. In contrast, its interior recaptures the style of Carlos IV, with paneled walls, marble floors, and bouquets of fresh flowers. Almost every film star shooting on location in Spain stays here. This luxury palace has plush but dignified rooms decorated in Louis XVI, English Regency, or Italian provincial style. Each comes with a neatly kept bathroom with a tub/shower combo.

Paseo de la Castellana 22, 28046 Madrid. (C) **800/223-1234** in the U.S. and Canada, or 91-587-12-34. Fax 91-575-95-04. www.madrid.hyatt.com. 182 units. 500€ double; from 750€ suite. AE, DC, MC, V. Parking

19€. Metro: Rubén Darío. **Amenities:** 2 restaurants; bar; gym; sauna; car rental; salon; room service; babysitting; laundry service; dry cleaning. *In room:* A/C, TV, minibar, hair dryer, safe.

The Ritz ☆☆☆   The Ritz is the most legendary hotel in Spain. With soaring ceilings and graceful columns, it offers all the luxury and pampering you'd expect of a grand hotel. Although the building has been thoroughly modernized, great effort was expended to retain its Belle Epoque character and architectural details.

No other Madrid hotel, except the Palace, has a more varied history. One of *Les Grands Hôtels Européens,* the Ritz was built in 1908 by King Alfonso XIII with the aid of César Ritz. It looks out onto the circular Plaza de la Lealtad in the center of town, near 120-hectare (300-acre) Retiro Park, facing the Prado, the Palacio de Villahermosa, and the Stock Exchange. The Ritz was constructed when costs were relatively low and when spaciousness and luxury were the standard. Its facade has even been designated a historic monument. The glory days of 1910 live on in the rooms with their spacious closets, luxury mattresses, antique furnishings, and hand-woven carpets. Bathrooms are spacious, with robes, dual basins, deluxe toiletries, and tub/shower combos. The hotel requests that male guests wear a jacket and tie after 11am in the public areas. Nonetheless, casual wear, even blue jeans, is seen at the hotel, but such guests are conspicuous by their lack of what the Spanish call *gracia.*

Plaza de la Lealtad 5, 28014 Madrid. © 800/225-5843 in the U.S. and Canada, or 91-701-67-67. Fax 91-701-67-76. www.ritz.es. 167 units. 570€ double; from 1,000€ junior suite. AE, DC, MC, V. Parking 24€. Metro: Banco de España. **Amenities:** Restaurant; bar; fitness center; sauna; car rental; room service; laundry service; dry cleaning. *In room:* A/C, TV, minibar, hair dryer, iron, safe.

EXPENSIVE

Hotel Adler ☆☆   At the intersection of Velázquez and Goya streets, this is one of the most elegant places to stay in Madrid. You're housed in grand comfort at a location nicknamed "the golden triangle of art" (near El Prado, Reina Sofía, and the Thyssen-Bornemisza collection). The exclusive shops of Serrano are also near at hand. The classic building has been carefully restored and offers gracious comfort in a setting that retains the evocation of the 1880s but with decidedly modern touches. The bedrooms are user friendly: You live and sleep in ultimate comfort with *luxe* furnishings and totally modernized bathrooms with tub/shower combinations. The on-site restaurant is one of the better hotel dining rooms in this upmarket section of Market.

Calle Velázquez 33, 28001 Madrid. © 888/58-586-87-40 in the U.S. and Canada, or 91-548-78-84. Fax 91-548-78-85. www.travel-in-madrid.com. 45 units. 268€–395€ double; 360€–395€ suite. AE, DC, MC, V. Metro: Velázquez. **Amenities:** Restaurant; bar; room service; babysitting; laundry service; dry cleaning. *In room:* A/C, TV, minibar, hair dryer, safe.

Hotel Emperatriz ☆   This hotel lies just off the wide Paseo de la Castellana. Built in the 1970s, it has been recently renovated in a combination of Laura Ashley and Spanish contemporary styles by Madrid's trendiest firm, Casa & Jardín. Rooms are comfortable and classically styled in cheery yellows and salmons, and come with neatly kept bathrooms containing tub/shower combos. Ask for a room on the seventh floor, where you get a private terrace at no extra charge.

López de Hoyos 4, 28006 Madrid. © 91-563-80-88. Fax 91-563-98-04. www.emperatrizhotel.com. 158 units. 172€–200€ double; 365€ junior suite. AE, DC, MC, V. Metro: Rubén Darío. **Amenities:** Restaurant; bar; salon; room service; babysitting; laundry service; dry cleaning. *In room:* A/C, TV, minibar, hair dryer, safe.

MODERATE

Fiesta Gran Hotel Colón ✦   East of Retiro Park, Gran Hotel Colón is just a few minutes from the city center by subway. Built in 1966, it offers comfortable yet reasonably priced accommodations in a modern setting. More than half of the accommodations have private balconies, and all contain traditional furniture, much of it built-in. Rooms vary in size but most offer roomy comfort, dark wood beds and adequate closet space. Bathrooms are small, with stall showers, but with suitable shelf space. Other perks include two dining rooms, a covered garage, and bingo games. One of the Colón's founders was an interior designer, which accounts for the unusual stained-glass windows and murals in the public rooms and the paintings by Spanish artists in the lounge.

Pez Volador 11, 28007 Madrid. ℂ **91-573-59-00**. Fax 91-573-08-09. www.fiesta-hotels.com. 359 units. 88€–194€ double; from 233€ junior suite. AE, DC, MC, V. Parking 13€. Metro: Sainz de Baranda. **Amenities:** Restaurant; bar; health club; sauna; salon; room service; babysitting; laundry service; dry cleaning. *In room:* A/C, TV, minibar, hair dryer, safe.

Gran Hotel Velázquez ✦   This is one of the most attractive medium-sized hotels in Madrid, with plenty of comfort and convenience. Opened in 1947 on an affluent residential street near the center of town, it has a 1930s-style Art Deco facade and a 1940s interior filled with well-upholstered furniture and richly grained paneling. Several public rooms lead off a central oval area. As in many hotels of its era, the rooms vary. Some are large enough for entertaining, with a small separate sitting area. All contain piped-in music and walk-in closets. Bathrooms are decorated in marble or tiles, with either stall showers or tubs.

Calle de Velázquez 62, 28001 Madrid. ℂ **91-575-28-00**. Fax 91-575-28-09. www.chh.es. 146 units. 115€–150€ double; from 175€–200€ junior suite. AE, DC, MC, V. Parking 17€. Metro: Velázquez. **Amenities:** 2 restaurants; bar; salon; room service; laundry service; dry cleaning. *In room:* A/C, TV, minibar, hair dryer, iron, safe.

⸢Kids⸥ Family-Friendly Hotels

Crowne Plaza Madrid City Centre (p. 98)   Safe and reliable, and located at the very heart of Madrid, this 26-story hotel offers roomy accommodations and good beds and attracts a large family trade to its precincts. It's got location, reasonable prices, and all the services, including laundry, that most family travelers need.

Hotel Preciados (p. 101)   Children are especially welcome at this historic 1861 hotel. Special facilities for kids, such as extra beds, can be added to the standard rooms, and there's even a special kid's menu in the restaurant.

Meliá Castilla (p. 108)   Children can spend hours and all their extra energy in the hotel's swimming pool and gymnasium. On the grounds is a showroom exhibiting the latest European automobiles. Hotel services include babysitting, providing fun for kids and parents, too.

The Tirol   This centrally located government-rated three-star hotel, at Marquez de Urquijo, 28008 Madrid (ℂ **91-548-19-00**; www.hotel-tirol. com) is a favorite of families seeking good comfort at moderate price. It has a cafeteria.

Jardín de Recoletos ⭐ *Value* Built in 1999, this hotel welcomes its guests to the chic Salamanca district of Madrid. The hotel lies close to both the financial district and the best shops. A contemporary apartment hotel, it stands on a street of little noise but close to the Plaza Colón, one of the major traffic arteries of Madrid. The lobby is inviting with its sleek marble floors resting under a stained-glass ceiling with its adjacent combined cafe and restaurant.

Most of the rooms are rather spacious and attractively decorated in a traditional style, with little sitting and dining areas, wood trim, creamy white walls, and comfortable furniture in yellow and champagne colors. Unusual for Madrid, the accommodations come with well-equipped kitchenettes. If you want to pay extra, you can book into either a unit rated "superior" or else a suite that offers hydromassage bathrooms and a big terrace. All accommodations have well-maintained and equipped bathrooms, each with tub and shower.

Gil de Santivañes 6, Madrid 28001. © 91-781-16-40. Fax 91-781-16-41. 36 units. 108€ double; 123€–231€ suite. Rates include buffet breakfast. AE, DC, MC, V. Parking 11€. Metro: Colón. **Amenities:** Restaurant; cafe; room service; laundry/dry cleaning. *In room:* TV, minibar, kitchenette, hair dryer, beverage maker, iron.

INEXPENSIVE

Hotel Claridge This contemporary building, last renovated in 1994, is beyond Retiro Park, about 5 minutes from the Prado by taxi or subway. The rooms are well organized and pleasantly styled, though small and compact. They include small, well-organized bathrooms containing tub/shower combos. You can take your meals in the hotel's cafeteria and relax in the modern lounge.

Plaza Conde de Casal 6, 28007 Madrid. © 91-551-94-00. Fax 91-501-03-85. 150 units. Mon–Thurs 112€ double; Fri–Sun 78€ double; 160€ suite. AE, DC, MC, V. Metro: Conde de Casal. **Amenities:** Restaurant; bar; laundry service; dry cleaning. *In room:* A/C, TV, safe.

CHAMBERI
VERY EXPENSIVE

Castellana Inter-Continental Hotel ⭐⭐ Solid, spacious, and conservatively modern, this is one of Madrid's most reliable hotels. Originally built in 1963, the Castellana Inter-Continental lies behind a barrier of trees in a neighborhood of apartment houses and luxury hotels. Its high-ceilinged public rooms are gorgeous, with terrazzo floors and giant abstract murals pieced together from multicolored stones and tiles. Most of the accommodations have private balconies and traditional furniture. Most rooms have generous living space with safes and very large beds, often king size. Bathrooms are tiled and well equipped with robes, phones, and tub/shower combos.

Paseo de la Castellana 49, 28046 Madrid. © 800/327-0200 in the U.S., or 91-700-73-00. Fax 91-319-58-53. 310 units. 365€–415€ double; from 935€ suite. AE, DC, MC, V. Parking 18€. Metro: Gregorio Marañón. **Amenities:** 3 restaurants; bar; health club; sauna; salon; room service; babysitting; laundry; solarium. *In room:* A/C, TV, minibar, coffeemaker, hair dryer, iron, safe.

Hotel Orfila ⭐⭐ *Finds* Though not as spectacular as Santo Mauro, this small 19th-century palace in a residential area is a gem and a classic example of elegant, tasteful decoration. Many visitors are deserting such old favorites as Villa Magna or the Westin Palace to stay here. In 1886, it was a family home but in the 1990s was converted to a luxury hotel that still pays homage to its Belle Epoque past. The midsize to spacious bedrooms are decorated in a rich 19th-century style that would make one of the old *gran señores* feel at home. The public lounges also evoke its former aristocratic associations, and the lobby is installed in what used to be the courtyard of the town house, where horse-drawn carriages pulled in. The hotel also offers an elegant restaurant serving an international cuisine. Diners usually savor an aperitif first in the palace garden.

Orfila 6, 28010 Madrid. ℭ 91-702-77-70. Fax 91-702-77-72. www.hotelorfila.com. 32 units. 296€–348€ double; from 593€–694€ suite. AE, DC, MC, V. Metro: Alonso Martinez. **Amenities:** Restaurant; bar; room service; babysitting; laundry service; dry cleaning. *In room:* A/C, TV, minibar, hair dryer, safe.

Santo Mauro Hotel ✸✸✸ This hotel offers even more style and elegance than the Inter-Continental (see above). It opened in 1991 in what was once a neoclassical villa built in 1894 for the duke of Santo Mauro. Set within a garden and done in a French style, it's decorated with rich fabrics and Art Deco accents and furnishings. Staff members outnumber rooms by two to one. Each of the rooms contains an audio system with a wide choice of tapes and CDs as well as many lovely details, like raw silk curtains, Persian carpets, antique prints, and parquet floors. Rooms are large and come in combinations ranging from studios to duplex suites, all containing bathrooms with tub/shower combos.

Calle Zurbano 36, 28010 Madrid. ℭ 91-319-69-00. Fax 91-308-54-77. www.ac-hoteles.com. 51 units. 289€–404€ double; from 440€ suite. AE, DC, MC, V. Parking 15€. Metro: Rubén Darío or Alonso Martínez. **Amenities:** Restaurant; bar; pool; health club; sauna; room service; massage; babysitting; laundry service; dry cleaning. *In room:* A/C, TV, minibar, hair dryer, safe.

EXPENSIVE

Miguel Angel ✸ Just off Paseo de la Castellana, this hotel is sleek and modern. It opened its doors in 1975 and has been renovated periodically ever since. It has a lot going for it: ideal location, contemporary styling, good furnishings, an efficient staff, and plenty of comfort. There's an expansive sun terrace on several levels, with clusters of garden furniture surrounded by paintings of semitropical scenes. The soundproof rooms are done in color-coordinated fabrics and carpets, and in many cases reproductions of classic Iberian furniture, each with a superbly comfortable bed and a bathroom containing a tub/shower combo.

Miguel Angel 29–31, 28010 Madrid. ℭ 91-442-81-99. Fax 91-442-53-20. www.occidentalmiguelangel. com. 270 units. 150€–211€ double; from 375€ suite. AE, DC, MC, V. Parking 15€–30€. Metro: Gregorio Marañón. **Amenities:** 2 restaurants; bar; pool; fitness center; sauna; salon; room service; babysitting; laundry service; dry cleaning. *In room:* A/C, TV, minibar, hair dryer, safe.

MODERATE

Hotel Orense ✸ At first glance, you might mistake this silver-and-glass tower for one of many upscale condominium complexes surrounding it on all sides. Stylish and streamlined, with a design inaugurated in the late 1980s and renovated in 1996, it offers reproduction Oriental carpets and conservatively contemporary furniture that's comfortable, tasteful, and upscale. Accommodations are appropriate for a stay of up to several weeks, equipped along the lines of a private apartment. (In fact, management rents some of them to international corporations for long-term lodging and office space.) All rooms contain private bathrooms with tubs.

Pedro Teixeira 5, 28020 Madrid. ℭ 91-597-15-68. Fax 91-597-12-95. www.hotelorense.com. 140 units. Mon–Thurs 144€ double; Fri–Sun 88€ double; from 110€ suite. AE, DC, MC, V. Metro: Santiago Bernabeu. **Amenities:** Restaurant; bar; room service; laundry service; dry cleaning. *In room:* A/C, TV, minibar, coffeemaker, hair dryer, safe.

INEXPENSIVE

Hostal Residencia Don Diego ✸ On the fifth floor of an elevator building, Don Diego is in a combination residential/commercial neighborhood that's relatively convenient to many of the city monuments. The vestibule contains an elegant winding staircase with iron griffin heads supporting its balustrade. The hotel is warm and inviting, filled with leather couches and comfortably angular but attractive furniture. Rooms are a bit small but comfortable for the price. Bathrooms are cramped but adequate, with shower stalls. The staff is very service oriented and keeps the place humming along efficiently.

Calle de Velázquez 45, 28001 Madrid. © 91-435-07-60. Fax 91-431-42-63. 58 units. 83€ double; 112€ triple. AE, MC, V. Metro: Velázquez. **Amenities:** Cafeteria; laundry service; dry cleaning. *In room:* A/C, TV, hair dryer, iron, safe.

CHAMARTIN
EXPENSIVE

Eurobuilding ⚘ Even while the Eurobuilding was on the drawing boards, the rumor was that this government-rated five-star sensation of white marble would provide "a new concept in deluxe hotels." It is actually two hotels linked by a courtyard, away from the city center, but right in the midst of apartment houses, boutiques, nightclubs, first-class restaurants, and the modern Madrid business world.

The more glamorous of the twin buildings is the main one, named Las Estancias de Eurobuilding. It contains only suites, all recently renovated in pastel shades. Ornately carved gold-and-white beds, large terraces for breakfast and cocktail entertaining—all are tastefully coordinated. Across the courtyard the neighbor Eurobuilding contains less impressive, but still very comfortable, double rooms, many with views from private balconies of the formal garden below. All accommodations have private bathrooms with tub/shower combos.

Calle Padre Damián 23, 28036 Madrid. © 91-353-73-00. Fax 91-345-45-76. 490 units. 118€–239€ double; from 319€–487€ suite. AE, DC, MC, V. Parking 20€. Metro: Cuzco. **Amenities:** Restaurant; bar; room service; babysitting; laundry service; dry cleaning. *In room:* A/C, TV, minibar, coffeemaker, hair dryer, iron, safe.

Meliá Castilla ⚘ *Kids* This mammoth hotel is one of the largest in Europe. Loaded with facilities and built primarily to accommodate conventions, Meliá Castilla also caters to the needs of the individual traveler. The lounges and pristine marble corridors are vast—there is even a landscaped garden as well as a showroom full of the latest-model cars. Each good-size room comes with excellent twin beds, contemporary furniture, and bathrooms containing tub/shower combos. The hotel has long been a family favorite because of its many facilities, including one of the few hotel swimming pools in Madrid. Note that some lower rooms are quite noisy. Meliá Castilla is in the north of Madrid, about a block west of Paseo de la Castellana, and a short drive from the Chamartín railway station.

Calle Capitán Haya 43, 28020 Madrid. © 800/336-3542 in the U.S., or 91-567-50-00. Fax 91-567-50-51. www.solmelia.com. 915 units. 175€–253€ double; from 350€–477€ suite. AE, DC, MC, V. Parking 19€. Metro: Cuzco. **Amenities:** 3 restaurants; bar; lounge; pool; salon; room service; laundry service; dry cleaning. *In room:* A/C, TV, minibar, hair dryer, iron, safe.

MODERATE

The Aristos ⚘ *Value* This hotel is in an up-and-coming residential area of Madrid not far from the Eurobuilding (see above). Its main advantage is a garden where you can lounge and have a drink. Each of the medium-sized rooms has a small terrace and modern furniture. All units contain bathrooms with tub/shower combos.

Av. Pío XII 34, 28016 Madrid. © 91-345-04-50. Fax 91-345-10-23. 23 units. 163€ double. AE, DC, MC, V. Parking 9€. Metro: Pío XII. **Amenities:** Restaurant; lounge; room service; laundry service; dry cleaning. *In room:* A/C, TV, minibar, hair dryer, safe.

Hotel Chamartín   This brick-sided hotel soars nine stories above the northern periphery of Madrid. It's part of the massive modern shopping complex attached to the Chamartín railway station, although once you're inside your soundproofed room, the noise of the railway station will seem far away. The owner of the building is RENFE, Spain's government railway system, but the nationwide chain that administers it is HUSA Hotels. The hotel lies 15 minutes by taxi from both the airport and the historic core of Madrid and sits atop one of the capital's busiest Metro stops. The well-appointed rooms are good-size, with cushiony furnishings, along with orderly bathrooms with stall showers. Especially oriented to the business traveler, the hotel offers a video screen that posts the arrival and departure of all of Chamartín station's trains.

Agustín de Foxá, 28036 Madrid. © **91-334-49-00.** Fax 91-733-02-14. www.hotelchamartin.com. 378 units. Mon–Thurs 134€ double; Fri–Sun 85€ double; Mon–Thurs 230€ suite; Fri–Sun 173€ suite. AE, DC, MC, V. Metro: Chamartín. Bus: 5. **Amenities:** Restaurant; lounge; car rental; room service; babysitting; laundry service; dry cleaning. *In room:* A/C, TV, minibar, coffeemaker, hair dryer, iron, safe.

4 Where to Dine

Madrid boasts the most varied cuisine and the widest choice of dining opportunities in Spain. At the fancy tourist restaurants, prices are just as expensive as in New York, London, or Paris, but there are lots of affordable taverns and family restaurants as well.

Many of Spain's greatest chefs have opened restaurants in Madrid, energizing the city's culinary scene. Gone are the days when mainly Madrileño food was featured, which meant Castilian specialties such as *cocido* (a chickpea-and-sausage stew) or roast suckling pig or lamb. Now you can take a culinary tour of the country while remaining in Madrid—from Andalusia with its gazpacho and braised bulls' tails to Asturias with its *fabada* (a rich pork stew) and *sidra* (cider) to the Basque country, which has the most sophisticated cuisine in Spain. There is also a host of Galician and Mediterranean restaurants in Madrid. Amazingly, although Madrid is a landlocked city surrounded by a vast arid plain, you can order some of the freshest seafood in the country here.

Follow the local custom and don't overtip. Theoretically, service is included in the price of the meal, but it's customary to leave an additional 10%.

One way to save money is to order the *menú del día* (menu of the day) or *cubierto* (fixed price)—both are fixed-price menus based on what is fresh at the market that day. They are the dining bargains in Madrid, although often lacking the quality of more expensive a la carte dining. Usually each includes a first course, such as fish soup or hors d'oeuvres, followed by a main dish, plus bread, dessert, and the wine of the house. You won't have a large choice. The *menú turístico* is a similar fixed-price menu, but for many it's too large, especially at lunch. Only those with large appetites will find it to be the best bargain.

In most cases service can seem perfunctory by U.S. standards. Waiters are matter-of-fact, do not fawn over you, nor do they return to the table to ask how things are. This can seem off-putting at first, but if you observe closely you'll see that Spanish waiters typically handle more tables than American waiters and that they generally work quickly and efficiently.

NEAR THE PLAZA DE LAS CORTES
MODERATE

El Espejo ⋆ INTERNATIONAL   Here you'll find good food and one of the most perfectly crafted Art Nouveau decors in Madrid. If the weather is good,

Dining in Central Madrid

you can sit at one of the outdoor tables and be served by uniformed waiters who carry food across the busy street to a green area flanked with trees. We prefer a table inside, within view of the tile maidens with vines and flowers entwined in their hair. Upon entering, you'll find yourself in a charming cafe/bar, where many visitors linger before heading toward the spacious dining room. Dishes include grouper ragout with clams, steak tartare, guinea fowl with Armagnac, and duck with pineapple. Try profiteroles with cream and chocolate sauce for dessert.

Paseo de Recoletos 31. ℂ **91-308-23-47.** Reservations required. *Menú del día* 22€. AE, MC, V. Daily 1–4pm and 9pm–midnight. Metro: Colón. Bus: 27 or 45.

Errota-Zar BASQUE   Next to the House of Deputies and the Zarzuela Theater, Errota-Zar means "old mill," a nostalgic reference to the Basque country, home of the Olano family, owners of the restaurant.

A small bar at the entrance displays a collection of fine cigars and wines, and the blue-painted walls are adorned with paintings of Basque landscapes. The restaurant has only about two dozen tables, which can easily fill up. The Basque country is long known as the gastronomic capital of Spain, and Errota-Zar provides a fine showcase for its cuisine.

Try such appetizers as the rare tolosa kidney bean or fried anchovies. Many Basques begin their meal with a *tortilla de bacalao* (salt cod omelet). For main dishes, sample the delights of *chuletón de buey* (oxtail), along with grilled vegetables, or *kokotxas de merluza en aceite* (cheeks of hake cooked in virgin olive oil). Hake cheeks may not sound appetizing, but Spaniards and many foreigners praise this dish. You might opt instead for *foie al Pedro Jiménez* (duck liver grilled and served with a sweet wine sauce). The best homemade desserts are *cuajada de la casa,* a thick yogurt made from sheep's milk, or *tarta de limón,* a lemon cake. You might also try rice ice cream in prune sauce.

Jovellanos 3, 1st floor. ℂ **91-531-25-64.** Reservations recommended. Main courses 6.60€–18€. AE, DC, MC, V. Mon–Sat 1–4pm and 9pm–midnight. Closed Aug 15–30 and Easter. Metro: Banco España or Sevilla.

NEAR PLAZA DE LA CIBELES
MODERATE

Bocaito SPANISH/TAPAS   Inside this 150-year-old house, four original columns of wood encircle the high ceiling, and bullfighting posters adorn the white-tile walls. Behind a bar shaped into two horseshoes, the staff cooks and prepares some of the most appreciated tapas in Madrid. The selection ranges from simple delights such as *ajos tiernos en aceite* (tender garlic in olive oil), cured Serrano ham, *gambas fritas* (fried shrimp), and green asparagus in scrambled eggs to some very sophisticated delicacies, such as *bacalao con caviar* (salt cod paté with caviar). The famous *mejimecha* (marinated mussels with ham and onions in béchamel sauce) is sublime, as are the anchovies of the house and tasty croquettes. The prices for the tapas range from 5.40€ to 7.20€. Don Miguel Benavente, the chef and owner for more than 3 decades, recommends the *plato combinado* (a combination platter of all tapas), which, together with a glass of their very palatable Rioja house wine, is available at a cost of 9€. A selection of the culinary treats on offer includes lentils with *chorizo* (Spanish sausage), *merluza* (hake), *osso buco al horno* (braised veal shank), and typical Andalusian and Castilian dishes.

Calle Libertad 4–6 (2 blocks north of *Las Cibeles*). ℂ **91-532-12-19.** Reservations recommended. Main courses 11€–20€. MC, V. Mon–Fri 1–4pm and 8:30pm–midnight; Sat 8:30pm–midnight. Closed last 2 weeks Aug. Metro: Banco de España.

Moments An Early Evening *Tapeo*

What's more fun than a pub-crawl in London or Dublin? In Madrid, it's a *tapeo*, and you can drink just as much or more than in those far northern climes. One of the unique pleasures of Madrid, a *tapeo* is the act of strolling from one bar to another to keep yourself amused and fed before the fashionable Madrileño dining hour of 10pm.

Most of the world knows that tapas are Spain's delectable appetizers, and restaurants around the world now serve them. In Madrid they're served almost everywhere, in *tabernas, tascas,* bars, and cafes.

Although Madrid took to tapas with a passion, they may have originated in Andalusia, especially around Jerez de la Frontera, where they were traditionally served to accompany the sherry produced there. The first tapa (which means a cover or lid) was probably *chorizo* (a spicy sausage) or a slice of cured ham perched over the mouth of a glass to keep the flies out. Later, the government mandated bars to serve a "little something" in the way of food with each drink to dissipate the effects of the alcohol. This was important when drinking a fortified wine like sherry, as its alcohol content is more than 15% higher than that of normal table wines. Eating a selection of tapas as you drink will help preserve your sobriety.

Tapas can be relatively simple: toasted almonds; slices of ham, cheese, or sausage; potato omelets; or the ubiquitous olives. They can be more elaborate too: a succulent veal roll; herb-flavored snails; *gambas* (shrimp); a saucer of peppery *pulpo* (octopus); stuffed peppers; *anguila* (eel); *cangrejo* (crabmeat salad); *merluza* (hake) salad; and even bull testicles.

Each bar in Madrid gains a reputation for its rendition of certain favorite foods. One bar, for example, specializes in very garlicky grilled mushrooms, usually accompanied by pitchers of sangria. Another will specialize in *gambas*. Most chefs are men in Madrid, but at tapas bars or *tascas,* the cooks are most often women—often the owner's wife.

For a selection of our favorite bars, see "Our Favorite *Tascas*," later in this chapter. There are literally hundreds of others, many of which you'll discover on your own during your strolls around Madrid.

Tocororo CUBAN   This is Madrid's finest Cuban restaurant. The nostalgia is evident in the pictures of Old Havana, and in the paintings of famous artists such as Lam y Mattos that adorn the walls. The waitstaff is as lively as the pop Cuban music playing on the stereo. The dishes are typical Caribbean dishes, such as *ceviche* (marinated fish), *ropa vieja* (shredded meat served with black beans and rice), or lobster enchilada. If you prefer a simpler repast, try a selection of *empanadas y tamales* (fried potato pastries and plantain dough filled with onions and ground meat). Special cocktails of the house include *mojito* (rum, mint, and a hint of sugar) and daiquiris. In winter there is live Cuban music. With a discreet but pleasant ambience, this restaurant is located in the zone of *La Marcha* (most of the bars and discos are in this area).

Calle del Prado 3 (at the corner of Echegaray). ℰ **91-369-40-00.** Reservations required Thurs–Sat. Main courses 8.75€–15€; fixed-price menu 9€. AE, DC, MC, V. Mon–Sat 1–4pm and 8:30pm–midnight. Fri–Sat close at 1am. Closed last 2 weeks Feb and last week Sept. Metro: Sevilla.

ON OR NEAR THE GRAN VIA
EXPENSIVE

Arce ⊀ BASQUE Arce has brought some of the best modern interpretations of Basque cuisine to Madrid, thanks to the enthusiasm of owner/chef Iñaki Camba and his wife, Theresa. Within a comfortably decorated dining room, you can enjoy dishes made of the finest ingredients using flavors designed to dominate your taste buds. Examples include a salad of fresh scallops and an oven-baked casserole of fresh boletus mushrooms, seasoned lightly so the woodsy vegetable taste comes through. Look for unusual preparations of hake and seasonal variations of such game dishes as pheasant and woodcock.

Augusto Figueroa 32. ℰ **91-522-59-13.** Reservations recommended. Main courses 15€–39€. AE, DC, MC, V. Mon–Fri 1:30–4pm; Mon–Sat 9pm–midnight. Closed Easter week and Aug 15–31. Metro: Chueca and Banco de España.

MODERATE

El Mentidero de la Villa ⊀ MEDITERRANEAN The Mentidero ("Gossip Shop" in English) is a truly multicultural experience. The owner describes the cuisine as "modern Spanish with Japanese influence and a French cooking technique." That may sound confusing, but the result is an achievement; each ingredient manages to retain its distinct flavor. The kitchen plays with such adventuresome combinations as veal liver in sage sauce; a spring roll filled with fresh shrimp and leeks; noisettes of veal with tarragon; filet steak with a sauce of mustard and brown sugar; and medallions of venison with purée of chestnut and celery. One notable dessert is the sherry trifle. The postmodern decor includes *trompe l'oeil* ceilings, exposed wine racks, ornate columns with unusual lighting, and a handful of antique carved merry-go-round horses.

Santo Tomé 6. ℰ **91-308-12-85.** Reservations required. Main courses 35€–45€. AE, DC, MC, V. Mon–Fri 1:30–4:30pm; Mon–Sat 9pm–midnight. Closed Aug. Metro: Alonso Martínez, Colón. Bus: 37.

NEAR THE PUERTA DEL SOL
VERY EXPENSIVE

La Terraza del Casino ⊀⊀⊀ SPANISH/INTERNATIONAL The city's most imaginative chef, Ferran Adrià, isn't in Madrid. He's still tending those pots and pans in the little town of Roses near Girona in Catalonia. But the innovative master of cuisine created all the dishes on the menu here and flies in regularly to see that his cooks are following his orders. His *luxe* restaurant in Madrid lies on the top floor of the Casino in Madrid, a historical building and a former gentlemen's club with a history going back to 1910. Even the grand dons of those days surely didn't dine as well as you can today.

His dishes are exquisite, and food critics (and we concur) are always writing about taste "explosions" in your mouth. His Catalán restaurant is El Bulli, meaning "innovative" in Spanish. The same name could apply to this Madrid dining hot spot that provides a panoramic view of the heart of Madrid and can be reached by an elevator or by a sweeping 19th-century staircase designed to impress. The decor is classically restrained with high ceilings and crystal chandeliers. The exquisite food uses fresh seasonal ingredients and reinterprets Spanish dishes. An example is raya in oil and saffron with parsley purée and nuts on a bed of finely diced fries. More traditional dishes include the succulent *merluza a la gallega* (Galician hake), *crema de la fabada asturiana* (creamed Asturian bean soup), and the steeply priced *jamón Jabugo* (cured ham from acorn-fed pigs) served with a *menestra* (mixed vegetables) al dente. Only French champagne and Spanish wines are listed, and one of the best is the rounded woody red, the Ribeira de Duero from the province of Valladolid.

Alcalá 15. © **91-521-87-00.** Main courses 25€–33€; fixed-price menu 87€. AE, DC, MC, V. Mon–Fri 1–3:30pm and 9–11:30pm; Sat 9–11:30pm. Closed Aug. Metro: Sevilla.

Lhardy ★★ SPANISH/INTERNATIONAL   This is Madrid's longest running culinary act. Lhardy has been a Madrileño legend since opening in 1839 as a gathering place for the city's literati and political leaders. At street level is what may be the most elegant snack bar in Spain. Within a dignified antique setting of marble and hardwood, cups of steaming consommé are dispensed from silver samovars into delicate porcelain cups, and rows of croquettes, tapas, and sandwiches are served to stand-up clients who pay for their food at a cashier's kiosk near the entrance. The ground-floor deli and take-out service is open daily from 9am to 3pm and 5 to 9:30pm.

The real culinary skill of the place, however, is on Lhardy's second floor, where you'll find a formal restaurant decorated in the ornate Belle Epoque style of Isabel Segunda. Specialties of the house include fish, pork, veal, tripe in a garlicky tomato and onion wine sauce, and *cocido*, the celebrated chickpea stew of Madrid. *Soufflé sorpresa* (baked Alaska) is the dessert specialty.

Carrera de San Jerónimo 8. © **91-521-33-85.** Reservations recommended in the upstairs dining room. Main dishes 12€–30€. AE, DC, MC, V. Mon–Sat 1–3:30pm and 8:30–11pm. Closed Aug. Metro: Puerta del Sol.

EXPENSIVE

Caripén ★ ITALIAN/FRENCH   This restaurant stands in a historic district near the Royal Opera House and the Spanish Senate. It was once El Tablao, the flamenco club of Lola Flores, one of the most famous of all Spanish dancers. Its Art Deco decor has been restored, and instead of flamenco, you get the inspired French bistro cookery of Daniel Boute. The restaurant is especially popular with the Madrid locals, or *gatos* (cats), because it serves until 3am when most other quality establishments are shuttered. (Local residents are called *gatos* because they like to roam about at night.) Go for the *mejillones de roca* (mussels in white wine and cream sauce), a perfectly prepared steak tartare, *foie* with *setas* (duck liver and mushrooms), or skate in black butter. You can finish off with such desserts as tiramisu, freshly made fruit tarts, or crepes.

Plaza de la Marina Española 4. © **91-541-11-77.** Reservations recommended on weekends. Main courses 11€–17€. MC, V. Mon–Sat 9pm–3am. Closed Aug. Metro: Opera/Santo Domingo.

Casa Ciriaco CASTILIAN   In business for more than 10 years, this longtime favorite Taberna-cum-Restaurant is still run by the same family. Lying only two blocks from the Palacio Real, it has on occasion served dinners to members of the royal family along with a list of other impressive guests, including bullfighters, artists, and scholars. These distinguished guests are drawn to the unpretentious family atmosphere and the time-tested recipes. Nouvelle cuisine here means anything being served in 1900, including the classic Madrid tripe, which is an acquired taste for many diners. One of the most enticing offerings is *perdiz* (partridge) served with fava beans. Hare is another good choice, this dish served with white beans. A good appetizer is a plate of the grilled prawns, or else you might start with one of the hearty soups of the day, including a specialty of Castile: *sopa castellana*. A few fish dishes appear, including mountain trout, and *conchinillo asado* (roast suckling pig) is a specialty. Wash everything down with a glass of Toledo wine.

Calle Mayor 84. © **91-559-50-66**. Reservations recommended. Main courses 12€–21€. MC, V. Thurs–Tues 1–4:30pm and 8pm–12:30am. Closed Aug. Metro: Puerta del Sol.

Casa Lastra Sidrería ASTURIAN   Some visitors come here because they've heard this establishment serves "Austrian cuisine." Actually, the food is inspired by the cuisine of Asturias, a province of Spain in the northwest. Since 1926, this tavern has attracted a devoted following, particularly among homesick Asturians. The decoration is in a regional style, with cowbells, dried sausages, "pigtails" of garlic, and wood clogs. This restaurant and cider house—the national drink of the province—is known for serving very big portions, which means you might skip the starters. However, if you do indulge, we'd recommend *fabes con almejas* (white beans with clams) and *chorizo a la sidra* (spicy Spanish sausage cooked in cider). As a main course, *merluza* (hake) is also cooked in cider. If you're here in winter, order a fabulous *fabada*, the meat, sausage and bean casserole of the province. Milk-fed lamb is also roasted to perfection, and goat meat is yet another specialty, as is a cheese made from a blend of milk from goats, sheep, and cows. For dessert, locals order *carbayón*, which is made from sweetened egg yolks and almonds, although this may be too sweet for most tastes. Everything is washed down with cider, which might be more potent than you think.

Calle Olivar 3. © **91-369-08-37**. Reservations not required. Main courses 15€–20€. Fixed-price menu (Mon–Thurs) 12€. AE, DC, MC, V. Thurs–Tues 1–5pm; Thurs–Sat and Mon–Tues 8pm–midnight. Closed July. Metro: Anton Martin.

MODERATE

Casa Paco ✸✸ STEAK   Madrileños defiantly name Casa Paco, just beside the Plaza Mayor, when someone dares to denigrate Spanish steaks. They know that here you can get the thickest, juiciest, tastiest steaks in Spain, priced according to weight. Señor Paco sears his steaks in boiling oil before serving them on plates so hot that the almost-raw meat continues to cook, preserving the natural juices. Located in the Old Town, this two-story restaurant has three dining rooms but reservations are imperative. If you face a long wait, sample the tapas at the bar in front. Around the walls are autographed photographs of notables.

Casa Paco isn't just a steakhouse; you can start with fish soup and proceed to grilled sole or baby lamb, or try *Casa Paco cocido,* the house version of Madrid's famous chickpea and pork soup. You might top it off with one of the luscious desserts, but Paco no longer serves coffee. It made customers linger, keeping tables occupied while potential patrons had to be turned away.

Plaza Puerta Cerrada 11. © **91-366-31-66**. Reservations required. Main courses 5€–30€; fixed-price menu 24€. DC, MC, V. Mon–Sat 1:30–4pm and 8:30pm–midnight. Closed Aug. Metro: Puerta del Sol, or La Latina. Bus: 3, 21, or 65.

Cornucopia EURO-AMERICAN   Set on a narrow side street adjacent to the medieval Plaza de Descalzas Reales, this restaurant occupies the mezzanine level of what was originally a 19th-century private palace. Its glamour and allure derive from its ownership by four partners, two of whom (Jennifer Cole and her cohort, Kimberly Manning) are American; the others include French-born François and Spanish-born Fernando. Within a pair of elegant and airy dining rooms whose gleaming parquet floors remain from the original decor, you can admire the frequently changing paintings, all available for sale. Menu items include mussels with fennel and a roasted red pepper sauce over black fettuccini; grilled baby hen with mushrooms and sherry sauce; and grilled pork tenderloin stuffed with brie and bacon, and served with a pomegranate-apple compote and a red wine reduction sauce. Desserts are sumptuous and might include a dollop of such original homemade ice creams as *mojito*. Named after a traditional Cuban cocktail, it's flavored with mint, lemon, and rum. All the food is well prepared, the ingredients are fresh, and the staff is among the most inviting in Madrid.

Calle Flora 1. ℂ **91-547-64-65.** Reservations recommended. Main courses 8.75€–16€; fixed-price lunch (Tues–Sat only) 10€. AE, DC, MC, V. Tues–Sat 1:30–4pm; Tues–Sun 9–11:30pm. Closed 1 week in Aug. Metro: Opera or Callao.

El Cenador del Prado ⚶ INTERNATIONAL   In this elegant restaurant's

anteroom, an attendant will check your coat into an elaborately carved armoire before the maitre d' ushers you into one of a trio of rooms. Two of the rooms have cove moldings, English furniture, and floor-to-ceiling gilded mirrors. A third room is ringed with lattices and flooded with sun from a skylight.

The imaginative food reflects a French influence with an occasional Asian flourish. You might enjoy such specialties as crepes with salmon and Iranian caviar; a salad of red peppers and salted anchovies; a casserole of snails and oysters with mushrooms; a ceviche of salmon and shellfish; potato-leek soup studded with tidbits of hake and clams; sea bass with candied lemons; veal scaloppine stuffed with asparagus and garlic sprouts; or medallions of venison served with pepper-and-fig chutney.

Calle del Prado 4. ℂ **91-429-15-61.** Reservations recommended. Main courses 8€–24€; fixed-price menu 17€; vegetarian menu 17€. AE, DC, MC, V. Mon–Fri 1:45–3:45pm; Mon–Sat 8:45pm–11:45pm. Closed Aug 12–19. Metro: Antón Martín.

La Esquina del Real FRENCH   Next to the Teatro Real you'll find this

restaurant in an impressive 17th-century building with an ancient stone facade, thick granite walls, and the original wooden beams supporting old ceilings. This place has a sophisticated atmosphere, yet prices are very reasonable. One Madrid food critic recently called this place one of the city's "best kept" culinary secrets. The hospitable owner and chef, Jesus Oliva, extends a hearty welcome to patrons and feeds them well. Fresh ingredients are transformed into tasty concoctions, like large prawns with a delicate flavoring of raspberry vinaigrette or roast oxtail with mashed potatoes and fresh mushrooms. A rather common dish, veal fricassee in mushroom sauce, is transformed into something sublime here. To end your repast, you might opt for a combination platter of warm cheese, or try tart tatin, ice cream with a crunchy caramel sauce flambéed at your table.

Calle de la Unión 8. ℂ **91-559-43-09.** Reservations recommended on weekends. Main courses 7€–18€. AE, MC, V. Mon–Fri 2–4pm and 9:15pm–midnight; Sat 9pm–midnight. Closed last 2 weeks of Aug. Metro: Opera.

INEXPENSIVE

Café del Círculo de Bellas Artes ⚶ *Finds*   This former members-only club

is now open to the general public. If you eat and drink here, you still get the feeling you're crashing a private party. (Incidentally, this is a time-honored tradition in Madrid.) With its 1920s style ceilings, chandeliers, artistic statues, and soaring pillars, this cafe lies in an arts center. It's the best place to take a refueling stop when you're so tired you confused van Gogh with the Goyas at the Thyssen or the Real Academia de Bellas Artes.

Locals don't even know the place by its formal name, having nicknamed it *la pecera,* or aquarium. The food and drink are served in a palatial hall. At lunchtime join politicians and bankers from the nearby parliament or the Banco d'España to enjoy a variety of pork, beef, fresh fish, and chicken dishes. The menu is rotated daily. With luck, you'll be here on the day the chef decides to prepare his robust *cocido,* the "granddaddy of Spanish stews." It will put hair on your chest even if you're a woman. At night a more artsy crowd flocks to the place, devouring the succulent tapas such as shrimp and fresh anchovies and the rum cocktails that make you think you're back in Barbados. Only tapas are served at night but if you order three or four they become meals unto themselves.

Calle Alcalá 42. (© **91-521-69-42.** Lunch main courses 11€ each; evening tapas 2€–3€. MC, V. Sun–Thurs 9:30am–1am; Fri–Sat 9:30am–3am. Metro: Banco de España.

Casa Alberto CASTILIAN   One of the oldest *tascas* in the neighborhood, Casa Alberto is from 1827 and has thrived ever since. On the street level of a house where Miguel de Cervantes lived briefly in 1614, it contains an appealing mixture of bullfighting memorabilia, engravings, and reproductions of Old Master paintings. Many visitors opt only for the tapas, continually replenished from platters on the bar, but there's a sit-down dining area for more substantial meals. Specialties include fried squid, shellfish in vinaigrette sauce, *chorizo* (sausage) in cider sauce, and several versions of baked or roasted lamb.

Huertas 18. (© **91-429-93-56.** Reservations recommended. Main courses 12€–30€. AE, DC, MC, V. Tues–Sat 1–4pm; Tues–Sat 9pm–midnight; Sun noon–4pm. Metro: Antón Martín.

Champagnería Gala MEDITERRANEAN   This restaurant makes its reputation on its Catalán paellas but also on *fideuàs,* which is similar to the more famous rice dish except noodles are used instead. The waiters will offer you a choice of more than a dozen *fideuàs* or paellas. Run by a group of women, the setting is inviting, airy, partially grass covered, and has a plant-filled patio. The restaurant is found on a little back street near the Reina Sofía and Calle Atocha. Regional bean stews and other items round out the menu. But most visitors come here just to sample the paellas or *fideuàs* which can be meat, half-meat, half-fish, or else with just meat, seafood, or chicken—your choice. In-the-know diners consume their meals with *cava,* the sparkling wine of Catalonia. At the end of the meal, you'll be expected to drink dessert wine from a *porrón,* a traditional "drinking bottle" rather than a glass.

Moratín 22. Santa Ana. (© **91-429-25-62.** Reservations required. Main courses 10€–15€. No credit cards. Daily 1–4:30pm and 9:30–11pm. Metro: Antón Martin.

La Boitika (*Finds* VEGETARIAN   Vegetarian cuisine doesn't get a lot of attention in most Madrid restaurants, but this discovery is a rare exception. Opening east of the landmark Plaza Santa Ana, it is intimate and charming. It serves the capital's best macrobiotic vegetarian cuisine, and does so exceedingly well. We always begin with one of the homemade soups, which are made fresh daily, then have one of the large, fresh salads. The bread is also made fresh daily. One specialty is a "meatball without meat" (made with vegetables but shaped like a meatball). Tofu with zucchini and many other offerings appear daily.

Amor de Dios 3. (© **91-429-07-80.** Main courses 6€–10€; *menú del día* 7€–8€. No credit cards. Daily 1–4pm and 8–11pm. Metro: Antón Martín.

Museo del Jamón SPANISH/TAPAS   The displays on the walls of this unique establishment explain the bewildering name: "The Museum of Ham."

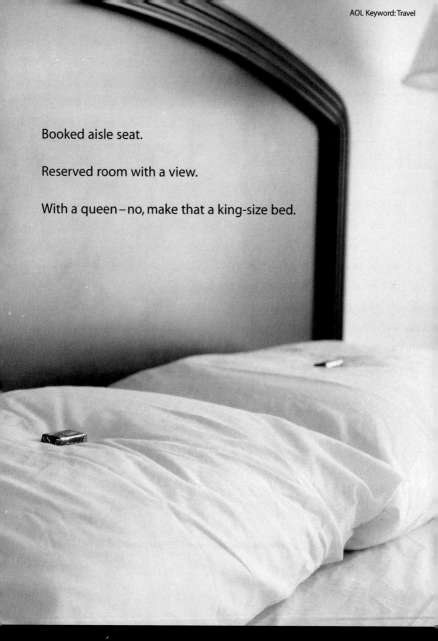

Booked aisle seat.

Reserved room with a view.

With a queen – no, make that a king-size bed.

th Travelocity, you can book your flights and hotels together, so
u can get even better deals than if you booked them separately.
u'll save time and money without compromising the quality of
ur trip. Choose your airline seat, search for alternate airports, pick your
tel room type, even choose the neighborhood you'd like to stay in.

Travelocity

Visit www.travelocity.com
or call 1-888-TRAVELOCITY

As in an art exhibition, large amounts of different kinds of hams—cured by a variety of methods—hang from the ceilings. The popular *chorizos* are hooked in rows reminiscent of one of those scenes in Golden Age paintings. This is indeed a real museum of the most celebrated fast food in Spain. On certain nights, the tavern offers live entertainment in the dining area upstairs, often a guitarist. The *paella* for two is reasonably priced. The aged *jamón Serrano* is a great delicacy now highly prized at tapas bars throughout Spain, Europe, and North America. You might try it in small sandwiches known as *bocattas* or as an always available tapa. The daily menu is varied and served in generous portions. Service is efficient, though not too friendly, but customers don't seem to mind.

Carrera de San Jerónimo 6 (2 blocks east of Puerta del Sol). © **91-521-03-46.** *Menú del día* 6.60€–12€; *platos combinados* 3€–4.50€. MC, V. Daily 9am–12:30am. Metro: Puerta del Sol.

Taberna del Alabardero BASQUE/SPANISH   In close proximity to the Royal Palace, this little Spanish classic is known for its selection of tasty tapas, ranging from squid cooked in wine to fried potatoes dipped in hot sauce. Photographs of famous former patrons, including Nelson Rockefeller and the race-car driver Jackie Stewart, line the walls. The restaurant in the rear is said to be one of the city's best-kept secrets. Decorated in typical tavern style, it serves a savory Spanish and Basque cuisine with market-fresh ingredients.

Felipe V 6. © **91-547-25-77.** Reservations required for restaurant only. Bar: tapas 3€–9.65€; glass of house wine 1.80€. Restaurant: main courses 8.70€–20€. AE, DC, MC, V. Daily 8am–1am. Metro: Opera.

RETIRO/SALAMANCA
VERY EXPENSIVE

Santceloni ★★★ MEDITERRANEAN   Santi Santamaria is ranked among the top three chefs of Spain, along with his chief rivals, Juan Mark Arzak and Ferrán Adriá. Santamaria gets our vote as the leader of the "troika," as these chefs are often called by food critics. He made his fame in his restaurant outside Barcelona. As his acclaim grew, he decided to open this branch of his fabled restaurant in Madrid. It's been hailed as an immediate success. Few chefs know how to present such an enticing and imaginative cuisine of the Mediterranean.

His cuisine is called *de mercado,* meaning that it's based on the freshest ingredients available that day in the marketplace. The same painstaking and fine care that goes into the selections of ingredients is also demonstrated when the produce hits those skillets, pots and pans. The taste of most dishes is sublime. Backed by an impressive, even daring, wine list, you can sample such starters as a terrine of tuna and foie gras, an unusual combination that is both appealing, startling, and a taste sensation. Large and well-flavored red prawns appear with sweet-tasting and lightly sautéed onions. The Atlantic fish, John Dory, is appetizingly wed with fennel. One of the best examples of Santamaria's wedding of ingredients is cream of pumpkin with crisp sweetbreads and black olives, a tasty "troika" unto itself. And, of course, his caviar with pork jowl and creamy potatoes is better than your mother made, as are his frogs' legs with garlic paste and a parsley emulsion.

In the Hotel Hesperia, Paseo de la Castellana 57. © **91-210-88-40.** Reservations required. Main courses 27€–36€. AE, DC, MC, V. Mon–Fri 2–4pm; Mon–Sat 9–11pm. Closed Aug. Metro Gregorio Marañón.

EXPENSIVE

Alkalde ★ BASQUE   For decades Alkalde has been known for serving top-quality Spanish food in an old tavern setting, and it continues to do so exceedingly well. Decorated like a Basque inn, it has beamed ceilings with hams hanging from the rafters. Upstairs is a large *típico* tavern; downstairs is a maze of stone-sided cellars that are pleasantly cool in summer (although the whole place is air-conditioned).

Basque cookery is the best in Spain, and Alkalde honors that noble tradition. Begin with the cream of crabmeat soup, followed by *gambas a la plancha* (grilled shrimp) or *cigalas* (crayfish). Other recommended dishes include *mero salsa verde* (brill in green sauce), trout Alkalde, stuffed peppers, and chicken steak. The dessert specialty is *copa Cardinal* (ice cream topped with fruit).

Jorge Juan 10. ℭ **91-576-33-59.** Reservations required. Main courses 25€–30€. AE, DC, MC, V. Daily 1:15pm–midnight. Metro: Retiro or Serrano. Bus: 8, 20, 21, or 53.

El Amparo ✿✿ BASQUE   Behind the cascading vines on El Amparo's facade is one of Madrid's most elegant gastronomic enclaves. Inside this converted carriage house, three tiers of rough-hewn wooden beams surround tables set with pink linens and glistening silver. A sloping skylight floods the interior with sun by day; at night, pinpoints of light from the high-tech hanging lanterns create intimate shadows. Polite, uniformed waiters serve well-prepared nouvelle cuisine versions of cold marinated salmon with a tomato sorbet, cold cream of vegetable and shrimp soup, bisque of shellfish with Armagnac, ravioli with crayfish dressed with balsamic vinegar and vanilla-scented oil, roast lamb chops with garlic purée, breast of duck, ragout of sole, steamed fish of the day, roulades of lobster with soy sauce, and steamed hake with pepper sauce.

Callejón de Puigcerdà 8 (at corner of Jorge Juan). ℭ **91-431-64-56.** Reservations required. Main courses 28€–30€. AE, DC, MC, V. Mon–Fri 1:30–3:30pm; Mon–Sat 9–11:30pm. Closed Easter week. Metro: Serrano. Bus: 19, 21, or 53.

El Pescador ✿ SEAFOOD   El Pescador is a popular spot, packing in crowds with more than 30 kinds of fish served, all prominently displayed in a glass case. Many of them are unknown in North America, and some originate off the coast of Galicia. The management airfreights them in and prefers to serve them *a la plancha* (grilled). You might start off with spicy fish soup and accompany it with one of the many good wines from northeastern Spain. If you're not sure what to order, try one of the many varieties and sizes of shrimp. They go under the names *langostinos, cigalas, santiaguinos,* and *carabineros.* Many of them are expensive and priced by weight, so be careful when you order.

Calle José Ortega y Gasset 75. ℭ **91-402-12-90.** Reservations required. Main courses 18€–24€. MC, V. Mon–Sat noon–4pm and 8pm–midnight. Closed Aug. Metro: Lista or Diego de León.

Horcher ✿ GERMAN/INTERNATIONAL   Horcher originated in Berlin in 1904. In 1943, prompted by a tip from a high-ranking German officer that Germany was losing the war, Herr Horcher moved his restaurant to Madrid. For years it was known as the best dining room in the city, but fierce competition has lately stolen that crown. Nevertheless, the restaurant is still going strong, continuing its grand European traditions, including excellent service.

You might try the skate or shrimp tartare or the distinctive warm hake salad. Both the venison stew with green pepper and orange peel and the crayfish with parsley and cucumber are typical of the elegant fare served with style. Spanish aristocrats often come here in autumn to sample game dishes, including venison, wild boar, and roast wild duck. Other main courses include veal scaloppine in tarragon and sea bass with saffron. For dessert, the house specialty is crepes Sir Holden, prepared at your table with fresh raspberries, cream, and nuts.

Alfonso XII 6. ℭ **91-532-35-96.** Reservations required. Jackets and ties for men. Main courses 30€–39€. AE, DC, MC, V. Mon–Fri 1:30–4pm; Mon–Sat 8:30pm–midnight. Metro: Retiro and Banco.

La Gamella ★★ CALIFORNIAN/CASTILIAN   La Gamella established its gastronomic reputation shortly after it opened several years ago in another part of town. In 1988, its Illinois-born owner Dick Stephens moved his restaurant into the 19th-century building where the Spanish philosopher Ortega y Gasset was born. The prestigious Horcher, one of the capital's legendary restaurants (see above), is just across the street, but the food at La Gamella is better. The russet-colored, high-ceilinged design invites customers to relax. Mr. Stephens has prepared his delicate and light-textured specialties for the king and queen of Spain, as well as for Madrid's most talked about artists and merchants, many of whom he knows and greets personally between sessions in his kitchen.

Typical menu items include a ceviche of Mediterranean fish, sliced duck liver in truffle sauce, a dollop of goat cheese served over caramelized endive, duck breast with peppers, and an array of well-prepared desserts, including an all-American cheesecake. Traditional Spanish dishes such as chicken with garlic have been added to the menu, plus what has been called "the only edible hamburger in Madrid."

Alfonso XII 4. ℭ **91-532-45-09.** Reservations required. Main courses 9.25€–19€. AE, DC, MC, V. Daily 1:30–4pm and 9pm–midnight. Closed 4 days around Easter. Metro: Retiro. Bus: 19.

La Trainera ★ SEAFOOD   This restaurant is more expensive, and more chic, than its sprawling, paneled interior might imply. Capable of seating up to 300 diners at a time, it occupies a quartet of dining rooms within a turn-of-the-20th-century building in the glamorous shopping neighborhood of Serrano. Look for vaguely Basque-inspired platters of very fresh seafood, which arrive steaming hot and drizzled with subtle combinations of herbs, wines, and olive oils. No meat of any kind is served here. Instead, you'll find spicy and garlic-enriched versions of fish soup, filet of sole prepared in any of several different versions, Cantabrian crayfish, and well-conceived versions of a *salpicón de mariscos* (a platter of shellfish). Other fish include red mullet, swordfish with capers, monkfish, and virtually anything else that swims. Any of them can be preceded with a heaping platter of shellfish set atop a bed of artfully arranged seaweed. Succulent shellfish, including lobster, shrimp, crab, and mussels, plus an array of other items, is market-priced by weight.

Calle Lagasca 60. ℭ **91-576-80-35.** Reservations recommended. Main courses 25€–50€. AE, DC, MC, V. Mon–Sat 1–4pm and 8pm–midnight. Metro: Serrano.

Pedro Larumbe ★ BASQUE/FRENCH   You dine in style here in an opulent section of La Castellana close to the Plaza de Colón. This century-old building was once the headquarters of the famous newspaper *ABC.* Today, it is the elegant restaurant of National Gastronomic Award winner Pedro Larumbe. There are three dining areas, each as elegant as the others: the classic Salón Pompeyano, the Art Deco Salón Fundador, and the beautifully tiled Patio Andalús. This Navarrese chef not only likes a fin-de-siècle decor, he prefers turn-of-the-20th-century cookery as well. His specialties are often from the tried-and-true recipes of yesterday, as evoked by his *solomillo a la mostaza,* or steak with mustard sauce. He also specializes in hake in green sauce with mussels, a favorite dish of the Basque country. One of his specialties is *ensalada de bocavante con salsa de almendras* (lobster salad with almond dressing), a true delight. The service is impeccable, the wine list well chosen, and the desserts something to write home about: tiramisu with a sweet wine and caramel sauce or "teardrops" of chocolate—that is dark and rich tear-shaped chocolate pieces.

Serrano 61. ☎ **91-575-11-12.** Reservations required. Main course 17€–25€. AE, DC, MC, V. Mon–Fri 1:30–4pm and 9pm–midnight; Sat 9pm–midnight. Closed Easter week and Aug 15–30. Metro: Rubén Darío and Núñez de Balboa.

Viridiana INTERNATIONAL Viridiana—named after the 1961 Luis Buñuel film classic—is praised as one of the up-and-coming restaurants of Madrid, known for the creative imagination of its chef and part-owner, Abraham García, who has lined the walls with stills from Buñuel films. (He is also a film historian, not just a self-taught chef.) Menu specialties are contemporary adaptations of traditional recipes, and they change frequently according to availability. Examples of the individualistic cooking include a salad of exotic lettuces served with smoked salmon, a chicken pastilla laced with cinnamon, baby squid with curry served on a bed of lentils, roasted lamb served in puff pastry with fresh basil, and the choicest langostinos from Cádiz. The food is sublime, and the inviting ambience makes you relax as you sit back to enjoy dishes that dazzle the eye, notably venison and rabbit arranged on a plate with fresh greens to evoke an autumnal scene in a forest.

Juan de Mena 14. ☎ **91-531-52-22.** Reservations recommended. Main courses 25€–33€. V. Mon–Sat 1:30–4pm and 9pm–midnight. Closed Easter week. Metro: Banco.

MODERATE

El Borbollón BASQUE/FRENCH The welcoming Castro family presides over this little charmer lying between Calle Serrano and Paseo de Recoletos, near both Plaza Cibeles and Plaza Colón. For two decades they have welcomed some of the more discerning palates in Madrid.

Eduardo Castro, the chef, is a local personality and a whiz in the kitchen. He is known for such dishes as a perfectly grilled *rape* (monkfish). Steak is cooked with savory green peppers, and a chateaubriand appears enticingly drenched in whiskey. Fresh turbot and hake appear regularly on the menu, and rich game dishes such as partridge are featured in the autumn. Choice cutlets of Segovian lamb are awakened with garlic cloves. Fresh flowers and bucolic art make for a soothing decor.

Paseo Recoletos 7. ☎ **91-431-41-34.** Main courses 15€–18€. AE, DC, MC, V. Daily Mon–Sat 1–4pm and 9pm–midnight. Metro: Retiro or Plaza Colón.

Gran Café de Gijón SPANISH If you want food and atmosphere like it was in Franco's heyday, drop in here. Each of the old European capitals has a coffeehouse that traditionally attracts the literati—in Madrid it's the Gijón, which opened in 1888 in the heyday of the Belle Epoque. Artists and writers still patronize this venerated old cafe, many of them spending hours over one cup of coffee. Open windows look out onto the wide paseo and a large terrace is perfect for sun worshippers and bird-watchers. Along one side of the cafe is a stand-up bar; on the lower level is a restaurant. In summer, sit in the garden to enjoy a *blanco y negro* (black coffee with ice cream) or a mixed drink.

Paseo de Recoletos 21. ☎ **91-521-54-25.** Reservations required for restaurant. Main courses 14€–21€; fixed-price menu 9.60€–22€. AE, DC, MC, V. Sun–Fri 7am–1:30am; Sat 7am–2am. Metro: Banco de España, Colón, or Recoletos.

Iroco ✦ INTERNATIONAL This well-run and popular Salamanca restaurant, known for its *nueva cocina* (nouvelle cuisine) attracts business women and men for its lunch and a trend-setting and younger crowd in the evening. Yes, that was Felipe, the crown prince of Spain, we spotted entering the restaurant with an entourage. Some of the more daring dishes, such as mixing apples with asparagus, may not be to your tastes. Other dishes may be more enticing, including our recently sampled tuna steak in a marinade (then grilled to perfection). The eggplant lasagna served here is also a delight, with fresh mushrooms and lots of creamy mozzarella. White fish salad is a good luncheon choice on a hot day, coming in a delightful sherry vinaigrette. Inspired by Asian fusion cuisine, the prawn rolls make a delightful beginning. Another good dish is *merluza* (hake) from the north coast, served in an asparagus sauce. Desserts are always tempting and made fresh daily.

Calle Velázquez 18. *C* **91-431-73-81.** Reservations required. Main courses 13€–17€. AE, DC, MC, V. Daily 1:30–4pm and 8:30pm–midnight. Metro: Goya.

CHAMBERI
VERY EXPENSIVE

Jockey ✦✦✦ INTERNATIONAL   This is a deluxe culinary citadel. For decades, this was the premier restaurant of Spain. A favorite of international celebrities, diplomats, and heads of state, it was once known as the Jockey Club, although "Club" was eventually dropped because it suggested exclusivity. The restaurant, with tables on two levels, isn't large. Wood-paneled walls and colored linen provide a cozy ambience—against the paneling are a dozen prints of jockeys mounted on horses—hence the name.

Since Jockey's establishment shortly after World War II, each chef who has come along has prided himself on coming up with new and creative dishes. You can still order Beluga caviar from Iran, but might settle happily for the goose-liver terrine or slices of Jabugo ham. Cold melon soup with shrimp is soothing on a hot day, especially when followed by grill-roasted young pigeon from Talavera or sole filets with figs in chardonnay. Stuffed small chicken Jockey style is a specialty, as is *tripa madrileña*, a local dish. Desserts are sumptuous.

Amador de los Ríos 6. *C* **91-319-24-35.** Reservations required. Main courses 24€–30€. AE, DC, MC, V. Daily 1–4pm and 9pm–midnight. Closed Aug. Metro: Colón.

EXPENSIVE

La Fuencisla ✦ SPANISH   Near El Museo Romántico is this small but comfortable restaurant that for nearly half a century has been serving meals in the traditional Spanish style. A family business, La Fuencisla (named as an offering to the Virgin of Segovia) is run by Señor and Señora de Frutos. Señor de Frutos greets the visitors in the front while the Señora creates tasty homemade meals in the kitchen. The dishes are typical of the Segovian kitchen, and ingredients are prepared according to time-tested recipes. No dish is more typical than the grilled chops of milk-fed lamb, praised by gastronomes. Begin with fresh asparagus in country butter and aromatic garlic or savory mussels in a marinara sauce. Filet of tuna freshly baked in the oven is another pleaser. For desserts, the cooks always prepare homemade tarts, which are especially good when the fresh fruit comes in. Otherwise, you might opt for the rice pudding or *flan de coco* (coconut pudding).

San Mateo 4. *C* **91-521-61-86.** Reservations recommended. Main courses 11€–20€. AE, DC, MC, V. Fri–Sat 2–4pm; Mon-Sat 9pm–1am. Closed Aug. Metro: Tribunal.

La Paloma ✦ BASQUE/FRENCH   In the exclusive Barrio Salamanca, this small but comfortable restaurant is the showcase for the culinary talents of chef/owner Segundo Alonso, who made a stellar reputation at the more exclusive El Amparo. Many of his fans followed him here and have since become regulars. His restaurant is in a nostalgic old restored house with high ceilings and wooden beams. His French and Basque dishes are some of the finest of their kind in Madrid. His food is robust, and he's known for what is called "variety meats," especially pigs' trotters. Even if you have never sampled this dish before, dare to here. You might be glad you did. You could settle instead for his equally celebrated wood pigeon stuffed with foie gras. He also does an excellent lasagna with crabmeat, spinach, and leeks, and a fine *rabo de toro* (bull's tail) stewed in red-wine sauce. The best fish dish is grilled turbot with tomato paste and thyme or sea urchin gratinéed and served with quail eggs. For dessert, try fresh dates with Chantilly cream or a velvety almond mousse with cinnamon ice cream.

Jorge Juan 39. ✆ **91-576-86-92.** Reservations recommended. Main courses 23€–51€. AE, DC, MC, V. Mon–Sat 1:30–4pm and 9pm–midnight. Metro: Vergara and Velázquez.

Las Cuatro Estaciones ✶✶✶ MEDITERRANEAN   Las Cuatro Estaciones is placed by gastronomes and horticulturists alike among their favorite Madrid dining spots, and is neck-and-neck with the prestigious Jockey. In addition to superb food, the establishment prides itself on decorating with masses of flowers that change with the season. Depending on the time of year, the mirrors surrounding the multilevel bar near the entrance reflect thousands of hydrangeas, chrysanthemums, or poinsettias. Each person involved in food preparation spends a prolonged apprenticeship at restaurants in France before returning home to try their talents on the taste buds of aristocratic Madrid.

Representative specialties include crab bisque; a petite marmite of fish and shellfish; and a nouvelle cuisine version of blanquette of monkfish so tender it melts in your mouth. The desserts include daily specials brought temptingly to your table.

General Ibáñez Ibero 5. ✆ **91-553-63-05.** Reservations required. Main courses 45€–54€. AE, DC, MC, V. Mon–Fri 1:30–4pm; Mon–Sat 9pm–midnight. Closed Easter week and Aug. Metro: Guzmán el Bueno.

MODERATE

La Bola MADRILEÑA   This is *the* taberna in which to savor the 19th century. Just north of the Teatro Real, it's one of the few restaurants (if not the only one) left in Madrid with a blood-red facade; at one time, nearly all fashionable restaurants were so coated. Time stands still inside this restaurant with its traditional atmosphere, gently polite waiters, Venetian crystal, and aging velvet. Ava Gardner, with her entourage of bullfighters, used to patronize this establishment. Grilled sole, filet of veal, and roast veal are regularly featured. Basque-style hake and grilled salmon are well recommended. Refreshing dishes to begin your meal include grilled shrimp, red pepper salad, and lobster cocktail.

Calle de la Bola 5. ✆ **91-547-69-30.** Reservations required. Main courses 20€–30€. No credit cards. Mon–Sat 1–4pm; Sun 1:30-4pm; daily 8:30–11pm. Metro: Opera. Bus: 25 or 34.

La Cava Real ✿ FRENCH/BASQUE   If your choice of wine is as important to you as the meal itself, this is the Madrid restaurant of choice for connoisseurs of *vino.* When the tavern opened in 1983, it was the first real wine bar Madrid had ever seen. Since then, there are many others, but La Cava Real remains the best. It's linked to Spain's largest wine club. Just don't mention the word *beer* here and you should do fine. There are more than 350 wines in the cellar, and you can order a staggering 50 of them by the glass, which allows you to sample more than one wine at the same meal if you so desire.

Turn to the skilled maitre d', Chema Gómez, for advice on wine. The chef, Javier Collar, hardly neglects the cuisine in favor of the wine, turning out a smooth and well-executed cuisine that weds two great kitchens, that of France and that of the Basque country. Our taste buds were enchanted with his pimientos stuffed with cod and his grilled and sweet-tasting *merluza* (hake) caught along the Basque coast. He also does wine, and in the autumn wild game such as partridge appears on the menu. The cheese selection deserves an award, and the chef also makes marvelous, really sumptuous, desserts fresh daily. It's worth it to save room for one.

Espronceda 34, Chaberi. ℂ **91-442-54-32.** Reservations required. Main courses 14€–21€; *menú de degustación* 46€. AE, DC, MC, V. Mon–Sat 1:30–4pm and 9pm–midnight. Closed Aug. Metro: Rio Rojas.

Teatriz ⭐ ITALIAN   Decorated by the famed French architect and designer Philippe Starck, this old theater is now transformed into a top-notch Italian restaurant. Theater seats have long given way to dining tables, but Starck kept many of the elements of the old theater. As you head for the restrooms, you encounter a stunning fountain of marble, silver, and gold, everything bathed in a bluish light, making you think you're in a nightclub. The kitchen closes at midnight, but the bar remains open until 3am. The dishes are genuine and cleverly crafted. Launch yourself with fresh mozzarella with tomatoes in virgin olive oil or raw salmon and turbot flavored with fresh dill. One of the best pastas is a tortellini filled with Parmesan-flavored ground meat. The desserts are worth saving room for, including cannelloni stuffed with dark chocolate or a fresh cheese mousse with mango ice cream. There is also a velvety smooth tiramisu.

Calle Hermosilla 15. ℂ **91-577-53-79.** Reservations recommended. Main courses 14€–16€; *menú completo* 21€. AE, DC, MC, V. Daily 1:30–4pm and 8:30pm–12:30am. Closed Aug. Metro: Serrano.

INEXPENSIVE

Foster's Hollywood AMERICAN   When your craving for Stateside food becomes overwhelming, head here. When Foster's opened its doors in 1971, it was not only the first American-style restaurant in Spain, but also one of the first in Europe. Since those early days, it has grown to 15 restaurants in Madrid and has even opened branches in Florida. A popular hangout for both locals and visiting Yanks, it offers a choice of dining rooms, ranging from classical club to a faux film studio with props. The varied menu includes Tex-Mex selections, ribs, steaks, sandwiches, freshly made salads, and, as its signature product, hamburgers grilled over natural charcoal. The *New York Times* once claimed that it had "probably the best onion rings in the world."

Paseo de la Castellana 116–118. ℂ **91-564-63-08.** Main courses 9€–20€. AE, DC, MC, V. Sun–Thurs 1–5pm and 8pm–midnight; Fri–Sat 1–5pm and 8pm–2am. Metro: Nuevo Ministerio.

NEAR ALONSO MARTINEZ
MODERATE

Café Balear PAELLA/SEAFOOD   Only a handful of other restaurants in Madrid focus as aggressively as this one on the national dish of Spain, paella, which here comes in 14 different versions with permutations that might surprise even the most jaded aficionado. Within a yellow-and-white dining room loaded with potted plants, you can order any of several paellas here, including versions with shellfish, with chicken and shellfish, with pork, with crabs, with lobster, and an all-black version that's tinted with squid ink for extra flavor. There's even a vegetarian version if you absolutely, positively hate fish. Lots of journalists, writers, poets, and artists seem to have adopted this place.

Calle Sagunto 18. ℂ **91-447-91-15.** Reservations recommended. Main courses 8€–16€. AE, MC, V. Daily 1:30–4pm; Tues–Sat 8:30–11:30pm. Metro: Iglesia.

Casa Vallejo SPANISH   This hardworking bistro with a not terribly subtle staff offers less exposure to international clients than some of its competitors. Despite that, you'll find a sense of culinary integrity that's based on a devotion to fresh ingredients and a rigid allegiance to time-tested Spanish recipes. Occupying a turn-of-the-20th-century building, it contains room for only 42 diners at a time. Menu items include garlic soup; tartlets layered with tomatoes, zucchini, and cheese; a ragout of clams and artichokes; croquettes of chicken; breast of chicken garnished with a fricassee of fresh wild mushrooms; pork filet; duck breast in orange or prune sauce; and creamy desserts. Budget gourmands in Madrid praise the hearty flavors here, the robust cookery, and the prices.

Calle San Lorenzo 9. ⓒ **91-308-61-58**. Reservations recommended. Main courses 11€–22€; fixed-price menu (available Mon–Fri only) 11€–18€. MC, V. Mon–Sat 2–4pm; Tues–Sat 9:30pm–midnight. Metro: Tribunal or Alonso Martínez.

Ciao Madrid ITALIAN   These two highly successful Italian restaurants are run by members of the extended Laguna family. The older of the two is the branch on Calle Apodaca, established about a dozen years ago; its cohort entered the scene in the early 1990s. Both maintain the same hours, prices, menu, and a decor inspired by the tenets of minimalist Milanese decor, with good-tasting food items that include risottos and pastas, such as ravioli or tagliatelle with wild mushrooms. No one will mind if you order a pasta as a main course (lots of clients here do, accompanying it with a green salad). If you're in the mood for a more substantial main course, consider osso buco, veal scaloppine, chicken or veal parmigiana, and any of several kinds of fish.

Calle Apodaca 20 (ⓒ **91-447-00-36**; Metro: Tribunal) and Calle Argensola 7 (ⓒ **91-308-25-19**; Metro: Alonso Martínez). Reservations recommended. Pastas 8€–10€; main courses 10€–20€. AE, DC, MC, V. Mon–Fri 1:30–3:45pm; Mon–Sat 9:30pm–12:30am. The branch at Calle Apodaca is closed in Sept; branch at Calle Argensola is closed in Aug.

CHAMARTIN
VERY EXPENSIVE

El Chaflán ✦ SPANISH   One of Madrid's hot new chefs, Juan Pablo Felipe Pablado, is a master in the kitchen. He can take almost any dish, including the classics, and give it a new flavor and texture. For example, he virtually deconstructs the most famous soup of Spain, gazpacho, and reassembles it into *glaces* and mousses. There's a firm hand in control here, and the chef personally selects the best produce, fish, and local meats to concoct his dishes. A recent mushroom risotto was perfectly prepared and full of flavor, as was the main course, a roast suckling pig that would rival any in Segovia, where they say this dish is prepared better than anywhere else in the world.

Av. Pío XII 34. ⓒ **91-350-61-93**. Reservations required. Main courses 26€–32€. AE, DC, MC, V. Tues–Sat 1:30–4pm and 9pm–midnight. Metro: Pío XII.

Zalacaín ★★★ INTERNATIONAL   Outstanding in both food and decor, Zalacaín is credited with bringing nouvelle cuisine to Spain when it opened its doors back in 1973. It is reached by an illuminated walk from Paseo de la Castellana and housed at the garden end of a modern apartment complex. It's within an easy walk of such deluxe hotels as the Castellana and the Miguel Angel. The name of the restaurant comes from the intrepid hero of Basque author Pío Baroja's 1909 novel, *Zalacaín El Aventurero*. Zalacaín is small, exclusive, and expensive. It has the atmosphere of an elegant old mansion: The walls are covered with textiles, and some are decorated with Audubon-type paintings. Men should wear jackets and ties.

The menu features many Basque and French specialties, often with nouvelle cuisine touches. It might offer a superb sole in a green sauce, but it also knows the glory of grilled pigs' feet. Among the best dishes are oysters with caviar and sherry jelly; crepes stuffed with smoked fish; ravioli stuffed with mushrooms, foie gras, and truffles; bouillabaisse; and veal escallops in orange sauce. For dessert, we'd suggest one of the custards, perhaps raspberry or chocolate.

Alvarez de Baena 4. ✆ **91-561-48-40**. Reservations required. Main courses 18€–48€. AE, DC, MC, V. Mon–Fri 1:15–4pm; Mon–Sat 9pm–midnight. Closed Easter week and Aug. Metro: Gregorio Marañón.

EXPENSIVE

El Olivo Restaurant ★★ MEDITERRANEAN   Locals praise the success of a non-Spaniard (in this case, French-born Jean Pierre Vandelle) in recognizing the international appeal of two of Spain's most valuable culinary resources: olive oil and sherry. Designed in tones of green and amber, this is the only restaurant in Spain that wheels a cart stocked with 40 regional olive oils from table to table. From the cart, diners select a variety to soak up with chunks of rough-textured bread seasoned with a dash of salt.

Menu specialties include grilled filet of monkfish marinated in herbs and olive oil, then served with black-olive sauce over compote of fresh tomatoes, and four preparations of cod arranged on a single platter and served with a *pil-pil* sauce (cod gelatin and herbs whipped into a mayonnaise-like consistency with olive oil). Dessert might be one of several different chocolate pastries.

Note: Many clients deliberately arrive early as an excuse to linger within El Olivo's one-of-a-kind sherry bar. Although other drinks are offered, the bar features more than 100 brands of vino de Jerez, more than practically any other establishment in Madrid. Priced at 1.50€ to 4.50€ per glass, they make the perfect aperitif. Also note that most main courses fall at the lower end of the price listing below.

General Gallegos 1. ✆ **91-359-15-35**. Reservations recommended. Main courses 20€–25€; fixed-price meals 45€. AE, DC, MC, V. Tues–Sat 1–4pm and 9pm–midnight. Closed Aug 15–31 and 4 days around Easter. Metro: Plaza de Castilla or Cusco.

La Broche ★★ CATALAN   The Catalán chef, Sergi Arola, is generating culinary excitement in Madrid, a Castilian city that in the past never paid a lot of respect to the cuisine of Barcelona. Arola trained under Catalonia's greatest chef, El Ferran Adrià of El Bulli. Arola learned from the master, but in Madrid he is creating his own magic with imaginative dishes. Forget the dull lobby of the Hotel Miguel Angel, a holdover from the 1970s, and enter this elegant dining enclave. Deluxe ingredients, personally selected by the chef and changed to take advantage of the best in any season, are fashioned into some of the capital's most flavor-filled dishes. Launch yourself into your repast with raw seafood and seawater gelée and then proceed across the heavenly menu, perhaps selecting a salmon risotto or a carpaccio of wild mushrooms. Even the bread placed on your table is freshly made and a delight, as are the creative desserts.

Calle Miguel Angel 29. ✆ **91-399-34-37**. Reservations required. Main courses 22€–33€. AE, DC, MC, V. Mon–Fri 2–3:15pm and 9–11:30pm. Closed Aug and Easter. Metro: Rubén Darío or Gregorio Marañón.

Príncipe de Viana ★ BASQUE   This place has gotten rave reviews. Fish is of course the most important staple of Basque cuisine, and there is a wide selection from which to choose. You might go the traditional route, with *bacalao ajoarriera* (cod with red peppers and tomatoes) and *merluza en salsa verde* (hake in parsley, garlic, and olive oil sauce). There are more adventurous modern concoctions, such as a salad with *chipirones* (baby squid) and *mollejas* (sweet meats) in a soy vinaigrette. Those with a sweet tooth will be more than satisfied with the dessert of cream cheese and mango sorbet. From the many Spanish and occasional foreign wines to choose from, the Albirino from Galicia is particularly recommended.

Calle Manuel de Falla 5. ✆ **91-457-15-49.** Reservations required. Main courses 18€–24€. AE, DC, MC, V. Mon–Fri 1–4pm and 9–11:30pm; Sat 9–11:30pm. Closed in Aug. Metro: Lima or Cuzco.

MODERATE

El Cabo Mayor ✿✿★ SPANISH   Near Chamartín train station, this is one of the best, most popular, and most stylish restaurants in Madrid, attracting on occasion the king and queen of Spain. An open-air staircase leading to the entranceway descends from a manicured garden on a quiet side street where a battalion of uniformed doormen stands ready to greet arriving taxis. The restaurant's decor is nautically inspired, with hardwood panels, brass trim, pulleys and ropes, a tile floor custom-painted with sea-green and blue replicas of waves, and hand-carved models of fishing boats. Some dozen bronze statues honoring fishers and their craft are displayed in brass portholes in illuminated positions of honor.

Menu choices include paprika-laden peppers stuffed with fish, a salad composed of Jabugo ham and foie gras of duckling, Cantabrian fish soup, stewed sea bream with thyme, asparagus mousse, salmon in sherry sauce, and loin of veal in cassis sauce. Desserts include a rice mousse with pine-nut sauce.

Juan Ramón Jiménez 37. ✆ **91-350-87-76.** Reservations recommended. Main courses 14€–44€. AE, DC, MC, V. Mon–Sat 1:30–4pm and 8:45–11:45pm. Closed Easter week and 1 week in Aug. Metro: Cuzco.

O'Pazo ✿ GALICIAN/SEAFOOD   This deluxe Galician restaurant is viewed by local cognoscenti as one of the top seafood places in the country. The fish is flown in daily from Galicia and mostly priced by weight at market rates. In front is a cocktail lounge and bar, all polished brass, with low sofas and paintings. Carpeted floors, cushioned Castilian furniture, soft lighting, and colored-glass windows complete the picture.

The fish and shellfish soup is delectable, although others gravitate to the seaman's broth as a beginning course. Natural clams are succulent, as are *cigalas* (a kind of crayfish), spider crabs, and Jabugo ham. Main dishes range from baby eels to sea snails, from Galician style scallops to *zarzuela* (a seafood casserole).

Calle Reina Mercedes 20. ✆ **91-553-23-33.** Reservations required. Main courses 17€–24€. MC, V. Mon–Sat 1–4pm and 8:30pm–midnight. Closed Aug. Metro: Nuevos Ministerios or Alvarado. Bus: 3 or 5.

CHUECA
INEXPENSIVE

Restaurante Salvador SPANISH/BASQUE   This is a robust, macho enclave of Madrid. The owner of this bustling restaurant, José Blásquez García, configured it as a mini-museum to his hobby and passion, the Spanish art of bullfighting. Inside, near a bar that stocks an impressive collection of sherries and whiskies, you'll find the memorabilia of years of bull-watching, including photographs of great matadors beginning in the 1920s, and agrarian artifacts used in the raising and development of fighting bulls. The menu is as robust and two-fisted as the decor, featuring macho-size platters of oxtail in red-wine sauce; different preparations of hake, one of which is baked delectably in a salt crust; stuffed peppers, fried calamari, and shrimp; and for dessert, the local version of *arroz con leche.*

Calle Barbieri 12. ✆ **91-521-45-24.** Reservations recommended. Main courses 11€–24€. AE, DC, MC, V. Mon–Sat 1:30–4pm and 9–11:30pm. Closed Aug. Metro: Chueca.

Taberna Carmencita ★ *Finds* SPANISH/BASQUE   Carmencita, founded in 1840 and exquisitely restored, is a street-corner enclave of old Spanish charm filled with 19th-century detailing and tile work. It was a favorite hangout for the poet Federico García Lorca, as well as a meeting place for intelligentsia in the pre–Civil War days. Meals might include entrecôte with green pepper sauce, escallop of veal, braised mollusks with port, filet of pork, cod with garlic, and Bilbao-style hake. Every Thursday the special dish is a complicated version of Madrid's famous *cocido*, which patrons wax lyrical over.

Libertad 16. ℂ 91-531-66-12. Reservations recommended. Main courses 6€–18€. AE, DC, MC, V. Mon–Fri 1–4pm; Mon–Sat 9pm–midnight. Metro: Chueca or Banco de España.

OFF THE PLAZA MAYOR
MODERATE

Casa Lucio CASTILIAN   Set on a historic street whose edges once marked the perimeter of Old Madrid, this is a venerable *tasca* with all the requisite antique accessories. Dozens of cured hams hang from hand-hewn beams above the well-oiled bar. Among the clientele is a stable of sometimes surprisingly well-known public figures—perhaps even the king of Spain. The two dining rooms, each on a different floor, have whitewashed walls, tile floors, and exposed brick. A well-trained staff offers classic Castilian food, which might include Jabugo ham with broad beans, shrimp in garlic sauce, hake with green sauce, several types of roasted lamb, and a thick steak served sizzling hot on a heated platter, called *churrasco de la casa*.

Cava Baja 35. ℂ 91-365-32-52. Reservations recommended. Main courses 12€–27€. AE, DC, MC, V. Sun–Fri 1–4pm; daily 9pm–midnight. Closed Aug. Metro: La Latina.

El Schotis ★ SPANISH   El Schotis was established in 1962 on one of Madrid's oldest and most historic streets. A series of large and pleasingly old-fashioned dining rooms is the setting for an animated crowd of Madrileños and foreign visitors, who receive ample portions of conservative, well-prepared vegetables, salads, soups, fish, and above all, meat. Specialties of the house include roast baby lamb, grilled steaks and veal chops, shrimp with garlic, fried hake in green sauce, and traditional desserts. Although one reader found everything but the gazpacho ho-hum, this local favorite pleases thousands of diners annually. There's a bar near the entrance for tapas and before- or after-dinner drinks.

Cava Baja 11. ℂ 91-365-32-30. Reservations recommended. Main courses 9€–20€; fixed-price menu 21€. AE, DC, MC, V. Mon–Sat 1–4pm and 8:30pm–midnight; Sun 1–4pm. Metro: Puerta del Sol or La Latina.

La Posada de la Villa SPANISH/GRILLED MEATS   This historic inn founded in 1642 offers a modern, more sanitized version of the earthy, grilled cuisine that fed the stonemasons who built the building's thick walls. Within a trio of dining rooms whose textured plaster and old stonework absolutely reeks of Old Castile, you'll find a hardworking staff and a menu that focuses on a time-honored specialty—roasted baby lamb—that's ordered more often than anything else on the menu. Other excellent choices include different versions of hake, Madrid-style tripe, and the rich, savory stew *(cocida madrileña)* that many local residents remember fondly from the days of their childhood. Notice that many of the chairs have brass plaques bearing the names of famous patrons—we saw one labeled "Janet Jackson" last time!

Cava Baja 9. ℂ 91-366-18-60. Reservations recommended. Main courses 11€–19€. AE, DC, MC, V. Daily 1–4pm; Mon–Sat 8pm–midnight. Closed Aug. Metro: La Latina.

Sobrino de Botín ★★ SPANISH   Ernest Hemingway made this restaurant famous. In the final two pages of his novel, *The Sun Also Rises,* Jake invites Brett to Botín for the Segovian specialty of roast suckling pig, washed down with Rioja Alta.

As you enter, you step back to 1725, the year the restaurant was founded. You'll see an open kitchen with a charcoal hearth, hanging copper pots, an 18th-century tile oven for roasting the suckling pig, and a big pot of soup whose aroma wafts across the tables. Painter Francisco Goya was once a dishwasher here. Your host, Antonio, never loses his cool—even when he has 18 guests standing in line waiting for tables.

The two house specialties are roast suckling pig and roast Segovian lamb. From the a la carte menu, you might try the fish-based "quarter-of-an-hour" soup. Good main dishes include baked Cantabrian hake and filet mignon with potatoes. The dessert list features strawberries (in season) with whipped cream. You can accompany your meal with Valdepeñas or Aragón wine, although most guests order sangria.

Calle de Cuchilleros 17. ⓒ **91-366-42-17**. Reservations required. Main courses 8.75€–25€; fixed-price menu 28€. AE, DC, MC, V. Daily 1–4pm and 8pm–midnight. Metro: La Latina or Opera.

INEXPENSIVE

El Cosaco RUSSIAN   One of the few Russian restaurants in Madrid sits adjacent to one of the most charming and evocative squares in town. Inside, you'll find a trio of dining rooms outfitted with paintings and artifacts from the former Soviet Union. Menu items seem to taste best when preceded with something from a long list of vodkas, many of them from small-scale distilleries you might not immediately recognize. Items include rich and savory cold-weather dishes that seem a bit disjointed from the sweltering heat of Madrid, but which you might find as satisfying alternatives from the all-Spanish restaurants in the same neighborhood. Examples include beef Stroganoff; quenelles of pike-perch with fresh dill; and thin-sliced smoked salmon or smoked sturgeon that's artfully arranged with capers, chopped onions, and chopped hard-boiled eggs. Red or white versions of borscht make a worthy starter, and blinis, stuffed with caviar or paprika-laced beef, are always excellent.

Plaza de la Paja 2. ⓒ **91-365-35-48**. Reservations recommended. Main courses 8€–15€. AE, DC, MC, V. Daily 9pm–midnight; Sat–Sun 2–3:30pm. Metro: La Latina.

La Chata SPANISH   The cuisine here is Castilian, Galician, and northern Spanish. Set behind a heavily ornamented tile facade, the place has a stand-up tapas bar at the entrance and a formal restaurant in a side room. Many locals linger in the darkly paneled bar, which is framed by hanging Serrano hams, cloves of garlic, and photographs of bullfighters. Full meals might include roast suckling pig, roast lamb, *calamares en su tinta* (squid in its own ink), grilled filet of steak with peppercorns, or omelets flavored with strips of eel.

Cava Baja 24. ⓒ **91-366-14-58**. Reservations recommended. Main dishes 12€–16€. AE, MC, V. Thurs–Mon 12:30–5pm; daily 8pm–1am. Metro: La Latina.

IN THE ARTURO SORIA DISTRICT
MODERATE

Nicomedes ★ *Finds* EXTREMADURAN   This is a real discovery. This colonial-style building has been completely refurbished by the charming Suárez sisters into a modern-looking château of five floors with beautiful, tall bay windows covering the full height of this impressive edifice. The immensity of the windows allows copious amounts of natural light to flood into the dining areas. The pervading atmosphere is one of openness combined with friendly hospitality. Customers often dine out in fine weather on a summer terrace. The modernity of the building is reflected in the style of the cuisine as well. The dishes from the western province of Extremadura are given a Madrid showcase here. Goat cheese with glazed onions is a tasty opener, as are *bolsitas rellenas de gamba y queso fresco* (crispy pasta balls stuffed with shrimp and freshly made cheese). *Rapa al horno con habitas y ajetes* (baked monkfish with beans and tender garlic) is a savory offering, although *solomillo de buey* (fondue of ox steak) is more typical of the region. For dessert, try the homemade cake of the day or a special sweet "biscuit" made with prunes and served with a caramel sauce.

Moscatelar 18. ✆ 91-388-78-28. Reservations recommended. Main courses 15€–19€. AE, DC, V. Tues–Sat 1:30–3:30pm and 9:30–11:30pm; Sun 1:30–3:30pm. Closed Aug. Metro: Esperanza or Arturo Soria.

NEAR PLAZA REPUBLICA ARGENTINA
MODERATE

Casa Benigna MEDITERRANEAN/SCANDINAVIAN   This small bistro lies in the northern sector of Madrid and has been run by the family of Jorge García for more than a decade. It is decorated in typically inviting Mediterranean style with blue walls and with murals of rural landscapes, even a library of books. The restaurant is the only one in Madrid that blends the cuisine of the far north of Europe with that of the sunny Mediterranean countries. The family has a close relative in Norway who contributes to their Scandinavian recipes. The dishes are exquisitely prepared and based on the finest ingredients. Here, you can order everything from Norwegian herring in delectable marinades to *arroz abanda,* a variation of traditional paella using different varieties of seafood. One especially good dish is the roast ribs of tender baby lamb. Many vegetarians appreciate their *parrillada de verduras,* or grilled fresh vegetables. For dessert, opt for the Norwegian cookies with wild berries or freshly made crepes with applesauce.

Benigno Soto 9. ✆ 91-413-33-56. Reservations required. Main courses 42€–48€. AE, DC, MC, V. Mon–Sat 1:30–3:30pm and 9–11pm; Sun 1:30–4pm. Metro: Concha Espino.

Príncipe y Serrano ✦ CASTILIAN   In an exclusive area of the Serrano district, this classic restaurant exudes distinction. Its sophisticated dining areas on both floors offer a warm and cozy atmosphere, and the outside lawns and flowered patios (one of them resembling a miniature golf course with small swimming

---

Moments Picnic, Anyone?

On a hot day, do as the Madrileños do: Secure the makings of a picnic lunch and head for Casa de Campo (Metro: El Batón), those once-royal hunting grounds in the west of Madrid across the Manzanares River. Children delight in this adventure, as they can also visit a boating lake, the Parque de Atracciones, and the Madrid zoo.

Your best choice for picnic fare is **Rodilla,** Preciados 25 (✆ 91-522-54-67; Metro: Callao), where you can find sandwiches, pastries, and take-out tapas. Sandwiches, including vegetarian, meat, and fish, begin at .75€. It's open Monday and Tuesday from 8:30am to 10:30pm; Wednesday, Thursday, and Sunday from 9am to 11pm; Friday and Saturday from 9am to midnight.

pools) make you forget you are in the center of a big city. There is the big *salón central,* two small dining areas for more private dinners, plus a bar downstairs. The cooking is simple, yet cosmopolitan, and always done to perfection. One especially good dish is roast potatoes with mussels. Also try the *manitas de ibérico rellenas de morcilla* (pork filled with chorizo sausage). We take delight in the freshly made apple tart with prune sauce or the crepes filled with mango and served in a fancy caramel cream sauce.

Serrano 240. (📞 **91-458-62-31.** Reservations recommended. Main courses 11€–21€. AE, DC, MC, V. Daily 1:30–4pm; Mon–Sat 9pm–midnight. Metro: Colombia or Concha Espino.

INEXPENSIVE

La Atalaya *(Value)* CANTABRIAN The owner of this pleasant restaurant, Gena Sánchez, hails from Santander in Northern Spain and, in the typical style of her hometown, has decorated the yellow walls of her establishment with a plethora of modern paintings. The food is also typical of Spain's green northern coast, with an emphasis on fresh fish. Every Thursday and Saturday the chefs prepare the most typical dish of Santander, a hearty cabbage soup. Called *cocido montanés,* it is also made with sausage, green beans, and black pudding. *Caracoles marucas,* or clams Santander style, prepared in a spicy sauce, is another good offering, as is *sopa de pescado,* or fish soup, one of the finest of its kind in Madrid. You might opt for a *torta de queso caliente,* a warm cheese soufflé. For dessert, traditional regional puddings are served.

Joaquín Costa 31. (📞 **91-562-87-45.** Reservations recommended. Main courses 8€–24€; fixed-price menu 12€. AE, DC, MC, V. Tues–Sat 1:30–4pm and 9pm–midnight. Metro: República de Argentina.

NEAR CIUDAD UNIVERSITARIA
EXPENSIVE

San Mamés 🍴 BASQUE/MADRILEÑA Situated in the north of the city in a historic building, this restaurant has been in the hands of the García family more than 50 years. The *tasca* (tavern) is decorated with colorful ceramic tiles and photographs of the celebrities who have dined here over the years. It is considered something of a secret address. With only two rooms, it has a homelike atmosphere of intimacy and good cheer. The cuisine offered is some of the best from both the Madrid and Basque kitchens. The owners shop carefully for the ingredients to prepare a repertoire of very tasty and well-flavored dishes. Their most typical dish is *callos a la madrileña,* a tripe stew with meat and chickpeas, beloved by their habitués. Otherwise, you might opt for *bacalao ajoarriero* (salt cod prepared with green peppers, tomatoes, and onions). Another dish favored in the Basque country is *cocochas de merluza,* which are the cheeks of the hake fish served with a bread sauce. For dessert, the owners recommend their *requesón con pasas* (cheesecake with raisins), or a hearty pudding called *tocino de cielo.*

Bravo Murillo 88. (📞 **91-534-50-65.** Reservations recommended. Main courses 14€–22€. AE, DC, MC, V. Mon–Fri 1:30–4pm and 8:30–11pm; Sat 1:30–4pm. Closed Aug. Metro: Cuatro Caminos.

INEXPENSIVE

Las Batuecas *(Value)* SPANISH This restaurant unpretentiously calls itself a *casa de comidas,* or "meal house." Since 1954, the little restaurant of José Pascual and his family has been located near the *ciudad universitaria.* Many of their customers originally came here as students, and over the years have become devotees of the homemade Spanish food, which is wholesome and good without being pretentious. The decoration is plain, with old paintings and newspaper articles intermixed with cartoons and reviews by travel and food magazines in different languages. It has two floors with tables, all in the rustic style. But no one comes here for decor; the food is the attraction. Come here with a big appetite and launch yourself into a fine meal with such dishes as *tortilla de callos* (omelet with tripe), or perhaps squid cooked in its ink. You can try their fresh artichokes cooked with white wine and ham or *berenjenas rebosadas* (sliced eggplant batter-fried). One of the tastiest main dishes is shoulder flank of lamb roast, perfectly done. Desserts include almond, vanilla, or chocolate cakes, or a fine selection of puddings. Note that dinner is served only 2 nights a week.

Av. Reina Victoria 17. ✆ **91-554-04-52**. Reservations required. Main courses 20€–25€; set menu 8€. No credit cards. Mon–Sat 1–4pm; Thurs–Fri 9–11pm. Closed Aug. Metro: Guzmán El Bueno and Cuatro Caminos.

OUR FAVORITE *TASCAS*

Don't starve waiting around for Madrid's fashionable 9:30 or 10pm dinner hour. Throughout the city you'll find *tascas*, bars that serve wine and platters of tempting hot and cold tapas. Below, we've listed our favorites. Keep in mind that you can often save pesetas by ordering at the bar rather than occupying a table.

Casa Mingo SPANISH   Casa Mingo has been known for decades for its cider, both still and bubbly. The perfect accompanying tidbit is a piece of the local Asturian *cabrales* (goat cheese), but the roast chicken is the specialty of the house, with a large number of helpings served daily. There's no formality here; customers share big tables under the vaulted ceiling in the dining room. In summer, the staff sets up tables and wooden chairs out on the sidewalk. This is not so much a restaurant as a *bodega/taverna* (bar/tavern) that serves food.

Paseo de la Florida 34. ✆ **91-547-79-18**. Main courses 20€–25€. No credit cards. Daily 11am–midnight. Metro: Principe Pío, then 5-min. walk.

Cervecería Alemania TAPAS   This place earned its name because of its long-ago German clients. Opening directly onto one of the liveliest little plazas in Madrid, it clings to its turn-of-the-20th-century traditions. Young Madrileños are fond of stopping in for a mug of draft beer. You can sit at one of the tables leisurely sipping beer or wine since the waiters make no attempt to hurry you along. To accompany your beverage, try the fried sardines or a Spanish omelet. Many of the *tascas* on this popular square are crowded and noisy— often with blaring loud music—but this one is quiet and a good place to have a conversation.

Plaza de Santa Ana 6. ✆ **91-429-70-33**. Beer 1.75€–2.10€; tapas 3.75€–8€. No credit cards. Sun–Thurs 11am–12:30am; Fri–Sat 11am–2am. Metro: Tirso de Molina or Puerta del Sol.

Cervecería Santa Bárbara TAPAS   Unique in Madrid, Cervecería Santa Bárbara is an outlet for a beer factory, and the management has done a lot to make it modern and inviting. Hanging globe lights and spinning ceiling fans create an attractive ambience, as does the black-and-white checkerboard marble floor. You go here for beer, of course: *cerveza negra* (black beer) or *cerveza dorada* (golden beer). The local brew is best accompanied by homemade potato chips or by fresh shrimp, lobster, crabmeat, or barnacles. You can either stand at the counter or go directly to one of the wooden tables for waiter service.

Plaza de Santa Bárbara 8. ✆ **91-319-04-49**. Beer 1.55€; tapas 6€–10€. MC, V. Daily 11:30am–midnight. Metro: Alonzo Martínez. Bus: 3, 7, or 21.

Taberna Toscana TAPAS   Many Madrileños begin their nightly *tasca* crawl here. The ambience is that of a village inn that's far removed from 20th-century Madrid. You sit on crude country stools, under sausages, peppers, and sheaves of golden wheat that hang from the age-darkened beams. The long, tiled bar is loaded with tasty tidbits, including the house specialties: *lacón y cecina* (boiled ham), *habas* (broad beans) with Spanish ham, and *chorizo* (a sausage of red peppers and pork)—almost meals in themselves. Especially delectable are the kidneys in sherry sauce and the snails in hot sauce.

Manuel Fernández y Gonzales 10. ℂ **91-429-60-31**. Beer 1€; glass of wine from .65€; tapas 3€–11€. MC, V. Tues–Sat noon–4pm and 8pm–midnight. Metro: Puerta del Sol or Sevilla.

5 Seeing the Sights

THE TOP ATTRACTIONS

In the heart of Madrid, near the Puerta del Sol Metro stop, the **Plaza Mayor** is the city's most famous square. It was known as the Plaza de Arrabal in medieval times, when it stood outside the city wall. The original architect of Plaza Mayor itself was Juan Gómez de Mora, who worked during the reign of Philip III. Under the Hapsburgs, the square rose in importance as the site of public spectacles, including the abominable *autos-da-fé*, in which heretics were burned. Bullfights, knightly tournaments, and festivals were also staged here.

Three times the buildings on the square burned—in 1631, 1672, and 1790—but each time the plaza bounced back. After the last big fire it was completely redesigned by Juan de Villanueva. Nowadays a Christmas fair is held around the equestrian statue of Philip III (dating from 1616) in the center of the square. On summer nights, the Plaza Mayor becomes the virtual living room of Madrid, as tourists sip sangria at the numerous cafes and listen to street musicians.

Monasterio de las Descalzas Reales ☆☆ In the mid–16th century, aristocratic women either disappointed in love or wanting to be the "bride of Christ" stole away to this convent to take the veil. Each brought a dowry, making this one of the richest convents in the land. By the mid–20th century, the convent sheltered mostly poor women. True, it still contained a priceless collection of art treasures, but the sisters were forbidden to auction anything, so they were literally starving. The state intervened, and the pope granted special dispensation to open the convent as a museum. Today, the public can look behind the walls of what was once a mysterious edifice on one of the most beautiful squares in Old Madrid.

In the Reliquary are the noblewomen's dowries, one of which is said to contain bits of wood from Christ's Cross; another, some of the bones of St. Sebastian. The most valuable painting is Titian's *Caesar's Money*. The Flemish Hall shelters other fine works, including paintings by Hans de Beken and Breughel the Elder. All the tapestries were based on Rubens's cartoons, displaying his chubby matrons. Be warned that the tours are not in English but there is much to see even if you don't speak Spanish.

Plaza de las Descalzas Reales s/n. ℂ **91-542-00-59**. Admission 4.80€ adults, 2.40€ children. Mon–Thurs and Sat 9:30am–5pm; Fri 10:30am–12:30pm; Sun 9am–2pm. Bus: 1, 2, 5, 20, 46, 52, 53, 74, M1, M2, M3, or M5. From Plaza del Callao, off Gran Vía, walk down Postigo de San Martín to Plaza de las Descalzas Reales; the convent is on the left.

Museo del Prado ☆☆☆ With more than 7,000 paintings, the Prado is one of the most important repositories of art in the world. It began as a royal collection and was enhanced by the Habsburgs, especially Charles V, and later the Bourbons. For paintings of the Spanish school, the Prado has no equal; on your first visit, concentrate on the Spanish masters (Velázquez, Goya, El Greco, and Murillo).

Goya Or Not, *The Milkmaid* & *The Colossus* Are Still Great Art

Spain's most fabled museum, the Prado, shocked the art world—and visitors, too—when it recently announced that two of its most famous paintings, *The Milkmaid of Bordeaux* and *The Colossus,* attributed to Francisco de Goya, are not in fact the work of this Spanish master. Goya specialists agree. The paintings still hang in the Prado, although their attribution has been changed to "attributed" to Goya instead of "by" Goya. Want to see some real Goyas? The Prado has some 150 actual paintings by the artist. At least we think that they do. Some Goya experts are questioning the authorship of some other "supposed" Goyas, especially several portraits. There was such a market for Goyas at the turn of the 19th century that many art dealers—surprise—kept turning up with "long lost" Goyas.

Major Italian works are exhibited on the ground floor. You'll see art by Italian masters—Raphael, Botticelli, Mantegna, Andrea del Sarto, Fra Angelico, and Correggio. The most celebrated Italian painting here is Titian's voluptuous Venus being watched by a musician who can't keep his eyes on his work.

The Prado is a trove of the work of El Greco (ca. 1541–1614), the Crete-born artist who lived much of his life in Toledo. You can see a parade of "The Greek's" saints, Madonnas, and Holy Families—even a ghostly *John the Baptist.*

You'll find a splendid array of works by the incomparable Diego Velázquez (1599–1660). The museum's most famous painting, in fact, is his *Las Meninas,* a triumph for its use of light effects and perspective. The faces of the queen and king are reflected in the mirror in the painting itself. The artist in the foreground is Velázquez, of course.

The Flemish painter Peter Paul Rubens (1577–1640), who met Velázquez while in Spain, is represented by the peacock-blue *Garden of Love* and by the *Three Graces.* Also worthy is the work of José Ribera (1591–1652), a Valencia-born artist and contemporary of Velázquez whose best painting is the *Martyrdom of St. Philip.* The Seville-born Bartolomé Murillo (1617–82)—often referred to as the "painter of Madonnas"—has three versions of the Immaculate Conception on display.

The Prado has an outstanding collection of the work of Hieronymus Bosch (1450?–1516), the Flemish genius. *The Garden of Earthly Delights,* the best-known work of "El Bosco," is here. You'll also see his *Seven Deadly Sins* and his triptych *The Hay Wagon. The Triumph of Death* is by another Flemish painter, Pieter Breughel the Elder (1525?–69), who carried on Bosch's ghoulish vision.

Francisco de Goya (1746–1828) ranks along with Velázquez and El Greco in the trio of great Spanish artists. Hanging here are his unflattering portraits of his patron, Charles IV, and his family, as well as the *Clothed Maja* and the *Naked Maja.* You can see the much-reproduced *Third of May* (1808), plus a series of Goya sketches (some of which, depicting the decay of 18th-century Spain, brought the Inquisition down on the artist) and his expressionistic "black paintings."

Paseo del Prado. ⓒ **91-330-28-00.** http://museoprado.meu.es. Admission 3€ adults, 1.50€ students and seniors. Free for kids 17 and under. Tues–Sat 9am–7pm; Sun and holidays 9am–7pm. Closed Jan 1, Good Friday, May 1, and Dec 25. Metro: Atocha or Cibeles. Bus: 10, 14, 27, 34, 37, or 45.

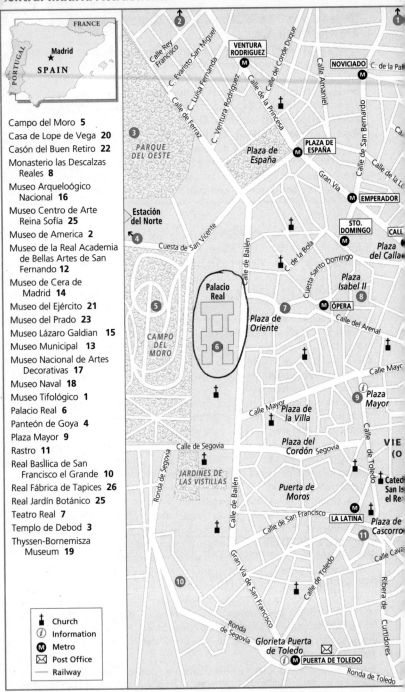

FRANCE

PORTUGAL

Madrid ★

SPAIN

Campo del Moro **5**

Casa de Lope de Vega **20**

Casón del Buen Retiro **22**

Monasterio las Descalzas Reales **8**

Museo Arqueloógico Nacional **16**

Museo Centro de Arte Reina Sofía **25**

Museo de America **2**

Museo de la Real Academia de Bellas Artes de San Fernando **12**

Museo de Cera de Madrid **14**

Museo del Ejército **21**

Museo del Prado **23**

Museo Lázaro Galdian **15**

Museo Municipal **13**

Museo Nacional de Artes Decorativas **17**

Museo Naval **18**

Museo Tifológico **1**

Palacio Real **6**

Panteón de Goya **4**

Plaza Mayor **9**

Rastro **11**

Real Basllica de San Francisco el Grande **10**

Real Fábrica de Tapices **26**

Real Jardín Botánico **25**

Teatro Real **7**

Templo de Debod **3**

Thyssen-Bornemisza Museum **19**

✝ Church
ⓘ Information
Ⓜ Metro
✉ Post Office
— Railway

0 1/5 mi
0 0.2 km

Calle de la Palma
Calle de Fuencarral
Calle de Genova
Paseo de la Castellana
Calle de Goya
Wax Museum
Plaza de Colón
SERRANO
Plaza de la Villa
Calle Fernando VI
COLÓN
JARDINES DEL DESCUBRIMIENTO
C. de El Escorial
Corredera Baja de San Pablo
del Pez
Hortaleza
Calle de Valverde
Calle de Fuencarral
Calle de Augusto Figueroa
Gravina
CHUECA
Calle Bárbara de Braganza
Calle de Serrano
Claudio Coello
San Marcos
Calle de Prim
Paseo de Recoletos
BARRIO DE SALAMANCA
Infantas
GRAN VÍA
Red. de San Luis
Gran Vía
Calle de Barquillo
Plaza de la Cibeles
Calle de Alcalá
Plaza de la Independencia
C. del Carmen
Calle Montera
Calle de
Preciados
Puerta del Sol
SOL
Calle de Alcalá
SEVILLA
BANCO DE ESPAÑA
Palacio de Villahermosa
Calle de Montalbán
~ Monestary
Carrera de San Jerónimo
Paseo del Prado
Plaza de la Lealtad
Calle A. Maura
Calle de la Cruz
Plaza de las Cortes
Plaza C. del Castillo
Calle de Alfonso XII
Plaza Jacinto Benavente
Calle del Prado
Calle de Cervantes
MADRID (MADRID)
Calle Atocha
Calle de las Huertas
Paseo del Prado
Museo del Prado
PARQUE DEL BUEN RETIRO
TIRSO DE MOLINA
Calle de la Magdalena
ANTÓN MARTÍN
Calle de la Cabeza
Calle de Santa Isabel
Calle Atocha
Calle de Gobernador
Calle de Espalter
REAL JARDÍN BOTÁNICO
Calle Jesús y María Lavapiés
Calle del Amparo
Calle Mesón de Paredes
Plaza Lavapiés
LAVAPIES
Reina Sofía
Calle de Alfonso XII
ATOCHA
Paseo de la Infanta Isabel
Calle de Embajadores
C. Miguel Servet
Estación de Atocha
Ronda de Atocha
Sta. María de la Cabeza

137

zaro Galdiano ★★   Imagine 37 rooms in a well-preserved 19th-
mansion bulging with artworks—including many by the most famous
old masters of Europe. Most visitors take the elevator to the top floor and work
down, lingering over 15th-century hand-woven vestments, swords and daggers,
royal seals, 16th-century Limoges crystal, Byzantine jewelry, Italian bronzes
from ancient times to the Renaissance, and medieval armor.

One painting by Bosch evokes his own peculiar brand of horror, the canvas
peopled with creepy fiends devouring human flesh. The Spanish masters are
the best represented: El Greco, Velázquez, Zurbarán, Ribera, Murillo, and
Valdés-Leál.

One section is devoted to works by the English portrait and landscape artists
Reynolds, Gainsborough, and Constable. Italian artists exhibited include
Tiepolo and Guardi. Salon 30—for many, the most interesting—is devoted to
Goya and includes paintings from his "black period." This off-the-beaten track
museum is a gem and usually enjoyably underpopulated, a nice contrast to the
overcrowded Prado, Thyssen, and Reina Sofía.

Serrano 122. ☎ **91-561-60-84.** Admission 3€. Tues–Sun 10am–2pm. Closed holidays and Aug. Metro:
Rubén Darío or Núñez de Balboa. Bus: 9, 16, 19, 27, 45, 51, 61, 89, or 114.

Museo Nacional Centro de Arte Reina Sofía ★

What the Prado is to tra-
ditional art, this museum is to modern art; the greatest repository of 20th-
century works in Spain. Set within the echoing, futuristically renovated walls of
the former General Hospital, originally built between 1776 and 1781, the
museum is a sprawling, high-ceilinged showplace. Once designated "the ugliest
building in Spain" by Catalán architect Oriol Bohigas, the Reina Sofía's design
hangs in limbo somewhere between the 18th and the 21st century. Inside are a
50,000-volume art library and database, a cafe, a theater, and a bookstore.

Special emphasis is paid to the great artists of 20th-century Spain: Juan Gris,
Salvador Dalí, Joan Miró, and Pablo Picasso (the museum has been able to
acquire a handful of his works). What many critics feel is Picasso's masterpiece,
Guernica, now rests at this museum after a long and troubling history of traveling. Banned in Spain during Franco's era (Picasso refused to allow it to be displayed here anyway), it hung until 1980 at New York's Museum of Modern Art.
The fiercely antiwar painting immortalizes the town's shameful blanket bombing by the German Luftwaffe, who were fighting for Franco during the Spanish
Civil War. Guernica was the cradle of the Basque nation, and Picasso's canvas
made it a household name around the world.

Santa Isabel 52. ☎ **91-467-50-62.** Admission 3€ adults, 1.50€ students; free after 2:30pm on Sat and all
day Sun. Mon and Wed–Sat 10am–9pm; Sun 10am–2:30pm. Free guided tours Mon and Wed at 5pm, Sat at
11am. Metro: Atocha.

Palacio Real (Royal Palace) ★★

This huge palace was begun in 1738 on
the site of the Madrid Alcázar, which burned to the ground in 1734. Some of its
2,000 rooms—which that "enlightened despot" Charles III called home—are
open to the public; others are still used for state business. The palace was last
used as a royal residence in 1931 before King Alfonso XIII and his wife, Victoria Eugénie, fled Spain.

Highlights of a visit include the Reception Room, the State Apartments, the
Armory, and the Royal Pharmacy. The Reception Room and State Apartments
should get priority here if you're rushed. They embrace a rococo room with a
diamond clock; a porcelain salon; the Royal Chapel; the Banquet Room, where
receptions for heads of state are still held; and the Throne Room.

The rooms are literally stuffed with art treasures and antiques—salon after salon of monumental grandeur, with no apologies for the damask, mosaics, Tiepolo ceilings, gilt and bronze, chandeliers, and paintings.

If your visit falls on the first Wednesday of the month, look for the changing of the guard ceremony, which occurs at noon and is free to the public.

In the Armory, you'll see the finest collection of weaponry in Spain. Many of the items—powder flasks, shields, lances, helmets, and saddles—are from the collection of Carlos V. From here, the comprehensive tour takes you into the Pharmacy. Afterward, stroll through the **Campo del Moro,** the gardens of the palace.

Plaza de Oriente, Calle de Bailén 2. ☏ **91-454-87-00.** Admission 7€ adults, 3.50€ students and children. Mon–Sat 9:30am–5pm; Sun 9am–2pm. Metro: Opera or Plaza de España.

Panteón de Goya (Goya's Tomb) ⭐⭐   In a remote part of town beyond the Norte train station lies Goya's tomb, containing one of his masterpieces: an elaborately beautiful fresco depicting the miracles of St. Anthony on the dome and cupola of the little hermitage of San Antonio de la Florida. This has been called Goya's Sistine Chapel. Already deaf when he began the painting, Goya labored dawn to dusk for 16 weeks, painting with sponges rather than brushes. By depicting common street life—stonemasons, prostitutes, and beggars—Goya raised the ire of the nobility who held judgment until the patron, Carlos IV, viewed it. When the monarch approved, the formerly outrageous painting was deemed acceptable.

The tomb and fresco are in one of the twin chapels (visit the one on the right) that were built in the latter part of the 18th century. Discreetly placed mirrors will help you see the ceiling better.

Glorieta de San Antonio de la Florida 5. ☏ **91-542-07-22.** Free admission. Tues–Fri 10am–2pm and 4–8pm; Sat–Sun 10am–2pm. Metro: Príncipe Pío. Bus: 41, 46, 75, or C.

Real Fábrica de Tapices (Royal Tapestry Factory)   In this factory, the age-old process of making exquisite (and very expensive) tapestries is still carried on with consummate skill. Nearly every tapestry is based on a cartoon of Goya, the factory's most famous employee. Many of these patterns, such as *The Pottery Salesman,* are still in production today. (Goya's original drawings are in the Prado.) Many of the other designs are based on cartoons by Francisco Bayeu, Goya's brother-in-law.

Fuenterrabía 2. ☏ **91-434-05-50.** Admission 2.50€. Mon–Fri 10am–2pm. Closed Aug and holidays. Metro: Menéndez Pelayo. Bus: 10, 14, 26, 32, 37, C, or M9.

Thyssen-Bornemisza Museum ⭐⭐⭐   Until 1985, the contents of this museum overflowed the premises of a legendary villa near Lugano, Switzerland; it was a hugely popular attraction there. The collection had been laboriously amassed over a period of about 60 years by the wealthy Thyssen-Bornemisza family, of Holland, Germany, and Hungary. Experts had proclaimed it one of the world's most extensive and valuable privately owned collections, rivaled only by the holdings of Queen Elizabeth II. For tax and insurance reasons, and because the collection had outgrown the boundaries of its lakeside villa, the collection was discreetly put on the market in the early 1980s to the world's major museums. Amid endless intrigue, glamorous supplicants from eight different nations came calling. Among them were Margaret Thatcher and Prince Charles; trustees of the Getty Museum in Los Angeles; the president of West Germany; and the duke of Badajoz, brother-in-law of King Carlos II. Even emissaries from

Walt Disney World came! Eventually, the collection was awarded to Spain for $350 million. Controversies over the huge public cost of the acquisition raged for months. Various estimates have placed the value of this collection between $1 billion and $3 billion.

To house the collection, an 18th-century building adjacent to the Prado, the Villahermosa Palace, was fitted with appropriate lighting and security devices, and renovated at a cost of $45 million. Rooms are arranged numerically so that by following the order of the rooms (nos. 1–48, spread out over 3 floors), a logical sequence of European painting can be traced from the 13th through the 20th century. The nucleus of the collection consists of 700 world-class paintings. They include works by, among others, El Greco, Velázquez, Dürer, Rembrandt, Watteau, Canaletto, Caravaggio, Hals, Memling, and Goya.

Unusual among the world's great art collections because of its eclecticism, the Thyssen group also contains 19th- and 20th-century paintings by many of the notable French Impressionists. It also houses works by Picasso, Sargent, Kirchner, Nolde, and Kandinsky—artists who had never been well represented in Spanish museums. In addition to European paintings, major American works can be viewed here, including paintings by Thomas Cole, Winslow Homer, Jackson Pollock, Mark Rothko, Edward Hopper, Robert Rauschenberg, Stuart Davis, and Roy Lichtenstein. There is an agreeable and moderately priced cafeteria and restaurant on-site.

Palacio de Villahermosa, Paseo del Prado 8. © **91-369-01-51.** Admission 4.80€ adults, 3€ students and seniors, free for children 12 and under. Tues–Sun 10am–7pm. Metro: Banco de España. Bus: 1, 2, 5, 9, 10, 14, 15, 20, 27, 34, 45, 51, 52, 53, 74, 146, or 150.

THE BULLFIGHT

Madrid draws the finest matadors in Spain. If a matador hasn't proved his worth in the **Plaza Monumental de Toros de las Ventas,** Alcalá 237 (© **91-356-22-00;** Metro: Ventas), he just hasn't been recognized as a top-flight artist. The major season begins during the Fiestas de San Isidro, patron saint of Madrid, on May 15. This is the occasion for a series of fights with talent scouts in the audience. Matadors who distinguish themselves in the ring are signed up for Majorca, Málaga, and other places.

The best way to get tickets to the bullfights is at the stadium's box office (open Fri–Sun 10am–2pm and 5–8pm). Alternatively, you can contact one of Madrid's most competent ticket agents, **Localidades Galicia,** Plaza del Carmen 1 (© **91-531-27-32;** Metro: Puerta del Sol). It's open Tuesday through Saturday from 9:30am to 1:30pm and 4:30 to 7pm, Sunday from 9:30am to 1:30pm. Regardless of where you buy them, tickets to bullfights range from 12€ to 126€, depending on the event and the position of your seat within the stadium. Concierges for virtually every reputable upper-bracket hotel in Madrid can acquire tickets, through inner channels of their own, to bullfights and other sought-after entertainment. Front-row seats at the bullfights are known as *barreras. Delanteras* (3rd-row seats) are available in both the *alta* (high) and the *baja* (low) sections. The cheapest seats sold, *filas,* afford the worst view and are in the sun *(sol)* during the entire performance. The best seats are in the shade *(sombra).* Bullfights are held on Sunday and holidays throughout most of the year, and every day during certain festivals, which tend to last around 3 weeks, usually in the late spring. Starting times are adjusted according to the anticipated hour of sundown on the day of a performance, usually 7pm from March to October and 5pm during late autumn and early spring. Late-night fights by neophyte matadors are sometimes staged under spotlights on Saturday around 11pm.

IF YOU HAVE MORE TIME
MUSEUMS

Museo Arqueológico Nacional ⭐⭐   This stately mansion is a storehouse of artifacts from the prehistoric to the baroque. One of the prime exhibits here is the Iberian statue *The Lady of Elche,* a piece of primitive carving (from the 4th c. B.C.) discovered on the southeastern coast of Spain. Finds from Ibiza, Paestum, and Rome are on display, including statues of Tiberius and his mother, Livia. The Islamic collection from Spain is outstanding. There are collections of Spanish Renaissance lusterware, Talavera pottery, Retiro porcelain, and some rare 16th- and 17th-century Andalusian glassware.

Many of the exhibits are treasures that were removed from churches and monasteries. A much-photographed choir stall from the palace of Palencia dates from the 14th century. Also worth a look are the reproductions of the Altamira cave paintings (chiefly of bison, horses, and boars), discovered near Santander in northern Spain in 1868.

Serrano 13. ℂ **91-577-79-12.** Admission 3€, free for children and adults over 65. Free on Sat 2:30–8:30pm and Sun. Tues–Sat 9:30am–8:30pm; Sun 9:30am–2:30pm. Metro: Serrano or Colón. Bus: 1, 9, 19, 51 or 74.

Museo de América (Museum of the Americas)   This museum, situated near the university campus, houses an outstanding collection of pre-Columbian, Spanish-American, and Native American art and artifacts. Various exhibits chronicle the progress of the inhabitants of the New World from the Paleolithic period to the present day. One exhibit, "Groups, Tribes, Chiefdoms, and States," focuses on the social structure of the various peoples of the Americas. Another display outlines the various religions and deities associated with them. Also included in the museum is an exhibit dedicated to communication, highlighting written as well as nonverbal expressions of art.

Av. de los Reyes Católicos 6. ℂ **91-549-26-41.** Admission 3€. Tues–Sat 9:30am–3pm; Sun 10am–2:30pm. Metro: Moncloa.

Museo de la Real Academia de Bellas Artes de San Fernando (Fine Arts Museum) ⭐   An easy stroll from Puerta del Sol, the Fine Arts Museum is located in the restored and remodeled 17th-century baroque palace of Juan de Goyeneche. The collection—more than 1,500 paintings and 570 sculptures, ranging from the 16th century to the present—was started in 1752 during the reign of Fernando VI (1746–59). It emphasizes works by Spanish, Flemish, and Italian artists. You can see masterpieces by El Greco, Rubens, Velázquez, Zurbarán, Ribera, Cano, Coello, Murillo, Goya, and Sorolla.

Alcalá 13. ℂ **91-524-08-64.** Admission 2.40€ adults, 1.50€ students, free for children under 18. Free on Wed. Tues–Fri 9am–7pm; Sat–Mon 9am–2pm. Metro: Puerta del Sol or Sevilla. Bus: 3, 15, 20, 51, 52, 53, or 150.

Museo del Ejército (Army Museum) ⭐   This museum in the Buen Retiro Palace houses outstanding exhibits from military history, including El Cid's original sword. In addition, you can see the tent used by Charles V in Tunisia, relics of Pizarro and Cortés, and an exceptional collection of armor. Look for the piece of the cross that Columbus carried when he landed in the New World. The museum had a notorious founder: Manuel Godoy, who rose from relative poverty to become the lover of María Luisa of Parma, wife of Carlos IV.

Méndez Núñez 1. ℂ **91-522-89-77.** Admission 1€ adults, free for children under 18 and adults over 65. Tues–Sun 10am–2pm. Metro: Banco de España or Retiro. Bus: 10, 19, 27, or 34.

Frommer's Favorite Madrid Experiences

Tasca **Hopping.** This is the quintessential Madrid experience and the fastest way for a visitor to tap into the local scene. *Tascas* are Spanish pubs serving tapas, those tantalizing appetizers. You can go from one to the other, sampling each tavern's special dishes and wines.

Eating Around Spain. The variety of gastronomic experiences is staggering: You can literally restaurant-hop from province to province without ever leaving Madrid.

Viewing the Works of Your Favorite Artist. Spend an afternoon at the Prado, savoring the works of your favorite Spanish artist.

Bargain Hunting at El Rastro. Madrid has one of the greatest flea markets in Europe, if not the world. Wander through its many offerings to discover that hidden treasure you've been searching for.

Enjoying a Night of Flamenco. Flamenco folk songs *(cante)* and dances *(baile)* are an integral part of the Spanish experience. Spend at least one night in a flamenco tavern listening to the heart-rending laments of gypsy sorrows and dreams.

Outdoor-Cafe Sitting. This is a famous experience for the summertime, when Madrileños come alive again on their *terrazas*. The drinking and good times can go on until dawn. From glamorous hangouts to lowly street corners, the cafe scene takes place mainly along the axis formed by the Paseo de la Castellana, Paseo del Prado, and Paseo de Recoletos (all of which make up one continuous street).

Museo Nacional de Artes Decorativas   In 62 rooms spread over several floors, this museum near the Plaza de la Cibeles displays a rich collection of furniture, ceramics, and decorative pieces. Emphasizing the 16th and 17th centuries, the eclectic collection includes Gothic carvings, alabaster figurines, festival crosses, dollhouses, baroque four-poster beds, a chapel covered with leather tapestries, and even kitchens from the 18th century. Two new floors focusing on the 18th and 19th centuries have recently been added to the museum.

Calle de Montalbán 12. ⓒ **91-532-64-99.** Admission 2.40€ adults, free for children and seniors. Tues–Fri 9:30am–3pm; Sat–Sun 10am–2pm. Metro: Banco de España or Retiro. Bus: 14, 27, 34, 37, or 45.

Museo Naval   The history of nautical science and the Spanish navy, from the time of Isabella and Ferdinand until today, comes alive at the Museo Naval. The most fascinating exhibit is the map made by the *Santa María's* first mate to show the Spanish monarchs the new discoveries. There are also souvenirs of the Battle of Trafalgar.

Paseo del Prado 5. ⓒ **91-379-52-99.** Free admission. Tues–Sun 10am–2pm. Closed Aug. Metro: Banco de España. Bus: 2, 14, 27, 40, 51, 52, or M6.

Museo Sorolla ⓐ   From 1912, painter Joaquín Sorolla and his family occupied this elegant Madrileño town house off Paseo de la Castellana. His widow turned it over to the government, and it is now maintained as a memorial. Much of the house remains as Sorolla left it, right down to his stained paintbrushes and pipes. The museum wing displays a representative collection of his works.

Although Sorolla painted portraits of Spanish aristocrats, he wa
interested in the common people, often depicting them in their nativ
view are the artist's self-portrait and the paintings of his wife an
Sorolla was especially fond of painting beach scenes of the Costa Bianca.

General Martínez Campos 37. © 91-310-15-84. Admission 2.40€. Tues–Sat 10am–3pm; Sun 10am–3pm.
Metro: Iglesia or Rubén Darío. Bus: 5, 16, 61, 40, or M3.

Real Basílica de San Francisco el Grande   Ironically, Madrid, the capital
of cathedral-rich Spain, does not possess a famous cathedral—but it does have
an important church, with a dome larger than that of St. Paul's in London. This
18th-century church is filled with a number of ecclesiastical works, notably a
Goya painting of St. Bernardinus of Siena. A guide will show you through.

Plaza de San Francisco el Grande, San Buenaventura 1. © 91-365-38-00. Admission 3€. Tues–Sat
11am–1pm and 4–6:30pm. Metro: La Latina or Puerta del Toledo. Bus: 3, 60, or 148.

PARKS & GARDENS

Casa de Campo (Metro: Lago or Batán) is the former royal hunting grounds—
miles of parkland lying south of the Royal Palace across the Manzanares River. You
can see the gate through which the kings rode out of the palace grounds, either
on horseback or in carriages, on their way to the tree-lined park. A lake contained within Casa de Campo is usually filled with rowers. You can have drinks
and light refreshments around the water or go swimming in a city run pool.
Children will love both the zoo and the Parque de Atracciones (see "Especially
for Kids," below). The Casa de Campo can be visited daily from 8am to 9pm.

Parque de Retiro (Metro: Retiro), originally a royal playground for the
Spanish monarchs and their guests, extends over 140 hectares (350 acres). The
huge palaces that once stood here were destroyed in the early 19th century; only
the former dance hall, the **Casón del Buen Retiro** (housing the modern works
of the Prado) and the building containing the Army Museum remain. The park
boasts numerous fountains and statues, plus a large lake. There are two exposition centers, the Velázquez and Crystal palaces (built to honor the Philippines
in 1887), and a lakeside monument, erected in 1922 in honor of King Alfonso
XII. In summer the rose gardens are worth a visit, and you'll find several places
for inexpensive snacks and drinks. The park is open daily 24 hours, but it is
safest from 7am to about 8:30pm.

Across Calle de Alfonso XII, at the southwest corner of Parque de Retiro, is
the **Real Jardín Botánico** (**Botanical Garden;** © 91-420-30-17; Metro:
Atocha; bus: 10, 14, 19, 32, or 45). Founded in the 18th century, the garden
contains more than 104 species of trees and 3,000 types of plants. Also on the
premises are an exhibition hall and a library specializing in botany. The park is
open daily from 10am to 6pm; admission is 1.50€.

Strung high above several of Madrid's verdant parks, the **Teleférico** (© 91-
541-74-50) was originally built in 1969 as part of a public fairgrounds (Parque de
Atracciones) that was modeled vaguely along the lines of Disneyland. Today, even
for visitors not interested in visiting the park, the Teleférico retains an allure of its
own as a high-altitude method of admiring the cityscape of Madrid. The cable
car departs from Paseo Pintor Rosales at the eastern edge of **Parque del Oeste**
(at the corner of Calle Marqués de Urquijo) and carries you high above two parks,
railway tracks, and over the Manzanares River to a spot near a picnic ground and
restaurant in Casa de Campo. Weather permitting, there are good views of the
Royal Palace along the way. The ride takes 11 minutes. The Teleférico is open
daily from 11am to 8pm; the trip costs 2.85€ one-way, or 4.10€ round-trip.

SPECIALLY FOR KIDS

Museo de Cera de Madrid (Wax Museum) *Kids*

The kids will enjoy seeing a lifelike wax Columbus calling on Ferdinand and Isabella, as well as Marlene Dietrich checking out Bill and Hillary Clinton. The 450 wax figures include heroes and villains of World War II. Two galleries display Romans and Arabs from the ancient days of the Iberian Peninsula; a show gives a 30-minute recap of Spanish history from the Phoenicians to the present.

Paseo de Recoletos 41. *©* **91-319-26-49.** Admission 12€ adults, 8€ children over 4, free for children 3 and under. Daily 10am–2pm and 4–8pm. Metro: Colón. Bus: 27, 45, or 53.

Parque de Atracciones *Kids*

The park was created in 1969 to amuse the young at heart with an array of rides and concessions. Here, you'll find a toboggan slide, a carousel, pony rides, an adventure into outer space, a walk through a transparent maze, a visit to jungle land, a motor-propelled series of cars disguised as a tail-wagging dachshund puppy, and a gyrating whirligig clutched in the tentacles of an octopus named El Pulpo. The most popular rides are a pair of roller coasters named 7 Picos and Jet Star.

The park has many diversions for adults. See the listing for the Auditorio del Parque de Atracciones under "Madrid After Dark," later in this chapter, for details.

Casa de Campo. *©* **91-463-29-00.** Admission 5€. Apr–May Tues–Fri noon–8pm, Sat–Sun noon–10pm (variable hours the rest of the year; call to check before going). Take the suburban train from Plaza de España and stop near the entrance to the park (Entrada de Batán).

Zoo Aquarium de la Casa de Campo *Kids*

This modern, well-organized facility allows you to see wildlife from five continents, with about 3,000 animals on display. Most are in simulated natural habitats, with moats separating them from the public. There's a petting zoo for the kids and a show presented by the Chu-Lin band. The zoo/aquarium complex includes a 520,000-gallon tropical marine aquarium, a dolphin aquarium, and an array of colorful parrots.

Casa de Campo. *©* **91-512-37-70.** Admission 13€ adults, 10€ seniors and children 3–8, free for children 2 and under. Daily 10am–sunset. Metro: Batán or Casa de Campo. Bus: 33.

ORGANIZED TOURS

A large number of agencies in Madrid book organized tours and excursions to sights and attractions both within and outside the city limits. Although it won't exactly be spontaneous, some visitors appreciate the convenience and efficiency of being able to visit so many sights in a single well-organized day.

Many of the city's hotel concierges, and all of the city's travel agents, will book anyone who asks for a guided tour of Madrid or its environs with one of Spain's largest tour operators, **Pullmantours,** Plaza de Oriente 8 (*©* **91-541-18-07**). Regardless of their destination and duration, virtually every tour departs from the Pullmantours terminal at that address. Half-day tours of Madrid include an artistic tour priced at 36€ per person, which includes entrance to a selection of the city's museums, and a panoramic half-day tour for 19€.

Toledo is the most popular full-day excursion outside the city limits. Trips cost 62€. These tours (including lunch) depart daily at 9:45am, last all day, and include ample opportunities for wandering at will through Toledo's narrow streets. You can, if you wish, take an abbreviated morning tour of Toledo, without stopping for lunch, for 41€.

Another popular tour stops briefly in Toledo and continues on to visit both the monastery at El Escorial and the Valley of the Fallen (Valle de los Caídos) before returning the same day to Madrid. With lunch included, this all-day excursion costs 87€.

The third major destination of bus tours from Madrid's center to the city's surrounding attractions is Pullmantours's full-day guided excursion to Avila and Segovia, which takes in a heady dose of medieval and ancient Roman monuments that are really very interesting. The price per person with lunch included is 66€.

The hop-off, hop-on **Madrid Vision Bus** lets you set your own pace and itinerary. A scheduled panoramic tour lasts a half-hour, provided that you don't get off the bus. Otherwise, you can opt for an unlimited number of stops, exploring at your leisure. The Madrid Vision makes four complete tours daily, two in the morning and two in the afternoon; on Sunday and Monday buses depart only in the morning. Call ℂ **91-541-18-07** for departure times, which are variable. You can board the bus at the Madrid tourist office.

6 Shopping

THE SHOPPING SCENE

Spain has always been known for its craftspeople, many of whom still work in the time-honored and labor-intensive traditions of their grandparents. It's hard to go wrong if you stick to the beautiful handcrafted objects—hand-painted tiles, ceramics, and porcelain; hand-woven rugs; handmade sweaters; and intricate embroideries. And, of course, Spain produces some of the world's finest leather. Jewelry, especially gold set with Majorca pearls, represents good value and unquestioned luxury.

Some of Madrid's art galleries are known throughout Europe for discovering and encouraging new talent. Antiques are sold in highly sophisticated retail outlets. Better suited to the budgets of many travelers are the weekly flea markets.

Spain continues to make inroads into the fashion world. Its young designers are regularly featured in the fashion magazines of Europe. Excellent shoes are available, some highly fashionable. But be advised that prices for shoes and quality clothing are generally higher in Madrid than in the United States.

GREAT SHOPPING AREAS

THE CENTER   The sheer diversity of shops in Madrid's center is staggering. Their densest concentration lies immediately north of Puerta del Sol, radiating out from Calle del Carmen, Calle Montera, and Calle Preciados.

CALLE MAYOR & CALLE DEL ARENAL   Unlike their more stylish neighbors to the north of Puerta del Sol, shops in this district to the west tend to be small, slightly dusty enclaves of coin and stamp dealers, family owned souvenir shops, clock makers, sellers of military paraphernalia, and an abundance of stores selling musical scores.

GRAN VIA   Conceived, designed, and built in the 1910s and 1920s as a showcase for the city's best shops, hotels, and restaurants, the Gran Vía has since been eclipsed by other shopping districts. Its Art Nouveau/Art Deco glamour still survives in the hearts of most Madrileños, however. The bookshops here are among the best in the city, as are outlets for fashion, shoes, jewelry, furs, and handcrafted accessories from all regions of Spain.

EL RASTRO   It's the biggest flea market in Spain, drawing collectors, dealers, buyers, and hopefuls from throughout Madrid and its suburbs. The makeshift stalls are at their most frenetic on Sunday morning. For more information, see the "Flea Markets" section, below.

PLAZA MAYOR   Under the arcades of the square itself are exhibitions of lithographs and oil paintings, and every weekend there's a loosely organized market for stamp and coin collectors. Within 3 or 4 blocks in every direction you'll find more than the average number of souvenir shops.

ON CALLE MARQUES   Viudo de Pontejos, which runs east from Plaza Mayor, is one of the city's headquarters for the sale of cloth, thread, and buttons. Also running east, on Calle de Zaragoza, are silversmiths and jewelers. On Calle Postas, you'll find housewares, underwear, soap powders, and other household items.

NEAR THE CARRERA DE SAN JERONIMO   Several blocks east of Puerta del Sol is Madrid's densest concentration of gift shops, crafts shops, and antiques dealers—a decorator's delight. Its most interesting streets include Calle del Prado, Calle de las Huertas, and Plaza de las Cortes. The neighborhood is pricey, so don't expect bargains here.

NORTHWEST MADRID   A few blocks east of Parque del Oeste is an upscale neighborhood that's well stocked with luxury goods and household staples. Calle de la Princesa, its main thoroughfare, has shops selling shoes, handbags, fashion, gifts, and children's clothing. Thanks to the presence of the university nearby, there's a dense concentration of bookstores, especially on Calle Isaac Peral and Calle Fernando el Católico, several blocks north and northwest, respectively, from the subway stop of Argüelles.

SALAMANCA DISTRICT   It's known throughout Spain as the quintessential upper-bourgeois neighborhood, uniformly prosperous; its shops are correspondingly exclusive. They include outlets run by interior decorators, furniture shops, fur and jewelry shops, several department stores, and design headquarters whose output ranges from the solidly conservative to the high-tech. The main streets of this district are Calle de Serrano and Calle de Velázquez. The district lies northeast of the center of Madrid, a few blocks north of Retiro Park. Its most central Metro stops are Serrano and Velázquez.

HOURS & SHIPPING

Major stores are open (in most cases) Monday through Saturday from 9:30am to 8pm. Many small stores take a siesta between 1:30 and 4:30pm. Of course, there is never any set formula, and hours can vary greatly from store to store, depending on the idiosyncrasies and schedules of the owner.

Many art and antiques dealers will crate and ship bulky objects for an additional fee. Whereas it usually pays to have heavy objects shipped by sea, it might surprise you that in some cases it's almost the same price to ship crated goods by airplane. Of course, it depends on the distance your crate will have to travel overland to the nearest international port, which, in many cases for the purposes of relatively small-scale shipments by individual clients, is Barcelona.

For most small and medium-sized shipments, airfreight isn't much more expensive than ocean shipping. **Iberia's Air Cargo Division (€ 800/221-6002** in the U.S.) offers airfreight service from Spain to New York, Chicago, Miami, or Los Angeles. What will you pay for this transport of your treasured art objects or freight? Here's a rule of thumb: For a shipment under 100 kilograms (220 lb.), from either Barcelona or Madrid to New York, the cost is approximately 5€ per pound. The per pound price goes down as the weight of the shipment increases, declining to, for example, 1€ per pound for shipments of more than 500 kilograms (1,100 lb.). Regardless of what you ship, there's a minimum charge enforced.

For an additional fee, Iberia or one of its representatives will pick up your package. For a truly precious cargo, ask the seller to build a crate for it. For information within Spain about air-cargo shipments, call Iberia's cargo division at Madrid's Barajas Airport (℃ **91-748-10-10**) or at Barcelona's airport (℃ **93-401-34-26**).

SHOPPING A TO Z
ANTIQUES

In addition to the shops listed below, the flea market (see **El Rastro,** below) is a source of antiques.

Centro de Anticuarios Lagasca   You'll find about a dozen antiques shops here, clustered into one covered arcade. They operate as individual businesses, although by browsing through each you'll find an impressive assemblage of antique furniture, porcelain, and whatnots. Open Monday through Saturday from 10am to 1:30pm and 5 to 8pm. Lagasca 36. ℃ **91-577-37-52.** Metro: Serrano or Velázquez.

Galería de Arte del Lubre   Housed in a mid-19th-century building are several unusual antiques dealers (and a large carpet emporium as well) many of whom specialize in antique, sometimes monumental paintings. Each establishment maintains its own schedule, although the center itself has overall hours. Open Monday through Friday from 11am to 2pm and 5 to 8:15pm. Serrano 5. ℃ **91-576-96-82.** Metro: Retiro. Bus: 9 or 15.

ART GALLERIES

Galería Kreisler   One successful entrepreneur on Madrid's art scene is Ohio-born Edward Kreisler, whose gallery, now run by his son, Juan, specializes in figurative and contemporary paintings, sculptures, and graphics. The gallery prides itself on occasionally displaying and selling the works of artists who are critically acclaimed and displayed in museums in Spain. Open Monday through Friday from 10:30am to 2pm and 5 to 9pm. Hermosilla 8. ℃ **91-431-42-64.** Metro: Serrano. Bus: 27, 45, or 150.

CAPES

Capas Seseña   Founded shortly after the turn of the 20th century, this shop manufactures and sells wool capes for both women and men. The wool comes from the mountain town of Béjar, near Salamanca. Celebrities who have been spotted donning Seseña capes include Picasso, Hemingway, and recently Hillary Rodham Clinton and daughter, Chelsea. Open Monday through Friday from 10am to 2pm and 4:30 to 8pm, Saturday from 10am to 2pm. Cruz 23. ℃ **91-531-68-40.** Metro: Sevilla or Puerta del Sol. Bus: 5, 39, 51, or 52.

CARPETS

Ispahan   In this 19th-century building, behind bronze handmade doors, are three floors devoted to carpets from around the world, notably Afghanistan, India, Nepal, Iran, Turkey, and the Caucasus. One section features silk carpets. It's open Monday through Saturday from 10am to 2pm and 4:30 to 8:30pm (till 8pm on Sat). Serrano 5. ℃ **91-575-20-12.** Metro: Retiro. Bus: 1, 2, 9, 19, and 15.

CERAMICS

Antigua Casa Talavera   "The first house of Spanish ceramics" has wares that include a sampling of regional styles from every major area of Spain, including Talavera, Toledo, Manises, Valencia, Puente del Arzobispo, Alcora, Granada, and Seville. Sangria pitchers, dinnerware, tea sets, and vases are all handmade. Inside one of the showrooms is an interesting selection of tiles painted with reproductions of scenes from bullfights, dances, and folklore. There's also a series of tiles depicting famous paintings in the Prado. At its present location since 1904, the shop is only a short walk from Plaza de Santo Domingo. This shop does not take credit cards but there are two ATMs within a block's walk. Open Monday through Friday from 10am to 1:30pm and 5 to 8pm, Saturday from 10am to 1:30pm. Isabel la Católica 2. ℭ **91-547-34-17.** Metro: Santo Domingo. Bus: 1, 2, 46, 70, 75, or 148.

CRAFTS
El Arco de los Cuchilleros Artesanía de Hoy   Set within one of the 17th-century vaulted cellars of Plaza Mayor, this shop is entirely devoted to unusual craft items from throughout Spain. The merchandise is one of a kind and in most cases contemporary; it includes a changing array of pottery, leather, textiles, woodcarvings, glassware, wickerwork, papier mâché, and silver jewelry. The hardworking owners deal directly with the artisans who produce each item, ensuring a wide inventory of handicrafts. The staff is familiar with applying for tax-free status of purchases here and speaks several different languages. It's open daily from 11am to 8pm, Sunday from 11am to 8pm. Plaza Mayor 9 (basement level). ℭ **91-365-26-80.** Metro: Puerta del Sol or Opera.

DEPARTMENT STORES
El Corte Inglés   This flagship of the largest department-store chain in Madrid sells hundreds of souvenirs and Spanish handicrafts—damascene steelwork from Toledo, flamenco dolls, and embroidered shawls. Some astute buyers report that it also sells glamorous fashion articles, such as Pierre Balmain designs, for about a third less than equivalent items in most European capitals. Services include interpreters, currency exchange windows, and parcel delivery either to a local hotel or overseas. Open Monday through Saturday from 10am to 10pm. Preciados 3. ℭ **91-379-80-00.** Metro: Puerta del Sol.

EMBROIDERIES
Casa Bonet   The intricately detailed embroideries produced in Spain's Balearic Islands (especially Majorca) are avidly sought for bridal chests and elegant dinner settings. A few examples of the store's extensive inventory are displayed on the walls. Open Monday through Friday from 10:45am to 2pm and 5 to 8pm, Saturday from 10:15am to 2pm. Núñez de Balboa 76. ℭ **91-575-09-12.** Metro: Núñez de Balboa.

FASHION
For the man on a budget who wants to dress reasonably well, the best outlet for off-the-rack men's clothing is one of the branches of El Corte Inglés department store chain (see above). Most men's boutiques in Madrid are very expensive and may not be worth the investment.

Herrero   The sheer size and buying power of this popular retail outlet for women's clothing make it a reasonably priced emporium for all kinds of feminine garb as well as various articles for gentlemen. It is open Monday through Saturday from 10:30am to 8:15pm. They are also open the first Sunday of each month from noon to 8:15pm. An additional outlet is on the same street at no. 16 (ℭ **91-521-15-24**), with the same hours. Preciados 7. ℭ **91-521-29-90.** Metro: Puerta del Sol or Callao.

Modas Gonzalo This boutique's baroque, gilded atmosphere evokes the 1940s, but its fashions are strictly up to date, well made, and intended for stylish adult women. No children's garments are sold. Open Monday through Saturday from 10am to 1:30pm and 4:30 to 8:30pm. Gran Vía 43. ✆ **91-547-12-39**. Metro: Callao or Santo Domingo.

Sybilla The fashionistas of Madrid are buzzing with excitement over the clothes displayed in the tiny atelier here. Fashion critics have hailed Sybilla's clothing as "wearable, whimsical, and inevitably original." Everything is stylish. The outlet also sells articles for the home like sheets, towels, and dishes. Open Monday through Friday from 10am to 2pm and 4 to 8:30pm, and Saturday from 11am to 3pm and 5 to 8:30pm. Jorge Juan 12. ✆ **91-578-13-22**. Metro: Serrano or Banco España.

FLEA MARKETS

El Rastro Foremost among markets is El Rastro (translated as either "flea market" or "thieves' market"), occupying a roughly triangular district of streets and plazas a few minutes' walk south of Plaza Mayor. Its center is Plaza Cascorro and Ribera de Curtidores. The market comes alive every Sunday morning and will delight anyone attracted to a mishmash of fascinating junk interspersed with antiques, bric-a-brac, and paintings. As for bargains, those days largely faded with the dictator, Franco himself. Today's vendors seem to know the price of everything, and on our latest visit we didn't find any El Grecos selling for $10. *Note:* Thieves are rampant here (hustling more than just antiques), so secure your wallet carefully and be alert. Plaza Cascorro and Ribera de Curtidores. Metro: La Latina. Bus: 3 or 17.

FOOD & WINE

Majorca Madrid's best-established gourmet shop opened in 1931 as an outlet selling a pastry called *ensaimada,* and this is still one of the store's most famous products. Tempting arrays of cheeses, canapés, roasted and marinated meats, sausages, and about a dozen kinds of paté accompany a spread of tiny pastries, tarts, and chocolates. Don't overlook the displays of Spanish wines and brandies. A stand-up tapas bar is always clogged with clients three deep, sampling the wares before they buy larger portions to take home. Tapas cost .90€ to 2.40€ per *ración* (portion). Open daily from 9:30am to 9pm. Velázquez 59. ✆ **91-431-99-09**. Metro: Velázquez or Nuñez de Balboa.

LEATHER

Loewe Since 1846 this has been the most elegant leather store in Spain. Its gold medal–winning designers have always kept abreast of changing tastes and styles, but the inventory still retains a timeless chic. The store sells luggage, handbags, and jackets for men and women (in leather or suede). Open Monday through Saturday from 9:30am to 8:30pm. There is another branch with the same hours, and much the same merchandise, at Serrano 26 (✆ **91-577-60-56**). Gran Vía 8. ✆ **91-522-68-15**. Metro: Banco de España or Gran Vía.

PERFUMES

Alvarez Gómez This is a marvelously old-fashioned *perfumería*. It's been around so long it's newly fashionable again. The shop markets its own fragrances, many based on almost long-forgotten formulas. Even if you're not specifically looking for perfume, you'll find an array of unusual merchandise here, including tortoise shell accessories, custom jewelry, and even women's handbags and belts. Open Monday through Friday from 10am to 8pm, Saturday from 10am to 2pm. Castellana 111. ℂ **91-555-59-61.** Metro: Cuzco.

Oriental Perfumeries Located at the western edge of the Puerta del Sol, this shop carries one of the most complete stocks of perfume in Madrid—both national and international brands. It also sells gifts, souvenirs, and costume jewelry. Open Monday through Friday from 10am to 9pm, and Saturday from 10am to 12:30pm and 5 to 9pm. Mayor 1. ℂ **91-521-59-05.** Metro: Puerta del Sol.

Perfumería Padilla This store sells a large and competitively priced assortment of Spanish and international scents for women. It maintains a branch at Calle del Carmen 8 (ℂ **91-522-66-83**). Both branches are open Monday through Saturday from 10am to 2:30 pm and 4:30 to 8:30pm. Metro: Puerta del Sol.

PORCELAIN

Lasarte This imposing outlet is devoted almost exclusively to Lladró porcelain, and the staff can usually tell you about new designs and releases the Lladró company is planning for the near future. Open Monday through Friday from 9:30am to 8pm, Saturday from 10am to 2:30 pm and 4:30 to 8pm. Gran Vía 44. ℂ **91-521-49-22.** Metro: Callao.

SHOPPING MALLS

ABC Serrano Set within what used to function as the working premises of a well-known Madrileño newspaper *(ABC)*, this is a complex of about 85 upscale boutiques that emphasize fashion, housewares, cosmetics, and art objects. Although each of the outfitters inside is independently owned and managed, most of them maintain hours of Monday through Saturday from 10am to midnight. On the premises, you'll find cafes and restaurants to keep you fed between bouts of shopping, lots of potted and flowering shrubbery, and acres and acres of Spanish marble and tile. Serrano 61 or Castellana 34. Metro: Serrano.

7 Madrid After Dark

Madrid abounds with dance halls, *tascas,* cafes, theaters, movie houses, music halls, and nightclubs. Because dinner is served late in Spain, nightlife doesn't really get under way until after 11pm, and it generally lasts until at least 3am—Madrileños are so fond of prowling around at night that they are known around Spain as *gatos* (cats). If you arrive at 9:30pm at a club, you'll have the place all to yourself, if it's even open.

In most clubs, a one-drink minimum is the rule: Feel free to nurse one drink through the entire evening's entertainment.

In summer, Madrid becomes a virtual free festival because the city sponsors a series of plays, concerts, and films. Pick up a copy of the *Guía del Ocio* (available at most newsstands) for listings of these events. This guide provides information about occasional discounts for commercial events, such as the concerts that are given in Madrid's parks. Also check the program of **Fundación Juan March,** Calle Castelló 77 (ℂ **91-435-42-40;** Metro: Núñez de Balboa). Tapping into funds bequeathed to it by a generous financier (Señor Juan March), it stages free concerts of Spanish and international classical music within a concert hall at its headquarters at Calle Castelló 77. In most cases, they are 90-minute events that are presented every Monday and Saturday at noon and every Wednesday at 7:30pm.

Flamenco in Madrid is geared mainly to prosperous tourists with fat wallets, and nightclubs are expensive. But since Madrid is preeminently a city of song and dance, you can often be entertained at very little cost—in fact, for the price of a glass of wine or beer if you sit at a bar with live entertainment.

Like flamenco clubs, discos tend to be expensive, but they often open for what are erroneously called afternoon sessions (7–10pm). Although discos charge entry fees, at an afternoon session the cost might be as low as 3€, rising to 15€ and beyond for a night session—that is, beginning at 11:30pm and lasting until the early morning hours. Therefore, if you're on a budget, go early, dance until 10pm, then proceed to dinner (you'll be eating at the fashionable hour).

Nightlife is so plentiful in Madrid that the city can be roughly divided into the following "night zones."

PLAZA MAYOR/PUERTA DEL SOL The most popular areas from the standpoint of both tradition and tourist interest, they can also be dangerous, so explore them with caution, especially late at night. They are filled with tapas bars and *cuevas* (drinking caves). Here it is customary to begin a *tasca* crawl, going to tavern after tavern, sampling the wine in each, along with a selection of tapas. The major streets for such a crawl are Cava de San Miguel, Cava Alta, and Cava Baja. You can order *pinchos y raciones* (tasty snacks and tidbits).

GRAN VIA This area contains mainly cinemas and theaters. Most of the after-dark action takes place on little streets branching off the Gran Vía.

PLAZA DE ISABEL II/PLAZA DE ORIENTE This is another area much frequented by tourists. Many restaurants and cafes flourish here, including the famous Café de Oriente.

CHUECA Along such streets as Hortaleza, Infantas, Barquillo, and San Lucas, this is the gay nightlife district, with dozens of clubs. Cheap restaurants, along with a few female striptease joints, are also found here. This area can be danger-ous at night, so watch for pickpockets and muggers. As of late, there has been greater police presence at night.

ARGÜELLES/MONCLOA For university students, this part of town sees most of the action. Many dance clubs are found here, along with alehouses and fast-food joints. The area is bounded by Pintor Rosales, Cea Bermúdez, Bravo Murillo, San Bernardo, and Conde Duque.

THE PERFORMING ARTS

Madrid has a number of theaters, opera companies, and dance companies. To discover where and when specific cultural events are being performed, pick up a copy of *Guía del Ocio* at any city newsstand. The sheer volume of cultural offer-ings might stagger you; for a concise summary of the highlights, see below.

Tickets to dramatic and musical events usually range in price from 5.50€ to 45€, with discounts of up to 50% granted on certain days of the week (usually Wed and matinees on Sun).

The concierges at most major hotels can usually get you tickets to specific concerts, if you are clear about your wishes and needs. They of course charge a considerable markup, part of which is passed along to whichever agency origi-nally booked the tickets.

You'll save money if you go directly to the box office. In the event your choice is sold out, you may be able to get tickets (with a reasonable markup) at **Local-idades Galicia,** Plaza del Carmen 1 (© **91-531-27-32;** Metro: Puerta del Sol). This agency also markets tickets to bullfights and sporting events. It is open Tuesday through Saturday from 9:30am to 1:30pm and 4:30 to 7pm, Sunday from 9:30am to 1:30pm, and daily from 9:30am to 8pm in May.

Here follows a grab bag of nighttime diversions that might amuse and entertain you. First, the cultural offerings:

MAJOR PERFORMING ARTS COMPANIES

For those who speak Spanish, the **Compañía Nacional de Nuevas Tendencias Escénicas** is an avant-garde troupe that performs new and often controversial works by undiscovered writers. On the other hand, the **Compañía Nacional de Teatro Clásico,** as its name suggests, is devoted to the Spanish classics, including works by the ever-popular Lope de Vega and Tirso de Molina.

Among dance companies, the national ballet of Spain—devoted exclusively to Spanish dance—is the **Ballet Nacional de España.** Their performances are always well attended. The national lyrical ballet company of the country is the **Ballet Lírico Nacional.**

World-renowned flamenco sensation Antonio Canales and his troupe, **Ballet Flamenco Antonio Canales,** offer spirited high-energy performances. Productions are centered on Canales's impassioned *Torero,* his interpretation of a bullfighter and the physical and emotional struggles within the man. For tickets and information, you can call Madrid's comprehensive ticket agency, the previously recommended **Localidades Galicia,** Plaza del Carmen 1 (② **91-531-27-32**), for tickets to cultural events and virtually any other event in Castile. Other agencies include **Casa de Cataluña** (② **91-538-33-00**) or **Corte Inglés** (② **91-432-93-00**). Both Casa de Cataluña and Cortes Inglés have satellite offices located throughout Madrid.

Madrid's opera company is the **Teatro de la Opera,** and its symphony orchestra is the outstanding **Orquesta Sinfónica de Madrid.** The national orchestra of Spain, widely acclaimed on the continent, is the **Orquesta Nacional de España,** which pays particular homage to Spanish composers.

CLASSICAL MUSIC

Auditorio del Parque de Atracciones   The schedule of this 3,500-seat facility might include everything from punk-rock musical groups to the more highbrow warm-weather performances of visiting symphony orchestras. Check with Localidades Galicia to see what's on at the time of your visit (see "The Performing Arts," above). Casa de Campo. Metro: Lago or Batán.

Auditorio Nacional de Música   Sheathed in slabs of Spanish granite, marble, and limestone and capped with Iberian tiles, this hall is the ultramodern home of both the National Orchestra of Spain and the National Chorus of Spain.

Standing just north of Madrid's Salamanca district, it ranks as a major addition to classical music in Europe. Inaugurated in 1988, it is devoted exclusively to performances of symphonic, choral, and chamber music. In addition to the Auditorio Principal (Hall A), whose capacity is almost 2,300, there's a hall for chamber music (Hall B), as well as a small auditorium (seating 250) for intimate concerts. Príncipe de Vergara 146. ② **91-337-01-39** or 91-337-01-40. Box office 91-337-03-07. Tickets 4.50€–48€. Metro: Cruz del Rayo.

Fundación Juan March   This foundation sometimes holds free concerts at lunchtime. The advance schedule is difficult to predict, so call for information. Calle Castelló 77. ② **91-435-42-40.** Metro: Núñez de Balboa.

La Fidula   Serving as a bastion of civility in a sea of rock 'n' roll and disco chaos, this club is a converted 1800s grocer. Today, it presents chamber music concerts nightly at 11:30pm with an additional show at 1am on weekends. The club offers the prospect of a tranquil, cultural evening on the town, at a moderate price. They take performances here seriously—late arrivals may not be seated for concerts. It is open Monday through Thursday and Sunday from 7pm to 3am, Friday and Saturday from 7pm to 4am. Calle Huerta 57. ✆ 91-429-29-47. Tickets 6€. Metro: Antón Martín.

Teatro Cultural de la Villa   Spanish-style ballet along with *zarzuelas* (operettas), orchestral works, and theater pieces are presented at this cultural center. Tickets go on sale 5 days before the event of your choice, and performances are usually presented at two evening shows (7 and 10:30pm). Plaza de Colón. ✆ 91-575-60-80. Tickets, depending on event, 8€–27€. Metro: Serrano or Colón.

Teatro Real   This theater is one of the world's finest acoustic settings for opera. Its extensive state-of-the-art equipment affords elaborate stage designs and special effects. Today the building is the home of the Compañía del Teatro Real, a company specializing in opera, and is a major venue for classical music. On November 19, 1850, under the reign of Queen Isabel II, the Royal Opera House opened its doors with Donizetti's *La Favorita*. Plaza Isabel II. ✆ 91-516-06-60. Tickets 24€–192€. Metro: Opera.

THEATER

Madrid offers many different theater performances, useful to you only if your Spanish is very fluent. If it isn't, check the *Guía del Ocio* for performances by English-speaking companies on tour from Britain or select a concert or subtitled movie instead.

In addition to the major ones listed below, there are at least 30 other theaters, including one devoted almost entirely to children's plays, the **Sala la Bicicleta** (no phone), in the Ciudad de los Niños at Casa de Campo. Nonprofessional groups stage dozens of other plays in such places as churches.

Teatro Calderón   This is the largest theater in Madrid, with a seating capacity of 2,000. In the past this venue included everything from dramatic theater to flamenco, but in recent years it has taken a more serious turn by presenting mostly opera, with performances beginning most evenings at 8pm. At press time, a long-running favorite was Bizet's *Carmen,* whose setting within Spain partly justifies its enduring popularity among Madrileños. Atocha 18. ✆ 91-429-58-90. Tickets 19€–48€. Metro: Tirso de Molina.

Teatro de la Comedia   This is the home of the Compañía Nacional de Teatro Clásico. Here, more than anywhere else in Madrid, you're likely to see performances from the classic repertoire of such great Spanish dramatists as Lope de Vega and Calderón de la Barca. There are no performances on Wednesday, and the theater is completely shut down during July and August. The box office is open daily from 11:30am to 1:30pm and 5 to 6pm, and for about an hour before the performances. Embajadores 9. ✆ 91-528-28-19. Tickets 8€–16€; 50% discount on Thurs. Metro: La Latina. Bus: 15, 20, or 150.

Teatro Español   This company is funded by Madrid's municipal government, its repertoire a time-tested assortment of great and/or favorite Spanish plays. The box office is open Tuesday through Sunday from 11:30am to 1:30pm and 5pm to the opening of the show. Príncipe 25. ✆ 91-429-62-97. Tickets 2€–16€; 50% discount on Wed. Metro: Sevilla.

Teatro Lírico Nacional de la Zarzuela   Near Plaza de la Cibeles, this theater of potent nostalgia produces ballet and an occasional opera in addition to *zarzuela.* Show times vary. The box office is open daily from noon to show time. Jovellanos 4. ✆ **91-524-54-00**. Tickets 10€–30€. Metro: Sevilla or Banco de España.

Teatro Nuevo Apolo   Nuevo Apolo is the permanent home of the renowned Antología de la Zarzuela company. It is on the restored site of the old Teatro Apolo, where these musical variety shows have been performed since the 1930s. Prices and times depend on the show. The box office is open Tuesday through Sunday from 11:30am to 1:30pm and 5pm till showtime. Plaza de Tirso de Molina 1. ✆ **91-369-06-37**. Cover usually 21€–36€. Metro: Tirso de Molina.

JAZZ & CABARET

Café Central   Off the Plaza de Santa Ana beside the famed Gran Hotel Victoria, the Café Central has a vaguely early-20th-century Art Deco interior, with an unusual series of stained-glass windows. Many of the customers read newspapers and talk at the marble-top tables during the day, but the ambience is far more animated during the nightly jazz sessions, which are ranked among the best in Spain, often drawing top artists. Open Sunday through Thursday from 1:30pm to 2:30am, Friday and Saturday from 1:30pm to 3am; live jazz is offered daily 10pm to midnight. Beer costs 2.40€. Plaza del Angel 10. ✆ **91-369-41-43**. Cover charge 10€–15€, depending on the show. Metro: Antón Martín or Puerta del Sol.

Café del Foro   This old-time favorite in the Malasaña district has suddenly become hip again. You never know exactly what the show for the evening will be, although live music of some sort generally starts at 11:30pm. Cabaret is often featured, along with live merengue, bolero, and salsa. There's a faux starry sky above the stage area, and Roman colonnades. Open daily from 7pm to 3am. Calle San Andres 38. ✆ **91-445-37-52**. No cover (but may be imposed for a specially booked act). Metro: Bilbao. Bus: 40, 147, 149, or N-19.

Café Jazz Populart   This club is known for its exciting jazz groups, which encourage the audience to dance. It specializes in Brazilian, Afro-bass, reggae, and new wave African music. When the music starts, usually around 11pm, the prices of drinks are nearly doubled. Open daily from 6pm to 3 or 4am. After the music begins, beer costs 4€, whiskey with soda 6€. Calle Huertas 22. ✆ **91-429-84-07**. Metro: Antón Martín or Sevilla. Bus: 6 or 60.

Clamores   With dozens of small tables and a huge bar in its dark and smoky interior, Clamores, which means noises in Spain, is the largest and one of the most popular jazz clubs in Madrid. Established in the early 1980s, it has thrived because of the diverse roster of American and Spanish jazz bands that have appeared here. The place is open daily from 7pm to around 3am, but jazz is presented only Tuesday through Saturday. Tuesday through Thursday, performances are at 11pm and again at 1am; Saturday, performances begin at 11:30pm, with an additional show at 1:30am. There are jam sessions on Sunday night, and no live performances on Monday night, when the format is recorded disco music. Regardless of the night of the week you consume them, drinks begin at around 5€ each. Albuquerque 14. ✆ **91-445-79-38**. Cover Tues–Sat usually 4.80€–24€, but varies with act; no cover Sun–Mon. Metro: Bilbao.

FLAMENCO

Café de Chinitas   One of the best flamenco clubs in town, Café de Chinitas is set one floor above street level in a 19th-century building midway between the Opera and Gran Vía. It features an array of (usually) gypsy flamenco artists from Madrid, Barcelona, and Andalusia, with acts and performers changing about once a month. You can arrange for dinner before the show, although many

The Sultry Sound of Flamenco

The lights dim and the flamenco stars clatter rhythmically across the dance floor. Their lean bodies and hips shake and sway to the music. The word *flamenco* has various translations, meaning everything from "gypsified Andalusian" to "knife," and from "blowhard" to "tough guy."

Accompanied by stylized guitar music, castanets, and the fervent clapping of the crowd, dancers are filled with tension and emotion. Flamenco dancing, with its flash, color, and ritual, is evocative of Spanish culture although its origins remain mysterious.

Experts disagree as to where it came from, but most claim Andalusia as its seat of origin. It was the gypsy artist who perfected both the song and the dance. Gypsies took to flamenco like "rice to paella," in the words of the historian Fernando Quiñones.

The deep song of flamenco represents a fatalistic attitude to life. Marxists used to say it was a deeply felt protest of the lower classes against their oppressors, but this seems unfounded. Protest or not, over the centuries rich patrons, often brash young men, liked the sound of flamenco and booked artists to stage *juergas,* or fiestas, where dancer-prostitutes became the erotic extras. By the early 17th century, flamenco was linked with pimping, prostitution, and lots and lots of drinking, both in the audience and by the artists.

By the mid–19th century, flamenco had gone legitimate and was heard in theaters and *café cantantes.* By the 1920s, even the pre–Franco Spanish dictator, Primo de Rivera, was singing the flamenco tunes of his native Cádiz. The poet Federico García Lorca and the composer Manuel de Falla preferred a purer form, attacking what they viewed as the degenerate and "ridiculous" burlesque of *flamenquismo,* the jazzed-up, audience-pleasing form of flamenco. The two artists launched a Flamenco Festival in Granada in 1922. Of course, in the decades since, their voices have been drowned out, and flamenco is more *flamenquismo* than ever.

In his 1995 book *Flamenco Deep Song,* Thomas Mitchell draws a parallel to flamenco's "lowlife roots" and the "orgiastic origins" of jazz. He notes that early jazz, like flamenco, was associated with despised ethnic groups, gangsters, brothels, free-spending blue bloods, and whoopee hedonism." By disguising their origins, Mitchell notes, both jazz and flamenco have entered the musical mainstream.

Madrileños opt for dinner somewhere else and then arrive just for drinks and the flamenco. Open Monday through Saturday, with dinner served from 9pm to midnight and the show lasting from 10:30pm to 2am. Reservations are recommended. Torija 7. © **91-559-51-35.** Dinner and show from 66€; cover charge for show without dinner (but with 1 drink included) 30€. Metro: Santo Domingo. Bus: 1 or 2.

Casa Patas This club is now one of the best places to see "true" flamenco as opposed to the more touristy version presented at Corral de la Morería (see below). It is also a bar and restaurant, with space reserved in the rear for

..amenco. Shows are presented at 10:30 pm Monday to Thursday, with a show at midnight on Thursday, Friday, and Saturday and more often during Madrid's major fiesta month of May. The best flamenco in Madrid is found here. Proof of the pudding is that flamenco singers and dancers often hang out here after hours. Tapas—priced at 2.70€ to 15€—are available at the bar. The club is open daily from 8pm to 2:30am. Calle Cañizares 10. ℂ **91-369-04-96.** Admission 22€–28€. Metro: Tirso de Molina or Anton Martín.

Corral de la Morería   In the old town, the Morería ("where the Moors reside") sizzles with flamenco, but it's definitely a tourist crowd. Colorfully costumed strolling performers warm up the audience around 11pm; a flamenco show follows, with at least 10 dancers. It's much cheaper to eat somewhere else first, paying only the one-drink minimum. Open daily from 8pm to 2am. Morería 17. ℂ **91-365-84-46.** Cover 1-drink minimum 30€; 70€–85€ with dinner. Metro: La Latina or Opera.

DANCE CLUBS

The Spanish dance club takes its inspiration from those of other Western capitals. In Madrid, most clubs are open from around 6pm to 9pm, later reopening around 11pm. They generally start rocking at midnight or thereabouts.

Cool   It's cool all right, among the coolest clubs in the capital. No club in Madrid seems to blend a gay and straight (or else bi) crowd as successfully as this major production set on two levels. Sometimes the most stunning drag queens in Madrid appear here (often billed as "more beautiful than actual girls"). Video projections are always enticing, and the crowd of patrons in their 20s and early 30s are a medley of Madrileños and international folk, especially Brits and Yanks. One special feature of the club is the heavily attended Shangay Tea Dance taking place on Sunday from 9am to 2am. If you're a "circuit queen" seeking out the hottest gay males in the Spanish capital, you're likely to encounter these "Urban Cowboys" here at this time. Open Friday and Saturday, from midnight to 6am and Sunday from 9pm to 2am. Isabel la Católica 6. ℂ 91-548-20-22. Cover 7€–10€. Metro: Callao.

Joy Eslava   Set near the Puerta del Sol, this place has survived the passing fashions of Madrileño nightlife with more style than many of its (now defunct) competitors. Virtually everyone in Madrid is likely to show up here, ranging from traveling sales reps in town from Düsseldorf to the youthful members of the Madrileño *movida*. Open nightly from 11:30pm to 6:30am. Drinks are 9€ each. Arenal 11. ℂ **91-366-37-33.** Admission 15€, including first drink. Metro: Puerta del Sol.

Kapital   This is the most sprawling, labyrinthine, and multicultural disco in Madrid at the moment. Set within what was originally a theater, it contains seven different levels, each sporting at least one bar and an ambience that's often radically different from the one you just left on a previous floor. Voyeurs of any age, take heart—there's a lot to see at the Kapital, with a mixed crowd that pursues whatever form of sexuality seems appropriate at the moment. Open Thursday through Sunday from midnight to 6am. Second drinks from 9€ each. Atocha 125. ℂ **91-420-29-06.** Admission 12€–15€, including first drink. Metro: Atocha.

Pasapoga   This club personifies the new Madrid of today, drawing the most sophisticated crowd of beautiful people in their 20s and 30s of almost any club in the capital. On many nights the clientele is about 90% gay. The interior is also sleek and beautiful, with the likes of such adornments as a grand staircase with ivory banisters. Under a mammoth and glittering chandelier, the princes and princesses of Madrid dance into the wee hours to recorded music to house, pop, and techno. The club is open Monday through Thursday from 6 to 10:30pm and Friday and Saturday from midnight to 6:30am. Gran Vía 37. © 91-547-5711. Cover 7€–12€. Metro: Callao.

Sweet Dance Club This club lives up to its name. It doesn't even open its doors until 1 o'clock in the morning. Even so, the place doesn't get rocking until 2 hours later. Once it does, it's the hottest scene in Madrid. Steel doors with steel vines open up to reveal a wildly campy scene that attracts a 90% gay clientele most nights. Look for suspended cages and a "disco ball" dance floor packed with some of the prettiest girls and handsomest men in Madrid. Wear your most daring apparel. Open only Friday and Saturday from 1am to daybreak. Calle Dr. Cortezo 1. © 91-869-40-38. Cover 7-12€, including first drink. Metro: Tirso de Molina.

Torero If you're not one of the *gente guapa* (beautiful people), head elsewhere. The tough bouncer at the door only admits those young men and women he judges to be beautiful; otherwise, it's away with you. If you can pass such a tough door policy, you'll find yourself in one of the city's most glamorous after dark rendezvous. The club is on two levels, with the top floor being more attractive and Iberian with its leather chairs. The downstairs is more functional and less desirable. Some entertainment is provided on most nights, with drag shows a feature on Thursday. The latest Spanish recordings are played here, especially "pop Español." Hours are Friday and Saturday from 11pm to 6am, Sunday to Thursday from 11pm to 5am. Calle Cruz 26. © 91-523-11-29. Cover: 12€. Metro: Sol or Tirso de Molina.

CUBAN SALSA

Café La Palma Live Cuban groups playing salsa dominate the agenda here. As in Paris, anything Cuban is suddenly chic in Madrid. This is a convivial club and one of the most happening clubs in the capital. It's open daily from 4pm to 3am, but go after 10pm for the most action. A group made up of people mainly in their 20s and 30s is attracted here by the live music. La Palma 62. © 91-522-50-31. Cover 5€–6€. Metro: Noviciado.

Negra Tomasa This is a Cuban music bar, drawing big crowds on the weekends. A Caribbean setting is evoked by fishermen and palm fronds. Pictures of Cuba on the walls also evoke the ambience. Cuban music and salsa attract a crowd in their 20s and 30s, and the place is very fashionable. The drinks served here—*mojitos,* daiquiris, and piña coladas—are familiar to barflies the world over. But have you ever had a Cubanito? It's tomato juice and lime with rum. Hours are daily from midnight to 3:30am. Calle Espoz y Mina and Calle Cádiz. © 01-523-5830. 6€ cover Fri–Sat only. Metro: Sol. Bus: 3, 15, 20, or 51.

PUBS & BARS

Balmoral Exposed wood and comfortable chairs here evoke a London club. The clientele tends toward journalists, politicians, army brass, owners of large estates, bankers, diplomats, and the occasional literary star. *Newsweek* magazine dubbed it one of the "best bars in the world." No food other than tapas is served. Open Monday through Saturday from 12:30pm to 2:30 or 3am. Beer is 3€; drinks are from 6€. Hermosilla 10. © 91-431-41-33. Metro: Serrano.

Balneario Clients enjoy potent drinks in a setting with fresh flowers, white marble, and a stone bathtub that might have been used by Josephine Bonaparte. Near Chamartín Station on the northern edge of Madrid, Balneario is one of the most stylish and upscale bars in the city. It is adjacent to and managed by one of Madrid's most elegant and prestigious restaurants, El Cabo Mayor, and often attracts that dining room's clients for aperitifs or after-dinner drinks. Tapas include endive with smoked salmon, asparagus mousse, and anchovies with avocado. Open Monday through Saturday from 6pm to 1:30am. Drinks are 3.90€ to 8€; tapas cost 3€ to 11€. Juan Ramón Jiménez 37. ✆ 91-350-87-76. Metro: Cuzco.

Bar Cock   This bar on two floors attracts some of the most visible artists, actors, models, and filmmakers in Madrid. The name comes from the word *cocktail,* or so they say. The decoration is elaborate and unique, in contrast to the hip clientele, and the martinis are Madrid's best. Open daily from 7pm to 3am; Friday and Saturday closed at 3:30 am. Closed on Sundays in summer; closed December 24 to 31. Drinks are 6€ to 10€. De la Reina 16. ✆ 91-532-28-26. Metro: Gran Vía.

Bar Taurino   This bar remains the top gathering spot for bullfight aficionados. A multitiered place, it is still a shrine to Manolete, the greatest matador of the 1950s who was praised by Hemingway. This is no rough-and-tumble bar, but a cultured space often attracting Madrid society. It reaches the peak of its excitement during the San Isidro bullfighting festival, when Spain's top bullfighters often make appearances here in their full death-in-the-afternoon suits of light. Hours are daily from 11am to midnight. In the Hotel Reina Victoria, Plaza Santa Ana. ✆ 91-531-45-00. Metro: Antón Martín.

Chicote   This is Madrid's most famous cocktail bar. It's classic retro chic, with the same 1930s interior design it had when the foreign press came to sit out the Civil War, although the sound of artillery shells along the Gran Vía could be heard at the time. Long a favorite of artists and writers, the bar became a haven for prostitutes in the late Franco era. No more. It's back in the limelight again, a sophisticated and much-frequented rendezvous. Open Monday through Saturday from 8am to 3am (until 4am Fri–Sat). Drinks cost from 7€ Monday through Saturday, but the waiters serve them with such grace you don't mind. Gran Vía 12. ✆ 91-532-67-37. Metro: Gran Vía.

Hispano Bar/Buffet   This establishment does a respectable lunch trade every day for members of the local business community who crowd in to enjoy the amply portioned *platos del día.* They might include a platter of roast duck with figs or orange sauce, or a supreme of hake. After around 5pm, however, the ambience becomes that of a busy after-office bar, patronized by stylishly dressed women and many local entrepreneurs. The hubbub continues on into the night. Open daily from 1:30pm to 2am. Full meals at lunchtime cost around 33€ to 40€, while beer, depending on the time of day you order it, costs about 1.80€. Paseo de la Castellana 78. ✆ 91-411-48-76. Metro: Gregorio Marañón.

La Venencia   On one of the traditional *tasca* streets in Old Madrid, this tavern has a distinct personality. It is dedicated to the art of serving Spain's finest sherry—and that's it. Don't come in here asking for an extra dry martini. Our favorite remains Manzanilla, a delicate fino with just a little chill on it. If Luis Buñuel were to need extras in a film, surely the patrons here would be an ideal backdrop. To go with all that sherry, the waiters (a little rough around the edges) will serve tapas, especially those garlicky marinated olives, *majoama* (cured tuna), and blue cheese canapés. Barrels form the decor, along with antique posters long turned tobacco-gold from the cigarette smoke. Open daily from 1 to 3pm and 7:30pm to 1:30am (until 2am Fri–Sat). Calle Echegarai 7. ✆ 91-429-73-13. Metro: Sevilla.

Los Gabrieles Located in the heart of one of Madrid's most visible warrens of narrow streets, in a district that pulsates with after-dark night life options, this historic bar served throughout most of the 19th century as the sales outlet for a Spanish wine merchant. Its cellar was once a fabled Gypsy bordello. In the 1980s its two rooms were transformed into a bar and cafe, where you can admire lavishly tiled walls with detailed scenes of courtiers, dancers, and Andalusian maidens peering from behind mantillas and fans. Open daily from noon to 12:30am. Beer costs 3€. Echegaray 17. ℂ 91-429-62-61. Metro: Puerta de Sol, Sevilla.

Palacio Gaviria Its construction in 1847 was heralded as the architectural triumph of one of the era's most flamboyant aristocrats, the marqués de Gaviria. Famous as one of the paramours of Queen Isabella II, he outfitted his palace with the ornate jumble of neoclassical and baroque styles that later became known as *Isabelino*. In 1993, after extensive renovations, the building was opened to the public as a concert hall for the occasional presentation of classical music and as a late-night cocktail bar. Ten high-ceilinged rooms now function as richly decorated, multipurpose areas for guests to wander in, drinks in hand, reacting to whatever, or whomever, happens to be there at the time. (One room is discreetly referred to as having been the bedroom-away-from-home of the queen herself.) No food is served, but the libations include a stylish list of cocktails and wines. The often-dull music doesn't match the elegance of the decor. Thursdays through Saturdays are usually dance nights, everything from the tango to the waltz. Cabaret is usually featured on most other nights. Open Monday through Wednesday from 10:30pm to 3am; Thursday from 10:30pm to 6am; Friday and Saturday from 11pm to 6am, and Sunday from 8:30pm to 2am. Second drinks start at 7.20€. Calle del Arenal 9. ℂ 91-526-60-69. Cover 7€–15€, including first drink. Metro: Puerta del Sol or Opera.

Teatriz Part of its function is as a restaurant where soft lighting and a decor by world-class decorator Philippe Starck create one of the most stylish-looking and avant-garde environments in Madrid. A meal averages around 25€ to 30€ at lunch and 21€ in the evening, but if it's just a drink you're looking for, consider an extended session at any of the site's three bars. Here, in a setting not quite like a disco but with a sound system almost as good, you'll find a music bar environment where stylish folk of all persuasions enjoy drinks and the gossip

---

⌒ *Moments* Summer *Terrazas*

At the first blush of spring weather, Madrileños rush outdoors to drink, talk, and sit at a string of open-air cafes, called *terrazas,* throughout the city. The best and most expensive ones are along Paseo de la Castellana between the Plaza de la Cibeles and the Plaza Emilio Castelar, but there are dozens more throughout the city.

You can wander up and down the boulevard, selecting one that appeals to you; if you get bored, you can go on later to another one. Sometimes these terrazas are called *chirinquitos.* You'll find them along other paseos, the Recoletos and the Prado, both fashionable areas but not as hip as the Castellana. For old traditional atmosphere, the terraces at the Plaza Mayor win out. The Plaza Santa Ana has several atmospheric choices within the old city. Friday and Saturday are the most popular nights for drinking; many locals sit here all night.

that seems to both originate and be magnified at a place like this. The restaurant is open daily from 8:30am to 12:30pm and 1:30 to 4pm. The bars are best appreciated every night from 11pm to 2:30am. Hermosilla 15. ℂ **91-577-53-79.** Metro: Serrano.

Viva Madrid A congenial and sudsy mix of students, artists, and tourists cram into this place, where antique tile murals and blatant Belle Epoque nostalgia contribute to an undeniable charm. Crowded and noisy, it's a place where lots of beer is swilled and spilled. It's set in a neighborhood of antique houses and narrow streets near the Plaza de Santa Ana. Open Friday and Saturday from 11am to 3am. Beer costs 3€; whiskey begins at 6€. Manuel Fernández y González 7. ℂ **91-429-36-40.** Metro: Sevilla or Puerta del Sol.

GAY & LESBIAN BARS

Black and White This is the major gay bar of Madrid, located in the center of the Chueca district. A guard will open the door to a large room—painted, as you might expect, black and white. There's a disco in the basement, but the street-level bar is the premier gathering spot, featuring drag shows beginning at 3am Thursday through Sunday, male striptease, and videos. Old movies are shown against one wall. *Warning:* This bar is frequented by young, potentially dangerous hustlers. Open Monday through Saturday from 10pm to 6am. Beer is 4€; whiskey costs 7€. Gravina (at corner of Libertad). ℂ **91-531-11-41.** Metro: Chueca.

Café Figueroa This turn-of-the-20th-century cafe attracts a diverse clientele, including a large number of gay men and lesbians. It's one of the city's most popular gathering spots for drinks and conversation. Open Sunday through Thursday from 4pm to midnight, Friday and Saturday from 4pm to 2:30am. Beer from 2.60€; whiskey costs from 4.80€. Augusto Figueroa 17 (at corner of Hortaleza). ℂ **91-521-16-73.** Metro: Chueca.

Cruising One of the landmark gay bars of Madrid, a center for gay consciousness-raising and gay cruising, this place has probably been visited at least once by every gay male in Castile. There are virtually no women inside, but always a hustler looking for a tourist john. It doesn't get crowded or lively until late at night. Open daily from 7pm to 3:30am. Beer costs from 3.30€; whiskey 6€. Perez Galdos 5. ℂ **91-521-51-43.** Metro: Chueca.

Leather Bar This is another of the premier bars for gay men in Madrid, but despite its supposed emphasis on leather and uniforms, only about 25% of the men who show up actually wear them. You'll find two bars on the establishment's street level and a disco in the basement where same-sex couples can dance. Beer costs 3€. It's open Sunday through Thursday from 7pm to 3am, Friday and Saturday from 8pm to 3:30am. Calle Pelayo 42. ℂ **91-308-14-62.** Metro: Chueca.

Rick's Rick's takes its name from *Everybody Comes to Rick's,* the original title of the Bogie classic, *Casablanca.* Many gay bars in the Chueca barrio are sleazy, but this is a classy joint, just like the fictional Rick's in Morocco. It's decorated with Bogie paraphernalia, including marble floors and gilt columns. The only thing missing is a piano player singing "As Time Goes By," and Bergman, of course. Gay men patronize the place, with the occasional woman showing up, too. Incongruously, it has a foosball table in the bar, but lavender walls. It's open daily "until some time in the morning." Calle Clavel 8. ℂ **91-531-91-86.** Cover 7€. Metro: Chueca or Gran Via.

CAVE CRAWLING

To capture a peculiar Madrid joie de vivre of the 18th century, visit s
and *cuevas* (taverns). From Plaza Mayor, walk down the Arco de
until you find a gypsylike cave that fits your fancy. Young people love to meet i..
the taverns of Old Madrid for communal drinking and songfests. The sangria
flows freely, the atmosphere is charged, and the room is usually packed with the
sounds of guitars wafting into the night air. Sometimes you'll see a strolling band
of singing students going from bar to bar, colorfully attired, with ribbons flut-
tering from their outfits.

Mesón de la Guitarra   Our favorite *cueva* in the area, Mesón de la Guitarra
is loud and exciting on any night of the week, and it's as warmly earthy as anything you'll find in Madrid. The decor combines terra-cotta floors, antique brick
walls, hundreds of sangria pitchers clustered above the bar, murals of gluttons,
old rifles, and faded bullfighting posters. Like most things in Madrid, the place
doesn't get rolling until around 10:30pm, although you can stop in for a drink
and tapas earlier. Don't be afraid to start singing an American song if it has a fast
rhythm—60 people will join in, even if they don't know the words. Open daily
from 7pm to 2am. Beer is 1.80€; wine is from 1€; tapas are 5.40€ to 9€. Cava
de San Miguel 13. ✆ **91-559-95-31.** Metro: Puerta del Sol or Opera.

Sésamo   In a class by itself, this *cueva* dating from the early 1950s draws a
clientele of young painters and writers with its bohemian ambience. Hemingway was one of those early visitors (a plaque commemorates him). At first, you'll
think you're walking into a tiny snack bar—and you are. But proceed down the
flight of steps to the cellar. Here, the walls are covered with contemporary paintings and quotations. At squatty stools and tables, an international assortment of
young people listens to piano music and sometimes piano or guitar playing.
Open daily from 6pm to 2:30am. A pitcher of sangria (for 4) is 8.50€; beer
costs 2€. Príncipe 7. ✆ **91-429-65-24.** Metro: Sevilla or Puerta del Sol.

A CASINO

The **Casino Gran Madrid** is at Km 29 along the Carretera La Coruña (the
A-6 highway running between Madrid and La Coruña), Apartado 62 (✆ **91-
856-11-00**). The largest casino in Madrid, it appeals to nongamblers with a roster of dining and entertainment facilities, including two restaurants, four bars,
and a nightclub. And if you happen to enjoy gambling, there are facilities for
French and American roulette, blackjack, punto y banco, baccarat, and chemin
de fer. Presentation of a passport at the door is essential—without it, you won't
be admitted. Entrance costs 3€, although that fee is often waived for residents
of some of Madrid's larger hotels who arrive with a ticket that's sometimes provided gratis by the hotel's management. The casino and all of its facilities are
open daily from 4pm to 5am.

An a la carte restaurant in the French Gaming Room offers international cuisine, with dinners costing from 38€ to 50€. A buffet in the American Gaming
Room will cost around 19€ to 21€. The restaurants are open daily from 9:15pm
to 2am. The casino is about 29km (18 miles) northwest of Madrid, along the
Madrid–La Coruña N-VI highway. If you don't feel like driving, the casino has
buses that depart from Plaza de España 6, every afternoon and evening at 4:30,
6, 7:30, 9, and 11pm, and 1am. Note that between October and June, men
must wear jackets and ties and must always carry passports; T-shirts and tennis
shoes are forbidden in any season. To enter, European visitors must present an
identity card and non-European visitors must present a passport.

Side Trips from Madrid

Madrid makes an ideal base for excursions because it's surrounded by some of Spain's major attractions. The day trips listed below to both New Castile and Old Castile range from 14km to 161km (9–100 miles) outside Madrid, allowing you to leave in the morning and be back by nightfall. In case you choose to stay overnight, however, we've included a selection of hotels in each town.

The satellite cities and towns around Madrid include Toledo, with its El Greco masterpieces; the wondrous El Escorial monastery; Segovia's castles that seem to float in the clouds; and the Bourbon palaces at La Granja. Cuenca, which is actually in La Mancha, is the longest excursion; so, unless you want to spend a good part of the day getting there and back, you should consider it an overnight trip. For a selection of other cities in Old Castile—each of which is better visited on an overnight stopover rather than a day trip from Madrid—see chapter 6, "Old Castile & León."

1 Toledo ✮✮✮

68km (42 miles) SW of Madrid, 137km (85 miles) SE of Avila

If you have only 1 day for an excursion outside Madrid, go to Toledo—a place made special by its Arab, Jewish, Christian, and even Roman and Visigothic elements. A national landmark, the city that so inspired El Greco in the 16th century has remained relatively unchanged. You can still stroll through streets barely wide enough for a man and his donkey—much less for an automobile.

Surrounded on three sides by a bend in the Tagus River, Toledo stands atop a hill overlooking the arid plains of New Castile—a natural fortress in the center of the Iberian Peninsula. It was a logical choice for the capital of Spain, but it lost its political status to Madrid in the 1500s. Toledo has remained the country's religious center, as the seat of the Primate of Spain.

If you're driving, the much-painted skyline of Toledo will come into view about 6km (3½ miles) from the city. When you cross the Tagus River on the 14th-century Puente San Martín, the scene is reminiscent of El Greco's moody, storm-threatened *View of Toledo*, which hangs in New York's Metropolitan Museum of Art. The artist reputedly painted that view from a hillside that is now the site of Parador Nacional de Conde Orgaz. If you arrive at the right time, you can enjoy an aperitif on the parador's terrace and watch one of the famous violet sunsets of Toledo (see "Where to Stay," later in this chapter).

ESSENTIALS

GETTING THERE RENFE **trains** run here frequently every day. Those departing Madrid's Atocha Railway Station for Toledo run daily from 6:45am to 8:45pm; those leaving Toledo for Madrid run daily from 7am to 9pm. Traveling time is approximately 2 hours, and a one-way fare costs 4.80€. RENFE also

Madrid Environs

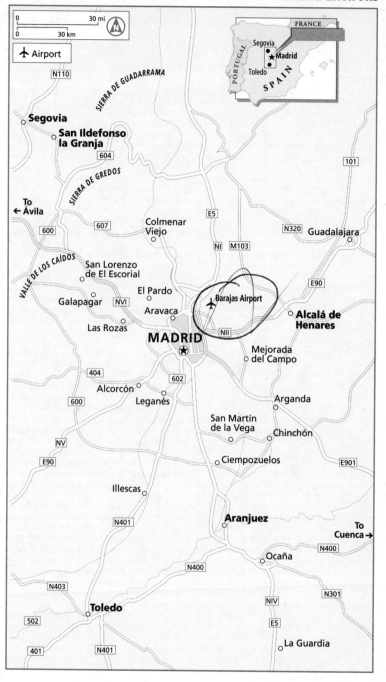

Toledo

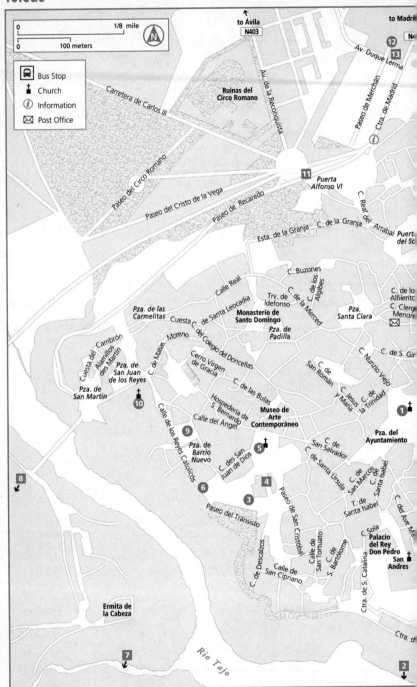

0 _____ 1/8 mile
0 _____ 100 meters

N

🚌 Bus Stop
⛪ Church
ⓘ Information
✉ Post Office

to Ávila
N403

to Madrid

Av. Duque Lerma

Paseo de Merchán

Ctra. de Madrid

Ruinas del Circo Romano

Carretera de Carlos III

Av. de la Reconquista

Paseo del Circo Romano

Paseo del Cristo de la Vega

Paseo de Recaredo

Puerta Alfonso VI

Esta. de la Granja

C. de la Granja

C. Real del Arrabal

Puerta del So

C. Buzones

Calle Real

Cuesta C. de Santa Leocadia

Trv. de Idefonso

C. de los Algibes

C. de la Merced

Pza. Santa Clara

C. de lo Alfilerito

C. Clérig Menore

Pza. de las Carmelitas

Cuesta C. del Colegio del Doncellas

Monasterio de Santo Domingo

Pza. de Padilla

C. de S. Gir

Cuesta del Cambrón

Alamillos des Martín

Moreno

C. de Matías

Cerro Virgen de Gracia

C. de las Bulas

C. de San Román

C. de Nunzio Viejo

C. de Jesús y María

C. de la Trinidad

Pza. de San Juan de los Reyes

Pza. de San Martín

⟨10⟩

Calle de los Reyes Católicos

Hospedería S. Bernardo

Calle del Ángel

Museo de Arte Contemporáneo

Pza. del Ayuntamiento

⟨1⟩

⟨9⟩

Pza. de Barrio Nuevo

C. des San Juan de Dios

⟨5⟩

C. de San Salvador

⟨8⟩

⟨6⟩

⟨4⟩

⟨3⟩

Paseo del Tránsito

Paseo de San Cristóbal

C. de Santa Úrsula

C. de San Marcos

C. de Santa Isabel

T. de Santa Isabel

C. del Ave Ma

Calle de San Tortuato

C. de S. Bartolomé

C. de S. Catalina

Ctra. de S. Catalina

C. Sola

Palacio del Rey Don Pedro

San Andrés

Calle de San Cipriano

C. de Descalzos

Ermita de la Cabeza

⟨7⟩

Rio Tajo

Ctra. d

⟨2⟩

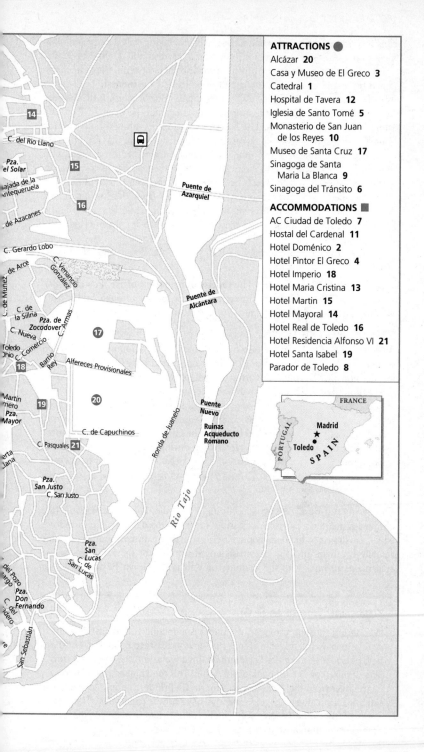

ATTRACTIONS ●

Alcázar **20**

Casa y Museo de El Greco **3**

Catedral **1**

Hospital de Tavera **12**

Iglesia de Santo Tomé **5**

Monasterio de San Juan
de los Reyes **10**

Museo de Santa Cruz **17**

Sinagoga de Santa
Maria La Blanca **9**

Sinagoga del Tránsito **6**

ACCOMMODATIONS ■

AC Ciudad de Toledo **7**

Hostal del Cardenal **11**

Hotel Doménico **2**

Hotel Pintor El Greco **4**

Hotel Imperio **18**

Hotel Maria Cristina **13**

Hotel Martin **15**

Hotel Mayoral **14**

Hotel Real de Toledo **16**

Hotel Residencia Alfonso VI **21**

Hotel Santa Isabel **19**

Parador de Toledo **8**

runs two express trains a day to and from Toledo, taking only 1 hour and making a stop at Aranjuez. For train information in Madrid, call © **90-224-02-02.**

It's actually easier to take the **bus** from Madrid than the train. Buses are maintained by several companies, the largest of which is **Continental.** They depart from Madrid's Estación Sur de Autobuses (South Bus Station), Calle Méndez Alvaro (© **91-468-42-00** for information), every day between 6:30am and 10pm at 30-minute intervals. The fastest leave Monday through Friday on the hour. Those that depart weekdays on the half hour, and those that run on weekends, take a bit longer. Travel time, depending on whether the bus stops en route, is between 1 hour and 1 hour 20 minutes. One-way transit costs 3.70€.

Once you reach Toledo, you'll be deposited at the Estación de Autobuses, which lies beside the river, about 1.2km (¾ mile) from the historic center. Although many visitors opt to walk, be ready to climb a hill. Bus nos. 5 and 6 run from the station uphill to the center, charging .80€ for the brief ride. Pay the driver directly.

If you're driving, exit Madrid via Cibeles (Paseo del Prado) and take the N-401 south.

VISITOR INFORMATION The **tourist information office,** Puerta de Bisagra (© **92-522-08-43;** www.jccm.es), is open Monday through Friday from 9am to 6pm, Saturday from 9am to 7pm, and Sunday from 9am to 3pm.

EXPLORING THE TOWN

Alcázar The Alcázar, at the eastern edge of the old city, dominates the Toledo skyline, but because of renovations will not open until early 2005 even though it's traditionally been the major attraction of Toledo. It became world famous at the beginning of the Spanish Civil War when it underwent a 70-day siege that almost destroyed it (see "The Siege of the Alcázar," below). Today it has been rebuilt and turned into an army museum housing such exhibits as a plastic model of what the fortress looked like after the Civil War, electronic equipment used during the siege, and photographs taken during the height of the battle. A walking tour gives a realistic simulation of the siege. Allow an hour for a visit.

Cuesta de Carlos V 2, near the Plaza de Zocodover. © **92-522-16-73.** Admission to be announced when open. Tues–Sun 9:30am–2pm. Bus: 5 or 6.

Casa y Museo de El Greco ✮ Located in Toledo's *antiguo barrio judío* (the old Jewish quarter, a labyrinth of narrow streets on the old town's southwestern edge), the House of El Greco honors the great master painter, although he didn't actually live here. In 1585 the artist moved into one of the run-down palace apartments belonging to the marqués of Villena. Although he was to live at

---

⟨*Moments* Toledo as El Greco Saw It

Wandering through the heart of Toledo is a delight. It is almost as memorable to view Toledo from afar. It still looks as El Greco painted it. For the best perspective, take the **Carretera de Circunvalación,** the road that runs 3km (2 miles) on the far bank of the Tagus. This road makes a circular loop of the river from the Alcántara to San Martín Bridge. Clinging to the hillsides are rustic dwellings and extensive olive groves *(cigarrales).* The cigarrales of the Imperial City were immortalized by Tirso de Molina, the 17th-century dramatist, in his trilogy **Los Cigarrales de Toledo.**

other Toledan addresses, he returned to the Villena palace in 1604 and remained there until his death. Only a small part of the original residence was saved from decay. In time, this and a neighboring house became the El Greco museum; today it's furnished with authentic period pieces.

You can visit El Greco's so-called studio, where one of his paintings hangs. The museum contains several more works, including a copy of *A View of Toledo* and three portraits, plus many paintings by various 16th- and 17th-century Spanish artists. The garden and especially the kitchen also merit attention, as does a sitting room decorated in the Moorish style.

Calle Samuel Leví s/n. (*C*) **92-522-40-46**. Admission 2.40€ adults, free for children under 18, seniors, and students. Tues–Sat 10am–2pm and 4–6pm; Sun 10am–2pm. Bus: 5 or 6.

Catedral de Toledo ★★★
Ranked among the greatest Gothic structures, the cathedral actually reflects several styles, since more than 2½ centuries elapsed during its construction (1226–1493). Many historic events transpired here, including the proclamation of Joanna the Mad and her husband, Philip the Handsome, as heirs to the throne of Spain.

Among its art treasures, the *transparente* stands out—a wall of marble and florid baroque alabaster sculpture overlooked for years because the cathedral was too poorly lit. Sculptor Narciso Tomé cut a hole in the ceiling, much to the consternation of Toledans, and now light touches the high-rising angels, a *Last Supper* in alabaster, and a Virgin in ascension.

The 16th-century *Capilla Mozárabe,* containing works by Juan de Borgoña, is another curiosity of the cathedral. Mass is still held here using Mozarabic liturgy.

The Treasure Room has a 500-pound, 15th-century gilded monstrance—allegedly made with gold brought back from the New World by Columbus—that is still carried through the streets of Toledo during the feast of Corpus Christi.

Other highlights of the cathedral include El Greco's *Twelve Apostles* and *Spoliation of Christ* and Goya's *Arrest of Christ on the Mount of Olives.*

The cathedral shop, where you buy tickets to enter, is well organized and stocks a variety of quality souvenirs, including ceramics and damascene.

Cardenal Cisneros 1. (*C*) **92-522-22-41**. Free admission to cathedral; Treasure Room 4.95€. Mon–Sat 10:30am–6:30pm; Sun 2–6:30pm.

Hospital de Tavera
This 16th-century Greco-Roman palace north of the medieval ramparts of Toledo was originally built by Cardinal Tavera; it now houses a private art collection. Titian's portrait of Charles V hangs in the banqueting hall. The museum owns five paintings by El Greco: *The Holy Family, The Baptism of Christ,* and portraits of St. Francis, St. Peter, and Cardinal Tavera. Ribera's *The Bearded Woman* also attracts many viewers. The collection of books in the library is priceless. In the nearby church is the mausoleum of Cardinal Tavera, designed by Alonso Berruguete.

Hospital de Tavera 2. (*C*) **92-522-04-51**. Admission 3€. Daily 10:30am–1:30pm and 3:30–6pm.

Iglesia de Santo Tomé
This modest little 14th-century chapel, situated on a narrow street in the old Jewish quarter, might have been overlooked had it not possessed El Greco's masterpiece **The Burial of the Count of Orgaz** ★★★, created in 1586. To avoid the hordes, go when the chapel first opens.

Plaza del Conde 4, Vía Santo Tomé. (*C*) **92-525-60-98**. Admission 1.50€. Daily 10am–6:45pm (closes at 5:45pm in winter). Closed Dec 25 and Jan 1.

Monasterio de San Juan de los Reyes 🔥 Founded by King Ferdinand and Queen Isabella to commemorate their triumph over the Portuguese at Toro in 1476, the church was started in 1477 according to the plans of architect Juan Guas. It was finished, together with the splendid cloisters, in 1504, dedicated to St. John the Evangelist, and used from the beginning by the Franciscan friars. An example of Gothic-Spanish-Flemish style, San Juan de los Reyes was restored after the damage caused during Napoléon's invasion and after its abandonment in 1835; since 1954, it has been entrusted again to the Franciscans. The church is located at the extreme western edge of the old town, midway between the Puente (bridge) of San Martín and the Puerta (gate) of Cambrón.

Calle Reyes Católicos 17. ☎ **92-522-38-02**. Admission 1.50€ adults, free for children 8 and under. Winter daily 10am–5:45pm; summer daily 10am–6:45pm. Bus: 2.

Museo de Santa Cruz 🔥🔥 Today a museum of art and sculpture, this was originally a 16th-century Spanish Renaissance hospice, founded by Cardinal Mendoza, "the third King of Spain," who helped Ferdinand and Isabella gain the throne. The facade is almost more spectacular than any of the exhibits inside. It's a stunning architectural achievement in the classical Plateresque style. The major artistic treasure inside is El Greco's *The Assumption of the Virgin,* his last known work. Paintings by Goya and Ribera are also on display along with gold items, opulent antique furnishings, Flemish tapestries, and even Visigoth artifacts. In the patio of the museum you'll stumble across fragments of carved stone and sarcophagi lids. One of the major exhibits is of a large Astrolabio tapestry of the zodiac from the 1400s. In the basement you can see artifacts, including elephant tusks, from archaeological digs throughout the province. When there is an exhibition, there is a 3€ charge for a guided tour.

Calle Miguel de Cervantes 3. ☎ **92-522-10-36**. Free admission. Mon–Sat 10am–6pm; Sun 10am–2pm. Bus: 5 or 6. Pass beneath the granite archway on the eastern edge of the Plaza de Zocodover and walk about 1 block.

Sinagoga del Tránsito 🔥 One block west of the El Greco home and museum stands this once-important house of worship for Toledo's large Jewish population. A 14th-century building, it is noted for its superb stucco Hebrew inscriptions, including psalms inscribed along the top of the walls and a poetic description of the Temple on the east wall. The synagogue is the most important part of the **Museo Sefardí (Sephardic Museum),** which opened in 1971 and contains art objects as well as tombstones with Hebrew epigraphy, some of which are dated before 1492.

Calle Samuel Leví s/n. ☎ **92-522-36-65**. Admission 2.50€. Tues–Sat 10am–1:45pm and 4–5:45pm; Sun 10am–1:45pm. Closed Jan 1, May 1, Dec 24–25, and Dec 31. Bus: 2.

Sinagoga de Santa María La Blanca 🔥 In the late 12th century, the Jews of Toledo erected an important synagogue in the Almohada style, which employs graceful horseshoe arches and ornamental horizontal moldings. Although the synagogue had been converted into a Christian church by the early 15th century, much of the original structure remains, including the five naves and elaborate Mudéjar decorations, which are mosque-like in their effect. The synagogue lies on the western edge of the city, midway between the El Greco museum and San Juan de los Reyes.

Calle Reyes Católicos 2 ☎ **92-522-72-57**. Admission 1.50€. Apr–Sept daily 10am–1:45pm and 3:30–6:45pm; Oct–Mar daily 10am–2pm and 3:30–5:45pm. Bus: 2.

SHOPPING

In swashbuckling days, the swordsmiths of Toledo were renowned. They're still around and still turning out swords today. Toledo is equally renowned for its *damasquinado,* or damascene work, the Moorish art of inlaying gold, even copper or silver threads, against a matte black steel backdrop. Today Toledo is filled with souvenir shops hawking damascene. The price depends on whether the item is handcrafted or machine made. Sometimes machine-made damascene is passed off as the more expensive handcrafted item, so you have to shop carefully. Bargaining is perfectly acceptable in Toledo, but if you get the price down, you can't pay with a credit card—only cash.

Marzipan (called *mazapán* locally) is often prepared by nuns and is a local specialty. Many shops in town specialize in this treat made of sweet almond paste.

The province of Toledo is also renowned for its pottery, which is sold in so many shops at competitive prices that it's almost unnecessary to recommend specific branches hawking these wares. However, over the years we've found that the large roadside emporiums on the outskirts of town on the main road to Madrid often are better bargains than the shops within the city walls, where rents are higher.

Better yet, for the best deals, and if you're interested in buying a number of items, consider a trip to **Talavera la Reina,** 76km (47 miles) west of Toledo, where most of the pottery is made. Since Talavera is the largest city in the province, it is hardly a picture-postcard little potter's village. Most of the shops lie along the main street of town, where you'll find store after store selling this distinctive pottery in multicolored designs.

Pottery hunters also flock to **Puente del Arzobispo,** another ceramic center, known for its green-hued pottery. From Talavera drive west on the N-V to Oropesa, then south for 14km (9 miles) to a fortified bridge across the Tagus. In general, ceramics here are cheaper than those sold in Toledo.

Just past Oropesa at the turnoff to Lagartera is the village where the highly renowned and sought-after embroidery of La Mancha originates. Virtually every cottage displays samples of this free-form floral stitching, shaped into everything from skirts to tablecloths. Of course, shops in Toledo are also filled with samples of this unique embroidery.

Established in 1910, **Casa Bermejo,** Calle Airosas 5 (© **92-528-53-67**), is a factory and store that employs almost 50 artisans, and you can watch them at work. The outlet carries a wide array of damascene objects fashioned into Toledo's traditional Mudéjar designs—swords, platters, pitchers, and other gift items. But not all the items follow the inspiration of the medieval Arabs. This outfit engraves many of the ornamental swords awarded to graduates of West Point in the United States, as well as the decorative, full-dress military accessories used by the armies of various countries of Europe, including France. Open Monday through Friday from 9am to 1pm and 3 to 6pm, Saturday from 10am to 2pm. Closing times are later in August, determined solely by business traffic.

Around since the 1920s, **Felipe Suárez,** Circo Romano 8 (© **92-522-56-15**), has manufactured damascene work in various forms, ranging from unpretentious souvenir items to art objects of rare museum-quality beauty that sell for as much as 12,000€. You'll find swords, straight-edged razors, pendants, fans, and an array of pearls. The shop is open daily from 10am to 7pm year-round.

The Siege of the Alcázar

Although the Alcázar of Toledo has suffered many a siege, one particularly dramatic encounter in 1936 made world headlines. The Republicans were fighting to gain control of conservative, staunchly Catholic Toledo. Franco's rebel troops were commanded by one tough officer, Col. José Moscardó. Not only were his troops inside the Alcázar, but women and children were holed up here as well. The Alcázar, although under heavy attack, withstood 70 days of bombardment.

On July 23, a Republican officer reached Moscardó by telephone within the Alcázar. The colonel was informed that Nationalist forces had kidnapped Luis, his 16-year-old son. Moscardó was told that unless he immediately surrendered the fortress, Luis would be executed.

To show that they did indeed have the child, they put Luis on the phone to his father. "¡Papá!" he shouted, "They say they are going to shoot me if you don't surrender."

Without hesitation, Moscardó told his son: "Then commend your soul to God, shout '¡Viva España!' and die like a hero."

The Republicans were good to their word. Luis was shot in the head. The fortress was surrendered in September of that year. In the Alcázar today the wall phone on which the colonel spoke to his son for the last time still hangs.

You'll also find superb craftsmanship in damascene work at **Santiago Sánchez Martín,** Calle Río Llano 15 (© **92-522-77-57**), which specializes in the elaborately detailed arabesques whose techniques are as old as the Arab conquest of Iberia. Look for everything from decorative tableware (platters, pitchers, and so on) to mirror frames, jewelry, letter openers, and ornamental swords. It's open Monday through Friday from 9am to 2pm and 4 to 7pm.

Many long-time residents of Toledo remember **Casa Telesforo,** Plaza de Zocodover 13 (© **92-522-33-79**), as the outfit that supplied the marzipan consumed at their childhood birthday parties and celebrations. A specialist in this almond-and-sugar confection, it sells the best marzipan in town, made into such whimsical shapes as hearts, diamonds, flowers, and fish. It's open daily from 9am to 10pm, later in summer, depending on the crowds.

WHERE TO STAY
EXPENSIVE
AC Ciudad de Toledo ★★   Opened in 1998, this is the first hotel in years to challenge the government-run parador. On a beltway south of the city—follow the directions to the parador—this deluxe property is a member of a chain that also includes the swanky Santo Mauro in Madrid. The epitome of luxury living, this hotel across the river from the city is entered at the third floor. You move down through the spiraling architectural design to reach the rest of the hotel. Bedrooms are spacious and luxuriously furnished, all in contemporary styling, with tiled bathrooms and tub/shower combos. The suites have oversize bathtubs and hydromassage.

Carretera De Circumvalación 15, 45005 Toledo. (✆ **92-528-51-25.** Fax 92-528-47-00. www.ac-hoteles.com. 49 units. 122€–156€ double; 196€–250€ suite. AE, DC, MC, V. Free parking. Bus: 5. **Amenities:** Restaurant; bar; gym; sauna; room service; babysitting; laundry service; dry cleaning. *In room:* A/C, TV, minibar, hair dryer.

Parador de Toledo ★★★   You'll have to make reservations well in advance to stay at this parador, which is built on the ridge of a rugged hill where El Greco is said to have painted his *View of Toledo.* That view is still here, and it is without a doubt one of the grandest in the world. The main living room/lounge has fine furniture—old chests, leather chairs, and heavy tables—and leads to a sunny terrace overlooking the city. On chilly nights you can sit by the fireplace. The guest rooms are the most luxurious in all of Toledo, far superior to those at María Cristina. They are spacious and beautifully furnished with reproductions of regional antique pieces. Most of the rooms come with roomy modern bathrooms clad in marble (others are tiled) and equipped with tub/shower combos and robes.

Cerro del Emperador, 45002 Toledo. (✆ **92-522-18-50.** Fax 92-522-51-66. www.parador.es. 76 units. 102€–132€ double; 165€ suite. AE, DC, MC, V. Free parking. Drive across Puente San Martín and head south for 4km (2½ miles). **Amenities:** Restaurant; bar; pool; room service; babysitting; laundry service; dry cleaning. *In room:* A/C, TV, minibar, hair dryer, safe.

MODERATE

Hostal del Cardenal ★★   This place has long been acclaimed as the best restaurant in Toledo (see below), but we'll let you in on a secret: You can rent rooms here, too. They're not as grand as those at the Parador, but they're wonderful nevertheless, especially if you want an old Toledan atmosphere. The entrance to this unusual hotel is set into the stone of the ancient city walls, a few steps from the Bisagra Gate. To enter the hotel you must climb a series of terraces to the top of the crenellated walls of the ancient fortress. Here, grandly symmetrical and very imposing, is the hostal, the former residence of the 18th-century cardinal of Toledo, Señor Lorenzana. Just beyond the entrance, still atop the city wall, you'll find flagstone walkways, Moorish fountains, rose gardens, and cascading vines. The building has tiled walls, long, narrow salons, dignified Spanish furniture, and a smattering of antiques. Bedrooms are small to medium, each one well appointed with a firm mattress and quality linen, plus a tidily organized bathroom with a stall shower and tub. The only parking is what's available free on the street. A member of the hotel staff will call you a taxi if you don't want to walk the steep ascent (on narrow to nonexistent sidewalks) into the historic district.

Paseo de Recaredo 24, 45004 Toledo. (✆ **92-522-49-00.** Fax 92-522-29-91. www.cardenal.asernet.es. 27 units. 78€–98€ double; 105€–135€ suite. AE, DC, MC, V. Parking 12€. Bus: 2 from rail station. **Amenities:** Restaurant; bar; laundry service; dry cleaning. *In room:* A/C, TV, hair dryer, safe.

Hotel Doménico ★   One of the finest hotels in Toledo, Doménico is located among Los Cigarrales, the typical country houses lying south of the city and offering panoramic views. The building, although modern, is constructed in a traditional style. Launched in 1993, the hotel is only a 5-minute drive to the historic core of Toledo. Bedrooms are medium in size and comfortably furnished. Some of the rooms have windows in the roof for greater light. The beds have excellent mattresses, plus bathrooms with showers and tubs. The second- and third-floor units have terraces opening onto breathtaking views of the city.

Cerro del Emperador, 45002 Toledo. (✆ **92-528-01-01.** Fax 92-528-01-03. www.hoteldomenico.com. 50 units. 81€–110€ double; 175€ suite. AE, MC, V. Free parking. Bus: 7. **Amenities:** Restaurant; bar; pool; room service; babysitting; laundry service; dry cleaning. *In room:* A/C, TV, minibar, hair dryer, safe.

Hotel María Cristina   Adjacent to the historic Hospital de Tavera and near the northern perimeter of the old town, this stone-sided, awning-fronted hotel resembles a palatial country home. If you're willing to forgo the view from the parador and the charm of Hostal del Cardenal, this hotel is a good backup. Originally built as a convent in 1560 and later used as a hospital, it was turned into this comfortable hotel in the late 1980s. Sprawling and historic, it contains clean, attractively furnished bedrooms, each with a comfortable bed and an immaculate bathroom, often with a tub/shower combo.

Marqués de Mendigorría 1, 45003 Toledo. © 92-521-32-02. Fax 92-521-26-50. www.hotelesmayoral.com. 73 units. 90€ double; 149€ suite. AE, DC, MC, V. Parking 9€. **Amenities:** Restaurant; bar; room service; laundry service; dry cleaning. *In room:* A/C, TV, minibar, hair dryer.

Hotel Pintor El Greco ⭐   In the old Jewish quarter, one of the most traditional and historic districts of Toledo, this hotel was converted from a typical *casa toledana*, which had once been used as a bakery. With careful restoration, especially of its ancient facade, it was transformed into one of Toledo's best and most atmospheric small hotels—the only one to match the antique charm of Hostal del Cardenal, although it remains relatively unknown. Decoration in both the public rooms and bedrooms is in a traditional Castilian style. Bedrooms come in a variety of shapes and sizes, as befits a building of this age, but all are equipped with firm mattresses and small bathrooms with tub/shower combos and adequate shelf space. At the doorstep of the hotel are such landmarks as the Monasterio de San Juan de los Reyes, Sinagoga de Santa María la Blanca, Sinagoga del Tránsito, Casa y Museo de El Greco, and Iglesia de Santo Tomé. Public parking is available for 5€ per day.

Alamillos del Tránsito 13, 45002 Toledo. © **92-528-51-91.** Fax 92-521-58-19. www.hotelpintorelgreco.com. 33 units. 110€–120€ double. AE, DC, MC, V. Parking 12€. **Amenities:** Lounge; babysitting; laundry service; dry cleaning. *In room:* A/C, TV, minibar, hair dryer, safe.

Hotel Residencia Alfonso VI   Built in the early 1970s, this hotel has been kept up to date with frequent renovations. Run by the same management as the Carlos V, it is a superior hotel with better appointments and comfort, although a few of the public rooms appear so faux Castilian they look like movie sets. It sits near a dense concentration of souvenir shops in the center of the old city, at the southern perimeter of the Alcázar. Inside you'll discover a high-ceilinged, marble-trimmed decor with a scattering of Iberian artifacts, copies of Spanish provincial furniture, and dozens of leather armchairs. Rooms, for the most part, are medium in size, each well appointed with cushiony furnishings, including comfortable mattresses on the Spanish beds. Bathrooms are tiled and a bit small containing tub/shower combos.

Calle General Moscardó 2, 45001 Toledo. © **92-522-26-00.** Fax 92-521-44-58. www.hotelalfonsovi.com. 83 units. 100€–110€ double; 175€–185€ suite. AE, MC, V. Bus: 5 or 6. **Amenities:** Restaurant; bar; room service; babysitting; laundry service; dry cleaning. *In room:* A/C, TV, minibar, hair dryer, safe.

INEXPENSIVE

Hotel Imperio   Long a budget favorite, this modest hotel lies a few yards from the Alcázar and Cathedral. Built in the 1980s, the hotel was recently renovated (and just in time), adding more comfort to the small rooms. The furnishings are rather severe, but the beds are comfortable and renewed. However, for the price this is one of the city's best choices. Rooms on the second floor have balconies overlooking the street. And all units contain private bathrooms with tub/shower combos.

Cadena 5, 45001 Toledo. ✆ **92-522-76-50.** Fax 92-525-31-83. www.terra.es/personal/himperio. 21 units. 40€ double. AE, DC, MC, V. **Amenities:** Bar; lounge; laundry service. *In room:* A/C, TV.

Hotel Martín   A good, serviceable choice, the two-story Martín opened in 1992 near the Bisagra Gate, the main medieval doorway to the city of Toledo. It lies only a 10-minute walk from the historic center. The hotel has a homey atmosphere, with a red-brick facade, old streetlights out front, and vertical windows. The interior is decorated in wood and pastel colors. The rooms are medium in size and furnished comfortably. Bathrooms are impeccably maintained, with showers. A continental breakfast is served (but is not included in the room rate).

Calle Espino 10, 45003 Toledo. ✆ **92-522-17-33.** www.hotelesmartin.com. 29 units. 49€–55€ double. MC, V. Parking 8€. **Amenities:** Bar; laundry service. *In room:* A/C, TV, hair dryer, safe.

Hotel Mayoral   In front of the walls of Toledo next to the bus station, this hotel dates from 1989. A rather formal entrance followed by a severe hallway leads to comfortable, well-furnished, medium-sized bedrooms with good beds and well-maintained bathrooms equipped with tub/shower combos. Most of the guest rooms have balconies with views of interior patios, although a few have a panoramic view of Toledo.

Av. de Castilla–La Mancha 3, 45003 Toledo. ✆ **92-521-60-00.** Fax. 92-521-69-54. www.hotelesmayoral. com. 110 units. 90€ double. AE, DC, MC, V. Parking 9€. Bus: 5 or 6. **Amenities:** Restaurant; bar; room service; babysitting; laundry service; dry cleaning. *In room:* A/C, TV, minibar.

Hotel Santa Isabel   In a building dating from the 15th century, Santa Isabel lies in the heart of Toledo, close to the cathedral and most sights of historic interest. Opposite the Convent of Santa Isabel from which it takes its name, the hotel still has much of its original character. The interior, however, has been austerely modernized. Bedrooms are small and spartan, but immaculately kept with comfortable beds and bathrooms containing showers. Some units have fine views of the interior patio; others open onto the street. Overflow guests are housed in a recently acquired building next door, which offers an additional 19 comparable bedrooms in a mixture of modern and antique.

Calle Santa Isabel 24, 45002 Toledo. ✆ **92-525-31-20.** Fax. 92-525-31-36. www.santa-isabel.com. 42 units. 42€–48€ double. AE, DC, MC, V. Parking 6€. Bus: 546. **Amenities:** Breakfast room, lounge. *In room:* A/C, TV.

WHERE TO DINE
MODERATE

Asador Adolfo ⭐   Located less than a minute's walk north of the cathedral, at the corner of Calle Hombre de Palo behind an understated sign, Asador Adolfo is one of the finest restaurants in town (although we still prefer the Hostal del Cardenal). Sections of the building were first constructed during the 1400s, but the thoroughly modern kitchen has recently been renovated. Massive beams support the dining room ceiling, and here and there the rooms contain faded frescoes dating from the original building.

Game dishes are a house specialty, with partridge with white beans and venison consistently rating among the best anywhere. Nongame offerings include hake flavored with local saffron as well as a wide array of beef, veal, or lamb dishes. To start, try the *pimientos rellenos* (red peppers stuffed with pulverized shellfish). The house dessert is marzipan, prepared in a wood-fired oven and noted for its lightness.

Calle Hombre de Palo 7. ✆ **92-522-73-21.** Reservations recommended. Main courses 18€–26€. AE, DC, MC, V. Tues–Sat 1–4pm and 8pm–midnight; Sun 1–4pm. Bus: 5 or 6.

Casón de los López ★★ CASTILIAN   A short walk from the heartbeat Plaza de Zocodover, this charmer of a restaurant serves the lightest and most sophisticated cuisine in Toledo. Its setting alone would make it an enticing choice. In an antique building, it's a virtual museum, furnished with antiques, some from as far back as the 16th century. Castilian iron bars, Mudéjar-style wooden ceilings, Arab stucco decorations, a patio ringed with marble statues, a splashing fountain, and caged birds create this mellow atmosphere. And get this: much of the furniture is for sale. Hope that some other diner won't buy the table out from under you when your main course is being served.

In such a mellow ambience, you can plunge into a cuisine that sees us return-ing again and again to sample the bounty of the countryside, especially such game as hare, rabbit, partridge, and pigeon. A recent specialty we enjoyed, loin of venison with fresh, garlic-flecked spinach in a velvety smooth mushroom cream sauce, was irresistibly juicy and a combination of blissful contrasts. Launch yourself with the garlic-ravioli soup, a first for many diners, and top the meal with an extravagant cheese and fresh plum mousse.

Sillería 3. ✆ **92-525-47-74.** Reservations required. Main courses 15€–22€. Set-price menus 33€–45€. Daily 1:30–4pm; Mon–Sat 9–11:30pm. AE, DC, MC, V.

Hostal del Cardenal ★★ SPANISH   Treat yourself to Toledo's best-known restaurant, owned by the same people who run Madrid's Sobrino de Botín (see chapter 4). The chef prepares regional dishes with flair and originality. Choos-ing from a menu very similar to that of the fabled Madrid eatery, begin with "quarter of an hour" (fish) soup or white asparagus, then move on to curried prawns, baked hake, filet mignon, or smoked salmon. Roast suckling pig is a specialty, as is partridge in casserole. Arrive early to enjoy a sherry in the bar or in the courtyard.

Paseo de Recaredo 24. ✆ **92-522-08-62.** Reservations required. Main courses 8€–18€; fixed-price menu 18€. AE, DC, MC, V. Daily 1–4pm and 8:30–11:30pm. Bus: 2 from rail station.

La Abadía CASTILIAN   The "Abbey" (its English name) started life as a *cervecería,* or alehouse, before it was turned into a convivial restaurant and tapas bar. Next to San Nicolás church, it stands at the intersection of Núñez de Arce and Calle de Alfileteros. It is ideal for a huge Castilian meal or for wine drink-ing and tapas eating. The decor is a tasteful combination of modern and rustic styles, and the interior is separated into two sections—with separate restaurant and bar areas. In honor of its old function as a *cervecería,* a wide variety of inter-national beers is offered. One of the best dishes—and one beloved by many Toledanos—is a partridge casserole with white wine, bay leaves, and onions. Filet of venison in a mushroom sauce is another worthy choice, as is *ensalada de verdura a la parrilla,* or a salad of freshly grilled vegetables. Some of the most delightful tapas include croquettes, roasted red peppers, and such meats as veni-son and Serrano ham. The most unusual dessert is an ice cream made of Manchego cheese.

Plaza de San Nicolás 3. ✆ **92-525-07-46.** Reservations recommended. Main courses 10€–15€; set menu 9€. DC, MC, V. Mon–Fri 8am–11pm; Sat–Sun noon–2:30am.

INEXPENSIVE

El Catavinos ★ *(Finds* SPANISH/CASTILIAN   El Catavinos means "wine taster" in Spanish, and indeed this charming restaurant started its life as a wine cellar. On the periphery of the center, a 10-minute walk from the Puerta de Bis-agra, the restaurant has a convivial bar downstairs and a restaurant upstairs decorated with old photographs of Peru. In fair weather, guests often eat out on the terrace. The menu is filled with exciting dishes, including such delicacies as partridge salad, bell peppers with a stuffing of hare, and grilled venison and veal meatballs in a savory tomato sauce. The *menú de degustación* is a cornucopia of seven different plates, each accompanied by a different wine. The desserts offered include a cheesecake made from goat milk with a sweet white wine.

Av. Reconquista 10. ⓒ **92-522-22-56.** Reservations recommended. Main courses 9€–19€; *menú de degustación* 25€. AE, DC, MC, V. Tues–Sat noon–midnight; Sun noon–4pm.

La Perdiz CASTILIAN   La Perdiz is named from the favorite dish of Toledans, partridge. That bird is best showcased here in a dish called *perdiz esto-fada a la toledana* (partridge stew with white wine, bay leaf, and onions). Another excellent choice is venison in a mushroom sauce. The menu has some imaginative offerings, such as a fresh fried cheese tossed in an orange dressing.

The best dessert and a local favorite is a marzipan tart with almond biscuits. On occasion a roast suckling pig is featured. The location is in the center of the old Jewish ghetto, about midpoint between two synagogues, Santa María la Blanca and Tránsito. The restaurant has two floors with views of the historic district. Locals, with good reason, cite the place for its good-quality cuisine at an affordable price. The same people who run La Perdiz also operate **Asador Adolfo** (see above), Toledo's premier restaurant, but prices at La Perdiz are far more reasonable.

Calle Reyes Católicos 7. ⓒ **92-521-46-58.** Reservations recommended. Main courses 12€–16€; set menu 21€. AE, MC, DC, V. Tues–Sat noon–11pm; Sun noon–4pm.

La Tarasca CASTILIAN   This restaurant, the domain of the Martín brothers, serves good food but is mainly recommended for its convenience, as it lies only a couple of blocks north of the cathedral. With two dining rooms and a cafeteria, it is also open throughout the day, even serving breakfast. The decor, although plain, still evokes the 19th century. Walls are painted green with wood paneling resting under beams, and the rooms are joined by archways. The cuisine consists of the hearty, robust fare that Toledans feast on, including the traditional opener, *sopa castellana,* a hearty soup made with various meats and beans. You can opt for such standard dishes as grilled steak and potatoes, but braised game hen would be more traditional, or perhaps local trout. Two of our favorite dishes are *pimientos rellenos* (stuffed peppers) and *cordoniz a la toledana* (roast quail with savory brown sauce). All desserts, including the puddings, are homemade.

Calle Hombre de Palo 8. ⓒ **92-522-43-42.** Main courses 9€–16€; set menu 9€–15€. AE, DC, MC, V. Daily 7:30am–11pm.

TOLEDO AFTER DARK

Begin your nighttime crawl through Toledo with a stop at **Bar Ludeña,** Plaza de la Magdalena 13, Corral de Don Diego 10 (ⓒ **92-522-33-84**), where a loyal clientele comes for delectable tapas. Fixed-price menus range from 9€ to 15€. Glasses of wine are sometimes passed through a small window to clients standing outside enjoying the view of the square. The bar is little more than a narrow corridor, serving *raciones* of tapas that are so generous they make little meals, especially when served with bread. The roasted red peppers in olive oil are quite tasty, along with the stuffed crabs and *calamares* (squid). Huge dishes of pickled cucumbers, onions, and olives are available. They also have a tiny dining room behind a curtain at the end of the bar serving inexpensive fare.

Despite the many tourists that throng its streets during the day, Toledo is quiet at night, with fewer dance clubs than you'd expect from a town of its size. If you want to hear some recorded music, head for **Bar La Abadía,** Plaza San Nicolas 3 (© 92-525-11-40), where crowds of local residents, many of them involved in the tourism industry, crowd elbow to elbow for pints of beer, glasses of wine, and access to the music of New York, Los Angeles, or wherever. Other spots to hit include **O'Brien's Irish Pub,** Calle Armas 12 (© 92-521-26-65), which seems more appropriate for the streets of Dublin than old Toledo. A crowd in its 20s flocks here, and there's live music every Thursday at 10:30pm. Drop in to **Trébol,** Calle Santa Fe 1 (© 92-521-37-02), to sample their wine, their excellent tapas, and their *bombas* (stuffed potato bombs). Another wine bar hangout is **Enebro,** on the postage stamp–size Plaza Santiago Balleros, off Calle Cervantes (© 92-522-21-11).

2 Aranjuez ★★

47km (29 miles) S of Madrid, 48km (30 miles) NE of Toledo

This Castilian town at a confluence of the Tagus and Jarama rivers was once home to Bourbon kings in the spring and fall. With the manicured shrubbery, stately elms, fountains, and statues of the Palacio Real and surrounding compounds, Aranjuez remains a regal garden oasis in what is otherwise an unimpressive agricultural flatland known primarily for its strawberries and asparagus.

ESSENTIALS
GETTING THERE **Trains** depart about every 20 minutes from Madrid's Atocha Railway Station to make the 50-minute trip to Aranjuez, a one-way fare costing 3€. Twice a day you can take an express train from Madrid to Toledo, which makes a brief stopover at Aranjuez. This trip takes only 30 minutes. Trains run less often along the east-west route to and from Toledo (a 40-min. ride). The Aranjuez station lies about a mile outside town. For information and schedules, call © 90-224-02-02. You can walk it in about 15 minutes, but taxis and buses line up on Calle Stuart (2 blocks from the city tourist office). The bus that makes the run from the center of Aranjuez to the railway station is marked N–Z.

Buses for Aranjuez depart every 30 minutes from 7:30am to 10pm from Madrid's Estación Sur de Autobuses, Calle Méndez Alvaro. In Madrid, call © 91-530-46-05 for information. Buses arrive in Aranjuez at the City Bus Terminal, Calle Infantas 8 (© 91-891-01-83).

Driving is easy and takes about 30 minutes once you reach the southern city limits of Madrid. To reach Aranjuez, follow the signs to Aranjuez and Granada, taking highway N-IV.

VISITOR INFORMATION The **tourist information office,** Plaza de San Antonio 9 (© 91-891-04-27; www.aranjuez.net), is open Tuesday through Sunday from 10am to 2pm and 4 to 6pm.

EXPLORING ARANJUEZ
Casa del Labrador ★★ "The Little House of the Worker," modeled after the Petit Trianon at Versailles, was built in 1803 by Charles IV, who later abdicated in Aranjuez. The queen came here with her youthful lover, Godoy (whom she had elevated to the position of prime minister), and the feeble-minded Charles didn't seem to mind a bit. Surrounded by beautiful gardens, the "bedless" palace is lavishly furnished in the grand style of the 18th and 19th

centuries. The marble floors represent some of the finest workmanship of that day; the brocaded walls emphasize the luxurious lifestyle, and the royal toilet is a sight to behold (in those days, royalty preferred an audience). The clock here is one of the treasures of the house. The *casita* lies .8km (½ mile) east of the Royal Palace; those with a car can drive directly to it through the tranquil Jardín del Príncipe.

Calle Reina, Jardín del Príncipe. © **91-891-03-05.** Admission 5€ adults, 2€ students and children. Apr–Sept Tues–Sun 10am–6:30pm; Oct–Mar Tues–Sun 10am–5:30pm.

Jardín de la Isla ★   After the tour of the Royal Palace, wander through the Garden of the Island. Spanish Impressionist Santiago Rusiñol captured its evasive quality on canvas, and one Spanish writer said that you walk here "as if softly lulled by a sweet 18th-century sonata." A number of fountains are remarkable: the "Ne Plus Ultra" fountain, the black-jasper fountain of Bacchus, the fountain of Apollo, and the ones honoring Neptune (god of the sea) and Cybele (goddess of agriculture).

You may also stroll through the Jardín del Parterre, located in front of the palace. It's much better kept than the Garden of the Island but not as romantic.

Directly northwest of the Palacio Real. No phone. Free admission. Apr–Sept daily 8am–8:30pm; Oct–Mar daily 8am–6:30pm.

Palacio Real ★★   As you enter a cobblestone courtyard, you can tell just by the size of the palace that it's going to be spectacular. Ferdinand and Isabella, Philip II, Philip V, and Charles III all made their way through here. The structure you see today dates from 1778 (the previous buildings were destroyed by fire). Its salons show the opulence of a bygone era, with room after room of royal extravagance. Many styles are blended: Spanish, Italian, Moorish, and French. And, of course, no royal palace would be complete without a room reflecting the rage for chinoiserie that once swept over Europe. The Porcelain Salon is also of special interest. A guide conducts you through the huge complex (a tip is expected).

Plaza Palacio. © **91-891-07-40.** Admission 5€ adults, 2.40€ students and children. Tues–Sun 10am–6:15pm. Bus: Routes from the rail station converge at the square and gardens at the westernmost edge of the palace.

WHERE TO STAY

Hostal Castilla *Value*   On one of the town's main streets north of the Royal Palace and gardens, the Castilla consists of the ground floor and part of the first floor of a well-preserved early-18th-century house. Most of the accommodations overlook a courtyard with a fountain and flowers. All come equipped with neatly kept bathrooms with tub/shower combos. Owner Martín Soria speaks English. There are excellent restaurants nearby, and the hostal has an arrangement with a neighboring bar to provide guests with an inexpensive lunch. This is a good location from which to explore either Madrid or Toledo on a day trip. Parking is available along the street.

Carretera Andalucía 98, 28300 Aranjuez. © **91-891-26-27.** 19 units. 45€ double. Rates include breakfast. AE, MC, V. **Amenities:** Lounge; laundry service; dry cleaning. *In room:* A/C, TV.

WHERE TO DINE

Casa José ★★ SPANISH/INTERNATIONAL   Set near Town Hall and the Church of Antonio, this well-managed restaurant occupies two ground-floor rooms of a 300-year-old house in the heart of town. It is the premier restaurant of the entire area, and local gastronomes drive for miles around to dine here. The regional food is prepared with intelligence, and any of the daily offerings is well worth ordering. Look for a menu of fresh local ingredients that changes at least four times a year, with an emphasis on pork, veal, fish, chicken, and shellfish. Of special note are braised lamb chops in a fresh tomato and cilantro sauce, Jabugo ham with broad beans, shrimp in garlic sauce, hake with green sauce, and thick juicy steaks.

Calle Abastos 32. ℂ **91-891-14-88.** Reservations recommended. Main courses 17€–18€. AE, DC, MC, V. Tues–Sun 1–4pm; Tues–Sat 9pm–midnight.

Casa Pablo SPANISH   An unpretentious restaurant near the bus station in the town center, Casa Pablo is from 1941. At tables set outside under a canopy, you can enjoy red and pink geraniums along the tree-lined street; in cooler weather you eat either upstairs or in the cozy and clean rear dining room. The fixed-price menu includes four courses, a carafe of wine, bread, and gratuity. If it's hot and you don't want a heavy dinner, try a shrimp omelet or half a roast chicken; once we ordered just a plate of asparagus in season, accompanied by white wine. If you want a superb dish, try a fish called *mero* (Mediterranean pollock of delicate flavor), grilled over an open fire.

Almibar 42. ℂ **91-891-14-51.** Reservations recommended. Main courses 15€–30€. AE, MC, V. Daily 1–4:30pm and 8pm–midnight. Closed Aug.

La Rana Verde SPANISH   "The Green Frog," lies just east of the Royal Palace next to a small bridge spanning the Tagus. Opened in 1905 by Tomás Díaz Heredero, it is owned and run by a third-generation member of his family, who has decorated it in 1920s style. The restaurant looks like a summerhouse, with its high-beamed ceiling and soft drooping ferns. The best tables overlook the river. As in all the restaurants of Aranjuez, asparagus is a special feature. Game, particularly partridge, quail, and pigeon, can be recommended in season; fish, too, including fried hake and fried sole, makes a good choice. Strawberries are served with sugar, orange juice, or ice cream.

Plaza Santiago Rusignol s/n. ℂ **91-891-32-38.** Reservations recommended. Main courses 7€–15€; fixed-price menus 12€–20€. MC, V. Daily 9pm–midnight.

3 San Lorenzo de El Escorial

48km (30 miles) W of Madrid, 52km (32 miles) SE of Segovia

Aside from Toledo, the most important excursion from Madrid is to the austere royal monastery of San Lorenzo de El Escorial. Philip II ordered the construction of this granite-and-slate behemoth in 1563, 2 years after he moved his capital to Madrid. Once the haunt of aristocratic Spaniards, El Escorial is now a resort where hotels and restaurants flourish in the summer as hordes come to escape the heat of the capital. Aside from the appeal of its climate, the town of San Lorenzo itself is not very noteworthy. But because of the monastery's size, you might decide to spend a night or two at San Lorenzo—more if you have the time.

San Lorenzo makes a good base for visiting nearby Segovia and Avila, the royal palace at La Granja, the Valley of the Fallen—and the even more distant university city of Salamanca.

ESSENTIALS
GETTING THERE   More than two dozen **trains** depart daily from Madrid's Atocha, Nuevos Ministerios, and Chamartín train stations. During the summer

extra coaches are added. For schedules and information, call ℰ **90-224-02-02.** A one-way fare costs 2.70€, and trip time is a little more than 1 hour.

The railway station is about a mile outside town along Carretera Estación (ℰ **91-890-07-14**). The Herranz bus company meets all arriving trains with a shuttle bus that ferries arriving passengers to and from the Plaza Virgen de Gracia, about a block east of the entrance to the monastery.

Empresa Herranz, Calle Del Rey 27, in El Escorial (ℰ **91-890-41-22** or 91-890-41-25), runs some 40 **buses** per day back and forth between Madrid and El Escorial. On Sunday service is curtailed to 10 buses. Trip time is an hour, and a round-trip fare costs 5.50€. The same company also runs one bus a day to **El Valle de los Caídos (The Valley of the Fallen).** It leaves El Escorial at 3:15pm with a return at 5:30pm. The ride takes only 15 minutes, and a round-trip fare is 8€, El Valle only.

If you're driving, follow the N-VI highway (marked on some maps as A-6) from the northwest perimeter of Madrid toward Lugo, La Coruña, and San Lorenzo de El Escorial. After about a half hour, fork left onto the C-505 toward San Lorenzo de El Escorial. Driving time from Madrid is about an hour.

VISITOR INFORMATION   The **tourist information office,** Calle Grimaldi 2 (ℰ **91-890-53-13;** www.sanlorenzodeelescorial.org), is open Monday through Thursday from 11am to 6pm, Friday through Sunday from 10am to 7pm.

SEEING THE SIGHTS

Casa de Príncipe (Prince's Cottage) ⭐   This small but elaborately decorated 18th-century palace near the railway station was originally a hunting lodge built for Charles III by Juan de Villanueva. Most visitors stay in El Escorial (see listing below) for lunch, visiting the cottage in the afternoon.

Calle Reina s/n. ℰ **91-890-59-03.** Admission included in comprehensive ticket to El Escorial, see below. Sat–Sun and holidays 10am–6:30pm.

El Valle de los Caídos (Valley of the Fallen) ⭐   This is Franco's El Escorial, an architectural marvel that took 2 decades to complete, dedicated to those who died in the Spanish Civil War. Its detractors say it represents the worst of neofascist design; its admirers say they have found renewed inspiration by coming here.

A gargantuan cross nearly 150m (500 ft.) high dominates the Rock of Nava, a peak of the Guadarrama Mountains. Directly under the cross is a basilica with a mosaic vault, completed in 1959. When José Antonio Primo de Rivera, the founder of the Falange party and a Nationalist hero, was buried at El Escorial, many, especially influential monarchists, protested that he was not a royal. Infuriated, Franco decided to erect another monument—this one. Originally it was slated to honor the dead on the Nationalist side only, but the intervention of several parties led to a decision to include all the *caídos* (fallen). In time, the mausoleum claimed Franco as well; his body was interred behind the high altar.

A funicular extends from near the basilica entrance to the base of the gigantic cross on the mountaintop above (where there's a superb view). The fare is 2€, and the funicular runs daily from 10:30am to 1:15pm and 4 to 6pm.

On the other side of the mountain is a Benedictine monastery that has sometimes been dubbed "the Hilton of monasteries" because of its seeming luxury.

ℰ **91-890-56-11.** Admission 5€ adults, 2.90€ students and children. Apr–Sept Tues–Sun 9:30am–6pm; Oct–Mar Tues–Sun 10am–7pm. Bus: Tour buses from Madrid usually include an excursion to the Valley of the Fallen on their 1-day trips to El Escorial (see "Getting There," above). Car: Drive to the valley entrance, about 8km (5 miles) north of El Escorial in the heart of the Guadarrama Mountains. Once here, drive 6km (3½ miles) west along a wooded road to the underground basilica.

Real Monasterio de San Lorenzo de El Escorial ✶✶✶   This huge granite fortress houses a wealth of paintings and tapestries and serves as the burial place for Spanish kings. Intimidating both inside and out because of its sheer size and institutional look, El Escorial took 21 years to complete, a remarkably short time considering the bulk of the building and the primitive construction methods of the day. After his death, the original architect, Juan Bautista de Toledo, was replaced by Juan de Herrera, the greatest architect of Renaissance Spain, who completed the structure.

Philip II, who collected many of the paintings exhibited here in the **New Museums** ✶✶, did not care for El Greco but favored Titian instead. Still, you'll find El Greco's *The Martyrdom of St. Maurice,* rescued from storage, and also his St. Peter. Other superb works include Titian's *Last Supper* and Velázquez's *The Tunic of Joseph.*

The **Royal Library** ✶✶ houses a priceless collection of 60,000 volumes— one of the most significant in the world. The displays range from the handwriting of St. Teresa to medieval instructions on playing chess. See, in particular, the Muslim codices and a Gothic *Cantigas* from the 13th-century reign of Alfonso X ("The Wise").

You can also visit the **Philip II Apartments** ✶✶; they are strictly monastic, and Philip called them the "cell for my humble self" in this "palace for God." Philip became a religious fanatic and requested that his bedroom be erected overlooking the altar of the 90m-high (300-ft.) basilica, which has four organs and a dome based on Michelangelo's drawings for St. Peter's. The choir contains a crucifix by Cellini. By comparison the Throne Room is simple. On the walls are many ancient maps. The Apartments of the Bourbon Kings are lavishly decorated, in contrast to Philip's preference for the ascetic.

Under the altar of the church you'll find one of the most regal mausoleums in the world, the **Royal Pantheon** ✶✶✶, where most of Spain's monarchs from Charles I to Alfonso XII, including Philip II, are buried. In 1993 Don Juan de Borbón, the count of Barcelona and the father of King Juan Carlos (Franco passed over the count and never allowed him to ascend to the throne) was interred nearby. On a lower floor is the "Wedding Cake" tomb for children.

Allow at least 3 hours for a visit. The guided tour doesn't take you to all the sites, but you are free to explore on your own afterward.

Calle Juan de Borbón s/n. ℂ 91-890-59-03. Comprehensive ticket 7€ adults, 3€ children, guided tour 8€. Apr–Sept Tues–Sun 10am–7pm; Oct–Mar Tues–Sun 10am–6pm.

WHERE TO STAY
MODERATE
Hotel Botánico ✶✶   True to its name, the hotel stands in a lovely manicured garden of both indigenous and exotic shrubbery. Although the building is traditionally Castilian, the decor seems vaguely alpine, with wood paneling and beams in the reception rooms. The clean, well-lit rooms are large and comfortable, with especially good beds and bathrooms containing tub/shower combos.

Calle Timoteo Padros 16, 28200 San Lorenzo de El Escorial. ℂ 91-890-78-79. Fax 91-890-81-58. 20 units. 106€–139€ double; 145€–206€ suite. Rates include breakfast. AE, MC, DC, V. Free parking. **Amenities:** Restaurant; bar; pool; room service; babysitting; laundry service; dry cleaning. *In room:* A/C, TV, minibar, hair dryer.

Hotel Victoria Palace ✶   The Victoria Palace, with its view of El Escorial, is a traditional establishment that has been modernized without losing its special aura of style and comfort. It is surrounded by beautiful gardens and has an outdoor swimming pool. The good-size rooms (some with private terraces) are well furnished and maintained, each with a quality mattress plus a small, tiled, and immaculately kept bathroom, often with a tub and shower combo. The rates are reasonable enough, and a bargain for a government-rated four-star hotel.

Calle Juan de Toledo 4, 28200 San Lorenzo de El Escorial. ℂ **91-896-98-90.** Fax 91-896-98-96. www.hotel victoriapalace.com. 87 units. 112€–130€ double; 148€–215€ suite. AE, DC, MC, V. Parking 11€. **Amenities:** Restaurant; bar; pool; room service; babysitting; laundry service; dry cleaning. *In room:* TV, hair dryer, safe.

INEXPENSIVE

Hostal Cristina   An excellent budget choice, this hotel is run by the Delgado family, which opened it in the mid-1980s. It doesn't pretend to compete with comfort and amenities of the Victoria Palace or even the Miranda & Suizo (see below), but it has its devotees nonetheless. About 45m (50 yd.) from the monastery, it stands in the center of town, offering clean and comfortable but simply furnished rooms. The beds have firm mattresses, and accommodations range from small to medium, each equipped with a small tiled bathroom with a tub/shower combination. The helpful staff will direct you to the small garden. Parking is available along the street.

Juan de Toledo 6, 28200 San Lorenzo de El Escorial. ℂ **91-890-19-61.** Fax 91-890-12-04. 16 units. 41€– 45€ double. MC, V. **Amenities:** Lounge. *In room:* TV.

Miranda & Suizo ℱ   On a tree-lined street in the heart of town within easy walking distance of the monastery, this excellent middle-bracket establishment ranks as a leading government-rated two-star hotel. It's the second choice in town, with rooms not quite as comfortable as those at the Victoria Palace. The Victorian-style building has good guest rooms nevertheless, some with terraces. Many of the rooms are rather spacious and each comes with a well-maintained private bathroom with tub/shower combo. The furnishings are comfortable, the beds often made of brass; sometimes you'll find fresh flowers on the tables. In summer, there is outside dining. Parking is available nearby for 6€ per day.

Calle Floridablanca 20, 28200 San Lorenzo de El Escorial. ℂ **91-890-47-11.** Fax 91-890-43-58. www.miranda suizo.com. 52 units. Sun–Thurs 81€ double; Fri–Sat 84€ double; Sun–Thurs 120€ junior suite; Fri–Sat 128€ junior suite. AE, DC, MC, V. **Amenities:** Restaurant; bar; laundry service; dry cleaning. *In room:* A/C, TV, mini-bar, hair dryer.

WHERE TO DINE
MODERATE

Charolés   SPANISH/INTERNATIONAL   The thick, solid walls of this establishment date, according to its managers, "from the monastic age"—and probably predate the town's larger and better-known monastery of El Escorial. The restaurant within was established around 1980 and has been known ever since as the best dining room in town. It has a flower-ringed outdoor terrace for use during nice weather. The cuisine doesn't quite rate a star, but chances are you'll be satisfied. The wide choice of menu items based entirely on fresh fish and meats includes grilled hake with green or hollandaise sauce, shellfish soup, pepper steak, a *pastel* (pie) of fresh vegetables with crayfish, and herb-flavored baby lamb chops. A strawberry or kiwi tart is a good dessert choice.

Calle Floridablanca 24. ℂ **91-890-59-75.** Reservations required. Main courses 18€–25€. AE, DC, MC, V. Daily 1–4pm and 9pm–midnight.

EL ESCORIAL AFTER DARK

No longer the dead place it was during the long Franco era, the town now comes alive at night, fueled by the throngs of young people who pack into the bars and taverns, especially those along Calle Rey and Calle Floridablanca. Some of our favorite bars, offering vats of wine or kegs of beer, include the **Piano Bar Regina,** Floridablanca (© **91-890-68-43**); **Abadía,** Leindro Rubio 3 (© **91-890-47-10**); and **Don Felipe II,** Floridablanca (© **91-896-07-65**). The hottest disco is **Move it,** Plaza de Santiago 11 (© **91-890-54-91**), which rarely imposes a cover unless some special group is featured.

4 Segovia ⟨★⟨★⟨★

87km (54 miles) NW of Madrid, 68km (42 miles) NE of Avila

Less commercial than Toledo, Segovia more than anywhere else typifies the glory of Old Castile. Wherever you look, you'll see reminders of a golden era, whether it's the most spectacular Alcázar on the Iberian Peninsula or the well-preserved, still-functioning Roman aqueduct.

Segovia lies on the slope of the Guadarrama Mountains, where the Eresma and Clamores rivers converge. This ancient city stands in the center of the most castle-rich part of Castile. Isabella herself was proclaimed queen of Castile here in 1474.

The narrow, winding streets of this hill city must be covered on foot to fully view the Romanesque churches and 15th-century palaces along the way.

ESSENTIALS

GETTING THERE   Nine **trains** leave Madrid's Chamartín Railway Station every day, arriving 2 hours later in Segovia, where you can board bus no. 3, departing every quarter hour for the Plaza Mayor. The trains that leave from Chamartín first travel through Atocha station, making it closer to some travelers' hotels. A one-way rail fare costs 5€. The station at Segovia is on the Paseo Obispo Quesada s/n (© **90-224-02-02**), a 20-minute walk southeast of the town center.

Buses arrive and depart from the Estacionamiento Municipal de Autobuses, Paseo de Ezequiel González 10 (© **92-142-77-07**), near the corner of the Avenida Fernández Ladreda and the steeply sloping Paseo Conde de Sepúlveda. There are 10 to 15 buses a day to and from Madrid (which depart from Paseo de la Florida 11; Metro: Norte), and about four a day traveling between Avila and Segovia. One-way tickets from Madrid cost 5.35€.

If you're driving, take the N-VI (on some maps it's known as the A-6) or the Autopista del Nordeste northwest from Madrid, toward León and Lugo. At the junction with Route 110 (signposted SEGOVIA), turn northeast.

VISITOR INFORMATION   The **tourist information office,** Plaza Mayor 10 (© **92-146-03-34;** www.infosegovia.com), is open Monday through Friday from 9am to 3pm and 5 to 7pm, Saturday and Sunday from 10am to 2pm and 5 to 8pm.

EXPLORING SEGOVIA

You'll find the best **shopping** between the Roman aqueduct, the cathedral, and the Alcázar. Head especially for Calle de Juan Bravo, Calle Daoiz, and Calle Marqués del Arco. Although their merchandise is mirrored by other shops nearby, two of the most appealing shops for ceramic pottery, woodcarvings, wrought iron, and art objects include **Salvador Lucio,** Calle Marqués del Arco 30 (© **92-146-05-52**), and **Kokul Artesanía,** Calle Marqués del Arco 20 (© **92-146-04-50**).

Cabildo Catedral de Segovia ✿✿ Constructed between 1515 and 1558, this is the last Gothic cathedral built in Spain. Fronting the historic Plaza Mayor, it stands on the spot where Isabella I was proclaimed queen of Castile. Affectionately called *la dama de las catedrales,* it contains numerous treasures, such as the Blessed Sacrament Chapel (created by the flamboyant Churriguera), stained-glass windows, elaborately carved choir stalls, and 16th- and 17th-century paintings, including a reredos portraying the deposition of Christ from the cross by Juan de Juni. The **cloisters** ✿ are older than the cathedral, dating from an earlier church that was destroyed in the so-called War of the Communeros. Inside the cathedral museum you'll find jewelry, paintings, and a collection of rare antique manuscripts.

Plaza Catedral, Marqués del Arco. ✆ **92-146-22-05.** Admission to cathedral, cloisters, museum, and chapel room 2€ adults, free for children under 12. Spring and summer daily 9am–7pm; off-season daily 9:30am–6pm.

El Alcázar ✿ View the Alcázar first from below, at the junction of the Clamores and Eresma rivers. It is on the west side of Segovia, so you may not spot it when you first enter the city. But that's part of the surprise.

The castle dates from the 12th century, but a large segment containing its Moorish ceilings was destroyed by fire in 1862. Restoration has continued over the years.

Royal romance is associated with the Alcázar. Isabella first met Ferdinand here, and today you can see a facsimile of her dank bedroom. Once married, she wasn't foolish enough to surrender her royal rights, as replicas of the thrones attest—both are equally proportioned. Philip II married his fourth wife, Anne of Austria, here as well.

Walk the battlements of this once-impregnable castle, from which its occupants hurled boiling oil onto the enemy below. Ascend the hazardous stairs of the tower, originally built by Isabella's father as a prison, for a panoramic view of Segovia.

Plaza de La Reina Victoria Eugenia. ✆ **92-146-07-59.** Admission 3.10€ adults, 2.20€ children 6–16, free for children 5 and under. Apr–Sept daily 10am–7pm; Oct–Mar daily 10am–6pm. Bus: 3. Take either Calle Vallejo, Calle de Velarde, Calle de Daoiz, or Paseo de Ronda.

Esteban Vicente Contemporary Art Museum In the heart of the city in a newly renovated 15th-century palace, a permanent collection of some 142 works by the abstract-expressionist artist Esteban Vicente has opened. The Spanish-born artist, now in his late 90s, has described himself as "an American painter, with very deep and loving Spanish roots." Born in a small town outside Segovia in 1903, he remained in Spain until 1927, eventually (since 1936) residing in New York where he played a pivotal role in the development of American abstract art. Today he is one of the last surviving members of the New York school, whose members included Rothko, de Kooning, and Pollock. Vicente's paintings and collages convey his sense of structure and feelings of luminous serenity with colors of astonishing vibrancy, brilliance, and range. His paintings are shown at the Metropolitan Museum of Art, the Museum of Modern Art, and the Whitney, all in New York—and now Segovia.

Plazuela de las Bellas Artes. ✆ **92-146-20-10.** Admission 2.40€ adults, 1.20€ seniors and students, free for children under 12. Admission free on Thurs. Tues–Sat 11am–2pm and 4–7pm; Sun 11am–2pm.

Iglesia de la Vera Cruz Built in either the 11th or 12th century by the Knights Templar, this is the most fascinating Romanesque church in Segovia. It stands in isolation outside the walls of the old town overlooking the Alcázar. Its unusual 12-sided design is believed to have been copied from the Church of the Holy Sepulchre in Jerusalem. Inside you'll find an inner temple, rising two floors, where the knights conducted nightlong vigils as part of their initiation rites.

Carretera de Zamarramala. ℂ **92-143-14-75**. Admission 1.50€. Apr–Sept Tues–Sun 10:30am–1:30pm and 3:30–7pm; Oct–Mar Tues–Sun 10:30am–1:30pm and 3:30–6pm. Closed Nov.

Monasterio del Parral ✦   The restored "Monastery of the Grape" was established for the Hieronymites by Henry IV, a Castilian king (1425–74) known as "The Impotent." The monastery lies across the Eresma River about a half mile north of the city. The church is a medley of styles and decoration—mainly Gothic, Renaissance, and Plateresque. The facade was never completed, and the monastery itself was abandoned when religious orders were suppressed in 1835. Today, it's been restored and is once again the domain of the *jerónimos,* Hieronymus priests and brothers. Inside, a robed monk will show you the various treasures of the order, including a polychrome altarpiece and the alabaster tombs of the Marquis of Villena and his wife—all the work of Juan Rodríguez.

Calle del Marqués de Villena (across the Eresma River). ℂ **92-143-12-98**. Free admission. Mon–Sat 10am–2:30pm and 4–6:30pm; Sun 10–11:30am and 4–6:30pm. Take Ronda de Santa Lucía, cross the Eresma River, and head down Calle del Marqués de Villena.

Roman Aqueduct (Acueducto Romano) ✦✦✦   This architectural marvel was built by the Romans nearly 2,000 years ago. Constructed of mortarless granite, it consists of 118 arches, and in one two-tiered section it soars 28.5m (95 ft.) to its highest point. The Spanish call it El Puente. It spans the Plaza del Azoguejo, the old market square, stretching nearly 720m (800 yd.). When the Moors took Segovia in 1072, they destroyed 36 arches, which were later rebuilt under Ferdinand and Isabella in 1484.

Plaza del Azoguejo.

WHERE TO STAY
EXPENSIVE
Parador de Segovia ✦✦✦   This 20th-century tile-roofed parador sits on a hill 3km (2 miles) northeast of Segovia (take the N-601). It stands on an estate called El Terminillo, which used to be famous for its vines and almond trees, a few of which still survive. If you have a car and can get a reservation, book in here; you'll pay more, but it's much more comfortable here than at either Los Arcos or Los Linajes (see below). The good-size rooms are deluxe, containing such extras as tiled bathrooms with shower/tub combos. Furnishings are tasteful, and large windows open onto panoramic views of the countryside. Some of the older rooms here are a bit dated, however, with lackluster decor.

The parador has one of the better restaurants in Segovia; its windows open onto a panoramic view of the mountains of Sierra de Guadarrama. A complete meal here, of either regional specialties or international dishes, costs around 25€.

Carretera Valladolid s/n (N-601), 40003 Segovia. ℂ **92-144-37-37**. Fax 92-143-73-62. 113 units. 116€ double; from 185€ suite. AE, DC, MC, V. Covered parking 6€ free outside. **Amenities:** Restaurant; bar; 2 pools; tennis courts; fitness center; sauna; room service; babysitting; laundry service; dry cleaning. *In room:* A/C, TV, minibar, hair dryer, safe.

MODERATE
Hotel Infanta Isabel ✦   Named after Queen Isabel, the great-grandmother of the present king, the hotel stands overlooking the charming central square and is within a stone's throw of the majestic cathedral. This is where the queen

would stay when on her way to the nearby summer palace of La Granja. The present owners have modernized the interior considerably but a good deal of the building's 19th-century grandeur, such as the staircase, remains. Each room is decorated in its own style with an eye to comfort. The hotel has every convenience, including modern bathrooms containing tub/shower combos.

Plaza Mayor, 40001 Segovia. ✆ 92-146-13-00. Fax 92-146-22-17. www.hotelinfantaisabel.com. 37 units. 71€–98€ double. AC, DC, MC, V. Parking 9€. **Amenities:** Bar; lounge; room service; babysitting; laundry service; dry cleaning. In room: A/C, TV, minibar, hair dryer, safe.

Hotel Los Arcos   This concrete-and-glass five-story structure opened in 1987 and is generally cited as the second-best in town. Well run and modern, it attracts the business traveler, but tourists frequent the place in droves as well. Rooms are generally spacious but furnished in a standard international bland way, except for the beautiful rug-dotted parquet floors. There are built-in furnishings and tiny bathrooms with tub/shower combos. Rooms are well kept, with good beds, although some furnishings look worn.

Even if you don't stay here, consider dining at the hotel's La Cocina de Segovia, which is the only hotel dining room that competes successfully with Mesón de Cándido (see "Where to Dine," below). As at the nearby competitors, roast suckling pig and roast Segovia lamb—perfectly cooked in specially made ovens—are the specialties. In all, it's a smart, efficiently run, and pleasant choice, if not a terribly exciting one.

Paseo de Ezequiel González 26, 40002 Segovia. ✆ 92-143-74-62. Fax 92-142-81-61. 59 units. 80€–96€ double; 126€–144€ suite. AE, DC, MC, V. Parking 8€. **Amenities:** Restaurant; bar; lounge; health club; room service; babysitting; laundry service; dry cleaning. In room: A/C, TV, minibar, hair dryer, safe.

Hotel Los Linajes ✿   In the historical district of St. Stephen at the northern edge of the old town stands this hotel, the former home of a Segovian noble family. While the facade dates from the 11th century, the interior is modern, except for some Castilian decorations. Following a 1996 renovation, the hotel looks a bit brighter and fresher than Los Arcos. Bedrooms, in a range of sizes and shapes, are comfortable with fine beds and tidily kept tiled bathrooms with showers. One of the best hotels in town, Los Linajes has gardens and patios where guests can enjoy a panoramic view over the city.

Doctor Velasco 9, 40003 Segovia. ✆ 92-146-04-75. Fax 92-146-04-79. 53 units. 76€–92€ double; from 108€–119€ suite. AE, DC, MC, V. Parking 9.60€. Bus: 1. **Amenities:** Cafe; bar; lounge; room service; laundry service; dry cleaning. In room: A/C, TV.

INEXPENSIVE

Las Sirenas   Standing on the most charming old plaza in Segovia opposite the Church of St. Martín, this hotel is from 1950 and has been renovated several times. However, it has long since lost its Franco-era supremacy to Los Arcos (see above). Modest and well maintained, it is decorated in a conservative style. Each room is filled with functional, simple furniture, good beds, and neatly kept bathrooms with showers. However, rooms are somewhat small. Breakfast is the only meal served, but the staff at the reception desk can direct clients to cafes and *tascas* nearby.

Juan Bravo 30, 40001 Segovia. ✆ 92-146-26-63. Fax 92-146-26-57. 39 units. 55€–65€ double. AE, DC, MC, V. **Amenities:** Breakfast salon. In room: A/C, TV.

WHERE TO DINE

El Bernardino CASTILIAN   El Bernardino, a 3-minute walk west of the Roman aqueduct, is built like an old tavern. Lanterns hang from beamed ceilings, and the view over the red-tile rooftops of the city is delightful. There is also a summer terrace. The *menú del día* may include roast veal with potatoes, flan or ice cream, plus bread and wine. You might begin your meal with *sopa castellana* (soup made with ham, sausage, bread, egg, and garlic). The roast dishes are exceptional here, including roast suckling pig from a special oven and roast baby lamb. You can also order grilled rib steak or stewed partridge.

Cervantes 2. ℂ **92-146-24-74.** Reservations recommended. Main courses 6€–16€; fixed-price menu 21€. AE, DC, MC, V. Daily 1–4pm and 8–11pm.

Mesón de Cándido ⋆⋆ CASTILIAN   It's still the best. For years this beautiful old Spanish inn, standing on the eastern edge of the old town, has maintained a monopoly on the tourist trade. Apart from the hotel restaurants—specifically La Cocina de Segovia at Los Arcos—it is the town's finest dining choice. The Cándido family took it over in 1905, and fourth- and fifth-generation family members still run the place, having fed, over the years, everybody from Hemingway to Nixon. The oldest part of the restaurant dates from 1822, and the restaurant has gradually been enlarged since then. The proprietor of the House of Cándido is known as *mesonero mayor de Castilla* (the major innkeeper of Castile). He's been decorated with more medals and honors than paella has grains of rice. The restaurant's popularity can be judged by the crowds of hungry diners who fill every seat in the six dining rooms. The a la carte menu includes those two regional staples: *cordero asado* (roast baby lamb) and *cochinillo asado* (roast suckling pig). Some of the seating areas are cramped and confining. Opt for a table on the second floor, facing the Aqueduct, or one of the outdoor cafe tables in front.

Plaza del Azoguejo 5. ℂ **92-142-59-11.** Reservations recommended. Main courses 9€–16€. AE, DC, MC, V. Daily 12:30–4:30pm and 8pm–midnight.

Mesón de José María SEGOVIAN   This centrally located bar and restaurant 1 block east of the Plaza Mayor serves quality regional cuisine in a rustic stucco-and-brick dining room. Before dinner, locals crowd in for tapas at the bar, then move into the dining room for such Castilian specialties as roast suckling pig, rural-style conger eel, and freshly caught sea bream. Try the cream of crabmeat soup, roasted peppers, salmon with scrambled eggs, house-style hake, or grilled veal steak. For dessert, a specialty is ice-cream tart with a whiskey sauce.

Cronista Lecea 11. ℂ **92-146-11-11.** Reservations recommended. Main courses 5.50€–19€; fixed-price menu 24€–36€. AE, DC, MC, V. Daily 1–4pm and 8:30–11:30pm.

Restaurante Duque CASTILIAN   Set on the street that links Segovia's ancient Roman aqueduct with the city's medieval core, this restaurant is from 1895. It has fed many successive generations of local residents ever since. The severely dignified interior looks as though it hasn't changed since it was built. The decor includes heavy ceiling beams, exposed stone, rough-textured plaster, and battered 19th-century farming artifacts. Come here for the kind of cuisine that was in vogue when the restaurant was built, with very few concessions to modern tastes. There's an excellent cream of crabmeat soup; roasted suckling pig slow-cooked on a spit; savory roasted lamb with aromatic rosemary, thyme, and garlic; and different preparations of grilled chicken, veal, beef, and pork. An excellent accompaniment for any of these would be kidney beans cooked with chunks of salted cod, fresh spinach, and mounds of mashed potatoes or rice.

Calle Cervantes 12. ℂ **92-146-24-87.** Reservations recommended. Main courses 12€–21€. AE, DC, MC, V. Daily 12:30–5pm and 8–11:30pm.

A SIDE TRIP TO LA GRANJA

To reach La Granja, 11km (7 miles) southeast of Segovia, you c[...] minute bus ride from the center of the city. Six to 10 buses a d[...] Paseo Conde de Sepulveda at Avenida Fernández Ladreda. A one-way fare [...] .70€. For information, call © **92-142-77-07.**

Palacio Real de La Granja   San Ildefonso de la Granja was the summer palace of the Bourbon kings of Spain who attempted to replicate the grandeur of Versailles in the province of Segovia. In that ambition, they fell far from the mark, as today's slightly unkempt grounds reveal. Set against the snowcapped Sierra de Guadarrama, the slate-roofed palace dominates the village that grew up around it (a summer resort these days).

The builder of La Granja was Philip V, grandson of Louis XIV and the first Bourbon king of Spain (his body, along with that of his 2nd queen, Isabel de Fernesio, is interred in a mausoleum in the Collegiate Church). Philip V was born at Versailles on December 19, 1683, which may explain why he wanted to re-create that atmosphere at Segovia.

At one time a farm stood on the grounds of what is now the palace—hence its totally incongruous name, *la granja,* meaning "the farm." The palace was built in the first part of the 18th century. Inside you'll find valuable antiques (many in the Empire style), paintings, and a remarkable collection of Flemish tapestries, as well as those based on Goya cartoons from the Royal Factory in Madrid.

Most visitors seem to find a stroll through the **gardens** more pleasing, so allow adequate time for that. The fountain statuary is a riot of cavorting gods and nymphs hiding indiscretions. The gardens are studded with chestnuts and elms.

Plaza de España 17, San Ildefonso (Segovia). © **92-147-00-19.** Admission 5€ adults, 2.50€ children 5–14, free for children 4 and under. Apr–Sept Tues–Sun 10am–6pm; Oct–Mar Tues–Sat 10am–1:30pm and 3–5pm, Sun 10am–2pm.

SEGOVIA AFTER DARK

Just head for the Plaza Mayor, Plaza Azoguejo, and the busy Calle del Carmen that runs into the Plaza Azoguejo. You're sure to find some fun in the scattering of simple bars and cafes that grow more crowded at night as the days grow hotter. If you want to go dancing, two of the most popular discos include **Mansión,** Calle de Juan Bravo (no phone), which is open nightly from 11pm till dawn for dancing, drinking, and flirting with the 20- to 30-year-old crowd, and the somewhat more stylish competitor, **Sabat,** Paseo del Salón (no phone), which is open nightly from 8pm till dawn, a bit more atmospheric and frequented by people from age 25 to around 50.

5 Alcalá de Henares

29km (18 miles) E of Madrid

History hasn't been kind to this ancient town, which once flourished with colleges, monasteries, and palaces. When a university was founded here in the 15th century, Alcalá became a cultural and intellectual center. Europe's first polyglot Bible (supposedly with footnotes in the original Greek and Hebrew) was published here in 1517, but the town declined during the 1800s when the university moved to Madrid. Today, Alcalá is one of the main centers of North American academics in Spain, cooperating with the Fulbright Commission, Michigan State University, and Madrid's Washington Irving Center. Overall, the city has taken on new life. Commuters have turned it into a virtual suburb, dubbing it "the bedroom of Madrid."

SSENTIALS

GETTING THERE   **Trains** travel between Madrid's Atocha or Chamartín station and Alcalá de Henares every day and evening. Service is every 15 minutes (trip time: 30 min.) and round-trip fare from Madrid costs 3.35€. The train station (© 90-224-02-02) in Alcalá is at Paseo Estación.

Buses from Madrid depart from Av. América 18 (Metro: América), every 15 minutes. A one-way fare is 1.75€. Bus service is provided by Continental-Auto, and the Alcalá bus station is on Av. Guadalajara 36 (© 91-888-16-22), 2 blocks past Calle Libreros.

Alcalá lies adjacent to the main national highway (N-11), connecting Madrid with eastern Spain. As you leave central Madrid, follow signs for Barajas Airport and Barcelona.

VISITOR INFORMATION   The **tourist information office,** Callejón de Santa María 1 (© 91-889-26-94; www.alcaladehenares-turismo.com), provides a map showing all the local attractions. It is open daily from 10am to 2pm and 4 to 6:30pm (until 7:30pm July–Sept).

EXPLORING ALCALA DE HENARES

Capilla de San Ildefonso
Next door to the Colegio is the Capilla de San Ildefonso, the 15th-century chapel of the old university. It also houses the Italian marble tomb of Cardinal Cisneros, the founder of the original university. This chapel also has an *artesonado* (artisan's) ceiling and intricately stuccoed walls.

Plaza San Diego. © 91-882-13-54 or 91-885-40-00. Admission included in tour of Colegio (see below). Hours same as Colegio (see below).

Colegio Mayor de San Ildefonso
Adjacent to the main square, Plaza de Cervantes, is the Colegio Mayor de San Ildefonso, where Lope de Vega and other famous Spaniards studied. You can see some of their names engraved on plaques in the examination room. The old university's Plateresque **facade** ✪ dates from 1543. From here you can walk across the Patio of Saint Thomas (from 1662) and the Patio of the Philosophers to reach the Patio of the Three Languages (from 1557), where Greek, Latin, and Hebrew were once taught. Here is the *Paraninfo* (great hall or old examination room), now used for special events. The hall has a Mudéjar carved-panel ceiling. The Paraninfo is entered through a restaurant, Hostería del Estudiante (see "Where to Dine," below).

Plaza San Diego. © 91-993-94. Admission 2.10€. Tours (mandatory) Mon–Fri 11:30am, 12:30, 1:30, 5, and 6pm; Sat–Sun 11 and 11:45am, 12:30, 1:15, 2, 4:30, 5:15, 6, 6:45, and 7:30pm.

Museo Casa Natal de Cervantes
Visitors come to see the birthplace of Spain's literary giant Miguel de Cervantes, the creator of *Don Quixote,* who may have been born here in 1547. This 16th-century Castilian house was reconstructed in 1956 around a beautiful little courtyard, which has a wooden gallery supported by pillars with Renaissance-style capitals, plus an old well. The house contains many Cervantes manuscripts and, of course, copies of *Don Quixote,* one of the world's most widely published books (available here in many languages).

Calle Mayor 50. © 91-889-96-54. Free admission. Tues–Sun 10:15am–1:30pm and 4:15–6:30pm.

WHERE TO DINE

Hostería del Estudiante ✪ CASTILIAN
Located within the university complex, this remarkable 1510 building is an attraction in its own right. It opened as a restaurant in 1929, and its typically Castilian recipes haven't been

altered since. In the cooler months, if you arrive early you can lounge in front of a 4.5m (15-ft.) open fireplace. Oil lamps hang from the ceiling, pigskins are filled with local wine, and rope-covered chairs and high-backed carved settees capture the spirit of the past. Run by the Spanish parador system, the restaurant offers a tasty (and huge) three-course set-price lunch or dinner featuring such regional specialties as roast suckling lamb, *huevos comigos* (3 eggs fried with mushrooms), and trout Navarre style. For dessert, try the cheese of La Mancha.

Calle Colegios 3. ☎ **91-888-03-30.** Reservations recommended. Main courses 21€–30€; fixed-price menus 23€. AE, DC, MC, V. Daily 1–4pm; Mon–Sat 9–11:30pm; Sun 9–10:30pm. Closed Aug.

6 Chinchón ⭐

52km (32 miles) SE of Madrid, 26km (16 miles) NE of Aranjuez

The main attraction of Chinchón is the *cuevas* **(caves),** where Anís de Chinchón, an aniseed liqueur, is manufactured. You can buy bottles of the liqueur in Plaza Mayor, at the center of town. **Plaza Mayor** ⭐⭐ or the main square of town is the architectural highlight of Chinchón. Dominated by its church, the arcaded square is surrounded by three-story frame houses with wooden balconies. In summer bullfights are presented on the square.

Wander along the town's steep and narrow streets, past houses with large bays and spacious carriageways. Although closed to the public, the 15th-century **Chinchón Castle,** seat of the Condes of Chinchón, can be viewed from outside. The most interesting church, **Nuestra Señora de la Asunción,** dating from the 16th and 17th centuries, contains a painting by Goya.

GETTING THERE   Chinchón is most often visited from Aranjuez (see earlier in this chapter), which is only a 15-minute ride away. **Buses** run twice a day from Aranjuez but only Monday through Friday, leaving from Calle Almibar next to the Plaza de Toros in Aranjuez. Schedules tend to be erratic, so call for information (☎ **91-891-01-83**). A one-way fare is 1.10€.

You can drive from Alcalá to Toledo, bypassing Madrid by taking the C-300 in a southwesterly arc around the capital. About halfway there, follow signs to CUEVAS DE CHINCHON. Another option is to take the E-901 southeast of Madrid toward Valencia, turning southwest at the turnoff for Chinchón.

WHERE TO STAY

Hotel Nuevo Chinchón *Value*   On the outskirts, this is the town's second-best address, rated just under the parador. This is a relatively new hotel, built in 1994, whose owners have invested lots of time and money in making it appear older and more nostalgic than it is. Low slung and modern from the outside, it contains small bedrooms whose headboards are painted in old-fashioned folkloric patterns. All units contain bathrooms equipped with showers. The overall effect is cozy, with a sense of low-key charm.

Urbanización Nuevo Chinchón, Carretera a Titulcia, Km 1.5, 28370 Chinchón. ☎ **91-894-05-44.** Fax 91-893-51-28. nuevochinchon@teleline.es. 17 units. 59€–66€ double. AE, MC, V. Free parking. **Amenities:** Restaurant; bar; pool; room service; babysitting; laundry service; dry cleaning. *In room:* A/C, TV, hair dryer, safe.

Parador de Chinchón ⭐⭐⭐   Set near the town center, this hotel lies within the carefully restored 17th-century walls of what was originally an Augustinian convent. After a stint as both a civic jail and a courthouse, it was transformed in 1972 into a government-run parador and is the best place to stay in town. A team of architects and designers converted it handsomely, with glass-walled hallways opening onto a stone-sided courtyard. The hotel has two bars and two dining halls. Severely dignified rooms still manage to convey their ecclesiastical origins. Rooms range from small to medium, each with a quality mattress and fine linen along with well-maintained tiled bathrooms with showers.

Av. Generalísimo 1, 28370 Chinchón. (C) **91-894-08-36.** Fax 91-894-09-08. 38 units. 110€ double; 148€ suite. AE, DC, MC, V. Parking 9€. **Amenities:** Restaurant; bar; pool; room service; babysitting; laundry service; dry cleaning. *In room:* A/C, TV, minibar, hair dryer, safe.

WHERE TO DINE

Mesón Cuevas del Vino ⟨✦⟩ SPANISH   This establishment is known for its wine cellars, and you can sample the stock at lunch or dinner. Hanging from the rafters are hams cured by the owners, along with flavorful homemade spiced sausages. Chunks of ham and sausage cooked in oil, plus olives and crunchy bread, are served. Your meal might begin with sliced *chorizo* (Spanish sausage); blood pudding; slices of La Mancha cheese; *sopa castellana* made with garlic, ham, and eggs; and thin-sliced cured ham. Main courses place heavy emphasis on roast suckling lamb and pig that emerge crackling from a wood-burning oven. Desserts include flan, biscuits coated in cinnamon and sugar, and liquefied and sweetened almonds presented in a soupy mixture in a bowl.

Benito Horteliano 13. (C) **91-894-02-85.** Reservations recommended on holidays. Main courses 5€–16€. No credit cards. Wed–Mon 1:30–4pm and 8–11pm. Closed Aug 1–20.

7 Avila ⟨✦⟩⟨✦⟩

109km (68 miles) NW of Madrid, 67km (41½ miles) SW of Segovia

The ancient city of Avila is completely encircled by well-preserved 11th-century walls, which are among the most important medieval relics in Europe. The city has been declared a national landmark, and there is little wonder why. The walls aren't the only attraction, however. Avila has several Romanesque churches, Gothic palaces, and a fortified cathedral. It is among some 80 cities designated by UNESCO as World Heritage Sites (6 of these are in Spain; the other 5 are Santiago de Compostela, Segovia, Toledo, Cáceres, and Salamanca).

Avila's spirit and legend are most linked to St. Teresa, born here in 1515. This Carmelite nun, who helped defeat the Reformation and founded a number of convents, experienced visions of the devil and angels piercing her heart with burning hot lances. She was eventually imprisoned in Toledo. Many legends sprang up after her death, including the belief that a hand severed from her body could perform miracles. Finally, in 1622, she was declared a saint.

Note: Bring warm clothes if you're visiting in the early spring.

ESSENTIALS

GETTING THERE   There are more than two dozen **trains** leaving daily from Madrid for Avila, about a 1½- to 2-hour trip each way. Depending on the schedule, trains depart from Chamartín, Atocha, and Príncipe (Norte) railway stations. The 8am train from Atocha, arriving in Avila at 9:26am, is a good choice, considering all there is to see. Tickets cost 5€ to 14€. The Avila station is at Avenida José Antonio ((C) **90-224-02-02**), about a mile east of the Old City. You'll find taxis lined up in front of Avila's railway station and at the more central Plaza Santa Teresa. For taxi information, call (C) **92-025-09-00.**

Buses leave Madrid daily from Paseo Florida 11 (Metro: Norte), in front of the Norte railway station. In Avila the bus terminal ((C) **92-025-65-05**) is at the corner of Avenida Madrid and Avenida Portugal, northeast of the center of town. A one-way ticket from Madrid costs 6€.

To drive there, exit Madrid from its northwest perimeter and head northwest on highway N-VI (A-6), toward La Coruña, eventually forking southwest to Avila. Driving time is around 1½ hours.

VISITOR INFORMATION   The **tourist information office,** Plaza Catedral 4 (© **92-021-13-87**), is open Monday through Friday from 9am to 2pm and 5 to 7pm, Saturday and Sunday from 10am to 2pm and 5 to 8pm.

EXPLORING THE TOWN

Begun on orders of Alfonso VI as part of the general reconquest of Spain from the Moors, the 11th-century **Walls of Avila** ★★, built over Roman fortifications, took 9 years to complete. They average 10m (33 ft.) in height and have 88 semicircular towers and more than 2,300 battlements. Of the nine gateways, the two most famous are the St. Vincent and the Alcázar, both on the eastern side. In many respects the walls are best viewed from the west. Whatever your preferred point of view, you can drive along their entire length: 2km (1½ miles).

Basílica de San Vicente ★★   Outside the city walls at the northeast corner of the medieval ramparts, this Romanesque-Gothic church in faded sandstone encompasses styles from the 12th to the 14th century. It consists of a huge nave and a trio of apses. The eternal struggle between good and evil is depicted on a cornice on the southern portal. The **western portal** ★★, dating from the 13th century, contains Romanesque carvings. Inside is the tomb of St. Vincent, martyred on this site in the 4th century. The tomb's medieval carvings, which depict his torture and subsequent martyrdom, are fascinating.

Plaza de San Vicente. © **92-025-52-30.** Admission 1.20€. Daily 10am–2pm and 4–6:30pm.

Carmelitas Descalzas de San José (Barefoot Carmelites of St. Joseph)
Also known as the *Convento de las Madres* (Convent of the Mothers), this is the first convent founded by St. Teresa, who started the Reform of Carmel in 1562. Two churches are here—the primitive one, where the first Carmelite nuns took the habit, and one built by Francisco de Mora, architect of Philip III, after the saint's death. The museum displays many relics, including, of all things, St. Teresa's left clavicle.

Las Madres 4. © **92-022-21-27.** Admission to museum 1€. Apr–Oct daily 10am–1:30pm and 4–7pm; off-season daily 10am–1:30pm and 3–6pm. From Plaza de Santa Teresa and its nearby Church of San Pedro, follow Calle del Duque de Alba for about 2 blocks.

Catedral de Avila ★★   Built into the old ramparts of Avila, this cold, austere cathedral and fortress (begun in 1099) bridges the gap between the Romanesque and the Gothic, and, as such, enjoys a certain distinction in Spanish architecture. One local writer compared it to a granite mountain. The interior is unusual, built with a mottled red-and-white stone.

Like most European cathedrals, Avila lost its purity of design through the years as new chapels and wings—one completely in the Renaissance mode—were added. A Dutch artist, Cornelius, designed the seats of the choir stalls, also in Renaissance style, and the principal chapel holds a reredos showing the life of Christ by Pedro Berruguete, Juan de Borgoña, and Santa Cruz. Behind the chapel the tomb of Bishop Alonso de Madrigal—nicknamed "El Tostado" ("The Parched One") because of its brownish color—is Vasco de Zarza's masterpiece. The Cathedral Museum contains a laminated gold ceiling, a 15th-century triptych, a copy of an El Greco painting, as well as vestments and 15th-century songbooks.

Plaza Catedral. © **92-021-16-41.** Admission 2.50€ adults, free for children under 10. May–Sept daily 9:30am–1:30pm and 3:30–8pm; Oct–Apr daily 10am–1:30pm and 3:30–6pm.

Convento de Santa Teresa   This 17th-century convent and baroque church, 2 blocks southwest of the Plaza de la Victoria, is at the site of St. Teresa's birth. To the right of the convent is the tiny Sala de Reliquias exhibiting some of her relics, including a finger from her right hand, the sole of one of her sandals, and a cord she used to flagellate herself.

Plaza de la Santa 2. ℂ **92-021-10-30.** Admission 2€. Convent May–Sept daily 9:30am–1:30pm and 3:30–9pm; Oct–Apr daily 9:30am–1:30pm and 3:30–8:30pm. Sala de Reliquias daily 9:30am–1:30pm and 3:30–7:30pm. Bus: 1, 3, or 4

Monasterio de Santo Tomás ★   This 15th-century Gothic monastery was once the headquarters of the Inquisition in Avila. For 3 centuries it housed the tomb of Torquemada, the first general inquisitor, whose zeal in organizing the Inquisition made him a notorious figure in Spanish history. Legend has it that after the friars were expelled from the monastery in 1836, a mob of Torquemada-haters ransacked the tomb and burned the remains somewhere outside the city walls. His final burial site is unknown.

Prince John, the only son of Ferdinand and Isabella, was also buried here, in a sumptuous sepulcher in the church transept. The tomb was desecrated during a French invasion; now, only an empty crypt remains.

Visit the Royal Cloisters, in some respects the most interesting architectural feature of the place. In the upper part of the third cloister, you'll find the Museum of Far Eastern Art, which exhibits Vietnamese, Chinese, and Japanese art and handicrafts.

Plaza Granada 1. ℂ **92-035-22-37.** Admission to museum 1.50€; cloisters 1€. Museum Tues–Sun 11am–12:45pm and 4–6pm; cloisters Mon–Sun 10am–1pm and 4–8pm. Bus: 1, 2, or 3.

WHERE TO STAY

Avila is a summer resort—a refuge from Castilian heat—but the hotels are few in number, and the Spanish book nearly all the hotel space in July and August. Make sure to have a reservation in advance. Las Cancelas (see "Where to Dine," below) also rents rooms.

MODERATE

Gran Hotel Palacio de Valderrábanos   Set immediately adjacent to the front entrance of the cathedral behind an entryway that is a marvel of medieval stonework, this is one of the most elegant and historic hotels of Castile. Originally built in the 1300s as a private home by an early bishop of Avila (and a member of the Valderrábanos family), it contains a once-fortified lookout tower (whose circumference encloses one of the suites), high-beamed ceilings, and intricately chiseled stonework. The public rooms have a somber elegance, with slightly faded baronial furniture that adds to the old-fashioned feeling. If possible, ask for a bedroom overlooking the cathedral. Rooms come in a variety of shapes, but each is usually medium in size, well furnished with comfortable beds and firm mattresses. Bathrooms are well organized, with tub/shower combos.

Plaza Catedral 9, 05001 Avila. ℂ **92-021-10-23.** Fax 92-025-16-91. www.palaciovalderranoshotel.com. 73 units. 106€ double; 152€ suite. AE, DC, MC, V. Parking 8€ per day. Bus: 1, 2, or 3. **Amenities:** Restaurant; bar; room service; babysitting; laundry service; dry cleaning. *In room:* A/C, TV, minibar, hair dryer, safe.

Hostería Ayala Berganza ★★ *(Finds)*   This 15th-century building was once the abode of one of Spain's most famous painters, Ignacio Zuloaga (1870–1945). It has been turned into one of the most atmospheric little inns in Castile. Part of the hotel is the original Castilian palace, dating from the 15th century and declared a historic monument, plus a modern structure completed in 1998. The location is next to the Romanesque church of San Millán, only a few minutes walk from the Aqueduct. The hotel lies just outside the ramparts of the center of Segovia, a 5-minute walk to the heart of town and the cathedral. Care and attention went into the design of the modernized bedrooms and two suites, each individually decorated and containing a private bathroom with tub and shower. In a stone-columned central patio, an excellent Castilian cuisine based on seasonal dishes and roasted meats from a wood-fired oven are served.

Calle Carretas 5, 40001 Segovia. ✆ **92-146-04-48.** Fax 92-146-23-77. www.innsofspain.com. 18 units. 110€–133€ double; 165€–190€ suite. Rates include breakfast. AE, MC, V. **Amenities:** Restaurant; coffee shop; bar; business facilities; babysitting; laundry service; garden. *In room:* A/C, TV, minibar, hair dryer, safe.

Hotel Reina Isabel ✦ Cited for its elegant decoration, this hotel stands behind a severe facade but warms considerably once you're inside. Rated four stars by the government, it lies about a 6-minute walk outside the walls of the old city. The interior is classically designed, with separate areas depicting various epochs in Spanish history, complete with furnishings and objets d'art from the 14th to the 18th century, including a magnificent altarpiece from the 15th century. The spacious bedrooms are similarly decorated and furnished with classical motifs, with marble floors and comfortable beds. All have state-of-the-art bathrooms; each unit contains a tub/shower combo, and each suite has a whirlpool tub. The hotel also operates an excellent restaurant, nearby **Copacabana,** San Millán 9 (✆ **92-021-11-10**).

Paseo de la Estación 17, 05001 Avila. ✆ **92-025-10-22.** Fax 92-025-11-73. www.reinaisabel.com. 60 units. 81€–102€ double; 150€ suite. AE, DC, MC, V. Parking 8€. **Amenities:** Restaurant; bar; room service; laundry service; dry cleaning. *In room:* A/C, TV, minibar, hair dryer, safe.

Palacio de Los Velada ✦✦✦ When the Spanish chain Meliá opened this splendid gem to guests in 1995, it quickly became the most sought-after accommodation in the province, surpassing even the government-run paradors. Four centuries ago, this palace sheltered the likes of Charles V and Philip II. Arrayed around a central courtyard, today's hotel offers a luxury that was unimaginable when those kings spent the night.

The styling in the public rooms and the luxuriously furnished guest rooms make even the paradors look like they need a face-lift. Enjoying the best location in town—right in the center near the cathedral—the hotel receives guests in the setting of a medieval palace, with massive stones and antiques throughout. All the modern conveniences, including wide, comfortable beds have been installed, along with state-of-the-art plumbing. Each of the tiled bathrooms is equipped with a combination tub and shower. A shopping arcade is nearby.

Plaza de la Catedral 10, 05001 Avila. ✆ **92-025-51-00.** Fax 92-025-49-00. www.veladahoteles.com. 145 units. 125€ double; 262€ suite. AE, MC, V. Parking 12€. **Amenities:** Restaurant; bar; room service; laundry service; dry cleaning. *In room:* A/C, TV, minibar, hair dryer, safe.

Parador de Avila ✦ Two blocks northwest of Plaza de la Victoria, this parador stands on a ridge overlooking the banks of the Adaja River. Once it was known as the Palace of Benavides, from the 15th century; its facade forms part of the square. The palace has a dignified entranceway with most of its public lounges opening onto a central courtyard with an inner gallery of columns. The recently refurbished rooms contain tasteful furnishings: stone fireplaces, highly polished tile floors, old chests, leather armchairs, paintings, and sculptures. The rooms, generally medium-sized, come with all the modern comforts, including good mattresses and tiled bathrooms equipped with showers.

Marqués de Camales de Chozas 2, 05001 Avila. ℂ **92-021-13-40.** Fax 92-022-61-66. www.parador.es. 61 units. 100€–110€ double; 252€ suite. AE, DC, MC, V. Free outside parking; garage 10€. **Amenities:** Restaurant; bar; room service; laundry service; dry cleaning. *In room:* A/C, TV, minibar, hair dryer, safe.

INEXPENSIVE

El Rastro *(Value)*　Situated near the junction of Calle Caballeros and Calle Cepadas, this is the best choice for the bargain hunter. Few visitors know that they can spend the night at this old Castilian inn built into the city walls. The small guest rooms are basic and clean containing private bathrooms with tubs.

Plaza del Rastro 1, 05001 Avila. ℂ **92-021-12-18.** Fax 92-025-16-26. 10 units. 35€–41€ double. AE, MC, DC, V. **Amenities:** Restaurant; bar; lounge. *In room:* TV, no phone.

Gran Hostal San Segundo　This small hotel and restaurant is just outside the immense walls surrounding the historic center of Avila. The elegant 19th-century building itself has just been renovated with a mind to both maintaining its historical charm and incorporating modern comfort. The soft salmon-hued reception rooms have high ceilings, and the medium-sized guest rooms are spotlessly clean, simple, and unpretentious. All units contain neatly kept bathrooms with tubs.

San Segundo 28, 05001 Avila. ℂ **92-025-25-90.** Fax 92-025-27-90. 14 units. 42€–48€ double. AE, DC, MC, V. Free parking on the street. **Amenities:** Restaurant; bar; laundry service; dry cleaning. *In room:* TV, hair dryer.

Hostería de Bracamonte *(★★) (Finds)*　The most tranquil spot in town is this little gem decorated in a classic Castilian style. It lies 1 block north of Plaza de Victoria, the main square within the city walls. A restful and quiet oasis, it has a number of charming features, including a lovely patio and a dark-wood Castilian motif throughout. Converted to a small inn in 1989, the *hostería* retains some of its aristocratic origins as the town house of Gov. Don Juan Teherán y Monjaraz. Rooms are spacious and have whitewashed walls; some have fireplaces and four-poster beds. All contain neatly kept bathrooms with tubs.

Bracamonte 6, 05001 Avila. ℂ **92-025-12-80.** 22 units. 61€–73€ double. MC, V. Parking available along the street. **Amenities:** Restaurant; bar; lounge. *In room:* TV, minibar.

WHERE TO DINE
MODERATE

El Molino de la Lasa *(★) (Finds)* SEGOVIAN　A mill dating from the 1400s and standing near the Adaja River has been turned into one of the best restaurants in Segovia. Instead of disguising the building's former functions, the owners decided to preserve and display the machinery. Try to arrive before your reservations to enjoy a drink in the animated and charming bar, filled with a mixture of both locals and visitors. The chef uses top-quality ingredients that he fashions into a savory cuisine with both fish and meat dishes. Try his garlic-studded roast pork or his *merluza* (hake) in a zesty marinara sauce. Some excellent, tender, and well-flavored lamb dishes are also served along with tasty veal chops. The trout served is caught in the Adaja River. Try for a side dish of *judías de El Barco,* from the nearby village of El Barco, whose farmers are said to produce the tastiest beans in Old Castile. In the garden is a little playground for the kids.

Bajada de la Losa 12. ℂ **92-021-11-01.** Reservations required. Main courses 19€–20€. AE, DC, MC, V. Tues–Sun 1:30–4:30pm and 9–11:30pm.

INEXPENSIVE

El Rastro CASTILIAN　An old inn built into the 11th-century town walls, El Rastro serves typical Castilian dishes, with more attention given to freshness and preparation than to culinary flamboyance. Specialties include roast baby lamb and tender white veal, raised in the region and known for its succulence. It is prepared at least four different ways. Dessert recipes have been passed down from Avila's nuns. Try, if you dare, the highly touted *yemas de Santa Teresa* (St. Teresa's candied egg yolk); when we dined here with travel expert Arthur Frommer, he found it a particularly horrible dessert—and we agree. Yet Avila residents keep praising it as a specialty. To our taste, there are far better selections on the menu. They also maintain a small hotel with 10 comfortable rooms (see "Where to Stay," above).

Plaza del Rastro 1. ✆ **92-021-12-19.** Reservations required on weekends only. Main courses 11€–14€; fixed-price menu 14€. AE, DC, MC, V. Daily 1–4pm and 9–11pm.

Hostería de Bracamonte SPANISH/CASTILIAN   Parts of the building that contain this place are 400 years old, but even in recent remodelings, every effort was made to duplicate the original ceiling beams, rough-textured plaster, and artfully chiseled stone of the original design. The kitchen focuses on grills and old-fashioned roasts, many of which are remembered fondly from the childhood of the regular guests. Examples include roasted tender baby lamb with herbs and garlic, grilled pork or veal chops, roasted chicken, and all manner of steaks, cutlets, ribs, and, to a lesser degree, seafood. The largest of the restaurant's four dining rooms is usually devoted to the care and feeding of busloads of groups traveling together, so you might find a bit more intimacy in one of the three smaller dining areas.

Bracamonte 6. ✆ **92-025-12-80.** Reservations recommended. Main courses 7€–16€. MC, V. Wed–Mon 11:30–4pm and 9–11:30pm.

Las Cancelas ✆ *Value* CASTILIAN   A recent discovery for us, Las Cancelas is where the locals go, whereas tourists crowd into several restaurants nearby. You get good food, regional specialties, a time-mellowed Castilian ambience, and affordable prices, a rather unbeatable combination. We begin our evenings in Avila at the restaurant's tapas bar up front. Tasty tidbits, almost mystical conversations, and good wine flow freely. Later you can head back to the dining room where simple paper covers the old wooden tables. A carafe of regional wine arrives at your table as you tear off hunks of the freshly baked bread. The restaurant itself is in a stone-columned patio where seasonal dishes emerge from the kitchen. Meats are roasted in a wood-fired oven and are the house specialties. We can never resist the *chuletón de Avila,* a mammoth T-bone steak and the chef's specialty. Platters of roast chicken, baked lamb, and other delights will also tempt you.

The Castilian inn is also one of the bargain places to stay in Avila, offering 14 small but modernized and comfortable bedrooms, each with a private shower, costing only 57€ a night for a double. Each has a TV and phone and in some cases air conditioning as well.

Cruz Viejo 6. ✆ **92-021-22-49.** Reservations recommended. Main courses 11€–18€. AE, DC, MC, V. Daily 1:30–4pm and 8:30–10:30pm.

8 Cuenca ★★

161km (100 miles) E of Madrid, 325km (202 miles) SW of Zaragoza

This medieval town once dominated by the Arabs is a spectacular sight with its *casas colgadas,* the cliff-hanging houses set on multiple terraces that climb up the impossibly steep sides of a ravine. The Júcar and Huécar rivers meet at the bottom.

ESSENTIALS

GETTING THERE **Trains** leave Madrid's Atocha Railway Station about eight times throughout the day. Trains arrive in Cuenca at Paseo del Ferrocarril in the new city (© **90-224-02-02**), after a journey lasting anywhere from 2½ to 3 hours. A one-way ticket from Madrid costs 9€.

There are also about eight **buses** from Madrid every day. Buses arrive at Calle Fermín Caballero s/n (© **96-922-70-87** or 96-922-11-84 for information and schedules). A one-way fare costs 11€.

Cuenca is the junction for several highways and about a dozen lesser roads that connect it to towns within its region. From Madrid, take the N-III to Tarancón, then the N-400, which leads directly into Cuenca.

VISITOR INFORMATION The city **tourist information office,** Plaza Mayor 1 (© **96-923-21-19;** www.aytocuenca.org), next to the cathedral off Plaza Mayor, is open Monday through Saturday from 9am to 2pm and 4 to 9pm.

EXPLORING THE AREA

The chief sight of Cuenca is the **Old Town** 🌟🌟 itself. Isolated from the rest of Spain, it requires a northern detour from the heavily traveled Valencia-Madrid road. Deep gorges give it an unreal quality, and eight old bridges spanning two rivers connect the ancient parts of town with the growing new sections. A foot-bridge is suspended over a 60m (200-ft.) drop.

Cuenca's streets are narrow and steep, often cobbled, and even the most athletic visitor will tire quickly. But you shouldn't miss it, even if you have to stop and rest periodically. At night you're in for a special treat when the *casas colgadas* 🌟 are illuminated. Also, try to drive almost to the top of the castle-dominated hill. The road gets rough as you approach the end, but the view makes the effort worthwhile.

If you have the time, you can make a side trip to the not that enchanting **Ciudad Encantada (Enchanted City),** Carretera de la Sierra, about 40km (25 miles) to the northeast of Cuenca. Storms and underground waters have created a city here out of large rocks and boulders, shaping them into bizarre designs: a seal, an elephant, a Roman bridge. Take CU-912, turning northeast onto CU-913. Ciudad Encantada is signposted.

Catedral de Cuenca Begun in the 12th century, this Gothic cathedral was influenced by England's Norman style, becoming the only Anglo-Norman cathedral in Spain. Part of it collapsed in the 20th century but has been restored. A national monument filled with religious art treasures, the cathedral dominates Plaza Mayor in the center of town. The cathedral's *museo diocesano* exhibits two canvases by El Greco, a collection of Flemish tapestries (some beautifully designed), and a statue of the Virgin del Sagrario from the 1100s.

Plaza Mayor. © **96-922-46-26.** Free admission to cathedral, 1.15€ to museum. Daily 9:30am–2pm and 4–6pm. Bus: 1 or 2.

⎛Moments The Hanging Houses of Cuenca

One of the most thrilling sites of Cuenca is to walk at night along the streets and admire the hanging houses, or *casas colgadas,* of the town. They are illuminated. Dating from the 14th century, these famous houses literally seem to hang over the deep Huécar ravine. At times they are built so close to the edge that you feel they are about to plunge overboard.

Museo de Arte Abstracto Español ★★   North of Plaza Mayor housed in a cliff-hanging dwelling, this ranks as one of the finest museums of its kind in Spain. It was conceived by painter Fernando Zóbel, who donated it in 1980 to the Juan March Foundation. The most outstanding abstract Spanish painters are represented, including Rafael Canogar (especially his *Toledo*), Luis Feito, Zóbel himself, Tàpies, Eduardo Chillida, Gustavo Torner, Gerardo Rueda, Millares, Sempere, Cuixart, and Antonio Saura (see his grotesque Geraldine Chaplin and his study of Brigitte Bardot, a vision of horror, making the French actress look like an escapee from Picasso's *Guernica*).

Calle los Canónigos s/n. ℭ **96-921-29-83**. Admission 3€ adults, 1.50€ students. Tues–Fri 11am–2pm and 4–6pm; Sat 11am–2pm and 4–8pm; Sun 11am–2:30pm. Bus: 1 or 2.

WHERE TO STAY

Hotel NH Ciudad de Cuenca ★   Since you can't always get into the parador, consider this stellar selection the second-best choice in town. In operation since the mid-1990s, it lies in a rapidly developing residential area close to the old town. Its exterior design is severe and clinical, but its interior is filled with comfort and grace notes. The wooden floored rooms are comfortable and well appointed, with well-selected upholstery, comfortable beds, and fully equipped bathrooms with tub/shower combos. The sole suite has a hydromassage.

Ronda de San José 1, 16004 Cuenca. ℭ **96-923-05-02**. Fax 96-923-05-03. www.nh-hoteles.es. 74 units. 67€–86€ double; 105€–133€ suite. AE, DC, MC, V. Parking 9€. Bus: 2. **Amenities:** Restaurant; bar; fitness center; sauna; room service; babysitting; laundry service; dry cleaning. *In room:* A/C, TV, minibar, hair dryer.

Leonor de Aquitania   Perched high up on the hillside above an almost sheer drop, the hotel enjoys spectacular views of both the old city of Cuenca from one angle and the narrow valley rising from the harsh though beautiful precipice opposite. The reception rooms have been maintained in extremely good, conservative taste, and the hotel evokes an elegantly restrained and comfortable charm. The medium-sized rooms are exceedingly well cared for, and each comes with an immaculate tile bathroom with shower. The Hebrea Hermosa (the beautiful Jewish maiden) suite is one of the most charming in this quiet medieval city. The staff is friendly and helpful, but we'd recommend that you skip the on-site restaurant, perhaps dining instead at the parador's restaurant.

Calle San Pedro 60, 16001 Cuenca. ℭ **96-923-10-00**. Fax 96-923-10-04. www.hotelleonordeaquitania.com. 46 units. 95€–108€ double; 152€–170€ suite. AE, DC, MC, V. **Amenities:** Restaurant; bar; gym; sauna; room service; babysitting; laundry service; dry cleaning. *In room:* TV, hair dryer, safe.

Parador de Cuenca ★★★   This government-sponsored hotel occupies the dignified premises of what was originally built in 1523 as a Dominican monastery. A noteworthy example of late Gothic architecture, it lies on a hillside above Cuenca, about a half mile northwest of the town's historic center. It is clearly the town's prestige address. Opened for business after extensive renovations in 1992, its timeless three stories contain masses of intricately chiseled 16th-century stonework (some enhanced with glass panels overlooking the river), a church, and a severely beautiful cloister. There are two floors of medium-sized rooms that are comfortably traditional and contain modern bathrooms with tub/shower combos.

Subida a San Pablo, Paseo de la Hoz del Huécar, 16001 Cuenca. ℭ **96-923-23-20**. Fax 96-923-25-34. www.parador.es. 63 units. 109€–118€ double; 218€–235€ suite. AE, DC, MC, V. Parking 11€. **Amenities:** Restaurant; bar; pool; fitness center; sauna; room service; babysitting; laundry service; dry cleaning. *In room:* A/C, TV, minibar, hair dryer, safe.

Posada de San José 🌟 Posada de San José stands in the oldest part of Cuenca, a short walk north of the cathedral. The 17th-century cells that used to shelter the sisters of this former convent now house overnight guests who consider its views of the old city the best in town. It sits atop a cliff overlooking the forbidding depths of a gorge. Accommodations are small but are still quite comfortable. Bathrooms are also small, with shower stalls. Owners Antonio and Jennifer Cortinas renovated this place into one of the best bargain hotels of the region. Parking is available along the street.

Julián Romero 4, 16001 Cuenca. ℭ **96-921-13-00.** Fax 96-923-03-65. www.posadasanjose.com. 30 units, 22 with bathroom. 29€–33€ double without bathroom; 58€–64€ double with bathroom. AE, DC, MC, V. Bus: 1 or 2. **Amenities:** Bar; lounge; laundry service; dry cleaning. *In room:* No phone.

WHERE TO DINE

El Figón de Pedro 🌟 CASTILIAN   Set in the business section of the new town at the foot of the hills that lead you to the wonders of medieval Cuenca, this restaurant belongs to one of Spain's most celebrated restaurateurs, Pedro Torres Pacheco. Given this, and by turning a quick blind eye to the abundance of late 1960s concrete, the location is well worth a visit. The air-conditioned restaurant is relatively intimate, with 13 tables and the traditional Castilian decor of plates on walls and folkloric memorabilia. The cuisine, however, is not half as predictable. The *morteruelo* (local paté made from partridge, pork, ham, and hare) should definitely be sampled, as should the gazpacho and *bacalao ajo arriero* (a purée of cod, garlic, eggs, and olive oil). The desserts here are interesting, unlike those in many Spanish restaurants, especially the original Moorish *alajú* (almonds, bread crumbs, honey, and orange water) and the Miguelito, a flat almond cake. When sated, you can then toast the meal with a glass of resoli, the strong local liquor.

Cervantes 13. ℭ **96-922-68-21.** Reservations recommended. Main courses 12€–18€; *menú del día* 20€–24€. AE, DC, MC, V. Daily 1:30–4pm; Mon–Sat 9–11pm.

Mesón Casa Colgadas 🌟🌟 SPANISH/INTERNATIONAL   One of the most spectacular dining rooms in Spain stands on one of the most precarious precipices in Cuenca. Established in the late 1960s, it occupies a five-story 19th-century house with sturdy supporting walls and beams. Pine balconies and windows overlook the ravine below and the hills beyond. In fact, it's the most photographed "suspended house" in town, and dinner here is worth every peseta. The menu includes regional dishes and a wide variety of well-prepared international favorites. Drinks are served in the tavern room on the street level, so even if you're not dining here, you may want to drop in for a drink and the view. You'll find the Mesón Casa Colgadas just south of the cathedral and near the Museum of Spanish Abstract Art.

Canónigos 3. ℭ **96-922-35-09.** Reservations recommended. Main courses 12€–22€; fixed-price menus 21€–26€. AE, DC, MC, V. Daily 1:30–4pm; Tues–Sun 9–11pm

Togar SPANISH   Rich with local flavor and aggressively cost conscious, this is a simple but likable *tasca* on the southwestern periphery of town. Established in 1955, and set within an angular building erected the same year, it offers homemade cookery whose inspiration derives from the various regions of Spain. One of the specialties is *revuelto Togar,* an egg, ham, and shrimp dish served with herbs and crusty bread. Also available are well-peppered versions of pork, several kinds of rich soups, and various beef and fish dishes.

Av. República Argentina 1. ℭ **96-922-01-62.** Reservations required. Main courses 6€–14€; fixed-price menu 10€–20€. AE, DC, MC, V. Daily 1–4pm and 8pm–midnight. Closed 2 weeks in July (dates vary). Bus: 1 or 6.

6

Old Castile & León

Spain owes much to Castile, Aragón, and León, since these three kingdoms helped unify the various regions of the country. Modern Spain was conceived when Isabella of Castile married Ferdinand of Aragón on October 19, 1469. Five years later she was proclaimed queen of Castile and León. The Moors were eventually driven out of Granada, the rest of Spain was conquered, and Columbus sailed to America—all during the reign of these two Catholic monarchs.

This proud but controversial queen and her unscrupulous husband fashioned an empire whose influence extended throughout Spain, Europe, and the New World. The power once held by Old Castile shifted long ago to Madrid, but there remain many reminders of its storied past.

In the ancient kingdom of León, which was eventually annexed to Castile, you'll find Salamanca, Zamora, and the provincial capital of León. Today the region is known for its many castles.

In Old Castile, we'll cover the inland provincial capital of Valladolid, where Isabella married Ferdinand and where a brokenhearted Columbus died on May 19, 1506. From here we'll move on to Burgos, once the capital of Old Castile. Vivar, a small town near here, produced Spain's greatest national hero, El Cid, who conquered the Moorish kingdom of Valencia.

For other destinations in the region, refer to chapter 5, "Side Trips from Madrid."

1 Ciudad Rodrigo ★

87km (54 miles) SW of Salamanca, 285km (177 miles) W of Madrid

A walled town dating from Roman days, **Ciudad Rodrigo** is known for its 16th- and 17th-century town houses, built by the conquistadors. It was founded in the 12th century by Count Rodriguez González and is today a national monument. Located near the Portuguese frontier, it stands high on a hilltop and is known for the familiar silhouette of the square tower of its Alcázar. This walled part of the city is referred to as the Casco Viejo.

The ramparts were built in the 12th century along Roman foundations. Several stairways lead up to a 1.5km (1-mile) long sentry path. You can wander these ramparts at leisure and then walk through the streets with their many churches and mansions. It is not one chief monument that is the allure, but rather the city as a whole.

The **Plaza Mayor** ★ is a showpiece of 17th-century architecture, with two Renaissance palaces. This is the main square of the city.

The town's major attraction is its **Cathedral** ★, which combines Romanesque and Gothic styles with a neoclassical tower. It was mostly built between 1170 and 1230, although subsequent centuries have seen more additions. It can be reached going east of Plaza Mayor through Plaza de San Salvador. The **Renaissance altar** ⭐ on the north aisle is an acclaimed work of ecclesiastical art; look also for the **Virgin Portal** ⭐ at the west door, which dates from the 1200s. For 2€ you'll be admitted to the **cloisters** ⭐, which are in a variety of architectural styles, including a Plateresque door. Hours are daily from 10am to 1pm and 4 to 6:30pm.

Your transportation in Ciudad Rodrigo will be your trusty feet, as walking is the only way to explore the city. Pick up a map at the tourist office (see below).

ESSENTIALS

GETTING THERE   The only real way to get here is from Salamanca. Because **train** service is infrequent and the train station is a long way from the walls of the old city, it's easier to take the bus from Salamanca; you'll get off at the Ciudad Rodrigo station at Calle Campo de Toledo (✆ **92-346-02-17**). Monday through Friday, 11 **buses** arrive from Salamanca; on Saturday and Sunday, five buses (trip time: 1 hr.). The cost is 4.75€ one-way.

The N-620 is the main road from both Salamanca and Portugal. Driving time from Salamanca is about 1¼ hours.

VISITOR INFORMATION   The **tourist office,** Plaza Amayuelas 5 (✆ **92-346-05-61;** www.ciudadrodrigo.net), is open Monday through Friday from 9am to 2pm and 5 to 7pm, Saturday and Sunday from 10am to 2pm and 5 to 8pm.

SPECIAL EVENTS   Carnival festivities in February in Ciudad Rodrigo feature a running of the bulls, traditional dances, and costumes.

WHERE TO STAY

Conde Rodrigo I   Its central location next to the cathedral is a big plus for this government-rated two-star hotel; try for a room opening onto the square. The recently renovated rooms are small and totally devoid of style, but they're comfortable. Bathrooms have tub/shower combos. The building itself has some medieval flavor, with its thick walls of chiseled stone. Public parking is available off-street.

Plaza de San Salvador 9, 37500 Ciudad Rodrigo. ✆ **92-346-14-04.** Fax 92-346-14-08. www.conde rodrigo.com. 34 units. 56€–64€ double. DC, MC, V. Parking 6€. **Amenities:** Restaurant; bar; babysitting; laundry service; dry cleaning. *In room:* A/C, TV, minibar, hair dryer, safe.

Parador de Ciudad Rodrigo ⭐⭐   Now restored, this government-affiliated hostelry is easily the town's leading inn. It is constructed on the site of an embattled castle from the 12th century that was built on command of Enrique II of Trastamara on a hill overlooking Río Agueda. The Torre del Homenaje defines the profile of Ciudad Rodrigo, and once it was the seat of the feudal court. The parador has several gates and what the Spanish call *miradores*—platforms offering panoramic views. Sunset-watching is a popular pastime. The Gothic entrance bears the royal coat-of-arms and a plaque in Gothic letters. The tastefully furnished rooms offer more style and comfort than any other hotel in town, including the Conde Rodrigo. There is a below-floor heating system in all the bathrooms, each with a tub/shower combo. Try for a room overlooking the garden that runs down to the Agueda River. The food in the restaurant is well prepared, and the service polite. The only parking available is on-street.

Plaza del Castillo s/n, 37500 Ciudad Rodrigo. ✆ **92-346-01-50.** Fax 92-346-04-04. www.parador.es. 35 units. 89€–102€ double; 123€ suite. AE, DC, MC, V. **Amenities:** Restaurant; bar; room service; laundry service; dry cleaning. *In room:* A/C, TV, minibar, hair dryer, safe.

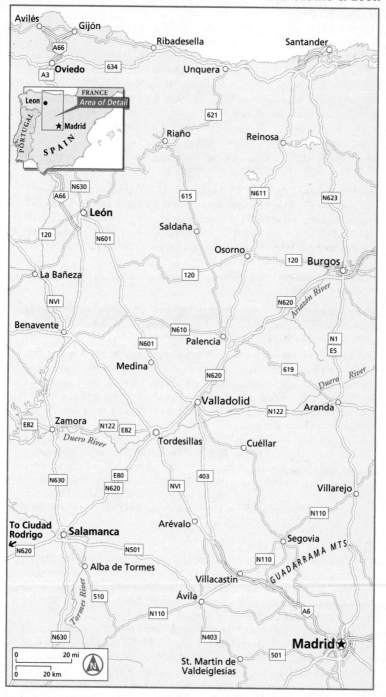

WHERE TO DINE

Estoril CASTILIAN/BASQUE   This is not only one of the most centrally located restaurants in town, but it's also one of the finest dining rooms, topped only by Mayton. A short walk from Plaza Mayor, this popular restaurant was built and founded in 1967. The air-conditioned interior is decorated in typical regional style with bullfight photographs. Specialties of the house include roasted meats, such as roast suckling pig, with a special emphasis on roasted goat. Seafood, such as sole and hake, is presented in the Basque style. The seafood soup is particularly good. Everything is accompanied by a variety of regional wines, including Cosechero Rioja.

Traversia Talavera 1. ℂ **92-346-05-50.** Reservations recommended. Main courses 9€–11€; *menú del día* 9€. DC, MC, V. Sun–Thurs noon–midnight; Fri–Sat noon–3 or 4am.

Mayton 📍 *Value* CASTILIAN   Adjacent to Plaza Mayor in a 17th-century building, Mayton is the best restaurant in the city. Its antique walls reverberate with atmosphere and legend. The menu is mostly fresh fish and shellfish, done exceedingly well. Try the *sopa castellana* (Castilian soup) for an appetizer, followed by *merluza* (hake) in green sauce. You can also order veal, as tender as that of Avila. The place is air-conditioned.

La Colada 9. ℂ **92-346-07-20.** Reservations recommended. Main courses 5€–15€. AE, DC, MC, V. Daily 1–3:30pm and 8–11:30pm.

2 Salamanca 📍📍📍

204km (127 miles) NW of Madrid, 118km (73 miles) E of Portugal

This ancient city, famous for its university founded by Alfonso IX in the early 1200s, is well preserved, with turreted palaces, faded convents, Romanesque churches, and colleges that have attracted scholars from all over Europe. The only way to explore **Salamanca** conveniently is on foot, so arm yourself with a good map and set out to explore. Nearly all the attractions are within walking distance of the Plaza Mayor.

In its day, Salamanca was ranked with Oxford, Paris, and Bologna as one of "the four leading lights of the medieval world." The intellectual life continues to this day, and a large invasion of American students brings added life to the town in summer. Its population has swelled to 180,000 but a provincial aura lingers.

Still a youthful, spirited place because of the venerable Salamanca University, the city has been named a "World Heritage City" by UNESCO, one of six such cities in Spain. No country has more.

ESSENTIALS

GETTING THERE   Three **trains** travel directly from Madrid's North Station to Salamanca daily (trip time: 2½ hr.), arriving northeast of the town center on the Paseo de la Estación de Ferrocarril (ℂ **90-224-02-02**). The fare is 14€. More frequent are the rail connections between Salamanca, Avila, Ciudad Rodrigo, and Valladolid (around 6 trains each per day).

There's frequent daily **bus** service from Madrid (trip time: 2½ hr.). Salamanca's bus terminal is at Av. Filiberto Villalobos 71 (ℂ **92-323-67-17**), northwest of the center of town. There are also buses to Salamanca from Avila, Zamora, Valladolid, León, and Cáceres (2–13 per day, depending on the point of departure).

Salamanca isn't on a national highway, but a good network of roads converges there from such nearby cities as Avila, Valladolid, and Ciudad Rodrigo. One of the most heavily trafficked highways is the N-620, leading into Salamanca from

both Barcelona and Portugal. From Madrid, take the N-VI northwest, forking off to Salamanca on the N-501.

VISITOR INFORMATION   The **tourist office,** Plaza Mayor 32 (© **92-321-83-42;** www.aytosalamanca.es), is open Monday through Saturday from 9am to 2pm and 4:30 to 6:30pm, Sunday from 10am to 2pm and 4:30 to 6:30pm.

EXPLORING SALAMANCA

To start, spend as much time as you can at the **Plaza Mayor** ✿✿✿, an 18th-century baroque square widely acclaimed as the most beautiful public plaza in Spain. No trip to this university town is complete unless you walk through the arcade of shops and feast your eyes on the honey-colored buildings. After this you'll understand why the *plaza mayor,* a town's main square, is an integral part of Spanish life. If it's a hot day and you want what everybody else in Plaza Mayor is drinking, stop in a cafe and order *leche helada,* a vanilla and almond concoction that's very refreshing.

Even before reaching the Plaza Mayor, you may want to stop and admire the facade of the landmark **Casa de las Conchas (House of Shells)** ⭐, which appears as you walk north from the Patio de las Escuelas (site of the Universidad de Salamanca; see below) on Calles de Libreros and San Isidro. This much-photographed building is at the corner of Rua Mayor and Calle de la Compañía 2 (© **92-326-93-17**). The restored 1483 house is noted for its facade of 400 simulated scallop shells. A professor of medicine at the university and a doctor at the court of Isabella created the house as a monument to Santiago de Compostela, the renowned pilgrimage site. The shell is the symbol of the Order of Santiago. You can visit the courtyard Monday through Friday from 9am to 9pm, Saturday from 9am to 2pm and 4 to 7pm, and Sunday from 10am to 2pm. Admission is free.

Casa Museo Unamuno   The poet and philosopher Miguel de Unamuno lived from 1900 to 1914 in this 18th-century home beside the university. Here he wrote many of the works that made him famous. You can see some of his notebooks and his library, along with many personal mementos.

Calle de Libreros 25. © **92-329-44-00**. Admission 1.80€. Tues–Fri 9:30am–1:30pm and 4–6pm; Sat–Sun 10am–1:30pm. July 7–Sept 30 open mornings only. Last tours leave 30 min. before closing time. Bus: 1.

Catedral Nueva (New Cathedral) ⭐⭐   The "new" cathedral dates from 1513. It took more than 200 years to complete it, so the edifice represents many styles: It's classified as late Gothic, but you'll see baroque and Plateresque features as well. José Churriguera contributed some rococo elements, too. Its single most enthralling architectural feature is its **west front** ⭐⭐, which is divided below the windows into a quartet of wide bays corresponding to the ground plan. These bays are distinguished by pierced stonework carved as intricately as the keystones in the arches. The building has a grand gold-on-beige sandstone facade, elegant chapels, the best-decorated dome in Spain, and bas-relief columns that look like a palm-tree cluster. Unfortunately, its stained glass is severely damaged. The cathedral lies in the southern section of the old town, about 5 blocks south of the Plaza Mayor at the edge of the Plaza de Anaya.

Plaza Juan XXII. © **92-321-74-76**. Free admission. Daily 9:30am–1pm and 4–7:30pm. Bus: 1.

Catedral Vieja (Old Cathedral) ⭐⭐   Adjoining the New Cathedral is this older Spanish Romanesque version, begun in 1140. Its simplicity provides a dramatic contrast to the ornamentation of its younger but bigger counterpart. In the main apsidal chapel is an **altarpiece** ⭐⭐ painted by Nicholas of Florence in the mid–15th century, consisting of 53 different beautifully decorated compartments. Even today this work of art remains fresh and vivid. After viewing the interior, stroll through the enclosed cloisters with their Gothic tombs of long-forgotten bishops. The chapels are of special architectural interest. In the Capilla de San Martín the frescoes date from 1242, and in the Capilla de Santa Bárbara, final exams for Salamanca University students were given. The Capilla de Santa Catalina is noted for its gargoyles.

Plaza Juan XXIII. © **92-321-74-76**. Admission 3€. Apr–Sept daily 10am–1:30pm and 4–8pm; Oct–Mar daily 9am–1pm and 4–7:30pm. Bus: 1.

Museo Art Nouveau–Art Deco   This museum contains more than 1,500 pieces, all part of the collection of the Manuel Ramos Andrade Foundation. From the late 19th century to the 1930s, the collection includes bronze and marble figurines, jewelry, furniture, paintings, and a collection of some 300 porcelain dolls. Numerous works by Emile Gallé and René Lalique are also on display.

Calle Gibraltar 14. (C) **92-312-14-25**. Admission 2.10€ adults, 1.50€ students, free for children 14 and under. Apr–Oct 15 Tues–Fri 11am–2pm and 5–9pm; Sat–Sun 11am–9pm. Oct 16–Mar 31 Tues–Fri 11am–2pm and 4–7pm; Sat–Sun 11am–8pm.

Museo de Salamanca (Casa de los Doctores de la Reina)
Built in the late 15th century by Queen Isabella's physician, this structure—located near the university—is a fine example of the Spanish Plateresque style. The Fine Arts Museum is here, boasting a collection of paintings and sculptures dating from the 15th to the 20th century.

Plaza Fray Luis de León 2. (C) **92-329-44-00**. Admission 1.20€. Tues–Sat 10am-2:30pm and 5–8pm; Sun 10am–2pm. Bus: 1.

Convento de las Dueñas
Across Calle Buenaventura from Convento de San Esteban (see below), this is one of the most popular sights of Salamanca, a former Mudéjar palace of a court official. The cloisters date from the 16th century, and are, in the opinion of some architectural critics, the most beautiful in Salamanca. Climb to the upper gallery for a close inspection of the carved capitals covered with demons and dragons, saints and sinners, and animals of every description—some from the pages of *The Divine Comedy*. There's also a portrait of Dante.

Plaza del Concilio de Trento. (C) **92-321-54-42**. Admission 1.50€. June–Sept daily 10:30am–1pm and 4:30–7pm; Oct–May daily 10:30am–1pm and 4:30–5:30pm.

Convento de San Esteban
Of all the old religious sites of Salamanca, St. Stephen's Convent is one of the most dramatic. The golden-brown Plateresque facade of this late Gothic church competes with the cathedral in magnificence. Inside, José Churriguera in 1693 created a **high altar** 🌟 that is one of Salamanca's greatest art treasures. The Claustro de los Reyes (Cloister of the Kings) is both Plateresque and Gothic in style. The convent lies 2 blocks east of the New Cathedral on the opposite side of busy Calle San Pablo at the southern terminus of Calle de España (Gran Vía).

Plaza del Concilio de Trento. (C) **92-321-50-00**. Admission 1.50€. Daily 9am–1:30pm and 4–8pm.

Universidad de Salamanca
The oldest university in Spain was once the greatest in Europe. No other university in Spain has such a **grand entrance** 🌟🌟🌟. A work from 1534, the entryway is a splendid piece of sculpture, intricate in its detail. It is said the architects carved this "doorway to heaven" as if they were aping a goldsmith's art. The main medallion in the first register depicts the Catholic Monarchs, Isabella and Ferdinand, who supplied the cost of creating this work of art. Other medallions depict everybody from Venus and Hercules to popes with cardinals. You can visit a dim 16th-century classroom, cluttered with crude wooden benches. The library upstairs can't be entered, but can be viewed through a glass door, and it's an impressive sight. The university is 2 blocks from the cathedral in the southern section of the old town.

(Fun Fact The Undaunted Fray Luis

In front of the Plateresque facade of the University of Salamanca, a statue honors Hebrew scholar Fray Luis de León. Arrested for heresy, Fray Luis was detained for 5 years before being cleared. When he returned, he began his first lecture: "As I was saying yesterday . . ." Fray Luis's remains are kept in the chapel, which is worth a look.

Patio de las Escuelas 1. ⓒ **92-329-44-00**. Admission 4€. Mon–Sat 9:30am–1pm and 4–7:30pm; Sun 9am–1pm. Enter from Patio de las Escuelas, a widening of Calle de Libreros.

SHOPPING

The town's two main shopping neighborhoods extend around Calle Meléndez and the historic borders of the Plaza Mayor 29. Both areas are good bets for fashion and housewares. You may also want to head for the town's largest department store, **Corte Fiel,** Plaza Mayor (ⓒ **92-321-92-40**), or the menswear branch at Calle Doro 24 (ⓒ **92-321-52-90**). And if you're looking for handicrafts, head for **Artesanía Hernández,** Calle Conde de Cadarrus 21 (ⓒ **92-312-07-98**), whose inventories represent most of the trades that used to proliferate in the region around Salamanca.

WHERE TO STAY
EXPENSIVE

AC Palacio de San Esteban   ✿   This government-rated four-star hotel has been installed in the former convent dedicated to San Esteban, which dates from the 1600s. It lies within the heart of monumental Salamanca. The hotel has been totally rejuvenated but the traditional style and luxury of its architectural past has been honored. Bedrooms are midsize and attractively and conservatively furnished with handsome bathrooms with both tub and shower. The location is close to many sightseeing attractions, including the cathedrals.

Arroyo de Santonio de Salamanca, 37008 Salamanca. ⓒ **92-326-22-96**. Fax 92-326-88-72. www.ac-hotels. com. 51 units. 140€–161€ double; 185€ suite. AE, DC, MC, V. **Amenities:** Restaurant; bar; fitness center; room service; baby-sitting; laundry/dry cleaning. *In room:* A/C, TV, minibar, hair dryer.

Gran Hotel   ✿   Because of its location and the legends that surround it, this hotel remains the favorite choice of traditionalists, a position it's held since it opened in 1930. However, the more elegant Palacio de Castellanos has come along to replace it as *número uno* in Salamanca. Set on the southeast corner of the Plaza Mayor, it remains the favorite of bull breeders and matadors, as well as of the literati of this ancient university town. Because its owners have kept it up-to-date, the hotel is still going strong. In 1994 it was completely renovated, with modern plumbing added, but with much of the old-fashioned charm left intact. Rooms are well maintained, with handsome bathrooms equipped with tub/shower combos.

Plaza Poeta Iglesias 6, 37001 Salamanca. ⓒ **92-321-35-00**. Fax 92-321-35-00. www.helcom.es/granhotel. 136 units. 105€–156€ double; 173€–204€ suite. AE, DC, MC, V. Parking 14€. **Amenities:** Restaurant; bar; room service; babysitting; laundry service; dry cleaning. *In room:* A/C, TV, minibar, hair dryer, safe.

Hotel Rector   ✿✿   *(Finds*   Far better than either the parador or the Gran Hotel, this little inn has become the most charming place to stay in Salamanca; nothing matches it in either atmosphere or tranquillity, although the far larger Palacio de Castellanos remains the most substantial deluxe palace. The Rector is a mere boutique hotel. Located just beyond the Roman bridge, it was a private mansion until the owners converted it into a hotel in 1990. Rooms are elegantly appointed with luxury mattresses and beautifully kept bathrooms complete with tub/shower combos. Don't expect all the luxuries found in a full-service hotel, but the staff here is extremely professional and polite. Since this place is such a gem, you have to reserve well in advance.

Rector Esperabé 10, 37008 Salamanca. ⓒ **92-321-84-82**. Fax 92-321-40-08. 13 units. 108€–127€ double; 139€ suite. AE, DC, MC, V. Parking 10€. **Amenities:** Room service; babysitting; laundry service; dry cleaning. *In room:* A/C, TV, minibar, hair dryer, safe.

NH Palacio de Castellanos ⭐⭐⭐   The grandest palace in Salamanca, this deluxe hotel was built on the site of the original 15th-century Palacio de Castellanos and lies in old Salamanca near the Plaza Mayor with good views in most directions. We like it much better than the parador. The good-size rooms are state-of-the-art, with sleek modern furnishings and deluxe bedding and bedside controls. Bathrooms have tub/shower combos.

San Pablo 58–64, 37008 Salamanca. (℡ **92-326-18-18.** Fax 92-326-18-19. www.nh-hoteles.es. 62 units. 136€ double; from 183€ suite. AE, DC, MC, V. Parking 13€. **Amenities:** Restaurant; bar; room service; babysitting; laundry service; dry cleaning. *In room:* A/C, TV, minibar, hair dryer, safe, bathrobes.

Parador Nacional de Salamanca   Usually, a parador in a town in western Spain is the leading hotel choice. Not so in Salamanca. The Palacio de Castellanos is the market leader, but this hostelry is an elegant choice and you can count yourself lucky to book into a room here. Situated just across the Tormes River, this multilevel parador with a modern facade opened in the early 1980s. It sits less than a mile south of the historic center of town. It's a fine choice, but isn't as special as some of Spain's other paradors (the public areas are looking a bit worn, for example). Each of the well-furnished and comfortable midsize rooms has a mirador-style balcony and a bathroom with a tub/shower combo.

Teso de la Feria 2, 37008 Salamanca. (℡ **92-319-20-82.** Fax 92-319-20-87. www.parador.es. 108 units. 110€ double; 155€ suite. AE, DC, MC, V. Free parking outside; 12€ garage. **Amenities:** Restaurant; bar; pool; room service; babysitting; laundry service; dry cleaning. *In room:* A/C, TV, minibar, hair dryer, safe.

MODERATE

Hotel Las Torres   Dignified and well maintained, and with a congenial staff, this hotel occupies a good spot near the northwest corner of the Plaza Mayor. A recent restoration of a historic monument, the hotel may look a little seedy, but it's not. The modern, comfortable rooms, although not overly large, contain excellent beds. Many have plaza views. Bathrooms have tub/shower combos. Additional seating from the unpretentious restaurant spills over beneath the arcades of the plaza, allowing indoor/outdoor dining and lots of opportunities for people-watching.

Plaza Mayor 26 (at the intersection of Calle Concejo), 37002 Salamanca. (℡ **92-321-21-00.** Fax 92-321-21-01. http://usuarios.iponet.es/htorres. 44 units. 85€–110€ double; 118€–152€ suite. AE, DC, MC, V. Parking 10€. **Amenities:** Restaurant; bar; lounge; room service; babysitting; laundry service; dry cleaning. *In room:* A/C, TV, minibar, hair dryer, safe.

Hotel San Polo ⭐   In the historic center, this hotel was built upon the ruins of an 11th-century church in the mid-1990s. Some of the Romanesque architectural elements have been incorporated into the contemporary building, which makes it more atmospheric. The midsize to spacious rooms are comfortably and tastefully furnished. Many open onto views of the cathedral. Bathrooms have tub/shower combos. The hotel lies at the intersection of Paseo del Rector Esperabé and Avenida Reyes de España.

Calle Arroyo de Santodomingo 2–4, 37008 Salamanca. (℡ **92-321-11-77.** Fax 92-321-11-54. 37 units. 84€–98€ double; 150€–180€ suite. AE, MC, V. Parking 6€. **Amenities:** Restaurant; bar; room service; babysitting; laundry service; dry cleaning. *In room:* A/C, TV, minibar, hair dryer, safe.

INEXPENSIVE

Hostal Plaza Mayor *Value*   If you're in town mainly to sightsee and dine out, and don't want to spend much on a room, make this hostal your number-one choice. A modest establishment, it offers good value for clean, comfortable, small rooms. Each has an immaculately maintained private bathroom with a shower.

The location is one of the finest in the city, right at the Plaza Mayor opposite the church of St. Martin. The hotel is quickly being discovered by bargain hunters.

Plaza del Corrillo 20, 37002 Salamanca. (✆) **92-326-20-20.** Fax 92-321-75-48. 19 units. 60€ double. MC, V. Parking 6€. **Amenities:** Restaurant; bar; room service; babysitting; laundry service; dry cleaning. *In room:* A/C, TV, hair dryer.

Hotel Don Juan ★ *(Finds)*   For the serious budget traveler, this little family hotel right off the Plaza Mayor is a gem. The decade-old hotel in a restored 200-year-old landmark building has a completely modernized interior that is light and airy. You're given a warm welcome by the owners, the Berrocal family. Rooms are small but clean and comfortable with tasteful decor. Bathrooms are well maintained with tub/shower combos. If available, opt for a room with a balcony overlooking the cathedral.

Calle Quintana 6, 37001 Salamanca. (✆) **92-326-14-73.** Fax 92-326-24-75. hoteldonjuan@wanadoo.es. 16 units. 60€–75€ double. MC, V. Parking 10€ nearby. **Amenities:** Cafeteria; bar; room service; babysitting; laundry service; dry cleaning. *In room:* A/C, TV, minibar, hair dryer, safe.

WHERE TO DINE

Chez Victor ★★★ FRENCH BASQUE   Set within the historic center of town, this is the most glamorous and best restaurant around. The owner-chef Victoriano Salvador spent some 15 years in France learning and perfecting his innovative cuisine. He returned home to open this restaurant, which won the only star Michelin has ever granted to a Salamanca restaurant. Specialties include freshly prepared fish—perhaps sea wolf in black squid sauce, broiled turbot in a hot vinaigrette sauce, or, even better, bluefin tuna steak in sesame seeds. Try the veal medallions in lemon sauce or, if it's offered, ribs of pork stuffed with prunes and served with a honey-mustard sauce. Despite the modernity of the cuisine, the portions are ample and well suited to Spanish tastes.

Espoz y Mina 26. (✆) **92-321-31-23.** Reservations required. Main courses 12€–22€. AE, DC, MC, V. Tues–Sun 2–3:30pm; Tues–Sat 9–11:30pm. Closed Aug.

El Candil CASTILIAN   This is a much-patronized Castilian tavern that has more than its share of devotees, often attracting a university crowd. Students of Salamanca consider it an ideal place to take their dates for the evening. That's because the food is good but also affordable. The location is in the center of town right off the Plaza Mayor. It's been in business for 6 decades, and the chefs cook as they always did, turning out regional fare that includes stuffed pimientos (a real treat) or else fried *merluza* (hake) served with a side order of sweet peppers. The roast suckling pig is perfectly done and fork tender. The chefs also make some very appetizing dishes with *bacalao* (dried cod). Their *marucha* steak is one of the best items they've ever offered. As an appetizer, you might try an order of their *farinato*, a sausage made from "secret ingredients" (we tasted pork and onion). They also do an *ensalada de perdiz* (partridge salad) very well.

Ventura Ruiz Aguilera 14–16. (✆) **92-321-72-39.** Reservations required. Main courses 8€–18€; fixed-price menu 35€. AE, DC, MC. Daily 9:30am–1am.

La Hoja ★ CASTILIAN   In the center of town, right off the landmark Plaza Mayor, one of the town's most outstanding chefs, Alberto López Oliva, prepares dishes with an imaginative twist, although drawing upon time-tested recipes from the province. The location is in a narrow passage lying right off the main square. In a setting of tall ceilings and paintings, you are presented the menu for the evening. The chef uses the freshest of ingredients at the market, and he fashions them into dishes with style, flair, and flavor. He prefers, whenever possible, to use regional produce. Among his more savory offerings are a mushroom risotto and an octopus salad with a cider vinaigrette. One of the most local of dishes is ribs of lamb served with fried potatoes. One of his special dishes is partridge cooked in chocolate. It's an acquired taste for some, as are his pig trotters cooked with slices of apples and prawns in a Balsamic vinaigrette.

Pasaje Coliseum 19. ℭ **92-326-40-28.** Reservations required. Main courses 14€–19€; fixed-price menu 28€. AE, MC, V. Tues–Sat 2–4:30pm and 9–11:30pm. Closed Aug 12–28.

Restaurant Chapeau ✿INTERNATIONAL   Set on the main street of Salamanca in a stone-sided building erected around 1900, this is a well-managed, socially prominent restaurant that has hosted most of the political and business dignitaries of town at one time or another. A tactful uniformed staff works hard presenting dishes that cater to conservative Castilian tastes as well as to more international kinds of palates. In the high-ceilinged dining room you're likely to find fish imported from the coast of Cantabria, including hake, sole, and mullet, either baked, fried, roasted, or added as the main components of a savory roster of stews and soups. Meat dishes include grilled, roasted, and stewed versions of veal, pork, beef, and chicken, any of which might be preceded with salads, pastas, soups, or an Iberian version of carpaccio (raw, thin-sliced beef) drizzled with olive oil and fresh herbs.

Gran Vía 20. ℭ **92-326-57-95.** Reservations recommended. Main courses 15€–20€; fixed-price menu 19€. AE, DC, MC, V. Mon–Sat 1–4pm and 8:30pm–midnight.

Trento ✿✿ CASTILIAN/BASQUE/NAVARRESE   The town's grandest palace, the Palacio de Castellanos (see above), also contains Salamanca's most stylish restaurant, operating since 1993. The decor was inspired by 19th-century France, with old rugs and paintings of Parisian street scenes. You can savor the subtle balance of imaginative flavors in dishes like a heart of lettuce served with filet of whitefish and fresh vegetables. That Spanish reliable, sweet peppers stuffed with salt cod, is especially good here, served with salmon sauce. Also of note is filet of veal with a Périgord sauce.

San Pablo 58–64. ℭ **92-326-18-18.** Reservations recommended. Main courses 12€–17€; set menu 18€. AE, DC, MC, V. Daily 1:30–4pm and 8:30–11:30pm.

SALAMANCA AFTER DARK

Don't expect a huge variety of nightlife options; this is a small-scale university town with an emphasis on undergraduate shenanigans. Your best bet is a stroll around the Plaza Mayor, where you'll pass cafes and bars that lend themselves to lingering or loitering, depending on your point of view. Usually a group of singing "tuna" dressed in medieval costumes perform for free nightly at 10pm, although these students appreciate tips. You might also wander onto such neighboring medieval streets as the Calle de Bordadores, Calle San Vicente, Calle Rua Mayor, and Calle Varillas, any of which offer tucked away spots for a quick caffeine or alcohol fix. Two Salamanca discos of particular note are **Disco Morgana,** Calle Iscar Peira (ℭ **92-321-41-78**), and its better-established, more historic competitor, **Camelot,** Calle Bordadores 3 (ℭ **92-321-21-82**). The latter occupies a stone monastery whose occupants 400 years ago would undoubtedly have been horrified at the goings-on within these premises that long ago echoed only with prayer and plainsong. And for a more modern spin on Salamanca's nightlife, head for the **Pub Rojo y Negro,** Calle Espoz y Mina 22 (no phone), where bouts of karaoke are interspersed with chatter, wine, whisky, and foaming mugs of Spanish beer.

3 Zamora ⊛

64km (40 miles) N of Salamanca, 238km (148 miles) NW of Madrid

Little known to North American visitors, **Zamora** (pronounced "thah-*moh*-rah") is the quintessential city of Old Castile, blending ancient and modern, but noted mainly for its Romanesque architecture. In fact, Zamora is often called a "Romanesque museum." A medieval frontier city, it rises up starkly from the Castilian flatlands, a reminder of the era of conquering monarchs and forgotten kingdoms.

You can explore Zamora's highlights in about 4 hours. Stroll along the main square, dusty Plaza Canovas; cross the arched Romanesque bridge from the 1300s; and take in at least some of the Romanesque churches for which the town is known, many of which date from the 12th century. The cathedral is the best example, but others include **Iglesia de la Magdalena,** Rua de los Francos, and **Iglesia de San Ildefonso,** Calle Ramos Carrión. You might also want to look at **Iglesia de Santa María la Nueva,** Plaza de Santa María, and **Iglesia de Santiago el Burgo,** Calle Santa Clara.

The crowning achievement, however, at the far west end of Zamora, is the **Cathedral San Salvador** ⊛, Plaza de la Catedral (© **98-053-06-44**). It is topped by a gold-and-white Eastern-looking **dome** ⊛. Inside, you'll find rich hangings, interesting chapels, two 15th-century Mudéjar pulpits, and intricately carved **choir stalls** ⊛⊛. Later architectural styles, including Gothic, have been added to the original Romanesque features, but this indiscriminate mixing of periods is typical of Spanish cathedrals. Inside the cloister, the Museo de la Catedral features ecclesiastical art, historical documents, church documents, and an unusual collection of **"Black Tapestries"** ⊛⊛ dating from the 1400s. These priceless Flemish tapestries tell the story of the Trojan War and are called "black" because some of their subjects are persons about to be decapitated. The cathedral is free, but admission to the museum costs 2€. The cathedral can generally be visited throughout the day. The museum is open April through September, Tuesday through Sunday from 11am to 2pm and 5 to 8pm. Off-season hours are Tuesday through Sunday from 11am to 2pm and 4 to 6pm.

ESSENTIALS

GETTING THERE   There are four **trains** to and from Madrid every day and two to and from La Coruña (trip time: 3 hr. and 6 hr., respectively). The railway station is at Calle Alfonso Peña (© **98-052-11-10**), about a 15-minute walk from the edge of the old town. Follow Avenida de las Tres Cruces northeast of the center of town. One-way fare from Madrid to Zamora is 23€.

Thirteen to 21 **bus** connections a day from Salamanca make this the easiest way to get in and out of town (trip time: 1 hr.). There are seven buses a day from Madrid (3½ hr.) for 15€. The town's bus station lies a few paces from the railway station, at Calle Alfonso Peña 3 (© **98-052-12-81**). Call © **98-052-09-52** for bus schedules and price information.

Zamora is at the junction of eight different roads and highways. Most of the traffic from northern Portugal into Spain comes through Zamora. Highways headed north to León, south to Salamanca, and east to Valladolid are especially convenient. From Madrid, take the A-6 superhighway northwest toward Valladolid, cutting west on the N-VI and west again at the turnoff onto 122.

VISITOR INFORMATION   The **tourist office,** Calle Santa Clara 20 (© **98-053-18-45;** www.jcy1.es/cau), is open Monday through Friday from 9am to 3pm and 5 to 7pm, Saturday and Sunday from 10am to 2pm and 5 to 8pm.

SPECIAL EVENTS   **Holy Week** in Zamora, the week before Easter, is a celebration known throughout the country. Street processions, called *pasos,* are among the most spectacular in Spain. If you plan to visit at this time, make your hotel reservations well in advance.

WHERE TO STAY

Hostería Real de Zamora 🦋   This most charming small hotel in town, sporting walls that date from the 1400s, occupies the long-ago headquarters of Zamora's dreaded Inquisition. (Before that, ironically, this was the site of a Jewish-owned building reputed to have been the home of the explorer Pizarro.) Today, the outstanding historical features of the building include a medieval reservoir, a patio perfect for enjoying a cup of tea or coffee, and a verdant garden along the city's medieval fortifications. An excellent example of a tastefully modernized aristocratic villa, it stands a few steps to the west of the northern embankment of the city's most photographed bridge, the Stone Bridge. The medium-sized rooms contain good beds. The well-maintained bathrooms are equipped with tub/shower combos. If you drive to the hotel, you'll have to rely on street parking.

Cuesta de Pizarro 7, 49027 Zamora. ©/fax **98-053-45-45.** www.hosteriasreales.com/hosteria4.htm. 23 units. 60€–72€ double. Rates include breakfast. AE, DC, MC, V. **Amenities:** Restaurant; bar; room service; babysitting; laundry service; dry cleaning. *In room:* A/C, TV, minibar, hair dryer, safe.

Parador de Zamora 🦋🦋   This is the grand address for Zamora, a parador of tranquillity and charm. The site has always held a legendary role in Zamora. Originally fortified as an *Alcazaba* by the Moors during their occupation of Zamora, it was rebuilt in 1459 by the Count of Alva y Aliste, and today the structure retains the severe, high-ceilinged dignity of its 15th-century Gothic form. Renovated by the Spanish government in the late 1960s, it is today one of the most beautiful paradors in Spain, and obviously the best and most tranquil place to stay in town.

Set 2 blocks south of the Plaza Mayor, near the junction of the Plaza de Viriato and Calle Ramos Carrión, the parador is richly decorated with medieval armor, antique furniture, tapestries, and potted plants. In winter, glass partitions close off a large inner patio centered on an antique well; baronial fireplaces provide much-appreciated warmth. Midsize rooms are white walled, well maintained, and tastefully decorated with conservative furniture, including beds with firm mattresses. The tidy bathrooms are equipped with tub/shower combos.

Plaza de Viriato 5, 49001 Zamora. © **98-051-44-97.** Fax 98-053-00-63. www.parador.es. 52 units. 95€–118€ double; 118€–140€ suite. AE, DC, MC, V. Parking 6€. **Amenities:** Restaurant; bar; pool; health club; sauna; room service; babysitting; laundry service; dry cleaning. *In room:* A/C, TV, minibar, hair dryer, safe.

WHERE TO DINE

París SPANISH/INTERNATIONAL   This elegantly decorated, air-conditioned restaurant is known for its fish, often made with a regionally inspired twist. Specialties include vegetable flan, braised oxtail, Zamora-style clams, and a delectable hake. Dishes, of course, change with the seasons. Most critics rate this restaurant number one in town. It is on the main traffic artery (Av. de Portugal) that funnels traffic south to Salamanca.

Av. de Portugal 14. ℭ **98-051-43-25**. Reservations recommended. Main dishes 10€–16€; *menú del día* 12€. AE, DC, MC, V. Mon–Sat 1–6pm and 8pm–midnight; Sun 1–6pm.

Serafín SPANISH   At the northeast edge of the old town, about a block south of the busy traffic hub of Plaza Alemania and Avenida de Alfonso IX, this air-conditioned haven with an attractive bar makes a relaxing retreat from the sun. The specialties change with the season but might include seafood soup Serafín, paella, fried hake, Iberian ham, and a savory *cocido* (stew).

Plaza Maestro Haedo 10. ℭ **98-053-14-22**. Main courses 12€–32€; fixed-price menus 16€–25€. AE, DC, MC, V. Daily 1–4:30pm and 8:30pm–midnight.

ZAMORA AFTER DARK

Calle Los Herreros, also called Calle de Vinos, contains more bars per square foot than any street in Zamora—about 16 of them in all. Each is willing to accommodate a stranger with a leisurely glass of wine or beer and a selection of tapas. Calle Los Herreros is a narrow street at the southern end of the old town, about 2 blocks north of the Duero River, within the shadow of the Ayuntamiento Viejo (Old Town Hall), a block south of the Plaza Mayor.

4 León ★★

327km (203 miles) NW of Madrid, 196km (122 miles) N of Salamanca

Once the leading city of Christian Spain, this old cathedral town was the capital of a centuries-old empire that declined after uniting with Castile. **León** today is the gateway from Old Castile to the northwestern routes of Galicia. It is a sprawling city, but nearly everything of interest to visitors—monuments, restaurants, and hotels—can be covered on foot once you arm yourself with a good map.

Once the heartbeat of a great kingdom, today León is a sleepy provincial city off the beaten track. But its wealth of old monuments, its top-notch accommodations, and a certain regal quality in the air still make the town feel like a capital.

Outlying mountain villages offer their own architectural gems, fine ski runs, and tasty concoctions of local trout and meat. Also, the region is particularly renowned for its soft-spoken, pristine Castilian accent. In sum, León is an

---

Moments **Luminous in León**

In the church-building sweepstakes of the Middle Ages, every Gothic cathedral vied to distinguish itself with some superlative trait. Milan Cathedral was the biggest, Chartres had the most inspiring stained-glass windows, Palma de Majorca had the largest rose window, and so on.

Structurally speaking, the boldest cathedral was at León. This edifice set the record for the highest proportion of window space, with stained-glass windows soaring 34m (110 ft.) to the vaulted ceiling, framed by the slenderest of columns, occupying 1,672 sq. m (18,000 sq. ft.), or almost all the space where you'd expect the walls to be.

The roof is held up not by walls, but by flying buttresses on the exterior. Inside, the profusion of light and the illusion of weightlessness astonish even medievalists. The architects Juan Pérez and Maestro Enrique, who designed the cathedral in the 13th century, were, in effect, precursors of Mies van der Rohe, 7 centuries before the age of steel girders draped with plate-glass curtain walls.

---

excellent place to experience the tranquillity of the Spanish heartland, as well as an obligatory stop for students of medieval architecture.

ESSENTIALS

GETTING THERE   León has good rail connections to the rest of Spain—11 **trains** daily from Madrid (trip time: 4–5 hr.). The station, Estación del Norte, Av. de Astorga 2 (© **90-224-02-02**), is on the western bank of the Bernesga River. Cross the bridge near the Plaza de Guzmán el Bueno. A one-way ticket from Madrid is 21€ to 28€, but travelers should be aware there are many different types of tickets, which change regularly.

Most of León's **buses** arrive and depart from the Estación de Autobuses, Paseo Ingeniero Saenz de Miera (© **98-721-10-00**). Three to five buses per day link León with Zamora and Salamanca, and there are 11 per day from Madrid (trip time: 4½ hr.). A one-way ticket on a direct regular bus from Madrid is 16€ to 26€ for the *supra* (comfortable) service.

León lies at the junction of five major highways coming from five different regions of Spain. From Madrid's periphery, head northwest on the N-VI super-highway toward La Coruña. At Benavente, bear right onto the N-630.

VISITOR INFORMATION   The **tourist office,** Plaza de Regla 4 (© **98-723-70-82;** www.jeyl.es/turismo), is open Monday through Friday from 9am to 2pm and 5 to 7pm, Saturday and Sunday from 10am to 2pm and 5 to 8pm.

EXPLORING THE TOWN

Catedral de León (Santa María de Regla) ★★★   The usual cathedral elements are virtually eclipsed here by the awesome **stained-glass windows** ★★★— some 125 in all (plus 57 oculi), dating from the 13th century. They are so heavy they have strained the cathedral's walls. Look for a 15th-century **altarpiece** ★ depicting the Entombment in the Capilla Mayor, as well as a Renaissance trascoro by Juan de Badajoz. The nave dates from the 13th and 14th centuries; the Renaissance vaulting is much later. Almost as interesting as the stained-glass windows are the **cloisters** ★, dating in part from the 13th and 14th centuries and containing faded frescoes and Romanesque and Gothic tombs; some capitals are carved with starkly lifelike scenes. Visitors can also tour a museum containing valuable art and artifacts, including a 10th-century Bible, notable sculptures, and a collection of romantic images of the Virgin Mary. The cathedral is on the edge of the old city, 7 blocks east of the town's most central square, the Plaza de Santo Domingo.

Plaza de Regla. © **98-787-57-70.** Admission to cathedral 1.70€ (also includes cloisters); museum 3.50€; cloisters only 1€. Cathedral, daily 8:30am–1:30pm and 4–8pm; cloisters and museum, Mon–Sat 9:30am–1:30pm and 4–7pm. Bus: 4.

Panteón y Museos de San Isidoro ★   This church, a short walk northwest of the cathedral, was dedicated to San Isidoro de Sevilla in 1063 and contains 23 tombs of Leonese kings. One of the first Romanesque buildings in León and Castile, it was embellished by Ferdinand I's artists. The columns are magnificent, the capitals splendidly decorated, and the vaults covered with murals from the 12th century. Unique in Spain, the Treasury holds rare finds—a 10th-century Scandinavian ivory, an 11th-century chalice, and an important collection of 10th- to 12th-century cloths from Asia. The library contains many ancient manuscripts and rare books, including a Book of Job from 951, a Visigothic Bible, an 1162 Bible, plus dozens of miniatures.

Plaza San Isidoro 4. ✆ **98-787-61-61**. Admission 3€. Sept–June Mon–Sat 10am–1:30pm and 4–6:30pm; Sun 10am–1:30pm. July–Aug Mon–Sat 9am–2pm and 3–8pm; Sun 9am–2pm. Bus: 4 or 9.

SHOPPING

Something about the city's antique architecture seems to encourage the acquisition of old-time handicrafts made from time-honored material like terra cotta, stone, copper, wrought iron, and leather. The Plaza de la Catedral and the streets that radiate out from it are particularly rich in battered, overcrowded kiosks with this type of artifact, and part of the fun of a trip within the city's historic core involves acquiring several pieces of it. For a more up-to-date roster of shopping options, consider a quick march through the vast stacks within León's biggest department store, **Corte Inglés,** Fray Luis de León 21 (✆ **98-726-31-00**). Inside, look for men's and women's clothing, books and gift items, and hints of the high-fashion priorities of cities as far away as Barcelona and Madrid.

WHERE TO STAY

Guzmán El Bueno   The most inexpensive accommodation we recommend in León is the no-frills Guzmán El Bueno, on the second floor of a centrally located boardinghouse. In all, it's a safe destination, widely known among international student travelers drawn to its low prices. Rooms are clean with decent beds; bathrooms contain tub/shower combos. Be warned in advance that the staff speaks only Spanish. Parking is available along the streets within walking distance of the hotel.

López Castrillón 6, 24003 León. ✆ **98-723-64-12**. 29 units. 37€–43€ double. MC, V. Walk up Calle Generalísimo from Plaza de Santo Domingo, turn left onto Calle de Cid; López Castrillón is a pedestrian-only street, branching off to the right. **Amenities:** Lounge; laundry service; dry cleaning. In room: TV.

Hotel Alfonso V ✪   Although we infinitely prefer the parador, this hotel in the heart of the city is less expensive and is famed for its classic contemporary decor. The pre-Franco hotel has been dramatically modernized with a stunning sculpture-filled lobby that rises seven wavy floors to a glass roof. Rooms, mostly medium in size, are a study in postmodernism, fitted with French windows, and excellent soundproofing. Bathrooms have tubs and showers.

Padre Isla 1, 24002 León. ✆ **98-722-09-00**. Fax 98-722-12-44. www.iova-sa.com. 62 units. 118€ double; 187€ suite. AE, DC, MC, V. Parking 12€. **Amenities:** Restaurant; bar; room service; babysitting; laundry service; dry cleaning. In room: A/C, TV, minibar, hair dryer, safe.

Hotel París ⓥ𝑎𝑙𝑢𝑒   Lying between the old and new towns, this hotel east of the Plaza Santo Domingo lures with Belle Epoque touches and a warm, inviting atmosphere. Consider it a cozy nest for your León sightseeing. Rooms are more intimate than spacious, but comfortable. Bathrooms have showers. Those old photographs in the public areas are not just of Paris—the hotel's namesake—but other European cities as well, including León.

Calle Ancha 18, 24003 León. ✆ **98-723-86-00**. Fax 98-727-15-72. www.hotelparisleon.com. 56 units. 69€ double; 85€ suite. AE, MC, V. **Amenities:** Restaurant; bar; room service; laundry service; dry cleaning. In room: A/C, TV, minibar, hair dryer.

Parador San Marcos ✪✪✪   This 16th-century former monastery with its celebrated Plateresque facade is one of the most acclaimed paradors in all of Spain. The government has remodeled it at great expense, installing extravagant authentic antiques and quality reproductions as well as improving the facade. Before its monastery days, the old *hostal* used to put up pilgrims bound for Santiago de Compostela in the 12th century. The parador also contains a church with a scallop-shell facade and an archaeological museum. The good-size rooms are sumptuous, each with a bathroom equipped with a tub/shower combo. The parador is northwest of the cathedral on the outskirts of the old town, on the east bank of the Bernesga River.

Plaza de San Marcos 7, 24001 León. ℂ 98-723-73-00. Fax 98-723-34-58. 230 units. 120€–136€ double; 220€–410€ suite. AE, DC, MC, V. Free parking. **Amenities:** Restaurant; bar; room service; babysitting; laundry service; dry cleaning. In room: TV, minibar, hair dryer, safe.

WHERE TO DINE

Alborada SPANISH   This contemporary restaurant much favored by local residents is outside the city center, a 15-minute walk northwest of the cathedral adjacent to the Parador San Marcos. Within a modern interior the owner supervises the preparation of fresh fish and meat dishes loosely based on French and Spanish models. Signature dishes include *lubina al horno* (baked whitefish), filet steak with pepper, hake casserole, and roast duck in orange sauce. A long wine list is available, and the room is air-conditioned.

Condesa de Sagasta 24. ℂ 98-722-19-12. Reservations recommended. Main courses 8€–15€; *menú del día* 12€. AE, DC, MC, V. Daily 1–4pm and 8:30pm–midnight. Bus: 4 or 9.

Bodega Regia CASTILIAN   Our favorite bodega in León lies within an easy walk of the cathedral in a restored 14th-century building. There is a central garden patio, with a rustic stone and clay floor emphasized by stone arches. A variety of tropical plants make for a warm, inviting atmosphere where architectural touches of the medieval period have been retained. The menu includes *embutidos de León*, a local sausage that is extremely tasty, as well as *pimientos de Bierzo con vinagre de Jerez*, red peppers grilled in a sherry-vinegar dressing. Another popular sausage is *morcilla de León y picadillo*, an exceptional treat. *Bacalao a la leonesa* is salt cod cooked with herbs and proper seasonings, and *alubias con espinaca* is an exceptional vegetable dish of white beans and spinach.

9–11 Regidores. ℂ 98-721-31-73. Main courses 12€–18€; set menu 18€. AE, DC, MC, V. Mon–Sat 1:45–4pm and 9pm–midnight. Closed Jan 6–17 and 15 days in Sept.

Casa Pozo ★ (Finds SPANISH   Two blocks south of the busy traffic hub of the Plaza Santo Domingo and across from city hall, this restaurant is a longtime favorite with locals who appreciate its unassuming style and flavor-filled cuisine. Regulars call owner Gabriel del Pozo Alvarez "Pin," and he's the reason behind the success of the place. Specialties include peas with salty ham, shrimp with asparagus, *estofados* (stews), roast pork or lamb with herbs and spices, and a delicate smothered sole. Twelve varieties of fresh fish are available. The restaurant offers an excellent selection of Rioja wines.

Plaza San Marcelo 15. ℂ 98-722-30-39. Reservations recommended. Main courses 12€–16€; fixed-price menus 12€. AE, DC, MC, V. Mon–Sat 1–4pm and 8–11:30pm. Bus: 4 or 9.

Formela ★★ CASTILIAN   Five minutes from the historical district and next to the Parador San Marcos, La Formela serves the finest cuisine in León, and has the best service, too. It is the smaller of two restaurants in Hotel Quindós. Located on the second floor, this restaurant is warm and inviting. The owner, Jaime Quindós, is a well-known art collector and former gallery owner. Walls are hung with contemporary paintings and a collection of antique Italian ornaments. There is an extensive collection of wines from throughout Spain but it is the cuisine that keeps diners happy. The menu includes *cesina de León*, one of the most delectable of local sausages, along with *revuelto de León con patatas,* or sautéed fresh vegetables with potatoes. The *ciervo estofado,* or venison casserole, is an alluring choice, as is *lubina a la espalda,* or filet of grilled whitefish. For dessert, the chefs will prepare you a crêpe Suzette or serve you *natillas caseras,* a Castilian-style pudding.

Gran Vía San Marcos 36. © 98-722-45-34. Reservations recommended. Main courses 12€–18€; set menu 15€. AE, DC, MC, V. Mon–Sat 1:30–3:30pm and 9–11:30pm.

LEON AFTER DARK

Few other cities in Spain evoke the mystery of the Middle Ages like León. To best appreciate the old-fashioned eloquence of the city, after dark wander around the Plaza Mayor, the edges of which are peppered with simple cafes and bars. None is particularly different from its neighbor, but overall the effect is rich, evocative, and wonderfully conducive to conversation and romance. Our favorite of the lot is the **Bar Universale,** Plaza Mayor (no phone), which serves tapas, sherries, wines, and beers in a setting that's particularly evocative and mellow.

5 Valladolid ⭐

201km (125 miles) NW of Madrid, 134km (83 miles) SE of León

From the 13th century until its eventual decay in the early 17th century, **Valladolid** was a royal city and an intellectual center attracting saints and philosophers. Isabella and Ferdinand were married here, Philip II was born here, and Columbus died here on May 19, 1506, broken in spirit and body after Isabella had died and Ferdinand refused to reinstate him as a governor of the Indies.

Valladolid is bitterly cold in winter, sweltering in summer. Today, after years of decline, the city is reviving economically and producing, among other things, flour, ironware, and cars. Consequently, it's polluted and noisy, and many of the older buildings have been replaced by more modern, utilitarian ones, although there are still many attractions remaining.

From the tourist office (see below), you can pick up a map that marks all the major monuments. These attractions can be covered on foot, although you may want to take a taxi to the two most distant points recommended: the Museo Nacional de Escultura and the Museo Oriental.

ESSENTIALS

GETTING THERE **Flights** to Valladolid land at **Vallanubla Airport,** Highway N-601 (© 98-341-55-00), a 15-minute taxi ride from the center of town. Aviaco routes daily flights to and from Barcelona.

Valladolid is well serviced by 14 daily **trains** to and from Madrid (trip time: 3–4½ hr.). A one-way fare is 12€ to 21€. Another city with train links to Valladolid is Burgos (16 trains per day). The train station (Estación del Norte), Calle Recondo s/n, by the Plaza Colon (© 90-224-02-02), is about a mile south of the historic center of town, 1 block southwest of the Campo Grande park.

The **bus** station is an 8-minute walk from the railway station, at Puente Colgante (© 98-323-63-08), at the southern edge of town. There are more than a dozen buses every day to and from Madrid (trip time: 2¼ hr.). Eight buses per day arrive from Zamora (1¼ hr.), and three buses per day from Burgos (1½ hr.).

Valladolid lies at the center of the rectangle created by Burgos, León, Segovia, and Salamanca and is connected to each with good highways. From Madrid, driving time is about 2¼ hours. Take superhighway A-6 northwest from Madrid, turning north on 403.

VISITOR INFORMATION   The **tourist office,** Calle de Santiago 19B (© **98-334-40-13;** www.jcyl.es/turismo), is open daily from 9am to 2pm and 5 to 7pm.

SEEING THE SIGHTS

Casa de Cervantes   Now a museum, this house was once occupied by Miguel de Cervantes, author of *Don Quixote,* who did much of his writing in Valladolid and remained here for the last years of his life. Behind its white walls the house is simply furnished, as it was in the author's day. It's half a block south of the cathedral, 2 blocks north of the city park, Campo Grande.

Calle del Rastro s/n. © **98-330-88-10.** Admission 2.50€; free on Sun. Tues–Sat 9:30am–3:30pm; Sun 10am–3pm.

Catedral ⊛   In 1580, Philip II commissioned Juan de Herrera, architect of El Escorial, to construct this monument in the city where he was born. When Philip died in 1598, work came to a stop for 18 years. Alberto Churriguera resumed construction, drawing up more flamboyant plans, especially for the exterior, in an unharmonious contrast to the severe lines of his predecessor. The classical, even sober, interior conforms more to Herrera's designs. A highlight is the 1551 altar-piece in the main apsidal chapel, the work of Juan de Juni. Art critics have commented that his polychrome figures seem "truly alive." The cathedral is in the heart of the city, east of the Plaza Mayor and north of the Plaza de Santa Cruz.

Calle Arrive 1. © **98-330-43-62.** Free admission to Cathedral; museum 2.50€. Cathedral and museum Tues–Fri 10am–1:30pm and 4:30–7pm; Sat–Sun 10am–2pm.

Iglesia de San Pablo   Once a 17th-century Dominican monastery, San Pablo is very impressive with its Isabelline-Gothic facade. Flanked by two towers, the main entrance supports levels of lacy stone sculpture. The church lies 6 blocks north of the cathedral, 1 block south of busy Avenida Santa Teresa. Mass is held daily, with eight Masses on Sunday.

Plaza San Pablo 4. © **98-335-17-48.** Free admission. Daily 7:30–9:30am, 12:30–2pm, and 7–9:30pm.

Museo Nacional de Escultura (National Museum of Sculpture) ⊛★★★
Located near Plaza de San Pablo, this museum displays a magnificent collection of gilded polychrome sculpture, an art form that reached its pinnacle in Valladolid. The figures were first carved from wood, then painted with consummate skill and grace to assume lifelike dimensions. See especially the works by Alonso Berruguete (1480–1561), son of Pedro, one of Spain's great painters. From 1527 to 1532 the younger Berruguete labored over the altar of the Convent of San Benito—a masterpiece now housed here. In particular, see his *Crucifix with the Virgin and St. John* in Room II and his *St. Sebastian and the Sacrifice of Isaac* in Room III. Works by Juan de Juni and Gregorio Fernández are also displayed.

After visiting the galleries, explore the two-story cloisters. The upper level is florid, with jutting gargoyles and fleurs-de-lis. See the chapel where the confessor to Isabella I (Fray Alonso de Burgos) was buried—and be horrified by the gruesome sculpture *Death.*

Colegio de San Gregorio, Calle Cadenas de San Gregorio 1. © **98-325-03-75.** Admission 2.40€, free for children under 18 and adults over 65. Tues–Sat 10am–2pm and 4–6pm; Sun 10am–2pm.

Museo Oriental   Located in the Royal College of the Augustinian Fathers, near Campo Grande park, the museum has 14 rooms: 10 Chinese and four Filipino. It has the best collection of Asian art in Spain, with bronzes from the 7th century B.C. to the A.D. 18th century, wooden carvings, 100 fine porcelain pieces, paintings on paper and silk from the 12th century to the 19th, and ancient Chinese coins, furniture, jade, and ivory. In the Filipino section, ethnological and primitive art is represented by shields and arms. Eighteenth-century religious art can be admired in extraordinary ivories, embroideries, paintings, and silversmiths' work. Popular art of the 19th century includes bronzes, musical instruments, and statuary.

Paseo de Filipinos 7. 🕐 **98-330-68-00**. Admission 3€; free for children 9 and under. Mon–Sat 4–7pm; Sun and holidays 10am–2pm.

WHERE TO STAY

Enara *Value*　About a quarter mile south of the cathedral, near the junction of Avenida 2 de Mayo and Paseo Miguel Iscar, Enara is arguably the best inexpensive accommodation in Valladolid. Its central location is backed up by contemporary, pleasantly furnished rooms, which are small but offer good comfort because of the fine beds and the immaculately kept bathrooms containing tub/shower combos. The decoration is in the typical Castilian style with some antiques. Built in the 19th century as a private house, it was converted into a hotel in the mid-1970s. Two of its three stories are devoted to simple but well-maintained rooms, and the ground floor contains the breakfast area. Parking is available along the Plaza de España.

Plaza de España 5, 47001 Valladolid. 🕐 **98-330-02-11**. Fax 98-330-03-11. 24 units. 45€ double. MC, V. Closed Dec 24–25. **Amenities:** Babysitting; laundry service; dry cleaning. *In room:* TV.

Felipe IV 🌟　When it was built the Felipe IV was one of the grandest hotels in the city, although the Olid Meliá (see below) now enjoys that position. Each of its midsize rooms is modernized, guaranteeing its ranking as a solidly acceptable establishment. All units have bathrooms containing tub/shower combos. A garage provides parking for motorists. The hotel is south of the busy traffic hub of Plaza de Madrid, a few blocks north of the rail station, near the eastern edge of the city park, Campo Grande. It attracts many business travelers.

Calle de Gamazo 16, 47004 Valladolid. 🕐 **98-330-70-00**. Fax 98-330-86-87. www.hfelipeIV.com. 131 units. 115€ double; 175€ suite. AE, DC, MC, V. Parking 11€. **Amenities:** Restaurant; bar; health club; room service; babysitting; laundry service; dry cleaning. *In room:* A/C, TV, minibar, hair dryer, safe.

Hotel Olid Meliá 🌟🌟　Set in the heart of the historic zone about 5 blocks northwest of the cathedral, this is a modern hotel whose original construction in the early 1970s has been upgraded throughout the public areas with a postmodern gloss. This is the town's leading choice, dwarfing the competition. The good-size rooms are the most comfortable in town. Each unit comes with an immaculate bathroom with a tub/shower combo.

Plaza San Miguel 10, 47003 Valladolid. 🕐 **800/336-3542** in the U.S., or 98-335-72-00. Fax 98-333-68-28. www.solmelia.com. 211 units. 115€–142€ double; from 205€–323€ suite. AE, DC, MC, V. Parking 15€. **Amenities:** Restaurant; bar; health club; salon; room service; babysitting; laundry service; dry cleaning. *In room:* A/C, TV, minibar, hair dryer, safe.

Hotel Parque　Completed in 1982, this modern chain hotel is 2 blocks west of the rail station on the city outskirts. It's popular with business travelers unwilling to negotiate the labyrinth of Valladolid's central streets. Although an acceptable choice in every way, it is not as luxuriously appointed or as comfortable as the Olid Meliá (see above). The good-size rooms are comfortable and functionally furnished with no surprises and few disappointments. All units contain spacious appointed bathrooms with tub/shower combos. It also offers special rooms and facilities for people with disabilities.

Joaquín García Morato 17, 47007 Valladolid. ℭ 800/336-3542 in the U.S., or 98-322-00-00. Fax 98-347-50-29. 186 units. 109€ double; 164€ suite. AE, DC, MC, V. Parking 11€. **Amenities:** Restaurant; bar; room service; babysitting; laundry service; dry cleaning. In room: A/C, TV, minibar, hair dryer, safe.

WHERE TO DINE

La Corte ⚑ CASTILIAN   In the center of the city, this restaurant, launched in 2001, is one of your best bets for the cookery of Old Castile. The building and appointments are modern although the interior is decorated in the old style, with wooden beamed ceilings and plaster white walls. The restaurant since its opening has drawn a list of distinguished patrons, including on occasion royal "personages." One of the best dishes is baked *rape,* or monkfish, served with pine nuts, fresh mussels, and prawns. *Bacalao* (cod) is prepared with virgin olive oil and garlic and served with a freshly made mushroom sauce. Oxtail is roasted and served with fried potatoes and sweet peppers, a winning combination, and you can also order tongue coated in pine nuts. Dessert could include a cheese tart of a melt-in-your-mouth chocolate truffle. At the tavern downstairs you can stop off for some of the house's regional Castilian wine, along with a savory list of tapas prepared fresh nightly.

Paseo Zorrilla 10. ℭ 98-333-87-85. Reservations not required. Main courses 9€–18€. DC, MC, V. Daily 9am–5pm and Mon–Sat 7:30pm–midnight.

La Parrilla de San Lorenzo ⚑ *Finds* CASTILIAN/INTERNATIONAL   The word for grill in Spanish is *parrilla,* and this restaurant serves some of the finest grilled fish and meat dishes in town. As a curiosity note, it honors St. Lawrence, who was burned to death over a grill. The setting was once a monastery from 1596 that has undergone many roles over the centuries before being converted into this successful restaurant. You dine in an elegant setting of yesterday with gilded mirrors, wrought iron, stained-glass windows depicting biblical themes, and stone arches, a very medieval atmosphere. You might begin with a *rape*—in this case an *ensalada de rape* or monkfish salad—with little red pimientos. The chef also does an excellent capon salad as well. Duck paté is another tantalizing appetizer. The house specialty is milk-fed lamb cooked to tender perfection in a wood oven. The bonito tuna is among the best fish offerings. It's marinated in sea salt before being lightly sautéed in virgin olive oil.

Calle Pedro Niño 1. ℭ 98-333-50-88. Reservations recommended. Main courses 12€–17€. AE, DC, MC, V. Daily 1:30–3:30pm and Mon–Sat 9pm–midnight.

Mesón Cervantes ⚑⚑ SPANISH/INTERNATIONAL   Opened in 1973, this restaurant is the finest in the city. The owner, Alejandro, works the dining room and is capably complemented in the kitchen by his wife, Julia. Neighborhood residents favor this place for its lack of pretension and its delectable cuisine. Two particular favorites are sole with pine nuts and seasonal river crabs. Many other fish dishes, including hake and monkfish, are available. Roast suckling pig and roast lamb are also popular. Other specialties include peppers stuffed with crabmeat; tender veal scaloppini "Don Quixote," served with a piquant sauce; and *arroz con liebre* (herb-laden rice studded with chunks of roasted wild rabbit, in season). The restaurant stands beside the Casa de Cervantes, .8km (½ mile) south of the cathedral.

Rastro 6. ℭ 98-330-61-38. Reservations recommended. Main courses 12€–20€. AE, DC, MC, V. Mon–Sat noon–4pm and 9pm–midnight. Closed Aug.

Mesón Panero ⑂ CASTILIAN/FRENCH The chef of this imaginative restaurant, Angel Cuadrado, can turn even the most austere traditional Castilian recipes into sensual experiences. Set near the water, this 1960s establishment lures diners with fresh fish, including a succulent brochette of sole and hake with fresh asparagus. One weekly favorite is *cocido castellano,* the famous regional stew. Roast lamb and suckling pig are also available, plus a selection of well-chosen wines. The Mesón Panero is near the Casa de Cervantes, a short walk from the tourist office.

Marina Escobar 1. ⓒ **98-330-70-19.** Reservations required. Main courses 15€–19€. AE, DC, MC, V. Daily 1:30–4pm; Mon-Sat 9pm–midnight. Closed Sun July–Aug.

VALLADOLID AFTER DARK

There are no great clubs to recommend in Valladolid, but that doesn't mean that the city isn't a lively, bustling place when darkness falls. Instead of grand clubs, it becomes a town of bars and pubs. **Calle del Paraíso** is in itself a virtual street of bars, with action overflowing later on to the pubby **Plaza del San Miguel.** Just enter the pub or bar that looks the most amusing with the most convivial crowd, and chances are you won't go wrong. Most of these pubs and bars cater to a younger crowd, often from the university. If you're 30 or older, you might want to patronize one of the cafes along **Calle de Vincente Meliner,** especially those near Plaza Dorado.

Just off the Plaza Mayor, the liveliest bar in town is **El Corcho,** Calle Correo 2 (ⓒ **98-333-08-61**), which also serves some of the tastiest Castilian tapas in town. It offers a very rustic atmosphere, with brick walls and sawdust sprinkled over the much-used floor. Over the marble-topped bar copperware and pig haunches are displayed. The cook rightly boasts of his *tostada de gambas,* which is shrimp drizzled with virgin olive oil and sprinkled over toasted bread. Other specialties include fish croquettes and Iberian ham and codfish. Tapas range in price from 1.20€ to 5€. Open daily from 1 to 4pm and 8pm to midnight.

6 Burgos ⑂⑂⑂

242km (150 miles) N of Madrid, 121km (75 miles) NE of Valladolid

Founded in the 9th century, this Gothic city in the Arlanzón River valley lives up to its reputation as the "cradle of Castile." Just as the Tuscans are credited with speaking the most perfect Italian, so the citizens of **Burgos,** with their distinctive lisp ("El Theed" for "El Cid"), supposedly speak the most eloquent Castilian.

El Cid Campeador, Spain's greatest national hero immortalized in the epic *El Cantar de Mío Cid,* is forever linked to Burgos. He was born near here and his remains lie in the city's grand cathedral.

Like all the great cities of Old Castile, Burgos declined seriously in the 16th century, only to be revived later. In 1936 during the Civil War, the right-wing city was Franco's Nationalist army headquarters.

Today, Burgos no longer enjoys its historical glory, but is a provincial city along the *meseta,* or plateau, of Spain. Dry as a desert and burning hot during the summer days, it comes alive at night and is filled with smoky cafes and dance clubs. Most of the bars, frequented by students, are in the area around the cathedral. Many of them don't start to party seriously until after 10pm, so it's a late-night town.

ESSENTIALS

GETTING THERE   Burgos is well connected by **train** from Madrid (trip time: 3½ hr.), Barcelona (8–9 hr.), the French border, and Valladolid. Fares from Madrid range from 19€ to 23€; from Barcelona, 34€ to 43€; and from Valladolid, 6€ to 13€. The Burgos railway station is at the terminus of Avenida de Conde Guadalhorce, .8km (½ mile) southwest of the center. To get here, head for the major traffic hub in the Plaza Castilla, then walk due south across the Arlanzón River. For train information or tickets, call © **90-224-02-02.**

Between 12 and 17 **buses** a day make the 3-hour trip up from Madrid. A one-way fare costs 13€. The bus depot in Burgos is at Calle Miranda (© **94-726-20-17**), which intersects the large Plaza de Vega, due south of (and across the river from) the cathedral.

Burgos is well connected to its neighbors by a network of highways, but its routes to and from Barcelona (6 hr.) are especially wide and modern. The road from Barcelona changes its name several times, from the A-2 to the A-68 to the E-4, but it is a superhighway all the way. From Madrid, follow the N-I north for about 3 hours; the highway is fast but less modern than the road from Barcelona.

VISITOR INFORMATION   The **tourist office,** Plaza Alonso Martínez 7 (© **94-720-18-46**), is open Monday through Saturday from 9am to 2pm and 5 to 7pm, Sunday from 10am to 2pm and 5 to 8pm.

EXPLORING THE TOWN

Casa de Cordón, the historical 15th-century palace on Plaza de Calvo Sotelo, has been restored and is now a bank. However, you can go by and take a look. History records that on April 23, 1497, Columbus met with Queen Isabella and King Ferdinand here after his second voyage to the New World. It was in this building that Philip the Handsome suffered a heart attack after a game of jai alai. His wife, Juana, dragged his body through the streets of Burgos, earning forever the name of Juana *la Loca* (the Crazy One).

Cartuja de Miraflores ✦   Lying 4km (2½ miles) east of the center of Burgos, this florid Gothic charterhouse was founded in 1441. King Juan II selected it as the royal tomb for himself and his queen, Isabel of Portugal. By 1494, the **church** ✦ was finished, its facade in a rather sober style, not suggesting the treasure trove of decoration inside. The stunning attraction of the interior is the **sculptured unit** ✦✦✦ in the apse, said to have been built with the first gold brought back from the New World. This is a masterpiece of design, and the faithful often stand here for an hour or 2 taking in its stunning beauty. It was the work of Gil de Siloé in the late 1400s. Siloé also designed the polychrome altar wood altarpiece. The remains of the king and queen (see above) lie in the white marble mausoleum designed like an eight-pointed star. The tomb's decorators gave these parents of Isabel the Catholic a fine sendoff with exuberant and flamboyant Gothic decorations such as cherubs, pinnacles, canopies, and scrolls.

Miraflores. © **94-720-31-25.** Free admission. Mon–Sat 10:15am–3pm and 4–6pm; Sun 11:30am–12:30pm, 1–3pm, and 4–6pm.

Catedral de Santa María ✦✦✦   Begun in 1221, this cathedral was one of the most celebrated in Europe. Built in diverse styles, predominantly Flamboyant

Gothic, it took 300 years to complete. Ornamented 15th-century bell towers flank the three main doorways by John of Cologne. The 16th-century Chapel of Condestable, behind the main altar, is one of the best examples of Isabelline-Gothic architecture, richly decorated with heraldic emblems, a sculptured filigree doorway, figures of apostles and saints, balconies, and an eight-sided star stained-glass window.

Equally elegant are the two-story 14th-century cloisters, filled with fine Spanish Gothic sculpture. The cathedral's tapestries, including one well-known Gobelin, are rich in detail. In one of the chapels you'll see an old chest linked to the legend of El Cid—it was filled with gravel and used as collateral by the warrior to trick moneylenders. The remains of El Cid himself, together with those of his wife, Doña Ximena, lie under Santa María's octagonal lanternlike dome. Finally, you might want to see the elaborate 16th-century Stairway of Gold in the north transept, the work of Diego de Siloé.

The cathedral is across the Arlanzón River from the railway station, midway between the river and the Citadel.

Plaza de Santa María. ℂ **94-720-47-12.** Admission to chapels, cloisters, and treasury 3.60€ adults, 2.40€ students and seniors. Daily 9:30am–1pm and 4–7pm.

Monasterio de las Huelgas 𝕬𝕬   This cloister outside Burgos has seen a lot of action. Built in the 12th century in a richly ornamented style, it was once a summer place for Castilian royalty, as well as a retreat for nuns of royal blood. Inside, the Gothic church is built in the shape of a Latin cross. Despite some unfortunate mixing of Gothic and baroque, it contains much of interest—notably some 14th-and 17th-century French tapestries. The tomb of the founder Alfonso VIII and his queen, the daughter of England's Henry II, lie in the Choir Room.

Thirteenth-century doors lead to the cloisters, dating from that century and blending Gothic and Mudéjar styles. Despite severe damage to the ceiling, the remains of Persian peacock designs are visible. The beautiful Chapter Room contains the standard of the 12th-century Las Navas de Tolora (war booty taken from the Moors), and the Museo de Ricas Telas is devoted to 13th-century costumes removed from tombs. These remarkably preserved textiles give a rare peek at medieval dress.

The monastery is 1.6km (1 mile) off the Valladolid Road (the turnoff is clearly marked). From the Plaza Primo de Rivera in Burgos, buses for Las Huelgas leave every 20 minutes.

Calle Compás de Adentro. ℂ **94-720-16-30.** Admission 5€ adults, 2.50€ students and children. Oct–Mar Tues–Sat 11am–2pm and 4–6pm; Sun 10:30am–3pm. Apr–Sept Tues–Sat 10:30am–2pm and 3:30–5:45pm; Sun 10:30am–3pm.

SHOPPING

A city as old and historic as Burgos is chock-a-block with emporia selling almost infinite volumes of ceramics, woodcarvings, and artifacts that include fireplace bellows crafted from leather, wood, and brass or copper. Many of these shops line the edges of the city's most central square, the Plaza Mayor, and the streets radiating out from it. Two in particular are especially worthwhile, with an appealing mixture of old and new artifacts inside. Consider **Antigüedades Javor,** Plaza Santiago s/n (ℂ **94-723-51-60**), and its most visible competitor, **Antigüedades Isla,** Calle Aparicio y Ruiz (ℂ **94-726-06-36**).

WHERE TO STAY
EXPENSIVE
Landa Palace ✧✧✧   One of the greatest hotels of Castile, a member of Relais & Châteaux, this hotel is some 3km (2 miles) south of Burgos on N-I. A romantic getaway, it is in a handsomely restored castle from the 1300s with later additions. Pilgrims once stopped here en route to Santiago de Compostela in Galicia, but they wouldn't recognize the grandeur of the place today. Decorated with tasteful antiques, the lobby sets the tone with its white marble and ornate coffered ceiling. Rooms are spacious and cozily inviting with antique decorations and tile floors. Marble bathrooms are state of the art with all the extras, including plush towels and tub/shower combos. Although parts of the hotel look a little worn, the graciousness of the staff compensates.

Carretera Madrid-Irún (at Km 235), 09001 Burgos. ℂ 94-725-77-77. Fax 94-726-46-76. www.landapalace.es. 42 units 165€–195€ double; 195€–225€ suite. MC, V. Free parking. **Amenities:** Restaurant; bar; pool; fitness center; room service; babysitting; laundry service; dry cleaning; currency exchange. *In room:* A/C, TV, minibar, hair dryer, safe.

MODERATE
Hotel Almirante Bonifaz   Book in here more for the price than for any grand comfort. It is clean and decent, however, though the small rooms don't invite lingering. They are more suitable for an overnight stay. In lieu of air conditioning, guests open their windows at night, although this subjects one to the noise of traffic. Rooms are comfortable; bathrooms have showers. The hotel lies near the river in the commercial part of town.

Vitoria 22–24, 09004 Burgos. ℂ **94-720-69-43.** Fax 94-725-64-04. www.grupojeda.com. 79 units. 82€–125€ double; 103€–140€ triple. AE, DC, MC, V. Parking 8.50€. **Amenities:** Restaurant; bar; car-rental desk; room service; babysitting; laundry service; dry cleaning. *In room:* A/C, TV, minibar, hair dryer, safe.

Hotel del Cid   Built in 1983 by the Alzaga family, who still own and operate it, this establishment stands in front of the cathedral and beside their restaurant. The restaurant is better known than the hotel, which grew up on the site of one of the first printing presses in Spain. Decorated like a 15th-century house, it boasts 20th-century luxuries, including extra-large beds and bathrooms with tub/shower combos, which were refurbished in 1992. A well-respected restaurant, **Mesón del Cid,** serves Spanish and regional cuisine, much to the delight of its frequently returning diners.

Plaza de Santa María 8, 09003 Burgos. ℂ **94-720-87-15.** Fax 94-726-94-60. 55 units. 115€ double; 135€ suite. AE, DC, MC, V. Parking 10€. **Amenities:** Restaurant; lounge; room service; babysitting; laundry service; dry cleaning. *In room:* A/C, TV, minibar, hair dryer, safe.

Hotel Rice ✧✧ *Finds*   This hotel, .8km (½ mile) north of the center, is the town's leading boutique hotel. It is imbued with charm, grace, and character, almost like a London town house. Once you enter the British-style lobby, you'll feel snug, cozy, and comfortable, taking in the Queen Anne chairs, the marble surfaces, the antique cabinets, and the elegant fabrics. Rooms have elegant touches, with luxury mattresses and the best bathrooms in Burgos.

Av. Reyes Católicos 30, 09005 Burgos. ℂ **94-722-23-00.** Fax 94-722-35-50. www.hotelrice.com. 50 units. 99€ double; 121€ triple. AE, DC, MC, V. **Amenities:** Restaurant; bar; room service; babysitting; laundry service; dry cleaning. *In room:* A/C, TV, minibar, hair dryer, safe.

INEXPENSIVE
Hotel España   The best budget choice in town is a 5-minute walk southeast of the cathedral and a block south of the Plaza Mayor on a leafy promenade

filled with sidewalk cafes and Castilians taking early evening strolls. The small rooms lack style and imagination but are completely comfortable, with good beds and tidy bathrooms containing tub/shower combos. The management is helpful to visitors. When the España is full, they have been known to call around to other hostelries for stranded tourists.

Paseo del Espolón 32, 09003 Burgos. ① **94-720-63-40.** Fax 94-720-13-30. www.hotelespana.net. 69 units. 65€–70€ double; 70€–80€ triple. MC, V. Closed Dec 20–Jan 20. **Amenities:** Restaurant; lounge; babysitting; laundry service; dry cleaning. *In room:* TV.

Hotel Norte y Londres   On a pleasant square a short walk northeast of the cathedral, this hotel is imbued with traces of faded grandeur, with its leaded stained-glass windows and crystal chandeliers. The building dates from the early 20th century; it was converted into a hotel in the 1950s and has flourished ever since. Rooms are good size, with basic furnishings, good beds, and large bathrooms equipped with yesteryear's finest plumbing and tub/shower combos. Breakfast is the only meal served.

Plaza de Alonso Martínez 10, 09003 Burgos. ① **94-726-41-25.** Fax 94-727-73-75. 50 units. 58€–70€ double. AE, MC, V. Parking 11€. **Amenities:** Breakfast room; lounge. *In room:* TV, hair dryer.

WHERE TO DINE

The restaurants in the heart of Burgos, surrounding the cathedral, usually feature prices that soar as high as a Gothic spire. Every menu contains the roast lamb and suckling pig known throughout the area, or you might order *entremeses variados,* an appetizer sampler of many regional specialties.

Casa Ojeda ★ BURGALESE   This top-notch restaurant combines excellent Burgos fare, cozy decor, attentive service, and moderate prices. Moorish tiles and low ceilings create an inviting ambience enhanced by intimate nooks, old lanterns, and intricate trelliswork. Upstairs the restaurant is divided into two sections: one overlooking the street and the other, the Casa del Cordón, where Ferdinand and Isabella received Columbus after his second trip to America (1497). The cookery is the best in town. A la carte dishes include roast lamb, Basque-style hake, sole Harlequin, and chicken in garlic. A house specialty is *alubias con chorizo y morcilla* (small white beans with spicy sausages).

Vitoria 5. ① **94-720-90-52.** Reservations required. Main courses 13€–20€. AE, DC, MC, V. Daily 1:15–4pm; Mon–Sat 9–11:30pm.

Mesón de los Infantes CASTILIAN/BASQUE   Just below the gate leading into the Plaza de Santa María, this restaurant serves good food amid elegant Castilian decor. Many of the chef's specialties are based on recipes in use in Castile for centuries. The roast suckling pig is everybody's favorite, and you can also order *cocido madrileño,* assorted shellfish, river crabs Burgalese style, and beef tail with potatoes. Kidneys are sautéed in sherry, and a wide list of game is often featured, including hare, partridge, rabbit, and pigeon. Grills and roasts are also crowd-pleasers.

Calle Corral de los Infantes. ① **94-720-59-82.** Reservations recommended. Main courses 6€–19€; fixed-price menu 12€. AE, DC, MC, V. Daily noon–4:30pm and 8pm–midnight.

Rincón de España *Value* SPANISH   This restaurant, about 1 block southwest of the cathedral, draws many discerning visitors. You can eat in a rustic dining room or outdoors under a large awning closed off by glass when the weather threatens. The restaurant offers *platos combinados,* as well as a more extensive a la carte menu. Some special dishes include black pudding sausage with peppers, barbecued lamb cutlets with potatoes, and roast chicken with sweet peppers. The food here is good, the portions are large, and the vegetables are fresh.

Nuño Rasura 11. ℭ **94-720-59-55.** Reservations recommended. Main courses 6€–18€; fixed-price menus 10€. AE, DC, MC, V. Daily 1–4pm and 8pm–midnight; closed Mon and Tues nights Oct–Apr.

A SIDE TRIP TO SANTO DOMINGO DE LA CALZADA ⋆

Some 68km (42 miles) east of Burgos, and easily visited on a day trip, lies Santo Domingo de la Calzada. The crowning achievement of the town, which grew as a stopover for pilgrims en route to Santiago de Compostela, is the 13th-century **cathedral** (ℭ **94-134-00-33**), a national landmark. For the most part Gothic in style, it nevertheless contains a hodgepodge of architectural elements— Romanesque chapels, a Renaissance choir, and a freestanding baroque tower. St. Dominic, for whom the city is named, is buried in the crypt. A centuries-old legend is attached to the cathedral: Supposedly a rooster stood up and crowed after it had been cooked to protest the innocence of a pilgrim who had been accused of theft and sentenced to hang. To this day, a live cock and hen are kept in a cage up on the church wall, and you can often hear the rooster crowing at Mass. The cathedral is open Monday through Saturday from 9am to 6pm and on Sunday from 5 to 7pm to avoid the Masses. It costs 1.80€ adults, .60€ children. Free admission for everyone on Sunday. Motorists can reach Santo Domingo de la Calzada by following either of the traffic arteries paralleling the river, heading east from Burgos Cathedral until signs indicate N-120.

7

Extremadura

This remote westernmost region of Spain extends from the Gredos and Gata mountain ranges all the way to Andalusia, and from Castile to the Portuguese frontier. Extremadura has a varied landscape of plains and mountains, meadows with holm and cork oaks, and fields of stone and lime. Spanish Extremadura (not to be confused with the Portuguese province of Extremadura) includes the provinces of Badajoz and Cáceres.

The world knows Extremadura best as the land of the conquistadors. Famous sons included Cortés, Pizarro, Balboa, and many others less well known but also important, such as Francisco de Orellana and Hernando de Soto. These men were mostly driven by economic necessity, finding it hard to make a living in this dry, sun-parched province. The money they sent back to their native land financed mansions and public structures that stand today as monuments to their long-ago American adventures.

Many of Extremadura's older civilizations have monuments, too, like the Roman ruins in Mérida, Arab ruins found in Badajoz, and medieval palaces in Cáceres.

Extremadura is a popular destination for outdoor fun. Spaniards come here to hunt, to enjoy the fishing and watersports popular in the many reservoirs, and to ride horses along ancient trails. Because summer is intensely hot here, spring and fall are the best times to visit.

1 Guadalupe ★★

188km (117 miles) W of Toledo, 225km (140 miles) SW of Madrid

Guadalupe lies in the province of Cáceres, 450m (1,500 ft.) above sea level. The village has a certain beauty and a lot of local color. Everything of interest lies within a 3-minute walk from the bus drop-off point at Avenida Don Blas Pérez, also known as Carretera de Cáceres.

Around the corner and a few paces downhill is the Plaza Mayor, which contains the Town Hall (where many visitors go to ask questions in lieu of a tourist office).

The village is best visited in spring, when the balconies of its whitewashed houses burst into bloom with flowers. Wander at your leisure through the twisting, narrow streets, some no more than alleyways. The buildings are so close together that in summer you can walk in the shade of the steeply pitched sienna-colored tile roofs. Celebrated for its shrine to the Virgin, Guadalupe is packed with vendors and is a major outlet of the religious-souvenir industry.

GETTING THERE

There is one bus every day to and from Madrid's Estación Sur (trip time: 3 hr.). The road is poor, but the route through the surrounding regions is full of savage beauty. In Guadalupe the buses park a few paces uphill from the Town Hall. Call **Empresa La Sepulvedana,** Madrid (© **91-530-48-00**), for schedules.

One narrow highway goes through Guadalupe. Most maps don't give it a number; look on a map in the direction of the town of Navalmoral de la Mata. From Madrid, take the narrow, winding C-401 southwest from Toledo, turning north in the direction of Navalmoral de la Mata after seeing signs for Navalmoral de la Mata and Guadalupe. Driving time from Madrid is between 3½ and 4½ hours, depending on how well you fare with the bad roads.

SEEING THE SIGHTS

Except for a handful of your basic souvenir shops around the Plaza Mayor, don't expect a lot of particularly interesting shopping in Guadalupe. Two exceptions to this rule are the small but personalized **Cacharro Tienda,** Plaza Mayor 12 (no phone), with an unusual collection of brass, copper, and iron, and the gift shop within the Hotel Lujuan, Calle Gregorio López 19 (© **92-736-71-70**), which sells local handcrafted items, often in brass and copper.

Land of the Conquistadors

It's estimated that some 15,000 Extremeños (from a total pop. of 400,000) went to seek gold in the New World. The most fabled of these adventurers were Hernán Cortés (from Medellín) in Mexico; Francisco Pizarro (from Trujillo) in Peru; Vasco Núñez de Balboa (from Jerez de los Caballeros) in Panama, where he first sighted the Pacific Ocean; Hernando de Soto (from Barcarrota) in Florida and beyond, discovering the Mississippi River; and Francisco Orellana (also from Trujillo) in Ecuador and the Amazon.

Thanks to these conquistadors, the names of Extremaduran villages are sprinkled through the Americas, as exemplified by the Guadalupe Mountains (Texas), Albuquerque (New Mexico), Trujillo (Peru), Mérida (Mexico), and Medellín (Colombia).

Because Extremeños faced such a hard time making a living in the harsh land of their birth, they often turned elsewhere to seek their fortune. One of the reasons for the poverty was that huge ranches were owned by absentee landlords, as many still are today. These ranches are called *latifundios,* and often farmers and their families live on these ranches, paying the owners for the privilege of grazing a few goats or growing some slight crops in the dry climate. A system of *mayorazgo* (still in effect) granted all the family property to the eldest son. The other sons, called *secundinos,* were left penniless, and often chose to set sail for the New World to seek their gold.

Many of the conquistadors died or stayed in the New World, but others who had grown rich there returned to the land of their birth and built magnificent homes, villas, and ranches, many of which still stand today.

Bernal Díaz, who joined the Cortés expedition to Mexico, put the situation very bluntly. "We came here to serve God and the king," he wrote, "and to get rich."

Real Monasterio de Santa María de Guadalupe ★★   In 1325, a farmer searching for a stray cow reportedly spotted a statue of the Virgin in the soil. In time, this statue became venerated throughout the world, honored in Spain by Queen Isabella, Columbus, and Cervantes. Known as the Dark Virgin of Guadalupe, it is said to have been carved by St. Luke. A shrine was built to commemorate the statue and tributes poured in from all over the world, making Guadalupe one of the wealthiest foundations in Christendom. The statue is found in the 18th-century chapel, **Camarín** ★. Surrounding the Virgin of Guadalupe is a treasure trove of riches, including jasper, marble, and precious woods, plus nine paintings by Luca Giordano.

The church is noted for the wrought-iron railings in its naves and a magnificently decorated **sacristy** ★★ with eight richly imaginative 17th-century masterpieces by Zurbarán. Be sure to see the museum devoted to ecclesiastical vestments and to the choir books produced by 16th-century miniaturists. The 16th-century Gothic cloister is also flamboyant, with two galleries. The pièce de résistance is the stunning **Mudéjar cloister,** with its brick-and-tile

Gothic-Mudéjar shrine dating from 1405 and a Moorish fountain from the 14th century.

Plaza de Juan Carlos 1. ✆ **92-736-70-00.** Admission to museum and sacristy 3€ adults, 1.50€ children 7–14, free for children 6 and under. Daily 9:30am–1pm and 3:30–6:30pm.

WHERE TO STAY

Hospedería del Real Monasterio ★   Here's your chance to live in a converted antique monastery. Once a way station for pilgrims visiting the shrine, the Hospedería used to provide lodging for a small donation. Times have changed, but the prices remain moderate at this government-rated two-star hotel in the center of town, which is the second-best place to stay after the parador, and a whole lot cheaper. Since the place is installed in an antique monastery, the accommodations come in various shapes and sizes, but each is tastefully furnished and fitted with firm mattresses and well-maintained bathrooms with showers.

Plaza Juan Carlos 1, 10140 Guadalupe. ✆ **92-736-70-00.** Fax 927-36-71-77. 47 units. 51€ double; 129€ suite. MC, V. Closed Jan 12–Feb 12. **Amenities:** Restaurant; bar; room service; laundry service; dry cleaning. *In room:* A/C, hair dryer.

Parador de Guadalupe ★★   Located in a scenic spot in the center of the village, the area's most luxurious accommodation is housed in a 16th-century building with a beautiful garden. Queen Isabella once stayed here, and the place often saw meetings between royal representatives and explorers, who signed their contracts here before setting out for the New World. The house is named after Francisco de Zurbarán, the great 17th-century painter who was born in the nearby town of Fuente de Cantos. There is a Zurbarán painting in one of the salons, along with ancient maps and engravings—many of them valuable works of art. Most of the comfortable rooms are quite spacious, and all have excellent beds with firm mattresses and bathrooms with tub/shower combos.

Marqués de la Romana 12, 10140 Guadalupe. ✆ **92-736-70-75.** Fax 927-36-70-76. www.parador.es. 41 units. 102€ double; 125€ suite. AE, DC, MC, V. Parking 6€. **Amenities:** Restaurant; bar; pool; tennis court; room service; babysitting; laundry service; dry cleaning. *In room:* A/C, TV, minibar, hair dryer, safe.

WHERE TO DINE

Both of the hotels recommended above also have good restaurants.

Mesón el Cordero SPANISH   Miguel and Angelita run Guadalupe's best independent restaurant, named for their specialty, *asado de cordero* (roast lamb flavored with garlic and thyme). The couple has operated this restaurant for more than 20 years and enjoys a devoted local following, which is recommendation enough. You might begin with another of their specialties, *sopa guadalupana,* then follow with partridge "from the countryside" if you have a taste for game. The house dessert is a creamy custard, *flan casero.*

Alfonso Onceno 27. ✆ **92-736-71-31.** Reservations recommended. Main courses 12€–16€; fixed-price menu 16€. AE, DC, MC, V. Tues–Sun 1–4pm and 7–11pm. Closed Feb 1–15.

2 Trujillo ★

245km (152 miles) SW of Madrid, 45km (28 miles) E of Cáceres

Dating from the 13th century, the walled town of **Trujillo** is known for the colonizers and conquerors born here. Among its famous natives were Francisco Pizarro, the conqueror of Peru, whose family palace on the Plaza Mayor was built with gold from the New World, and Francisco de Orellana, the founder of

Guayaquil, Ecuador, and the first European to explore the Amazon. Other Tru-jillano history-makers were Francisco de las Casas, who accompanied Hernán Cortés in his conquest of Mexico and founded the city of Trujillo in Honduras; Diego García de Paredes, who founded Trujillo in Venezuela; Nuño de Chaves, founder of Santa Cruz de la Sierra in Bolivia; and several hundred others whose names are found throughout the Americas. There is a saying that 20 American countries were born here.

Celts, Romans, Moors, and Christians have inhabited Trujillo over the cen-turies. The original town, lying above today's modern one, was built on a gran-ite ledge on the hillside. It is centered on the Plaza Mayor, one of the artistic landmarks of Spain. A Moorish castle and a variety of 16th- and 17th-century palaces, manor houses, towers, churches, and arcades encircle the plaza and over-look a bronze equestrian statue of Pizarro by American artists Mary Harriman and Charles Runse. Steep, narrow streets and shadowy little corners evoke the bygone times when explorers set out from here on their history-making adventures.

ESSENTIALS

GETTING THERE   There are nine **buses** per day to and from Madrid (trip time: 3½ or 4½ hr.). There are also six buses running daily from Cáceres (45 min.), and six from Badajoz. A one-way ticket from Madrid costs 13€; from Cáceres, 2.45€; and from Badajoz, 8€. Trujillo's bus station, Calle Marqués Albayda (© **92-732-12-02**), is on the south side of town on a side street that intersects with Calle de la Encarnación.

Trujillo lies at a network of large and small roads connecting it to Cáceres via the N-521 and to Lisbon and Madrid via the N-V superhighway. **Driving** time from Madrid is around 4 hours.

VISITOR INFORMATION   The **tourist office,** on the Plaza Mayor (© **92-732-26-77**; www.ayto-trujillo.com), is open April through October, daily from 9am to 2pm and 4 to 7pm, off season, daily from 9am to 2pm and 4:30 to 6:30pm.

EXPLORING THE PLAZA & BEYOND

In the heart of Trujillo, the **Plaza Mayor** ✸✸ is one of the outstanding archi-tectural sights in Extremadura. A statue honoring Francisco Pizarro, who almost single-handedly destroyed the Inca civilization of Peru, dominates it. The statue is an exact double of one standing in Lima. Many of the buildings on this square were financed with wealth brought back from the New World.

The most prominent structure on the square is the **Ayuntamiento Viejo (Old Town Hall),** with three tiers of arches, each tier squatter than the one below.

Iglesia de San Martín stands behind the statue dedicated to Pizarro. This granite church, originally from the 15th century, was reconstructed in the 16th century in Renaissance style. Inside are an impressive nave, several tombs, and a rare 18th-century organ still in working condition.

While you are on the square, observe the unusual facade of the **Casa de las Cadenas,** a 12th-century house draped with a heavy chain, a symbol that Philip II had granted the Orellana family immunity from heavy taxes.

You can then visit the **Palacio de los Duques de San Carlos,** a 16th-century ducal residence turned into a convent. Ring the bell to gain entry any time daily from 9:30am to 1pm and 4:30 to 6:30pm. A donation of at least 1.20€ is appreciated, and a resident will show you around; appropriate dress (no shorts or bare shoulders) is required. The facade has Renaissance sculptured figures, and the two-level courtyard inside is even more impressive.

Palacio de la Conquista, also on the square, is one of the most grandiose mansions in Trujillo. Originally constructed by Hernán Pizarro, the present structure was built by his son-in-law to commemorate the exploits of this explorer, who accompanied his half brother, Francisco, to Peru.

The stores that ring the Plaza Mayor have the town's best shopping; they stock stonework, leather, brass, copper, and ironwork. The best is **Bazar Sant'Olaria,** Plaza Mayor 6 (© **92-732-33-18**), which has a selection of the best of virtually everything produced in the region. Handcrafted woodcarvings are available from a small-scale artisan, **Artesanía Del Mimbre,** Plazuela de San Judas 3 (© **92-732-10-66**), whose intensely detailed effigies of saints and characters from Spanish literature are nothing short of charming.

Castillo   Constructed by the Arabs on the site of a Roman fortress, this castle stands at the summit of the granite hill on which Trujillo was founded. Once at the castle, you can climb its battlements and walk along the ramparts enjoying a panoramic view of the austere countryside of Extremadura. Later, you can go below and see the dungeons. It is said that the Virgin Mary appeared here in 1232, giving the Christians renewed courage to free the city from Arab domination. Many visitors find it most dramatic at sunset.

Crowning the hilltop. Admission 1.25€. Daily 10am–2pm and 4–6:30pm.

Iglesia de Santa María   This Gothic building with an outstanding Renaissance choir is the largest church in Trujillo, having been built over the ruins of a Moorish mosque. Ferdinand and Isabella once attended Mass here. The proudest treasure is an altar *retablo* (gradine) with two dozen panels painted by Fernando Gallego. Also here is the tomb of Diego García de Paredes, the "Samson of Extremadura," who is said to have single-handedly defended a bridge against an attacking French army with only a gigantic sword. To reach the church, go through the gate of the Plaza Mayor at Puerta de San Andrés and take Calle de las Palomas through the old town.

Calle de Ballesteros. © **92-732-02-11.** Admission 1.20€. Daily 10am–2pm and 4:30–7:30pm.

WHERE TO STAY

Hotel Victoria ★ *Finds*   This small, delightful hotel lies a 5-minute walk from the Plaza Mayor in an ornate 19th-century colonial mansion. The interior is light and airy, and the rooms surround what was once the courtyard of the house. Each level is adorned with a filigree design of pillars and ornate wrought-iron balustrades and capitals. The accommodations are spacious, with wooden ceilings, tiled marble floors, and comfortable beds, along with modern conveniences such as private well-equipped bathrooms with tub/shower combos.

Plaza del Campillo 22, 10200 Trujillo. © **92-732-18-19.** Fax 927-32-30-84. 27 units. 61€ double; 97€ suite. AE, MC, V. Parking 5€. **Amenities:** Restaurant; bar; cafe; laundry service; dry cleaning. *In room:* A/C, TV, hair dryer.

Las Cigüeñas   Located east of the town center and convenient if you're driving, this is the second-best place to stay in Trujillo. It doesn't have the charm of the parador (see below), but it's cheaper. A roadside hotel with a garden, it offers functional but clean and comfortable rooms, which, though small, are equipped with firm mattresses and bathrooms with showers. You'll find Las Cigüeñas on the main highway from Madrid, about a mile before Trujillo.

Av. de Madrid s/n, Carretera N-V, 10200 Trujillo. ✆ **92-732-12-50.** Fax 927-32-13-00. 78 units. 72€ double; 96€ suite. AE, DC, MC, V. Free parking. **Amenities:** Restaurant; bar; room service; babysitting; laundry service; dry cleaning. *In room:* A/C, TV, minibar, hair dryer, safe.

Meliá Trujillo 🌟 *Finds* The popular Spanish chain hotel, Meliá, has moved into Trujillo and taken over a former monastery from the 1600s, with its adjoining cloisters, and converted it into a hotel of charm. The grace note is a lovely old courtyard with a swimming pool that's the greatest place to be at midday in the August heat of Trujillo. Bedrooms come in various shapes and sizes, ranging from small to spacious, and each is equipped with a first-rate bathroom with tub or shower (or both). The on-site restaurant is installed in the former refectory. Like the building itself, the refectory has been handsomely converted in keeping with the spirit of the building. Regional and Spanish specialties are served, and the cookery is exceptional for the area.

Plaza del Campillo 1, Trujillo 10200. ✆ **92-745-89-00.** Fax 927-32-30-46. www.solmelia.com. 77 units. 125€ double; 175€ junior suite; 315€ suite. AE, DC, MC, V. **Amenities:** Restaurant; bar; pool; room service; laundry/dry cleaning. *In room:* A/C, TV, minibar, hair dryer, safe.

Parador de Trujillo 🌟🌟🌟 Housed in the 1533 Convent of Santa Clara, this centrally located parador, about a block south of Avenida de la Coronación, is a gem of Trujillo-style medieval and Renaissance architecture that's been faithfully restored since being converted into a parador in 1984. The beautifully decorated rooms, once nuns' cells, have canopied beds and spacious bathrooms with tub/shower combos. The gardens and fruit trees of the Renaissance cloister are inviting, and a courtyard in its new section blends with the original convent architecture.

Calle de Santa Beatriz de Silva 1, 10200 Trujillo. ✆ **92-732-13-50.** Fax 927-32-13-66. trujillo@parador.es. 46 units. 94€ double; 152€ suite. AE, DC, MC, V. Parking in garage 12€. **Amenities:** Restaurant; bar; room service; babysitting; laundry service; dry cleaning. *In room:* A/C, TV, minibar, hair dryer, safe.

WHERE TO DINE

The hotels recommended above also have good restaurants serving regional cuisine.

Mesón la Troya EXTREMADURAN Locals and visitors alike are drawn to this centrally located restaurant featuring regional cuisine and doing the province proud. Have a dry sherry in the bar that resembles the facade of a Spanish house. This cozy provincial theme also flows into the dining rooms, with their white walls decorated with ceramic plates, potted plants, and red tiles. Few people leave hungry after devouring the set menu, with its more than ample portions; food items change daily. Local dishes include *prueba de cerdo* (garlic-flavored pork casserole) and *carne con tomate* (beef cooked in tomato sauce). A table is always reserved for the village priest, who comes here for breakfast, lunch, and dinner and has done so for more than 27 years.

Plaza Mayor 10. ✆ **92-732-13-64.** Reservations recommended. Main courses 5.50€–12€; fixed-price menu 15€. MC, V. Daily 1–4:30pm and 8:45pm–midnight.

Pizarro EXTREMADURAN Locals cite this central hostal as the best place to go for regional Extremaduran cookery. Built in 1864, the inn is set on the town's main square and named for its famous son. The same family has owned and operated the place since 1919. Regional wines accompany meals that invariably include ham from acorn-fed pigs. You might begin with asparagus with mayonnaise sauce, then follow with *asado de cordero* (roast lamb flavored with herbs and garlic) or Roman-style fried *merluza* (hake). The kitchen's game specialty is *estofado de perdices* (partridge casserole).

Plaza Mayor 13. ✆ **92-732-02-55.** Reservations recommended. Main courses 6€–17€; *menú del día* 12€. AE, DC, MC, V. Daily 1:30–4pm and 8:30–10:30pm.

3 Cáceres ✶✶

298km (185 miles) SW of Madrid, 256km (159 miles) N of Seville

A national landmark and the capital of Extremadura, **Cáceres** is encircled by old city walls and has several palaces and towers, many financed by gold sent from the Americas by the conquistadors.

One of six cities in Spain designated World Heritage Sites by UNESCO, Cáceres was founded in the 1st century B.C. by the Romans as Norba Caesarina, but its present-day name is derived from *alcázares,* an Arab word meaning fortified citadel. After the Romans, it was settled by all the cultures that have made the south of Spain the unique cultural melting pot of influences it is today. The contemporary city offers a unique blend of the traces these successive invaders left behind.

ESSENTIALS

GETTING THERE   Cáceres has the best **rail** connections in the province, with five trains per day from Madrid (trip time: 4–5 hr.). A one-way ticket costs 16€ to 27€. There is also one train per day from Lisbon (4½ hr.); the fare is 32€ to 67€. One train per day also runs from Seville (4 hr.); the fare is 15€.

The station in Cáceres is on Avenida Alemania (✆ **92-723-37-61**) near the main highway heading south (Carretera de Sevilla). A green-and-white bus shuttles passengers about once an hour from the railway and bus stations (across the street from one another; board the shuttle outside the bus station) to the busiest traffic junction in the new city, the Plaza de América. From there it's just a 10-minute walk to the edge of the old town.

Bus connections to Cáceres are more frequent than railway connections. From the city bus station (✆ **92-723-25-50**) on the busy Carretera de Sevilla, about a half mile south of the city center, buses arrive and depart for Madrid (trip time: 5 hr.) and Seville (4½ hr.) every 2 to 3 hours. There's also bus transport to Guadalupe (1 per day); Trujillo (6 or 7 a day); Mérida (2 a day); Valladolid (3 a day); and Córdoba (2 a day). Many travelers opt to walk the short distance from the Cáceres bus station to the city center.

Driving time from Madrid is about 4 hours. Most people approach Cáceres from eastern Spain via the N-V superhighway until they reach Trujillo. Here they exit onto the N-521, driving another 45km (28 miles) west to Cáceres.

VISITOR INFORMATION   The **tourist office,** Plaza Mayor 20 (✆ **92-701-08-34;** www.turismoextremadura.com), is open Monday through Friday from 9am to 2pm and 4 to 6:15pm, Saturday and Sunday from 9:30am to 2pm.

EXPLORING THE OLD CITY

The modern city lies southwest of the *barrio antiguo,* **Cáceres Viejo** ✶✶✶, which is enclosed by massive **ramparts.** The heart of the old city lies between the Plaza de Santa María and, a few blocks to the south, the Plaza San Mateo. The **Plaza de Santa María** ✶ is an irregularly shaped, rather elongated square. On each of its sides are the honey-brown facades of buildings once inhabited by the nobility. On a casual stroll through the city's cobblestone streets, your attention will surely be drawn at first to the walls that enclose the old upper town. These are a mixture of Roman and Arab engineering, and their state of preservation is excellent. About 30 towers remain from the city's medieval walls, all of them heavily restored. Originally much taller, the towers reflected the pride and independence of their builders; when Queen Isabella took over, however, she ordered them cut down to size. The largest tower is at the Plaza del General Mola. Beside it stands the Estrella Arco (Star Arch), constructed by Manuel Churriguera in the 18th century. To its right you'll see the Torre del Horno, a mud-brick adobe structure left from the Moorish occupation.

On the far side of the Plaza de Santa María rises the **Catedral de Santa María,** which is basically Gothic in style, although many Renaissance embellishments have been added. Completed sometime in the 1500s, this is the cathedral of Cáceres and it contains the remains of many conquistadors. It has three Gothic aisles of almost equal height and a carved retablo at the high altar dating from the 16th century. (Insert coins to light it up.)

La Casa de los Toledo-Montezuma was built by Juan Cano de Saavedra with money from the dowry of his wife, the daughter of Montezuma. The house is set into the northern corner of the medieval ramparts, about a block to the north of Plaza de Santa María. It is now a public records office.

The **Plaza Mayor** is remarkably free from most of the blemishes and scarring effects that city planning and overregulation have made so common in other historically important sites. Passing through **El Arco de la Estrella (Arch of the Star),** you will then catch the most advantageous angle of Santa María Cathedral.

Some of the most appealing shops in Cáceres are on the streets radiating outward from the Plaza Mayor, with a particularly good selection of artifacts along either side of **Calle Pintores.**

Cuesta de la Compañía leads to the Plaza San Mateo and the 14th-century **Iglesia de San Mateo,** which has a Plateresque portal and a rather plain nave—except for the Plateresque tombs, which add a decorative touch.

Two adjoining plazuelas near here embody the flavor of old Cáceres. The first of them, the **Plaza de las Veletas,** on the site of the old Alcázar, is the **Casa de las Veletas (Weather Vane House;** © **92-724-72-34**), which houses a provincial archaeological museum with priceless prehistoric and Roman pieces, along with a famous *aljibe* (Arab well). Its baroque facade, ancient Moorish cistern, five naves with horseshoe arches, and patio and paneling from the 17th century have been preserved. The museum displays Celtic and Visigothic remains, Roman and Gothic artifacts, and a numismatic collection. Admission is 1.50€, and the museum is open Tuesday through Saturday from 9:30am to 2:30pm, and Sunday from 10am to 2:30pm and 4 to 6pm. At the second plazuela, **San Pablo,** sits the **Casa de las Cigüeñas (House of the Storks),** the only palace whose tower remains intact despite the order by Queen Isabella at the turn of the 15th century to reduce the height of all such strategic locations for military reasons. The building now serves as a military headquarters and is not open to the public.

You'll probably notice lots of storks nesting on most of the rooftops and bell towers in the town. This is a revealing sign of how Cáceres has managed to preserve not only its landmarks but also an environmentally sound balance between people and nature.

Church of Santiago was begun in the 12th century and restored in the 16th century. It has a reredos carved in 1557 by Alonso de Berruguete and a 15th-century figure of Christ. The church is outside the ramparts, about a block to the north of Arco de Socorro. To reach it, exit the gate, enter the Plaza Socorro, and then walk down Calle Godoy. It is on your right.

If you want to see a more modern face of the region, and shop for housewares and fashion while you're at it, drive 15 minutes west of the town center to the **Centro Comercial Ruta de la Plata,** Carretera Portugal, where you'll find a scattering of boutiques, plus a number of simple snack bars and cafes.

WHERE TO STAY

Hotel Extremadura   This 1960s hotel offers straightforward rooms. They're a bit boxy and functionally furnished but are well maintained and very comfortable, with good beds and immaculate bathrooms with tub/shower combos. It is located about half a mile southwest of the historic center in a bustling commercial district. Prices are fair for what you get.

Av. Virgen de Guadalupe 28, 10001 Cáceres. ℂ **92-762-96-39**. Fax 92-762-92-49. 151 units. 146€ double; 172€ suite. AE, DC, MC, V. Parking 9€. **Amenities:** Restaurant; bar; pool; health spa; room service; babysitting; laundry service; dry cleaning. *In room:* A/C, TV, minibar, hair dryer, safe.

Meliá Cáceres ★★   The Meliá hotel chain continues to show up the government parador system by opening superior lodgings in towns long dominated by a parador. Although the Parador de Cáceres is fine in every way, the Meliá is superior in service. This converted Renaissance palace is just south of the Plaza del General Mola beside the entrance to the old town. Its rooms are better appointed, sunnier, and more spacious than those at the parador. Bathrooms are roomy and have tub/shower combos. Everything is tastefully converted, and there's a lot of exposed stone, along with indirect lighting and sleek modern furnishings.

Plaza San Juan 11, 10003 Cáceres. ℂ **92-721-58-00**. Fax 927-21-40-70. 86 units. 155€ double; 182€ suite. AE, DC, MC, V. **Amenities:** Restaurant; bar; room service; babysitting; laundry service; dry cleaning. *In room:* A/C, TV, minibar, hair dryer, safe.

Parador de Cáceres ★★   This state-operated parador is set within what was originally a 15th-century palace. Built in a severe style, it enjoys a tranquil location and a well-scrubbed, durable format of exposed stone, white plaster, and tile or stone floors. Pristine white corridors lead to dignified rooms outfitted in a starkly appealing combination of white walls and dark-grained, somewhat bulky furniture inspired by the austere decorative traditions of Extremadura. All the modern extras have been installed here, including excellent bathrooms with tub/shower combos. Suits of armor adorn some of the public areas, giving the place a vaguely feudal feel, but the patios that open onto masses of potted plants and flowers are quite welcoming.

Moments **The Flavor of the Land**

The cuisine offered at the parador and at many other places in Cáceres affords a novel experience to even seasoned travelers. You might try the famous *cuchifrito,* a suckling pig stewed in pepper, orange, and vinegar sauce, or the *caldereta de cordero,* lamb with pepper and almonds. A more daring choice would be *jabalí a la cacereña,* a wild boar dish marinated in red wine and herbs. The most characteristic dessert in all of Extremadura is *técula mécula,* an ancient example of the region's marzipan confectionery, which like most things in Cáceres has been passed down from one generation to the next for centuries.

Calle Ancha 6, 10003 Cáceres. ☎ 92-721-17-59. Fax 927-21-17-29. 33 units. 109€–116€ double; 169€–175€ suite. AE, DC, MC, V. Free parking on streets; garage parking 9€. **Amenities:** Restaurant; bar; room service, babysitting; laundry service; dry cleaning. *In room:* A/C, TV, minibar, hair dryer, safe.

WHERE TO DINE

Atrio ✿✿✿ SPANISH/CONTINENTAL   Atrio serves the finest cuisine in the entire province. Even hard-to-please Michelin grants this place a star. Situated in a shopping mall cul-de-sac, the inside decor is elegant and somewhat unusual for this part of Spain—streamlined and sleek in white and sunflower yellow. The chef steers a skillful course between rich, regional flavors and more Continental fare. The menu changes frequently to take advantage of the best of the various seasons. Prices can go much higher than those indicated below if truffles are added to your dish. Service is the finest in the area—in all, it's a professional and deluxe operation.

Av. de España 30. ☎ 92-724-29-28. Reservations recommended. Main courses 17€–30€; fixed-price menu 59€. DC, MC, V. Daily 1:30–4pm; Mon–Sat 9pm–midnight.

El Figón de Eustaquio ✿ EXTREMADURAN   El Figón is a pleasant place serving regional cuisine that has been satisfying locals since 1948. You'll notice the four Blanco brothers who run the place doing practically everything. This includes preparing the amazingly varied dishes—for example, honey soup, *solomillo* (filet of beef), and trout Extremaduran style (covered in ham), as well as typical Spanish specialties. The air-conditioned interior has a rustic decor. El Figón is west of the western ramparts of the old city near the intersection of Avenida Virgen de Guadalupe and the Plaza San Juan.

Plaza San Juan 12. ☎ 92-724-81-94. Reservations recommended. Main courses 15€–22€; fixed-price menus 12€–18€. AE, DC, MC, V. Daily 1:30–4pm and 8pm–12:30am.

Torre de Sande ✿ NOUVELLE SPANISH   A 15th-century palace at the highest point in the city at the Plaza de San Mateo, this restaurant features a trio of separate dining rooms and a beautiful terraced garden in use as weather permits. The chef and owner, Cesar Raez, has been here since 1996. The view of the city from the garden is panoramic, and wonderful at night. The chefs combine regional flavors with the best of modern recipes, with palate-pleasing and marvelously succulent results. Try such delights as *boletus con foie* (mushrooms with duck liver), *ensalada de mango y salmon* (mango and salmon salad), *solomillo de retinto* (a prized local beefsteak), or *perdiz a la cantara con salsa* (partridge stuffed with liver and truffles in a port wine sauce). Desserts include *tapita de tres chocolates* (layer cake of 3 types of chocolate) and a sheep's-milk pudding.

Calle de los Condes 3. ☎ 92-721-11-47. Reservations recommended. Main courses 12€–21€. AE, DC, MC, V. Daily 1–5pm; Mon–Sat 9pm–midnight.

4 Mérida ✿

71km (44 miles) S of Cáceres, 56km (35 miles) E of Badajoz

Founded in 25 B.C., **Mérida** is at the crossroads of the Roman roads linking Toledo and Lisbon and Salamanca and Seville. At one time the capital of Lusitania (the Latin name for ancient Portugal, which included parts of southwestern Spain), Mérida was one of the most splendid cities in Iberia, ranking as a town of major importance in the Roman Empire; in fact, it was once called a miniature Rome. Its monuments, temples, and public works make it the site of some of the finest Roman ruins in Spain, and as such it is the tourist capital of

Extremadura. Old Mérida can be covered on foot—in fact, that is the only way to see it. Pay scant attention to the dull modern suburb across the Guadiana River, which skirts the town with its sluggish waters.

ESSENTIALS

GETTING THERE   **Trains** depart and arrive from the RENFE station on Calle Cardero (© **90-224-02-02**), about a half mile north of the Plaza de España. Each day there are four trains to and from Cáceres (trip time: 1 hr.), five trains to and from Madrid (4 hr.), one to and from Seville (3 hr.), and seven to and from Badajoz (1 hr.). The fare from Madrid is 19€ to 30€.

The **bus** station is on Avenida de la Libertad (© **92-437-14-04**) near the train station. Every day, there are three buses to and from Madrid (5½ hr.), six to eight buses to and from Seville (3 hr.), two buses to and from Cáceres (2 hr.), and five to 10 buses to Badajoz (1 hr.). From Mérida to Madrid, the fare is 18€ to 22€; Mérida to Seville, 11€; Mérida to Cáceres, 4€; and Mérida to Badajoz, 3.65€.

To **drive,** take the N-V superhighway from Madrid or Lisbon. Driving time from Madrid is approximately 5 hours; from Lisbon, about 4½ hours. Park in front of the Roman theater and explore the town on foot.

VISITOR INFORMATION   The **tourist office,** at Av. José Sáez de Buruaga (© **92-400-97-30;** www.turismoextremadura.com), is open April through October, Monday through Friday from 9:30am to 1:45pm and 5 to 7:30pm, Saturday from 9:15am to 1:45pm. Off-season hours are Monday through Friday from 9:30am to 2pm and 4 to 6pm, Saturday and Sunday from 9:15am to 1:45pm. Those are the official hours, but don't expect the staff to interpret them too literally.

EXPLORING MERIDA

The **Roman bridge** ✦ over the Guadiana was the longest in Roman Spain—about half a mile—and consisted of 64 arches. It was constructed of granite under Trajan or Augustus, then restored by the Visigoths in 686. Philip II ordered further refurbishment in 1610; work was also done in the 19th century. The bridge crosses the river south of the center of Old Mérida, its length increased because of the way it spans two forks of the river, including an island in midstream. In 1993, it was restored and turned into a pedestrian walkway. A semicircular suspension bridge for cars was constructed to carry the heavy traffic and save the bridge for future generations. Before the restoration and change, this bridge served as a main access road into Mérida, witnessing transportation evolve from hooves and feet to trucks and automobiles.

Another sight of interest is the old hippodrome, or **Circus Maximus,** which could seat about 30,000 spectators for chariot races. The original Roman masonry was carted off for use in other buildings, and today the site looks more like a parking lot. Excavations have uncovered rooms that may have housed gladiators. The former circus is at the end of Avenida Extremadura on the northeastern outskirts of the old town, about half a mile north of the Roman bridge and a 10-minute walk east of the railway station.

Arco Trajano (Trajan's Arch) lies near the heart of the Old Town beside Calle Trajano, about a block south of the Parador Vía de la Plata. An unadorned triumphal arch, it measures 15m high by 9m across (48 ft. by 30 ft.).

Acueducto de los Milagros is the most intact of the town's two remaining Roman aqueducts; this one brought water from Proserpina, 5km (3 miles) away.

From the aqueducts, water was fed into two artificially created lakes, Cornalvo and Proserpina. The aqueduct is northwest of the old town, lying to the right of the road to Cáceres, just beyond the railway tracks. Ten arches still stand.

The latest monument to be excavated is the **Temple of Diana** (dedicated to Caesar Augustus). Squeezed between houses on a narrow residential street, it was converted in the 17th century into the private residence of a nobleman, who used four of the original Corinthian columns in his architectural plans. The temple lies at the junction of Calle Sagasta and Calle Romero Leal in the center of town.

While in the area, you can also explore the 13th-century **Iglesia de Santa María la Mayor,** Plaza de España. It has a 16th-century chapel graced with Romanesque and Plateresque features. It stands on the west side of the square.

Alcazaba   On the northern bank of the Guadiana River beside the northern end of the Roman bridge (which it was meant to protect) stands the Alcázar, also known as the Conventual or the Alcazaba. Built in the ninth century by the Moors, who used fragments left over from Roman and Visigothic occupations, the square structure was later granted to the Order of Santiago.

Plaza Del Rastro, Calle Graciano s/n. © **92-431-73-09.** Admission 2.55€. June–Sept daily 9:30am–1:45pm and 5–7:15pm; Oct–May daily 9:30am–1:45pm and 4–6:15pm.

Anfiteatro Romano   At the height of its glory, in the 1st century B.C., the amphitheater could seat 14,000 to 15,000 spectators. Chariot races were held here, along with gladiator combats and mock sea battles, for which the arena would be flooded. Many of the seats were placed dangerously close to the bloodshed. You can visit some of the rooms that housed the wild animals and gladiators waiting to go into combat.

Calle José Ramón Melida s/n. © **92-431-25-30.** Admission included in Teatro Romano ticket (see above). Daily 9:30am–1:45pm and 4–6pm.

Museo Arqueológico de Arte Visigodo   In front of Trajan's Arch is this archaeological museum housing a treasure trove of artifacts left by the conquering Visigoths. Look especially for the two statues of Wild Men in one of the alcoves.

Calle Santa Julio, Plaza de España. © **92-430-01-06.** Free admission. July–Sept Tues–Sat 10am–2pm and 5–7pm, Sun 10am–2pm; Oct–June Tues–Sat 10am–2pm and 4–6pm, Sun 10am–2pm.

Museo Nacional de Arte Romano   Located in a modern building adjacent to the ancient Roman amphitheater, to which it is connected by an underground tunnel, this museum is acclaimed as the greatest repository of Roman artifacts in Spain. Not only does it contain more than 30,000 artifacts from Augusta Emerita, capital of the Roman province of Lusitania, but it also incorporates part of a Roman road discovered in the early 1980s during the construction of the building. Many of the museum's sculptures came from the excavations of the Roman theater and amphitheater. You'll see displays of mosaics, figures, pottery, glassware, coins, and bronze objects. The museum is built of red brick in the form of a Roman basilica.

Calle José Ramón Melida s/n. © **92-431-16-90.** Admission 2.40€ adults, 1.20€ students, free for children. Tues–Sat 10am–1:45pm and 4–6pm; Sun 10am–2pm.

Teatro Romano   This Roman theater, one of the best-preserved Roman ruins in the world, was built by Agrippa (Augustus's son-in-law) in 18 B.C. to house an audience of 6,000 people. Modeled after the great theaters of Rome, it was constructed by dry-stone methods, a remarkable achievement. During the reign of Hadrian (2nd c.), a tall stage wall was adorned with statues and colon-nades. Behind the stage, visitors today can explore excavations of various rooms. From the end of June to early July, they can also enjoy a season of classical plays.

José Ramón Melida s/n. ℰ **92-431-25-30**. Admission 5€ adults (includes admission to Anfiteatro Romano), free for children. Daily 9:30am–1:45pm and 4–6pm.

WHERE TO STAY

Nova Roma (Value)   Lacking the old-world charm of the Parador de Mérida (see below), the 1991 Nova Roma wins hands-down for those with more modern taste. Clean, comfortable, and functionally furnished, it's a good value for this heavily frequented tourist town. Rooms range from small to medium, and each comes with firm mattresses and a compact bathroom with a tub/shower combo. The Nova Roma is west of the Teatro Romano and north of the Plaza de Toros (bullring).

Suárez Somonte 42, 06800 Mérida. ℰ **92-431-12-61**. Fax 924-30-01-60. www.novaroma.com. 55 units. 77€–84€ double. AE, DC, MC, V. Parking 9€. **Amenities:** Restaurant; bar; room service; laundry service; dry cleaning. *In room:* A/C, TV.

Parador de Mérida ⭐⭐   This parador is in the heart of town on the Plaza de la Constitución, in the former Convento de los Frailes de Jesús (dating from the 16th c.). Although it has had a long and turbulent history and was once a prison, a salon has been installed in the cloister, and a central garden is studded with shrubbery and flowers. Old stone stairs lead to the rooms, which come in various shapes and sizes, each beautifully kept and furnished. Bathrooms are lux-urious, the best in town. Each unit comes with a tub/shower combo. In the 1960s two dictators met here: Franco of Spain and Salazar of Portugal.

Plaza de la Constitución 3, 06800 Mérida. ℰ **92-431-38-00**. Fax 924-31-92-08. merida@parador.es. 82 units. 104€ double; 185€ suite. AE, DC, MC, V. Parking 9€. **Amenities:** Restaurant; bar; pool; health spa; sauna; room service; babysitting; laundry service; dry cleaning. *In room:* A/C, TV, minibar, hair dryer, safe.

Tryp Medea ⭐   A 15-minute walk west of the town's historic center on the opposite bank of the Guadiana River, this hotel, which opened in 1993, is equaled only by the parador. Lots of mirrors, stylish postmodern furniture crafted from locally made wrought iron, and numerous modern accessories dec-orate the rooms, many of which offer views over the historic core of Mérida. Ranging from small to medium, each unit is well appointed, with tidily arranged bathrooms containing tub/shower combos.

Av. de Portugal s/n, 06800 Mérida. ℰ **92-437-24-00**. Fax 924-37-30-20. www.solmelia.com. 126 units. 130€–150€ double; 169€–188€ triple. AE, DC, MC, V. Garage parking 8€; free parking on street. Bus: 4 or 6. **Amenities:** Restaurant; bar; pool; squash courts; health club; sauna; room service; babysitting; laundry service; dry cleaning. *In room:* A/C, TV, minibar, hair dryer, safe.

WHERE TO DINE

In addition to the listings below, all the hotels recommended above have good restaurants.

Altair EXTRAMADURAN   On the banks of the Guadiana River, this restau-rant is known for its rendering of classic dishes of the province which have been updated for the contemporary palate. A wall opening onto the river provides a vista of the famous Roman Bridge. Generous portions of good-tasting regional specialties predominate, including the local favorite of neighboring Castile, roast sucking pig with creamed potatoes. A roast duckling is succulently baked with honey and figs, a dish that may have originated with the Arab conquerors centuries ago. Another excellent dish is baked cod or else loin of beef with fresh mushrooms. Instead of ordering a la carte, we opt for the daily changing four-course menu, which is filled with delightful surprises. Good quality ingredients and a skillful handling of the produce bring out the flavor characterized in the cooking here.

Av. José Fernández López. (✆ **92-430-45-12.** Reservations recommended. Main courses 12€–17€. Fixed price 4-course menu 30€. AE, DC, MC, V. Mon–Sat 2–4pm and 7pm–midnight.

Briz *Value* EXTREMADURAN   There is almost universal agreement, even among the locals, that the set menu at Briz represents the best value in town—not only reasonable in price but also very filling. Briz has been known for its Extremaduran regional dishes since 1949. Main dishes include heavily flavored lamb stew and *perdiz* in salsa (a gamy partridge casserole), which might be preceded by an appetizer of peppery sausage mixed into a medley of artichokes. Peppery veal steak and fried filet of goat are other specialties. Strong, hearty wines accompany the dishes. You'll find Briz across from the post office.

Félix Valverde Lillo 5. (✆ **92-431-93-07.** Main courses 8€–18€; fixed-price menu 10€. MC, V. Mon–Sat 1–4pm and 9pm–midnight.

Restaurante Nicolás SPANISH   Transformed from an old, run-down house in 1985, Nicolás is the most charming restaurant in town. If the lower dining room isn't to your liking, you'll find seating upstairs, as well as a pleasant garden for outdoor meals. You might enjoy roast baby goat, carefully seasoned roast lamb, and flavorful concoctions of sole, salmon, or monkfish. Roast partridge is the game specialty. Nicolás is located opposite the post office.

Félix Valverde Lillo 13. (✆ **92-431-96-10.** Reservations recommended. Main courses 9€–18€; fixed-price menu 12€. AE, DC, MC, V. Daily noon–5pm; Mon–Sat 8:30pm–midnight.

5 Zafra

61km (38 miles) S of Mérida, 172km (107 miles) N of Seville

One of the most interesting stopovers in lower Extremadura, the white-walled town of **Zafra** is filled with old Moorish streets and squares. The 1457 **castle** of the dukes of Feria, the most important in the province, boasts both a sumptuous 16th-century Herreran patio and the Sala Dorada with its richly paneled ceiling. The place is now a government parador (see below). You'll want to spend time on the central square, the arcaded 18th-century **Plaza Mayor** ✦, and its satellite, the 16th-century **Plaza Vieja (Old Square)** ✦. These are the two most important sights in Zafra, along with **Nuestra Señora de la Candelaria,** a church with nine panels by Zurbarán, displayed on the retablo in a chapel designed by Churriguera. The church, constructed in the Gothic-Renaissance style, has a red-brick belfry. Admission is free, and it's open Monday through Friday from 10:30am to 1pm and 7 to 8:30pm, Sunday from 11am to 12:30pm.

ESSENTIALS
GETTING THERE   Five **buses** a day arrive from Mérida; a one-way ticket costs 3.60€. For schedules, call (✆ **92-455-39-07.**

Zafra lies at the point where the highway from Seville (E-803) splits, heading east to Mérida and Cáceres and west to Badajoz. **Driving** there is easy. From Mérida to Zafra, allow an hour; from Seville, allow about 2½ hours. There's also a direct road from Córdoba.

VISITOR INFORMATION   The **tourist office** at Plaza de España 8B ((✆ **92-455-10-36;** www.zaftraturismo.com or www.ayto-zaftra.com), is open Monday through Friday from 11am to 2pm and 5 to 8pm, Saturday and Sunday from 10am to 2pm.

WHERE TO STAY

Huerta Honda ⭐ *Finds*   From the modern, recently renovated rooms of this hotel in front of the Plaza del Alcázar, you'll get views of the citadel and the old town. Living space here is a bit tight, but the beds are good and the bathrooms immaculately kept and equipped with tub/shower combos. Under the same management, at no. 36 on the same street, is the restaurant **Barbacana,** a well-recommended dining room offering Castilian cuisine.

López Asme 32, 06300 Zafra. ☎ **92-455-41-00.** Fax 924-55-25-04. www.hotelhuertahonda.com. 47 units. 72€–130€ double; 150€–240€ suite. AE, MC, V. **Amenities:** 2 restaurants; bar; pool; room service; laundry service; dry cleaning. *In room:* A/C, TV, minibar, hair dryer, safe.

Parador de Zafra ⭐⭐   The namesake of this parador in a restored castle near the Plaza de España stayed here with the dukes of Feria before his departure for the New World. The interior, beautiful but restrained, contains the chapel of the Alcázar, with an octagonal Gothic dome. Although not the finest parador in Extremadura, the hotel is decorated in splendid taste and quite comfortable, boasting a patio, and a garden. Rooms are medium in size or even spacious. Bathrooms are fairly roomy and equipped with tub/shower combos.

Plaza Corazón de María 7, 06300 Zafra. ☎ **92-455-45-40.** Fax 924-55-10-18. www.parador.es. 45 units. 94€–110€ double; 169€–220€ suite. AE, DC, MC, V. Free parking along the Plaza Corazón de María. **Amenities:** Restaurant; bar; pool; room service; babysitting; laundry service; dry cleaning. *In room:* A/C, TV, minibar, hair dryer.

WHERE TO DINE

Barbacana ⭐ CASTILIAN   Next to the previously recommended Huerta Honda in the center of town, this is the city's most elegantly decorated restaurant. It just happens to serve the finest cuisine as an added bonus. The atmosphere is chic and sophisticated. Visitors will find the second-floor dining room more relaxed and salubrious. This restaurant has operated here for more than a decade, earning an enviable reputation throughout the region. The owner is an aficionado of the bullfight and has adorned the walls with many paintings depicting scenes from this sport. The cuisine is firmly rooted in the region, and you'll stuff yourself with well-prepared specialty after specialty. Such delicacies appear on the menu as *revuelto de trigeros* (sautéed green asparagus) or *trugas revueltas en ajo* (truffles sautéed in garlic). From there, you can proceed to such main courses as *merluza con almejas* (hake in clam sauce) or *cochinillo* (suckling pig).

Av. López Asme 30. ☎ **92-455-41-00.** Main courses 13€–18€; set menu 27€. MC, V. Mon–Sat 1:30–4pm and 8:30–11:30pm; Sun 1:30–4pm.

8

Andalusia

This once-great stronghold of Muslim Spain is rich in history and tradition, containing some of the country's most celebrated treasures: the world-famous Mezquita (mosque) in Córdoba, the Alhambra in Granada, and the great Gothic cathedral in Seville. It also has many smaller towns just waiting to be discovered—Ubeda, Jaén, gorge-split Ronda, Jerez de la Frontera, and the gleaming white port city of Cádiz. Give Andalusia at least a week and you'll still have only skimmed the surface.

This dry mountainous region also embraces the Costa del Sol (Málaga, Marbella, and Torremolinos), a popular coastal strip covered in the following chapter. Go to the Costa del Sol for beach resorts, nightlife, and relaxation; visit Andalusia for its architectural wonders and beauty.

Crime alert: Anyone driving south into Andalusia and the Costa del Sol should be wary of thieves. Daylight robberies are commonplace, especially in Seville, Córdoba, and Granada. It's not unusual for a car to be broken into while tourists are enjoying lunch in a restaurant. Some establishments have hired guards (a service for which you should tip, of course). Under no circumstances should you ever leave passports, traveler's checks, or other valuables unguarded in a car.

1 Jaén, Baeza & Ubeda

International tourists discovered the province of Jaén, with three principal cities—**Jaén,** the capital, **Baeza,** and **Ubeda**—in the 1960s. For years, visitors whizzed through Jaén on the way south to Granada or bypassed it altogether on the southwest route to Córdoba and Seville. But the government improved the province's hotel outlook with excellent paradors, which now provide some of the finest accommodations in Andalusia.

JAEN

97km (60 miles) E of Córdoba, 97km (60 miles) N of Granada, 338km (210 miles) S of Madrid

In the center of Spain's major olive-growing district, **Jaén** is sandwiched between Córdoba and Granada and has always been a gateway between Castile and Andalusia.

Jaén's bustling modern section is of little interest to visitors, but the **Moorish old town,** where narrow cobblestone streets hug the mountainside, is reason enough to visit. A hilltop castle, now a first-rate parador, dominates the city. On a clear day you can see the snow-covered peaks of the Sierra Nevada.

The city of Jaén is the center of a large province of 13,491 sq. km (5,189 sq. miles) framed by mountains: the Sierra Morena to the north, the Segura and Cazorla ranges to the east, and those of Huelma, Noalejo, and Valdepeñas to the south. To the west, plains widen into the fertile Guadalquivir Valley. Jaén province comprises three well-defined districts: the Sierra de Cazorla, a land of

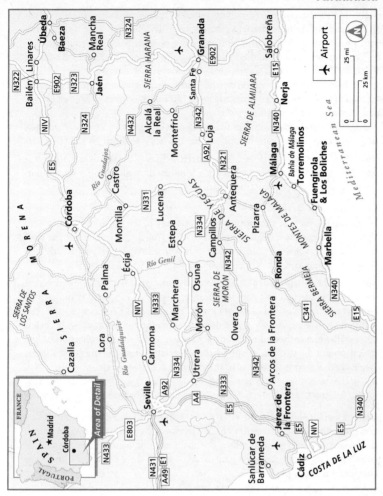

wild scenery; the plains of Bailén, Ajona, and Arjonilla, filled with wheat fields, vineyards, and old olive trees; and the valleys of the tributaries of the Guadalquivir.

ESSENTIALS

GETTING THERE   It's easier to leave Jaén than it is to get there. **Trains** to Jaén run only from south to north. Northbound trains—including four daily to Madrid's Atocha Station—arrive and depart from Jaén's RENFE station on the Paseo de la Estación (© **90-224-02-02**) north of the center of town. The trip to Madrid takes 4 to 5 hours depending on the type of train. If you're traveling from north to south, however, it isn't quite so easy. Most southbound trains from Madrid, and all trains heading south to Seville and the rest of Andalusia, stop only at a larger rail junction that's inconveniently in the hamlet of Espeluy, 35km (22 miles) to the north. From Espeluy, trains are sometimes funneled a short ride to the east to the railway junction midway between Linares 50km (31 miles from Jaén) and Baeza (the Estación de Linares-Baeza). Consult the Jaén tourist office or the rail station for advice on your particular routing.

The **bus** terminal is at the Plaza Coca de la Piñera (© **95-325-01-06**), a block south of the central Parque de la Victoria. Either directly or after a transfer at Baeza, 48km (30 miles) to the north, buses travel 13 times a day to Granada (1½ hr. away), 10 times to Ubeda (30 min.), 4 times to Málaga (3 hr.), and 10 times to Baeza (1 hr.).

Four important highways, plus several provincial roads, converge on Jaén from four directions. From Madrid, follow the N-IV (E-5) to N-323 (E-902).

VISITOR INFORMATION   The **tourist office,** Calle Maestra 13 (© **95-324-26-24;** www.andalusia.org), is open Monday through Friday from 10am to 7pm, Saturday and Sunday from 10am to 1pm.

EXPLORING JAÉN

Jaén produces some of the most appealing pottery in the south of Spain, as well as some of the most intricately crafted baskets. You'll find outlets for the stuff all over the city's historic core, but one store whose inventory is particularly well chosen is **Antanyo,** Calle Virgen de la Capilla 7 (© **95-324-37-35**).

Catedral de Santa María   The formality and grandeur of Jaén's cathedral stand witness to the city's past importance. Begun in 1555 and completed in 1802, it's a honey-colored blend of Gothic, baroque, and Renaissance styles, but mainly Renaissance. A huge dome dominates the interior with its richly carved choir stalls. The **cathedral museum** 𝒜 contains an important collection of historical objects in two underground chambers, including paintings by Ribera. The cathedral stands southwest of the Plaza de la Constitución.

Plaza de Santa María. © **95-323-42-33.** Free admission to cathedral; museum 3€. Cathedral daily 8:30am–1pm and 4:30–8pm (closes at 7pm in winter); museum Sat–Sun 10am–1pm and 5–7pm. Bus: 8, 10, or 16.

Centro Cultural Palacio de Villardompardo   This is a three-in-one attraction, including some former Arab baths (known as *hamman*) and two museums, the Museo de Artes y Costumbres Populares and the Museo Internacional de Arte Naif. The hours (see below) are the same for all three attractions, and none charges admission.

Underneath the palace, near Calle San Juan and the Chapel of Saint Andrew (San Andrés), are the former Arab baths. They represent some of the most important Moorish architecture from the 11th century ever discovered in Spain. You can visit a warm room, a hot room, and a cold room—the last with a barrel vault and 12 star-shaped chandeliers.

The Museo de Artes y Costumbres Populares houses a collection of primarily 19th-century folkloric artifacts, including costumes, dolls, ceramics, and even photographs documenting former days in Andalusia. The Museo Internacional de Arte Naif features a changing art exhibit that includes the work of artists from around the globe who have been able to create professional, skilled paintings without any formal art instruction.

Plaza de Santa Luisa de Marillac s/n. © **95-323-62-92.** Free admission. Tues–Fri 9am–8pm; Sat–Sun 9:30am–2:30pm. You must go on foot: In the old quarter of Jaén, follow signs indicating either BAÑOS ARABES or BARRIO DE LA MAGDALENA.

Iglesia de la Magdalena   Of the many churches worth visiting in Jaén, La Magdalena is the oldest and most interesting. This Gothic church was once an

Arab mosque. The minaret of the former mosque is now the bell tower of the church. If you wander to the back of the church you can see a courtyard that was used by Arab worshippers for their ritualized ablutions. In the cloisters are several tombstones from the era of the Roman occupation of Andalusia.

Calle de la Magdalena. 🕿 **95-319-03-31.** Free admission. Tues–Sat 6am–8pm and Sun 6am–1pm.

Museo Provincial 🖈   The Provincial Museum's collection includes Roman mosaics, a Mudéjar arch, and many ceramics from the early Iberian, Greek, and Roman periods. On the upper floor is an exhibit of Pedro Berruguete paintings, including *Christ at the Column.* Look for a Paleo-Christian sarcophagus from Martos. The museum is between the bus and train stations.

Paseo de la Estación 27. 🕿 **95-325-06-00.** Admission 1.50€. Tues 3–8pm; Wed–Sat 9am–8pm; Sun 9am–2:30pm.

WHERE TO STAY

Hotel Condestable Iranzo *Value*   No old-fashioned Andalusian charm here— what you see is what you get in this large hotel occupying an entire corner of the main square. The building is no beauty, but it is well located, has a good view of the castle and the mountains, and offers a wide range of facilities. The mid-size rooms are functional and comfortable, all with bathrooms containing tub/shower combos.

Paseo de la Estación 32, 23008 Jaén. 🕿 **95-322-28-00.** Fax 95-326-38-07. www.estoyen.com/condestable. 165 units. 74€–85€ double; 121€–131€ suite. AE, MC, V. Parking 7€. **Amenities:** Restaurant; bar; lounge; room service; babysitting; laundry service; dry cleaning. *In room:* A/C, TV.

Hotel Europa *Value*   In the commercial and historical center of Jaén, this little hotel is a winner following a massive renovation, which brought everything up to date. Although the avant-garde decor is a little severe, it manages to be cozy and contemporary at the same time. The medium-size rooms have been spruced up, with sparkling clean bathrooms equipped with tub/shower combos.

Plaza de Belén 1, 23003 Jaén. 🕿 **95-322-27-00.** Fax 95-322-26-92. www.husa.es. 37 units. 53€ double; 63€ triple. AE, DC, MC, V. Parking 7€. **Amenities:** Bar; lounge. *In room:* A/C, TV, hair dryer, safe.

Parador Castillo de Santa Catalina 🖈🖈   Five kilometers (3 miles) to the east on the hill overlooking the city, this castle is one of the government's showplace paradors. In the 10th century, the castle was a Muslim fortress surrounded by high protective walls and approached only by a steep winding road. The castle is still reached by the same road; you enter through a three-story-high baronial hallway, and a polite staff will show you to your balconied midsize room (doubles only), tastefully furnished and comfortable, with a spick-and-span tile bathroom equipped with a tub/shower combo.

Castillo de Santa Catalina, 23001 Jaén. 🕿 **95-323-00-00.** Fax 95-323-09-30. jaen@parador.es. 45 units. 110€ double; 139€ suite. AE, DC, MC, V. Free parking. Follow Carretera al Castillo y Neveraol. **Amenities:** Restaurant; bar; pool; room service; laundry service; dry cleaning. *In room:* A/C, TV, minibar, hair dryer, safe.

WHERE TO DINE

Consider a meal in the luxurious hilltop parador commanding a view of Jaén (see above). It's one of the loveliest spots in the area.

Casa Antonio ANDALUSIAN/INTERNATIONAL   Some of the best Andalusian food in the province is served here in a typical and traditional setting. A trio of tiny dining rooms is decorated with contemporary paintings and dark wood paneling. The accomplished cooking is full of local charm, as evoked by such specialties as mushrooms in a well-flavored cream sauce served with prawns and black olives. Scallops are served with mashed potatoes, and a tender roast sucking pig is baked with potatoes, in the Castilian style.

Calle Fermin Palma 3. (②) **95-327-02-62**. Reservations recommended. Main courses 14€–19€. AE, DC, MC, V. Tues–Sun 1–4:30pm and 8pm–midnight. Closed Aug.

Casa Vicente ANDALUSIAN   Near the cathedral in the historic district, this restaurant is part of a palace dating from the 16th century, complete with a central patio ringed by the dining areas. The "casa" is praised locally for the quality of its tapas and its good wine. The area surrounding the town is known for its vegetables, which are showcased here in such dishes as *espinaca esparragada* (spinach with vegetable sauce) and *alcachofa natural* (artichokes in garlic). For a main dish, we recommend the *lomo de orsa mozárabe* (lamb in sweet-and-sour sauce) or *bacalao encebollado* (salt cod sautéed with onions and sweet peppers). Two local desserts are rice pudding and *manjarblanco mozárabe* (Moorish-style fudge).

Francisco Martín Mora 1. (②) **95-323-22-22**. Reservations recommended. Main courses 12€–15€; set menu 21€. DC, MC, V. Mon–Sat noon–5pm and 8pm–midnight; Sun noon–5pm. Closed Aug.

Mesón Río Chico (Value) ANDALUSIAN   Serving authentic regional cuisine, this charming restaurant has been around since 1962 in a simple modern building in the heart of Jaén. Menu items include strongly flavored versions of hake, beefsteak, roasted pork, and chicken. Because there's room for only 45 diners at a time, it's important to reserve in advance. In spite of its informality and simplicity, many locals claim this is their favorite dining room in town, even though many recipes and dishes haven't been changed since the 1960s.

Calle Nueva 12. (②) **95-324-08-02**. Reservations recommended. Main courses 8€–16€. AE, MC, V. Tues–Sat noon–3:30pm and 9–11:30pm; Sun noon-3:30pm.

BAEZA ✹✹
45km (28 miles) NE of Jaén, 308km (191 miles) S of Madrid

Historic Baeza (known to the Romans as Vilvatia), with its Gothic and Plateresque buildings and cobblestone streets, is one of the best-preserved old towns in Spain. At twilight, lanterns hang on walls of plastered stone, lighting the narrow streets. The town had its heyday in the 16th and 17th centuries and in the Visigothic period was the seat of a bishop.

ESSENTIALS
GETTING THERE   The nearest important rail junction, receiving **trains** from Madrid and most of Andalusia, is the Estación Linares-Baeza (② **90-224-02-02**), 14km (8½ miles) west of Baeza's center. For information about which trains arrive there, refer to the section on Jaén, above.

There are 10 **buses** a day to Ubeda; the ride is 15 minutes long, costing .75€ one-way. From Jaén, there are seven buses per day (trip time: 1 hr.), costing 3.10€ one-way. For more information, call ② **90-202-09-99**.

Baeza lies east of the N-V, the superhighway linking Madrid with Granada. Highway 321/322, which runs through Baeza, links Córdoba with Valencia.

VISITOR INFORMATION   The **tourist office,** at the Plaza del Pópulo (② **95-374-04-44;** www.andalusia.org), is open Monday through Friday from 10am to 2:30pm and 5 to 7pm.

EXPLORING BAEZA

Baeza's main square, the **Plaza del Pópulo** ✿, is a two-story open colonnade. The buildings here date in part from the 16th century and one of the most interesting houses the tourist office (see above), where you can get a map to help guide you through the town. Look for the fountain containing four half-effaced lions, the Fuente de los Leones, which may have been brought here from the Roman town of Cantulo.

Head south along the Cuesta de San Gil to reach the Gothic and Renaissance **cathedral** ✿, Plaza de la Fuente de Santa María ((©) **95-374-41-57**), built in the 16th century on the foundations of an earlier mosque. Look for the Puerta de la Luna (Moon Door), and in the interior, remodeled by Andrés de Vandelvira and his pupils, the carved wood and the brilliant painted *rejas* (iron screens). The Gold Chapel is especially outstanding. The cathedral is open daily from 10:30am to 1pm and 4 to 7pm; admission is free.

After leaving the cathedral, continue up the Cuesta de San Felipe to the **Palacio de Jabalquinto** ✿, a beautiful example of civil architecture in the Flamboyant Gothic style, built by Juan Alfonso de Benavides, a relative of King Ferdinand. Its facade is filled with interesting decorative elements, and there's a simple Renaissance-style courtyard with marble columns. Inside, two lions guard the heavily decorated baroque stairway.

WHERE TO DINE

Casa Juanito ✿ ANDALUSIAN/LA MANCHA   Owners Juan Antonio and Luisa Salcedo are devotees of the lost art of Jaén cookery and revive ancient recipes in their frequently changing suggestions for the day. The hotel owners run a small olive oil outlet and use only their own produce when cooking. Game is served in season, and many vegetable dishes are made with ham. Among the savory and well-prepared menu items are *habas* (beans), filet of beef with tomatoes and peppers, partridge in pastry crust, and house-style cod.

In the Hotel Juanito, Plaza del Arca del Agua s/n. (©) **95-374-00-40**. Reservations required Fri–Sat. Main courses 8€–18€. MC, V. Daily 1–4pm; Tues–Sat 8–11pm. Closed the 1st week of July.

El Sali SPANISH/ANDALUSIAN   This restaurant is set in a modern building erected in the 1980s in the town center, adjacent to the Plaza del Pópulo. In air-conditioned comfort, you can enjoy what many locals regard as the most reasonable set menu in town, and in summer you can sit on a terrace overlooking the city's Renaissance monuments. The owners serve not only the cuisine of Andalusia, but also certain dishes from around Spain. They're known for their fresh vegetables, as exemplified by *la pipirana,* a cold medley of vegetables with tuna, accented with boiled eggs, tomatoes, onions, and spices (only in summer). The atmosphere is relaxed, the service is cordial, and the portions are generous.

Pasaje Cardenal Benavides 15. (©) **95-374-13-65**. Main courses 8€–16€; fixed-price menu 12€. AE, DC, MC, V. Daily 1–4pm; Thurs–Tues 8:30–11:30pm. Closed Sept 20–Oct 31.

Vandelvira ✿ *Finds* ANDALUSIAN   A 16th-century former convent has been converted into this citadel of good cooking and affordable prices. Similar to a cathedral in size, the building still contains much of its original architecture and conventual furnishings. The summer terrace becomes one of the most popular night bars and taverns in town. The chefs have learned their craft well, and they choose their ingredients with care. They have a few fish dishes, including *bacalao* (cod), but mostly they excel with their meats. Milk-fed lamb is one of their finest deals, and they handle their veal dishes very well, too. One of their more exotic specialties is pigs' knuckles stuffed with *perdiz* (partridge) and spinach. They also prepare an excellent appetizer of partridge paté with virgin olive oil.

Calle de San Francisco 14. © **95-374-81-72**. Reservations recommended. Main courses 12€–15€. AE, DC, MC, V. Tues–Sun 11am–5pm; Tues–Sat 8–11pm.

UBEDA ✦
10km (6 miles) NE of Jaén, 312km (194 miles) S of Madrid

A former stronghold of the Arabs often called the "Florence of Andalusia," Ubeda is a Spanish National Landmark filled with golden-brown Renaissance palaces and tile-roofed whitewashed houses. The best way to discover Ubeda's charm is to wander its narrow cobblestone streets. The government long ago created a parador here in a renovated ducal palace—you might stop for lunch if you're not pressed for time. Allow time for a stroll through Ubeda's shops, which specialize in leather craft goods and esparto grass carpets.

ESSENTIALS
GETTING THERE The nearest **train** station is the Linares-Baeza station (© **90-224-02-02**). For information on trains to and from the station, refer to the Jaén section (see above).

There are 15 **buses** daily to Baeza, less than 10km (6¼ miles) away, and to Jaén. Seven buses per day go to the busy railway station at Linares-Baeza, where a train can take you virtually anywhere in Spain. Bus service to and from Córdoba, Seville, and Granada is also available. Ubeda's bus station is in the heart of the modern town, on Calle San José (© **95-375-21-57**), where signs will point you on a downhill walk to the *zona monumental.*

To drive here, turn off the Madrid-Córdoba road and head east for Linares, then on to Ubeda, a detour of 42km (26 miles). The turnoff is at the junction with Route 322.

VISITOR INFORMATION The **tourist office,** Calle Baja del Marques 4 (© **95-375-08-97;** www.andalusia.org), is open Monday through Friday from 8:30am to 7:30pm, Saturday and Sunday from 10am to 2pm.

EXPLORING UBEDA
You might begin your tour at the centrally located **Plaza de Vázquez de Molina** ✦✦, which is flanked by several mansions, including the Casa de las Cadenas, now the Town Hall. The mansions have been decaying for centuries, but many are now finally being restored.

Hospital de Santiago On the western edge of town off Calle del Obispo Coros stands the Hospital of Santiago, completed in 1575 and still in use today. It was built by Andrés de Vandelvira, "the Christopher Wren of Ubeda." Today the hospital is a cultural venue, hosting concerts and containing a minor modern art museum.

Av. Cristo Rey. © **95-375-08-42**. Admission free. Mon–Fri 8am–2pm and 4–10pm; Sat–Sun 11am–3pm and 6–10pm.

Iglesia de San Pablo ✦ This church in the center of the old town is almost as fascinating as the Iglesia El Salvador (below). The Gothic San Pablo is famous for its 16th-century south portal in the Isabelline style and for its chapels.

Plaza 1 de Mayo. © **95-375-06-37**. Free admission. Mon–Sat 5:30–8:15pm; Sun 11am–1:45pm.

Iglesia El Salvador ★★ One of the grandest examples of Spanish Renaissance architecture, this church was designed in 1536 by Diego de Siloé. The richly embellished portal is mere window dressing for the wealth of decoration inside the church, including a sacristy designed by Andrés de Vandelvira and a single nave with gold-and-blue vaulting. The many sculptures and altarpieces and the spectacular rose windows are of special interest.

Plaza de Vázquez de Molina. © **95-375-81-50.** Admission 2.50€. Daily 10am–2pm and 5–7:30pm.

WHERE TO STAY

María de Molina ★ *Finds* The parador (below) is still the number-one place to stay, but this new hotel gives it serious competition. In a beautifully restored and once-decaying palace, the three-story hotel lies in the center of the historic district. Much of the past, including stone vaulted ceilings downstairs, was maintained by the modern architects. The hotel opens onto a marble columned atrium in which chairs are placed in the center, with a skylight overhead. Wherever you look you'll find architectural grace notes such as hand-carved wooden doors and marble arches over stairwells. In contrast, the bedrooms are thoroughly modernized, ranging from rather cramped but still comfortable to spacious suites. We prefer the room with a terrace or at least one of four units with a balcony, but these are booked well in advance. Each room comes with a small bathroom covered in Andalusian tiles and equipped with tub and shower. Try to have at least one dinner at the restaurant, enjoying not only its fine Andalusian cuisine, but also its mellow ambience, which is particularly inviting at night.

Plaza del Ayuntamiento, 23400 Ubeda. © **95-379-53-56.** Fax 95-379-36-94. www.hotel-maria-de-molina. com. 20 units. Sun–Thurs 70€ double, Fri–Sat 92€ double; Sun–Thurs 92€ suite, Fri–Sat 122€ suite. AE, DC, MC, V. **Amenities:** Restaurant; cafeteria; bar; room service; babysitting; laundry service. *In room:* A/C, TV, hair dryer, safe.

Palacio de la Rambla ★★★ *Finds* When the Marquesa de la Rambla arrives in town, she stays here at her ancestral 16th-century home. Eight of its rooms are open to paying guests, who prefer the Renaissance *palacio* style. The spacious manorial rooms boast many of their original furnishings, but everything has been supplemented with modern conveniences. Each has a bathroom with a tub/shower combo and is individually furnished, often with tapestries, objets d'art, and other remnants of old Spain's aristocratic life. The cloistered courtyard, an ideal retreat on a hot day, is surrounded by granite columns.

Plaza del Marqués 1, 23400 Ubeda. © **95-375-01-96.** Fax 95-375-02-67. 8 units. 99€ double; 111€ suite. Rates include buffet breakfast. AE, MC, V. Parking 5€. Closed July 15–Aug 15. **Amenities:** Laundry service; dry cleaning. *In room:* A/C, TV, minibar, hair dryer.

Parador Nacional del Condestable Dávalos ★★ In the heart of town on the most central square stands this 16th-century palace turned parador, which shares an old paved plaza with the Iglesia El Salvador and its dazzling facade. The formal entrance to the Renaissance palace leads to an enclosed patio, encircled by two levels of Moorish arches, where palms and potted plants stand on the tile floors. The rooms are nearly two stories high, with beamed ceilings, tall windows, and antiques and reproductions; the beds are comfortable, and the bathrooms come with tub/shower combos.

Plaza de Vázquez de Molina 1, 23400 Ubeda. © **95-375-03-45.** Fax 95-375-12-59. www.ubedaroma paradores.es. 36 units. 103€–116€ double; 175€ suite. AE, DC, MC, V. **Amenities:** Restaurant; bar; room service; babysitting; laundry service; dry cleaning. *In room:* A/C, TV, minibar, hair dryer, safe.

WHERE TO DINE

Parador Restaurante Nacional del Condestable Dávalos ★ SPAN-ISH/ANDALUSIAN   This parador is the best place to dine for miles around. Although the cuisine isn't the most creative, it's made with market-fresh ingredients prepared from recipes handed down through decades. The menu is wide ranging. Start with a typical dish of the area, such as cold soup with almonds, delightful on a hot day. Partridge is a local favorite—appetizers might include stuffed green peppers with partridge, stewed partridge with plums, or a refreshing salad with marinated partridge. The best fish dishes are the grilled monkfish in saffron sauce and the grilled sole with garlic and apple-vinegar sauce. Meat eaters might be tempted by the regional dishes, such as oxtail in red-wine sauce and stewed kid with pine nuts. The *menú del parador* is a good bet, including an appetizer plus fish or meat for a main course and then dessert. The tasting menu for two showcases four typical regional dishes nightly.

Plaza de Vazques de Molina 1. © 95-375-03-45. Reservations recommended. Main courses 14€–21€; *menú del parador* 25€; tasting menu 44€ for 2 people. AE, DC, MC, V. Daily 1:30–4pm and 8:30–11pm.

2 Córdoba ★★★

105km (65 miles) W of Jaén, 419km (260 miles) SW of Madrid

Ten centuries ago, Córdoba was one of the greatest cities in the world, with a population of 900,000. The capital of Muslim Spain, it was Europe's largest city and a cultural and intellectual center. It flourished with public baths, mosques, a great library, and palaces. Later, greedy hordes sacked the city, tearing down ancient buildings and carting off many art treasures. Despite these assaults, Córdoba still retains traces of its former glory—enough to challenge Seville and Granada as the most fascinating city in Andalusia.

Today this provincial capital is known chiefly for its mosque, but it abounds with other artistic and architectural riches, especially its lovely homes. The old Arab and Jewish quarters are famous for their narrow streets lined with whitewashed houses boasting flower-filled patios and balconies, and it's perfectly acceptable to walk along gazing into the courtyards. This isn't an invasion of privacy: The citizens of Córdoba take pride in showing off their patios as part of the city's tradition. And don't forget to bring along a good pair of walking shoes, as the only way to explore the monumental heart of the city is on foot.

Córdoba has recently joined the ranks of UNESCO's World Heritage sites, so you'll want to spend at least a couple of days here.

ESSENTIALS

GETTING THERE   Córdoba is a rail junction for routes to the rest of both Andalusia and Spain. There are about 22 TALGO and AVE **trains** daily between Córdoba and Madrid (1½–2 hr.). Other, slower trains *(tranvías)* take 5 to 8 hours for the same transit. There are also 25 trains from Seville every day (1½ hr.). The main rail station is on the town's northern periphery, at Av. de América 130, near the corner of Avenida de Cervantes. For information, call © **90-224-02-02.** To reach the heart of the old town from the station, head south on Avenida de Cervantes or Avenida del Gran Capitán. While you're staying in Córdoba, if you want to buy a ticket or to get departure times and prices, you can go to the RENFE office at Ronda de los Tejares 10 (© **90-224-02-02**).

Several **bus** companies serve Córdoba, each of which maintains a separate terminal. For all general information on bus routes, call © **90-202-09-99.**

ATTRACTIONS ●

Alcázar de los Reyes Cristianos **2**
Conjunto Arqueológico Madinat Al-Zahra **7**
Mezquita-Catedral de Córdoba **20**
Museo Arqueológico Provincial **14**
Museo de Bellas Artes de Córdoba **12**
Museo de Julio Romero de Torres **12**
Museo Municipal de Arte Táurino **3**
Palacio Museo de Viana **10**
Sinagoga **4**
Torre de la Calhorra **1**

ACCOMMODATIONS ■

Armistad Córdoba **5**
El Conquistador Hotel **17**
Hotel Averroes **11**
Hotel El Califa **6**
Hotel Macia Alfaros **13**
Hotel Maimónides **18**
Hotel Marisa **19**
Hotel Mezquita **16**
Los Omeyas **15**
Parador Nacional de la Arruzafa **9**
Tryp Gallos **8**

Córdoba lies astride the N-IV (E-5) connecting Madrid with Seville. Don't think of entering the complicated maze of streets in the old town with a car, though. You'll inevitably get lost and find no place to park. There are two small public parking lots outside the old town, one on Calle Robledo and the other on Calle Aeropuerto. Both are well positioned, well marked, and easy to find.

VISITOR INFORMATION The **tourist office,** Calle Torrijos 10 (© **95-747-12-35;** www.andalusia.org), is open Monday through Saturday from 9:30am to 7pm, Sunday from 10am to 2pm.

EXPLORING THE CITY

Among Córdoba's many sights is the **Puente Romano (Roman bridge),** dating from the time of Augustus and crossing the Guadalquivir River about 1 block south of the Mezquita. It's hardly Roman anymore because not one of its 16 supporting arches is original. The sculptor Bernabé Gómez del Río erected a statue of St. Raphael in the middle of the bridge in 1651.

Plaza de Toros, on Gran Vía del Parque, stages its major bullfights in May, although fights are presented at other times of the year. Watch for local announcements. Most hotels will arrange tickets for you, ranging in price (in general) from 20€ to 95€. Call © **95-741-49-99** for information.

Alcázar de los Reyes Cristianos ⭐ Commissioned in 1328 by Alfonso XI, the Alcázar of the Christian Kings is a fine example of military architecture. Ferdinand and Isabella governed Castile from this fortress on the river as they

Moments   A Peeping Tom in Córdoba

As you walk through the narrow streets of the ancient **Judería,** the so-called Jewish section that hasn't been that in 5 centuries, you may think your fellow strollers are being rude by spying in on the various courtyards. Join them. The owners of these old-fashioned town houses, evocative of North Africa, deliberately leave their front doors ajar, hoping that the passing public will peer in at their tree-shaded and flower-filled patios. They are preening proud of their Andalusian courtyards and like to show them off to the world. Every owner seemingly tends with loving care to these courtyards, and water burbling from hoses keeps the plants green in the blistering heat of a summer day. White and blue patterned ceramic tiled floors add to the allure. During spring festivals, Cordobans abandon their pretense at privacy and throw their doors wide open, letting the public fully enjoy their carefully cultivated oases of beauty.

prepared to reconquer Granada, the last Moorish stronghold in Spain. Columbus journeyed here to fill Isabella's ears with his plans for discovery.

Two blocks southwest of the Mezquita, this quadrangular building is notable for powerful walls and a trio of towers—the Tower of the Lions, the Tower of Allegiance, and the Tower of the River. The Tower of the Lions contains intricately decorated ogival ceilings that are the most notable example of Gothic architecture in Andalusia. The beautiful gardens and the Moorish baths are celebrated attractions. The Patio Morisco is another lovely spot, its pavement decorated with the arms of León and Castile. A Roman sarcophagus is representative of 2nd- and 3rd-century funeral art and the Roman mosaics are outstanding—especially a unique piece dedicated to Polyphemus and Galatea.

Caballerizas Reales. ✆ 95-742-01-51. Admission 2€ adults, 1€ children. May–Sept Tues–Sat 10am–2pm and 6–8pm, Sun 10am–2pm; Oct–Apr Tues–Sat 9:30am–3pm and 4:30–6:30pm, Sun 9:30am–3pm. Gardens illuminated May–Sept 10pm–1am. Bus: 3 or 12.

Mezquita-Catedral de Córdoba ✶✶✶   From the 8th century, the Mezquita was the crowning Muslim architectural achievement in the West. It's a fantastic labyrinth of red-and-white-striped arches. To the astonishment of visitors, a cathedral now sits awkwardly in the middle of the mosque, disturbing the purity of the lines. The 16th-century cathedral, a blend of many styles, is impressive in its own right, with an intricately carved ceiling and baroque choir stalls. Additional ill-conceived annexes later turned the Mezquita into an architectural oddity. Its most interesting feature is the **mihrab** ✶✶, a domed shrine of Byzantine mosaics that once housed the Koran. After exploring the interior, stroll through the Courtyard of the Orange Trees, which has a beautiful fountain. The hardy can climb a 16th-century tower to catch a panoramic view of Córdoba and its environs.

Torrijos and Calle Cardenal Herrero s/n (south of the train station, just north of the Roman bridge). ✆ 95-747-05-12. Admission 6.50€ adults, 3.25€ children under 10. June–Sept daily 10am–7pm; Oct–Apr daily 10am–6pm. Closed Jan and May.

Museo Arqueológico Provincial ✶   Córdoba's Archaeological Museum, 2 blocks northeast of the Mezquita, is one of the most important in Spain. Housed in a palace dating from 1505, it displays artifacts left behind by the various peoples and conquerors who have swept through the province. There are Paleolithic and Neolithic items, Iberian hand weapons and ceramics, and Roman sculptures, bronzes, ceramics, inscriptions, and mosaics. Especially interesting are the Visigothic artifacts. The most outstanding collection, however, is devoted to Arabic art and spans the entire Muslim occupation. Take a few minutes to relax in one of the patios with its fountains and ponds.

Plaza Jerónimo Páez 7. ✆ **95-747-40-11**. Admission 1.50€. Tues 3–8pm; Wed–Sat 9am–8pm; Sun and public holidays 9am–3pm.

Museo de Bellas Artes de Córdoba   As you cross the Plaza del Potro to reach the Fine Arts Museum, notice the fountain at one end of the square. Built in 1557, it shows a young stallion with forelegs raised, holding the shield of Córdoba. Housed in an old hospital on the plaza, the Fine Arts Museum contains medieval Andalusian paintings, examples of Spanish baroque art, and works by many of Spain's important 19th- and 20th-century painters, including Goya. The museum is east of the Mezquita, about a block south of the Church of St. Francis (San Francisco).

Plaza del Potro 1. ✆ **95-747-13-14**. Admission 1.50€ adults, free for children 11 and under. Tues 3–8pm; Wed–Sat 9am–8pm; Sun and public holidays 9am–3pm. Bus: 3, 4, 7, or 12.

Museo de Julio Romero de Torres   Across the patio from the Fine Arts Museum, this museum honors Julio Romero de Torres, a Córdoba-born artist who died in 1930. It contains his celebrated *Oranges and Lemons,* and other notable works such as *The Little Girl Who Sells Fuel, Sin,* and *A Dedication to the Art of the Bullfight.* A corner of Romero's Madrid studio has been reproduced in one of the rooms, displaying the paintings left unfinished at his death.

Plaza del Potro. ✆ **95-749-19-09**. Free admission (there are occasional exhibitions that will charge a fee). Mon–Fri 10am–7pm; Sat–Sun 10am–4pm.

Museo Municipal de Arte Taurino   Memorabilia of great bullfights are housed here in the Jewish Quarter in a 16th-century building, inaugurated in 1983 as an appendage to the Museo Municipal de Arte Cordobesa. Its ample galleries recall Córdoba's great bullfighters with suits of light, pictures, trophies, posters, even stuffed bulls' heads. You'll see a wax likeness of Manolete in repose and the blood-smeared uniform of El Cordobés—both of these famous matadors came from Córdoba. The museum is about a block northwest of the Mezquita, midway between the mosque and the synagogue.

Plaza de las Bulas (also called Plaza Maimónides). ✆ **95-720-10-56**. Admission 3€, free for children under 18. May–Sept Tues–Sat 10:30am–2pm and 6–8pm, Sun 9:30am–3pm; Oct–Apr Mon–Sat 10am–2pm and 4:30–6:30pm, Sun 9:30am–2:30pm. Bus: 3 or 12.

Palacio Museo de Viana 🌟🌟 *Finds*   The public has seldom had access to Córdoba's palaces, but that's changed with the opening of this museum. Visitors are shown into a carriage house, where the elegant vehicles of another era are displayed. Note the intricate leather decoration on the carriages and the leather wall hangings, some of which date from the period of the Reconquest; there's also a collection of leather paintings. You can wander at leisure through the garden and patios. The palace is 4 blocks southeast of the Plaza de Colón on the northeastern edge of the old quarter.

Plaza de Don Gome 2. ✆ **95-749-67-41**. Palace admission 6€; patios 3€. June–Sept Mon–Sat 9am–2pm; Oct–May Mon–Fri 10am–1pm and 4–6pm, Sat 10am–1pm. Closed June 1–15.

Sinagoga   In Córdoba you'll find one of Spain's few remaining pre-Inquisition synagogues, built in 1350 in the Barrio de la Judería (Jewish Quarter), 2 blocks west of the northern wall of the Mezquita. The synagogue is noted particularly for its stuccowork; the east wall contains a large orifice where the Tabernacle was once placed (inside, the scrolls of the Pentateuch were kept). After the Jews were expelled from Spain, the synagogue was turned into a hospital, until it became a Catholic chapel in 1588.

Calle de los Judíos 20. ℂ **95-720-29-28**. Admission .30€. Tues–Sat 10am–2pm and 3:30–5:30pm; Sun 10am–1:30pm. Bus: 3.

Torre de la Calahorra   The Tower of Calahorra stands across the river at the southern end of the Roman bridge. Commissioned by Henry II of Trastamara in 1369 to protect him from his brother, Peter I, it now houses a town museum where visitors can take a self-guided tour with headsets. One room houses wax figures of Córdoba's famous philosophers, including Averro and Maimónides. Other rooms exhibit a miniature model of the Alhambra at Granada, complete with water fountains; a miniature Mezquita; and a display of Arab musical instruments. Finally, you can climb to the top of the tower for some panoramic views of the Roman bridge, the river, and the cathedral/mosque.

Av. de la Confederación, Puente Romano. ℂ **95-729-39-29**. Admission to museum 4€ adults, 2.50€ children. May–Sept daily 10am–2pm and 4:30–8:30pm; Oct–Apr daily 10am–6pm. *Multivisión* 11am, noon, 3pm, 4pm. Last tour 1 hr. before closing time. Bus: 16.

SHOPPING

In Moorish times, Córdoba was famous for its leather workers. Highly valued in 15th-century Europe, their leather was studded with gold and silver ornaments, then painted with embossed designs (*guadamaci*). Large panels of it often served in lieu of tapestries. Today the industry has fallen into decline, and the market is filled mostly with cheap imitations. You might want to seek out the following shop, especially if you're interested in Cordoban handicrafts: **Artesanía Andaluza,** Tomás Conde 3 (no phone), near the bullfight museum, features a

---

Finds **A Caliph's Pleasure Palace: the Moorish Versailles**

The **Conjunto Arqueológico Madinat Al-Zahra,** a kind of Moorish Versailles just outside Córdoba, was constructed in the 10th century by the first caliph of al-Andalús, Abd ar-Rahman III. He named it after the favorite of his harem, nicknamed "the brilliant." Thousands of workers and animals slaved to build this mammoth pleasure palace, said to have contained 300 baths and 400 houses. Over the years the site was plundered for building materials; in fact, it might have been viewed as a quarry for the entire region. Some of its materials, so it's claimed, went to build the Alcázar in Seville. The Royal House, rendezvous point for the ministers, has been reconstructed. The principal salon remains in fragments, though, so you have to imagine it in its majesty. Just beyond the Royal House are the ruins of a mosque constructed to face Mecca. The Berbers sacked the place in 1013.

It's at Carretera Palma de Río, Km 8 (ℂ **95-732-91-30**). Admission is 1.50€. Hours are from May 1 to September 15, Tuesday through Saturday from 10am to 8:30pm, Sunday from 10am to 2pm; from October 1 to April 30, Tuesday through Saturday from 10am to 6:30pm, Sunday from 10am to 2pm. A bus leaves from the station on Calle de la Bodega, but it lets you off about 3km (2 miles) from the site.

vast array of Córdoban handicrafts, especially filigree silver from the mines of Sierra Morena and some excellently crafted embossed leather, a holdover from the Muslim heyday. Lots of junk is mixed in with the good stuff, though, so beware. The shop is open Monday through Saturday from 9am to 5pm.

Arte Zoco, Calle de los Judíos s/n (no phone), is the largest association of craftspeople in Córdoba. Established in the Jewish Quarter in the mid-l980s, it assembles on one site the creative output of about a dozen artisans whose mediums include leather, wood, silver, crystal, terra cotta, and iron. About a half dozen of the artisans maintain their studios on the premises, so you can visit and check out the techniques and tools they use to pursue their crafts. You'll find everything from new, iconoclastic, and avant-garde designs to pieces that honor centuries-old traditions. Of special interest is the revival of the Califar pottery first introduced to Córdoba during the regimes of the Muslim caliphs. The shop is open Monday through Friday from 9:30am to 8pm, Saturday and Sunday from 9:30am to 2pm. The workshops and studios of the various artisans open and close according to the whims of their occupants but are usually maintained Monday through Friday from 10am to 2pm and 5:30 to 8pm.

Librería Seferad, Calle Romero 4 (© **95-729-88-95**), across from Córdoba's only synagogue, is a cubbyhole-size place selling articles that hark back to the Sephardic culture of medieval Europe. You'll find tapes of Sephardic music and chants, pottery fashioned in traditional Sephardic designs, filigreed silver ornaments, and reference works to Ladino, the medieval Iberian dialect spoken by Jews throughout the Diaspora. Inventory is limited, and hours are erratic, usually daily from 10:30am to 8:30pm.

Alejandro and Carlos López Obrero run **Meryan,** Calleja de Las Flores 2 (© **95-747-59-02**), on one of the most colorful streets in the city. In this 250-year-old building you can see artisans plying their crafts; although most items must be custom-ordered, some ready-made pieces are for sale, including cigarette boxes, jewel cases, attaché cases, book and folio covers, and ottoman covers. It's open Monday through Friday from 9am to 8pm, Saturday from 9am to 2pm.

Córdoba has a branch of Spain's major department store, El Corte Inglés, at Ronda de los Tejares 32 (© **95-722-28-81**). At least some of the staff speaks English. It's open Monday through Saturday from 10am to 10pm.

WHERE TO STAY

At the peak of its summer season, Córdoba has too few hotels to meet the demand, so reserve as far in advance as possible.

EXPENSIVE

Amistad Córdoba ★★ In the heart of the Judería (old Jewish Quarter) a 4-minute walk from the mosque, this hotel is the most desirable in town. It opened in 1992 after renovations combined two existing 18th-century mansions. The houses face each other and are linked by a small patio of beautiful Andalusian arches and colorful Spanish tiles. The spacious rooms come with modern comforts like excellent beds, and the design is a tasteful combination of wood and fabric. In 1998, a more modern wing opened. All units come with neat bathrooms containing tub/shower combos.

Plaza de Maimónides 3, 14004 Córdoba. © **95-742-03-35.** Fax 95-742-03-65. www.nh-hoteles.com. 84 units. 100€–133€ double; 110€–146€ suite. Parking 12€. AE, DC, MC, V. **Amenities:** Restaurant; bar; room service; babysitting; laundry service; dry cleaning. *In room:* A/C, TV, minibar, hair dryer, safe.

El Conquistador Hotel ✿ Built centuries ago as a private villa, this hotel is tastefully renovated and one of the most attractive in town, with triple rows of stone-trimmed windows and ornate iron balustrades. It sits opposite an unused rear entrance to the Mezquita. The marble-and-granite lobby opens into an interior courtyard filled with seasonal flowers, a pair of splashing fountains, and a symmetrical stone arcade. The quality, size, and comfort of the rooms—each with a black-and-white marble floor and a private bathroom—earn the hotel four government-granted stars.

Magistral González Francés 15, 14003 Córdoba. ✆ **95-748-11-02.** Fax 95-747-46-77. 130 units. 160€ double; from 218€ suite. AE, DC, MC, V. Parking 12€. Bus: 12. **Amenities:** Bar; lounge; car rental; room service; babysitting; laundry service; dry cleaning. *In room:* A/C, TV, minibar, hair dryer.

Parador Nacional de la Arruzafa ✿✿ *Value* Found 4km (2½ miles) outside town in a suburb called El Brillante, this parador, named after an Arab word meaning "palm grove," offers the conveniences and facilities of a luxurious resort hotel at reasonable rates. Occupying the site of a former caliphate palace, it's one of the finest paradors in Spain. The spacious guest rooms have been furnished with fine dark-wood pieces, and some have balconies for eating breakfast or relaxing over a drink. All have bathrooms with tub/shower combos.

Av. de la Arruzafa 33, 14012 Córdoba. ✆ **95-727-59-00.** Fax 95-728-04-09. www.parador.es. 94 units. 109€–126€ double; 151€ suite. AE, DC, MC, V. Free parking. **Amenities:** Restaurant; bar; pool; tennis court; fitness center; sauna; room service; babysitting; laundry service; dry cleaning. *In room:* A/C, TV, minibar, hair dryer, safe.

MODERATE

Hotel El Califa *Value* Attracting a mainly Spanish crowd, this central hotel is a short walk northwest of the Mezquita. Though rather impersonal and a bit austere, it's generally a good value. It has russet-colored marble floors, velour wall coverings, a spacious lounge, and a TV that seems to broadcast nonstop soccer matches. The midsize rooms are reasonably comfortable and furnished in a functional modern style. The bathrooms come with tub/shower combos. Parking is available along the street.

Lope de Hoces 14, 14003 Córdoba. ✆ **95-729-94-00.** Fax 95-729-57-16. www.gsmhoteles.es. 66 units. 110€ double; 122€ suite. AE, DC, MC, V. Bus: 12. **Amenities:** Bar; lounge; room service; babysitting; laundry service; dry cleaning. *In room:* A/C, TV, hair dryer.

Tryp Gallos Half a block from a wide tree-shaded boulevard on the western edge of town, this aging 1970s hotel stands eight floors high, crowned by an informal roof garden. The hotel is a favorite of both groups and commercial travelers. The comfortable but small rooms have many extra comforts, such as balconies, and neat bathrooms with tub/shower combos.

Medina Azahara 7, 14005 Córdoba. ✆ **888/956-3542** in the U.S., or 95-723-55-00. Fax 95-723-16-36. www.solmelia.com. 115 units. 100€ double; 122€ triple. AE, DC, MC, V. **Amenities:** Restaurant; bar; lounge; pool; laundry service; dry cleaning. *In room:* A/C, TV, minibar, hair dryer, safe.

INEXPENSIVE

Hotel Averroes ✿ This hotel expanded in 1999, adding 20 more rooms after renovating the house next door, and now the two buildings are linked by an impressive patio *cordobés*. With its characteristic tiled walls and classic arches, the patio is a social area with tables where you can relax after a day of sightseeing. The medium-size rooms are comfortable, with marble floors, pastel walls, and good-size beds with firm mattresses. All have bathrooms with tub/shower combos. The bus that stops in front will take you to the town center in just 5 minutes, or you can count on a 15-minute stroll.

Campo Madre de Dios 38, 14002 Córdoba. ⓒ **95-743-59-78**. Fax 95-743-59-81. www.geocities.com/Vienna/Choir/6063/2. 72 units. 69€–84€ double. AE, DC, MC, V. Bus: 3. **Amenities:** Restaurant; bar; lounge; pool; laundry service; dry cleaning. *In room:* A/C, TV, hair dryer, safe.

Hotel Marisa (Value) In front of the Mezquita, this modest hotel is not only one of the most centrally located in Córdoba but also one of the city's best values. Completed in the early 1970s, it has had continuing renovations to keep it in good shape. Most recent improvements have been to the bathrooms with showers, where the plumbing was renewed. The rooms are small but cozily comfortable. It's possible to reserve one with a balcony overlooking either the statue of the Virgin of Rosales or the Patio de los Naranjos (orange trees). The architecture and furnishings are in a vague Andalusian style.

Cardenal Herrero 6, 14003 Córdoba. ⓒ **95-747-31-42**. Fax 95-747-41-44. 28 units. 57€–60€ double. AE, DC, MC, V. Parking 12€. **Amenities:** Bar; room service; babysitting; laundry service; dry cleaning. *In room:* A/C.

Hotel Mezquita This hotel faces the east side of the mosque and is the lodgings closest to the Mezquita. In 1998, it was constructed on the site of two old houses, which are now connected by a patio. The decor includes a display of antiques arranged tastefully throughout. The architecture is typically Andalusian—arches, interior patios, and hand-painted tiles, along with old mirrors and chandeliers. The small but comfortable rooms are painted pastels to contrast with the dark oak furnishings. The bathrooms come with tub/shower combos. Naturally, the rooms overlooking the Mezquita are the first to be booked.

Plaza Santa Catalina 1, 14003 Córdoba. ⓒ **95-747-55-85**. Fax 95-747-62-19. 21 units. 41€–66€ double. AE, DC, MC, V. Parking 12€. **Amenities:** Cafeteria; laundry service; dry cleaning. *In room:* A/C, TV.

Los Omeyas ⓐ If you want to stay in the very heart of Córdoba, you couldn't be better located than this hotel, lying nestled in what was the Jewish Quarter. The name comes from the Umayyad dynasty that ruled the Muslim empire of al-Andalús (the Arab tradition is still clearly visible in white marble and latticework). The hotel is naturally lit by a central colonnaded patio furnished with tables. Although in no way grand, the rooms are extremely comfortable and tastefully decorated and have bathrooms with tub/shower combos; those on the top floor offer a panoramic view of the ancient tower of the Mosque, which is literally around the corner.

Calle Encarnación 17, 14003 Córdoba. ⓒ **95-749-22-67**. Fax 95-749-16-59. 36 units. 52€–64€ double; 62€–74€ triple; 72€–84€ quad. AE, DC, MC, V. Parking 12€. **Amenities:** Bar; lounge; room service; babysitting. *In room:* A/C, TV, safe.

WHERE TO DINE

By all means, shake free of your hotel for at least one meal a day in Córdoba. The restaurants are not just places at which to have a quick bite but may combine food with flamenco—so make an evening of it.

EXPENSIVE

Campos de Córdoba ⓐ SPANISH/ANDALUSIAN Owned/run by Javier Campo, this restaurant, with a welcoming rustic atmosphere, is a 10-minute walk from the mosque. Since 1908 it has been both a wine cellar (bodega) and an Andalusian tavern. The walls are adorned with old fiesta posters, and there's an intriguing tapas bar at the entrance. Or you can retreat to the cozy Sacristy, a bar in back, past a wall of wine vats autographed by celebrity visitors. In honor of its former role as a bodega, the restaurant offers one of the best selections of wine in town—try the house wine, *montilla viejo.* The well-chosen menu prepared from fresh ingredients consists of local fare, such as a salt cod salad with orange dressing and *frituritas de la casa con salmorejo* (tiny fried fish eaten whole and served with thick Andalusian gazpacho). Locals come here to sample the *escabeche de perdiz* (pickled pieces of partridge), but you may find the *lubina al horno* (baked whitefish) more to your liking. Other specialties are *merluza rellena con verduritas* (hake stuffed with julienne vegetables) and *rabo de toro en salsa* (bull's tail in savory tomato sauce). For a tiny selection of a variety of sweets from the dessert cart, ask for a *surtido de la casa.*

Calle de los Lineros 32. ℂ **95-749-75-00**. Reservations recommended. Main courses 12€–18€. AE, DC, MC, V. Daily noon–5pm; Mon–Sat 8pm–midnight.

La Almudaina ★★★ SPANISH/FRENCH The owners of this historic restaurant near the Alcázar deserve as much credit for their renovations of a decrepit 15th-century palace as they do for the excellent cuisine produced in their bustling kitchen. Fronting the river in the old Jewish Quarter, La Almudaina is one of the most attractive eateries in Andalusia, where you can dine in one of the lace-curtained salons or on a glass-roofed central courtyard. Specialties include salmon crepes; a wide array of fish, such as hake with shrimp sauce; and meats, such as pork loin in wine sauce. For dessert, try the not-too-sweet chocolate crepe.

Plaza de los Santos Mártires 1. ℂ **95-747-43-42**. Reservations required. Main courses 16€–45€; fixed-price menu 20€. AE, DC, MC, V. Daily noon–5pm; Mon–Sat 8:30pm–midnight. Closed Sun July–Aug. Bus: 12.

Mesón el Burlaero ✿ SPANISH/ANDALUSIAN In a 16th-century house that belonged to the first bishops of Córdoba, this restaurant in the Jewish Quarter is in the center of the tourist area. The *mesón* offers seven dining areas, along with balconies and a central patio adorned with antique-style murals. The whole place has been lovingly restored and tastefully decorated. The most lavish way to dine here is to order the *menú gastronómico de degustación,* a selection of various house specialties. From the a la carte menu you can begin with *salmorejo* (thick Andalusian gazpacho), and then follow with *rabo de toro en salsa* (bull's tail in savory tomato sauce) or *dorada a la sal* (gilthead sea bream that has been salted to retain its juices and then baked). On a hot day, the best dessert is the cold soufflé with vanilla ice cream.

Calle de la Hoguera 5. ℂ **95-747-27-19**. Reservations recommended. Main courses 11€–17€; set menus 18€–30€. AE, DC, MC, V. Daily 11am–4pm and 7:30pm–midnight.

MODERATE
Casa Pepe de la Judería ✿ CORDOBAN Around the corner from the mosque, this is one of the best-located restaurants in this ancient city. It lies on the route to the Judería, the old Jewish ghetto—hence, its name. A series of little rooms, decorated in a typical Andalusian style, are spread over three floors. From May to October, tables are placed on the rooftop where meats such as chicken and pork are barbecued, and an Andalusian guitarist entertains. The fare is in the hearty regional style, both good tasting and using first-rate ingredients. Some of the combinations of dishes, such as cod cooked with raisins, pine nuts, and mussels, may actually be based on recipes from the days when the Arabs controlled Córdoba. The chef prepares excellent soups such as a typical Andalusian gazpacho or a soup made with fresh fish and shellfish. We are especially

fond of the *merluza* (hake) prepared Cordobesa style with sweet peppers, garlic, and onions. Rape of monkfish appears in a tangy shellfish sauce. The baked lamb is another special dish, well recommended.

Calle Romero 1 ✆ **95-720-07-44.** Reservations recommended. Main courses 11€–18€ Daily 1:30–6pm and 8:30pm–1am.

El Blasón *Value* ANDALUSIAN   Opened in the late 1980s in a relatively modern building near the Gran Teatro that's been accessorized to commemorate old Andalusia, this is a restaurant where the tab, without wine, rarely exceeds 30€. You'll dine in any of four separate rooms, each evoking the mid–19th century, thanks to formal crystal chandeliers and a scattering of antiques. Especially appealing is an enclosed patio where ivy creeps up walls and the noises from the city outside are muffled. The cuisine is well prepared and in some cases described in terms that verge on the poetic. Examples are salmon with oranges from the mosque, and goose thigh in fruited wine. Braised oxtail is always a good bet, as well as any of the roasted lamb dishes redolent with the scent of olive oil and herbs.

José Zorrilla 11. ✆ 95-748-06-25. Reservations recommended. Main courses 12€–21€. AE, DC, MC, V. Daily noon–4:30pm and 8pm–midnight.

El Caballo Rojo ★★ SPANISH   Within walking distance of the Mezquita in the old town, this restaurant is the most popular in Andalusia, and except for La Almudaina (see above), it remains the best in Córdoba. The place has a noise level no other restaurant here matches, but the skilled waiters seem to cope with all demands. Stop in the restaurant's popular bar for a pre-dinner drink, then take the iron-railed stairs to the upper dining room, where a typical meal might include gazpacho, a main dish of chicken, then ice cream and sangria. (The ice cream, incidentally, is likely to be homemade pistachio.) Try a variation on the usual gazpacho—almond-flavored broth with apple pieces. In addition to Andalusian dishes, the chef offers both Sephardic and Mozarabic specialties, an example of the latter being monkfish prepared with pine nuts, currants, carrots, and cream. Real aficionados come here for the *rabo de toro* (stew made with the tail of an ox or a bull). The cookery is robust and flavorsome.

Cardinal Herrero 28, Plaza de la Hoguera. ✆ **95-747-53-75.** Reservations required. Main courses 12€–19€. AE, DC, MC, V. Daily 1–4:30pm and 8pm–midnight. Bus: 12.

INEXPENSIVE

El Churrasco ★ SPANISH   Housed in an ancient stone-fronted building in the Jewish Quarter northwest of the Mezquita, El Churrasco serves elegant meals in five dining rooms. You'll pass a bar and an open grill before reaching a ground-floor dining room that resembles a Moorish courtyard with rounded arches and a fountain. Upstairs, more formal rooms display the owner's riveting collection of paintings. You can enjoy such specialties as grilled filet of beef with whiskey sauce, succulent roast lamb, grilled salmon, and monkfish in pine-nut sauce—all accompanied by good service—but the signature dish is the charcoal-grilled pork loin.

Romero 16. ✆ 95-729-08-19. Reservations required. Main courses 10€–25€. AE, DC, MC, V. Daily 1–4pm and 8pm–midnight. Closed Aug. Bus: 12.

CORDOBA AFTER DARK

Nighttime fun in the oldest part of Córdoba usually means visiting several tapas bars surrounding the Mezquita. Foremost among them is **Casa Pepe,** Calle

Romero 1 (© **95-720-07-44**), an atmospheric old hideaway in an antique building where many generations have lifted a glass before you. It's open daily from 1 to 4pm, and like most of the other places, reopens from 8 to 11:30pm. Nearby is **Casa Salinas,** Puerto de Almodóvar s/n (© **95-729-08-46**), offering glasses of sherry and plates of tapas. Bar **El Juramento,** Calle Juramento 6 (© **95-748-54-77**), is old-fashioned enough to be cozy and crowded enough to be convivial. The oldest bodega in Córdoba (opened around 1812) is the **Casa Miguel,** Plaza San Miguel 7 (no phone). And for a bar where discussions about the relative merits of Andalusian bullfighters always seem more passionate than anywhere else in town, head for **Bar Círculo Taurino,** Calle Manuel María Arcona 1 (© **95-748-18-62**). Small, cramped, and loaded with memorabilia from bullfights past, it's near the Plaza Colón.

La Canoa, Pasaje Ronda Los Tejares 18–20 (© **95-747-17-61**), has a rustic interior decorated with wine-barrel tables and Carthusian cellar decor. A glass of wine or beer will be more of a rapid pick-me-up than something to linger over for hours. You can order a ration of Serrano ham or a hefty platter of cheese if you're hungry. **La Canoa,** between the Plaza de Colón and the Paseo de la Victoria, is open Monday through Saturday from noon to 4pm and 8pm to midnight (closed 2 weeks in Aug). Push back a thick curtain to enter the dimly lit **Casa Rubio,** Puerta de Almodóvar 5 (© **95-742-08-53**), where you'll find a gruff but accommodating welcome at the rectangular bar or in one of a pair of rooms partially covered with Andalusian tiles. We like the leafy inner courtyard where iron tables and a handful of chairs wobble only slightly on the uneven flooring. Casa Rubio is open daily 9am to midnight.

The city's most popular flamenco club is **El Cardenal,** Calle Torijos 10 (© **95-748-31-12**). Shows are presented at 10:30pm Monday through Saturday, with a cover of 18€, which includes the first drink. If you want to shake your booty, head for the popular **Disco Cahira,** Calle Conde de Roblado s/n (no phone), which holds court nightly after 11pm within a busy commercial neighborhood of modern Córdoba. For more formal entertainment, check out the listings at the city's theatrical grande dame, the early-1900s **Gran Teatro de Córdoba,** Av. Gran Capitán 3 (© **95-748-02-37**), site of most of the ballet, opera, chamber-music, and symphony performances in town.

3 Seville (★(★(★

549km (341 miles) SW of Madrid, 217km (135 miles) NW of Málaga

Sometimes a city becomes famous simply for its beauty and romance. Seville (*Sevilla* in Spanish), the capital of Andalusia, is such a place. In spite of its sultry summer heat and its many problems, such as high unemployment and street crime, it remains one of the most charming Spanish cities. Don Juan and Carmen—aided by Mozart and Bizet—have given Seville a romantic reputation. Because of the acclaim of *Don Giovanni* and *Carmen,* not to mention *The Barber of Seville,* debunkers have risen to challenge this reputation. But if a visitor can see only two Spanish cities in a lifetime, they should be Seville and Toledo.

All the images associated with Andalusia—orange trees, mantillas, lovesick toreros, flower-filled patios, and castanet-rattling gypsies—come to life in Seville. But it's not just a tourist city; it's a substantial river port, and it contains some of the most important artistic works and architectural monuments in Spain.

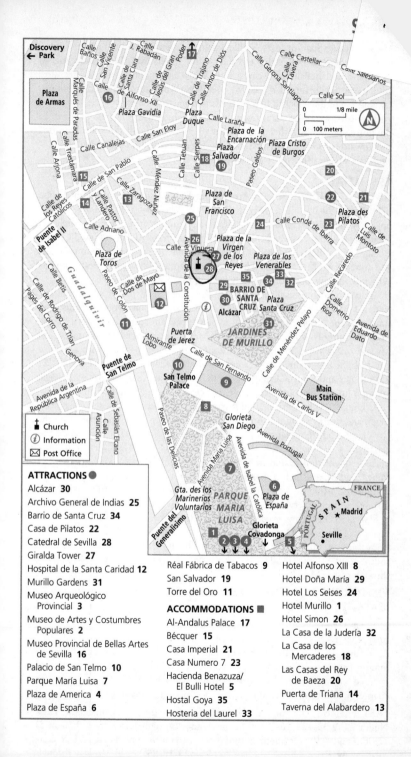

Discovery
← **Park**

Plaza de Armas

Calle Baños
Calle J. Rabadán
Calle San Vicente
Calle del Gran Poder
Calle de Santa Clara
Calle de Alfonso XII
Calle de Trajano
Calle Amor de Diós
Calle Gerona
Calle Castellar
Calle Tavera
Santiago
Calle Salesianos
Calle Marqués de Paradas
Plaza Gavidia
Plaza Duque
Calle Laraña
Calle Sol
Calle Canalejas
Calle San Eloy
Plaza de la Encarnación
Plaza Cristo de Burgos
Calle Trastámara
Calle Arjona
Calle de San Pablo
Calle Tetuán
Calle Sierpes
Plaza Salvador
Calle de los Reyes Católicos
Calle Zaragoza
Calle Pastor y Landero
Calle Méndez Nuñez
Paseo Galdós
Calle Adriano
Plaza de San Francisco
Puente de Isabel II
Plaza de Toros
Paseo de Colón
Calle de Dos de Mayo
Calle Vinuesa
Avenida de la Constitución
Plaza de la Virgen de los Reyes
Calle Condé de Ibarra
Plaza des Pilatos
Calle de Luis Montoto
Plaza de los Venerables
Guadalquivir
Calle Betis
Calle de Rodrigo de Trian
Pagés del Corro
Genova
Puente de San Telmo
Almirante Lobo
Puerta de Jerez
BARRIO DE SANTA CRUZ
Plaza Santa Cruz
Alcázar
JARDINES DE MURILLO
Calle Recaredo
Calle Demetrio Rios
Avenida de Eduardo Dato
Calle de San Fernando
Calle de Menéndez Pelayo
Avenida de la República Argentina
Calle de Sebastián Elcano
Calle Asunción
San Telmo Palace
Main Bus Station
Avenida de Carlos V
Glorieta San Diego
Avenida Portugal
Paseo de las Delicias
Gloria San Diego
Avenida Maria Luisa
Avenida de Isabel la Católica
Gta. des los Marinerios Voluntarios
PARQUE MARIA LUISA
Plaza de España
FRANCE
Puente del Generalisimo
Glorieta Covadonga
SPAIN
PORTUGAL
★ Madrid
Seville

0 ____ 1/8 mile
0 ____ 100 meters

✝ Church
ⓘ Information
✉ Post Office

ATTRACTIONS ●

Alcázar **30**
Archivo General de Indias **25**
Barrio de Santa Cruz **34**
Casa de Pilatos **22**
Catedral de Sevilla **28**
Giralda Tower **27**
Hospital de la Santa Caridad **12**
Murillo Gardens **31**
Museo Arqueológico Provincial **3**
Museo de Artes y Costumbres Populares **2**
Museo Provincial de Bellas Artes de Sevilla **16**
Palacio de San Telmo **10**
Parque María Luisa **7**
Plaza de America **4**
Plaza de España **6**

Réal Fábrica de Tabacos **9**
San Salvador **19**
Torre del Oro **11**

ACCOMMODATIONS ■

Al-Andalus Palace **17**
Bécquer **15**
Casa Imperial **21**
Casa Numero 7 **23**
Hacienda Benazuza/ El Bulli Hotel **5**
Hostal Goya **35**
Hosteria del Laurel **33**

Hotel Alfonso XIII **8**
Hotel Doña María **29**
Hotel Los Seises **24**
Hotel Murillo **1**
Hotel Simon **26**
La Casa de la Judería **32**
La Casa de los Mercaderes **18**
Las Casas del Rey de Baeza **20**
Puerta de Triana **14**
Taverna del Alabardero **13**

Unlike other Spanish cities, Seville has fared rather well under most of its conquerors—the Romans, Arabs, and Christians. Rulers from Pedro the Cruel to Ferdinand and Isabella held court here. When Spain entered its 16th-century golden age, Seville funneled gold from the New World into the rest of the country, and Columbus docked here after his journey to America.

Be warned, however, that driving here is a nightmare: Seville was planned for the horse and buggy rather than for the car, and nearly all the streets run one way toward the Guadalquivir River. Locating a hard-to-find restaurant or a hidden little square will require patience and luck.

ESSENTIALS

GETTING THERE   Seville's **Aeropuerto San Pablo,** Calle Almirante Lobo (© **95-444-90-00**), is served by Iberia (© **90-240-05-00** toll free within Spain), which flies several times a day to and from Madrid (and elsewhere via Madrid). It also flies several times a week to and from Alicante, Grand Canary Island, Lisbon, Barcelona, Palma de Majorca, Tenerife, Santiago de Compostela, and (once a week) Zaragoza. The airport is about 10km (6¼ miles) from the center of the city along the highway leading to Carmona.

Train service into Seville is now centralized into the Estación Santa Justa, Av. Kansas City s/n (© **90-224-02-02**). Buses C1 and C2 take you from this train station to the bus station at Prado de San Sebastián, and bus EA runs to and from the airport. The high-speed AVE train has reduced travel time from Madrid to Seville to 2½ hours. The train makes 17 trips daily with a stop in Córdoba. Sixteen trains a day connect Seville and Córdoba; the AVE train takes 45 minutes and a TALGO takes 1½ hours. Three trains a day run to Málaga, taking 3 hours; there are also three trains per day to Granada (4 hr.).

Although Seville confusingly has several satellite **bus** stations servicing small towns and nearby villages of Andalusia, most buses arrive at and depart from the city's largest bus terminal on the southeast edge of the old city, at Prado de San Sebastián, Calle José María Osborne 11 (© **95-441-71-11**). Several companies make frequent runs to and from Córdoba (2½ hr.), Málaga (3½ hr.), Granada (4 hr.), and Madrid (8 hr.). For information and ticket prices, call Alsina Graells at © **95-453-60-82.** A newer bus station is at Plaza de Armas (© **95-490-80-40**), but it usually services destinations beyond Andalusia, including Portugal.

Several major highways converge on Seville, connecting it with all the rest of Spain and Portugal. During periods of heavy holiday traffic, the N-V (E-90) from Madrid through Extremadura—which, at Mérida, connects with the southbound N-630 (E-803)—is usually less congested than the N-IV (E-5) through eastern Andalusia.

VISITOR INFORMATION   The **tourist office,** Av. de la Constitución 21 (© **95-422-14-04;** www.andalusia.org), is open Monday through Saturday from 9am to 7pm, Sunday and holidays from 10am to 2pm.

SPECIAL EVENTS   The most popular times to visit Seville are during the April Fair—the most famous *feria* in Spain, with bullfights, flamenco, and folklore on parade—and during Holy Week when wooden figures called *pasos* are paraded through streets by robed penitents. See the "Calendar of Events" in chapter 3, and contact the tourist office for more information.

FAST FACTS   The American Express office, in the Hotel Inglaterra, Plaza Nueva 7 (© **95-421-16-17**), is open Monday through Friday from 9:30am to 1:30pm and 4:30 to 7:30pm, Saturday from 10am to 1pm. There's a U.S. consulate at Av. Paseo de las Delicias 7 (© **95-423-18-85**), open Monday through

Friday from 10am to 1pm. For medical emergencies, go to the Hospital Universitario y Provincial, Av. Doctor Fedriani s/n (𝒞 **95-455-74-00**).

With massive unemployment, the city has been hit by a crime wave in recent years. María Luisa Park is especially dangerous, as is the highway leading to Jerez de la Frontera and Cádiz. Dangling cameras and purses are especially vulnerable. Don't leave cars unguarded with your luggage inside. Regrettably, some daring attacks are made when passengers stop for traffic signals—as happens in some U.S. cities.

If you need a cab, call Tele Taxi at 𝒞 **95-462-22-22** or Radio Taxi at 𝒞 **95-458-00-00.** Cabs are metered and charge .30€ per kilometer.

SEEING THE SIGHTS

The only way to explore Seville is on foot, with a good map in hand—but remember to be alert to muggers.

THE TOP ATTRACTIONS

Alcázar ⋆⋆⋆   Pedro the Cruel built this magnificent 14th-century Mudéjar palace north of the cathedral. It's the oldest royal residence in Europe still in use: On visits to Seville, King Juan Carlos and Queen Sofía stay here. From the Dolls' Court to the Maidens' Court through the domed Ambassadors' Room, it contains some of the finest work of Sevillian artisans. In many ways it evokes the Alhambra at Granada. Ferdinand and Isabella, who at one time lived in the Alcázar and influenced its architectural evolution, welcomed Columbus here on his return from America. On the top floor, the Oratory of the Catholic Monarchs has a fine altar in polychrome tiles made by Pisano in 1504. The well-kept **gardens** ⋆ filled with beautiful flowers, shrubbery, and fruit trees, are alone worth the visit.

Plaza del Triunfo s/n. 𝒞 **95-450-23-23.** Admission 5€. Oct–Mar Tues–Sat 9:30am–5pm, Sun 9:30am–1:30pm; Apr–Sept Tues–Sat 9:30am–7pm, Sun 9:30am–5pm.

Archivo General de Indias   The great architect of Philip II's El Escorial, Juan de Herrera, was also the architect of this building next to the cathedral, originally the Lonja (Stock Exchange). Construction on the Archivo General de Indias lasted from 1584 to 1646. In the 17th century it was headquarters for the Academy of Seville, which was founded in part by the great Spanish artist Murillo. In 1785, during the reign of Charles III, the building was turned over for use as a general records office for the Indies. That led to today's Archivo General de Indias, said to contain some four million antique documents, even letters exchanged between patron Queen Isabella and explorer Columbus (he detailing his discoveries and impressions). These very rare documents are locked in air-conditioned storage to keep them from disintegrating. Special permission has to be acquired before examining some of them. On display in glass cases are fascinating documents in which the dreams of the early explorers come alive.

> **Go with the Gold**
>
> Many treasure-hunters come to the Archivo General de Indias hoping to learn where Spanish galleons laden with gold went down off the coasts of the Americas.

Av. de la Constitución 3. 𝒞 **95-421-12-34.** Free admission. Mon–Fri 8am–3pm.

Casa de Pilatos ⋆⋆   This 16th-century Andalusian palace of the dukes of Medinaceli recaptures the splendor of the past, combining Gothic, Mudéjar, and

que styles in its courtyards, fountains, and salons. According to tradition, is a reproduction of Pilate's House in Jerusalem. Don't miss the two
old carriages or the rooms filled with Greek and Roman statues. The collection
of paintings includes works by Carreño, Pantoja de la Cruz, Sebastiano del
Piombo, Lucas Jordán, Batalloli, Pacheco, and Goya. The museum's first floor is
seen by guided tour only, but the ground floor, patios, and gardens are self-
guided. The palace is about a 7-minute walk northeast of the cathedral on the
northern edge of Barrio de Santa Cruz, in a warren of labyrinthine streets whose
traffic is funneled through the nearby Calle de Aguilas.

Plaza Pilatos 1. ℂ **95-422-52-98**. Admission museum 8€; patio and gardens 5€. Daily 9am–7pm.

Catedral de Sevilla and Giralda Tower ★★★   The largest Gothic building
in the world and the third-largest church in Europe after St. Peter's in Rome and
St. Paul's in London, the Catedral de Sevilla was designed by builders with a
stated goal—that "those who come after us will take us for madmen." Construction began in the late 1400s on the site
of an ancient mosque and took centuries to complete. The cathedral
claims to contain the remains of
Columbus, with his tomb mounted on
four statues. Works of art abound,
many of them architectural, such as the
15th-century stained-glass windows,
the iron screens *(rejas)* closing off the
chapels, the elaborate 15th-century choir stalls, and the Gothic reredos above
the main altar. During Corpus Christi and Immaculate Conception observances, altar boys with castanets dance in front of the high altar. In the Treasury
are works by Goya, Murillo, and Zurbarán as well as a touch of the macabre in
a display of skulls. After touring the dark interior, emerge into the sunlight of
the Patio of Orange Trees, with its fresh citrus scents and chirping birds.

> **Cathedral Alert**
>
> Shorts and T-shirts are not
> allowed in the cathedral.
> Remember to dress appropri-
> ately before you set out so
> you're not turned away.

La Giralda, a Moorish tower next to the cathedral, is the city's most famous
monument—it conjures up Seville. Erected as a minaret in the 12th century, it
has seen later additions, such as 16th-century bells. To climb it is to take the
walk of a lifetime. There are no steps—you ascend a seemingly endless ramp. If
you can make it to the top you'll have a dazzling view of Seville. Entrance is
through the cathedral.

Plaza del Triunfo, Av. de la Constitución. ℂ **95-421-49-71**. Admission to cathedral and tower 6€ adults,
1.50€ children and students. Free admission Sun. Daily 11am–5pm.

Hospital de la Santa Caridad ✦   This 17th-century hospital is intricately
linked to the legend of Miguel Manara, portrayed by Dumas and Mérimée as
the scandalous Don Juan. It was once thought that he built this institution to
atone for his sins, but this has been disproved. The death of Manara's beautiful
young wife in 1661 caused such grief that he retired from society and entered
the "Charity Brotherhood," burying corpses of the sick and diseased as well as
condemned and executed criminals. Today the members of this brotherhood
continue to look after the poor, the old, and invalids who have no one else to
help them. Nuns will show you through the festive orange-and-sienna courtyard. The baroque chapel contains works by the 17th-century Spanish painters
Murillo and Valdés-Leal. As you're leaving the chapel, look over the exit door for
the macabre picture of an archbishop being devoured by maggots.

Calle Temprado 3. ℭ **95-422-32-32**. Admission 3€. Mon–Sat 9am–1:30pm and 3:? 9am–1pm.

Museo Provincial de Bellas Artes de Sevilla ★★ This lovely oïu ~ off Calle de Alfonso XII houses one of the most important Spanish art collections. A whole gallery is devoted to two paintings by El Greco, and works by Zurbarán are on exhibit; however, the devoutly religious paintings of the Seville-born Murillo are the highlight. An entire wing is given over to macabre paintings by the 17th-century artist Valdés-Leal. His painting of John the Baptist's head on a platter includes the knife—in case you don't get the point. The top floor, which displays modern paintings, is less interesting.

Plaza del Museo 9. ℭ **95-422-07-90**. Admission 1.50€, free for students. Tues 3–8pm; Wed–Sat 9am–8pm; Sun 9am–2pm. Bus: C4.

Torre del Oro The 12-sided Tower of Gold, dating from the 13th century, overlooks the Guadalquivir River. Originally it was covered with gold tiles, but someone long ago made off with them. The tower has been recently restored and turned into a maritime museum, the Museo Náutico, displaying drawings and engravings of the port of Seville in its golden heyday.

Paseo de Cristóbal Colón. ℭ **95-422-24-14**. Admission 1€. Tues–Fri 10am–2pm; Sat–Sun 11am–2pm.

MORE ATTRACTIONS
BARRIO DE SANTA CRUZ ★★★ What was once a ghetto for Spanish Jews, who were forced out of Spain in the late 15th century in the wake of the Inquisition, is today the most colorful district of Seville. Near the old walls of the Alcázar, winding medieval streets with names like Vida (Life) and Muerte (Death) open onto pocket-size plazas. Flower-filled balconies with draping bougainvillea and potted geraniums jut out over this labyrinth, shading you from the hot Andalusian summer sun. Feel free to look through numerous wrought-iron gates into patios filled with fountains and plants. In the evening it's common to see Sevillians sitting outside drinking icy sangria under the glow of lanterns.

To enter the Barrio Santa Cruz, turn right after leaving the Patio de Banderas exit of the Alcázar. Turn right again at the Plaza de la Alianza, going down Calle Rodrigo Caro to the Plaza de Doña Elvira. Use caution when strolling through the area, particularly at night; many robberies have occurred here.

⎛ Moments *Olé:* A Day at the Bullfight

From Easter until late October, some of the best bullfighters in Spain appear at the Maestranza bullring, on the Paseo de Colón (ℭ **95-450-13-82**). One of the leading bullrings, the stadium attracts matadors whose fights often get television and newspaper coverage throughout Iberia. Unless there's a special festival going on, bullfights *(corridas)* occur on Sunday. The best are staged during April Fair celebrations. Tickets tend to be pricey and should be purchased in advance at the ticket office *(despacho de entradas)* on Calle Adriano, beside the Maestranza. You'll find many unofficial kiosks selling tickets placed strategically along the main shopping street, Calle Sierpes, but they charge a 20% commission—a lot more if they think they can get it.

ARQUE MARIA LUISA 😊😊   This park, dedicated to María Luisa, sister of Isabella II, was once the grounds of the **Palacio de San Telmo.** The palace, whose baroque facade is visible behind the deluxe Alfonso XIII Hotel, today houses a seminary. The former private royal park is now open to the public. In 1929, Seville was to host the Spanish American Exhibition, and many pavilions from around the world were erected here. The worldwide depression put a damper on the exhibition, but the pavilions still stand.

Running south along the Guadalquivir River, the park attracts those who want to take boat rides, walk along flower bordered paths, jog, or go bicycling. The most romantic way to traverse it is by rented horse and carriage, but this can be expensive, depending on negotiation with the driver.

Exercise caution while walking through this park, as many muggings have been reported.

PLAZA DE AMERICA   Another landmark Sevillian square, the Plaza de América represents city planning at its best: Here you can walk through gardens planted with roses, enjoying the lily ponds and the fountains and feeling the protective shade of the palms. And here you'll find a trio of elaborate buildings left over from the world exhibition that never materialized—in the center, the home of the government headquarters of Andalusia; on either side, two minor museums worth visiting only if you have time to spare.

The **Museo Arqueológico Provincial,** Plaza de América s/n (© **95-423-24-01**), contains many artifacts from prehistoric times and the days of the Romans, Visigoths, and Moors. It's open Tuesday through Saturday from 9am to 8pm, and Sunday from 9am to 2pm. Admission is 1.50€ for adults and free for students and children. Bus nos. 30, 31, and 34 go there. Nearby is the **Museo de Artes y Costumbres Populares,** Plaza de América s/n (© **95-423-25-76**), displaying folkloric costumes, musical instruments, Córdoban saddles, weaponry, and farm implements that document the life of the Andalusian people. It's open Tuesday through Saturday from 9am to 8pm, and Sunday from 9am to 2pm. Admission is 1.50€ for adults and free for children and students.

PLAZA DE ESPAÑA   The major building left from the exhibition at the Parque María Luisa (see above) is the half-moon–shaped Renaissance-style structure set on this landmark square. The architect, Aníbal González, not only designed but also supervised the building of this immense structure; today it's a government office building. At a canal here you can rent rowboats for excursions into the park, or you can walk across bridges spanning the canal. Set into a curved wall are alcoves focusing on the characteristics of Spain's 50 provinces, as depicted in tile murals.

REAL FABRICA DE TABACOS   When Carmen waltzed out of the tobacco factory in the first act of Bizet's opera, she made its 18th-century original in Seville world-famous. This old tobacco factory was constructed between 1750 and 1766, and 100 years later it employed 10,000 *cigarreras,* of which Carmen was one in the opera. (She rolled cigars on her thighs.) In the 19th century, these tobacco women made up the largest female workforce in Spain. Many visitors arriving today, in fact, ask guides to take them to "Carmen's tobacco factory." The building, located on Calle San Fernando near the city's landmark luxury hotel, the Alfonso XIII, is the second largest in Spain and is still here. But the Real Fábrica de Tabacos is now part of the Universidad de Sevilla. Look for signs of its former role, however, in the bas-reliefs of tobacco plants and Indians over the main entrances. You'll also see bas-reliefs of Columbus and Cortés. Then you can wander through the grounds for a look at student life, Sevillian style. The factory is directly south of the Alcázar gardens.

SHOPPING

ART One of the most respected galleries in Seville, **Rafael Ortíz,** Marmolles 12 (© **95-421-48-74**), specializes in contemporary paintings, usually from Iberian artists. Exhibitions change frequently and inventories sell out quickly. It's open Monday through Saturday from 11am to 1:30pm and 6 to 9pm, Sunday from 11am to 1:30pm.

BOOKS **The English Bookshop,** Eduardo Dato 36 (© **95-465-57-54**), is the kind of place where you can find tomes on gardening, political discourse, philosophy, and pop fiction. It's open Monday through Friday from 10am to 1:45pm and 5 to 8:30pm, Saturday from 10am to 1:30pm. Close to Seville's university, the **Librería Vértice,** San Fernando 33 (© **95-421-16-54**), stocks books in a variety of languages. The polyglot inventory ranges from the professorial to Spanish romances of the soap-opera genre. It's open Monday through Friday from 9:30am to 2pm and 5:30 to 8:30pm, Saturday from 11am to 2pm.

CERAMICS Near the cathedral, **El Postigo,** Arfe s/n (© **95-456-00-13**), has a wide selection of Andalusian ceramics. Some of the pieces are much too big to fit into your suitcase; others—especially the hand-painted tiles—make charming souvenirs that can easily be transported. It's open Monday through Saturday from 10am to 2pm and Monday through Friday from 5:30 to 8:30pm. Near the town hall, **Martian,** Calle Sierpes 74 (© **95-421-34-13**), sells a wide array of painted tiles and ceramics: vases, plates, cups, serving dishes, and statues, all made in or near Seville. Many of the pieces use ancient geometric patterns of Andalusia. Other floral motifs are rooted in Spanish traditions of the 18th century. It's open Monday through Saturday from 10am to 2pm and 5 to 8:30pm.

DEPARTMENT STORES **El Corte Inglés,** Plaza Duque 10 (© **95-422-09-31**), is the best of the several department stores clustered in Seville's commercial center. It features multilingual translators and rack after rack of every conceivable kind of merchandise for the well-stocked home, kitchen, and closet. If you're in the market for the brightly colored *feria* costumes worn by young girls during Seville's holidays, there's an impressive selection of the traditional regional fashion, along with all the latest designer fashions for everyday. It's open Monday through Saturday from 10am to 10pm.

FANS Carmen fluttered her fan and broke hearts. You can, too, if you pick up a traditional Andalusian fan at **Casa Rubio,** Sierpes 56 (© **95-422-68-72**). It stocks one of the city's largest selections, from the austere and dramatic to the florid and fanciful. It's open Monday through Saturday from 9:30am to 1:30pm and 5 to 8:30pm.

FASHION See also "Department Stores," above. **Iconos,** Av. de la Constitución 21A (© **95-422-14-08**), is an idiosyncratic boutique loaded with fashion accessories that can be used by everyone from teenage girls to mature women. Silk scarves, costume jewelry, and an assortment of T-shirts with logos lettered in varying degrees of taste—it's all here. It's open Monday through Saturday from 10am to 9pm, Sunday from noon to 5pm. Head for **Victorio & Lucchino,** Sierpes 87 (© **95-422-79-51**), for chic upscale fashions sold Monday through Saturday from 10am to 2pm and Monday through Friday from 5 to 8:30pm. For traditional regional costumes, try **Pardales,** Cuna 23 (© **95-421-37-09**), which outfits many of the region's professional flamenco performers. Much of its merchandise is akin to couture; other items are less expensive and sold off the rack. It's open Monday through Saturday from 10am to 2pm and Monday through Friday from 5 to 8pm.

GIFTS   Souvenirs of the city, T-shirts, hammered wrought-iron whatnots, and ceramics are available at **Matador,** Av. de la Constitución 28-30 (© **95-422-62-47**), open Monday through Saturday from 10am to 2pm and Monday through Friday from 5 to 8:30pm. More upscale gifts, such as crystal and art objects, can be found at **Venecia,** Cuna 51 (© **95-422-99-94**), open Monday through Saturday from 10am to 2pm and Monday through Friday from 5 to 8:30pm.

WHERE TO STAY

During Holy Week and the Seville Fair, hotels often double, even triple, their rates. Price increases are often not announced until the last minute. If you're going to be in Seville at these times, arrive with an ironclad reservation and an agreement about the price before checking in.

VERY EXPENSIVE

Hotel Alfonso XIII ✦✦✦   At the southwestern corner of the gardens fronting the Alcázar, this rococo building is one of Spain's three or four most legendary hotels and Seville's premier address. Built in the Mudéjar/Andalusian revival style as a shelter for patrons of the Ibero-American Exposition of 1929 and named after the then-king of Spain, it reigns as a super-ornate and super-expensive bastion of glamour. Its rooms and hallways glitter with hand-painted tiles, acres of marble and mahogany, antique furniture embellished with intricately embossed leather, and a spaciousness nothing short of majestic. All rooms are beautifully kept, with bathrooms containing tub/shower combos.

San Fernando 2, 41004 Sevilla. © **800/221-2340** in the U.S. and Canada, or 95-491-70-00. Fax 95-491-70-99. 147 units. 363€–433€ double; 841€–895€ suite. AE, DC, MC, V. Parking 14€. **Amenities:** 2 restaurants; bar; pool; tennis courts; car rental; room service; babysitting; laundry service; dry cleaning. *In room:* A/C, TV, minibar, hair dryer, safe.

EXPENSIVE

Al-Andalús Palace ✦✦   No hotel in Seville has a more avant-garde design than this palace just 5 minutes from the center in the Heliópolis district, an upmarket residential area. The front public rooms are suspended by cable, and the glass facade reflects both the blue skies of Seville and the marble floors. The large guest rooms are elegantly appointed, with large windows and excellent mattresses; some have balconies. The decor and furnishings are minimalist—functional but modern. Many accommodations have small living rooms and suites with their own breakfast bars. The bathrooms have showers, large tubs, and mirrors; the suites contain hydromassage.

Av. Palmera s/n, 41012 Sevilla. © **95-423-06-00.** Fax 95-423-02-00. www.sol-1.com/hotel/al-andalus. 632 units. 112€–237€ double; 220€–450€ suite. AE, DC, MC, V. Parking 9€. Bus: 34. **Amenities:** Restaurant; bar; pool; health spa; room service; babysitting; laundry service; dry cleaning. *In room:* A/C, TV, minibar, hair dryer, safe.

Casa Imperial ✦✦✦   In the historic center, this hotel was launched in the mid-1990s near Casa Pilatos and dates from the 15th century, when it was the home of the butler to the marquis of Tarifa. The interior is refined, and there are four Andalusian patios adorned with exotic plants. The beamed ceilings are original, and sparkling chandeliers hang from the ceilings. The rooms are large—many have small kitchens and ample terraces. The bathrooms are tastefully decorated with showers and luxurious tubs, some of which are antiques.

Calle Imperial 29, 41003 Sevilla. ℂ 95-450-03-00. Fax 95-450-03-30. www.casaimperial.com. 24 units. 175€–225€ double; 225€–295€ suite. AE, DC, MC, V. Rates include breakfast buffet. Free parking. **Amenities:** Restaurant; bar; room service; babysitting; laundry service; dry cleaning. *In room:* A/C, TV, minibar, hair dryer, safe.

Casa Número 7 ★★ *Finds* This is as close as you can get to staying in an elegant private home in Seville. Next to the Santa Cruz *barrio,* the little inn is in a beautiful, sensitively restored 19th-century mansion where you live in style, as evoked by the butler who serves you breakfast. Small in dimension, Casa No. 7 is big on style and grace notes, recapturing the aura of Old Seville. It thinks of itself, with justification, as a civilized oasis in the midst of a bustling city. In 2001 it won the prestigious Tatler Travel Award as the world's "best small hotel." Rooms are individually decorated in old Sevillano style, with impeccable taste and an eye to comfort. Called more "Chelsea (London) town house than Seville hacienda," the building envelops an old atrium, and is filled with such touches as family photographs, Oriental area rugs, a marble fireplace, and floral print love seats. All come with good-size bathrooms with tub and shower. We prefer the spacious Yellow Room, with its "Juliet balcony" overlooking the street.

Vírgenes 7, 41004 Sevilla. ℂ **95-422-15-81.** Fax 95-421-45-27. www.casanumero7.com. 6 units. 170€–275€ double. Rates include breakfast. **Amenities:** "Honesty" bar; laundry service. *In room:* A/C.

Las Casas del Rey de Baeza ★ Less luxurious than its sibling, La Casa de la Judería (see below), this antique hotel close to the Casa de Pilatos is still a winning choice with its stone floors and 19th-century Andalusian architecture. A hotel since 1998, it has an interior patio surrounded by a cozy coterie of rooms and a long Andalusian balcony. Some of the beautifully furnished rooms have living rooms, and the decor is finely honed in marble and wood with comfortable furnishings. The bathrooms contain tub/shower combos.

Calle Santiago, Plaza Jesús de la Redención 2, 41003 Seville. ℂ **95-456-14-96.** Fax 95-456-14-41. www. hostes.es. 41 units. 127€–162€ double; 180€–220€ suite. AE, DC, MC, V. Parking 12€. **Amenities:** Bar; lounge; pool; babysitting; laundry service; dry cleaning. *In room:* A/C, TV, minibar, hair dryer, safe.

Taverna del Alabardero ★★ *Finds* This tavern now houses one of the single most charming places to stay in the city. Close to the bullring and a 5-minute walk from the cathedral, this is a restored 19th-century mansion with a spectacular central patio and a romantic atmosphere. The units on the third floor have balconies overlooking street scenes as well as whirlpool tubs. All the rooms are spacious and comfortable, each individually decorated in a specific regional style. The bathrooms contain tub/shower combos.

Zaragoza 20, 41001 Sevilla. ℂ **95-456-06-37.** Fax 95-456-36-66. 7 units. 145€–235€ double; 178€–274€ suite. Rates include continental breakfast. AE, DC, MC, V. Parking 15€. **Amenities:** Restaurant; bar; lounge; room service; babysitting; laundry service; dry cleaning. *In room:* A/C, TV, minibar, hair dryer, safe.

MODERATE

Bécquer A short walk from the action of the Seville bullring and only 2 blocks from the river, Bécquer is on a street full of cafes where you can order tapas and drink Andalusian wine. The Museo Provincial de Bellas Artes is also nearby. Built in the 1970s, the hotel was enlarged and much renovated in the late 1980s. It occupies the site of a former mansion and retains many objets d'art rescued before that building was demolished. You register in a wood-paneled lobby before being shown to one of the functionally furnished rooms—a good value in a pricey city. All have bathrooms with tub/shower combos.

Calle Reyes Católicos 4, 41001 Sevilla. ℃ **95-422-89-00.** Fax 95-421-44-00. www.hotelbecquer.com. 139 units. 125€–162€ double; 250€–324€ suite. AE, DC, MC, V. Parking 11€. Bus: 21, 24, 30, or 31. **Amenities:** Restaurant; bar; lounge; room service; babysitting; laundry service; dry cleaning. *In room:* A/C, TV, minibar, hair dryer, safe.

Hotel Doña María ⭐ Staying at this hotel is a worthwhile investment, partly because of the Iberian antiques in the stone lobby and upper hallways. And the location a few steps from the cathedral creates a dramatic view from the Doña María's rooftop terrace. An ornate neoclassical entryway is offset with a pure white facade and iron balconies, which hint at the building's origin in the 1840s as a private villa. Amid the flowering plants on the upper floor you'll find garden-style lattices and antique wrought-iron railings. Each of the one-of-a-kind rooms has a bathroom with a tub/shower combo and is well furnished and comfortable, though some are rather small. A few have four-poster beds, others a handful of antique reproductions. Light sleepers might find the noise of the church bells jarring. Breakfast is the only meal served.

Don Remondo 19, 41004 Sevilla. ℃ **95-422-49-90.** Fax 95-421-95-46. www.hdmaria.com. 64 units. 99€–165€ double. AE, DC, MC, V. Parking 12€. **Amenities:** Breakfast room; bar; pool; room service; babysitting; laundry service; dry cleaning. *In room:* A/C, TV, minibar, hair dryer, safe.

Hotel Los Seises Once the 16th-century palace of the archbishop of Seville, this hotel is behind the cathedral in the old Jewish Quarter of Santa Cruz. Renovations have added modern amenities but many of the Andalusian touches have been retained. In this category of antique hotels, we still prefer the Casa Imperial, but what you get here isn't bad. At least it was the pope's choice when he visited Seville. Traditional stucco walls are adorned with modern paintings in contrast to the antique tiles. The rooms range from small to spacious, each with a good bed and a restored bathroom with a tub/shower combo. Be sure to check out the stunning vista of La Giralda you can enjoy while sunbathing on the rooftop.

Calle Segovias 6, 41004 Sevilla. ℃ **95-422-94-95.** Fax 95-422-43-34. www.hotellosseises.com. 42 units. 128€–181€ double. AE, DC, MC, V. Parking 15€. **Amenities:** Restaurant; bar; pool; room service; babysitting; laundry service; dry cleaning. *In room:* A/C, TV, minibar, hair dryer, safe.

La Casa de la Judería ⭐⭐ Ⓥⁿˡᵘᵉ In the Santa Cruz district, this hotel is installed in a palace from the 1600s once owned by the duke of Beja, a great character in the history of Spain's aristocracy and known as the patron of Cervantes. Within easy walking distance of the cathedral and other sights, the building has been a hotel since 1991. It's now one of the best places to stay in Seville, offering an excellent bang for your euro. All the rooms, medium in size, are individually decorated and furnished in an antique style, sometimes with four-poster beds; all have balconies, some facing street scenes and others opening onto one of the four interior patios in the classic Andalusian style. Many units have living rooms, and all the suites contain whirlpool tubs. The bathrooms are beautifully maintained, with tub/shower combos.

Plaza Santa María la Blanca, Callejón de Dos Hermanas 7, 41004 Sevilla. ℃ **95-441-51-50.** Fax 95-442-21-70. www.casasypalacios.com. 116 units. 124€–150€ double; 142€–240€ suite. AE, DC, MC, V. Parking 13€. **Amenities:** Dining room; bar; room service; babysitting; laundry service; dry cleaning. *In room:* A/C, TV, minibar, hair dryer, safe.

Las Casas de los Mercaderes ⭐ In the business center of Seville, this restored mansion lies close to the cathedral between the squares of San Francisco and

Salvador. Its name reflects the history of the area, which was once home to many immigrant merchants. The 19th-century original has been fully renovated—at the time, an 18th-century patio was discovered. Much of the original style and grace notes were retained. Most of the medium-sized rooms have balconies and classic Spanish furnishings. The modern bathrooms come with tub/shower combos.

Calle Alvarez Quintero 9–13, 41004 Sevilla. ✆ **95-422-58-58.** Fax 95-422-98-84. www.casasypalacios.com. 47 units. 99€–122€ double. AE, DC, MC, V. Parking 14€. **Amenities:** Bar; lounge; room service; babysitting; laundry service; dry cleaning. *In room:* A/C, TV, minibar, hair dryer, safe.

Puerta de Triana *(Value)* This budgeteer's dream is a 5-minute walk from the cathedral in the Paseo Colón district. Last renovated in 1992, it was constructed in the early 1970s in neoclassic style. Antique styles are mixed with modern features, and the interior is surprisingly elegant for a place charging such low prices. The hotel offers simply but comfortably furnished rooms, each with a bath containing a tub/shower combo. If you're driving to this location near the Plaza de Toros, you can ask the staff to direct you to one of the nearby garages where discounts for hotel guests are available.

Reyes Católicos 5, 41001 Sevilla. ✆ **95-421-54-04.** Fax 95-421-54-01. www.hotelpuertadetriana.com. 62 units. 75€–120€ double. AE, DC, MC, V. **Amenities:** Laundry service; dry cleaning. *In room:* A/C, TV, hair dryer.

INEXPENSIVE

Hostal Goya Its location in a narrow-fronted town house in the oldest part of the barrio is one of the Goya's strongest virtues. The building's gold-and-white facade, ornate iron railings, and picture-postcard demeanor are all noteworthy. The rooms are cozy and simple. Guests congregate in the marble-floored ground-level salon, where a skylight floods the couches and comfortable chairs with sunlight. No meals are served. Reserve well in advance. Parking is often available along the street.

Mateus Gago 31, 41004 Sevilla. ✆ **95-421-11-70.** Fax 95-456-29-88. 20 units (15 with bathroom). 58€–68€ without bathroom, 65€–75€ with bathroom. MC, V. *In room:* No phone.

Hostería del Laurel ⭐ *(Finds)* Long one of our favorite dining taverns in Santa Cruz, this traditional inn, whose downstairs is hung with cured Andalusian hams and strings of fresh garlic, also offers bargain rooms. During his stay here in 1844, Don José Zorrilla, Spain's most romantic writer of the time, was so inspired by the atmosphere of the inn that he created his famous character, Don Juan Tenorio. Bedrooms are simply furnished and immaculately kept, opening onto one of the barrio's most delightful and time-mellowed squares. All units come with a small bathroom equipped with tub and shower. The rooms are spread across several floors of restored old houses with their tiny patios and bubbling fountains. When you're hungry, just follow the wafting aromas of well-flavored food to the restaurant downstairs (see "Where to Dine," below).

Plaza de los Venerables 5, 41004 Sevilla. ✆ **95-422-02-95.** Fax 95-421-04-50. www.hosteriadellaurel.com. 21 units. 70€–97€ double. Rates include breakfast. AE, DC, MC, V. **Amenities:** Restaurant; bar. *In room:* A/C, TV.

Hotel Murillo Tucked away on a narrow street in the heart of Santa Cruz, the Residencia Murillo (named after the artist who used to live in this district) is almost next to the gardens of the Alcázar. Inside, the lounges harbor some fine architectural characteristics and antique reproductions; behind a grilled screen is a retreat for drinks. Many of the rooms we inspected were cheerless and gloomy, so have a look before checking in. All units do contain bathrooms with tub/shower combos. You can reach this *residencia* from the Menéndez y Pelayo, a wide avenue west of the Parque María Luisa, where a sign leads you through the **Murillo Gardens** on the left. Motorists should try to park in the Plaza de Santa Cruz. Then walk 2 blocks to the hotel, which will send a bellhop back to the car to pick up your suitcases. If there are two in your party, station a guard at the car, and if you're going out at night, call for an inexpensive taxi to take you instead of strolling through the streets of the old quarter—it's less romantic but a lot safer.

Calle Lope de Rueda 7–9, 41004 Sevilla. © 95-421-60-95. Fax 95-421-96-16. www.hotelmurillo.com. 57 units. 50€–63€ double; 62€–79€ triple. AE, DC, MC, V. Parking 12€ nearby. **Amenities:** Room service; laundry service; dry cleaning. *In room:* A/C, hair dryer.

WHERE TO STAY NEARBY

Hacienda Benazuza/El Bulli Hotel ★★★   On a hillside above the agrarian hamlet of Sanlúcar la Mayor, 19km (12 miles) south of Seville, this legendary manor house is surrounded by 16 hectares (40 acres) of olive groves and farmland. Its ownership has been a cross section of every major cultural influence that has swept through Andalusia since the Moors laid its foundations in the 10th century. After the Catholic conquest of southern Spain, the site became a stronghold of the fanatically religious Caballeros de Santiago. In 1992, Basque-born entrepreneur Rafael Elejabeitia bought the property and spent millions of pesetas to transform it into one of Andalusia's most charming hotels. Careful attention was paid to preserving the ancient Moorish irrigation system, whose many reflecting pools nourish the gardens. All but a few of the rooms are in the estate's main building, each individually furnished with Andalusian antiques and Moorish trappings. All units contain neatly kept bathrooms with tub/shower combos. The kitchen is now under the culinary influence of Ferran Adria, the famous chef of Catalonia who is hailed as one of the top two or three best chefs in the country. He's rarely on the premises but his recipes and style of cookery are used. Even if you're not staying here, you might want to call for a dinner reservation. Chances are it'll be one of your finest meals in Seville.

Calle Virgen de las Nieves s/n, 41800 Sanlúcar la Major, Sevilla. © 95-570-33-44. Fax 95-570-3410. www.hbenazuza.com. 44 units. 310€–390€ double; 415€–1,130€ suite. AE, DC, MC, V. Free parking. Closed Jan. From Seville, follow the signs for Huelva and head S on the A-49 Hwy., taking exit no. 16. **Amenities:** 2 restaurants; bar; pool; tennis courts; room service; babysitting; laundry service; dry cleaning. *In room:* A/C, TV, minibar, hair dryer, safe.

WHERE TO DINE
VERY EXPENSIVE

Egaña Oriza ★★★ BASQUE/INTERNATIONAL   Seville's most stylish restaurant is set within the conservatory of a restored mansion adjacent to the Murillo Gardens. Much of its reputation stems from its role as one of the few game specialists in Andalusia—a province otherwise devoted to seafood. The restaurant was opened by Basque-born owner/chef José Mari Egaña, who manages to combine his passion for hunting with his flair for cooking. Many of the ingredients have been trapped or shot within Andalusia, a region whose potential for sports shooting is underutilized, according to Sr. Egaña. The view from the dining room encompasses a garden and a wall that formed part of the fortifications of Muslim Seville. Specialties depend on the season but might include ostrich carpaccio, gazpacho with prawns, steak with foie gras in grape sauce, casserole of wild boar with cherries and raisins, duck *quenelles* in a potato nest with apple purée, and woodcock flamed in Spanish brandy. The wine list provides an ample supply of hearty Spanish reds to accompany these dishes. Dessert might feature a chocolate tart slathered with freshly whipped cream. Sr. Egaña's wife, Mercedes, runs the dining room.

San Fernando 41. ℂ **95-422-72-11.** Reservations required. Main courses 24€–48€. AE, DC, MC, V. Restaurant Mon–Fri 1:30–3:30pm; Mon–Sat 9–11:30pm; bar daily 9am–midnight. Closed Aug.

La Isla ✪ SPANISH/ANDALUSIAN   This choice is in two large Andalusian dining rooms (thick plaster walls, tile floors, and taurine memorabilia). Its seafood is trucked or flown in from either Galicia or Huelva, one of Andalusia's major ports, and is always fresh. Menu items include *merluza a la primavera* (hake with young vegetables), *solomillo a la castellana* (grilled beefsteak with strips of Serrano ham), chicken croquettes, and shellfish soup. The restaurant is a short walk from the cathedral within a very old building erected, the owners say, on foundations laid by the ancient Romans.

Arfe 25. ℂ **95-421-26-31.** Reservations recommended. Main courses 27€–41€. AE, DC, MC, V. Daily 1–5pm and 8pm–midnight. Closed Aug.

EXPENSIVE

El Burladero ✪ CONTINENTAL   This restaurant in one of Seville's most prominent hotels is awash with the memorabilia and paraphernalia of bullfighting. The wall tiles were removed from one of the pavilions at the 1929 Seville world's fair, and the photographs adorning the walls are a veritable history of bullfighting. (The restaurant is named after the wooden barricade behind which bullfighters in an arena can escape from the charge of an enraged bull.) It boasts a popular bar, where Sevillanos meet and mingle before their meals. Menu specialties include upscale interpretations of local country dishes, with an attractive mix of items from other regions of Spain as well. Examples include *bacalao al horno con patatas* (baked salt cod with potatoes and saffron sauce), roasted shoulder of lamb stuffed with a deboned oxtail and served in a richly aromatic sauce, clams with white kidney beans, *cocido* (a boiled amalgam of sausages, meats, chickpeas, and vegetables), and a stew of eel meat laced with garlic and spices. Dishes from other parts of Europe include duck liver, truffled filet steak in puff pastry, and salmon cooked in lemon-flavored dill sauce.

In the Hotel Tryp Colón, Canalejas 1. ℂ **95-450-55-99.** Reservations recommended. Main courses 13€–19€; fixed-price menus from 35€. AE, DC, MC, V. Daily 1:30–4:30pm and 9pm–midnight. Closed Aug.

La Albahaca ✪✪ ANDALUSIAN/BASQUE   In the Barrio de Santa Cruz, the most typical and evocative quarter of Seville, this elegant restaurant holds forth. The house itself was constructed by Juan Talavera, a celebrated architect of his day, and many of the original architectural features have been preserved. Over the years the restaurant has attracted European royalty such as the king and queen of Spain or of Denmark, along with visiting celebrities such as Charlton Heston.

From the patio you can enter one of three beautiful dining rooms, or else you can in fair weather enjoy a table on the front terrace. High quality ingredients go into the first-rate cuisine. Appetizers likely to intrigue you are the fresh goose liver and apple terrine in a pheasant jelly or baked sea bass with stir-fried plums, raisins, and almonds. Main courses that have met with ever-lasting approval are the roasted wild boar with fig marmalade or the pheasant breast roasted with Iberian bacon. One of the most delectable offerings is veal sirloin with fresh goose liver served with a red-wine sauce. Desserts are among the best in town, especially the fig soufflé or the bitter orange mousse, and most definitely the cottage cheesecake with walnuts.

Plaza Santa Cruz 12. © **95-422-07-14.** Reservations required. Main courses 16€–20€. AE, DC, MC, V. Mon–Sat 1–4pm and 8pm–midnight. Closed Mon July–Aug.

La Judería ANDALUSIAN/SPANISH   Founded in 1982, the restaurant has long been a local favorite in Seville, attracting everybody from bullfighters to politicians. The decoration is in a typically Sevilian style, with brick walls. The chefs use all of Spain as a giant shopping cart, serving traditional meats such as lamb from the province of Avila or fresh fish from the Basque coast of northern Spain. We always like to launch our repast here with a savory kettle of mussels cooked and flavored with wine. The baked baby lamb of Avila is the choice dish for meat fanciers, and it's served with fresh vegetables. A whole fish is also baked in salt here, the casing then peeled off. That way, the fish retains its moistness during the cooking process. Other white fish dishes are served in a tangy tomato sauce.

Cano y Cueto 13, Jardines de Murillo. © **95-441-20-52.** Reservations recommended. Main courses 12€–15€. AE, DC, MC, V. Daily 1–5pm and 8pm-midnight.

Poncio ★★ *Finds* ANDALUSIAN   Even though your cabbie may tell you that this relatively new dining room in the Triana district doesn't exist, press on to discover some of the finest food in Seville. Eat in style with the Spanish dons who know of this place, even the sherry-makers from Jerez de la Frontera who journey to Seville on business. Chef Willy Moya might have studied with some of the grand cooks of Paris, but when he got back home, he invented his own dishes. Yes, there's still a Parisian influence, but as one faithful diner said, "Moya's roots lay buried deep in the soil of Andalusia." We concur. We always like to start with a platter of the tender, flavorful Jabugo ham, preceded, as always, with a glass of sherry. On our last visit our party ordered an array of tapas so all of us got to share in such delights as baby broad beans with quail eggs and ham; fresh, salted anchovies; and steamed peppers stuffed with prawns and orange cream. Only the croquettes were disappointing, a bit heavy. That "thick tomato soup" on the English menu turns out to be one of Seville's most delightful gazpachos. Ask the waiter to describe the dish of the day (often the best choice on the menu) or stick to such favorites as tender lamb, aromatically roasted in the oven in a wood-burning stove or else salt-encrusted sea bass in a delicate prawn oil served with olive caviar (not caviar, but minced olives that resemble caviar in look, not texture). None of the desserts sampled have ever disappointed. Would you believe hot apple pie with ice cream? The wine list is short but refined and tastefully selected.

Calle Victoria 8. © **95-434-00-10.** Reservations required. Main courses 14€–2€. AE, DC, MC, V. Mon–Sat 2–4:30pm and 9:30pm–1am.

Porta Coeli ★★ MEDITERRANEAN   With one of Seville's most sophisticated decors, this is the finest hotel dining in the city. Even if you're not a hotel guest, consider reserving one of the 15 beautifully laid tables set against a backdrop of tapestry-hung walls. The flavor combinations are contemporary, and you'll relish the freshest ingredients. The menu boasts a wide variety of dishes featuring duck, including a delectable duck with fried white beans laced with ham. Another savory offering is *ensalada de bacalao con tomate* (salt cod salad with tomatoes) and *arroz marinero con bogavante* (rice with crayfish). The locals rave about the *corazón de solomillo al foie con zetas al vino* (beef heart with liver and mushroom in red-wine sauce), though this might be an acquired taste. For dessert, nothing is more luscious than the napoleon with fresh fruit.

In the Hotel Hesperia Sevilla, Eduardo Dato 49. ✆ **95-453-35-00.** Reservations recommended. Main courses 11€–29€. AE, DC, MC, V. Daily 1:30–3:30pm and 9pm–midnight. Closed Aug. Bus: 23.

MODERATE

Casa Robles ANDALUSIAN   This restaurant is praised by locals and visitors alike. It began life as an unpretentious bar and bodega in 1954. Over the years, thanks to a staff directed by owner/chef Juan Robles and his children, it developed into a bustling restaurant on two floors of a building a short walk from the cathedral. Amid an all-Andalusian decor, you can enjoy such dishes as fish soup in the Andalusian style, *lubina con naranjas* (whitefish with Sevillana oranges), hake baked with strips of Serrano ham, and many kinds of fresh fish. The dessert list is long and very tempting.

Calle Alvarez Quintero 58. ✆ **95-421-31-50.** Reservations recommended. Main courses 12€–20€. AE, DC, MC, V. Daily 1–4:30pm and 8:30pm–1am.

Enrique Becerra ✷ ANDALUSIAN   Near the cathedral, this is a cozy retreat in a whitewashed house with wrought-iron window grilles, and its home-cooked dishes are prepared with flair. This popular tapas bar and dining spot has an intimate setting that welcomes you with the feeling that your business is really appreciated. While perusing the menu, you can sip dry Tío Pepe and nibble herb-cured olives with lemon peel. The gazpacho is among the city's best, and the sangria is served ice cold. Specialties include hake *real,* sea bream Bilbao style, and a wide range of well-prepared meat and fish dishes. The wine list is one of the best in Seville.

Gamazo 2. ✆ **95-421-30-49.** Reservations recommended. Main courses 12€–20€; fixed-price menus 42€–54€. AE, DC, MC, V. Mon–Sat 1–5pm and 8pm–midnight.

Rincón de la Casana ✷ *Finds* ARGENTINEAN/ANDALUSIAN   Close to the old town, this landmark wins new converts every year. Converted from an old building, it has a main door of intricate carving and craftsmanship, and its roof is red tiled in the traditional style. The two-story interior has one of the most interesting decors in the city, with antique tiles and typical Andalusian artifacts. At the entrance is the mounted head of the last bull killed by the famous matador José Luis Vásquez. The chefs know their ingredients right down to the last olive. On our last visit we savored *chuletón de buey* (ox steak) and *carne con chimichurri* (steak with chopped parsley and garlic dressing in virgin olive oil). Desserts are freshly made every day, including traditional puddings and tasty tarts, most often with fresh fruit.

Santo Domingo de la Calzada 13. ✆ **95-453-17-10.** Reservations required. Main courses 11€–18€; set menu 27€. AE, DC, MC, V. Mon–Sat 1–4:30pm and 8:30pm–12:30am.

Taverna del Alabardero ✷✷ ANDALUSIAN   One of Seville's most prestigious restaurants occupies a 19th-century town house 3 blocks from the cathedral. Famous as the dining choice of nearly every politician and diplomat who visits Seville, it has recently hosted the king and queen of Spain, the king's mother, the Spanish president and members of his cabinet, and dozens of well-connected but merely affluent visitors. Amid a collection of European antiques and oil paintings, you'll dine in any of two main rooms or three private ones, and perhaps precede your meal with a drink or tapas on the flowering patio. There's a garden in back with additional tables. Menu items include spicy peppers stuffed with pulverized thigh of bull, Andalusian fish *(urta)* on a compote of aromatic tomatoes with coriander, cod filet with essence of red peppers, and Iberian beefsteak with foie gras and green peppers.

Calle Zaragoza 20, 41001 Seville. © 95-450-27-21. Fax 95-456-36-66. Reservations recommended. Main courses 9€–23€. AE, DC, MC, V. Daily 1–3:30pm and 8pm–midnight. Closed Aug. Bus: 13, 25, or 26.

INEXPENSIVE

Hostería del Laurel ★ *Finds* ANDALUSIAN   In one of the most charming buildings on tiny, difficult-to-find Plaza de los Venerables in the labyrinthine Barrio de Santa Cruz, this is a hideaway. It has iron-barred windows stuffed with plants. Inside, amid Andalusian tiles, beamed ceilings, and more plants, you'll enjoy good regional cooking. Many diners stop for a drink and tapas at the ground-floor bar before going into one of the dining rooms. The *hostería* is attached to a well-recommended hotel.

Plaza de los Venerables 5. © 95-422-02-95. Reservations recommended. Main courses 8€–22€; fixed-price menu 22€–42€. AE, DC, MC, V. Daily noon–4pm and 7:30pm–midnight.

Río Grande ANDALUSIAN   This classic Sevillian restaurant is named for the Guadalquivir River, which its panoramic windows overlook. It sits against the bank of the river near the Plaza de Cuba in front of the Torre del Oro. Some diners come here just for a view of the city monuments. Most dishes are priced at the lower end of the scale. A meal might include stuffed sweet pepper *flamenca*, fish-and-seafood soup seaman's style, salmon, chicken-and-shellfish paella, bull tail Andalusian-style, or garlic chicken. A selection of fresh shellfish is brought in daily. Large terraces contain a snack bar, the Río Grande Pub, and a bingo room. You can often watch sports events on the river in this pleasant (and English-speaking) spot.

Calle Betis s/n. © 95-427-39-56. Reservations required. Main courses 12€–18€. AE, DC, MC, V. Daily 1–4pm and 8pm–midnight. Bus: 41 or 42.

SEVILLE AFTER DARK

When the sun goes down, think sherry, wine, and tapas. After a couple of drinks have got you going, you might venture to a flamenco club or even try to learn the intricate steps of one of southern Spain's most addictive dances, the *sevillana*.

DRINKS & TAPAS   Tapas are said to have originated in Andalusia, and the old-fashioned **Casa Román,** Plaza de los Venerables 1 (© 95-421-64-08), in the Barrio de Santa Cruz, looks as if it has been dishing them up since day one, but it's actually been around only since 1934. Definitely include this place on your tasca hopping through the old quarter. At the deli counter in front you can make your selection; you might even pick up the fixings for a picnic in the Parque María Luisa. It's open daily from 9:30am to 4pm and 7pm to midnight. Tapas are priced from 3.50€.

As you make the rounds of tapas bars, you discover *pata negra* ham, made from the black-hoofed Iberian breed of pig of the same name. Surely one of the world's great hams, the flavor is subtle and sweet instead of salty like Virginia ham. The pigs are fed on acorns. **Casa Ruitz,** Calle Francos 59 (© 95-422-86-24), serves the best *pata negra* in Seville. The wine, too, is good here.

El Rinconcillo, Gerona 40 (© 95-422-31-83), at the northern edge of the Barrio de Santa Cruz, has a 1930s ambience, partly because of its real age and partly because of its owners' refusal to change one iota of the decor. It may actually be the oldest bar in Seville, with a history dating from 1670. Amid dim lighting, heavy ceiling beams, and marble-topped tables, you can enjoy a beer or a full meal along with the rest of the easygoing crowd. The bartender will mark your tab in chalk on a well-worn wooden countertop. El Rinconcillo is especially known for its salads, omelets, hams, and selection of cheeses. Look for the Art Nouveau tile murals. It's open daily from 1pm to 2am, and a meal costs around 20€.

The best seafood tapas in town are served at **La Alicantina,** Plaza del Salvador 2 (© **95-422-61-22**), amid the glazed-tile decor typical of Seville. Both the bar and the sidewalk tables are always filled to overflowing. The owner serves generous portions of clams marinara, fried squid, grilled shrimp, fried cod, and clams in béchamel sauce. La Alicantina, about 5 blocks north of the cathedral, is open daily from noon to midnight. Tapas range upward from 1.80€.

At the northern end of Murillo Gardens, opening onto a quiet square with flower boxes and an ornate iron railing, **Modesto,** Cano y Cueto 5 (© **95-441-68-11**), also serves fabulous seafood tapas. In the bar you can choose your appetizers just by pointing. Upstairs is a good-value restaurant offering a meal for 20€, including such dishes as fried squid, baby sole, grilled sea bass, and shrimp in garlic sauce. Modesto is open daily from 8am to 2am. Tapas are priced from 3€.

Our favorite bar in town is **Abades,** Calle Abades 13 (© **95-422-56-22**), where a 19th-century Santa Cruz mansion has been turned into something resembling the living room on a luxurious movie set. It evokes the style of the Spanish Romantic era. Drinks and low-key conversations are the style here, and though you might spot the occasional celeb, you'll see lots of folks in jeans enjoying the comfort of the sofas and wicker armchairs. The ingredients of the special house drink called *aqua de Sevilla* are a secret, but we suspect sparkling white wine, pineapple juice, and eggs (the whites and yolks mixed in separately, of course). Classical music is played in the background. Take a taxi to get here at night, as it might not be safe to wander late along the narrow streets of the barrio. In summer, it's open daily from 4pm to 4am; in winter, hours are daily from 4pm to 2:30am.

FLAMENCO When the moon is high in Seville and the scent of orange blossoms is in the air, it's time to wander the alleyways of Santa Cruz in search of the sound of castanets. Or take a taxi to be on the safe side.

Consider a visit to **Club Los Gallos,** Plaza de Santa Cruz 11 (© **95-421-69-81**), a reputable nightclub where male and female performers stamp, clap, and exude rigidly controlled Iberian passion on a small stage in front of appreciative observers. A cover charge of 27€ includes the first drink. No meals are served, and advance reservations are a good idea. Its leading competitor, charging roughly the same prices with more or less the same program, is **El Arenal,** Calle Rodó 7 (© **95-421-64-92**), where you'll sit at tiny, cramped tables with

---

Moments **Dancing the *Sevillanas***

Flamenco is danced in solitary grandeur, but everyone joins in with the communal but complicated dance steps of the *sevillanas.* The best place to check it out is **El Simpecao,** Calle Betis s/n (no phone). Beginning at 11pm every night of the year, recorded music presents four distinctly different facets of the complicated and old-fashioned dance steps in which dozens of everyday folk strut their Andalusian style in a way you rarely see outside Spain. The setting is modern and just a wee bit battered. Entrance is free.

barely enough room to clap—but you will, because of the smoldering emotions conveyed in the performances here.

In central Seville on the riverbank between two historic bridges, **El Patio Sevillano,** Paseo de Cristóbal Colón 11 (© **95-421-41-20**), is a showcase for Spanish folk song and dance performed by exotically costumed dancers. The presentation includes a wide variety of Andalusian flamenco and songs, as well as classical pieces by composers such as Falla, Albéniz, Granados, and Chueca. From March to October there are three shows nightly, beginning at 7:30 and 10pm. Admission, including one drink, is 29€.

DANCE CLUBS   If you're interested in the latest dance tunes, Seville's most popular club is **Disco Antigüedades,** Calle Argote de Molina (no phone). About 2 blocks north of the cathedral in a much-renovated antique building, it opens nightly at 11pm, charging around 5€ entrance, which includes the first drink. Expect lots of salsa and merengue in addition to more international fare from across Europe and the United States.

GAY BARS   Seville has a large gay and lesbian population, much of it composed of foreigners, including Americans, Germans, and British, and of Andalusians who fled here for a better life, escaping less tolerant towns and villages. Gay life thrives in such bars as **Isbiliyya Café-Bar,** Paseo de Colón (© **95-421-04-60**), which is usually open daily from 4pm to 4am. The bar is found across the street from the Puente Isabel II bridge, near Bar Capote. Outdoor tables are a magnet in summer.

THE PERFORMING ARTS   To keep abreast of what's happening in the arts and after dark in Seville, pick up a copy of the free monthly leaflet *El Giraldillo* or consult the listings in the local press, *Correo de Andalucía, Sudoeste, Nueva Andalucía,* or *ABC Sevilla.* Everything is listed here, from jazz to classical music concerts and from art exhibits to dance events. You can also call a cultural hot line at © **010** to find out what's happening. Most of the staff at the other end speaks English.

Keep an eye out for classical concerts that are sometimes presented in the cathedral of Seville, the church of **San Salvador,** and the Conservatorio Superior de Música at Jesús del Gran Poder. Variety productions, including some plays for the kids, are presented at **Teatro Alameda,** Crédito (© **95-438-83-12**). The venerable **Teatro Lope de Vega,** Avenida María Luisa (© **95-459-08-53**), is the setting for ballet performances and classical concerts, among other events. Near Parque María Luisa, this is the leading stage of Seville, but knowledge of Spanish is necessary.

It wasn't until the 1990s that Seville got its own opera house, but **Teatro de la Maestranza,** Paseo de Colón 22 (© **95-422-65-73**), quickly became one of the world's premier venues for operatic performances. Naturally, the focus is on works inspired by Seville, including Verdi's *La Forza del Destino* or Mozart's *Marriage of Figaro,* although jazz, classical music, and even the quintessentially Spanish *zarzuelas* (operettas) are also performed here. The opera house may be visited only during performances. Tickets (which vary in price, depending on the event staged) can be purchased daily from 10am to 2pm and 5 to 8pm at the box office in front of the theater.

SIDE TRIPS FROM SEVILLE

CARMONA ☞   An easy hour-long bus trip from the main terminal in Seville, Carmona is an ancient city dating from Neolithic times. Thirty-four kilometers

The Legacy of al-Andalús

The Moors who once occupied Andalusia—notably Seville, Granada, and Córdoba—left more than such architectural treasures as the Giralda Tower in Seville, the great mosque in Córdoba, and the Alhambra in Granada. Their intellectual and cultural legacy still influences modern life throughout the Western world.

The celebrated Arab princesses and sultans with their harems are long gone, encountered today only in the tales of Washington Irving and others. Yet from A.D. 711, the Moors (Muslims who were an ethnic mixture of Berbers, Hispano-Romans, and Arabs) occupied southern Spain for nearly 8 centuries and turned it into a seat of learning. It was a time of soaring achievements in philosophy, medicine, and music.

Moorish rule brought the importation of the eggplant and the almond, as well as the Arabian steed—not to mention such breakthroughs in academia as astronomy (including charting the positions of the planets) and a new and different view of Aristotle. Arab numerals replaced the more awkward Roman system, and from the Arabs came the gift of algebra. Ibn Muadh of Jaén wrote the first European treatise on trigonometry.

Intellectual giants emerged, like the Córdoba-born Jewish philosopher Maimónides. It's said that Columbus evolved his theories about a new route to the East after hours and hours of studying the charts of Idrisi, an Arabian geographer who drew up a world map as early as 1154. Arabs relied upon the compass as a navigational aid long before its use among Portuguese explorers.

Córdoba desired to shine brighter than Baghdad as a center of science and the arts. In time it attracted Abd ar-Rahman II, who introduced the fifth string to the Arab lute, leading to the development of the six-string guitar. He also ordained the way food should be eaten at mealtimes, a legacy that lives to this day. Before, everybody just helped himself randomly to whatever had been prepared; but he devised a method where courses were served in a regimented order, ending with dessert, fruit, and nuts. Today, Andalusian chefs are reviving many of the old recipes from the Arab cupboard, such as lamb cooked with honey.

Arab poetry may have inspired the first ballads sung by European troubadours, who had an enormous impact on later Western literature. Also, many Spanish words today have their origins in the Arabic language, including *alcázar* for fortress, *arroz* for rice, *naranja* for orange, and *limón* for lemon.

The Moors brought an irrigation system to Andalusia, increasing crop production; many of today's systems follow those 1,000-year-old channels. And paper first arrived in Europe through Córdoba.

Although the fanatical Isabel la Católica may have thrown a fit at the heretical idea, it was really a trio of peoples who shaped modern Spain as a nation: the Jews, the Christians, and most definitely the Arabs. The Arabs and the Jews were ousted by Isabella and Ferdinand at the close of the 15th century, but their influence still lingers.

(21 miles) east of Seville, it grew in power and prestige under the Moors, establishing ties with Castile in 1252.

Surrounded by fortified walls, Carmona has three Moorish fortresses—one a parador, and the other two, the Alcázar de la Puerta de Córdoba and Alcázar de la Puerta de Sevilla. The top attraction is Seville Gate, with its double Moorish arch opposite St. Peter's Church. Note, too, Córdoba Gate on Calle Santa María de Gracia, which was attached to the ancient Roman walls in the 17th century.

The town itself is a virtual national landmark, filled with narrow streets, whitewashed walls, and Renaissance mansions. The Plaza San Fernando is the most important square, with many elegant 17th-century houses. The most important church is dedicated to Santa María and stands on Calle Martín López. You enter a Moorish patio before exploring the interior with its 15th-century white vaulting.

In the area known as Jorge Bonsor (named for the original discoverer of the ruins) is a Roman amphitheater as well as a Roman necropolis containing the remains of 1,000 families who lived in and around Carmona 2,000 years ago. Of the two important tombs, the Elephant Vault consists of three dining rooms and a kitchen. The other, the Servilia Tomb, was the size of a nobleman's villa. On-site is a Museo Arqueológico (© **95-423-24-01**) displaying artifacts found at the site. From April to October, hours are Tuesday through Saturday from 9am to 5pm; off-season hours are Tuesday through Saturday from 10am to 2pm. Admission is 1.50€.

If you're driving to Carmona, exit from Seville's eastern periphery onto the N-V superhighway, following the signs to the airport, then to Carmona on the road to Madrid. The Carmona turnoff is clearly marked.

If you want to stay overnight, try the **Casa de Carmona** ★★, Plaza de Lasso 1, 41410 Carmona (© **95-419-10-00**, or 212/686-9213 in the U.S. and Canada; fax 95-419-01-89; www.casadecarmona.com), one of the most elegant hotels in Andalusia. It was built as the home of the Lasso family during the 1500s. Several years ago, a team of entrepreneurs turned it into a luxury hotel yet retained the marble columns, massive masonry, and graceful proportions of the original. Each of the 32 units is a cozy enclave of opulent furnishings, with a theme inspired by ancient Rome, medieval Andalusia, or Renaissance Spain. Rates are 210€ to 310€ for a double and 600€ to 900€ for a suite. American Express, Diners Club, MasterCard, and Visa are accepted.

ITALICA Lovers of Roman history will flock to Itálica (© **95-599-82-62**), the ruins of an ancient city 9km (5½ miles) northwest of Seville on the major road to Lisbon, near the small town of Santiponce.

After the battle of Ilipa, Publius Cornelius Scipio Africanus founded Itálica in 206 B.C. Two of the most famous of Roman emperors, Trajan and Hadrian, were born here. Indeed, master builder Hadrian was to have a major influence on his hometown. In his reign the amphitheater, the ruins of which can be seen today, was among the largest in the Roman Empire. Lead pipes that carried water from the Guadalquivir River still remain. A small museum displays some of the Roman statuary found here, although the finest pieces have been shipped to Seville. Many mosaics are on exhibit, depicting beasts, gods, and birds, and others are constantly being discovered. The ruins, including a Roman theater, can be explored for 1.50€, or for free if you're an E.U. citizen. From April to September, the site is open Tuesday through Saturday from 9am to 8pm, Sunday from 9am to 3pm. From October to March, it's open Tuesday through Saturday from 9am to 5:30pm, Sunday from 10am to 4pm.

If you're driving, exit from the northwest periphery of Seville following the signs for highway E-803 in the direction of Zafra and Lisbon. But if you don't have a car, the Empresa CASAL bus company has a bus that leaves the Plaza de Armas station for Santiponce every hour. A gas station next to the main gates of Itálica is the last stop on the route.

4 Jerez de la Frontera ⋆

87km (54 miles) S of Seville, 593km (368 miles) SW of Madrid, 34km (21 miles) NE of Cádiz

The charming little Andalusian town of Jerez de la Frontera made a name for itself in England for the thousands of casks of golden sherry it has shipped there over the centuries. Nearly 3,000 years old, Jerez is nonetheless a modern, progressive town with wide boulevards, although it does have an interesting old quarter. Busloads of visitors pour in every year to get free drinks at one of the bodegas where wine is aged and bottled.

The name of the town is pronounced "heh-*res*" or "heh-*reth*," in Andalusian or Castilian, respectively. The French and the Moors called it various names, including Heres and Scheris, which the English corrupted to Sherry.

ESSENTIALS

GETTING THERE   Iberia and Avianco offer **flights** to Jerez Monday through Friday from Barcelona and Zaragoza; daily flights from Madrid; and several flights a week to and from Germany, London, and Grand Canary Island. The airport at Carretera Jerez-Sevilla is about 11km (7 miles) northeast of the city center (follow the signs to Seville). Call ⓒ **95-615-00-00** for information.

Trains from Madrid arrive daily. A ticket from Madrid to Jerez on the TALGO costs 58€ to 86€, and the trip takes 4½ hours. The railway station in Jerez is at the Plaza de la Estación (ⓒ **90-224-02-02**) at the eastern end of Calle Medina.

Bus connections are more frequent than train connections, and the location of the bus terminal is more convenient. You'll find it on Calle Cartuja at the corner of Calle Madre de Dios, a 12-minute walk east of the Alcázar. About 17 buses arrive daily from Cádiz (1 hr. away) and three buses per day travel from Ronda (2¾ hr.). Seven buses a day arrive from Seville (1½ hr.). Phone ⓒ **95-634-52-07** for more information.

Jerez lies on the highway connecting Seville with Cádiz, Algeciras, Gibraltar, and the ferryboat landing for Tangier, Morocco. There's also an overland road connecting Jerez with Granada and Málaga.

VISITOR INFORMATION   The **tourist office** is at Alameda de Cristina s/n (ⓒ **95-633-11-50;** www.webjuarez.com). It's open Monday through Friday from 9:30am to 2:30pm and 4:30 to 6:30pm, Saturday and Sunday from 9:30am to 3:30pm. To reach it from the bus terminal, take Calle Medina to Calle Honda and continue along as the road turns to the right. The English-speaking staff can provide directions, transportation suggestions, open hours, and so on for any bodega you might want to visit. You'll also be given a map pinpointing the location of various bodegas.

EXPLORING THE AREA
TOURING THE BODEGAS ⋆⋆

Jerez is not surrounded by vineyards as you might expect. Instead, the vineyards lie to the north and west in the "Sherry Triangle" marked by Jerez, Sanlúcar de Barrameda, and El Puerto de Santa María (the latter 2 towns on the coast). This

Moments   The Dancing Horses of Jerez

A rival of sorts to Vienna's famous Spanish Riding School is the **Escuela Andaluza del Arte Ecuestre (Andalusian School of Equestrian Art)**, Av. Duque de Abrantes s/n (© 95-631-96-35). In fact, the long, hard schooling that brings horse and rider into perfect harmony originated in this province. The Viennese school was started with Hispano-Arab horses sent from this region, the same breeds you can see today. Every Thursday at noon, crowds come to admire the **Dancing Horses of Jerez** ★★ as they perform in a show that includes local folklore. Lanes 1 and 2 sell for 21€, lanes 3 and 4 sell for 18€, and lanes 5 and 6 go for 13€. When performances aren't scheduled, you can visit the stables and tack room, observing as the elegant horses are being trained. Hours are Monday through Wednesday and Friday from 10am to 1pm, costing 6€. Bus 18 goes here.

is where top-quality *albariza* soil is found, the highest quality containing an average of 60% chalk, which is ideal for the cultivation of grapes used in sherry production, principally the white Palomino de Jerez. The ideal time to visit is September. However, you can count on the finest in hospitality year-round since Jerez is widely known for the warm welcome it bestows.

In and around Jerez there must be more than 100 bodegas where you can not only see how sherries are made, bottled, and aged but also get free samples. Among the most famous producers are Sandeman, Pedro Domecq, and González Byass, the maker of Tío Pepe. On a typical visit to a bodega, you'll be shown through several buildings in which sherry and brandy are manufactured. In one building, you'll see grapes being pressed and sorted; in another, the bottling process; in a third, thousands of large oak casks. Then it's on to an attractive bar where various sherries—amber, dark gold, cream, red, sweet, and velvety—can be sampled. If either is offered, try the very dry La Ina sherry or the Fundador brandy, one of the most popular in the world. **Warning:** These drinks are more potent than you might expect!

Most bodegas are open Monday through Friday from 10:30am to 1:30pm. Regrettably, many of them are closed in August, but many do reopen by the third week of August to prepare for the wine festival in early September.

Of the dozens of bodegas you can visit, the most popular are listed below. Some of them charge an admission fee and require a reservation.

A favorite among British visitors is Harveys of Bristol, Calle Pintor Muñoz Cebrian s/n (© 95-634-60-00), which doesn't require a reservation. An English-speaking guide leads a 2-hour tour except for the first 3 weeks of August. Visit Monday through Friday for tours at noon, costing 4.50€. You'll definitely want to visit Williams & Humbert Limited, Carretera Nacional IV, Km 641.75, Punto Santa María (© 95-635-34-06), which offers tours at noon and 1:30pm Monday through Friday, charging 4€. Their premium brands include the world-famous Dry Sack Medium Sherry, Canasta Cream, Fino Pando, and Manzanilla Alegría, in addition to Gran Duque de Alba Gran Reserva Brandy. It's wise to reserve in advance.

Another famous name is González Byass, Manuel María González 12 (© 95-635-70-16); admission is 7€, and reservations are required. Tours depart at 10:30 and 11:30am, and 12:30, 1:30, 3:30 and 4:30pm Monday through Saturday. Equally famous is Domecq, Calle San Ildefonso 3 (© 95-615-15-00).

Reservations are required, and admission is 5€. Tours depart at 9, 10, and 11am, noon, and 1pm Monday through Friday.

Since many people go to Jerez specifically to visit a bodega, August or weekend closings can be very disappointing. If this happens to you, make a trip to the nearby village of Lebrija, about halfway between Jerez and Seville, 14km (8½ miles) west of the main highway. Lebrija, a good spot to get a glimpse of rural Spain, is a local winemaking center where some very fine sherries originate. At one small bodega, that of Juan García, you're courteously escorted around by the owner. There are several other bodegas in Lebrija, and the local citizens will gladly point them out to you. It's all very casual, and much more informal than the bodegas of Jerez.

WHERE TO STAY
EXPENSIVE
Guadalete ✪   In a tranquil exclusive area north of Jerez, this first-class hotel lies a 15-minute walk from the historic core. It may not be as good as the Royal Sherry Park but is still one of the town's leading hotels, often hosting business travelers dealing with the sherry industry. A marble-floored lobby, spacious and contemporary public rooms, and palm tree gardens give this place somewhat of a resort aura. The rooms are medium in size to spacious and have state-of-the-art bathrooms with tub/shower combos. The hotel is decorated with original watercolors and lithographs painted by local artists in the 1970s.

Av. Duque de Abrantes 50, 11407 Jerez de la Frontera. ✆ **95-618-22-88.** Fax 95-618-22-93. www.hotel-guadalete.com. 137 units. 105€–145€ double; 200€–305€ suite. AE, MC, V. Free parking. **Amenities:** Restaurant; bar; 2 pools; room service; babysitting; laundry service; dry cleaning. *In room:* A/C, TV, minibar, hair dryer, safe.

Hotel Avenida Jerez ✪   Very close to the commercial heart of Jerez, this hotel occupies a modern balconied structure and is the best hotel within Jerez itself, although Montecastillo (see below) on the outskirts is a serious challenger. Inside, cool polished stone floors, leather armchairs, and a variety of potted plants create a restful haven. The good-size rooms are discreetly contemporary and decorated in neutral colors, with big windows, comfortable beds, and private bathrooms equipped with tub/shower combos.

Av. Alcalde Alvaro Domecq 10, 11405 Jerez de la Frontera. ✆ **95-634-74-11.** Fax 95-633-72-96. www.nh-hoteles.es. 95 units. 99€–199€ double. AE, DC, MC, V. Parking 9€. **Amenities:** Restaurant; bar; room service; babysitting; laundry service; dry cleaning. *In room:* A/C, TV, minibar, hair dryer.

Hotel Royal Sherry Park ✪✪   Especially noted for its setting within a palm-fringed garden whose tiled edges attract many sun-loving guests, this is one of the best modern hotels in Jerez. It's located on a wide boulevard north of the historic center of town and contains a marble-floored lobby, modern public rooms, and fairly standard but comfortable guest rooms, each with a bathroom containing a tub/shower combo. The uniformed staff lays out a copious breakfast buffet and serves drinks at several hideaways, both indoors and within the garden.

Av. Alcalde Alvaro Domecq 11 bis, 11405 Jerez de la Frontera. ✆ **95-631-76-14.** Fax 95-631-13-00. www.sherryparkhotel.com. 173 units. 117€–250€ double; 212€–327€ suite. AE, DC, MC, V. Free parking. **Amenities:** Restaurant; bar; 2 pools; health club; sauna; car rental; room service; babysitting; laundry service; dry cleaning. *In room:* A/C, TV, minibar, hair dryer, safe.

Montecastillo ✪✪   Giving the Hotel Avenida Jerez serious competition is this deluxe country club in the rolling hills of the sherry *campiña* (wine country).

The area's most tranquil retreat, it has rooms with scenic-view balconies overlooking a plush landscape. The hotel, a 10-minute ride from the center of Jerez, is elegantly furnished and professionally run. The spacious rooms are decorated in a provincial French style with elegant fabrics, beautiful linens, and large beds. The marble bathrooms come with tub/shower combinations.

Carretera De Arcos, 11406 Jerez de la Frontera. ✆ **95-615-12-00.** Fax 95-615-12-09. 121 units. 151€–281€ double; 216€–311€ suite. AE, DC, MC, V. Free parking. **Amenities:** Restaurant; bar; 3 pools; golf course; health spa; sauna; room service; babysitting; laundry service; dry cleaning. *In room:* A/C, TV, minibar, hair dryer.

MODERATE

La Cueva Park   This charming hotel in a century-old building 6.5km (4 miles) from the center of town attracts motorists, though it's just half a mile from the bus station. The architecture is typical of Andalusia, with a tiled roof overhanging thick brick walls. Gardens surround the hotel. All the medium-sized units are comfortably furnished. There are nine white-walled bungalow-style apartments classified as suites, each with its own cooking area, living room, and terrace. All units come with bathrooms containing tub/shower combos.

Carretera de Arcos, Km 6.5, Apartado 536, 11406 Jerez de la Frontera. ✆ **95-618-91-20.** Fax 95-618-91-21. www.hotellacueva.com. 58 units. 70€–120€ double; 168€–210€ suite. AE, DC, MC, V. Parking 6€. **Amenities:** Restaurant; bar; pool; room service; babysitting; laundry service; dry cleaning. *In room:* A/C, TV, minibar, hair dryer, safe.

INEXPENSIVE

El Coloso *Value*   A few steps from the Plaza de las Angustias in the historic center, this is one of the best bargains in town, modest but recommendable. The decor is in the conventional local style with whitewashed walls and a trio of Andalusian-style patios with balconies opening onto street scenes of Jerez. The hotel opened in 1969 and was last renovated in 1998. The rooms are a bit cramped but beautifully maintained, with good beds and bathrooms containing tub/shower combos. Breakfast is the only meal served.

Pedro Alonso 13, 11402 Jerez de la Frontera. ✆/fax **95-634-90-08.** 25 units. 42€–75€ double. MC, V. Parking 5€. *In room:* A/C, TV, hair dryer.

Hotel Avila   One of the better bargains in Jerez, the Avila is a modern building erected in 1968 and renovated in 1987. It's near the post office and the Plaza del Arenal in the commercial center of town. Its rooms are clean, comfortable, and well maintained, although not special in any way. The beds, however, are quite comfortable and the bathrooms are equipped with shower stalls.

Calle Avila 3, 11401 Jerez de la Frontera. ✆ **95-633-48-08.** Fax 95-633-68-07. 32 units. 53€–73€ double. AE, DC, MC, V. Parking 7€–10€ nearby. **Amenities:** Bar; lounge; laundry service; dry cleaning. *In room:* A/C, TV, hair dryer.

WHERE TO DINE

El Bosque ⊛ SPANISH/INTERNATIONAL   Less than a mile northeast of the city center, El Bosque is the city's most elegant restaurant and opened after World War II. A favorite of the sherry-producing aristocracy, it retains a strong emphasis on bullfighting memorabilia, which makes up most of the decor. Order the excellent *rabo de toro* (bull's tail stew) if you want to dine like a native. You might begin with a soothing gazpacho, then try one of the fried fish dishes, such as hake Seville style. Rice with king prawns and baby shrimp omelets are popular. Occasionally, Laguna duck in honey with chestnuts and pears is a feature. Desserts are usually good, especially the pistachio ice cream.

Alcalde Alvaro Domecq 26. (© **95-630-33-33**. Reservations required. Main courses 16€–26€. AE, DC, MC, V. Mon–Sat 1:30–5pm and 8:30pm–midnight.

Gaitán ANDALUSIAN Owner Juan Hurtado continues to win acclaim for the food served here at his small restaurant near the Puerta Santa María. Surrounded by celebrity photographs, you can enjoy such Andalusian dishes as garlic soup, various stews, duck a la Sevillana, and fried seafood. One special dish is lamb cooked with honey, based on a recipe so ancient it dates from the Muslim occupation of Spain. For dessert, the almond tart is a favorite.

Calle Gaitán 3. (© **95-634-58-59**. Reservations recommended. Main courses 12€–16€; fixed-price menu 14€. AE, DC, MC, V. Daily 1–4:30pm; Mon–Sat 1–4:30pm and 8:30–11:30pm.

Mesa Redonda ★★ *Finds* TRADITIONAL SPANISH This restaurant is a rare treat. Owner/chef José Antonio Romero and his wife, Margarita, have sought out the traditional recipes once served in the homes of the aristocratic sherry dons of Jerez. They present them to you in winning combinations in a setting like a private residence, complete with a library filled with old recipe books and literature about food and wine. Only 10 tables are available and easily filled. The menu is ever changing, as is the culinary repertoire of this couple. Try the *albondiguillas marineras* (fish meatballs in shellfish sauce) and *hojaldre de rape y gambas* (a pastry filled with monkfish and prawns). Most recommendable are the *filetes de lenguado con zetas* (filet of sole with mushrooms) and *cordero asado* (grilled lamb). For dessert, there's nothing finer than the lemon-and-almond cake.

Manuel de la Quintana 3. (© **95-634-00-69**. Reservations required. Main courses 12€–15€. AE, DC, MC, V. Mon–Sat 1:30–4pm and 9–11pm. Closed last week in July and 1st 3 weeks in Aug.

5 Cádiz ★

122km (76 miles) S of Seville, 625km (388 miles) SW of Madrid

Cádiz is the oldest inhabited city in the Western world, founded in 1100 B.C. This modern, bustling Atlantic port is a kind of Spanish Marseille, a melting pot of Americans, Africans, and Europeans who are docking or passing through. The old quarter teems with local characters, little dives, and seaport alleys. But despite its thriving life, the city doesn't hold major interest for visitors, except for the diverse cultures that have shaped it. Phoenicians, Arabs, Visigoths, Romans, and Carthaginians all passed through Cádiz and left their imprints. Throughout the ages this ancient port city has enjoyed varying states of prosperity, especially after the discovery of the New World.

At the end of a peninsula, Cádiz separates the Bay of Cádiz from the Atlantic, and from numerous sea walls around the town you have views of the ocean. It was here that Columbus set out on his second voyage.

ESSENTIALS

GETTING THERE **Trains** arrive from Seville (taking 2 hr.), Jerez de la Frontera (40 min.), and Córdoba (5 hr.). The train station is located on Avenida del Puerto (© **90-224-02-02**), on the southeast border of the main port.

If you're taking a **bus** from Madrid, you'll probably have to transfer in Seville. Buses arrive in Cádiz at two separate terminals. From Seville (12 per day; 2 hr.), Jerez de la Frontera (6 per day; 1 hr.), Málaga, Córdoba, and Granada, buses arrive at the Estación de Comes terminal, Plaza de la Hispanidad 1 (© **95-680-70-59**), on the north side of town, a few blocks west of the main port. Far less prominent is the terminal run by the Transportes Los Amarillos, Av. Ramón de Carranza 31 (© **95-629-08-00**), several blocks to the south, which runs frequent buses to several nearby towns and villages, most of which are of interest only for local residents and workers.

Driving from Seville, the A-4 (also called E-5), a toll road, or N-IV, a toll-free road running beside it, will bring you into Cádiz.

VISITOR INFORMATION The **tourist office,** Av. Ramón de la Carranza s/n (© **95-625-86-46;** www.cadizturismo.com), is open Tuesday through Friday from 9am to 7pm, Saturday from 9am to 2pm.

EXPLORING CADIZ

Despite being one of the oldest towns in Europe, Cádiz has few remnants of antiquity. It is still worth visiting, however, especially to wander through the old quarter, which retains a special charm.

The Plaza de San Juan de Dios is the ideal place to sit at a sidewalk cafe and people-watch in the shadow of the neoclassical Isabelino Ayuntamiento (Town Hall), with its outstanding chapter house. The Oratorio de San Felipe Neri, Santa Inés (© **95-621-16-12**), where the Cortés (Parliament) met in 1812 to proclaim its constitution, has an important Murillo *(Conception)* and a history museum. Admission is 1.50€, and it's open August through June daily from 8:30 to 10am and 7:30 to 9:45pm. The Hospital de Mujeres (Women's Hospital) has a patio courtyard dating from 1740 and a chapel with El Greco's *Ecstasy of St. Francis.*

Catedral de Cádiz This magnificent 18th-century baroque building by architect Vicente Acero has a neoclassical interior dominated by an outstanding apse. The tomb of Cádiz-born composer Manuel de Falla lies in its splendid crypt; music lovers from all over the world come here to pay their respects. Haydn composed *The Seven Last Words of Our Savior on the Cross* for this cathedral.

Plaza Catedral. © **95-628-61-54.** Admission 3€. Tues–Fri 10am–2pm and 4:30–7pm; Sat–Sun 10am–1pm.

Museo de Cádiz ✦ This fully restored museum contains one of Spain's most important Zurbarán collections, as well as paintings by Rubens and Murillo (including the latter's acclaimed picture of Christ). The archaeology section displays Roman, Carthaginian, and Phoenician finds, and ethnology exhibits include pottery, baskets, textiles, and leather works.

Plaza de Mina s/n. © **95-621-22-81.** Admission 1.50€, free Sun. Tues 2:30–8pm; Wed–Sat 9am–8pm; Sun 9:30am–2:30pm.

WHERE TO STAY

Cádiz has a number of inexpensive accommodations, some of which are quite poor. However, for a moderate price you can afford some of the finest lodgings in the city. Note that rooms are scarce during the February carnival season.

Parador Hotel Atlántico ✦✦ Actually a modern resort hotel, this national parador is built on one of the loveliest beaches of the Bay of Cádiz at the western edge of the old town. It's clearly the outstanding accommodation choice. The white building has a marble patio, a salon decked in rattan and cane, and spacious rooms that feature balconies with tables and chairs for relaxed ocean viewing. More than half of the rooms were renovated in 1995. All have bathrooms with tub/shower combos.

Duque de Nájera 9, 11002 Cádiz. © **95-622-69-05.** Fax 95-621-45-82. cadiz@parador.es. 95€–111€ double; 218€–237€ suite. AE, DC, MC, V. Rates include breakfast. Parking 6€ for garage. **Amenities:**

Restaurant; bar; pool; health club; sauna; room service; babysitting; laundry service; dry cleaning. *In room:* A/C, TV, minibar, hair dryer, safe.

Regio 1   Built in 1978, this aging hotel is about a block inland from the harbor and the Paseo Marítimo. The small rooms are simple but airy and comfortable—nowhere near the equal of the Atlántico (see above), but then its prices are much more reasonable. Each unit comes with a small bathroom with tub/shower combo. Breakfast is the only meal served. The overflow from this hotel is sometimes directed to the hotel's twin, the superior Regio 2 (see below).

Ana de Viya 11, 11009 Cádiz. © **95-627-93-31.** Fax 95-627-91-13. www.hotelregiocadiz.com. 42 units. 55€–76€ double. AE, DC, MC, V. Parking in garage 5€. **Amenities:** Bar; room service; babysitting; laundry service; dry cleaning. *In room:* A/C, TV, hair dryer.

Regio 2   Business was successful enough in the late 1970s to justify the construction of this twin of an already existing hotel, the Regio 1 (see above). Run by the same management and sharing some of their staff and luxuries in common, it was built in 1981 about 183m (200 yd.) from its twin. It offers bathrooms with tub/shower combos in each of its simple but pleasant rooms, which are more comfortable and in better shape than those of Regio 1. Both hotels are a very short walk from the ocean.

Av. Andalucía 79, 11008 Cádiz. © **95-625-30-08.** Fax 95-625-30-09. www.guiadecadiz.com. 40 units. 60€–72€ double. AE, DC, MC, V. Parking 6€. **Amenities:** Bar; lounge; room service; laundry service; dry cleaning. *In room:* A/C, TV, hair dryer.

WHERE TO DINE

Achuri ⓖ BASQUE/ANDALUSIAN   Achuri, a block behind the Palace of Congress in the historic district, is one of the best-loved restaurants in this old port city. It's been in the same family for half a century, earning a fine reputation for its good food. The interior is in a typical Mediterranean port style, its white stucco walls adorned with paintings interspersed with windows letting in plenty of sunshine. The menu includes fresh anchovies in virgin olive oil with a green leaf salad, *merluza al achuri* (hake casserole with green asparagus sauce), and *pardo al brandy* (red snapper in brandy sauce). Another excellent dish is *bacalao en rosa verde* (salt cod in tomato-and-vegetable sauce). Desserts include lemon mousse or *tocinillo de cielo* (a hearty regional pudding).

Calle Plocia 15. © **95-625-36-13.** www.achuri.net. Reservations recommended. Main courses 10€–16€. AE, MC, V. Sun–Wed 1–4:30pm; Thurs–Sat 1–4:30pm and 8pm–midnight. Closed Dec 24–Jan 7.

El Faro SEAFOOD   Unless you're a devotee of seafood, this might not be your preferred restaurant. There's only a limited selection of meat, with the main emphasis on the array of fresh fish and shellfish available in its large dining room. (There's an additional, much smaller room to the side, usually reserved for groups of locals.) El Faro occupies the white-walled premises of one of the simple houses near the harbor front in Cádiz's oldest neighborhood. Menu items include fried lamb chops and beefsteak and a long list of seafood, such as seafood soup, roulades of sole with spinach, hake with green sauce, monkfish with strips of Serrano ham, and lobster.

Calle San Félix 15. © **95-621-10-68.** Reservations recommended. Main courses 12€–16€; fixed-price menu 25€. AE, DC, MC, V. Daily 1–4:30pm and 8:30pm–midnight.

El Ventorillo del Chato ⓖ *Finds* ANDALUSIAN   El Chato ("pug nose") is the nickname of the original founder of this inn launched in 1780 on the isthmus linking the port city to the mainland. Once a hostelry for wayfarers, it still has its old wooden floors, ceramic tiles, and a large collection of keys and muskets from the Napoleonic era. There are two floors, including the basement, where flamenco shows are sometimes performed on the original *tablao* (special flamenco dance floor). The food is excellent, the ingredients well chosen, and the chefs skilled at their time-tested recipes. Try the *arroz del señorito* (a paella of shellfish that has been taken from the shells and cleaned before cooking), *arroz negro con chocos* (squid with rice colored by its own ink), or *dorada en berenjena confitada al vino tinto* (gilthead sea bream with eggplant cooked with red-wine sauce). Desserts are tempting, especially ice cream with three types of chocolate or homemade cake with orange sauce.

Carretera de Cádiz a San Fernando, Km 2. ℂ 95-625-00-25. Reservations recommended. Main courses 10€–18€; tasting menu 30€. AE, DC, MC, V. Mon–Sat 1–4pm and 9pm–midnight.

CADIZ AFTER DARK

As night falls, most revelers wander from bar to bar. There's no one outstanding venue. The bar scene is like a floating crap game. The district enveloping the Plaza Mina in the heart of the city is very animated, as is Calle de Manuel Rances, the best street in the old town for barhopping, as visitors devour tapas and wine along the way. The principal artery that runs along the Playa Victoria (Victorian Beach) is the Paseo Marítimo. In summer, this strip contains some of the liveliest bars. We're especially fond of **Bar Jarra** (ℂ 95-626-57-74), lying along Calle José Agullo. It offers both Hispanic and Stateside music. As the night wears long and streaks of dawn cut through the night, the joints along Punto de San Felipe come awake. To reach this sector, go north along the seafront from the Plaza España.

6 Costa de la Luz ✸

Isla Cristina, one of the coast's westernmost cities, is 55km (34 miles) west of Huelva, 649km (403 miles) southwest of Madrid; Tarifa, at the opposite end of the coast, lies 95km (59 miles) southeast of Cádiz, 691km (429 miles) southwest of Madrid.

West of Cádiz, near Huelva and the Portuguese frontier, is the rapidly developing Costa de la Luz (Coast of Light), which hopes to pick up the overflow from Costa del Sol. The Luz coast stretches from the mouth of the Guadiana River, forming the boundary with Portugal, to Tarifa Point on the Straits of Gibraltar. Dotting the coast are long stretches of sand, pine trees, fishing cottages, and lazy whitewashed villages.

The Huelva district forms the northwestern half of the Costa de la Luz. The southern half stretches from Tarifa to Sanlúcar de Barrameda, the spot from which Magellan embarked in 1519 on his voyage around the globe. Columbus also made this the home port for his third journey to the New World. Sanlúcar today is widely known in Andalusia for its local sherry, Manzanilla, which you can order at any of the city's bodegas.

If you make it to Sanlúcar, you'll find the tourist office at Calzada de Ejército (ℂ 95-636-61-10), just a block inland from the beach. It's open Monday through Friday from 10am to 2pm and Saturday and Sunday from 10am to 2pm and 6 to 8pm. Don't count on a great deal of guidance, however. To travel between the northern and southern portions of the Costa de la Luz, you must go inland to Seville, since no roads go across the Coto Doñana and the marshland near the mouth of the Guadalquivir.

ESSENTIALS

GETTING THERE   Huelva, the coast's most prominent city, is serviced by **trains** from Seville 2 hours away. If you're going on to Portugal from here, you can take a bus to Ayamonte where you can board a ferry to the gateway of Vila Real de San Antonio, the beginning of Portugal's Algarve coast. **Buses** run several times a day from Seville, where connections can be made to all parts of Spain. From Huelva, about eight buses a day depart for Ayamonte and the Portuguese frontier. Huelva is easily reached by car in about an hour from Seville, 89km (55 miles) to the east, via a broad and modern highway, the E-01.

VISITOR INFORMATION   The **tourist office** is in Huelva at Av. de Alemania 12 (© **95-925-74-03;** www.andalusia.org), and is open Monday from 9am to 2:30pm, Tuesday through Friday from 9am to 7pm, and Saturday from 10am to 2pm.

EXPLORING THE AREA

At Huelva, a large statue on the west bank of the river commemorates the departure of Christopher Columbus on his third voyage of discovery. About 7km (4½ miles) up on the east bank of the Tinto River, a monument marks the exact spot where his ships were anchored while they were being loaded with supplies before departure.

South of Huelva is the Monasterio de la Rábida, Palos de la Frontera (© **95-935-04-11**), in whose little white chapel Columbus prayed for success on the eve of his voyage. Even without its connections to Columbus, the monastery would be worth a visit for its paintings and frescoes. A guide will show you around the Mudéjar chapel and a large portion of the old monastery, which is open Tuesday through Sunday from 10am to 1pm and 4 to 6:15pm. Admission is 2.50€. The monastery is on the east bank of the Tinto. Take bus no. 1 from Huelva.

WHERE TO STAY & DINE

Accommodations are severely limited along the Costa de la Luz in summer, so it's crucial to arrive with a reservation. You can stay at a government-run parador east of Huelva in Mazagón (see below) or in Ayamonte, near the Portuguese frontier. Where you're unlikely to want to stay overnight is the dreary industrial port of Huelva itself.

Ayamonte was built on the slopes of a hill on which a castle stood. It's full of beach high-rises, which, for the most part, contain vacation apartments for Spaniards in July and August. Judging by their license plates, most of these visitors come from Huelva, Seville, and Madrid, so the Costa de la Luz is more Spanish in flavor than the overrun and more international Costa del Sol.

Ayamonte has clean, wide, sandy beaches and mostly calm waves. Portions of the beaches are even calmer because of sandbars 50m to 100m (55–110 yd.) from the shore, which become virtual islands at low tide. The nearest beaches to Ayamonte are miles away at Isla Canela and Moral.

Parador Nacional Costa de la Luz ★★   The leading accommodation in Ayamonte is this parador that opened in 1966. Commanding a sweeping view of the river and the surrounding towns along its banks—sunsets are memorable here—the parador stands about 30m (100 ft.) above sea level on the site of the old castle of Ayamonte. It was built in a severe modern style and boasts Nordic-inspired furnishings. Most rooms are medium-sized and comfortably appointed, with good beds and bathrooms with tub/shower combos.

Av. de la Constitución s/n, 21400 Ayamonte. ℂ **95-932-07-00.** Fax 95-902-20-19. 53 units. 89€–110€ double; 137€–173€ suite. Rates include breakfast. AE, DC, MC, V. Free parking. From the center of Ayamonte, signs for the parador lead you up a winding road to the hilltop, about 1km (½ mile) SE of the center. **Amenities:** Restaurant; bar; pool; room service; babysitting; laundry service; dry cleaning. *In room:* A/C, TV, minibar, hair dryer, safe.

Parador Nacional Cristóbal Colón ★★ One of the best accommodations in the area is 23km (14 miles) from Huelva and 6km (3½ miles) from the center of Mazagón. A rambling 1960s structure, the parador has comfortable, spacious rooms with balconies and terraces overlooking an expansive garden and pine groves that slope down to the white-sand beach of Mazagón. All units have bathrooms with tub/shower combos.

Carretera de San Juan del Puerto a Matalascañas s/n, 21130 Mazagón. ℂ **95-953-63-00.** Fax 95-953-62-28. 63 units. 105€–120€ double; 140€–165€ suite. AE, DC, MC, V. Free parking. Exit from Magazón's eastern sector, following the signs to the town of Matalascañas. Take the coast road (Hwy. 442) to the parador. **Amenities:** Restaurant; bar; lounge; pool; babysitting; laundry service; dry cleaning. *In room:* A/C, TV, minibar, hair dryer, safe.

7 Ronda ★★★

102km (63 miles) NE of Algeciras, 97km (60 miles) W of Málaga, 147km (91 miles) SE of Seville, 591km (367 miles) S of Madrid

This little town high in the Serranía de Ronda Mountains (698m/2,300 ft. above sea level) is one of the oldest and most aristocratic places in Spain. The main tourist attraction is a 150m (500-ft.) gorge, spanned by a Roman stone bridge, the Puente San Miguel, over the Guadelevín River. On both sides of this hole in the earth are cliff-hanging houses, which look as though they would plunge into the chasm with the slightest push.

Ronda is an incredible sight. The once difficult road here is now a wide highway with guardrails. The town and the surrounding mountains were legendary hideouts for bandits and smugglers, but today the Guardia Civil has just about put an end to that occupation. The gorge divides the town into an older part, the Moorish and aristocratic quarter, and the newer section south of the gorge, built principally after the Reconquest. The old quarter is by far the more fascinating; it contains narrow, rough streets and buildings with a marked Moorish influence (watch for the minaret). After the lazy resort living of the Costa del Sol, make a side excursion to Ronda; its unique beauty and refreshing mountain air are a tonic.

Note that local children may attach themselves to you as guides. For a few euros, it might be worth it to hire one, since it's difficult to weave your way in and out of the narrow streets.

ESSENTIALS

GETTING THERE There are three **trains** daily from Málaga (2 hr.), three per day from Seville (3½ hr.), and three per day from Granada (3 hr.). Most rail routes into Ronda require a change of train in the railway junction of Bobadilla several miles to the northeast. Ronda's rail station is in the western edge of the new city, on Avenida Andalucía (ℂ **95-287-16-73**).

The main **bus** company in Ronda is Los Amarillos, which runs daily service from both Málaga and Seville. Buses arrive and depart from the station on the western edge of the new town, at Plaza Concepción García Redonda 2 (ℂ **95-218-70-61**). To Málaga, there are six buses a day Monday through Friday and four on weekends. To Seville, there are five buses a day Monday through Friday, three on Saturday, and four on Sunday.

Five highways converge on Ronda from all parts of Andalusia. All five head through mountainous scenery, but the road south to Marbella through the Sierra Palmitera is one of the most winding and dangerous.

VISITOR INFORMATION   The **tourist office,** Plaza de España 9 (© **95-287-12-72;** www.andalusia.org), is open Monday through Friday from 9am to 7pm, Saturday and Sunday from 10am to 2pm.

EXPLORING RONDA

The still-functioning Baños Arabes are reached from the turnoff to Puente San Miguel. Dating from the 13th century, the baths have glass roof-windows and hump-shaped cupolas. They're generally open Tuesday through Sunday from 9:30am to 2pm and 4 to 6pm. Admission is free, but you should tip the care-taker who shows you around.

The Palacio de Mondragón, Plaza de Mondragón (© **95-287-84-50**), was once the private home of one of the ministers to Charles III. Flanked by two Mudéjar towers, it now has a baroque facade. Inside are Moorish mosaics. It's open Monday through Friday from 10am to 7pm, Saturday and Sunday from 10am to 3pm; admission is 2€, and free for children under 14.

The Casa del Rey Moro, Marqués de Parada 17, is misnamed, as this House of the Moorish King was actually built in the early 1700s. However, it's believed to have been constructed over Moorish foundations. The interior is closed, but from the garden you can take an underground stairway, called La Mina, which leads you to the river, a distance of 365 steps. Christian slaves cut these steps in the 14th century to guarantee a steady water supply in case Ronda came under siege.

Ronda has the oldest bullring in Spain. Built in the 1700s, the Plaza de Toros is the setting for the yearly Goyesque Corrida in honor of Ronda native son Pedro Romero, one of the greatest bullfighters of all time. If you want to know more about Ronda bullfighting, head for the Museo Taurino (© **95-287-41-32**), reached through the ring. It's open daily: June through September from 10am to 8pm and October through May from 10am to 6pm. Admission is 4€. Exhibits at the museum document the exploits of the noted Romero family. Francesco invented the killing sword and the muleta, and his grandson, Pedro (1754–1839), killed 5,600 bulls during his 30-year career. Pedro was the inspi-ration for Goya's famous Tauromaquia series. There are also exhibits devoted to Cayetano Ordóñez, the matador immortalized by Hemingway in *The Sun Also Rises.*

WHERE TO STAY
EXPENSIVE
Parador de Ronda ★★   On opening in 1994, this parador surpassed the Reina Victoria (see below) and remains the finest accommodation in the area. It sits on a high cliff overlooking the fantastic gorge that cuts a swath more than 150m (500 ft.) deep and 90m (300 ft.) wide through the center of this moun-tain town. Stretching along the edge of the gorge to a bridge, the Puente Nuevo, built over the Tajo in 1761, the parador is surrounded by a footpath with scenic overlooks offering views of the gorge and the torrents of the Guadalevín River below. The good-size rooms are beautifully furnished, each containing a bath-room with a tub/shower combo; many open onto views of the peaks surround-ing Ronda.

> *Finds* **Prehistoric Cave Paintings**
>
> Near Benaoján, the **Cueva de la Pileta** ⍟ (© **95-216-73-43**), 25km (16 miles) southwest of Ronda, plus a 2km (1¼-mile) hard climb, has been compared to the Caves of Altamira in northern Spain, where prehistoric paintings were discovered toward the end of the 19th century. In a wild area known as the Serranía de Ronda, José Bullón Lobato, grandfather of the present owners, discovered this cave in 1905. More than a mile in length and filled with oddly and beautifully shaped stalagmites and stalactites, the cave was found to contain five fossilized human skeletons and two animal skeletons.
>
> In the mysterious darkness, prehistoric paintings have been discovered depicting animals in yellow, red, black, and ocher, as well as mysterious symbols. One of the highlights of the tour is a trip to the chamber of the fish, containing a wall painting of a great black seal-like creature about 1m (3 ft.) long. This chamber, the innermost heart of the cave, ends in a precipice that drops vertically nearly 75m (250 ft.). In the valley just below the cave lives a guide who'll conduct you around the chambers, carrying artificial light to illuminate the paintings. Plan to spend at least an hour here. Tours are given daily from 10am to 1pm and 4 to 5pm. Admission, including the hour tour, is 6.50€ adults and 2.50€ children.
>
> You can reach the cave most easily by car from Ronda, but those without private transport can take the train to Benaoján. The cave, whose entrance is at least 6.5km (4 miles) uphill, is in the rocky foothills of the Sierra de Libar midway between two tiny villages: Jimera de Libar and Benaoján. The valley that contains the cave is parallel to the valley holding Ronda, so the town of Ronda and the cave are separated by a steep range of hills requiring a rather complicated detour to either the south or the north of Ronda, then doubling back.

Plaza de España 29400 Ronda. © **95-287-75-00**. Fax 95-287-81-88. www.parador.es. 78 units. 116€–136€ double; 179€–215€ suite. AE, DC, MC, V. Parking 9€. **Amenities:** Restaurant; bar; pool; room service; babysitting; laundry service; dry cleaning. *In room:* A/C, TV, minibar, hair dryer, safe.

MODERATE

Hotel Reina Victoria ⍟   On the eastern periphery of town, this country-style hotel dates from 1906, when it was built by an Englishman in honor of his recently departed monarch, Queen Victoria. It's near the bullring, with terraces that hang right over a 147m (490-ft.) precipice. Hemingway frequently visited, but the Reina Victoria is known best as the place where poet Rainer María Rilke wrote *The Spanish Trilogy.* His third-floor room has been set aside as a museum with first editions, manuscripts, photographs, and even a framed copy of his hotel bill. A life-size bronze statue of him stands in a corner of the garden. The rooms are big and airy, some with living rooms and many with private terraces. The beds are sumptuous, and the bathrooms boast tub/shower combos.

Paseo Doctor Fleming 25, 29400 Ronda. © **95-287-12-40**. Fax 95-287-10-75. 89 units. 95€–118€ double; 132€–152€ suite. AE, DC, MC, V. Free parking. **Amenities:** Restaurant; bar; pool; room service; babysitting; laundry service; dry cleaning. *In room:* A/C, TV, minibar, hair dryer, safe.

INEXPENSIVE
Hotel Don Miguel ★ *Value* From the narrow street leading to it, this hotel presents a severely dignified white facade very similar to that of its neighbors. From the back, however, the hotel looks out over the river gorge of a steep ravine, adding drama to those rooms overlooking it. Set a few steps east of the Plaza de España and composed of several interconnected houses, it offers a vine-strewn patio above the river, a modernized interior accented with exposed brick and varnished pine, and simple but comfortable small rooms. All bathrooms come with tub/shower combos.

Plaza de España 4, 29400 Ronda. ℂ **95-287-77-22**. Fax 95-287-83-77. 30 units. 66€ double. AE, DC, MC, V. Parking 8€. Closed Jan 10–24. **Amenities:** Restaurant; bar; lounge. *In room:* A/C, TV, hair dryer.

Hotel San Gabriel ★★ *Finds* This charming 1736 mansion stands in the historic core a short walk from the gorge. The building was painstakingly renovated by the owner and his sons and daughter, who give you Ronda's warmest welcome. Inside, all is stylish and homelike, filled with antiques, stained-glass windows, a Spanish-style billiard table, a *cine* salon (with seats taken from the city's old theater), and even an old library. Each room is spacious and well appointed, all with exterior views, individual decoration, and bathrooms with tub/shower combos. Try for no. 15, a cozy top-floor nest on two levels. On the patio guests can relax and take in the beauty of the place.

Marqués de Moctezuma 19 (just off Calle Armiñán), 29400 Ronda. ℂ **95-219-03-92**. Fax 95-219-01-17. www.hotelsangabriel.com. 16 units. 79€ double; 92€ suite. AE, MC, V. **Amenities:** Bar; room service; babysitting. *In room:* A/C, TV, minibar, hair dryer, safe.

Maestranza ★ *Finds* This modern hotel grew up on the site of a villa once lived in by Pedro Romero, one of Spain's most legendary bullfighters. In the center of town, it faces the oldest bullring in the world. Today all traces of the former villa are gone. In its place is one of the best and most contemporary hotels in town. The bedrooms are small to midsize, but have been designed for comfort, with modern furnishings, carpets, and draperies, each accommodation coming with a private bathroom with tub and shower. The public rooms are both tasteful and graceful, and the staff is helpful and the service excellent.

Calle Virgen de la Paz 24, 29400 Ronda. ℂ **95-218-70-72**. Fax 952-19-01-70. www.hotelmaestranza.com. 54 units. 89€–107€ double; 124€–143€ suite. AE, DC, MC, V. **Amenities:** Restaurant; bar; limited room service; babysitting; laundry/dry cleaning. *In room:* A/C, TV, minibar, hair dryer, safe.

WHERE TO DINE
Casa Santa Pola INTERNATIONAL/ANDALUSIAN Constructed in the 19th century but altered and rebuilt over the years, this building on the outskirts of the city opens onto views of the gorge. It's composed of three levels built onto the mountainside; access is through the third floor. The interior is a mix of Moorish, rococo, and contemporary, with a decor of antique ornaments, wooden floors, archways, terra-cotta walls, and red bistro-style tablecloths. Many of the good-tasting meals are cooked in a traditional brick oven, especially the *cochinillo* (roast suckling pig). Other excellent dishes are the *lomo asado* (grilled filet beef steak) and the savory *rabo de toro* (roast bull's tail). Desserts are homemade and traditional to the area. On certain nights, diners are treated to shows organized by owner Tomás Mayo.

Calle Santo Domingo 3. ℂ **95-287-92-08**. Main courses 10€–20€; set menu 19€. AE, DC, MC, V. Fri–Wed noon–4:30pm and 7:30–11pm.

Pedro Romero ⓖ SPANISH/ANDALUSIAN   Named after the famed bull-fighter, this restaurant attracts aficionados of that sport. In fact, it stands oppo-site the bullring and gets extremely busy on bullfighting days, when it's almost impossible to get a table. While seated under a stuffed bull's head, surrounded by photographs of young matadors, you might begin your meal with the classic garlic soup, then follow with a well-prepared array of meat or poultry dishes.

Virgen de la Paz 18. ⓒ **95-287-11-10.** Reservations required on day of *corrida* and/or Sat–Sun. Main courses 13€–18€. AE, DC, MC, V. Daily 12:30–4pm and 7:30–11pm.

Tragabuches ⓖⓖⓖ MODERN SPANISH   Chef/owner Sergio López, hailed by many Spanish gastronomes as the most talented young chef in Spain, has clearly staked out his role as the provider of the finest and most creative cuisine in Ronda. There are two dining rooms, each with a stylish contemporary decor. Against a typical backdrop of white walls, tables are decked out with pastel cloths and seat covers. The inventive menu is likely to feature well-crafted dishes like *cochinillo asado* (grilled suckling pig) or *rape en salsa de vinagreta, pulpo y ver-dura* (monkfish in a vinaigrette sauce with octopus and fresh vegetables). Begin perhaps with a cheese taco or the tasty liver paté. The excellent desserts include a range of homemade cakes and ice cream.

Calle José Aparicio 1 (between Plaza de España and Plaza de Toros). ⓒ **95-219-02-91.** Reservations rec-ommended on weekends. Main courses 13€–20€; set menu 50€. AE, DC, MC, V. Daily 1–4pm; Mon–Sat 7:30pm–midnight.

8 Granada ⭐⭐⭐

415km (258 miles) S of Madrid, 122km (76 miles) NE of Málaga

About 660m (2,200 ft.) above sea level in the foothills of the snowcapped Sierra Nevada, Granada sprawls over two main hills, the Alhambra and the Albaicín, and is crossed by two rivers, the Genil and the Darro. This former stronghold of Moorish Spain is full of romance and folklore. Washington Irving *(Tales of the Alhambra)* used the symbol of this city, the pomegranate *(granada)*, to conjure up a spirit of romance. In fact, the name probably derives from the Moorish word *Karnattah.* Some historians have suggested that it comes from Garnatha Alyehud, the name of an old Jewish ghetto.

Washington Irving may have helped publicize the glories of Granada to the English-speaking world, but in Spain the city is known for its ties to another writer: Federico García Lorca. Born in 1898, this Spanish poet/dramatist, whose masterpiece was *The House of Bernarda Alba,* was shot by soldiers in 1936 in the first months of the Spanish Civil War. During Franco's rule, García Lorca's works were banned in Spain, but that situation has changed and he's once again honored in Granada, where he grew up.

Cuesta de Gomérez is one of the most important streets in Granada. It climbs uphill from the Plaza Nueva, the center of the modern city, to the Alhambra. At the Plaza Nueva the east-west artery, Calle de los Reyes Católicos, goes to the heart of the 19th-century city and the towers of the cathedral. The main street of Granada is the Gran Vía de Colón, the principal north-south artery.

Calle de los Reyes Católicos and the Gran Vía de Colón meet at the circular Plaza de Isabel la Católica, graced by a bronze statue of the queen offering Columbus the Santa Fe agreement, which granted the rights to the epochal voy-age to the New World. Going west, Calle de los Reyes Católicos passes near the cathedral and other major sights in the downtown section of Granada. The

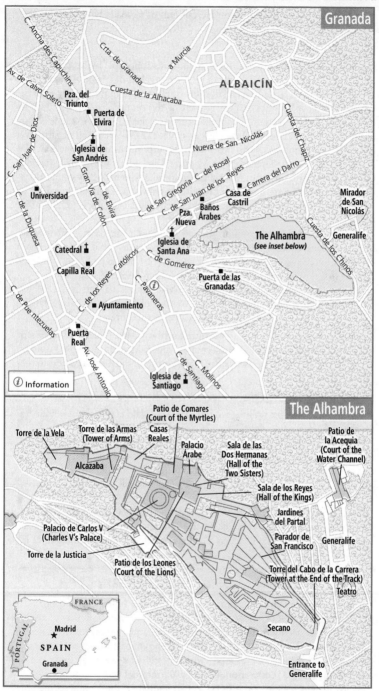

Granada & the Alhambra

Granada

C. Ancha des Capuchins
Crta. de Granada
a Murcia
Av. de Calvo Soleto
Cuesta de la Alhacaba
ALBAICÍN
Pza. del Triunto
Puerta de Elvira
C. San Juan de Dios
Nueva de San Nicolás
Cuesta del Chapiz
Iglesia de San Andrés
Gran Via de Colón
C. de Elvira
C. de San Gregoria
C. del Rosal
C. de San Juan de los Reyes
Carrera del Darro
Mirador de San Nicolás
Universidad
Casa de Castril
C. de la Duquesa
Baños Árabes
Pza. Nueva
Generalife
The Alhambra
(see inset below)
Cuesta de los Chinos
Catedral
Iglesia de Santa Ana
C. de los Reyes Católicos
C. de Gomérez
Capilla Real
C. Pavaneras
Puerta de las Granadas
C. de Pue ntezuelas
Ayuntamiento
Puerta Real
Av. José Antonio
C. de Santiago
C. Molinos
Iglesia de Santiago
ⓘ Information

The Alhambra

Patio de Comares (Court of the Myrtles)
Torre de las Armas (Tower of Arms)
Casas Reales
Torre de la Vela
Patio de la Acequia (Court of the Water Channel)
Palacio Árabe
Sala de las Dos Hermanas (Hall of the Two Sisters)
Alcazaba
Sala de los Reyes (Hall of the Kings)
Palacio de Carlos V (Charles V's Palace)
Jardines del Partal
Torre de la Justicia
Parador de San Francisco
Generalife
Patio de los Leones (Court of the Lions)
Torre del Cabo de la Carrera (Tower at the End of the Track)
Teatro
Secano
Entrance to Generalife

FRANCE
PORTUGAL
Madrid ★
SPAIN
Granada ●

street runs to Puerta Real, the commercial hub of Granada with many stores, hotels, cafes, and restaurants.

ESSENTIALS

GETTING THERE **Iberia** flies to Granada once or twice daily from Barcelona and Madrid, several times a week from Palma de Majorca, three times a week from Valencia, and every Thursday from Tenerife in the Canary Islands. Granada's airport is 16km (10 miles) west of the center of town; call © **95-824-52-00** for information. A convenient Iberia ticketing office is 2 blocks east of the cathedral at Plaza Isabel Católica 2 (© **95-822-75-92**). A bus departs several times daily connecting this office with the airport, costing 3€ one-way.

Two **trains** connect Granada with Madrid's Atocha Rail Station daily (taking 6 hr.). Overnight trains from Madrid generally take 8 hours. Many connections to the rest of Spain are funneled through the railway junction at Bobadilla, a 2-hour ride to the west. The train station is at Avenida Andalucía (© **90-224-02-02**).

Most **buses** pull into a station on the fringe of Granada at Carretera de Madrid. Alsina Graells (© **95-818-54-80**) is the most useful company here, offering 6 buses per day from Córdoba (3 hr.), 12 from Jaén (1½ hr.), 9 from Madrid (5 hr.), 15 from Málaga (2 hr.), and 6 from Seville (3 hr.).

Granada is connected by superhighway to Madrid, Málaga, and Seville. Many sightseers prefer to make the **drive** from Madrid to Granada in 2 days, rather than one. If that is your plan, Jaén makes a perfect stopover.

VISITOR INFORMATION The **tourist office,** Calle de Mariana Pineda s/n (© **95-822-59-90;** www.otgranada.com), is open Monday through Saturday from 9am to 7pm. There's also a small tourist office in the Alhambra next to the Puerto Vino.

EXPLORING GRANADA

Try to spend some time walking around Old Granada. Plan on about 3 hours to see the most interesting sights.

The Puerta de Elvira is the gate through which Ferdinand and Isabella made their triumphant entry into Granada in 1492. It was once a grisly place, with the rotting heads of executed criminals hanging from its portals. The quarter surrounding the gate was the Arab section *(morería)* until all the Arabs were driven out of the city after the Reconquest.

One of the most fascinating streets is Calle de Elvira; west of it the Albaicín, or old Arab quarter, rises on a hill. In the 17th and 18th centuries, many artisans occupied the shops and ateliers along this street and those radiating from it.

Moments Strolling Andalusia's Most Romantic Street

The most-walked street in Granada is Carrera del Darro, running north along the Darro River. It was discovered by the Romantic artists of the 19th century; many of their etchings (subsequently engraved) of scenes along this street were widely circulated, doing much to spread the fame of Granada throughout Europe. You can still find some of these old engravings in the musty antiques shops. Carrera del Darro ends at Paseo de los Tristes (Avenue of the Sad Ones), so named for the funeral corteges that used to go by here on the way to the cemetery.

Come here if you're looking for antiques. On Calle de Elvira stands the Iglesia de San Andrés, begun in 1528, with its Mudéjar bell tower. Much of the church was destroyed in the early 19th century, but several interesting paintings and sculptures remain. Another old church in this area is the Iglesia de Santiago, constructed in 1501 and dedicated to St. James, patron saint of Spain. Built on the site of an Arab mosque, it was damaged in an 1884 earthquake. The church contains the tomb of architect Diego de Siloé (1495–1563), who did much to change the face of the city.

Despite its name, the oldest square is the Plaza Nueva, which, under the Muslims, was the site of the bridge of the woodcutters. The Darro was covered over here, but its waters still flow underneath the square (which in Franco's time was named the Plaza del General Franco). On the east side of the Plaza Nueva is the 16th-century Iglesia de Santa Ana, built by Siloé. Inside its five-nave interior you can see a Churrigueresque reredos and coffered ceiling.

The *corrida* isn't really very popular here, but if you want to check out a bull-fight anyway, they're usually limited to the week of the Fiesta de Corpus Christi from May 29 to June 6 or the Día de la Cruz (Day of the Cross) observed on May 3. There's also a fight on the last Sunday in September. The Plaza de Toros, the bullring, is on Avenida de Doctor Olóriz, close to the soccer stadium. For more information, call © **95-827-24-51.**

Albaicín ★ This old Arab quarter on one of the two main hills of Granada doesn't belong to the city of 19th-century buildings and wide boulevards. It, and the surrounding gypsy caves of Sacromonte, are holdovers from an older past. The Albaicín once flourished as the residential section of the Moors, even after the city's reconquest, but it fell into decline when the Christians drove them out. This narrow labyrinth of crooked streets escaped the fate of much of Granada, which was torn down in the name of progress. Fortunately it has been preserved, as have its cisterns, fountains, plazas, whitewashed houses, villas, and the decaying remnants of the old city gate. Here and there you can catch a glimpse of a private patio filled with fountains and plants, a traditional elegant way of life that continues.

Bus: 7 to Calle de Pagés.

Alhambra and Generalife ★★★ Later enriched by Moorish occupants into a lavish palace, the Alhambra was originally constructed for defensive purposes on a rocky hilltop outcropping above the Darro River. The modern city of Granada was built across the river from the Alhambra, about half a mile from its western foundations.

When you first see the Alhambra, you may be surprised by its somewhat somber exterior. You have to walk across the threshold to discover the true delights of this Moorish palace. Tickets are sold in the office at the Entrada del Generalife y de la Alhambra. Enter through the incongruous 14th-century **Gateway of Justice** ★. Most visitors don't need an expensive guide but will be content to stroll through the richly ornamented open-air rooms, with their lace-like walls and courtyards with fountains. Many of the Arabic inscriptions translate as "Only Allah is conqueror."

The most-photographed part of the palace is the **Court of Lions** ★★★, named after its highly stylized fountain. This was the heart of the palace, the most private section where the sultan enjoyed his harem. Opening onto the court are the Hall of the Two Sisters, where the favorite of the moment was kept, and the Gossip Room, a factory of intrigue. In the dancing room in the Hall of

⌒ **Tips** **Reserving for the Alhambra**

Because of the overwhelming crowds, the government limits the number of people who can enter the Alhambra. Go as early as possible, but even if you get there at 10am you may not be admitted until 1:30pm. If you arrive after 4pm, it's unlikely you'll get in at all. Your best bet is to make arrangements for tickets before you arrive by calling the Banco Bilbao Vizcaya at ℭ **90-222-44-60** within Spain. You can charge tickets to your MasterCard or Visa (plus 7€ surcharge) and then pick them up from any BBV office in Spain. Most visitors go to the BBV branch in Granada, at Plaza Isabel Católica 1, in the heart of the modern town.

Kings, entertainment was provided nightly to amuse the sultan's party. Eunuchs guarded the harem but apparently not very well—according to legend, one sultan beheaded 36 Moorish princes here because one of them was suspected of having been intimate with his favorite.

You can see the room where Washington Irving lived (in the chambers of Charles V) while he was compiling his *Tales of the Alhambra*. The best-known tale is the legend of Zayda, Zorayda, and Zorahayda, the three beautiful princesses who fell in love with three captured Spanish soldiers outside "La Torre de las Infantas." Irving credits the French with saving the Alhambra for posterity, but in fact they were responsible for blowing up seven of the towers in 1812, and it was a Spanish soldier who cut the fuse before more damage could be done. When the duke of Wellington arrived a few years later, he chased out the chickens, the gypsies, and the transient beggars who were using the Alhambra as a tenement and set up housekeeping here himself.

Charles V may have been horrified when he saw the cathedral in the middle of the great mosque at Córdoba, but he's responsible for architectural meddling here, building a Renaissance palace at the Alhambra—which, although quite beautiful, is terribly out of place. Today it houses the Museo Bellas Artes en la Alhambra (ℭ **95-822-48-43**), open Tuesday through Saturday from 9am to 8pm, Sunday from 9am to noon. Of minor interest, it displays mostly religious paintings and sculpture from the 1500s to the present. It also shelters the Museo de la Alhambra (ℭ **95-822-75-27**), devoted to Hispanic-Muslim art and open Tuesday through Saturday from 8am to 7:30pm, and Sunday from 9am to 2pm.

Exit from the Alhambra via the Puerta de la Justicia, then circumnavigate the Alhambra's southern foundations until you reach the gardens of the summer palace, where Paseo de los Cipreses quickly leads you to the main building of the **Generalife** ✿✿, built in the 13th century to overlook the Alhambra. The sultans used to spend their summers in this palace (pronounced "heh-neh-rah-*lee*-feh"), safely locked away with their harems. The Generalife's glory is its gardens and courtyards. Don't expect an Alhambra in miniature: The Generalife was always meant to be a retreat, even from the splendors of the Alhambra. This palace was the setting for Irving's story of the prince locked away from love.

Palacio de Carlos V. ℭ **95-822-09-12.** Comprehensive ticket, including Alhambra and Generalife (below), 7€; Museo Bellas Artes 1.50€; Museo de la Alhambra 1.50€; illuminated visits 6.75€. Mar–Oct daily 9am–7:45pm, floodlit visits daily 10pm–midnight; Nov–Feb daily 9am–5:45pm, floodlit visits daily 8–10pm. Bus: 2.

Baños Arabes The Moors called them the "baths of the walnut tree." Among the oldest buildings still standing in Granada, and among the best-preserved

Muslim baths in Spain, they predate the Alhambra. Visigothic and Roman building materials are supposed to have gone into their construction, and it is remarkable that they escaped destruction during the reign of the Reyes Católicos (Ferdinand and Isabella).

Carrera del Darro 31. ⓒ 95-822-23-39. Free admission. Tues–Sat 10am–2pm.

Casa de Castril This building has always been one of the most handsome Renaissance palaces in Granada. The Plateresque facade of 1539 has been attributed to Diego de Siloé. In 1869, it was converted into a museum with a collection of minor artifacts found in the area. The most outstanding exhibit here is a collection of Egyptian alabaster vases that were dug up in a necropolis in Almuñécar. Look especially for the figure of a bull from Arjona. There is also a selection of decorative Moorish art that the Arabs left behind as they retreated from Granada.

Museo Arqueológico, Carrera del Darro 41. ⓒ 95-822-56-40. Admission 1.50€. Tues 3–8pm; Wed–Sat 9am–8pm; Sun 9am–2:30pm. Bus: Neptuno-Albaicín.

Casa-Museo de Manuel de Falla The famous Spanish composer Manuel de Falla, known for his strongly individualized works, came to live in Granada in 1919, hoping to find a retreat and inspiration. He moved into a *carmen* (local dialect for a small white house) just below the Alhambra and in time befriended García Lorca. In 1922, on the grounds of the Alhambra, they staged the Cante Jondo Festival, the purest expression of flamenco. Today, you can walk through the gardens of the man who wrote such works as *Nights in the Gardens of Spain* and see his collection of handicrafts and ceramics, along with other personal memorabilia. Despite the posted hours, a caretaker isn't always present to guide you about—it's better to call in advance to see if someone is actually here. The location is about a block from the Alhambra Palace Hotel.

Antequeruela Alta 11. ⓒ 95-822-94-21. Admission 1.80€. Apr–Sept Mon–Fri noon–2pm and 6–8pm, Sat noon–2pm; Oct–Mar Mon–Sat 10am–4pm.

Casa-Museo Federico García Lorca ⭐ *Finds* Poet/dramatist Federico García Lorca spent many happy summers with his family here at their vacation home. He moved to Granada in 1909, a dreamy-eyed schoolboy, and was endlessly fascinated with its life, including the Alhambra and the gypsies, whom h was later to describe compassionately in his *Gypsy Ballads*. The house is decorated with green trim and grillwork and filled with family memorabilia,

---

⎛Tips⎞ Walking to the Alhambra

Many visitors opt for a taxi or the bus to the Alhambra, but some hardy souls enjoy the uphill climb from the cathedral at the Plaza de la Lonja (signs indicate the winding roads and the steps that lead to the Alhambra). If you decide to walk, enter the Alhambra via the Cuesta de Gómerez, which, although steep, is the quickest and shortest pedestrian route. It begins at the Plaza Nueva, about 4 blocks east of the cathedral, and goes steeply uphill to the Puerta de las Granadas, the first of two gates to the Alhambra. The second, another 183m (200 yd.) uphill, is the Puerta de la Justicia, which accepts 90% of the touristic visits to the Alhambra. Beware of self-styled guides milling around the parking lot; they may just be interested in picking your pocket.

including furniture and portraits. You can look out at the Alhambra from one of its balconies. You may inspect the poet's upstairs bedroom and see his oak desk stained with ink. Look for the white stool that he carried to the terrace to watch the sun set over Granada. The house is in the Fuentevaqueros section of Granada, near the airport.

Virgen Blanca 6, Parque Federico García Lorca. ✆ **95-825-84-66**. Admission 1.80€. Oct 7–Mar 31, 10am–7pm and 4–6pm; Apr 1–June 30, 10am–1pm and 5–7pm; July–Aug 10am–2:30pm; Sept 10am–1pm and 6–8pm.

Catedral and Capilla Real 🌟🌟　This richly ornate Renaissance cathedral with its spectacular altar is one of the country's architectural highlights, acclaimed for its beautiful facade and gold-and-white interior. It was begun in 1521 and completed in 1714. Behind the cathedral (entered separately) is the Flamboyant Gothic **Royal Chapel** 🌟🌟, where the remains of Queen Isabella and her husband Ferdinand lie. It was their wish to be buried in recaptured Granada, not Castile or Aragón. The coffins are remarkably tiny—a reminder of how short they must have been. Accenting the tombs is a wrought-iron grille, itself a masterpiece. Occupying much larger tombs are the remains of their daughter, Joanna the Mad, and her husband, Philip the Handsome. In the sacristy you can view Isabella's personal **art collection** 🌟🌟, including works by Rogier Van der Weyden and various Spanish and Italian masters such as Botticelli. The cathedral is in the center of Granada off two prominent streets, Gran Vía de Colón and Calle de San Jerónimo. The Capilla Real abuts the cathedral's eastern edge.

Plaza de la Lonja, Gran Vía de Colón 5. ✆ **95-822-29-59**. Admission to cathedral 2.50€; chapel 2.50€. Cathedral and chapel daily 10:30am–1:30pm and 3:30–6:30pm (4–7pm in winter).

Monasterio Cartuja 🌟　This 16th-century monastery, off the Albaicín on the outskirts of Granada, is sometimes called the "Christian answer to the Alhambra" because of its ornate stucco and marble and the baroque Churrigueresque fantasy in the sacristy. Its most notable paintings are by Bocanegra, its outstanding sculpture by Mora. The church of this Carthusian monastery was decorated with baroque stucco in the 17th century, and its 18th-century sacristy is an excellent example of latter-day baroque style. Napoléon's armies killed St. Bruno here, and La Cartuja is said to be the only monument of its kind in the world. Sometimes one of the Carthusian monks will take you on a guided tour.

Camino de Alfacar s/n. ✆ **95-816-19-32**. Admission 2.50€. Daily 10am–1pm and 4–8pm (closes at 6pm in winter). Bus: 8 from cathedral.

SHOPPING

Alcaicería, once the Moorish silk market, is next to the cathedral in the lower city. The narrow streets of this rebuilt village of shops are filled with vendors selling the arts and crafts of Granada province. For the souvenir hunter, the Alcaicería offers one of the most splendid assortments in Spain of tiles, castanets, and wire figures of Don Quixote chasing windmills. Lots of Spanish jewelry can be found here, comparing favorably with the finest Toledan work. For the window-shopper in particular, it makes a pleasant stroll.

Handicrafts stores virtually line the main shopping arteries, especially those centered around Puerta Real, including Gran Vía de Colón, Reyes Católicos, and Angel Ganivet. For the best selection of antiques stores, mainly selling furnishings of Andalusia, browse the shops along Cuesta de Elvira.

At **Tejidos Artísticos Fortuny,** Plaza Fortuny 1 (© **95-822-43-27**), you can buy curtains, knotted carpets, nubby-textured draperies, tablecloths, place mats, and fabrics. Much of the merchandise is hand-woven. It's open Monday through Friday from 9am to 2pm and 5 to 8pm.

WHERE TO STAY
EXPENSIVE
Hotel Alhambra Palace ✦
Evoking a Moorish fortress complete with a crenellated roofline, a crowning dome, geometric tile work, and the suggestion of a minaret, this legendary hotel is a good choice. It was built in 1910 in a sort of Mudéjar Revival style in a secluded spot midway up the slope toward the Alhambra, a 10-minute walk from that attraction. The private rooms don't live up to the drama of the public areas. Try for a room with a balcony opening onto a view of the city of Granada. The court rooms are less desirable because they lack double-glazing. Most rooms are spacious and quite comfortable, but a few small ones are in need of restoration. All contain bathrooms with tub/shower combos. Most readers like its old-world aura, but a few have found the hotel so unsatisfactory they didn't want to check in after seeing their room. If at all possible, ask to see your room before agreeing to a booking.

Peña Partida 2, 18009 Granada. © **95-822-14-68**. Fax 95-822-64-04. www.h-alhambrapalace.es. 130 units. 178€ double; 252€ suite. Rates include breakfast. AE, DC, MC, V. Free parking. Bus: Destination Alhambra. **Amenities:** Restaurant; bar; room service; babysitting; laundry service; dry cleaning. *In room:* A/C, TV, minibar, hair dryer, safe.

Parador Nacional de San Francisco ✦✦✦
This most famous parador in Spain—and the hardest to get into—is within the grounds of the Alhambra. The decor is tasteful and the place evokes a lot of history with its rich Andalusian ambience. The parador itself is within a former convent founded by the Catholic monarchs after they conquered the city in 1492. Before that the building was part of the Muslim complex that included the Alhambra and a mosque built in the mid-1300s by Caliph Yusuf I. The bodies of Ferdinand and Isabella were once placed here until their tombs could be readied in the cathedral. From its terrace you have views of the Generalife gardens and the Sacromonte caves. The guest rooms are generally roomy and comfortable, receiving their last renovation in 1992. The bathrooms with tub/shower combos add to the allure. Try for a room in the older section, which is furnished with antiques; rooms in the more modern wing are less inspired.

Alhambra, 18009 Granada. © **95-822-14-40**. Fax 95-822-22-64. 36 units. 208€ double. AE, DC, MC, V. Free parking. Bus: 30 or 32. **Amenities:** Restaurant; bar; room service; laundry service; dry cleaning; currency exchange. *In room:* A/C, TV, minibar, hair dryer.

MODERATE
Carmen de Santa Inés ✦ *Value*
You can go Carmen crazy in Granada, although the sultry, fictional gypsy is more commonly associated with Seville. You could stay at the parent hotel, the first-class **Hotel Carmen** at Acera del Darro 62 (© **95-825-83-00**), with its 283 rooms. Or else, if you like the charm and grace of an intimate inn, you could go to its gracious stepchild, Carmen de Santa Inés, an *antigua casa*. Because it's more tranquil, this inn has a slight edge on its sibling, Palacio de Santa Inés, which is only 2 blocks away (see below for recommendation).

Graciously restored, Carmen de Santa Inés will house you in style and comfort, all at an affordable price. Lying in the historical Albayzin section, this was an old Moorish house on a quiet street. Much of yesterday has been retained, including original wooden beams, a private patio, Arab fountains, a marble stair-case and columns—all very romantic. Bedrooms are small but filled with com-fort and character. If you've got a few extra bucks to spare, rent "El Mirador," with its balcony terrace opening onto panoramic views of the Alhambra and the cityscape. There is no elevator, and only breakfast is served.

Placeta de Porras 7, 18018 Granada. © **95-822-63-80.** Fax 95-822-44-04. 9 units. 100€ double; 195€ suite. AE, DC, MC, V. **Amenities:** Laundry. *In room:* A/C, TV, minibar, hair dryer, safe.

Casa Morisca ★★ *(Finds* We thought we couldn't top the charms of the two Inéses: Carmen de Santa Inés and Palacio de Santa Inés. Then we lept at Casa Morisca and fell in love again, fickle us. In the historic lower district of Albayzin, at the foot of the Alhambra, this house dates from the end of the 15th century. In the patio you can still see the remains of a Moorish pool, and galleries sup-ported by pilasters and columns evoke Granada long before Washington Irving arrived to write about it. The interior was kept and restored, although the facade was given a 17th-century overlay. Bedrooms are individually decorated in an old style but with all modern comforts such as private bathrooms equipped with showers and tubs. No hotel in Granada has been restored with such respect for its past life. For example, a turret lookout above the upper floor, which appeared in an 1859 photograph, was reconstructed accurately in 1998. All the 17th-cen-tury iron and carpentry work has been cleaned and restored. Local craftsmen worked only with the original materials of the building, including clay tiles and lime mortar.

Cuesta de la Victoria 9, 18010 Granada. © **95-822-11-00.** Fax 95-821-57-96. www.hotelcasamorisca.com. 14 units. 140€ double; 190€ suite. AE, DC, MC, V. **Amenities:** Breakfast room; room service; laundry/drycleaning. *In room:* A/C, TV, minibar, hair dryer, safe.

Hotel América ★★ This small hotel is within the Alhambra's walls. Walk through the covered entryway of this former villa into the shady patio that's lively yet intimate, with large trees, potted plants, and ferns. Other plants cas-cade down white plaster walls entwined with ornate grillwork. The living room of this homey little retreat has a collection of regional decorative objects; some of the rooms have Andalusian reproductions. Although small, the rooms are comfortably furnished and well maintained, with compact bathrooms with shower stalls.

Real de la Alhambra 53, 18009 Granada. © **95-822-74-71.** Fax 95-822-74-70. 14 units. 110€ double; 125€ suite. DC, MC, V. Parking nearby 9€. Closed Dec–Feb. Bus: 32. *In room:* A/C, hair dryer.

Hotel Inglaterra The NH chain runs this old hotel 2 blocks northeast of the cathedral and 5 minutes from the Alhambra. In 1992, they completely refur-bished the run-down place. Its five floors stand back from the thundering traf-fic of the main drag, Gran Vía de Colón. The large central patio is encircled by rooms in the typical Andalusian style. The decor is classical, but there are plenty of modern touches. The rooms are moderately spacious and comfortably fur-nished with good beds and bright decorations. The bathrooms come with tub/shower combos. Although the elevator goes up only four floors, the fifth-floor rooms open onto panoramic views of the Alhambra.

Cettie Meriem 4, 18010 Granada. © **95-822-15-59.** Fax 95-822-71-00. www.nh-hoteles.es. 36 units. 120€ double. AE, DC, MC, V. Parking 11€. **Amenities:** Bar; laundry service; dry cleaning. *In room:* A/C, TV, minibar, hair dryer.

Hotel Palacio Santa Inés ★★ This *antigua casa* is one of the most enchant-ing places to stay in Granada. It's in the colorful Albaicín district, about a

5-minute walk from the Alhambra. The painstakingly restored little palace was in complete ruins until the mid-1990s. Now it's a lovely, graceful inn, even a bit luxe. A 16th-century courtyard, time-aged wooden beamed ceilings, and silver chandeliers take you back to yesterday, as do the restored frescoes on the walls of the patio (said to have been painted by a student of Raphael). The rooms are medium-sized, some have small sitting rooms, and several open onto views of Granada. Much of the furniture is antique, and the modern bathrooms have tub/shower combos. The hotel is a block northwest of Carrera del Darro and Iglesia de Santa Ana.

Cuesta de Santa Inés 9, 18010 Granada. ☎ **95-822-23-62**. Fax 95-822-24-65. www.lugaresdivinos.com. 35 units. 100€–120€ double; 150€–225€ suite. AE, DC, MC, V. Parking 16€. **Amenities:** Bar; babysitting; laundry service; dry cleaning. *In room:* A/C, TV, minibar, hair dryer, safe.

Hotel Reina Cristina   It's in the center of the city, a 3-minute walk from the cathedral in a renovated 19th-century mansion called a *casa granadina*. Part of the lore and tragic legend of the city of Granada, this hotel shared a moment in Spanish history. One of the nation's greatest writers and Granada's favorite son, the poet/playwright Federico García Lorca, was arrested here by the right-wing forces of Generalísimo Franco and abducted. He was taken 3km (2 miles) away and executed. The family-operated hotel now exudes grace, charm, and tranquillity, with helpful service. All the small rooms have undergone extensive renovation, and much of the original furnishings have been retained. The bathrooms have been renewed, all with tub/shower combos.

Calle Tablas 4, 18002 Granada. ☎ **95-825-32-11**. Fax 95-825-57-28. www.hotelreinacristina.com. 43 units. 96€–102€ double; 117€–125€ triple. Rates include breakfast buffet. AE, DC, MC, V. Parking 12€. **Amenities:** Restaurant; bar; room service; babysitting; laundry service; dry cleaning. *In room:* A/C, TV, minibar, hair dryer, safe.

INEXPENSIVE

Casa del Aljarife ★ *Finds*   In the Albaicín district 4 blocks from the Plaza Santa Ana, this is a little nugget known only to a few discerning travelers. In a recently renovated 17th-century structure, it has a large patio with trees and a Moorish fountain with views of the Alhambra. A family concern, the *casa* is well cared for and has a welcoming atmosphere. Each medium-sized or spacious room has its own unique style, with a tasteful Andalusian style. The bathrooms have shower stalls. Owner Christian Most is gracious, apologizing for the lack of luxuries by pointing out that "everything you need" is virtually outside the door.

Placeta de la Cruz Verde 2, 18010 Granada. ☎/fax **95-822-24-25**. www.granadainfo.com/most. 4 units. 84€ double; 168€ suite. MC, V. *In room:* A/C.

Hotel Guadalupe   This building sits beside an inclined road leading up to the Alhambra. It was built in 1969 but seems older, with thick stucco walls, rounded arches, and jutting beams. The hotel is continuously being renovated, and the comfortably furnished but rather small rooms overlook the Alhambra. The compact bathrooms are equipped with tub/shower combos.

Av. de la Sabika s/n, 18009 Granada. ☎ **95-822-34-23**. Fax 95-822-37-98. www.eel.es/guadalupe. 58 units. 65€–95€ double. AE, DC, MC, V. Parking 11€. Bus: 30 or 32. **Amenities:** Restaurant; bar; room service; babysitting; laundry service; dry cleaning. *In room:* A/C, TV, minibar, hair dryer.

WHERE TO DINE
EXPENSIVE

Las Tinajas ★ ANDALUSIAN   This restaurant a short walk from the cathedral is named for the huge amphorae depicted on the facade of the building. For more than 3 decades it has been the culinary showcase of José Alvarez. His decor is classical Andalusian, with wood walls adorned with ceramic tiles and pictures of old Granada. Diners are surrounded by antique ornaments interspersed with modern elements and fixtures. There's a convivial but crowded bar where locals and visitors alike order Andalusian wines and a wide variety of delicious tapas. Señor Alvarez is proud of his Mediterranean culinary traditions and uses only the freshest ingredients. Begin with such delights as the cold zucchini-and-almond cream soup or the white beet stuffed with ham and cheese. Follow with a delectable monkfish cooked with local herbs or the peppered sirloin steak. Desserts include Moorish cake with almonds and raspberries, made from a recipe left over from the days of the sultan, and a hearty regional pudding with coffee-flavored cream.

Martínez Campos 17. ⓒ **95-825-43-93.** Reservations recommended. Main courses 8€–22€; set menu 28€–32€. AE, DC, MC, V. Daily noon–5pm and 8pm–midnight. Closed July 15–Aug 15.

MODERATE

Alhabaca ⭐ *Finds* ANDALUSIAN/SPANISH   You'd have to live in Granada for quite a while to learn of this little bistro in a century-old building, since locals don't exactly share the secret. It's owned by Javier Jiménez, who seats 30 diners at 10 tables in this old-fashioned restaurant decorated in a rustic style with bare white walls. The traditional dishes he serves are unpretentious and tasty, especially the *salmorejo* (creamy tomato gazpacho) and *ensalada de dos salsas* (a green salad with 2 dressings). The stuffed salmon is marvelous, as is *pastel de berenjena con salmon marinado* (layered pastry with eggplant and marinated salmon). For dessert, we recommend the velvety yogurt mousse.

Calle Varela 17. ⓒ **95-822-49-23.** Reservations recommended on weekends. Main courses 7€–13€. MC, V. Tues–Sun 1–4pm; Tues–Sat 8–11pm. Closed Aug.

Carmen de San Miguel ANDALUSIAN   On the sloping incline leading up to the Alhambra, this likable restaurant offers spectacular views over the city center. The restaurant is proud of its glassed-in dining room and patio-style terrace, whose banks of flowers are changed seasonally. Specialties include grilled hake, a paté of partridge with a vinaigrette sauce, Iberian ham with Manchego cheese, and a casserole of monkfish and fresh clams. The food, although good, doesn't quite match the view. The wines are from throughout the country, with a strong selection of Riojas.

Plaza de Torres Bermejas 3. ⓒ **95-822-67-23.** Reservations recommended. Main courses 15€–20€; *menú del día* 40€. AE, DC, DISC, MC, V. Mon–Sat 1:30–4pm and 8:30–11:30pm; winter Sun 1:30-4pm.

Parador Nacional San Francisco ⭐⭐ ANDALUSIAN/SPANISH   Even if you can't afford to stay at this luxurious parador (see "Where to Stay," above), the most famous in Spain, consider heading here for a tranquil retreat after you've battled the tourist hordes in the Alhambra itself. The dining room is spacious, the service is polite, and you gaze upon the rose gardens and a distant view of the Generalife. At this 16th-century convent built by the Reyes Católicos, you get not only atmosphere but also a cuisine that features regional dishes of Andalusia and Spanish national specialties. Lunch is the preferred time to dine here, because the terrace overlooking the palace is open then. A light outdoor lunch of sandwiches and salads can be ordered on the a la carte menu if you don't want to partake of the heavy major Spanish repast in the heat of the day. The cuisine is competent in every way, although at no point rising to any culinary achievement. When in doubt, order the Andalusian specialties instead of the Spanish national dishes, as most of the chefs are Andalusian.

Real de la Alhambra. © 95-822-14-40. Main courses 9€–17€; fixed-price menu 24€. AE, DC, MC, V. Daily 1–4pm and 8:30–11pm. Bus: 30 or 32.

Restaurante Cunini SEAFOOD   The array of seafood specialties served at Cunini, perhaps 100 selections, extends even to the tapas served at the long stand-up bar. Many guests move on after a drink or two to the paneled ground-floor restaurant, where the cuisine reflects the whole of Spain. Meals often begin with soup—perhaps *sopa sevillana* (with ham, shrimp, and whitefish). Also popular is a deep fry of small fish called a *fritura Cunini,* with other specialties including rice with seafood, *zarzuela* (seafood stew), smoked salmon, and grilled shrimp. The Plaza de la Pescadería is adjacent to the Gran Vía de Colón just below the cathedral.

Plaza de la Pescadería 14. © 95-825-07-77. Reservations recommended. Main courses 13€–33€; fixed-price menu 18€. AE, DC, MC, V. Tues–Sat noon–4pm and 8pm–midnight; Sun noon–4pm.

Ruta del Valleta ★★ ANDALUSIAN   Granada lacks a really first-class restaurant within its historic core. Despite its origins in 1976 as an unpretentious roadhouse restaurant, this place rapidly evolved into what's usually acclaimed as the best restaurant in or around Granada. It's in the hamlet of Cenés de la Vega, about 6km (3½ miles) northwest of Granada's center, and has six dining rooms of various sizes, each decorated with a mix of English and Andalusian furniture and accessories. (They include a worthy collection of hand-painted ceramics from the region, many of which hang from the ceilings.) The owners are a pair of Granada-born brothers, Miguel and José Pedraza, who direct the impeccable service rituals. Menu items change with the season but are likely to include roast suckling pig; roasted game birds like pheasant and partridge, often served with Rioja wine sauce; preparations of fish and shellfish, including monkfish with Andalusian herbs and strips of Serrano ham; filet steak in morel-studded cream sauce; and a dessert specialty of frozen rice pudding on a bed of warm chocolate sauce. The wine list is said to be the most comprehensive in the region.

Carretera Vieja de la Sierra Nevada, Km 5.5, Cenés de la Vega. © 95-848-61-34. Reservations recommended. Main courses 12€–22€; fixed-price menus 36€ without wine. AE, DC, MC, V. Daily 1–4pm; Mon–Sat 8pm–midnight.

INEXPENSIVE

Antigua Bodega Castanede ★ *Finds* ANDALUSIAN   More and more discerning visitors are going to Andalusia wanting to dine in *típico* joints that rarely see a foreigner. Our nomination for the most rustic local bodega in Granada is the Castanede. It's been here for more than a century and is the oldest of its type in the colorful Albaicín *barrio,* only a 10-minute walk from the Alhambra, just off the Plaza Nueva. A convivial spot, it's crowded with locals who know they can get tasty but unpretentious food here at low, low prices. On clay floors resting under wooden beams, there are only 11 tables for a proper sit-down meal, but many patrons crowd in at the bar placing their order. The place is praised locally for its wide ranges of tapas—there are 18 stuffed versions of the humble potato alone. Other meals include a variety of thick stews served in traditional clay bowls, ideal if you're visiting on a cold day. You can order a *tabla ibérica,* a selection of small dishes featuring cheese, ham, crab, shrimp, and venison. For the sweet tooth, go for the chocolate mousse or one of the homemade tarts.

Calle Elvira 5. © 95-822-63-62. Main courses 6€–10€. MC, V. Daily 12:30–5pm and 8pm–1:30am.

Chikito SPANISH Chikito is across from the famous tree-shaded square where García Lorca met with other members of El Rinconcillo (The Little Corner), a dozen young men considered the best and the brightest in the 1920s, when they brought a brief but dazzling cultural renaissance to their hometown. The cafe where they met has now changed its name, but it's the same building. The present-day Chikito is a bar/restaurant. In fair weather, guests enjoy drinks and snacks on tables placed in the square; in winter they retreat inside to the tapas bars. There's also a complete restaurant, offering *sopa sevillana,* shrimp cocktail, Basque hake, baked tuna, oxtail, *zarzuela* (seafood stew), grilled swordfish, and Argentine-style veal steak. Regrettably, this literary shrine has barely civil waiters, who obviously lack patience with newcomers. You may want to skip dinner here and settle for tapas and a glass of sherry at the bar.

Plaza del Campilio 9. ℂ 95-822-33-64. Reservations recommended. Main courses 12€–19€; fixed-price menu 18€. AE, DC, MC, V. Thurs–Tues 1–4pm and 8–11:30pm. Bus: 1, 2, or 7.

Restaurant Mirador de Moraima ANDALUSIAN/SPANISH Facing the Alhambra in an antique house, this is a large, rambling restaurant with a half dozen dining rooms and three outdoor terraces. The hardworking staff prepares large quantities of such dishes as gazpacho, roasted goat in wine sauce, slabs of beefsteak with a sauce of aromatic herbs, several preparations of cod, grilled Spanish sausages, and roasted lamb. Don't expect subtlety or big-city sophistication here—what you'll get is generous portions of good cooking and a deep pride in the region's rural traditions.

Calle Pianista García Carrillo 2. ℂ 95-822-82-90. Reservations recommended. Main courses 8€–16€. AE, MC, V. Mon–Sat 1:30–3:30pm and 8:30–11:30pm.

Restaurant O Caña SPANISH Behind a mosaic-sheathed facade in an antique building in Granada's Jewish Quarter, this restaurant offers a long bar, a salon where you might be tempted to sit down before a meal with a glass of sherry, and a well-managed dining room. The portions are generous, well flavored, and authentic to the old-time traditions of Andalusia. Since it opened in 1905, the site has turned out endless versions of its specialties (oxtail, grilled *solomillo* of beefsteak, Spanish sausages, grilled duck breast, and endless amounts of suckling pig and roasted lamb). It has earned the loyalty of generations of local families, many of whom arrive en masse to dine together, especially on Sunday.

Plaza de Realejo 1. ℂ 95-825-64-70. Main courses 6€–12€; fixed-price menu 8€. AE, DC, MC, V. Daily 7pm–midnight.

Restaurante Sevilla SPANISH/ANDALUSIAN Attracting a mixed crowd of all ages, the Sevilla is definitely *típico,* but with an upbeat elegance. In the past you might have seen El Cordobés (when he was Spain's leading bullfighter), Brigitte Bardot, or even Andrés Segovia dining here. Even before them, the place was discovered by García Lorca, a patron in the 1930s, and Manuel de Falla. Most dishes are at the lower end of the price scale. Our most recent meal here included gazpacho, Andalusian veal, and caramel custard, plus bread and the wine of Valdepeñas. To break the gazpacho monotony, try *sopa virule,* made with pine nuts and chicken breasts. For a main course, we recommend the *cordero a la pastoril* (lamb with herbs and paprika). The best dessert is bananas flambé. You can dine inside, where it's pleasantly decorated, or on the terrace. You'll find the place opposite the Royal Chapel, near the Plaza Isabel Católica.

Calle Oficios 12. ℂ 95-822-12-23. Reservations recommended. Main courses 10€–24€. AE, DC, MC, V. Daily 1–4pm; Mon–Sat 8–11pm.

GRANADA AFTER DARK

DRINKS & TAPAS   A good place to begin your night is along the Campo del Príncipe, where at least seven old-fashioned tapas bars do a rollicking business during the cool of the evening. Our favorite is **La Esquinita,** Campo del Príncipe s/n (© **95-822-71-06**). Small, atmospheric, and sometimes claustrophobic, it serves a crowd that mostly eats standing up, sometimes spilling into the street, rather than sitting at any of the trio of small tables. A specialty tapas here is a *ración* of fried fish that tastes absolutely sublime when accompanied by wine or cold beer.

A perennial favorite directly in front of the cathedral is **Antigua Bodega Cartañeda,** Elvira 5 (© **95-822-97-06**). Inside, rows of antique wine barrels and exposed masonry bring to mind many generations of wine connoisseurs, whose ranks you'll be tempted to join, thanks to the fact that virtually nothing has been changed in this place in years. Another contender for your bar business is **Casa Henrique,** Calle Acero de Darro 8 (© **95-812-35-08**), an old-fashioned masonry-sided hole-in-the-wall lined with antique barrels of wine and sherries. Its specialty tapas consist of thin-sliced Serrano ham and heaping platters of steamed mussels with herbs and white wine.

One of the most popular tapas bars in Granada (at least with us) is **Casa Vino del Agua,** Calle Algibe de Trillo 7 (© **95-822-43-56**), a well-maintained bar with an adjoining restaurant in a small garden in the heart of the Albaicín. Everyone agrees that the cooling nighttime breezes show this convivial spot off to best advantage. Don't expect full-fledged platters; its strength is small-scale portions of cheeses, patés, and salads, which go especially well with glasses of wine and beer. An equally historic spot with a verdant patio loaded with plants and shrubs is **Bar Pilar del Toro,** Calle Hospital de Santa Ana 12 (© **95-822-38-47**), near the cathedral and the Plaza Nueva. An even larger competitor, **La Gran Taverna,** Plaza Nueva 12 (© **95-822-88-46**), is a modern and irreverent site that attracts coffee- and wine-tasters as well as lovers of sliced Serrano ham, fondues, and liqueurs. **Bar La Mancha,** Calle Joaquín Costa 10 (© **95-822-89-68**), is a roughly equivalent nearby site.

THE GYPSY CAVES OF SACROMONTE *Overrated*   These inhabited gypsy caves are the subject of much controversy. Admittedly, they're a tourist trap, one of the most obviously commercial and shadowy rackets in Spain. Still, the caves are a potent enough attraction if you follow some rules.

Once, thousands of gypsies lived on the "Holy Mountain," so named because of several Christians martyred here. However, many of the caves were heavily damaged by rain in 1962, forcing hundreds of the occupants to seek shelter elsewhere. Nearly all the gypsies remaining are in one way or another involved with tourism. (Some don't even live here—they commute from modern apartments in the city.)

When evening settles over Granada, loads of visitors descend on these caves near the Albaicín, the old Arab section. In every cave, you'll hear the rattle of castanets and the strumming of guitars, while everybody in the gypsy family struts his or her stuff. Popularly known as the *zambra,* this is intriguing entertainment only if you have an appreciation for the grotesque. Whenever a gypsy boy or girl comes along with genuine talent, he or she is often grabbed up and hustled off to the more expensive clubs. Those left at home can be rather pathetic in their attempts to entertain.

One of the main reasons for going is to see the caves themselves. If you're expecting primitive living, you may be in for a surprise—many are quite

---

> ### *Tips* No, Gracias
>
> During the *zambra,* refuse to accept a pair of castanets, even if offered under the friendly guise of having you join in the fun. If you accept them, chances are you'll later be asked to pay for them. Buying anything in these caves isn't recommended. Leave your jewelry at your hotel and don't take more money than you're prepared to lose.

---

comfortable, with conveniences like telephones and electricity. Often they're decorated with copper and ceramic items—and the inhabitants need no encouragement to sell them to you.

If you want to see the caves, you can walk up the hill by yourself. Your approach will already be advertised before you get here. Attempts will be made to lure you inside one or another of the caves—and to get money from you. Alternatively, you can book an organized tour arranged by one of the travel agencies in Granada. Even at the end of one of these group outings—with all expenses theoretically paid in advance—there's likely to be an attempt by the cave dwellers to extract more money from you. As soon as the *zambra* ends, hurry out of the cave as quickly as possible. Many readers have been critical of these tours.

A visit to the caves is almost always included as part of the morning and (more frequently) afternoon city tours offered every day by such companies as Grana Visión (② **95-853-58-75**). Night tours of the caves (when the caves are at their most eerie, most evocative, and most larcenous) are usually offered only to those who can assemble 10 or more people into a group. This might have changed by the time of your visit, so phone a reputable tour operator such as Grana Visión to learn if any newly developed options are available.

FLAMENCO　The best flamenco show in Granada is staged at **Sala de Fiesta Alhambra,** Carretera de Jaén, Polígono Industrial Olinda (② **95-841-22-69**), nightly at 10:15pm. The acts are a bit racy, even though they've been toned down considerably for today's audiences. In addition to flamenco, performers attired in regional garb do folk dances and give guitar concerts. The show takes place in a garden setting. There's a high cover charge of 23€, which includes a drink you can nurse all evening. It's best to take a taxi here.

DANCE CLUBS　If you eventually tire of bodega-crawling, you might be tempted as the night progresses to go dancing in the town's most popular disco: **Granada 10,** Calle Carcel Baja 10 (② **95-822-40-01**), open daily from 12:30am to 5am. It charges 6€ entrance, including the first drink.

GAY BARS　Granada has a number of bars that aren't exclusively gay but draw a mixed crowd of homosexual and straight locals and foreigners. One of the best bets is **Al Pie de la Vela,** Calle del Darro 35 (② **95-822-85-39**), a cruisy bar attracting a mostly male clientele of mixed ages, though the 18-to-28 set seems to predominate. The club is open nightly from 9:30pm to 4am.

9

The Costa del Sol

The mild winter climate and almost-guaranteed summer sunshine have made this razzle-dazzle stretch of Mediterranean shoreline known as the **Costa del Sol** a year-round attraction. From the harbor city of Algeciras it stretches east to the port city of Almería. Sandwiched in between is a steep, rugged coastline set against the Sierra Nevada. You'll find poor to fair beaches, sandy coves, whitewashed houses, olive trees, lots of new apartment houses, fishing boats, golf courses, souvenir stands, fast-food outlets, and widely varied populations—both human and vegetable.

This coastal strip, quite frankly, no longer enjoys the chic reputation it had in Franco's day. It's overbuilt and spoiled, though you can still find pockets of posh (including Puerto Banús, with its yacht-clogged harbor). One advantage of the area is that, thanks to European Union money, it's easier to get around than ever before. The infamous N-340 highway from Málaga to Estepona has become a fast, safe six-lane road. In days of yore, it was the most dangerous highway in Spain.

The coast is even better for **golf** than for beaches. The best resorts are **Los Monteros** (© **95-277-17-00**), in Marbella, which is the leading course; **Parador Nacional del Golf** (© **95-238-12-55**), between Málaga and Torremolinos; **Hotel Atalaya Park** in Estepona (© **95-288-90-00**); and **Golf Hotel Guadalmina** in Marbella (© **95-288-22-11**). To learn more, pick up a copy of the monthly magazine *Costa Golf* at any newsstand. Many golfers prefer to play a different course at every hotel. Usually, if you notify your hotel reception desk a day in advance, a staff member will arrange a playing time.

Water-skiing and windsurfing are available in every resort, and all types of boats can be rented from various kiosks at all the main beaches. You don't have to search hard for these outfitters—chances are they'll find you.

From June to October the coast is mobbed, so make sure you have a reservation in advance. And keep in mind that October 12 is a national holiday—visitors should make doubly sure of their reservations. At other times, innkeepers are likely to roll out the red carpet.

Many restaurants close around October 15 for a much-needed vacation. Remember, too, that many supermarkets and other facilities are closed on Sunday.

1 Algeciras

679km (422 miles) S of Madrid, 132km (82 miles) W of Málaga

Not really a destination in and of itself, **Algeciras** is the jumping-off point for Africa—it's only 3 hours to Tangier, Morocco. If you're planning an excursion, there's an inexpensive baggage storage depot at the ferry terminal. Algeciras is also a base for day trips to **Gibraltar.** For information, check with the Gibraltar

Tourist Office, Casemates Square ((C) **95-677-49-82**). It's open Monday through Friday from 9am to 5pm, Saturday and Sunday from 10am to 4pm. If you don't have time to visit "the Rock," you can at least see it from Algeciras—it's only 10km (6 miles) away.

ESSENTIALS

GETTING THERE & DEPARTING   The local RENFE office is at Calle Juan de la Cierva ((C) **90-224-02-02**). From Madrid, five **trains** daily make the 6-hour trip; the fare is 32€. From Málaga, you have to transfer in Bobadillo; the fare is 16€. The trip takes 3½ hours and runs along most of the Costa del Sol, including Marbella and Torremolinos.

Various independent **bus companies** serve Algeciras. Empresa Portillo, Av. Virgen de Carmen 15 ((C) **95-665-10-55**), 1½ blocks to the right when you exit the port complex, runs nearly a dozen buses a day along the Costa del Sol to Algeciras from Málaga. It also sends two buses a day to Córdoba (6 hr.) and two buses a day to Granada (5 hr.). To make connections to or from Seville, use Line Sur, Calle Juan de la Cierva 5 ((C) **95-665-34-56**). Six buses a day go to Jerez de la Frontera, and eleven to Seville. **Transportes Generales Comes,** Hotel Octavio, Calle San Bernardo 1 ((C) **95-665-34-56**), sells tickets to **La Línea,** the border station for the approach to Gibraltar.

⎛Tips   Beaches: The Good, the Bad & the Ugly

We'd like to report that the Costa del Sol is a paradise for swimmers. Surprisingly, it isn't, although it was the allure of beaches that origi- nally put the "sol" in the Costa del Sol beginning in the 1950s.

The worst beaches—mainly pebbles and shingles—are at Nerja, Málaga, and Almuñécar. Moving westward, you encounter the gritty, grayish sands of Torremolinos. The best beaches here are at El Bajondillo and La Carihuela (which borders an old fishing village). Another good stretch of beach is along the meandering strip between Carvajal, Los Boliches, and Fuengirola. In addition, two good beaches—El Fuerte and La Fontanilla—lie on either side of Marbella. However, all these beaches tend to be overcrowded, especially in July and August when mama and papa from the hinterlands take the kids to the beach. Crowding is worst on Sundays May through October when beaches are overrun with family picnickers as well as sunbathers.

All public beaches in Spain are free, and you shouldn't expect changing facilities. There might be a cold shower on the major beaches, but that's it.

Although it's not sanctioned or technically allowed by the govern- ment, many women go topless on the beaches. Nudity is common on some of the less frequented beaches, although it is against the law; if you indulge, you will be subject to arrest by the civil guard. Many bathers flout the law and go nude anyway, but it's not advised. If you want to bare it all, head for the Costa Natura, about 3km (2 miles) west of Estepona. This is the site of the only official nudist colony along the Costa del Sol.

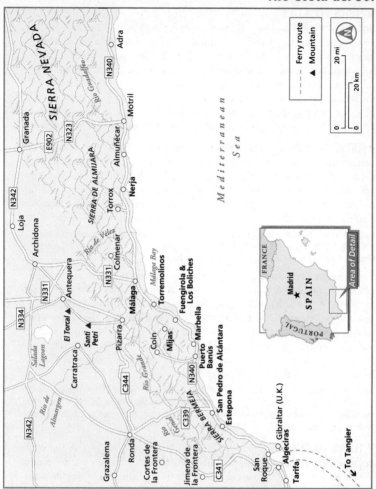

Most visitors in Algeciras plan to cross to Tangier, Morocco. **Ferries** leave every hour on the hour daily from 8am to 10pm. A Class A ticket costs 28€ per person, a Class B ticket 23€. To transport a **car** costs at least 72€ per vehicle, and cars aren't transported in stormy weather. Discounts are available: 20% for Eurailpass holders, 30% for InterRail pass holders, and 50% for children. The price of tickets is the same at the dozens of travel agencies scattered throughout the town; don't bother shopping around. For more ferry information call *©* **95-666-60-61** or 90-245-46-45.

Carretera de Cádiz (E-15/N-340) runs from Málaga west to Algeciras. If you're driving south from Seville (or Madrid), take highway N-IV to Cádiz, then connect with the N-340/E-5 southwest to Algeciras.

VISITOR INFORMATION   The **tourist office** at Juan de la Cierva (*©* **95-657-26-36;** www.andalusia.org) is open Monday through Friday from 9am to 2pm.

WHERE TO STAY

Hotel Alarde ★★★ *Value* If you want to get away from the tacky, noisy port area, consider staying at this hotel near the Parque María Cristina. It's a central location in a quiet commercial section of town. The small double rooms have balconies and Andalusian-style furnishings, including bathrooms with tub/shower combos. During our most recent stay we were impressed with both the staff and the inviting atmosphere.

Alfonso XI 4, 11201 Algeciras. ⓒ **95-666-04-08.** Fax 95-665-49-01. 68 units. 67€–80€ double. AE, DC, MC, V. Parking 6€. **Amenities:** Restaurant; bar; babysitting; laundry service; dry cleaning. *In room:* A/C, TV, safe.

Hotel Al-Mar ★★★ The government-rated three-star Al-Mar is one of the best choices in town, with better rooms than the Alarde. It's near the port, where the ferries embark for Ceuta and Tangier. This large hotel boasts blue-and-white Sevillian and Moorish decor. The midsize guest rooms are well maintained, furnished in an Andalusian style, with good beds and bathrooms with tub/shower combos. A fourth-floor drawing room provides a panoramic view of the Rock.

Av. de la Marina 2, 11201 Algeciras. ⓒ **95-665-46-61.** Fax 95-665-45-01. www.eh.etursa.es/almar. 192 units. 72€–74€ double; from 75€–77€ suite. Rates include breakfast. AE, DC, MC, V. Parking 7€. **Amenities:** Restaurant; bar; babysitting; laundry service; dry cleaning. *In room:* A/C, TV, hair dryer, safe.

Hotel Reina Cristina ★★ In its own park on the southern outskirts of the city (a 10-min. walk south of the rail and bus stations), this is the town's leading hotel. A Victorian building accented with turrets, ornate railings, and a facade appropriately painted with pastels, the Reina Cristina offers a view of the faraway Rock of Gibraltar. On the premises are a small English-language library and a semitropical garden held in place with sturdy retaining walls. The comfortable, high-ceilinged rooms have excellent furnishings, including comfortable beds and bathrooms with tub/shower combos.

Paseo de la Conferencia, 11207 Algeciras. ⓒ **95-660-26-22.** Fax 95-660-33-23. www.reinacristina.com. 187 units. 62€–97€ double; from 209€–310€ suite. Rates include breakfast. AE, DC, MC, V. Free parking. **Amenities:** 2 restaurants; 2 bars; 2 pools; tennis courts; health spa; sauna; room service; babysitting; laundry service; dry cleaning. *In room:* A/C, TV, hair dryer, safe.

WHERE TO DINE

Because Algeciras is not distinguished for its restaurants, many visitors dine at their hotels instead of taking a chance at the dreary little spots along the waterfront.

Asador Iruña SPANISH Your most reliable meal will be at the Reina Cristina (see hotel recommendation, above), but if you'd like to chance an independent eatery, this is the best of the lackluster lot. It provides a soothing respite from the industrial port's dust, noise, and heat with a menu that incorporates some of Spain's most popular dishes. Dishes are hearty and filling, but not a lot more. Expect hearty soups, grilled beefsteak, roast chicken, Spanish sausages, and veal. Fish is fresh and flavorful, and local fish includes hake, swordfish, squid, octopus, red snapper, mullet, and cod.

Alfonso XI 11, 11100 Algeciras. ⓒ **95-665-21-49.** Main courses 12€–24€. AE, DC, MC, V. Daily 11am–4:30pm and 8pm–1am.

2 Tarifa

23km (14 miles) W of Algeciras, 713km (443 miles) S of Madrid, 98km (61 miles) SE of Cádiz

Instead of heading east from Algeciras along the Costa del Sol, we suggest a visit west to **Tarifa.** This old Moorish town is the southernmost point in Europe.

After leaving Algeciras, the roads climb steeply and the drive to Tarifa is along one of Europe's most splendid coastal routes. In the distance you'll see Gibraltar, the straits, and the green hills of Africa—in fact, you can sometimes get a glimpse of houses in Ceuta and Tangier on the Moroccan coastline.

Named for the Moorish military hero Tarik, Tarifa has retained more of its Arab character than any other town in Andalusia. Narrow cobblestone streets lead to charming patios filled with flowers. The main square is the Plaza San Mateo.

Two factors have inhibited the development of Tarifa's beautiful 5km (3-mile) white beach, the Playa de Lances: It's still a Spanish military zone, and the wind blows almost half the time. For windsurfers, though, the strong western breezes are unbeatable. Tarifa is filled with shops that rent windsurfing equipment and give advice about the best locales.

Many visitors also come to see Tarifa's historical artifacts and wander the crumbling city ramparts. The **Castello Tarifa,** site of a famous struggle in 1292 between Moors and Christians, dominates the town. The castle was held by Guzmán el Bueno ("the Good"). When Christians captured his 9-year-old son and demanded surrender of the garrison, Guzmán tossed the Spanish a dagger, saying he preferred "honor without a son, to a son with dishonor." The execution was carried out. Sadly, the castle is not open to the public.

 Teeing Off: A Golden Triangle of Golf

Faced with more than 40 places to take a swing on the Costa del Sol, golfers are often overwhelmed by the choice of courses, as many are championship venues. Depending on where you're staying, it may take some driving time to get to them, but here is a trio of courses that rank among the greatest in Europe, with no apologies to Scotland.

- **San Roque Club,** Urbanización San Roque, Carretera N-340, Km 126.5, Sotogrande-San Roque (℗ **95-661-30-30**), was created by two Englishmen, former Ryder Cup players Tony Jacklin and Dave Thomas, on the grounds of the summer palace of the Domecq sherry dynasty. The back nine features two of the finest holes along the coast.

- **Club de Golf Valderrama,** Av. de los Cortijos 1, Sotogrande-San Roque (℗ **95-679-12-00**), is in our view *número uno* among the golf courses of continental Europe. Daring, dramatic, demanding, according to *Golf World,* as we concur, the course was first designed by the grand old man himself, Robert Trent Jones Sr. Steve Ballesteros, called "the Arnold Palmer of Spain," designed the most notorious 17th hole, called by Ryder Cup players "one of the most strategically challenging holes in the world." Pines and cork trees keep the par-72 course wickedly challenging.

- **Real Club de Golf Sotogrande,** Paseo del Parque, Sotogrande (℗ **95-678-50-14**) is a par-72 course also laid out originally by Robert Trent Jones Sr. Its 11th hole is buffeted by two prevailing winds blowing in different directions. Many of the fairways are 40 yards to 50 yards long, and the course is riddled with shimmering lakes evocative of Florida.

From Algeciras, **Transporres Generales Comes,** Calle San Bernardo 1 (✆ **95-665-34-56**), under the Hotel Octavio runs several buses daily to Tarifa. The trip takes 30 minutes and costs 2€. To drive, take the Cádiz highway, N-340/E-5, west from Algeciras.

WHERE TO STAY & DINE

Balcón de España   For food and overnight comfort, no inn in the area matches "the balcony of Spain." A surrounding park envelops the inn lying 8km (5 miles) north of Tarifa. The bedrooms are midsize and well kept with tidy bathrooms with tub and shower. Some guests prefer to stay in one of the equally comfortable outlying bungalows. The staff can arrange horseback riding from a stable nearby if you picture yourself an Andalusian equestrian. The hotel offers the best Andalusian cuisine in the area, even better than its leading rival, Mesón de Sancho. If you're traveling through the area by day, you can stop in here for lunch.

La Peña 2, Carretera Cádiz-Málaga Km 77, 11380 Tarifa. ✆ **95-668-09-63**. Fax 95-668-04-72. www.balcondespana.com. 38 units. 66€–100€. AE, MC, V. Free parking. Closed Oct 25, Nov–Apr 24. **Amenities:** Restaurant; bar; pool; tennis courts; room service; laundry. In room: TV.

Mesón de Sancho   We'd give a slight edge to the Balcón de España because of its beautiful garden and situation. Other than that competition, this hacienda is the second best in the area, housing you in style and comfort at a point 16km (10 miles) southwest of Algeciras and 10.5km (6½ miles) northeast of Tarifa on the road to Cádiz. An informal inn with good beds and excellent regional food, it also offers a pool surrounded by olive trees and terraces. The hotel still evokes the era (1955) in which it was built, but it was last renovated in 1995. The small rooms are modest but streamlined, each with a small tiled bathroom with tub and shower. The provincial dining room overlooks the garden.

N-340, Km 94, 11380 Tarifa. ✆ **95-668-49-00**. Fax 95-668-47-21. www.mesondesancho.com. 40 units. 43€–66€. AE, DC, MC, V. Free parking. **Amenities:** Restaurant; bar/cafe; pool; tennis; room service; laundry service; garden terrace. In room: TV, minibar, hair dryer.

3 Estepona

85km (53 miles) W of Málaga, 639km (397 miles) S of Madrid, 46km (29 miles) E of Algeciras

A town of Roman origin, Estepona is a budding beach resort, less developed than Marbella or Torremolinos and more likable for that reason. Estepona contains an interesting 15th-century parish church, with the ruins of an old aqueduct nearby (at Salduba). Its recreational port is an attraction, as are its **beaches:** Costa Natura, Km 257 on the N-340, the first legal nude beach of its kind along the Costa del Sol; La Rada, 3km (2 miles) long; and El Cristo, only 550m (600 yd.) long. After the sun goes down, stroll along the Paseo Marítimo, a broad avenue with gardens on one side, beach on the other.

In summer, the cheapest places to eat in Estepona are the *merenderos,* little dining areas set up by local fishers and their families right on the beach. Naturally they feature seafood, including sole and sardine kebabs grilled over an open fire. You can usually order a fresh salad and fried potatoes; desserts are simple.

After your siesta, head for the tapas bars. You'll find most of them—called *freidurías* (fried-fish bars)—at the corner of Calle de los Reyes and La Terraza. Tables spill onto the sidewalks in summer, and *gambas a la plancha* (shrimp) are the favorite (but not the cheapest) tapas to order.

ESSENTIALS

GETTING THERE   The nearest rail links are in Algeciras. However, Estepona is on the bus route from Algeciras to Málaga. If you're driving, head east from Algeciras along the E-5/N-340.

VISITOR INFORMATION   The **tourist office,** Av. San Lorenzo 1 (© **95-280-20-02;** www.infoestepona.com), is open Monday through Friday from 9am to 6pm, Saturday 9am to 1:30pm.

WHERE TO STAY

Atalaya Park Golf Hotel & Resort ✦✦   Located midway between Estepona and Marbella, this modern resort complex attracts sports and nature lovers. Its tranquil beachside location sits amid 8 hectares (20 acres) of subtropical gardens. Spacious rooms furnished in elegant modern style are well maintained and inviting. All units have neatly kept bathrooms with tub/shower combos. Guests have complimentary use of the hotel's extensive sports facilities. Many guests from northern Europe check in and almost never leave the grounds.

Carretera de Cádiz, Km 168.5, 29688 Estepona. © **95-288-90-00.** Fax 95-288-90-02. www.atalaya-park.es. 469 units. 119€–181€ double; 189€–271€ suite. Rates include breakfast. AE, DC, MC, V. Free parking. **Amenities:** 4 restaurants; 2 bars; nightclub; 2 pools; golf course; tennis courts; health club; sauna; solarium; car rental; room service; babysitting; laundry service; dry cleaning. *In room:* A/C, TV, minibar, hair dryer, safe.

Buenavista   This comfortable if modest little *residencia* beside the coastal road opened in the 1970s. The tiny rooms are likely to be noisy in summer because of heavy traffic nearby. Beds are comfortable, and the little bathrooms have shower stalls. Buses from Marbella stop nearby.

Av. de España 180, 29680 Estepona. © **95-280-01-37.** Fax 95-280-55-93. 38 units. 45€–60€ double. AE, MC, V. **Amenities:** Restaurant. *In room:* TV.

Kempinski Resort Hotel ✦✦✦   One of the most luxurious retreats in this part of the Costa del Sol, this modern resort hotel offers a lush and elegant way of life. Situated between the main coastal route and the beach, this resort borrowed heavily from nearby Morocco in Africa to create this oasis of charm and grace with hanging gardens adding the most dramatic touch. A member of "The Leading Hotels of the World," the property opens onto beautifully landscaped and luxuriant palm-studded gardens fronting the ocean. Bedrooms are airy and spacious, furnished in grand comfort with balconies or private terraces overlooking the sea. Each comes with a deluxe bathroom with tub and shower and all the fixings. Many expats who live in the area flock here for the Sunday afternoon jazz brunch, the most elaborate at the western part of the Costa del Sol, with a live band playing that New Orleans sound. Some top European chefs create a cuisine that is ever changing and ever good, with carefully crafted regional specialties and well-executed international dishes.

Carretera de Cádiz, Km 159, Playa el Padrón, 29680 Estepona. © **95-280-95-00.** Fax 95-280-95-50. 148 units. 315€–495€ double; 575€–685€ junior suite; from 735€ suite. AE, DC, MC, V. **Amenities:** 3 restaurants; 3 bars; 4 pools (1 indoor); tennis court; fitness center; gym; spa; sauna; salon; 24-hr. room service; babysitting; laundry/dry cleaning. *In room:* A/C, TV, minibar, hair dryer.

Las Dunas ✦✦✦   One of the great hotels of the Costa del Sol and a member of the "Leading Hotels of the World," Las Dunas attracts fashionable Europeans pursuing the pampered life. Site of a world-class spa and one of the area's newest resorts, the five-star government-rated hotel is constructed in a U-shape, evocative of a gigantic hacienda. It stands in the midst of gardens and fountains; regrettably, the beach nearby is mediocre. Suites outnumber standard doubles, and most units have balconies overlooking the Mediterranean. All are sumptuously comfortable and equipped with roomy bathrooms containing tub/shower combos.

Urbanización La Boladilla Baja-Noreste, Carretera de Cádiz, Km 163.5, 29689 Estepona. (C) **95-279-43-45.** Fax 95-279-48-25. www.las-dunas.com. 73 units. 180€–355€ double; 305€–370€ junior suite; from 880€ suite. Free parking. **Amenities:** 2 restaurants; bar; pool; health club; sauna; whirlpool; spa; room service; babysitting; laundry service; dry cleaning; library. *In room:* A/C, TV, minibar, hair dryer, safe.

WHERE TO DINE

La Alcaria de Ramos *(Finds* SPANISH   Your best meal in Estepona is awaiting you at this restaurant on the outskirts of the resort en route to San Pedro. This country retreat has been decorated in the style of an old summerhouse along the Spanish coast. There's a beautiful terrace garden where customers may dine as weather permits. The chef and owner, José Ramos, has won many national gastronomic competitions, and has been creating intriguing variations on traditional recipes since the early 1990s. He will regale you with such dishes as *tortas de patatas* (potato cakes—yes, potato cakes, and how good they are!). Try also his *crepes de aguacate con gambas* (avocado crepes with shrimp) and his *pato asado con puré de manzana y col roja* (grilled duck with apple purée and red cabbage). Also worth ordering is the *parrillada de pescado y mariscos* (assorted grilled fish and shellfish). For dessert try his clever concoction *helado frito con frambuesa* (fried ice cream with raspberry sauce).

Urbanización El Paraíso Vista al Mar 1, N-340 Km 167. (C) **95-288-61-78.** Reservations recommended. Main courses 9€–18€. MC, V. Mon–Sat 7:30pm–midnight.

Lido INTERNATIONAL   In the deluxe Hotel Las Dunas (see above), one of the grandest and most elegant restaurants along the Costa del Sol holds forth. With panoramic views, romantic piano tunes, and savory food, you are launched into your dinner with a rousing yet nuanced cuisine. The main part of the restaurant is octagonal, with floor-to-ceiling windows opening onto a sheltered terrace. Carefully chosen artwork and a mammoth crystal chandelier set a tony texture. Expect nothing but culinary delights on the ever-changing menu. Some of the dishes evoke the Pacific Rim, others draw upon inspiration from Europe—a sort of "Euro-Asiatique" cuisine.

Only the finest products are used: duck from Nantes, lamb from Provence, beef and veal from Spain's Basque country, or tender and delectable chicken from Bresse (in our view, Europe's best). Picture it: sea bass carpaccio in a basil vinaigrette, fresh lobster in delicate saffron sauce, veal sweetbreads with *fines herbs.* Can you resist the crepes with a Grand Marnier froth filling and a sauce made from blood-red oranges? If memory serves, the chilled lemon grass crème brûlée with chilled mocha cream and fat, juicy raspberries is better than our grandma made.

Urbanización La Boladilla Baja-Noreste, Carretera de Cádiz Km 163.5. (C) **95-279-43-45.** Reservations required. Main courses 25€–29€; set menus 50€ for 3 courses, 70€ for 5 courses. AE, DC, MC, V. Daily 8–11pm. Closed mid-Jan to mid-Feb.

4 Puerto Banús

8km (5 miles) E of Marbella, 782km (486 miles) S of Madrid

A favorite resort for international celebrities, the coastal village of **Puerto Banús** was created almost overnight in the traditional Mediterranean style. It's a dreamy place, the very image of what a Costa del Sol fishing village should look like, but rarely does. Yachts can be moored nearly at your doorstep. Along the harbor front you'll find an array of expensive bars and restaurants. Wandering through the quiet back streets, you'll pass archways and patios with grilles.

To reach the town, you can take one of 15 buses that run daily from Marbella or drive east from Marbella along the E-15.

WHERE TO DINE

Antonio ✦ SEAFOOD/INTERNATIONAL   There's no better place to sit and watch the chic port life of Puerto Banús than this long-time favorite. One day we spotted at least two chicly but casually dressed women getting off yachts who were dead ringers for the late Jackie O. Opt for a table on the terrace if the weather's right and watch the parade of beautiful people who live in the elegant pages of *Departures* magazine—that is, those who believe in traveling the world in style and have the money to do so. Fortunately, the first-class cuisine here matches the setting, with lots of modern paintings on the wall, an abundance of greenery, and predominant colors of black and white.

The chefs know how to balance colors, textures, and flavors, creating such tasty fare as the best filet mignon we've tasted in the area along with old favorites such as well-flavored pork chops with fries and vegetables. The loin of veal is tender, moist, and perfectly seasoned, but our all-time favorite here is sea bass baked in salt to retain its moisture and aroma. A lot depends on the catch of the day. Perhaps it'll be a delectable sea bream or else *rape* (monkfish) fashioned into a tantalizing kabob over the grill.

Muella de Ribera. ✆ **95-281-35-36**. Reservations required. Main courses 11€–23€. AE, DC, MC, V. Daily 1–4pm and 7:30–11pm (until 1:30am July–Sept).

Dalli's Pizza Factory *Value* PASTA   The California-inspired philosophy at Dalli's offers a new way to save pesetas in high-priced Puerto Banús. Its specialty is pasta, pasta, and more pasta—served with a portion of garlic bread and a carafe of house wine, it's a great bargain. In a setting that's a cross between high-tech and Art Deco, you can order nutmeg-flavored ravioli with spinach filling, *penne all'arrabbiata*, lasagna, and several kinds of spaghetti. More filling are the chicken cacciatore and scaloppine of chicken and veal. They are served with—guess what?—pasta as a side dish. The owners, incidentally, are a trio of Roman-born brothers who were reared in England and educated in California.

Muelle de Rivera. ✆ **95-281-86-23**. Pastas 10€–15€; meat platters 13€–20€. AE, MC, V. Daily 1pm–1am.

Don Leone INTERNATIONAL   Many residents in villas around Marbella drive to this luxuriously decorated dockside restaurant for dinner, and it gets crowded at times. Begin with the house minestrone, then follow with pasta in clam sauce; lasagna is also a regular treat. Meat specialties include veal parmigiana and roast baby lamb, and the fish dishes are also worth a try, especially the *frita mixta de pescados* (mixed fish fry). The food is competently prepared with fresh ingredients, although at times it fails to capture authentic Spanish flavor. The wine list is one of the best along the coast.

Muelle de Rivera 44. ✆ **95-281-17-16**. Reservations recommended. Main courses 16€–20€. AE, MC, V. Daily 1–4pm and 8pm–midnight, only open for dinner Oct–Nov 21. Closed Nov 21–Dec 21.

5 Marbella ⧆

60km (37 miles) W of Málaga, 45km (28 miles) W of Torremolinos, 80km (50 miles) E of Gibraltar, 76km (47 miles) E of Algeciras, 600km (373 miles) S of Madrid

Although it's packed with tourists and only slightly less popular than Torremolinos, **Marbella** is still the nicest resort along the Costa del Sol, with some of the region's best upscale resorts coexisting with budget hotels. Despite the hordes, Marbella remains what it has always been, a pleasant Andalusian town at the foot of the Sierra Blanca. Traces of its past survive in its palatial town hall, medieval ruins, and ancient Moorish walls. Marbella's most charming area is the **old quarter,** with narrow cobblestone streets and Arab houses, centered on the Plaza de los Naranjos.

The biggest attractions in Marbella, however, are **El Fuerte** and **La Fontanilla,** the two main beaches. There are other, more secluded beaches, but you need your own transportation to get there.

A long-ago visitor, Queen Isabella, was said to have exclaimed, *"¡Qué mar tan bello!"* ("What a beautiful sea!"), and the name stuck.

ESSENTIALS

GETTING THERE   Twenty **buses** run between Málaga and Marbella daily. Three buses each come from Madrid and Barcelona. The bus station is located on the outskirts of Marbella on Avenida Trapiche, a 5-minute ride from the center of town.

If you're driving, Marbella is the first major resort as you head east on the N-340/E-15 from Algeciras.

VISITOR INFORMATION   The **tourist office,** Glorieta de la Fontanilla s/n (© **95-277-14-42;** www.turismomarbella.com), is open Monday through Friday from 9:30am to 9pm, Saturday from 10am to 2pm. Another tourist office with the same hours is on the Plaza de los Naranjos (© **95-282-35-50**).

SHOPPING

Some other Andalusian village may inspire you to buy handicrafts (particularly pottery, woodcarvings, or wrought iron), but Marbella's international glamour might just incite so much insecurity about your wardrobe that you'll want to rush out to accessorize. Should you suddenly feel underdressed, head for the old town. The cornucopia of fashion outlets includes, among many top European designers, every Hollywood starlet's favorite emporium, **Versace,** in the Centro Commercial Benabola 8, Puerto Banús (© **95-281-02-96**).

If art is your passion, tour the art galleries that pepper the town. You'll spot high-rolling investors picking up contemporary treasures as part of a holiday shopping spree. Two of Marbella's most appealing art galleries lie in the old town: the **Galleria d'Arte Van Gestel,** Plaza de los Naranjos 11 (© **95-277-48-19**), and **Galleria H,** Calle 3D (© **95-281-12-60**). And if your search for fine art carries over to **Puerto Banús,** consider an overview of the contemporary artwork displayed at the **Sammer Gallery,** Av. de Rivera, Las Terrazas de Banús, Local 10–16 (© **95-281-29-95**). If you'd like to purchase some of Andalusia's regional ceramics, your best bet is **Cerámica San Nicolás,** Plaza de la Iglesia 1 (© **95-277-05-46**).

On Saturday morning, forget the shops and head with the locals to **Nueva Andalucía flea market.** Everything is likely to be on sale, from Spanish leather goods to local pottery and embroideries.

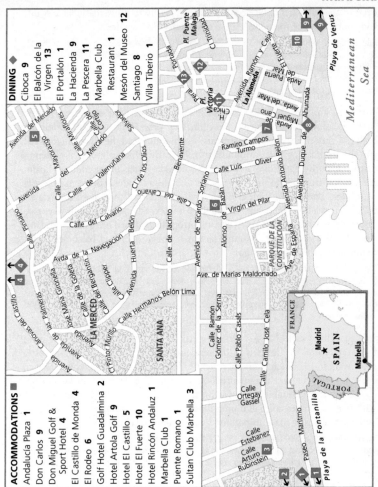

DINING ◆
Ciboca **9**
El Balcón de la
Virgen **13**
El Portalón **1**
La Hacienda **9**
La Pescera **11**
Marbella Club
Restaurant **1**
Mesón del Museo **12**
Santiago **8**
Villa Tiberio **1**

ACCOMMODATIONS ■
Andalucía Plaza **1**
Don Carlos **9**
Don Miguel Golf &
Sport Hotel **4**
El Castillo de Monda **4**
El Rodeo **6**
Golf Hotel Guadalmina **2**
Hotel Artola Golf **9**
Hotel El Castillo **5**
Hotel El Fuerte **10**
Hotel Rincón Andaluz **1**
Marbella Club **1**
Puente Romano **1**
Sultan Club Marbella **3**

WHERE TO STAY

Because the setting is ideal, some of the best hotels along the Costa del Sol are in Marbella.

VERY EXPENSIVE

Marbella Club ★★★   This is the grande dame of all Costa del Sol resorts. Until a few equally chic hotels were built along the Costa del Sol, the snobbish Marbella Club reigned almost without equal as the exclusive hangout of aristocrats and tycoons. Established in 1954, the resort sprawls over a landscaped property that slopes from its roadside reception area down to the private beach. Composed of small, ecologically conscious clusters of garden pavilions, bungalows, and small-scale annexes, the Marbella Club has some of the loveliest gardens along the coast. Hotel rooms along the Costa del Sol don't come much better than these varied and spacious choices, often with canopy beds. Most of the bathrooms are roomy, with dual basins and tub/shower combos. Rooms have private balconies or terraces. The clientele is discreet, international, elegant, and appreciative of the resort's small scale and superb service.

Bulevar Príncipe Alfonso von Hohenlohe s/n, 29600 Marbella. ✆ 800/448-8355 in the U.S., or 95-282-22-11. Fax 95-282-98-84. www.marbellaclub.com. 160 units. 240€–620€ double; 330€–1,720€ suite; 990€–3,500€ bungalow. AE, DC, MC, V. Free parking. **Amenities:** Restaurant (see "Where to Dine," later in this chapter); bar; 2 pools; room service; massage; babysitting; laundry service; dry cleaning; private beach. *In room:* A/C, TV, minibar, hair dryer, safe.

Puente Romano ⭐⭐   Its devotees rank this resort right up there with the Marbella Club, but we'd give it the runner-up prize. This hotel was originally built as a cluster of vacation apartments, which influenced the attention to detail and the landscaping that surrounds it. In the early 1970s, a group of entrepreneurs transformed it into one of the most unusual hotels in the south of Spain. Although it sits close to the frenetic coastal highway midway between Marbella and Puerto Banús, and some critics have dismissed it as "more flash than class," it still enjoys a loyal following. Inside the complex, arbor-covered walkways pass cascading water, masses of vines, and a subtropical garden. The spacious Andalusian-Mediterranean-style accommodations have semisheltered balconies. Bathrooms have tub/shower combos.

Carretera de Cádiz, Km 177, 29600 Marbella. ✆ 800/448-8355 in the U.S., or 95-282-09-00. Fax 95-277-57-66. www.puenteromano.com. 274 units. 205€–460€ double; 244€–2,300€ suite. AE, DC, MC, V. Free parking. By car, take the E-15 4km (2½ miles) west of Marbella. **Amenities:** Restaurant; bar; pool; tennis courts; health club; sauna; room service; babysitting; laundry service; dry cleaning; solarium. *In room:* A/C, TV, minibar, hair dryer, safe.

Sultan Club Marbella ⭐   On the outskirts of Marbella a 10-minute drive from the center, this hotel is in the residential district of Milla de Oro, just a short walk to the beach. This apartment hotel opened in 1997 and is meant to evoke luxury living like the sultans of old enjoyed. The interior brims with tropical plants and fountains. The apartments contain one or two bedrooms, each with large balconies, a small dining room, and a fully equipped kitchen, along with such extras as spacious bathrooms with tub/shower combos.

Av. Arturo Rubenstein, 29600 Marbella. ✆ 95-277-15-62. Fax 95-277-55-58. www.monarquehoteles.es. 76 units. 90€ 1-bedroom apt; 290€ 2-bedroom apt. AE, DC, MC, V. Parking 8€. **Amenities:** Restaurant; bar; pool; health club; sauna; whirlpool; children's center; room service; massage; babysitting; laundry service; dry cleaning. *In room:* A/C, TV, minibar, hair dryer, safe.

EXPENSIVE

Don Carlos ⭐⭐   One of the most dramatic hotels on the coast, the Don Carlos rises on a set of angled stilts above a pine forest. Between the hotel and its manicured beach, the best in Marbella, are 53 hectares (130 acres) of award-winning gardens. With cascades of water and thousands of subtropical plants, they require a full-time staff of 22 gardeners. The hotel's low-lying terraces attract high-powered conferences from throughout Europe. Each of the roomy accommodations has lacquered furniture, and bathrooms boast tub/shower combos.

Carretera de Cádiz, Km 192, 29600 Marbella. ✆ 95-283-11-40. Fax 95-283-34-29. www.hotel-doncarlos.com. 153€–315€ double; 231€–915€ suite. AE, DC, MC, V. Free parking. **Amenities:** 2 restaurants; 2 bars; 2 pools; 11 tennis courts; health club; sauna; room service; babysitting; laundry service; dry cleaning. *In room:* A/C, TV, minibar, hair dryer, safe.

Don Miguel Golf & Sport Hotel ⭐⭐   At the foot of the mountain overlooking Marbella, this deluxe hotel with an 18-hole golf course rises over a scenic location a 20-minute walk from Marbella's center. It's giving other government-rated four-star hotels serious competition. From the terrace of the rooms and suites, the sea or mountain view is panoramic. The subtropical gardens are among the most spectacular along the coast, and swimming pools and golf dominate the activity calendar. The tennis club is the best along the coast, as is a state-of-the-art sports center. Rooms are beautifully styled and spacious; bathrooms have tub/shower combos.

The restaurants serve first-class Andalusian and international food, with top rated chefs in the kitchen.

Camino del Trapiche, 29600 Marbella. © 95-105-90-00. Fax 95-105-90-03. www.don-miguel.net. 501 units. 262€–344€ double; 332€–414€ suite. Rates include breakfast. AE, DC, MC, V. **Amenities:** 3 restaurants; 5 bars; nightclub/disco; 2 pools; golf course; 16 tennis courts; gym; sauna; room service; babysitting; laundry service; dry cleaning. *In room:* A/C, TV, minibar, hair dryer, safe.

Golf Hotel Guadalmina *Kids*   In the residential area of Guadalmina, right outside Marbella, this resort hotel is surrounded by two scenic golf courses and the Mediterranean. The hotel has long been a landmark on the coast, but was closed at the turn of the millennium for a wholesale renovation and expansion. Today it is better than ever. All the accommodations, both in the original building and in a new 91-wing, are midsize to spacious. Bedrooms are comfortable and well furnished, and the decor is typical Andalusian. Rooms open onto the sea (the most desirable), the golf courses, or the hotel's gardens. Both a Spanish and an international cuisine are served at the first-class La Terraza. Golfers check in here in droves, as Guadalmina is one of the golf pioneers along the coast. Many families have taught their children to swim in the hotel's impressively large pool. If that fails, there is also a kiddie pool that's securely shallow. Movie-goers might already recognize the resort. The film *A Touch of Class* was filmed here, starring Glenda Jackson, who received an Oscar for best actress.

Urb. Guadalmina Baja, 29678 Marbella. © 95-288-22-11. Fax 95-288-22-91. www.hotelguadalmina.com. 179 units. 192€ double; 276€ junior suite; 602€ suite. AE, DC, MC, V. **Amenities:** Restaurant; bar; 2 pools; fitness center; babysitting; laundry/dry cleaning; room service. *In room:* A/C, TV, minibar, hair dryer, safe.

MODERATE

Hotel Artola Golf   Between Fuengirola and Marbella, .8km (½ mile) from the beach, this charming place was originally an old staging post for travelers en route to Gibraltar. In the 1970s it was converted into an inn. The architecture is typically Andalusian, with a stucco and wood facade under a terra-cotta roof. A garden and patio surround the building. The interior decoration has retained some of its historical aura with colorful tiles plus decorative wooden wall panels and beams. The midsize rooms are comfortably furnished and tastefully decorated, often with Moorish details. All units have balconies and fully equipped bathrooms with tub/shower combos.

Carretera de Cádiz, Km 194, 29600 Marbella. © 95-283-13-90. Fax 95-283-04-50. 35 units. 77€–100€ double; 123€–146€ suite. AE, MC, V. Free parking. **Amenities:** Bar; pool; golf course; room service; babysitting. *In room:* A/C (in some), TV, minibar, hair dryer.

Hotel Rincón Andaluz   In a stylish area of Marbella close to Puerto Banús, this government-rated four-star hotel is built to evoke a *pueblo andaluz* or Andalusian village. Lying in a park, the low-level rustic-style buildings form an ideal retreat. The large rooms are tastefully decorated and fully equipped, and all units have at least a small living room (larger in the suites). Ground-floor rooms have direct access to the gardens; others open onto balconies.

Carretera de Cádiz, Km 173, 29660, Marbella. © 95-281-15-17. Fax 95-281-41-80. www.riv.com. 300 units. 68€–104€ double; 94€–145€ suite. Rates include breakfast. AE, DC, MC, V. Free parking. **Amenities:** Restaurant; 2 bars; room service; laundry service; dry cleaning. *In room:* A/C, TV, minibar, hair dryer, safe.

INEXPENSIVE

El Rodeo *(Value)*   Even though this modern hotel stands just off the main coastal road of Marbella, within walking distance of the bus station, the beach, and the old quarter, it is quiet and secluded. The facilities include a newly renovated piano bar where many guests and locals gather. The midsize rooms are functional. All contain bathrooms with tub/shower combos. The hotel is open year-round; peak season rates run June through October.

Victor de la Serna s/n, 29600 Marbella. **℃ 95-277-51-00.** Fax 95-282-33-20. 99 units. 70€–110€ double. AE, DC, MC, V. **Amenities:** Restaurant; pool. *In room:* A/C, TV, safe.

Hostal El Castillo   At the foot of the castle in the narrow streets of the old town, this small hotel opens onto a minuscule triangular area used by the adjoining convent and school as a playground. There's a small, covered courtyard. The spartan rooms are scrubbed clean and have bathrooms with tub/shower combos. No breakfast is served, and only a little English is spoken.

Plaza San Bernabé 2, 29600 Marbella. **℃ 95-277-17-39.** 25 units. 29€–42€ double. MC, V. Free parking. *In room:* No phone.

A NEARBY PLACE TO STAY

El Castillo de Monda *(Finds)*   In 1996, a group of entrepreneurs transformed the crumbling ruins of an 8th-century Moorish fortress into this showplace, which lies in a sleepy village 12km (7½ miles) north of Marbella. El Castillo de Monda adds a soothing note of calm and quiet to a region that grows glitzier by the year. Rooms are beautifully maintained, generous in size, and traditionally furnished. Bathrooms have tub/shower combos.

Monda, 29110 Málaga. **℃ 95-245-71-42.** Fax 95-245-73-36. www.costadelsol.spa.es/hotel/monda. 26 units. 98€–113€ double. AE, MC, V. Free parking. **Amenities:** Restaurant; bar; pool; babysitting; laundry service; dry cleaning. *In room:* A/C, TV, hair dryer.

WHERE TO DINE
EXPENSIVE

El Portalón *✦* SPANISH/INTERNATIONAL   This is one of Marbella's most stylish dining enclaves. Its staff is one of the most urbane in town, serving patrons from throughout Europe with aplomb and obvious pride. Menu selections include some time-honored Iberian dishes, such as suckling lamb and pig slowly roasted in a wood-burning oven, grilled meats, and impeccably fresh fish imported daily. Low-fat dishes are like those you might expect to find at a California spa—lobster salad, grilled sea bass with a julienne of fresh vegetables, and entrecôte of beef with fresh vegetables and red-wine sauce. A recent addition is an Art Deco–style pavilion called the "vinoteca," which serves an excellent selection of wines from all over Spain. The restaurant is about a mile west of town beside the road leading to Puerto Banús, across from the beach and adjacent to the entrance to the Marbella Club.

Carretera de Cádiz, Km 178. **℃ 95-282-78-80.** Reservations recommended. Main courses 22€–32€; tasting menu 65€. AE, DC, MC, V. Mon–Sat 1–3:30pm and 8–11:30pm.

La Hacienda *✦✦✦* INTERNATIONAL   La Hacienda, a tranquil choice 13km (8 miles) east of Marbella, serves some of the best food along the Costa del Sol. In cooler months you can dine in the rustic tavern before an open fireplace. In fair weather, meals are served on a patio partially encircled by open Romanesque arches. The chef is likely to offer foie gras with lentils, lobster croquettes (as an appetizer), and roast guinea hen with cream, minced raisins, and port. The flavorful food is prepared with the freshest ingredients and presented with style. An iced soufflé finishes the meal nicely.

Urbanización Hacienda Las Chapas, Carretera de Cádiz, Km 193. ✆ **95-283-12-67.** Reservations recommended. Main courses 15€–42€; fixed-price menu 50€. AE, DC, MC, V. Summer daily 8:30pm–midnight; winter Wed–Sun 1–3:30pm and 8:30–11:30pm. Closed Nov 15–Dec 20.

La Meridiana ✿✿✿ ITALIAN/ANDALUSIAN   If not the most sophisticated restaurant along the Costa del Sol, La Meridiana certainly has the most romantic setting, with a garden terrace, and arguably serves the best cuisine as well. A sweep of a glass-enclosed porch has been added to the original restaurant. La Notte, a nightclub, has opened on a nearby terrace and has become the hot spot along the coast for late-night revelers. The menu of Italian and Andalusian specialties changes four times a year. You don't just get the routine gazpacho here but such cold soups as curried pumpkin or chilled white almond and garlic with melon and grapes. Tiny boneless chicken comes stuffed with couscous, raisins, almonds, and spices, and all the favorites of rich people as well: foie gras, Beluga caviar, lobster, and fine Ibérico ham.

Camino de la Cruz. ✆ **95-277-61-90.** Reservations required. Main courses 14€–42€; fixed-price menu 42€. AE, DC, MC, V. Daily 8:30pm–midnight. Closed Jan 9–Feb 10.

Marbella Club Restaurant ✿✿ INTERNATIONAL   Our favorite meals here have been whenever the staff moves the action onto the terrace in good weather. Lunch is traditionally an overflowing buffet served in the beach club. Dinners are served amid blooming flowers, flickering candles, and the strains of live music—perhaps a Spanish classical guitarist, a small chamber orchestra playing 19th-century classics, or a South American vocalist. Menu items, inspired by European cuisines, change with the season. You might begin with beef carpaccio or lobster salad delicately flavored with olive oil. Specialties include one of the coast's most savory paellas, and tender veal cutlets from Avila.

In the Marbella Club, Bulevar Príncipe Alfonso von Hohenlohe s/n. ✆ **95-282-22-11.** Reservations recommended. Lunch buffet 52€; dinner main courses 19€–29€. AE, DC, MC, V. Open year-round 1:30–4pm; summer daily 9pm–12:30am; winter daily 8:30–11:30pm.

Villa Tiberio ✿ ITALIAN   Villa Tiberio's proximity to the upscale Marbella Club (a 5-min. walk away) ensures a flow of visitors from that elite hotel. In what was originally built as a private villa during the 1960s, it serves the most innovative Italian food in the region, and attracts the many north European expatriates living nearby. Appetizers include thinly sliced smoked beef with fresh avocados and oil-and-lemon dressing, and *fungi fantasia* (a large wild mushroom stuffed with seafood and lobster sauce). Especially tempting is the *pappardelle alla Sandro*—large flat noodles studded with chunks of lobster, tomato, and garlic. Other versions come with cream, caviar, and smoked salmon. Main dishes include sea bass with cherry tomatoes, basil, and black truffle oil; duck baked with orange and Curaçao liqueur; and *osso buco* (braised veal shanks).

Carretera de Cádiz, Km 178.5. ✆ **95-277-17-99.** Reservations recommended. Main courses 10€–22€; fixed-price menus 42€–47€. AE, DC, MC, V. Mon–Sat 7:30pm–12:30am.

MODERATE

Ciboca SPANISH   This restaurant is sometimes recommended as a valuable and attractive middle-bracket choice by the concierges and desk clerks of hotels as prestigious and upscale as the also-recommended Marbella Club. Set in the heart of Marbella's historic medieval core, it occupies a 500-year-old building ringed with vines and flowers, whose tables are moved onto the historic square outside whenever the weather is balmy. A full roster of Spanish wines can accompany dishes that include virtually any kind of fish, especially sea bass, baked in a salt crust. Also appealing is roasted lamb scented with Andalusian herbs, and tournedos served with a perfectly made béarnaise sauce. Staff is cooperative and hardworking.

Plaza de las Naranjas 6. ℂ **95-277-37-43.** Reservations recommended. Main courses 20€–26€. MC, V. Daily noon–11pm.

Mesón del Museo FRENCH   Mesón del Museo is on the upper floor of an 18th-century building that contains one of the oldest art and antique galleries in Marbella. The dining room is decorated with Iberian accessories and Andalusian antiques. The chef focuses on French dishes. Try delicious fried Camembert, followed by filet of sole in a champagne and truffle sauce. A selection of French and Spanish wines complements the menu.

Plaza de los Naranjos 11 (1st floor). ℂ **95-282-56-23.** Reservations recommended. Main courses 15€–19€. MC, V. Tues–Sun 7:30–11pm. Closed July.

Santiago ⟨★⟩ SEAFOOD/INTERNATIONAL   As soon as you enter Santiago, the bubbling lobster tanks give you an idea of what's in store. The decor, the tapas bar near the entrance, and the summertime patio together with fresh fish dishes make this one of the most popular eating places in town. Savory fish soup is well prepared and well spiced. Follow with a generous serving of sole in champagne or grilled or sautéed turbot. On a hot day, the seafood salad, garnished with lobster, shrimp, and crabmeat and served with a sharp sauce, is especially recommended. In addition to seafood, the menu offers many meat dishes. For dessert, we suggest a serving of manchego cheese.

Duque de Ahumada 5. ℂ **95-277-00-78.** Reservations required. Main courses 12€–22€. AE, DC, MC, V. Daily 1–5pm and 7pm–1am.

INEXPENSIVE

La Pescera ANDALUSIAN   Beside a historic square in the heart of old Marbella, this is a bustling, well-managed restaurant. It has loyal local clientele and a reputation for serving well-prepared fish and seafood. There's a worthwhile roster of meat dishes, such as grilled steaks and pork filets, but most diners opt for fish. Specialties range from working-class dishes such as *bacalao frito* (fried cod) to more esoteric versions of shellfish and crayfish—kept alive and healthy until the last moment in big on-site holding tanks.

Plaza de la Victoria s/n. ℂ **95-276-41-74.** Reservations recommended Thurs–Sat night. Main courses 15€–30€. AE, DC, MC, V. Daily 10:30am–1am.

MARBELLA AFTER DARK

There's more international wealth hanging out in the watering holes of Marbella, and a wider choice of glam (or pseudo-glam) discos, than you'll find virtually anywhere else in the south of Spain. Foremost among these is the chic **Oliva Valer,** in the Hotel Puente Romano, N-340, Km 177 (ℂ **95-282-88-61**). A worthwhile, very stylish alternative is **O! Marbella,** N-340, Km 192 (ℂ **95-283-54-77**), adjacent to the Hotel Don Carlos. For a nightclub with a bit of Italian flair, consider **La Notte,** "Las Lomas" de Marbella Club (ℂ **95-282-60-24**), where people often come for an after-dinner drink from the upscale restaurant La Meridiana nearby.

A Marbella Tasca Crawl

To really rub shoulders with the locals and experience a taste of Spain, take your meals in the tapas bars. You can eat well in most places, and Marbella boasts more hole-in-the-wall tapas bars than virtually any other resort town in southern Spain. Even if you set out with a specific place in mind, you'll likely be waylaid en route by a newer, older, bigger, smaller, brighter, or more mysterious joint you want to try. That's half the fun.

Prices and hours are remarkably consistent: The coffeehouse that opens at 7am will switch to wine and tapas when the first patron asks for it (sometimes shortly after breakfast), then continue through the day dispensing wine, sherry, and, more recently, bottles of beer to accompany the food. On average, tapas cost 3€ to 8€ per *ración,* but some foreign visitors configure them into *platos combinados.*

Tapas served along the Costa del Sol are principally Andalusian in origin, with an emphasis on seafood. The most famous plate, *fritura malagueña,* consists of fried fish based on the catch of the day. Sometimes *ajo blanco,* a garlicky local version of gazpacho, is served, especially in summer. Fried squid or octopus is another favorite, as are little Spanish-style herb-flavored meatballs. *Tortilla* (an omelet, often with potatoes) is the most popular egg dish. Other well-known tapas selections include pungent tuna, grilled shrimp, *piquillos rellenos* (red peppers stuffed with fish), *bacalao* (salt cod), and mushrooms sautéed in olive oil and garlic.

Tapas bars line many of the narrow streets of Marbella's historic core, with rich pickings around Calle del Perral and, to a somewhat lesser extent, Calle Miguel Cana. In August especially, when you want to escape wall-to-wall people and the heat and noise of the old town, head for one of the shoreline restaurants and tapas bars called *chiringuitos.* All serve local specialties, and you can order a full meal, a snack, tapas, or a drink. One of our favorites is **Los Sardinales,** Playa de los Alicates (✆ 95-283-70-12), which serves some of the best sangria in the area. You might return later for a succulent seafood dinner. Another favorite hangout is **Chiringuito La Pesquera,** Playa Marbellamar (✆ 95-277-03-38), where you can order a plate of fresh grilled sardines.

If you're in the heart of historic Marbella, enjoy a night in the bodegas and taverns of the old town. One that's conveniently located adjacent to one of the town's widest thoroughfares is **Bodega La Venensia,** Plaza de los Olivos s/n (✆ 95-277-99-63). Its wide choice of sherries, wines, and tapas welcomes lots of chattering patrons. In the old town, you might check out **Bar El Estrecho,** Calle San Lázaro s/n (no phone), or its nearby competitor, **Bar Mattutte,** in the Calle Arte s/n (no phone). One with a particularly large assortment of wines is **Vinacoteca,** Calle Peral s/n (no phone). Dedicated to the inventory of as many Spanish wines as possible, it provides the opportunity to compare the vintages produced in the surrounding region.

The best flamenco club in town is **Ana María,** Plaza del Santo Cristo 4–5 (ⓒ **95-277-56-46**). We think it's simultaneously the most authentic place and the safest for foreign visitors with a limited knowledge of Spanish. The long, often-crowded bar area sells tapas, wine, sherry, and a selection of more international libations. On the stage, singers, dancers, and musicians perform flamenco and popular songs. This is late-night entertainment—the doors don't open till 11pm, and the crowd really gets going between midnight and 4am. It's closed November through March. Drink prices start at 20€, including cover.

Ten kilometers (6 miles) west of Marbella, near Puerto Banús, **Casino Marbella,** Andalucía Plaza, Urbanización Nueva Andalucía (ⓒ **95-281-40-00**), is on the lobby level of the Andalucía Plaza resort complex (see "Where to Stay," above). Unlike the region's competing casino, at the Hotel Torrequebrada, the Marbella does not offer cabaret or nightclub shows. The focus is on gambling, and mobs of visitors from northern Europe engage with abandon. Individual games include French and American roulette, blackjack, punto y banco, craps, and chemin de fer.

You can dine before or after gambling in the Casino Restaurant, a few steps above the gaming floor. Meals go for about 26€ per person, including wine. Jackets are not required for men, but shorts and T-shirts will be frowned on. The casino is open daily from 7pm to 4 or 5am. There's a cover charge of 3.60€. A passport is required for admission.

6 Fuengirola & Los Boliches

32km (20 miles) W of Málaga, 104km (64 miles) E of Algeciras, 574km (356 miles) S of Madrid

The fishing towns of **Fuengirola** and **Los Boliches** lie halfway between the more famous resorts of Marbella and Torremolinos. A promenade along the water stretches some 4km (2½ miles). Less developed Los Boliches is just .8km (½ mile) from Fuengirola.

These towns don't have the facilities or drama of Torremolinos and Marbella, but except for two major luxury hotels, Fuengirola and Los Boliches are cheaper. This has attracted hordes of budget-conscious European tourists.

The ruins of **Castello San Isidro** can be seen from a promontory overlooking the sea. The **Santa Amalja, Carvajal,** and **Las Gaviotas beaches** are broad, clean, and sandy. Everybody goes to the big **flea market** at Fuengirola on Tuesdays.

ESSENTIALS

GETTING THERE From Torremolinos, take the Metro at La Nogalera station (under the RENFE sign). **Trains** depart every 30 minutes. The fare is 1.15€.

Fuengirola is on the main Costa del Sol **bus** route from either Algeciras in the west or Málaga in the east.

If you're driving from Marbella, take the N-340/E-15 east from Marbella.

VISITOR INFORMATION The **tourist office,** Av. Jesús Santos Rein 6 ⓒ 95-246-74-57; www.fuengirola.org), is open Monday through Friday from 9:30am to 2pm and 4:30 to 7pm, Saturday from 10am to 1pm.

WHERE TO STAY

Byblos Andaluz 👍👍👍 This luxurious resort with excellent recreational facilities is in a golf club setting 5km (3 miles) from Fuengirola and 10km (6 miles) from the beach. The grounds contain a white minaret, Moorish arches, tile-adorned walls, and an orange-tree patio inspired by the Alhambra grounds. The large rooms and suites are elegantly and individually designed and furnished in Roman, Arabic, Andalusian, and rustic styles. Private sun terraces and lavish bathrooms with tub/shower combos add to the comfort.

Urbanización Mijas Golf, 29650 Mijas Costa Málaga. © **95-246-02-50.** Fax 95-247-67-83. www.byblos-andaluz.com. 144 units. 250€–312€ double; from 440€–1,230€ suite. Rates include breakfast. AE, DC, MC, V. Free parking. **Amenities:** 3 restaurants; 2 bars; 5 pools; 2 golf courses; tennis courts; health spa; sauna; room service; babysitting; laundry service; dry cleaning; solarium. *In room:* A/C, TV, minibar, hair dryer, safe.

Las Pirámides This resort, a favorite of northern Europeans and tour groups, is a citylike compound about 45.5m (50 yd.) from the beach. All the good-size rooms have slick modern styling, as well as terraces. Bathrooms have tub/shower combos.

Miguel Marquez, 29640 Fuengirola. © **95-247-06-00.** Fax 95-258-32-97. www.hotellaspiramides.com. 316 units. 120€–148€ double; 147€–162€ suite. AE, MC, V. Parking 10€. **Amenities:** Cafe; 2 bars; lounge; 2 pools; car rental; room service; babysitting; laundry service; dry cleaning. *In room:* A/C, TV, minibar, hair dryer, safe.

Villa de Laredo ☆ *finds* Enjoying A panoramic site on the waterfront promenade, this good value inn lies a block east of the main port. One of the newest hotels to be built in town, it benefits from a central location without even attempting to equal the luxury offered on the periphery at such resorts as Byblos Andaluz. Bedrooms are newly styled and comfortably furnished, containing small bathrooms with tub and shower. Try, if possible, for one of the rooms with a small terrace opening onto the seafront promenade. The featured attraction of the villa is its rooftop pool, opening onto views of the Paseo Marítimo.

Paseo Marítimo Rey de España 42, 29640 Fuengirola. © **95-247-76-89.** Fax 95-247-79-50. 50 units. 53€–118€ double. Rates include half board. AE, DC, MC, V. **Amenities:** Restaurant; bar; pool; room service; laundry service. *In room:* A/C, TV, minibar, hair dryer, safe.

WHERE TO DINE

Casa Vieja FRENCH Inside the thick stone walls of a cottage built in the 1870s for a local fisherman, this restaurant is on the main street of Los Boliches, a short walk east of the center of Fuengirola. It recently underwent extensive renovations, gaining a covered garden for year-round outside dining as well as a blues and jazz bar. New owners David (who can help you select a wine) and Bernard have gone to great lengths to create a soft, romantic ambience. The extensive menu contains one sumptuous option after another. For starters, try warm goat cheese salad with honey vinaigrette or sea bass and salmon terrine. Follow with beef *carbonnades falmandes,* fish duo with white butter sauce, or pork filet with caramelized mustard sauce. For desserts, don't pass up the signature chocolate fondant.

Av. de Los Boliches 27, Fuengirola. © **95-258-38-30.** Reservations recommended. Fixed-price 4-course menu 30€. MC, V. Tues–Sat 7:30–10:45pm (last orders).

Don Pé CONTINENTAL In hot weather, Don Pé patrons dine in a courtyard where the roof can be adjusted to allow in light and air. In cold weather, a fire on the hearth illuminates the heavy ceiling beams and rustic accessories. The menu features a selection of game dishes, including medallions of venison, roast filet of wild boar, and duck with orange sauce. The ingredients are imported from the forests and plains of Andalusia.

Calle de la Cruz 17 (off the Av. Ramón y Cajal), Fuengirola. © **95-247-83-51.** Reservations recommended. Main courses 9€–18€. V, MC. Mon–Sat 7pm–midnight.

La Langosta ⭐ SPANISH/SEAFOOD   Just a stone's throw from Fuengirola, La Langosta is one of the most-recommended restaurants in the area. The stylish Art Deco dining room is a welcome relief from the ever-present Iberian rustic style of so many other restaurants in the region. The menu features a variety of seafood (it is just 2 blocks from the beach), as well as Spanish dishes that include *gazpacho andaluz* and prawns *al ajillo* (in olive oil and garlic). Lobster is prepared thermidor style or virtually any way you want; among the beef offerings is an especially succulent version of *chateaubriand*. The staff seems particularly well trained and helpful.

Calle Francisco Cano 1, Los Boliches. ⓒ **95-247-50-49**. Main courses 12€–29€; fixed-price menu 30€. AE, DC, MC, V. Mon–Sat 7pm–midnight. Closed Dec–Jan.

7 Mijas ⭐

30km (18½ miles) W of Málaga, 585km (363 miles) S of Madrid

Just 8km (5 miles) north of coastal road N-340/E-15, this village is known as "White Mijas" because of its marble-white Andalusian-style houses. **Mijas** is at the foot of a mountain range near the turnoff to Fuengirola, and from its lofty height—450m (1,476 ft.) above sea level—you get a panoramic view of the Mediterranean.

Celts, Phoenicians, and Moors preceded today's intrepid tourists to Mijas. The town itself, rather than a specific monument, is the attraction. The easiest way to get around its cobblestone streets is to rent a burro taxi. If you consider Mijas overrun with souvenir shops, head for the park at the top of Cuesta de la Villa, where you'll see the ruins of a **Moorish fortress** dating from 833. If you're in town for a fiesta, you'll be attending events in the country's only square bullring (a bullsquare?).

There's frequent bus service to Mijas from the terminal at Fuengirola, 30 minutes away. To drive from Fuengirola, take the Mijas road north.

WHERE TO STAY

Hotel Mijas ⭐⭐   One of the most charming hotels on the Costa del Sol dates from 1970 when it was built on steeply sloping land in the center of town. This Andalusian-inspired block of white walls and flowering terraces is sun flooded and comfortable throughout. There are sweeping views over the Mediterranean from most of the public areas and the tiny but comfortable rooms. Bathrooms have tub/shower combos. The staff is tactful and hardworking. There is no elevator.

Urbanización Tamisa 2, 29650 Mijas. ⓒ **95-248-58-00**. Fax 95-248-58-25. 103 units. 80€–110€ double; 155€–216€ suite. AE, DC, MC, V. Free parking. **Amenities:** Restaurant; bar; pool; health club; sauna; salon; room service; babysitting; laundry service; dry cleaning. *In room:* A/C, TV, hair dryer, safe.

La Cala Resort ⭐⭐   Golfers specifically journey to Mijas just to stay at this stylishly contemporary resort, which is inland. The two golf courses at La Cala are its main attraction, including La Cala North (par 73) and La Cala South (par 72). Both courses were designed by the noted golf architect, Cabell B. Robinson, who cited the Costa del Sol terrain as his most challenging project. Even if you're not a golfer, you'll find one of the finest and most first-rate accommodations in the area, unless you prefer to be right on the sea. This course is 7km (4⅓ miles) from a good beach. Bedrooms are midsize to spacious, each attractively furnished in a contemporary mode, with superb bathrooms with tub and shower. Every accommodation opens onto a large balcony overlooking the fairways and greens and the Mijas hills beyond. Since most visitors stay on-site at night, it's good to know that the cuisine, a medley of Spanish and Continental dishes, is first rate, using quality ingredients.

La Cala de Mijas, 29649 Mijas-costa. (℃) **95-266-90-00.** Fax 95/266-90-39. www.lacala.com. 104 units. 146€–220€ double; 219€–292€ suite. Rates include breakfast. AE, DC, MC, V. **Amenities:** 2 restaurants; 2 bars; 2 pools (1 indoor); 2 tennis courts; squash; sauna; fitness center; 24-hr. room service; babysitting; laundry/dry cleaning. *In room:* A/C, TV, minibar, hair dryer, safe.

WHERE TO DINE

Restaurante El Padrastro INTERNATIONAL   Part of the fun of dining at the town's best restaurant is getting here. You go to the cliff side of town and, if you're athletic, walk up 77 steps; if you're not, take the elevator to the highest point. El Padrastro serves international cuisine on its covered terraces with panoramic views of the coast. You can choose whether to eat inexpensively (stick with the regional dishes) or elaborately (break the bank and go for the chateaubriand with a bottle of the best Spanish wine).

Paseo del Compás 22. (℃) **95-248-50-00.** Reservations recommended. Main courses 12€–24€. AE, DC, MC, V. Daily 11am–4pm and 7–11pm.

Villa Paradiso INTERNATIONAL   This restaurant deserves its immense popularity especially among the British expats and others now living permanently in the area. Lamb shanks are aromatically baked in the oven until fork tender and served with a fresh fruit sauce. Lubina or sea bass is baked in a salt crust, its aromas bursting into flavor when peeled back. Every day different specialties are featured. On our most recent visit, the delight of the evening was tender medallions of baby pork with a well-made sauce. In the autumn, venison is likely to appear on the menu.

Centro Comercial El Zoco. (℃) **95-293-12-24.** Reservations recommended. Main courses 6€–22€. AE, DC, MC, V. Daily 1pm–midnight.

8 Torremolinos

15km (9 miles) W of Málaga, 122km (76 miles) E of Algeciras, 568km (353 miles) S of Madrid

This Mediterranean beach resort is the most famous in Spain. It's known as a melting pot for international visitors, mostly Europeans and Americans. Many relax here after a whirlwind tour of Europe—the living is easy, the people are fun, and there are no historical monuments to visit. Once a sleepy fishing village, **Torremolinos** has been engulfed in a cluster of cement-walled resort hotels. Prices are on the rise, but it remains one of Europe's vacation bargains.

ESSENTIALS

GETTING THERE   The nearby Málaga airport serves Torremolinos, and frequent **trains** also run from the terminal at Málaga. For train information, call (℃) **90-224-02-02. Buses** run frequently between Málaga and Torremolinos; call (℃) **95-235-00-61** for schedules.

If you're driving, take the N-340/E-15 west from Málaga or the N-340/E-15 east from Marbella.

VISITOR INFORMATION   The **tourist office** at the Plaza de la Independencia ((℃) **95-237-42-31;** www.visitetorremolinos.com) is open daily from 9:30am to 2pm.

WHERE TO STAY
EXPENSIVE

Hotel Tropicana ✦   Nearly a kilometer (½ mile) from Torremolinos on the beach, this hotel is still going strong after 4 decades. Management prides itself on the friendly atmosphere and service offered, and the interior decor reflects the bright, breezy atmosphere of the place. The reception area is graced with tropical plants, wicker chairs, and a marble floor; the midsize to spacious rooms are well furnished with sea views. Bathrooms have tub/shower combos.

Calle Trópico 6, 29620 Torremolinos. ✆ **95-238-66-00.** Fax 95-238-05-68. www.hotel-tropicana.net. 84 units. 96€–148€ double. Rates include buffet breakfast. AE, DC, MC, V. Free parking. **Amenities:** Restaurant; bar; pool; game room; room service; babysitting; laundry service; dry cleaning. *In room:* A/C, TV, hair dryer, safe.

Meliá Costa del Sol ✦   There are two Meliá hotels in Torremolinos, both operated by the popular Spanish hotel chain. This one is more centrally located; the other is more luxurious. The midsize rooms are modern and well maintained, and each has a well-kept bathroom with a tub/shower combo. However, the hotel is popular with package tour groups, so you may not feel a part of things if you're here alone.

Paseo Marítimo 11, 29620 Torremolinos. ✆ **800/336-3542** in the U.S., or 95-238-66-77. Fax 95-238-64-17. www.solmelia.es. 533 units. 88€–128€ double; 227€–310€ suite. AE, DC, MC, V. Free parking. **Amenities:** Restaurant; bar; pool; salon; room service; babysitting; laundry service; dry cleaning. *In room:* A/C, TV, minibar, hair dryer, safe.

Meliá Torremolinos ✦✦   This is the more luxurious of the two Meliá hotels at the resort, but farther removed from the center. This hotel has deliberately lowered its official government rank from five stars to four, which means you can enjoy the better service at lower prices. The hotel stands in its own gardens on the western outskirts of town on the road to Cádiz. Rooms range from small to spacious. Bathrooms are well furnished and have tub/shower combos.

Carlota Alessandri 109, 29620 Torremolinos. ✆ **800/336-3542** in the U.S., or 95-238-05-00. Fax 95-238-05-38. www.solmelia.com. 289 units. 99€–131€ double; from 168€–220€ suite. AE, DC, MC, V. Free parking. Closed Nov–Feb. **Amenities:** Restaurant; 2 bars; pool; tennis courts; aerobics classes; room service; babysitting; laundry service; dry cleaning. *In room:* A/C, TV, minibar, hair dryer, safe.

Sol Don Pablo   One of the most desirable hotels in the center of Torremolinos, Don Pablo is in a modern building a minute from the beach, surrounded by its own garden and playground areas. The surprise is the glamorous interior, which borrows heavily from Moorish palaces and medieval castle themes. Arched-tile arcades have splashing fountains, and the grand staircase features niches with life-size stone statues of nude figures. The comfortably furnished rooms have sea-view terraces, and bathrooms have tub/shower combos.

Paseo Marítimo s/n, 29620 Torremolinos. ✆ **95-238-38-88.** Fax 95-238-37-83. 443 units. 85€–144€ double. Rates include buffet breakfast. AE, DC, MC, V. **Amenities:** Restaurant; bar; lounge; 2 pools; room service; babysitting; laundry service; dry cleaning. *In room:* A/C, TV, minibar, hair dryer, safe.

MODERATE

Hotel Cervantes ✦   The government-rated four-star Cervantes is a 7-minute walk from the beach. It has a garden and is adjacent to a maze of patios and narrow streets of boutiques and open-air cafes. Rooms have modern furniture, piped-in music, and spacious terraces; many have balconies with sea views. Bathrooms have tub/shower combos. In midsummer this hotel is likely to be booked with tour groups from northern Europe.

Calle las Mercedes s/n, 29620 Torremolinos. ✆ **95-238-40-33**. Fax 95-238-48-57. 397 units. 75€–115€ double. Full board 36€ per person. AE, DC, MC, V. **Amenities:** Restaurant; 2 bars; 2 pools; health club; sauna; room service; babysitting; laundry service; dry cleaning. *In room:* A/C, TV, hair dryer, safe.

Hotel Las Palomas Built at the height of Torremolinos's construction boom (1968), this well-managed hotel is one of the town's most attractive, surrounded by carefully tended gardens. Located near the coastal road, it's a 1-minute walk from the beach and a 10-minute walk south of the center of town. It has a clientele of repeat visitors who hail mostly from France, Belgium, and Holland. Each of the midsize rooms has a private balcony and a bathroom with tub/shower combo. There's no air-conditioning, but open windows and balcony doors catch the sea breezes.

Carmen Montés 1, 29620 Torremolinos. ✆ **95-238-50-00**. Fax 95-238-64-66. 303 units. 42€–96€ double. AE, DC, MC, V. **Amenities:** Restaurant; bar; 2 pools; salon; babysitting; laundry service; dry cleaning. *In room:* A/C, TV, hair dryer.

Sidi Lago Rojo ★ *Finds* In the heart of the fishing village of La Carihuela, Sidi Lago Rojo is the finest place to stay. It stands only 45m (150 ft.) from the beach and has its own gardens and sunbathing terraces. Built in the 1970s and renovated at least once since then, it offers tastefully decorated studio-style rooms. All rooms have terraces with views. Bathrooms have showers. In the late evening there is disco dancing.

Miami 1, 29620 Torremolinos. ✆ **95-238-76-66**. Fax 95-238-08-91. 144 units. 85€–104€ double. AE, DC, MC, V. **Amenities:** Restaurant; bar; pool; babysitting; laundry service; dry cleaning. *In room:* A/C, TV, safe.

INEXPENSIVE

Hotel El Pozo *Value* This hotel isn't for light sleepers—it's in one of the liveliest sections of town, a short walk from the train station. It's usually filled with budget travelers, including many students from northern Europe. The lobby level has professional French billiards, heavy Spanish furniture, and a view of a small courtyard. From your window or terrace you can view the promenades below. The small rooms, which contain tub/shower combos, are furnished in a simple, functional style—nothing special, but the price is right.

Casablanca 2, 29620 Torremolinos. ✆ **95-238-06-22**. Fax 95-238-71-17. 28 units. 36€–60€ double. DC, MC, V. **Amenities:** Bar. *In room:* A/C, TV, safe.

Hotel Los Jazmines Located on one of the best beaches in Torremolinos, Los Jazmines faces a plaza at the foot of the shady Avenida del Lido. Sun-seekers will find it replete with terraces, lawns, and an irregularly shaped swimming pool. The small rooms (all doubles) seem a bit impersonal, but have their own little balconies and compact bathrooms with tub/shower combos. From here it's a good hike up the hill to the town center.

Av. de Lido 6, 29620 Torremolinos. ✆ **95-238-50-33**. Fax 95-237-27-02. 100 units. 50€–60€ double. AE, DC, MC, V. **Amenities:** Bar; pool. *In room:* TV, safe.

Miami ★ *Finds* The Miami, near the Carihuela section, might remind you of a 1920s Hollywood movie star's home. High walls and private gardens surround the property. Fuchsia and bougainvillea climb over the rear patio's arches, and a tile terrace is used for sunbathing and refreshments. The country-style living room contains a walk-in fireplace, and the compact rooms are furnished in a traditional, comfortable style and contain bathrooms with tub/shower combos. Each has a balcony. Breakfast is the only meal served.

Aladino 14, 29620 Torremolinos. (C) **95-238-52-55.** 27 units. 38€–56€ double. No credit cards. Free parking. **Amenities:** Bar; babysitting; laundry service; dry cleaning. *In room:* No phone.

NEARBY PLACES TO STAY

Where Torremolinos ends and Benalmádena-Costa to the west begins is hard to say. Benalmádena-Costa is packed with hotels, restaurants, and tourist facilities.

Hotel Torrequebrada ★★   In the late 1980s this became one of the largest government-rated five-star luxury hotels along the Costa del Sol. Five kilometers (3 miles) west of Torremolinos, it opens onto its own beach and offers a wide range of facilities and attractions. The spacious, handsomely furnished rooms have large terraces with sea views. Bathrooms have tub/shower combos.

Av. del Sol s/n, 29630 Benalmádena. (C) **95-244-60-00.** Fax 95-244-27-46. www.torrequebrada.com. 350 units. 145€–191€ double; 212€–935€ suite. Discounts for stays of 5 or more days. AE, DC, MC, V. Free parking. **Amenities:** 3 restaurants; 2 bars; pool; tennis courts; health club; sauna; room service; babysitting; laundry service; dry cleaning; casino. *In room:* A/C, TV, minibar, hair dryer, safe.

WHERE TO DINE

The cuisine in Torremolinos is more American and Continental European than Andalusian. The hotels often serve elaborate four-course meals, but you might want to sample more casual local offerings. A good spot to try is the food court **La Nogalera,** the major gathering place between the coast road and the beach. Head down Calle del Cauce to this compound of modern whitewashed Andalusian buildings. Open to pedestrian traffic only, it's a maze of passageways, courtyards, and patios for eating and drinking. You can find anything from sandwiches to Belgian waffles to scrambled eggs to pizza.

AT LA NOGALERA

El Gato Viudo SPANISH   El Gato Viudo is a tradition with local diners for almost 40 years. Simple and amiable, this old-fashioned tavern occupies the street level and cellar of a building off Calle San Miguel and offers sidewalk seating. The menu includes such good dishes as grilled fish; marinated hake; roasted pork, steak, and veal; calamari with spicy tomato sauce; grilled shrimp; and shellfish or fish soup. The atmosphere is informal, and the staff is accustomed to coping with diners from virtually everywhere.

La Nogalera 11. (C) **95-238-51-29.** Main courses 8€–18€. AE, DC, MC, V. May–Oct daily 1–4pm and 6–11:30pm; Nov–Apr Thurs–Tues 1–4pm and 6–11:30pm.

AT LA CARIHUELA

If you want to get away from the high-rises and honky-tonks, head to nearby La Carihuela. In the old fishing village on the western outskirts of Torremolinos you'll find some of the best bargain restaurants. Walk down a hill toward the sea to reach the village.

Casa Juan ★ SEAFOOD   In a modern-looking building in La Carihuela, this seafood restaurant is about a mile west of Torremolinos's center. Menu items include selections from a lavish display of fish and shellfish prominently positioned near the entrance. You might try *mariscada de mariscos* (shellfish), a fried platter of mixed fish, cod, kebabs of meat or fish, or paella. Of special note is *lubina a la sal*—sea bass packed in layers of roughly textured salt, broken open at your table, and deboned in front of you. When the restaurant gets busy, as it often does, the staff is likely to rush around hysterically—something many local fans think adds to its charm.

Calle san Jines 18–20, La Carihuela. ℂ **95-237-35-12.** Reservations recommended. Main courses 10€–22€. AE, DC, MC, V. Tues–Sun 12:30–4:30pm and 7:30pm–midnight. Closed Dec.

El Roqueo SEAFOOD Established in 1975 in the heart of the village, El Roqueo is the perfect place for a seafood dinner near the sea. Begin with savory *sopa de mariscos* (shellfish soup). Then try a specialty of the chef, a delectable fish baked in rock salt; you can also order grilled sea bass or shrimp. Top everything off with soothing caramel custard. Some of the more expensive fish courses are priced by the gram, so order carefully.

Calle del Carmen 35, La Carihuela. ℂ **95-238-49-46.** Reservations recommended. Main courses 14€–33€. AE, DC, MC, V. Wed–Mon 1–4pm and 8pm–midnight. Closed Dec 15–Jan 15.

AT BENALMADENA-COSTA

Mar de Alborán ★★ BASQUE/ANDALUSIAN This restaurant's elegantly airy decor seems appropriate for its location near the sea, just a short walk from the resort's Puerto Marina. It serves the specialties of both Andalusia and the Basque region of northern Spain. Menu items might include cold terrine of leeks; or *bacalao* (salt cod) "Club Ranero," served with garlic and red-pepper cream sauce. You can also try *kokotxas,* the Basque national dish of hake cheeks in green sauce with clams; anglerfish with prawns; or foie gras served with sweet Málaga wine and raisins. The restaurant's game dishes (available in season) are renowned. Dessert might be a frothy version of peach mousse with purée of fruit and dark-chocolate sauce.

Alay 5. ℂ **95-244-64-27.** Reservations recommended. Main courses 10€–20€; *menú del día* 30€. AE, DC, MC, V. Sun and Tues–Fri 1:30–4pm; Tues–Sat 8:30pm–midnight. Closed Dec 22–Jan 22.

TORREMOLINOS AFTER DARK

Torremolinos has more nightlife than any other spot along the Costa del Sol. The earliest action is always at the bars, which are lively most of the night, serving drinks and tapas. Sometimes it seems that in Torremolinos there are more bars than people, so you shouldn't have trouble finding one you like. Note that some bars are open during the day as well.

We like the **Bar Central,** Plaza Andalucía, Bloque 1 (ℂ **95-238-27-60**), for coffee, brandy, beer, cocktails, limited sandwiches, and pastries, served indoors or on a large, French-style covered terrace. It's a good spot to meet people. Prices begin at 1.15€ for a beer, 3€ for a hard drink. Open Monday through Saturday from 8am to 11:30pm (later in summer).

La Bodega, San Miguel 40 (ℂ **95-238-73-37**), relies on its colorful clientele and the quality of its tapas to draw customers, who seem to rank this place above the dozens of other *tascas* in this popular tourist zone. You'll be fortunate to find space at one of the small tables because many consider the bar food plentiful enough for a satisfying lunch or dinner. Once you begin to order—platters of fried squid, pungent tuna, grilled shrimp, tiny brochettes of sole—you might not be able to stop. Most tapas cost 1.50€. A beer costs 1.15€, a hard drink at least 3€. Open daily from 12:30pm to midnight.

Ready to dance off all those tapas? **El Palladium,** Palma de Mallorca (ℂ **95-238-42-89**), a well-designed nightclub in the town center, is one of the most convivial in Torremolinos. Strobes, spotlights, and a sound system (described as loud and distortion-free) set the scene. There's even a swimming pool. Expect to pay 2.15€ or more for a drink; cover is 6€, including one drink after 11pm. Open from 11pm to 6am in summer months only.

Gay men and women from throughout northern Europe are almost always in residence in Torremolinos; if you want to meet some of them, consider a drink or two at **Abadía,** La Nogalera 9 (no phone). Other options, all around La Nogalera, include **Contactos,** La Nogalera 204 (no phone), which does not get busy till well after 10pm, and **Morbos,** La Nogalera 113 (no phone), which is open till 5am. The most popular gay disco in town is the **Tensión,** La Nogalera 524 (no phone), which plays popular dance music for a very cruisy crowd.

One of the Costa del Sol's major casinos, **Casino Torrequebrada,** Carretera de Cádiz, Benalmádena-Costa (© 95-244-60-00), is on the lobby level of the Hotel Torrequebrada (see "Where to Stay," above). It has tables devoted to blackjack, chemin de fer, punto y banco, and two kinds of roulette. The casino is open daily from 8am to 4am. The nightclub offers a flamenco show year-round, at 11pm on Thursday, Friday, and Saturday nights; in midsummer, there might be more glitz and more frequent shows (ask when you get there or call). Nightclub acts begin at 10:30pm (Spanish revue) and 11:30pm (Las Vegas revue). The restaurant is open nightly from 8:30 to 11pm. Casino admission is 3.60€; with one drink, both shows, casino and cabaret/nightclub admission, it's 29€, with dinner, 60€. Bring your passport to be admitted.

9 Málaga ⭐

548km (340 miles) S of Madrid, 132km (82 miles) E of Algeciras

Málaga is a bustling commercial and residential center whose economy does not depend exclusively on tourism. Its chief attraction is the mild off-season climate. Summer can be sticky.

Málaga's most famous citizen was Pablo Picasso, born in 1881 at the Plaza de la Merced, in the center of the city. The artist unfortunately left little of his spirit—and only a small selection of his work—in his birthplace.

ESSENTIALS

GETTING THERE   Travelers from North America must transfer for Málaga in Madrid or Barcelona. From within Europe, some airlines (including British Airways from London) offer nonstop flights to Málaga. **Iberia** has frequent service, and even more flights offered through its affiliate airlines, which include **Binter, Viva,** and **Aviaco.** Flights can be booked through Iberia's reservations line (© 800/772-4642 in the U.S., or 90-240-05-00 in Spain).

At least five **trains** a day serve Málaga from Madrid (trip time: 4 hr.). Three trains a day connect the Andalusian city of Seville with Málaga (3 hr.). For ticket prices and rail information in Málaga, call RENFE (© 90-224-02-02).

Buses from all over Spain arrive at the terminal on the Paseo de los Tilos, behind the RENFE offices. Buses run to all the major Spanish cities, including eight buses per day from Madrid (trip time: 7 hr.), five per day from Córdoba, and 10 per day from Seville. Call © 95-235-00-61 in Málaga for bus information.

From the resorts in the west (such as Torremolinos and Marbella), you can drive east along the N-340/E-15 to Málaga. If you're in the east at the end of the Costa del Sol (Almería), take the N-340/E-15 west to Málaga, with a stopover at Nerja.

VISITOR INFORMATION   The **tourist office** at Pasaje de Chinitas 4 (© 95-221-34-45; www.andalusia.org) is open Monday through Friday from 9am to 1pm, Saturday and Sunday from 10am to 2pm.

SPECIAL EVENTS   The most festive time in Málaga is the first week in August, when the city celebrates its reconquest by Ferdinand and Isabella in 1487. The big *feria* (**fair**) is an occasion for parades and bullfights. A major tree-shaded boulevard, the Paseo del Parque, is transformed into a fairground featuring amusements and restaurants.

EXPLORING MALAGA

Unlike the rest of the Costa del Sol, Málaga has several historical sites of interest to the average visitor.

Alcazaba ⟨★⟩   The remains of this ancient Moorish palace are within easy walking distance of the city center, off the Paseo del Parque. Plenty of signs point the way up the hill. The fortress was erected in the 9th or 10th century, although there have been later additions and reconstructions. Ferdinand and Isabella stayed here when they reconquered the city. With government-planted orange trees and purple bougainvillea making the grounds even more beautiful, the view overlooking the city and the bay is among the most panoramic on the Costa del Sol.

Plaza de la Aduana, Alcazabilla. ✆ **95-221-60-05.** Admission 1.80€. Museum Tues–Fri 9:30am–8pm; Sat 10am–1pm; Sun 10am–2pm. Bus: 4, 18, 19, or 24.

Castillo de Gibralfaro   On a hill overlooking Málaga and the Mediterranean are the ruins of an ancient Moorish castle-fortress of unknown origin. It is near the government-run parador, and might easily be tied in with a luncheon visit.

Warning: Do not walk to Gibralfaro Castle from town. Readers have reported muggings along the way, and the area around the castle is dangerous. Take the bus from the cathedral.

Cerro de Gibralfaro. Admission 1.80€. Daylight hours. Microbus: 35, leaving hourly from cathedral.

Málaga Cathedral   This 16th-century Renaissance cathedral in Málaga's center, built on the site of a great mosque, suffered damage during the Spanish Civil War. However, it remains vast and impressive, reflecting changing styles of interior architecture. Its most notable attributes are the richly ornamented choir stalls by Ortiz, Mena, and Michael. The cathedral has been declared a national monument.

Plaza Obispo. ✆ **95-221-59-17.** Admission 2€. Mon–Sat 10am–6:30pm. Closed holidays. Bus: 14, 18, 19, or 24.

Picasso House-Museum   A well-told tale concerns the birth of Picasso: In October 1891, when the artist was born, he was unable to draw breath until his uncle blew cigar smoke into his lungs. Whether this rather harsh entry into the world had any effect on his work is mere speculation. What cannot be denied is the effect he was to have on the world. He was born in a five-story building in the heart of Málaga's historic quarter; this is where he spent the first 17 months of his life. The house is now more of a museum, with about 200 works on display. The museum mounts monthly exhibitions featuring avant-garde works from Picasso's time.

Plaza de la Merced. ✆ **95-206-02-15.** Free admission. Mon–Sat 10am–2pm and 5–8pm; Sun 10am–2pm. In summer, closing time is 9pm.

SHOPPING

The region around Málaga produces artfully rustic pottery, which makes a worthwhile souvenir. A handful of highly appealing outlets are scattered throughout the city's historic core. The best include **Almazul,** Calle Beatas 53 (© **95-221-28-43**); and **Los Artesanos,** Cister 13 (© **95-260-45-44**). Outside the town limits, the most comprehensive collection of ceramics and pottery can be found at **La Vistillas,** Carretera Mijas, Km 2 (© **95-245-13-63**), about 2km (1¼ miles) from Málaga's center.

WHERE TO STAY

For such a large city in a resort area, Málaga has a surprising lack of hotels. Book well in advance, especially if you want to stay in a parador.

EXPENSIVE

AC Málaga Palacio ⭐ The leading hotel in the town center, the Palacio opens onto a tree-lined esplanade near the cathedral and the harbor. Most balconies offer views of the port, and below you can see horses pulling century-old carriages. The midsize rooms are traditionally furnished and have firm beds and bathrooms with tub/shower combos. The street-floor lounges mix antiques with more modern furnishings.

Cortina del Muelle 1, 29015 Málaga. © **95-221-51-85**. Fax 95-222-51-00. www.ac-hoteles.com. 214 units. 124€–186€ double; from 237€ suite. AE, DC, MC, V. Parking 12€ nearby. Bus: 4, 18, 19, or 24. **Amenities:** Restaurant; bar; pool; fitness center; sauna; room service; babysitting; laundry service; dry cleaning. *In room:* A/C, TV, minibar, hair dryer.

Hotel Larios ⭐ On the main street of the old town, this hotel ranks just under the parador as the most desirable place to stay. The interior is contemporary and stylish, with a terrace opening onto a panoramic view of the city. The midsize rooms are decorated in a minimalist but stylish way. All have comfortable furnishings, including bathrooms with tub/shower combos, and the suites come with whirlpool tubs. Because of the popularity of the hotel, it is advised to book well in advance.

Calle Marqués de Larios 2, 29005 Málaga. © **95-222-22-00**. Fax 95-222-24-07. www.hotel-larios.com. 40 units. 111€–131€ double; 130€–180€ suite. AE, DC, MC, V. Free parking. **Amenities:** Restaurant; bar; room service; laundry service; dry cleaning. *In room:* A/C, TV, minibar, hair dryer, safe.

Parador de Málaga-Gibralfaro ⭐⭐ Restored in 1994, this is one of Spain's oldest, most tradition-laden paradors. It enjoys a scenic location high on a plateau near an old fortified castle. Overlooking the city and the Mediterranean, it has views of the bullring, mountains, and beaches. Rooms have private entrances, living-room areas, and wide glass doors opening onto private sun terraces. Bathrooms have tub/shower combos.

Monte Gibralfaro, 29016 Málaga. © **95-222-19-02**. Fax 952-22-19-04. www.parador.es. 38 units. 119€–160€ double. AE, DC, MC, V. Free parking. Take the coastal road, Paseo de Reding, which becomes Av. de Pries and then Paseo de Sancha. Turn left onto Camino Nuevo and follow the small signs. **Amenities:** Restaurant (see "Where to Dine," below); bar; pool; room service; babysitting; laundry service; dry cleaning; currency exchange. *In room:* A/C, TV, minibar, hair dryer, safe.

Tryp Guadalmar ⭐ Drenched in sunlight, this nine-story modern hotel sits across from a private beach 3km (2 miles) west of the center of Málaga. It benefited from a radical renovation in 1996 and a takeover by the well-respected Tryp chain. Accommodations are spacious, airy, and simply furnished; each room has a private sea-view balcony and a bathroom with tub/shower combo. You're likely to get heavy doses of families with children at this hotel. An air of anonymity prevails as the staff struggles with constant exposure to the comings and goings of large numbers of vacationers.

Calle Mobydick 2, Urbanización Guadalmar, 29004 Málaga. ☎ **95-223-17-03.** Fax 95-224-03-85. 194 units. 164€ double; 410€ suite. Children under 12 stay half price in parent's room. AE, DC, MC, V. Free parking. **Amenities:** Restaurant; bar; pool; health club; sauna; room service; babysitting; laundry service; dry cleaning. *In room:* A/C, TV, minibar, hair dryer, safe.

MODERATE

Los Naranjos *Value*   The well-maintained Los Naranjos is one of the more reasonably priced choices in the city. It's 1.6km (1 mile) from the heart of town on the eastern side of Málaga, past the Plaza de Toros (bullring), near the best beach in Málaga, the Baños del Carmen. The hotel offers midsize rooms in contemporary style. Some bathrooms have only showers. Breakfast (which costs extra) is the only meal served.

Paseo de Sancha 35, 29016 Málaga. ☎ **95-222-43-19.** Fax 95-222-59-75. www.hotel-losnaranjos.com. 41 units. 102€ double; 126€ suite. AE, DC, MC, V. Parking 10€. Bus: 11. **Amenities:** Restaurant; bar; room service; babysitting; laundry service; dry cleaning. *In room:* A/C, TV, minibar, hair dryer, safe.

Parador Nacional del Golf ★★   A tasteful resort hotel created by the Spanish government, this hacienda-style parador is flanked by a golf course on one side and the Mediterranean on another. It's less than 3km (2 miles) from the airport, 11km (6½ miles) from Málaga, and 4km (2½ miles) from Torremolinos. Rooms have private balconies with water views. Some units have whirlpool tubs, others just tiled showers. The furnishings are attractive, and the beds excellent.

Carretera de Málaga, Apartado 324, 29080 Torremolinos, Málaga. ☎ **95-238-12-55.** Fax 95-238-89-63. www.paradores.es. 60 units. 110€ double. AE, DC, MC, V. Free parking. **Amenities:** Restaurant (see "Where to Dine," below); bar; lounge; pool; golf course; tennis courts; room service; babysitting; laundry service; dry cleaning. *In room:* A/C, TV, minibar, hair dryer, safe.

INEXPENSIVE

El Cenachero   Opened in 1969, this modest little hotel is 5 blocks from the park near the harbor. The nicely carpeted rooms are simply and functionally furnished; half have showers, the rest full bathrooms. No meals are served.

Barroso 5, 29001 Málaga. ☎ **95-222-40-88.** 14 units. 39€–46€ double. No credit cards. Bus: 4 or 14. **Amenities:** Lounge. *In room:* TV.

Hostal Derby ★ *Finds*   Not to be redundant, but the Derby is a real find. A fourth-floor boardinghouse, it's in the heart of town, on a main square directly north of the train station. Some of the rather basic, cramped rooms have excellent views of the Mediterranean and the port of Málaga. Most units have a shower only. No breakfast is served, and the hotel is very light on extras.

San Juan de Dios 1, 29015 Málaga. ☎ **95-222-13-01.** 16 units, 12 with bathroom. 33€ double with sink; 36€–43€ double with bathroom. No credit cards. Bus: 7, 9, 12, 14, 15, 16, or 17. **Amenities:** Lounge.

Hotel Residencia Carlos V   This hotel is in a central location near the cathedral, with an interesting facade decorated with wrought-iron balconies and *miradores* (viewing stations). This remains a reliable, conservative choice. The small rooms are furnished in a no-frills style, but are well maintained and equipped with bathrooms containing tub/shower combos.

Cister 10, 29015 Málaga. ☎ **95-221-51-20.** Fax 95-221-51-29. 50 units. 52€–59€ double. AE, DC, MC, V. Parking 9.50€. Bus: 3 from the rail station. *In room:* A/C, TV.

A LUXURIOUS PLACE TO STAY NEARBY

La Bobadilla ★★★   An hour's drive northeast of Málaga, La Bobadilla is the most luxurious retreat in southern Spain. It is a secluded oasis in the foothills of the Sierra Nevada near the town of Loja, which is 71km (44 miles) north of Málaga. La Bobadilla is a 21km (13-mile) drive from Loja.

The hotel complex is built like an Andalusian village, a cluster of whitewashed *casas* constructed around a tower and a white church. Every *casa* has a roof terrace and a balcony overlooking the olive grove–studded district. Each sumptuous accommodation is individually designed, from the least expensive doubles to the most expensive King's Suite (which has plenty of room for bodyguards). All rooms have sumptuous bathrooms containing tub/shower combos. The hotel caters to a pampered coterie of international guests, and the service is perhaps the finest in Spain.

The hotel village stands on a hillside, on 708 hectares (1,750 acres) of private, unspoiled grounds. If you get bored in this lap of luxury, you can always drive to Granada, an hour away. Should you decide to marry your companion at the resort, the chapel has a 9m (30-ft.) high organ with 1,595 pipes.

Finca La Bobadilla, Apartado 144, 18300 Loja (Granada). ✆ **95-832-18-61.** Fax 95-832-18-10. www. la-bobadilla.com. 62 units. 247€–283€ double; from 317€–362€ suite. Rates include breakfast. AE, DC, MC, V. Free parking. From the Málaga airport, follow signs toward Granada, but at Km 175 continue through the village of Salinas. Take road marked SALINAS/RUTE; after 3km (2 miles), follow signposts for hotel to the entrance. **Amenities:** 2 restaurants; bar; pool; health club; sauna; whirlpool; horseback riding; salon; room service; babysitting; laundry service; dry cleaning. *In room:* A/C, TV, minibar, hair dryer, safe.

WHERE TO DINE
EXPENSIVE
Café de París ★★ FRENCH/SPANISH   Café de París, Málaga's best restaurant, is in La Malagueta, the district surrounding the Plaza de Toros (bullring). Proprietor and chef de cuisine José García Cortés worked at many important dining rooms before carving out his own niche. Much of Cortés's cuisine has been adapted from classic French dishes to please the Andalusian palate. You might be served crepes gratinées filled with baby eels or local whitefish baked in salt (it doesn't sound good but is excellent). Stroganoff is made not with the usual beef but with ox meat. Save room for the creative desserts, such as citrus-flavored sorbet made with champagne or custard-apple mousse.

Vélez Málaga 8. ✆ **95-222-50-43.** Reservations required. Main courses 18€–26€; *menú del día* 45€. AE, DC, MC, V. Mon–Sat 1–4pm; Tues–Sat 8pm–midnight. Closed July 1–15. Bus: 13.

Escuela de Hostelería ★ *Finds* MEDITERRANEAN   This restaurant comes as a surprise: a hotel and catering school that is housed in a villa from the 1800s, lying at a point 8km (5 miles) outside Málaga and 3km (1¾ miles) from the international airport. In business since the early 1990s, this is a secret address known mainly to discerning locals with a palate for good food. The menu is changed monthly. Dishes are not student "experiments" but carefully crafted dishes based on the use of first-class ingredients. Freshly caught *merluza* (hake) is perfectly prepared with zesty mussels and mushrooms in a parsley-laced sauce. In autumn, loin of deer might appear on the menu with a chestnut purée. An excellent dish we recently sampled was loin of beef broiled and served with a red-wine sauce. Another specialty that frequently appears throughout the year is ham-covered filet of pork served with a Málaga wine sauce. The desserts are made fresh daily and are sumptuous. The villa is old but the dining room adjoining it is modern, opening onto a garden.

Finca La Cónsula, Churriana. ✆ **95-262-25-62.** Reservations required. Main courses 17€–22€; fixed-price lunch 27€. AE, DC, MC, V. Mon–Fri 1:30–3:30pm. No dinner. Closed Aug.

MODERATE

El Chinitas ✶ SPANISH/MEDITERRANEAN   In the heart of Málaga a short walk from the tourist office, this is one of the most established restaurants in town. Many regular patrons consume a round of tapas and drinks at the associated Bar Orellana next door (which maintains the same hours, minus the midafternoon closing), then head to Chinitas for a meal. The place is often filled with local residents, which is a good sign. The menu changes but might include a mixed fish fry, grilled red mullet, shrimp cocktail, grilled sirloin, or shellfish soup. The service is both fast and attentive.

Moreno Monroy 4. ℰ **95-221-09-72**. Reservations recommended. Main courses 8€–18€. DC, MC, V. Daily 1–4pm and 8pm–midnight.

Parador de Málaga-Gibralfaro ✶ SPANISH   This government-owned restaurant, on a mountainside high above the city, is especially notable for its view. You can look down into the heart of the Málaga bullring, among other sights. Meals are served in the attractive dining room or under the arches of two wide terraces, which provide views of the coast. Featured dishes include *hors d'oeuvres parador*—your entire table covered with tiny dishes of tasty tidbits. Two other specialties are an omelet of *chanquetes,* tiny whitefish popular in this part of the country, and chicken Villaroi.

Monte Gibralfara. ℰ **95-222-19-02**. Main courses 11€–23€; fixed-price menu 25€. AE, DC, MC, V. Daily 1–4pm and 8:30–11pm. Microbus: H, by the cathedral.

Parador Nacional del Golf ✶ SPANISH   This government-owned restaurant has an indoor/outdoor dining room that opens onto a circular swimming pool, golf course, and private beach. The interior room, furnished with reproductions of antiques, has a refined country-club atmosphere. Before-lunch drinks at the sleek modern bar tempt golfers, among others, who then proceed to the covered terrace for their Spanish meals.

Autovía Del Mediterráneo, Apartado 324, Málaga. ℰ **95-238-12-55**. Main courses 12€–24€; fixed-price menu 22€. AE, DC, MC, V. Daily 1:30–4pm and 8:30–11pm.

INEXPENSIVE

La Cancela ✶ *Finds* ANDALUSIAN/INTERNATIONAL   A charming little bistro, relatively unknown, is run with warmth and hospitality. It lies in a hard-to-find alleyway, right off a main artery, Calle Granada, 1 block from the landmark Palacio Episcopal at the top of Molina Larrios. The regular patrons like to sit out on a summer day enjoying a table on the sidewalk (it's sheltered). You can also retreat indoor at any time of the year to enjoy a repertoire of standard and well-prepared dishes. Nothing is too fancy here. If Franco were to return to Málaga, he'd be familiar with all the fare offered.

The restaurant has been in business for half a century, and the kitchen pretty much cooks as it did when the place first opened. All kinds of fresh fish is brought in here daily from local waters, and most of the regular customers, and we concur, prefer it grilled which the cooks do to perfection. Another preparation is deep fried. A tender loin of veal, well seasoned, is served with fried potatoes, or else you may prefer a skewer of pork with tomatoes, red peppers, and fried potatoes. Another specialty is a pork dish served with a Málaga wine sauce.

Calle Denís Belgrano 5. ℰ **95-223-31-25**. Reservations not required. Main courses 6€–15€. AE, DC, MC, V. Thurs–Tues 1–4:30pm; Tues and Thurs–Sun 8–11:30pm.

Refectorium SPANISH   Located behind the Málaga bullring, this place becomes hectic during any bullfight. It fills with aficionados and often, after the fight, with the matadors too. But you can dine here anytime, especially when the pace is less frantic. The cuisine has an old-fashioned flair, and the servings are generous. The typical soup of the Málaga area is *ajo blanco con uvas* (cold almond soup flavored with garlic and garnished with big muscatel grapes). For a classic opener, try a plate of garlic-flavored mushrooms seasoned with bits of ham. The fresh seafood is a delight, including *rape* (monkfish) and angler; lamb might be served with a saffron-flavored tomato sauce. Desserts are like Mama made, including rice pudding.

Calle Cervantes 8. (✆ **95-221-89-90.** Reservations recommended on weekends and at bullfights. Main courses 6€–18€. AE, DC, MC, V. Mon–Sat 1–6pm and 9pm–1am.

MALAGA AFTER DARK

The fun of nightlife in Málaga is wandering (although a few destinations do stand out). More than just about any other city in the region, Málaga offers night owls the chance to stroll a labyrinth of inner-city streets, drinking wine at any convenient *tasca,* and talking with friends and new acquaintances.

We suggest that you start out along the town's main thoroughfare, **Calle Larios,** which runs adjacent to the city's port. Off Calle Larios, you can gravitate to any of the *tascas,* discos, and pubs lining the edges of the **Calle Granada.** Of particular interest, in terms of the fun and atmosphere you're likely to find inside, are **Bar Pimpil,** Calle Granada s/n (no phone), and **La Posada,** Calle Granada s/n (no phone).

We'll let you in on a secret: If you want to eat well and cheaply, do as the locals do and head for either or both of the taverns below. Although nothing is refined, the food is some of the finest in Málaga, and some of the least expensive. You can easily fill up on two or three orders of tapas because portions are extremely generous.

The entrance to **Bar Logüeno,** Marín García 9 (✆ **95-222-30-48**), is behind a wrought-iron-and-glass door. It leads into a stucco-lined room decorated in a local tavern style with a vengeance. There are enough hams, bouquets of garlic, beer kegs, fishnets, and sausages to feed an entire village for a week. However, there's hardly enough room to stand, and you'll invariably be jostled by a busy waiter shouting "Calamari!" to cooks in the back kitchens.

Nearby, an all-pedestrian street, **Calle Compagnía,** and a square, the **Plaza Uncibaj,** are home to simpler *tascas.* Completely unpretentious (and in some cases without any discernable name), they serve glasses of wine and tapas similar to those available from their neighbors.

Two popular dance bars are **Saloma,** Calle Luis de Velázquez s/n, and **Cosa Nuestra,** Calle Las Lazcano 5. Don't even think of heading to either before 11pm, but once you're there, the music will probably continue till at least 4am.

10 Nerja ★★

52km (32 miles) E of Málaga, 168km (104 miles) W of Almería, 548km (340 miles) S of Madrid

Nerja is known for its good beaches and small coves, its seclusion, its narrow streets and courtyards, and its whitewashed flat-roofed houses. Nearby is one of Spain's greatest attractions, the Cave of Nerja (see below).

At the mouth of the Chillar River, Nerja gets its name from the Arabic word *narixa,* meaning "bountiful spring." Its most dramatic spot is the **Balcón de**

Europa ★★, a palm-shaded promenade that juts out into the Mediterranean. The walkway was built in 1885 in honor of a visit from the Spanish king Alfonso XIII in the wake of an earthquake that had shattered part of nearby Málaga. The phrase "Balcón de Europa" (Balcony of Europe) is said to have been coined by the king during one of the speeches he made in Nerja praising the beauty of the panoramas around him. To reach the best beaches, head west from the Balcón and follow the shoreline.

ESSENTIALS

GETTING THERE   At least 10 **buses** per day make the 1½-hour trip from Málaga. From Almería, four buses a day make the 3-hour trip. Call the bus station, Avenida Pescia s/n (✆ **95-252-15-04**), for information and schedules.

If you're driving, head along the N-340/E-15 east from Málaga or take the N-340/E-15 west from Almería.

VISITOR INFORMATION   The **tourist office** at Puerta del Mar 2 (✆ **95-252-15-31;** www.nerja.org) is open Monday through Friday from 10am to 2pm and 5:30 to 8:30pm, Saturday from 10am to 1pm.

SPECIAL EVENTS   A **cultural festival** takes place here in July. In the past it has drawn leading artists, musicians, and dancers from around the world, including Yehudi Menuhin, Maya Plisetskaya, and the Bolshoi Ballet.

EXPLORING THE CUEVA DE NERJA

The most popular outing from Málaga and Nerja is to the **Cueva de Nerja (Cave of Nerja)** ★★, Carretera de Maro s/n (✆ **95-252-96-35**). Scientists believe this prehistoric stalactite and stalagmite cave was inhabited from 25,000 to 2000 B.C. It was undiscovered until 1959, when a handful of boys found it by chance. When fully opened, it revealed a wealth of treasures left from the days of the cave dwellers, including Paleolithic paintings. They depict horses and deer, but as of this writing the room with cave paintings is not open to the public. The archaeological museum in the cave contains a number of prehistoric artifacts. You can walk through stupendous galleries where ceilings soar to a height of 60m (200 ft.).

The cave is in the hills near Nerja. From here you get panoramic views of the countryside and sea. The cave is open daily from 10am to 2pm and 4 to 6:30pm. Admission is 5€ adults, 2.50€ for children 6 to 12, free for children under 6. Buses to the cave leave from Muelle de Heredia in Málaga hourly from 7am to 8:15pm. Return buses are also hourly until 8:15pm. The journey takes about 1 hour.

WHERE TO STAY
EXPENSIVE

Hotel Mónica   This government-rated four-star hotel opened in 1986 in an isolated beachfront location about a 10-minute walk from the Balcón de Europa. The comfortable, good-size rooms have private balconies and bathrooms with tub/shower combos.

Playa de la Torrecilla s/n, 29780 Nerja. ✆ **95-252-11-00**. Fax 95-252-11-62. www.riu.com. 257 units. 85€–165€ double. AE, DC, MC, V. Free parking. **Amenities:** Restaurant; bar; pool; room service; babysitting; laundry service; dry cleaning. *In room:* A/C, TV, minibar, hair dryer, safe.

Parador de Nerja ★★   This government-owned hotel is on the outskirts of town a 5-minute walk from the center. On the edge of a cliff, the hotel centers on a flower-filled courtyard with splashing fountain. The spacious rooms are furnished in understated but tasteful style, and bathrooms have tub/shower combos.

Calle Almuñécar 8, Playa de Burriana-Tablazo, 29780 Nerja. ✆ **95-252-00-50.** Fax 95-252-19-97. www.parador.es. 98 units. 116€–146€ double. AE, DC, MC, V. Free parking. **Amenities:** Restaurant; bar; pool; tennis courts; room service; babysitting; laundry service; dry cleaning. *In room:* A/C, TV, minibar, hair dryer, safe.

MODERATE

Hotel Balcón de Europa   Occupying the best position in town, at the edge of the Balcón de Europa, this 1970s hotel offers guest rooms with private balconies overlooking the water and the rocks. At a private beach nearby, parasolshielded tables offer a place for a peaceful vista. The comfortable, midsize rooms have modern furniture and firm beds. Bathrooms have tub/shower combos. There's a private garage a few steps away.

Paseo Balcón de Europa 2, 29780 Nerja. ✆ **95-252-08-00.** Fax 95-252-44-90. www.hotel-balconeuropa.com. 110 units. 103€–141€ double; 126€–164€ suite. AE, DC, MC, V. Parking 7.50€. **Amenities:** 2 restaurants; bar; pool; sauna; room service; babysitting; laundry service; dry cleaning. *In room:* A/C, TV, minibar, hair dryer, safe.

Plaza Cavana ★ *Finds*   In the center of town, just behind El Balcón de Europa and a short walk from the beach, this two-story hotel is imbued with an oldfashioned Andalusian charm. It lies behind a typical white facade with wooden balconies. The lobby has a classic decor with marble floors, and there is a garden patio where guests can relax. Rooms are elegant, spacious, and comfortable, and open onto balconies with either sea or mountain views. The neatly kept bathrooms have tub/shower combos.

Plaza Cavana 10, 29780 Nerja. ✆ **95-252-40-00.** Fax 95-252-40-08. 35 units. 75€–110€ double. AE, DC, MC, V. Parking 9€. **Amenities:** Restaurant; bar; 2 pools; sauna; room service; babysitting; laundry service; dry cleaning. *In room:* A/C, TV, minibar, hair dryer, safe.

INEXPENSIVE

Hostal Miguel   The family-run Miguel is a pleasant, unpretentious inn on a quiet back street about a 3-minute walk from the Balcón de Europa, across from the well-known Pepe Rico Restaurant. The simply furnished, somewhat small rooms have been renovated to add more Andalusian flavor. Bathrooms have shower stalls. Breakfast is the only meal served, usually on a lovely roof terrace with a view of the mountains and sea.

Almirante Ferrándiz 31, 29780 Nerja. ✆ **95-252-15-23.** Fax 95-252-65-35. 9 units. 32€–42€ double. MC, V. **Amenities:** Breakfast room. *In room:* No phone.

Paraíso del Mar ★ *Finds*   Next door to the more upmarket Parador de Nerja, this little hacienda also offers a panoramic view of the coastline. The former home of a wealthy expatriate has been turned into this comfortable villa lying near the edge of a cliff opening onto the fabled Balcón de Europa or "balcony of Europe." Bedrooms are tastefully furnished but not luxurious, and four of them come with tub baths, the others having showers. Because of the view, most people request a sea-view accommodation. As a compensation, the rooms in the rear are more spacious or else come with a Jacuzzi so you don't feel deprived. You can absorb that view from one of the hotel's public terraces.

Prolongación del Carabeo 22, 29780 Nerja. ✆ **95-252-16-21.** Fax 95-252-23-09. www.interhotel.com/spain/es/hoteles/4680.html. 12 units. 58€–100€ double; 100€–132€ suite. Rates include breakfast. DC, MC, V. **Amenities:** Pool; laundry/dry cleaning. *In room:* A/C, TV, minibar, safe.

WHERE TO DINE

Casa Luque *Value* ANDALUSIAN   With its impressive canopied and balconied facade near the heart of town, Casa Luque looks like a dignified private
villa. The interior has an Andalusian courtyard, and in summer there's a sea-view
terrace. Dishes are tasty and helpings quite filling—you'll find good value here.
Meals change according to the season and might include Andalusian gazpacho,
pork filet, hot-pepper chicken Casanova, or grilled meats. The limited selection
of fish includes grilled Mediterranean grouper.

Plaza Cavana 2. © **95-252-10-04.** Reservations required. Main courses 10€–18€. DC, MC, V. Daily
noon–4pm and 7–11pm.

Pepe Rico Restaurant ⚐ INTERNATIONAL   Opened in 1966, Pepe Rico
is one of Nerja's finest restaurants. Dine in a tavern room or on the patio, where
you can order meals alfresco. The specialty of the day, which might be a Spanish, German, Swedish, or French dish, ranges from almond-and-garlic soup to
duck in wine. The impressive list of hors d'oeuvres includes smoked swordfish,
salmon mousse, and prawns *pil-pil* (with hot chile peppers). Main dishes include
filet of sole, roast leg of lamb, prawns Café de Paris, and steak dishes. Considering the quality of the food, the prices are reasonable.

Almirante Ferrándiz 28. © **95-252-02-47.** Reservations recommended. Main courses 12€–18€; fixed-price
menu 10€ at lunch, 24€ at dinner. MC, V. Mon–Sat 12:30–3pm and 7–11pm. Closed Dec 10–20 and Jan
10–Feb 17.

Restaurante de Miguel ⚐⚐ INTERNATIONAL   This restaurant is the
best in town. Established in 1986 by a Nerja resident, at first it drew only local
families hoping for their friend to succeed. Since then the place has attracted a
devoted crowd of foreign visitors and expatriate residents of the Costa del Sol. It
is in the center of town near the busiest traffic intersection. Its small air-conditioned interior is one of the most upscale places in Nerja. The well-prepared
menu includes cream of shrimp soup flavored with cognac, tournedos with goat-
cheese sauce, and sea bass with Pernod and fennel. There's a wide selection of
beef and steak dishes and, of course, fresh fish from the tank.

Pintada 2. © **95-252-29-96.** Reservations recommended. Main courses 11€–15€. MC, V. Daily 8pm–midnight. Winter hours: Daily 7:30–11pm. Closed 2 Mon each month.

Restaurante Rey Alfonso ⚐ SPANISH/INTERNATIONAL   Few visitors
to the Balcón de Europa realize that they're standing directly above one of the
most unusual restaurants in town. The restaurant's menu and decor don't hold
many surprises, but the close-up view of the crashing waves makes dining here
worthwhile. Have a drink at the bar if you don't want a full meal. Specialties
include a well-prepared *paella valenciana*, Cuban-style rice, five preparations of
sole (from grilled to meunière), several versions of tournedos and entrecôte, beef
Stroganoff, crayfish in whisky sauce, and crêpes Suzettes for dessert. You enter
from the bottom of a flight of stairs that skirts the rocky base of a late-19th-cen-
tury *mirador* (viewing station), which juts seaward as an extension of the town's
main square.

Paseo Balcón de Europa s/n. © **95-252-09-58.** Reservations recommended. Main courses 9€–18€. MC, V.
Mon–Sat 11am–4pm and 7–11pm. Closed Nov.

10

Valencia & the Costa Blanca

Spain's third-largest city, Valencia—celebrated for oranges and paella—lies in the midst of a *huerta*, a fertile crescent of alluvial plain that's irrigated by a centuries-old system. The area is a breadbasket of Spain, a place where "the soil never sleeps."

For such a major city, Valencia is relatively unexplored by tourists, even though it has some rewarding treasures, including a wealth of baroque architecture, fine museums, good cuisine, and a proud, if troubled, history.

The Costa Blanca (White Coast) begins rather unappealingly at Valencia but improves considerably as it winds its way south toward Alicante. The overbuilt route south is dotted with fishing ports and resorts known chiefly to Spanish and other European vacationers. The success of **Benidorm** began in the 1960s, when this fishing village was transformed into an international resort. **Alicante,** the official capital of the Costa Blanca, enjoys a reputation as a winter resort because of its mild climate. **Murcia** is inland but on the main road to the Costa del Sol, so hordes of motorists pass through it.

1 Valencia ★★

351km (218 miles) SE of Madrid, 361km (224 miles) SW of Barcelona, 650km (404 miles) NE of Málaga

Valencia's charms—or lack thereof—are much debated. Some claim that the city where El Cid faced the Moors is one of the most beautiful on the Mediterranean. Others write it off as drab, provincial, and industrial. The truth lies somewhere in between.

Set amid orange trees and rice paddies, Valencia's reputation as a romantic city seems more justified by its past than by its present. Hidden between modern office buildings and monotonous apartment houses, remnants of an illustrious past do remain. However, floods and war have been cruel to Valencia, forcing Valencianos to tear down buildings that today would be architectural treasures.

Valencia has a strong cultural tradition. Its most famous son was writer Vicente Blasco Ibáñez, best known for his novel about bullfighting, *Blood and Sand,* and for his World War I novel, *The Four Horsemen of the Apocalypse.* Both were filmed twice in Hollywood, with Rudolph Valentino starring in the first version of each. Joaquín Sorolla, the famous Spanish Impressionist, was another native of Valencia. You can see his works at a museum dedicated to him in Madrid.

ESSENTIALS
GETTING THERE   **Iberia** flies to Valencia from Barcelona, Madrid, Málaga, and many other cities. There are also flights between Palma de Majorca and Valencia. You'll land 14.5km (9 miles) southwest of the city. Cercanías trains run between the airport and the main train station within Valencia every half hour during the day. The cost of a 1-way ticket is 1€. For flight information, contact the Iberia Airlines office, Calle Paz 14 (© **90-240-05-00**).

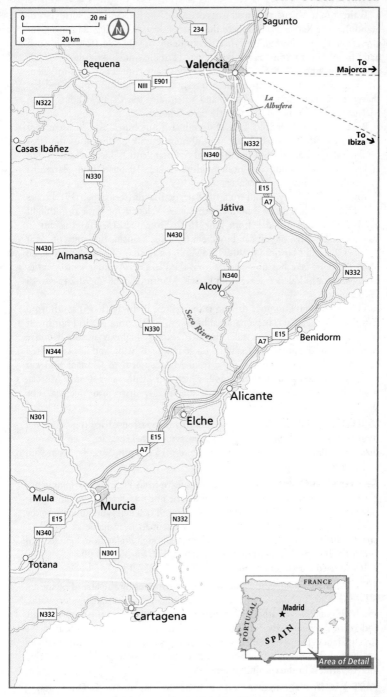

The Costa Blanca

Trains run to Valencia from all parts of Spain. The Estación del Norte (North Station), Calle Xátiva 24, is close to the heart of the city, making it a convenient arrival point. Its information office, Calle Renfe (© **90-224-02-02**), is open daily from 7am to 9pm. From Barcelona, 11 trains—including the TALGO, which takes 4 hours—arrives daily. Nine trains daily connect Madrid to Valencia. The new Alaris high-speed train travels at 221kmph (137 mph) and has shaved travel time between Madrid and Valencia to less than 3½ hours. From Málaga, on the Costa del Sol, the trip takes 9 hours.

Buses arrive at Valencia's Estació Terminal d'Autobuses, Av. de Menéndez Pidal 15 (© **96-346-62-66**), about a 30-minute walk northwest of the city's center. Take bus no. 8 from the Plaza del Ayuntamiento. Thirteen buses a day, at least one every hour, run from Madrid (4 hr.), 10 buses from Barcelona (5 hr.), and five buses from Málaga (8 hr.).

You can take a **ferry** to and from the Balearic Islands (see chapter 19). Ferries to Palma de Majorca take 6 hours. Ferries leave Valencia for Ibiza at midnight Thursday through Tuesday from June 15 to September 15. Travel agents in Valencia sell tickets, or you can buy them from the Transmediterránea office at the port, Estació Marítim (© **90-245-46-45**), on the day of your departure. To reach the port, take bus no. 4 or 19 from the Plaza del Ayuntamiento. Ferries from Majorca to Valencia leave from Estació Marítim 2. Call © **90-245-46-45** for details.

The easiest route if you're driving is the express highway (E-15) south from Barcelona. You can also use a national highway, E-901, from Madrid northwest of Valencia. From Alicante, take the E-15 express highway north. If you're coming from Andalusia, the roads are longer, more difficult, and not connected by express highways. You can drive from Málaga north to Granada and cut across southeastern Spain on the 342, which links with the 340 into Murcia. From there, take the road to Alicante for an easy drive into Valencia. The Barcelona-Valencia toll is 18€.

VISITOR INFORMATION   The **tourist information office** is at Plaza del Ayuntamiento 1 (© **96-351-04-17;** www.ayto-valencia.es). It's open Monday through Friday from 8:30am to 2:15pm and 4:15 to 6pm, Saturday from 9am to 12:45pm.

GETTING AROUND   Most local buses leave from Plaza del Ayuntamiento 22. You can buy tickets at any newsstand. The one-way fare is .90€ and a 10-ride booklet sells for 4.70€. Bus no. 8 runs from Plaza del Ayuntamiento to the bus station at Avenida Menéndez Pidal. A bus map is available at the EMT office, Calle Correo Viejo 5. It's open Monday through Friday from 8am to 1pm and from 4:30 to7pm. For bus information, call © **96-352-83-99.**

If you need a taxi, call © **96-370-33-33** or 96-357-13-13.

SPECIAL EVENTS   The **Fallas de San José,** honoring the arrival of spring, is held in March (dates vary). It is a time for parades, street dancing, fireworks, and bullfights. Neighborhoods compete to see who can erect the most intricate and satirical papier-mâché effigy, or *ninot.* Some 300 *ninots* then appear in the street parades. The festival ends with *la nit del foc,* or "fire night," when effigies are burned. Historically, this inferno was to exorcise social problems and bring luck to farmers in the coming summer.

FAST FACTS   The local **American Express** representative is **Duna Viajes,** Calle Cirilo Amorós 88 (© **96-374-15-62**). It's open Monday through Friday from 10am to 2pm and 5 to 7:30pm, Saturday from 9am to 1:30pm.

Valencia

ACCOMMODATIONS ■

Catalonia Excelsior **8**
Hostal Residencia Bisbal **12**
Hotel Ad Hoc **18**
Hotel Astoria Palace **9**
Hotel Consul del Mar **2**
Hotel Reina Victoria **7**
Melía Comfort Inglés **10**
Melía Rey Don Jaime **2**
Melía Valencia Palace **1**
Monte Picayo **19**
NH Hotel Vilacarlos **2**
Sidi Saler **4**
Sorolla **6**

ATTRACTIONS ●

Catedral **16**
Cuidad de las Artes y de las Ciencias **3**
Instituto Valenciano de Arte Moderno **13**
Jardines del Real **21**
La Lonja de la Seda **11**
Museo San Pio **20**
Palau de la Generalitat **15**
Plaza de Toros **5**
Torres de Quart **14**
Torres de Serranos District **17**

‡ Church
ⓘ Information

The **U.S. Consular Agency** is at Calle Doctor Romagosa #1, 2nd floor (© 96-351-69-73); it's open Monday through Friday from 10am to 1pm.

In a medical emergency, call © **112** or © **091,** or go to the **Hospital Clínico Universitario,** Av. Blasco Ibáñez 17 (© **96-386-26-00**).

Don't be surprised if you see signs in a language that's not Spanish or Catalán. It is *Valenciano,* a dialect of Catalán. Often you'll be handed a "bilingual" menu in Castilian Spanish and in *Valenciano.* Many citizens of Valencia are not caught up in this cultural resurgence, and view the promotion of the dialect as possibly damaging to the city's economic goals. Most street names appear in *Valenciano.*

The self-service laundry **Lavandería El Mercat,** Plaza del Mercado 12 (© **96-391-20-10**), is open Monday through Friday from 10am to 2pm and 4:30 to 8:30pm, Saturday from 10am to 2pm.

EXPLORING VALENCIA

Corridas (bullfights) are staged for a week during the *fallas* observances in the summer (see "Spain Calendar of Events," in chapter 3). Today locals seem more interested in soccer than in bullfighting. Nevertheless, Valencia's **Plaza de Toros,** one of the largest rings in Spain, is adjacent to the rail station at Calle de Xátiva 28 (© **96-351-93-15**).

Catedral (Seu) ★ For 500 years, this cathedral has claimed to possess the Holy Grail, the chalice Jesus used at the Last Supper; it's on display in a side chapel. The subject of countless legends, the Grail was said to have been used by Joseph of Arimathea to collect Jesus's blood as it fell from the cross. It looms large in Sir Thomas Malory's *Morte d'Arthur,* Tennyson's *Idylls of the King,* and Wagner's *Parsifal.*

Although this 1262 cathedral represents a number of styles, including Romanesque and baroque, Gothic predominates. Its huge arches have been restored, and in back is a handsome domed basilica. It was built on the site of a mosque torn down by the Catholic monarchs.

After seeing the cathedral, you can scale an incomplete 47m (155-ft.) high Gothic tower—known as **Miguelete** ★ (or Micalet in local dialect). It affords a panoramic view of the city and the fertile huerta beyond. Or visit the **Museo de la Catedral,** where works by Goya and Zurbarán are on exhibit.

Plaza de la Reina. © **96-391-81-27.** Admission to cathedral free; to Miguelete 1.20€; to Museo de la Catedral 1.20€. Cathedral daily 7:30am–1pm and 4:30–8:30pm; Miguelete Mon–Sat 10am–12:30pm and 4:30–7:30pm; Sun 10am–1pm and 5–7:30pm; Museo de la Catedral Mon–Sat 10am–1pm and 4–6pm. Bus: 9, 27, 70, or 71.

Ciudad de las Artes y de las Ciencias (City of the Arts and Sciences) ★★★ In a bid to rival Seville's Expo and Barcelona's redeveloped port, Valencia competes with what has been billed as "the largest urban complex in Europe for cultural, educational, and leisure expansion." It's in the southern part of the city, on a 36-hectare (90-acre) site in a carefully landscaped park of lush greenery and peaceful lagoons, and should be complete sometime in 2004. The point of the complex is to make learning fun. The state-of-the-art educational center consists of four main buildings:

L'Hemisferic ★: Designed by award-winning architect Santiago Calatrava, this building offers documentaries and an exploration of the universe. A laser show (with changing programs) runs on a 47-sq.-m (900-sq.-ft.) concave IMAX screen, with the soundtrack in four languages, and six-channel stereo.

Museo de las Ciencias Príncipe Felipe ★: Devoted to science and discovery, the building takes the form of a vast roof supported by a transparent glazed north facade and an opaque south facade. At the center, the visitor will be able to not only look at, but also touch and feel in this "museum of sensations." The museum is filled with special exhibitions demonstrating the high technology of companies in the 21st century.

Two other major sections include the following:

L'Oceanografic: Eight hectares (20 acres) of the complex are devoted to lagoons and leisure pavilions arranged into an underwater city that will re-create marine habitats from every ocean. There's also a dolphinarium for aquatic shows and a miniport for playing with remote-controlled boats. Submarine glass walkways connect the areas. An underwater restaurant is also on-site.

Palacio de las Artes: A seemingly weightless 45m (150-ft.) high glass and metal construction will contain one outdoor and two indoor auditoriums. All three will have the latest technology for the performance of plays, opera, and music. It is scheduled for completion in early 2004.

Instituto Obreno s/n. ℂ **90-210-00-31.** www.cac.es. Admission to L'Hemisferic 6.60€ adults, 4.30€ children, students, and seniors. Admission to L'Oceanografic 19€ adults, 13€ children students, and seniors. Admission to Museo de las Ciencias Príncipe Felipe 6€ adults, 3.60€ children, students, and seniors. L'Hemisferic Mon–Fri 10am–8pm, Sat–Sun 10am–1pm. Museo de las Ciencias Príncipe Felipe and L'Oceanografic Mon–Fri 10am–8m, Sat–Sun 10am–9pm. Bus: 13, 14, or 15 to Centro Comercio de Saler.

Instituto Valencia de Arte Moderno (IVAM) ★★   This giant complex consists of two sites: an ultramodern building and a 13th-century former convent. Its opening gained Valencia prime status among the world's art capitals.

Julio González Center is named for the avant-garde Spanish artist whose paintings, sculptures, and drawings form the nucleus of the permanent collection. Much influenced by Picasso, González was a pioneer in iron sculpture. His work in turn exerted a profound influence on the American sculptor David Smith, among others.

The other site is the nearby **Center del Carmen,** the old convent, with cloisters from the 14th and the 16th centuries. It devotes three halls to changing exhibits of contemporary art. Permanent displays include works of Ignacio Pinazo, whose paintings and drawings mark the beginning of modernism in Valencia. The institute is on the western edge of the old quarter, near the **Torres de Quart,** 15th-century towers that guard the entrance to the city.

Calle Guillém Castro 118. ℂ **96-386-30-00.** Admission 2.10€ adults, free for children. Hours for both centers Tues–Sun 10am–8pm. Bus: 5.

La Lonja de la Seda ★   This former silk exchange, completed in 1498, is the most splendid example of secular Gothic architecture in Spain. A beautiful building, La Lonja has twisted spiral columns inside and stained-glass windows.

Plaza del Mercado. ℂ **96-352-54-78.** Free admission. Tues–Sat 9am–2pm and 5:30–8pm; Sun 9am–1:30pm. Closed holidays. Bus: 4, 7, 27, 60, or 81.

Museo San Pío (Museu Sant Píus V) ★   This treasure house of paintings and sculptures, which stands on the north bank of the Turia River, contains a strong collection of Flemish and native Valencian art. Of particular note are those by the **14th- and 15th-century Valencian "primitives"** ★★. The most celebrated painting is a 1640 self-portrait by Velázquez, and a whole room is devoted to Goya. Other artists exhibited include Bosch, Morales, El Greco *(St. John the Baptist),* Ribera, Murillo, Pinturicchio, and Sorolla. Of special interest is a salon displaying the works of contemporary Valencian painters and an important sculpture by Mariano Benlliure. The ground-floor archaeological collection encompasses early Iberian, Roman (including an altar to a pagan emperor), and early Christian finds.

San Pío V 9. ℂ **96-393-20-46.** Free admission. Tues–Sun 10am–8pm. Bus: 1, 5, 6, 8, 11, 18, 26, 29, 36, or 79. Metro: Alameda.

Palau de la Generalitat ☆   In the old aristocratic quarter of Valencia, this Gothic palace built in the 15th and 16th centuries is one of the most fascinating edifices in Spain. It has two square towers (one constructed as recently as 1952), carved wooden ceilings and galleries, and frescoes. It now serves as the headquarters of the regional government (Generalitat).

Caballeros 2. © **96-386-34-61**. Free admission. By appointment only. Bus: 5.

BEACHES & MORE

BEACHES   The beaches to the north and south of the port, Playa de la Punta and Playa de Levante, are too polluted for swimming. To go to the beach, head south in the direction of **El Saler,** where you'll find cleaner waters.

BOATING   **Club Náutico Valencia,** Camí del Canal 91 (© **96-367-90-11**), has a sailing school that rents boats for scuba diving, and snorkeling. It maintains a full yacht service facility.

GOLF   There are four major golf courses in the area. One of the best is **Golf El Saler** at the Parador Nacional El Saler (© **96-161-03-84**), 18km (11 miles) south of Valencia in a setting of pine dunes. Another good course is the **Club de Campo del Bosque,** Carretera Godelleta, Km 4.1, Chiva (© **96-180-41-42**), 4km (2½ miles) from Valencia. Or try the **Club de Golf Escorpión at Bétera** (© **96-160-12-11**), 19km (12 miles) northwest en route to Liria. All three are 18-hole courses. There's a nine-hole course, the **Manises Golf Club** (© **96-152-18-71**), on the Carretera Riba Roja, Km 4 at Manises, 12km (7½ miles) west of Valencia.

SHOPPING

There are fewer souvenir shops and tourist facilities in workaday Valencia than in any other Spanish city its size. Instead, you're likely to find everyday reality in the form of middlebrow department stores and food and wine emporiums. The best shopping streets include the **Plaza del Ayuntamiento, Calle Don Juan de Austria, Calle Colón,** and the streets thereabouts. For a peek at what aging Valencian *duennas* are storing in their cellars and attics, head for the *rastro* (flea market) in the Avenida de Suecia near the soccer stadium, beginning around 8:30am every Sunday. The city's largest department store, **El Corte Inglés,** Calle Pintor Sorolla 26 (© **96-315-95-00**), sells a wide array of anything you might need, including local handicrafts, crystal and porcelain, and other luxury items.

Valencia is home to some of Spain's best pottery. The region produces Lladró porcelain, Manises stoneware, and glassware. Local craftspeople take pride in their *azulejos*—brightly colored ceramic tiles, first developed during the Muslim occupation of Andalusia.

One worthy detour is to **Manises,** 9km (5½ miles) west of Valencia. It's known as a center for ceramics and for its *azulejos.* As a pottery center, Manises dates from the Middle Ages. Representatives from all the major kingdoms of Europe came here to purchase the wares, which are characterized by their distinctive blue-and-white patterns. The town is packed with ceramics factories and retail outlets. From the center of Valencia, several buses run frequently to Manises. The tourist office will give you a bus schedule.

Another good stop for the serious shopper is nearby **Paterna,** about 6.5km (4 miles) northwest of Valencia off C-234 (it's signposted all the way). It has dozens of pottery stores with prices far below those in the center of Valencia.

Continuing farther north to the province of Castellón, you'll find the towns of **Alcora** and **Onda.** They're justly celebrated for their pottery, much of which is reasonably priced because the "middleperson" is often eliminated. In addition to pottery, several shops in Onda sell some of the best-crafted *azulejos* in this part of Spain. **Alcora** is 19km (12 miles) northwest of Castellón de la Plana along the C-232; **Onda,** 15km (9 miles) west along the C-223.

In the city of Valencia itself, head for **Lladró,** Calle Poeta Querol 9 (*©* **96-351-16-25**), where prices are consistent with those at other retail outlets. Or seek out the shop adjacent to the factory, **Casa de Lladró,** Carretera de Alborraya s/n, in the suburb of Tavernas Blanques (*©* **96-318-70-00**), 5km (3 miles) north of the city center. The factory retail outlet sells slightly damaged or irregular pieces at lower prices. To visit the factory itself, call 1 month in advance (use the Casa de Lladró number, above).

WHERE TO STAY

In July and August, when Valencia can be uncomfortably hot and humid, some hoteliers lower prices significantly if business is slow. It never hurts to ask.

EXPENSIVE

Hotel Astoria Palace *☆*   On a small, charming square in the heart of town, this modern business hotel offers some of the best-furnished public and private rooms in Valencia. A favorite of such Spanish stars as opera singer Montserrat Caballé, bullfighter Manuel Benítez ("El Cordobés"), and an impressive roster of writers and politicians, the Astoria is plush, well managed, and appealing. Many of the tastefully furnished guest rooms overlook a statue of Grecian maidens and swans in the square outside. The highest prices are for three premium floors, which have a private lounge and separate check-in. Each of the tiled bathrooms is equipped with a tub/shower combination. The hotel is 5 short blocks south of the cathedral.

Plaza Rodrigo Botet 5, 46002 Valencia. *©* **96-398-10-00.** Fax 96-398-10-11. www.hotel-astoria-palace.com. 203 units. 139€–218€ double; 204€–310€ junior suite; 310€ suite. AE, DC, MC, V. Parking 14€ nearby. Bus: 9, 10, 27, 70, or 71. **Amenities:** Restaurant; bar; health club; sauna; whirlpool; car rental; room service; babysitting; laundry service; dry cleaning. *In room:* A/C, TV, minibar, hair dryer, safe.

Hotel Reina Victoria *☆*   Although it has lost some of its charm and luster in recent years, the Reina Victoria enjoys a reputation as the most architecturally glamorous hotel in Valencia. Built in 1913, the hotel has welcomed many distinguished guests, including Alfonso XIII and its namesake Queen Victoria herself, as well as Dalí, Manolete, Picasso, Falla, García Lorca, and Miró. Bristling with neoclassical detailing and wrought-iron accents, it overlooks the flower gardens and fountains of Valencia's central square, the Plaza del País Valenciano. Rooms range from small to medium (only a few are really spacious) and have tiny bathrooms that contain both tubs and showers. The hotel is in the heart of town, a 5-minute walk from the railway station.

Barcas 4, 46002 Valencia. *©* **96-352-04-87.** Fax 96-352-27-21. www.husa.es. 97 units. 105€–132€ double; 157€ triple. Weekend prices include breakfast. AE, DC, MC, V. Parking 12€. Bus: 4, 7, or 27. **Amenities:** Restaurant; bar; room service; babysitting; laundry service; dry cleaning. *In room:* A/C, TV, minibar, hair dryer, safe.

Meliá Rey Don Jaime *☆☆*   A respected member of one of Spain's largest hotel chains, the Meliá towers over the urban landscape about .8km (½ mile) southeast of the cathedral. Many guests appreciate the hotel's proximity to the convention and concert hall (Palau de la Música) midway between the Old Town and the port. The stylish public rooms are sheathed in marble, rough stone, and tile work, whereas the guest rooms are sunny, well-maintained enclaves of contemporary style. The best units—more spacious and better furnished—are on the third floor. However, all rooms come with fine mattresses, and bathrooms containing tub/shower combos. Many of the accommodations on the upper floors open onto panoramic views of the port and the sea.

Av. de Baleares 2, 46023 Valencia. © **800/336-3542** in the U.S., or 96-337-50-30. Fax 96-337-15-72. 319 units. 146€–182€ double; 351€ suite. AE, DC, MC, V. Parking 11€. Bus: 19, 41, 89, or 90. **Amenities:** Restaurant; bar; pool; car rental; room service; babysitting; laundry service; dry cleaning; solarium. *In room:* A/C, TV, minibar, hair dryer, safe.

Meliá Valencia Palace 😊😊 This deluxe hostelry is part of Valencia's ongoing attempts to revamp its tourism image. At last the city has a world-class hotel to compete with the firmly established Meliá Rey Don Jaime and the Astoria Palace. This newly opened hotel is currently the most sought-after reservation in the city. A sleek, modern building, this government-rated five-star choice overlooks the Turia Gardens and the imposing Palau de la Música. The word "palace" within the hotel's name is apt, as it evokes a Grand Hotel of long ago, but with all the modern amenities. Bedrooms are spacious and luxuriously furnished, with double-glazing—in other words, you get the view but not the traffic noise. Roomy bathrooms are state-of-the-art, with deep tubs, power showers, and *luxe* toiletries. One of the hotel's most attractive features is the rooftop swimming pool—unusual for Valencia. The split-level restaurant with its regional specialties and international dishes is so excellent that you may want to dine here even if you're not a guest.

Paseo de la Alameda 32, 46023 Valencia. © **96-337-50-37.** Fax 96-337-55-32. www.solmelia.es. 243 units. 217€ double; 247€ suite. AE, DC, MC, V. Parking 14€. **Amenities:** Restaurant; bar; pool; gym; sauna; room service; babysitting; laundry service; dry cleaning. *In room:* A/C, TV, minibar, hair dryer, safe.

Monte Picayo 😊😊 Built in a classic Castilian style, this luxurious government-rated five-star retreat lies 18km (11 miles) north of Valencia. Enjoying a scenic and well-landscaped hillside location, it is an especially good choice in summer when you want to escape the heat of central Valencia, one steamy city. The public rooms are bright, airy and spacious, as are the well-furnished double rooms, done with traditional styling and class, each of them comfortable with a complete bathroom with tub and shower. Each of the accommodations comes with a private terrace opening onto a view, and nine of the units also have a small private pool. You don't have to go into Valencia at night, as the cuisine at this resort is first rate, an international repertoire with many Valencian specialties. The resort also has some of the best amenities in the area. The hotel lies 6km (3¾ miles) from the sandy beaches of Puig, Canet, and Puebla de Farnals, and also is close to a trio of golf courses.

Urbanización Monte Picayo, Autopista Valencia-Barcelona, 46530 Puzol, Valencia. © **96-142-01-00.** Fax 96-142-21-68. www.hvsl.es. 83 units. 130€–225€ double; 160€–280€ junior suite; from 300€ suite. AE, DC, MC, V. **Amenities:** Restaurant, bar, pool, 2 tennis courts, miniature golf, casino. *In room:* A/C, TV, minibar, hair dryer.

Sidi Saler If it's summer, and you want a location right on the beach, head for the coastal strip 12km (7½ miles) south of Valencia at Playa El Saler, one of the best sandy beaches in the area. Open year-round, and built in 1975, this hotel is at its best in the warm months. A golf course is close at hand should you grow bored with the sands. Bedrooms are midsize, and most of them have a midsize balcony overlooking the sea. The junior suites are even better, not only with that large balcony but a separate living room as well. Furnishings are modern but traditional in styling, with well-maintained bathrooms with tubs and showers. If you don't want to travel far afield for your meals, you'll find good dining on-site, not only Valencian paella but an array of regional and international dishes.

Playa del Saler, 46012 Valencia. © **96-161-04-11**. Fax 96-161-08-38. www. hotelessidi.es. 276 units. 203€–229€ double; 298€ junior suite; 475€ suite. AE, DC, MC, V. **Amenities:** 2 restaurants; 2 bars; 2 pools; fitness center; sauna; room service; summer-only babysitting; laundry/dry cleaning. *In room:* A/C, TV, minibar, hair dryer, safe, trouser press.

MODERATE

Catalonia Excelsior ✦ *(Value)*   This 1930s building has been sensitively restored and turned into one of the most welcoming and affordable hotels in the central part of town. The public rooms of this seven-floor structure are refreshing, especially the Art Deco–style restaurant with its adjacent bar. A spiral marble stairwell climbs up to a mellow salon—paneled in a dark cherry wood—which opens onto a terrace. Bedrooms range from small to midsize and have new carpeting and very comfortable beds, most often with a brass headboard. The other furnishings are comfortable as well, and each opens onto a well-maintained private bathroom with both shower and tub.

Barcelonina 5, 46002 Valencia. © **96-351-46-12**. Fax 963-523478. www.hoteles-catalonia.es. 81 units. 124€–155€ double. **Amenities:** Breakfast lounge; pool; sauna; laundry/dry cleaning. *In room:* A/C, TV, minibar, hair dryer.

Hotel Ad Hoc ✦ *(Finds)*   The owner, Luís García Alarcón, an antiques dealer, is the inspiration behind this choice government-rated, three-star hotel in a sensitively restored building from the 1880s. Occupying a bull's-eye center position—in fact, one of Valencia's best located hotels—it lies near the old source of the Turía River between the 1391 Torres Serranos and the 1763 Civil Government building. Bedrooms, often with exposed brick walls, are soundproofed against traffic noise and are simply but tastefully furnished, with small tiled bathrooms with tubs and showers. Don't judge the hotel by its facade, which is rather impersonal and ordinary. The interior of the building will warm your heart. On a small street, the hotel is difficult to reach if you're driving because of a series of one-way streets.

Boix 4, 46003 Valencia. © **96-391-91-40**. Fax 96-391-36-67. www.jpmoser.com/l-adhoc.html. Mon–Thurs 113€ double, 141€ triple; Fri–Sun 80€ double, 108€ triple. AE, DC, MC, V. **Amenities:** Restaurant; bar; laundry; room service. *In room:* A/C, TV, hair dryer, safe.

Meliá Comfort Inglés ✦✦   This turn-of-the-20th-century hotel, the former palace of the duke and duchess of Cardona, has aged well. In the heart of old Valencia, it stands opposite another Churrigueresque palace. Guest rooms vary in size, with most overlooking the tree-lined street. They offer comforts such as sofa beds with fine linens and immaculately kept bathrooms equipped with tub/shower combos. Ask for a room with a view of one of the city's many palaces. The service is discreet and polite.

Marqués de Dos Aguas 6, 46002 Valencia. © **96-351-64-26**. Fax 96-394-02-51. 63 units. 112€–163€ double. AE, DC, MC, V. Parking 13€. Bus: 6, 9, 11, 31, or 32. **Amenities:** Restaurant; bar; room service; laundry service; dry cleaning. *In room:* A/C, TV, minibar, hair dryer, safe.

NH Hotel Villacarlos   Located close to the river, this hotel is within easy walking distance of most of the city's monuments. Following Barcelona's lead, Valencia has been keen to adopt the new, and the Hotel Villacarlos is a prime example. It has a simple postmodern facade that makes the reception area's bright orange decor all the more surprising. Abstract paintings in orange and blue (the hotel's color scheme) adorn the walls—remember your sunglasses if you have a headache. In the guest rooms, blue and orange are kept to a minimum. The furniture is functional and new, including comfortable beds and full-length mirrors. Bathrooms are well stocked, with tub/shower combos.

Av. del Puerto 60, 46023 Valencia. © 96-337-50-25. Fax 96-337-50-74. 51 units. Mon–Thurs 90€–120€ double; Fri–Sun 64€ double. AE, DC, MC, V. Parking 11€. Bus: 19. **Amenities:** Restaurant; lounge; room service; babysitting; laundry service; dry cleaning. *In room:* A/C, TV, minibar, hair dryer.

INEXPENSIVE

Hostal Residencia Bisbal Conveniently located in the old city, this husband-and-wife operation offers simply furnished rooms. They're a bit small, but tidy and comfortable. In most units you'll find bathrooms with showers. No meals are served, and the hotel offers no real luxuries, but you'll find many bars and restaurants nearby. The English-speaking staff is very helpful.

Pie de la Cruz 9, 46001 Valencia. © 96-391-70-84. Fax 96-392-37-37. 10 units. 31€–37€ double. MC, V. Parking 13€. Bus: 8, 27, 29, or 81. *In room:* No phone.

Sorolla In the city center, this six-story hotel built in the 1960s is named after Valencia's most famous artist. The guest rooms have narrow balconies and compact, utilitarian furnishings, including good beds and bathrooms with shower-tub combos. Comfort, not style, is the key. No meals are served.

Convento de Santa Clara 5, 46002 Valencia. © 96-352-33-92. Fax 96-352-14-65. 58 units. 90€–130€ double. AE, DC, MC, V. Parking nearby 12€. Bus: Any route from the rail station. **Amenities:** Lounge; babysitting; laundry service; dry cleaning. *In room:* A/C, TV, minibar, hair dryer, safe.

WHERE TO DINE
EXPENSIVE

Civera ⭐ SPANISH/MEDITERRANEAN/SEAFOOD In the stylish Torres de Serrano district, a modern part of town near the Bellas Artes Museum, this traditional restaurant is the domain of the Civera brothers. Since the 1970s, they have offered high-quality, good-tasting seafood here. You have a choice of six dining sections, all evoking the atmosphere of a ship with blue-and-white-painted walls, high-beamed ceilings, and sailing artifacts such as navigators, ropes, nets, and knots. The menu includes such dishes as *salpicón de mariscos,* a seafood combination, or oysters flavored with garlic or fresh calamari with vegetables. Lobster can be ordered broiled or boiled. Meat courses worthy of note are a variety of different Levante sausages or round top sirloin steak. The desserts range from fresh fruit to homemade cakes.

Calle Lerida 11. © 96-347-59-17. Reservations recommended. Main courses 12€–42€; set menu 110€. AE, DC, MC, V. Tues–Sun 1–4pm; Tues–Sat 8–11pm. Closed Aug. Bus: 6, 8, or 16.

El Ceibo ⭐ VALENCIAN This restaurant was once hailed by local food critics as "El Rey de Arroz" or "the king of paella." To some extent that is still true. A variation on paella, the world famous dish of Valencia, is concocted by the chefs every day. In a rustic, country style setting, you can order not only rice dishes but a number of fish and meat selections as well. The cooks are good at turning out tender and well-flavored loin of beef in a peppery sauce or else delectable broiled entrecôtes. The chef's specialty is *picada del Ceibo,* a local dish made with various grilled sausages and topped with a layer of provolone cheese. The white walls are decorated with contemporary artwork and various ceramics made in the province.

Ciscar 3. © 96-395-32-76. Reservations recommended on Fri–Sat. Main courses 20€–25€. AE, DC, MC, V. Tues–Sat 2:30–5pm and 8:30pm–midnight. Closed Aug.

Joaquín Schmidt ⭐⭐ *Kids* MEDITERRANEAN Of German parents but born in Madrid, the chef here, Joaquín Schmidt Río-Valle, is becoming one of the best known in Valencia. His restaurant shines brightly because of his philosophy of "preparing each menu as if I'm cooking for cherished friends." His ever-changing repertoire of delights is based on shopping for the most market-fresh ingredients. With an impressive wine list to back up his culinary creations, his food always rises above the merely routine or even the merely competent. As classical music plays in the background, a waiter presents the menu. From his series of menu surprises, anticipate an explosion of unexpected aromas and tastes. All dishes are prepared using only extra-virgin olive oils, the best of balsamic vinegars, and special salts he imports from Brittany and Great Britain. "Menu of all Faiths" is four dishes plus dessert, but his Gourmand Menu brings you five dishes plus dessert. The extravaganza is the Joaquín Schmidt menu, seven dishes plus cheese and dessert.

Calle Vistacion N7. (C) **96-340-17-10**. Reservations required. 4-course fixed price menu 35€; 5-course fixed price menu 41€, 7-course fixed price menu 56€; 2-course children's menu 23€. MC, V. Tues–Sat 1:30-3:30pm; Mon–Sat 9–10:30pm.

La Pepica ⚝ SEAFOOD/VALENCIAN   This old Hemingway haunt looks a little worse for wear, but it's still going strong, after having been established in 1898. Royalty no longer dines here, and Don Ernesto is also long gone, but the same recipes that used to entice such personages are still practiced with skill at this typical old Valencian hideaway. The place is still famous for its paella dishes. The favorite rice dish is made with fresh lobster but this is, of course, the most expensive selection. Grilled or fried seafood share equal billing with the various kinds of paella. The chef is skilled at preparing calamari, among other dishes. Finish off with one of the desserts of the region, including flans, puddings, or fresh fruit tarts.

El Paseo Neptuno, north 6, La Playa de las Arenas. (C) **96-371-03-66**. Reservations recommended. Main courses 25€–30€. AE, DC, MC, V. Daily 1–5pm; Mon–Sat 9pm–midnight. Closed last 2 weeks of Nov.

La Riuà ⚝ _Finds_ VALENCIAN   Set in Valencia's historic core, a short walk from the Plaza de la Reina and the cathedral, this well-managed restaurant has done a booming business with local residents ever since it was established in 1982. There's no outdoor terrace (the congestion of the urban neighborhood around it prevents that), but you'll get a good view of traditional local decorative styles from the tiles and ceramics that adorn the walls of its trio of cozy dining rooms. Menu items read like a lexicon of traditional _valenciano_ dishes, including virtually every kind of fish (grilled, fried, or baked in the oven, in some cases within a salt crust) that exists in the western Mediterranean. There are also well-flavored versions of _paella,_ and fish that's served with at least three distinctly different seasonings of rice. (This includes versions flavored with squid ink.) Meats include _chuletas_ (spicy sausages), roasted pork, and tender, well-flavored veal. Locals appreciate stewed octopus _(pulpitos guisados),_ a dish that many of them seem to remember from their childhood. The restaurant's name, incidentally, translates from the _Valenciano_ dialect as "the spot where the river meets the sea."

Calle del Mar 27. (C) **96-391-45-71**. Reservations recommended. Main courses 22€–30€. AE, DC, MC, V. Mon–Sat 2–4pm; Tues–Sat 9–11:30pm. Closed Aug. Bus: 4.

La Sucursal ⚝⚝ _Finds_ VALENCIAN   Located in the Instituto Valencia de Arte Moderno (IVAM), this restaurant lies in the _barrio antiguo,_ the ancient quarter of this historic city. Its location is unusual in that it's housed in a modern art museum. With a minimalist decor, it invites with its innovative cuisine, backed up with an impressive wine list of regional vintages such as a fruity red Ceremonia made from a blend of cabernet sauvignon and tempranillo grapes. The chef is known for his soupy rice dishes prepared in deep pots instead of paella pans. Of these dishes, the specialty that wins local raves is *arroz caldoso de bogavante,* made with bits of lobster and seasoned with saffron and paprika. Unusual dishes include a carpaccio made of deer and an "octopus cake" seasoned with Brie and fresh herbs. You can also order a loin of beef in a rosemary *jus* sauce, followed by a platter featuring cheese made from both sheep and goat milk from the nearby mountains of Espadán. Begin with grilled squid and small onions in a light cream and mayonnaise sauce, or else the house foie gras, finishing off with a smooth tasting sorbet made of fresh quince. You can also order a winning pistachio sorbet.

La Sucursal, 118 Guillén de Castro. **(℃) 96-374-66-65.** Reservations required. Main courses 15€–18€. DC, MC, V. Mon–Fri 2–4pm; Mon–Sat 9–11pm.

Oscar Torrijos ★★★ MEDITERRANEAN/INTERNATIONAL   This stellar restaurant serves the best cuisine in Valencia. The menu, described by owner and chef Josep Quintana as Mediterranean, displays the knowledge of French and German cooking he acquired while working in Switzerland. Specialties include rice dishes (for which Valencia is famous)—in particular, paella. Rice with *rape* and artichokes is excellent, as is rice with king prawns. Fish from the Mediterranean and the Atlantic features heavily on the menu. Señor Quintana also makes delicious foie gras. Wine buffs should note that there are some 25,000 quality bottles in his cellar. The restaurant is centrally located in the Barrio Carmen.

Calle Dr. Sumsi 4. **(℃) 96-373-29-49.** Reservations required. Main courses 18€–25€; *menú del día* 35€; tasting menu 48€. AE, DC, MC, V. Tues–Sat 1–4pm and 9–11:30pm; Sun 1–4pm. Closed Aug 15–Sept 15. Metro: Colón.

MODERATE

Eladio ★★ SPANISH/INTERNATIONAL   Borrowing from culinary teaching he learned during his apprenticeship in Switzerland, Eladio Rodríguez prepares flavor-filled cuisine based on seasonal ingredients. The menu changes daily depending on what is fresh and available. Some diners particularly praise his shellfish and fish from his native Galicia, which might include hake, monkfish, or sea wolf, prepared as simply or as elaborately as you want. Many order fish grilled simply over charcoal and served with garlic butter sauce. Noteworthy dishes include octopus and ragout of shellfish, anglerfish, and salmon. Pastries, prepared by Eladio himself, make a suitable finish. The setting is calm and pleasant.

Calle Chiva 40. **(℃) 96-384-22-44.** Reservations recommended. Main courses 12€–30€. AE, DC, MC, V. Mon–Sat 1–4pm and 8–11:30pm. Closed Aug. Bus: 3, 70, or 72.

El Bermell ★ *Finds* VALENCIAN   In a lovely old 1600s building, this restaurant lies in the Barrio del Carmen, the oldest district in Valencia. In such a beautiful tavern setting, Emili Bermell has built up a reputation as one of the best chefs in the city. Each day he personally goes to the sprawling marketplace to select only the best and freshest of local ingredients, which he fashions into carefully crafted and good tasting dishes. Dig into his first tempting specialty, a superb mushroom salad made with fresh fruit grown and ripened in the surrounding region. For a main course, we suggest cod, which is stuffed with onions and served with a tangy green pepper sauce. Duck breast is an immensely appealing dish, and it's served with a Riojo wine sauce.

Calle Santo Tomás 18. **(℃) 96-391-02-88.** Reservations recommended. Main courses 12€–18€. AE, DC, MC, V. Mon 8–11:45pm; Tues–Sat 9:30am–4pm and 8–11:45pm. Closed Aug. Metro: Angel Guimera.

El Timonel ★ MEDITERRANEAN/SEAFOOD   Since 1997, discerning diners have headed for the domain of chef/owner Jaime Sauz, whose restaurant lies 2 blocks east of the Plaza de Toros. A comfortable and cozy interior is decorated in style of a yacht, evocative of the chef's use of fresh fish and seafood. Expect bass, flounder, red mullet, and a delectable local white fish called *lliva*. The fish is usually grilled. Señor Sauz believes if the product is fresh enough, it doesn't have to be mucked up with a lot of sauces. One of the best dishes is *dorada a la sal*, gilthead sea bream baked in a coating of salt to seal in its juices. Rice dishes blended with seafood (similar to paella) have always been one of the mainstays of the local diet, and excellent ones are served here—none better than *arroz de bogavante*, or rice with prawns and lobster. For meat eaters, we recommend the *chuletón de buey* (breaded oxtail steaks) or the *chuleticas de cordero lechal* (small spring lamb cutlets).

Felix Pizcueta 13. ✆ **96-352-63-00.** Reservations recommended. Main courses 10€–20€; set menu 26€. AE, DC, MC, V. Tues–Sun 1:30–4pm and 8:30pm–midnight. Metro: Corte Inglés.

INEXPENSIVE

El Gourmet SPANISH/INTERNATIONAL   This restaurant is an honest establishment where well-trained waiters serve good-quality, reasonably priced food. Set in the center of Valencia, it serves up such dishes as hake with clams, partridge with herbs in puff pastry, oxtail stew, fried filets of veal or pork, scrambled eggs with eggplant and shrimp, and seasonal vegetables.

Calle Taquígrafo Martí 3. ✆ **96-395-25-09.** Reservations recommended. Main courses 10€–15€; fixed-priced menu 22€. AE, DC, MC, V. Tues–Sat 1–4pm and 9–11:30pm; Sun 1–4pm. Closed Easter week and 1 week in Aug. Metro: Colón.

Palace Fesol ✿ MEDITERRANEAN   This is an old lunch favorite. In the years after World War I, the Palace Fesol became famous for its namesake specialty, lima beans. Today many more excellent dishes grace the menu at the "bean palace," with typical Valencian paella high on the list at lunch. You can also order several chicken dishes served with rice (included under the general name *paella* because they are cooked in paella pans). Other selections include *zarzuela de mariscos* (shellfish medley), grilled red mullet and baby hake, baby lamb cutlets, and chateaubriand. Photos of film stars, bullfighters, and other celebrities line the walls. The restaurant is cooled by old-fashioned ceiling fans and decorated with beamed ceilings, lanterns, and a hand-painted tile mosaic.

Hernán Cortés 7. ✆ **96-352-93-23.** Reservations recommended. Main courses 12€–25€. AE, DC, MC, V. Tues–Sun 1–4pm. Bus: 5. Metro: Colón.

Patos SPANISH   In a slightly battered turn-of-the-20th-century town house, this restaurant lies in the town center and has thrived since the early 1980s. At least part of its reputation derives from its daily preparations of *patos* (duck), which is better here than anywhere else in town. Expect pressed and grilled versions with orange, cherry, or herb sauce, usually accompanied by fresh vegetables and potatoes. There are two dining rooms plus an outdoor terrace overlooking a garden. Other choices include pizza, pasta, steak, grilled pork loin, and such desserts as flan and freshly baked pastries.

Calle del Mar 28. ✆ **96-392-15-22.** Reservations recommended. Main courses 12€–18€; fixed-price lunch 11€; fixed-price dinner 16€. MC, V. Daily 1–4pm and 8:30pm–midnight. Metro: El Corte Inglés.

VALENCIA AFTER DARK

Where you go at night in Valencia depends on when you visit. The best area in the cooler months is in the center, in the historic **Barrio Carmen.** Valencia is famous for its *marcha* (nightlife) and for its bohemian bars. The **Calle Alta** is a good street to start your barhopping *tasca* crawl.

An evening out in Valencia might also involve a series of *tasca* crawls that focus on the historic core around the **Plaza del Ayuntamiento.** Some of the most evocative *tascas* don't even have clear signs—your best bet involves jumping in and out of whichever appeals to you. Among our favorites, a short walk from Town Hall and Valencia's tourism office, are the **Bar Canovas,** Plaza de Canovas del Castillo s/n (no phone), and the **Bar Zaena,** Calle Antiguo Reino de Valencia s/n (no phone).

Another longtime local favorite is **Barcas,** Barcas 7 (© **96-352-12-33**), among banks and office buildings in the heart of town directly north of the Estación del Norte. It serves drinks and tapas (including small servings of paella) at the stand-up bar. You could conceivably stop here for your first cup of coffee at 7am and for your final nightcap at 1am. In the evening there is often live music. The establishment is more popular as a bar than as a restaurant. It's open daily from 7am to 1am. Drink prices start at 1.45€, and tapas cost 3€.

In summer, the emphasis switches to the beach, Playa de Malvarrosa. Valencia is hot and steamy, and the cooling night breezes blowing in from the sea are especially welcome. Everyone from teens to 40-somethings congregate around open-air bars. The bars play music, often have dance floors, and are open from late May to September. Drinks usually cost 3€ to 5€. There are also discos in this part of town, one of which is the **Disco Caballito de Mar,** Calle Eugenia Vines 22. They are more expensive, and drinks are several euros more than in the open-air bars.

Valencia is Spain's third-biggest city and, after Madrid and Barcelona, the country's biggest gay center. Most of the action is in the historic center in the **Barrio Carmen,** particularly along Calle Quart. Valencia is a progressive, liberal city, and visitors need have no fear about being "out" on the street. For more information, interested parties can stop in at or call the **Lambda organization,** Calle San Dionisio 8I (© **96-391-20-84**). There are many clubs, bars, coffee shops, saunas, hotels, and restaurants from which to choose. The best publication for what's happening when is Madrid-based *Shangay,* distributed free in gay establishments.

The latest offering on the club scene is **Le Goulou,** Calle Quart 30 (no phone), open nightly from 10pm to 3am. The long-established **Venial,** Calle Quart 26 (© **96-391-73-56**), is a few doors down. It opens at 12:30am and closes at 5am Sunday through Thursday, and 6:30am on Friday and Saturday, when there is a charge of 12€ with a drink included.

If you want to forget dancing and concentrate on late-night naughtiness, head to **La Guerra,** Calle Quart 47 (© **96-391-36-75**). It has five action-packed floors, a labyrinth, and the latest Californian "movies" nightly from 8pm to 3am.

As in many cities, gay men have to some degree elbowed lesbian interests out of the way, but Valencianas are fighting back. Women wanting a boy-free zone can try **Donna Donna,** Calle Portal Valldigna 2 (no phone), open Thursday through Sunday from 6pm to 2am. The lesbian disco **Mogambo,** Sangre 2 (no phone), is more mixed and attracts a youngish crowd. Entry is 7€, which covers one drink. Mogambo is open Thursday through Sunday from 11pm to 4am. As in the rest of Spain, the night starts late, and 10pm is considered quite early. At this time, one of the best places to go is the **Café de la Seu,** Calle Santo Caliz 7 (© **96-391-57-15**). All shades of pinkdom can have a relaxing drink for 2€ to 4.50€ from 6pm to 2am, daily.

On the cultural front, **Palau de la Música,** Paseo de la Alameda 30 (© **96-337-50-20**), is a contemporary concert hall in a dried-out bed of the Turia River, between the Aragón and Angel Custudio bridges. Opened in 1987, it occupies a sort of Hispano-Muslim venue, with palm trees, "temples," and reflecting pools. Call to find out the day's program or ask at the tourist office (see "Essentials," earlier in this chapter). Details of major concerts are also published in the newspapers. Ticket prices vary from 6€ to 30€.

For additional ideas, consult a recent copy of *Qué y Dónde,* a magazine available at any news kiosk for around 1.20€.

2 Benidorm

43km (27 miles) NE of Alicante, 135km (84 miles) S of Valencia

Before tourists discovered its 6km (3½ miles) of beaches, Benidorm was a tiny fishing village. But now summer vacationers pour in, and a new concrete hotel seems to be built every day. With its heavy northern European influence, Benidorm has become the most overrun beach town east of Torremolinos. It has both ardent fans and determined detractors.

According to an 1890s guidebook, Benidorm was a "very tranquil place where drunkenness was unknown." What a change had come over the resort by the 1970s and 1980s, when it attracted a rowdy, beer-drinking crowd. Today, some 180,000 people a day visit the long beach strip.

After the bad press of the past, city officials are trying to clean up Benidorm and make it more of an upmarket (rather than package-tour) destination. The Aiguera Park and its amphitheater exemplify the change. It offers such free cultural activities as dancing, jazz, soul music, and even a Russian choir.

Despite efforts to upgrade its image, Benidorm still has high-rises and economical package tourists. In winter, pensioners from all over Europe, even Russia, fill the villas and small hotels. In summer, however, the place takes on a much more youthful aura. The resort has two fine white-sand beaches.

ESSENTIALS

GETTING THERE   From Alicante, there are hourly **train** departures for Benidorm. **Buses** from Valencia and Alicante leave almost hourly, too.

If you're driving, take the E-15 expressway south from Valencia or north from Alicante. The one-way toll from Alicante to Benidorm is 4.20€; the one-way toll from Valencia to Benidorm is 9€.

VISITOR INFORMATION   The **tourist information office** is at Av. Martínez Alejos 16 (© **96-585-32-24**). It's open Monday through Saturday from 9:30am to 1:30pm and 4:30 to 7:30pm.

WHERE TO STAY

Make sure you reserve in advance between mid-June and September. If you arrive without a reservation, you'll be out of luck. During this time hotel managers often slap the full-board requirement onto their rates. To beat this, book one of the rare *residencias,* which serve breakfast only.

Don Pancho   One of the best hotels in Benidorm, Don Pancho is a high-rise a short distance from the beach. Each of the well-furnished, well-maintained guest rooms opens onto a small balcony. The midsize rooms are doubles but can be rented for single use. The tiled bathrooms have tub/shower combos.

Av. del Mediterráneo 39, 03503 Benidorm. © **96-585-29-50**. Fax 96-586-77-79. www.don-pancho.com. 252 units. 82€–127€ double; 111€–158€ suite. AE, DC, MC, V. Parking 10€. **Amenities:** Restaurant; bar; tennis courts; room service; babysitting; laundry service; dry cleaning. *In room:* A/C, TV, minibar, hair dryer, safe.

Gran Hotel Delfín ✦   About 3km (2 miles) west of the center of town, away from the traffic-clogged mayhem that sometimes overwhelms the center of Benidorm, this 1960s hotel is beside the very popular Poniente Beach. It is the resort's finest hotel, catering to a sun-loving crowd of vacationers who appreciate its airy spaciousness and lack of formality. Guest rooms are sparsely decorated, with masonry floors and much-used furniture, some in a darkly stained Iberian style. Nonetheless, the accommodations are quite comfortable, and the tiled bathrooms are well maintained and contain tub/shower combos.

Playa de Poniente (La Cala), 03502 Benidorm. ✆ **96-585-34-00.** Fax 96-585-71-54. www.webic.com. 93 units. 106€–132€ double; 143€–179€ suite. AE, DC, MC, V. Free parking. Closed Nov–Mar. **Amenities:** Restaurant; bar; pool; tennis courts; health club; sauna; room service; babysitting; laundry service; dry cleaning. *In room:* A/C, TV, minibar, hair dryer, safe.

Hotel Brisa   Just across from one of the town's most popular beaches, this hotel is a five-story modern building with a swimming pool and a small garden. The sunny guest rooms, simply furnished with sturdy furniture, have good beds and tile floors. All rooms come with a neatly kept bathroom with a tub/shower combination. This is very much a beach hotel, where many guests bring uncomplicated wardrobes, and, in some cases, their children, in anticipation of lazy days on the beach. Many summer guests are from northern Europe.

Av. de Madrid 31, Playa de Levante, 03503 Benidorm. ✆/fax **96-585-54-00.** 70 units. 64€–85€ double; 87€–100€ junior suite. Rates include breakfast. MC, V. **Amenities:** Restaurant; bar; pool; laundry service; dry cleaning. *In room:* A/C, TV, minibar, hair dryer, safe.

Hotel Canfali ✦ *(Finds)*   A seaside villa between the Playa de Levante and the Playa de Poniente, the Canfali is one of the best small hotels in town. Originally built in 1950, it was enlarged in 1992. Its position is a scene-stealer—on a low cliff at the end of the esplanade, with a staircase winding down to the beach. The best rooms have balconies with sea views. All units have bathrooms with tub/shower combos. Although the hotel is spacious and comfortable, its decor is undistinguished, its guest rooms functional. Terraces overlook the sea, a perfect spot for morning coffee.

Plaza de San Jaime 5, 03501 Benidorm. ✆ **96-585-08-18.** Fax 96-585-00-66. 38 units. 18€–68€ double. Rates include full board when you stay a minimum of 7 nights. No credit cards. **Amenities:** Restaurant; bar; babysitting; laundry. *In room:* A/C, TV, safe.

WHERE TO DINE

I Fratelli ITALIAN/INTERNATIONAL   Now into its third decade of business in a resort where many restaurants last only a season, this eatery must be doing something right. What it does is offer a finely honed Italian cuisine, and does so exceedingly well. It's an affordable choice, as most of its dishes are at the lower end of the price scale. Although most of the cuisine is Italian, there are also some dishes inspired by recipes from France or even from the international kitchen.

Our favorite dish here is fresh fish baked in a salt casing so it will retain its moisture. The cooks also prepare a succulent loin of lamb and also fresh turbot steaks to perfection. The best pasta here? It's ravioli in a savory Neapolitan tomato sauce. The setting is attractive and inviting with crisp white linen contrasting with black chairs.

Calle Dr. Orts Llorca, #20. ✆ **96-585-39-79.** Reservations recommended. Main courses 9€–30€. AE, DC, MC, V. Daily 1–4pm and 7:30pm–midnight. Closed Nov.

Pérgola SPANISH/INTERNATIONAL   Of the many buildings along the sea at the Playa de Levante, this is the one nearest the center of Benidorm. Established in 1979, it offers a sweeping view over the bay, an airy, stylish interior, and a flower-strewn terrace for warm-weather lunches and dinners. Skillfully prepared choices include seafood crepes with clams; a combination platter of hake and salmon drizzled with crabmeat sauce; stuffed crabs; stewed cod with garlic confit; duck breast with pears; and rack of beef with mustard sauce.

Acantillado-Edificio Coblanca 10, Calle Hamburgo, Rincón de Loix. (✆) **96-585-38-00.** Reservations recommended. Main courses 12€–18€. MC, V. Tues–Sun 1–3:30pm and 8pm–midnight.

Tiffany's ⍟ SPANISH/INTERNATIONAL   One of the town's better restaurants, Tiffany's has basked in its popularity since the 1970s, serving meals with well-rehearsed dignity. A live pianist plays occasionally. The food offerings change with the seasons and the availability of the ingredients, but might include a roulade of filet of sole stuffed with caviar and shrimp, tournedos Tiffany (with foie gras and truffles), a fish or veal dish, and a dessert of homemade chocolate éclairs with warm chocolate sauce.

Av. del Mediterráneo 51. (✆) **96-585-44-68.** Reservations recommended. Main courses 15€–20€. AE, DC, MC, V. Daily 7:30pm–midnight. Closed Jan 7–Feb 7.

BENIDORM AFTER DARK

The best nightclub in the region is the **Benidorm Palace,** Carretera Dr. Severo Ochoa s/n, Rincón de Loix (✆ **96-585-16-60**). The cover (including 1 drink) is a steep 23€ to 37€, but the place features the latest music, a large dance floor, and the biggest stage in Europe (40m/130 ft. wide). The stage fills with 50 international artists, often entertaining an audience of 1,500. Shows have ranged from "Hurrah for Hollywood" to Russian dancers. Always count on glamorous dancing women as part of the show. There are expansive bars and ample seating. It's open Friday through Wednesday from 9pm to 2am; shows start at 10pm. Drinks cost 3€.

Casino Mediterráneo, N-332, Km 141 (✆ **96-589-07-00**), offers gambling in a modern building surrounded by the rolling hills of the Costa Blanca. Most visitors come to try their hand at roulette (French and American), blackjack, and *boules.* An on-site restaurant serves a la carte Spanish meals ranging from 12€ to 25€ per person every evening from 9pm to 2am. The casino is open nightly from 8pm to 4am. It's about 7km (4½ miles) from Benidorm, beside the highway to Alicante. Casino admission is 2€; a passport is required for admission.

3 Alacant or Alicante ⍟

80.5km (50 miles) N of Murcia, 40km (25 miles) S of Benidorm, 172km (107 miles) S of Valencia, 417km (259 miles) SE of Madrid

Alicante, capital of the Costa Blanca, is popular in both summer and winter. Many consider it the best all-around city in Spain. As you amble about its esplanades, you almost feel as if you were in Africa: Women in caftans and peddlers hawking carvings from Senegal or elsewhere often populate the waterfront.

San Juan, the largest beach in Alicante, is a short distance from the capital. It's lined with villas, hotels, and restaurants. The bay of Alicante has two capes, and on the bay is **Postiguet Beach.** The bay stretches all the way to the **Cape of Santa Pola,** a town with two good beaches, a 14th-century castle, and several seafood restaurants.

ESSENTIALS

GETTING THERE   Alicante's **Internacional El Altet Airport** (✆ **96-691-90-00**) is 19km (12 miles) from the city. There are as many as six daily flights from

Madrid, about three flights per week from Seville, and three weekly from Barcelona. Three flights arrive weekly from Ibiza and Málaga (on the Costa del Sol). Thirteen buses daily connect the city to the airport; the fare is 1.05€. The Iberia Airlines ticket office (© 96-691-91-88) is at the airport.

Five **trains** a day make the 3-hour trip from Valencia. Five trains a day come from Barcelona (11 hr.), and six a day from Madrid (9 hr.). The RENFE office is at the Estación Término, Avenida Salamanca (© 90-224-02-02).

Different **bus** lines from various parts of the coast converge at the terminus, Calle Portugal 17 (© 96-513-07-00). There is almost hourly service from Benidorm (see above) and from Valencia (4 hr.). Buses also run from Madrid, a 5- to 6-hour trip.

To drive here, take the E-15 expressway south along the coast from Valencia. The expressway and N-340 run northeast from Murcia.

Valearia runs three **ferries** a day to and from Ibiza (4 hr.). Flebasa, Estació Marítim, Puerto de Denia (© 96-642-86-00), offers service to Ibiza (7 hr.) daily, and to Formentera (10 hr.) twice weekly.

VISITOR INFORMATION   The **tourist information office** is at Av. Rambla de Méndez Núñez 23 (© 96-520-00-00; www.comunidadvalenciana.com). It's open Monday through Friday from 10am to 8pm, Saturday from 10am to 2pm and 3 to 8pm.

FAST FACTS   For medical assistance, go to the **Hospital General,** Calle Maestro Alonzo 109 (© 96-593-89-99). In an emergency, dial © **091;** to reach the city police, call © **96-510-72-00.**

EXPLORING ALICANTE

With its wide, palm-lined avenues, this town was made for walking—and that's just what you'll do! The magnificent **Explanada d'Espanya** ✺, extending around part of the yacht harbor, includes a great promenade of mosaic sidewalks under the palms. All the boulevards are clean and lined with unlimited shopping options. At Alicante's leading department store, El Corte Inglés, you can find bargains without being trampled by mobs, as in Madrid. Alicante is known for its parks, gardens, and lines of palm trees, and it boasts several old plazas, some paved with marble.

High on a hill, the stately **Castell de Santa Bárbara** (© 96-526-31-31) towers over the bay and provincial capital. The Greeks called the fort Akra Leuka (White Peak). Its original defenses, erected by the Carthaginians in 400 B.C., were later used by the Romans and the Arabs. The fortress's grand scale is evident in its moats, drawbridges, tunneled entrances, guardrooms, bakery, cisterns, underground storerooms, hospitals, batteries, powder stores, barracks, high breastworks, deep dungeons, and the Matanza Tower and the Keep. From the top of the castle is a panoramic view over land and sea. The castle is accessible by road or elevator (board at the Explanada d'Espanya). Admission by elevator is 2.40€. In summer it's open daily from 10am to 7:30pm, in winter, daily from 9am to 6:30pm.

It is also possible to drive to the top. A paved road off Avenida Vásquez de Mella leads directly to a parking lot beside the castle. If you drive, admission is free.

On the slopes of the Castillo de Santa Bárbara behind the cathedral is the **Barrio de Santa Cruz** ✺. Forming part of the **Villa Vieja** (the old quarter), it is a colorful section with wrought-iron window grilles, banks of flowers, and a view of the entire harbor.

Alicante isn't all ancient. Facing the Iglesia Santa María is the **Museu Colecció Art del Segle XX** ✺, Plaza de Santa María 3 (© 96-514-07-68). Housed in the city's oldest building, it contains modern art. Constructed as a granary in 1685, the restored building features works by Miró, Calder, Cocteau, Vasarély, Dalí, Picasso, and Tàpies. Other notable artists include Braque, Chagall, Giacometti, Kandinsky, and Zadkine. You'll also see a musical score by Manuel de Falla. The museum was formed in 1977 with the donation of a private collection by the painter and sculptor Eusebio Sempere, whose works are on display. It is open Tuesday through Saturday from 10am to 2pm and 4 to 8pm, Sunday from 10:30am to 2:30pm. Admission is free. Check its status before heading here. Closed for renovations at press time, it is slated to open late in 2004.

SHOPPING

Despite the hurly-burly of tourism that unfolds around you at almost every street corner, there are many worthwhile shopping opportunities. Some of the best involve handmade artifacts—ceramics, hand-tooled leather, woodcarvings, ornamental boxes, candleholders, and small-scale mosaics. One of the best all-purpose shops is **Fran Holuba,** Calle Jaime Segarra 16 (C **96-524-45-95**), which carries examples of each of the major artisanal forms described above. For modern (not religious) sculpture crafted from wood and such stones as marble, head for the studio of **Pedro Soriano,** Plaza San Antonio 2 (C **96-520-78-54**). For general merchandise, head for the town's largest department store, **El Corte Inglés,** Av. Maison Nave 53 (C **96-592-50-01**).

WHERE TO STAY
EXPENSIVE

Hotel Meliá Alicante   Built in 1973 on a spit of landfill jutting into the Mediterranean, this massive hotel almost dwarfs every other establishment in town. Midsize guest rooms are painted in sunny colors and have balconies, usually with sweeping panoramas of sailboats in the nearby marina or over the beach. All rooms have neatly kept bathrooms with tub/shower combos. The public rooms are contemporary, with lots of marble. The hotel is midway between the main harbor and the very popular El Postiguet beach.

Plaza Puerta Del Mar 3, 03002 Alicante. C **800/336-3542** in the U.S., or 96-520-50-00. Fax 96-520-47-56. 545 units. 112€–155€ double; 153€–197€ suite. Weekend room rates include breakfast. AE, DC, MC, V. Parking 11€. **Amenities:** Restaurant; bar; pool; room service; fitness center; sauna; babysitting; laundry service; dry cleaning. *In room:* A/C, TV, minibar, hair dryer, safe.

Hotel Tryp Gran Sol   In the heart of the tourist zone a block from the beachfront Paseo Marítimo, this 1970 hotel towers above most of the buildings in town. A member of the widely known Tryp chain, it offers simple guest rooms with unimaginative but comfortable furnishings. Bathrooms have tile or marble accents and tub/shower combos. One-third of the rooms were recently renovated.

Rambla de Méndez Núñez 3, 03002 Alicante. C **800/336-3542** in the U.S., or 965-20-30-00. Fax 965-21-14-39. 123 units. 117€ double; 149€ suite. AE, DC, MC, V. Parking 6€. **Amenities:** Restaurant; bar; room service; babysitting; laundry service; dry cleaning. *In room:* A/C, TV, minibar, hair dryer, safe.

MODERATE

Abba Eurhotel Hesperia   This eight-floor modern hotel is one of the most convenient in Alicante, lying 320m (350 yd.) from the harbor and convenient to both the rail and bus depots. Opening in 1992, it underwent renovations in 2003, retaining its contemporary ambience and inviting quality. Its bedrooms are midsize for the most part and attractively decorated and furnished, each adjoined by a well-maintained bathroom with tub and shower. The on-site restaurant is a good choice for its fresh Mediterranean fish platters, rice dishes, and various grilled meats. Some of its food is inspired by the Basque kitchen.

Calle Pinto Lorenzo Casanova 33, 03003 Alicante. ☎ **96-513-04-40.** Fax 96-592-83-23. 117 units. Fri–Sat 60€ double; Sun–Thurs 104€ double. From 122€ suite. AE, DC, MC, V. **Amenities:** Restaurant (Mon–Fri); bar; room service; laundry/dry cleaning. *In room:* A/C, TV, minibar.

Hotel Residencia Leuka *Value*   The Leuka is best booked for the weekend, when it offers good value and is free of packs of businesspeople. Although it's about a 15-minute walk from the sea, it is close to the station and two of the city's main thoroughfares. Guests have easy access to almost all destinations by bus. The 10-story building has an anonymously ugly 1970s facade. However, all the rooms have good-size balconies, and units above the third floor offer wonderful views of the castle. Guest rooms are quite plain, but spacious and reasonably comfortable. All come with neatly kept bathrooms with tub/shower combos.

Calle Segura 23, 03004 Alicante. ☎ **96-520-27-44.** Fax 965-14-12-22. 106 units. Mon–Thurs 62€ double; Fri–Sun 42€ double. AE, DC, MC, V. Parking 7.50€. Bus: 22. **Amenities:** Bar; lounge; room service; babysitting; laundry service; dry cleaning. *In room:* A/C, TV, hair dryer, safe.

INEXPENSIVE

Hostal Les Monges Palace *Value*   A building dating from 1912 and a hotel since 1989 has been restored and turned into a good stopover in the oldest and most historic district of the inner city. A family run boarding B&B-type hotel, it offers small and rather simply furnished bedrooms, each comfortably furnished and equipped with traditional, old-styled furnishings. Rooms are decorated with good taste with an eye toward elegance. All of them contain antiques and paintings which make this hotel more exceptional than the standard *moderno* choices in the area. The suite is special in that it's decorated with Japanese furnishings and with a bathroom that offers both a private Jacuzzi and a sauna.

Calle San Augustín 4, 03002 Alicante. ☎ **96-521-50-46.** 18 units. 35€ single; 80€ suite. DC, MC, V. Parking 8€. **Amenities:** Laundry/dry cleaning. *In room:* A/C, minibar, hair dryer.

Pensión Portugal   The two-story Portugal is 1 block from the bus station, about 4 blocks from the railway station, and a 3-minute walk from the harbor. The small accommodations, furnished in tasteful modern style, are immaculate but basic. Guests in units with private bathrooms and showers will find their rooms a bit cramped but serviceable. For those who share, the corridor bathrooms are adequate.

Calle Portugal 26, 03003 Alicante. ☎ **96-592-92-44.** 16 units, 8 with bathroom. 27€–29€ double without bathroom, 32€–34€ double with bathroom. No credit cards. Parking 7€. **Amenities:** Lounge. *In room:* No phone.

NEARBY ACCOMMODATIONS

Meliá Altea Hills Resort 🌟🌟🌟   Long deprived of a government-rated five-star hotel, the Costa Blanca around Alicante now has a world-class resort. It fills a gap that has existed for decades in the luxury market. Bearing one of the highest price tags along the coast, the *luxe* resort is opulent, elegant, tasteful, and exceedingly comfortable. All rooms are suites, opening onto the foothills of the Mascaret mountain range facing south with panoramic views over the Bay of Altea. The skyscrapers of Benidorm can be seen in the distance. Polished mahogany, brass, and subtropical gardens, along with tile floors create the ambience of a Spanish hacienda. The bathrooms are the best of any hotel in the province, luxurious retreats unto themselves. Everything is on-site from a deluxe restaurant to a fully equipped gym. You can dine on an open-air terrace, enjoying a first-rate Mediterranean menu.

Urbanización Altea Hills, N-332, Km 163.5, 03590 Altea, near Alicante. ✆ **96-688-10-06.** Fax 96-688-10-24. www.solmelia.es. 101 units. 180€–232€ double; 215€–507€ suite. AE, DC, MC, V. Lies 45km (28 miles) north of Alicante on Carretera de Valencia. **Amenities:** Restaurant; 2 bars, pool; tennis court; gym; sauna; room service; babysitting; laundry service; dry cleaning. *In room:* A/C, TV, minibar, hair dryer, safe.

WHERE TO DINE

The characteristic dish of Alicante is rice, served many different ways. The most typical sauce is aioli, a kind of mayonnaise made from oil, egg yolks, and garlic. Dessert selections are the most varied on the Costa Blanca; *turrón de Alicante* (Spanish nougat) is the most popular.

La Dársena SPANISH   Established in the 1960s, this is a famous waterfront restaurant along the Costa Blanca, celebrated for offering a staggering 148 different paellas. Everything you thought didn't go into paella goes into the different versions here, even cauliflower, chicken livers, and lamb kidneys. You can also order all the more conventional paellas as well, including succulent morsels like shellfish. You can work up a big appetite just reading the long menu. We'd recommend that you start by ordering an appetizer, *fritura de la Bahía,* a crisp fish fry of local fish (similar to red mullet) and *boquerón* (fresh anchovies). You can also order a velvety smooth crab soup flavored with Armagnac or a refreshing tart composed of tuna and fresh spinach. One of the more memorable paellas is *arroz con bacalao y costar de ajo,* which is made with salt cod, thinly sliced garlic, and potatoes, the medley crowned by a light, airy egg crust.

Muelle de Levante 6. ✆ **96-520-75-89.** Reservations required at lunch. Main courses 14€–21€. AE, DC, MC, V. Mon–Sun 1–4pm; Tues–Sat 8:30–11pm.

Nou Manolín ✪ *(Finds* TAPAS/SPANISH   This is the kind of place locals will tell you about if they like you. The place is fabled locally for its array of some 50 tapas served daily, everything from shrimp in garlic sauce to batter-fried fresh anchovies. When he established it in 1972, the founder of this restaurant named it after an almost-forgotten neighborhood bar (El Manolín), which his grandfather had maintained before the Spanish Civil War. Nou Manolín's street level contains a busy bar area, but diners usually gravitate to the upstairs dining room, where tiled walls and uniformed waiters contribute to the ambience of an elegant *tasca.* Menu items focus mainly on paellas, but include many kinds of fish cooked in a salt crust, several kinds of stew, fresh shellfish, and a wide selection of Iberian wines. An unusual rice dish is *arroz con kokotxas,* which is made with fresh cod "cheeks"— that is, the arrowhead-shaped flesh of the lower jaw. It has a gelatinous texture. The rice is studded with such fresh vegetables as sweet red peppers, artichokes, cauliflowers, and green beans.

Calle Villegas 3. ✆ **96-520-03-68.** Reservations recommended. Main courses 12€–22€. AE, DC, MC, V. Daily 1–4pm and 8:30pm–midnight.

Restaurante El Jumillano SPANISH   This place has changed so little you might think one of Franco's soldiers is about to stroll into this time capsule. This was a humble wine bar when it opened in 1936 near the old city. The original wine-and-tapas bar is still going strong, but the food has improved immeasurably. Today the original owner's sons (Juan José and Miguel Pérez Mejías) offer a cornucopia of succulent food, including fresh fish laid out in the dining room on the sun-bleached planks of an antique fishing boat. Many menu items derive from locally inspired recipes. The specialties include a "festival of canapés," slices of cured ham served with fresh melon, shellfish soup with mussels, Alicante stew, pigs' trotters, a savory filet of beef seasoned with garlic, and a full gamut of grilled hake, sea bass, and shellfish.

César Elhuezabal 64. (C) **96-521-17-64.** Reservations recommended. Main courses 11€–17€. AE, DC, MC, V. Mon–Sat 1–4pm and 8pm–midnight; Sun noon–4pm. Closed Sun July–Sept. Bus: D or F.

ALICANTE AFTER DARK

A town devoted to the pursuit of hot times, Alicante never seems to lack for a bar. You can find alcohol and socializing at almost any time of the day or night. One of the town's densest concentrations of watering holes lies adjacent to the port. Night owls wander from one bar to the next along the length of the **Muelle del Puerto** (a stretch of pavement that's also known as the Explanada d'Espanya). There are at least 20 nightspots that rock through the night. Three of the most popular and visible are **Bar Potato; Casa Yum-Yum,** where tapas are consumed with something approaching vigor; and **Mesón del Puerto.** Their addresses are all Muelle del Puerto s/n, and they have no phones. Also consider the bar at one of our favorite restaurants, **La Dársena** (see "Where to Dine," above), even if you don't wish to dine.

Alternatively, consider walking through the narrow streets of Alicante's **Casco Antiguo.** Streets particularly rich in bodegas and *tavernas* include **Calle Laboradores, Calle Cien Fuegos,** and the **Plaza Santa Face.** We usually prefer to wander aimlessly through this district, popping in and out wherever we feel most comfortable. If you want to plan ahead, consider **El Mesón,** in the Calle Laboradores 23; **La Tapería,** Plaza Santa Face s/n; and **El Pote Gallego,** Plaza Santa Face s/n. Again, no phones.

Alicante has a well-established and relatively large gay scene for a city of its size. The numbers swell in July and August, with tourists from the rest of Spain and Madrid in particular. For information, contact the Lambda organization, Calle Doctor Santa Oblaya 7, in the San Blas area (© **96-513-26-10**). It's open Wednesday from 7 to 9pm, Saturday from 7 to 10pm.

The evening starts at one of several bars. A popular haunt is **Missing** (© **96-521-67-28**), Calle Gravina 4, which is open daily from 9pm to 3:30am.

4 Elx or Elche ⧉

21km (13 miles) SW of Alicante, 56km (35 miles) NE of Murcia, 406km (252 miles) SE of Madrid

Sandwiched between Alicante and Murcia, the little town of Elche is famous for its age-old mystery play, lush groves of date palms, and shoe- and sandal-making.

On August 14 and 15 for the past 6 centuries, the **Misteri d'Elx (Mystery of Elche)** has celebrated the Assumption of the Virgin. It is reputedly the oldest dramatic liturgy in Europe. Songs are performed in an ancient form of Catalán. Admission is free, but it's hard to get a seat unless you book in advance through the tourist office (see "Essentials," below). The play takes place at the Church of Santa María, which dates from the 17th century.

Unless you visit at the time of the mystery play, the town's **Palm Grove** ⧉⧉ holds the most appeal. The 600,000-tree palm forest is unrivaled in Europe. It's said that Phoenician (or perhaps Greek) seafarers originally planted the trees. A thousand years ago, the Moors created the irrigation system that still maintains the palms. Stroll through the **Huerto del Cura (Priest's Grove)** ⧉⧉, open daily from 9am to 6pm, to see the palm garden and collection of tropical flowers and cacti. In the garden, look for the **Palmera del Cura (Priest's Palm),** from the 1840s, with seven branches sprouting from its trunk. In the grove you will see one of the most famous ladies of Spain, *La Dama de Elche*. This is a replica—the original 500 B.C. limestone bust, discovered in 1897, is on display in the National Archaeological Museum in Madrid.

ESSENTIALS

GETTING THERE The central train station is the Estación Parque, Avenida del Ferrocarril. **Trains** arrive almost hourly from Alicante. Call ☎ **96-545-62-54** for schedules.

The bus station (☎ **96-661-50-50**) is at Avenida de la Libertat. **Buses** travel between Alicante and Elche on the hour.

Take the N-340 highway from Alicante and proceed southwest if you're driving.

VISITOR INFORMATION The **tourist information office** is at Parque Municipal, Portell de Granyana (☎ **96-545-38-31;** www.ayto-elche.es). It's open Monday through Friday from 10am to 7pm, Saturday and Sunday from 10am to 2pm.

WHERE TO STAY

Huerto del Cura ★★★ *Finds* Staying here is a unique experience. Huerto del Cura stands in the so-called Priest's Grove, and you'll have panoramic views of the palm trees from your room. The privately owned parador consists of a number of immaculately kept cabins in the grove. Each is well furnished and roomy, with efficiently organized, tiled bathrooms equipped with tub/shower combos. Service is impeccable.

Porta de La Morera 14, 03203 Elche. ☎ 96-661-00-11. Fax 96-542-19-10. interhotel.com/spain/es/hoteles/239.html. 86 units. 80€–122€ double; 136€–148€ suite. AE, DC, MC, V. Free parking. **Amenities:** Restaurant; bar; pool; tennis courts; fitness center; sauna; solarium; room service; babysitting; laundry service; dry cleaning. *In room:* A/C, TV, minibar, hair dryer, safe.

WHERE TO DINE

Parque Municipal INTERNATIONAL A large open-air restaurant and cafe in the middle of a public park, the Parque Municipal is a good place to go for decent food and relaxed service. Many regional dishes appear on the menu; try one of the savory rice dishes as a main course, followed by "cake of Elche." Two specialties are paella and Mediterranean sea bass, sailor's style.

Paseo La Estación. ☎ 96-545-34-15. Reservations recommended. Main courses 10€–15€; fixed-price menu 12€; tasting menu 18€. MC, V. Daily 1–4pm and 9–11pm.

Restaurante La Finca ★ MEDITERRANEAN In the countryside near the Elche football (soccer) stadium, this restaurant lies 5km (3 miles) south of town along the Carretera de El Alted. La Finca opened in 1984, and its good food has attracted customers ever since. The menu changes frequently, based on the season and what's fresh. Both fish and meat are prepared in creative ways, although time-tested recipes are used as well. Try tuna-stuffed peppers or veal kidneys with potatoes. Chocolate mousse might be available for dessert.

Partida de Perleta, Poligano #7. ☎ 96-545-60-07. Reservations recommended. Main courses 14€–20€. AE, MC, V. Daily 1–5pm; Mon–Sat 8:30pm–midnight.

5 Murcia ★

84km (52 miles) SW of Alicante, 394km (245 miles) SE of Madrid, 256km (159 miles) SW of Valencia

This ancient Moorish city of sienna-colored buildings is an inland provincial capital on the main road between Valencia and Granada. It is on the Segura River.

ESSENTIALS

GETTING THERE   From Alicante, 9 to 17 **trains** daily make the 1½-hour trip. From Barcelona (7–10 hr.), there are three trains daily; from Madrid (4–5 hr.), three or four trains daily. From the Estació del Carmen, Calle Industria s/n (© **90-224-02-02**), take bus no. 11 to the heart of the city.

Buses arrive at Calle San Andrés (© **96-829-22-11**), behind the Museo Salzillo. The information window is open daily from 7am to 10pm. There's frequent service from Granada (4–5 hr.), Cádiz (12½ hr.), Córdoba (9 hr.), Valencia (3¾ hr.), and Seville (7–9 hr.).

If you're driving, take the N-340 southwest from Alicante.

VISITOR INFORMATION   The **tourist information office** is at Calle San Cristóbal (© **90-210-10-70**). It's open Monday through Saturday from 9:30am to 1:30pm and 5 to 7pm.

SPECIAL EVENTS   Murcia's **Holy Week celebration,** from Palm Sunday to Easter Sunday, is an ideal time to visit. Its processions are spectacular, with about 3,000 people taking part, and some sculptures of Salzillo (see below) are carried through the streets. Musicians blow horns so big they have to be carried on wheels.

EXPLORING MURCIA

Although it suffered much from fire and bombardment during the Spanish Civil War, the city abounds in grand 18th-century houses.

One of the other major sights is the **Museo de Salzillo** *, Plaza San Agustín 3 (© **96-829-18-93**). The son of an Italian sculptor father and a Spanish mother, Francisco Salzillo won fame with his sculptures in polychrome wood. This museum displays his finest work, plus many terra-cotta figurines based on biblical scenes. It is open Tuesday through Saturday from 9:30am to 1pm and 4 to 7pm, Sunday from 11am to 1pm. Admission is 3€.

Another attraction is the **Museo de Arqueología,** Calle Gran Vía Alfonso X, El Sabio 9 (© **96-823-46-02**), one of the best in Spain. Through artifacts— mosaics, pottery fragments, Roman coins, ceramics, and other objects—it traces life in Murcia province from prehistoric times. The two most important collections are devoted to objects from the Hispano-Moorish period between the 12th and the 14th centuries and to Spanish ceramics of the 17th and 18th centuries. Hours in July and August are Monday through Friday from 9am to 1:30pm; September through June, it's open Monday through Friday from 9am to 2pm and 5 to 8pm, Saturday from 11am to 2pm. Admission is 1€.

WHERE TO STAY

Catalonia Conde de Floridablanca *Value*   Rising from the center of the Barrio del Carmen near the cathedral, this hotel is ideally situated for exploring the old city. Originally built in 1972, it was thoroughly renovated and enlarged in 1992. The building is attractively decorated in conservative modern style, with comfortable and appealing midsize guest rooms. Units also contain neatly kept bathrooms with tub/shower combos.

Princesa 18, 30002 Murcia. © **96-821-46-26.** Fax 96-821-32-15. www.hoteles-catalonia.es. 82 units. 68€–120€ double. AE, DC, MC, V. Parking 10€. Bus: 2, 5, 6, or 11. **Amenities:** Restaurant; bar; room service; laundry service; dry cleaning. *In room:* A/C, TV, minibar, hair dryer, safe.

Hotel Hispano 1   An older version of Hispano 2 (see below), run by the same people, this solid choice hotel is still reliable after all these years. It stands right next to the cathedral. The well-kept guest rooms are functional and homey, but a bit small. Bathrooms are neatly kept with tub/shower combos.

Calle Trapería 8, 30001 Murcia. © **96-821-61-52**. Fax 96-821-68-59. 46 units. 36€ double. AE, DC, MC, V. Bus: 2, 5, 6, or 11. **Amenities:** Bar; laundry service; dry cleaning. *In room:* No phone.

Hotel Hispano 2 *(Value)*

The older Hispano 1 (see above) proved so successful that the owners inaugurated this property in 1976. The comfortably furnished guest rooms are superior to those at the older sibling. All are equipped with bathrooms containing tub/shower combos.

Calle Radio Murcia 3, 30001 Murcia. © **96-821-61-52**. Fax 96-821-68-59. 35 units. 60€ double. AE, DC, MC, V. Parking 7€. Bus: 2, 5, 6, or 11. **Amenities:** Bar; babysitting; laundry service; dry cleaning. *In room:* A/C, TV, minibar, hair dryer, safe.

Hotel Meliá 7 Coronas ★★

A member of the well-recommended nation-wide chain, this is the finest hotel in town. The angular 1971 building offers comfortable midsize guest rooms and a cool, refreshing terrace with bar service and a legion of flowering plants. All rooms have tidy bathrooms with tub/shower combos. The hotel is within a 15-minute walk east of the cathedral, near the gardens abutting the northern edge of the Río Segura.

Paseo de Garay 5, 30003 Murcia. © **800/336-3542** in the U.S., or 96-821-77-71. Fax 96-822-12-94. 153 units. 137€–166€ double; 168€–202€ suite. AE, DC, MC, V. Parking 12€. Bus: 2, 5, 6, or 11. **Amenities:** Restaurant; bar; room service; babysitting; laundry service; dry cleaning. *In room:* A/C, TV, minibar, hair dryer, safe.

NH Rincón de Pepe ★

This modern hotel hidden on a narrow street in the heart of the old quarter is attached to a well-known restaurant, Rincón de Pepe (see below). The small to medium guest rooms are up-to-date, with many built-in conveniences and bathrooms equipped with tub/shower combos.

Calle de Apóstoles 34, 30001 Murcia. © **96-821-22-39**. Fax 96-822-17-44. 148 units. 110€–141€ double; 160€–190€ suite. AE, DC, MC, V. Parking 9.50€. **Amenities:** Restaurant; bar; room service; babysitting; laundry service; dry cleaning; casino. *In room:* A/C, TV, minibar, hair dryer, safe.

A NEARBY RESORT

Hyatt Regency La Manga ★★★

One of the best resorts in Spain is away from the coast near the eastern part of Andalusia. Nestled on 567 hectares (1,400 acres; the grounds are larger than the land controlled by the Principality of Monaco), it features a comprehensive array of sports facilities. The decor is inspired by the aristocratic private villas of Andalusia. Families usually opt for one of the functional four-star apartments in the airy Los Lomos complex. Fifty apartments (as well as about 20 time share units not accessible to the public) make up a re-creation of an Andalusian pueblo. Couples and clients staying for a week or less tend to gravitate toward the luxurious doubles. All units contain immaculately kept bathrooms equipped with tub/shower combos. The grand five-star accommodations occupy the resort's architectural showcase, the Príncipe Felipe, named for the son of King Juan Carlos.

Los Belones, 30385 Cartagena, Murcia. © **800/223-1234** in the U.S., or 96-833-12-34. Fax 96-833-12-35. www.lamanga.hyatt.com. 192 units. 207€–315€ double; 377€–485€ suite; 87€–201€ studio apt; 135€–315€ 1- to 3-bedroom apt. AE, DC, MC, V. Free parking. **Amenities:** Restaurant; bar; pool; 3 golf courses; 18 tennis courts; health club; sauna; salon; room service; babysitting; laundry service; dry cleaning. *In room:* A/C, TV, minibar, hair dryer, safe.

WHERE TO DINE

Acuario REGIONAL/INTERNATIONAL   This restaurant near the cathedral allows you to dine in air-conditioned comfort. Since it opened in 1987, it has been known for excellent Murcian cuisine and its selection of international dishes. You might begin with paté of salmon, following with *merluza* (hake) in sherry sauce, a tender tournedos, or the chef's specialty, eggplant cooked with Serrano ham and mushrooms. If it's available, the lemon soufflé is delectable.

Plaza Puxmarina 1. ✆ **96-821-99-55**. Reservations recommended. Main courses 12€–24€; tasting menu 27€. DC, MC, V. Mon–Sat 1–4pm and 8:30pm–midnight. Closed 2 weeks in Aug. Bus: 2, 5, 6, or 11.

Rincón de Pepe SPANISH/INTERNATIONAL Established in the mid-1920s, this is the best restaurant in town. Many visitors won't leave town without going to this culinary landmark. You can spend a lot or a little, depending on what you order. Specialties change frequently, and the menu varies seasonally. You may enjoy pigs' trotters and white beans, spring lamb kidneys in sherry, or white beans with partridge. Shellfish selections include Carril clams, a platter of assorted grilled seafood and fish, and grilled red prawns. Among the meat and poultry specialties are roast spring lamb Murcian style and duck in orange sauce.

Plaza de Apóstoles 34. ✆ **96-821-22-39**. Reservations recommended. Main courses 12€–28€. AE, DC, MC, V. Daily noon–4pm; Mon–Sat 8pm–midnight. Bus: 3, 4, or 8.

11

Barcelona

Blessed with rich and fertile soil, an excellent harbor, and a hardworking population, Barcelona has always prospered. When Madrid was still a dusty Castilian backwater, Barcelona was a powerful, diverse capital, influenced by the Mediterranean empires that conquered it. Carthage, Rome, and Charlemagne-era France overran Catalonia, and each left an indelible mark on the region's identity.

The Catalán people have clung fiercely to their unique culture and language, both of which Franco systematically tried to eradicate. But Catalonia has endured, becoming a semiautonomous region of Spain (with Catalán its official language). And Barcelona, the region's lodestar, has truly come into its own. The city's most powerful monuments open a window onto its history: the intricately carved edifices of the medieval Gothic Quarter; the curvilinear modernismo (Catalán Art Nouveau) that inspired Gaudí's **La Sagrada Família;** and the seminal works of Picasso and Miró, in museums that mark Barcelona as a crucial incubator for 20th-century art.

As if those attractions weren't enough, Barcelona is on the doorstep of some of Europe's great playgrounds and vacation retreats. The Balearic Islands lie to the east, the Costa Brava to the north, the Penedés wine country to the west, and to the south, the Roman city of Tarragona, the

monastery at Montserrat, and such Costa Dorada resort towns as Sitges.

Despite its allure, Barcelona grapples with problems common to many major cities—the increasing polarization of rich and poor, rising drug abuse, and an escalating crime rate, mostly theft. But city authorities have, with some degree of success, brought crime under control in the tourist zones.

A revitalized Barcelona eagerly prepared for and welcomed thousands of visitors as part of the 1992 Summer Olympic Games, but the action didn't end when the last medal was handed out. Barcelona turned its multimillion-dollar building projects into permanently expanded facilities for sports and tourism. Its modern 151 million euro ($150 million) terminal at El Prat de Llobregat Airport can accommodate 12 million passengers a year, and ever-pragmatic Barcelona races to the 21st century with a restructuring program called "Post Olympic." The city is fast emerging as one of the hottest tourist cities in Europe.

Landmark buildings and world-class museums fill the historic city. And an array of nightlife (Barcelona is a *big* bar town) and shopping possibilities, plus nearby wineries, ensure that you'll be entertained round the clock. It makes for some serious sightseeing; you'll need plenty of time to take it all in—in fact, almost as much time as it takes to see Madrid.

1 Catalonian Culture

Barcelona has always thrived on contact and commerce with countries beyond Spain's borders. From its earliest days, the city has been linked more closely to

France and the rest of Europe than to Iberia. Each of the military and financial empires that swept through Catalonia left its cultural imprint.

LANGUAGE

Catalonia lies midway between France and Castilian Spain. The province is united by a common language, **Catalán.** Modern linguists attribute the earliest division of Catalán from Castilian to two phenomena. The first was the cultural links and trade ties between ancient Barcina and the neighboring Roman colony of Provence, which shaped the Catalán tongue along Provençal and Languedocian models. The second major event was the invasion of the eastern Pyrenees by Charlemagne in the late 800s, and the designation of Catalonia as a Frankish march (buffer zone) between Christian Europe and Moorish-dominated Iberia.

Although Catalán is closely related to Castilian Spanish, even those travelers who are fluent in Spanish are occasionally confronted with unfamiliar words in Barcelona. Don't be surprised if maps or brochures have addresses in Castilian, but then you find signs in Catalán on the street.

Today, Catalán is the most widely spoken nonnational language in Europe.

ARCHITECTURE

Like many other cities in Spain, Barcelona claims its share of Neolithic dolmens and ruins from the Roman and Moorish periods. Monuments survive from the Middle Ages, when the Romanesque solidity of no-nonsense barrel vaults, narrow windows, and fortified design were widely used.

In the 11th and 12th centuries, religious fervor swept through Europe, and pilgrims began to flock to Barcelona on their way west to Santiago de Compostela, bringing with them French building styles and the need for new and larger churches. The style that emerged, called Catalonian Gothic, had softer lines and more elaborate ornamentation than traditional Gothic. Appropriate for both civic and religious buildings, it used *ogival* (pointed) arches, intricate stone carvings, large interior columns, exterior buttresses, and vast rose windows set with colored glass. One of Barcelona's purest and most-loved examples of this style is the Church of **Santa María del Mar,** north of the city's harbor.

The Barcelona visitors best remember, however, is the Barcelona of modernismo, an Art Nouveau movement that, from about 1890 to 1910, put the city on the architectural map. It blends pre-Raphaelite voluptuousness and Catalonian romanticism, heavily laced with curved lines and organic forms easily recognized in nature.

The movement's most famous architect was Antoni Gaudí. The chimneys of his buildings look like half-melted mounds of chocolate twisted into erratic spirals; his horizontal lines flow over vertical supports. Some of Gaudí's most distinctive creations include Casa Milá, Casa Batlló, Parc Güell, and the landmark Temple Expiatori de la Sagrada Família (left incomplete at his death).

Other modernist architects of this era looked for inspiration to medieval models. Examples include Doménech i Montaner and Puig i Cadafalch, whose elegant mansions and concert halls seemed perfectly suited to the enlightened, sophisticated prosperity of the 19th-century Catalonian bourgeoisie. A 19th-century economic boom neatly coincided with the profusion of geniuses that suddenly emerged in the building business. Entrepreneurs who had made their fortunes in the fields and mines of the New World commissioned some of the beautiful and elaborate villas in Barcelona and nearby Sitges.

Initiated in 1858, the expansion of Barcelona into the northern **Eixample district** laid the groundwork for the modernismo architects' designs. The gridlike pattern of streets in the Eixample was intersected with broad diagonals. Although opposed by local landowners and never endowed with the detail of its original design, it provided a carefully planned, elegant path in which a growing city could showcase its finest buildings.

A city competition conducted in the late 1850s was to decide the final architect to draw up the plans for the Eixample. Antoni Rovira won the competition and produced a radical plan. The apartment buildings, which surrounded park areas, were to be democratically occupied—"by the people of Barcelona." The plan was never carried out. The Spanish Ministry of Works approved a rectangular grid plan devised by Ildefons Cerdà, and Catalán officials felt that Madrid centralism had quashed their grand new scheme. The gardens in Cerdà's more conservative plan were never built, and the property passed to greedy landlords who constructed more buildings. Ruthless property speculation came immediately after work on the Eixample began in 1860. This dramatic story of failed hopes and dreams is told in Eduardo Mendoza's novel *The City of Marvels* and Robert Hughes's *Barcelona*.

Consistent with the general artistic stagnation in Spain during the Franco era (1939–75), the 1950s saw a tremendous increase in the number of anonymous housing projects around the periphery of Barcelona. Since the death of Franco, a cultural renaissance has ensued: New and more creative designs for buildings are again being executed.

ART

From the cave paintings discovered at Lérida to several true giants of the 20th century—Picasso, Dalí, and Miró—Catalonia has had a long and significant artistic tradition. It is the Spanish center of the plastic arts.

The first art movement to attract attention in Barcelona was **Catalonian Gothic sculpture,** which held sway from the 13th to the 15th century and produced such renowned masters as Bartomeu and Pere Johan. Sculptors working with Italian masters brought the Renaissance to Barcelona, but few great Catalonian legacies remain from this period. The rise of baroque art in the 17th and 18th centuries saw Catalonia filled with several impressive examples, but nothing worth a special pilgrimage.

In the neoclassical period of the 18th century, Catalonia, and particularly Barcelona, arose from an artistic slumber. Art schools opened and foreign painters arrived, exerting considerable influence. The 19th century produced many Catalonian artists who followed the general European trends of the time without forging any major creative breakthroughs.

The 20th century brought renewed artistic ferment in Barcelona, as reflected by the arrival of Málaga-born Pablo **Picasso.** (The Catalán capital today is the site of a major Picasso museum.) The great surrealist painters of the Spanish school, Joan **Miró** (who also has an eponymous museum in Barcelona) and Salvador **Dalí** (whose fantastical museum is along the Costa Brava, north of Barcelona), also came to the Catalonian capital.

⌐ Fun Fact Picasso & *Les Demoiselles*

Biographers of the 20th century's greatest artist, Spanish-born Pablo Picasso, claim that the artist was inspired to paint one of his masterpieces, *Les Demoiselles d'Avignon*, after a "glorious night" spent in a notorious bordello on Carrer D'Avinyó.

Many Catalán sculptors achieved acclaim in this century, including Casanovas, Llimon, and Blay. The Spanish Civil War brought cultural stagnation, yet against all odds many Catalán artists continued to make bold statements. Antoni Tàpies was one of the principal artists of this period (1 of the newest museums in Barcelona is devoted to his work). Among the various schools formed in Spain at the time was the neofigurative band, which included such artists as Vásquez Díaz and Pancho Cossio.

Today, many Barcelona artists are making major names for themselves, and their works are sold in the most prestigious galleries of the Western world. Outstanding among these is sculptor **Susana Solano,** who ranks among the most renowned names in Spanish contemporary art.

2 Orientation

ARRIVING

BY PLANE   Most travelers to Barcelona fly to Madrid and change planes there, although there are direct flights to Barcelona on Delta. Iberia offers many daily shuttle flights between Barcelona and Madrid—at 15-minute intervals during peak hours on weekdays—plus service from Valencia, Granada, Seville, and Bilbao. Generally cheaper than Iberia, both **Air Europa** (© **93-298-33-28**) and **Spanair** (© **93-298-33-62**) run shuttles between Madrid and Barcelona. Shuttle schedules depend on demand, with more frequent service in the early morning and late afternoon. For more information on flying into Madrid, refer to "Getting There," in chapter 3.

The airport, **El Prat de Llobregat,** 08820 Prat de Llobregat (© **93-298-38-38;** www.Barcelona-Airport.com), is 12km (7½ miles) southwest of the city. The route to the center of town is carefully signposted. A train runs between the airport and Barcelona's Estació Central de Barcelona-Sants every day from 6:14am (the 1st airport departure) to 10:13pm (from Sants) or 10:43pm (the last city departure). The 30-minute trip costs 2.30€ Monday through Friday, 2.30€ Saturday and Sunday. If your hotel is near Plaça de Catalunya, you might opt for an Aerobús. It runs daily every 15 minutes between 6am and midnight from the airport and 11:15pm from the Plaça de Catalunya. The fare is 3.30€. A taxi from the airport into central Barcelona costs 22€ to 35€.

BY TRAIN   A train called the **Barcelona-TALGO** provides rail service between Paris and Barcelona in 11½ hours. For many other routes from the rest of Europe, you change trains at Port Bou, on the French-Spanish border. Most trains issue seat and sleeper reservations.

Trains arrive at the **Estació de França,** Avenida Marqués de L'Argentera (Metro: Barceloneta, L3), from points throughout Spain as well as from international cities. From Madrid there are five TALGOS trains per day that make the trip in 7 hours, and three night trains that take 9½ hours; from Seville, there are two trains daily making the 12-hour trip; and from Valencia, there are 15 trains daily making the 3½-hour trip. There are express night trains to and from Paris, Zurich, Milan, and Geneva.

The modernized 1929 station has a huge screen with updated information on train departures and arrivals, personalized ticket dispatching, a passenger attention center, a tourism information center, showers, internal baggage control, a first-aid center, and centers for hotel reservations and car rentals. It is much more than a departure point: The station also has an elegant restaurant, a cafeteria, a book-and-record store, a jazz club, and even a disco. Estació de França is steps from Ciutadella Park, the zoo, and the port, and is near Vila Olímpica. RENFE also has a terminal at **Estació Central de Barcelona-Sants,** Plaça de Països Catalanes (Metro: Sants-Estació). For general RENFE information, call ✆ **90-224-02-02.**

BY BUS Bus travel to Barcelona is possible but not popular—it's pretty slow. Barcelona's Estació del Nord is the arrival and departure point for **Enatcar** (✆ **90-242-22-42**) buses to and from southern France and Italy. Enatcar also operates 24 buses per day to and from Madrid (trip time: 7½ hr.) and 25 buses per day to and from Valencia (4½ hr.). A one-way ticket from Madrid costs 22€; from Valencia, 20€.

Linebús (✆ **93-265-07-00**) offers six trips a week to and from Paris. **Julià Vía,** Carrer Viriato (✆ **93-490-40-00**), operates seven buses a week to and from Frankfurt and another seven per week to and from Marseille.

For bus travel to the beach resorts along the Costa Brava (see chapter 13, "Girona & the Costa Brava"), go to **Sarfa,** Estació del Nord (✆ **93-265-11-58**). Trip time is usually 1 hour, 20 minutes.

BY CAR From **France** (the usual European road approach to Barcelona), the major access route is at the eastern end of the **Pyrenees.** You have a choice of the express highway (E-15) or the more scenic coastal road. But be warned: If you take the coastal road in July and August, you will often encounter bumper-to-bumper traffic. You can also approach Barcelona via **Toulouse.** Cross the border into Spain at **Puigcerdà** (where there are frontier stations), near the principality of Andorra. From there, take the N-152 to Barcelona.

From **Madrid,** take the N-2 to Zaragoza, then the A-2 to El Vendrell, followed by the A-7 motorway to Barcelona. From the **Costa Blanca** or **Costa del Sol,** follow the E-15 north from Valencia along the eastern Mediterranean coast.

BY FERRY **Transmediterránea,** Moll Sant Bertran s/n (✆ **90-245-46-45**), operates daily trips to and from the Balearic islands of Majorca (trip time: 8 hr.) and Minorca (9 hr.). In summer, it's important to have a reservation as far in advance as possible.

VISITOR INFORMATION

Barcelona has two types of tourist offices. The local government office deals with Spain in general and Catalunya in particular, with basic information about Barcelona. This organization has an office at the airport, **El Prat de Llobregat** (✆ **93-478-47-04**), which you'll pass as you clear customs. Summer hours are Monday through Saturday from 9am to 9pm; off-season hours are Monday through Saturday from 9:30am to 8pm; year-round, it's open Sunday from 9:30am to 3pm. There is another large office in the center of Barcelona at the **Palau de Rubert,** Passeig de Gràcia 107 (✆ **93-238-40-00**), where there are often exhibitions. It's open daily from 10am to 7pm.

The other organization, the **Oficina de Informació de Turisme de Barcelona,** Plaça de Catalunya 17-S (✆ **90-630-12-82** from inside Spain), deals exclusively with the city of Barcelona. This is also where you can get detailed information about the city and the Barcelona card for tourist discounts. The office is open daily from 9am to 9pm. The same organization has an office at the **Estació Central de Barcelona-Sants** (Sants railway station), Plaça de Països Catalanes (no phone; Metro: Sants-Estació). In summer, it is open daily from 8am to 8pm; off season, it is open Monday through Friday from 8am to 8pm, Saturday and Sunday from 8am to 2pm.

The Barcelona Card

An ideal way to appreciate Barcelona better and save money at the same time is with the Barcelona card. It's definitely a bargain if you stay in the city for more than an afternoon and do any sightseeing at all. For adults, it costs 15€ for 1 day and 19€ for 2 days. For children, the card costs 9€ for 1 day and 12€ for 2 days.

The 24-hour card covers the Metro or bus, and unlimited travel on all public transport.

Culture vultures who hold the card can get discounts of 15% to 50% in 28 museums. Eleven theaters and shows grant a 10% to 25% discount, which also applies at 16 leisure and night venues. You also get a 12% discount at 23 leading stores. Finally, there is an 8% discount in 11 restaurants. The cards specify where they can be used. They're for sale at the tourist offices at the airport, at Sants station, and in the Plaça de Catalunya (see "Visitor Information," above).

CITY LAYOUT

MAIN SQUARES, STREETS & ARTERIES   **Plaça de Catalunya** (Plaza de Cataluña in Spanish) is the city's heart; the world-famous **Rambles** (Ramblas) are its arteries. Les Rambles begins at the Plaça Portal de la Pau, with its 49m (164-ft.) high monument to Columbus and stretches north to the Plaça de Catalunya. Along this wide promenade you'll find bookshops and newsstands, stalls selling birds and flowers, and benches or cafe tables and chairs, where you can sit and watch the passing parade.

At the end of the Rambles is the **Barri Xinés** (Barrio Chino, or **Chinese Quarter**). It has long-enjoyed notoriety as a haven of prostitution and drugs. Still a dangerous district, it is best viewed during the day, if at all.

Off the Rambles lies **Plaça Reial (Plaza Real),** the most harmoniously proportioned square in Barcelona. Come here on Sunday morning to see the stamp and coin collectors peddle their wares.

The major wide boulevards of Barcelona are the **Avinguda** (Avenida) **Diagonal** and **Passeig** (Paseo) **de Colom,** and an elegant shopping street, the **Passeig de Gràcia.**

A short walk from the Rambles will take you to the **Passeig del Moll de la Fusta,** a waterfront promenade developed in the 1990s. It's home to some of the best (but not the cheapest) restaurants in Barcelona. If you can't afford the prices, come here at least for a drink in the open air and a view of the harbor.

To the east is the old port, **La Barceloneta,** which dates from the 18th century. This strip of land between the port and the sea has traditionally been a good place for seafood. **Barri Gòtic** (Barrio Gótico, or **Gothic Quarter**) is east of the Rambles. This is the site of the city's oldest buildings, including the cathedral.

North of Plaça de Catalunya, the **Eixample** unfolds. An area of wide boulevards, it contains two major roads that lead out of Barcelona: the Avinguda Diagonal and Gran Vía de les Corts Catalanes. Another major neighborhood, working-class **Gràcia,** is north of the Eixample.

Montjuïc, one of the city's mountains, begins at Plaça d'Espanya, a traffic rotary, beyond which are Barcelona's famous fountains. Montjuïc was the setting for the principal events of the 1992 Summer Olympic Games. The other mountain is **Tibidabo,** in the northwest, which boasts great views of the city and the Mediterranean. It has an amusement park.

FINDING AN ADDRESS/MAPS   Finding a Barcelona address can be a problem. The city abounds with long boulevards and a complicated maze of narrow, twisting streets. Knowing the street number, if there is one, is essential. The designation s/n *(sin número)* means that the building has no number. It's crucial to learn the cross street if you're seeking a specific address.

The rule about street numbers is that there is no rule. On most streets, numbering begins on one side and runs up that side until the end, then runs in the opposite direction on the other side. Number 40 might be opposite 408. But there are many exceptions. Sometimes street numbers on buildings in the older quarters have been obscured by the patina of time.

Arm yourself with a good map before setting out. Free maps from tourist offices and hotels aren't adequate because they don't label the little streets. The best map for exploring Barcelona, published by **Falk,** is available at most bookstores and newsstands, such as those found along the Rambles. This pocket map includes all the streets, with an index of how to find them.

NEIGHBORHOODS IN BRIEF

Barri Gòtic   This section rises to the north of Passeig de Colom, with its **Columbus Monument.** Its eastern border is a major artery, Vía Laietana, which begins at La Barceloneta at Plaça d'Antoni López and runs north to Plaça d'Urquinaona. Les Rambles forms the western border of the Gothic Quarter, and on the northern edge is the Ronda de Sant Pere, which intersects with **Plaça de Catalunya** and the **Passeig de Gràcia.** The heart of this medieval quarter is the **Plaça de Sant Jaume,** which was a major crossroads in the old Roman city. Many of the structures in the old section are ancient, including the ruins of a Roman temple dedicated to Augustus. Antiques stores, restaurants, cafes, museums, some hotels, and bookstores fill the area today. It is also the headquarters of the **Generalitat,** seat of the Catalán government.

Les Rambles   Also commonly known as **La Rambla.** The most famous promenade in Spain, ranking with Madrid's Paseo del Prado, it was once a drainage channel.

These days, street entertainers, flower vendors, news vendors, cafe patrons, and strollers flow along its length. The gradual 1.5km (1-mile) descent toward the sea has often been called a metaphor for life because its bustling action combines cosmopolitanism and crude vitality.

Les Rambles actually consists of five sections, each a particular *rambla*—Rambla de Canaletes, Rambla dels Estudis, Rambla de Sant Josep, Rambla dels Caputxins, and Rambla de Santa Mónica. The shaded pedestrian esplanade runs from the Plaça de Catalunya to the port—all the way to the Columbus Monument. Along the way you'll pass the **Gran Teatre del Liceu,** on Rambla dels Caputxins, one of the most magnificent opera houses in the world until it caught fire in 1994 and had to be rebuilt. Miró did a sidewalk mosaic at the Plaça de la Boquería. During the stagnation of the Franco era, this street grew seedier and seedier, but the opening of the Ramada Renaissance hotel and the restoration of many buildings have brought energy and hope for the street.

Barri Xinés Despite the name ("Chinese Quarter"), this isn't Chinatown—historians are unsure how the neighborhood got its name. For decades it's had an unsavory reputation. Petty thieves, prostitutes, drug dealers, and purse-snatchers are just some of the neighborhood characters. Nighttime is dangerous, so exercise caution; still, most visitors like to take a quick look to see what all the excitement is about. Just off Les Rambles, the area is primarily between the waterfront and Carrer de l'Hospital. Although Barri Xinés has a long way to go, an urban renewal program has led to the destruction of some of the seedier parts of the *barrio*. The opening of the **Museu d'Art Contemporani** at Plaça dels Angels has led to a revitalization of the area and the opening of a lot more art galleries. The official name Barcelona has given to this district is **El Raval.**

Barri de la Ribera Another neighborhood that stagnated for years but is now well into a renaissance, the Barri de la Ribera is adjacent to the Barri Gòtic, going east to Passeig de Picasso, which borders the Parc de la Ciutadella. The centerpiece of this district is the **Museu Picasso,** housed in the 15th-century Palau Agüilar, Montcada 15. Numerous art galleries have opened around the museum, and the old quarter is fashionable. Many mansions in this area were built during one of Barcelona's major maritime expansions, principally in the 1200s and 1300s. Most of these grand homes still stand along **Carrer de Montcada** and other nearby streets.

La Barceloneta & the Harbor Front Although Barcelona has a long seagoing tradition, its waterfront was in decay for years. Today, the waterfront promenade, **Passeig del Moll de la Fusta,** bursts with activity. The best way to get a bird's-eye view of the area is to take an elevator to the top of the Columbus Monument in Plaça Portal de la Pau.

Near the monument were the **Reials Drassanes,** or royal shipyards, a booming place during the Middle Ages. Years before Columbus landed in the New World, ships sailed around the world from here, flying the traditional yellow-and-red flag of Catalonia.

To the east is a mainly artificial peninsula, **La Barceloneta (Little Barcelona).** Formerly a fishing district dating mainly from the 18th century, it's now filled with seafood restaurants. The blocks here are long and surprisingly narrow—architects planned them that way so that each room in every building fronted a street. Many bus lines terminate at the Passeig Nacional, site of the **Barcelona Aquarium.**

The Eixample To the north of the Plaça de Catalunya is the Eixample, or Ensanche, the section of Barcelona that grew beyond the old medieval walls. This great period of enlargement (*eixample* in Catalán) came mainly in the 19th century. Avenues form a grid of perpendicular streets, cut across by a majestic boulevard—**Passeig de Gràcia,** a posh shopping street ideal for leisurely promenades. The area's main traffic artery is **Avinguda Diagonal,** which links the expressway and the heart of the congested city.

The Eixample was the center of Barcelona's modernismo movement, and it possesses some of the most original buildings any architect ever designed. Gaudí's Sagrada Família is one of the major attractions.

Montjuïc & Tibidabo Montjuïc, called Hill of the Jews after a Jewish necropolis there, gained prominence in 1929 as the site of the World's Fair and again in 1992 as the site of the

Summer Olympic Games. Its major attractions are the Joan Miró museum, the Olympic installations, and the **Poble Espanyol (Spanish Village),** a 2-hectare (5-acre) site constructed for the World's Fair. Examples of Spanish art and architecture are on display against the backdrop of a traditional Spanish village. Tibidabo (503m/1,650 ft.) is where you should go for your final look at Barcelona. On a clear day you can see the mountains of Majorca, some 209km (130 miles) away. Reached by train, tram, and cable car, Tibidabo is the most popular Sunday excursion in Barcelona.

Pedralbes Pedralbes is where wealthy Barcelonans live in either stylish blocks of apartment houses, 19th-century villas behind ornamental fences, or stunning modernismo structures. Set in a park, the **Palau de Pedralbes** (Avinguda Diagonal 686) was constructed in the 1920s as a gift from the city to Alfonso XIII, the grandfather of King Juan Carlos. Today it has a new life, housing a museum of carriages and a group of European paintings called the **Colecció Cambó.**

Vila Olímpica This seafront property contains the tallest buildings in the city. The revitalized site, in the post–Olympic Games era, is the setting for many imported-car showrooms, designer clothing stores, restaurants, and business offices. The "village" was where the athletes lived during the 1992 games. A miniature city is taking shape, complete with banks, art galleries, nightclubs, bars, and even pastry shops.

3 Getting Around

To save money on public transportation, buy a card that's good for 10 trips. **Tarjeta T-1,** for 5.90€, is good for the Metro and the bus. Passes *(abonos temporales)* are available at **Transports Metropolita de Barcelona,** Plaça de la Universitat. It's open Monday through Friday from 8am to 5pm, Saturday from 8am to 1pm.

To save money on sightseeing tours during the summer, ride on **Bus Turistic,** which passes by 24 of the most popular sights. You can get on and off the bus as you please, and the price covers the Tibidabo funicular and the Montjuïc cable car and funicular. Tickets, which can be purchased on the bus or at the tourist office at Plaça de Catalunya, cost 15€ for 1 day, 19€ for 2 days; for children, 9€ for 1 day and 12€ for 2 days.

BY SUBWAY

Barcelona's Metro system consists of five main lines; it crisscrosses the city more frequently and with greater efficiency than the bus network. Two commuter trains run between the city and the suburbs. Service operates Monday through Thursday from 5am to midnight, Saturday from 5am to 2am, and Sunday and holidays from 6am to 2am. The one-way fare is 1.10€. Each Metro station entrance is marked with a red diamond. The major station for all subway lines is **Plaça de Catalunya.**

BY BUS

Some 100 bus lines traverse the city, and as always, you don't want to ride them at rush hour. The driver issues a ticket as you board at the front. Most buses operate daily from 6:30am to 10pm; some night buses go along the principal arteries from 11pm to 4am. Buses are color-coded—red ones cut through the city center during the day, and yellow ones do the job at night. The one-way fare is 1.10€.

Barcelona Metro

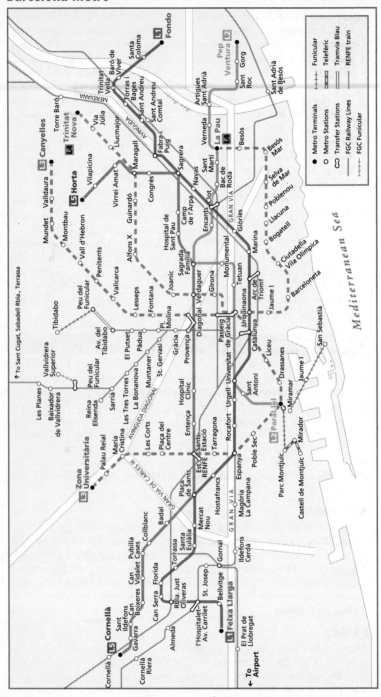

BY TAXI

Each yellow-and-black taxi bears the letters SP *(servicio público)* on its front and rear. A lit green light on the roof and a LIBRE sign in the window indicate the taxi is free to pick up passengers. The basic rate begins at 1.15€. Check to make sure you're not paying the fare of a previously departed passenger; taxi drivers have been known to "forget" to turn back the meter. Each additional kilometer in slow-moving traffic costs .70€. Supplements might apply—.85€ for a large suitcase placed in the trunk, for instance. Rides to the airport sometimes carry a supplement of 2.10€. For a taxi, call © **93-330-08-04.**

BY CAR

Driving in congested Barcelona is frustrating and potentially dangerous. Besides, it's unlikely you'd ever find a place to park. Try other means of getting around. Save your car rentals for excursions and for when you're ready to move on.

All three of the major U.S.-based car-rental firms are represented in Barcelona, both at the airport and (except for Budget) downtown.

Avis, Calle Corcega 293 (© **93-487-87-54**), is open Monday through Friday from 8am to 1pm and 4 to 9pm, Saturday from 8am to 8pm. **Hertz** is at Tuset 10 (© **93-217-80-76**); it's open Monday through Friday from 9am to 2pm and 4 to 7pm, Saturday from 9am to 2pm. Hertz is closed on Sunday except in the airport, where it is open from 7am to midnight daily. This forces clients of those companies to trek out to the airport to pick up or return their cars; however, after-hours arrangements can be made.

Remember that it's usually cheaper and easier to arrange your car rental before leaving the United States. For more information on car rentals in Spain, refer to "Getting Around," in chapter 3.

BY FUNICULAR & RAIL LINKS

At some point in your journey, you may want to visit Tibidabo or Montjuïc (or both). A train called **Tramvía Blau (Blue Streetcar)** goes from Plaça Kennedy to the bottom of the funicular to Tibidabo. It operates every 15 to 20 minutes from 9:05am to 9:35pm on weekends only. The fare is 2€ one-way, 3€ round-trip. During the week, buses run from the Plaça Kennedy to the bottom of the funicular from approximately 10am to 9:30pm daily. The bus costs 1€ one-way.

At the end of the run, you can go the rest of the way by funicular to the top, at 503m (1,650 ft.), for a stunning panoramic view of Barcelona. The funicular operates only when the Fun Fair at Tibidabo is open. Opening times vary according to the time of year and the weather conditions. As a rule, the funicular starts operating 20 minutes before the Fun Fair opens, then every half hour. During peak visiting hours, it runs every 15 minutes. The fare is 2€ one-way, 3€ round-trip.

The **Tibibus** (© **93-211-79-42**) goes from the Plaça de Catalunya, in the center of the city, to Tibidabo from June 24 to September 15 on Saturday and Sunday. It runs every 40 minutes from 11am to 6:30pm and sometimes 8:30pm, depending on when the park closes. The one-way fare is 1.90€. To reach Montjuïc, the site of the 1992 Olympics, take the **Montjuïc funicular** (© **93-318-70-74**). It links with subway line 3 at Parallel. The funicular operates daily, from 8am to 8pm. In winter it operates daily from 8am to 8pm. The round-trip fare is 2.10€.

A **cable car** linking the upper part of the Montjuïc funicular with Castell de Montjuïc is in service in winter, daily from 11:15am to 7:15pm (until 7:30pm on weekends). The one-way fare is 3.40€; the round-trip fare is 4.80€ for adults. From June 28 to September 15 and holidays, it operates Monday through Friday from 11:15am to 8pm, until 9pm on weekends.

The **Montjuïc teléferic** (cable car) runs from Barceloneta to Montjuïc. Service from June 20 to September 15 is daily from 10:30am to 7pm, and from noon to 5pm in winter. The fare is 3.20€ one-way, 4.50€ round-trip.

 FAST FACTS: Barcelona

American Express The office is at Passeig de Gràcia 101 (℃ **93-255-00-00;** Metro: Diagonal), near the corner of Carrer del Rosselló. It's open Monday through Friday from 9:30am to 6pm, Saturday from 10am to 1:30pm.

Consulates For information on embassies, see "Fast Facts: Spain," in chapter 3. The **U.S. Consulate,** Reina Elisenda 23 (℃ **93-280-22-27;** train: Reina Elisenda), is open Monday through Friday from 9am to 1pm. The **Canadian Consulate,** Calle Elisenda de Pinos (℃ **93-204-27-00;** Metro: Reina Elisenda), is open Monday through Friday from 10am to noon. The **U.K. Consulate,** Avinguda Diagonal 477 (℃ **93-366-62-00;** Metro: Hospital Clinic), is open Monday through Friday from 9:30am to 1:30pm and 4 to 5pm. The **Australian Consulate** is at Gran Vía Carlos III 98, ninth floor (℃ **93-330-94-96;** Metro: María Cristina), and is open Monday through Friday from 10am to noon.

Currency Exchange Most banks exchange currency Monday through Friday from 8:30am to 2pm and—in the downtown area, except in the summer—on Saturday from 8:30am to 1pm and 4 to 8pm. A major *oficina de cambio* (exchange office) is at the Estació Central de Barcelona-Sants, the principal rail station. It's open Monday through Saturday from 8:30am to 10pm, Sunday from 8:30am to 2pm and 4:30 to 10pm. Exchange offices at Barcelona's airport are open daily from 6:30am to 11pm.

Dentist Call the **Clínica Dental Beonadex,** Passeig Bonanova 69, 3rd floor (℃ **93-418-44-33**), for an appointment. It's open Monday from 3 to 9pm, Tuesday through Friday from 8am to 3pm and 4 to 7pm.

Doctors See "Hospitals," below.

Drugstores The most centrally located one is **Farmacia Manuel Nadal i Casas,** Rambla de Canaletes 121 (℃ **93-317-49-42;** Metro: Plaça de Catalunya). It's open daily from 9am to 10pm. Pharmacies take turns staying open late at night. Those that aren't open post the names and addresses of pharmacies in the area that are.

Emergencies Fire, ℃ **080;** police, ℃ **092;** ambulance, ℃ **061.**

Hospitals Barcelona has many hospitals and clinics, including **Hospital Clinic** and **Hospital de la Santa Creu i Sant Pau,** at the intersection of Carrer Cartagena and Carrer Sant Antoni María Claret (℃ **93-291-90-00;** Metro: Hospital de Sant Pau).

Internet Access **Conéctate,** Calle Pau Claris 134 (℃ **93-467-04-43**), is open 7 days a week, 24 hours a day; the minimum cost for access is 1.20€.

Newspapers & Magazines The *International Herald-Tribune* is sold at major hotels and nearly all the news kiosks along Les Rambles. Sometimes you can buy *USA Today* or one of the London newspapers, such as the

Times. Barcelona's leading daily newspapers, which often list cultural events, are *El Periódico* and *La Vanguardia*.

Police In an emergency, call ✆ **092.**

Post Office The main post office is at Plaça d'Antoni López (✆ **93-486-80-50;** Metro: Jaume I). It's open Monday through Saturday from 8:30am to 9:30pm for sending letters and telegrams.

Safety Be particularly careful with cameras, purses, and wallets, all favorite targets of thieves and pickpockets in Barcelona, and particularly on the world-famous Rambles. The southern part of Les Rambles, near the waterfront, is the most dangerous section, especially at night. Proceed with caution.

Taxis See "Getting Around," earlier in this chapter.

Telephone Dial ✆ **1003** for information in Barcelona. For elsewhere in Spain, dial ✆ **1009.** Most local calls cost .40€. Hotels impose surcharges on phone calls, especially long distance, either in Spain or abroad. There is no longer a central telephone office, but calls can be made in comfort and security from phone centers on Les Rambles.

Transit Information For general RENFE (train) information, dial ✆ **90-224-02-02.**

4 Where to Stay

Barcelona may be one of the most expensive cities in Spain, but prices at Barcelona's first-class and deluxe hotels are completely in line with those in other major European cities—and they even look reasonable compared to prices in Paris and London.

Safety is an important factor when choosing a hotel. Some of the least expensive hotels are not in good locations. A popular area for budget-conscious travelers is the **Barri Gòtic (Gothic Quarter),** in the heart of town. You'll live and eat less expensively here than in any other part of Barcelona, but you should be careful when returning to your hotel late at night.

More modern, but more expensive, accommodations can be found north of the Barri Gòtic in the **Eixample district,** centered on the Metro stops Plaça de Catalunya and Universitat. Many buildings are in the modernismo style, from the first 2 decades of this century—and sometimes the elevators and plumbing are of the same vintage. The Eixample is a desirable and safe neighborhood, especially along its wide boulevards. Noise is the only problem you might encounter.

Farther north, above the Avinguda Diagonal, you'll enter the **Gràcia** area, where you can enjoy distinctively Catalán neighborhood life. The main attractions are a bit distant but reached easily by public transportation.

Many of Barcelona's hotels were built before the invention of the automobile, and even those that weren't rarely found space for a garage. When parking is available at the hotel, the price is indicated; otherwise, the hotel staff will direct you to a garage. Expect to pay upward of 14€ for 24 hours, and if you do have a car, you might as well park it and leave it there, because we'd never recommend driving around the city.

Barcelona Accommodations

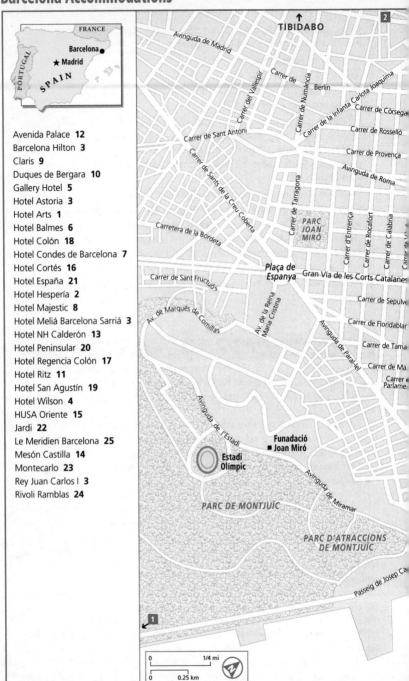

Avenida Palace **12**
Barcelona Hilton **3**
Claris **9**
Duques de Bergara **10**
Gallery Hotel **5**
Hotel Astoria **3**
Hotel Arts **1**
Hotel Balmes **6**
Hotel Colón **18**
Hotel Condes de Barcelona **7**
Hotel Cortés **16**
Hotel España **21**
Hotel Hespería **2**
Hotel Majestic **8**
Hotel Meliá Barcelona Sarriá **3**
Hotel NH Calderón **13**
Hotel Peninsular **20**
Hotel Regencia Colón **17**
Hotel Ritz **11**
Hotel San Agustín **19**
Hotel Wilson **4**
HUSA Oriente **15**
Jardi **22**
Le Meridien Barcelona **25**
Mesón Castilla **14**
Montecarlo **23**
Rey Juan Carlos I **3**
Rivoli Ramblas **24**

Plaça de
Francesc Macia

Carrer de Buenos Aires

Carrer de Londres

Carrer de Paris

Travessara de Gràcia

Gran de Gràcia

Avinguda Diagonal

Travessara de Gràcia

Av. de Sant Antoni Maria Claret

Carrer de la Industria

Carrer de Còrsega

EIXAMPLE

i

Carrer de Rosselló

Plaça de la
Sagrada
Família

Carrer de Roger de Flor

Carrer de Provença

Carrer Enric Granados

Carrer de Balmes

Rambla de Catalunya

Passeig de Gràcia

Carrer de Pau Claris

Avinguda Diagonal

Carrer de Mallorca

Carrer de València

Carrer d'Aragó

Carrer de R. de Llúria

Carrer del Bruc

Carrer de Girona

Carrer de Bailèn

Passeig de Sant Joan

Carrer de Napols

Carrer de Sicilia

Carrer del Consell de Cent

Carrer de la Diputació

Carrer de Comte Borrell

Carrer del Comte d'Urgell

Carrer de Villarroel

Carrer de Casanova

Carrer de Muntaner

Carrer d'Aribau

Gran Via de les Corts Catalanes

Plaça de la
Universitat

Ronda Universitat

Plaça de
Tetuan

Plaça
Catalunya

i

Ronda de Sant Antoni

Carrer de Pelai

RAVAL

Plaça
Urquinaona

Ronda de Sant Pere

Carrer de Casp

Carrer d'Ausias Marc

Carrer d'Ali Bei

Carrer de Ribes

Carrer de Sardenya

Ronda Sant Pau

Carrer de Hospital

Av. Portal
de l'Angel

La Rambla

BARRI GÒTIC

Via Laietana

Palau de la
Música Catalana

Passeig de Lluís Companys

Carrer de la Marina

Carrer de Sant Pau

Gran Teatre
del Liceu

Cathedral

C. de   Ferran   C. de la Princesa

Carrer de Wellington

Carrer Nou de la Rambla

Avda. de les Drassanes

La Rambla

LA RIBERA

Museu
Picasso

Carrer del Comerç

Passeig de Picasso

PARC DE LA
CIUTADELLA

Carrer Ample

Plaça Portal
de la Pau

Passeig de Colom   Pg. Isabel II

Moll de la Fusta

Moll d'Espanya

Port
Vell

Avinguda d'Icaria

PARC
ZOOLOGIC

Villa
Olímpica →

BARCELONETA

Passeig   Marítim

CIUTAT VELLA

The Ciutat Vella (Old City) forms the monumental center of Barcelona, taking in Les Rambles, Plaça de Sant Jaume, Vía Laietana, Passeig Nacional, and Passeig de Colom. It contains some of the city's best hotel bargains. Most of the glamorous, and more expensive, hotels are in Sur Diagonal (see below).

VERY EXPENSIVE

Le Meridien Barcelona ★★★ Originally built in 1956, this is the finest hotel in the old town, as the roster of famous guests (such as Michael Jackson) can surely attest. It's superior in comfort to its two closest rivals in the area, the Colón and the Rivoli Ramblas (and also more expensive). Guest rooms are spacious and comfortable, with extra-large beds and heated bathroom floors with tub/shower combos. All rooms have double-glazed windows, but that doesn't fully block out noise from Les Rambles. The Renaissance Club, an executive floor popular with businesspeople, provides extra luxuries.

Les Rambles 111, 08002 Barcelona. ℭ 800/543-4300 in the U.S., or 93-318-62-00. Fax 93-301-77-76. www.meridienbarcelona.com. 212 units. 175€–350€ double; from 325€–500€ suite. AE, DC, MC, V. Parking 20€. Metro: Liceu or Plaça de Catalunya. **Amenities:** Restaurant; bar; health club; room service; babysitting; laundry service; dry cleaning. *In room:* A/C, TV, minibar, hair dryer, safe.

EXPENSIVE

Hotel Colón ★★ *Kids* The Colón is an appropriate choice if you plan to spend a lot of time exploring Barcelona's medieval neighborhoods. Blessed with what might be the most dramatic location in the city, opposite the main entrance to the cathedral, this hotel sits behind a dignified neoclassical facade. Inside, you'll find conservative and slightly old-fashioned public rooms, a helpful staff, and good-size guest rooms filled with comfortable furniture. Despite recent renovations, they retain an appealingly dowdy charm. Each room comes with a bathroom containing a tub/shower combo. Not all rooms have views, and units in back are quieter. Sixth-floor rooms with balconies overlooking the square are the most desirable. Some of the lower rooms are rather dark. Upon request, families can often be given more spacious rooms.

Avinguda de la Catedral 7, 08002 Barcelona. ℭ 800/845-0636 in the U.S., or 93-301-14-04. Fax 93-317-29-15. www.hotelcolon.es. 147 units. 220€–245€ double; from 350€ suite. AE, DC, MC, V. Bus: 16, 17, 19, or 45. **Amenities:** Restaurant; bar; room service; babysitting; laundry service; dry cleaning. *In room:* A/C, TV, minibar, hair dryer, safe.

Hotel NH Calderón ★ Efficient, well maintained, and well staffed with a multilingual corps of employees, this hotel delivers exactly what it promises: safe and comfortable accommodations in a well-conceived, standardized format that's akin to many other modern hotels around the world. Originally built in the 1960s, this 10-story hotel wasn't particularly imaginative then, but was greatly improved in the early 1990s after its acquisition by NH, with frequent renovations ever since. Accommodations have comfortable, contemporary-looking furnishings with hints of high-tech design, good lighting, lots of varnished hardwood, and colorful fabrics. All units have bathrooms with tub/shower combos.

Rambla de Catalunya 26, 08007 Barcelona. ℭ 93-301-00-00. Fax 93-412-41-93. www.nh-hoteles.es. 252 units. Mon–Thurs 220€ double; Fri–Sun 166€ double. AE, DC, MC, V. Parking 15€. Metro: Passeig de Gràcia. **Amenities:** Restaurant; bar; pool; health club; sauna; room service; laundry service; dry cleaning. *In room:* A/C, TV, minibar, hair dryer, safe.

Rivoli Ramblas ★ Behind a dignified Art Deco town house on the upper section of the Rambles, a block south of the Plaça de Catalunya, this recently renovated hotel incorporates many fine examples of avant-garde Catalán design in its stylish interior. The Colón has more tradition and style, and the Meridien more modern comfort; this is choice number three in the old town. The minimalist public rooms glisten with polished marble. Guest rooms are carpeted, soundproofed, and elegant, but rather cramped. Guest rooms all have neatly kept bathrooms with tub/shower combos.

Les Rambles 128, 08002 Barcelona. ✆ 93-302-66-43. Fax 93-317-50-53. www.rivolihotels.com. 129 units. 246€ double; from 300€–696€ suite. Rates include breakfast. AE, DC, MC, V. Metro: Plaça de Catalunya or Liceu. **Amenities:** Restaurant; bar; health spa; sauna; car rental; room service; babysitting; laundry service; dry cleaning; solarium. *In room:* A/C, TV, minibar, coffeemaker, hair dryer, iron, safe.

MODERATE

Duques de Bergara ✷   This upscale hotel occupies an 1899 town house built for the Duke of Bergara. In 1998, the original five-story structure more than doubled in size with the addition of a new seven-story tower. Guest rooms throughout have the same conservative, traditional comforts. Each unit has large, comfortable beds with first-rate mattresses, elegant fabrics, and good lighting. The roomy marble bathrooms are equipped with tub/shower combos. Public areas contain most of the paneling, stained glass, and decorative accessories originally installed by modernismo architect Emilio Salas i Cortes, a professor of the movement's greatest luminary, Gaudí. In the reception area, look for stained-glass panels displaying the heraldic coat of arms of the building's original occupant and namesake, the duke of Bergara.

Bergara 11, 08002 Barcelona. ✆ 93-301-51-51. Fax 93-317-34-42. 149 units. 171€–235€ double; 201€–259€ triple. AE, DC, MC, V. Public parking nearby 18€. Metro: Plaça de Catalunya. **Amenities:** Restaurant; cafe; bar; pool; room service; laundry service; dry cleaning. *In room:* A/C, TV, minibar, hair dryer, safe.

Hotel Regencia Colón ⓥ𝘃𝘢𝘭𝘶𝘦   This stately stone six-story building stands directly behind the pricier Hotel Colón and in the shadow of the cathedral. The Regencia Colón attracts tour groups because it's a good value for Barcelona. The formal lobby seems a bit dour, but the well-maintained rooms are comfortable and often roomy, albeit worn. Rooms are insulated against sound, and 40 have full bathrooms with tubs (the remainder have showers only). All have comfortable beds and piped-in music. The hotel's location is a plus.

Sagristans 13–17, 08002 Barcelona. ✆ 93-318-98-58. Fax 93-317-28-22. www.hotelregenciacolon.com. 50 units. 148€ double; 170€ triple. AE, DC, MC, V. Metro: Plaça de Catalunya or Urquinaona. **Amenities:** Bar; babysitting; laundry service; dry cleaning. *In room:* A/C, TV, minibar, hair dryer, safe.

Montecarlo ✷   This hotel beside the Rambles dates from 200 years ago when it was built as an opulent private home. In the 1930s it was transformed into the comfortably unpretentious hotel you'll find today. It offers a level of comfort superior to that of most competitors. Each of the midsize guest rooms is efficiently decorated and comfortable. Double-glazed windows help keep out some of the noise. Public areas include some of the building's original accessories, with carved doors, a baronial fireplace, and crystal chandeliers.

La Rambla 124, 08002 Barcelona. ✆ 93-412-04-04. Fax 93-318-73-23. hotel@montecarloben.com. 55 units. 172€–300€ double; 374€ suite. AE, DC, MC, V. Parking 15€. Metro: Plaça de Catalunya. **Amenities:** Lounge; sauna; room service; babysitting; laundry service; dry cleaning. *In room:* A/C, TV, minibar, hair dryer, iron, safe.

INEXPENSIVE

Hotel Cortés   A short walk from the cathedral, the Cortés dates from 1910 and was, like many of its competitors, thoroughly renovated in time for the 1992 Olympics; since then it has been improved again. It competes effectively with the Continental. Midsize to small guest rooms are scattered over five floors. About half overlook a quiet central courtyard, the other half open onto the street. All have private bathrooms, most of which contain tub/shower combos.

Santa Ana 25, 08002 Barcelona. © **93-317-91-12.** Fax 93-412-66-08. 44 units. 98€ double. Rates include breakfast. AE, DC, MC, V. Metro: Plaça de Catalunya. **Amenities:** Restaurant; bar; babysitting. *In room:* A/C, TV, safe.

Hotel España   Although the rooms at this cost-conscious hotel have none of the architectural grandeur of Barcelona's modernist age, they're well scrubbed, comfortably sized, and outfitted with functional furniture and neatly kept bathrooms containing tub/shower combos. The building itself is a relic of the city's turn-of-the-20th-century splendor, as it was constructed in 1902 by fabled architect Doménech i Montaner, designer and architect of the Palau de la Música. It was once patronized by the likes of Salvador Dalí. There's an elevator for the building's four floors, a facade that still evokes the past, and a hard-working staff that's comfortable with non-Spanish-speaking visitors. The lower Rambla, near where this hotel sits, evokes either cultural fascination or indignation, depending on how urbanized you are, but overall, it's an acceptable and well-managed choice at a relatively reasonable price.

Carrer Sant Pau 11, 08001 Barcelona. © **93-318-17-58.** Fax 93-317-11-34. 60 units. 86€ double. AE, DC, MC, V. Metro: Liceu or Drassanes. **Amenities:** 3 restaurants. *In room:* A/C, TV, hair dryer, safe.

Hotel Peninsular *(Value)*   In a converted nunnery just off Les Rambles, this converted hotel in the Art Nouveau style is a welcoming haven for the budget traveler. Constructed within the shell of a former monastery that had a passageway connecting it to Sant Agusti church, the hotel was thoroughly modernized in the early 1990s. Its use of wicker furnishings still lends somewhat of a colonial aura, and its inner courtyard, lined with plants, is its most attractive grace note. In the typical Modernist style of its era, the Peninsular still has long hallways and high doorways and ceilings. The bedrooms are well maintained but rather simply, though comfortably furnished, each with a bathroom with shower.

Sant Pau 34–36, 08001 Barcelona. © **93-302-31-38.** Fax 93-412-36-99. 59 units. 70€. Rates include breakfast. MC, V. Metro: Liceu. **Amenities:** Cafeteria; bar. *In room:* A/C.

Hotel San Agustín   This tastefully renovated five-story hotel stands in the center of the old city, near the covered produce markets overlooking the brick walls of an unfinished Romanesque church. The small guest rooms are comfortable and modern, with such luxuries as piped-in music, and tiled bathrooms with tub/shower combos. Some units are equipped for travelers with disabilities.

Plaça de San Agustín 3, 08001 Barcelona. © **93-318-16-58.** Fax 93-317-29-28. 76 units. www.hotelsa.com. 116€–158€ double; 158€–174€ triple; 131€ quad; 174€–220€ 2-bedroom family unit. Rates include breakfast. AE, DC, MC, V. Metro: Liceu. **Amenities:** Restaurant; lounge; room service; laundry service; dry cleaning. *In room:* A/C, TV, hair dryer, safe.

HUSA Oriente   Right on the bustling Rambles, this hotel, a government-rated, three-star, was once one of the original "grand hotels" of Barcelona. On the site of a Franciscan monastery, the hotel dates from 1842. It was so prominent in its day that it attracted the likes of Toscanini and Maria Callas. It even became part of Hollywood legend when Errol Flynn checked in. He became so drunk he passed out in the bar. The manager ordered two bartenders to carry him upstairs where they were instructed to strip the swashbuckling star. The manager then sent word to guests down below that they could see the star in the nude. They filed in one by one for the viewing all night. When Flynn woke up with a hangover the next morning, he was none the wiser. Renovations have improved the hotel but it lacks the character of its former glory, today attracting mainly frugal travelers. The arched ballroom of yesterday has been turned into an atmospheric lounge, and the dining room still has a certain grandeur. Each simple but comfortable room has a tiled bathroom with shower.

Les Rambles 45, 08002 Barcelona. © **93-302-25-58.** Fax 93-412-38-19. www.husa.es. 142 units. 131€ double. AE, MC, V. Metro: Liceu. **Amenities:** Restaurant, bar. *In room:* A/C, TV, safe.

Jardí *(Value)*   Sought out for its location, this little hotel opens onto the tree-shaded Plaça Sant Josep Oriols with its many cafes and the severe Gothic architecture of the medieval church of Santa María del Pi. The building in the heart of Barcelona's Gothic quarter rests on ancient Roman foundations. The five-floor hotel has recently been upgraded and improved, with the installation of an elevator. Under separate management, Bar del Pi, on the ground floor, is a favorite of artists and students who live nearby. In the modernization, much of the original architectural charm was maintained, although rooms remain rather basic but are comfortable with bathrooms with tub and with shower. The quieter units are on top, of course. Five of the accommodations have private terraces, and 26 of them open onto private but rather small balconies.

Plaça Sant Josep Orio 1, 08002 Barcelona. © **93-301-59-00.** Fax 93-342-57-33. 42 units. 70€–75€ double; 85€ triple. AE, DC, MC, V. Metro: Liceu. **Amenities:** Bar. *In room:* A/C, TV, safe.

Mesón Castilla ★ *(Value)*   This government-rated two-star hotel, a former apartment building, has a Castilian facade with a wealth of Art Nouveau detailing. Owned and operated by the Spanish hotel chain HUSA, the Castilla is charming and well maintained, and it certainly has a fantastic location, right in the center of the city close to Les Rambles. Its nearest rival is the Regencia Colón, to which it is comparable in atmosphere and government ratings. It is far superior to the Cortés and the Continental. The midsize rooms are comfortable—beds have ornate Catalán-style headboards—and some open onto large terraces. The tiled bathrooms are equipped with tub/shower combos.

Valldoncella 5, 08001 Barcelona. © **93-318-21-82.** Fax 93-412-40-20. 57 units. 117€ double. AE, DC, V. Parking 18€. Metro: Plaça de Catalunya or Universitat. **Amenities:** Breakfast room; lounge; babysitting; laundry service; dry cleaning. *In room:* A/C, TV, minibar, hair dryer, safe.

SUR DIAGONAL
VERY EXPENSIVE

Barcelona Hilton ★★   This government-rated five-star property, opposite the gates to the fairgrounds (beyond that, to the Olympic Stadium), is a huge 11-floor corner structure. It is part of a huge commercial complex with an adjoining office tower. The lobby is sleek with lots of velvet chairs. Most rooms are rather large and finely equipped. Furnishings are Hilton-standardized, but the rooms are filled with thick carpeting, rich wood furnishings and some of the best combination bathrooms in the city with all the extras, including dual basins and robes. Some units are smoke-free, and others are reserved exclusively for women.

Avinguda Diagonal 589–591, 08014 Barcelona. © **800/445-8667** in the U.S. and Canada, or 93-495-77-77. Fax 93-495-77-00. www.hilton.com. 288 units. 305€–365€ double; 320€–435€ suite. AE, DC, MC, V. Parking 21€. Metro: María Cristina. **Amenities:** 2 restaurants; cafe; bar; health club; business center; 24-hr. room service; babysitting; laundry service; dry cleaning. *In room:* A/C, TV, minibar, coffeemaker, hair dryer, iron, safe.

Claris ★★   One of the most unusual hotels in Barcelona, this postmodern lodging is the only government-rated five-star deluxe property in the city center. It incorporates vast quantities of teak, marble, steel, and glass behind the historically important facade of a landmark 19th-century building (the Verdruna Palace). Although we prefer the Ritz (see below), many hail the Claris as the city's top choice. Opened in 1992 (in time for the Olympics), it's a seven-story structure with a swimming pool and garden on its roof. There's a small museum of Egyptian antiquities from the owner's collection on the second floor. The blue-violet guest rooms contain state-of-the-art electronic accessories as well as unusual art objects—Turkish kilims, English antiques, Hindu sculptures, Egyptian stone carvings, and engravings. The spacious rooms are among the most opulent in town, with wood marquetry and paneling, custom furnishings, safes, and some of the city's most sumptuous beds. Bathrooms are roomy and filled with deluxe toiletries, and tub/shower combos. If money is no object, book one of the 20 individually designed duplex units.

Carrer de Pau Claris 150, 08009 Barcelona. (𝄯 **800/888-4747** in the U.S., or 93-487-62-62. Fax 93-215-79-70. www.hotelclaris.com. 120 units. 175€–355€ double; from 319€–483€ suite. Fri–Sun rates include breakfast. AE, DC, MC, V. Parking 19€. Metro: Passeig de Gràcia. **Amenities:** 2 restaurants; 2 bars; pool; fitness center; sauna; room service; babysitting; laundry service; dry cleaning; private museum. *In room:* A/C, TV, minibar, hair dryer, safe.

Hotel Ritz ⭐⭐⭐   Acknowledged by many as the finest, most prestigious, and most architecturally distinguished hotel in Barcelona, the Art Deco Ritz dates from 1919. Richly remodeled during the late 1980s, it has welcomed more millionaires, famous people, and aristocrats (and their official and unofficial consorts) than any other hotel in northeastern Spain. One of the finest features is a cream-and-gilt neoclassical lobby, where afternoon tea is served to the strains of a string quartet. The sumptuous guest rooms are as formal, high ceilinged, and richly furnished as you'd expect. Some have Regency furniture, bathrooms accented with mosaics, and showers with bathtubs inspired by those in ancient Rome. You get all the luxuries here: elegant fabrics, deluxe mattresses, and plush towels.

Gran Vía de les Corts Catalanes 668, 08010 Barcelona. (𝄯 **93-318-52-00.** Fax 93-318-01-48. www.ritz-barcelona.com. 122 units. 380€ double; from 475€ suite. AE, DC, MC, V. Parking 21€. Metro: Passeig de Gràcia. **Amenities:** 2 restaurants; bar; fitness center; car rental; room service; babysitting; laundry service; dry cleaning. *In room:* A/C, TV, minibar, hair dryer, safe.

Rey Juan Carlos I ⭐⭐⭐   Named for the Spanish king who attended its opening and has visited several times, this government-rated five-star hotel competes effectively against the Ritz, Claris, and Hotel Arts. Opened just before the Olympics, it rises 17 stories at the northern end of the Diagonal, in a wealthy neighborhood known for corporate headquarters, banks, and upscale stores. Note that it's a bit removed, however, from many of Barcelona's top attractions. The design includes a soaring inner atrium with glass-sided elevators. Midsize to

---

(Kids Family-Friendly Hotels

Hotel Colón (p. 386)   Opposite the cathedral in the Gothic Quarter, this hotel has been compared to a country home. Families ask for, and often get, spacious rooms.

Hotel Hesperia (p. 392)   At the northern edge of the city, this hotel enjoys a safe neighborhood setting. Rooms are large enough to hold an extra bed.

spacious guest rooms contain many electronic extras, conservatively comfortable furnishings, and oversize beds. Many have views over Barcelona to the sea. Thoughtful touches include good lighting, adequate workspace, spacious closets, and blackout draperies, plus marble bathrooms with tub/shower combos.

Avinguda Diagonal 671, 08028 Barcelona. ℂ **800/445-8355** in the U.S., or 93-364-40-40. Fax 93-364-42-64. www.hrjuancarlos.com. 412 units. 350€ double; 450€–665€ suite. Occasional weekend discounts. AE, DC, MC, V. Free parking. Metro: Zona Universitària. **Amenities:** 2 restaurants; 2 bars; 2 pools; fitness center; car rental; salon; room service; laundry service; dry cleaning. *In room:* A/C, TV, minibar, hair dryer, safe.

EXPENSIVE

Avenida Palace ⭐ In an enviable 19th-century neighborhood filled with elegant shops and apartment buildings, this hotel is behind a pair of mock-fortified towers. Despite its relative modernity (it dates from 1952), it evokes an old-world sense of charm, partly because of the attentive staff, scattering of flowers and antiques, and 1950s-era accessories that fill its public rooms. Guest rooms are solidly traditional and quiet, with some set aside for nonsmokers. The soundproofed rooms range from midsize to spacious, with comfortable beds, and mostly wood furnishings. Bathrooms are well equipped, with dual basins, tub/shower combos, and heat lamps.

Gran Vía de les Corts Catalanes 605 (at Passeig de Gràcia), 08007 Barcelona. ℂ **93-301-96-00.** Fax 93-318-12-34. 160 units. 205€–235€ double; 314€ suite. AE, DC, MC, V. Parking 16€. Metro: Passeig de Gràcia. **Amenities:** 2 restaurants; bar; salon; room service; babysitting; laundry service; dry cleaning; currency exchange. *In room:* A/C, TV, minibar, hair dryer, safe.

Hotel Condes de Barcelona ⭐ Off the architecturally splendid Passeig de Gràcia, this government-rated four-star hotel, originally a private villa (1895), is one of Barcelona's most glamorous. Business was so good it opened a 74-room extension across the street (Carrer Majorca), which regrettably lacks the flair of the original. It boasts a unique neo-medieval facade, influenced by Gaudí's modernismo. All the comfortable midsize guest rooms contain marble bathrooms, with tub/shower combos, reproductions of Spanish paintings, and soundproofed windows. Some rooms are already beginning to show post-Olympic wear and tear.

Passeig de Gràcia 73–75, 08008 Barcelona. ℂ **93-488-22-00.** Fax 93-467-47-81. www.condesde barcelona.com. 183 units. 136€–290€ double; 360€–504€ suite. AE, DC, MC, V. Parking 16€. Metro: Passeig de Gràcia. **Amenities:** Restaurant; cafe; bar; pool; room service; babysitting; laundry service; dry cleaning. *In room:* A/C, TV, minibar, hair dryer, safe.

Hotel Majestic ⭐ This hotel is one of Barcelona's most visible landmarks and has been since the 1920s, when it was built in a sought-after location within a 10-minute walk from Plaça de Catalunya. In the early 1990s it was radically renovated and upgraded into four-star status while retaining the dignified stateliness of the public areas, but with an added sense of color and contemporary drama in the bedrooms. Today, each is outfitted in a different, usually monochromatic, color scheme, with carpets, artwork, and upholsteries. All units come equipped with bathrooms containing tub/shower combos. Staff is hardworking and conscientious, albeit sometimes swamped with tour buses containing dozens of clients arriving all at once.

Passeig de Gràcia 68, 08007 Barcelona. ℂ **93-488-17-17.** Fax 93-488-18-80. www.hotelmajestic.es. 322 units. 175€–320€ double; 360€–535€ suite. AE, DC, MC, V. Parking 22€. Metro: Passeig de Gràcia. **Amenities:** 2 restaurants; bar; pool; fitness center; sauna; room service; laundry service; dry cleaning. *In room:* A/C, TV, minibar, hair dryer, safe.

Hotel Meliá Barcelona Sarrià ⭐ One block from the junction of the Avinguda Sarrià and the Avinguda Diagonal in the heart of the business district, this hotel still earns its five-star government rating, which was granted when it opened its doors back in 1976. Some rooms were renovated in the early to mid-1990s, but others look a bit worn. It offers comfortably upholstered, carpeted guest rooms done in neutral international modern. They have wide beds with firm mattresses and bathrooms with tub/shower combos. A member of the Meliá chain, the hotel caters to both the business traveler and the vacationer.

Avinguda Sarrià 50, 08029 Barcelona. © **800/336-3542** in the U.S., or 93-410-60-60. Fax 93-410-77-44. www.solmelia.com. 314 units. 197€–273€ double; 333€–446€ suite. AE, DC, MC, V. Parking 18€. Metro: Hospital Clinic. **Amenities:** Restaurant; bar; health club; sauna; room service; babysitting; laundry service; dry cleaning. *In room:* A/C, TV, minibar, hair dryer, safe.

MODERATE

Hotel Balmes Set in a seven-story structure built in the late 1980s, this chain hotel successfully combines a conservative decor with modern accessories and a well-trained staff. Bedrooms are vaguely English in their inspiration, with a warm color scheme of yellows and browns, marble-trimmed bathrooms, equipped with tub/shower combos and enough space to allow residents, many of whom are in town on business, to live and work comfortably. If you're looking for a maximum of peace and quiet, rooms overlooking the back of the hotel—site of a small garden—are quieter and calmer than those facing the busy street.

Carrer Mallorca 216, 08008 Barcelona. © **93-451-19-14.** Fax 93-451-00-49. www.derbyhotels.es. 100 units. 136€–186€ double. AE, DC, MC, V. Parking 15€. Metro: Diagonal. **Amenities:** Restaurant; bar; pool; room service; laundry service; dry cleaning. *In room:* A/C, TV, minibar, hair dryer, safe.

INEXPENSIVE

Hotel Astoria ⭐ *Value* One of our favorite hotels, and an excellent value, the Astoria is near the upper part of the Rambles and the Diagonal. It has an Art Deco facade that makes it appear older than it is. The high ceilings, geometric designs, and brass-studded detail in the public rooms could be Moorish or Andalusian. The comfortable midsize guest rooms are soundproofed; half have been renovated, with slick louvered closets and glistening white paint. The more old-fashioned units have warm textures of exposed cedar and elegant, pristine modern accessories. All units come equipped with private bathrooms containing showers.

París 203, 08036 Barcelona. © **93-209-83-11.** Fax 93-202-30-08. www.derbyhotels.es. 115 units. 80€–160€ double; 130€–260€ suite. AE, DC, MC, V. Parking nearby 18€. Metro: Diagonal. **Amenities:** Bar; lounge; room service; laundry service; dry cleaning. *In room:* A/C, TV, minibar, hair dryer, safe.

NORTE DIAGONAL
EXPENSIVE

Gallery Hotel ⭐ *Finds* This is a winning, modern choice lying between the Passeig de Gràcia and Rambla de Catalunya. In business for a decade, it was completely remodeled in 2002. The name, Gallery, comes from its location close to a district of major art galleries. The stylishly decorated hotel lies in the upper district of the Eixample, just below the Diagonal. Bedrooms are midsize for the most part and tastefully furnished, each with a small bathroom with tub and shower. The on-site restaurant is known for its savory Mediterranean cuisine.

Calle Rosello 249, 08008 Barcelona. © **93-415-99-11.** Fax 93-415-91-84. www.galleryhotel.com. 115 units. Mon–Thurs 162€–224€ double, 240€–300€ suite; Fri–Sun 105€ double, 142€ suite. AE, DC, MC, V. Parking: 15€. Metro: Diagonal. **Amenities:** Restaurant; bar; sauna; fitness center; room service; baby-sitting; laundry/dry cleaning. *In room:* A/C, TV, minibar, coffeemaker, hair dryer, safe.

MODERATE

Hotel Hesperia ⭐ *Kids* This hotel on the northern edge of the city, a 10-minute taxi ride from the center, sits in one of Barcelona's most pleasant residential neighborhoods. Built in the late 1980s, the hotel was last renovated before the 1992 Olympics. You'll pass a Japanese rock formation to reach the stone-floored reception area with its adjacent bar. Sunlight floods the monochromatic guest rooms (all doubles—prices for singles are the same). Although most rooms are medium-sized, they have enough room for an extra bed, which makes this a good choice for families. Beds have quality mattresses and fine linen; bathrooms have a generous assortment of good-size towels and tub/shower combos. The uniformed staff offers fine service.

Los Vergós 20, 08017 Barcelona. © **93-204-55-51.** Fax 93-204-43-92. www.hoteles-hesperia.es. 134 units. 142€–198€ double; 175€–230€ suite. AE, DC, MC, V. Parking 12€. Metro: Tres Torres. **Amenities:** Restaurant; bar; room service; laundry service; dry cleaning. In room: A/C, TV, minibar, hair dryer, safe.

INEXPENSIVE

Hotel Wilson   This comfortable hotel in an architecturally rich neighborhood is a member of the HUSA chain. The small lobby isn't indicative of the rest of the building. The second floor opens into a large, sunny lounge. The guest rooms are well kept, generally spacious, and furnished in traditional style. All units contain bathrooms with tub/shower combos.

Avinguda Diagonal 568, 08021 Barcelona. © **93-209-25-11.** Fax 93-200-83-70. www.husa.es. 57 units. 123€–170€ double; 152€–218€ suite. AE, DC, DISC, MC, V. Parking 18€. Metro: Diagonal. **Amenities:** Restaurant; bar; laundry service; dry cleaning. In room: A/C, TV, minibar, hair dryer, iron, safe.

VILA OLIMPICA
VERY EXPENSIVE

Hotel Arts ★★★   Managed by the Ritz-Carlton chain, this hotel occupies 33 floors of one of the tallest buildings in Spain, and one of Barcelona's only skyscrapers. (The upper floors of the 44-floor postmodern tower contain the private condominiums of some of the country's most gossiped-about aristocrats and financiers.) The hotel is about 2.5km (1½ miles) southwest of Barcelona's historic core, near the sea and the Olympic Village. Its decor is contemporary and elegant. The spacious, well-equipped guest rooms have built-in furnishings, generous desk space, and large, sumptuous beds. Clad in pink marble, the deluxe bathrooms have fluffy robes, Belgian towels, dual basins, and phones. Views take in the skyline and the Mediterranean, and the hotel possesses the city's only beachfront pool. The young staff is polite and hardworking, the product of months of Ritz-Carlton training.

Carrer de la Marina 19–21, 08005 Barcelona. © **800/241-3333** in the U.S., or 93-221-10-00. Fax 93-221-10-70. www.ritzcarlton.com. 482 units. 310€–450€ double; 415€–575€ suite. AE, DC, MC, V. Parking 20€. Metro: Ciutadella–Vila Olímpica. **Amenities:** 4 restaurants; cafe; 2 bars; pool; fitness center; room service; laundry service; dry cleaning. In room: A/C, TV, minibar, hair dryer, iron, safe.

5 Where to Dine

If money is no object, you'll find some of the grandest culinary experiences in Europe here. Diverse Catalán cuisine reaches its pinnacle in Barcelona, but you don't get just Catalán fare—the city is rich in the cuisines of all the major regions of Spain, including Castile and Andalusia. Because of Barcelona's proximity to France, many of the finer restaurants serve French or French-inspired dishes.

On the other end of the spectrum, finding an affordable restaurant in Barcelona is easier than finding an inexpensive, safe hotel. Reservations are seldom needed, except in the most expensive and popular places. The **Barri Gòtic** offers the cheapest meals. There are many budget restaurants in and around the

Barcelona Dining

Plaça de Francesc Macià

Carrer de Buenos Aires

Carrer de Londres

Carrer de Paris

Travessara de Gràcia

Travessara de Gràcia

Av. de Sant Antoni Maria Claret

Carrer de la Industria

Avinguda Diagonal

Carrer de Còrsega

EIXAMPLE

Carrer de Provença

Carrer de Rosselló

Gran de Gràcia

Plaça de la Sagrada Familia

Avinguda Diagonal

Carrer Enric Granados

Carrer de Balmes

Rambla de Catalunya

Passeig de Gràcia

Carrer de Pau Claris

Carrer de Mallorca

Carrer de València

Carrer d'Aragó

Passeig de Sant Joan

Carrer de Roger de Flor

Carrer de Nàpols

Carrer de Sicilia

Carrer del Comte d'Urgell

Carrer de Villarroel

Carrer de Casanova

Carrer de Muntaner

Carrer d'Aribau

Carrer del Consell de Cent

Carrer de la Diputació

Gran Via de les Corts Catalanes

Carrer de R. de Llúria

Carrer del Bruc

Carrer de Girona

Carrer de Bailèn

Carrer de Sardenya

Plaça de la Universitat

Ronda Universitat

Plaça Catalunya

Plaça de Tetuan

Carrer de Casp

Carrer d'Ausias Marc

Carrer d'Ali Bei

Carrer de Ribes

Ronda de Sant Antoni

Carrer de Pelai

Av. Portal de l'Àngel

Plaça Urquinaona

Ronda de Sant Pere

RAVAL

Carrer de Hospital

La Rambla

BARRI GÒTIC

Via Laietana

Palau de la Música Catalana

Passeig de Lluís Companys

Carrer de la Marina

Carrer de Sant Pau

Gran Teatre del Liceu

C. de

Cathedral

Ferran

C. de la Princesa

Carrer del Comerç

Passeig de Picasso

Passeig de Pujades

PARC DE LA CIUTADELLA

Carrer de Wellington

Carrer Nou de la Rambla

La Rambla

Avda. de les Drassanes

Carrer Ample

LA RIBERA

Museu Picasso

Pg. Isabel II

Passeig de Colom

Moll de la Fusta

PARC ZOOLOGIC

Villa Olímpica →

Plaça Portal de la Pau

Avinguda d'Icaria

Moll d'Espanya

Port Vell

BARCELONETA

Passeig Martím

395

Carrer de Montcada, site of the Picasso museum. Dining rooms in the **Eixample** tend to be more formal and expensive, but less adventurous.

CIUTAT VELLA
EXPENSIVE

Agut d'Avignon ☆ CATALAN   One of our favorite restaurants in Barcelona is in a tiny alleyway near the Plaça Reial. The city's restaurant explosion has toppled Agut d'Avignon from its position as best in the city, but it's still going strong after 40 years and has a dedicated following. It attracts politicians, writers, journalists, financiers, industrialists, and artists—and even the king and cabinet ministers, along with visiting dignitaries. Since 1983 Mercedes Giralt Salinas and her son, Javier Falagán Giralt, have run the restaurant. A small 19th-century vestibule leads to the multilevel dining area, which has two balconies and a main hall evoking a hunting lodge. You may need help translating the Catalán menu. The traditional specialties are likely to include acorn-squash soup served in its shell; fisherman's soup with garlic toast; haddock stuffed with shellfish; sole with *nyoca* (a medley of nuts); large shrimp with aioli; duck with figs; and filet beefsteak in sherry sauce.

Trinitat 3 (at Carrer d'Avinyó). ☎ **93-302-60-34.** Reservations required. Main courses 11€–21€. AE, DC, MC, V. Daily 1–4:30pm and 9pm–12:30am. Metro: Jaume I or Liceu.

Casa Leopoldo ☆ *Finds* SEAFOOD   An excursion through the somewhat seedy streets of the Barri Xinés is part of the Casa Leopoldo experience. At night it's safer to come by taxi. This colorful restaurant founded in 1939 serves some of the freshest seafood in town to a loyal clientele. There's a popular stand-up tapas bar in front, and two dining rooms. Specialties include eel with shrimp, barnacles, cuttlefish, seafood soup with shellfish, and deep-fried inch-long eels.

Sant Rafael 24. ☎ **93-441-30-14.** Reservations required. Main courses 25€–38€; fixed-price menu 38€. AE, DC, MC, V. Tues–Sun 1:30–4pm; Tues–Sat 9–11pm. Closed Aug and Easter week. Metro: Liceu.

Quo Vadis ☆ SPANISH/CATALAN/CONTINENTAL   Elegant and impeccable, this is one of the finest restaurants in Barcelona. In a century-old building near the open stalls of the Boquería food market, it was established in 1967 and has done a discreet but thriving business ever since. The four paneled dining rooms exude conservative charm. Culinary creations include a ragout of seasonal mushrooms, fried goose liver with prunes, filet of beef with wine sauce, and a variety of grilled or flambéed fish. There's a wide choice of desserts made with seasonal fruits imported from all over Spain.

Carme 7. ☎ **93-302-40-72.** Reservations recommended. Main courses 16€–24€. AE, DC, MC, V. Mon–Sat 1:15–4pm and 8:30–11:30pm. Metro: Liceu.

Restaurant Hoffmann ☆☆ CATALAN/FRENCH/INTERNATIONAL   This restaurant in the Barri Gòtic is one of the most famous in Barcelona, partly because of its creative cuisine, partly because of its close association with a respected school that trains employees for Catalonia's hotel and restaurant industry. The culinary and entrepreneurial force behind it is German/Catalán Mey Hoffmann, whose restaurant overlooks the facade of one of Barcelona's most beloved Gothic churches, Santa María del Mar. In good weather, three courtyards hold tables. Menu items change every 2 months and often include French ingredients. Examples include a superb *fine tarte* with deboned sardines, foie gras wrapped in puff pastry, baked John Dory with new potatoes and ratatouille, a ragout of crayfish with green risotto, succulent pigs' feet with eggplant, and rack of lamb with grilled baby vegetables. Especially flavorful, if you appreciate beef, is a filet steak cooked in Rioja and served with shallot confit and potato gratin. Fondant of chocolate makes a worthy dessert.

Carrer Argenteria 74–78. ✆ **93-319-58-89**. Reservations recommended. Main courses 14€–36€; fixed-price lunch (includes water and coffee) 30€. AE, DC, MC, V. Mon–Fri 1:30–3:15pm and 9–11:15pm. Metro: Jaume I.

MODERATE

Agut ✷ *Finds* CATALAN   In a historic building in the Barri Xinés, 3 blocks from the harbor front, Agut epitomizes the bohemian atmosphere surrounding this fairly seedy area. For three quarters of a century, this has been a family-run business, with María Agut García the current reigning empress. (Don't confuse Agut with the more famous Agut d'Avignon nearby.) The aura is of the 1940s and '50s, with a cozy little bar to the right as you enter. Paintings on the walls are from well-known Catalán artists from the 1940s to the '60s. The cuisine is solid and time-tested fare. It is vigorous cookery served at moderate prices. Begin with *mil hojas de butifarra amb zets* or layers of pastry filled with Catalán sausage and mushrooms, or the *terrine de albergines amb fortmage de cabra* (terrine of eggplant with goat cheese gratinée). One of our favorite dishes is *soufle de rape amb gambes* (soufflé of monkfish with shrimp). For gastronomes only, try the *pie de cerdo relleno con foie amb truffles* (pork feet stuffed with duck liver and truffles). For dessert, if you order *sortido,* you'll get a combination plate with an assortment of the small homemade cakes of the house.

Gignas 16. ✆ **93-315-17-09**. Reservations required. Main courses 6€–18€; fixed-price lunch 8.10€. MC, V. Tues–Sun 1:30–4pm; Tues–Sat 9pm–midnight. Closed Aug. Metro: Jaume I.

Can Culleretes CATALAN   Founded in 1786 as a *pastelería* (pastry shop) in the Barri Gòtic, this oldest Barcelona restaurant retains many original architectural features. All three dining rooms are decorated with tile dadoes and wrought-iron chandeliers. The well-prepared food features authentic dishes of northeastern Spain, including sole Roman style, *zarzuela a la marinera* (shellfish medley), cannelloni, and paella. From October to January, special game dishes, including *perdiz* (partridge), are available. Signed photographs of celebrities, flamenco artists, and bullfighters who have visited decorate the walls.

Quintana 5. ✆ **93-317-64-85**. Reservations recommended. Main courses 5.50€–16€; *menú del día* 11€–14€. MC, V. Tues–Sun 1:30–4pm; Tues–Sat 9–11pm. Closed in July. Metro: Liceu. Bus: 14 or 59.

Comerç 24 ✷ *Finds* CATALAN   View a dining visit here as an opportunity to experience the culinary vision of a rare aesthete and artist. The chef is Carles Abellan, who has given his imaginative, distinctive interpretation to all the long-time favorite dishes of Catalonia. With his avant-garde and minimalist design, he offers a soothing backdrop for his cuisine. The restaurant lies close to the waterfront along Barceloneta, the Parc de la Ciutadella, and the old Gothic *barrio*. The chef uses fresh seasonal ingredients, balanced sauces, and bold but never outrageous combinations, and he believes in split-second timing. Begin perhaps with his freshly diced tuna marinated in ginger and soy sauce, and Abellan will immediately win you over. Perhaps you'll sample his fresh salmon "perfumed" with vanilla and served with yogurt. His baked eggplant with Roquefort, pine nuts, and fresh mushrooms from the countryside is a vibrant and earthly feast. Only the great star Marlene Dietrich could make a better potato omelet than Abellan. Believe it or not, he serves that old-fashioned snack that Catalan children used to be offered when they came home from school, a combination of chocolate, salt, and bread flavored with olive oil. It's surprisingly good, but who would dare order it except a food writer on assignment?

Carrer Comerç 24, La Ribera. ✆ **93-319-21-02**. Reservations required. Main courses 5€–16€; tasting menu 42€. MC, V. Tues–Sat 1:30–3:30pm and 8:30pm–12:30am. Closed 10 days in Dec, 10 days in Aug. Metro: Arco de Triompho.

Coses de Menjar ★ *Finds* FUSION/MEDITERRANEAN   In Catalán, the name of this restaurant translates as "things to eat." That name hardly does justice to the wacky fusion cuisine—first popularized in Madrid—that has spread to Barcelona in all its oddball madness. The Parellada family has launched what's known as a dining dynasty in Barcelona, and daughter Ada is the guiding light behind this fun place with its wine glass chandeliers, napkin rings made from bent forks, spoon-shaped lamps, cheese-grater candleholders, and other touches of quirkiness.

A hip hangout for the golden youth of Barcelona's New Age, Coses de Menjar may sound gimmicky—and it is—but its cuisine is superb. If you want beautifully presented and savory Mediterranean cookery, you can get that too, including a meal recently enjoyed of red mullet in almond sauce with a side of fresh figs. The fresh pumpkin salad came with cherries and soft cheese. But the piece de resistance was the grilled foie gras with Parmesan ice cream. Don't knock it until you've tried it. The cheesy ice cream is a taste treat and tour de force of the clever chef. A chestnut ice cream also appears in the most delicious pineapple soup we've sampled this side of Asia. Whatever your final verdict, this place works.

Pla de Palau 7. ℂ **93-310-60-01.** Reservations required. Main courses 11€–14€. MC, V. Mon–Thurs 1:30–4pm and 9–11:30pm; Fri–Sat 1:30–4pm and 9pm–midnight. Metro: Jaume I.

Els Quatre Gats CATALAN   This is a Barcelona legend since 1897. The "Four Cats" (in Catalán slang, "just a few people") was a favorite of Picasso, Rusiñol, and other artists, who once hung their works on its walls. On a narrow cobblestone street in the Barri Gòtic near the cathedral, the fin-de-siècle cafe has been the setting for poetry readings by Joan Maragall, piano concerts by Isaac Albéniz and Ernie Granados, and murals by Ramón Casas. It was a base for members of the modernismo movement and figured in the city's intellectual and bohemian life.

Today the restored bar is a popular meeting place. The fixed-price meal is one of the better bargains in town, considering the locale. The unpretentious Catalán cooking here is called *cucina de mercat* (based on whatever looked fresh at the market). The constantly changing menu reflects the seasons. No hot food is served on Sunday.

Montsió 3. ℂ **93-302-41-40.** Reservations required Sat–Sun. Main courses 12€–22€; fixed-price menu (Mon–Fri) 10€. AE, DC, MC, V. Daily 1pm–1am. Cafe daily 8am–2am. Metro: Plaça de Catalunya.

Espai Sucre ★★ *Finds* DESSERTS   Espai Sucre ("Sugar Space" in English) is Barcelona's most unusual dining room, with a minimalist decor and seating for 30. For the dessert lover, it is like entering a heaven created by the sugar fairy himself. The place has a gimmick, and it works. The menu is devoted to desserts. There is a short list of so-called "salty" dishes for those who want to cool it with the sugar. Actually it's quite good and imaginatively prepared, including the likes of ginger couscous with pumpkin and grilled stingray or artichoke cream with a poached quail egg and Serrano ham. The lentil stew with foie gras is first rate, as are the spicy veal "cheeks" with green apples.

Forget all about those tearoom concoctions you'd find in a pastry cafe. The desserts here are original creations. Your "salad" is likely to be small cubes of spicy milk pudding resting on matchsticks of green apple with baby arugula leaves, peppery caramel, dabs of lime kefir and lemon curd, and a straight line of toffee. Smoky tea cream with chocolate, black sesame, and yogurt appears. Even when

---

Finds **Calling All Chocoholics!**

Established in 1930, **Dulcinea,** Vía Petrixol 2 (📞 **93-302-68-24**), is the most famous chocolate shop in Barcelona. The specialties are *melindros* (sugar-topped soft-sided biscuits), and the regulars who flock here love to dunk them into the very thick hot chocolate—so thick, in fact, that drinking it feels like eating a melted chocolate bar. A cup of hot chocolate with cream costs 2.55€, and a *ración* of *churros* (a deep-fried pastry), which is dipped in the hot chocolate, goes for 1.10€; no credit cards. Dulcinea is open daily from 9am to 1pm and 5:30 to 9:30pm; closed in August. Take the Metro to Liceu.

---

your platter holds a tiny phyllo pyramid, no bigger than a pencil eraser, you bite in to discover it's filled with lemon and rosemary marmalade. Ever had a soup of litchi, celery, apple, and eucalyptus? If some of the concoctions frighten your palate, you'll find comfort in the more familiar—vanilla cream with coffee sorbet and caramelized banana. Every dessert comes with a recommendation for the appropriate wine to accompany it.

Princesa 53. 📞 **93-268-16-30.** Reservations required. Main courses 8.50€–11€. 3-dessert platter 21€, 5-dessert platter 32€. DC, MC, V. Tues–Sat 9–11:30pm. Metro: Arco de Triompho.

La Cuineta *Value* CATALAN   This restaurant near the Catalán government offices is a culinary highlight of the Barri Gòtic. Decorated in typical regional style, it favors local cuisine. The fixed-price menu is a good value, or you can order a la carte. The most expensive appetizer is *bellota* (acorn-fed ham), but we suggest a market-fresh Catalán dish, such as *favas* (broad beans) stewed with *butifarra,* a tasty, spicy local sausage.

Pietat 12. 📞 **93-315-01-11.** Reservations recommended. Main courses 15€–38€; fixed-price menu 28€–33€. AE, DC, MC, V. Daily 1–4pm and 8pm–midnight. Metro: Jaume I.

INEXPENSIVE

Café de L'Academia ✸ *Value* CATALAN/MEDITERRANEAN   In the center of Barri Gòtic a short walk from Plaça Sant Jaume, this 28-table restaurant looks expensive but is really one of the best and most affordable in the medieval city. The building dates from the 15th century, but the restaurant was founded only in the mid-1980s. Owner Jordí Casteldi offers an elegant atmosphere in a setting of brown stone walls and ancient wooden columns. At a small bar you can peruse the varied menu and study the wines offered. Dishes of this quality usually cost three times as much in Barcelona. The chef is proud of his "kitchen of the market," suggesting that only the freshest ingredients from the day's shopping are featured. Try such delights as *lassanye de butifarra i ceps* (lasagna with Catalán sausage and flap mushrooms), *bacalla gratinado i musselina de carofes* (salt cod gratinée with an artichoke mousse), or *terrina d'berengeras amb fortmage de cabra* (terrine of eggplant with goat cheese). A delectable specialty is *codorniz rellena en cebollitas tiernas y foie de pato* (partridge stuffed with tender onions and duck liver).

Carrer Lledó 1 (Barri Gòtic), Plaça Sant Just. 📞 **93-315-00-26.** Reservations required. Main courses 8.25€–13€; fixed-price menu (lunch only) 9.75€. AE, MC, V. Mon–Fri 9am–noon, 1:15–4pm, and 9–11:30pm. Closed last 2 weeks Aug. Metro: Jaume I.

Garduña CATALAN   This is the most famous restaurant in Barcelona's covered food market, La Bouquería. Originally conceived as a hotel, it has concentrated on food since the 1970s. Battered, somewhat ramshackle, and a bit claustrophobic, it's fashionable with an artistic set that might have been designated as bohemian in an earlier era. It's near the back of the market, so you'll pass endless rows of fresh produce, cheese, and meats before you reach it. You can dine downstairs, near a crowded bar, or a bit more formally upstairs. Food is ultrafresh—the chefs certainly don't have to travel far for the ingredients. You might try "hors d'oeuvres of the sea," cannelloni Rossini, grilled hake with herbs, *rape* (monkfish) *marinera,* paella, brochettes of veal, filet steak with green peppercorns, seafood rice, or a *zarzuela* (stew) of fresh fish with spices.

Jerusalem 18. ℂ **93-302-43-23.** Reservations recommended. Main courses 6€–25€; fixed-price lunch 9€; fixed-price dinner 12€. AE, DC, MC, V. Mon–Sat 1–4pm and 8pm–midnight. Metro: Liceu.

La Rosca CATALAN/SPANISH   For more than half a century, owner Don Alberto Vellve continues to welcome customers into this little Barri Gòtic eatery, close to Plaça de Catalunya. On a short street, the place is easy to miss, except to devotees who have been coming here for decades. Go here if you'd like to see the type of place where people dined inexpensively in the Franco era. A mixture of Catalán and modern Spanish cuisine is served in this house, which is small and in an old rustic style with high ceilings and white walls. The decor has nostalgic touches, such as old bullfighting posters and pictures of Barcelona in the mid–20th century. There are 60 unadorned tables, which diners fill quickly to take advantage of the cheap three-course luncheon menu. Dig into such hearty fare as veal stew or assorted fish and shellfish grilled. Baby squid is cooked in its own ink, and one of the best and most typical dishes is white beans sautéed with ham and Catalán sausage. For a true treat, ask for the *rape a la planate* (grilled monkfish).

Juliá Portet 6. ℂ **93-302-51-73.** Reservations recommended. Main courses 6€–12€; fixed-price menu 7.50€–10€. No credit cards. Sun–Fri 9am–4pm and 8–9:30pm. Closed Aug 20–30. Metro: Urquinaona and Catalunya.

Pla de la Garsa ✿ MEDITERRANEAN/CATALAN   In Barrio Ribera close to the cathedral, this historic building is fully renovated but still retains some 19th-century fittings, such as a cast-iron spiral staircase used to reach another dining area upstairs. However, the ground floor is more interesting. Here you'll encounter the owner, Ignacio Sulle, an antiques collector who has filled his establishment with an intriguing collection of objets d'art. He boasts one of the city's best wine lists, and features a daily array of traditional Catalán and Mediterranean favorite dishes. Begin with one of the patés, especially the goose, or a confit of duck thighs. You can also order meat and fish patés. One surprise is a terrine with black olives and anchovies. For a main course you can order a perfectly seasoned beef bourguignon or *fabetes fregides amb menta i pernil* (beans with meat and diced Serrano ham). The cheese selection is one of the finest we've found in town, especially bountiful in Catalán goat cheese, including Serrat Gros from the Pyrenees.

Assaonadors 13. ℂ **93-315-24-13.** Reservations recommended for weekends. Main courses 5€–10€. AE, MC, V. Daily 8pm–1am. Metro: Jaume I.

Senyor Parellada CATALAN   The glossy contemporary-looking interior of this place is in distinct contrast to a battered-looking facade of a building that's at least a century old. Inside, in a pair of lemon-yellow and blue dining rooms, you'll find menu items such as Italian-style cannelloni, stuffed cabbage, cod "as it was prepared by the monks of the Poblet monastery," baked monkfish with mustard and garlic sauce, roasted duck served with figs, and roasted rack of lamb with red-wine sauce. Patrons flock faithfully to this bistro, knowing they'll be served a traditional cuisine of northeast Spain with fine local produce. The chefs seem to know how to coax the most flavor out of the premium ingredients. The restaurant also has 43 double rooms available for rent for 95€.

Carrer Argenteria 37. ② **93-310-50-94.** Reservations recommended. Main courses 2.85€–11€. AE, MC, V. Daily 1–4pm and 8:30pm–midnight. Metro: Jaume I.

SUR DIAGONAL
VERY EXPENSIVE

Beltxenea ★★ BASQUE/INTERNATIONAL   In a building originally designed in the late 19th century as an apartment building, this restaurant celebrates Basque cuisine. The Basques are noted as the finest chefs in Spain, and this is indeed grand cuisine. It's served here in one of the most elegantly and comfortably furnished restaurants in the city. Schedule a meal for a special night—it's worth the money. The menu might include hake fried with garlic or garnished with clams and served with fish broth. Roast lamb, grilled rabbit, and pheasant are well prepared and succulent, as are the desserts. There's dining outside in the formal garden during the summer.

Majorca 275. ② **93-215-30-24.** Reservations recommended. Main courses 16€–45€; tasting menu 50€. AE, DC, MC, V. Mon–Fri 1:30–3:30pm; Mon–Sat 8:30–11:30pm. Closed 3 weeks in Aug. Metro: Passeig de Gràcia and Diagonal.

Drolma ★★★ INTERNATIONAL   In business since 1999, this is one of Barcelona's best haute cuisine restaurants. Fermin Puig is one of Spain's most celebrated chefs, his culinary showcase found in the Hotel Majestic. The restaurant's name is Sanskrit for Buddha's female side. We don't know what this has to do with anything. He might as well have called his restaurant "Majestic," as his food certainly is. Only the freshest of ingredients go into his carefully balanced cookery based on the market's seasonal bounty. We especially like the personal spin he gives to seasonal dishes along with the luxurious foodstuffs presented nightly. What diner could not love the chef who presents pheasant-stuffed cannelloni in a velvety foie gras sauce, the dish delicately sprinkled with the rare black truffle? His wild turbot is enhanced with fresh mushrooms from the Catalán countryside, and his prawns with fresh asparagus tips in a virgin olive oil sauce preserves the natural flavor of each ingredient. Though simple, this dish is in a word divine. The lamb is aromatically grilled with fresh herbs, giving the meat a pungent and refreshing dimension. The baked goat with potatoes and mushrooms is bold yet delicate in flavor.

In the Hotel Majestic, Passeig de Gràcia 70, Eixample. ② **93-496-77-10.** Reservations required. Main courses 38€–60€. AE, DC, MC, V. Mon–Sat 1–3:30pm and 8:30–11pm. Closed: Aug. Metro: Passeig de Gràcia.

Jaume de Provença ★★★ CATALAN/FRENCH   A few steps from the Estació Central de Barcelona-Sants railway station, at the western end of the Eixample, this is a small, cozy restaurant with rustic decor. It is the only restaurant along the Diagonal that can compare to La Dama. Named after its owner and chef, Jaume Bargués, it features modern interpretations of traditional Catalán and southern French cuisine. Examples include gratin of clams with spinach, a salad of two different species of lobster, foie gras and truffles, and pigs' trotters with plums and truffles. Or you might order crabmeat lasagna, cod with saffron sauce, sole with mushrooms in port wine sauce, or an artistic dessert specialty of orange mousse.

Provença 88. ℂ **93-430-00-29.** Reservations recommended. Main courses 12€–29€. AE, DC, MC, V. Tues–Sun 1–4pm; Tues–Sat 9–11:30pm. Closed Easter week and Aug. Metro: Entença.

La Dama ✿✿✿ CATALAN/INTERNATIONAL This is one of the few restaurants in Barcelona that deserves, and gets, a Michelin star. In one of the grand 19th-century buildings for which Barcelona is famous, this stylish and well-managed restaurant serves a clientele of local residents and civic dignitaries. You take an Art Nouveau elevator (or the sinuous stairs) up one flight to reach the dining room. Specialties include salmon steak served with vinegar derived from *cava* (sparkling wine) and onions, cream of potato soup flavored with caviar, a salad of crayfish with orange-flavored vinegar, an abundant platter of autumn mushrooms, and succulent preparations of lamb, fish, shellfish, beef, goat, and veal. The building, designed by Manuel Sayrach, is 3 blocks west of the intersection of Avinguda Diagonal and Passeig de Gràcia.

Diagonal 423. ℂ **93-202-06-86.** Reservations required. Main courses 14€–35€; fixed-price menu 50€. AE, DC, MC, V. Daily 1:30–3:30pm and 8:30–11:30pm. Metro: Provença.

EXPENSIVE

Can Isidre ✿ CATALAN In spite of its seedy location (take a cab at night!), this is perhaps the most sophisticated Catalán bistro in Barcelona. Opened in 1970, it has served King Juan Carlos and Queen Sofía, Julio Iglesias, and the famous Catalán bandleader, Xavier Cugat. Isidre Gironés, helped by his wife, Montserrat, is known for his fresh cuisine beautifully prepared and served. Try spider crabs and shrimp, a foie gras salad, sweetbreads with port and flap mushrooms, or carpaccio of veal Harry's Bar style. The selection of Spanish and Catalán wines is excellent.

Les Flors 12. ℂ **93-441-11-39.** Reservations required. Main courses 15€–42€. AE, DC, MC, V. Mon–Sat 1:30–4pm and 8:30–11pm. Closed Sat–Sun July and Aug. Metro: Paral.lel.

Casa Calvet ✿ MEDITERRANEAN This is one of the most visible and sought-after restaurants of the Eixample district, with a reputation and cachet that has attracted everyone from the Mayor of Barcelona to Queen Sofía and her daughter, the Infanta Cristina. It is on the ground floor of one of the great modernist apartment buildings of Barcelona, a stained-glass and wood-trimmed fantasy designed by Antoni Gaudí in 1899. Menu items are artful and sophisticated, reflecting influences from both Catalonia and France. Stellar examples might include fresh pan-fried duck liver served in a bitter orange sauce; ravioli stuffed with oysters and clams and served in a sparkling *cava* sauce; and grilled filet of pork with chestnuts and cider sauce.

Carrer Casp 48. ℂ **93-412-40-12.** Reservations recommended. Main courses 19€–28€. AE, MC, V. Mon–Sat 1–3:30pm and 8:30–11pm. Closed 3 weeks in Aug. Metro: Passeig de Gràcia.

Jean Luc Figueras ✿✿✿ CATALAN For a *Kama Sutra*–like dining experience, head for this hip Gràcia town house that was once the studio of Balenciaga. Even if food critics narrowed the list of Barcelona restaurants down to five, the chef and owner, Jean Luc Figueras, would likely appear on the list. The setting is modern and refined, and the cookery is both traditional and innovative, as Figueras stamps every dish with his own personal touch. Highly dedicated to staying on top, Figueras is a seeker of the finest raw materials on the Barcelona market, and his menu is adjusted to take advantage of the best produce in any season. The emphasis is on fresh seafood, although his meat dishes are also sublime. His fried prawn and ginger-flecked pasta in a mango and mustard sauce would make the gods weep, and his sea bass with cod and blood sausage was no less brilliant. Your tongue will fall in love with you if you're wise enough to select such nouvelle-inspired dishes as shrimp with a velvety smooth and golden pumpkin cream sauce or the pork with a zesty goat cheese enlivened with peach honey. The desserts are homemade and inevitably sumptuous, and we took particular delight in the seven varieties of freshly made bread.

Santa Teresa 10. ✆ **93-415-28-77**. Reservations required. Main courses 19€–32€. AE, DC, MC, V. Mon–Sat 1:30–4:30pm and 8:30pm–midnight. Metro: Diagonal.

MODERATE

L'Olive ✮ CATALAN/MEDITERRANEAN   You assume that this two-floor restaurant is named for the olive that figures so prominently into its cuisine, but actually it's named for the owner, Josep Olive. You can be born with no more apt a name for a Mediterranean restaurateur. The building is designed in a modern Catalán style with walls adorned with reproductions of famous Spanish painters, such as Miró, Dalí, or Picasso. The tables are topped in marble, the floors impeccably polished. There are sections on both floors where it's possible to have some privacy, and overall the feeling is one of elegance with a touch of intimacy. You won't be disappointed by anything on the menu, especially *bacalla cache* (raw salt cod) or *filet de vedella al vi negre al forn* (veal filets cooked in the oven in a red-wine sauce), and especially the *salsa maigret* of duck with strawberry sauce. One specialty is *amanida de col llombarda amb seitons* (a salad of finely shredded red cabbage that has been parboiled in sherry vinegar and tossed with a purée of olive oil and a small fish similar to white anchovies). Monkfish flavored with roasted garlic is always a palate pleaser, and you can finish with a *crema catalán* (a flan), or one of the delicious Catalán pastries.

Calle Balmes 47 (corner of Concéjo de Ciento). ✆ **93-452-19-90**. Reservations recommended. Main courses 14€–19€; *menú completo* 36€. AE, DC, MC, V. Daily 1–4pm; Mon–Sat 8:30pm–midnight; Sun 1–4pm. Metro: Passeig de Gràcia.

Rosalert ✮ CATALAN/SEAFOOD   At the corner of Carrer Napols close to La Sagrada Família, this restaurant has been the domain of Jordí Alert for more than 4 decades. He specializes in *comida de mar a la plancha,* or grilled seafood, and does so in a typical setting of hardwood floors and tile-covered walls. His seafood and crustaceans are grilled on a heated iron plate without any additives. There is no more awesome glass tank of live shellfish in Barcelona. You choose your meal, and the poor victim is extracted with a net and thrown on the grill. Of course, you find all the typical offerings, such as tiny octopus, succulent mussels, fat shrimp, squid, fresh oysters, and langoustines. If you're daring, you can

---

⒦Kids Family-Friendly Restaurants

Dulcinea (p. 399)   This makes a great refueling stop any time of the day—guaranteed to satisfy any chocoholic.

Poble Espanyol (p. 422)   A good introduction to Spanish food. All the restaurants in the "Spanish Village" serve comparable food at comparable prices—let the kids choose what to eat.

order such unusual seafood as *dátiles* ("dates" in English). This is a delicious shellfish whose shape resembles a date. Begin with one of the freshly made tapas, such as salt cod in vinaigrette or broad beans laced with garlic and virgin olive oil. Your best bet might be the *parrillada,* or assorted fish and shellfish from the grill. One of the best offerings is turbot cooked on the grill with potatoes and fresh mushrooms.

Avinguda Diagonal 301. © 93-207-10-19. Reservations recommended. Main courses 10€–24€. AE, DC, MC, V. Tues–Sun 9am–5pm and 8pm–2am. Closed Aug 10–30. Metro: Verdaguer/Sagrada Família.

INEXPENSIVE
El Caballito Blanco SEAFOOD/INTERNATIONAL   This is a Barcelona standby famous for seafood and popular with the locals. The fluorescent-lit dining area does not offer much atmosphere, but the food is good, varied, and relatively inexpensive (unless you order lobster or other expensive shellfish). The "Little White Horse," in the Passeig de Gràcia area, features a huge selection, including monkfish, mussels marinara, and shrimp with garlic. If you don't want fish, try the grilled lamb cutlets. Several different patés and salads are offered. There's a bar to the left of the dining area.

Mallorca 196. © 93-453-10-33. Main courses 8€–28€. AE, MC, V. Tues–Sun 1–3:45pm; Tues–Sat 9–10:45pm. Closed Aug. Metro: Hospital Clinic and Diagonal.

La Dentellière ⭐ (Finds) FRENCH/MEDITERRANEAN   Charming, and steeped in the French aesthetic, this bistro is imbued with a modern, elegant decor. Inside, you'll find a small corner of provincial France, thanks to the dedicated effort of Evelyne Ramelot, the French writer who owns the place. After an aperitif at the sophisticated cocktail bar, you can order from an imaginative menu that includes a lasagna made from strips of salted cod, peppers, and tomato sauce, and a delectable carpaccio of filet of beef with pistachios, lemon juice, vinaigrette, and Parmesan cheese. The wine list is particularly imaginative, with worthy vintages mostly from France and Spain.

Calle Balmes 165, corner Paris. © 93-218-74-79. Reservations recommended. Main courses 8€–14€; set-price lunch 8.10€; set-price dinner 18€. MC, V. Tues–Sat 1:30–4pm and 8:30–11:30pm. Metro: Diagonal.

Tragaluz ⭐ MEDITERRANEAN   Named after the turn-of-the-20th-century modernist building that contains it, this well-respected restaurant offers three very contemporary-looking beige dining rooms on separate floors. Menu items are derived from fresh ingredients that vary with the season. Depending on the month of your visit, you might find terrine of duck liver, Santurce-style hake (with garlic and herbs), filet of sole stuffed with red peppers, and beef tenderloin in a Rioja wine sauce. One of the best desserts is a semisoft slice of deliberately underbaked chocolate cake. Diners seeking low-fat dishes will find solace here, as will vegetarians. The vegetables served are the best and freshest in the market that day. You'll find a sushi restaurant downstairs. The Tragaluz chefs are adept at taking local products and turning them into flavorful, carefully prepared dishes. Most dishes are at the lower end of the price scale.

Pasaje Concepción 5, Eixample. © 93-487-66-21. Reservations recommended. Main courses 15€–28€. AE, DC, MC, V. Daily 1:30–4pm and 8:30pm–midnight; Thurs–Sat closes at 1am. Metro: Diagonal or Provença.

NORTE DIAGONAL
VERY EXPENSIVE
Botafumeiro ⭐⭐⭐ SEAFOOD   Although the competition is strong, this classic *marisquería* consistently puts Barcelona's finest seafood on the table. Much of the allure comes from the attention of the white-jacketed staff. If you

like, you can eat at the bar. If you do venture to the rear, you'll find a series of attractive dining rooms noted for the ease with which business deals seem to be arranged during the lunch hour. International businesspeople often rendezvous here, and the king of Spain is sometimes a patron.

Menu items include fresh seafood prepared in a glistening modern kitchen visible from parts of the dining room. The establishment prides itself on its fresh and saltwater fish, clams, mussels, lobster, crayfish, scallops, and several varieties of crustaceans that you may never have seen before. Stored live in holding tanks or in enormous crates near the entrance, many of the creatures are flown in daily from Galicia, home of owner Moncho Neira. With the 100 or so fish dishes, the menu lists only four or five meat dishes, including three kinds of steak, veal, and a traditional version of pork with turnips. The wine list offers a wide array of *cavas* from Catalonia and highly drinkable choices from Galicia.

Gran de Gràcia 81. © **93-218-42-30**. Reservations recommended for dining rooms. Main courses 22€–40€. AE, DC, MC, V. Daily 1pm–1am. Metro: Fontana.

Gaig ★★★ MODERN CATALAN   One of the shining culinary showcases of Barcelona, Gaig was founded some 130 years ago by the great-grandmother of present owner Carlos Gaig. Back then it was known as a *fonda,* or small inn for travelers. Despite the age of the building, the interior design is both modern and luxurious, having recently been restyled. The restaurant is celebrated locally for the quality and freshness of its food. If you order a meal with eggs, those eggs will have been contributed by chickens seen wandering about the patio where customers often dine alfresco in the summer months. The cuisine of Gaig centers on traditional Catalán recipes transformed and altered to suit lighter and more modern palates. Among the stellar dishes to order are *arroz del delta con pichón y zetas* (rice with partridge and mushrooms), *rape asado a la catalana* (grilled monkfish with local herbs), and *els petits filet de vedella amb prunes i pinyons* (small veal filets with prunes and pine nuts). One of the tastiest dishes is marinated roast pork thigh. Desserts include *crema de Sant Joseph* (a warm flan with wild strawberries on top), homemade chocolates, and a selection of tarts.

Passeig de Maragall 402. © **93-429-10-17**. Reservations recommended. Main courses 25€–40€; *menú gastronómico* 68€. AE, DC, MC, V. Tues–Sun 1:30–4pm; Tues–Sat 9–11pm; Sun 1:30–4pm. Closed 3 weeks in Aug. Metro: Horta.

EXPENSIVE

Gorría ★ *Finds* BASQUE/NAVARRE   If you're a devotee of the cookery of Navarre and of the coastal Basque country in northern Spain, as we are, then make a date in Barcelona to head for this quite wonderful discovery. On two levels, this restaurant has been in business since the mid-70s, lying only 200m (656 ft.) from La Sagrada Família and just 50m (164 ft.) from Plaza de Toros, the bullring. Javier Gorría, who learned to cook from his more famous father, the chef, Fermin Gorría, is in charge, and he's as good as his old man. In a location in the Eixample, Gorría holds forth nightly tempting your taste buds with his creations. He pampers his regular clientele, mainly homesick expats from Navarre and the Basque country, with memories of home. No dish is finer than the herb-flavored baby lamb baked in a wood-fired oven. The classic Basque dish, hake, comes in a garlic-laced green herbal sauce with fresh mussels and perfectly cooked asparagus on the side. His grilled turbot is fresh and straightforward, perfection itself with its flavoring of garlic, virgin olive oil, and a dash of vinegar. His braised pork also emerges from the wood-fired oven, and we could make a meal out of his *pochas* or white beans. Another favorite is a platter of artichokes stuffed with shrimp and wild mushrooms.

Diputació 421, Eixample. ✆ **93-245-11-64.** Reservations recommended. Main courses 15€–27€. AE, DC, MC, V. Mon–Sat 1–3:30pm and 9–11:30pm. Closed: Aug. Metro: Monumental.

Neichel ★★★ FRENCH/MEDITERRANEAN Alsatian-born owner Jean Louis Neichel is called "the most brilliant ambassador French cuisine has ever had within Spain." Neichel is almost obsessively concerned with gastronomy—the savory presentation of some of the most talked-about preparations of seafood, fowl, and sweets in Spain.

Your meal might include a "mosaic" of foie gras with vegetables, strips of salmon marinated in sesame and served with *escabeche* (vinaigrette) sauce, or slices of raw and smoked salmon stuffed with caviar. The prize-winning terrine of sea crab floats on a lavishly decorated bed of cold seafood sauce. Move on to *escalope* of turbot served with *coulis* (purée) of sea urchins, fricassee of Bresse chicken served with spiny lobsters, sea bass with a mousseline of truffles, Spanish milk-fed lamb served with the juice of Boletus mushrooms, or rack of lamb gratinéed in an herb-flavored pastry crust. The selection of European cheeses and the changing array of freshly made desserts are nothing short of spectacular.

Pedralbes 16. ✆ **93-203-84-08.** Reservations required. Main courses 20€–40€. AE, DC, MC, V. Tues–Sat 1:30–3:30pm; Mon–Sat 8:30–11pm. Closed holidays and Aug. Metro: Palau Reial or María Cristina.

Reno ★ CATALAN One of the finest and most enduring haute cuisine restaurants in Barcelona, Reno sits behind sidewalk-to-ceiling windows hung with fine-mesh lace to shelter diners from prying eyes on the octagonal plaza outside. The impeccably mannered staff is formal but not intimidating. Seasonal specialties might include partridge simmered in wine or port sauce, a platter of assorted fish smoked on the premises, hake with anchovy sauce, or filet of sole stuffed with foie gras and truffles or grilled with anchovy sauce. An appetizing array of pastries wheels from table to table on a cart. Dessert might also be crepes flambéed at your table.

Tuset 27. ✆ **93-200-91-29.** Reservations required. Main courses 13€–28€. AE, DC, MC, V. Mon–Sat 1–4pm and 8:30–11:30pm, Sat closes from 1–4pm. Metro: Diagonal.

Roig Robí ★ INTERNATIONAL This restaurant—the name means "ruby red" (the color of a perfectly aged Rioja) in Catalán—serves excellent food from an imaginative kitchen with a warm welcome. Although we're not as excited about this restaurant as we once were, it does remain one of the city's most dependable choices. Order an aperitif at the L-shaped oak bar, then head down a long corridor to a pair of flower-filled dining rooms. In warm weather, glass doors open onto a verdant walled courtyard. Menu items include fresh beans with pine nut sauce, *hake al Roig Robí*, fresh mushroom salad with green beans and fresh tomatoes, and shellfish from Costa Brava. Monkfish comes with clams and onion confit, ravioli stuffed with spring herbs, and chicken stuffed with foie gras. Cockscomb salad is available for those with adventuresome palates.

Séneca 20. ✆ **93-218-92-22.** Reservations required. Main courses 16€–36€; fixed-price menu 56€. AE, DC, MC, V. Mon–Fri 1:30–4pm; Mon–Sat 9–11:30pm. Metro: Diagonal.

Via Veneto ★★ INTERNATIONAL/CATALAN Consistently well-prepared cuisine attracts diners to this conservatively decorated restaurant a short walk from the Plaça de Francesc María. The kitchen is always inventing imaginative Catalán recipes based on fresh local ingredients, such as tartare of fresh fish with caviar, roasted salt cod with potatoes, and veal kidney with truffle sauce. Loin of roast suckling pig comes with seasonal baby vegetables, and filet steak is served in a brandy, cream, and peppercorn sauce. There's a wide array of wines. Dessert might be a richly textured combination of melted chocolate, cherries, Armagnac, and vanilla ice cream.

Ganduxer 10. ✆ **93-200-72-44.** Reservations required. Main courses 18€–30€. AE, DC, MC, V. Mon–Fri 1:15–4pm; Mon–Sat 8:30–11:30pm. Closed Aug 1–20. Metro: La Bonanova.

MOLL DE LA FUSTA & BARCELONETA
EXPENSIVE

Abac ✲✲ *Finds* INTERNATIONAL   This is the showcase of a personality chef, Xavier Pellicer, who creates a self-termed *cuisine d'auteur,* meaning a menu of completely original dishes. Inside the 1948 Park Hotel, his minimalist restaurant has even attracted members of the Spanish royal family, eager to see what Pellicer is cooking on any given night. Some of his dishes may be too experimental for most tastes, but we've found his daring palate pleasing to us. He is a master in balancing flavors, and his dishes perk up the taste buds and even challenge them at times. His plates emphasize color and texture, and his sauces are perfectly balanced. You never know on any given night where his culinary inspiration has led him. Perhaps a mushroom tartare will be resting on your plate or else a velvety smooth steamed foie gras. Roasted sea bass appears with sweet pimientos and oyster plant or salsify. Iberian suckling pig is cooked and flavored to perfection, as is his fennel ravioli with "fruits of the sea."

Carrer del Rec. 79–89, La Ribera. ✆ **93-319-66-00.** Reservations required. Main courses 23€–33€; tasting menu 76€. AE, DC, MC, V. Tues–Sat 1:30–3:30pm; Mon–Sat 8:30–10:30pm. Closed Aug. Metro: Barceloneta.

Can Costa ✲ SEAFOOD   This is one of the oldest seafood restaurants in this seafaring town. Established in the late 1930s, it has two busy dining rooms, a practiced staff, and an outdoor terrace, although a warehouse blocks the view of the harbor. Fresh seafood prepared according to traditional recipes rules the menu. It includes the best baby squid in town—sautéed in a flash so that it has a nearly grilled flavor, almost never overcooked or rubbery. A long-standing chef's specialty is *fideuá de peix,* a relative of the classic Valencian shellfish paella, with noodles instead of rice. Desserts are made fresh daily.

Passeig Don Joan de Borbò 70. ✆ **93-221-59-03.** Reservations recommended. Main courses 16€–30€. MC, V. Daily 12:30–4pm; Thurs–Tues 8–11:30pm. Metro: Barceloneta.

Can Solé CATALAN   In Barceloneta at the harbor, Can Solé still honors the traditions of this former fishing village. Many of the seafood joints here are too touristy for our tastes, but this one is authentic and delivers good value. The decor is rustic and a bit raffish, with wine barrels, lots of noise, and excellent food. Begin with the sweet tiny clams or the cod cakes, perhaps some bouillabaisse. Little langoustines are an eternal but expensive favorite, and everything is aromatically perfumed with fresh garlic. You might also sample one of the seafood-rich dishes. Desserts are so good they're worth saving room for, especially the orange pudding or the praline ice cream.

Carrer Sant Carles 4. ✆ **93-221-50-12.** Reservations required. Main courses 9€–40€. AE, DC. MC, V. Tues–Sun 1–4pm; Tues–Sat 8:30–11pm. Metro: Barceloneta.

7 Portes ✲ SEAFOOD   This is a lunchtime favorite for businesspeople (the Stock Exchange is across the way) and an evening favorite for many in-the-know diners who have made it their preferred restaurant in Catalonia. Festive and elegant, it's been going since 1836, making it one of the oldest restaurants in Barcelona. Regional dishes include fresh herring with onions and potatoes, a different paella daily (sometimes with shellfish, for example, or with rabbit), and a wide array of fresh fish. You might order succulent oysters or an herb-laden stew of black beans with pork or white beans with sausage. Portions are enormous. The restaurant's name means "Seven Doors," and it really does have seven doors. Waiters wear the long white aprons of the Belle Epoque era.

Passeig d'Isabel II 14. ℭ **93-319-30-33.** Reservations required. Main courses 18€–32€. AE, DC, MC, V. Daily 1pm–1am. Metro: Barceloneta.

MODERATE

Cal Pep ⭐ *Finds* CATALAN   One of the dining secrets of Barcelona, Cal Pep lies close to the Picasso Museum and is a slice of local life. On a tiny postage-stamp square, it's generally packed, and the food is some of the tastiest in the old town. There's actually a Pep himself, and he's a great host, going around to see that everybody is one happy family. In the rear is a small dining room, but most patrons like to occupy one of the counter seats up front. From the pans in the rear emerge a selection of perfectly cooked dishes that might launch you into your meal. Try the fried artichokes or the mixed medley of seafood that includes small sardines. Tiny clams come swimming in a well-seasoned broth given extra spice by a sprinkling of hot peppers. A delectable tuna dish comes with a sesame sauce, and fresh salmon is flavored with such herbs as basil—sublime.

Plaça des les Olles 8. ℭ **93-310-79-61.** Reservations required. Main courses 12€–20€. AE, MC, V. Mon 8:30–11:30pm; Tues–Sat 1–4:30pm and 8:30–11:30pm. Closed Aug. Metro: Barceloneta or Jaime I.

Can Majó ⭐⭐ SEAFOOD   This is one of the best seafood restaurants in Barcelona, lying close to the harbor life. In summer one of the most desirable tables at the port is found on the terrace of this restaurant. The decoration inside is in the rustic tavern style, most inviting. Art lines the walls, and the staff exudes a hospitable, friendly aura as they give excellent, sometimes rushed service. The food plows fairly familiar ground, but when it's good, it's good, and it can be very good indeed. The fish is very fresh tasting, as it was just brought in that morning. Now almost into its fourth decade, the restaurant still serves some of the best *sopa de pescado y marisco* (fish and shellfish soup) in the area. Its sautéed squid is a heavenly meal in itself, or in the words of one diner: "A day without calamari is a day in hell." *Bacalao* (dried cod) appears in a savory green sauce with little baby clams n their shells. Its paellas are as good as those served in the famed restaurants of Valencia, and their lobster bouillabaisse is extremely gratifying.

Almirall Aixada 23, Barceloneta. ℭ **93-221-54-55.** Reservations required. Main courses 12€–24€. AE, DC, MC, V. Tues–Sun 1–4pm; Tues–Sat 8:30–11:30pm. Metro: Barceloneta.

Ramonet ⭐ SEAFOOD   In a Catalán-style villa near the seaport, this rather expensive restaurant serves a large variety of fresh seafood and has done so since 1763. The front room, with stand-up tables for seafood tapas, beer, and regional wine, is often crowded. In the two dining rooms, you can choose from a variety of seafood—shrimp, hake, and monkfish are almost always available. Other specialties include pungent anchovies, grilled mushrooms, black rice, braised artichokes, tortilla with spinach and beans, and mussels "from the beach."

Carrer Maquinista 17. ℭ **93-319-30-64.** Reservations recommended. Main courses 10€–25€. AE, DC, MC, V. Daily 10am–4pm; Mon–Sat 8pm–midnight; Sun 10:30am–4:30pm. Usually closed Aug 19–Sept 1. Metro: Barceloneta.

INEXPENSIVE

Agua ⭐ MEDITERRANEAN/ITALIAN   It bustles, it's hip, and it serves well-prepared fish and shellfish in a hyper-modern setting overlooking the beach. A terrace beckons anyone who wants an in-your-face view of the water, but if the wind is blowing with a bit too much chill, you can retreat into the big-windowed blue-and-yellow dining room. Here, amid display cases showing the catch of the day, you can order heaping portions of meats and fish to be grilled over an open fire. Excellent examples include grilled versions of chicken, fish, shrimp, crayfish, and an especially succulent version of stuffed squid. Most of them are served with as little culinary fanfare, and as few sauces, as possible, allowing the freshness and flavor of the raw ingredients to shine through the chargrilled coatings. Risottos, some of them studded with fresh clams and herbs, are usually winners, with many versions suitable for vegetarians.

Passeig Marítim de la Barceloneta 30 (Port Marítim). (€) **93-225-12-72.** Reservations recommended. Main courses 5€–15€. AE, MC, V. Daily 1–4pm and 8:30pm–midnight (1am Fri–Sat). Metro: Ciutadella.

El Túnel SPANISH This long-established restaurant serves delectable fish soup, cannelloni with truffles, kidney beans with shrimp, roast kid, fish stew, and filet of beef with peppers. The food is uncomplicated but delicious. The service is eager, the wine cellar extensive. El Túnel is close to the general post office.

Ample 33–35. (€) **93-315-27-59.** Reservations recommended for lunch. Main courses 8.30€–15€. MC, V. Tues–Sun 6pm–1am; Fri–Sat 6pm–2am. Closed Aug. Metro: San Jaume.

NEAR ESTACIO DE SANTS

La Llauna *Finds* CATALAN The name of this restaurant is a reference to the pot in which *calcots* are cooked. Available only in the spring, this rare dish is similar to a spring onion but twice or more the size with an almost meaty taste. It isn't easy to find this delicacy in Barcelona, but this restaurant specializes in *calcots,* cooking them over an open charcoal grill. It has two floors for diners, each decorated in a Catalán rustic style with white walls and posters of local country life. Prices are very reasonable. The menu includes a selection of well-prepared regional dishes based on local products and fresh ingredients. Locals begin with *pa amb tomaquet* (toasted bread with tomatoes and olive oil), going on to sample such hearty fare as various grilled meats with fried potatoes or *gambas a la Llauna o con conejo* (shrimp or rabbit with *calcots* in wine sauce).

Plaça D'Osca 2. (€) **93-422-32-25.** Reservations recommended on weekends. Main courses 5€–16€; *menú del día* (at lunch) 7.50€. MC, V. Thurs–Tues noon–midnight. Metro: Plaça de Sants and Estació de Sants.

VILA OLIMPICA

Talaia Mar MEDITERRANEAN This is not only the best restaurant at Olympic Port, but has one of the most innovative menus in Catalonia. Giordi Samper, the chef, devises unique menus and turns out food that is both amusing and savory. The presentations are often simple yet always elegant. To discover this chef's talent, sample his set menu, which he calls, quite appropriately, *festival gastronómico.* For a main course, sample his tuna tartare with guacamole and salmon eggs or his brochettes of lobster. The increasingly rare black truffle appears in some of his smooth and velvety risottos. He does a marvelous steamed hake in a balsamic reduction as well as a grilled sea bass with shrimp, which is flavored with asparagus juice among other delights. Fresh fish arrives from the market daily and is grilled to perfection, as is the aromatically roasted rack of lamb. We could return here night after night and always find some new dish to tempt the palate. Rising above the port, the restaurant is beside two towers, Hotel Arts and Torée Mapfre.

Marina 16. (€) **93-221-90-90.** Reservations required. Main courses 15€–27€. Set menu 51€. AE, DC, MC, V. Daily 1–4pm and 8pm–midnight. Metro: Ciutadella–Vila Olímpica.

WEST OF TIBIDABO

La Balsa INTERNATIONAL   On the uppermost level of a circular tower built as a cistern, La Balsa offers a view over most of the surrounding cityscape. To reach it, you climb to the structure's original rooftop where you're likely to be greeted by owner and founder Mercedes López. Food emerges from a cramped but well-organized kitchen several floors below. (The waiters are reputedly the most athletic in Barcelona, because they must run up the stairs carrying steaming platters.) The restaurant serves such dishes as a *judías verdes* (salad of broad beans) with strips of salmon in lemon-flavored vinaigrette, stewed veal with wild mushrooms, a salad of warm lentils with anchovies, and pickled fresh salmon with chives. Undercooked maigret (breast) of duck is served with fresh, lightly poached foie gras, and baked hake (flown in from Galicia) is prepared in squid-ink sauce. The restaurant is 2km (1¼ miles) north of the city's heart—you'll need a taxi—in the Tibidabo district, close to the Science Museum (Museu de la Ciéncia). It's often booked several days in advance.

Infanta Isabel 4. ✆ **93-211-50-48.** Reservations required. Main courses 12€–27€. AE, MC, V. Tues–Sat 2–3:30pm; Mon–Sat 9–11:30pm. Closed Easter week. No buffet in Aug.

ON THE OUTSKIRTS

El Racó de Can Fabes ★★★ MEDITERRANEAN   This is one of the greatest restaurants of Spain—maybe the greatest. If you don't mind the 30-minute drive or the 45-minute train ride from Barcelona, a distance of 52km (32 miles), you will be transported to a gourmet citadel, housed in a 3-century-old building in the center of the Catalán village of 1,700 people. Santi Santamaría and Angels Serra, who founded the restaurant in the '80s, seemed rather immune to press acclaim, continuing to show their discipline and craftsmanship in spite of all the raves. They don't let a single platter reach their dining room without getting their keen-eyed sense of approval. This Michelin three-star restaurant (its highest rating) is run with exquisite care and dedication. The restaurant is refined and elegant yet retains a rustic aura. Recent strokes of their inspiration included hot and cold mackerel with cream of caviar and tender pigeon with duck tartare. A heavenly concoction is spicy foie gras with Sauterne and a coulis (essence) of sweet red and green peppers. Two different preparations of crayfish, each one a delight, come both raw and cooked. Roast pigeon is prepared in ways that correspond to the seasons and the "mood of the chef." For dessert, there's nothing finer than their "Festival de chocolate."

Sant Joan 6, Sant Ceoloni. ✆ **93-867-28-51.** Reservations required. Main courses 29€–55€. Set menus 120€. AE, DC, MC, V. Tues–Sun 1:30–3:30pm; Tues–Sat 8:30–10:30pm. Closed Jan 28–Feb 11 and June 24–July 8. Take any RENFE train from the Passeig de Gràcia station, heading for France, disembarking at Sant Celoni.

OUR FAVORITE *TASCAS*

The bars listed below are known for their tapas; for more recommendations, refer to the "Barcelona After Dark" section, later in this chapter.

Alt Heidelberg GERMAN/TAPAS   A Barcelona institution since the 1930s, Alt Heidelberg serves German beer on tap, a good selection of German sausages, and Spanish tapas. You can also order full meals—sauerkraut garni is a specialty.

Ronda Universitat 5. ✆ **93-318-10-32.** Tapas 2€–6€; combination plates 6€–9€. MC, V. Mon–Fri 8:30am–1:30am; Sat–Sun noon–2am. Metro: Universitat.

Bar del Pi TAPAS   One of the most famous bars in the Barri Gòtic, this establishment is midway between two medieval squares opening onto the church of Pi. Tapas are limited; most visitors come to drink coffee, beer, or wine. You can

Moments **A Wine Taster's Secret Address**

It doesn't get much better in Barcelona than an afternoon spent on the terrace of **La Vinya del Senyor,** Plaça Santa María 5 (© **93-310-33-79**), taking in the glorious Gothic facade of Santa María del Mar. You could even take a wine connoisseur like Mel Brooks (when not counting his take on *The Producers*), and we think even this hard-to-please man would be pleased. The wine list will inspire awe. Imagine, for example, 13 Priorats, 31 Riojas, and more than a dozen vintages of the legendary Vega Sicilia. In all, there are more than 300 wines and selected *cavas,* sherries, and *moscatells,* and the list is constantly rotated so you can always expect some new surprise on the *carte.* If you don't want a bottle, you'll find some two dozen wines offered by the glass, including a sublime 1994 Jané Ventura Cabernet Sauvignon. To go with your wine, tantalizing tapas are served, including walnut rolls drizzled in olive oil, cured Iberian ham, and French cheese. Tapas cost from 1.65€ to 5.85€. American Express, Diners Club, MasterCard, and Visa are accepted. Hours are Tuesday through Saturday from noon to 1:30am and Sunday from noon to midnight. Metro: Jaume I or Barceloneta.

sit inside at one of the cramped bentwood tables, or stand at the crowded bar. In warm weather, take a table beneath the single plane tree on the landmark square. The plaza usually draws an interesting group of young bohemian sorts and travelers.

Plaça Sant Josep Oriol 1. © **93-302-21-23.** Tapas 2€–5€. No credit cards. Mon–Fri 9am–11pm; Sat 9:30am–10:30pm; Sun 10am–10pm. Metro: Liceu.

Bar Turò TAPAS In an affluent residential neighborhood north of the old town, Bar Turò serves some of the best tapas in town. In summer you can sit outside or retreat to the narrow confines of the bar. You select from about 20 kinds of tapas, including Russian salad, fried squid, and Serrano ham.

Tenor Viñas 1. © **93-200-69-53.** Tapas 2€–12€. V. Mon–Sat 8:30am–midnight; Sun 8:30am–4pm. Metro: Hospital Clinic.

Bodega la Plata TAPAS Established in the 1920s, La Plata is one of a trio of famous bodegas on this narrow medieval street. It occupies a corner building whose two open sides allow aromatic cooking odors to permeate the neighborhood. This bodega contains a marble-topped bar and overcrowded tables. The culinary specialty is *raciones* (small plates) of deep-fried sardines—head and all. You can make a meal with two servings coupled with the house's tomato, onion, and fresh anchovy salad.

Mercé 28. © **93-315-10-09.** Tapas 1.50€–3€. No credit cards. Mon–Sat 9am–3:30pm and 6–11pm. Metro: Barceloneta.

Bodegueta TAPAS Founded in 1940, this old wine tavern specializes in Catalán sausage. Wash it all down with inexpensive Spanish wines. Beer costs .90€ to 1.80€; wine goes for 1€.

Rambla de Catalunya 100. © **93-215-48-94.** Tapas from 2€–5€. No credit cards. Mon–Sat 9am–1:45am; Sun 7pm–1:30am. Metro: Diagonal.

Casa Alfonso TAPAS Spaniards love their ham, which comes in many forms. The best of the best is *jamón Jabugo,* the only one sold at this traditional establishment. Entire hams hang from steel braces. They're taken down, carved, and trimmed before you into paper-thin slices. This particular form of cured ham, generically called *jamón Serrano,* comes from pigs fed acorns in Huelva, in deepest Andalusia. Devotees of all things porcine will ascend to piggy-flavored heaven.

Roger de Lluria 6. **☎ 93-301-97-83.** Tapas 4€–9€. MC, V. Mon–Tues 9am–midnight; Wed–Sat 9am–1am. Metro: Urquinaona.

Casa Tejada TAPAS   Covered with rough stucco and decorated with hanging hams, Casa Tejada (established in 1964) offers some of the best tapas. Arranged behind a glass display case, they include such dishes as marinated fresh tuna, German-style potato salad, ham salad, and five preparations of squid (including one that's stuffed). For variety, quantity, and quality, this place is hard to beat. There's outdoor dining in summer.

Tenor Viñas 3. **☎ 93-200-73-41.** Tapas 2.10€–15€. MC, V. Daily 10am–1:30am. Metro: Muntaner or Hospital Clinic.

Las Campanas (Casa Marcos) TAPAS   From the street (there's no sign), Las Campanas looks like a storehouse for cured hams and wine bottles. Patrons flock to the long, stand-up bar for *chorizo* pinioned between two pieces of bread. Sausages are usually eaten with beer or red wine. The place opened in 1952, and nothing has changed since. A tape recorder plays nostalgic favorites, from Edith Piaf to the Andrews Sisters.

Mercé 21. **☎ 93-315-06-09.** Tapas 2€–11€. No credit cards. Thurs–Tues 12:30–4pm and 7pm–2am. Metro: Jaume I.

Quimet & Quimet ★ TAPAS/CHEESE   This is a great tapas bar, especially for cheese, of which it offers the finest selection in Barcelona. Built at the turn of the 20th century, the tavern in the Poble Sec sector is still run by the fifth generation of Quimets. Their wine cellar is one of the best stocked of any tapas bar, and their cheese selection is varied. One night we sampled four on the same plate, including *nevat,* a tangy goat cheese; *cabrales,* an intense Spanish blue; *zamorano,* a hardy, nutty sheep's milk cheese, and *torta del Casar,* a soft, creamy farm cheese. Of course, you can also order other delights such as mussels with tomato confit and caviar, razor clams, and even sturgeon.

Poeta Cabanyes 25. **☎ 93-442-3142.** Tapas 1.50€–10€. MC, V. Tues–Sat noon–4pm and 7–10:30pm; Sun noon–4pm. Metro: Paral.lel.

Rey de la Gamba SHELLFISH   The "King of Prawns" could also be called the House of Mussels, since it sells more of that shellfish. In the 18th-century fishing village of Barceloneta, this place packs them in, especially on weekends. A wide array of seafood accompanies cured ham—the combination is a tradition.

Mall Mestval 23. **☎ 93-221-00-12.** Main courses 15€–22€. MC, V. Daily 11am–1am. Metro: Calle Marina.

6 Seeing the Sights

Spain's second-largest city is also its most cosmopolitan and avant-garde. Barcelona is filled with landmark buildings and world-class museums offering many sightseeing opportunities. These include Antoni Guadí's Sagrada Família, Museu Picasso, Barcelona's Gothic cathedral, and Les Rambles, the famous tree-lined promenade cutting through the heart of the old quarter.

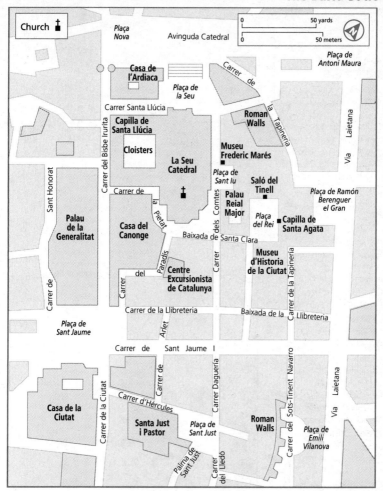

Church ✝

Plaça Nova

Avinguda Catedral

0   50 yards

0   50 meters

Plaça de Antoni Maura

Casa de l'Ardiaca

Plaça de la Seu

Carrer de

Carrer Santa Llúcia

Roman Walls

la Tapineria

Via Laietana

Capilla de Santa Llúcia

Carrer del Bisbe Irurita

Cloisters

La Seu Catedral

Museu Frederic Marés

Sant Honorat

Carrer de

la Pietat

Plaça de Sant Iu

Saló del Tinell

Plaça de Ramón Berenguer el Gran

Palau de la Generalitat

Casa del Canonge

Palau Reial Major

Plaça del Rei

Capilla de Santa Agata

Carrer dels Comtes

Baixada de Santa Clara

Carrer de

Paradís

Centre Excursionista de Catalunya

del

Carrer

Museu d'Historia de la Ciutat

Carrer de la Tapineria

Carrer de

Plaça de Sant Jaume

Carrer de la Llibreria

Baixada de la Llibreteria

Arlet

Carrer de Sant Jaume I

Casa de la Ciutat

Carrer de la Ciutat

Carrer d'Hércules

Carrer de

Santa Just i Pastor

Plaça de Sant Just

Carrer Dagueria

Roman Walls

Carrer del Sots-Tinent Navarro

Via Laietana

Plaça de Emili Vilanova

Palma de Sant Just

Carrer del Lledó

SIGHTSEEING SUGGESTIONS FOR FIRST-TIME VISITORS

If You Have 1 Day   Spend the morning exploring the Barri Gòtic. In the afternoon visit Antoni Gaudí's unfinished masterpiece, La Sagrada Família, before returning to the heart of the city for a walk down Les Rambles. To cap your day, take the funicular to the fountains at Montjuïc or go to the top of Tibidabo for a panoramic view of Barcelona and its harbor.

If You Have 2 Days   On Day 2, visit the Museu Picasso in the Gothic Quarter. Then stroll through the surrounding district, the Barri de la Ribera, which is filled with Renaissance mansions and is the site of the gorgeous church Santa María del Mar. Follow this with a ride to the top of the Columbus Monument for a panoramic view of the harbor front. Have a seafood lunch at La Barceloneta and in the afternoon, stroll up Les Rambles again. Explore Montjuïc and visit the Museu d'Art de Catalunya if time remains. End the day with a meal at Los Caracoles, a famous restaurant in the old city, just off Les Rambles.

Barcelona Attractions

Plaça de
Francesc Macia

Carrer de Buenos Aires

Carrer de Londres

Carrer de Paris

Travessara de Gràcia

Avinguda Diagonal

Gran de Gràcia

Travessara de Gràcia

Av. de Sant Antoni Maria Claret

Carrer de Còrsega

EIXAMPLE

Carrer de la Industria

Carrer de Provença

Carrer Enric Granados

Carrer de Balmes

Rambla de Catalunya

Passeig de Gràcia

Carrer de Pau Claris

Carrer de Rosselló

8

9

10

Carrer de Roger de Flor

Plaça de la
Sagrada
Família

7

Avinguda Diagonal

Carrer de Mallorca

Carrer de València

Carrer del Comte d'Urgell

Carrer de Villarroel

Carrer de Casanova

Carrer de Muntaner

Carrer d'Aribau

11 12

13

Carrer del Consell de Cent

14

Carrer de R. de Llúria

Carrer del Bruc

Carrer de Girona

Carrer de Bailén

Passeig de Sant Joan

Carrer d'Aragó

Carrer de Napols

Carrer de Sicília

Carrer de la Diputació

Gran Via de les Corts Catalanes

Plaça de la
Universitat

Ronda de Sant Antoni

Carrer de Pelai

Ronda Universitat

Plaça
Catalunya

Plaça de
Tetuan

Carrer   de Casp

Carrer   d'Ausias Marc

Carrer de Sardenya

RAVAL

15

Plaça
Urquinaona

Carrer   d'Ali Bei

Carrer de Ribes

Carrer de Hospital

La Rambla

Av. Portal
de l'Angel

Ronda de Sant Pere

Palau de la
Música Catalana

Via Laietana

Passeig de
Lluís Companys

Carrer de la Marina

Carrer de Sant Pau

BARRI GÒTIC

24

16

26 25

27

Passeig de Pujades

21

PARC DE LA
CIUTADELLA

C. de   Ferran   C. de la Princesa

Carrer Nou de la Rambla

Avda. de les Drassanes

La Rambla

23

22

LA RIBERA

Carrer del Comerç

Passeig de Picasso

Carrer de Wellington

Carrer Ample

Pg. Isabel II

20

19

Villa
Olímpica →

17

Plaça Portal
de la Pau

Passeig de Colom

Moll de la Fusta

18

Moll d'Espanya

Avinguda d'Icaria

Port
Vell

BARCELONETA

Passeig   Marítim

If You Have 3 Days On Day 3, make a pilgrimage to the monastery of Montserrat, about 45 minutes outside of Barcelona, to see the venerated Black Virgin and a host of artistic and scenic attractions. Try to time your visit to hear the 50-member boys' choir.

If You Have 4 or 5 Days On Day 4, take a morning walk along the harbor front, or in the modernist Eixample section of Barcelona, the planned urban expansion area from 1860. Have lunch on the pier. In the afternoon visit Montjuïc again to tour the Fundació Joan Miró and walk through the Poble Espanyol, a miniature village with reproductions of representative regional architecture, created for the 1929 World's Fair. On Day 5, take another excursion from the city. If you're interested in history, visit the former Roman city of Tarragona to the south. If you want to unwind on a beach, head south to Sitges.

THE TOP ATTRACTIONS

One of Barcelona's greatest attractions is not a single sight but an entire neighborhood, the **Barri Gòtic (Gothic Quarter)** ✦✦. This is the old aristocratic quarter, parts of which have survived from the Middle Ages. Spend at least 2 or 3 hours exploring its narrow streets and squares, which continue to form a vibrant, lively neighborhood. Start by walking up the Carrer del Carme, east of Les Rambles. A nighttime stroll takes on added drama, but exercise caution—safety is an issue here. The buildings are austere and sober for the most part, the cathedral being the crowning achievement. Roman ruins and the vestiges of 3rd-century walls add further interest. This area is intricately detailed and filled with many attractions that are easy to miss (see map, above).

Catedral de Barcelona ✦✦✦   Barcelona's cathedral is a celebrated example of Catalonian Gothic architecture. Construction began at the end of the 13th century and was nearly completed in the mid–15th century (although the west facade dates from the 19th c.). The three naves, cleaned and illuminated, have splendid Gothic details. With its large bell towers, blending of medieval and Renaissance styles, beautiful **cloister** ✦, high altar, side chapels, handsomely sculptured choir, and Gothic arches, it ranks as one of the most impressive cathedrals in Spain. Vaulted galleries in the cloister, enhanced by forged iron grilles, surround a garden of magnolias, medlars, and palm trees. The historian Cirici called this "the loveliest oasis in Barcelona." The cloister, illuminated on Saturday and during fiestas, also contains a museum of medieval art. Its most notable work is the 15th-century *La Pietat* of Bartolomé Bermejo. You can take an elevator to the roof where you can see a wonderful view of Gothic Barcelona but only Monday through Saturday from 10:30am to 1:30pm and 4:30 to 6pm. At noon on Sunday, you can see the *sardana*, a Catalonian folk dance, performed in front of the cathedral.

Plaça de la Seu s/n. ✆ **93-315-15-54.** Admission to cathedral free; to museum 1€. Global ticket to museum, choir, rooftop terraces, and towers 4€. Cathedral daily 9am–1pm and 5–7pm; cloister museum daily 10am–1pm and 4–7pm. Metro: Jaume I.

Fundació Joan Miró ✦   Born in 1893, Joan Miró was one of Spain's greatest artists, known for his whimsical abstract forms and brilliant colors. Some 10,000 works by the Catalán surrealist, including paintings, graphics, and sculptures, are collected here. The building has been greatly expanded in recent years, following the design of Catalán architect Josep Lluis Sert, a close friend of Miró's. An exhibition in a modern wing charts (in a variety of media) Miró's artistic evolution, from his first drawings at the age of 8 to his last works. The museum frequently mounts temporary exhibitions of contemporary art.

Plaça de Neptú, Parc de Montjuïc. ℭ **93-443-94-70**. Admission 7.20€ adults, 3.60€ students; free for children under 15. July–Sept Tues–Wed and Fri–Sat 10am–8pm, Thurs 10am–9:30pm, Sun 10am–2:30pm; Oct–June Tues–Wed and Fri–Sat 10am–7pm, Thurs 10am–9:30pm, Sun 10am–2:30pm. Bus: 50 at Plaça d'Espanya and 55.

La Sagrada Família 🌟🌟

Gaudí's incomplete masterpiece is one of the country's more idiosyncratic creations—if you have time to see only one Catalán landmark, make it this one. Begun in 1882 and incomplete at the architect's death in 1926, this incredible cathedral—the Church of the Holy Family—is a bizarre wonder. The languid, amorphous structure embodies the essence of Gaudí's style, which some have described as Art Nouveau run wild. Admission includes a 12-minute video on Gaudí's religious and secular works. Work continues on the structure, but without any sure idea of what Gaudí intended. Some say that the cathedral will be completed by the mid–21st century.

Majorca 401. ℭ **93-207-30-31**. Admission 8€; video guide 3€; elevator to the top (about 60m/200 ft.) 1.50€. Nov–Mar daily 9am–6pm; Apr and Sept–Oct daily 9am–8pm. Metro: Sagrada Família.

Museu Nacional d'Art de Catalunya 🌟🌟🌟

This museum, which recently underwent massive renovations, is the major depository of Catalán art. The National Art Museum of Catalonia is perhaps the most important center for Romanesque art in the world. More than 100 pieces, including sculptures, icons, and frescoes, are on display. The highlight is the collection of murals from various Romanesque churches. The frescoes and murals are displayed in apses much like those in the churches in which they were found. They're in sequential order, giving the viewer a tour of Romanesque art from its primitive beginnings to the more advanced, late Romanesque and early Gothic eras.

Palau Nacional, Parc de Montjuïc. ℭ **93-622-03-60**. Admission 4.80€ adults, 3.30€ youths 7–20, free for children under 7. Tues–Sat 10am–7pm; Sun 10am–2:30pm. Metro: Espanya.

Museu Picasso 🌟

Two old palaces on a medieval street contain this museum of the work of Pablo Picasso (1881–1973). He donated some 2,500 of his paintings, engravings, and drawings to the museum in 1970. Picasso was particularly fond of Barcelona, where he spent much of his youth. In fact, some of the paintings were done when he was only 9. One portrait dating from 1896 depicts his stern aunt, Tía Pepa. Another, completed when Picasso was 16, depicts *Science and Charity* (his father was the model for the doctor). Many works, especially the early paintings, show the artist's debt to van Gogh, El Greco, and Rembrandt; a famous series, *Las Meninas* (1957), is said to "impersonate" the work of Velázquez (if you've just been to the Prado in Madrid, or are about to go, this is a particularly interesting comparison). The *La Vie* drawings from the blue period are perhaps the most interesting. His notebooks contain many sketches of Barcelona scenes. Because the works are arranged in rough chronological order, you can get a wonderful sense of Picasso's development and watch as he discovered a trend or had a new idea, mastered it, grew bored with it, and then was off to something new. You'll learn that Picasso was a master portraitist and did many traditional representational works before his flights of fancy took off. In 1999 the museum acquired two more medieval mansions to its exhibition space, increasing the museum's size by a third. This additional space is used for temporary exhibitions.

Montcada 15–19. ℭ **93-319-63-10**. Admission 5€ adults, 2.50€ students and people under 25, free for children under 16. Tues–Sat 10am–7:30pm; Sun 10am–2:30pm. Metro: Jaume I.

Frommer's Favorite Barcelona Experiences

A Walk Through the Barri Gòtic. You'll pass through 15 centuries of history in one labyrinthine district.

Watching the *Sardana.* The national dance of Catalonia is performed at noon on Sunday at the Plaça de San Jaume in front of the cathedral.

A Trip to the Top of Montjuïc. Barcelona spreads out at your feet. This stop will provide enough amusement to fill 3 days.

Soaking Up Designer Bar Culture. Bars of all shapes and sizes are the chic places to go at night—Barcelona has more than any other city in Spain. Catalán design is paramount.

Drinking *Cava* in a Xampanyería. Enjoy a glass of bubbly, Barcelona style. The wines are excellent, and Cataláns swear that their *cavas* taste better than French champagne.

A Tour of Barcelona's Harbor. Stroll from the pier in front of the Columbus Monument to the breakwater.

Exploring the Museu Picasso. Examine the evolution of the world's greatest 20th-century artist from the age of 9.

Marveling at La Sagrada Família. Gaudí's "sand-castle cathedral" is a testimony to the architect's talent and religious belief.

A Visit to Poble Espanyol. Artificial village, to be sure, but it gives you a chance to see the architecture of all of Spain without leaving Barcelona.

Parc Güell ✸✸   Gaudí began this idiosyncratic park as a real-estate venture for a friend, the well-known Catalán industrialist Count Eusebi Güell, but it was never completed. Although only two houses were constructed, it makes for an interesting excursion. The city took over the property in 1926 and turned it into a public park. One of the houses, **Casa-Museu Gaudí,** Carrer del Carmel 28 (✆ **93-219-38-11**), contains models, furniture, drawings, and other memorabilia of the architect. (Ramón Berenguer, not Gaudí, designed the house.) Admission to the house is 4€; open daily from 10am to 6pm. Gaudí completed several of the public areas, which today look like a surrealist Disneyland, complete with a mosaic pagoda and a lizard fountain spitting water. Gaudí had planned to make this a model community of 60 dwellings, arranged somewhat like a Greek theater. A central grand plaza was built above a market, as well as an undulating bench decorated with ceramic fragments. The bizarre Doric columns of the would-be market are hollow, part of Gaudí's drainage system.

At end of Carrer de Llarrard. ✆ **93-424-38-09.** Free admission. May–Sept daily 10am–9pm; Oct–Apr daily 10am–6pm. Bus 24, 25, 31, or 74.

IF YOU HAVE MORE TIME

Fundació Antoni Tàpies ✸   When it opened in 1990 this became the third Barcelona museum devoted to the work of a single artist. In 1984, the Catalán artist Antoni Tàpies set up a foundation bearing his name, and the city of Barcelona donated an ideal site: the old Montaner i Simon publishing house, near the Passeig de Gràcia in the Eixample district. One of the city's landmark buildings, the brick-and-iron structure was built between 1881 and 1884 by that exponent of Catalán Art Nouveau, architect Lluis Doménech i Montaner. The core of the museum is a collection of works by Tàpies (most contributed by the artist), covering stages of his career as it evolved into abstract expressionism. Here, you can see the entire spectrum of media in which he worked: painting, assemblage, sculpture, drawing, and ceramics. His associations with Picasso and Miró are apparent. The largest of the works is on top of the building: a controversial gigantic sculpture, *Cloud and Chair,* made from 2,700m (9,000 ft.) of metal wiring and tubing.

Aragó 255. ℂ 93-487-03-15. Admission 4.20€ adults, 2.10€ students, free for children under 16. Tues–Sun 10am–8pm. Metro: Passeig de Gràcia.

Fundación Francisco Godia *Finds*   In the heart of Barcelona, this new museum showcases the famous art collection of Francisco Godia Sales, the Catalán art collector and entrepreneur. He amassed one of the great private collections of art in the country. Godia (1921–90) combined a love of art with a head for business and a passion for motor racing. When he wasn't driving fast ("the most wonderful thing in the world"), he was amassing his art collection. As a collector, he showed exquisite taste and great artistic sensibility.

He gathered a splendid array of medieval sculpture and ceramics, but showed a keener instinct for purchasing great paintings, Godia acquired works by some of the most important artists of the 20th century, including Julio González, María Blanchard, Joan Ponç, Antoni Tàpies, and Manolo Hugué, the latter a great friend of Picasso. From its earliest stages, Godia realized the artistic importance of Catalán modernismo and collected works by sculptors like Josep Llimona and painters like Santiago Rusiñol and Ramon Casas. Godia also dipped deeper into the past, acquiring works, for example, of two of the most important artists of the 17th century: Jacob van Ruysdael and Luca Giordano.

Carrer Valencia 284. ℂ 93-272-31-80. Admission 4.50€ adults, 2.10€ children and students, free for children 4 and under. Wed–Mon 10am–8pm. Metro: Passeig de Gràcia.

L'Aquarium de Barcelona   One of the most impressive testimonials to sea life anywhere opened in 1996 in Barcelona's Port Vell, a 10-minute walk from the bottom of the Rambles. The largest aquarium in Europe, it contains 21 glass tanks positioned along either side of a wide curving corridor. Each tank depicts a different marine habitat, with emphasis on everything from multicolored fish and corals to seagoing worms to sharks. The highlight is a huge "oceanarium" representative of the Mediterranean as a self-sustaining ecosystem. You view it from the inside of a glass-roofed, glass-sided tunnel that runs along its entire length, making fish, eels, and sharks appear to swim around you.

Port Vell. ℂ 93-221-74-74. Admission 12€ adults, 7.70€ children 4–12 and students, free for children under 4. July–Aug daily 9:30am–11pm; June and Sept daily 9:30am–9:30pm; Oct–May daily 9:30am–9pm. Metro: Drassanes or Barceloneta.

Mirador de Colón   This monument to Christopher Columbus was erected at the Barcelona harbor on the occasion of the Universal Exhibition of 1888. It consists of three parts, the first being a circular structure raised by four stairways (6m/19½ ft. wide) and eight iron heraldic lions. On the plinth are eight bronze bas-reliefs depicting Columbus's principal feats. (The originals were destroyed; these are copies.) The second part is the base of the column, consisting of an eight-sided polygon, four sides of which act as buttresses; each side contains sculptures. The third part is the 50m (167-ft.) column, which is Corinthian in style. The capital boasts representations of Europe, Asia, Africa, and America—all linked together. Finally, over a princely crown and a hemisphere recalling the newly discovered part of the globe, is a 7.5m (25-ft.) high bronze statue of Columbus—pointing, ostensibly, to the New World—by Rafael Ataché. Inside the iron column, an elevator ascends to the *mirador.* From here, a panoramic view of Barcelona and its harbor unfolds.

Portal de la Pau. (🕐 **93-302-52-24.** Admission 2€ adults, 1.30€ children 4–12, free for children under 4. Sept 25–Mar Mon–Fri 10am–1:30pm and 3:30–6:30pm, Sat–Sun and holidays 10am–6:30pm; Apr–May Mon–Fri 10am–2pm and 3:30–7pm, Sat–Sun 10am–7pm; June–Sept 24 daily 9am–8:30pm. Closed Jan 1, Oct 12, and Dec 25–26. Metro: Drassanes. Bus: 14, 18, 36, 57, 59, or 64.

Monestir de Pedralbes 🕸

One of the oldest buildings in Pedralbes (the city's wealthiest residential area) is this monastery founded in 1326 by Elisenda de Montcada, queen of Jaume II. Still a convent, the establishment is the mausoleum of the queen, who is buried in its Gothic church. Walk through the cloisters, with nearly two dozen arches on each side, rising three stories high. A small chapel contains the chief treasure of the monastery, murals by Ferrer Bassa, who was the major artist of Catalonia in the 1300s.

This monastery was a minor attraction until 1993, when 72 paintings and eight sculptures from the famed Thyssen-Bornemisza collection went on permanent display. Among the outstanding works of art are Fra Angelico's *The Virgin of Humility* and 20 paintings from the early German Renaissance period. Italian Renaissance paintings range from the end of the 15th century to the middle of the 16th century. They include works by Dosso Dossi, Lorenzo Lotto, Tintoretto, Veronese, and Titian. Such old masters as Rubens, Zurbarán, and Velázquez represent the baroque era.

Baixada del Monestir 9. (🕐 **93-203-92-82.** Admission 5.50€ adults, 3.50€ students and seniors over 64, free for children under 16. Tues–Sun 10am–2pm. Metro: Reina Elisenda. Bus: 22, 63, 64, 75, or 114.

Museu Arqueològic

The Museu Arqueològic occupies the former Palace of Graphic Arts built for the 1929 World's Fair. It reflects the long history of this Mediterranean port city, beginning with prehistoric Iberian artifacts. The collection includes articles from the Greek, Roman (glass, ceramics, mosaics, bronzes), and Carthaginian periods. Some of the more interesting relics were excavated in the ancient Greco-Roman city of Empúries in Catalonia; other parts of the collection came from the Balearic Islands.

Passeig de Santa Madrona 39–41, Parc de Montjuïc. (🕐 **93-423-21-49.** Admission 2.40€ adults, 1.80€ students, free for children under 16. Tues–Sat 9:30am–7pm; Sun 10am–2:30pm. Metro: Espanya. Bus: 55.

Museu Barbier-Mueller Art Precolombí 🕸🕸

Inaugurated by Queen Sofía in 1997, this is one of the most important collections of pre-Columbian art in the world. In the restored Palacio Nadal, which was built during the Middle Ages, the collection contains almost 6,000 pieces of tribal and ancient art. Josef Mueller (1887–1977) acquired the first pieces by 1908. Pre-Columbian cultures created religious, funerary, and ornamental objects of great stylistic variety with relatively simple means. Stone sculpture and ceramic objects are especially outstanding. For example, the Olmecs, who settled on the Gulf of Mexico at the beginning of the 1st millennium B.C., executed notable monumental sculpture in stone and magnificent figures in jade. Many exhibits focus on the Mayan culture, the most homogenous and widespread of its time, dating from 1000 B.C. Mayan artisans mastered painting, ceramics, and sculpture. Note the work by the pottery makers of the Lower Amazon, particularly those from the island of Marajó.

Carrer de Montcada 12–14. ℭ **93-310-45-16.** Admission 3€ adults, 1.50€ students, free for children under 12. Free to all first Sun of every month. Tues–Sat 10am–6pm; Sun and holidays 10am–3pm. Metro: Jaume I. Bus: 14, 17, 19, 39, 40, 45, or 51.

Museu d'Art Contemporani de Barcelona ✿

A soaring white edifice in the once-shabby but rebounding Raval district, the Museum of Contemporary Art is to Barcelona what the Pompidou Center is to Paris. Designed by the American architect Richard Meier, the building is a work of art itself, manipulating sunlight to offer brilliant, natural interior lighting. On display in the 6,875 sq. m (74,000 sq. ft.) of exhibit space is the work of modern luminaries such as Tàpies, Klee, Miró, and many others. The museum has a library, bookshop, and cafeteria.

Plaça dels Angels 1. ℭ **93-412-08-10.** Admission 7€ adults, 5.50€ students, free for children under 14. Wed–Sat 11am–7:30pm; Sun 10am–3pm. Metro: Plaça de Catalunya.

Museu d'Art Modern

This museum shares a wing of the Palau de la Ciutadella with the Catalán parliament. Constructed in the 1700s, it was once used as an arsenal. It later became a royal residence before being turned into a museum early in this century. Its collection of art focuses on the early 20th century and features the work of Catalán artists, including Martí Alsina, Vayreda, Casas, Fortuny, and Rusiñol. The collection encompasses some 19th-century Romantic and neoclassical works, as well as modernismo furniture (including designs by architect Puig i Cadafalch).

Plaça d'Armes, Parc de la Ciutadella. ℭ **93-319-57-28.** Admission 3€ adults, 2.10€ students, free for children under 7. Tues–Sat 10am–7pm; Sun 10am–2:30pm. Closed Jan 1, Dec 24, and May 1. Metro: Arc de Triomf. Bus: 14, 16, 17, 39, 40, 41, 51, 57, 59, or 64.

Museu d'Història de la Ciutat

Connected to the Royal Palace (see below), this museum traces the history of the city from its early days as a Roman colony to its role in the 1992 Summer Olympics. The museum is in a 15th-century mansion, the Padellás House. Many exhibits date from Roman days, with much else from medieval times.

Plaça del Rei. ℭ **93-315-11-11.** Admission 6€ adults, 2.50€ children and students. Tues–Sat 10am–2pm and 4–8pm; Sun 10am–2pm. Bus: 17, 19, or 45.

Museu Egipci de Barcelona

Spain's only museum dedicated specifically to Egyptology contains more than 250 pieces from the personal collection of founder Jordí Clos (owner of the Hotel Claris). On display are sarcophagi, jewelry, hieroglyphics, sculptures, and artwork. Exhibits focus on ancient Egyptians' everyday life, including education, social customs, religion, and food. The museum has its own lab for restorations. A library with more than 3,000 works is open to the public.

Calle Valencia 284. ℭ **93-488-01-88.** Admission 5.50€ adults, 4.50€ students and children. Mon–Sat 10am–8pm; Sun 10am–2pm. Guided tours Sat. Closed holidays. Metro: Passeig de Gràcia.

Museu Frederic Marés ✿✿

One of the biggest repositories of medieval sculpture in the region is the Frederic Marés Museum, just behind the cathedral. It's in an ancient palace with impressive interior courtyards, chiseled stone, and soaring ceilings, an ideal setting for the hundreds of polychrome sculptures. The sculpture section dates from pre-Roman times to the 20th century. In the same building is the Museu Sentimental, a collection of everyday items that help to illustrate life in Barcelona during the past 2 centuries. The ticket price includes admission to both museums.

Plaça de Sant Iú 5–6. ℭ **93-310-58-00.** Admission 3€ adults, free for children under 12. Tues–Sat 10am–7pm; Sun 10am–3pm. Metro: Jaume I. Bus: 17, 19, or 45.

useu Marítim ★★   In the former Royal Shipyards (Drassanes Reials), this 13th-century Gothic complex was used to construct ships for the Catalán-Aragonese rulers. The most outstanding exhibition is a reconstruction of *La Galería Real* of Don Juan of Austria, a lavish royal galley. Another special exhibit features a map by Gabriel de Vallseca that belonged to explorer Amerigo Vespucci.

Avinguda de las Drassanes s/n. (© **93-342-99-20**. Admission 5.40€ adults, 2.70€ children 7–16 and seniors, free for children under 7. Daily 10am–7pm. Metro: Drassanes. Bus: 14, 18, 36, 38, 57, 59, 64, or 91.

Palau Reial (Royal Palace) ★   The former palace of the counts of Barcelona, this later became the residence of the kings of Aragón. It is believed that Isabella and Ferdinand received Columbus here when he returned from his first voyage to the New World. Here, some say, the monarchs got their first look at a Native American. The Saló del Tinell, a banquet hall with a wood-paneled ceiling held up by half a dozen arches, dates from the 14th century. Rising five stories above the hall is the Torre del Reí Martí, a series of porticoed galleries.

Plaça del Rei. (© **93-315-11-11**. Admission 4€. Summer Tues–Sat 10am–8pm; off season Tues–Sat 10am–2pm and 4–8pm; year-round Sun 10am–3pm. Bus: 16, 17, 19, 22, 40, or 45.

oble Espanyol ★ *Kids*   In this re-created Spanish village built for the 1929 World's Fair, various regional architectural styles are reproduced. From the Levant to Galicia, 115 life-size reproductions of buildings and monuments represent the 10th to the 20th centuries. At the entrance, for example, stands a facsimile of the gateway to the walled city of Avila. The center of the village has an outdoor cafe where you can sit and have drinks. Numerous shops sell provincial crafts and souvenir items, and in some of them you can see artists at work, printing fabric and blowing glass. Since the 1992 Olympics, the village has included 14 restaurants, one disco, and eight musical bars. In addition, visitors can see an audiovisual presentation about Barcelona and Catalonia. Many families delight in the faux Spanish atmosphere, but the more discriminating find it a bit of a tourist trap—overly commercialized and somewhat cheesy. It's a matter of personal taste. You'll find lots of mediocre places to eat here.

Marqués de Comillas, Parc de Montjuïc. (© **93-325-78-66**. Admission 7€ adults, 3.70€ children 7–12, free for children under 7. Audiovisual hall free. Mon 9am–8pm; Tues–Thurs 9am–2am; Fri–Sat 9am–4am; Sun 9am–midnight. Metro: Espanya.

MORE ARCHITECTURAL HIGHLIGHTS

Architecture enthusiasts will find a wealth of fascinating sights in Barcelona. Primary among them, of course, are the fantastical creations of Antoni Gaudí and his modernismo cohorts.

Casa Amatller   Constructed in a cubical design with a Dutch gable, this building was created by Puig i Cadafalch in 1900. It stands in sharp contrast to its neighbor, the Gaudí-designed Casa Batlló (see below). The architecture of the Casa Amatller, imposed on an older structure, is a vision of ceramic, wrought iron, and sculptures. The structure combines grace notes of Flemish Gothic—especially on the finish of the facade—with elements of Catalán architecture. The gable outside is in the Flemish style. Inside, be sure to view the original Gothic revival interior, now the headquarters of the Institut Amatller d'Art Hispanic.

Passeig de Gràcia 41. (© **93-216-01-75**. Free admission. Mon–Sat 10am–7pm; Sun 10am–2pm. Metro: Passeig de Gràcia.

Casa Batlló   Next door to the Casa Amatller, Casa Batlló was designed by Gaudí in 1905. Using sensuous curves in iron and stone, the architect gave the facade a lavish baroque exuberance. The balconies have been compared to "sculpted waves." The upper part of the facade evokes animal forms, and delicate tiles spread across the design. The downstairs building is the headquarters of an insurance company. Many tourists walk inside for a view of Gaudí's interior, which is basically as he designed it. This is a place of business, so be discreet.

Passeig de Gràcia 43. (℗ **93-488-06-66.** Admission 10€ adults, 8€ children and students, free for children under 5. Mon–Sat 9am–2pm; Sun 9am–8pm. Metro: Passeig de Gràcia.

Casa de la Ciutat/Ayuntamiento   Constructed at the end of the 14th century, the building that houses the municipal government is one of the best examples of Gothic civil architecture in the Catalán Mediterranean style. Across the landmark square from the Palau de la Generalitat, it has been endlessly renovated and changed. Behind a neoclassical facade, the building has a splendid courtyard and staircase. Its major architectural highlights are the 15th-century Salón de Ciento (Room of the 100 Jurors) and the black marble Salón de las Crónicas (Room of the Chronicles). The Salón de Ciento, in particular, represents a medley of styles.

Plaça de Sant Jaume. (℗ **93-402-70-00.** Free admission. Sun 10am–3:30pm. Metro: Jaume I or Liceu.

Casa Lleó Morera   Between the Carrer del Consell de Cent and the Carrer d' Aragó stands one of the most famous buildings of the modernismo movement. It is one of the trio of structures called the Mançana de la Discòrdia (Block of Discord), an allusion to the mythical judgment of Paris. Three of Barcelona's most famous modernismo architects, including Gaudí, competed with their works along this block. Florid Casa Lleó, designed by Doménech i Montaner in 1905, was revolutionary in its day. That assessment still stands. The building is private, and the interior is closed to the public.

Passeig de Gràcia 35. No phone. Metro: Passeig de Gràcia.

Centre Cultural Caixa Catalunya   Commonly called La Pedrera or Casa Milà, this is the most famous apartment complex in Spain. Antoni Gaudí's imagination went wild when he planned its construction; he even included vegetable and fruit shapes in his sculptural designs. Controversial and much criticized upon its completion, today it stands as a classic example of modernismo architecture. The entire building was restored in 1996. The ironwork around the balconies forms an intricate maze, and the main gate has windowpanes shaped like turtle shells. Phantasmagorical chimneys known in Spanish as *espantabrujas* (witch-scarers) fill the rooftop. From the rooftop, you'll have a view of Gaudí's unfinished cathedral, **La Sagrada Família.** The Espai Gaudí (Gaudí Space) in the attic has an intriguing multimedia display of the controversial artist's work.

Passeig de Gràcia 92. (℗ **93-484-59-80** or 93-484-59-00. Admission and tour 6€ adults, 3€ students, free for children under 12. Rooftop tours daily 10am–6pm; English tours Mon–Fri 5pm. Metro: Diagonal.

OLYMPIC MEMORIES
Galería Olímpica   An enthusiastic celebration of the 1992 Olympic Games in Barcelona, this is one of the few museums in Europe exclusively devoted to sports and statistics. Exhibits include photos, costumes, and memorabilia, with heavy emphasis on the events' pageantry, the number of visitors who attended, and the fame the events brought to Barcelona. Of interest to statisticians, civic planners, and sports buffs, the gallery contains audiovisual information about the building programs that prepared the city for the onslaught of visitors. There are conference facilities, an auditorium, video recordings of athletic events, and archives. In the cellar of the Olympic Stadium's southeastern perimeter, the museum is most easily reached by entering the stadium's southern gate (Porta Sud).

Passeig Olímpic s/n, lower level. (📞) **93-426-06-60**. Admission 2.50€. Apr–Sept Mon–Fri 10am–1pm and 4–6pm; Oct–Mar Tues–Sat 10am–1pm and 4–6pm. Metro: Espanya. Bus: 13 or 50.

BULLFIGHTING

Cataláns do not pursue this art form, or sport, with as much fervor as Castilians. Nevertheless, you may want to attend a *corrida* (bullfight) in Barcelona. Bullfights are held from April to September, usually on Sunday at 6:30pm at Plaça de Toros Monumental, Gran Vía de les Corts Catalanes (📞) **93-245-58-04**). Buy tickets in advance from the office at Muntaner 24 (📞) **93-453-38-21**). Tickets cost 13€ to 95€.

PARKS & GARDENS

Barcelona isn't just museums; much of its life takes place outside, in its unique parks and gardens. See the entry on Parc Güell under "The Top Attractions," earlier in this chapter.

Tibidabo Mountain (⭐), north of the port, offers the finest panoramic view of Barcelona. A funicular takes you up 488m (1,600 ft.) to the summit. The ideal time to visit this summit (the culmination of the Sierra de Collserola) is at sunset, when the city lights are on. At the time of the Olympics, a 255m (850-ft.) communications tower, Mirador Torre de Collserola, was built. Although attacked by traditionalists for destroying the natural beauty of the mountain, Torre de Collserola offers the most panoramic views in all of Catalonia. It costs 3€ to go up the tower. From Plaça de Catalunya, take bus no. 58 to Avinguda del Tibidabo, where you can board a special bus to the funicular. Hop aboard to scale the mountain. The funicular runs daily when the park is open, starting 20 minutes before the Fun Fair. The fare is 2.70€ each way.

In the southern part of the city, the mountain park of **Montjuïc** has splashing fountains, gardens, outdoor restaurants, and museums, making for quite an outing. A re-created Spanish village, the Poble Espanyol, and the Joan Miró museum are also in the park. (See individual listings, above, for information.) There are many walks and vantage points for viewing the Barcelona skyline.

The park was the site of several Olympic events. An illuminated fountain display, the **Fuentes Luminosas,** is on view at Plaça de la Font Magica, near the Plaça d'Espanya. It runs from 8 to 11pm every Saturday and Sunday from October to May, from 9pm to midnight on Thursday, Saturday, and Sunday from June to September.

To reach the top, take bus no. 61 from Plaça d'Espanya or the Montjuïc funicular. The funicular is open from June 13 to September 30 daily from 11am to 10pm. In winter it operates daily from 10:45am to 8pm. The round-trip fare is 3.60€.

Parc de la Ciutadella, Avinguda Wellington s/n (📞) **93-225-67-80**), gets its name (Park of the Citadel) because it is the site of a former fortress. After Philip V won the War of the Spanish Succession (Barcelona was on the losing side), he got his revenge: He ordered that the "traitorous" residential suburb be leveled. In its place rose a citadel. In the mid–19th century it, too, was leveled, but some architectural evidence survives in a governor's palace and an arsenal. Today lakes, gardens, and promenades fill most of the park, which also holds a **zoo** (see "Especially for Kids," below) and the **Museu d'Art Modern** (see "If You Have More Time," earlier in this chapter). Gaudí contributed to the monumental fountain in the park when he was a student; the lampposts are also his. The park is open daily from May to September from 8am to 9pm; from October to April from 10am to 5pm. Admission is 12€ adults, 7.50€ children 3 to 12. To reach the park, take the Metro to Ciutadella.

Parc de Joan Miró, near the Plaça de Espanya, is dedicated to one of Catalonia's most famous artists. It dates to the 1990s and occupies an entire block. One of Barcelona's most popular parks, it is often called Parc de l'Escorxador (slaughterhouse), a reference to its former occupant. Its main features are an esplanade and a pond from which a giant sculpture by Miró, *Woman and Bird,* rises. Palm, pine, and eucalyptus trees, as well as playgrounds and pergolas, complete the picture. To reach the park, take the Metro to Espanya. It is open throughout the day.

ESPECIALLY FOR KIDS

The Catalán people have great affection for children, and although many of the attractions of Barcelona are for adults, an array of amusements is designed for the young—and the young at heart.

Children from 3 to 7 have their own place at the **Museu de la Ciéncia,** Teodor Roviralta 55 (© **93-212-60-50**). "Clik del Nens" is a science playground just for them where they can walk on a giant piano, make bubbles, lift a hippopotamus, and enter an air tunnel. They observe, experiment, and examine nature in an environment created just for them. Special 1-hour guided sessions take place daily. (See "If You Have More Time," earlier in this chapter.)

At the **Poble Espanyol,** Marqués de Comillas, Parc de Montjuïc (© **93-325-78-66**), kids find a Spanish version of Disneyland. Frequent fiestas enliven the place, and it's fun for everybody, young and old. (See "If You Have More Time," earlier in this chapter.)

Only an hour's drive from Barcelona and most often visited from the city of Tarragona (see chapter 12), **Port Aventura** (© **90-220-22-20**) lies at Autovéia Salou/Vila-Seca Km 2, outside the town of Salou, which is 11km (7 miles) south of Reus, reached after an 13km (8-mile) drive northwest of Tarragona. This park from 1995 promises "the adventure of one's life" in a series of dangerous-appearing rides, plus steam engine trips, water slides, and simulated boat trips through places as exotic as the American West or Polynesia. The cost is 32€ to 34€ adults or 25€ to 27€ kids 11 and under. From June 23 to September 16, it is open daily from 10am to midnight. Off-season hours are daily from 10am to 7pm.

Parc d'Atraccions (Tibidabo)   On top of Tibidabo, this park combines tradition with modernity—rides from the beginning of the century complete with 1990s novelties. In summer the place takes on a carnival-like atmosphere.

Plaça Tibidabo 3–4, Cumbre del Tibidabo. © **93-211-79-42**. Ticket for all rides 20€, 8€ adults over 60, free for children under 4. May to mid-June Wed–Sun noon–7pm; mid-June to Sept Tues–Sun noon–8pm; off season Sat–Sun and holidays 11am–10pm. Transit: Bus no. 58 to Avinguda del Tibidabo to Tramvía Blau, then take funicular.

Parc Zoològic ⭐   Modern, with barless enclosures, this ranks as Spain's top zoo. One of the most unusual attractions is the famous albino gorilla Snowflake (Copito de Nieve), the only one of its kind in captivity in the world. The main entrances to the Ciutadella Park are on the Passeig de Pujades and Passeig de Picasso.

Parc de la Ciutadella. © **93-225-67-80**. Admission 12€ adults, 7.50€ students and children, 6.60€ seniors, free for children under 3. Summer daily 10am–7pm; off season daily 10am–5pm. Metro: Ciutadella.

ORGANIZED TOURS

Pullmantur, Gran Vía de les Corts Catalanes 645 (© **93-317-12-97;** Metro: Plaça de Catalunya), offers a number of tours and excursions with English-speaking guides. For a preview of the city, you can take a morning tour. They depart from the company's terminal at 9:30am, and take in the cathedral, the Gothic Quarter, the monument to Columbus, and the Spanish Village and the Olympic Stadium. Tickets cost 33€. An afternoon tour leaves at 3:30pm and visits some of the most outstanding architecture in the Eixample, including Gaudí's La Sagrada Família, Parc Güell, and a stop at the Picasso Museum. This tour costs 33€.

Pullmantur also offers several excursions outside Barcelona. The daily tour of the monastery of Montserrat includes a visit to the Royal Basilica to view the famous sculpture of the Black Virgin. This tour, which costs 42€ to 50€ departs at 9:30am and returns at 2:30pm to the company's terminal. A full-day Girona-Figueres tour includes a visit to Girona's cathedral and its Jewish quarter, plus a trip to the Dalí museum. This excursion, which costs 85€, leaves Barcelona at 8:30am and returns at approximately 6pm (June–Sept only). Call ahead—a minimum number of participants is required or the tour isn't conducted.

Another company that offers tours of Barcelona and the surrounding countryside is **Juliatours,** Ronda Universitat 5 (© **93-317-64-54**). Itineraries and prices are similar to Pullmantur's. One tour, the "Visita Ciudad Artística," focuses on the city's artistic significance. The tour also passes Casa Lleó Morera, designed in 1905 by Doménech i Montaner in a floral modernist mode, and takes in many of Gaudí's brilliant buildings, including the Casa Milá (La Pedrera) and La Sagrada Família. Also included is a visit to the Museu Picasso, depending on the day of your tour. This tour, which leaves at 3:30pm and returns at 7pm, costs 33€.

7 Active Pursuits

AN OUTSTANDING FITNESS CENTER

The city's main fitness center is adjacent to the Olympic Stadium in an indoor/outdoor complex whose main attractions are its two beautifully designed swimming pools. Built for the 1992 Summer Olympics, the facility contains a health club and gym. It's open to the public for 8€ for a full day's pass. For the address and hours, see the Piscina Bernardo Picornell listing in "Swimming," below.

GOLF

One of the city's best courses, **Club de Golf Vallromanas,** Afueras s/n, Vallromanas, Barcelona (© **93-572-90-64**), is 20 minutes north of the center by car. Nonmembers who reserve tee times in advance are welcome to play. The greens fee is 75€ on weekdays, 125€ on weekends. The club is open Wednesday through Monday from 9am to 9pm. Established in 1972, it is the site of Spain's most important golf tournament.

Reial Club de Golf El Prat, El Prat de Llobregat (© **93-379-02-78**), is a prestigious club that allows nonmembers to play under two conditions: They must have a handicap issued by the governing golf body in their home country; and they must prove membership in a golf club at home. The club has two 18-hole par-72 courses. Greens fees are 60€ Monday through Friday. Weekends are for members only. From Barcelona, follow Avinguda Once de Septiembre past the airport to Barrio de San Cosme. From there follow the signs along Carrer Prat to the golf course.

SWIMMING

Most city residents head to the beaches near the Vila Olímpica or Sitges when they feel like swimming. If you're looking for an uncrowded pool, you'll find one at the **Esportiu Piscina DeStampa,** Carrer Rosich 12, in the Hospitalet district

(© **93-334-56-00**). It's open Monday through Friday from 7:30am to 10pm, Saturday from 10am to 2pm and 4 to 8pm, and Sunday from 10am to 2pm. Weekday admission is 2.38€; Saturday and Sunday, it's 3.75€.

A much better choice, however, allows you to swim where some Olympic events took place, at **Piscina Bernardo Picornell,** Avinguda de Estadi 30–40, on Montjuïc (© **93-423-40-41**). Adjacent to the Olympic Stadium, it incorporates two of the best swimming pools in Spain (1 indoors, 1 outdoors). Custom-built for the Olympics, they're open to the public Monday through Friday from 7am to midnight, Saturday from 7am to 9pm, and Sunday from 7am to 4pm. Admission costs 8.10€ and allows full use throughout the day of whichever pool is open, plus the gymnasium, the sauna, and the whirlpools. Bus no. 61 makes frequent runs from the Plaça d'Espanya.

8 Shopping

For fashion and style, Barcelonans look more to Paris and their own sense of design than to Madrid. *Moda joven* (young fashion) is all the rage.

If your time and budget are limited, you may want to patronize Barcelona's major department store, **El Corte Inglés,** for an overview of Catalán merchandise at reasonable prices. Barcelona is filled with boutiques, but clothing is expensive, even though the city has been a textile center for centuries.

Markets (see below) are very popular and are suitable places to search for good buys.

THE SHOPPING SCENE

If you're a window shopper, stroll along the **Passeig de Gràcia** from the Avinguda Diagonal to the Plaça de Catalunya. Along the way, you'll see some of the most elegant and expensive shops in Barcelona, plus an assortment of splendid turn-of-the-20th-century buildings and cafes, many with outdoor tables. Another prime spot is the **Rambla de Catalunya** (upper Rambles).

Another shopping expedition is to the **Mercat de la Boquería,** Rambla 91 (© **93-318-25-84**), near Carrer del Carme. Here you'll see a wide array of straw bags and regional products, along with a handsome display of the food you're likely to eat later: fruits, vegetables (artfully displayed), breads, cheeses, meats, and fish. Vendors sell their wares Monday through Saturday from 8am to 8pm.

In the **old quarter** not far from Plaça de Catalunya, the principal shopping streets are all five Rambles, plus Carrer del Pi, Carrer de la Palla, and Avinguda Portal de l'Angel, to cite some major thoroughfares. Moving north in the **Eixample** are Passeig de Catalunya, Passeig de Gràcia, and Rambla de Catalunya. Even farther north, **Avinguda Diagonal** is a major shopping boulevard. Other prominent shopping streets include Bori i Fontesta, Vía Augusta, Carrer Muntaner, Travessera de Gràcia, and Carrer de Balmes.

In general, shopping hours are Monday through Saturday from 9am to 8pm. Smaller shops may close from 1:30 to 4pm.

The **American Visitors Bureau,** Gran Vía 591 (© **93-301-01-50**), between Rambla de Catalunya and Carrer de Balmes, will pack and ship your purchases and gifts, and even handle excess luggage and personal effects. The company operates a travel agency that books flights and hotel accommodations. It's open Monday through Friday from 9am to 1pm and 4 to 7pm, Saturday by appointment only.

Watch for sales (*rebajas,* or *rebaixes* in Catalán) in mid-January, late July, and August. Stores getting rid of their winter or summer stock often offer heavy discounts.

SHOPPING A TO Z

Prices in Barcelona tend to be slightly lower than in London, Paris, and Rome.

You'll find stylish, attractively designed **clothing** and **shoes. Decorative objects** are often good buys. In the city of Miró, Tàpies, and Picasso, **art** is a major business and the reason gallery owners from around the world visit. You'll find dozens of galleries, especially in the Barri Gòtic and around the Picasso Museum. Barcelona is also noted for its **flea markets,** where good purchases are always available if you search hard enough.

Antiques abound, but rising prices have put many of them beyond the means of the average shopper. However, the list below includes some shops where you can at least look. Most shoppers from abroad settle happily for handicrafts, and the city is rich in offerings, ranging from pottery to handmade furniture. Barcelona has been in the business of creating and designing **jewelry** since the 17th century, and its offerings and prices are of the widest possible range.

What follows is only a limited selection of some of the hundreds of shops in Barcelona.

ANTIQUES

El Bulevard des Antiquaris   This 70-unit complex just off one of the town's most aristocratic avenues has a huge collection of art and antiques assembled in a series of boutiques. There's a cafe/bar on the upper level. Summer hours are Monday through Friday from 9:30am to 8:30pm; winter hours are Monday from 4:30 to 8:30pm, Tuesday through Saturday from 10:30am to 8:30pm. Some boutiques keep shorter hours. Passeig de Gràcia 55. No phone. Metro: Passeig de Gràcia.

Sala d'Art Artur Ramón   One of the finest antiques and art dealers in Barcelona can be found at this three-level emporium. Set on a narrow flagstone-covered street near Plaça del Pi (the center of the antiques district), it stands opposite a tiny square, the Placeta al Carrer de la Palla. The store, which has been operated by four generations of men named Artur Ramón, also operates branches nearby and is known for its 19th- and 20th-century painting and sculpture, 19th and 20th century drawings and engravings, and 18th and 19th century decorative arts and objets d'art along with rare ceramics, porcelain, and glassware. Prices are high, as you'd expect, for items of quality and lasting value. Open Monday through Saturday from 10am to 1:30pm and 5 to 8pm. Palla 23. ✆ **93-302-59-70.** Metro: Jaume I.

Urbana   Urbana sells an array of architectural remnants (usually from torn-down mansions), antique furniture, and reproductions of brass hardware. There are antique and reproduction marble mantelpieces, wrought-iron gates and garden seats, even carved wood fireplaces with the modernismo look. It's an impressive, albeit costly, array of merchandise. Open Monday through Friday from 10am to 2pm and 4:30 to 8pm. Còrsega 258. ✆ **93-218-70-36.** Metro: Hospital Sant Pau.

BOOKS

LAIE   The best selection of English-language books, including travel maps and guides, is at LAIE, a block from the Gran Vía de les Corts Catalanes. It's open Monday through Friday from 10am to 9pm, Saturday from 10:30am to 9pm. The bookshop has an upstairs cafe with international newspapers and a little terrace. It serves breakfast, lunch (salad bar), and dinner. The cafe is open Monday through Saturday from 9am to 1am. The shop also schedules cultural events, including art exhibits and literary presentations. Pau Claris 85. ✆ **93-318-17-39.** Metro: Plaça de Catalunya or Urquinaona.

DEPARTMENT STORES

El Corte Inglés   One of the local representatives of the largest and most glamorous department store chain in Spain, this branch sells a wide variety of merchandise. It ranges from Spanish handicrafts to high-fashion items, from Catalán records to food. The store has restaurants and cafes and offers consumer-related services, such as a travel agent. It has a department that will mail your purchases home. Not only that, but you can have shoes reheeled, hair and beauty treatments, and food and drink in the rooftop cafe. Open Monday through Saturday from 10am to 10pm. El Corte Inglés has two other Barcelona locations: Avinguda Diagonal 617–619 (✆ **93-366-71-00;** Metro: María Cristina), and Avinguda Diagonal 471 (✆ **93-493-48-00;** Metro: Hospital Clinic). Plaça de Catalunya 14. ✆ **93-306-38-00.** Metro: Plaça de Catalunya.

DESIGNER HOUSEWARES

Vinçón   Fernando Amat's Vinçón is the best in the city, with 10,000 products—everything from household items to the best in Spanish contemporary furnishings. Its mission is to purvey good design, period. Housed in the former home of artist Ramón Casas—a contemporary of Picasso's during his Barcelona stint—the showroom is filled with the best Spain has. The always-creative window displays alone are worth the trek: Expect *anything.* Open Monday through Saturday from 10am to 8:30pm. Passeig de Gràcia 96. ✆ **93-215-60-50.** Metro: Diagonal.

FABRICS & WEAVINGS

Coses de Casa   Appealing fabrics and weavings are displayed in this 19th-century store, called simply "Household Items." Many are hand-woven in Majorca, their boldly geometric patterns inspired by Arab motifs of centuries ago. The fabric, for the most part, is 50% cotton, 50% linen; much of it would make excellent upholstery material. Open Monday through Friday from 10am to 2pm and 4:30 to 8pm, Saturday from 10am to 2pm and 5 to 8pm. Plaça de Sant Josep Oriol 5. ✆ **93-302-73-28.** Metro: Jaume I or Eliceo.

FASHION

Adolfo Domínguez   This shop, one of many outlets spread across Spain and Europe, displays fashion that has earned for the store the appellation of "The Spanish Armani." There's one big difference. Domínguez's suits for both women and men, unlike Armani, are designed for those with some hips. They cover all ages at their stores including the youth market. As one fashion critic said of their latest offerings, "They are austere but not strict, forgivingly cut in urbane earth tones." Open Monday through Saturday from 10am to 8:30pm. Passeig de Gràcia 32. ✆ **93-487-41-70.**

Antonio Miró   This shop is devoted exclusively to the clothing design of Miró, but without the Groc label (see below). It carries fashionable men's and women's clothing. Before buying anything at Groc, survey the wares at this store, which seems even more stylish. Open Monday through Saturday from 10am to 2pm and 4:30 to 8:30pm. Consejo de Ciento 349. ✆ **93-487-06-70.** Metro: Passeig de Gràcia.

Groc   One of the most stylish shops in Barcelona, Groc is expensive but filled with high-quality men's and women's apparel made from the finest natural fibers. The men's store is downstairs, the women's store one flight up. Open Monday through Saturday from 10am to 2pm and 4:30 to 8:30pm (the men's department stays open all day). August hours are Monday through Friday from 11am to 2pm and 5 to 8pm. Rambla de Catalunya 100. ✆ **93-215-74-74.** Metro: Plaça de Catalunya.

Textil i d'Indumentaria Operated as a showcase for Catalonian design and ingenuity by Barcelona's Museum of Textile and Fashion, and set on a medieval street across from the Picasso Museum, this shop proudly displays and sells clothing for men, women, and children, all of which is either designed or at least manufactured within the region. Inventories include shoes, men's and women's sportswear and formal wear, jewelry, teddy bears, suitcases and handbags, umbrellas, and towels, each shaped and cut by up-and-coming Cataláns. Two of the most famous designers include menswear specialist Antonio Miró (no relation to the 1950s and '60s artist Joan Miró) and women's clothing designer Lydia Delgado. Open Tuesday through Saturday from 10am to 8:30pm, and Sunday from 10am to 3pm. Carrer Montcada 12. (℗ **93-310-74-04**. Metro: Jaume I.

GALLERIES

Art Picasso Here you can get good lithographic reproductions of works by Picasso, Miró, and Dalí, as well as T-shirts emblazoned with the masters' designs. Tiles often carry their provocatively painted scenes. Open Monday through Saturday from 10am to 7:30pm, Sunday from 10am to 7:30pm. Tapinería 10. (℗ **93-310-49-57**. Metro: Jaume I.

Sala Parés Established in 1840, this is a Barcelona institution. The Maragall family recognizes and promotes the work of Spanish and Catalán painters and sculptors, many of whom have gone on to acclaim. Paintings are displayed in a two-story amphitheater, with high-tech steel balconies supported by a quartet of steel columns evocative of Gaudí. Exhibitions of the most avant-garde art in Barcelona change about every 3 weeks. Open Monday through Saturday from 10:30am to 2pm and 4:30 to 8:30pm. Petritxol 5. (℗ **93-318-70-20**. Metro: Plaça de Catalunya.

LEATHER

Loewe Barcelona's biggest branch of this prestigious Spanish leather-goods chain is in one of the best-known modernismo buildings in the city. Everything is top-notch, from the elegant showroom to the expensive merchandise to the helpful salespeople. The company exports its goods to branches throughout Asia, Europe, and North America. Open Monday through Saturday from 10am to 8:30pm. Passeig de Gràcia 35. (℗ **93-216-04-00**. Metro: Passeig de Gràcia.

MARKETS

El Encants antiques market is held every Monday, Wednesday, Friday, and Saturday in Plaça de les Glòries Catalanes (Metro: Glòries). Go anytime during the day to survey the selection.

Coins and postage stamps are traded and sold in **Plaça Reial** on Sunday from 10am to 8pm. It's off the southern flank of Les Rambles (Metro: Drassanes). A book and coin market is held at the Ronda Sant Antoni every Sunday from 10am to 2pm (Metro: Universitat).

MUSIC

Casa Beethoven Established in 1920, this store carries the most complete collection of sheet music in town. The collection naturally focuses on the works of Spanish and Catalán composers. Music lovers might make some rare discoveries. Open Monday through Friday from 9am to 2pm and 4 to 8pm, Saturday from 9am to 1:30pm and 5 to 8pm. Les Rambles 97. (℗ **93-301-48-26**. Metro: Liceu.

PORCELAIN

Kastoria This large store near the cathedral is an authorized Lladró dealer, and stocks a big selection of the famous porcelain. It also carries many kinds of leather goods, including purses, suitcases, coats, and jackets. Open Monday through Saturday from 10am to 7pm, Sunday from 10am to 2pm. Avinguda Catedra 6–8. ☏ **93-310-04-11.** Metro: Plaça de Catalunya.

POTTERY

Artesana i Coses   Here you'll find pottery and porcelain from every major region of Spain. Most of the pieces are heavy and thick-sided—designs in use for centuries. Open Monday through Saturday from 10:30am to 8pm, Sunday from 11am to 3pm. Placeta de Montcada 2. ☏ **93-319-54-13.** Metro: Jaume I.

Itaca   Here you'll find a wide array of handmade pottery from Catalonia and other parts of Spain, plus Portugal, Mexico, and Morocco. The merchandise has been selected for its basic purity, integrity, and simplicity. Open Monday through Saturday from 10am to 8:30pm. Carrer Ferran 26. ☏ **93-301-30-44.** Metro: Liceu.

SHOPPING CENTERS & MALLS

The landscape has exploded since the mid-1980s with the construction of several American-style shopping malls. Some are too far from the city's historic core to be convenient for most foreign visitors, but here's a description of some of the city's best.

Centre Comercial Barcelona Glòries   Built in 1995, this is the largest shopping center in downtown Barcelona, a three-story emporium of the good life. It's based on the California model but is crammed into a distinctly urban neighborhood. It has more than 100 shops, some posh, others much less so. Although there's a typical shopping mall anonymity to some aspects of this place, you'll still be able to find almost anything you might have forgotten while packing. Open Monday through Saturday from 10am to 10pm. Avinguda Diagonal 208. ☏ **93-486-04-04.** Metro: Glòries.

Diagonal Center (Lilla Diagonal)   This two-story mall contains stores devoted to luxury products, as well as a scattering of bars, cafes, and simple but cheerful restaurants favored by office workers and shoppers. It has about half the number of shops the Centre Comercial Barcelona Glòries (see above) offers. Built in the early 1990s, it even has an area devoted to video games where teenagers can make as much electronic noise as they want while their guardians shop. Open Monday through Saturday from 10am to 9:30pm. Avinguda Diagonal 557. ☏ **93-444-00-00.** Metro: María Cristina.

Maremagnum   The best thing about this place is its position adjacent to the waterfront on Barcelona's historic seacoast; it's also well suited to outdoor promenades. Built in the early 1990s near the Columbus Monument, it contains many shops, 12 cinemas, an IMAX, and a wide variety of restaurants, pubs, and discos catering to a very young crowd. Nightlife here begins at 11pm, lasting until dawn. You might get the idea that only a few of the people who come here are interested in shopping. Open Monday through Saturday from 11am to 10pm. Moll d'Espanya s/n. ☏ **93-225-81-00.** Metro: Drassanes.

Poble Espanyol   This is not technically a shopping mall but a "village" (see "If You Have More Time," earlier in this chapter). It has about 35 stores selling typical folk crafts from every part of Spain: glassware, leather goods, pottery, paintings, carvings, and so forth. Store hours vary, but you can visit any time during the day. Marqués de Comillas, Parc de Montjuïc. ☏ **93-325-78-66.** Metro: Espanya, then take free red double-decker bus to Montjuïc, or bus no. 13 or 50 (1.05€).

9 Barcelona After Dark

Barcelona comes alive at night, and the array of nighttime diversions is staggering. There is something to interest almost everyone and to fit most pocketbooks. The **funicular ride** to Tibidabo and the illuminated **fountains** of Montjuïc are especially popular, and fashionable **clubs** operate in nearly every major district of the city. For families, the **amusement parks** are the busiest venues.

Locals sometimes opt for an evening in the *tascas* **(taverns),** or perhaps settling in for a bottle of wine at a cafe, an easy and inexpensive way to spend an evening people-watching. Serious drinking in pubs and cafes begins by 10 or 11pm. But for the most fashionable bars and discos, Barcelonans delay their entrances until at least 1am.

Your best source of local information is a little magazine called *Guía del Ocio,* which previews "La Semana de Barcelona" (This Week in Barcelona). It's in Spanish, but most of its listings will probably be comprehensible. Almost every news kiosk along Les Rambles carries it.

Nightlife begins for many Barcelonans with a **promenade** *(paseo)* along Les Rambles in the early evening, usually from 5 to 7pm. Then things quiet down a bit until a second surge of energy brings out the crowds again, from 9 to 11pm. After that the esplanade clears out quite a bit, but it's always lively.

If you're very young, you might want to check out the nightlife scene at **Maremagnum** (see "Shopping Centers & Malls," above).

If you've been scared off by press reports about Les Rambles between the Plaça de Catalunya and the Columbus Monument, know that the area's really been cleaned up in the past decade. Still, you will feel safer along the Rambla de Catalunya, in the Eixample, north of the Plaça de Catalunya. This street and its offshoots are lively at night, with many cafes and bars. During the Franco era the center of club life was the cabaret-packed district near the south of Les Rambles, but the area is known for nighttime muggings—use caution if you go there.

Cultural events are also big in the Catalonian repertoire, and old-fashioned **dance halls** survive in some places. Although **disco** has waned in some parts of the world, it is still going strong in Barcelona. Decaying movie houses, abandoned garages, and long-closed vaudeville theaters have been taken over and restored as nightlife venues.

Flamenco isn't the rage here that it is in Seville and Madrid, but it still has its devotees. The city is also filled with **jazz** aficionados. Best of all, the old tradition of the **music hall** with vaudeville lives on.

In the summer you'll see plenty of free entertainment—everything from opera to monkey acts—just by walking the streets. The Rambles is a particularly good place to watch.

THE PERFORMING ARTS

Culture is deeply ingrained in the Catalán soul, and the performing arts are strong. In fact, some take place on the street, especially along Les Rambles. Crowds often gather around a singer or a mime. A city square will suddenly come alive on Saturday night with a spontaneous festival; "tempestuous, surging, irrepressible life and brio," is how the writer Rose MacCauley described it.

Long a city of the arts, Barcelona experienced a cultural decline during the Franco years, but now it is filled once again with the best opera, symphonic, and choral music. At the venues listed here, unless otherwise specified, ticket prices depend on the event.

CLASSICAL MUSIC

La Casa dels Músics   Pianist Luis de Arquer has established a small chamber company in his 19th-century Gràcia home. Here in an intimate atmosphere, small-scale productions of *opera buffa* and *bel canto* are presented, usually beginning at 9pm (but you must call to confirm if presentations will go on and to make reservations). For the true music lover, this could be your most charming evening in Barcelona. Carrer Encarnació 25. © **93-284-99-20.** Tickets 20€. Metro: Fontana.

Palau de la Música Catalana   In a city chock-full of architectural highlights, this one stands out. In 1908 Lluis Doménech i Montaner, a Catalán architect, designed this structure using stained glass, ceramics, statuary, and ornate lamps, among other elements. It stands today, restored, as a classic example of modernismo. Concerts and leading recitals take place here. Open daily from 10am to 3:30pm; box office open Monday through Saturday from 10am to 9pm. Sant Francesc de Paula 2. © **93-295-72-00.** Metro: Urquinaona.

THEATER

Theater is presented in the Catalán language and therefore will not be of interest to most visitors. For those who do speak the language, or perhaps are fluent in Spanish (even then, though, you're unlikely to understand much), here are some recommendations.

Gran Teatre del Liceu   This monument to Belle Epoque extravagance, a 2,700-seat opera house, is one of the grandest theaters in the world. It was designed by the Catalán architect Josep Oriol Mestves. On January 31, 1994, fire gutted the opera house, shocking Catalonians, many of whom regarded this place as the very citadel of their culture. The government immediately vowed to rebuild, and the new Liceu was reopened in 1999, well before the millennium deadline set by the cultural czars. Rambla dels Caputxins. © **93-485-99-13.** Metro: Liceu.

Mercat de Los Flors   Housed in a building constructed for the 1929 International Exhibition at Montjuïc, this is the other major Catalán theater. Peter Brook first used it as a theater for a 1983 presentation of *Carmen.* The theater focuses on innovators in drama, dance, and music, as well as European modern dance companies. The 999-seat house has a restaurant overlooking the city rooftops. Lleida 59. © **93-426-18-75.** Tickets 6€–12€. Metro: Espanya or Pueblo Seco.

Teatre Lliure   This self-styled free theater is the city's leading Catalán-language playhouse. Once a workers' union, the building has been the headquarters of a theater cooperative since 1976. Its directors are famous in Barcelona for their bold presentations, including works by Bertolt Brecht, Luigi Pirandello, Jean Genet (who wrote about Barcelona), and even Molière and Shakespeare. New dramas by Catalán playwrights are also presented. Montseny 47. © **93-218-92-51.** Tickets 12€–19€. Metro: Fontana.

Teatre Nacional de Catalunya   Josep María Flotats heads this major company. The actor-director trained in the tradition of theater repertory, working in Paris at Théâtre de la Villa and the Comédie Française. His company presents both classic and contemporary plays. The theater is closed in August. Plaça de les Arts 1. © **93-306-57-06.** Tickets 18€–21€. Metro: Plaza de las Glorias.

FLAMENCO

El Tablao de Carmen   This club presents a highly rated flamenco cabaret in the re-created village. You can go early and explore the village, and even have dinner. This place has long been a tourist favorite. The club is open Tuesday through Sunday from 8pm to past midnight—around 1am on weeknights, often until 2 or 3am on weekends, depending on business. The first show is always at 9:30pm; the second show is at 11:30pm on Tuesday, Wednesday, Thursday, and Sunday, and midnight on Friday and Saturday. Reservations are recommended. Poble Espanyol de Montjuïc. ℂ **93-325-68-95**. Dinner and show 53€–75€; drink and show 28€. Metro: Espanya.

Los Tarantos Established in 1963, this is the oldest flamenco club in Barcelona, with a rigid allegiance to the tenets of Andalusian flamenco. Its roster of artists changes regularly. They often come from Seville or Córdoba, stamping out their well-rehearsed passions in ways that make the audience appreciate the arcane nuances of Spain's most intensely controlled dance idiom. No food is served. The place resembles a cabaret theater, where up to 120 people at a time can drink, talk quietly, and savor the nuances of a dance that combines elements from medieval Christian and Muslim traditions. Each show lasts around 1¼ hours. Shows are Monday through Saturday at 10pm and midnight. Plaça Reial 17. ℂ **93-318-30-67**. Cover (includes 1 drink) 24€. Metro: Liceu.

Tablao Flamenco Cordobés At the southern end of Les Rambles, a short walk from the harbor front, you'll hear the strum of the guitar, the sound of hands clapping rhythmically, and the haunting sound of the flamenco, a tradition here since 1968. Head upstairs to an Andalusian-style room where performances take place with the traditional *cuadro flamenco*—singers, dancers, and guitarist. Cordobés is said to be the city's best flamenco showcase. The show with dinner begins at 8:30pm, the show without dinner at 10pm. Three shows are offered nightly with dinner, at 8pm and 9:45pm; without dinner at 10pm. Reservations are required. Les Rambles 35. ℂ **93-317-57-11**. Dinner and show 50€; 1 drink and show 29€. Metro: Drassanes.

CABARET, JAZZ & MORE

Barcelona Pipa Club If you find the Harlem Jazz Club (below) small, wait until you get to the "Pipe Club." Long beloved by jazz aficionados, this is for true devotees. Ring the buzzer and you'll be admitted (at least we hope you will), then climb two flights up in a run-down building. This is hardly a trendy nightclub, with five rooms decorated with displays or photographs of pipes. Music ranges from New Orleans jazz to Brazilian rhythms. The club and its comfortable bar are open daily from 10pm to 4am. Plaça Reial 3. ℂ **93-302-47-32**. Metro: Liceu.

Espai Barroc One of Barcelona's most culture-conscious nightspots occupies some of the showplace rooms of the Palau Dalmases, a stately palace in the Barri Gòtic. In a room lined with grand art objects, you can listen to recorded opera arias and sip glasses of beer or wine. The most appealing night is Thursday—beginning at 11pm, 10 singers perform a roster of arias from assorted operas, one of which is invariably *Carmen*. Since its establishment in 1996, the place has thrived. Almost everyone around the bar apparently has at least heard of the world's greatest operas, and some can even discuss them more or less brilliantly. Open Tuesday through Sunday from 8pm to 2am. Carrer Montcada 20. ℂ **93-310-06-73**. Cover on Thurs only (includes 1 drink) 18€. Metro: Jaume I.

Harlem Jazz Club On a nice street in the Ciutat Vella, this is one of Barcelona's oldest and finest jazz clubs. It's also one of the smallest, with just a handful of tables. No matter how many times you've heard "Black Orpheus" or "The Girl from Ipanema," they always sound new again here. Music is viewed with a certain reverence; no one talks when the performers are on. Live jazz, blues, tango, Brazilian music—the sounds are always fresh. Open Tuesday through Thursday and Sunday from 8pm to 4am, until 5am Friday and Saturday. Live music begins at 10:30pm on Tuesday through Thursday and Sunday, and 11:30pm and 1am on Friday and Saturday. The second set is at midnight (1am Fri–Sat). Comtessa de Sobradiel 8. © **93-310-07-55.** 1 drink minimum. Closed 2 weeks in Aug. Metro: Jaume I.

Jamboree   In the heart of the Barri Gòtic, this has long been one of the city's premier locations for good blues and jazz, although it doesn't feature jazz every night. Sometimes a world-class performer will appear here, but most likely it'll be a younger group. The crowd knows its stuff and demands only the best talent. On our last visit, we were entertained by an evening of Chicago blues. Or you might find that a Latin dance band has been scheduled. Open daily from 10:30pm to 5am; shows begin at midnight. Plaça Reial 17. © **93-301-75-64.** Cover 6€–12€. Metro: Liceu.

Luz de Gas   This theater and cabaret has the hottest Latino jazz on weekends. On weeknights there is cabaret. The place is an Art Nouveau delight, with colored glass lamps and enough voluptuous nudes to please Rubens himself. The club was once a theater, and its original seating has been turned into different areas each with its own bar. The lower two levels open onto the dance floor and stage. If you'd like to talk, head for the top tier, which has a glass enclosure. Call to see what the lineup is on any given night: jazz, pop, soul, rhythm and blues, salsa, bolero, whatever. Open Friday through Wednesday from 11pm to 4am, Thursday 11pm to 5am. Carrer de Muntaner 246. © **93-209-77-11.** Cover (includes 1 drink) 15€. Bus: 6, 27, 32, 34.

DANCE CLUBS & DISCOS

La Paloma   Those feeling nostalgic may want to drop in on Barcelona's most famous dance hall. Remember the fox trot? The mambo? If not, learn about them here, along with the tango, the cha-cha, and the bolero. Live orchestras provide the music. The ornate old hall is open Thursday through Sunday. Matinees are from 6 to 9:30pm; night dances are from 11:30pm to 5am. Drink prices start at 7€. Tigre 27. © **93-301-68-97.** Cover 7€. Metro: Universitat.

Up and Down   The chic atmosphere here attracts elite Barcelonans of all ages. The more mature patrons, specifically the black-tie, postopera crowd, head upstairs, leaving the downstairs section to loud music and flaming youth. Up and Down is the most cosmopolitan disco in Barcelona, with impeccable service, sassy waiters, and a welcoming atmosphere. Technically, this is a private club—you can be turned away at the door. The restaurant is open Tuesday through Saturday from 10pm to 2am, and prices for meals run 30€ and up. The disco is open Tuesday through Saturday from midnight to 6am. Drinks in the disco cost 12€ for a beer and at least 17€ for a hard drink. Numancia 179. © **93-205-51-94.** Cover (includes 1 drink) 12€–17€. Metro: María Cristina.

CAFES

Integral to the time-honored tradition of Catalonia is the cafe where everything from politics to art is debated in the traditional format of a *tertulia,* a semiformalized combined argument and conversation. Picasso once frequented some of these cafes, as did many Catalán leaders in the dark days of the Franco era.

Café de la Opera   Standing across from the Liceu opera house, this is Barcelona's most famous cafe, having opened more than a century ago. It has remained the favorite stopover not only for opera-goers and performers but for those strolling along the Ramblas. Since it opens at 8:30am daily, many locals come here for a traditional breakfast. At any time of the day you can enjoy tapas, drinks, and people-watching. La Rambla 74. © **93-317-75-85**. Metro: Liceu.

Café Paris Even Prince Felipe, heir to the Spanish throne, comes here when he's in Barcelona. Poets and pundits, bullfighters and the transgendered, everyone is welcome here. A Catalán tradition since 1935, it even opened its doors to Hemingway during the dark days of Barcelona under siege from Franco's troops. Opening at 7am, the place usually closes at midnight except on Friday to Sunday when it keeps going until 3am with drinkers and revelers. Carrer Aribau 184 and Calle Paris. © **93-209-85-30**. Metro: Rosello.

Café Zurich At the top of the Ramblas, this is a traditional meeting point in Barcelona, and it's also great for the passing parade around Catalonia's most fabled boulevard. If the weather is fair, opt for an outdoor table, enjoying the excellent tapas (all kinds), the cold beer, and the gaiety. Launched in the early 1920s, it's been going strong ever since, with its dark wood furnishings and columns. Try one of the little sandwiches here—called *bocadillos.* Those with the Serrano ham are especially good. Plaça de Catalunya 1. © **93-317-91-53**. Metro: Plaça de Catalunya.

El Bosc de las Fades This is the most bizarre cafe in Barcelona, evoking a fairytale forest, or at the least trying to. It's brought to you by the same people who created Museu de Cera de Barcelona or the waxworks. Expect "unreal trees" and the whispering sound of waterfalls, plus a "gnome" or two. The cafe attracts essentially a young crowd who enjoy the faux woodland dell, the background music, and the drinks. Open 11am to 1am daily. Passaje de la Banca 7. © **93-317-26-49**. Metro: Drassanes.

Espaci Barroc The name of this cafe means "baroque space," and so it is, lying in one of Barcelona's loveliest patios, the Palau Dalmases whose origins go back to the 1400s. Along the stairway is a bas-relief depicting the "Rape of Europa." The building is the headquarters of Omnium Cultural, devoted to the spread of the history and culture of Catalonia province. The patio itself is a study in the baroque with sculpted fruits and flowers. In the background the music of the baroque era is gently played. The cafe is closed Monday but open Tuesday through Saturday from 8pm to 2am and Sunday from 6 to 10pm. Carrer Montcada 20, La Ribera. © **93-310-06-73**. Metro: Jaume I.

BARS & PUBS

Hivernacle This is a wine tavern luring a young, hip crowd to a setting of towering palms in a 19th-century greenhouse. The location is just inside the gates of the city's most centrally located park. A fashionable crowd likes to come here to "graze" upon the tapas. A restaurant adjoins. Open Monday through Saturday from 10am to midnight, Sunday from 9am to 4pm. Parc de la Ciutadella. © **93-295-40-17**. Metro: Arco del Triunfo.

Café Bar Padam The clientele and decor here are modern and hip. The bar, which attracts many gay patrons, is on a narrow street in the Ciutat Vella, about 3 blocks east of the Rambla dels Caputxins. The only color in the black-and-white rooms comes from fresh flowers and modern paintings. French music is sometimes featured as well as art expositions. Open Monday through Saturday from 7pm to 2:30am. Rauric 9. © **93-302-50-62**. Metro: Liceu.

Cocktail Bar Boadas This intimate, conservative bar is usually filled with regulars. Established in 1933, it is near the top of Les Rambles. Many visitors stop in for a predinner drink and snack before wandering to one of the district's many restaurants. It stocks a wide array of Caribbean rums, Russian vodkas, and English gins, and the skilled bartenders know how to mix them all. The place is especially well known for its daiquiris. Open daily from noon to 2am (till 3am Fri–Sat). Tallers 1. © 93-318-95-92. Metro: Plaça de Catalunya.

Dirty Dick's An English-style pub in a residential part of town, Dirty Dick's has lots of dark paneling and exposed brick, with banquettes for quiet conversation. If you sit at the bar you'll be faced with a tempting array of tiny sandwiches that taste as good as they look. The pub is at the crossing of Vía Augusta, a main thoroughfare through the district. Open daily from 6pm to 2:30am. Taberna Inglesa, Carrer Marc Aureli 2. © 93-200-89-52. Metro: Muntaner.

El Born Facing a rustic-looking square, this former fish store has been cleverly converted. There are a few tables near the front, but our preferred spot is the inner room decorated with rattan furniture and modern paintings. The music might be anything from Louis Armstrong to classic rock 'n' roll. The upstairs buffet serves dinner. The room is somewhat cramped, but you'll find a simple, tasty collection of fish, meat, and vegetable dishes, all carefully laid out. A full dinner without wine costs around 16€ to 27€. Beer and wine are quite cheap. Open Monday through Saturday from 6pm to 3am. Passeig del Born 26. © 93-319-53-33. Metro: Jaume I or Barcelona.

Molly's Fair City The hangout of expats, plus visiting Brits and Irishmen, this is as close as Barcelona gets to having a Dublin beer hall. The sound of English voices is heard throughout the pub, growing louder as the evening wears on, and that can be very late. The pub opens at 8pm nightly but stays open until 2:30am Monday through Friday and until 3am on Saturday and Sunday. Expect blaring music, loud voices, and beer flowing like a river. The location is in the heart of the old city adjoining Plaça Reial. Carrer Ferran 7. © 93-342-40-26. Metro: Liceu.

New York Talk about late, late night life in Barcelona. The gang of patrons who like this club, the largest in the Gothic barrio, don't show up until 3am. The bar, a former strip joint, is open only Thursday through Saturday from midnight to 5am. The red lights and black walls still evoke its heyday when the women took it all off. Recorded music—mainly British pop—is heard in the background. Young people, mostly in their 20s and often from the university, patronize this joint. After 2am, a cover charge of 9€, including one drink, is imposed. Carrer Escudellers 5. © 93-318-87-30. Metro: Drassanes.

Schilling A young and stylish crowd can be seen crossing Plaça Reial with its Gaudí lampposts, heading for this old cafe to sample its drink, its succulent pastas, savory tapas, and panini. Forsaking Barcelona's fabled modernism, Schilling gleefully lingers in another era, with its iron columns, marble tables, and wall of wine bottles. A large gay crowd often dominates the night along with some hip, supposedly straight young things and a few aging pensioners. On a recent visit, we noted three models that would give Jennifer Lopez competition and at least two young Catalán versions of Brad Pitt. A waiter confided to us, "We're famous for our slow service." His appraisal was right on the mark. Open Monday through Saturday from 10am to 2:30am, Sunday from noon to 2am. Carrer Ferran 23. © 93-317-67-87. Metro: Liceu.

CHAMPAGNE BARS

The Cataláns call their own version of sparkling wine *cava*. In Catalán, champagne bars are called *xampanyerías*. The Spanish wines are often excellent, and some consider them better than their French counterparts. With more than 50 Spanish companies producing *cava,* and each bottling up to a dozen grades of wine, the best way to learn about Spanish champagne is to visit the vineyard or to sample the products at a *xampanyería.*

Champagne bars usually open at 7pm and stay open into the wee hours of the morning. They serve tapas, ranging from caviar to smoked fish to frozen chocolate truffles. Most establishments sell only a limited array of house *cavas* by the glass, and more esoteric varieties by the bottle. You'll be offered a choice of *brut* (slightly sweeter) or *brut nature.* The most acclaimed brands include Mont-Marçal, Gramona, Mestres, Parxet, Torello, and Recaredo.

El Xampanyet   This little champagne bar, our favorite in Barcelona, has been operated by the same family since the 1930s. When the Picasso Museum opened nearby, its popularity was assured. On this ancient street, the tavern is adorned with colored tiles, antique curios, marble tables, and barrels. With your sparkling wine, you can order fresh anchovies in vinegar or other tapas. If you don't want the *cava,* you can order fresh cider at the old-fashioned zinc bar. Open Tuesday through Saturday from noon to 4pm and 7 to 11:30pm and Sunday from noon to 4pm. Closed in August. Carrer Montcada 22. ℂ **93-319-70-03.** Metro: Jaume I.

Xampanyería Casablanca   Someone had to fashion a champagne bar after the Bogart-Bergman film, and this is it. It serves four kinds of house *cava* by the glass, plus a good selection of tapas, especially patés. Open Monday through Saturday from 8am until 3am. Bonavista 6. ℂ **93-237-63-99.** Metro: Passeig de Gràcia.

Xampú Xampany   At the corner of the Plaça de Tetuan, this *xampanyería* offers a variety of hors d'oeuvres in addition to wine. Abstract paintings, touches of high tech, and bouquets of flowers break up the pastel color scheme. Open Monday through Saturday from 8pm to 1:30am. Gran Vía de les Corts Catalanes 702. ℂ **93-265-04-83.** Metro: Girona.

Moments Piaf, Drag Queens & a Walk on the Wild Side

Do you long to check out the seedy part of Barcelona that writers such as Jean Genet brought so vividly to life in their books? Much of it is gone forever, but *la Vida* nostalgically lives on in pockets like the **Bar Pastis.**

Valencianos Carme Pericás and Quime Ballester opened this tiny bar just off the southern end of Les Rambles in 1947. They made it a shrine to Edith Piaf, and her songs still play on an old phonograph in back of the bar. The decor consists mostly of paintings by Ballester, who had a dark, rather morbid vision of the world. You can order four kinds of pastis in this dimly lit "corner of Montmartre."

Outside the window, check out the view—usually a parade of transvestite hookers. The crowd is likely to include almost anyone, especially people who used to be called bohemians. The bar features live music: French music on Sunday, tango music on Tuesday, and *canta autor* on Wednesday where the performer both writes and sings his or her own songs. Open Monday through Thursday from 7:30pm to 2:30am, Friday, Saturday, and Sunday until 3am. Carrer Santa Mónica 4. ℂ **93-318-79-80.** Metro: Drassanes.

GAY & LESBIAN BARS

Café Dietrich   As if you didn't already know by its namesake, this cafe stages the best drag strip shows in town, a combination of local and foreign divas "falling in love again" like the great Marlene herself. It remains Barcelona's most popular gay haunt. The scantily clad bartenders are hot, and the overly posh decor lives up to its reputation as a "divinely glam musical bar/disco." Many of the drag queens like to fraternize with the handsomest of the patrons, to whom they offer deep kisses on the mouth. Open Sunday through Thursday from 10pm to 2am and Friday and Saturday from 10pm to 3am. Consell de Cent 255. ℂ 93-451-77-07. Metro: Gràcia or Universidad.

Medusa   This minimalist decorated bar draws a trendy young crowd, mainly of cute boys. "The cuter you are, the better your chances of getting in if we get crowded as the night wears on," we were assured by one of the staff. A super trendy place, Medusa draws the fashionistas. We prefer its DJs to all others in town. The place gets very cruisy after 1am. Open Sunday through Thursday from 11pm to 3am, Friday through Saturday from 11pm to 3:30am. Casanova 75. ℂ 93-454-53-63. Metro: Urgell.

Metro   Still one of the most popular gay discos in Barcelona, Metro attracts a diverse crowd—from young fashion victims to more rough-and-ready macho types. One dance floor plays contemporary house and dance music, and the other traditional Spanish music mixed with Spanish pop. This is a good opportunity to watch men of all ages dance the "Sevillanas" together in pairs with a surprising degree of grace. The gay press in Barcelona quite accurately dubs the backroom here as a "notorious, lascivious labyrinth of lust." One interesting feature appears in the bathrooms, where videos have been installed in quite unexpected places. Open Monday through Thursday from midnight to 5am; Friday and Saturday from midnight to 6am. Sepúlveda, 185. ℂ 93-323-52-27. Cover 10€. Metro: Universitat.

New Chaps   Gay Barcelonans refer to this saloon-style watering hole as Catalonia's premier leather and denim bar. In fact, the dress code usually is leather of a different stripe: more boots and jeans than leather and chains. Behind a pair of swinging doors evocative of the old American West, Chaps contains two different bar areas. Some of Barcelona's horniest guys flock to the downstairs darkroom in the wee hours. Open daily from 9pm to 3am. Avinguda Diagonal 365. ℂ 93-215-53-65. Metro: Diagonal.

Punto BCN   Barcelona's largest gay bar attracts a mixed crowd of young "hotties" and foreigners. Always crowded, it's a good base to start out your evening. There is a very popular happy hour on Wednesday from 6 to 9pm. Open daily from 6pm to 2am. Muntaner 63–65. ℂ 93-453-61-23. Metro: Eixample.

Salvation   This leading gay dance club has been going strong since 1999. It's still the flashiest dive on the see-and-be-seen circuit, and a good place to wear your see-through clothing, especially as the hour grows late. There are two rooms devoted to a different type of music, the first with house music and DJs and the other with more commercial and "soapy" themes. An habitué told us, "I come here because of the sensual waiters," and indeed they are the handsomest and most muscular in town. Look your most gorgeous, buffed self if you want to get past the notoriously selective doorman. On Friday and Saturday nights, women need special passes to gain entrance. These can be requested at Dietrich (see above). Open Friday to Saturday from midnight to 5am. Ronda de Sant Pere 19–21. ℂ 93-318-06-86. Metro: Urquinaona.

12

Catalonia

You can take several noteworthy day trips from Barcelona. The most popular is to the Benedictine monastery of **Montserrat,** northwest of Barcelona. To the south, the Roman city of **Tarragona** has been neglected by visitors but is particularly interesting to those who appreciate ancient history. Beach lovers and gays and lesbians should head for the resort town of **Sitges.**

About six million people live in Catalonia, and twice that many visit every year. It's one of Europe's playgrounds, with its beaches along the **Costa Brava** (see chapter 13) and the **Costa Dorada,** centered on Sitges. Tarragona is the capital of its own province, and Barcelona, of course, is the political, economic, and cultural center of Catalonia (see chapter 12).

The province of Catalonia forms a triangle bordered by the French frontier to the north, the Mediterranean Sea to the east, and the province of Aragón to the west. The northern coastline is rugged, whereas the Costa Dorada is flatter, with miles of sandy beaches as well as a mild, sunny climate.

Pilgrims may go to Montserrat for its scenery and religious associations, and history buffs to Tarragona for its Roman ruins, but just plain folks head to the Costa Dorada for fun. Named for its strips of golden sand, this seashore extends along the coastlines of Barcelona and Tarragona provinces.

Avid beachcombers sometimes traverse the entire coast.

One popular stretch is **La Maresme,** extending from Río Tordera to Barcelona, a distance of 64km (40 miles). Allow at least 2½ hours to cover it without stops. The Tarragonese coastline extends from Barcelona to the Ebro River, a distance of 193km (120 miles); a trip along it will take a whole day. Highlights along this coast include **Costa de Garraf,** a series of creeks skirted by the corniche road after Castelldefels, Sitges, and Tarragona. One of the most beautiful stretches of the coast is **Cape Salou,** south of Tarragona in a setting of pinewoods.

We begin our tour through this history-rich part of Catalonia by going not along the coast but rather inland to the Sierra de Montserrat, which has more spectacular views than any location along the coast. Wagner used it as the setting for his opera *Parsifal.* The serrated outline made by the sierra's steep cliffs led the Catalonians to call it *montserrat* (saw-toothed mountain). Today it remains the religious center of Catalonia. Thousands of pilgrims annually visit the town's monastery with its Black Virgin.

The **Monestir de Poblet** in Tarragona is the other major monastery of Catalonia. It, too, is a world-class attraction.

1 Montserrat ★★

56km (35 miles) NW of Barcelona, 592km (368 miles) E of Madrid

The monastery at **Montserrat,** which sits atop a 1,200m (4,000-ft.) high mountain, 11km (7 miles) long and 5.5km (3½ miles) wide, is one of the most

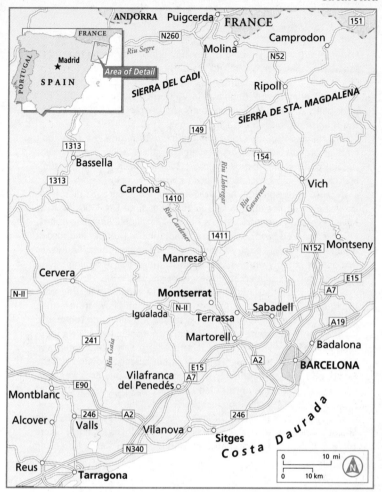

important pilgrimage spots in Spain. It ranks alongside Zaragoza and Santiago de Compostela. Thousands travel here every year to see and touch the medieval statue of La Moreneta (The Black Virgin), the patron saint of Catalonia. Many newly married couples flock here for her blessing.

Avoid visiting on Sunday, if possible, as thousands of locals pour in, especially if the weather is nice. Remember that the winds blow cold up here even in summer, so visitors should take along warm sweaters, jackets, or coats. In winter, thermal underwear might not be a bad idea.

ESSENTIALS

GETTING THERE The best and most exciting way to go is via the Catalán railway, **Ferrocarrils de la Generalitat de Catalunya** (Manresa line), with 10 trains a day leaving from the Plaça d'Espanya in Barcelona. The central office is at Plaça de Catalunya 1 (© **93-205-15-15**). The train connects with an aerial cable way (Aeri de Montserrat), which is included in the fare of 12€ round-trip.

A Journey to Andorra

You might never have heard of the tiny principality of **Andorra** ★★, sandwiched between Spain and France high in the eastern Pyrenees. Charlemagne gave this country its independence in A.D. 784, and with amused condescension, Napoléon let Andorra keep its autonomy. The principality is now ruled by two co-princes, the president of France and the Spanish archbishop of La Seu d'Urgell.

Less than 464 sq. km (288 sq. miles) in size, Andorra is a storybook land of breathtaking scenery—cavernous valleys, snowcapped peaks, rugged pastureland, and deep gorges. It's long been popular for summer excursions and, more recently, as a winter ski resort.

Because of its isolation, Andorra retained one of Europe's most insular peasant cultures until as late as 1945. But since the 1950s, tourists have increased from a trickle to a flood—12 million every year, in fact. This has wreaked havoc on Andorra's traditional way of life and turned a huge part of the country into one vast shopping center. Andorrans live almost entirely on monies earned from tax-free shopping, along with the thriving ski market in the winter months.

Some suggest that Andorra has ruined its mountain setting with urban sprawl because taxis, crowds, and advertising have transformed the once-rustic principality into a busy center of trading and commerce. At first glance, the route into the country from Spain looks like a used-car lot, and its mile-long traffic jams are legendary. New hotels and hundreds of shops have opened in the past decade to accommodate the French and Spanish pouring across the frontiers to buy duty-free merchandise. A magazine once called Andorra "Europe's feudal discount shopping center." In addition, gasoline is cheap here.

Most people make their base in the capital, **Andorra-la-Vella** (in Spanish, Andorra-la-Vieja), or the adjoining town, **Les Escaldes,** where there are plenty of shops, bars, and hotels. Shuttles run between the

The train, with its funicular tie-in, has taken over as the preferred means of transport. However, a long-distance **bus** service is provided by **Autocars Julià** in Barcelona. Daily service from Barcelona to Montserrat is generally available, with departures near the Estació Central de Barcelona-Sants on the Plaça de Països Catalánes. One bus makes the trip at 9am, returning at 5pm; the round-trip ticket costs 8.70€. Contact the Julià company at Carrer Viriato (© **93-490-40-00**).

To drive here, take the N-2 southwest of Barcelona toward Tarragona, turning west at the junction with the N-11. The signposts and exit to Montserrat will be on your right. From the main road, it's 14.5km (9 miles) up to the monastery through eerie rock formations and dramatic scenery.

VISITOR INFORMATION The **tourist office** is at the Plaça de la Creu (© **93-877-77-77**), open daily from 10am to 6pm.

EXPLORING MONTSERRAT

One of the monastery's noted attractions is the 50-member **Escolanía** ★★, one of the oldest and most renowned boys' choirs in Europe, dating from the 13th towns, but most shoppers prefer to walk. Most of the major hotels and restaurants are on the main street of Andorra-la-Vella (Avinguda Meritxell) or on the main street of Les Escaldes (Avinguda Carlemany).

But unless you've come just to shop, you'll want to leave the capital for a look at this tiny principality. Two nearby villages, **La Massana** and **Ordino,** can be visited by car or by bus (leaving about every 30 min. from the station in Andorra-la-Vella). Buses cross the country from south to north and vice versa. The drive to Andorra takes you through some of the finest mountain scenery in Europe, with a backdrop of peaks, vineyards, and rushing brooks. From Barcelona, drive via Puigcerdà to La Seu d'Urgell. From here on the C-145, it's a quick 10km (6 miles) to the border of this autonomous principality, one of the world's smallest countries.

Although no one ever accused the Pyrenees of being more dramatic than the Alps, they are, in fact, far more rugged. The climate of dry air is brisk in winter, and some of Europe's best skiing can be found here. There's abundant snow from November lasting (usually) to April. **Pas de la Casa-Grau Roig** is the oldest resort, located just within the French border. Along with a slalom course, it has 18 trails for advanced skiers, plus some tame slopes for neophytes, and 25 lifts. The largest complex, however, is **Soldeu-El Tarter,** with 28 slopes (some designed for children) and a 12km (7½-mile) cross-country course. There are 22 ski lifts. The resort of **Pals** features 20 trails, 14 lifts, and a forest slalom course. **Arinsal** offers 25 slopes serving both the experienced skier and the beginner. But the most beautiful and dramatic resort of all is **Ordino Arcalis,** with 11 lifts and 16 slopes. Many British visitors flock here in winter, as Andorran ski packages are, in general, far more reasonable than those offered in Switzerland or Austria.

Warning: Border guards check very carefully for undeclared goods.

century. At 1pm daily you can hear them singing "Salve Regina" and the "Virolai" (hymn of Montserrat) in the basilica. The basilica is open daily from 8 to 10:30am and noon to 6:30pm. Admission is free. To view the Black Virgin, a statue from the 12th or 13th century, enter the church through a side door to the right.

At the Plaça de Santa María you can also visit the **Museu de Montserrat** (© **93-877-77-77**), known for its collection of ecclesiastical paintings, including works by Caravaggio and El Greco. Modern Spanish and Catalán artists are also represented (see Picasso's early *El Viejo Pescador,* 1895). Works by Dalí and such French Impressionists as Monet, Sisley, and Degas are shown. The collection of ancient artifacts is quite interesting, and make sure to look for the crocodile mummy, which is at least 2,000 years old. The museum is open Monday through Friday from 10am to 6pm, Saturday and Sunday from 9:30am to 6:30pm, charging 4.50€ adults and 3€ children and students.

The 9-minute **funicular ride** to the 1,236m (4,119-ft.) high peak, Sant Jeroni, makes for a panoramic trip. The funicular operates about every 20 minutes daily from 10am to 6pm. The cost is 6.10€ round-trip. From the top, you'll see not only the whole of Catalonia but also the Pyrenees and the islands of Majorca and Ibiza.

You can also make an excursion to **Santa Cova (Holy Grotto),** the alleged site of the discovery of the Black Virgin. The grotto dates from the 17th century and was built in the shape of a cross. You go halfway by funicular but must complete the trip on foot. April through October, the grotto is open daily from 9am to 6:30pm; off-season hours are daily from 10am to 5:30pm. The funicular operates April through October, every 20 minutes daily from 10am to 6pm, and November through March daily from 11am to 4:45pm, at a cost of 2.50€ round-trip.

WHERE TO STAY & DINE

Few people spend the night here, but most visitors want at least one meal. If you don't want to spend a lot, buy a picnic in Barcelona or ask your hotel to pack a meal.

Abat Cisneros ★   This modern hotel on the main square of Montserrat offers few pretensions and a history of family management from 1958. The small rooms are simple and clean, each with a comfortable bed, and the bathrooms come with tub/shower combos. Many regional dishes of Catalonia are served in the in-house restaurant. The hotel's name is derived from a title given to the head of any Benedictine monastery during the Middle Ages.

Plaça de Monestir, 08199 Montserrat. ✆ **93-877-77-01.** Fax 93-877-77-24. interhotel.com/spain/es/hoteles/ 1829.html. 56 units. 44€–81€ double. Rates include breakfast. AE, DC, MC, V. Parking 3€. **Amenities:** Restaurant; bar; lounge; laundry service; dry cleaning. *In room:* TV, safe.

2 Tarragona ★★

97km (60 miles) S of Barcelona, 554km (344 miles) E of Madrid

The ancient Roman port city of **Tarragona,** on a rocky bluff above the Mediterranean, is one of the grandest but most neglected sightseeing centers in Spain. Despite its Roman and medieval remains, it's merely the second oldest city of Catalonia.

The Romans captured Tarragona in 218 B.C., and during their rule the city sheltered one million people behind 64km (40-mile) long city walls. One of the four capitals of Catalonia when it was an ancient principality and once the home of Julius Caesar, Tarragona today consists of an old quarter filled with interesting buildings, particularly the houses with connecting balconies. The upper walled town is mainly medieval, the town below newer.

In the new town, walk along the **Ramble Nova,** a fashionable wide boulevard that's the main artery of life. Running parallel with Ramble Nova to the east is the **Ramble Vella,** which marks the beginning of the old town. The city has a bullring, good hotels, and even beaches. The Romans were the first to designate Tarragona a resort town.

After seeing the attractions listed below, cap off your day with a stroll along the **Balcó del Mediterráni (Balcony of the Mediterranean),** where the vistas are especially beautiful at sunset.

ESSENTIALS

GETTING THERE   Daily, 30 to 40 **trains** make the 1½-hour trip to and from the Barcelona-Sants station. Five trains per day make the 8-hour trip from Madrid. In Tarragona, the RENFE office is in the train station, the Plaza Pedrera s/n (✆ **90-224-02-02**).

Catalonia Remembers Pablo Casals

Fleeing from Franco and the fascist regime, the world's greatest cellist, Pablo Casals, left his homeland in 1939. Today his body has been returned to El Vendrell, 72km (45 miles) south of Barcelona, where he is remembered with a museum in his honor. The museum is installed in the renovated house where he lived until he went into self-imposed exile.

In 17 rooms it is filled with Casals memorabilia, including his first cello, photographs and films of his performances, the Peace Medal awarded by the United Nations in 1971, and photographs of the artist with such famous men as John F. Kennedy, who awarded him the Medal of Freedom.

Casals died in Puerto Rico in 1973 at the age of 96, and he was finally returned to his beloved Catalonia in 1979, where he is buried at the El Vendrell graveyard.

Casa Pau Casals lies at Av. Palfuriana 59–61, in El Vendrell (✆ **97-768-42-76**). From September 16 to June 14 it is open Tuesday through Friday from 10am to 2pm and 4 to 6pm, Saturday from 10am to 2pm and 4 to 7pm, and Sunday from 10am to 2pm. From June 15 to September 15 Tuesday through Saturday from 10am to 2pm and 5 to 9pm, and Sunday from 10am to 2pm. Admission is 5€ for adults and 3€ for children. Allow 1 hour.

To reach El Vendrell from Barcelona, head southwest along A-19 until you come to C-246. Continue along this route, which will lead you into El Vendrell.

From Barcelona, there are 11 **buses** per day to Tarragona (1½ hr.); from Valencia, 11 buses (3½ hr.), and from Alicante, six buses (6½ hr.). Call ✆ **97-722-91-26** in Tarragona for more information.

To drive, take the **A-2** southwest from Barcelona to the **A-7,** then take the **N-340.** The route is well marked. This is a fast toll road. The one-way cost of the toll road from Barcelona to Tarragona is 8€.

VISITOR INFORMATION The **tourist office** is at Fortuny 4 (✆ **97-723-34-15;** www.catalunyaturisme.com), open Monday through Friday from 9am to 2pm and 4 to 6:30pm, Saturday from 9am to 2pm.

EXPLORING THE TOWN

Amfiteatre Romà   At the foot of Miracle Park and dramatically carved from a cliff that rises from the beach, this Roman amphitheater recalls the days in the 2nd century when thousands gathered here for amusement.

Parc del Milagro. ✆ **97-724-25-79**. Admission 1.90€. Mar–Sept Tues–Sat 9am–9pm, Sun 9am–3pm. Oct–Feb Tues–Sat 9am–5pm, Sun 10am–3pm. Bus: 2.

Catedral ★   At the highest point of Tarragona is this 12th-century cathedral, whose architecture represents the transition from Romanesque to Gothic. It has an enormous vaulted entrance, fine stained-glass windows, Romanesque cloisters, and an open choir. In the main apse, observe the altarpiece of St. Thecla, patron of Tarragona, carved by Pere Joan in 1430. Two flamboyant doors open into the chevet. The east gallery is the **Museu Diocesà,** with a collection of Catalán art.

Plaça de la Seu. ℂ **97-723-86-85.** Admission to cathedral and museum 2.40€. Mar 16–Oct 15 daily 10am–12:30pm and 4–7pm; Oct 16–Nov 15 daily 10am–12:30pm and 3–5pm; Nov 16–Mar 15 daily 10am–2pm. Bus: 1.

Museu Nacional Arqueològic Overlooking the sea, the Archaeology Museum houses a collection of Roman relics—mosaics, ceramics, coins, silver, sculpture, and more. The outstanding attraction here is the mosaic *Head of Medusa* ★★, with its penetrating stare.

Plaça del Rei 5. ℂ **97-723-62-09.** Admission 2.40€. June 1–Sept 30 Tues–Sat 10am–8pm, Sun 10am–2pm; off season Tues–Sat 10am–1:30pm and 4–7pm, Sun 10am–2pm. Bus: 8.

Museu Necròpolis ★ This is one of the most important burial grounds in Spain, used by the Christians from the 3rd to the 5th century. It stands outside town next to a tobacco factory whose construction led to its discovery in 1923. While on the grounds, visit the **Museu Paleocristià,** which contains a number of sarcophagi and other objects discovered during the excavations.

Paleocristians, Avinguda de Ramón y Cajal 80. ℂ **97-723-62-09.** Admission to Necròpolis plus museum 2.40€. June 1–Sept 30 Tues–Sat 10am–8pm, Sun and holidays 10am–2pm; off season Tues–Sat 10am–1:30pm and 3–5:30pm, Sun and holidays 10am–2pm. Bus: 4.

Passeig Arqueològic ★ At the far end of the Plaça del Pallol, an archway leads to this .8km (½-mile) walkway along the ancient ramparts, built by the Romans on top of gigantic boulders. The ramparts have been much altered over the years, especially in medieval times and in the 1600s. There are scenic views from many points along the way.

El Portal del Roser. ℂ **97-724-57-96.** Admission 1.90€. Oct–Mar Tues–Sat 9am–5pm, Sun and holidays 9am–3pm; Apr–Sept Tues–Sat 10am–9pm, Sun and holidays 9am–3pm. Bus: 2.

SHOPPING

You'll find a scattering of handicraft shops throughout Tarragona's historic core, with a particularly dense concentration along the Ramble Nova. (Its central section is an all-pedestrian zone.) Any of them might provide a handcrafted souvenir of your visit. But for the densest concentration of shops and boutiques, head for the **Centro Commercial Parc Central,** on Avinguda Roma. Although the main focus here revolves around a supermarket, the site has at least 40 shops selling whatever you'd need in terms of clothing, sundries, and household goods.

NEARBY THEME PARK THRILLS

A 10-minute ride from the heart of Barcelona, the **Port Aventura Amusement Park,** Port Aventura (ℂ **97-777-90-90**), is Spain's biggest theme park. Universal Studios has acquired a prime stake in it and has plans to make it even larger. On a vast 809 hectares (2,000 acres), it'll be expanded to become Europe's largest entertainment center. Since its inauguration in 1995, it has already become one of the Mediterranean's favorite family destinations.

The park is a microcosm of five distinct worlds, with full-scale re-creations of classic villages ranging from Polynesia to Mexico, from China to the old American West. It also offers a thrilling variety of roller coaster and white-water rides, all centered on a lake you can travel via the deck of a Chinese junk.

The park is open daily: March 26 to June 19 from 10am to 8pm; June 20 to September 13 from 10am to midnight; September 14 to January 11 from 10am to 8pm. Closed January 12 to March 25. Admission costs 34€ adults, 27€ children. Nighttime admission is 23€ adults, 18€ children. The fee includes all shows and rides.

Some 50% of the trains on the Barcelona-Sitges-Tarragona line stop at Port Aventura. From Barcelona, the trip takes 1½ hours, and a one-way fare costs about 5.25€. A taxi from the center of Tarragona costs about 12€ one-way.

WHERE TO STAY
EXPENSIVE
Hotel Imperial Tarraco ⭐⭐   About .4km (¼ mile) south of the cathedral, atop an oceanfront cliff whose panoramas include a sweeping view of both the sea and the Roman ruins, this hotel is the finest in town. It was designed in the form of a crescent and has guest rooms that may angle out to sea and almost always include small balconies. The accommodations, all with bathrooms containing tub/shower combos, contain uncomplicated plain modern furniture. The public rooms display lots of polished white marble, Oriental carpets, and leather furniture. The staff responds well to the demands of both traveling businesspeople and art lovers on sightseeing excursions.

Paseo de las Palmeras/Rambla Vella, 43003 Tarragona. ℂ **97-723-30-40.** Fax 97-721-65-66. www.fut.es/~imperial. 170 units. 109€–150€ double; 160€–203€ suite. Rates include breakfast. AE, DC, MC, V. Free parking. Bus: 1. **Amenities:** Restaurant; bar; pool; tennis court; room service; babysitting; laundry service; dry cleaning. *In room:* A/C, TV, minibar, hair dryer, safe.

MODERATE TO INEXPENSIVE
Hotel Astari   Travelers in search of peace and quiet on the Mediterranean come to the Astari, which opened in 1959 and was last renovated in 1992. This resort hotel on the Barcelona road offers fresh and airy though rather plain accommodations. Most rooms are small, but each comes with a good bed and a bathroom with a tub/shower combo. The Astari has long balconies and terraces, one favorite spot being the outer flagstone terrace with its umbrella-shaded tables set among willows, orange trees, and geranium bushes. This is the only hotel in Tarragona with garage space for each guest's car.

Vía Augusta 95, 43003 Tarragona. ℂ **97-723-69-00.** Fax 97-723-69-11. www.gsmhoteles.es. 81 units. 63€–85€ double. AE, DC, MC, V. Parking 7€. Bus: 9. **Amenities:** Restaurant; bar; pool; room service; laundry service; dry cleaning. *In room:* A/C, TV, minibar, hair dryer, safe.

Hotel Lauria ⭐   Less than half a block north of the town's popular seaside promenade (Passeig de les Palmeres), beside the tree-lined Rambla, this government-rated three-star hotel offers unpretentious clean rooms, each of which has been recently modernized. Rooms range from small to medium, and each bathroom is equipped with a tub/shower combo. Long considered the leading hotel in town until the arrival of some newcomers, it still draws loyal repeat visitors. The rooms in back open onto a view of the sea.

Rambla Nova 20, 43004 Tarragona. ℂ **97-723-67-12.** Fax 97-723-67-00. www.hlauria.es. 72 units. 56€–66€ double. AE, DC, MC, V. Parking 9€. Bus: 1. **Amenities:** Bar; pool; room service; laundry service; dry cleaning. *In room:* A/C, TV, minibar, hair dryer, safe.

WHERE TO DINE
Barquet ⭐ CATALAN/SEAFOOD   In the center of town, a 5-minute walk from the cathedral, this restaurant specializes in seafood and shellfish prepared in the Catalán style. It opened in 1950 in the cellar of a relatively modern building and today is run by the third generation of its original owners. Within a pair of nautical-themed dining rooms you can enjoy *sopa de pescados* (fish soup) Tarragona style, *romesco* (ragout) of sea bass with herbs, an assemblage of fried finned creatures called *fideos rossejats,* and several preparations of sole and hake. If you're not interested in seafood, a choice of grilled veal, chicken, or beef is

offered. The list of Spanish and Catalán wines will complement any meal. The staff is well trained, polite, and proud of their Catalán antecedents.

Gasometro 16. ⓒ **97-724-00-23**. Reservations recommended. Main courses 8€–18€; *menú del día* 9€. AE, DC, MC, V. Mon–Sat 1–3:30pm; Tues–Sat 8–11pm. Closed Aug.

Epicurí ★★ *(Value)* CATALAN/CONTINENTAL In 2002, this long-established restaurant was bought by chef Javier Andrieu, who poured years of experience into a site in the heart of town, a very short walk from the archaeological treasures of medieval Tarragona. Within a cozy dining room whose decor falls midway between the organic modernism of Gaudí and the Art Nouveau opulence of turn-of-the-20th-century Paris, you'll be presented with a choice of two set menus, one at 17€ that includes three courses; and a much more lavish one, priced at 35€ that features an aperitif plus six courses. Cuisine is based on securing the best market-fresh ingredients in town. The most intriguing dishes include half-cooked foie gras served with grapes; a succulent entrecôte of veal with artichokes; steamed veal cutlets with lemon or Madeira sauce; magret of duckling with tiny Catalán mushrooms known as *moixernons;* and a heaven-sent filet of turbot with an almond-flavored saffron sauce. If the ingredients are available in the market, you might find such other dishes as a ragout of squid cooked in black beer.

Calle Mare de Deú de la Mercè. ⓒ **97-724-44-04**. Reservations required. Set lunch menu 10€; set dinner menu 18€–36€. DC, MC, V. Tues–Sun 1:30–4pm; Wed–Sat 8:30–11pm.

Les Coques ★ *(Finds)* MEDITERRANEAN This is a real discovery in the historic core of old Tarragona. Sophisticated Les Coques specializes in fare from both land and sea and does so exceedingly well. The specialties depend on whatever is good in any season. For example, their selection of mushrooms, called *zetas,* can be prepared in almost any style and have a marvelously woodsy taste. They also prepare the best grilled octopus (the miniature variety) in town. We tasted virgin olive oil and garlic, but the chef prefers to keep his other flavors "secret." Among meat selections they do marvelously tender and succulent lamb chops flavored with rich burgundy sauce.

Bajada Nueva del Patriarca 2. ⓒ **97-722-83-00**. Reservations required. Main courses 17€–21€. AE, DC, MC, V. Mon–Sat 1–3:45pm and 9–10:45pm.

Les Voltes ★ *(Finds)* MEDITERRANEAN This excellent restaurant lies within the vaults of Roman Circus Maximus. Chiseled stone from 2,300 years ago abides harmoniously with thick plate glass and polished steel surfaces. A large 250-seat restaurant, Les Voltes offers a kitchen of skilled chefs turning out a flavorful and well-seasoned Mediterranean cuisine. The menu features time-tested favorites such as a succulent baked lamb from the neighboring hills. *Rape,* or *monkfish,* deserves special billing, served with roasted garlic in a cockle and mussel sauce. Showing sure-handed spicing, the loin of veal is peppery and served with broiled eggplant.

Carrer Trinquet Vell 12. ⓒ **97-723-06-51**. Reservations recommended. Main courses 6€–18€. DC, MC, V. Tues–Sun 1–3:30pm; Tues–Sat 8:30–11:30pm.

Sol-Ric CATALAN/INTERNATIONAL Many guests remember the service here long after memories of the good cuisine have faded. Dating from 1859, the place has a rustic ambience replete with antique farm implements hanging from the walls. There's an outdoor terrace as well as a central fireplace, usually blazing in winter. The chef prepares oven-baked hake with potatoes, tournedos with Roquefort, seafood stew, and several exotic fish dishes, among other specialties.

Vía Augusta 227. ⓒ **97-723-20-32**. Main courses 6€–22€; fixed-price menu 11€. AE, MC, V. Tues–Sun 1–4pm; Tues–Sat 8:30–11pm. Closed mid-Dec to mid-Jan.

The Beaches of the Costa Dorada

Running along the entire coastline of the province of Tarragona, for some 211km (131 miles) from Cunit as far as Les Cases d'Alcanar, is a series of excellent beaches and impressive cliffs, along with beautiful pine-covered headlands. In the city of Tarragona itself is **El Milagre** beach, and a little farther north are the beaches of **L'Arrabassade, Savinosa, dels Capellans,** and the **Llarga.** At the end of the latter stands **La Punta de la Mora,** which has a 16th-century watchtower. The small towns of **Altafulla** and **Torredembarra,** both complete with castles, stand next to these beaches and are the location of many hotels and urban developments.

Farther north again are the two magnificent beaches of **Comarruga** and **Sant Salvador.** The first is particularly cosmopolitan; the second is more secluded. Last comes the beaches of **Calafell, Segur,** and **Cunit,** all with modern tourist complexes. You'll also find the small towns of **Creixell, Sant Vicenç de Calders,** and **Clarà,** which have wooded hills in the background.

South of Tarragona, the coastline forms a wide arc that stretches for miles and includes **La Piñeda** beach. **El Recó** beach fronts the Cape of Salou where, in among its coves, hills, and hidden-away corners, many hotels and residential centers are located. The natural port of **Salou** is nowadays a center for international tourism.

Continuing south toward Valencia, you next come to **Cambrils,** a maritime town with an excellent beach and an important fishing port. In the background stand the impressive Colldejou and Llaberia mountains. Farther south are the beaches of **Montroig** and **L'Hospitalet,** as well as the small town of **L'Ametlla de Mar** with its small fishing port.

After passing the Balaguer massif, you eventually reach the delta of the River Ebro, a wide lowland area covering more than 483km (300 miles), opening like a fan into the sea. This is an area of rice fields crisscrossed by branches of the Ebro and by an enormous number of irrigation channels. There are also some lagoons that because of their immense size are ideal as hunting and fishing grounds. Moreover, there are some beaches over several miles in length and others in small hidden estuaries. Two important towns in the region are **Amposta,** on the Ebro itself, and **Sant Carles de la Ràpita,** a 19th-century port town favored by King Carlos III.

The Costa Dorada extends to its most southwesterly point at the plain of **Alcanar,** a large area given over to the cultivation of oranges and other similar crops. Its beaches, along with the small hamlet of **Les Cases d'Alcanar,** mark the end of the Tarragona section of the Costa Dorada.

TARRAGONA AFTER DARK

Rambla Nova contains a handful of sleepy-looking bars, any of which might serve a cup of coffee or bottle of beer throughout the day and evening.

There's a little more action at the convivial **Club Náutico,** Passeig Marítim s/n (no phone), where tapas, wines, and drinks are served to an often-crowded room overlooking the sea. Similar bars in the town's medieval core include **Bar Anticuario,** Carrer Santa Ana s/n (no phone).

You might also try **Cucudrulus,** Carrer del Protectorado/Pau de Protectorat s/n (no phone), which is a pub with heavy English overtones, an international crowd, and a knack for presenting emerging rock bands of varying degrees of talent. At **Bar Poetes,** Carrer Sant Llorenç 15 (no phone), live bands sometimes perform in a cellar a very short walk from the cathedral.

Concerts and theatrical productions are staged in the city's cultural centerpiece, the **Teatro Metropol,** Rambla Nova 46 (© **97-724-47-95**). Because of the language problem, you might skip theatrical events presented in Catalán in favor of some of the musical and dance presentations.

SIDE TRIPS FROM TARRAGONA

If you rent a car, you can visit two attractions within a 30- to 45-minute drive from Tarragona. The first stop is the **Monestir de Poblet** ★★★, Plaça Corona d'Aragó 11, E-43448 Poblet (© **97-787-02-54**), 47km (29 miles) northwest of Tarragona, one of the most intriguing monasteries in Spain. Its most exciting features are the oddly designed tombs of the old kings of Aragón and Catalonia. Constructed in the 12th and 13th centuries and still in use, Poblet's cathedral-like church reflects both Romanesque and Gothic architectural styles. Cistercian monks still live here, passing their days writing, studying, working a printing press, farming, and helping to restore the building, which suffered heavy damage during the 1835 revolution. Admission to the monastery costs 4.20€ adults and 2.40€ children 13 and under and students. March through October, it's open Monday through Saturday from 10am to 12:30pm and 3 to 6pm; November through February, it's open daily from 10:30am to 12:30pm and 3 to 5:30pm. Except for Monday, when no guide service is available, visits to the monastery are usually set up as a part of tours, mostly in Spanish but with occasional English translations. They depart at 75-minute intervals throughout the monastery's open hours.

About 4.8km (3 miles) farther you can explore an unspoiled medieval Spanish town, **Montblanch.** At its entrance, a map pinpoints the principal artistic and architectural treasures—and there are many. Walk, don't drive, along the narrow, winding streets.

3 Sitges ★★

40km (25 miles) S of Barcelona, 596km (370 miles) E of Madrid

Sitges is one of the most popular resorts of southern Europe, the brightest spot on the Costa Dorada. It's especially crowded in summer, mostly with affluent young northern Europeans, many of them gay. For years the resort largely drew prosperous middle-class industrialists from Barcelona, but those staid days have gone; Sitges is as swinging today as Benidorm and Torremolinos down the coast, but nowhere near as tacky.

Sitges has long been known as a city of culture, thanks in part to resident artist, playwright, and Bohemian mystic Santiago Rusiñol. The 19th-century modernismo (aka *modernisme*) movement began largely at Sitges, and the town remained the scene of artistic encounters and demonstrations long after the movement waned. Sitges continued as a resort of artists, attracting such giants as Salvador Dalí and poet Federico García Lorca. The Spanish Civil War (1936–39) erased what has come to be called the "golden age" of Sitges. Although other artists and writers arrived in the decades to follow, none had the name or the impact of those who had gone before.

ESSENTIALS

GETTING THERE RENFE runs **trains** from Barcelona-Sants to Sitges, a 30-minute trip that costs 2€. Call Ⓒ **90-224-02-02** in Barcelona for information about schedules. Four trains leave Barcelona per hour.

Sitges is a 45-minute drive from Barcelona along the **C-246,** a coastal road. An express highway, the **A-7,** opened in 1991. The coastal road is more scenic, but it can be extremely slow on weekends because of the heavy traffic, as all of Barcelona seemingly heads for the beaches.

VISITOR INFORMATION The **tourist office** is at Carrer Simea Morera 1 (Ⓒ **93-894-42-51;** www.sitges.org). From June to September 15, it's open daily from 9am to 9pm; from September 16 to May, hours are Monday through Friday from 9am to 2pm and 4 to 6:30pm, Saturday from 10am to 1pm.

SPECIAL EVENTS The **Carnaval** at Sitges is one of the outstanding events on the Catalán calendar. For more than a century, the town has celebrated the days before the beginning of Lent. Fancy dress, floats, feathered outfits, and sequins all make this an exciting event. The party begins on the Thursday before Lent with the arrival of the king of the Carnestoltes and ends with the Burial of a Sardine on Ash Wednesday. Activities reach their flamboyant best on Sant Bonaventura, where gay people hold their own celebrations.

FUN ON & OFF THE BEACH

The old part of Sitges used to be a fortified medieval enclosure. The castle is now the seat of the town government. The local parish church, called **La Punta (The Point)** and built next to the sea on top of a promontory, presides over an extensive maritime esplanade, where people parade in the early evening. Behind the side of the church are the Museu Cau Ferrat and the Museu Maricel (see "Museums," below).

 We'll Have a Gay Old Time

Along with Ibiza, Key West, and Mikonos, Sitges has established itself firmly on the "A" list of gay resorts. It's a perfect destination for those who want a ready-made combination of beach and bars, all within a few minutes' walk of each other. It works well as a temporary, calmer alternative to Barcelona, which is about 30 minutes away by train, and so is great for a day trip or a few days out of the city. Off-season, it's pretty quiet on the gay front apart from the carnival in February, when hordes of gays and lesbians descend from Barcelona and the party really begins.

Summer, however, is pure hedonistic playtime, and the town draws the boys in from all over Europe. Sitges is never going to tax the intellect, but it might well exhaust the body. There's a gay beach crammed with the usual overload of muscles and summer accessories in the middle of the town in front of the Passeig Marítim. The other beach is nudist and farther out of town, between Sitges and Vilanova. The best directions are to go as far as the L'Atlántida disco and then follow the train track to the farther of the two beaches. The woods next to it are unsurprisingly packed with playful wildlife sporting short hair and deep tans.

Most people are here to hit the beach. The beaches have showers, bathing cabins, and stalls; kiosks rent motorboats and watersports equipment. Beaches on the eastern end and those inside the town center are the most peaceful—for example, **Aiguadoiç** and **Els Balomins. Playa San Sebastián, Fragata Beach,** and the **"Beach of the Boats"** (below the church and next to the yacht club) are the area's family beaches. A young, happening crowd heads for the **Playa de la Ribera** to the west.

All along the coast, women can and certainly do go topless. Farther west are the most solitary beaches, where the scene grows more racy, especially along the **Playas del Muerto,** where two tiny nude beaches lie between Sitges and Vilanova i la Geltrú. A shuttle bus runs between the cathedral and Golf Terramar. From Golf Terramar, go along the road to the club L'Atlántida, then walk along the railway. The first beach draws nudists of every sexual persuasion, and the second is almost solely gay. Be advised that lots of action takes place in the woods in back of these beaches.

MUSEUMS

Beaches aside, Sitges has some choice museums, which really shouldn't be missed.

Museu Cau Ferrat   The Catalán artist Santiago Rusiñol combined two 16th-century cottages to make this house, where he lived and worked; upon his death in 1931 he willed it to Sitges along with his art collection. More than anyone else, Rusiñol made Sitges a popular resort. The museum collection includes two paintings by El Greco and several small Picassos, including *The Bullfight.* A number of Rusiñol's works are on display. See the box on Rusiñol and his house/museum, above.

Carrer del Fonollar. ☎ **93-894-03-64.** Admission 3€ adults, 1.50€ students, free for children under 16; combination ticket for the 3 museums listed in this section: 5€ adults, 3€ students and children. June 15–Sept 30 Tues–Sun 10am–2pm and 5–9pm; Oct 1–June 14 Tues–Fri 10am–1:30pm and 3–6:30pm, Sat 10am–7pm, Sun 10am–3pm.

Museu Maricel   Opened by the king and queen of Spain, the Museu Maricel contains art donated by Dr. Jesús Pérez Rosales. The palace, owned by American Charles Deering when it was built right after World War I, is made up of two parts connected by a small bridge. The museum has a good collection of Gothic and Romantic paintings and sculptures, as well as many fine Catalán ceramics. There are three noteworthy works by Santiago Rebull and an allegorical painting of World War I by José María Sert.

Carrer del Fonallar. ☎ **93-894-03-64.** Admission 3€ adults, 1.50€ students, free for children under 16; admission included in combination ticket (see Museu Cau Ferrat, above). Same hours as Museu Cau Ferrat.

Museu Romàntic ("Can Llopis")   This museum re-creates the daily life of a Sitges land-owning family in the 18th and 19th centuries. The family rooms, furniture, and household objects are most interesting. You'll find wine cellars and an important collection of antique dolls (upstairs).

Sant Gaudenci 1. ☎ **93-894-29-69.** Admission (including guided tour) 3€ adults, 1.50€ students, free for children under 16; admission included in combination ticket (see Museu Cau Ferrat, above). All museums have the same hours and dates.

WHERE TO STAY

In spite of a building spree, Sitges just can't handle the large numbers of tourists who flock here in July and August. By mid-October just about everything—including hotels, restaurants, and bars—slows down considerably or closes altogether.

EXPENSIVE

Meliá Gran Sitges ⭐   Designed with steeply sloping sides reminiscent of a pair of interconnected Aztec pyramids, this hotel dates from 1992, when it housed spectators and participants in the Barcelona Olympics. The hotel has a marble lobby with what feels like the largest window in Spain, overlooking a view of the mountains. Each midsize room comes with a large furnished veranda for sunbathing, and each bathroom has a tub/shower combo. Many guests are here to participate in the conferences and conventions held frequently in the battery of high-tech convention facilities. It's about a 15-minute walk east of the center of Sitges, near the access roads leading to Barcelona.

El Puerto de Aiguadoiç, 08870 Sitges. ☎ **800/336-3542** in the U.S., or 93-811-08-11. Fax 93-894-90-34. 307 units. 150€–224€ double; 170€–242€ suite. Rates include breakfast. AE, DC, MC, V. Parking 8€. **Amenities:** Restaurant; bar; pool; health club; sauna; room service; babysitting; laundry service; dry cleaning. *In room:* A/C, TV, minibar, hair dryer, safe.

San Sebastián Playa ⭐⭐   The best choice in Sitges, opposite San Sebastián beach, this four-star hotel with its wedding cake facade has been in operation since 1990. The functional Art Deco interior is the most beautifully decorated of any hotel in Sitges. A lot of attention has gone into the guest rooms, which are spacious and comfortable, with bathrooms containing tub/shower combos. Each has a balcony opening onto the sea.

Port Alegre 53, 08070 Sitges. ☎ **93-894-86-76.** Fax 93-894-04-30. www.hotelsansebastian.com. 51 units 113€–176€ double; 190€–256€ suite. Rates include breakfast. Parking: 13€. **Amenities:** Restaurant; bar; pool; room service; babysitting; laundry service; dry cleaning; private garden. *In room:* A/C, TV, minibar, hair dryer, safe.

Subur Marítim ⭐   In a residential area on the seafront facing a good beach, this government-rated four-star hotel is only a 5-minute walk from the center. It's a winning choice, made up of a traditional Catalán building and a more modern functional structure. The interior is cozy, with a traditional Catalán decor of wood fittings and cast-iron adornments on doors and windows. The amply sized rooms are comfortably furnished and tastefully decorated, each with a balcony and neatly kept bathroom with a tub/shower combo.

Passeig Marítim, 08870 Sitges. ☎ **93-894-15-50.** Fax 93-894-04-27. www.hotelsuburmaritim.com. 42 units. 140€–171€ double; 187€–203€ suite. Rates include breakfast buffet. AE, DC, MC, V. Free parking. **Amenities:** Restaurant; bar; pool; jet ski rental; room service; babysitting; laundry service; dry cleaning. *In room:* A/C, TV, minibar, hair dryer, safe.

Terramar ⭐   Facing the beach in a residential area of Sitges, about half a mile from the center, this modern resort hotel with its balconied front evokes a many-tiered yacht. The interior, however, is designed in a classical Mediterranean style with marble floors and white walls. The spacious guest rooms are comfortable, with carpeted floors, colorful wall coverings, and bathrooms with tub/shower combos.

Passeig Marítim 80, 08870 Sitges. ☎ **93-894-00-50.** Fax 93-894-56-04. www.hotelterramar.com. 209 units. 92€–147€ double; 147€–178€ suite. Rates include breakfast buffet. AE, DC, MC, V. Closed Nov–Mar. Bus: 1. **Amenities:** 2 restaurants; 2 bars; pool; 2 tennis courts; room service; babysitting; laundry service; dry cleaning; private garden. *In room:* A/C, TV, minibar, hair dryer, safe.

MODERATE

El Galeón   A leading choice only a short walk from both the beach and the Plaça d'Espanya, this well-styled hostelry blends a bit of the old Spain with the new. The small public rooms feel cozy; the good-size guest rooms, accented with wood grain, have a more streamlined aura. Each comes with a comfortable bed, plus a bathroom with a shower stall.

Sant Francesc 44, 08870 Sitges. (C) **93-894-06-12**. Fax 93-894-63-35. 74 units. 47€–82€ double. Rates include breakfast. MC, V. Parking 11€. Closed Oct 20–Apr. **Amenities:** Restaurant; bar; pool; babysitting. *In room:* A/C, TV, safe.

Hotel Romàntic de Sitges ★ (Finds)

Made up of three beautifully restored 19th-century villas, this hotel is only a short walk from the beach and the train station. The romantic bar is an international rendezvous, and the public rooms are filled with artworks. You can have breakfast in the dining room or in a garden filled with mulberry trees. The rooms, reached by stairs, range from small to medium and are well maintained, with good beds and bathrooms with shower stalls. Overflow guests are housed in a nearby annex, the Hotel de la Renaixença.

Carrer de Sant Isidre 33, 08870 Sitges. (C) **93-894-83-75**. Fax 93-894-81-67. www.hotelromantic.com. 60 units. 75€–95€ double. Rates include breakfast. AE, MC, V. Closed Nov–Mar 15. **Amenities:** Bar; lounge; babysitting. *In room:* Hair dryer, safe.

INEXPENSIVE

Hotel El Cid El Cid's exterior suggests Castile and inside, appropriately enough, you'll find beamed ceilings, natural stone walls, heavy wrought-iron chandeliers, and leather chairs. The same theme is carried out in the rear dining room and in the pleasantly furnished rooms, which, though small, are still quite comfortable, with fine beds and bathrooms containing shower stalls. Breakfast is the only meal served. El Cid is off the Passeig de Vilanova in the center of town.

San José 39 bis, 08870 Sitges. (C) **93-894-18-42**. Fax 93-894-63-35. 77 units. 38€–65€ double. Rates include continental breakfast. MC, V. Closed Nov–Apr. **Amenities:** Bar; pool; babysitting; solarium. *In room:* No phone.

Hotel El Xalet ★ (Finds)

Right in the town center, this little charmer lies about a 10-minute stroll from the nearest good beach. Pronounced like "chalet," it's a happy blend of contemporary comfort and traditional styling. The Modernist building is from the early 20th century, with both Gothic and art nouveau architectural adornments. Some visitors strolling by at first think it's a Gothic church with its ornate stonework, intricate carvings, and towering spires. Antique mosaics and marble decorate the lobby and reception. Grace notes are the small pool in the hotel's well-manicured gardens and an inviting roof terrace where you can order breakfast. Bedrooms are small to midsize, with comfortable furnishings and pastel shades of salmon and yellow, along with small, neat bathrooms, some with tubs, the others with showers. The summer only restaurant serves succulent Catalonia specialties.

Isla de Cuba 21, 08870 Sitges. (C) **93-811-00-70**. Fax 93-894-55-79. 12 units. 60€–72€ double; 90€ suite. Rates include breakfast. AE, DC, MC, V. **Amenities:** Restaurant; roof terrace; pool. *In room:* A/C, TV, minibar, hair dryer, iron, safe.

Hotel Noucentista (Value)

Owned by the same family that owned El Xalet, this is another winning choice and stands across the road from their sibling property. After undergoing 3 years of renovation in the 21st century, it is now better than ever. The name, Noucentista, in Spanish means 1900, the year of the building's original construction. The interior is quite stunning, a statement of Modernism with much use of antiques. The small to midsize bedrooms are stylishly and comfortably furnished with ample closet space and bathrooms, each with a shower. Some of the accommodations open onto small private balconies.

The inn lies a 10-minute walk from the beach. The hotel is also graced with a small courtyard garden, and guests have access to Xalet's swimming pool.

Isla de Cuba 21, 08870 Sitges. ☏ **93-8110070.** Fax 93-894-5579. 12 units. 60€–72€ double; 90€ suite. AE, DC, MC, V. *In room:* A/C, TV, minibar, hair dryer, safe.

Hotel Subur   This old-time favorite stands in prominent position in the center of town on the seafront. The first hotel built in Sitges (in 1916), the Subur was torn down and reconstructed in 1960 and last renovated in 1992. Its small rooms are well furnished, its bathrooms equipped with tub/shower combos, and balconies open onto the Mediterranean. The hotel remains open year-round, even during the cooler months.

Passeig de la Ribera s/n, 08870 Sitges. ☏ **93-894-00-66.** Fax 93-894-69-86. 96 units. 88€–105€ double. Rates include breakfast. AE, DC, MC, V. Parking 11€. **Amenities:** Restaurant; bar; room service; babysitting; laundry service; dry cleaning. *In room:* A/C, TV, minibar, safe.

WHERE TO DINE
EXPENSIVE

El Velero ⭐ SEAFOOD   This is one of Sitges's leading restaurants, positioned along the beachfront promenade. The most desirable tables are found on the glass greenhouse terrace, opening onto the esplanade, though there's a more glamorous restaurant inside. Try a soup, such as clam and truffle or whitefish, followed by a main dish such as paella marinara (with seafood) or suprême of salmon in pine-nut sauce.

Passeig de la Ribera 38. ☏ **93-894-20-51.** Reservations required. Main courses 18€–36€; fixed-price menu 24€. AE, DC, MC, V. Tues-Sun 1:30–4pm and 8:30–11:30pm.

MODERATE

Els Quatre Gats ⭐ CATALAN   Its cuisine is called *cocina del mercado,* based on whatever produce is fresh that day in the markets. When it opened in the early 1960s as a bar/cafe, it adopted the name of one of Catalonia's most historic cafes, Els 4 Gats, a Barcelona hangout that had been a Picasso favorite. In a setting accented with paintings and varnished paneling, you can enjoy fresh grilled fish, garlic soup, lamb cutlets with local herbs, roast chicken in wine sauce, and veal kidneys in sherry sauce. On a side street near the sea, the restaurant is a few steps from the beachfront Passeig de la Ribera.

Sant Pau 13. ☏ **93-894-19-15.** Reservations recommended. Main courses 12€–18€; *menú del día* 18€. AE, DC, MC, V. Thurs–Tues 1–4pm and 8–11pm. Closed Nov–Mar.

Fragata ⭐ SEAFOOD   Though its simple interior offers little more than well-scrubbed floors, tables with crisp napery, and air-conditioning, some of the most delectable seafood specialties in town are served here, and hundreds of loyal customers come to appreciate the authentic cuisine. Specialties include seafood soup, a mixed grill of fresh fish, cod salad, mussels marinara, several preparations of squid and octopus, plus some flavorful meat dishes, such as grilled lamb cutlets.

Passeig de la Ribera 1. ☏ **93-894-10-86.** Reservations recommended. Main dishes 12€–24€. AE, DC, MC, V. Daily 1–4:30pm and 8:30–11:30pm.

La Masía CATALAN   A provincial decor complements the imaginative regional specialties for which this place has been known since 1972. They include several preparations of cod, roast suckling lamb well seasoned with herbs, *pollo ajillo* (garlic chicken, a regional dish), a wide array of fresh fish and shellfish, and monkfish with aioli—the chef's pride. Every Catalonian's favorite dessert is *crema catalana* (caramel pudding). If you prefer to dine outdoors, you can sit in the pleasant garden adjacent to the main dining room.

Passeig Vilanova 164. ☎ **93-894-10-76**. Reservations required. Main courses 6€–20€; *menú del día* 12€. AE, DC, MC, V. Daily 1–4pm and 8:30–11:30pm.

Mare Nostrum SEAFOOD   This landmark dates from 1950, when it opened in what had been a private home in the 1890s. The dining room has a waterfront view, and in warm weather tables are placed outside. The menu includes a full range of seafood dishes, among them grilled fish specialties and steamed hake with champagne. The fish soup is particularly delectable. Next door, the restaurant's cafe serves ice cream, milkshakes, sandwiches, tapas, and three varieties of sangria, including one with champagne and fruit.

Passeig de la Ribera 60. ☎ **93-894-33-93**. Reservations required. Main courses 9€–15€. AE, DC, MC, V. Thurs–Tues 1–4pm and 8–11pm. Closed Dec 15–Feb 1.

SITGES AFTER DARK

One of the best ways to pass an evening in Sitges is to walk the waterfront esplanade, have a leisurely dinner, then retire about 11pm to one of the open-air cafes for a nightcap and some serious people-watching. Few local dives can compete with the scene taking place on the streets.

If you're straight, you may have to hunt to find a bar that isn't predominantly gay. There are so many gay bars, in fact, that a map is distributed pinpointing their locales. Nine of them are concentrated on **Carrer Sant Bonaventura** in the center of town, a 5-minute walk from the beach (near the Museu Romàntic). If you grow bored with the action in one place, you just have to walk down the street to find another. Drink prices run about the same in all the clubs.

Mediterráneo, Sant Bonaventura 6 (no phone), is the largest gay disco/bar. It sports a formal Iberian garden and sleek modern styling. And upstairs in this restored 1690s house just east of the Plaça d'Espanya are pool tables and a covered terrace. On summer nights, the place is filled to overflowing.

Other gay bars include **Bourbon's,** Sant Bonaventura 13 (☎ **93-894-33-47**), which appeals to a predominately youngish crowd, and **El Candil,** Carrer de la Carreta 9 (☎ **93-894-78-36**), with a wider age range and a darkroom and video shows. **El Horno,** Joan Tarrida 6 (☎ **93-894-09-09**), with slight leather overtones that grow more prominent as the night progresses, opens earlier, at 5:30pm, and also features a darkroom.

Another of the town's most popular and crowded nightspots, with DJs spinning the latest dance hits, is **Ricky's Disco,** Sant Pau 25 (☎ **93-894-96-81**), which charges a cover of 9€ to 12€. This place caters to an international mix of gay and straight visitors. It's set back from the beach on a narrow street noted for its inexpensive restaurants and folkloric color. **Trailer,** Angel Vidal 36 (no phone), is an extremely popular club—the hottest in town—and the best place to end the night. It closes at 5:30am, and the 9€ cover includes a drink.

13

Girona & the Costa Brava

The **Costa Brava,** the so-called wild coast, is a 153km (95-mile) stretch of coastline—the northernmost Mediterranean seafront in Spain—beginning north of Barcelona at Blanes and stretching toward the French border. Visit this area in May, June, September, or October and avoid July and August, when tour groups from northern Europe book virtually all the hotel rooms.

Undiscovered little fishing villages along the coast long ago bloomed into resort towns. **Tossa de Mar** is the most delightful of them. **Lloret de Mar** is immensely popular but too commercial and overdeveloped for many tastes. The most unspoiled spot is remote **Cadaqués.** Some of the smaller villages make excellent stops.

If you want to visit the Costa Brava but simply can't secure a room in high season, consider taking a day trip by car from Barcelona or booking one of the daily organized tours that leave from that city. Allow plenty of time for driving. In summer, the traffic jams can be fierce and the roads between towns difficult and winding.

If you visit the coast in summer without a hotel reservation, you'll stand a fair chance of getting a room in **Girona,** the capital of the province and one of the most interesting medieval cities in Spain.

1 Girona ★ ★

97km (60 miles) NE of Barcelona, 90km (56 miles) S of the French city of Perpignan

Founded by the Romans, **Girona** is one of the most important historical sites in Spain. Later, it became a Moorish stronghold. Later still, it reputedly withstood three invasions by Napoléon's troops (1809). For that and other past sieges, Girona is often called the "City of a Thousand Sieges."

Split by the Onyar River, this sleepy medieval city attracts crowds of tourists darting inland from the Costa Brava for the day. For orientation purposes, go to the ancient stone footbridge across the Onyar. From here, you'll have the finest view. Bring good walking shoes, as the only way to discover the particular charm of this medieval city is on foot. You can wander for hours through the **Call,** the labyrinthine old quarter, with its narrow, steep alleyways and lanes and its ancient stone houses, which form a rampart chain along the Onyar. Much of Girona can be appreciated from the outside, but it does contain some important attractions you'll want to see on the inside.

ESSENTIALS

GETTING THERE   More than 26 **trains** per day run between Girona and Barcelona from 6:08am to 9:26pm, including two TALGOS. Trip time is 1 to 2 hours, depending on the train. Trains arrive in Girona at the Plaça Espanya (© **97-220-70-93** for information).

From the Costa Brava, you can take one of the SARFA **buses** (© **97-220-17-96** in Girona) to Girona. Three per day depart from Tossa de Mar (see "Tossa de Mar," later in this chapter). Barcelona Bus (© **97-220-24-32** in Girona) also operates express buses between Girona and Barcelona at the rate of 6 to 13 per day, depending on the season and demand.

From Barcelona or the French border, drivers connect with the main north-south route (A-7), taking the turnoff to Girona. From Barcelona, take the A-2 north to reach the A-7.

VISITOR INFORMATION   The **tourist office** at Rambla de la Libertat (© **97-222-65-75;** www.ajuntament.gi) is open Monday through Friday from 8am to 8pm, Saturday from 8am to 2pm and 4 to 8pm, and Sunday from 9am to 2pm.

EXPLORING THE MEDIEVAL CITY

Banys Arabs   These 12th-century Arab baths, an example of Romanesque civic architecture, are in the old quarter of the city. Visit the **caldarium** (hot bath), with its paved floor, and the **frigidarium** (cold bath), with its central octagonal pool surrounded by pillars that support a prism-like structure in the overhead window. Although the Moorish baths were heavily restored in 1929, they give you an idea of what the ancient ones were like.

Carrer Ferran el Católic. © **97-221-32-62.** Admission 1.50€. Apr–Sept Mon–Sat 10am–7pm, Sun 10am–2pm; Oct–Mar Tues–Sun 10am–2pm. Closed Jan 1, Jan 6, Easter, and Dec 25–26.

Catedral   Girona's major attraction is its magnificent cathedral, reached by climbing a 17th-century baroque staircase of 90 steep steps. The 14th-century cathedral represents many architectural styles, including Gothic and Romanesque, but it's most notably Catalán baroque. The facade you see as you climb those long stairs dates from the 17th and 18th centuries; from a cornice on top rises a bell tower crowned by a dome with a bronze angel weather vane. Enter the main door of the cathedral and go into the nave, which, at 23m (75 ft.), is the broadest in the world of Gothic architecture.

The cathedral contains many works of art, displayed for the most part in its museum. Its prize exhibit is a **tapestry of the Creation,** a unique piece of 11th- or 12th-century Romanesque embroidery depicting humans and animals in the Garden of Eden. The other major work displayed is one of the world's rarest manuscripts—the 10th-century *Códex del Beatus,* which contains an illustrated commentary on the Book of the Apocalypse. From the cathedral's **Chapel of Hope,** a door leads to a **Romanesque cloister** from the 12th and 13th centuries, with an unusual trapezoidal layout. The cloister gallery, with a double colonnade, has a series of biblical scenes that are the prize jewel of Catalán Romanesque art. From the cloister you can view the 12th-century **Torre de Carlemany** (Charlemagne's Tower).

Plaça de la Catedral. © **97-221-44-26.** Free admission to cathedral; cloister and museum 3€. Cathedral daily 9am–1pm and during cloister and museum visiting hours. Cloister and museum: July–Sept Tues–Sat 10am–8pm, Sun 10am–2pm; Oct–Feb Tues–Sat 10am–2pm and 4–6pm, Sun 10am–2pm; Mar–June Tues–Sat 10am–2pm and 4–7pm, Sun 10am–2pm.

Església de Sant Feliu   This 14th- to 17th-century church was built over what may have been the tomb of Feliu of Africa, martyred during Diocletian's persecution at the beginning of the 4th century. Important in the architectural history of Catalonia, the church has pillars and arches in the Romanesque style and a Gothic central nave. The **bell tower**—one of the Girona skyline's most characteristic features—has eight pinnacles and one central tower, each supported on a solid

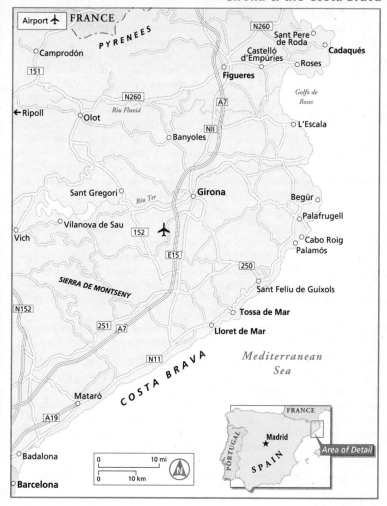

octagonal base. The main facade of the church is baroque. The interior contains some exceptional works, including a 16th-century **altarpiece** and a 14th-century alabaster *Reclining Christo.* Notice the eight pagan and Christian **sarcophagi** set in the walls of the presbytery, the two oldest of which are from the 2nd century A.D. One shows Pluto carrying Persephone off to the depths of the earth.

Pujada de Sant Feliu. ☎ **97-220-14-07.** Free admission. Daily 7am–1pm and 4–6:30pm; holidays 4–6:30pm.

Museu Arqueològic Housed in a Romanesque church and cloister from the 11th and 12th centuries, this museum illustrates the history of the country from the Paleolithic to the Visigothic periods, using artifacts discovered in nearby excavations. The monastery itself ranks as one of the best examples of Catalán Romanesque architecture. In the cloister, note some Hebrew inscriptions from gravestones of the old Jewish cemetery.

Sant Pere de Galligants, Santa Llúcia 1. ☎ **97-220-26-32.** Admission 1.80€ adults, 1.35€ students, free for seniors and children under 10. Tues–Sat 10am–2pm and 4–6pm; Sun 10am–2pm.

Museu d'Art ⭐ In a former Romanesque and Gothic Episcopal palace (Palau Episcopal) next to the cathedral, this museum displays artworks spanning 10 centuries (once housed in the old Diocesan Museum and the Provincial Museum). Stop in the throne room to view the **altarpiece of Sant Pere of Púbol** by Bernat Martorell and the **altarpiece of Sant Miguel de Crüilles** by Luis Borrassa. Both of these works, from the 15th century, are exemplary pieces of Catalán Gothic painting. The museum is also proud of its **altar stone** of Sant Pere de Roda, from the 10th and 11th centuries; this work in wood and stone, depicting figures and legends, was once covered in embossed silver. The 12th-century *Crüilles Timber* is a unique piece of Romanesque polychrome wood. *Our Lady of Besalù,* from the 15th century, is one of the best Virgins carved in alabaster.

Pujada de la Catedral 12. © **97-220-95-36**. Admission 2€ adults, 1.40€ students, children, and adults over 65. Mar–Sept Tues–Sat 10am–7pm (June–Aug Wed hours are 10am–2pm), Sun 10am–2pm; Oct–Feb Tues–Sat 10am–6pm, Sun 10am–2pm. Closed Jan 1, Jan 6, Easter, and Dec 25–26.

Museu de Cinema ⭐ Film buffs are flocking to this recently opened film museum, the only one of its kind in Spain. It houses the Tomàs Mallol collection of some 25,000 cinema artifacts, going all the way up to films shot as late as 1970. Many objects are from the "precinema" era, plus other exhibits from the early days of film. The museum even owns the original camera of the pioneering Lumière brothers. Fixed images such as photographs, posters, engravings, drawings, and paintings are exhibited along with some 800 films of various styles and periods. There's even a library with film-related publications.

Sèquia 1. © **97-241-27-77**. Admission 3€ adults, 1.50€ children and students. May–Sept Tues–Sun 10am–8pm; off season Tues–Fri 10am–6pm, Sat 10am–8pm, Sun 11am–3pm.

Museu d'Història de la Ciutat Housed in the old 18th-century Capuchin Convent de Sant Antoni, this collection dates from the time of Puig d'en Roca (Catalonia's oldest prehistoric site) to the present. It includes Girona's (and Spain's) first electric streetlights. Additional displays of tools, technical materials, and the accouterments of passing lifestyles make up a kind of municipal résumé. From the original Capuchin convent, there remains the cemetery used for drying corpses before mummifying them (1 of 3 of this type left in the world).

Carrer de la Força. © **97-222-22-29**. Admission 2€. Tues–Sat 10am–2pm and 5–7pm; Sun 10am–2pm.

SHOPPING

Consistent with its role as an international seaside resort, Girona has a network of shops catering to everything from sportswear to formal wear. The most appealing shopping street is **Carrer Santa Clara.** At **Adolfo Domínguez,** Carrer Santa Clara 36 (© **97-222-29-61**), the inventories of men's and women's clothing derive from Spain and the rest of Europe. For men's and women's sportswear, try **Tommy,** Rambla de la Libertat 28 (© **97-222-36-93**), or its almost-adjacent neighbor specializing only in women's clothing, **Casual,** Rambla de la Libertat 32 (tel. **97-222-36-93**). Finally, consider **Zara,** Carrer Joan Maragall s/n (© **97-222-13-05**), a stylish but very affordable emporium for both men and women.

If handicrafts appeal to you, consider a 32km (20-mile) eastward trek from Girona to the hamlet of **La Bispal,** more or less midway between Girona and the town of Palamos. (From Girona, follow the signs pointing to Palamos.) Here, rows of simple shops display and sell the output of dozens of artisans who labor to produce artfully rustic ceramics, some of which are too bulky to ship, others that can be packed and carried as part of your carry-on luggage.

WHERE TO STAY
MODERATE

Hotel Carlemany ✦   In a commercial area only 10 minutes from the historic core, this 1995 hotel is the city's best. A favorite of business travelers, it's contemporary with an ultramodern design and a cavernous interior of marble, polished wood, Oriental carpets, and tropical plants. The midsize to spacious rooms are soundproofed and airy, with bathrooms containing tub/shower combos.

Plaça Miguel Santalo, 17002 Girona. © **97-221-12-12.** Fax 97-221-49-94. www.carlemany.com. 90 units. 105€ double; 140€ suite. AE, MC, V. Parking 11€. **Amenities:** Restaurant; 2 bars; room service; babysitting; laundry service; dry cleaning. *In room:* A/C, TV, hair dryer, safe.

Hotel Ultonia   Restored in 1993 and now better than ever, this small hotel lies a short walk from the Plaça de la Independencia. Since the late 1950s it has been a favorite with business travelers, but today it attracts more visitors, as it's close to the historical district. The rooms are compact and furnished in modern style, with comfortable beds and bathrooms, most of which have tub/shower combos. Double-glazed windows keep out the noise. Some of the rooms opening onto the avenue have tiny balconies. In just 8 to 12 minutes, you can cross the Onyar into the medieval quarter. Guests can enjoy a breakfast buffet (not included in the rates quoted below), but no other meals are served.

Avinguda Jaume I 22, 17001 Girona. © **97-220-38-50.** Fax 97-220-33-34. 45 units. 77€–94€ double. AE, DC, MC, V. Parking 8€ nearby. **Amenities:** Laundry service; dry cleaning. *In room:* A/C, TV, minibar.

Meliá Girona ✦   This modern and functional runner-up to the Carlemany is a member of the large Spanish chain opened in 1990 and attracts mostly business travelers. About 20 minutes from the resorts of the Costa Brava, it's often used as an emergency accommodation in summer when the beach hotels are packed. It lacks a personal touch in decorations, but the rooms are spacious and comfortable, with bathrooms with tub/shower combos.

Calle Barcelona 112, 17003 Girona. © **97-240-05-00.** Fax 97-224-32-33. www.solmelia.com. 120€ double; 160€ suite. AE, DC, MC. V. Parking: 8.50€. **Amenities:** Restaurant; bar; room service; babysitting; laundry service; dry cleaning. *In room:* A/C, TV, minibar, hair dryer, safe.

INEXPENSIVE

Bellmirall ✦ *Value*   Across the Onyar River, this little discovery lies in the heart of the old Jewish ghetto. It's one of the best values in the old town. The building itself, much restored and altered over the years, dates originally from the 14th century. Christina Vach took control of the venerated old building and proceeded to restore it and convert it to a hotel. She has succeeded admirably in her task. Bedrooms are small to midsize, and are decorated in part with antiques set against brick walls. Some of these walls are adorned with paintings, others with carefully selected ceramics. Each room comes with a small bathroom with shower. In summer, it's possible to order breakfast outside in the courtyard.

Carrer Bellmirall 3, 17004, Girona. © **97-220-40-09.** 7 units. 56€ double; 75€ triple. Rates include breakfast. No credit cards. Free parking (hotel provides permit). Closed Jan–Feb. *In room:* No phone.

Condal *Value*   Near the rail and bus stations west of the old town, this third-class 1960s hotel is, in the words of one frequent visitor, "aggressively simple." As such, it's recommended to bargain hunters only. The lounge and reception area is small; there's no elevator; and no meals are served—but these are minor concerns. The small rooms are clean and functional, and some open onto pleasant views. Each comes with a comfortable bed and a bathroom with a tub/shower combination. The attendants speak only a little English, but they're more than willing to try.

Joan Maragall 10, 17002 Girona. (C) 97-220-44-62. 38 units. 48€ double. AE, MC, V. *In room:* TV, hair dryer.

Hotel Peninsular Devoid of any significant architectural character, this modest hotel provides clean but uncontroversial accommodations near the cathedral and the river. The small rooms, which benefited from a 1990 renovation, are scattered over five floors. All units contain neatly kept bathrooms with showers. The hotel is better for short-term stopovers than for prolonged stays. Breakfast is the only meal served (and is not included in the rates quoted below).

Carrer Nou 3, 17001 Girona. (C) **97-220-38-00.** Fax 97-221-04-92. www.novarahotels.com. 45 units. 56€–66€ double. AE, DC, MC, V. Parking 6€ nearby. **Amenities:** Laundry service; dry cleaning. *In room:* TV, hair dryer, safe.

NEARBY PLACES TO STAY

Hostal de la Gavina ✦✦✦ This is the grandest address in the northeast corridor of Spain. Since it opened in the early 1980s, the Hostal de la Gavina has attracted the rich and glamorous, including King Juan Carlos, Elizabeth Taylor, and a host of celebrities from northern Europe. It's on a peninsula jutting seaward from the center of S'Agaro, within a thick-walled Iberian villa built as the home of the Ansesa family (the owners of the hotel) in 1932. Most of the accommodations are in the resort's main building, which has been enlarged and modified. The spacious rooms are the most sumptuous in the area, with elegant appointments, deluxe fabrics, plush towels, toiletries, and tub/shower combos.

Plaça de la Rosaleda, 17248 S'Agaro (Girona). (C) **97-232-11-00.** Fax 97-232-15-73. www.lagavina.com. 74 units. 165€–250€ double; from 250€–355€ suite. AE, DC, MC, V. Parking 17€ garage; free outside. Closed Nov–Apr. **Amenities:** 2 restaurants; 2 bars; pool; tennis courts; health club; sauna; whirlpool; room service; massage; babysitting; laundry service; dry cleaning. *In room:* A/C, TV, minibar, hair dryer, safe.

Mas de Torrent ✦✦✦ An hour's drive north of Barcelona and a 15-minute drive from the beaches of Costa Brava, this is a Relais & Châteaux member that was elegantly created from a 1751 farmstead *(masía)*. In the hamlet of Torrent, Mas de Torrent is one of the most artful and best hotels in Spain. Try for one of the 10 rooms in the original farmhouse, with its massive beams and spacious bathrooms with deep tubs and power showers. The rooms in the more modern bungalow-style annex are just as comfortable but lack the mellow old atmosphere. From the stone balconies of the rooms, vistas of the countryside come into view with Catalonian vineyards in the distance. In the restaurant, the chef focuses mainly on the classic dishes of Catalonia, including monkfish in saffron or fine noodles simmered in fish consommé and served with fresh shellfish. You can also migrate over to an independent nearby restaurant, El Bulli (see below). Shoppers can take the 10-minute drive to La Bispal, one of the largest potterymaking towns on the continent.

Afueras de Torrent, Torrent 17123 Girona. (C) **97-230-32-92.** Fax 97-230-32-93. www.mastorrent.com. 39 units. 250€–280€ double; from 280€–340€ suite. AE, DC, MC, V. Free parking. Lies 37km (23 miles) north of Girona. **Amenities:** Restaurant; bar; pool; room service; babysitting; laundry. *In room:* A/C, TV, minibar, safe.

WHERE TO DINE

Bronsoms ✦ CATALAN In the heart of the old town, within an 1890s building that was a private home, this restaurant is one of the most consistently reliable in Girona. The subject of praise from newspapers as far away as Madrid, it has been under its present management since 1982, perfecting the art of serving a Catalán-based *cocina del mercado*—that is, cooking with whatever market-fresh ingredients are available. The house specialties include fish paella, *arroz negro* (black rice, tinted with squid ink and studded with shellfish), white beans, and several preparations of Iberian ham.

Sant Francesc 7. © **97-221-24-93.** Reservations recommended. Main courses 6€–12€; fixed-price menu 8€. AE, MC, V. Mon–Sat 1–4pm and 8–11:30pm; Sun 1–4pm.

Cal Ros CATALAN   In the oldest part of Girona, near the Plaza de Cataluña, this restaurant thrives as a culinary staple and has done so since the 1920s. It was named after a long-ago light-haired owner (Cal Ros translates from the Catalán as "the blond person"), although exactly who that was, no one today seems to remember. You'll be seated in one of four rustic dining rooms, each with heavy ceiling beams, exposed stone and plaster, and a sense of old Catalonia. Menu items include savory *escudilla,* made with veal, pork, and local herbs and vegetables; at least four kinds of local fish, usually braised with potatoes and tomatoes; tender fried filets of veal with mushrooms; and flaky homemade pastries, some of them flavored with anise-flavored cream.

Calle Cort Reial 9. © **97-221-73-79.** Reservations recommended. Main courses 6€–18€. MC, V. Nov–Mar Tues–Sun 1–4pm, Tues–Sat 8–11pm; Apr–Oct Sun–Mon 1–4pm and 8–11pm.

El Cellar de Can Roca ☆☆☆ CATALAN   Just 2km (1¼ miles) from the center of Girona, El Cellar de Can Roca is the best of the new spate of restaurants appearing in Girona and represents the success of the campaign to transform Girona into one of the more fashionable cities in Spain. Run by three young brothers, the restaurant is intimate, with only 12 tables. The cuisine is an interesting combination of traditional Catalán dishes creatively transformed into contemporary Mediterranean fare. Start with an avocado purée, and for dessert you can't pass up the mandarin orange sorbet with pumpkin compote.

Carrer Taiala 40. © **97-222-21-57.** Reservations recommended. Main courses 17€–26€; fixed-price menus 46€. AE, DC, MC, V. Tues–Sat 1–4pm and 9–11pm.

NEARBY PLACES TO DINE

El Bulli ☆☆☆ SPANISH/CATALAN   Chef Fernando Adrià is hailed as the most exciting in Spain. The press has dubbed him the "Salvador Dalí of the kitchen" because of his creative approach to cookery. Joël Robuchon, hailed as the world's best chef before his retirement in Paris, has announced that Adrià is the best chef in the world. He operates his *luxe* eatery in the little hamlet of Roses, but many of the most discerning palates of Catalonia seek out this restaurant. Michelin grants it three stars, an accolade most often reserved for the top restaurant of Paris. El Bulli, which means "innovative" in Spanish, lives up to its name. Most guests order a 12-course tasting menu that's finer than you'll be served in any of Barcelona's top restaurants. You never know what's going to appear, but anticipate the most delightful surprises, based on what's the finest produce in any given season. You anticipate you're in for a delightful evening at the beginning when you're given addictive little dishes of polenta chips and caramelized sunflower seeds. Your *amuse-bouche* might be a "cappuccino" of guacamole. One dish alone should give Adrià culinary immortality: his lasagna of calamari. *Travel & Leisure* has hailed El Bulli as "the world's most outrageously creative kitchen," and we concur, at least in Spain, if not the world.

Cala Montjoi, Roses. © **97-215-04-57.** www.elbulli.com. Reservations required. Main courses 24€–32€; *menú de degustación* 130€. AE, MC, V. July–Sept daily 8pm–10:30pm; Oct–June Wed–Sun 8–10:30pm. From Girona, take N-1 north to Figueres, then route 260 east to Roses, a total of 56km (35 miles).

Sant Pau ★★★ CATALAN   If Picasso were around today, we bet he'd be hitting the culinary trail to the doorstep of Carme Ruscalleda, the leading female chef of Spain. Even some of the top chefs of France are crossing the Spanish border to sample her cuisine. Michelin grants her two stars, but we feel she richly deserves three. She has a virtuoso technique, bringing finesse to food and even a touch of fantasy to some of her dishes. We marvel at her ability to take the freshest of produce and add just the right spice or seasoning to bring out the item's greatest flavor.

Carrer Nou 10, in St. Pol de Mar. ✆ 93-760-06-62. Reservations required. Main courses 30€–40€. AE, DC, MC, V. Tues–Sun 1:30–3:30pm; Tues–Sat 9am–1pm. From Girona, take N-1 55km (34 miles) south.

GIRONA AFTER DARK

Central Girona has a good number of tapas bars and cafes, some of which don't have easily distinguishable names. Many of them are scattered along **La Rambla,** around the edges of the keynote **Plaça de Independencia,** and within the antique boundaries of the **Plaça Ferrán el Católic.** Moving at a leisurely pace from one to another is considered something of an art form in the sultry heat of Girona's early evenings. Some animated tapas bars in the city center are **Bar de Tapes,** Carrer Barcelona 13 (✆ 97-241-01-64), near the rail station, and **Tapa't,** Plaça de l'Oli (no phone), which is noteworthy for its old-fashioned charm. Also appealing for its crowded conviviality and its impressive roster of shellfish and seafood tapas is **Bar Boira,** Plaça de Independencia 17 (✆ 97-220-30-96).

Beginning around 11pm, you might want to drop into one or another of the town's discos, the most popular of which is **Disco/Sala de Fiestas Platea,** Carrer Reial de Fontclara s/n (✆ 97-222-72-88). In the city's oldest core, it's open Wednesday through Sunday beginning at 11pm. (Be warned that your greatest difficulty will be finding the place; the street it's on is a narrow alley just behind Girona's main post office.) Newer, with less of a track record but a rapidly evolving style that appeals to everyone between 23 and 45, is **Discoteca 7 Artes,** Carrer Sant'Narcis s/n (no phone), open Wednesday through Saturday from 11pm until at least 4am.

One of the most appealing things to do in Girona after dark, at least between June and September, is to cross to the opposite side of the river into the verdant precincts of the **Parque de la Devesa.** This park is an artfully landscaped terrain of stately trees, flowering shrubs, kiosk-style refreshment stands, and open-aired bars, which in some cases have disco music and patrons dancing on wooden decks. Our favorite is **Disco Glops,** Parque de la Devesa (no phone), which rocks in the open air every Wednesday from around 10:30pm till dawn.

2 Lloret de Mar

100km (62 miles) S of the French border, 68km (42 miles) N of Barcelona

Although it has a good half moon–shaped sandy beach, **Lloret de Mar** is neither chic nor sophisticated, and most people who come here are Europeans, on package tours, looking for an inexpensive vacation. The competition for cheap rooms is fierce.

Lloret de Mar has grown at a phenomenal rate from a small fishing village with just a few hotels to a bustling resort with more hotels than anyone can count. And more keep opening, though there never seem to be enough in July and August. The accommodations are typical of those in other Costa Brava towns, running the gamut from impersonal modern box-type structures to vintage flowerpot-adorned whitewashed buildings on the narrow streets of the old town. There are even a few pockets of posh, including the Hotel Roger de Flor (see below). The area has rich vegetation, attractive scenery, and a mild climate.

ESSENTIALS

GETTING THERE   From Barcelona, take a **train** to Blanes, then take a **bus** 8km (5 miles) to Lloret. If you **drive,** head north from Barcelona along the A-19.

VISITOR INFORMATION   The **tourist office** at Plaça de la Vila 1 (© **97-236-47-35;** www.lloret.org) is open Monday through Friday from 10am to 1pm and 4 to 8pm, Saturday from 10am to 1pm.

WHERE TO STAY

Many of the hotels—particularly the government-rated three-star places—are booked solidly by tour groups. Here are some possibilities if you reserve in advance.

EXPENSIVE

Gran Hotel Monterrey ★★   Ranked just under the Roger de Flor, this government-rated four-star hotel is like a deluxe country club in a large park, a short walk from the casino, town center, and beaches. The hotel opened in the 1940s and has been partly renovated almost every year since. It's well known as a retreat for those who want to recharge their batteries. The interior areas have big windows with expansive views. The rooms are spacious and luxuriously decorated, with bathrooms containing tub/showers; most have balconies or lounge areas.

Carretera de Tossa, 17310 Lloret de Mar. © 97-236-40-50. Fax 97-236-35-12. www.ghmonterrey.com. 224 units. 105€–152€ double; 120€–171€ suite. AE, DC, MC, V. Free parking. Closed Oct–Mar. **Amenities:** Restaurant; 2 bars; 2 pools; 3 tennis courts; health club; sauna; whirlpool; beauty spa; room service; massage; babysitting; laundry service; dry cleaning. *In room:* A/C, TV, minibar, hair dryer, safe.

Hotel Roger de Flor ★★★   This much-enlarged older hotel, some of which is reminiscent of a private villa, is a pleasant diversion from the aging slabs of concrete filling other sections of the resort. Set at the eastern edge of town, the hotel offers the most pleasant and panoramic views of any hotel. Potted geraniums, climbing bougainvillea, and evenly spaced rows of palms add elegance to the combination of new and old architecture. The midsize rooms are high-ceilinged, modern, and filled with excellent furnishings, including well-maintained bathrooms with tub/shower combos. The public rooms contain plenty of exposed wood and spill out onto a partially covered terrace.

Turó de l'Estelat s/n, 17310 Lloret de Mar. © 97-236-48-00. Fax 97-237-16-37. www.rogerdeflor.com. 100 units. 109€–246€ double; 208€–350€ suite. AE, DC, MC, V. Free parking. **Amenities:** Restaurant; 2 bars; pool; tennis courts; fitness center; car rental; room service; babysitting; laundry service; dry cleaning. *In room:* TV, minibar, safe.

Hotel Santa Marta ★★ *Finds*   This tranquil hotel, a short walk above a crescent-shaped bay favored by swimmers, is nestled amid a sun-flooded grove of pines. Both the public rooms and the guest rooms are attractively paneled and filled with traditional furniture. The spacious rooms offer private balconies overlooking the sea or a pleasant garden, and all contain bathrooms with tub/shower combos. The neighborhood is quiet but desirable, about 2km (1½ miles) west of the commercial center of town.

Playa de Santa Cristina, 17310 Lloret de Mar. © 97-236-49-04. Fax 97-236-92-80. www.hstamarta.com. 78 units. 95€–252€ double. AE, DC, MC, V. Free parking. Closed Dec 23–Jan 31. **Amenities:** 2 restaurants; 2 bars; pool; sauna; car rental; room service; babysitting; laundry service; dry cleaning; solarium. *In room:* A/C, TV, minibar, hair dryer, safe.

MODERATE

Hotel Vila del Mar   This century-old hotel is a short walk from the beach, close to the heart of town near the bus station. Behind its exterior is a rather mundane but well-maintained interior with a nautical feel. The soundproof rooms are pleasantly decorated and well equipped, and the bathrooms have hydromassage and tub/shower combos.

Calle de la Vila 55, 17310 Lloret de Mar. © **97-236-50-08.** Fax 97-237-11-68. www.6tems.com/viladelmar. 36 units. 106€–169€ double. AE, DC, MC, V. Parking 12€. **Amenities:** Restaurant; bar; pool; health club; sauna; room service; babysitting; laundry service; dry cleaning. *In room:* A/C, TV, minibar, hair dryer, safe.

INEXPENSIVE

Hotel Excelsior   This hotel attracts a beach-oriented clientele from Spain and northern Europe. The Excelsior sits almost directly on the beach, rising six floors above the esplanade. All but a handful of the rooms offer either frontal or lateral views of the sea, and all are equipped with bathrooms that mostly contain tub/shower combos. The furniture is modern but uninspiring. During midsummer, half-board is obligatory. Even though it is a modest hotel, one of the greatest restaurants of the Costa Brava, Les Petxines, is located here (see below).

Passeig Mossèn Jacinto Verdaguer 16, 17310 Lloret de Mar. © **97-236-61-76.** Fax 97-237-16-54. www. gna.es/lloret. 45 units. July–Sept (including obligatory ½-board) 51€ per person double; Oct–June (including breakfast) 32€–38€ per person double. AE, DC, V. Parking 9€. Closed Oct 31–Apr 1. **Amenities:** 2 restaurants; bar; babysitting; laundry. *In room:* A/C, TV, safe.

WHERE TO DINE

El Trull SEAFOOD   This restaurant attracts hordes of Spanish who appreciate the beautiful scenery of the 3km (2-mile) trek north of Lloret into the hills. Set in the modern suburb of Urbanización Playa Canyelles and known for its enduring popularity, El Trull positions its tables within view of a well-kept garden and a (sometimes crowded) pool. The food is some of the best in the neighborhood. Menu items focus on seafood and include fish soup; fish stew heavily laced with lobster; many variations of hake, monkfish, and clams; and an omelet "surprise." (The waiter will tell you the ingredients if you ask.)

Cala Canyelles s/n. © **97-236-49-28.** Main courses 12€–36€; fixed-price menu 20€. AE, DC, MC, V. Daily 1–4pm and 8–11:30pm (till midnight on weekends).

Les Petxines ✮✮✮ MEDITERRANEAN   This is a near-perfect dining experience at a resort that until the arrival of chef Paula Casanovas never had a premier dining room. It does now. The most carefully orchestrated food in this resort is served within the Franco-era (ca. 1954) confines of the dining room of the Hotel Excelsior, a relatively simple 45-room hotel directly on the seafront. Thirty diners at a time sit in relative intimacy within a big-windowed dining room, enjoying the sophisticated specialties of Casanovas. Her food varies with the season, her inspiration, and the availability of ingredients in local markets, but you can always expect superlatively fresh fish and shellfish (*petxines* in Catalán) after which the restaurant is named. Her best examples include several versions of fish soup, some of them with a confit of lemons and shrimp-stuffed ravioli, and a ragout of fish and shellfish that's extremely succulent. Meat-eaters appreciate the flavorful versions of pigeon, one of them stuffed with foie gras, that sometimes appear on the menu.

In the Hotel Excelsior, Passeig Mossèn J. Verdaguer 16. © **97-236-41-37.** Reservations required. Main courses 18€–24€; set-price menus 25€ and 50€ for 6-course "surprise menu." AE, DC, MC, V. Tues–Sun 1:15–3:35pm; Tues–Sat 8:30–11pm. Open Sun night July–Aug.

Restaurante Santa Marta ✯ INTERNATIONAL/CATALAN   Set in the previously recommended 40-year-old hotel about 2km (1½ miles) west of the commercial center of town (see "Where to Stay," above), this pleasantly sunny enclave offers well-prepared food and a sweeping view of the beaches and the sea. Menu specialties vary with the seasons but might include paté of wild mushrooms in a special sauce, smoked salmon with hollandaise on toast, medallions of monkfish with a mousseline of garlic, ragout of giant shrimp with broad beans, filet of beef Stroganoff, and a regionally inspired cassoulet of chicken prepared with cloves.

In the Hotel Santa Marta, Playa de Santa Cristina. ℂ 97-236-49-04. Reservations recommended. Main courses 16€–28€; fixed-price menu 40€. AE, DC, MC, V. Daily 1:30–3:30pm and 8:30–10:30pm. Closed Dec 15–Jan 31.

LLORET DE MAR AFTER DARK

At the **Casino Lloret de Mar,** Carrer Esports 1 (ℂ **97-236-61-16**), games of chance include French and American roulette, blackjack, and chemin de fer. There's a restaurant, buffet dining room, bar-boîte, and dance club, along with a pool. The casino is southwest of Lloret de Mar, beside the coastal road leading to Blanes and Barcelona. Drive or take a taxi at night and bring your passport for entry. Hours are Sunday through Thursday from 5pm to 4am, Friday and Saturday from 5pm to 5am. (The casino closes 30 min. later in summer.) Admission is 3.50€.

The dance club **Hollywood,** Carretera de Tossa (ℂ **97-236-74-63**), at the edge of town, is the place to be and be seen. Look for it on the corner of Carrer Girona. It's open nightly from 10pm to 5am.

3 Tossa de Mar ✯✯

90km (56 miles) N of Barcelona, 12km (7½ miles) NE of Lloret de Mar

The gleaming white town of **Tossa de Mar,** with its 12th-century walls, labyrinthine old quarter, fishing boats, and fairly good sand beaches is perhaps the most attractive base for a Costa Brava vacation. It seems to have more joie de vivre than its competitors. The battlements and towers of Tossa were featured in the 1951 Ava Gardner and James Mason movie *Pandora and the Flying Dutchman,* still sometimes seen on TV.

In the 18th and 19th centuries, Tossa survived as a port center, growing rich on the cork industry. But that declined in the 20th century, and many of its citizens emigrated to America. In the 1950s, thanks in part to the Ava Gardner movie, tourists began to discover the charms of Tossa and a new industry was born.

To experience these charms, walk through the 12th-century walled town, known as **Vila Vella,** built on the site of a Roman villa from the 1st century A.D. Enter through the Torre de les Hores.

Tossa was once a secret haunt for artists and writers—Marc Chagall called it a blue paradise. It has two main beaches, **Mar Gran** and **La Bauma.** The coast near Tossa, north and south, offers even more possibilities.

As one of few resorts to have withstood exploitation and retained most of its allure, Tossa enjoys a broad base of international visitors—so many, in fact, that it can no longer shelter them all. In spring and fall, finding a room may be a snap, but in summer it's next to impossible unless reservations are made far in advance.

ESSENTIALS

GETTING THERE   Direct **bus** service is offered from Blanes and Lloret. Tossa de Mar is also on the main Barcelona-Palafrugell route. Service from Barcelona is daily from 7:40am to 7:10pm, taking 1½ hours. For information, call © **90-226-06-06** or 93-265-65-08. **Drive** north from Barcelona along the A-19.

VISITOR INFORMATION The **tourist office** is at Av. El Pelegrí 25 (© **97-234-01-08;** www.infotossa.com). From April to October, it's open Monday through Saturday from 10am to 8pm, Sunday from 10:30am to 1:30pm; off-season hours are Monday through Saturday from 10am to 1pm and 4 to 7pm.

WHERE TO STAY
VERY EXPENSIVE
Grand Hotel Reymar ⭐ A triumph of engineering a 10-minute walk southeast of the historic walls—the hotel occupies a position on a jagged rock above the sea edge—this graceful building was constructed in the 1960s and renovated in the early 1990s. The Reymar has several levels of expansive terraces ideal for sunbathing away from the crowds below. Each good-size room has a balcony, a sea view, a bathroom with a tub/shower combo, and a mix of modern wood-grained and painted furniture.

Platja de Mar Menuda, 17320 Tossa de Mar. © **97-234-03-12.** Fax 97-234-15-04. www.ghreymar.com. 166 units. 57€–116€ double; 82€–176€ per person in suite. Rates include breakfast. AE, DC, MC, V. Parking 8€. Closed Nov–Apr. **Amenities:** 4 restaurants; 3 bars; pool; tennis courts; health club; sauna; whirlpool; car rental; room service; babysitting; laundry service; dry cleaning; solarium. *In room:* A/C, TV, minibar, hair dryer, safe.

MODERATE
Mar Menuda ⭐⭐ *Finds* This hotel is a gem, a real Costa Brava hideaway surviving amid tawdry tourist traps and fast-food joints. Its terrace is the area's most panoramic, overlooking the sea and the architectural highlights of the town. The rooms range from midsize to spacious, each tastefully furnished and containing a good-size bathroom with tub/shower. The staff is also helpful in arranging many watersports, such as scuba diving, windsurfing, and sailing. The cuisine served here is also first class.

Platja de Mar Menuda, 17320 Tossa de Mar. © **800/528-1234** in the U.S., or 97-234-10-00. Fax 97-234-00-87. 50 units. 124€–138€ double with breakfast; 162€ suite. AE, DC, MC, V. Free parking. Closed Nov–Dec. **Amenities:** Restaurant; bar; tennis courts; room service; babysitting; laundry service; dry cleaning. *In room:* A/C, TV, hair dryer, safe.

INEXPENSIVE
Canaima *Kids* Lacking the charm of Hotel Diana, this little inn is the bargain of the resort. It lies in a tranquil zone in a residential area 150m (492 ft.) from the beach. The palm trees in this sector of Tossa evoke a real Mediterranean setting. Built in 1963, the hotel bounced back with a series of restorations that lasted from 1997 to 2001. Most of the midsize guest rooms, each with a tiled bathroom with shower and tub, have a balcony opening onto a view. Since some of the accommodations have three beds, the Canaima is also a family favorite. In lieu of its lack of amenities, it has a public phone, a bar with television, and a hotel safe.

Avigunda La Palma 24. 17320 Tossa de Mar. © **97-234-09-95.** hotelcanaima@telephine.es. 55€ double. Rates include continental breakfast. AE, MC, V. **Amenities:** Terrace bar. *In room:* No phone.

Hotel Cap d'Or ⭐ *Finds* Perched on the waterfront on a quiet edge of town, this 1790s building nestles against the stone walls and towers of the village castle. Built of rugged stone itself, the Cap d'Or is like an old country inn and seaside hotel combined. The rooms come in different shapes and sizes but are decently maintained, each with a good bed and a small bathroom with a shower stall. Although the hotel is a bed-and-breakfast, it does have a terrace on the promenade offering a quick meal.

Passeig de Vila Vella 1, 17320 Tossa de Mar. ℂ/fax **97-234-00-81**. hcapdor@terra.es. 11 units. 62€–68€ double. Rates include breakfast. MC, V. Closed Nov–Mar. **Amenities:** Restaurant; bar; laundry service; dry cleaning. *In room:* TV.

Hotel Diana ★ Set back from the esplanade, this government-rated two-star hotel is a former villa designed in part by students of Gaudí. It boasts the most elegant fireplace on the Costa Brava. An inner patio—with towering palms, vines and flowers, and fountains—is almost as popular with guests as the sandy front yard beach. The spacious rooms contain fine traditional furnishings and bathrooms with shower stalls; many open onto private balconies.

Plaça de Espanya 6, 17320 Tossa de Mar. ℂ **97-234-18-86**. Fax 97-234-18-86. 21 units. 75€–125€ double. AE, DC, MC, V. Closed Nov–Apr. **Amenities:** Restaurant; bar; room service. *In room:* A/C, TV, minibar, hair dryer.

Hotel Neptuno The popular Neptuno sits on a quiet residential hillside northwest of Vila Vella, somewhat removed from the seaside promenade and the bustle of Tossa de Mar's inner core. Built in the 1960s, the hotel was renovated and enlarged in the late 1980s. Inside, antiques are mixed with modern furniture; the beamed-ceiling dining room is charming, and the guest rooms are tastefully lighthearted and modern, each with a good bed and a small bathroom containing a shower. This place is a longtime favorite with northern Europeans, who often book it solid during July and August.

La Guardia 52, 17320 Tossa de Mar. ℂ **97-234-01-43**. Fax 97-234-19-33. neptune@ghthotels.com. 124 units. June–Sept 42€–48€ per person double; off season (including breakfast) 25€–34€ per person double. Rates include breakfast. AE, DC, MC, V. Free parking. Closed Nov–Mar. **Amenities:** Restaurant; bar; pool; laundry service; dry cleaning. *In room:* No phone.

Hotel Tonet Opened in the early 1960s, in the earliest days of the region's tourist boom, this simple family-run pension is one of the resort's oldest. Renovated since then, it's on a central plaza surrounded by narrow streets and maintains the ambience of a country inn, with upper-floor terraces where you can relax amid potted vines and other plants. The small rooms are rustic, with wooden headboards, simple furniture, and bathrooms equipped with shower stalls. Tonet maintains its own brand of Iberian charm.

Plaça de l'Església 1, 17320 Tossa de Mar. ℂ **97-234-02-37**. Fax 97-234-30-96. www.tossa.com/hoteltonet. 36 units. 40€–51€ double. Rates include breakfast. AE, DC, MC, V. Parking 10€ nearby. **Amenities:** Bar. *In room:* TV.

WHERE TO DINE

Bahía ★ CATALAN Adjacent to the sea, Bahía is well known for a much-awarded chef and a history of feeding hungry vacationers since 1953. Menu favorites are for the most part based on time-honored Catalán traditions and include *simitomba* (a grilled platter of fish), *brandade* of cod, baked monkfish, and an array of grilled fish—including *salmonete* (red mullet), *dorada* (gilthead sea bream), and *calamares* (squid)—depending on what's available.

Passeig del Mar 19. ℂ **97-234-03-22**. Reservations recommended. Main courses 10€–30€; *menú del día* 15€–26€. AE, DC, MC, V. Daily 1–4:30pm and 7:30–11:30pm.

La Cuina de Can Simon ★★★ CATALAN Some of the most sought after dining tables in Tossa de Mar are within this charming, cozy, and intimate establishment containing only 18 seats. The small size allows the hardworking staff to prepare some extremely esoteric courses, each of which is served in an antique, elegantly rustic stone-sided dining room originally built in 1741. During the colder months, a fire might be burning in the stately looking fireplace. Most diners select the *menu gastronómico*, consisting of six small courses that combine into meals that are memorable. If you dine here, expect to be delivered a refined, brilliantly realized repertoire of foodstuff. Expect seductive, modern dishes that display unerring technique and imaginative flavors. Individual components might include oven-roasted duckling with a sweet-and-sour sauce; crayfish-stuffed ravioli with Beluga caviar and truffle oil; a monkfish supreme with scalloped potatoes and golden-fried sweet onions. Desserts that we particularly fancied include an artfully arranged platter of ice cream, pastries, sauces, and tarts, each of which factored seasonal red fruits (strawberries, whortleberries, and currants) into its composition.

Portal 24. ℭ **97-234-12-69**. Reservations required. Main courses 16€–40€; set-price menus 42€–58€. AE, DC, MC, V. Wed–Mon 1–4pm and 8–11pm.

TOSSA DE MAR AFTER DARK

In Tossa de Mar's fast-changing nightlife, there's little stability or reliability. However, one place that's been in business for a while is the **Ely Club,** Carrer Bernat 2 (ℭ **97-234-00-09**). Fans from all over the Costa Brava come here to dance to up-to-date tunes. Daily hours are from 10pm to 5am between March 15 and October 15 only. In July and August, there's a one-drink minimum. The Ely Club is in the center of town between the two local cinemas.

4 Figueres

219km (136 miles) N of Barcelona, 37km (23 miles) E of Girona

In the heart of Catalonia, **Figueres** once played a role in Spanish history. Philip V wed María Luisa of Savoy here in 1701 in the church of San Pedro, thereby paving the way for the War of the Spanish Succession. But that historical fact is nearly forgotten today: The town is better known as the birthplace of surrealist artist Salvador Dalí in 1904.

There are two reasons for visiting Figueres: one of the best restaurants in Spain and the Dalí Museum.

ESSENTIALS

GETTING THERE RENFE, the national railway of Spain, has hourly **train** service between Barcelona and Figueres. All trains between Barcelona and France stop here. It's better and faster to take the train if you're coming from Barcelona. But if you're in Cadaqués (see the section later in this chapter), there are five daily SARFA **buses** making the 45-minute trip.

Figueres is a 40-minute **drive** from Cadaqués. Take the excellent north-south highway, the A-7, either south from the French border at La Jonquera or north from Barcelona, exiting at the major turnoff to Figueres.

VISITOR INFORMATION The **tourist office** is at the Plaça del Sol (ℭ **97-250-31-55;** www.figueresciutat.com). From June to October, the office is open Monday through Friday from 9am to 8pm; from November until Easter, hours are Monday through Friday from 9am to 3pm; and from Easter to June 20, hours are Monday through Friday from 9am to 3pm and 4:30 to 8pm, Saturday from 9am to 2pm.

VISITING DALI

Castell de Púbol ✦✦ For additional insights into the often bizarre aesthetic sensibilities of Spain's most famous surrealist, consider a 40km (25-mile) trek from Figueres eastward along highway C-252, following the signs to Parlava. In the village of Púbol, whose permanent population almost never exceeds 200, you'll find the Castell de Púbol. Dating from 1000, it was partially ruined when bought by Dalí as a residence for his estranged wife, Gala, in 1970, on the condition that he'd come only when she invited him. (She almost never did.) After her death in 1982, Dalí moved in for 2 years, moving on to other residences in 1984 after his bedroom mysteriously caught fire one night. Quieter, more serious, and much less surrealistically flamboyant than the houses in Port Lligat and Figueres, the castle is noteworthy for its severe Gothic and Romanesque dignity and for furniture and decor that follow the tastes of the surrealist master. (Don't expect a lot of paintings—that's the specialty of the museum at Figueres.)

Carrer Gala Salvador Dalí s/n. ✆ **97-248-86-55.** Admission 5.50€ adults, 4€ students, free for children under 9. June 15–Sept 15 daily 10:30am–8pm; Mar 13–June 14 and Sept 16–Nov 1 Tues–Sun 10:30am–6pm.

Teatre Museu Dalí ★★★   The internationally known Dalí was as famous for his surrealist and often erotic imagery as he was for his flamboyance and exhibitionism. At the Figueres museum, in the center of town beside the Rambla, you'll find his paintings, watercolors, gouaches, charcoals, and pastels, along with graphics and sculptures, many rendered with seductive and meticulously detailed imagery. His wide-ranging subject matter encompassed such repulsive issues as putrefaction and castration. You'll see, for instance, *The Happy Horse,* a grotesque and lurid purple beast the artist painted during one of his long exiles at Port Lligat. A tour of the museum is an experience. When a catalog was prepared, Dalí said with a perfectly straight face, "It is necessary that all of the people who come out of the museum have false information."

Plaça de Gala-Dalí 5. ✆ **97-267-75-00.** Admission 9€ adults, 6.50€ students and adults over 65, free for children under 9. July to mid-Sept daily 9am–7:45pm; mid-Sept to June Tues–Sun 10:30am–5:45pm. Visits available various nights in July and Aug; call for information.

WHERE TO STAY

Hotel Pirineos   This pleasant hotel near the main road leading to the center of town is a 5-minute walk from the Dalí Museum. Many of the comfortable but small rooms have balconies, but furnishings are rather plain, although the beds are good and the bathrooms are neat, with shower stalls.

Ronda de Barcelona 1, 17600 Figueres. ✆ **97-250-03-12.** Fax 97-250-07-66. 55 units. 60€–63€ double; 110€ suite. Rates include breakfast. AE, DC, MC, V. Parking 6€. **Amenities:** 2 restaurants; bar; room service; laundry service; dry cleaning. *In room:* A/C, TV, safe.

Hotel President   Since 1970, this has been one of the most desirable accommodations in town, lying in the center, a 5-minute walk from the Dalí Museum. An austere exterior belies the welcoming comfort inside. The midsize rooms are neutrally decorated, with comfortable beds and new mattresses, and the bathrooms have either showers or combo tub/showers.

Ronad Ferial 33, 17600 Figueres. ✆ **97-250-17-00.** Fax 97-250-19-97. 76 units. 65€ double. AE, DC, MC, V. Free parking. **Amenities:** Restaurant; bar; room service; laundry. *In room:* A/C, TV, hair dryer, safe.

Hotel Ronda *(Value*   A 10-minute walk from the Dalí Museum, this hotel continues to welcome travelers as it has done since the 1970s. They're housed in comfort at a very low price in a typically Catalán building with an unpretentious facade; the building has conventional Mediterranean-style white walls, ample balconies, and simple decorations. The small rooms are clean and simple, each with a plain bathroom with a tub/shower combo. The hotel is popular with budget-minded Europeans, so reservations in summer are important.

Ronda Barcelona 104, 17600 Figueres. ✆ **97-250-39-11.** Fax 97-250-16-82. 52 units. 42€–56€ double. AE, MC, V. Free parking. **Amenities:** Restaurant; bar. *In room:* A/C, TV.

The Mad, Mad World of Salvador Dalí

Salvador Dalí (1904–89) became one of the leading exponents of surrealism, depicting irrational imagery of dreams and delirium in a unique, meticulously detailed style. Famous for his eccentricity, he was called "outrageous, talented, relentlessly self-promoting, and unfailingly quotable." At his death at age 84, he was the last survivor of the three famous *enfants terribles* of Spain (the poet García Lorca and the filmmaker Luis Buñuel were the other two).

For all his international renown, Dalí was born in Figueres and died in Figueres. Most of his works are in the eponymous Theater-Museum there, built by the artist himself around the former theater where his first exhibition was held. Dalí was also buried in the Theater-Museum, next door to the church that witnessed both his christening and his funeral—the first and last acts of a perfectly planned scenario.

Salvador Felipe Jacinto Dalí i Domènech, the son of a highly respected notary, was born on May 11, 1904, in a house on Carrer Monturiol in Figueres. In 1922, he registered at the School of Fine Arts in Madrid and went to live at the prestigious Residencia de Estudiantes. There his friendship with García Lorca and Buñuel had a more enduring effect on his artistic future than his studies at the school. As a result of his undisciplined behavior and the attitude of his father, who clashed with the Primo de Rivera dictatorship over a matter related to elections, the young Dalí spent a month in prison.

In the summer of 1929, the artist René Magritte, along with the poet Paul Eluard and his wife, Gala, came to stay at Cadaqués, and their visit caused sweeping changes in Dalí's life. The young painter became enamored of Eluard's wife; Dalí left his family and fled with Gala to Paris, where he became an enthusiastic member of the surrealist movement. Some of his most famous paintings—*The Great Masturbator,* *Lugubrious Game,* and *Portrait of Paul Eluard*—date from his life at Port

WHERE TO DINE

Durán ✿ CATALAN   This is a popular place for a top-notch meal in the provinces and had Dalí as a loyal patron. You might start with the Catalán salad, made with radishes, boiled egg, ham paté, tuna fish, tomato, and fresh salad greens. Other specialties are steak with Roquefort, *zarzuela* (fish stew), and *filetes de lenguado a la naranja* (sole in orange sauce). Like the Empordá (see below), the Durán specializes in game. Try, if it's available, the grilled rabbit on a plank, served with white wine. The french fries here, unlike those in most of Spain, are crisp and excellent. Finish off with a rich dessert or at least an espresso. You can also stay at the Durán, in one of its 65 well-furnished rooms, each with a bathroom, air-conditioning, a TV, and a phone. A double goes for 59€ to 72€.

Carrer Lasauca 5, 17600 Figueres. © **97-250-12-50.** Fax 97-267-70-46. Reservations required. Main courses 12€–26€; fixed-price menu 9.50€. AE, DC, MC, V. Daily 12:30–4pm and 8:30–11pm.

Empordá ✿✿✿ CATALAN   A stop at this restaurant just might provide you with your finest meal in the entire area. Don't judge the place by its appearance, which is ordinary if not institutional; there's nothing ordinary about the cuisine,

Lligat, the small Costa Brava town where he lived and worked off and on during the 1930s.

Following Dalí's break with the tenets of the surrealist movement, his work underwent a radical change, with a return to classicism and what he called his mystical and nuclear phase. He became one of the most fashionable painters in the United States and seemed so intent on self-promotion that the surrealist poet André Breton baptized him with the anagram "Avida Dollars." Dalí wrote a partly fictitious autobiography titled *The Secret Life of Salvador Dalí* and *Hidden Faces,* a novel containing autobiographical elements. These two short literary digressions earned him still greater prestige and wealth, as did his collaborations in the world of cinema (such as the dream set for Alfred Hitchcock's *Spellbound,* 1945) and in those of theater, opera, and ballet.

On August 8, 1958, Dalí and Gala were married according to the rites of the Catholic church in a ceremony performed in the strictest secrecy at the shrine of Els Àngels, just a few miles from Girona.

During the 1960s, Dalí painted some very large works, such as *The Battle of Tetuán.* Another important work painted at this period is *Perpignan Railway Station,* a veritable revelation of his paranoid-critical method that relates this center of Dalí's mythological universe to his obsession with painter Jean-François Millet's *The Angelus.*

In 1979, Dalí's health began to decline, and he retired to Port Lligat in a state of depression. When Gala died, he moved to Púbol, where, obsessed by the theory of catastrophes, he painted his last works, until he suffered severe burns in a fire that nearly cost him his life. Upon recovery, he moved to the Torre Galatea, a building he had bought as an extension to the museum in Figueres. Here he lived for 5 more years, hardly ever leaving his room, until his death in 1989.

as all the food-loving French who cross the border to dine here will tell you. This family-run restaurant, .8km (½ mile) north of the town center, gained an early reputation among U.S. military personnel in the area for subtly prepared game and fish dishes. Salvador Dalí (who wrote his own cookbook) and Josep Pla, perhaps the country's greatest 20th-century writer, were fans. The appetizers are the finest along the Costa Brava, including duck foie gras with Armagnac, warm paté of *rape* (monkfish) with garlic mousseline, and fish soup with fennel. The outstanding fish and seafood dishes include cuttlefish in Catalán sauce, suprême of sea bass with flan made with fennel and anchovy, and a brochette of grilled baby squids in vinaigrette. Among the meat selections are the chef's special *lievre à la royale* (hare), beef filet in red wine sauce with onion marmalade, and goose in a delectable mushroom sauce. You can also stay in one of the 42 midsize rooms here, each with a bathroom, air-conditioning, and a TV. Doubles run 116€ to 135€, while suites are 135€ to 180€.

Antigua Carretera de Francia s/n (N-II). © **97-250-05-62.** Reservations required. Main courses 15€–36€; fixed-price menu 30€–45€. AE, DC, MC, V. Daily 12:45–3:30pm and 8:30–10:30pm.

5 Cadaqués ⭐⭐

196km (122 miles) N of Barcelona, 31km (19 miles) E of Figueres

Cadaqués is still unspoiled and remote, despite the publicity it received when Salvador Dalí lived in the next-door village of Lligat in a split-level house surmounted by a giant egg. The last resort on the Costa Brava before the French border, Cadaqués is reached by a small winding road, twisting over the mountains from Rosas, the nearest major center. When you get to Cadaqués, you really feel you're off the beaten path. The village winds around half a dozen small coves, with a narrow street running along the water's edge. This street has no railing, so exercise caution.

Scenically, Cadaqués is a knockout: crystal-blue water, fishing boats on the sandy beaches, old whitewashed houses, narrow twisting streets, and a 16th-century parish up on a hill.

ESSENTIALS

GETTING THERE Three to five **buses** per day run from Figueres to Cadaqués. Trip time is 1¼ hours. The service is operated by SARFA (✆ **97-225-87-13**).

VISITOR INFORMATION The **tourist office,** Cotxe 2 (✆ **97-225-83-15**), is open Monday through Saturday from 10:30am to 1pm and 4:30 to 7:30pm.

WHERE TO STAY

Hostal S'Aguarda *Value* On the road winding above Cadaqués on the way to Port Lligat, this hostal has a panoramic view of the village's harbor and medieval church. Each of the modern, airy rooms opens onto a flower-decked terrace. They have tile floors and simple furniture, as well as bathrooms with tub/shower combos.

Carretera de Port Lligat 30, 17488 Cadaqués. ✆ **97-225-80-82**. Fax 97-225-10-57. www.hotelsaguarda.com. 28 units. 48€–88€ double. AE, DC, MC, V. Free parking. Closed Nov. **Amenities:** Bar; pool; laundry service; dry cleaning. *In room:* A/C, TV.

Hotel Playa Sol In a relatively quiet section of the port along the bay, this 1950s hotel offers the best view of the stone church at the distant edge of the harbor. The balconied building is constructed of brick and terra-cotta tiles. The small rooms are comfortably furnished, most of their bathrooms with tub/shower combos. The hotel doesn't have an official restaurant, but it does offer lunch from June 15 to September 15.

Platja Planch 3, 17488 Cadaqués. ✆ **97-225-81-00**. Fax 97-225-80-54. www.playasol.com. 50 units. 83€–146€ double. AE, DC, MC, V. Parking 7€. Closed Jan–Feb. **Amenities:** Bar; pool; room service; garden. *In room:* A/C, TV.

Llane Petit *Value* This is a little inn of considerable charm lying below the better known Hotel Rocamar opening right onto the beach. A hospitable place, it offers decent-sized and well-maintained bathrooms with both tubs and showers. All accommodations open onto a little terrace. The owners keep the hotel under constant renovation during the slow months so that is always fresh again when the summer hordes descend. A good idea would be to patronize the hotel's little dinner-only restaurant, as the cuisine is well prepared and most affordable.

Doctor Bartomeus 37, 17488 Cadaqués. ✆ **97-225-10-20**. Fax 97-225-87-78. 37 units. 60€–100€. AE, DC, MC, V. Rates include breakfast off season. Free parking. **Amenities:** Restaurant; bar; room service; laundry/dry cleaning. *In room:* A/C, TV, safe.

Rocamar At the beach, this government-rated three-star hotel is one of the better choices in town, attracting a fun-loving crowd of young northern Europeans in summer. All the accommodations are well furnished, with rustic yet comfortable pieces, along with small and neatly kept bathrooms with both tubs and showers. The rooms in front have balconies opening onto the sea; those in back have balconies, their windows with views of the mountains and beyond. The hotel is known for its good food served at affordable prices.

Doctor Bartomeus, 17488 Candaqués. ℭ **97-225-81-50.** Fax 97-225-86-50. 70 units. 62€–145€ double; 110€–124€ suite. Rates include breakfast. AE, DC, MC, V. Restaurant; bar; 2 pools; tennis court; room service; babysitting; laundry/dry cleaning. *In room:* A/C, TV, safe.

WHERE TO DINE

Don Quijote ✯ CATALAN   On the road leading into the village, this intimate bistro features a large vine-covered garden in front. You can dine either inside or alfresco. The well-prepared a la carte specialties include lamb chops, pepper steak, *zarzuela* (seafood stew), and gazpacho. The Don Quijote cup, a fruit and ice-cream dessert, is the best way to end a meal.

Caridad Seriñana 5. ℭ **97-225-81-41.** Reservations recommended. Main courses 8€–18€; fixed-price menus 16€–30€. MC, V. Daily noon–4pm and 7pm–midnight. Closed Nov–Mar.

Es Trull SEAFOOD   On the harborside street in the center of town, this cedar-shingled cafeteria is named for the ancient olive press dominating the interior. A filling fixed-price meal is served. According to the chef, if it comes from the sea and can be eaten, he'll prepare it with that special Catalán flair. You might try mussels in marinara sauce, grilled hake, or natural baby clams. Rice dishes are a specialty, not only paella but also black rice colored with squid ink and rice with calamari and shrimp.

Port Ditxos s/n. ℭ **97-236-49-28.** Reservations recommended. Main courses 8€–24€; fixed-price menus 15€. AE, DC, MC, V. Daily 12:30–4pm and 7–11pm. Closed Nov–Easter.

La Galiota ✯✯ CATALAN/FRENCH   Dozens of surrealist paintings, including some by Dalí, adorn the walls of this award-winning restaurant, the finest in town. On a sloping street below the cathedral, the place has a downstairs sitting room and a dining room converted from what was a private house. The chef's secret is in selecting only the freshest of ingredients and preparing them in a way that enhances their natural flavors. The roast leg of lamb, flavored with garlic, is a specialty. The marinated salmon is excellent, as are the sea bass and the sole with orange sauce.

Carrer Narciso Monturiol 9. ℭ **97-225-81-87.** Reservations required. Main courses 16€–24€; fixed-price menu 30€. AE, DC, MC, V. Daily 1:30–3:30pm and 8:30–10:30pm. Closed Oct to mid-June.

CADAQUES AFTER DARK

The distinctive **L'Hostal,** Paseo 8A (ℭ **97-225-80-00**), has attracted some of the most glamorous names of the art and music worlds. Some music critics have called it the second-best jazz club in Europe, and it certainly rates as the best club along the coast. It's a Dixieland bar par excellence, run by the most sophisticated entrepreneurial team in town. Habitués still remember when Salvador Dalí escorted Mick Jagger here, much to the delight of Colombian writer Gabriel García Márquez. In fact, the bar's logo was designed by Dalí himself. Heightening the ambience are the dripping candles, the high ceilings, and the heavy Spanish furniture. The best music is usually performed late at night. It's open daily from 11am to 5am. Entrance is free.

14

Aragón

Landlocked **Aragón,** along with Navarre, forms the northeastern quadrant of Spain. It is an ancient land composed of three provinces: Zaragoza; remote Teruel, which is farther south; and Huesca, in the north as you move toward the Pyrenees. These are also the names of the provinces' three major cities.

Most of Aragón constitutes terra incognita for the average tourist— which is unfortunate, since it is one of the most history-rich regions of the country. You can visit it as an extension of your trip to Castile, to the west, or as a segment of your trek through Catalonia, to the east. Huesca, close to the mountains, is ideal for a summer visit—unlike most of Aragón, especially the fiercely hot southern section, which has Spain's worst climate. Winter is often bitterly cold, but spring and autumn are ideal.

Aragón is known best for two former residents: Catherine of Aragón, who foolishly married Henry VIII of England, and Ferdinand of Aragón, whose marriage to Isabella, queen of Castile and León in the 15th century, led to the unification of Spain.

Aragón also prides itself on its exceptional Mudéjar architecture and on its bullfighting tradition. In September many villages in the region have their own festivals, when bulls run through the streets. What they don't have is the good promotion that Hemingway gave the festival at Pamplona, in the neighboring province of Navarre. On the other hand, they aren't plagued with wine-drunk tourists—the curse of the Pamplona festival. In folklore, Aragón is known for the *jota,* a bounding, leaping dance performed by men and women since at least the 1700s.

Aragón's capital, Zaragoza, is the most-visited destination in the region because it lies on the main route between Madrid and Barcelona. If you're driving from Madrid to Barcelona (or vice versa), make a detour to Zaragoza. If you get interested in Aragón while there, stick around to explore this ancient land.

1 Zaragoza ★★

322km (200 miles) NE of Madrid, 306km (190 miles) W of Barcelona

Zaragoza (pronounced "thah-rah-*goh*-thah") lies halfway between Madrid and Barcelona. This provincial capital, the seat of the ancient kingdom of Aragón, is a bustling, prosperous, commercial city of wide boulevards and arcades.

Zaragoza has not one but two cathedrals and, like Santiago de Compostela in Galicia, was a major pilgrimage center. According to legend, the Virgin Mary appeared to St. James, patron saint of Spain, on the banks of the Ebro River and ordered him to build a church there.

Zaragoza is at the center of a rich *huerta,* or plain. Its history dates from the Romans, who called it Caesar Augusta. Today, Zaragoza is a city of more than

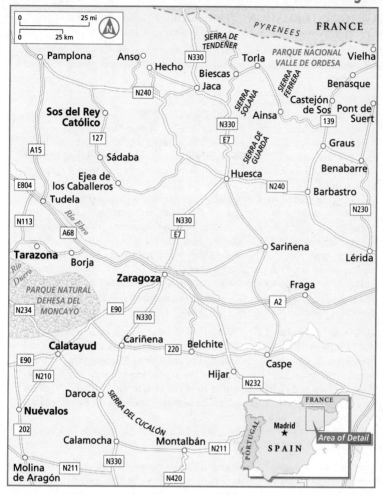

three quarters of a million people, just less than 75% of the entire population of Aragón.

The 40,000 students at the University of Zaragoza have livened up this once-staid city. Cafes, theaters, restaurants, music bars, and *tascas* have boomed in recent years, and more monuments have been restored and opened to the public.

ESSENTIALS

GETTING THERE **Aviaco** has direct **flights** to Zaragoza from Madrid and Barcelona. From the airport in Zaragoza, you can get a bus to the Plaza de San Francisco. The Iberia office in Zaragoza is at Calle Bilbao 11 (© **97-621-82-56**).

Eight **trains** arrive daily from Barcelona (trip time: 4 hr.) and eight from Madrid (3½–5 hr.). The RENFE office in Zaragoza is at Calle San Clemente 13 (© **90-224-02-02**), just off the Paseo de la Independencia.

There is one direct **bus** a day running between Zaragoza and Barcelona (7 hr.).

Zaragoza is easily reached on the E-90 (A-2) east from Madrid or west from Barcelona.

VISITOR INFORMATION   The **tourist office** at Plaza del Pilar s/n (© 97-639-35-37; www.turismozaragosa.com) is open daily from 10am to 8pm.

SPECIAL EVENTS   One of the city's big festivities is the **Fiesta de la Virgen del Pilar,** held the week of October 12, with top-name bullfighters, religious processions, and general merriment.

SEEING THE SIGHTS

Basílica de Nuestra Señora del Pilar ★   This 16th- and 17th-century basilica on the bank of the Ebro River is in an almost Oriental style with its domes and towers. Thousands of the faithful travel here annually to pay homage to the tiny statue of the *Virgen del Pilar* in the Holy Chapel. The name of the cathedral, El Pilar, comes from the pillar upon which the Virgin is supposed to have stood when she asked Santiago (St. James) to build the church.

During the second week of October the church is a backdrop for an important festival devoted to Our Lady of the Pillar, with parades, bullfights, fireworks, flower offerings, and street dancing. Also of interest within the church are frescoes painted by Goya, who was born nearby.

You can also visit the **Museo del Pilar,** which houses the jewelry collection used to adorn the Pilar statue as well as sketches by Goya and other artists, including both Bayeu brothers. Much of the collection is ancient.

Plaza de las Catedrales. © **97-639-74-97.** Free admission to cathedral; museum 1.50€. Cathedral Tues–Sun 6am–9:30pm; museum daily 9am–2pm and 4–6pm. Bus: 22 or 23.

La Seo del Salvador ★★   This Gothic-Mudéjar church, built between 1380 and 1550, is more impressive than El Pilar (see above). It has a rich baroque and Plateresque facade and is a particularly fine example of Aragonese Gothic architecture. Among its more important features are the main altar and a fine collection of French and Flemish tapestries from the 15th to the 17th century, which are housed in the adjacent museum. The baroque cupolas in the Temple of Pilar were decorated by Goya and Bayeu.

Plaza de la Seo. © **97-629-12-38.** Museum admission 1.50€. Museum daily 10am–2pm and 4–7pm. Bus: 21, 22, 29, 32, 35, 36, 43, 44, or 45.

Museo Camón Aznar   Occupying a Renaissance palace a block from El Pilar (see above), this museum has three floors and 23 rooms filled with artwork. On the second floor is a sketch of María Sarmiento that Velázquez made for his masterpiece *Las Meninas* (The Maids of Honor), which hangs in the Prado in Madrid. The Bayeu brothers (Francisco and Ramón) are represented by several works, as is Goya. His collection includes an important self-portrait, a version of his *Los Caprichos* (The Whims), *La Tauromaqía* (The Tauromachy), *Los Desastres de la Guerra* (The Disasters of War), and *Los Disparates* (The Follies).

Espoz y Mina 23. © **97-639-73-28.** Admission 1€. Tues–Fri 9am–2:30pm and 6–9pm; Sat 10am–2pm and 6–9pm; Sun 10am–2pm. Bus: 22 or 23.

Museo de Zaragoza   This museum is installed in a 1908 building with 10 ground-floor rooms devoted to exhibits from the prehistoric to the Muslim period. The Roman legacy (nos. 4–8) has sculptures (a bust of Augustus), mosaics, and ceramics. The fine arts section includes paintings by Goya (no. 20); you can see his self-portrait there. In the next room, you'll find his drawings *Los Caprichos* (The Whims). Also displayed is a Goya portrait of Carlos IV and his wife. The museum is directly north of Paseo de Marino Moreno.

Plaza de los Sitios 6. ✆ **97-622-21-81**. Free admission. Tues–Sat 10am–2pm and 5–8pm; Sun 10am–2pm. Bus: 30, 35, or 40.

Museo Pablo Gargallo   This museum honors sculptor Pablo Gargallo, born in Maella in 1881. It is installed in a beautiful Aragonese Renaissance-style palace (1659) that was declared a national monument in 1963. Gargallo, influential in the art world of the 1920s, is represented by 100 original works, ranging from *Dr. Petit's Fireplace* (1904) to *Great Prophet,* a bronze piece from 1933. The museum is located in the center, a 5-minute walk south of El Pilar.

Plaza de San Felipe 3. ✆ **97-672-49-22**. Free admission. Tues–Sat 10am–2pm and 5–9pm; Sun 10am–2pm. Bus: 22 or 23.

Palacio de la Aljafería ⭐   This most unusual sight, a Moorish palace in Aragón, has been restored by the parliament and preserved as a national monument. Reminiscent of Córdoban architecture, it was built in the 11th century for Moorish kings but has seen considerable alterations and additions since then, particularly when Ferdinand and Isabella lived here.

Calle Los Diputados. ✆ **97-628-95-28**. Admission 3€ adults, 1€ students, free for children under 12. Sat–Wed 10am–2pm and 4–8pm; Fri 4–8pm. Bus: 21 or 33.

WHERE TO STAY
EXPENSIVE

Boston ⭐⭐   This hotel, which opened in 1992, lies in the heart of Zaragoza's modern business district, a 15-minute walk from the medieval neighborhoods that most visitors want to explore. Named in honor of Boston, Massachusetts, where the building's architect earned his degree, it's the city's best hotel and one of the tallest buildings in town. Throughout, the style is ultramodern, even futuristic, strongly infused with postmodern design and American ideas. Rooms are the town's finest—usually spacious, with all the modern comforts such as well-maintained bathrooms equipped with tub/shower combos.

Camino de las Torres 28, 50008 Zaragoza. ✆ **97-659-91-92**. Fax 97-659-01-96. www.hotelboston.es. 313 units. 105€–150€ double; 177€–233€ suite. AE, DC, MC, V. Parking 13€. Bus: 29. **Amenities:** Restaurant; bar; health club; sauna; room service; babysitting; laundry service; dry cleaning. *In room:* A/C, TV, minibar, hair dryer, safe.

Hotel Palafox ⭐   One of the top hotels in town, the Palafox looks somewhat like an apartment house. It was inaugurated in 1982 and rates five stars from the government. A favorite of business travelers, it frequently hosts local events such as fashion shows. The midsize rooms have sleek traditional styling and are well maintained and comfortable, with quality beds and neatly organized bathrooms with tub/shower combos.

Calle Casa Jiménez s/n, 50004 Zaragoza. ✆ **97-623-77-00**. Fax 97-623-47-05. www.palafoxhoteles.com/htmls/es/palafox. 179 units. 103€–154€ double; 314€–519€ suite. AE, MC, V. Parking 12€. Bus: 22. **Amenities:** Restaurant; bar; pool; health club; sauna; room service; massage; babysitting; laundry service; dry cleaning. *In room:* A/C, TV, minibar, hair dryer, safe.

MODERATE

Hespería Zaragoza   This hotel in the historical center, a 5-minute walk from the basilica of El Pilar, has welcomed guests since 1994. A plain, modern exterior opens to reveal a marble-floored lobby where you'll encounter an efficient staff. There is no great stylishness here, but your comfort is ensured. Rooms are small but well furnished and inviting, each with a fully equipped bathroom containing a tub/shower combo.

Conde de Aranda 48, 50003 Zaragoza. ✆ **97-628-45-00.** Fax 97-628-27-17. www.hoteles-hesperia.es. 86 units. 90€–120€ double. AE, DC, MC, V. Parking 9€. **Amenities:** Restaurant; bar; room service; babysitting; laundry service; dry cleaning. *In room:* A/C, TV, minibar, hair dryer.

NH Gran Hotel ✿ *Value*　　Nearly a kilometer (½ mile) south of the cathedral, behind one of the most beautiful Hispano–Art Deco facades in town, this hotel is the most historic and charming in Zaragoza and a good value. Established by King Alfonso XIII in 1929, the Gran has a domed rotunda for conversation and an array of formal public areas and conference facilities. Rooms have been restored into a neutral, traditional international style. All contain neatly kept bathrooms equipped with tub/shower combos. A favorite of the business community, the hotel offers excellent service. Hemingway and one of his biographers, A. E. Hotchner, stayed at the Gran when they were in Zaragoza.

Joaquín Costa 5, 50001 Zaragoza. ✆ **97-622-19-01.** Fax 97-623-67-13. www.nh-hoteles.com. 134 units. 127€ double; from 188€ suite. AE, DC, MC, V. Parking 13€. **Amenities:** Restaurant; bar; room service; babysitting; laundry service; dry cleaning. *In room:* A/C, TV, minibar, hair dryer, safe.

Rey Alfonso I　　This well-maintained hotel is a favorite with businesspeople, who prefer its location in the commercial heart of town. A prominent arcade marks the entrance. The small rooms are comfortable and modern, with especially good beds and bathrooms equipped with tub/shower combos.

Calle Coso 17–19, 50003 Zaragoza. ✆ **97-639-48-50.** Fax 97-639-96-40. http://interhotel.com/spain/es/hoteles/4499.html. 117 units. 79€–130€ double. AE, DC, MC, V. Parking 11€. Bus: 22. **Amenities:** Restaurant; bar; room service; laundry service; dry cleaning. *In room:* A/C, TV, minibar, hair dryer, safe.

Vía Romana ✿ *Finds*　　This is a real find in the old quarter, a government-rated three-star hotel that is welcoming and comfortable, especially if you want to cover the town on foot. The hotel has been beautifully restored, with a well-trained staff and inviting midsize rooms with good furnishings and comfortable beds, plus immaculately kept bathrooms that are mostly equipped with tub/shower combos. For some reason, this hotel always seems fully booked in October, but you can make a reservation easily during other months.

Calle de Don Jaime 1, 50001 Zaragoza. ✆ **97-639-82-15.** Fax 97-629-05-11. www.husa.es. 66 units. 67€–114€ double. AE, DC, MC, V. Parking 9€ nearby. **Amenities:** Restaurant; bar; room service; babysitting; laundry service; dry cleaning. *In room:* A/C, TV, minibar, hair dryer, safe.

INEXPENSIVE

Don Yo *Value*　　Of course, you have to check this place out because of its intriguing name. Right in the center of town at the Plaza de Aragón and Plaza de la Independencia, it is a favorite among local journalists and draws a large repeat clientele among the business communities of Madrid and Barcelona. The hotel offers quiet, personal service, but it's not strong on atmosphere. The medium-size rooms are well furnished, not particularly stylish, but well maintained and relaxing, with especially good beds and bathrooms mostly with tub/shower combos. For comfort and good value, Don Yo is an appealing choice.

Juan Bruil 4–6, 50001 Zaragoza. ✆ **97-622-67-41.** Fax 97-621-99-56. 147 units. Mon–Thurs 86€ double; Fri–Sun 73€ double. AE, DC, MC, V. Parking 10€. **Amenities:** Restaurant; lounge; room service; babysitting; laundry service; dry cleaning. *In room:* A/C, TV, minibar, hair dryer, safe.

Hotel Gran Vía *Value*　　This hotel on the Paseo Gran Vía, near the Church of Santa Engracia and close to the main shopping district, is modern and lacks character but is welcoming and comfortable, with rooms at a very reasonable price. You don't get a lot of frills here, as the rooms are small and functional but the white walls, carpeted floors, excellent beds, and tidy bathrooms with showers make for a restful overnight stopover.

Calle Gran Vía 38, 50005 Zaragoza. © **97-622-92-13.** Fax 97-622-07-07. www.granviahotel.com. 44 units. 79€–120€ double; 90€–144€ suite. AE, DC, MC, V. Parking 12€. **Amenities:** Cafeteria; bar; room service; laundry service; dry cleaning. *In room:* A/C, TV, minibar.

Ramiro I   If you don't care about style and just want a comfortable place to sleep at a moderate price, head for the Ramiro I. It's an older establishment with much comfort. A government-rated three-star hotel at the edge of the old town, it offers small rooms that are contemporary and functional, often booked by businesspeople, and, surprisingly, by very few tourists. All units have been totally refurbished for supreme comfort; each has a well-kept bathroom with a tub/shower combo.

Coso 123, 50001 Zaragoza. © **97-629-82-00.** Fax 976-39-89-52. www.pretur.es. 69 units. 85€–113€ double. AE, DC, MC, V. Parking 11€. Take Calle San Vincente de Paul south from the west end of the Cathedral. After 4 blocks, follow Calle San Jorge west for 1 block to reach the hotel. **Amenities:** Restaurant; bar; lounge; room service; babysitting; laundry service; dry cleaning. *In room:* A/C, TV, minibar, hair dryer.

WHERE TO DINE

La Mar 🏵🏵 SEAFOOD   This is the top seafood restaurant in town. Service is leisurely, but if you're in the mood for a prolonged meal, the menu might include a full range of seasonal vegetables, peppers stuffed with seafood mousse, *dorada* (gilthead sea bream) cooked in a salt crust, baked sea bream, turbot with clams, grilled hake or monkfish, grilled squid, shellfish soup, or shellfish rice. If you're not in the mood for fish, try the grilled beefsteak with several kinds of sauces.

Plaza Aragón 12. © **97-621-22-64.** Reservations recommended. Main courses 15€–23€; fixed-price menu 40€; tasting menu 54€. AE, DC, MC, V. Mon–Sat 1:30–4pm and 9pm–midnight.

La Rinconada de Lorenzo 🏵 ARAGONESE   One of the best in town, this restaurant offers such unusual dishes as fried rabbit with snails. Oven-roasted lamb or lamb hock can be ordered in advance, but lamb skewers are always available. The chef prepares several versions of *migas* (fried bread crumbs) flavored with a number of different ingredients, including grapes and ham. Even though Zaragoza is inland, fresh fish is always on the menu: hake, grilled sole, sea bream, and salmon, for example. Veal is featured on the menu with wild boar and veal ribs, as well as veal meatballs served in a bean stew. Desserts are all homemade. Regional wines make fine accompaniments.

Calle La Salle 3. © **97-655-51-08.** Reservations required. Main courses 12€–27€. AE, DC, MC, V. Daily noon–4pm and 8–11:30pm. Bus: 40 or 45.

Los Borrachos SPANISH/FRENCH   Committed to preserving an old-fashioned kind of service, this restaurant occupies a formal set of dining rooms near the heart of town. Menu items may include a combination platter of hake with lobster, wild boar with wine sauce, filet of beef with a pepper-cognac sauce, roasted pheasant or rabbit, and an asparagus mousse accented with strips of Serrano ham. This restaurant's name, incidentally, translates as "The Drunkards," taken from the characters in a famous Velázquez painting.

Paseo de Sagasta 64. © **97-627-50-36.** Reservations recommended. Main courses 10€–21€; tasting menu 30€. AE, DC, MC, V. Daily 1–4pm and 8pm–midnight.

Risko Mar BASQUE/SPANISH   One of Zaragoza's most consistently reliable restaurants occupies a circa 1970s building that sits in the heart of the city's busiest commercial zone, a short walk from El Corte Inglés Department store and lots of other shops and boutiques. Within a pair of wood-paneled, red-toned dining rooms, you'll rub elbows with a busy workaday crowd of Spaniards, some of whom memorized the menu long ago and simply tell the waiters what they feel like eating that day. The best items include fresh fish, pork, veal, and beefsteaks and a popular version of roasted suckling lamb prepared with herbs, vegetables, and drippings. *Merluza Risko Mar* (house-style hake served with fresh clams, baby eels, and green sauce) is a justifiably celebrated house specialty.

Calle Francisco de Vitoria 16–18. © **97-622-50-53.** Reservations recommended. Main courses 16€–22€. DC, MC, V. Daily 1:30–3:30pm; Mon–Sat 9–11:30pm. Closed Aug. Bus: 33.

ZARAGOZA AFTER DARK

Zaragoza seems sleepy and low-key until after around 11pm, when things perk up a bit. A good place to begin an evening's bar and pub crawl is the Plaza Santa Cruz, site of one of the city's most funky bars, **Embajada de Jamaica** (no phone), which will tempt you with party-colored drinks. A particularly animated bar belongs to a restaurant, the **Club Náutico,** Plaza Pilar (no phone), which overlooks the muddy waters of the Ebro River.

A popular hangout near the Plaza del Pilar is **Casa Amadico,** Jordán de Urriés 3 (© **97-629-10-41**), where local government and business types congregate after work for tasty seafood tapas. Temptations include oysters, smoked salmon, lobster, and Serrano ham. It's open Tuesday through Sunday from 1 to 4pm and 7pm to midnight, and is closed in August. Another tapas bar worth a look is **Casa Luis,** Romea 8 (© **97-629-11-67**), whose array of shellfish tapas includes oysters, shrimp, and razor clams in little bundles. It's open year-round, Tuesday through Sunday from noon to 5pm and 8pm to midnight. A glass of wine costs 1€, and the selection of tapas ranges from .90€ to 3.60€.

A disco that doesn't even begin to function until most of the others have closed is **Discoteca Kit,** Calle Fernando el Católico 70 (no phone), which begins to rock and roll around 6am. Another option is **Café Hispano,** Camino de las Torres 42 (© **97-622-21-61**), a bar where singers (either professional or members of the crowd who've just gotta sing) croon danceable and drinkable songs. It's open Tuesday through Sunday from 8pm to 3:30am.

If you just want to barhop and try different *tascas,* most of which aren't even identified with individual signs, consider a promenade along the Calle Dr. Cerrada (near the Plaza Pamplona), the nearby Calle Dr. Casas, or Calle La Paz, where neighborhood residents usually duck inside at regular intervals for a quick fix of wine or sherry.

SIDE TRIPS FROM ZARAGOZA

Goya aficionados (male ones only, that is) can visit the **Cartuja de Aula Dei** ✦ (© **97-671-49-34**), a 16th-century Carthusian monastery 11km (7 miles) north of Zaragoza in Montañana. The young Goya, an Aragonese, completed one of his first important commissions here in 1774, a series of 11 murals depicting scenes from the lives of Christ and Mary. During the Napoleonic invasion, the murals suffered badly but have since been restored. Only men are admitted to this strictly run Carthusian community. The monastery is open the last Saturday of every month only from 9am to 3pm. Call ahead to arrange a time. From Zaragoza, bus 28 departs about every half hour to the site (trip time: 20 min.), with a one-way ticket costing .65€. Catch the bus at the stop near the Roman walls. You can also drive; take E-90 east out of town and follow the signs for Montañana.

Goya fans of both genders can go south from Zaragoza to the little village of **Fuendetodos,** where the artist was born in 1746. A small two-room cottage in the village (not his actual birthplace, however) was restored in 1985 and turned into a museum, **Casa de Goya,** Zuloaga 3 (© **97-614-38-30**). You're shown transparencies of his most important works. It is open Tuesday through Sunday from 11am to 2pm and 4 to 7pm. Admission is 1.80€. Take the N-330 south to the town of Muel, then go 18km (11 miles) south to Villanueva del Huerve. Bear east on the A-220 and continue for 8km (5 miles) to Fuendetodos. From Zaragoza, Autobuses Samar Buil, Calle Borao 13 (© **97-643-43-04**) carries passengers to the village.

2 Tarazona

88km (54½ miles) W of Zaragoza, 293km (182 miles) NE of Madrid

To call **Tarazona** the "Toledo of Aragón" may be a bit much, but it does deserve the name "Mudéjar City." Lying about halfway along the principal route connecting Zaragoza to the province of Soria, it is laid out in tiers above the quays of the Queiles River. Once the kings of Aragón lived here, and before that, the city was known to the Romans. You can walk through the old barrio with its tall facades and narrow medieval streets.

ESSENTIALS
GETTING THERE   From Zaragoza, four **buses** leave daily for Tarazona (1½ hr. away). If you're **driving,** head west from Zaragoza along the A-68, connecting with the N-122 to Tarazona.

VISITOR INFORMATION   The **tourist office** at Plaza San Francisco 1 (© **97-664-00-74;** www.terrazona.org) is open daily from 9am to 1:30pm and 4:30 to 7pm.

EXPLORING TARAZONA
Tarazona's major attraction is its Gothic **cathedral,** begun in 1152 but essentially reconstructed in the 15th and 16th centuries. However, the Aragonese Mudéjar style is still much in evidence, especially as reflected in the lantern tower and belfry. The dome resembles that of the old cathedral in Zaragoza.

The town is also known for its 16th-century **Ayuntamiento (Town Hall),** which has reliefs across its facade depicting Ferdinand and Isabella retaking Granada. The monument stands on the Plaza de España in the older upper town, on a hill overlooking the river. Take the Ruta Turística from here up to the church of **Santa Magdalena,** with a Mudéjar tower that forms the chief landmark of the town's skyline; its mirador opens onto a panoramic view. Continuing up the hill, you reach **La Concepción,** another church with a narrow brick tower.

WHERE TO STAY & DINE
Brujas de Bécquer   Nearly a kilometer (½ mile) southeast of town beside the road leading to Zaragoza you'll find this unpretentious modern hotel, built in 1972 and renovated 20 years later. Rooms are modest but comfortable and bathrooms are neatly kept with shower stalls. The dining room serves delicious fixed-price meals. Reservations are almost never needed. The hotel, incidentally, was named in honor of a 19th-century Seville-born patriot and poet (Gustavo Adolfo Bécquer) who praised the beauties of Aragón in some of his writing.

Teresa Cajal 30, 50500 Tarazona. © **97-664-04-00** or 97-664-04-04. Fax 97-664-01-98. 57 units. 43€–47€ double. AE, DC, MC, V. Parking garage 6€. **Amenities:** Restaurant; laundry service; dry cleaning. *In room:* A/C, TV, hair dryer.

3 Calatayud

85km (53 miles) W of Zaragoza, 235km (146 miles) NE of Madrid

The Romans founded **Calatayud** only to abandon it some time during the 2nd century, and it wasn't until the arrival of the Muslims in the 8th century that it was repopulated. The Moors were routed in 1120 by the conquering Catholic forces, which allowed some of the inhabitants to stay. But they were made virtual slaves and forced to live in a *morería* (Moorish ghetto). Some of the Moorish influence can still be seen in the town. Many 14th- and 15th-century church towers in Calatayud are reminiscent of minarets.

ESSENTIALS

GETTING THERE   Calatayud lies on the main rail line linking Madrid to Zaragoza. There are 12 **trains** a day from Madrid, nine from Zaragoza, and three from Barcelona. There are three to four **buses** a day from Zaragoza (1½ hr. away). Calatayud is on the E-90 linking Madrid with Zaragoza.

VISITOR INFORMATION   The **tourist office** at Plaza del Fuerte s/n (© 97-688-63-22) is open Tuesday through Sunday from 10am to 1pm and 4 to 7pm.

EXPLORING CALATAYUD

The major attraction of Calatayud is **Santa María la Mayor,** Calle de Obispo Arrué, a brick church built in Aragonese style with an ornate Plateresque-Mudéjar facade and an exceptionally harmonious octagonal belfry. Nearby, on the Calle Datao, **Iglesia de San Pedro de los Francos** is the leaning tower of Calatayud. It is a fine example of the Mudéjar style.

A walk along Calle Unión leads to **La Parraguía de San Andrés,** with an elegant and graceful Mudéjar belfry. Strike a path through the old Moorish quarter up the hill to the ruins of the castle that dominated Qal'at Ayyub (the old Arab name for the town). Once you're there, a panoramic view unfolds.

East of Calatayud, excavations continue to uncover the **Roman city of Bibilis,** on the Mérida–Zaragoza highway. It was the birthplace of Roman satirist Martial (ca. A.D. 40–104).

WHERE TO STAY & DINE

Hospedería Mesón de la Dolores ★★ *Value*   Calatayud now offers an elegant, tranquil place to stay. A 15th-century Aragonese palace has been converted into a classic hotel of pristine beauty and rural charm. Rooms are midsize to spacious, and each is beautifully furnished and equipped with roomy bathrooms with deep tub/shower combos. On site is a little Museum of Wine, as the town is famous for wine. Considering the quality of this hotel, prices in this remote part of Spain are most reasonable. The on-site restaurant is the finest place in town at which to dine, even if you're a nonresident.

Plaza de Mesones 4, 50300 Calatayud. © **97-688-90-55.** Fax 97-688-90-59. 34 units. www.mesonla dolores.com. 52€–59€ double; 68€–81€ suite. AE, MC, V. Parking 4.50€. **Amenities:** Restaurant; bar; laundry service; dry cleaning. *In room:* A/C, TV, hair dryer, safe.

Hotel Calatayud   About 1.6km (1 mile) east of Calatayud, on the N-II highway to Zaragoza, the hotel contains acceptable rooms with simple furnishings, plus good beds and well-maintained private bathrooms equipped with tub/shower combos.

Autovía de Aragón Salida Km 237, 50300 Calatayud. © **97-688-13-23.** Fax 97-688-54-38. www. calatayud.com. 78 units. 56€–64€ double; 87€ suite. AE, DC, MC, V. **Amenities:** Restaurant; bar; lounge; laundry service; dry cleaning. *In room:* A/C, TV.

4 Nuévalos/Piedra

117.5km (73 miles) W of Zaragoza, 230km (143 miles) E of Madrid

The town of **Nuévalos,** with its one paved road, isn't much of a lure, but thousands of visitors from all over the world flock to the **Monasterio de Piedra,** called the garden district of Aragón (see review below).

GETTING THERE

From Madrid, **train** connections reach Alhama de Aragón. Take a taxi from there to the monastery.

From Zaragoza, head southwest on the N-II through Calatayud. At the little town of Ateca, take the left turnoff, which is marked for Nuévalos and the Monasterio de Piedra, and drive for 23km (14 miles). If you're driving from Madrid, take the N-II and turn east at the spa town of Alhama de Aragón.

TOURING THE MONASTERY

In Nuévalos, the major attraction is the **Monasterio de Piedra** ★★ (© **97-684-90-11**). *Piedra* means rock in Spanish, and after the badlands of Aragón, you expect bleak, rocky terrain. Instead, you have a virtual Garden of Eden, with a 60m (197-ft.) waterfall. It was here in 1194 that Cistercian monks built a Charterhouse on the banks of the Piedra River. The monks are long gone, having departed in 1835, and their former quarters have been reconstructed and turned into a hotel (see below).

Two pathways, marked in blue or red, meander through the grounds, and views are offered from any number of levels. Tunnels and stairways, dating from the 19th century, are the work of Juan Federico Mutadas, who created the park here. Slippery steps lead down to an iris grotto, just one of many quiet, secluded retreats. It is said the original monks inhabited the site because they wanted a "foretaste of paradise." To be honest, they were escaping the court intrigues at the powerful Monestir de Poblet in Tarragona province. The monastery at Piedra is only 3km (2 miles) from the hillside village of Nuévalos. You can wander through the grounds daily from 9am to 8pm in summer (closes at 5pm in winter) for an admission charge of 9€ adults, 6€ children.

WHERE TO STAY & DINE

Monasterio de Piedra ★★ *(Finds*   This is one of the showplaces of Aragón. The grounds include a beautiful garden, with little log bridges and masses of flowering plants and trees. The beautifully maintained rooms, which you should reserve well in advance, have phones and TV but no other in-room luxuries. Some open onto terraces and all contain neatly kept bathrooms with tub/shower combos.

50210 Nuévalos. © **97-684-90-11.** Fax 97-684-90-54. 60 units. 99€–110€ double. Rates include breakfast and admission to the monastery. AE, DC, MC, V. **Amenities:** Restaurant; bar; pool; tennis courts; room service; laundry service; dry cleaning. *In room:* TV, hair dryer.

5 Sos del Rey Católico ★

422km (262 miles) N of Madrid, 60km (37 miles) SW of Pamplona

In northern Aragón, **Sos del Rey Católico** formed one of the Cinco Villas of Aragón, stretching along a 90km (56-mile) frontier with Navarre. These villages, in the far-distant part of northern Aragón, also included Tauste, Ejea, Uncastillo, and Sabada. Despite their small size, they were raised to the status of towns by Philip V, who was grateful for their assistance and loyalty in the War of Spanish Succession (1701–13).

The most visited town is Sos del Rey Católico, so named because it was the birthplace of Ferdinand, the Catholic king, in 1452. He entered the world's history books after his marriage to Isabella of Castile and León. Locals will point out the Palacio de Sada, where the king is said to have been born. The town is more interesting than its minor monuments, and you can explore it at will, wandering its narrow, cobbled streets and stopping at any place that attracts your fancy. The kings of Aragón fortified this village on the Navarre border with a thick wall. Much of that medieval character has been preserved—enough so that the village has been declared a national monument.

GETTING THERE

From Zaragoza to Sos, a 2½-hour ride away, there is a daily **bus** at 6:30pm, returning at 7am the next morning.

To **drive** from Zaragoza, take the N-330 to Huesca. Continue on N-330 to Jaca, then bear west on the N-240 toward Pamplona. Turn south at the cutoff to Sanguesa.

WHERE TO STAY & DINE

Parador de Sos del Rey Católico ★★　This member of the government-owned parador network is unusual because of the care that was taken to blend a six-story building into its medieval setting. Built in 1975, it's composed mostly of stone and wood timbers, with lots of interior paneling and antique-looking accessories. Despite its location in the heart of the village, sweeping views open from some of the windows onto the nearby countryside. Coming in various shapes and sizes, the accommodations are well maintained and beautifully furnished, with quality beds and immaculately kept private bathrooms with tub/shower combos. Hearty Aragonese food is served in the restaurant.

Sainz de Vicuña 1, 50680 Sos del Rey Católico. ✆ **94-888-80-11.** Fax 94-888-81-00. www.parador.es. 65 units. 84€–109€ double; 169€–249€ suite. AE, DC, MC, V. Parking 6€. Closed Jan–Feb. **Amenities:** Restaurant; lounge; room service; laundry service; dry cleaning. *In room:* A/C, TV, minibar, hair dryer.

15

Navarre & La Rioja

The ancient land of **Navarre** (*Navarra* in Spanish, *Nafarroa* in Basque) shares a 130km (81-mile) frontier with France, with nine crossing points. This province with a strong Basque tradition is an important link between Iberia and the rest of the continent.

As a border region, Navarre has seen its share of conflict, and to this day the remains of lonely castles and fortified walled towns bear witness to that. But somehow this kingdom, one of the most ancient on the peninsula, has managed to preserve its own government and identity. Romans, Christians, Muslims, and Jews have all left their stamp on Navarre, and its architecture is as diverse as its landscape. It is also a province rich in folklore. Pagan rites were blended into Christian traditions to form a mythology that lives even today in Navarre's many festivals. Dancers and singers wear the famous red berets, the *jota* is the most celebrated folk dance, and the best-known sport is *pelota*—sometimes called jai alai in other parts of the world.

Navarre is also rich in natural attractions, but most foreign visitors miss them when they just visit for the Fiesta de San Fermín in July to see the running of the bulls through the streets of Pamplona, Navarre's capital and major city. Even if you do visit for the festival, try to explore some of the panoramic Pyrenean landscape.

Adjoining Navarre is **La Rioja,** the smallest region of mainland Spain—bordered not only by Navarre but also by Castile and Aragón. Extending along the Ebro River, this province has far greater influence than its tiny dimensions would suggest because it is one of the most important wine-growing districts in Europe. The land is generally split into two sections: Rioja Alta, which gets a lot of rainfall and has a mild climate, and Rioja Baja, which is much hotter and more arid, more like Aragón. The capital of the province is Logroño, a city of some 200,000 that links the two regions.

The most visited towns are **Logroño** and **Haro,** the latter known for its wineries. **Santo Domingo de la Calzada** was a major stop on the ancient pilgrims' route on the way to Santiago de Compostela, while **Nájera** once served as capital for the kings of Navarre. Now little more than a village, it lies along the Najerilla River.

1 Pamplona (Iruña)

90km (56 miles) SE of San Sebastián, 385km (239 miles) NE of Madrid, 168km (104 miles) NE of Zaragoza

Ernest Hemingway's descriptions of the running of the bulls in his 1927 novel, *The Sun Also Rises,* made **Pamplona** known throughout the world. The book's glamour remains undiminished for the crowds who read it and then rush off to Pamplona to see the *encierros* (bull running) during the Fiesta de San Fermín. Attempts to outlaw this world-famous ceremony have failed so far, and it remains a superstar attraction, particularly among bullfighting aficionados. The riotous festival usually begins on July 6 and lasts to the 14th. Fireworks and

Basque flute concerts are only some of the spectacles giving added color to the fiesta. Wine flows and people party nonstop for the duration. Those who want to know they'll have a bed after watching the *encierro* should reserve a year in advance at one of the city's handful of hotels or boardinghouses, or stay in San Sebastián or some other neighboring town and visit Pamplona during the day.

But Pamplona is more than just a city where an annual festival takes place. Long the most significant town in Spain's Pyrenean region, it was also a major stopover for those traveling either of two frontier roads: the Roncesvalles Pass or the Velate Pass. Once a fortified city, it was for centuries the capital of the ancient kingdom of Navarre.

In its historic core, the Pamplona of legend lives on, but the city has been engulfed by modern real-estate development. The saving grace of new Pamplona is La Taconera, a spacious green swath of fountain-filled gardens and parkland west of the old quarter where you will see students from the University of Navarre.

Pamplona became the capital of Navarre in the 10th century. Its golden age was during the reign of Charles III (called "the Noble"), who gave it its cathedral, where he was eventually buried. Over the years, the city has been the scene of many battles, with various factions struggling for control. Those who lived in the old quarter, the Navarrería, wanted to be allied with Castile, whereas those on the outskirts favored a French connection. Castile eventually won out, although some citizens of Navarre today want Pamplona to be part of a newly created country of the Basque lands.

ESSENTIALS

GETTING THERE   Pamplona is the air hub of the Navarre region. The city is served by two weekday **Aviaco** flights from both Madrid and Barcelona; international connections can be made from either city. Arrivals are at Aeropuerto de Noaín (© **94-816-87-00**), 6.5km (4 miles) from the city center and accessible only by taxi, about 10€.

Three **trains** a day arrive from Madrid (trip time: 5–6 hr.) and two to three from Barcelona (7–9 hr.). Pamplona also has three daily train connections from San Sebastián to the north (1¼ hr.) and four to seven daily from Zaragoza to the south (2–3 hr.). For information, call © **90-242-02-02.**

Buses connect Pamplona with several major Spanish cities: four per day from Barcelona (6 hr.), five to seven per day from Zaragoza (3½ hr.), and nine per day from San Sebastián (1½ hr.). Instead of being able to call for information, you'll have to consult the bulletin board's list of destinations at the **Estación de Autobuses** (© **94-822-38-54**) at Calle Conde Oliveto (corner of Calle Yanguas and Miranda). Nearly 20 privately owned bus companies converge here, and it's a mass of confusion.

The A-15 Navarra national highway begins on the outskirts of Pamplona and runs south to join A-68, midway between Zaragoza and Logroño. N-240 connects San Sebastián with Pamplona.

VISITOR INFORMATION   The **tourist office** at Calle Eslava 1 (© **94-820-65-40;** www.cfnavarra.es) is open Monday through Saturday from 10am to 2pm and 4 to 7pm, and Sunday from 10am to 2pm.

EXPLORING PAMPLONA

The heart of Pamplona is the **Plaza del Castillo,** formerly the bullring, built in 1847. Today it is the seat of the autonomous provincial government. This elegant

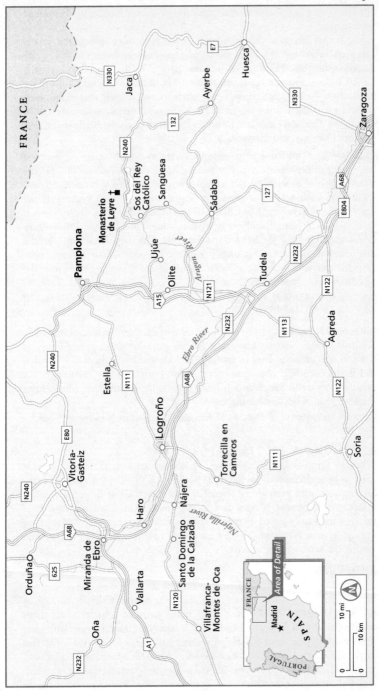

tree-lined paseo becomes a virtual communal bedroom during the Festival of San Fermín.

The narrow streets of the old quarter extend from three sides of the square. The present bullring, the **Plaza de Toros,** is just east and south of this square alongside the Paseo Hemingway. Running parallel to the east of the square is **Calle Estafeta,** a narrow street that is the site of the running of the bulls. With its bars and *tascas,* it attracts university students and is lively year-round, even without a festival. During the festival it is the most frequented place in town next to the Plaza del Castillo. The bulls also run through the barricaded streets of Santo Domingo and Mercaderes.

Catedral ★ This is the most important sight in Pamplona, dating from the late 14th century on the site of a former Romanesque basilica. The present facade, a mix of neoclassical and baroque, was the work of Ventura Rodríguez, architect to Charles III. The interior is Gothic with lots of fan vaulting. In the center is the alabaster tomb of Charles III and his Castilian wife, Queen Leonor, done in 1416 by Flemish sculptor Janin de Lomme. The 14th- and 15th-century Gothic cloisters are a highlight of the cathedral. The Barbazán Chapel, off the east gallery, is noted for its vaulting. The Museo Diocesano, housed in the cathedral's refectory and kitchen, displays religious objects, spanning the era from the Middle Ages to the Renaissance.

Calle Curia. © **94-822-56-79.** Free admission to cathedral; museum 3.60€. July 15–Sept 15 Mon–Sat 10am–7pm; Mon–Sat 11am–1:30pm.

Museo de Navarra ★ The major museum of Pamplona is housed in a 16th-century hospital, Nuestra Señora de la Misericordia, located close to the river. It has rich collections of Roman artifacts, including some 2nd-century mosaics, and Romanesque art, plus an important Goya portrait of the Marqués de San Adrián. Gothic and Renaissance paintings are on the second floor. Murals from the 13th century are another highlight.

Cuesta de Santa Domingo s/n. © **94-842-64-92.** Admission 1.80€. Tues–Sat 9:30am–2pm and 5–7pm; Sun 11am–2pm.

ATTENDING A PELOTA MATCH

While in Pamplona, you might want to head about 6km (3½ miles) outside town to **Frontón Euskal–Jai Berri** (© **94-833-11-59**), along Avenida de Francia, to check out a professional *pelota* (jai alai) match. Game times are Tuesday, Saturday, and Sunday at 4pm and on regional and national holidays. Four matches are usually played on game days, and tickets can be purchased any time during the sets. Admission to the bleachers is 12€ to 15€. We'd recommend leaving the betting to the experts.

SHOPPING

You'll find lots of Navarese handicrafts in kiosks scattered through the old city, but for a particularly well-inventoried outlet, head for **Echeve,** Calle Mercadores 14 (© **94-822-42-15**); it sells such handcrafted items as vests, ceramics, hats, woodcarvings, and *botas* (wineskins), which locals use to squirt wine, with great dexterity, into their open mouths. A roughly equivalent competitor is **Las Tres 222,** Calle Comedias 7 (© **94-822-44-38**), which sells wineskins, neckerchiefs, and wide belts known as *gerrikos,* favored by weight lifters and sports enthusiasts who feel a twinge in their backs whenever they're called upon to perform heavy-duty lifting.

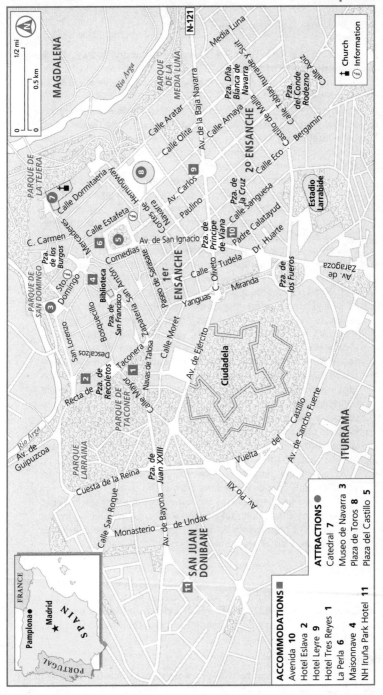

Pamplona

N-121

N

1/2 mi
0.5 km

✝ Church
ⓘ Information

MAGDALENA

PARQUE DE
LA MEDIA LUNA

Media Luna

Rio Arga

Calle Aratar

Calle Olite

Av. Calle Amaya

Calle de la Baja Navarra

Pza. Dña.
Blanca de
Navarra

Pza.
del Conde
Rodezno

Calle Avoz

Castillo de Maia y Tablas murrado y Sur

Calle Eco. C. Bergamin

8

Calle Dormitaeria

Cortes de Navarra

Av. Carlos

9

2º ENSANCHE

Estadio
Larrabide

PARQUE DE
LA TEJERA

✝ ■ 7

Calle Estafeta

Hemingway

ⓘ

Paulino

Pza. de
la Cruz

Calle Sanguesa

C. Carmen

Mercaderes

6

5

Av. de San Ignacio

Pza. de
Principe
de Viana

Padre Calatayud

Pza. de
los Burgos

Comedias

Paseo de Sarasate

10

Calle

Dr. Huarte

PARQUE DE
SAN DOMINGO

3

Sto. ⓘ
Domingo

Biblioteca

4

Pza. de
San Francisco

Zapateria

San Anton

1er
ENSANCHE

C. Oliveto

Tudela

Miranda

Pza. de
los Fueros

Av. de
Zaragoza

San Lorenzo

Bosquecillo

Descalzos

Yanguas

Calle Moret

Rio Arga

Recta de

2

Pza. de
Recoletos

Taconera

Navas de Tolosa

Taconera

Calle Mayor

Calle Navarra

Av. de Ejército

Ciudadela

ITURRAMA

Av. de
Guipuzcoa

PARQUE DE
TACONERA

PARQUE
LARRAINA

Pza. de
Juan XXIII

Cuesta de la Reina

Av. de Bayona

Av. de Undax

Calle San Roque

Monasterio

Av. Pio XII

Vuelta   del

Av. de Sancho Fuerte

SAN JUAN
DONIBANE

11

FRANCE

SPAIN

Pamplona ●

★ Madrid

PORTUGAL

ACCOMMODATIONS ■
Avenida 10
Hotel Eslava 2
Hotel Leyre 9
Hotel Tres Reyes 1
La Perla 6
Maisonnave 4
NH Iruña Park Hotel 11

ATTRACTIONS ●
Catedral 7
Museo de Navarra 3
Plaza de Toros 8
Plaza del Castillo 5

491

The Running of the Bulls

Beginning at noon on July 6 and continuing nonstop to July 14, the **Fiesta de San Fermín** is one of the most popular events in Europe, drawing thousands of tourists who overtax the severely limited facilities of Pamplona.

Get up early (or don't go to bed at all), since the bulls run every day at 8am sharp. To watch, be in position behind the barricades along Calle Estafeta no later than 6am. Only the able-bodied and sober should plan to run. Women are officially not permitted to run, although many defy this ban each year.

There simply aren't enough beds or bullfight tickets to go around, and scalpers have a field day. Technically, tickets for a good seat in the ring go on sale at 8pm the night before the *corrida* (bullfight), and tickets for standing room go on sale at 4pm on the day of the bullfight. But all the tickets are sold out, and since it is impossible to get them through a travel agent beforehand, tourists have to use scalpers.

The fiesta draws half a million visitors, many of whom camp in the city parks. Temporary facilities are set up, but there are never enough beds. Hotel reservations should be confirmed *at least* 6 months beforehand. If you look respectable, some *Pamplónicos* may rent you a room. Be aware, however, that they may gouge you for the highest price they think you're willing to pay, and your room might turn out to be a dirty floor shared with others in a slumlike part of the city. The tourist office will not make any recommendations during the festival—you're basically on your own. Many young visitors sleep on the grounds of the Ciudadela and Plaza Fueros traffic ring, but you could be mugged. Longtime visitors to Pamplona advise that it's better to sleep in a group, on top of your belongings, and during the day when it's safer than under cover of darkness. If you can't find a room, check your valuables at the bus station on Calle Conde Oliveto (where there are also showers—free, but cold).

As for bars and restaurants, ignore all the times given below. Most establishments operate around the clock at this time.

Warning: Some people go to the festival not to watch the bulls but to pick pockets. And don't take needless risks, such as leaping from a building in the hope friends below will catch you. Many people do this each year, and not all are caught.

If you're looking for fashion or accessories, head for a boutique called **Zara,** Av. Carlos III 7 (© **94-822-75-04**), which is closed on Monday, or explore the aisles of Pamplona's biggest department store, **Unzu,** Calle Mercaderes 3 (© **94-820-91-00**).

WHERE TO STAY

During the Festival of San Fermín, prices are three to four times higher than those listed below. In some instances, a hotel commits itself to prices it will charge at *Fiesta* (the original name of *The Sun Also Rises* when it was first published in Britain). Other owners charge pretty much what they think they can get, and they can get a lot. Therefore, agree on the price when making a reservation, if you've been able to get a reservation in the first place. At other times of the year, Pamplona is a reasonably priced tourist destination.

EXPENSIVE

Avenida ⭐ *Finds*   One of the best inns in town, this small, well-run place opened in 1989. The midsize rooms are well furnished and contain bathrooms with tub/shower combos; some are even better than the government's three-star rating suggests. Furnishings tend toward the sleek and modern, and local watercolors add a warm touch.

Zaragoza 5, 31003 Pamplona. ℂ 94-824-54-54. Fax 94-823-23-23. 27 units. Mon–Thurs 94€ double; Fri–Sun 60€ double; July 6–14 220€ double. AE, DC, MC, V. Parking 9€. **Amenities:** Restaurant; bar; room service; babysitting; laundry service; dry cleaning. *In room:* A/C, TV, minibar, hair dryer.

Hotel Tres Reyes ⭐   A short walk west of the old town, just 2 blocks north of the ancient citadel, this is one of the finest hotels in town, surpassed only by Iruña Park. It provides tasteful airy rooms with contemporary furnishings, lots of sunlight, and private bathrooms equipped with tub/shower combos. Many rooms have balconies, and all are welcome refuges from the intensity of the local festivities.

Jardines de la Taconera 1, 31001 Pamplona. ℂ 800/448-8355 in the U.S., or 94-822-66-00. Fax 94-822-29-30. www.hotel3reyes.com. 160 units. 171€–460€ double; 376€–684€ suite. AE, DC, MC, V. Parking 15€ indoors; free outside. **Amenities:** Restaurant; cafeteria; bar; pool; health club; sauna; squash courts; room service; massage; babysitting; laundry service; dry cleaning. *In room:* A/C, TV, minibar, hair dryer, safe.

NH Iruña Park Hotel ⭐⭐   A short walk west of the Parque de la Ciudadela, this is the largest and best hotel in town, often the site of conventions. A large staff maintains the blandly furnished but comfortable rooms, some suitable for people with disabilities, and bathrooms are equipped with tub/shower combos. Public areas are modern and glossy, with deep armchairs and big windows.

Arcadio María Larraona 1, 31008 Pamplona. ℂ 94-817-32-00. Fax 94-817-23-87. www.nh-hoteles.com. 225 units. 128€–335€ double; 342€–450€ suite. AE, DC, MC, V. Parking 13€. **Amenities:** Restaurant; bar; exercise room; sauna; solarium; car rental; room service; babysitting; laundry service; dry cleaning. *In room:* A/C, TV, minibar, hair dryer, safe.

MODERATE

Hotel Eslava ⭐ *Finds*   Right off the Plaza de Recoletas, and a 10-minute walk from the bus station, this renovated hotel manages to combine the spirits of old and new Spain. Its small living room resembles the drawing room of a distinguished Spanish house. All the average-size rooms are tastefully decorated; some have balconies with views of the city walls and the vistas beyond. All come with comfortable beds and bathrooms which for the most part contain tub/shower combos.

Plaza Virgen de la O 7, corner with Calle Recoletas 20, 31001 Pamplona. ℂ 94-822-22-70. Fax 94-822-51-57. www.hotel-eslava.com. 28 units. 56€–115€ double. AE, DC, MC, V. Bus: 9. **Amenities:** Lounge; laundry service; dry cleaning. *In room:* TV.

La Perla   Opened in 1880 and last renovated long ago, this is not exactly the most outstanding hotel in town. But during the festival it becomes *the* place to stay, because it opens onto the main square of Pamplona and overlooks Calle Estafeta, the straightaway of the *encierro* through which the bulls run. The small rooms are furnished with an old-fashioned flair. All contain neatly kept bathrooms, most of which contain tub/shower combos. In days of yore they sheltered everybody from Ernest Hemingway to U.S. Sen. Henry Cabot Lodge.

Plaza del Castillo 1, 31001 Pamplona. ✆ **94-822-77-06.** Fax 94-822-15-19. 67 units. 55€–98€ double; 130€ suite. AE, DC, MC, V. **Amenities:** Lounge.

Maisonnave Located in the historic old town of Pamplona, west of the Plaza del Castillo and within easy walking distance of the *tascas* and restaurants, this place is solidly booked for the fiesta. You must reserve at least 6 months in advance—and even then, say a prayer. The small rooms have been completely renovated, each well furnished, well maintained, and comfortably though blandly standardized. Bathrooms have tub/shower combos.

Nueva 20, 31001 Pamplona. ✆ **94-822-26-00.** Fax 94-822-01-66. www.hotelmaisonnave.es. 138 units. 89€ double. AE, DC, MC, V. Parking 9€. Bus: 9 or 15. **Amenities:** 2 restaurants; bar; lounge; room service; babysitting; laundry service; dry cleaning. *In room:* A/C, TV, minibar, hair dryer.

WHERE TO DINE
EXPENSIVE
Alhambra REGIONAL/SPANISH   One of the best-known and most stable restaurants in Pamplona, and just a 15-minute walk from the cathedral, Alhambra dates from the end of World War II. In 1995 the restaurant was renovated and enlarged. Set within two paneled dining rooms, it features a complete selection of local wines and regional specialties, including carefully deboned sardines, grilled and served with truffles; grilled filet of hake with local herbs; and selected cuts of filet steak with sauces made from local mushrooms and garlic.

Calle Bergamín 7. ✆ **94-824-50-07.** Reservations recommended. Main courses 18€–25€. AE, DC, MC, V. Mon–Sat 1–4pm and 9–11:30pm.

Europa ★★★ SPANISH   Located in the center of Pamplona near the Plaza del Castillo, this is, along with Josetxo (see below), the best restaurant in the entire region. Both have Michelin stars, which are rarely doled out in this part of Europe. The chef and culinary artist is Pamplona-born Pilar Idoate, who prepares a seasonal menu. Examples include baked potatoes stuffed with truffles and minced crayfish, roulades of sole with mountain herbs, filet steaks with Roquefort dressing, and such game dishes as venison and pheasant. Desserts include an orange mousse with a *marquesa de chocolate*.

Calle Espoz y Mina 11. ✆ **94-822-18-00.** Reservations recommended. Main courses 18€–25€; business menu 35€. AE, DC, MC, V. Mon–Sat 1–3:30pm and 9–11pm.

Hartza ★ REGIONAL/INTERNATIONAL   One of the oldest bodegas in town, a popular restaurant has flourished at this location near the bullring since the 1870s. Even though it doesn't have a Michelin star, it manages to give Josetxo and Europa (see above and below) serious competition. The chef's touch is delicate, and although Hartza doesn't attempt as many dishes as Josetxo, what it does create is sublime and inventive. There's a summer garden for outdoor dining, plus a street-level bar. The portions are generous (but expensive); specialties change with the seasons but might include well-seasoned vegetable soup, stuffed peppers, tournedos, hake and eel, and a selection of regional cheeses. The interior is air-conditioned during the hottest summer months.

Juan de Labrit 19. ✆ **94-822-45-68.** Reservations recommended. Main courses 19€–30€. AE, DC, MC, V. Tues–Sun 1:30–3:30pm; Tues–Sat 9–11:30pm. Closed Aug and 10 days at Christmas.

Josetxo ★★★ BASQUE   The finest and grandest restaurant in town, Josexto is run by a civic-minded local family with more than 30 years' experience in the restaurant trade. The chef has a magic combination: inventiveness and solid technique, backed up by the very freshest ingredients. Specialties vary with the seasons but might include puff pastry stuffed with shellfish, a *panaché* (medley) of fresh vegetables with Serrano ham, sea bass cooked in white wine, variations of goose paté, and several rabbit and trout dishes. Dessert might be a chocolate truffle tart layered with orange-flavored cream. The restaurant is beside a busy traffic circle, 4 blocks south of the Plaza del Castillo.

Plaza Príncipe de Viana 1. ✆ **94-822-20-97.** Reservations recommended on weekends. Main courses 15€–28€. AE, DC, MC, V. Mon–Sat 1:30–3:30pm and 9–11pm. Closed Holy Week and Aug.

MODERATE
Casa Otano NAVARRESE/SPANISH   In the oldest part of town, on a narrow street that empties into the Plaza de Castillo, this is a busy and popular tavern-style restaurant with three dining rooms and a reputation for feeding generations of Pamplona residents. Established in the 1950s, the menu includes house-style hake (baked with garlic, green sauce, herbs, and clams), many different kinds of succulent grilled meats and fish, chicken roasted in sherry sauce, and thick cuts of delicious pork chops.

Calle San Nicolás 5. ✆ **94-822-50-95.** Reservations recommended. Main courses 6€–22€; set lunch 11€–30€. AE, MC, V. Mon–Sat 1–4pm and 9–11:30pm; Sun 1–4pm.

INEXPENSIVE
Erburu ⭑ *Finds* REGIONAL   There's absolutely nothing fancy or artificial about this restaurant, which has been serving well-conceived, old-fashioned food for the past 30 years. It contains only 45 seats, staffed by a crew that seems to have been here since the day the place opened. Many of the regular clients don't even ask for a menu. Examples include snails in garlic sauce, braised oxtail, steaming bowls of kale and potato soup, hake in garlic-flavored green sauce, and several kinds of beef, pork, and chicken. Dessert might be an old-time portion of flan, accompanied, according to your wishes, with fresh fruit and/or ice cream.

Calle San Lorenzo 19. ✆ **94-822-51-69.** Reservations recommended. Main courses 7€–17€; fixed-price menu lunch 10€. AE, MC, V. Tues–Sun 10am–midnight. Closed the last week in July.

PAMPLONA AFTER DARK
In a city famous for the way bulls run through its streets, there's something consistent about the local habit of wandering through the city's streets, particularly within the historic *casco antiguo*. Two streets in particular, **Calle San Nicolás** and **Calle de Jarauta,** are lined with *tascas,* bars, bodegas, and pubs. Lots of them don't even have signs, so just wander and drop in and out of whichever strikes your fancy.

The town's most popular club is **Marengo,** avenue Bayona 2 (✆ **94-826-55-42**), a huge enclave which is a nightspot where a crowd in their 20s and 30s come to dance the night away to recorded music. Your dress code must pass inspection by a team of hardened doormen before you are allowed inside. Tickets to enter cost 8€, and hours are Thursday through Saturday from 11pm to 6am. At a Celtic import, **O'Connor's Irish Pub,** Paseo Sarasate s/n (no phone), pints of Guinness and recorded Irish ballads enliven the old town.

Looking for a dance club to let off some late-night steam? Head for Pamplona's most popular disco, **Reverendos,** Monasterio de Velate 5 (✆ **94-826-15-93**), where 20- and 30-somethings dance, flirt, and drink till all hours. The cover charge is 6€, which includes the price of a drink.

Dating from 1888, the Art Deco **Café Iruña,** Plaza del Castillo 44 (✆ **94-822-20-64**), has an outdoor terrace that's popular in summer. The winter crowd is likely to congregate around the bar, ordering combination plates and snacks in addition to drinks. The place thrives as a cafe/bar daily from 8am to 1am; however, it becomes more of a restaurant during the lunch hour. Platters of hot food are served to many of the local office workers and day laborers. The *menú del día* is 10€, and a full lunch, served daily from 1 to 3:30pm, costs 9€ to 12€. Beer goes for 1.50€ at the bar, slightly more at a table.

Cafetería El Molino, Bayona 13 (*©* **94-825-10-90**), centrally located in the commercial Barrio San Juan, doubles as a popular tapas bar. Late in the evening, the action really heats up. The huge assortment of tapas includes fried shrimp, squid, anchovies, fish croquettes, and Russian salad. Most tapas don't exceed 1.35€, although some of the more expensive ones go for 2.50€. Open Monday through Saturday (except Wed) from 8am to 1am, Sunday from 9am to 1am.

2 Olite ⟨★⟩

44km (27 miles) S of Pamplona, 369km (229 miles) N of Madrid

A historical city, Olite sits in a rich agricultural belt with a Mediterranean climate of short winters and long hot summers. Cornfields and vineyards, along with large villages, pepper the countryside. It is also the center of a winemaking industry carried on by cooperative cellars. These wine merchants hold a local festival each year from September 14 to September 18.

ESSENTIALS

GETTING THERE   Two to four **trains** per day from Pamplona run to Olite, taking 35 minutes one-way. For rail information, call *©* **94-870-06-28.**

Two **bus** companies, **Conda** (*©* **94-882-03-42**) and **La Tafallesa** (*©* **94-822-28-86**), run from Pamplona to Olite at the rate of 6 to 12 per day. The trip takes 45 minutes.

By **car,** take the A-15 expressway south from Pamplona.

VISITOR INFORMATION   The **tourist office** at Plaza Carlos II el Noble s/n (*©* **94-874-17-03;** www.cfnavarra.es) is open Monday through Saturday from 10am to 2pm and 4 to 7pm, and Sunday from 10am to 2pm.

EXPLORING OLITE

In the 15th century, this Gothic town was a favorite address of the kings of Navarre. Charles III put Olite on the map, ordering that the **Palacio Real,** Plaza Carlos III el Noble, be built in 1406. The towers and lookouts make visiting it an adventure. April through September, hours are daily from 10am to 2pm and 5 to 8pm; October through March, daily from 10am to 6pm. Admission is 2.10€ adults, 1.20€ children and students.

Next to the castle stands a Gothic church, **Iglesia de Santa María la Real,** with a splendid 12th-century doorway decorated with flowers.

WHERE TO STAY & DINE

Parador Príncipe de Viana ⟨★★⟩   This state-run parador in the center of town is in one of the wings of the Palacio Real (see above). Surrounded by watchtowers, thick walls, and massive buttresses, the building is one of the most impressive sights in town. Only 12 accommodations, however, are in the parador's medieval core, and they go for a premium over their comfortable counterparts, which are in a new wing added in 1963 when the castle became a parador. Regardless of their location in the compound, the rooms are dignified and quite comfortable, each with a bathroom with a tub/shower combo.

> **Finds** **Rustic Lodgings in the Navarre Countryside**
>
> If you have some time to spend in the area, consider a rental at one of the government-sponsored rustic home stays, ranging from rooms in old farmhouses in the mountains to simple lodgings in homes in the region's small hamlets. Sometimes fully equipped apartments in the region are available. In nearly all cases, these lodgings are extremely reasonable in price and very affordable to families who'd like to experience the great outdoors in this often neglected part of Spain. Called *casas rurales,* the lodgings are documented in detail in a helpful guide called *Guía de Alojamientos de Turismo Rural.* These guides are distributed free at any of the tourist offices in Navarre, including the one at Pamplona. For more information, call the office at © **94-820-65-41,** where some members of the staff speak English.

Plaza de los Teobaldos 2, 31390 Olite. © **94-874-00-00.** Fax 94-874-02-01. www.parador.es. 43 units. 91€–103€ double. AE, DC, MC, V. **Amenities:** Restaurant; room service; laundry service; dry cleaning. *In room:* A/C, TV, minibar, hair dryer, safe.

SIDE TRIPS TO UJUE & A HISTORIC MONASTERY

High up on a mountain of the same name, a short drive east along a secondary road from Olite, **Ujúe** seems plucked from the Middle Ages. Built as a defensive town, it has cobbled streets and stone houses clustered around its fortress **Church of Santa María,** dating from the 12th to the 14th century. The heart of King Charles II ("the Bad") was placed to rest here. The church towers open onto views of the countryside, extending to Olite in the west and the Pyrenees in the east.

On the Sunday after St. Mark's Day (Apr 25), Ujúe is an important pilgrimage center for the people of the area, many of whom, barefoot and wearing tunics, carry large crosses. They come to Ujúe to worship Santa María, depicted on a Romanesque statue dating from 1190. It was plated in silver in the second half of the 15th century.

If you have a car, you might also check out the **Monasterio de la Oliva** ★, 34km (21 miles) south of Olite. It was founded by King García Ramírez in 1164 and is an excellent example of Cistercian architecture. This monastery, one of the first to be constructed by French monks outside France, once had great influence; today the most notable feature is its 14th-century Gothic cloisters. The late 12th-century church is even more impressive than the cloisters. It has a distinguished portal and two rose windows. Pillars and pointed arches fill its interior. It's open daily from 9:30am to 1:30pm and 3:30 to 6:30pm.

3 Tudela ★

84km (52 miles) S of Pamplona, 316km (196 miles) N of Madrid

In the center of the food belt of the Ribera or Ebro Valley with a population of only 30,000, the ancient city of **Tudela** is the second largest in Navarre. Situated on the right bank of the Ebro, it had a long history as a city where Jews, Arabs, and Christians lived and worked together. The Muslims made it a dependency of the caliphate at Córdoba, a period of domination that lasted until 1119. The city had a large Moorish quarter, the *morería,* and many old brick houses are in the Mudéjar style. King Sancho VII ("the Strong"), who defeated the Saracens, chose Tudela as his favorite residence in 1251. It has been a bishopric since the 18th century.

ESSENTIALS

GETTING THERE   Tudela lies on the southern rail line south of Pamplona. Two RENFE **trains** pass through here, one connecting La Rioja to Zaragoza via Castejón de Ebro. Another train links Zaragoza to Vitoria-Gasteiz via Pamplona. For more information and schedules (subject to change), call ℭ **94-882-06-46.**

Conda buses (ℭ **94-882-03-42**) go to Tudela from Pamplona at the rate of six to nine per day (trip time: 1½ hr.).

Take A-15 south from Pamplona, if you're driving.

VISITOR INFORMATION   The **tourist office** at Plaza Vieja (ℭ **94-884-80-58;** www.cfnavarra.es) is open Monday through Saturday from 10am to 2pm and 4 to 7pm, and Sunday from 10am to 2pm.

TOURING THE CATHEDRAL

Begin your exploration at the central Plaza de los Fueros, from where you can wander through a maze of narrow alleys laid out during the Moorish occupation.

At the square called Plaza Vieja, visit Tudela's most important monument, **Catedral de Santa Ana** ⭐, renovated in 2003, and open Tuesday through Saturday from 9am to 1pm and 4 to 7pm, Sunday from 9am to 2pm. Constructed in the 12th and 13th centuries, it has an outstanding work of art on its facade, the Doorway of the Last Judgment, with about 120 groups of figures. Creation is depicted, but the artisans were truly inspired in showing the horrors of hell. The church contains many Gothic works of art, such as choir stalls from the 1500s. Several chapels are richly decorated, including one dedicated to Our Lady of Hope with masterpieces from the 15th century. The main altar contains an exceptional *retablo* painted by Pedro Díaz de Oviedo. The small but choice cloisters are the highlight of the tour, however, and cost .75€ to enter. Dating from the 12th and 13th centuries, they contain many Romanesque arches. Capitals on the columns include scenes from the New Testament.

WHERE TO STAY & DINE

Morase ⭐   Not only is this one of the best places to stay in town, but it's also a leading restaurant. Built in 1963, it's small but very comfortable. The midsize rooms are modern and well maintained, each with a bathroom containing a tub/shower combo. With the finest dining room in town, the Morase is a special delight when the first of the asparagus comes in, praised by gastronomes all over Spain. The specialties sound conventional but are well prepared, including a *pastel* of vegetables and hake baked with garlic. The lamb from Navarre is delectable, as is roast pork with herbs or red peppers stuffed with purée of seafood. On the bank of the Ebro, the restaurant offers a garden, an air-conditioned dining room, and adequate parking. Reservations are recommended.

Paseo de Invierno 2, 31500 Tudela. ℭ 94-882-17-00. Fax 94-882-17-04. 7 units. 60€ double. AE, DC, MC, V. Closed Aug 1–15. Parking 9€. **Amenities:** Restaurant; bar; room service; babysitting; laundry service; dry cleaning. *In room:* A/C, TV, hair dryer.

Tudela Bardenas ⭐   This is one of the best choices for an overnight stop-over. Directly in front of the bullring (Plaza de Toros), this hotel was built in the 1930s and tripled in size by 1992. Today it is modern and functional, with a polite and helpful staff. Rooms, though a bit boxy and standardized, are nevertheless comfortable, with well-maintained bathrooms equipped with tub/shower combos. The in-house restaurant is one of the best in the city. It draws a lively crowd, especially before and after bullfights, and serves well-prepared food. It offers typical fresh products of the Ribera region, along with some magnificent fish and grilled meat. Try the omelet with cod or the baked monkfish. You can also order beefsteak, followed by homemade pastries and desserts. And sample such wines as Viña Magaña. Reservations are recommended.

Av. Zaragoza 60, 31500 Tudela. ⓒ 94-841-08-02. Fax 94-841-09-72. www.tudelabardenas.com. 46 units. 59€–83€ double. AE, DC, MC, V. Parking 9€. **Amenities:** Restaurant; lounge; babysitting; laundry service; dry cleaning. *In room:* A/C, TV, minibar, hair dryer.

4 Sangüesa ★

407km (253 miles) N of Madrid, 47km (29 miles) SE of Pamplona

Sangüesa is on the left bank of the Aragón River, at the Aragonese frontier. A monumental town in its own right, Sangüesa can also serve as a base for excursions in the area, including visits to some of Navarre's major attractions, such as the monastery at Leyre and Javier Castle.

Long known to the Romans, Sangüesa was later involved in the battle against Muslim domination in the 10th century. It has seen many wars, including occupation by supporters of Archduke Charles of Austria in 1710 and many a skirmish during the Carlist struggles of the 19th century. On several occasions it has been the seat of the parliament of Navarre. Pilgrims crossing northern Spain to Santiago de Compostela stopped at Sangüesa.

ESSENTIALS
GETTING THERE   Two to three **buses** bound for Sangüesa leave from Pamplona daily (trip time: 45 min.). For information, call ⓒ **94-887-02-09.**

If you're driving from Pamplona, take the secondary road N-240 to Sangüesa.

VISITOR INFORMATION   The **tourist office** at Calle Mayor 2 (ⓒ **94-887-14-11;** www.cfnavara.es) is open Monday through Saturday from 10am to 2pm and 4 to 7pm, and Sunday from 10am to 2pm.

VISITING THE CHURCHES
Iglesia de Santa María ★ lies on Calle Mayor (ⓒ **94-887-01-32**) and stands at the far end of town beside the river. Begun in the 12th century, it has a doorway from the 12th and 13th centuries that is an outstanding work of Romanesque art. The south portal, filled with remarkably carved sculptures, is Santa María's most outstanding feature. The vestry contains a 1.5m (4½-ft.) high processional monstrance from the 15th century.

The nearby **Iglesia de Santiago** (ⓒ **94-887-01-32**) on Calle Santrago 18 is a late traditional Romanesque structure from the 12th and 13th centuries. It has a battlement-type tower and contains an impressive array of Gothic sculpture, discovered under the church only in 1964. Look for the bizarre statue of St. James atop a big conch. Both churches are only open for Mass.

WHERE TO STAY & DINE
If after visiting the town you want to spend the night in the area, you can check in at the hotel reviewed below or drive 14.5km (9 miles) across the border south to one of the most charming towns of Aragón, Sos del Rey Católico (see chapter 14). It features an excellent parador.

Yamaguchy   The best place to stay among extremely limited choices is this hotel .4km (¼ mile) outside town on the road to Javier. The small rooms are functional, modern, clean, and comfortable, each with a good bed and bathroom with tub/shower combo. The many Navarrese dishes served in the restaurant include lamb stew and steak. You can also sample award-winning wines from local wine cellars.

Carretera de Javier s/n, 31400 Sangüesa, ℂ **94-887-01-27**. Fax 94-887-07-00. www.hotelyamaguchy.com. 41 units. 48€–52€ double; 52€ suite. AE, DC, MC, V. Free parking. **Amenities:** Restaurant; lounge; pool; babysitting. *In room:* TV.

SIDE TRIPS TO LEYRE & JAVIER CASTLE

LEYRE   The **Monasterio de San Salvador of Leyre** ℛ (ℂ **94-888-40-11**) is 16km (10 miles) east of Sangüesa, perched on the side of a mountain of the same name, overlooking the Yesa Dam. Of major historic and artistic interest, the main body of the monastery was constructed between the 11th and the 15th centuries on the site of a primitive pre-Romanesque church; in time, it became the spiritual center of Navarre. Many kings, including Sancho III, made it their pantheon. Its **crypt,** consecrated in 1057, ranks as one of the country's major works of Romanesque art.

When the church was reconstructed by the Cistercians in the 13th century, they kept the bays of the old Romanesque church. The outstanding and richly adorned 12th-century west portal is called the **Porta Speciosa,** and is covered with intricate carvings. In one section, Jesus and his disciples are depicted atop mythical creatures. Some of the other artistic treasures of this once-great monastery are displayed at the Museo de Navarra in Pamplona.

The monastery is 4km (2½ miles) from Yesa, which itself is on N-240, the major road linking Pamplona, Sangüesa, and Huesca. Take the N-240 into Yesa, then follow an uphill road marked LEYRE 4km (2½ miles) to the monastery. Visits are possible Monday through Friday from 10:30am to 2pm and 4 to 7pm, Sunday from 10:30 to 11:15am, 1 to 2pm, and 4 to 7pm. Admission is 1.80€ for adults and free for children.

At Leyre you'll also find one of the most unusual accommodations in Navarre, the **Hospedería,** Monasterio de Leyre, 31410 Leyre (ℂ **94-888-41-00**). This two-star inn with 32 units (all with bathrooms and phones) was created from the annexes constructed by the Benedictines in the 1700s. Guest rooms open onto views of the Yesa Reservoir. The rate is 50€ to 60€ for a double room (MasterCard and Visa accepted), and parking is free. The hotel restaurant serves good Navarrese food in a rustic setting. The restaurant is open daily from 8:30 to 10am, 1 to 3:30pm, and 8 to 10pm. The Hospedería is closed from December 10 to March 1.

JAVIER CASTLE   The second major excursion possible in the area is to **Castillo de Javier** ℛ (ℂ **94-888-40-00**), 8km (5 miles) from Sangüesa. The castle dates from the 11th century, but owes its present look to restoration work carried out in 1952. Francisco Javier (Xavier), patron of Navarre, was born here on April 7, 1506. Along with Ignatius Loyola, he founded the order of the Society of Jesus (the Jesuits) in the mid–16th century. The castle houses a magnificent 13th-century crucifix, and thousands of the faithful congregate at Javier on two consecutive Sundays in March. This is the most popular pilgrimage in Navarre. Known as the Javierada, it pays homage to Francisco Javier, who was canonized in 1622.

During your visit to the castle, visit the oratory, the guard chamber, the great hall, and the saint's bedroom. The castle is teeming with interesting art, including a 15th-century fresco called the *Dance of Death.* To get to the castle, take

N-240 to Yesa, then follow an unmarked road that's signposted CASTILLO DE JAVIER. It's open daily from 9am to 1pm and 4 to 6pm. Admission is free but donations are requested.

For food and lodging, go to the tranquil **Hotel El Mesón,** Explanada, 31411 Javier (© **94-888-40-35;** fax 94-888-42-26), right in the center of the hamlet of Javier on the same unmarked road the castle is on. Management rents eight comfortably furnished rooms, but the hotel is closed from December 15 to February. Doubles go for 52€, and parking is free. The hotel's restaurant offers the best food in the area, with a fixed-price menu going for 13€. American Express, MasterCard, and Visa are all accepted.

5 Logroño (★)

330km (205 miles) N of Madrid, 92km (57 miles) W of Pamplona

The capital of the province of La Rioja, **Logroño** is also the major distribution center for the area's wines and agricultural products. Because La Rioja is so small, Logroño could serve as your base for touring all the major attractions of the province. Although much of Logroño is modern and dull, it does have an old quarter known to the pilgrims crossing this region to visit the tomb of St. James at Santiago de Compostela.

ESSENTIALS
GETTING THERE   There are four daily RENFE **trains** from Barcelona (trip time: 7 hr.) and one per day from Madrid (5¼ hr.). From Bilbao in the north, two to three trains arrive per day (3 hr.). For information, call © **90-224-02-02.**

Five **buses** arrive daily from Pamplona (trip time: 2 hr.) and four to five from Madrid (5 hr.). For information, call © **94-123-59-83.**

Take N-111 southwest from Pamplona by **car** or A-68 northwest from Zaragoza.

VISITOR INFORMATION   The **tourist office** at Paseo del Espolón (© **94-129-12-60;** www.larioja.org/turismo) is open Monday through Saturday from 10am to 2pm and 5 to 8pm, Sunday from 10am to 2pm.

EXPLORING LOGROÑO
Catedral de Santa María de la Redonda, Plaza del Mercado (© **94-125-76-11**), has vaulting from the 1400s, although the baroque facade dates from 1742. Inside, you can visit its 1762 Chapel of Our Lady of the Angels, built in an octagonal shape with rococo adornments. Constructed on top of an earlier Romanesque church, today's cathedral is known for its broad naves and twin towers. It's open daily from 8am to 1pm and 6 to 8:30pm.

From the square on which the cathedral sits, walk up Calle de la Sagasta until you reach the 12th-century **Iglesia de Santa María de Palacio,** on Marqués de

---

⌒Tips   A Special Event

About a third of all Rioja wine production comes from the Najerilla River's valleys. From September 20 to September 26, the **Wine Harvest Festival** (© **94-129-12-60**) takes place throughout the region of La Rioja. Barefoot locals stomp upon grapes spilling from oak casks, and area vineyards showcase their wares. Other activities include dances, parades, music, and bullfights.

San Nicolás, once part of a royal palace. The palace part dates from 1130 when Alfonso VII offered his residence to the Order of the Holy Sepulchre. Most of what he left is long gone, of course, but there is still a pyramid-shaped spire from the 13th century.

Walk through the heart of Logroño, exploring the gardens of the broad **Paseo del Espolón.** In the late afternoon, all the residents turn out for their paseo.

While in Logroño, you can visit the **Bodegas Olarra,** Polígono de Cantabria s/n (© **94-123-52-99**), open Thursday through Tuesday from 9am to 1pm and 3 to 7pm, Wednesday 3:30 to 7:00pm, closed August. Reserve in advance for a tour. It produces wines under the Otonal and Olarra labels.

WHERE TO STAY

Hotel Marqués de Vallejo   In the center of town near the cathedral, close to the Plaza del Espolón, this little hotel is surrounded by restaurants and wine bars serving Rioja vintages. A warm traditional atmosphere awaits you. The style is modest but functional, well maintained, and welcoming. Rooms are midsize and furnished in neutral modern, but they are comfortable and have small bathrooms with shower stalls.

Marqués de Vallejo 8, 26001 Logroño. © **94-124-83-33.** Fax 94-124-02-88. 31 units. 76€ double. AE, MC, V. **Amenities:** Bar; laundry service; dry cleaning. *In room:* A/C, TV.

Hotel Murrieta *(Value)*   At the western border of the historic part of town, a block north of the Gran Vía, is this 1980s hotel offering midsize, comfortable, pristine rooms at a relatively good value. Rooms contain private bathrooms, most of which have tub/shower combos.

Marqués de Murrieta 1, 26005 Logroño. © **94-122-41-50.** Fax 94-122-32-13. www.pretur.es. 111 units. 71€ double. AE, MC, V. Parking 10€. **Amenities:** Restaurant; cafeteria; room service; babysitting; laundry. *In room:* A/C, TV, minibar.

La Numantina *(Value)*   This rather simple hotel, one of the best bargains in town, is on a street central to both the historic core and the commercial district. Its small and basic rooms are clean and reasonably comfortable, each with a good bed and a tidy bathroom with shower. No breakfast is served, but you can buy pastries at a shop across the street.

Calle Sagasta 4, 26001 Logroño. © **94-125-14-11.** Fax 94-125-16-45. 19 units. 44€–46€ double. MC, V. Closed Dec 22–Jan 7. **Amenities:** Lounge. *In room:* TV.

Tryp Los Bracos *(★)*   This landmark government-rated four-star hotel is the finest in town, according to many wine merchants who journey here frequently on business. The town's toniest address offers an elegant reception hall and the most helpful staff in town. The street on which it sits is one of the best known in the city, and although it used to lie outside the walls, Logroño has now caught up with it. The midsize rooms are handsomely furnished, if rather monotonous in style. All come equipped with neatly kept bathrooms with tub/shower combos. Many good restaurants and cafes are within an easy walk.

Bretón de los Herreros 29, 26001 Logroño. © **94-122-66-08.** Fax 94-122-67-54. www.solmelia.com. 71 units. 110€ double; 133€ suite. AE, DC, MC, V. Parking 11€. **Amenities:** Restaurant; bar; room service; babysitting; laundry service; dry cleaning. *In room:* A/C, TV, minibar, hair dryer, safe.

WHERE TO DINE

Asador La Chata *(★)* REGIONAL   Founded in 1821 in a building close to the town's cathedral, this delightful choice exudes a sense of Old Navarre. Its tactful owners define it as an *asador,* which means it specializes in wood-roasted meat dishes. Lunch is an everyday event, and much patronized by workers in the local wine trade, but dinner is served only 4 evenings a week. Because of the establishment's small size (only 60 seats), advance reservations are essential. You can enjoy the two house specialties: fresh asparagus prepared with strips of locally cured ham, and *cabrito asado* (roast baby goat with herbs). Meats are succulently tender.

Carnicerías 3. © **94-125-12-96**. Reservations required. Main courses 12€–18€. AE, DC, MC, V. Daily 1–4pm; Fri–Sat 9–11pm.

Casa Emilio REGIONAL   An ample bar greets you as you enter Casa Emilio, which serves primarily roasts, especially goat and beef. In air-conditioned comfort, you can also enjoy peppers stuffed with cod or baked hake. From the well-stocked wine cellar come some of the finest Rioja wines. Casa Emilio is south of the old town, directly west of the major boulevard, Vara de Rey.

República Argentina 8. © **94-125-88-44**. Reservations recommended. Main courses 12€–18€; *menú del día* 8€. AE, DC, MC, V. Mon–Sat 1:30–4pm and 9–11pm. Closed Aug.

6 Haro ⊛

359km (223 miles) N of Madrid, 48km (30 miles) NE of Logroño

Center of the wine tours of the Rioja Alta district, the region around **Haro** has been compared to Tuscany. Come here to taste the wine at the bodegas, as international wine merchants do year-round (but especially after the autumn harvest).

ESSENTIALS

GETTING THERE   Four to five RENFE **trains** (© **94-131-15-97**) run daily from Logroño (trip time: 1 hr.). There are also four to five connections per day from Zaragoza (3½ hr.).

Five to six **buses** per day run to Haro from Logroño (trip time: 45 min.–1 hr.).

By **car,** follow the A-68 expressway (south of Logroño) northwest to the turnoff for Haro.

VISITOR INFORMATION   The **tourist office** at Plaza Monseñor Florentino Rodríguez s/n (© **94-130-33-66**) is open Tuesday through Sunday from 10am to 2pm and 4 to 7pm.

SPECIAL EVENTS   Every June 29, the **Battle of Wine** erupts. It's an amusing, mock-medieval brawl in which opposing teams splatter each other with wineskins filled with the output from local vineyards.

EXPLORING HARO & VISITING THE BODEGAS

The town itself deserves a look before you head for the bodegas. Its old quarter is filled with mansions, some from the 16th century; the most interesting ones lie along **Calle del Castillo.** At the center of the old quarter is the major architectural landmark of the town, the **Iglesia de San Tomás,** Plaza de la Iglesia. Distinguished by its wedding-cake tower and Plateresque south portal, the 16th-century church has a Gothic interior.

You could spend up to 3 days touring the wineries in town, but chances are that a few visits will satisfy your curiosity. **Bodegas Muga,** Barrio de la Estación s/n (© **94-131-04-98**), near the rail station, offers tours (usually in Spanish) of its wine cellars. A tour in English is offered Monday through Friday at 11am.

Finally, pay a visit to **Rioja Alta,** Av. Vizcaya s/n (© **94-131-03-46**), not far from Muga. It's open Monday through Friday from 9am to 2pm (closed from mid-Aug to mid-Sept). Visits must be arranged in advance.

If you arrive in Haro in August or the first 2 weeks in September, when many of the bodegas are closed, settle instead for drinking wine in the *tascas* that line the streets between Parroquia and Plaza de la Paz. After a night spent there, you'll forget all about the bodega tours. Some of the finest wines in Spain are sold at these *tascas,* along with tapas—all at bargain prices.

WHERE TO STAY

Hotel Ciudad De Haro   Nearly a kilometer (½ mile) southeast of the city on the highway, this is the second choice hotel in Haro. The small but comfortable rooms are attractively furnished, many with impressive views. Rooms contain neatly kept bathrooms that mostly contain tub/shower combos. Ample parking facilities are available.

Carretera N-124, Km 41 s/n, 26200 Haro. ℂ **94-131-12-13**. Fax 94-131-17-21. 59 units. 86€–121€ double; 136€–179€ suite. AE, DC, MC, V. Free parking. **Amenities:** Restaurant; bar; pool; room service; babysitting; laundry service; dry cleaning. *In room:* A/C, TV, minibar, hair dryer, safe.

Los Agustinos 🖈🖈   This former Augustinian convent is now a government-rated four-star hotel in the center of Haro. Since its restoration and reopening in 1990, it has become the most desirable place to stay in a town that has always had too few accommodations. Owned by a Basque chain of hotels, it is in a "zone of tranquillity" (pedestrian zone). Rooms are well appointed and comfortable, each equipped with a good bed. The tidily arranged bathrooms have tub/shower combos.

Calle San Agustín 2, 26200 Haro. ℂ **94-131-13-08**. Fax 94-130-31-48. www.aranzazu-hoteles.com. 62 units. 74€–92€ double; 160€ suite. AE, DC, MC, V. Parking 6€. **Amenities:** Restaurant; bar; room service; babysitting; laundry service; dry cleaning. *In room:* A/C, TV, hair dryer.

WHERE TO DINE

Beethoven I, II, y III 🖈 *Value* REGIONAL/BASQUE   This premier restaurant of Haro in the center of town is actually three restaurants, each standing beside one another. Each offers good food and value. They're justifiably famous for their platters of wild mushrooms, which chef María Angeles Fresno raises herself. Try the stuffed filet of sole, vegetable stew, or wild pheasant, finishing off with an apple tart. The interiors are air-conditioned. The wine cellars are among the finest in the area.

Santo Tomás 3–5. ℂ **94-131-11-81**. Reservations required in summer. Main courses 9€–23€; fixed-price menus 12€–15€. MC, V. Wed–Mon 1:30–4pm; Wed–Sun 8:30–11:30pm.

Terete 🖈 *Finds* REGIONAL   This place has been an *horno asado* (restaurant specializing in roasts) since 1867 and is beloved by locals for its roast suckling pig. The service is discreet, the food savory and succulent—the kitchen has had a long time to learn the secrets of roasting meats. The dishes are all prepared according to traditional regional recipes. When the fresh asparagus comes in, that is reason enough to dine here. The local peaches in season make the best dessert. Naturally, the finest of Rioja wines are served. Terete is in the center of Haro.

Lucrecia Arana 17. ℂ **94-131-00-23**. Reservations recommended. Main courses 14€–27€; fixed-price menu 11€. MC, V. Tues–Sun 1:15–4pm; Tues–Sat 8:30–11pm. Closed July 1–15 and Oct 15–31.

16

The Basque Country

The **Basque** people are the oldest traceable ethnic group in Europe. Their language, *Euskera* (also spelled *Euskara, Uskara,* or *Eskuara,* depending on the dialect), predates any of the commonly spoken Romance languages; its origins, like that of the Basque race itself, are lost in obscurity. There are many competing theories. One is that the Basques descended from the original Iberians, who lived in Spain before the arrival of the Celts some 3,500 years ago. Conqueror after conqueror, Roman to Visigoth to Moor, may have driven these people into the Pyrenees, where they stayed and carved out a life for themselves—filled with tradition and customs practiced to this day.

The region is called Euskadi, which in Basque means "collection of Basques." In a very narrow sense it refers to three provinces of Spain: Guipúzcoa (whose capital, **San Sebastián,** the #1 sightseeing destination in Euskadi, features La Concha, one of Spain's best-loved stretches of sand); Viscaya (whose capital is the industrial city of **Bilbao**); and Alava (with its capital at **Vitoria**). But to Basque nationalists who dream of forging a new nation that'll one day unite all the Basque lands, Euskadi also refers to the northern part of Navarre and three provinces in France, including the famed resort of Biarritz.

The three Spanish Basque provinces occupy the eastern part of the Cantabrian Mountains, between the Pyrenees and the valley of the Nervión. They maintained a large degree of independence until the 19th century, when they finally gave in to control from Castile, which continued to recognize their ancient rights and privileges until 1876.

Geographically, the Basque country straddles the western foothills of the Pyrenees, so the Basque people live in both France and Spain—but mostly in the latter. During the Spanish Civil War (1936–39), the Basques were on the Republican side defeated by Franco. Oppression during the Franco years has led to deep-seated resentment against the policies of Madrid. The Basque separatist movement, ETA (*Euskadi ta Askatasuna,* or Basque Nation and Liberty) and the French organization Enbata (Ocean Wind) engaged unsuccessfully in guerrilla activity in 1968 to secure a united Basque state.

Many Basque nationalists still fervently wish that the Basque people could be united into one autonomous state instead of being divided between France and Spain.

The riddle of the Basque language has puzzled linguists and ethnologists for years; its grammar, syntax, and vocabulary are unrelated to those of any other European language. The language is known as Euskera (see above for other dialectical spellings). Although on the wane since the beginning of this century, the Basque language is now enjoying a modest renaissance; it's taught in schools, and autonomous TV stations in the region broadcast in the language.

Basques wear a *boina,* a beret of red, blue, or white woolen cloth as a badge of pride and a political statement. You may see nationalist graffiti as you travel, slogans such as *Euskadi ta Askatasuna* ("Basque Nation and Liberty") painted everywhere. Although the separatist movement is still simmering, you'll find most of the people friendly, hospitable, and welcoming. Politics rarely intrudes on vacationers in this beautiful corner of Spain.

1 San Sebastián ★★

21km (13 miles) W of the French border, 483km (300 miles) N of Madrid, 100km (62 miles) E of Bilbao

San Sebastián (Donostia in the Basque language) is the summer capital of Spain, and here the Belle Epoque lives on. Ideally situated on a choice spot on the Bay of Biscay, it's surrounded by green mountains. From June to September, the population swells as hundreds of Spanish bureaucrats escape the heat and head for this tasteful resort—it has few of the tawdry trappings associated with major beachfront cities. San Sebastián is an ideal base for trips to some of the Basque country's most fascinating towns.

Queen Isabella II put San Sebastián on the map as a resort when she spent the summer of 1845 there. In time, it became the summer residence of the royal court. On July 8, 1912, Queen María Cristina inaugurated the grand hotel named after her, and the resort became very fashionable. In what's now the city hall, built in 1887, a casino opened, and European aristocrats gambled in safety here during World War I.

San Sebastián is the capital of the province of Guipúzcoa, the smallest in Spain, tucked in the far northeastern corner bordering France. It's said that Guipúzcoa has preserved Basque customs better than any other province. Half of the *donostiarras*—residents of San Sebastián—speak Euskera. The city is a major seat of Basque nationalism, so be advised that protests, sometimes violent, are frequent.

San Sebastián contains an old quarter, **La Parte Vieja,** with narrow streets, hidden plazas, and medieval houses, but it is primarily a modern city of elegant shops, wide boulevards, sidewalk cafes, and restaurants.

La Concha is the city's most famous beach—especially in July and August, when it seems as though half the population of Spain and France spends its days under striped canopies or dashing into the refreshingly cool waters of the bay. The shell-shaped La Concha is half-encircled by a promenade, where crowds mill during the evening. The adjoining beach is the **Playa de Ondarreta.** The climate here is decidedly more Atlantic than Mediterranean.

San Sebastián has a good, though insufficient, choice of hotels in summer, plus many excellent restaurants, most of which are expensive. Its chief drawback is overcrowding in July and August. Bullfights, art and film festivals, sporting events, and cultural activities keep San Sebastián hopping during summer.

ESSENTIALS

GETTING THERE   From Madrid, **Iberia Airlines** (© 94-342-35-86) offers six daily flights to San Sebastián, plus four daily flights from Barcelona. The domestic airport is at nearby Fuenterrabía. From Fuenterrabía, buses run to the center of San Sebastián every 12 minutes daily from 7:48am to 10pm.

From Madrid, **RENFE** runs trains to the French border at Irún, many of which stop in San Sebastián (a 6- to 7-hr. trip). An overnight train from Paris to Madrid stops in San Sebastián, just in time for breakfast (and San Sebastián's cafes serve the best croissants south of the Pyrenees). RENFE provides overnight train service from Barcelona to San Sebastián and on to Bilbao. For RENFE information, call © 90-224-02-02.

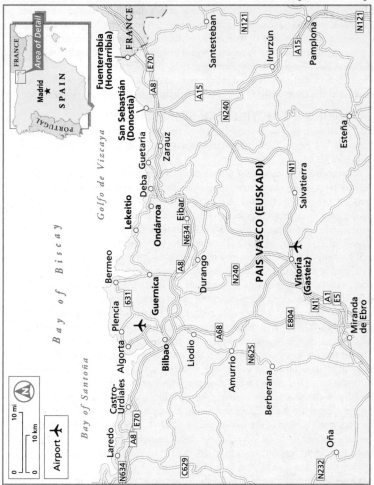

San Sebastián is well linked by a **bus** network to many of Spain's major cities, although if you're in Madrid, it's more convenient to take a train. Nine to 29 buses a day connect San Sebastián to Bilbao (trip time: 1¼ hr.); three daily buses arrive from Barcelona (7 hr.); and five buses run daily from Pamplona (1½ hr.). These routes are covered by several private bus companies. The tourist office (see below) distributes a pamphlet listing various routes, the companies that service these runs, and telephone numbers to call for schedules.

From Madrid, take the N-1 toll road north to Burgos, then follow A-1 to Miranda de Ebro. From here, continue on the A-68 north to Bilbao and then the A-8 east to San Sebastián. From Pamplona, take the A-15 north to the N-1 route, which leads right into San Sebastián.

VISITOR INFORMATION The **tourist office** is at Calle Reina Regente s/n (✆ **94-348-11-66**). From June to September, it's open Monday through Saturday from 8am to 8pm, Sunday from 10am to 2pm; off-season hours are Monday through Saturday from 9am to 2pm and 3:30 to 7pm, Sunday from 10am to 2pm.

SPECIAL EVENTS   Two weeklong events draw visitors from around the world. In mid-August, San Sebastián stages its annual carnival, **Aste Nagusia,** a joyous celebration of traditional Basque music and dance, along with fireworks, cooking competitions, and sports events. In mid-September, the San Sebastián **International Film Festival** draws luminaries from America and Europe. The actual dates of these festivals vary from year to year, so check with the tourist office (see above). In the second half of July, San Sebastián hosts a jazz festival, **Jazzaldia.**

EXPLORING & ENJOYING SAN SEBASTIAN

San Sebastián means beach time, excellent Basque food, and strolling along the Paseo de la Concha. The monuments, such as they are, can easily be viewed before lunch.

Museo de San Telmo, Plaza Zuloaga 1 (© **94-342-49-70**), housed in a 16th-century Dominican monastery, contains an impressive collection of Basque artifacts from prehistoric times. The museum includes works by Zuloaga (*Torreillos en Turégano,* for example), golden age artists such as El Greco and Ribera, and a large number of Basque painters. Standing in the old town at the base of Monte Urgull, the museum is open Tuesday through Saturday from 10:30am to 1:30pm and 4 to 7:30pm, Sunday from 10am to 2pm. Admission is free.

The wide promenade **Paseo Nuevo** almost encircles Monte Urgull, one of the two mountains between which San Sebastián is nestled (Monte Igueldo is the other one). A ride along this promenade opens onto panoramic vistas of the Bay of Biscay. The paseo comes to an end at the **Palacio del Mar** ⭐, Muelle 34 (© **94-344-00-99**), an oceanographic museum/aquarium. Like most cutting-edge aquariums, it boasts a mesmerizing collection of huge tanks containing myriad marine species. A transparent underwater walkway allows a 360-degree view of sharks, rays, and other fish as they swim around you. A maritime museum upstairs presents a fascinating synopsis of mankind's precarious relationship with the sea down through the ages through historical displays of fishing gear, naval artifacts, and marine fossils. Here you can also see the skeleton of the last whale caught in the Bay of Biscay, in 1878. The museum is open daily: January through May and October through December from 10am to 7pm and from June 15 to September 15 from 10am to 9pm. Admission is 8€ adults, 5€ students, and free for children 4 and under.

Other sights include the **Palacio de Miramar,** which stands on its own hill opening onto La Concha. In the background is the residential district of Antiguo. Queen María Cristina, after whom the grandest hotel in the north of Spain is named, opened this palace in 1893, but by the turbulent 1930s, it had fallen into disrepair. The city council took it over in 1971 and renovations continue. You can visit daily: in summer from 9am to 9:30pm, in winter from 10am to 5pm. Because you can't go inside the palace, you must settle for a look at the lawns and gardens. The palace stands on land splitting the two major beaches of San Sebastián: Playa de la Concha and Playa de Ondarreta.

Palacio de Ayete was constructed by the duke of Bailéen in 1878 and became the summer home of King Alfonso XIII and his queen, María Cristina, until their own Palacio de Miramar (see above) was completed. With 75,000 sq. m (250,000 sq. ft.) of parkland, the palace served as the summer home of Franco from 1940 until 1975. The residence remains closed to the public, but you can wander through the beautiful grounds daily: in summer from 10am to 8:30pm, in off season from 10am to 5pm. To reach it, take bus 19 to Ayete from Plaza de Guipúzcoa.

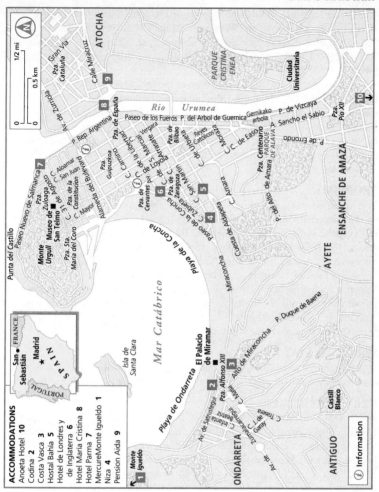

ACCOMMODATIONS
Anoeta Hotel 10
Codina 2
Costa Vasca 3
Hostal Bahía 5
Hotel de Londres y
  de Inglaterra 6
Hotel María Cristina 8
Hotel Parma 7
MercureMonte Igueldo 1
Niza 4
Pensión Aida 9

i Information

Museo Chillida-Leku, Caserío Zabalaga 66, Jáuregui Barrio, Hernani (© 94-332-71-80), is devoted to the artwork of Eduardo Chillida, a sculptor legendary in the Basque world and one whose work appears in many of the world museums. He's best known for his monumental steel *Comb of the Wind* rising from the rocks at the far end of the Bay of Biscay. A 10-minute drive from the heart of San Sebastián, the museum lies in the little mountain town of Hernani. The hillside around the museum is studded with some 40 Chillida monoliths set amongst beech trees, oaks, and magnolias.

In the center of the property is a farmhouse from the 1500s, which the artist designed to display some of his smaller pieces. These include hanging paper "gravitations" (not quite a collage, but not a mobile either), translucent alabaster sculpture, stone blocks that evoke the Mayan culture, as well as "jigsaw" sculptures of metal and marble. The aging sculptor refers to his museum as a "cathedral." Surprisingly and virtually unheard of in an art museum, he invites visitors to touch his sculpture, as he firmly believes that sculpture "should be touched." Hours in July and August are Wednesday through Monday from 10:30am to 7pm; September through June from 10:30am to 3pm. Admission is 6€ adults, 3.75€ ages 10 to 21, and free for those under 9. Take bus G2 from San Sebastián.

Finally, to get the best view of the city, take the funicular to the top of **Monte Igueldo** ★★★, where, from a gazebo, you get a panoramic view of the bay and the Cantabrian coastline. From June 25 to September 25, the funicular runs Monday through Friday from 10am to 9pm, Saturday and Sunday from 10am to 10pm. Off-season service is daily from 11am to 8pm. A round-trip fare costs 1.20€. It's also possible to drive up. In spring, the air is rich with the scent of honeysuckle.

SHOPPING

Your immersion into Basque culture will probably prompt you to buy some of the handicrafts and accessories from the region. Two of the best outlets are **Txapela,** Calle Puerto 3 (© **94-342-02-43**), and **Arriluzea,** Calle 31 de Agosto 13 (© **94-342-56-66**). Both sell souvenirs and the rough cotton shirts for which the Basques are famous. And if you're looking for a *boina* (beret) or any other form of headgear, consider a visit to the venerable shelves of San Sebastián's oldest hat manufacturer, **Ponsol,** Calle Narrica 4 (© **94-342-08-76**). For virtually anything else in the city, try the length of the most congested shopping district, **Paseo de Muelle,** where dozens of merchants hawk everything from T-shirts to cameras and film.

WHERE TO STAY

If you book well in advance, you'll find many good hotel values, but in season most hoteliers insist you take at least half-board (breakfast plus 1 main meal).

VERY EXPENSIVE

Hotel María Cristina ★★★   One of the most spectacular Belle Epoque hotels in Spain, enviably positioned in the heart of town midway between the bay and Río Urumea, this is the town's top choice. The Cristina opened in 1912 behind a facade of chiseled stone and ornate ironwork. The crowd is likely to include movie stars, film directors, and newly moneyed moguls; this is where the glitterati stay during San Sebastián's film festival. The hotel was richly remodeled in 1987. The public rooms are opulent with ormolu, mahogany, onyx and exotic marbles, and rosewood marquetry. The spacious guest rooms are appropriately lavish, with luxury beds and bathrooms with tub/shower combos.

Oquendo 1, 20004 San Sebastián. © **800/221-2340** in the U. S., or 94-343-76-00. Fax 94-343-76-76. www. westin.com. 136 units. 253€–415€ double; 644€–1,528€ suite. AE, DC, MC, V. Parking 17€. **Amenities:** Restaurant; bar; car rental; room service; babysitting; laundry service; dry cleaning. *In room:* A/C, TV, minibar, hair dryer, safe.

EXPENSIVE

Costa Vasca ★★   A large red-brick hotel rated four stars by the government, the Costa Vasca is 10 minutes from Ondarreta Beach and a 5-minute drive (or 10 min. on foot) from the center of town. The interior of the hotel is modern and businesslike with plenty of space for conferences and banquets; however, it's ideal for the individual traveler, too. The rooms are good-size and comfortably furnished, their bathrooms equipped with tub/shower combos. Many of the accommodations have balconies. The decoration is tasteful but discreet.

Av. de Pío Baroja, 20008 San Sebastián. ℂ **94-321-10-11.** Fax 94-321-24-28. www.aranzazu-hoteles.com. 203 units. 125€–140€ double; 310€–330€ suite. AE, DC, MC, V. Free parking. **Amenities:** Restaurant; bar; pool; room service; babysitting; laundry service; dry cleaning. *In room:* A/C, TV, minibar, hair dryer, safe.

Hotel de Londres y de Inglaterra ⭐   Beside the northern edge of the town's most popular beach, Playa de la Concha, this 19th-century hotel is one of the most stylish in town. It's not as plush as the María Cristina but is significantly more affordable. The views from many of the balconies encompass the beach and some rocky offshore islands. The traditional-style public rooms contain deep armchairs and big windows. Renovated in the past few years, the hotel has good-size guest rooms with a vaguely English decor and modern bathrooms with tub/shower combos.

Zubleta 2, 20007 San Sebastián. ℂ **94-344-07-70.** Fax 94-344-04-91. www.hlandres.com. 148 units. 125€– 192€ double; 167€–234€ suite. AE, DC, MC, V. Parking 12€ nearby. **Amenities:** Restaurant; bar; car rental; room service; babysitting; laundry service; dry cleaning. *In room:* A/C, TV, minibar, hair dryer, safe.

MODERATE

Anoeta Hotel   Close to the sports arena and a 5-minute drive from the town center, this government-rated three-star hotel is named for the old village that once stood here but was long ago absorbed by the growing boundaries of San Sebastián. Anoeta features cherrywood, marble fittings, and a modern decor behind its brick facade. With a welcoming atmosphere, it's one of the better choices in the middle-bracket range. The rooms are generally small but most inviting, with comfortable beds, wooden furniture, and bathrooms with tub/shower combos.

Paseo de Anoeta 30, 20014 San Sebastián. ℂ **94-345-14-99.** Fax 94-345-20-36. www.hotelanoeta.com. 26 units. 75€–97€ double; 92€–119€ suite. AE, DC, MC, V. Parking: 7€. Bus: 26 or 28. **Amenities:** Restaurant; bar; babysitting; laundry service; dry cleaning. *In room:* A/C, TV, minibar, hair dryer, safe.

Mercure Monte Igueldo ⭐   This first-class hotel is perched like a castle on the top of the mountain overlooking San Sebastián, a 10-minute drive from the center of town. The public rooms, guest rooms, and main terrace all boast panoramic coast views. Each of the streamlined modern rooms has a private balcony. The furnishings are standardized but reasonably comfortable; each room has a well-kept bathroom with a tub/shower combo.

Paseo del Faro 134, Monte Igueldo, 20008 San Sebastián. ℂ **94-321-02-11.** Fax 94-321-50-28. www. monteigueldo.com. 125 units. 115€–125€ double; 151€–164€ triple. AE, DC, MC, V. Free parking. Bus: Igueldo. **Amenities:** Restaurant; bar; pool; room service; babysitting; laundry service; dry cleaning. *In room:* TV, minibar, hair dryer, safe.

Niza ⭐ *(Finds)*   This little hotel, opening onto the Playa de la Concha, offers real character and a great location. It has modern furnishings in the small rooms and antiques in the public lounges. The petit salon, for example, contains an Oriental rug, Directoire chairs, a tall grandfather clock, and a rosewood breakfront. In direct contrast are the rather basic rooms, with wooden headboards, white walls, and wall-to-wall carpeting. All units have bathrooms with tub/shower combos.

Zubieta 56, 20007 San Sebastián. ℂ **94-342-66-63.** Fax 94-344-12-51. www.hotelniza.com. 41 units. 98€– 112€ double. AE, DC, MC, V. Parking 12€ nearby. Bus: 5 or 6. **Amenities:** Restaurant; bar; babysitting; laundry service; dry cleaning. *In room:* TV, hair dryer.

INEXPENSIVE

Hostal Bahía *(Value)*   A good-value hotel a block from the beach, the Bahía features guest rooms of varying sizes: Some are large enough to contain sofas and armchairs; others fall into the cubicle category. Each comes with a little bathroom with a shower stall. Many North Americans stay here and take public transportation to Pamplona for the running of the bulls.

Calle San Martín 54B, 20007 San Sebastián. (✆ **94-346-92-11**. Fax 94-346-39-14. 55 units. 60€–90€ double. Rates include breakfast. DC, MC, V. Parking 12€. Bus: 5, 6, 7, 8, or 9. **Amenities:** Bar; laundry service; dry cleaning. *In room:* TV, hair dryer, safe.

Pensión Aida *Value*   The resort's best bargain is this recently discovered nugget with a certain charm. *Travel & Leisure* called its rates "ridiculously low." At the film festival, Robert DeNiro won't be seen checking in here, heading for María Cristina instead. But struggling filmmakers who haven't made a distribution deal are likely to be found here. It is simply but comfortably decorated. Bedrooms are small to midsize, each with a little tiled bathroom with shower. Although the little boardinghouse itself is short on amenities, many facilities are just outside its doors, including a dry cleaning and laundry establishment across the street and several cafeterias and inexpensive restaurants nearby.

Calle Iztueta 9, 20001 San Sebastián. (✆ **94-332-78-00**. Fax 94-332-67-07. www.pensionesconencanto. com. 9 units. 45€–65€ double. MC, V. *In room:* TV, hair dryer, iron.

WHERE TO DINE
EXPENSIVE

Akelare ✺✺✺ BASQUE   A visit to Akelare became a must for serious foodies when owner/chef Pedro Subijana won the 1983 National Prize for Gastronomy as the best chef in Spain; his preparations have influenced a generation of chefs and defined the entire philosophy of *la nueva cocina vasca* (modern Basque cuisine). Opened in 1974, the restaurant is on the western edge of San Sebastián in a hexagonal villa built as a catering hall. Inside, a sweeping view through large windows encompasses the mists and raging currents of the Bay of Biscay far below. The plushly upholstered modern decor, with a hospitable fireplace, is an appropriate foil for dishes inspired by the Basque *caseríos* (farmsteads).

The perfect beginning to any meal is puff pastry filled with anchovy filets, accompanied by a glass of chilled *fino* sherry. Traditional dishes might include fish cooked on a griddle with garlic and parsley; beans with bacon, chorizo, and pork ribs; baked rice with clams; or a special *marmitako* (fisherman's stew). More innovative are the snails with watercress sauce; boiled cabbage stuffed with duck and served with purée of celery; warm salad of bonito fish served with basil, lemon, chervil, and vinegar sauce; and duck filet with exotic seasonal mushrooms. The name of the restaurant, incidentally, translates from the Basque as "Witches' Sabbath."

Paseo del Padre Orkolaga 56. (✆ **94-321-20-52**. Reservations strongly recommended. Main courses 28€–42€; tasting menu 75€. AE, DC, MC, V. Tues–Sun 1–3:30pm; Tues–Sat 8:30–11pm. Closed Jan 2–Mar 7 and Oct 15–Oct 29.

Arzak ✺✺✺ BASQUE   One of the most famous restaurants in the Basque world (an honor it shares with Akelare; see above), this legendary place occupies the lavishly renovated childhood home of owner/chef Juan Mari Arzak. Well known in San Sebastián for his role in preparing a meal for Queen Elizabeth II of Britain (for which he later received an invitation to Buckingham Palace), Arzak combines staples of the Basque culinary legacy with many new creations of his own. Begin with a selection of fresh oysters or natural foie gras. Crayfish is regularly featured as an appetizer, as is the chef's special *sopa de pescado* (fish soup). For a main course, consider *merluza* (hake) in vinaigrette with onions and small squid. On the back of the menu is a list of classic dishes that have won the most praise among visitors—everything from stuffed sweet peppers with fish mousse to pheasant or partridge. For dessert, the orange flan with cream might just be the best you've ever had. The restaurant is on the main road leading from the center of town to the French border.

Alto de Miracruz 21. © **94-328-55-93**. Reservations required. Main courses 35€–43€; fixed-price menu 102€ excluding drinks. AE, DC, MC, V. Tues–Sun 1–3:30pm; Tues–Sat 8:30–11:30pm. Closed June 15–July 3 and Nov 5–30.

Casa Nicolasa ⭐ BASQUE   Members of all-male eating clubs (a Basque tradition begun in the 19th c.) have assured us that Casa Nicolasa serves the best cuisine at San Sebastián. That would be difficult to prove, especially in a city where international food critics have rated Arzak and Akelare even higher (see above).

In the heart of the resort, at the edge of the old town by the Mercado la Brecha, the restaurant features refined cuisine and impeccable service. Master chef José Juan Castillo, greatly aided by his gracious wife, Ana María, seems to believe that gastronomy should be elevated to a high art. Many of the dishes served have stood the test of time; others reflect today's culinary imagination. The foie gras is homemade and the smoothest, albeit the most expensive, way to begin a meal. *Rape* (monkfish) is prepared in various creative ways and is one of the most satisfying main courses. Save room for dessert, as the pastry selections are one of the outstanding features of the kitchen. When business is at its peak in August and September, the restaurant is likely to open Monday night for dinner as well.

Calle Aldamar 4. © **94-342-07-55**. Reservations required. Main courses 21€–29€; *menú del chef* 42€. AE, DC, MC, V. Mon–Sat 1–3:30pm; Tues–Sat 8:30–11pm. Closed Jan 21–Feb 13.

Martín Berasategui ⭐ BASQUE   Just when you thought the dining situation in San Sebastián couldn't stand any more starred chefs, along comes Martín Berasategui, whose cooking excites food critics throughout Europe. Trained by his mother, who cooked for local fishers, Berasategui opened his restaurant on the outskirts of town. His cuisine is subtle and pure, and he uses butter and cream for desserts only. The hors d'oeuvres are among the best we've ever sampled in the region—from a curl of cider-marinated mackerel with fried anchovies in olive oil to morsels of rare tuna belly grilled over wooden charcoal. Starters include a rich lobster soup with barnacles. For a main dish, opt for such delectable choices as hake with baby clams or gazpacho of *langostinos.* If you try one of the tasting menus, you'll get a summation of Berasategui's cuisine—perhaps pan-seared lambs' brains with baby salad greens and a slice of duck liver. The chef's attention to detail is terrific: For a *porrusalda* (soup) made with, among other ingredients, fresh sea eel and ribbons of smoked eel, Berasategui collects the moisture the eels give off when smoked and mixes it back into the savory broth.

Loidi Kalea 4, Lasarte. © **94-336-64-71**. Reservations required. Main courses 26€–36€; tasting menu 94€. AE, MC, V. Wed–Sat 1–3pm and 8:30–11pm; Sun 1–3pm. Closed 3 weeks at Christmas.

Panier Fleuri ⭐⭐ BASQUE/INTERNATIONAL   Yet another celebrated restaurant in San Sebastián, this citadel of cuisine serves Basque dishes with a definite French flavor and flair. A third generation of the Fombellida family of chefs has had a long time to perfect their cuisine. The service is discreet and elegant, and diners have a chance to learn why Basque food preparation is regarded as among the finest in Europe. The setting alone is rewarding, in a formal dining room opening onto the pounding surf at the mouth of the Urumea River.

Chef Tatus Fombellida has won the National Prize for Gastronomy in Spain, and she's better than ever. Her *faisan* (pheasant) and *becada asada* (roast woodcock) have been hailed as among the finest game dishes at the resort. Another delectable offering is sole baked with spinach and presented with fresh hollandaise sauce. Finish off this rich fare with a lemon sorbet with champagne. Even better known than the cuisine here is the wine cellar, which contains many vintage bottles. The wine steward will guide you through an often perplexing selection, including mellow versions of such wines as Remelluri, Barón de Oña, and Viña Albina.

Paseo de Salamanca 1. ✆ **94-342-42-05.** Reservations required. Main courses 22€–52€; fixed-price menu 55€. AE, DC, MC, V. Thurs–Tues 1–3:30pm; Mon–Tues and Thurs–Sat 8:30–11:30pm. Closed June 1–24 and Dec 24–31.

MODERATE

Bodegón Alejandro ⭐ *Finds* BASQUE   In a pair of pale yellow dining rooms accented with tiles and a sense of nostalgia for years gone by, this bodega-style restaurant focuses exclusively on a set-price menu whose composition changes virtually every day. Many of the ingredients come from the nearby marketplace, reflecting the seasonality and bounty of the Basque country. Menu items are based on old recipes, including red peppers stuffed with salt cod and herbs; seafood stews with rice; artichokes with clams; and roasted veal or braised pork in wine sauce. Any of a rotating series of pastries and cakes are highly caloric but eminently satisfying desserts.

Calle Fermín Calbetón 4B. ✆ **94-342-71-58.** Reservations recommended. Set-price menu 25€. AE, MC, V. Tues–Sun 1–4pm; Tues–Sat 9–11pm.

Juanito Kojua ⭐ BASQUE/SEAFOOD   This little seafood restaurant in the old town, off the Plaza de la Constitución, has no decor to speak of, but it's famous throughout Spain. There are two dining areas on the main floor, behind a narrow bar (perfect for an appetizer while you're waiting for your table), and one downstairs—all air-conditioned in summer. Specialties may include paella, half a *besugo* (sea bream), *rape,* and *lubina* (sea bass). The meats are good, too, but it's best to stick to the fresh fish.

Puerto 14. ✆ **94-342-01-80.** Reservations required. Main courses 15€–20€; fixed-price menu 22€. AE, DC, MC, V. Tues–Sun 1–3:30pm; Tues–Sat 8:30–11:30pm.

Urepel ⭐ BASQUE/INTERNATIONAL   Close to its major competitor, Panier Fleuri (see above), Urepel is near the mouth of the Urumea River, at the edge of the old town. Its interior isn't as elegant as those of the restaurants above, but fans of this place aren't bothered by that at all. They come for the food. The restaurant is the domain of Tomás Almandoz, one of the outstanding chefs in the north of Spain. Seafood dominates the menu and is deftly handled, often served with delicate sauces. The main courses are made even better by an emphasis on perfectly prepared vegetables. *Rape, dorada* (gilthead sea bream), and *cigalas* (crayfish) are likely to turn up on the menu. You can also order goose or duck, somewhat rare in San Sebastián. One specialty is *pato de caserío fileteado a la naranja* (regional-style duck flavored with oranges). A local food critic got so carried away with the dessert cart and its presentation that she claimed, "It would take Velázquez to arrange a pastry so artfully"—an indication of how highly regarded this place is. We prefer it in the evening instead of at midday, when many of the tables are reserved by local businesspeople and government officials.

Paseo de Salamanca 3. ✆ **94-342-40-40.** Reservations required. Main courses 14€–35€. AE, DC, MC, V. Mon and Wed–Sat 1–3:30pm and 8:30–11pm. Closed Easter week, July 1–23, and Dec 24–Jan 6.

INEXPENSIVE

Casa Vallés *Value* SPANISH   Established in 1942 on an all-pedestrian street near the cathedral, this restaurant has survived government coups, civil wars, and the ongoing blur of many dozens of local residents who have come in hundreds of times for daily sustenance. You'll find a bustling tapas bar on the ground floor, where small plates of fish, vegetable, and meat-based tapas cost from 1.10€ to 2.10€ each. There's a simple but dignified-looking wood-paneled dining area upstairs. Menu items include lots of fresh fish, and succulent meats such as veal, steak, pork, and chicken that can—at your request—be grilled over charcoal. Hake, sole, and filet of eel are among the most justifiably popular fish, but since the menu is huge, and since a long list of seasonally based specials are often added to the menu, most tastes are abundantly satisfied.

Reyes Católicos 10. *©* **94-345-22-10**. Main courses 14€–28€. AE, DC, MC, V. Thurs–Tues 1–3:30pm and Thurs–Mon 8:30–11pm. Closed: 2 weeks in late June.

Rekondo BASQUE   This is one of the most substantial restaurants in town, with a location near the beach. The setting is a trio of formally decorated pale yellow dining rooms. Menu items include grilled chops and steaks, preparations of hake and flounder, and spicy garlic-laced versions of octopus and squids. The food is usually accompanied by any of a very large choice of vintages from around Europe. The chefs don't tax their imaginations but prepare reliable fare based on time-tested recipes.

Paseo Igueldo 57. *©* **94-321-29-07**. Reservations recommended. Main courses 18€–24€. AE, DC, MC, V. Thurs–Tues 1–3:30pm and 8:30–11pm. Closed 2 weeks in June and 3 weeks in Nov.

SAN SEBASTIAN AFTER DARK

The best evening entertainment in San Sebastián is to go **tapas-tasting** in the old quarter. Throughout the rest of Spain this is known as a *tapeo,* or tapas crawl. In San Sebastián it's called a *poteo-ir-de-pinchos,* or searching out morsels on toothpicks. In most of the Basque country, the tapas-eating ritual is different from that in the rest of Spain. A platter of tapas *(pinchos)* is placed out on the bar and patrons spear the tasty morsels with toothpicks; when they're done, servers tally up the toothpicks to determine how much is owed. A pale dry white wine, known as *xacoli,* is usually consumed chilled in a plain highball glass.

Groups of young people often spend their evenings on some 20 streets in the old town, each leading toward Monte Urgull, the port, or La Brecha marketplace. **Alameda del Bulevar** is the most upscale of these streets and **Calle Fermín Calveton** one of the most popular. You'll find plenty of these places on your own, but here are some to get you going.

Bar Asador Ganbara, Calle San Jerónimo 21 (*©* **94-342-25-75**), is decorated with a flair in light-colored wood and is a tapas lover's delight. The dishes are well prepared, using market-fresh ingredients. Try the house specialty: small melt-in-your-mouth croissants filled with cheese, egg, bacon, and Serrano ham. Also sample the spider crab and prawns with mayonnaise. In addition to its bar service, the establishment runs a restaurant in a separate section. The bar is open Tuesday through Sunday from 11am to 3:15pm, Tuesday through Saturday from 6 to 11:45pm. The restaurant is open Tuesday through Sunday from 1 to 3:30pm, Tuesday through Saturday from 8 to 11:15pm. Calle San Jerónimo runs at right angles to Calle Fermín Calveton.

The tasty tapas served at **Casa Alcalde,** Mayor 19 (*©* **94-342-62-16**), just a 5-minute walk from the Parque Alderdi Eder, are thinly sliced ham, cheese, and shellfish dishes. The different varieties are all neatly displayed. You can also have full meals in a small restaurant at the back. It's open daily from 10am to 11pm. The variety of tapas and wines offered at **Casa Vallés,** Reyes Católicos 10 (© **94-345-22-10**), seems endless. Go to hang out with the locals and feast on tidbits guaranteed to spoil your dinner. Casa Valles, in the center of town behind the cathedral, is open daily from 8:30 to 11:30pm (closed the last 2 weeks of Dec).

Many locals say that **La Cepa,** 31 de Agosto 7–9 (© **94-342-63-94**), on the northern edge of the old town, serves perhaps the best tapas, and the Jabugo ham is one proof of this claim. Try the grilled squid or the salt-cod-and-green pepper omelet. You can also order dinner here. It's open Wednesday through Monday from 11am to midnight. At **Aloña/Berri,** Berminghan 24, Nuevo Gros (© **94-329-08-18**), you can feast on the delights of silky salt cod *brandade,* pigeon in pastry, and anchovies in red pepper cream. At **Oñatz,** Urdaneta 22 (© **94-345-55-47**), they serve the city's most exquisite morsels, none better than a "haystack" of foie gras and apples. You can go on to the mussel-and-garlic flan or braised oxtail. At the family-run **Bar Juli,** Viteri 27, Renteria (© **94-351-28-87**), Igor, a graduate of Arzak (see "Where to Dine," above), lures and satisfies the most demanding palates of San Sebastián. Try his sushi-like tuna salad and what have been called "the best seafood *croquetas* on the northern shore of Spain."

San Sebastián has other nightlife possibilities, but they dim when compared to a *tapeo.* Nevertheless, if disco isn't too retro for you, head for **Kabutzia,** Muelle (no phone), where a cover and one drink costs 12€. The club opens at 8pm, with variable closing times, depending on business. The best live jazz is found at **Altxeri Galería,** Calle Reina Regente 2 (© **94-342-29-31**), where a cover charge may or may not be imposed, depending on the group. It's open Sunday through Thursday from 5pm to 1:30am, Friday and Saturday from 5pm to 3:30am.

San Sebastián's only venue for gambling is the **Casino de San Sebastián,** Mayor 1 (© **94-342-92-14**). The casino requires minimum bets of 1.50€ to 3€ for the roulette tables and 1.50€ for the blackjack tables. Entrance costs 3.75€ per person and requires the presentation of an ID card with a photograph or a passport. Jackets and ties for men aren't required. From September 16 to June 14, the casino is open daily from 6:30pm to 3am (until 4am on Sat and holidays), and between June 15 and September 15, it's open daily from 6:30pm to 4am (till 5am on Sat and holidays).

The big cultural center is the concert hall, **Kursaal Centre,** Av. de Zurriola 1 (© **94-300-30-00**), a daringly modern avant-garde building strategically positioned on the Bay of Concha. It is a cultural, sporting, and leisure center, which is the venue for almost any major event: "Basque Dixieland" band, a big salsa band from Madrid, or gospel singers from America's Deep South. The designer was famed Spanish architect, Rafael Moneno, who created what's been compared to two mammoth Noguchi lantern lamps.

Kursaal, along with the Guggenheim museum in Bilboa, has helped put the Basque country on the cultural maps of Europe. Many tradition-minded locals objected to the glaringly modern structure, feeling that it was out of style with the city's essential Belle Epoque architecture.

All the major festivals of San Sebastián, including the September film festival, are staged here. There is a 1,800-seat theater for plays, music, dance, and zarzuela performances. Even if there is no major event staged here during your visit to San Sebastián, you can take a guided tour daily at 11:30am, 12:30pm, and 1:30pm, costing 2.05€.

SIDE TRIPS FROM SAN SEBASTIAN

One of the reasons for coming to San Sebastián is to use it as a base for touring the surrounding area. Driving is best because bus connections are awkward or nonexistent.

PASAI DONIBANE   On the east bank of a natural harbor 10.5km (6½ miles) from San Sebastián, **Pasai Donibane** ⊛—formerly known by its Spanish name, Pasajes de San Juan—is one of the most typical of Basque fishing villages. In summer, don't take a car. Parking is difficult, the medieval streets are one-way, and the wait at traffic signals is long because all southbound traffic has to clear the street before northbound motorists have the right of way. A bus leaves every 15 minutes from the Calle Aldamar in San Sebastián for Pasajes de San Pedro, Pasai Donibane's neighboring fishing village. From here, it's possible to walk to Pasai Donibane. Buses head back to San Sebastián from Pasajes de San Pedro at a quarter to the hour all day long.

The village, with its cod-packing factories, is on a sheltered harbor with fishing boats tied up at the wharf. The architecture is appealing: five-and six-story balconied tenement-like buildings in different colors. Victor Hugo lived here in the summer of 1846 (it hasn't changed much since) at building no. 63 on the narrow main street, San Juan.

Many visitors come here to dine. On the waterfront, **Txulotxo** ⊛, San Juan 71 (© **94-352-39-52**), is an old stone building with a glass-enclosed dining room; it's one of the most authentic Basque restaurants. For openers, try the *sopa de pescado* (fish soup) or a mix of *entremeses variados* (hors d'oeuvres). Although pasta dishes are featured, most diners opt for one of the seafood selections, perhaps hake in green sauce, grilled shrimp, or grilled monkfish with clams and shrimp. It's open Wednesday through Monday from 1:30 to 4:30pm, Wednesday through Saturday and Monday from 8:30 to 11:30pm (closed Jan 1–15). American Express and Visa are accepted.

LOYOLA   Surrounded by mountain scenery, **Loyola,** 55km (34 miles) southwest of San Sebastián, is the birthplace of St. Ignatius, the founder of the Jesuits. He was born in 1491, died in 1556, and was canonized in 1622. The sanctuary at Loyola is the most visited attraction outside San Sebastián. Six buses a day leave from Plaza Guipúzcoa 2, San Sebastián, for Loyola (the first departing at 8:30am and the last at 8pm). Buses return about every 2 hours.

There are large pilgrimages to Loyola for the annual celebration on St. Ignatius Day, July 31. The activity is centered at the **Monasterio de San Ignacio de Loyola,** an immense structure built by the Jesuits in the 1700s around the Loyola family manor house near Azpeitia. An International Festival of Romantic Music is held here during the first week of August.

The **basilica** is the work of Italian architect Fontana. Surrounded by a 35m (118-ft.) high cupola by Churriguera, it's circular in design. From 12:30 to 3:30pm daily, you can enter the **Santa Casa,** with its 15th-century tower on the site of the former Loyola manor house. The rooms in which the saint was born and in which he convalesced have been converted into richly decorated chapels. At the entrance you can rent a tape detailing Loyola's life, and dioramas are shown at the end of the tour.

ONDARROA   **Ondárroa** ⊛, 48km (30 miles) west of San Sebastián, is described as a *pueblo típico*, a typical Basque fishing village. It's the area's largest fishing port. Lying on a spit of land, it stands between a hill and a loop of the Artibay River. Laundry hangs from the windows of the little plant-filled balconied houses, and most of the residents are engaged in canning and fish salting, if not fishing. The local church looks like a ship's prow at one end. Around the snug harbor you'll find many little places to drink and dine after taking a stroll through the village. From San Sebastián, Ondárroa is serviced by buses that run along the Costa Vasca. If you're driving, head west from San Sebastián along the coastal road.

2 Fuenterrabía ⟨⚲⟩

23km (14 miles) E of San Sebastián, 510km (317 miles) N of Madrid, 18km (11 miles) W of St-Jean-de-Luz (France)

A big seaside resort and fishing port, **Fuenterrabía** (Hondarrabía in Basque) is near the French frontier and, for that reason, has been subject to frequent attacks over the centuries. In theory, it was supposed to guard access to Spain, but sometimes it hasn't performed that task too well.

ESSENTIALS

GETTING THERE   Fuenterrabía doesn't have a **train** station, but it is serviced by the station in nearby Irún (© **90-224-02-02**). Buses depart Irún's Plaza de San Juan for Fuentarrabía at 10- to 15-minute intervals. Irún is the end of the line for trains in northern Spain. East of Irún, you must board French trains.

Buses run every 20 minutes from Plaza Guipúzcoa in San Sebastián to Fuenterrabía, 1 hour away. Call © **94-364-13-02** for information. By **car** take A-8 east to the French border, turning toward the coast at the exit sign for Fuenterrabía.

VISITOR INFORMATION   The **tourist office** at Calle Javier Ugarte 6 (© **94-364-54-58**) is open July through August, daily from 10am to 8pm; off-season hours are Monday though Friday from 9am to 1:30pm and 4 to 6:30pm, Saturday from 10am to 2pm.

EXPLORING FUENTERRABIA & ENVIRONS

The most interesting part of town is the **medieval quarter** in the upper market, where some of the villas date from the early 17th century. The fishing district in the lower part of town is called **La Marina;** old homes, painted boats, and marine atmosphere there attract many visitors. Because restaurants in Fuenterrabía tend to be very expensive, you can fill up here on seafood tapas in the many taverns along the waterfront. The beach at Fuenterrabía is wide and sandy, and many prefer it to the more famous ones at San Sebastián.

Wander for an hour or 2 around the old quarter, taking in Calle Mayor, Calle Tiendas y Pampinot, and Calle Obispo. The **Castillo de Carlos V,** standing at the Plaza de las Armas, has been turned into one of the smallest and most desirable paradors in Spain (see "Where to Stay," below). It's hard to get a room here unless you reserve well in advance, but you can visit the well-stocked bar over the entrance hall.

Sancho Abarca, a king of Navarre in the 10th century, is supposed to have founded the original castle that stood on this spot, but the present look owes more to Charles V in the 16th century. You can still see the battle scars on the castle that date from the time of the Napoleonic invasion of Spain.

The most impressive church in the old quarter is the **Iglesia de Santa María,** a Gothic structure that was vastly restored in the 17th century and given a baroque tower. The proxy wedding of Louis XIV and the Infanta María Teresa took place here in June 1660.

Moments **Sunset in the Basque Country**

You can head west out of town along the **Jaizkibel Road** ★★, which many motorists prefer at sunset. After going 5km (3 miles), you'll reach the shrine of the Virgin of Guadalupe, where another panoramic view unfolds. From here, you can see the French Basque coast. Even better views await if you continue along to the Hostal Jaizkibel. If you stay on this road, you will come to the little fishing village of Pasai Donibane (see "Side Trips from San Sebastián," above), 18km (11 miles) away.

If you have a car, you can take some interesting trips in the area, especially to **Cabo Higuer,** a promontory with panoramic views, reached by going 4km (2½ miles) north. Leave by the harbor and beach road. You can see the French coast and the town of Hendaye from this cape.

WHERE TO STAY

Hotel Pampinot ★★   This aristocratic mansion, built in 1587, housed the Infanta María Teresa for a night as she headed toward France to marry Louis XIV. Today, it presents a richly textured stone facade with Renaissance detailing and heraldic symbols on one of the most historic streets of the old town. Inside, an antique sense of elegance is conveyed by beamed ceilings, exposed stonework, parquet flooring, and ornate ironwork. The midsize rooms are traditional and charming, with a mix of antique and reproduction furniture. Each bathroom comes with a tub/shower combo. Although breakfast (not included in the rates) is the only meal served, the staff can direct you to a choice of nearby eateries.

Kale Nagusia 5, 20280 Hondarrabía. ℭ **94-364-06-00.** Fax 94-364-51-28. www.hotelpampinot.com. 8 units. 80€–118€ double; 115€–152€ suite. AE, DC, MC, V. Closed Nov. **Amenities:** Bar; car rental; babysitting; laundry service; dry cleaning. *In room:* A/C, TV, hair dryer, safe.

Jáuregui   Opened in 1981 in the center of the old village, this is a good choice for moderately priced accommodations. The modern interior boasts comfortable accessories, and the hotel has a garage—a definite plus, since parking in Fuenterrabía is virtually impossible. Each of the small rooms is well furnished and maintained; thoughtful extras include a shoeshine machine on each floor. All units contain bathrooms with tub/shower combos. Breakfast is the only meal served (but is not included in the rates quoted below).

Zuloaga 5, 20280 Hondarrabía. ℭ **94-364-14-00.** Fax 94-364-44-04. www.hoteljauregui.com. 42 units. 75€–102€ double; 100€–183€ apt. AE, MC, V. Parking 9€. **Amenities:** Restaurant; bar; room service; babysitting; laundry service; dry cleaning. *In room:* A/C, TV, minibar, hair dryer, safe.

Parador de Hondarrabía ★★   This beautifully restored 10th-century castle, on a hill in the center of the old town, was once used by Emperor Charles V as a border fortification. The building itself is impressive, and so are the taste and imagination of the restoration. Antiques, old weapons, and standards hang from the high-vaulted ceilings, and some of the comfortable provincial-style rooms open onto the Bay of Biscay. Units range from small to medium, each with a firm mattress and a bathroom with a tub/shower combo. Breakfast (not included in the rates) is the only meal served. It's best to reserve a room here well in advance.

Plaza de Armas, 20280 Hondarrabía. ℭ **94-364-55-00.** Fax 94-364-21-53. www.parador.es. 36 units. 121€–137€ double; 207€–237€ suite. Rates include breakfast. AE, DC, MC, V. Free parking. **Amenities:** Bar; room service; laundry service; dry cleaning. *In room:* TV, minibar, hair dryer, safe.

Río Bidasoa Five minutes from the center of town and only 5km (3 miles) west of the French border, this is an old mansion that was remodeled to become the modern hotel you see today. It's surrounded by one of the most beautiful gardens in the area. The exterior is crisp and white, with balustrades trimmed in wood. The rooms are midsize to spacious and furnished in various contrasting styles and fashions (even in the same room), with bathrooms that for the most part are equipped with tub/shower combos.

Nafarroa Behera 1, 20280 Hondarrabía. ℂ **94-364-54-08.** Fax 94-364-51-70. www.hotelriobidasoa.com. 44 units. 80€–103€ double; 100€–133€ suite. AE, DC, MC, V. Free parking. **Amenities:** Restaurant; bar; pool; room service; babysitting; laundry service; dry cleaning. *In room:* A/C, TV, minibar, hair dryer, safe (in some rooms).

WHERE TO DINE

Ramón Roteta BASQUE Named after its owner/founder, this attractive restaurant is one of Europe's most consistently respected purveyors of traditional Basque cuisine. Contained in what was a 1920s villa, it's on the southern outskirts of town, near the local parador and the city limits of Irún. Menu specialties include a terrine of green vegetables and fish served with red-pepper vinaigrette, baked sea crabs with tiny potatoes and onions, fresh pasta with seafood, and the dessert specialty, a mandarin orange tart flavored with rose petals. The villa is surrounded by a pleasantly unstructured garden you can appreciate from a table on the terrace.

Villa Ainara. ℂ **94-364-16-93.** Reservations recommended. Main courses 18€–23€. AE, MC, V. Wed–Mon 1–3:30pm and 8:30–11:30pm (closed Sun night).

Sebastián BASQUE In the oldest district of Fuenterrabía, close to the castle, this restaurant offers modern cuisine using top-notch ingredients appropriate to the season. The two floors of the restaurant feature thick masonry walls, among which are scattered an array of 18th-century paintings. Try one of the specialties: foie gras of duckling Basque style, terrine of fresh mushrooms, or medallions of sole and salmon with seafood sauce.

Mayor 9–11. ℂ **94-364-01-67.** Reservations required. Main courses 18€–24€; fixed-price menu 40€. AE, DC, DISC, MC, V. Tues–Sun 1–3:30pm and 8–11pm. Closed Nov.

3 Guernica

428km (266 miles) N of Madrid, 84km (52 miles) W of San Sebastián

The subject of Picasso's most famous painting (returned to Spain from the Museum of Modern Art in New York and now displayed at the Reina Sofía Museum in Madrid), **Guernica** or Gernika in Basque, the spiritual home of the Basques and the seat of Basque nationalism, was destroyed in a Nazi air raid on April 26, 1937, during the Spanish Civil War. It was the site of a revered oak tree, under whose branches Basques had elected their officials since medieval times. No one knows how many died during the 3½-hour attack—estimates range from 200 to 2,000. The bombers reduced the town to rubble, but a mighty symbol of independence was born. Although activists around the world attempted to rally support for the embattled Spanish Republicans, governments everywhere, including that of the United States, left the Spaniards to fend for themselves, refusing to supply them with arms.

The town has been attractively rebuilt close to its former style. The chimes of a church bell ring softly, and laughing children play in the street. In the midst of this peace, however, you'll suddenly come upon a sign: SOUVENIRS . . . REMEMBER.

The former Basque parliament, the **Casa de Juntas** (or **Juntetxea**) (© **94-625-11-38**), is the principal attraction in town. It contains a historical display of Guernica and is open daily from 10am to 2pm and 4 to 7pm, June through September (to 6pm in winter). Admission is free. Outside are the remains of the ancient communal oak tree, symbol of Basque independence; it wasn't uprooted by Hitler's bombs. From the train station, head up Calle Urioste.

The **Fundación Museo de la Paz de Guernica,** Foru Plaza 1 (© **94-627-02-13**), contains a permanent exhibition of the bombing as depicted in photographs in 1937 and in artifacts, including bomb fragments bearing Luftwaffe markings. We learn that the tragic bombing on a market day (greater casualties that way) began at 4:30pm and lasted for 3 hours, as Nazi bombers unloaded thousand-pound bombs and thousands of incendiary projectiles on the helpless Basque populace. On one wall of the museum is a framed letter from President Roman Herzog of Germany, dated March 27, 1997, acknowledging German responsibility for the indefensible act of aerial bombardment and calling for reconciliation and peace. Copies of Picasso's working drawings for *Guernica* are also displayed. An oil painting in the spirit of Picasso's *Guernica* covers an entire wall of the exhibition.

In July and August, it's open daily from 10am to 7pm; from September to June, hours are Monday through Saturday from 10am to 2pm and 4 to 7pm, Sunday from 10am to 2pm. Admission is 4€ but ages 10 and under are admitted free.

VISITOR INFORMATION The **tourist office** is at Calle Artecale 8, 48300 Guernica (© **94-625-58-92**). Summer hours are Monday through Saturday from 10am to 7pm, Sunday from 10am to 2pm; off-season hours are Monday through Friday from 10am to 1:30pm and 4 to 7pm, Saturday from 10am to 1:30pm.

GETTING THERE

From Bilbao, **trains** run five times daily to Guernica. Trip time is 50 minutes. Call © **94-625-11-82** for schedules. **Bizkaibus,** at Calle Iparraguirre 21, runs buses to Bilbao, with connections to Guernica. For information, call © **90-222-22-65.**

From Bilbao, head east along the A-8 superhighway; cut north on the 6315 and follow the signs for Guernica. From San Sebastián, **drive** west along A-8, and cut north on the 6315. A more scenic, but slightly longer, route involves driving west from San Sebastián on the A-8, and branching off on the coastal road to Ondárroa. Continue on as the road turns south and follow the signs to Guernica.

WHERE TO STAY

Boliña This little place is modesty itself but provides a decent shelter for the night for those who come to Guernica, wanting to absorb its regional atmosphere. It's a contemporary little structure with simply furnished and small rooms, each with a tiny bathroom with a shower stall. The staff is helpful and inviting, although English is hardly the tongue of the land around here.

Barrenkale 3, 48300 Guernica. © 94-625-03-00. Fax: 94-625-03-04. 16 units. 39€–46€ double. AE, DC, MC, V. **Amenities:** Restaurant; bar. *In room:* TV, hair dryer.

Hotel Gernika Because so many pilgrims flock to this scene of the notorious air raid massacre on the dawn of World War II, the town finally has a first-rate hotel. It's not the Ritz but suitable for its relatively modest comfort. Bedrooms are midsize and comfortably furnished, each with a small, tiled bathroom with shower. Breakfast is served but there is no on-site restaurant. Several good dining options lie close at hand, however.

Carlos Gangoit 17, 48300 Guernica. ℰ **94-625-03-50.** Fax 94-625-58-74. www.hotel-gernika.com. 15 units. 65€ double. AE, DC, MC, V. **Amenities:** Bar; room service; babysitting; laundry service; dry cleaning. *In room:* A/C, TV.

WHERE TO DINE

Baserri Maitea ★ *Finds* BASQUE   This is a 3-century-old Basque *caseríos* (farmhouse) that was skillfully converted to entertain diners with its imaginative home cookery. We know of no other place in the area that gives you such a sense of Basque tradition and food. The ceiling is as tall as many churches. Wooden beams hold the place together, the decorative note sounded by strings of garlic and red peppers grown in the countryside. The young pigeon in a caramelized glaze is a delight, as is the milk-fed lamb roasted in an oven fired by wood. From that same oven emerges a beautifully roasted *besugo* (sea bream). Look also for the catch of the day—on our last visit it was a white fish called *raya* caught in Basque waters and served with the aromatic green sauce so beloved by locals.

B635 to Bermeo, Km 2. ℰ **94-625-34-08.** Reservations recommended. Main courses 19€–30€. AE, DC, MC, V. Mon–Sat 1:30–4pm and 9–11pm; Sun 1:30–4pm.

A NEARBY PLACE TO DINE

Asador Zaldua BASQUE   Most of the specialties served here come from a blazing grill whose turning spits are visible from the dining room. A wide array of seafood and fish is available, some dishes baked to a flaky goodness in a layer of rock salt. The lobster salad alone is worth the trip, 9km (5½ miles) north of the center of town on the road to Bermeo.

Sabino Arana 10. ℰ **94-687-08-71.** Reservations required in summer. Main courses 15€–36€; *menú del día* 34€. AE, MC, V. June–Oct Mon–Sat 1:30–3:30pm and 9–11pm; Nov–May Fri–Sat 8:30–11pm only. Closed Dec 20–Jan 5.

4 Bilbao ★

396km (246 miles) N of Madrid, 100km (62 miles) W of San Sebastián

Bilbao, Spain's sixth-largest city and biggest port, has been described as an "ugly, gray, decaying, smokestack city," and so it is—in part. But it has a number of interesting secrets to reveal, as well as good food, and as a rail hub it serves as a center for exploring some of the best attractions in the Basque country. Most of the city's sights can be viewed in a day or 2. Many visitors flock here only to see the controversial new $100-million Guggenheim Museum, designed by American architect Frank Gehry and called "the beast" by some locals because of its bizarre shape. From afar, it resembles a gargantuan sculpture, with a tumbling boxes profile and a 131m (430-ft.) long ship gallery.

Bilbao is the industrial hub of the north and the political capital for the Basques. Shipping, shipbuilding, and steel-making have made it prosperous, so there's no shortage of bankers or industrialists. Its commercial heart, bursting with skyscrapers and sky cranes, hums with activity. Among cities of the Basque region, it has the highest population (around 450,000); the metropolitan area, including the suburbs and many surrounding towns, is home to over a million inhabitants.

Bilbao has a wide-open feeling, extending more than 8km (5 miles) across the valley of the Nervión River, one of Spain's most polluted waterways. Many buildings wear a layer of grime. Some visitors compare Bilbao to the sooty

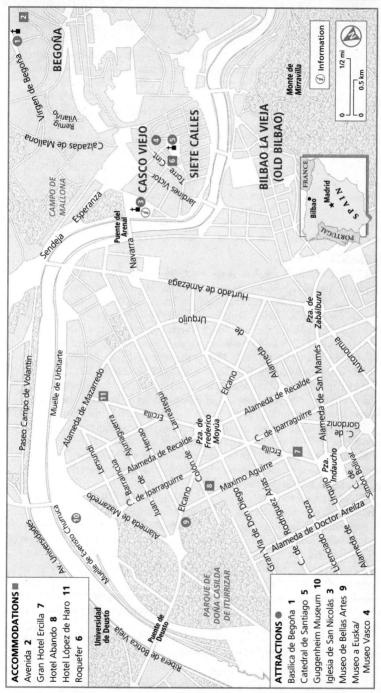

Bilbao

BEGOÑA

Virgen de Begoña

Remig Vilarío

Calzadas de Mallona

CASCO VIEJO

Torre Cinc.

Jardines Victor

SIETE CALLES

CAMPO DE MALLONA

Esperanza

Sendeja

Navarra

Puente del Arenal

Hurtado de Amézaga

Urquijo

de

Alameda

Pza. de Zabálburu

Autonomía

Elcano

Alameda de Recalde

Alameda de San Mamés

C. de Iparraguirre

Ercilla

Alameda de Mazarredo

Paseo Campo de Volantín

Muelle de Urbitarte

Ercilla

Larreategui

Licenciado Poza

Henao

Alameda de Recalde

C. de Barraincúa

Ajuriaguerra

C. de

Juan

Lersundi

Pza. Frederico Moyúa

Colón de Larreategui

Elcano

Gran Vía de Don Diego

Maximo Aguirre

Rodríguez Arias

Pza. Indaucho

Urquijo

C. de Iparraguirre

Alameda de Mazarredo

Alameda de Doctor Areilza

Alameda de Simón Bolívar

C. de Gordoniz

C. de

Muelle de Ibeiso Churruca

Av. Universidades

Universidad de Deusto

Puente de Deusto

Ribera de Botica Vieja

PARQUE DE DOÑA CASILDA DE ITURRIZAR

BILBAO LA VIEJA (OLD BILBAO)

Monte de Mirravilla

ⓘ Information

0   1/2 mi
0   0.5 km

FRANCE

SPAIN

Bilbao ● ★ Madrid

PORTUGAL

ACCOMMODATIONS ■
Avenida **2**
Gran Hotel Ercilla **7**
Hotel Abando **8**
Hotel López de Haro **11**
Roquefer **6**

ATTRACTIONS ●
Basílica de Begoña **1**
Catedral de Santiago **5**
Guggenheim Museum **10**
Iglesia de San Nicolás **3**
Museo de Bellas Artes **9**
Museo a Euska/
Museo Vasco **4**

postindustrial sprawl of an English port town. However, the extravagant Guggenheim Museum is cast as a symbol of Basque economic revival, and locals hope it will lead to a revitalization of their city. Bilbao was badly hit by the 1970s economic crisis, leading to a closure of shipyards and steelworks. It has benefited greatly from a $1.5-billion reconversion grant, of which the Guggenheim project is one of the main beneficiaries. Signs of revitalization are also seen in a flashy new Metro system designed by Sir Norman Foster of England and a new airport terminal, the work of Spanish architect Santiago Calatrava. In addition, many owners of local buildings are removing those layers of accumulated grime.

Bilbao was established by charter June 15, 1300, which converted it from a village *(pueblo)*, ruled by local feudal duke Don Diego López de Haro, into a city. Aided by water power and the transportation potential of the Nervión River, it grew and grew, most of its fame and glory coming during the industrial expansion of the 19th century. Many of the city's grand homes and villas for industrialists were constructed then, particularly in the wealthy suburb of Neguri. The most famous son of Bilbao was Miguel de Unamuno, the writer/educator more closely associated with Salamanca.

ESSENTIALS

GETTING THERE   **Bilbao Airport** (© 94-486-96-63) is 8km (5 miles) north of the city, near the town of Erandio. Flights arrive from Madrid, Barcelona, Alicante, Arrecife, Fuenteventura, Las Palmas, Málaga, Palma, Santiago de Compostela, Sevilla, Tenerife, Valencia, Vigo, Brussels, Frankfurt, Lisbon, London, Milan, Paris, and Zurich. **Iberia**'s main booking office in Bilbao is at the airport (© 94-486-98-30), open daily from 5am to 10pm. From the airport into town, take red bus A3247 to the heart of the city for 1€.

The **RENFE** station, the Estación de Abando (© 90-224-02-02), is on Plaza Circular 2, just off the Plaza de España. From here, you can catch short-distance trains within the metropolitan area of Bilbao and long-distance trains to most parts of Spain. Two trains per day run to and from Madrid (trip time: 6 hr. on the afternoon train, 7 hr. on the night train). Two trains per day run to and from Barcelona (11 hr.), and one train per day goes to and from Galicia (12 hr.). There are also two night trains per week to and from the Mediterranean Coast: one toward Alicante and Valencia (daily during the summer months) and the other toward Málaga (3 times a week in the summer).

PESA, at the Estación de Buses de Garillano (© 94-439-50-77), operates more than a dozen buses per day to and from San Sebastián (trip time: 1¼ hr.). **Continental,** Calle Gurtubay s/n (© 94-439-50-77), has nine buses per day from Madrid (trip time: 5 hr.). It has four buses per day to and from Barcelona (7 hr.). If you'd like to explore either Lekeitio or Guernica (see above) by bus, use the services of **Bizkaibus** (© 90-222-22-65). Fifteen buses per day go to Lekeitio Monday through Saturday and two on Sunday. Trip time is 45 minutes. Ten buses run each weekday to Guernica (trip time: 45 min.). On weekends, only five buses per day go to Guernica. For all general bus information call (© 94-439-50-77).

Bilbao is beside the A-8, linking the cities of Spain's northern Atlantic seacoast to the western edge of France. It is connected by superhighway to both Barcelona and Madrid.

VISITOR INFORMATION   The **tourist office** at Paseo del Arenal 1 (© 94-479-57-60; www.bilbao.net) is open Monday through Friday from 9am to 2pm and 4 to 7:30pm, Saturday from 9am to 2pm, and Sunday from 10am to 2pm.

SPECIAL EVENTS   Festivals often fill the calendar, the biggest and most widely publicized being **La Semana Grande,** dedicated to the Virgin of Begoña and lasting from mid-August until early September. During the celebration, the Nervión River is the site of many flotillas and regattas. July 25 brings the festival of Bilbao's patron saint, **Santiago (St. James),** and July 31 is the holiday devoted to the region's patron saint, **St. Ignatius.**

EXPLORING BILBAO

The **Nervión River** meanders through Bilbao, whose historic core was built inside one of its loops, with water protecting it on three sides. Most of the important shops, banks, and tourist facilities lie within a short walk of the **Gran Vía,** running east-west through the heart of town. The old quarter is east of the modern commercial center, across the river.

THE TOP ATTRACTIONS

Guggenheim Museum ★★★   The newest and biggest attraction in Bilbao is the Guggenheim Museum, at the intersection of the bridge called Puente de la Salve and the Nervión River. The 104,700 sq. m (349,000 sq. ft.) colossus is the focal point of a $1.5-billion redevelopment plan for the city. The internationally acclaimed Frank Gehry design features a 50m (165-ft.) high atrium—more than 1½ times the height of the rotunda of Frank Lloyd Wright's Guggenheim Museum in New York. Stretching under the aforementioned bridge and incorporating it in its design, the museum reanimates the promenade with a towering roof reminiscent of a blossoming metallic flower.

The Guggenheim isn't an encyclopedic museum, such as the Met in New York City. This museum features the works of some of the most towering artists of the latter half of the 20th century—including Picasso, Robert Motherwell, Robert Rauschenberg, Clyfford Still, Antoni Tàpies, Andy Warhol, Ives Klein, and (our personal favorite) Willem de Koonig. The beginning of the collection is marked by a 1952 Mark Rothko work, "Untitled." Recent European art is also exhibited (including some paintings from the 21st c.) along with an array of young Basque and Spanish artists. Artwork lent by the Guggenheims in New York and Venice will rotate, and Bilbao will also host temporary exhibits traveling here from New York.

Although some disgruntled Basque locals still call the museum "the colossal Californian cauliflower" or "a cheese factory," many architectural critics from around the world, including Paul Goldberger of the *New York Times,* have hailed

---

Tips   Warning: Parking Lot Robberies

Regrettably, the parking lot, where many patrons to the Guggenheim Museum park, is the scene of countless car robberies. The lot is not run by the museum and the museum is in no way responsible for the thefts that take place there. But many visitors stop off at the Guggenheim in cars filled with luggage, intending to spend the night elsewhere along the Basque coast.

Even if luggage is locked in the trunk, these thefts in broad daylight are commonplace. In most cases, the police seem to offer little assistance, and the lot seems relatively unguarded. Be warned that your property is at great risk if you leave your car unguarded in the lot while you spend 2 or 3 hours enjoying the museum.

Frank Gehry's unique structure as the first great building of the 21st century. The structure is said to have been inspired by the Fritz Lang film classic *Metropolis* and is viewed as a homage to Bilbao's industrial past and commitment to its future. The massive museum is clad in shimmering titanium, which many observers find sexy and unmistakably elegant. The building takes up 24,000 sq. m (28,700 sq. yd.) in the former dockyards beside the Nervión River, and about half of that space is devoted to the exhibition halls. The museum has virtually abolished right angles and flat walls. As one critic put it, "it was as if Gehry were working in pastry rather than concrete or steel."

Calle Abandoibarra 2. ✆ **94-435-90-00**. Admission 10€ adults, 5€ seniors and students, free for children 12 and under. Tues–Sun 11am–8pm. Closed Jan 1 and Dec 25. Bus: 1, 10, 13, or 18.

Museo a Euska/Museo Vasco Devoted to Basque archaeology, ethnology, and history, this museum is in the center of the old quarter, south of Calle Esperanza Ascao, housed in a centuries-old Jesuit cloister. Some of the exhibits showcase Basque commercial life during the 16th century. You can see everything from ship models to shipbuilding tools, along with reconstructions of rooms illustrating political and social life. Basque gravestones are also on view. In addition, you'll see the equipment used to play the popular Basque game of *pelota* (aka jai alai).

Plaza Miguel de Unamuno 4, 48005 Bilbao. ✆ **94-415-54-23**. Admission 3€ adults, 1.50€ children and students, free for children under 10. Tues–Sat 11am–5pm; Sun 11am–2pm.

Museo de Bellas Artes ✪ This is another one of Spain's important art museums, containing both medieval and modern works, including paintings by Velázquez, Goya, Zurbarán, and El Greco. Among the works of non-Spanish artists are *The Money Changers* by the Flemish painter Quentin Massys and *The Lamentation Over Christ* by Anthony Van Dyck. In its modern wing, the museum contains works by Gauguin, Picasso, Léger, Sorolla, and Mary Cassatt. The gallery is particularly strong in 19th- and 20th-century Basque artists, the foremost of which is the modern sculptor Eduardo Chillida, who created a massive piece titled *Monument to Iron.* If you tire of looking at the art, you can walk in the English-inspired gardens around the museum, 4 blocks south of the old quarter.

Plaza del Museo 2. ✆ **94-439-60-60**. Admission 4.50€ adults, 3€ seniors and students, free for children under 10; Wed free for all. Tues–Sat 10am–8pm and Sun 10am–2pm.

EXPLORING THE CASCO VIEJO (OLD QUARTER) ✪

Despite the fact that Bilbao was established around 1300, it has curiously few medieval monuments. It does have an intriguing old quarter, however, on the east side of Nervión River and the site of its most interesting bars and restaurants. The custom is to go here at night and barhop, ordering small cups of beer or wine. A small glass of wine is called a *chiquiteo.*

The old quarter of Bilbao is connected to the much larger modern section on the opposite bank by four bridges. A few paces north of the old quarter's center are **graceful arches,** 64 in all, enclosing the Plaza Nueva, also called the Plaza de los Mártires, completed in 1830.

The entire *barrio* has been declared a national landmark. It originally defined an area around seven streets, but it long ago spilled beyond that limitation. Its most important church is the **Iglesia de San Nicolás.** Behind this church you'll find an elevator on Calle Esperanza Ascao, which, if working, carries sightseers to the upper town. You can also climb 64 steps from the Plaza Unamuno. From here it's a short walk to the **Basílica de Begoña,** built largely in the early 1500s. Inside the dimly lit church is a brightly illuminated depiction of the Virgin, dressed in long, flowing robes. She's the patroness of the province. Also displayed are some enormous paintings by Luca Giordano. While in the old town, you might visit the **Catedral de Santiago,** Plaza Santiago, which was built in the 14th century and then restored in the 16th century after a fire. The cathedral's facade was rebuilt in the 19th century. These three churches are open daily from 9am to 5pm. On Sundays you may take in the **flea market,** starting at 8am, on the streets of the old quarter.

To reach the old town on foot, the only way to explore it, take the Puente del Arenal from the Gran Vía, the main street of Bilbao.

SHOPPING

Many visitors like to return from the Basque country with a chic beret, which locals call *txapelas.* The best selection is found at **Sombreros Gorostiada,** Calle Victor 9 (© **94-416-12-76**), a family-owned business since 1857. They also sell woolen caps, various hats, and also hunting caps. If you'd like to purchase Basque artisanal products, head for **Basandere,** Calle Iparraguirre 4 (© **94-423-63-86**), near the Guggenheim Museum. Their crafts are of high quality, and every three months they stage art exhibitions from local artists. In addition, the shop also sells gourmet Basque food items.

WHERE TO STAY
EXPENSIVE

Gran Hotel Ercilla ⭐ Soaring high above the buildings surrounding it in the heart of Bilbao's business district, this is a tastefully decorated bastion of attentive service and good living. The midsize to spacious guest rooms are conservative and comfortably furnished, all with roomy bathrooms with tub/shower combos. Completely renovated in 1989 and 1990, the Ercilla is one of Bilbao's most desirable hotels, usually the preferred choice of Spanish politicians, movie stars, and journalists.

Ercilla 37–39, 48011 Bilbao. © **94-470-57-00.** Fax 94-443-93-35. www.hotelercilla.es. 350 units. 127€–185€ double; 307€ suite. AE, DC, MC, V. Parking 14€. **Amenities:** Restaurant; bar; car rental; room service; babysitting; laundry service; dry cleaning. *In room:* A/C, TV, minibar, hair dryer, safe.

Hotel Abando ⭐ This government-rated four-star hotel isn't in the same class as the López de Haro, but it's a first-class property achieving a sudden fame. This new hotel lies in the city center, offering an array of well-furnished rooms with comfortable beds. The rooms also have roomy tiled bathrooms with tub/shower combos. If you don't want to go out at night, you can enjoy top Basque and international cuisine at the restaurant.

Colón de Larreautegui 9, 48001 Bilbao. © **94-423-62-00.** Fax 94-424-55-26. www.aranzazu-hoteles.com. 145 units. 94€–149€ double; 123€–175€ suite. AE, DC, MC, V. Parking 12€. All buses to Estación de Abando. **Amenities:** Restaurant; bar; room service; babysitting; laundry service; dry cleaning. *In room:* A/C, TV, minibar, hair dryer, safe.

Hotel López de Haro ⭐⭐⭐ This refined palace of pleasure is the ultimate in luxury living in the greater Bilbao area. Behind a discreet facade of chiseled gray stone, this 1990 hotel is filled with English touches and features marble flooring, hardwood paneling, and a uniformed staff. The comfortable midsize guest rooms contain flowered or striped upholstery, modern bathrooms with tub/shower combos, and wall-to-wall carpeting or hardwood floors.

Obispo Orueta 2–4, 48009 Bilbao. ℂ **94-423-55-00.** Fax 94-423-45-00. www.hotellopezdeharo.com. 53 units. 158€–197€ double; 310€ suite. AE, DC, MC, V. Parking 14€. **Amenities:** Restaurant; bar; room service; babysitting; laundry service; dry cleaning. *In room:* A/C, TV, minibar, hair dryer, safe.

MODERATE

Avenida   For those who want to be away from the center and don't mind a bus or taxi ride or two, this is a welcoming choice. It's in the Barrio de Begoña, near one of the major religious monuments of Bilbao, the Basílica de Begoña. The hotel was built in the late 1950s and its small rooms, furnished in a functional modern style, are well kept and maintained. All units contain bathrooms with tub/shower combos. During special fairs in Bilbao, rates increase by at least 10%.

Zumalacárregui 40, 48006 Bilbao. ℂ **94-412-43-00.** Fax 94-411-46-17. www.bchoteles.com. 143 units. 78€–140€ double; 113€–158€ suite. Rates include breakfast. AE, DC, MC, V. Free parking. Metro: Santutxu. **Amenities:** Restaurant; bar; room service; babysitting; laundry service; dry cleaning. *In room:* A/C, TV, minibar, hair dryer, safe.

INEXPENSIVE

Roquefer   If you'd like to stay in the old quarter and avoid the high prices of business hotels, this is a very basic choice, suitable if your main concern is only a place to lay your head. The small rooms are simple and furnished in a functional style, each with a good bed. If you're looking for any kind of amenities or extras, try another location. You'll be in the center of the *tasca* and restaurant district for nighttime prowls. To reach the hotel, take the bridge, Puente del Arenal, across the river to the old town.

Lotería 2–4, 48005 Bilbao. ℂ **94-415-07-55.** Fax 94-423-18-16. hotelripa@teleline.es. 18 units (6 with bathroom). 35€ double without bathroom; 40€ double with bathroom. No credit cards. Parking 6€. *In room:* TV.

WHERE TO DINE
EXPENSIVE

Bermeo ✦✦✦ BASQUE   One of the best hotel restaurants in all of Spain and one of the finest representatives of Basque cuisine anywhere in the world, Bermeo caters to the Basque world's most influential politicians, writers, and social luminaries. Within the modern walls of one of Bilbao's tallest hotels, the restaurant is decorated with glowing wood panels, crisp linens, and copies of 19th-century antiques. Service from the formal uniformed staff is impeccable. Menu items change with the seasons but might include a salad of lettuce hearts in saffron dressing with smoked salmon, homemade foie gras with essence of bay leaves, fresh thistles sautéed with ham, five preparations of cod, stewed partridge with glazed shallots, and duckling filets with green peppercorns. For dessert, try the truffled figs or a slice of bilberry pie with cream.

In the Gran Hotel Ercilla, Ercilla 37. ℂ **94-470-57-00.** Reservations required. Main courses 14€–27€; fixed-price menu 36€. AE, DC, MC, V. Sun–Fri 1–3:30pm; Mon–Sat 8:30–11:30pm. Closed Sat–Sun from July–Sept.

Club Náutico ✦✦✦ BASQUE/FRENCH   One of the top restaurants in the Basque world, the elegant Club Náutico is in the previously recommended Hotel López de Haro. Chef Alberto Velez is the former protégé of Alberto Zuluaga, who ran the kitchen here for years and was one of the most publicized culinary luminaries of northern Spain. The restaurant offers formal tables set with some of the finest china, crystal, and silverware. Specialties include succulent local artichokes stuffed with foie gras, poached eggs with beluga caviar and oyster sauce, lobster sautéed with artichokes and balsamic vinegar, baked sea bass with béarnaise sauce, sautéed scallops with truffle sauce, and roast beef with a purée of radishes. A superb selection of Spanish and international wines is available by either the glass or the bottle.

In the Hotel López de Haro, Obispo Orueta 2. © **94-423-55-00**. Reservations recommended. Main courses 18€–25€; fixed-price menus 29€–50€. AE, DC, MC, V. Mon–Fri 1–3:30pm; Mon–Sat 8:30–11:30pm.

Guría ⚑ BASQUE   One of Bilbao's most venerable restaurants, Guría is expensive and worth it. The chef shows care and concern for his guests by serving only market-fresh ingredients. He's celebrated for his *bacalao* (cod), which he prepares many ways. Try the sea bass with saffron or loin of beef cooked in sherry as an alternative. A slightly caloric but divine dessert is the *espuma de chocolat*. Guría is on the southern edge of one of the most monumental traffic arteries in town, 6 blocks west of Bilbao's most prominent square, the Plaza de Federico Moyúa, a block south of the sprawling Parque de Dr. Casilda Ituriza. Inside you'll find a modern decor of dark-stained wood, two dining rooms, and a monochromatic color scheme.

Gran Vía de López de Haro 66. © **94-441-85-64**. Reservations required. Main courses 18€–41€; fixed-price menu 41€–59€. AE, DC, MC, V. Mon–Sat 12:30–4pm and 9pm–midnight. Closed last week of July and first week of Aug.

Zortziko ⚑⚑⚑ BASQUE/CONTINENTAL   This is a bastion of refined cuisine and ranks near the top in all of the Basque country. It's convenient to the Guggenheim, which is a few steps away. In a multiroomed, vaguely French setting furnished in the late Victorian style, you'll find a formal environment. Lunches tend to focus on business discussions among clients; dinners tend to be more leisurely and recreational. One of the most unusual dining areas is the wine cellar, where the only table is reserved, sometimes many days in advance, by diners who appreciate the sense of being surrounded by valuable vintages. It's more likely, however, that your table will be on the restaurant's street level. In a city where the restaurant competition is fierce, this kitchen emerges at the very top. Menu items include most of the traditional Basque staples, like pigeon breast or sea bass marinated and roasted in red Rioja wine. The tasting menu presents a wide variety of Basque specialties.

Alameda de Mazarredo 17. © **94-423-97-43**. Reservations recommended. Main courses 15€–29€; set-price menu 60€. AE, V. Mon–Sat 1–3:30pm; Tues–Sat 9–11:30pm. Metro: Abando.

MODERATE

El Perro Chico ⚑ *Finds* BASQUE   In our view, this is the most unappreciated restaurant in Bilbao. It's true that the decor doesn't win any *Architectural Digest* awards. It could easily be turned into a gypsy den for telling fortunes. But patrons don't come here for that. It's the cuisine, an array of Basque classics, that counts. Many discerning celebrities have already found the place before us: Antonio Banderas, Dennis Hopper, and Jeremy Irons. Frank Gehry, architect of the Guggenheim, considers it his favorite Bilbao dining room. Start, perhaps, with the grilled fresh anchovies with a green sauce or long green peppers, which are fried and perfectly salted. Fresh tuna comes with a black liquid ink sauce from a squid that's rich and delectable. The dish of clams and artichokes would keep us coming back again and again. The hake (called *merluza*) has a natural sweetness only enhanced by the topping of a velvety béchamel sauce and scoops of freshly mashed potatoes.

Aretxaga 2. © **94-415-05-19**. Reservations required. Main courses 13€–21€. MC, V. Tues–Sat 1:30–3pm; Mon–Sat 9:15–11pm.

Etxanobe ⚑⚑ BASQUE/INTERNATIONAL   In the gleaming Palacio Euskalduna, this postmodern restaurant is the hottest dining ticket in Bilbao today. Part of the far-reaching waterfront development project, this bastion of grand cuisine is a showcase for the culinary talents of Fernando Canales. One Bilbao gourmet, whose tastes we respect, says he literally "swoons over" the innovative, tasty dishes emerging from the Canales kitchen. We didn't swoon or faint, but on our recent visit we enjoyed a rich, bountiful cuisine made from only the freshest of ingredients and handled with precision and skill among the kitchen staff. Just remembering the carpaccio of slightly unctuous crayfish (called *cigalas* locally), swirled with a robust bacon vinaigrette, makes us want to get back on the plane right away. The oxtail crépinette (a small, slightly flattened sausage) is so richly brown and succulently tasty, it's been compared to eating chocolate. Skate emerges from piping hot ovens cooked just right and covered with a porcini ravioli to die for. From the terrace is a view of the Guggenheim.

4 Av. de Abandoibarra 4. ℂ **94-442-10-23.** Reservations required. Main courses 11€–24€. AE, DC, MC, V. Mon–Sat 1:30–3:30pm and 8:30–11:30pm.

Matxinbenta ★ BASQUE   Serving some of the finest Basque food in the city since the 1950s, this restaurant is popular for business lunches or dinners. Specialties include fresh tuna in piquant tomato sauce and a local version of ratatouille known as *piperada*. You can order veal cutlets cooked in port wine and finish with a mint-flavored fresh-fruit cocktail. The service is excellent. Matxinbenta contains three dining rooms, each with contemporary furniture, potted plants, and lots of exposed wood. It's a block north of the Gran Vía, in the center of the city, adjacent to Bilbao's most visible department store, El Corte Inglés.

Ladesma 26. ℂ **94-424-84-95.** Reservations required. Main courses 15€–21€; *menú del día* 30€. AE, DC, MC, V. Daily 1–4pm; Mon–Sat 8–11:30pm.

Restaurante Guggenheim Bilbao ★★ INTERNATIONAL/BASQUE This museum is home not only to a world-class art collection but also to a world-class restaurant carved out of this architectural curiosity. The chef de cuisine, Bixenta Arrieta, is a master of *nueva cocina vasca*, and his fisherman's stew in an herb-laced green broth is award winning, as is his white salt cod with tomatoes stuffed with baby squid and black rice (colored by the squid's ink). Diners make a selection from the menu of the sea or the menu from the countryside *(del campo)*. Begin perhaps with a lobster salad or duck-stuffed cannelloni. A wide selection of Basque wines is served.

Abandoibarra Etorbidea 2. ℂ **94-423-93-33.** Reservations (as far in advance as possible). Main courses 12€–28€. AE, DC, MC, V. Tues–Sun 1:30–3:15pm; Wed–Sat 9–10:30pm. Metro: Moyúa. Bus: 1, 10, 13, or 18.

INEXPENSIVE

Aitxiar *Value* BASQUE   Well respected for its good food, low prices, and utter lack of pretension, this restaurant in the Casco Viejo serves Basque cuisine in two dining rooms in a house built in the 1930s. Expect a decor that includes lots of exposed stone and wood, a hardworking waitstaff, strong flavors, and lots of regional pride. Menu items include potato soup with chunks of fresh tuna and an array of fish hauled in that morning from nearby waters. Two of the most appealing are hake, which tastes marvelous in an herb-infused green sauce, and cod, prepared in at least two versions. Baby squid is a savory choice, as are the spicy sausages *(chuletas)*, which taste best when consumed as an appetizer.

Calle María Muñoz 8. ℂ **94-415-09-17.** Main courses 11€–30€. AE, DC, V. Wed–Mon 9am–1am. Metro: Plaza Unamuno.

Víctor Montes ★ *Finds* BASQUE/SPANISH   In the heart of Bilbao's oldest neighborhood, this restaurant maintains a handful of battered dining rooms—

some upstairs—where closely packed tables, racks of wine, and frantic waiters create a sense of good-natured hysteria, especially at lunchtime. Expect copious portions of old-fashioned roasts, stews, soups, and salads, usually with an emphasis on fresh vegetables and seafood such as grilled squid or fresh fava beans with nuggets of cod. Many locals, especially those in a hurry, tend to bypass a dining table altogether, opting for one or more *raciones* of tapas. They're lined up atop the bar, served to patrons on small plates, and taste wonderful when accompanied with sherry, wine, or beer.

Plaza Nueva 8. ⓒ **94-415-70-67.** Reservations recommended for full meals; not necessary for tapas bar. Tapas from 1.30€; main courses 12€–22€. AE, MC, V. Mon–Sat 1–3:30pm and 7:30pm–midnight. Metro: Casco Viejo.

BILBAO AFTER DARK

Basque cuisine is the finest in Spain, featuring *pintxos* (pronounced "*peen-chohs*")—tapas. The best place for tapas bars is **Calle Licenciado Poza,** between Alameda del Doctor Areilza and Calle Iparraguirre. Favorites include **Atlanta,** Calle Rodríguez Arias 28 (ⓒ **94-427-64-72**), famous locally for its *jamón Serrano* (cured ham) sandwiches, and **Busterri,** Calle Licenciado Poza 43 (ⓒ **94-441-50-67**), well known locally for its grilled anchovies and *jamón Jabugo* (a regional ham). **Gatz,** Calle Santa María 10 (ⓒ **94-415-48-61**), serves Bilbao's finest cod tartlets and their unique version of a Basque style ratatouille. The young Riojas and the crisp Navarra whites will help you wash everything down. **Café Bar Bilbao,** Plaza Nueva 6 (ⓒ **94-415-16-71**), has two tapas we delight in: silky anchovies (fresh, of course) curled around green olives and *bacalao al pil-pil* (salt cod with garlic emulsion).

During your nights in Bilbao, you might be happiest wandering through the old town's narrow alleyways, two of which (**Calle Pozas** and **Calle Barrencalle**) are dotted with all manner of bars, *tascas,* and bodegas. After a drink or two, you might opt to go out dancing, or at least visit any of three popular discos to watch how it's done in the Basque country. Favorites include **Disco Rock Star,** Gran Vía 89 (ⓒ **94-441-10-60**); **Disco-Pub Crystal,** Calle Buenos Aires 5 (no phone); and **El Palladium,** Calle Iparraguirre 11 (no phone). If you're looking for a gay bar, you'll find a scattering along the **Calle Barrencalle,** where the most popular of several nearby competitors includes **Bar Consorcio** (ⓒ **94-416-99-04**). On Friday and Saturday nights from 6:30pm to 6:30am, the bar that's jumping is **Cotton Club,** Calle Gregario de la Revilla 25 (ⓒ **94-410-49-51**), named after its early ancestor in New York's Harlem. More than 30,000 beer caps form part of the decor. A DJ spins the latest tunes for the mingling throngs in their 20s and 30s. The atmosphere is less hectic when the club is open Sunday from 6:30pm to 3am and Monday and Thursday from 4:30pm to 3am. Beer begins at 2€, whiskey at 4.50€, and there's no cover.

The boys of Bilbao (sounds like a film, doesn't it?) gather at **High Club,** Calle Naja 5 (no phone), the city's most visible gay club. Mostly young males show up here, but some women appear nightly as well. In the main room, Spanish dance music is played, and in a small theater upstairs, XXX-rated films are shown. There's a hyperactive "dark room" in the back.

The major cultural venue in Bilbao is the **Teatro Arriaga,** Plaza Arriaga s/n (ⓒ **94-479-20-56**), on the banks of the Nervión River. This is the setting for world-class opera, classical music concerts, ballet, and even *zarzuelas* (comic operas). Announcements of cultural events at the time of your visit are available at the tourist office (see "Visitor Information," earlier in this section).

5 Vitoria ⭑

66km (41 miles) S of Bilbao, 114km (71 miles) SW of San Sebastián, 351km (218 miles) N of Madrid

Quiet and sleepy until the early 1980s, **Vitoria** was chosen as headquarters of the Basque region's autonomous government. In honor of that occasion, it revived the name Gasteiz, by which it was known when founded in 1181 by King Sancho of Navarre. Far more enduring, however, has been the name Vitoria, a battle site revered by the English. On June 21, 1813, Wellington won here against the occupying forces of Napoléon. A statue dedicated to the Iron Duke stands today on the neoclassical Plaza de la Virgen Blanca.

Shortly after its founding, the city became a rich center for the wool and iron trades, and this wealth paid for the fine churches and palaces in the medieval quarter. Many of the city's buildings are made of gray-gold stone. Local university students keep the taverns rowdy until the wee hours.

ESSENTIALS

GETTING THERE   The **Aeropuerto Vitoria-Foronda** (© 94-516-35-00) is 8km (5 miles) northwest of the town center and has direct air links to Madrid on Iberia Airlines. For flight information, call **Iberia** at © 94-516-36-37 daily from 6am to 11pm.

From San Sebastián, seven to nine **trains** daily make the 2-hour trip to Vitoria. For information, call © 90-224-02-02. From San Sebastián, roughly four **buses** daily make the 1½-hour trip. Bus connections are also possible through Bilbao (8–12 buses daily make the 1-hr. trip).

Take the E-5 north from Madrid to Burgos, cutting northwest until you see the turnoff for Vitoria. (Note that along its more northerly stretches this super-highway is identified as both E-5 and A-1.)

VISITOR INFORMATION   The **tourist office,** at Plaza General Loma 1 (© 94-516-15-98), is open daily from 9am to 1pm and 3 to 7pm.

SPECIAL EVENTS   One of the major jazz festivals in the north of Spain takes place here annually in mid-July. It's the weeklong **Festival de Jazz de Vitoria-Gasteiz.** For the big-name performers, tickets range from 4€ to 12€, but spontaneous entertainment takes place on the street for free, although donations are appreciated. The tourist office can supply complete details.

EXPLORING VITORIA

The most important sight in Vitoria is the **medieval district** ⭑, whose Gothic buildings were constructed on a series of steps and terraces. Most of the streets, arranged in concentric ovals, are named after medieval artisan guilds. The northern end is marked by the Catedral de Santa María, its southern flank by the Iglesia de San Miguel.

One of the most interesting streets in the *barrio* is **Calle Cuchillaría,** which contains many medieval buildings. You can enter the courtyard at number 24, the **Casa del Cordón,** which was constructed in different stages from the 13th to the 16th century. Number 58, the **Bendana Palace,** built in the 15th century, has a fine ornate staircase set into its courtyard.

Catedral de Santa María (the "old" cathedral), Calle Fray Zacaras (© 94-525-51-35), was built in the 14th century in the Gothic style. It contains a good art collection, with paintings that imitate various schools, including those of Van Dyck, Caravaggio, and Rubens, as well as several tombs carved in a highly decorated Plateresque style. Santa María is at the northern edge of the old town.

The cathedral is closed for general visits not arranged in advance because of oncoming renovations, which may last for several years to come. However, you can call the number above and ask to be included in a group, as only group visits are allowed. Such tours are possible daily from 11am to 1pm and 5 to 7pm, costing 2€. Groups can be made up spontaneously if enough people are interested. For more details contact the tourist office (see above).

This cathedral is not to be confused with the town's enormous neo-Gothic "new cathedral," the **Catedral María Inmaculada,** Cadena y Eleta s/n (© **94-515-06-31**), just north of the Jardines la Florida. This cathedral is from the 20th century and can be skipped, although on-site is its **Diocesan Museum of Sacred Art,** a small but choice collection of ecclesiastical paintings gathered from various churches, including a minor work by El Greco. The cathedral is open Monday through Saturday from 11am to 2pm, charging no admission. The museum can be visited Tuesday through Friday from 10am to 2pm and 4 to 6:30pm, Saturday from 10am to 2pm, and Sunday from 11am to 2pm, also charging no admission.

The major historic square is the **Plaza de la Virgen Blanca,** a short walk south of the medieval quarter. Its neoclassical balconies overlook the statue of Wellington. The square is named after the late-Gothic polychrome statue of the Virgen Blanca (the town's patron) that adorns the portico of the 13th-century **Church of San Miguel,** which stands on the square's upper edge. The 17th-century altarpiece inside was carved by Gregorio Fernández. The church is open Monday through Friday from 11am to 3pm.

At the **Plaza de España** (also known as the Plaza Nueva), a satellite square a short walk away, the student population of Vitoria congregates to drink.

Vitoria has some minor museums, which are free. The **Museo de Arqueología de Alava,** Correría 116 (© **94-518-19-22**), behind a half-timbered facade, exhibits artifacts such as pottery shards and statues unearthed from digs in the area. Some of these date from Celto-Iberian days; others are from the Roman era. The museum is open Tuesday through Friday from 10am to 2pm and 4 to 6:30pm, Saturday from 10am to 2pm.

The **Museo de Bellas Artes de Alava,** Palacio de Agustín, Paseo de Fray Francisco 8 (© **94-518-19-18**), has a collection of several unusual weapons, a *Crucifixion* and portraits of Saints Peter and Paul by José Ribera, and a triptych by the Master of Avila. It's open Tuesday through Friday from 10am to 2pm and 4 to 6:30pm, Saturday from 10am to 2pm and 5 to 8pm, and Sunday from 11am to 2pm and 5 to 8pm.

WHERE TO STAY
EXPENSIVE

Hotel Barceló Gasteiz ★★   On the eastern flank of the broad, tree-lined boulevard that circumnavigates the old town, this is the most modern hotel around. Built in 1982, it was completely renovated in 1994. Although not architecturally distinguished, it serves as the preferred meeting point for the city's business community, offering good-size conservative rooms with uncomplicated furnishings and a series of comfortable (albeit not dramatic) public rooms. The tiled bathrooms are state-of-the-art, and each is equipped with a tub/shower combo.

Av. Gasteiz 45, 01009 Vitoria. © **94-522-81-00.** Fax 94-522-62-58. www.barceloclavelhoteles.com. 150 units. 99€–146€ double; 166€ suite. AE, DC, MC, V. Parking 11€. **Amenities:** Restaurant; bar; car rental; room service; babysitting; laundry service; dry cleaning. *In room:* A/C, TV, minibar, hair dryer.

MODERATE

Hotel General Alava ✰ Named after a local hero—a Spanish general who won an important battle against the French in 1815—this hotel is one of the best and most comfortably furnished in town. The rooms range from small to medium, each fitted with a small tiled bathroom with a shower stall. Built in 1975, it attracts scores of business travelers from throughout Spain. The hotel is a 10-minute walk west of the town center, near the junction of Calle Chile.

Gasteiz 79, 01009 Vitoria. ✆ **94-521-50-00.** Fax 94-524-83-95. www.sercotel.es. 114 units. 109€ double, breakfast included; 210€ suite. AE, DC, MC, V. Parking 9.50€. **Amenities:** Restaurant; bar; laundry service; dry cleaning. *In room:* A/C, TV, minibar, hair dyer, safe.

INEXPENSIVE

Achuri This attractively priced modern hotel provides a friendly welcome. A short walk from the train station, it offers tidy and comfortably furnished but small rooms and bathrooms equipped with tub/shower combos. Breakfast is the only meal available (and is not included in the room rates), but you'll find several places serving food in the vicinity.

Rioja 11, 01005 Vitoria. ✆ **94-525-58-00.** Fax 94-526-40-74. 40 units. 47€ double; 57€ triple. AE, DC, MC, V. **Amenities:** Laundry service; dry cleaning. *In room:* TV.

Hotel Dato ✰ *Finds* Three blocks south of the southern extremity of the old town in the pedestrian zone, this hotel is the best budget accommodation. It's known for its original regional decor. The rooms, ranging from small to medium, are well decorated, often with quite a bit of style, and each comes with a bathroom with a tub/shower combo. No breakfast is served.

Eduardo Dato 28, 01005 Vitoria. ✆ **94-514-72-30.** Fax 94-523-23-20. www.hoteldato.com. 41 units. 39€ double. AE, DC, MC, V. Parking meters on street. *In room:* TV, hair dryer.

WHERE TO DINE

As in Bilbao, *tasca* hopping before dinner with the consumption of many small glasses *(chiquiteos)* of beer or wine at many different bars and taverns is very popular and fun for visitors to Vitoria. There are a number of places on Avenida de Gasteiz.

El Portalón ✰✰ BASQUE This is the finest and most interesting restaurant in town. It was built in the late 1400s as a tavern and post office near what was, at the time, one of the only bridges leading in and out of Vitoria. Rich with patina and a sense of history, the restaurant prides itself on serving extremely fresh fish from the nearby Gulf of Biscay, always prepared in traditional style. Cream and butter are rarely used. Menu items include a salad of endive with shellfish, vegetarian crepes, a traditional hake dish known as *merluza koxkera,* ragout of fish and/or shellfish, and many variations of monkfish, turbot, and eel.

Correría 151. ✆ **94-514-27-55.** Reservations recommended. Main courses 14€–20€; fixed-price menu 20€. AE, DC, MC, V. Mon–Sat 1–4pm and 9–11pm. Closed Aug 10–Sept 1.

Mesa *Value* BASQUE For price and value, this ranks as one of the most worthwhile restaurants in town. You can partake of a number of Basque specialties, none better than the notable *merluza* (hake), the fish so beloved by Basque chefs. Fresh fish and a well-chosen selection of meats are presented nightly. The service is attentive. The setting is solid, sober, and severely dignified, with white walls and wood trim, and tables and chairs stained dark in the Iberian style.

Chile 1. ✆ **94-522-84-94.** Reservations recommended. Main courses 7€–13€; *menú de la casa* 15€. AE, MC, V. Thurs–Tues 1:30–3:30pm and 9–11:30pm. Closed Aug 10–Sept 10.

17

Cantabria & Asturias

The provinces of Cantabria and Asturias are historic lands that lay claim to attractions ranging from fishing villages along the coastlines to the Picos de Europa, a magnificent stretch of snowcapped mountains.

Cantabria was settled in prehistoric times and later colonized by the Romans. The Muslims were less successful in their invasion. Protected by the mountains, many Christians found refuge here during the long centuries of Moorish domination. Much religious architecture remains from this period, particularly Romanesque. Cantabria was once part of the Castilla y León district of Spain, but is now an autonomous region with its own government.

Most tourism is confined to the northern coastal strip; much of the inland mountainous area is poor and unpopulated. If you venture away from the coast, you usually need a rental car because public transport is inadequate at best. **Santander,** a rail terminus, makes the best center for touring the region; it also has the most tourist facilities. From Santander, you can get nearly anywhere in the province within a 3-hour drive.

The principality of Asturias lies between Cantabria in the east and Galicia in the west. It reaches its scenic (and topographical) summit in the **Picos de Europa,** where the first Spanish national park was inaugurated. With green valleys, fishing villages, and forests, Asturias is a land for all seasons.

The coastline of Asturias constitutes one of the major sightseeing attractions in northern Spain. Called the **Costa Verde,** it begins in the east at San Vicente de la Barquera and stretches almost 145km (90 miles) to Gijón. Allow about 6 hours to drive it without stops. The western coast, beginning at Gijón, goes all the way to Ribadeo, a border town with Galicia—a distance of 180km (112 miles). This rocky coastline, studded with fishing villages and containing narrow estuaries and small beaches, is one of the most spectacular stretches of scenery in Spain. It takes all day to explore.

Asturias is an ancient land, as prehistoric cave paintings in the area demonstrate. Iron Age Celtic tribes resisted the Romans, as Asturians proudly point out to this day. They also resisted the Moors, who subjugated the rest of Spain. The Battle of Covadonga in 722 represented the Moors' first major setback after their arrival in Iberia 11 years previously.

Asturians are still staunchly independent. In 1934, Francisco Franco, then an ambitious young general, arrived with his Moroccan troops to suppress an uprising by miners who had declared an independent Socialist republic. His Nationalist forces returned again and again to destroy such Asturian cities as Gijón for their fierce resistance during the Spanish Civil War.

1 Laredo

60km (37 miles) W of Bilbao, 48km (30 miles) E of Santander, 427km (265 miles) N of Madrid

To an American, "the streets of Laredo" means the gun-slinging Old West. To a Spaniard it means an ancient maritime town on the eastern Cantabrian coast that has been turned into a major summer resort, with hundreds of apartments and villas along its 5km (3 miles) of beach. Playa de la Salvé is to the west and Playa de Oriñón is to the east.

The medieval quarter, the **Puebla Vieja,** retains the traditional atmosphere of Laredo. It was walled on the orders of Alfonso VIII of Castile, who wanted to protect the town from pirate raids along the coast. The hillside **Iglesia de la Asunción,** dating from the 13th century, overlooks the harbor. It has five naves and rather bizarre capitals.

If you're driving west to Santoña, note the big monument honoring native son Juan de la Cosa, the cartographer who sailed with Columbus on his first voyage to America.

ESSENTIALS

GETTING THERE   From Bilbao, head west along the coastal highway (identified at various points as the A-8 or the E-70), and follow the signs to Laredo.

Bus service is available from both Bilbao and Santander. The station is in the town center at the Av. de José Antonio s/n (© **94-260-49-67**). There are at least 20 buses per day coming into Laredo from Bilbao, and as many as 24 per day coming into Laredo from Santander. Travel time to Laredo from Bilbao is 40 minutes, and the one-way fare is 3€. Travel time from Santander is 30 minutes, and the one-way fare is 2.65€.

VISITOR INFORMATION   The **tourist information office,** Alameda de Miramar s/n (© **94-261-10-96;** www.ayuntamientolaredo.com), is open daily from 9am to 2pm and 5 to 7pm.

SPECIAL EVENTS   On the last Friday of August, the annual **Battle of Flowers** draws thousands of visitors to watch bloom-adorned floats parade through the old town.

WHERE TO STAY

El Ancla del Laredo   Although hardly a thrill, this is the best place to stay in the area. In a residential area a short stroll from the beach, this hotel has operated successfully since 1965. The architectural style evokes an English chalet, and the interior is cozy, with nautical motifs and paraphernalia of the sea (*ancla* means "anchor"). Rooms are also equipped with bathrooms containing tub/shower combos. The decoration is light and airy with wooden beams and fittings, along with rattan furniture and carpeted floors.

Calle González Gallego 10, 39770 Laredo. © **94-260-55-00.** Fax 94-261-16-02. 40 units. 70€–108€ double; 86€–126€ suite. AE, DC, MC, V. Free parking. **Amenities:** Restaurant; bar; room service; babysitting; laundry service; dry cleaning. *In room:* TV, minibar, hair dryer, safe.

Risco   On a hillside overlooking Laredo, .8km (½ mile) southeast of the center of town, this aging 1960s hotel opens onto impressive views of the old town and of one of the nearby beaches. It offers simple, functionally furnished rooms, each clean and comfortable with a bathroom equipped with a tub/shower combo. In the garden are scattered tables for food service (see the restaurant recommendation below).

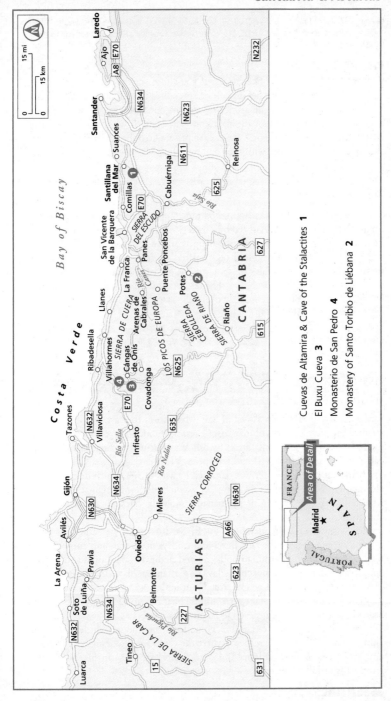

Cuevas de Altamira & Cave of the Stalactites **1**

El Buxu Cueva **3**

Monasterio de San Pedro **4**

Monastery of Santo Toribio de Liébana **2**

La Arenosa 2, 39770 Laredo. © 94-260-50-30. Fax 94-260-50-55. 26 units. 80€–103€ double; 103€–120€ suite. Rates include breakfast. AE, DC, MC, V. Free parking. **Amenities:** Restaurant; bar; room service; laundry service; dry cleaning. *In room:* TV.

WHERE TO DINE

Camarote SEAFOOD   The owner of Camarote (in the center of town) is Felipe Manjarrés, and his chef de cuisine specializes in seafood, especially fresh fish. The decor is tasteful and attractive, and the outdoor terrace makes a pleasant alternative to the indoor dining room. The spinach with crayfish and the cheese tarts are truly excellent. Original recipes are used for salads with ham and shrimp as well as for those with tuna and fresh fruit. Try the grilled sea bream or a filet steak Rossini.

Av. Vitoria s/n. © 94-260-67-07. Reservations recommended. Main courses 15€–18€. AE, DC, MC, V. Daily 1–4pm and 9pm–midnight.

Risco ★ SEAFOOD   This is Laredo's most appealing restaurant, known for innovative seafood dishes. Assisted by a battery of helpers, the chef prepares such items as marinated salmon with pink peppercorns, scrambled eggs with lobster, and peppers stuffed with minced pigs' trotters or crabmeat. For dessert, try a fresh-fruit sorbet. Some tables are set up in the garden, or you can dine in a traditional room with views of the sea. The restaurant is on the ground floor of the Risco hotel (see "Where to Stay," above). It's closed on Monday, except during the busy months of July and August.

La Arenosa 2. © 94-260-50-30. Reservations recommended. Main courses 12€–16€; *menú del día* 12€–22€. AE, DC, MC, V. Tues–Sun 1–3:30pm and 8:30–11pm; Mon 1–3:30pm and 8:30–11pm, July and Aug only.

2 Santander ★

393km (244 miles) N of Madrid, 116km (72 miles) NW of Bilbao

Santander has always been a rival of San Sebastián in the east, but it has never attained the premier status of that Basque resort. It did, however, become a royal residence from 1913 to 1930, after city officials presented an English-style Magdalena Palace to Alfonso XIII and his queen, Victoria Eugenia.

An ancient city, Santander was damaged by a 1941 fire, which destroyed the old quarter and most of its dwellings. It was rebuilt along original lines, with wide boulevards, a waterfront promenade, sidewalk cafes, shops, restaurants, and hotels.

Most visitors to Santander head for **El Sardinero** ★★, a resort less than 2.5km (1½ miles) from the city. Buses and trolleys make the short run between the city center and El Sardinero both day and night. Besides hotels and restaurants, Santander has three **beaches,** Playa de Castaneda, Playa del Sardinero, and Playa de la Concha, where people stretch out under candy-striped umbrellas. If they become too crowded, take a 15-minute boat ride to **El Puntal,** a beautiful beach that is rarely crowded, even in August.

If you don't like crowds or beaches, go up to the lighthouse, a little more than 2km (1¼ miles) from El Sardinero, where the views are wide-ranging. A restaurant serves snacks both indoors and outdoors. Here, you can hike along the green cliffs or loll in the grass.

ESSENTIALS

GETTING THERE   Daily flights from Madrid and Barcelona land at Aeropuerto de Santander (© 94-220-21-00), a little more than 6.5km (4 miles)

from the town center, accessible by taxi only, costing 12€. The local office of **Iberia** is at Paseo de Pereda 18 (© **94-222-97-00**).

There are three **trains** daily from Madrid (trip time: 7 hr.); a one-way fare costs 42€. Four trains a day travel from Bilbao (3 hr.). For rail information, call © **90-224-02-02**.

Buses arrive at Plaza Estaciones (© **94-221-19-95**). There are 24 connections a day to and from Bilbao (trip time: 2 hr.); a one-way ticket costs 6€ to 9€. Six to nine buses a day arrive from Madrid (6 hr.), costing from 27€.

N-634 continues west from Laredo to Santander, with an N-635 turnoff to reach the resort.

VISITOR INFORMATION   The **tourist information office** is at Jardines de Pereda (© **94-220-30-00**; www.ayto-santander.es). It's open Monday through Friday from 9am to 1pm and 4 to 7pm, Saturday from 9am to 1pm.

SPECIAL EVENTS   The **Music and Dance Festival** in August is one of the most important artistic events in Spain (accommodations are very hard to come by during this time). Occasionally, this festival coincides with religious celebrations honoring Santiago (St. James), the patron saint of Spain. Santander is an education center in summer as well. Courses are offered at the once-royal palace, now the Menéndez Pelayo International University. Students and teachers from North America and Europe come here to study and enjoy the area.

EXPLORING SANTANDER

Biblioteca Menéndez y Pelayo   Located in the same building as the Municipal Museum is this 45,000-volume library amassed by Menéndez y Pelayo and left to Santander upon his death in 1912. Guided tours are available. Opposite the building is the Casa Museo, which displays this great man's study and shows how modestly he lived.

Calle Rubio 6. © **94-223-45-34**. Free admission. Mon–Fri 9:30–11:30am and 4–9:30pm.

Catedral   Greatly damaged in the 1941 fire, this restored fortresslike 13th-century cathedral holds the tomb of historian/writer Marcelino Menéndez y Pelayo (1856–1912), Santander's most illustrious man of letters. The 12th-century crypt with a trio of low-slung aisles, untouched by fire, can be entered through the south portico. The Gothic cloister was restored after the fire. Roman ruins were discovered beneath the north aisle in 1983.

Somorrostro s/n. © **94-222-60-24**. Free admission. Daily 10am–1pm and 4–7:30pm.

Museo Municipal de Bellas Artes   Located near the Ayuntamiento (Town Hall), the Municipal Museum of Fine Arts has some interesting Goya paintings, notably his portrait of Ferdinand VII, commissioned by the city, and his series of etchings called *Disasters of War*. You can see some of his continuing series of *Caprichos* (Whims). See also Zurbarán's *Mystic Scene* and an array of works by Flemish, Spanish, and Italian artists, many of them contemporary.

Calle Rubio 6. © **94-223-94-85**. Free admission. Mon–Fri 10am–1pm and 5–8pm; Sat 10am–1pm.

Museo Regional de Prehistoria y Arqueología de Cantabria ✪   This museum has some interesting artifacts discovered in the Cantabrian province—not only Roman but also some unusual prehistoric finds. Since it is unlikely you'll be allowed to visit the Cuevas de Altamira (see "Santillana del Mar & Cuevas de Altamira," below), come here to see objects and photographs from these prehistoric caves with their remarkable paintings. Some of the items on display date from 15,000 years ago.

Calle Casimiro Sáinz 4. ✆ **94-220-71-09**. Free admission. June 16–Sept 16 Tues–Sat 10am–1pm and 4–7pm, Sun 11am–2pm; Sept 17–June 15 Tues–Sat 9am–1pm and 4–7pm, Sun 11am–2pm.

SHOPPING

True aficionados of pottery and the nuances of ceramics usually drive from Santander to **Santillana del Mar,** 29km (18 miles) away, where handcrafted ceramics are in great abundance. But if you want to see a pared-down version of what's available in Santillana del Mar yet stay within Santander's city limits, head for any of the retailers on the Calle Arrabal, in the city's commercial center. One of the most promising of them is **La Muralla,** Calle Arrabal 17 (no phone).

An antiques gallery richly stocked with old furniture and paintings with rich veneers is **Fundación Marcellino Botín,** Calle Pedrueca 1 (✆ **94-222-60-72**). Ironically, many of the boutiques and stores of Santander aren't in the city at all but within a 50-unit shopping center 3km (2 miles) from town, beside the road leading to the airport. Check out the **Centro Comercial Valle Real,** Carretera Bilbao, Km 2.

WHERE TO STAY

Santander is loaded with good-value hotels, from its year-round city hotels to its summer villas at El Sardinero. It gets crowded, so try to reserve well in advance.

IN TOWN

Hotel Central ★ *Finds*   The blue beaux arts facade of this hotel, built around 1900, is one of the most attractive and ornate in its neighborhood. Inside, the hotel is known for its original decor and cozy atmosphere. The rooms are midsize and done in a comfortable modern style, with many cozy, homelike touches like bedside reading lamps and armchairs. All units come equipped with bathrooms containing tub/shower combos. The location is about a block from the Plaza Fortificada and the sea-fronting Jardines de Pereda.

General Mola 5, 39004 Santander. ✆ **94-222-24-00**. Fax 94-236-38-29. www.elcentral.com. 41 units. 74€–106€ double; 122€–177€ suite. Discounts offered some weekends, depending on bookings. AE, DC, MC, V. Free parking. **Amenities:** Restaurant; bar; room service; babysitting; laundry service; dry cleaning. *In room:* A/C, TV, hair dryer.

Hotel México ★ *Value*   Only a block from the rail station, this is one of your best budget bets in the heart of the city, ideal for those without transportation who don't want to range far afield of the hotel, especially if they have luggage. The exterior may not be too enticing, but the atmosphere improves inside this family-operated inn. Even though it's in a congested area, street noises seem at a minimum, and the midsize rooms are well cared for and comfortably furnished, with bathrooms, which for the most part are equipped with tub/shower combos. Often the rooms are in the old-fashioned architectural style of northern Spain, with glassed-in balconies and tall ceilings. Breakfast is offered in a formal room with Queen Anne chairs and oak wainscoting.

Calderón de la Barca 3, 39002 Santander. ✆ **94-221-24-50**. Fax 94-222-92-38. www.hotel-mexico.com. 32 units. 72€–104€ double. MC, V. Free parking. **Amenities:** Restaurant; bar; room service; laundry service; dry cleaning. *In room:* TV, hair dryer.

NH Ciudad de Santander ★   About 8 blocks north of Santander's busiest seaside promenade (Paseo de Pereda) in the center of the city's commercial heartland, this white-sided five-story rectangular hotel dates from 1989. Although this is the best hotel in the city itself, for true luxury check into Hotel Real at El Sardinero (see below). A big-windowed lobby here has marble floors, honey-colored wooden paneling, and modern accessories. The midsize rooms are monochromatic, similar to the lobby, with fully equipped bathrooms equipped with tub/shower combos and convenient writing desks.

Menéndez Pelayo 13–15, 39006 Santander. ✆ **94-222-79-65.** Fax 94-221-73-03. www.nh-hoteles.es. 62 units. 105€–180€ double; 135€–196€ suite. AE, DC, MC, V. Parking 10€ outdoors; 8€ indoors. Bus: 5. **Amenities:** Restaurant; bar; car rental; room service; laundry service; dry cleaning. *In room:* A/C, TV, minibar, hair dryer, safe.

AT EL SARDINERO

Hotel Real ★★★   A grande dame, this is the most splendid and luxurious hotel in the entire area. Architecturally noteworthy—it was the first building in the region constructed of reinforced concrete—the Real was built in 1917 to house the entourage of courtiers who accompanied King Alfonso XIII on his midsummer vacations to Santander. Purchased and completely renovated by the prestigious HUSA chain in 1987, it is once again one of the most elegant hotels in northern Spain, filled with updated reminders of a more gracious age. Located about 3km (2 miles) east of the commercial center of town, near the site of the Royal Palace on a hillside above the Magdalena Beach, the Real contains richly conservative and spacious rooms, most with views of the sea and all with many comforts including a bathroom containing a tub/shower combo.

Paseo Pérez Galdós 28, 39005 Santander. ✆ **94-227-25-50.** Fax 94-227-45-73. www.hotelreal.es. 121 units. 167€–275€ double; from 343€–899€ suite. AE, DC, MC, V. Free parking. Bus: 1, 2, 5, or 7. **Amenities:** Restaurant; bar; room service; babysitting; laundry service; dry cleaning. *In room:* A/C, TV, minibar, hair dryer.

Las Brisas   A mansion from the 1920s, this building has been successfully converted into a well-run family style hotel by Teresa and Jesús Garcia, the friendly and hospitable owners. It's like an upmarket cottage style hotel opening onto the often chilly waters of northern Spain. Of all the hotels in town, Las Brisas features rooms in the widest range of sizes, from those more suited to one person to large family-size duplexes. Flowery curtains and blankets and dark wood furniture predominate. All the rooms are well maintained and come with small bathrooms with tubs and showers. Try if available for one of the accommodations with views over the water. The cozy breakfast room is a snug retreat.

Calle la Braña 14, 39005 Santander. ✆ **94-227-00-91.** Fax 942-281173. 13 units. 50€–100€ double; 65€–100€ triple. AE, DC, MC, V. Parking 10€. **Amenities:** Laundry/dry cleaning, breakfast room. *In room:* TV, coffeemaker.

Palacio del Mar ★   One of the city's most modern hotels dates from the mid-1990s when it was built near the La Sardinero beaches, a short drive north of Santander's commercial core. The decor features a sinuous series of postmodern lines that might have been inspired by a Joan Miró painting, accented with winding staircases and walls made from glass blocks. Each of the spacious accommodations is a suite, with comfortable and contemporary-looking furniture, three phone extensions, and cheerful upholstery. All rooms contain bathrooms equipped with tub/shower combos.

Av. de Cantabria 5, El Sardinero, 39012 Santander. ✆ **94-239-24-00.** Fax 94-239-22-20. 67 units. 144€–198€ double; 156€–276€ suite. Extra bed 36€ adults, 18€ children. AE, DC, MC, V. Parking 9€. **Amenities:** Restaurant; bar; room service; babysitting; laundry service; dry cleaning. *In room:* A/C, TV, minibar, hair dryer, safe.

WHERE TO DINE

Most visitors to Santander dine at their hotels or boardinghouses, which sometimes offer better value for the money and more efficient service than city restaurants. For variety, however, here are a few suggestions.

IN TOWN

Bodega Cigaleña REGIONAL   Popular with the young set in Santander, this Castilian bodega in the city center serves typical regional cuisine in a rustic setting amid hanging hams, large wine kegs, and provincial tables. The set menu changes every day. A sample meal might be *sopa de pescado* (fish soup), shellfish paella, fruit of the season, bread, and wine. The Cigaleña offers a good choice of wines from an old Castilian town near Valladolid. Ask to see its Museo del Vino.

Daoiz y Velarde 19. © **94-221-30-62.** Main courses 10€–22€; fixed-price menu 26€. AE, DC, MC, V. Mon–Sat noon–4pm and 8pm–midnight. Closed June 20–July 1 and Oct 20–Nov 20. Bus: 5.

Bodega del Riojano RIOJAN   Dating from the 1500s, this was once a wine cellar, the evidence of which can still be seen today in its time-blackened wooden beams and old tables. Locals call the bodega the "Round Museum" (Museo Redondo), because of its display of paintings on the ends of old wine barrels used in the decoration. Since 1940 this has been one of the favorite local taverns for both food and drink. Dishes are frequently changed on the menu—in fact they're adjusted daily and there are major seasonal variations. Your most reliable and consistent main dish is based on the local catch of the day. The fresh fish can be grilled or else baked to your specifications. Succulent pork chops also emerge fresh from the grill. One of the best dishes likely to be featured is sweet red peppers stuffed with ground meat. Codfish is also baked in a zesty tomato sauce, and the desserts are homemade daily.

Rio de la Pila 5. © **94-221-67-50.** Reservations recommended. Main courses 9€–14€. AE, DC, MC, V. Tues–Sun 1:30–4pm and 8:30pm–midnight. No dinner Sun Oct–May.

Zacarías ★★ *Finds* CANTABRIAN/SPANISH   Zacarías Puente Herboso is the best-known chef in Santander. Although a geologist by profession, his growing interest in gourmet food led to his opening of this first-class restaurant. As a well-known food writer, he is the local authority on Cantabrian recipes, which he fashions to his own desires and specifications instead of slavishly following the originals. The fresh flavors of the local countryside are enticingly showcased here. Try perhaps his fisherman's stew, a delectable kettle made with *merluza* (hake), clams, and potatoes. His *alubia rojas* (red beans with sausage) is another favorite. Yet another dish that enjoys local renown is *guiso pescadores,* boiled potatoes sautéed in garlic, olive oil, onion, fresh parsley, and red chile peppers. Nothing is quite as alluring as his *manganos encebollados* or calamari and caramelized onion. Hake also appears delightfully in a green sauce with fresh mussels.

General Mola 41. © **94-221-23-33.** Reservations required. Main courses 17€–24€. AE, DC, MC, V. Daily 1–4pm and 8pm–12:30am.

AT EL SARDINERO

La Sardina de Plata ★ SEAFOOD   In a warren of small streets in the center of the old city, this nautically designed restaurant serves imaginative cuisine highlighted by delicate sauces. Selections might include such enticing dishes as cheese mousse, beef filet with truffles and cognac, or a succulent fish salad. There is an extensive wine list. The service is courteous and efficient.

Doctor Fleming 3–4. © **94-227-10-35.** Reservations required. Main courses 13€–20€. AE, DC, MC, V. Tues–Sun 1:30–4pm; Tues–Sat 8:30pm–midnight. Closed Jan 7–Feb 7. Bus: 1, 2, 5, or 7.

SANTANDER AFTER DARK

The most exciting thing to do in the evening is to head for the gaming tables of the **Gran Casino del Sardinero,** Plaza de Italia (© **94-227-60-54**), which has a cover charge of 3€. It's open daily from 8pm to 4am; be sure to bring your passport for entry. In the same complex is a bar/restaurant/cafe called **Lisboa** (© **94-227-10-20**), a good place to celebrate your winnings or try to forget what you've lost. It serves moderately priced meals, and some locals even drop in for breakfast. In summer it's especially crowded. It's open daily from 9am to 2am.

3 Santillana del Mar (★(★ & Cuevas de Altamira (★(★

29km (18 miles) SW of Santander, 393km (244 miles) N of Madrid

THE VILLAGE OF SANTILLANA

Among the most perfectly preserved medieval villages in Europe, **Santillana del Mar,** a Spanish national landmark, was once a famous place of pilgrimage. A monastery housed the relics of St. Juliana, a martyr in Asia Minor who refused to surrender her virginity to her husband. Pilgrims, especially the *grandees* of Castile, came to worship at this site. The name *Santillana* is a contraction of "Santa Juliana." The "del Mar" is misleading, as Santillana is not on the water but inland.

Jean-Paul Sartre called Santillana "the prettiest village in Spain," and we wouldn't want to dispute his esteemed judgment. In spite of all the tour buses, Santillana still retains its medieval atmosphere and is very much a village of dairy farmers to this day.

Wander on foot throughout the village, taking in its principal sites, including **Plaza de Ramón Pelayo** (sometimes called Plaza Mayor). Here the Parador de Santillana (see below) has been installed in the old Barreda Bracho residence.

A 15th-century tower, facing Calle de Juan Infante, is known for its pointed arched doorway. A walk along Calle de las Lindas (Street of Beautiful Women) may not live up to its promise, but it does include many of the oldest buildings in Santillana and two towers dating from the 14th and 15th centuries. Calle del Río gets its name from a stream running through town to a central fountain.

ESSENTIALS

GETTING THERE   La Cantábrica (© **94-272-08-22**) operates six buses a day from Santander but cuts back to four between September and June. Trip time is 45 minutes.

By **car,** take the N-611 out of Santander to reach the C-6316 cutoff to Santillana.

VISITOR INFORMATION   The **tourist information office** is at Plaza Mayor (© **94-281-82-51;** www.turismo.cantabria.org). Hours are Monday through Saturday from 9:30am to 1pm and 4 to 7pm, Sunday from 10am to 1pm.

EXPLORING SANTILLANA

Visit the 800-year-old cathedral, the **Colegiata de Santillana** (★, Calle Santo Domingo (© **94-281-80-04**), which shelters the tomb of the village's patron saint, Juliana, and walk through its ivy-covered cloister. Other treasures displayed are 1,000-year-old documents and a 17th-century Mexican silver altarpiece. It's open April through October daily from 9:30am to 1pm and 4 to 7:30pm; off season daily from 10am to 1pm and 4 to 6pm. Admission, including entrance to the Convent of the Poor Clares, is 2.50€.

At the other end of the main street, the 400-year-old Convento de Regina Coelí, also called the **Convent of the Poor Clares** (Museo Diocesano; © **94-281-80-04**), houses a rich art collection inspired by a Madrid art professor who encouraged the nuns to collect and restore religious paintings and statues damaged or abandoned during the Spanish Civil War. The collection is constantly expanding. It's open daily from 10am to 2pm and 4 to 7:30pm (closing at 6pm in winter). Admission is 2.50€.

WHERE TO STAY
Moderate

Parador de Santillana Gil Blas/Parador de Santillana del Mar ★★
The best place to stay in town is at either of these two paradors. Although they occupy the same address and even the same telephone number, they are two different hotels, each with 28 units. The most expensive and with the better rooms is the government-rated four-star Parador de Santillana Gil Blas, followed by the government-rated three-star Parador de Santillana del Mar. Both hotels occupy a 400-year-old former palace filled with modern extensions. The twin paradors are filled with many antiques and have hand-hewn plank floors, old brass, chandeliers, and refectory tables. Large portraits of knights in armor hang in the main gallery. Most of the guest rooms are large, with antiques and windows on two sides, some opening onto views of a garden. Bathrooms have tub/shower combos. Several rooms in the three-star parador are much smaller (these tend to be on the top floor).

Plaza de Ramón Pelayo 8, 39300 Santillana del Mar. © **94-281-80-00.** Fax 94-281-83-91. www.parador.es. 56 units. Parador de Santillana del Mar: 95€–110€ double; 155€ suite. Parador Santillana Gil Blas: 126€–139€ double; 158€ suite. AE, DC, MC, V. Free parking. **Amenities:** Restaurant; bar; room service; babysitting; laundry service; dry cleaning. *In room:* A/C, TV, minibar, hair dryer, safe.

Inexpensive

Casa del Marqués ★★   Other than the town's two-in-one parador, this *antigua casa sensorial* or old manor house is the second best place to stay. It houses you in style, comfort, and atmosphere in the heart of town near Plaza Mayor. The present building stands on the foundation of a manor dating from the 12th century. Dripping with antiquity, the building still has its old stone walls. The midsize bedrooms are furnished comfortably but with a kind of rustic decoration to honor the building's long history, each accommodation coming with a well-kept, completely modernized bathroom with tub and shower. From the terraces or balconies of the hotel, a panoramic view unfolds.

Cantón 26, 39330 Santillana del Mar. © **94-281-88-88.** Fax 94-281-88-88. www.turismosantillanandelmar.com. 15 units. 107€–169€ double. AE, DC, MC, V. **Amenities:** Bar; room service; laundry; babysitting. *In room:* A/C, TV, minibar, hair dryer, safe.

Casa del Organista ★★ *Finds*   This 18th-century manor is a little secret we're revealing to you. In the old town, this gem discreetly receives paying guests and does so with a certain style. Of all the hotels in town, this one is the most tranquil and scenically located. We liked our most recent stay so well that we regretted packing up and shipping out to the next town. Most of the old architecture has been retained, including thick wooden beams evocative of a mountain house. Bedrooms are midsize, furnished with wood headboards under beamed ceilings. All the bathrooms have been refurbished with brand-new fixtures and tub/shower combinations. The three-story structure still retains its wooden balconies.

Calle Los Hornos 4, 39330 Santillana del Mar. © **94-284-03-52.** Fax 94-284-01-91. www.casadelorganista. com. 14 units. 48€–82€ double. MC, V. **Amenities:** Bar; room service; laundry. *In room:* TV, hair dryer.

Hotel Altamira ★   This government-rated three-star hotel in the center of the village is a 400-year-old former palace. Although not as impressive as the parador, it often takes the overflow in its comfortable, well-maintained rooms. All units contain bathrooms with tub/shower combos.

Calle Cantón 1, 39330 Santillana del Mar. © **94-281-80-25**. Fax 94-284-01-36. www.hotelaltamira.com. 32 units. 52€–89€ double. AE, DC, MC, V. Parking 2€. **Amenities:** Restaurant; bar; room service; babysitting; laundry service; dry cleaning. *In room:* A/C, TV, hair dryer.

Hotel Siglo XVIII ✪ *Finds*

This is a cozy nest. Located a 5-minute walk from the old town, this small three-star government-rated hotel has operated since 1996 in an old building behind a stone facade. Inside, the decoration is cozy and homelike, with a lingering aura of the 18th century, dominated by carved wood, high-beamed ceilings, white walls, and tile floors. The rooms, some of which have balconies opening onto the surrounding landscape, are midsize with plenty of comfort and light. All units contain neatly kept bathrooms equipped with tub/shower combos.

Revolgo 38, 39330 Santillana del Mar. © **94-284-02-10**. Fax 94-284-02-11. 16 units. 45€–71€ double. AE, DC, MC, V. Free parking. Closed Dec 12–Mar 1. **Amenities:** Bar; pool; room service; babysitting; laundry service; dry cleaning. *In room:* TV, hair dryer.

Los Infantes ✪

This government-rated three-star hotel is a comfortable choice, although not as charming as the Hotel Altamira (see above). Located in an 18th-century building on the main road leading into the village, Infantes has successfully kept the old flavor of Santillana: beamed ceilings and lounges furnished with tapestries, antiques, clocks, and paintings. The small rooms are cozy and well kept, with wall-to-wall carpeting; two have small balconies, and all have private bathrooms, mostly equipped with tub/shower combos.

Av. L'Dorat 1, 39330 Santillana del Mar. © **94-281-81-00**. Fax 94-284-01-03. www.grouppolosinfantes.com. 48 units. 60€–104€ double; 79€–120€ suite. AE, DISC, MC, V. Free parking 1.50€. **Amenities:** Restaurant; bar; laundry service; dry cleaning. *In room:* TV, hair dryer.

WHERE TO DINE

Dining isn't one of the compelling reasons to visit Santillana del Mar. Except for Los Blasones (see below), the only recommendable independent restaurant, your best bet is to dine at one of the previously recommended hotels. For atmosphere and quality of cuisine, the finest choice is Parador de Santillana (see above).

Los Blasones REGIONAL   Located in the center of town on the Plaza de la Gándara, this bar-restaurant, a local hangout, serves the best food in town among the independent restaurants. It's in a rustic building made of stone. Barbecue selections are featured, and the chef's specialty is *solomillo al queso de Treviso* (sirloin with cheese sauce). Try the perfectly grilled hake or the tasty stuffed peppers.

Plaza de la Gándara 8. © **94-281-80-70**. Reservations recommended. Main courses 9.50€–19€. AE, MC, V. Daily 1–4pm and 8–11:30pm. Closed Dec 10–Mar 10.

THE ALTAMIRA CAVES

About 2.5km (1½ miles) from Santillana del Mar are the **Cuevas de Altamira** ✪✪✪ (© **94-281-80-05**), famous for prehistoric paintings dating from the end of the Ice Age, paintings that have caused these caves to be called the "Sistine Chapel of prehistoric art." The cave paintings at Altamira are ranked among the finest prehistoric paintings ever discovered. They are rivaled but not matched by similar paintings discovered at Lascaux in the Dordogne Valley in France. These ancient depictions of bison and horses, painted vividly in reds and blacks on the caves' ceilings, were not discovered until the late 19th century. Once their authenticity was established, scholars and laypersons alike flocked to see these works of art, which provide a fragile link to our remote ancestors.

Severe damage was caused by the bacteria brought in by so many visitors, so now the Research Center and Museum of Altamira allows only 25 visitors per day June through September (no children under 13) and five visitors per day October through May. Admission is 2.40€. If you don't have a car, you have to walk from Santillana del Mar, as there is no bus service. From the center of Santillana, signs point the way to the cave. You walk past the abandoned Iglesia de San Sebastián, then cut through the streets of the hamlet of Herrán. Signs there direct you right across a farmer's field until you reach the cave. If you wish to visit, write to this address 1 year in advance asking permission to see the main cave and specifying the number in your party and the desired date: **Centro de Investigación y Museo de Altamira,** 39330 Santillana del Mar, Cantabria, Spain (© **94-281-80-05**).

Virtually everyone can get into the **Altamira Center** (© **94-281-80-05**), lying a few hundred feet from the original caves. King Juan Carlos and Queen Sofía officially opened the center, which can accommodate 200,000 visitors a year. On exhibit is a perfect replica of the cave, complete with precise copies of the murals. They are so realistic that they look like you're seeing the original caveman art. The replica of the cave, including "the Ceiling of the Polychromes" was created by computerized digital-transfer technology. The so-called "neocave" contains every crack and indentation of the original. The highlight, as in the original, is the array of 21 red bison in the Polychrome Chamber. Hours are Tuesday through Saturday from 9:30am to 7:30pm, Sunday from 9:30am to 5pm, costing 2.40€ for adults, 1.20€ for students, and free for kids under 18.

4 Los Picos de Europa ★★★

Potes: 114km (71 miles) W of Santander, 398km (247 miles) N of Madrid; Cangas de Onís: 147km (91 miles) W of Santander, 419km (260 miles) N of Madrid

These mountains are technically part of the Cordillera Cantábrica, which runs parallel to the northern coastline of Spain. In the narrow and vertiginous band known as Los Picos de Europa, they are by far at their most dramatic.

These "European Peaks" are the most famous and most legend-riddled mountains in Spain. Rising more than 2,590m (8,500 ft.), they are not high by alpine standards, but their proximity to the sea makes their height especially awesome. During the Middle Ages, they were passable only with great difficulty. (Much earlier, the ancient Romans constructed a north-south road whose stones are still visible in some places.) An abundance of wildlife, the medieval battles that occurred here, and dramatically rocky heights have all contributed to the twice-told tales that are an essential part of the entire principality of Asturias.

The position of Los Picos defined the medieval borders between Asturias, Santander, and León. Covering a distance of only 39km (24 miles) at their longest point, they are geologically and botanically different from anything else in the region. Thousands of years ago, busy glaciers created massive and forbidding limestone cliffs, which today challenge the most dedicated and intrepid rock climbers in Europe.

As you're touring the majestic Picos de Europa, be on the lookout for some of the rarest wildlife remaining in Europe. On the beech-covered slopes of these mountains and in gorges laden with jasmine, you might spot the increasingly rare Asturcon, a shaggy, rather chubby wild horse so small it first looks like a toy pony. Another endangered species is the Iberian brown bear—but if you see one, keep your distance. The park is also home of the surefooted chamois goat and some rare butterflies. Many bird-watchers flock here every year to see rare birds of prey, such as peregrine falcons, buzzards, and golden eagles. All wildlife is strictly protected by the government.

If you want to hike in this region, make sure you're well prepared. Many of the slopes are covered with loosely compacted shale, making good treads and hiking boots a must. Inexperienced hikers should definitely stick to well-established paths. In summer, temperatures can get hot and humid, and sudden downpours sweeping in from the frequently rainy coastline are common in any season. Hiking is not recommended between October and May, but you can drive or do the walk described below in Driving Tour 3 in any season.

The Picos are divided by swiftly flowing rivers into three regions: From east to west, they are Andara, Urrieles, and Cornión.

By far the best way to see this region is by car. Most drivers arrive in the region on the N-621 highway, heading southwest from Santander, or on the same highway northeast from the cities of north-central Spain (especially León and Valladolid). This highway connects many of the region's best vistas in a straight line. It also defines the region's eastern boundary. If you're driving east from Oviedo, you'll take the N-6312, in which case the first town of any importance will be Cangas de Onís.

Travel by bus is much less convenient but possible if you have lots of time and have had your fill of the rich architecture of the Spanish heartland. The region's touristic hubs are the towns of Panes and Potes; both have bus service (2 buses per day in summer, 1 per day in winter) from Santander and León. More frequent buses (5 per day) come to Potes from the coastal town of Unquera (which is along the coastal train lines). From Oviedo, there are two buses daily to the district's easternmost town of Cangas; they continue a short distance farther southeast to Covadonga. Within the region, a small local bus runs once a day, according to an erratic schedule, along the northern rim of the Picos, connecting Cangas de Onís with Las Arenas. Frankly, bus service in this region is too time consuming for most visitors.

EXPLORING THE REGION

If you have a car, the number and variety of tours in this region are almost endless, but for this guide, we have organized the region into three driving tours. Any of them, with their side excursions, could fill an entire day; if you're rushed and omit some of the side excursions, you'll spend half a day.

| DRIVING TOUR 1 | **PANES TO POTES** ✦✦ |

Distance: 29km (18 miles); 1 hour

Except for one optional detour, this drive extends entirely along one of the region's best roads, N-621, which links León and Valladolid to Santander. The drive is most noteworthy for its views of the ravine containing the Deva River, a ravine so steep that direct sunlight rarely penetrates it.

About two-thirds of the way to Potes, signs point you on a detour to the village of:

❶ Liébana

This village is .8km (½ mile) off the main road. Here you'll find the church of Nuestra Señora de Liébana, built in the 10th century in the Mozarabic style, surrounded by a copse of trees at the base of tall cliffs. Some people consider it the best example of Arabized Christian architecture in Europe, with Islamic-inspired geometric motifs.

If it isn't open, knock at the door of the first house you see as you enter the village—the home of the guardian, who will unlock the church if she's around. For this, she will expect a tip. If she's not around, content yourself with admiring the church from the outside, noting its spectacular natural setting.

Continuing for about another 8km (5 miles), you'll reach the village of:

❷ Potes

This is a charming place with well-kept alpine houses against a backdrop of jagged mountains.

Three kilometers (2 miles) southwest of Potes, near Turiano, stands the:

❸ Monastery of Santo Toribio de Liébana

The monastery dates from the 17th century. Restored to the style it enjoyed at the peak of its vast power, a transitional Romanesque, it contains what is reputed to be a splinter from the True Cross, brought from Jerusalem in the 8th century by the Bishop of Astorga. The monastery is also famous as the former home of Beatus de Liébana, the 8th-century author of *Commentary on the Apocalypse,* one of medieval Spain's most famous ecclesiastical documents. Today the building remains a functioning monastery. Ring the bell during daylight hours, and one of the brothers will let you enter if you are properly attired.

At the end of a winding and breathtakingly beautiful road to the west of Potes is the:

❹ Parador del Río Deva

You can spend the night here or just stop for lunch. The drive following the path of the Deva River for the most part will take you to:

❺ Fuente-Dé

Once you're here, a *teleférico* carries you 600m (2,000 ft.) up to an observation platform above a wind-scoured rock face. In summer this cable car operates daily in July and August from 9am to 8pm; September through June, hours are daily from 10am to 6pm. Round-trip fare is 10€. At the top you can walk 5km (3 miles) along a footpath to the rustic **Refugio de Aliva** (✆ **94-273-09-99**), open between June 15 and September 15. Doubles cost 55€ to 68€. If you opt for just a meal or a snack at the hostel's simple restaurant, remember to allow enough time to return to the *teleférico* before its last trip down. If you plan on taking the next driving tour (below), then head back to Potes.

DRIVING TOUR 2   **POTES TO CANGAS DE ONIS** ✪

Distance: **150km (93 miles); 4 hours**

This tour includes not only the Quiviesa Valley and some of the region's most vertiginous mountain passes, but also some of its most verdant fields and most elevated pastures. You might stop at an occasional village, but most of the time you will be going through deserted countryside. Your route will take you through several tunnels and high above mountain streams set deep into gorges. The occasional belvederes along the way always deliver on their promise of panoramic views.

The village of Potes (see "Driving Tour 1," above) is your starting point. Take N-621 southwest to Riaño. At Riaño, turn north for a brief ride on N-625. Then take a winding route through the heart of the region by driving northwest on N-637. Although it's beautiful all along the way, the first really important place you'll reach is:

① Cangas de Onís

This is the westernmost town in the region, where you can get a clean hotel room and a solid meal after a trek through the mountains. The biggest attraction in Cangas de Onís is an ivy-covered **Roman bridge,** lying west of the center, spanning the Sella River. Also of interest is the **Capilla de Santa Cruz,** immediately west of the center. One of the earliest Christian sites in Spain (and a holy spot many centuries before that), it was originally constructed in the 8th century over a Celtic dolmen and rebuilt in the 15th century.

About 1.5km (1 mile) northwest of Cangas de Onís, beside the road leading to Arriondas, stands the:

② Monasterio de San Pedro

This is a Benedictine monastery in the village of **Villanueva.** The church that you see was originally built in the 17th century, when it enclosed within its premises the ruins of a much older Romanesque church. Combining Baroque opulence and Romanesque simplicity, it has some unusual carved capitals showing the unhappy end of the medieval King Favila, supposedly devoured by a Cantabrian bear.

DRIVING TOUR 3 | **CANGAS DE ONIS TO PANES** ★★

Distance: 56km (35 miles); 1 hour

This tour travels along the relatively straight C-6312 from the western to the eastern entrance to the Picos de Europa region. A number of unusual excursions could easily stretch this into an all-day outing.

From Cangas de Onís (see "Driving Tour 2," above) heading west about 1.6km (1 mile), you'll reach the turnoff to:

① Cueva del Buxu

Inside the cave are a limited number of prehistoric rock engravings and charcoal drawings, somewhat disappointingly small. Only 25 people per day are allowed inside (respiration erodes the drawings), so unless you get there early, you won't get in. It's open Wednesday through Sunday from 10am to 2pm and 4 to 6:30pm. Admission is 2€.

Some 6.5km (4 miles) east, signs point south in the direction of:

② Covadonga

Revered as the birthplace of Christian Spain, it is about 9.5km (6 miles) off the main highway. A battle here in A.D. 718 pitted a ragged band of Christian Visigoths against a small band of Muslims. The resulting victory established the first niche of Christian Europe in Moorish Iberia. The town's most important monument is **La Santa Cueva,** a cave containing the sarcophagus of Pelayo (d. 737), king of the Visigothic Christians, and an enormous neo-Romanesque basilica, built between 1886 and 1901, commemorating the Christianization of Spain. At the end of the long boulevard that funnels into the base of the church stands a statue of Pelayo.

Return to the highway and continue east. You'll come to the village of Las Estazadas; then after another 11km (7 miles) you'll reach:

③ Las Arenas de Cabrales

Note that some maps refer to this town simply as Arenas. This is the headquarters of a cheese-producing region whose Cabrales, a blue-veined cheese made from ewes' milk, is avidly consumed throughout Spain.

Drive 5km (3 miles) south from Arenas, following signs to the village of:

④ Puente de Poncebos

This is shown on some maps simply as Poncebos. Here, the road ends abruptly (except, perhaps, for 4WD vehicles). This village is several miles downstream from the source of Spain's most famous salmon-fishing river, the Cares, which flows from its source near the more southerly village of Cain through deep ravines.

Beginning at Poncebos, a footpath has been cut into the ravine on either side of the Cares River. It is one of the engineering marvels of Spain, known for centuries as **"The Divine Gorge."** It crosses the ravine many times over footbridges and sometimes through tunnels chiseled into the rock face beside the water, making a hike along the banks of this river a memorable outing. You can climb up the riverbed from Poncebos, overland to the village of Cain, a total distance of 11km (7 miles). Allow between 3 and 4 hours. At Cain, you can take a taxi back to where you left your car in Poncebos if you don't want to retrace your steps.

After your trek up the riverbed, continue your drive on to the village of:

⑤ Panes

This village lies a distance of 23km (14 miles), to the eastern extremity of the Picos de Europa.

WHERE TO STAY & DINE IN THE AREA

Accommodations are extremely limited in these mountain towns. If you're planning an overnight stop, make sure you have a reservation. Most taverns will serve you food during regular opening hours without a reservation.

Lying directly north of Cangas de Onís is the little village of Arriondas. You come upon this situation only on the culinary maps of Europe. This unprepossessing village has not only one but two Michelin-starred restaurants. Nowhere in the Picos de Europa area can you dine as well as you can here. In fact, these are two of the best restaurants along the entire north coast of Spain.

IN ARRIONDAS

Casa Marcial ★★ ASTURIAN   Even though it's not quite as good as El Corral del Indiano, this is one of the great restaurants along the northern coast of Spain, an unexpected discovery in this remote pueblo. Here Chef Nacho Manzano creates a superlative cuisine in an antique farmhouse fronting rolling green foothills. On our last visit, we arrived on a hot day and found the perfect dish for our palate: an icy cucumber soup poured around a sorbet made of green pepper with swirls of virgin green olive oil poured over it.

From the River Stella comes a salmon served in a "pool" of melon gazpacho with fresh asparagus. It doesn't get much better than this. Manzano is a master at cooking and flavoring mountain lamb from the nearby hills. He can take any dish, perhaps locally grown chicken, and turn it into a masterpiece—in this case by braising it to an elegant mahogany and folding fresh gizzards into the mix to produce a bravura meal. Each of his dishes could rate a star. One of his most devoted regular patrons told us he knew the secret of the chef's success. "He can blur the borders between the sea and the forest."

Carretera AS-342, La Salgar 10, 3km (2 miles) north of Arriondas. ☎ **98-584-09-91.** Reservations required. Main courses 16€–26€; fixed-price menu 42€–45€. Tues–Sat 1–4pm and 9–11:30pm; Sun 1–4pm. Closed Feb.

El Corral del Indiano ★★★ ASTURIAN   In the middle of nowhere you come upon a restaurant worth the trip half way across Spain. In this little village at the foot of Los Picos de Europa, chef José Antonio Campo Viejo lures some of the greatest gastronomes of Europe to his restaurant, even though conversing with him might be difficult because of his heavy mountain accent. He can brighten one of those misty, gray days so common in the region.

As you enter, not really knowing what to expect, you notice at once that this is no rustic mountain tavern. Modernist tableware is placed on the stiff white tablecloths and the walls are an electric blue. Although the chef may draw inspiration from local recipes, he infuses every one of his dishes with his own hypercreative culinary sense.

The tastes are most often sensational. Since main courses are so very expensive, it's a greater value to order the tasting menu. A soup might combine clams tasting as fresh as if just plucked from the ocean with a velvety sea of freshly picked green peas, a sweet, briny taste that makes you wish it were June year-round. Many local homes are cooking smoked sausages and beans, but no kettle is better than that simmering on Viejo's stove. His *pote asturiano,* a blend of cabbage and pig parts, is the single best version of that dish we've ever tasted. If you ever get to rule the world, our recommendation is to kidnap Viejo as your own personal chef and spend the rest of your life enjoying the likes of nuggets of lamb sweetbreads glazed in a raisiny flavored sherry. By the time dessert comes around, you think you didn't hear right—foie gras and sweet peas. You go along with this mad, mad suggestion and end up loving it. Viejo is a self-taught genius.

Av. de Europa 14. ℂ 98-584-10-72. Reservations required. Main courses 30€–42€. Tasting menu 50€. AE, DC, MC, V. Fri–Wed 1:30–3:30pm; Fri–Sat and Mon–Tues 9–11pm.

IN CANGAS DE ONIS

Hotel Aultre Naray ⭐ *Finds*   A small hotel with character, this establishment is in an Asturian country house dating from 1873. Its robust masonry work is typical of the 19th century, and it has a beautiful stone archway in the entrance. The decoration came from an interior design workshop in Madrid, resulting in a harmonious blend of traditional architecture with current design trends. The hotel has well-furnished midsize bedrooms, each with a private tiled bathroom equipped with a tub/shower combo. Four rooms have sloping ceilings. There's a cozy sitting room with a fireplace for guests. The hotel is in the foothills of the Escapa mountain range, enjoying a panoramic view of the mountains and an oak forest on the banks of the River Sella. The area is a perfect place for fishing; hiking in the mountains and canoeing are other popular diversions.

Cangas de Onis, Peruyes, 33547 Asturias. ℂ 98-584-08-08. Fax 98-584-08-48. www.aultrenaray.com. 10 units. 62€–93€ double; 102€–133€ family room for 4 persons. AE, DC, MC, V. Free parking. **Amenities:** Restaurant; bar; room service; laundry service; dry cleaning. *In room:* TV, hair dryer, safe.

La Palmera REGIONAL   When the weather is right you can dine outside here, enjoying some mountain air with the food. Sometimes this place is overrun, but on other occasions you can have a meal in peace. The menu features game from the surrounding mountains, along with filet of beef, lamb chops, and salmon in green sauce. Try the local mountain cheese. La Palmera is 3km (2 miles) east of Cangas de Onís on the road to Covadonga.

Soto de Cangas. ℂ 98-594-00-96. Main courses 10€–15€. AE, DC, MC, V. Daily 1:30–4:30pm and 9–11:30pm.

IN COSGAYA

Hotel del Oso   This well-run little hotel is located in two buildings next to the Deva River, beside the road leading from Potes to the parador and cable car at Fuente-Dé. The place is ringed with natural beauty. Its small rooms are well furnished and maintained with bathrooms equipped with tub/shower combos. Meals are taken at the Mesón del Oso (see below).

Carretera Espinama s/n, 39582 Cosgaya. ✆ **94-273-30-18**. Fax 94-273-30-36. www.hoteldeloso.com. 50 units. 52€–60€ double. MC, V. Free parking. Closed Jan 7–Feb 15. From Potes, take the road signposted to Espinama 14.5km (9 miles) south. **Amenities:** Restaurant; bar; pool. *In room:* TV, hair dryer, safe.

Mesón del Oso ASTURIAN   Open to the public since 1981, this stone-built restaurant is named after the bear that supposedly devoured Favila, an 8th-century king of Asturias. Here, at the birthplace of the Christian warrior King Pelayo, you can enjoy Lebaniega cuisine, reflecting the bounty of mountain, stream, and sea. The portions are generous. Try trout from the Deva River, grilled tuna, roast suckling pig, or a mountain stew called *cocida lebaniego,* whose recipe derives from local lore and tradition. Dessert might be a fruit-based tart. There's an outdoor terrace.

Carretera Espinama s/n. ✆ **94-273-30-18**. Main courses 12€–19€. MC, V. Daily 1–4pm and 9–11pm. Closed Jan 7–Feb 15. From Potes, take the route south toward Espinama 14.5km (9 miles).

IN COVADONGA

Hotel Pelayo   There's no street address for this place, but it's in the shadow of the large 19th-century basilica that dominates the village. The view from its windows takes in a panoramic landscape. Guests come here to enjoy the mountain air, and many pilgrims check in while visiting religious shrines in the area. The place has a somewhat dated, but nevertheless appealing, family atmosphere. The small rooms are comfortable and well furnished with good beds and bathrooms, which are mostly equipped with tub/shower combos.

33589 Covadonga. ✆ **98-584-60-61**. Fax 98-584-60-54. 43 units. 50€–90€ double; 70€–115€ suite. AE, DC, MC, V. Free parking. Closed Dec 15–Feb 1. Drive east and then south from Cangas de Onís, following the signs for Covadonga and the hotel. **Amenities:** Restaurant; bar; room service; laundry service; dry cleaning. *In room:* TV, hair dryer.

IN FUENTE-DE

Parador de Fuente-Dé ★★   The finest place to stay in the area, this government-run parador faces the Picos de Europa. Opened in 1975, it is at the end of the major road through the Liébana region. Hunters in autumn and mountain climbers in summer often fill its attractively decorated and comfortably furnished bedrooms, which are midsize to spacious, each with a tub/shower combination.

At 3.5km de Espinama, 39588 Espinama. ✆ **94-273-66-51**. Fax 94-273-66-54. www.parador.es. 78 units. 72€–85€ double. AE, DC, MC, V. Free parking. Closed Nov 15–Mar 1. Drive 26km (16 miles) west of Potes. **Amenities:** Restaurant; bar; room service; laundry service; dry cleaning. *In room:* A/C, TV, minibar, hair dryer, safe.

IN POTES

Restaurant Martín REGIONAL   This family-run establishment in the center of Potes is filled with regional charm and spirit. They prepare garbanzos (chickpeas) with bits of *chorizo* (sausage), other vegetables, and the rich produce of the region, depending on the season. They serve game from the Picos and fish from the Cantabrian coast. The dessert choices comprise more than a dozen tarts and pastries.

Roscabao s/n. ✆ **94-273-02-33**. Main courses 8€–15€. AE, DC, MC, V. Daily 1–4:30pm and 8–11pm. Closed Jan.

5 Gijón (Xixón)

473km (294 miles) N of Madrid, 192km (119 miles) W of Santander, 29km (18 miles) E of Oviedo

The major port of Asturias and its largest city is a summer resort and an industrial center rolled into one. As a port, Gijón (pronounced "hee-*hohn*") is said to predate the Romans. The Visigoths came through here, and in the 8th century the Moors wandered through the area, but none of those would-be conquerors made much of an impression.

The best part of the city to explore is the *barrio* of **Cimadevilla,** with its maze of alleys and leaning houses. This section, jutting into the ocean to the north of the new town, spills over an elevated piece of land known as Santa Catalina. Santa Catalina forms a headland at the west end of the **Playa San Lorenzo,** stretching for about 2.5km (1½ miles); this sandy beach has good facilities. After time at the beach, you can stroll through the **Parque Isabel la Católica** at its eastern end.

Gijón is short on major monuments. The city was the birthplace of Gaspar Melchor de Jovellanos (1744–1811), one of Spain's most prominent men of letters, as well as an agrarian reformer and liberal economist. Manuel de Godoy, the notorious minister, ordered that Jovellanos be held prisoner for 7 years in Bellver Castle on Majorca. In Gijón his birthplace has been restored and turned into the **Museo-Casa Natal de Jovellanos,** Plaza de Jovellanos, open Tuesday through Saturday from 10am to 2pm and 4 to 8pm. Admission is free.

ESSENTIALS

GETTING THERE   Gijón doesn't have an airport, but **Iberia** flies to the airport at Ranón, 42km (26 miles) away, a facility it shares with Oviedo-bound passengers.

Gijón has good rail links and makes a good gateway into Asturias. Three **trains** a day make the 6½- to 8½-hour trip from Madrid. León is a convenient rail hub for reaching Gijón because nine trains per day make the 2- to 3-hour trip between these cities. You can also take the narrow-gauge **FEVE** from Bilbao.

Six **buses** a day, run by Alsa (© **90-242-22-42**), connect Gijón with Madrid (5½ hr. away), and two buses per day run to and from Santander (4½ hr. away). Four buses a day go to León (2 hr. away).

From Santander in the east, **drive** west along the N-634. At Ribadesella, you can take the turnoff to the 632, which is the coastal road that will take you to Gijón. This is the scenic route. To save time, continue on N-634 until you reach the outskirts of Oviedo, then cut north on A-66, the express highway to Gijón.

VISITOR INFORMATION   The **tourist information office** is at Marqués de San Esteban 1 (© **98-534-60-46;** www.infoasturias.com). It's open Monday through Friday from 9am to 2pm and 4 to 6:30pm, Saturday from 9am to 2pm.

SPECIAL EVENTS   The most exciting time to be in Gijón is on **Asturias Day,** the first Sunday in August. This fiesta is celebrated with parade floats, traditional folk dancing, and lots of music. But summers here tend to be festive even without a festival. Vacationers are fond of patronizing the cider taverns *(chigres),* eating grilled sardines, and joining in singalongs in the portside *tascas.* Be aware that you can get as drunk on cider as you can on beer, maybe somewhat faster.

WHERE TO STAY
EXPENSIVE

Hernán Cortés ★★   About 1 block east of Plaza del 6 de Agosto, midway between Playa San Lorenzo and the harbor, this hotel named after the conquistador is one of the finest in town. Although it was recently renovated, its midsize guest rooms still retain a bit of the allure of yesteryear and provide such thoughtful extras as shoeshine equipment. All units contain bathrooms with tub/shower combos. The Cortés doesn't have a restaurant. The proprietors will serve lunch or dinner in your room from a neighboring restaurant.

Fernández Vallín 5, 33205 Gijón. (C) **98-534-60-00.** Fax 98-535-56-45. www.hotelhernancortes.es. 56 units. 110€–171€ double; 127€–191€ suite. AE, DC, MC, V. Parking 9€ nearby. Bus: 4 or 11. **Amenities:** Bar; lounge; room service; laundry service; dry cleaning. In room: A/C, TV, minibar, hair dryer, safe.

Parador del Molino Viejo (Parador de Gijón) 🌟🌟🌟   Next to the verdant confines of Gijón's most visible park, about half a mile east of the town center and an easy walk from the popular beach Playa San Lorenzo, this is the premier place to stay. Awarded four stars by the government (which runs it), it was constructed around the core of an 18th-century cider mill. The parador is surrounded by a garden strewn with tables, beside a stream sheltering colonies of swans. It contains a marble-sheathed reception area, an unpretentious restaurant, and a cider bar that, on weekends, is quite popular with local residents. The guest rooms are somewhat cramped and surprisingly simple for a four-star hotel; however, they're tastefully restored with well-scrubbed wooden floors, thick shutters, traditional furniture, and larger-than-usual bathrooms with tub/shower combos.

Parque Isabel la Católica s/n, 33203 Gijón. (C) **800/223-1356** in the U.S., or 98-537-05-11. Fax 98-537-02-33. www.parador.es. 40 units. 95€–119€ double. AE, DC, MC, V. Free parking. Bus: 4 or 11. **Amenities:** Restaurant; bar; room service; laundry service; dry cleaning. In room: A/C, TV, minibar, hair dryer, safe.

MODERATE

Begoña   This functional modern hotel with much-appreciated parking offers small rooms that are well furnished and comfortable, plus efficient chamber service to keep everything clean. Each unit also comes equipped with a neatly kept bathroom, most of which contain tub/shower combos. Regional and national dishes, with many seafood concoctions, are served in the restaurant. The hotel is on the southern outskirts of the new town, 1 block north of Avenida Manuel Llaneza, the major traffic artery from the southwest.

Carretera de la Costa 44, 33205 Gijón. (C) **98-514-72-11.** Fax 98-539-82-22. www.hotelesbegona.com. 250 units. 68€–71€ double. AE, DC, MC, V. Parking 8€. Bus: 4 or 11. **Amenities:** Restaurant; bar; room service; babysitting; laundry service; dry cleaning. In room: TV.

La Casona de Jovellanos 🌟 *(Finds)*   This venerable hotel stands on the rocky peninsula that was the site of the oldest part of fortified Gijón, a short distance south of the Parque Santa Catalina. It contains only a few rooms, so reservations are imperative. The small rooms themselves are attractively furnished and well maintained, each with a comfortable bed and a bathroom containing a tub/shower combo. The hotel was built on foundations 3 centuries old. In 1794, the writer Jovellanos established the Asturian Royal Institute of Marine Life and Mineralogy here, and it was later transformed into this hotel within walking distance of the beach and yacht basin.

Plaza de Jovellanos 1, 33201 Gijón. (C) **98-534-12-64.** Fax 98-535-61-51. 13 units. 46€–76€ double. AE, DC, MC, V. Parking nearby 9€. Bus: 4 or 11. **Amenities:** Restaurant; bar; laundry service; dry cleaning. In room: TV, hair dryer, safe.

WHERE TO DINE

Casa Tino *(Value)* REGIONAL   Quality combined with quantity, at reasonable prices, is the hallmark of this restaurant near the police station, north of Manuel

Llaneza and west of the Paseo de Begoña. Each day the chef prepares a different stew—sometimes fish and sometimes meat. The place is packed with chattering diners every evening, many of them regulars. Sample the white beans of the region cooked with pork, stewed hake, or marinated beefsteak, perhaps finishing with one of the fruit tarts.

Alfredo Truan 9. ℂ **98-534-13-87.** Reservations recommended. Main courses 10€–15€; *menú del día* 9€. AE, DC, MC, V. Fri–Wed 1:15–3:30pm and 8:45–11:30pm. Bus: 4 or 11.

Casa Víctor SEAFOOD   Owner and sometime chef Víctor Bango is a bit of a legend. He oversees the buying and preparation of the fresh fish for which this place is famous. The successful young people of Gijón enjoy the tavernlike atmosphere here, as well as the imaginative dishes—a mousse made from the roe of sea urchins, for example, is all the rage in Asturias these days. Well-chosen wines accompany such other menu items as octopus served with fresh vegetables and grilled steak. Casa Víctor is located by the dockyards.

Carmen 11. ℂ **98-534-83-10.** Reservations recommended. Main courses 16€–22€; fixed-price menu 12€. AE, DC, MC, V. Mon–Sat 1–3:30pm and 8:30–11:30pm. Closed mid-Dec to mid-Jan. Bus: 4 or 11.

El Puerto SPANISH/CONTINENTAL   Set directly on the waterfront, with very large windows that overlook the fishing boats and pleasure craft bobbing at anchor in the nearby harbor, this restaurant has emerged since its debut in 1990 as the finest in Gijón. Sheathed in hardwood paneling, and accented with glittering crystal ornaments and lighting fixtures, it specializes in an upscale *cocina del mercado,* often based on very fresh fish, most of which was hauled out of nearby waters within a few hours of its preparation. An enduring specialty is sliced hake served with lobster claws, clams, and green sauce. Appropriate beginnings include homemade foie gras with grapes, and a succulent version of crepes stuffed with flake-fleshed spider crab. Most diners are accommodated on the street level, but there's additional seating available on the floors immediately below and above.

Calle Claudio Alvargonzález s/n. ℂ **98-534-90-96.** Reservations recommended. Main courses 15€–23€; *menú gastronómico* 36€. AE, DC, MC, V. Daily 1:30–4pm; Mon–Sat 9pm–midnight. Closed Easter week.

6 Oviedo (Uviéu)

203km (126 miles) W of Santander, 444km (276 miles) N of Madrid

Oviedo is the capital of Asturias. Despite its high concentration of industry and mining, the area has unspoiled scenery. Only 26km (16 miles) from the coast, Oviedo is very pleasant in summer, when much of Spain is unbearably hot. It makes an ideal base for excursions along the Costa Verde.

A peaceful city today, Oviedo has had a long and violent history. Razed in the 8th century during the Reconquest, it was rebuilt in an architectural style known as Asturian pre-Romanesque, which predated many of the greatest achievements under the Moors. Remarkably, this architectural movement was in flower when the rest of Europe lay under the black cloud of the Dark Ages.

As late as the 1930s, Oviedo was suffering violent upheavals. An insurrection in the mining areas on October 5, 1934, led to a seizure of the town by miners, who set up a revolutionary government. The subsequent fighting led to the destruction of many historical monuments. The cathedral was also damaged, and the university was set on fire. Even more destruction came during the Spanish Civil War.

ESSENTIALS

GETTING THERE Oviedo doesn't have an airport. The nearest one is at Ranón, 52km (32 miles) away, which it shares with Gijón-bound passengers. Call © **98-512-76-07** for information.

From Madrid, there are six **trains** per day. Call RENFE at © **90-224-02-02** for information.

One **bus** per day arrives from Santander (trip time: 1 hr.). Seven buses pull in daily from Madrid (6 hr.). For bus schedules, call © **90-242-22-42.**

From the east or west, take N-634 across the coast of northern Spain. From the south, take N-630 or A-66 from León.

VISITOR INFORMATION The **tourist information office** is at Calle Uria 64 (© **98-521-33-85;** www.infoasturias.com). Hours are daily from 9am to 2pm and 4:30 to 6:30pm.

EXPLORING OVIEDO

Oviedo has been rebuilt into a modern city around the Parque de San Francisco. It still contains some historical and artistic monuments, the most important being the **cathedral** ⚐ on the Plaza de Alfonso II el Casto (© **98-522-10-33**). The Gothic church was begun in 1348 and completed at the end of the 15th century (except for the spire, which dates from 1556). Inside is an altarpiece in the florid Gothic style, dating from the 14th and 15th centuries. The cathedral's 9th-century **Cámara Santa (Holy Chamber)** is famous for the Cross of Don Pelayo, the Cross of the Victory, and the Cross of the Angels, the finest specimens of Asturian art in the world. Admission to the cathedral is free, but entrance to the Holy Chamber is 2.50€ for adults and 1.80€ for children 10 to 15, free for children under 10. The cathedral is open May through October, Monday through Saturday from 10am to 1pm and 4 to 7pm; November through April, Monday through Saturday from 10am to 1pm and 4 to 6pm. Take bus no. 1.

Behind the cathedral, the **Museo Arqueológico,** Calle San Vicente 5 (© **98-521-54-05**), in a former convent dating from the 15th century, houses prehistoric relics discovered in Asturias, pre-Romanesque sculptures, a numismatic display, and old musical instruments. It's open Tuesday through Saturday from 10am to 1:30pm and 4 to 6pm, Sunday from 11am to 1pm. Admission is free.

Standing above Oviedo, on Monte Naranco, are two of the most famous examples of Asturian pre-Romanesque architecture. **Santa María del Naranco** ⚐⚐ (© **98-529-56-85**), originally a 9th-century palace and hunting lodge of Ramiro I, offers views of Oviedo and the snowcapped Picos de Europa. Once containing baths and private apartments, it was converted into a church in the 12th century. Intricate stonework depicts hunting scenes, and barrel vaulting rests on a network of blind arches. The open porticoes at both ends were 200 years ahead of their time architecturally. The church is open April through September, daily from 9:30am to 1pm and 3 to 7pm; October through March, daily from 10am to 1pm and 3 to 5pm. Admission is 2.20€.

About 90m (100 yd.) away is **San Miguel de Lillo** ⚐ (© **98-529-56-85**). It, too, was built by Ramiro I, as a royal chapel, and was no doubt a magnificent specimen of Asturian pre-Romanesque architecture until 15th-century architects marred its grace. The stone carvings that remain, however, are exemplary. Most of the sculptures have been transferred to the archaeological museum in town.

The church is open daily from 9:30am to 1pm, Monday through Saturday from 3 to 7pm. Admission is 2.20€ Tuesday through Sunday, free on Monday.

Ask at the tourist office for its 45-minute walking tour from the center of Oviedo to the churches. Check that the churches will be open at the time of your visit.

SHOPPING

Serious shoppers know that Oviedo offers some of the best outlets in Spain for handbags and shoes. For a number of the finest boutiques, head for the intersection of **Uria** and **Gil de Jaz.** In this district and on adjoining side streets you'll find some of the country's best-known designer boutiques, selling the same merchandise that goes at far higher prices in such cities as Madrid and Barcelona. Many artisans in this district make their own products—selling, for example, a variety of calfskin goods and hand-sewn leather. You'll also come across good sales on Asturian ceramic ware.

WHERE TO STAY

EXPENSIVE

Hotel Occidental de la Reconquista ★★★   Named after a subject dear to the hearts of the Catholic monarchs—the ejection of the Muslims from Iberia—this is one of the most prestigious hotels in Spain. Originally built between 1754 and 1777 as an orphanage and hospital, it received visits from Queen Isabella II in 1858 and a reworking of its baroque stonework during a restoration in 1958. The Reconquista was converted into a hotel in 1973 after the outlay of massive amounts of cash. Despite the growth of the city, it remains the second-largest building in Oviedo.

Today, the interior boasts a combination of modern and reproduction furniture, as well as a scattering of ecclesiastical paintings and antiques. The spacious guest rooms contain private bathrooms with tub/shower combos and are outfitted in antique styles, with views of the old town or of a series of elegantly antique interior courtyards. The hotel is 2 blocks north of the largest park in the town center, the Campo San Francisco.

Gil de Jaz 16, 33004 Oviedo. ✆ **98-524-11-00.** Fax 98-524-11-66. www.hoteldelareconquista.com. 142 units. 200€ double; from 625€ suite. AE, DC, MC, V. Parking 14€. Bus: 1, 2, or 3. **Amenities:** Restaurant; bar; sauna; salon; room service; laundry service; dry cleaning. *In room:* A/C, TV, minibar, hair dryer.

MODERATE

Clarín   This recently built modern hotel in the old quarter is noted for its tasteful decor, with comfortable, inviting, well-maintained small rooms equipped with tidily kept bathrooms, which contain mostly tub/shower combos. The hotel stands right in the middle of the historic district within walking distance of many of the attractions.

Caveda 23, 33002 Oviedo. ✆ **98-522-72-72.** Fax 98-522-80-18. www.hotelclarin.es. 47 units. 85€ double. AE, MC, V. Parking 9€. Bus: 1, 2, or 3. **Amenities:** Restaurant; bar; room service; babysitting; laundry service; dry cleaning. *In room:* A/C, TV, minibar, hair dryer.

El Magistral   In the commercial district of Uria, this six-story hotel—rated three stars by the government—is from 1997. The modern design in the public areas is dominated by glass and chrome with spot lighting and tiled floors. The midsize bedrooms are more traditional, with parquet floors, pastel walls, and fully equipped bathrooms with tub/shower combos. The hotel's restaurant is about 50m (165 ft.) from the main building and has a fine reputation locally for its regional cuisine.

Calle Jovellanos 3, 33003 Oviedo. ✆ **98-521-51-16.** Fax 98-521-06-79. www.elmagistral.com. 34 units. 96€ double. AE, DC, MC, V. Parking: 7.50€. **Amenities:** Restaurant; bar; room service; babysitting; laundry service; dry cleaning. *In room:* A/C, TV, minibar, hair dryer, safe.

Hotel Vetusta ★ *Finds*   In the center of the city, just a 5-minute walk from the cathedral, this four-story hotel takes its name from an imaginary fictional city invented by the author Clarín. It has been in operation since 1997, following the successful renovation of an old structure of wood and brick, split by wooden balconies. The interior has steel and wood fittings and is done in an ultra-contemporary style. The small bedrooms are very compact but comfortably furnished, with fully equipped bathrooms containing tub/shower combos. Some have balconies, and eight contain a hydromassage.

Calle Covadonga 2, 33002 Oviedo. ✆ **98-522-22-29.** Fax 98-522-22-09. www.hotelvetusta.com. 16 units. 75€–99€ double. DC, MC, V. Parking: 7€. **Amenities:** Bar, room service, laundry service; dry cleaning. *In room:* A/C, TV, minibar, hair dryer, safe.

WHERE TO DINE

Casa Conrado REGIONAL   Almost as solidly established as the cathedral nearby, this restaurant offers good-tasting, hearty Asturian stews, seafood platters, seafood soups, several preparations of hake, including one cooked in cider, escalopes of veal with champagne, and a full range of desserts. It is a local favorite and a long-established culinary tradition. The service is attentive.

Argüelles 1. ✆ **98-522-39-19.** Reservations required. Main courses 13€–25€; fixed-price menu 30€. AE, DC, MC, V. Mon–Sat 1–4pm and 9pm–midnight. Closed Aug. Bus: 1.

Casa Fermín ★ REGIONAL/INTERNATIONAL   The chef here prepares the best regional cuisine in town in a building near the university and the cathedral. To order the most classic dish, ask for *fabada asturiana,* a bean dish with Asturian black pudding and Avilés ham. A tasty hake cooked in cider is another suggestion. Venison is a specialty in season (Oct–Mar). Try the traditional Cabrales cheese of the province. The restaurant decor is in pink and granite. Although it's been around for half a century, it has a contemporary air to it because it's filled with plants and covered with skylights. Casa Fermín is directly east of the Parque de San Francisco.

Calle San Francisco 8. ✆ **98-521-64-52.** Reservations recommended. Main courses 13€–21€; *menú de degustación* 36€. AE, DC, MC, V. Mon–Sat 1:30–4pm and 9–11pm. Bus: 1 or 2.

El Raitán ★ *Finds* REGIONAL   This restaurant south of the cathedral serves a set menu and bases all its dishes on regional ingredients, with meals accompanied by wines from La Rioja. A large array of well-prepared choices is available for each course. Each day the chef presents nine classic regional dishes that change with the season. The place has a tavern setting with overhead beams—atmospheric and intimate.

Trascorrales 6. ✆ **98-521-42-18.** Reservations recommended. Main courses 17€–20€; *menú asturiano* 17€–25€. DC, MC, V. Wed–Mon 1:30–4pm and 9pm–midnight; Sun 1:30–4pm. Bus: 1 or 2.

La Máquina ★ *Finds* ASTURIAN   The entire province is known for one dish, fabada, made with white beans and sausage. This dish reaches the pinnacle of perfection at this little farmhouse-like place lying 6km (4 miles) outside of Oviedo and signposted on the road to Avilés. In front of the restaurant in the village of Lugones is a little locomotive. The recipes at this lunch only place are prepared from time-tested dishes, and they are regional, hearty, and full of flavor, especially that fabada. The fabada is prepared with white alubia beans, a sausage called morcilla, peppery chorizo, chopped bacon, and Serrano ham, and flavored with various seasonings such as saffron powder and oregano. Of course, plenty of fresh bread is served to mop up the juices. You can also order other delectable courses such as tender and well-seasoned *entrecôtes* of veal and various versions of freshly caught *merluza* (hake), often prepared with cured ham. The fresh vegetables are invariably fresh and prepared with skill to retain their natural flavors. The local favorite for dessert is rice pudding resting under a crisp layer of hot caramel.

Avenida Conde de Santa Bárbara 59. (© **98-526-00-19.** Reservations recommended. Main courses. 10€–13€. DC, MC, V. Mon–Sat 1:30–4pm. Closed mid-June to Mid-July.

OVIEDO AFTER DARK

Very few of the many bars of Oviedo's old town stand out as particularly unique, so most night owls make it a point to wander from one joint to another as part of an evening's entertainment. Your best bet involves the old town neighborhoods around the Plaza del Paraguas, the Plaza da Fontán, and the Plaza Riego, each of which offers lots of unusual architecture in addition to hole-in-the-wall bars, many of which aren't identified with any discernible name. If you really want to go dancing as part of your nocturne in Oviedo, consider the town's most popular disco, **Estilo,** Calle Pomarín s/n (© **98-529-67-38**), where clients from the ages of 21 to around 30 rock 'n' roll to recorded dance music, but never, ever, before midnight. It is open Friday through Sunday until around 6am each night. Admission is 6€.

18

Galicia

Extending above Portugal in the northwest corner of Spain, **Galicia** is a rain-swept land of grass and granite, much of its coastline gouged by fjord-like inlets. It is a land steeped in Celtic tradition—in many areas its citizens, called *Gallegos*, speak their own language (not a dialect of Spanish but a separate language, *Gallego*). Galicia consists of four provinces: La Coruña (including Santiago de Compostela), Pontevedra, Lugo, and Orense.

The Romans made quite an impression on the region. The Roman walls around the city of **Lugo** and the Tower of Hercules at **La Coruña** are part of that legacy. The Moors came this way, too, and did a lot of damage along the way. But finding the natives none too friendly and other battlefields more promising, they moved on.

Nothing did more to put Galicia on the tourist map than the **Camino de Santiago,** the Pilgrims' Route. It is the oldest, most traveled, and most famous route on the old continent. To guarantee a place in heaven, pilgrims journeyed to the supposed tomb of Santiago (St. James), patron saint of Spain. They trekked across the Pyrenees by the thousands, risking their lives in transit. The Camino de Santiago contributed to the development and spread of Romanesque art and architecture across Spain. Pilgrimages to the shrine lessened as medieval culture itself began its decline.

1 La Coruña ⟨★⟩

604km (375 miles) NW of Madrid, 155km (96 miles) N of Vigo

Despite the fact that **La Coruña** (*A Coruña* in Galician) is an ancient city, it does not have a wealth of historical and architectural monuments. Celts, Phoenicians, and Romans all occupied the port, and it is another of the legendary cities that claim Hercules as its founder.

The greatest event in the history of La Coruña occurred in 1588, when Philip II's Invincible Armada sailed from here to England. Only half the ships made it back to Spain. The following year, Sir Francis Drake and his ships attacked the port in reprisal.

ESSENTIALS

GETTING THERE　　There are seven flights a week from Madrid to La Coruña. Serviced only by Aviaco, the **Aeropuerto de Alvedro** (℡ **98-118-72-00**) is 10km (6 miles) from the heart of the city.

From Madrid (via Orense and Zamora), there is express **train** service two times a day (trip time: 8½ hr.). Arrivals are at the **La Coruña Station** on Calle Joaquín Planelles (℡ **90-224-02-02**). For the RENFE office, Calle Fonseca 3, call ℡ **98-118-43-35.**

From Santiago, there's frequent daily **bus** service leaving from the station on Calle Caballeros (℡ **98-118-43-35**). Four buses a day connect Madrid and

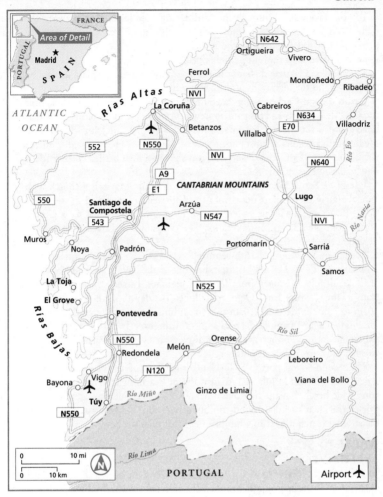

La Coruña (trip time: 7 hr.). A one-way ticket from Madrid costs from 32€ to 45€.

By **car,** La Coruña is reached from Madrid by the N-VI. You can also follow the coastal highway, the N-634, which runs all the way across the northern rim of Spain from San Sebastián to the east.

VISITOR INFORMATION   The **tourist office** at Dársena de la Marina s/n (✆ **98-122-18-22;** www.turgalicia.es) is open Monday through Friday from 9am to 2pm and 4:30 to 6:30pm, Saturday from 10:30am to 1pm.

EXPLORING LA CORUÑA

La Coruña's old town is ideal for strolling around. **Plaza de María Pita** divides the old town from the new. María Pita, a local housewife, was said to have spotted the approach of Drake's troops. Risking her own life, she fired a cannon shot to alert the citizens to an imminent invasion. For that act of heroism, she is revered to this day.

You can take a stroll through the **Jardines de Méndez Núñez,** between the harbor and Los Cantones (Cantón Grande and Cantón Pequeño). Facing the police station and overlooking the port, the gardens are in the very center of town and make for a restful interlude during your sightseeing.

The cobbled **Plazuela de Santa Bárbara**—a tiny tree-shaded plaza flanked by old houses and the high walls of the Santa Bárbara convent—also merits a visit.

Jardín de San Carlos, along Paseo del Parrote, dates from 1843 and is near the Casa de la Cultura. This garden grew up on the site of an old fortress that once guarded the harbor. It contains the tomb of Gen. Sir John Moore, who fought unsuccessfully against the troops of Napoléon. He retreated with his British forces to La Coruña, where he was shot in a final battle. These gardens now make an ideal picnic spot.

Iglesia de Santa María del Campo, Calle de Santa María, is a church with an elaborately carved west door from the 13th century, modeled in the traditional Romanesque-Gothic style. Beneath its rose window you'll see a Gothic portal from the 13th or 14th century. The tympanum is carved with a scene depicting the Adoration of the Magi.

Castillo de San Antón, a 16th-century fort, is now the **Museo Arqueológico e Histórico** (© 98-118-98-50), standing out in the bay on the southeast side of the peninsula. It is open from July to September, Tuesday through Saturday from 11am to 9pm; from October to June, Tuesday through Saturday from 10am to 7pm, and Sunday 10am to 2pm. Admission is 2€ for adults, and 1€ for children ages 13 and under and adults 66 and over. In addition to having a panoramic location on its own islet, it displays many unusual artifacts from La Coruña province. Take bus number 3 or 3A.

The second-largest port in Spain, La Coruña is a popular vacation resort, so it gets very crowded in July and August. Riazor Beach, right in town, is a good, fairly wide beach, but the best one is Santa Cristina, about 5km (3 miles) outside town. There's regular round-trip bus service, but the best way to go is via the steamer (catch it next to Club Náutico) that plies the bay.

WHERE TO STAY
EXPENSIVE

La Toja Hotel Finisterre ⭐⭐   Immediately above the port, a short walk east of the tourist information office at the edge of the old town, this high-rise hotel is one of the finest and most panoramic in town. Bedrooms are small but comfortable, with wall-to-wall carpeting; lots of exposed wood; bright, contemporary upholstery; and private bathrooms with tub/shower combos and plush towels. The hotel is the preferred choice of business travelers. Although it was built in 1947, it has been remodeled many times since, most recently in 2002.

Paseo del Parrote 20, 15001 La Coruña. © **98-120-54-00.** Fax 98-120-84-62. www.hotelfinisterre.com. 92 units. 150€–175€ double; 225€–450€ suite. AE, DC, MC, V. Free parking. Bus: 1, 2, 3, or 5. **Amenities:** Restaurant; bar; 4 pools; tennis court; health club; Jacuzzi; sauna; salon; room service; babysitting; laundry service; dry cleaning; skating rink; basketball court. *In room:* A/C, TV, minibar, hair dryer, safe.

Meliá María Pita ⭐⭐⭐   On Orzan beach, close to the historic district, this graceful government-rated four-star hotel is the city's finest. It's in an elegant building with extensive glass windows. A member of the Meliá chain, it offers a well-lit, marble-floored interior and one of the most efficient staffs in the city. Bedrooms are generally large, and all the units are comfortable, with wooden floors and tasteful decorations, including bathrooms equipped with tub/shower combos. The most desirable accommodations come with private balconies overlooking the ocean.

Av. Pedro Barrié de la Maza 1, 15003 La Coruña. ✆ **98-120-50-00.** Fax 98-120-55-65. www.solmelia.com. 183 units. 113€–160€ double; 260€–450€ suite. AE, DC, MC, V. Parking 12€. **Amenities:** Restaurant; bar; sauna; room service; massage; babysitting; laundry service; dry cleaning. *In room:* A/C, TV, minibar, hair dryer, safe.

MODERATE

Ciudad de La Coruña On the northwestern tip of the peninsula, surrounded by sea grasses and dunes, this government-rated three-star establishment is cordoned off from the apartment-house complexes that surround it by a wide swath of green. Built in the early 1980s, each attractively modern guest room has a private bathroom equipped with a shower unit. Accommodations are generally roomy and maintenance is excellent.

Ciudad Residencial La Torre, Paseo de Adormideras s/n, 15002 La Coruña. ✆ **98-121-11-00.** Fax 98-122-46-10. 131 units. 100€–140€ double; 116€–157€ suite. AE, DC, MC, V. Free parking. Bus: 3, 3A, or 5. **Amenities:** Restaurant; cafeteria; bar; health club; sauna; room service; babysitting; laundry service; dry cleaning. *In room:* TV, minibar, hair dryer, safe.

NH Atlántico This convenient, comfortable, and contemporary hotel contrasts with the lavishly ornate 19th-century park surrounding it, where crowds of Galicians promenade in fine weather. The Atlántico is in the building that houses the city's casino. Well-furnished guest rooms are among the most appealing in town, thanks to relatively spacious dimensions and comfortably contemporary furnishings a cut above less-expensive competitors. Each tiled bathroom is equipped with a tub/shower combination.

Jardines de Méndez Núñez s/n, 15006 La Coruña. ✆ **98-122-65-00.** Fax 98-120-10-71. www.nh-hoteles.com. 199 units. 115€–152€ double; 210€–300€ suite. AE, DC, MC, V. Parking 14€. Bus: 1, 2, or 3. **Amenities:** Restaurant; nightclub; bar; room service; laundry service; dry cleaning; casino. *In room:* A/C, TV, minibar, hair dryer.

INEXPENSIVE

Almirante There are few amenities here—just good, clean rooms, all doubles, at good prices. Room dimensions are a bit skimpy, but the price is right. All units are equipped with neatly kept bathrooms with shower stalls. There is no restaurant, but a continental breakfast is served in the cafeteria (for an extra charge). The location is a bonus: just 1 minute from the beach.

Paseo de Ronda 54, 15011 La Coruña. ✆ **98-125-96-00.** Fax 98-125-96-08. 20 units. 33€–48€ double. AE, MC, V. Parking 5.50€. Bus: 7, 14, or 14A. **Amenities:** Bar; room service; laundry service; dry cleaning. *In room:* TV.

Hotel España This pleasant but somewhat lackluster choice lies just a few steps from the gazebos and roses of the Jardines de Méndez Núñez. It has a narrow reception area, a comfortable series of long sitting rooms, and modern, simply furnished rooms. All units come equipped with neatly kept bathrooms containing shower stalls.

Juana de Vega 7, 15004 La Coruña. ✆ **98-122-45-06.** Fax 98-120-02-79. hotespa@deza.com. 84 units. 46€–75€ double. AE, DC, MC, V. Parking 8€. Bus: 1, 2, or 23. **Amenities:** Bar; laundry. *In room:* TV.

WHERE TO DINE

Two or so blocks from the waterfront, several restaurants specialize in Galician cuisine, all with competitive prices. It's customary to go window-shopping for food here. The restaurants along two of the principal streets—Calle de la Estrella and Calle de los Olmos—all have display counters up front.

Adega O Bebedeiró GALICIAN In business since the 1980s, this dining room looks much older and, in fact, evokes a rustic farmstead with its old stone walls, fireplace, and hardwood floors. Guests sit at pine tables and stools, taking in the backdrop of dust-covered wine bottles and farm equipment. In such a traditional setting, you expect old-fashioned, time-tested recipes—and that's what you get. The kitchen uses first rate and fresh ingredients in their hearty, regional fare such as local fish stuffed with shellfish and baked in a puff pastry. A side dish worth savoring is the mushrooms grown in the nearby countryside and served in olive oil with a green pepper sauce. An unusual concoction is prawns stewed with fresh avocado. The kitchen also turns out one of the best shellfish-laced paellas in town.

Calle Angel Rebollo 34. ℂ **98-121-06-09.** Reservations not required. Main courses 6€–14€. AE, DC, MC, V. Daily 1–4pm and 8pm–midnight. Closed last 2 weeks of Dec and June.

Casa Pardo ✦✦✦ GALICIAN Near the Palacio de Congresos south of the old town, this restaurant is justly acclaimed as the finest dining room in the city. Under the direction of Eduardo Pardo, it offers both a traditional cuisine and innovative seafood dishes. Fresh shellfish and fish dishes, everything from oysters to salmon, are prepared here with skill. The Galician turbot is delectable. Seafood items aren't the only selections on the menu—fresh meat and vegetable dishes are also well prepared. Patrons of this entrenched dining room prefer such wines as Terras Gauda and Viña Costeira. The restaurant is elegant but unstuffy. The fact that the first-rate staff is alert and informed about the graceful service rituals of old Spain makes this a subtle and relaxed, although undeniably formal, atmosphere.

Novoa Santos 15. ℂ **98-128-71-78.** Reservations recommended. Main courses 12€–21€. AE, DC, MC, V. Mon–Sat 1:30–4pm and 9pm–midnight.

El Coral ✦ GALICIAN/SEAFOOD/INTERNATIONAL This is our favorite and one of the most popular dining spots at the port. In business since 1954, it offers polite service, cleanliness, and Galician cookery prepared with distinction. This restaurant specializes in shellfish, fish, meats, and Galician wines. The chef's specialty is *turbante de mariscos* (shellfish). You might also try the *calamares rellenos* (stuffed squid). A popular main course is *lubina* (sea bass) *al horno.* A pitcher (1 liter) of Ribero wine makes a good choice; you can also order Condados and Rioja wines. The front window forms an altar of shellfish in infinite varieties, a tapestry of crustaceans and mollusks. Inside, the atmosphere is intimate and elegant, with formally dressed waiters, crisp white linens, dark wood-paneled walls, and glittering crystal chandeliers.

Av. De la Marina Callejón de la Estacada 9. ℂ **98-120-05-69.** Reservations recommended. Main courses 12€–18€. AE, DC, MC, V. Mon–Sat 1–4pm and 9pm–midnight. Bus: 1, 2, 5, or 17.

LA CORUÑA AFTER DARK

Some of the most appealing bars in La Coruña are atmospheric holes-in-the-wall with a local clientele and a decor that has remained virtually unchanged since the end of the Spanish Civil War. A good example of this is **La Traída,** Calle Torreiro 3 (ℂ **98-122-93-21**), whose *empanadas* and tapas are much sought after. The place's walls are lined with posters from past bullfights, political rallies, and art exhibitions. Don't look for a sign—there isn't one, at least not one marking the entrance. Equally appealing is **Bar La Bombilla,** Galera 7 (ℂ **98-122-46-91**), where flavorful tapas and strong red wines help a night go by faster.

A roughly equivalent competitor is **Bar Yeboles,** Calle Capitán Trancoso 14 (© **98-120-62-20**), set close to Town Hall and the Plaza de María Pita, the town's main square. If you want to go dancing after your drinks and tapas, and if it's after around 11pm, consider a run into the town's most appealing and most popular disco, **Disco Playa Club,** Av. Pedro Barrie de la Massa s/n (© **98-127-75-14**). Set on an oceanfront terrace, a few feet from the waves of Playa Riazor, it's open year-round Thursday through Saturday.

2 Santiago de Compostela ✮✮✮

614km (381 miles) NW of Madrid, 74km (46 miles) S of La Coruña

All roads in Spain once led to the northwestern pilgrimage city of **Santiago de Compostela.** In addition to being the third-largest holy city of the Christian world, Santiago de Compostela is a university town and a marketplace for Galician farmers.

But it was the medieval pilgrims who made the city famous. A pilgrimage to the tomb of the beheaded apostle, St. James, was a high point for the faithful—peasant and prince alike—who journeyed here from all over Europe.

Santiago de Compostela's link with legend began in A.D. 813, when an urn was discovered containing what were believed to be the remains of St. James. A temple was erected over the spot, but in the 16th century, church fathers hid the remains of the saint, fearing they might be destroyed in raids along the coast by Sir Francis Drake. Somewhat amazingly, the alleged remains—subject of millions of pilgrimages from across Europe—lay relatively forgotten.

For decades no one was exactly certain where they were. Then in 1879 a workman making repairs on the church discovered what were supposed to be the remains, hidden since the 1500s. Of course, skeptics seriously questioned their authenticity. To prove this was the actual corpse of St. James, church officials brought back a sliver of the skull of St. James from Italy. They claimed that it fit perfectly, like a puzzle piece, into the recently discovered skeleton.

Aside from its religious connections, Santiago de Compostela, with its flagstone streets, churches, and shrines, is one of the most romantic and historic of Spain's great cities. It has been declared a national landmark. Santiago has the dubious distinction of being the rainiest city in Spain, but the showers tend to arrive and end suddenly. Locals claim that the rain only makes their city more beautiful, and the rain-slick cobblestones might prompt you to agree.

ESSENTIALS

GETTING THERE   From Madrid, Iberia has daily **flights** to Santiago, and there are daily flights from Barcelona. The only international airport in Galicia is east of Santiago de Compostela at Lavacolla (© **98-154-75-01** for flight information), 11km (7 miles) from the center on the road to Lugo.

From La Coruña, 16 **trains** make the 1-hour trip daily at a cost of 3.30€ to 4€. Two trains arrive daily from Madrid. The 8-hour trip costs 38€. Call © **90-224-02-02** for information.

Buses leave on the hour, connecting La Coruña with Santiago (1 hr. away), and cost 5.50€. Three buses arrive in Santiago daily from Madrid (8–9 hr.). The trip costs 37€. Phone © **98-158-77-00** for schedules.

If you're **driving,** take the express highway (A-9/E-50) south from La Coruña to reach Santiago. From Madrid, N-VI runs to Galicia. From Lugo, head south along N-640.

VISITOR INFORMATION   The **tourist office,** at Rua del Villar 43 (© **98-158-40-81;** www.turgalicia.es.), is open Monday through Friday from 10am to 2pm and 4 to 7pm, Saturday from 11am to 2pm and 5 to 7pm, and Sunday from 11am to 2pm.

STROLLING THROUGH SANTIAGO

Santiago de Compostela's highlight is undoubtedly its storied cathedral, and you should take at least 2 hours to see it. Afterward, take a stroll through this enchanting town, which has a number of other interesting monuments as well as many stately mansions along Rua del Villar and Rua Nueva.

The **Catedral** ✮✮✮, Plaza del Obradoiro (© **98-158-35-48**), begun in the 11th century, is the crowning achievement of Spanish Romanesque architecture, even though it actually reflects a number of styles. Maestro Mateo's **Pórtico de la Gloria** ✮✮✮, carved in 1188, ranks among the finest produced in Europe at that time. The three arches of the portico are carved with biblical figures from the Last Judgment. In the center, Christ is flanked by apostles and the 24 Elders of the Apocalypse. Below the Christ figure is a depiction of St. James himself. He crowns a carved column that includes a portrayal of Mateo at the bottom. If you observe this column, you will see that a series of five deep indentations has been worn into it by pilgrims since the Middle Ages. Even today pilgrims line up here to lean forward to place their hands on the pillar and touch foreheads with Mateo.

The cathedral has three naves in cruciform shape and several chapels and cloisters. The altar, with its blend of Gothic simplicity and baroque decor, is extraordinary. You can visit the crypt, where a silver urn contains what are believed to be the remains of the Apostle St. James. A cathedral museum displays tapestries and archaeological fragments. Next door, the **Palacio de Gelmírez** (© **98-157-23-00**), an archbishop's palace built during the 12th century, is another outstanding example of Romanesque architecture.

Admission to the cathedral is free; to the cloisters, 3€; to the Palacio de Gelmírez, 1.20€. Hours for the cathedral are daily from 7am to 9pm; for the museum, from July to October, Monday through Saturday from 10am to 1:30pm and 4 to 7:30pm, Sunday from 10am to 1:30pm and 4 to 7pm; from November to June, Monday through Saturday from 11am to 1pm and 4 to 6pm, Sunday from 10am to 1:30pm and 4 to 6pm. For the Palacio de Gelmírez, the hours are from July to September, daily from 10:30am to 1:30pm and 4 to 7pm.

Most of the other impressive buildings are on Plaza del Obradoiro, also called Plaza de España. Next to the cathedral is **Hostal de los Reyes Católicos** ✮, now a parador (see "Where to Stay," below), formerly a royal hospice and, in the 15th century, a pilgrims' hospice. It was designed by Enrique de Egas, Isabella and Ferdinand's favorite architect. Tourists may visit the cloistered courtyard with its beautiful 16th- to 18th-century fountains and the main chapel; however, you must have a guide from the cathedral in attendance (© **98-158-22-00** for information). Hours are daily from 10am to 1pm and 4 to 7pm.

Monasterio de San Martín Pinario ✮, Plaza de la Immaculada, founded in 899 and rebuilt in the 17th century, remains one of the most important monasteries in Galicia. Its large facade was built in the Compostela baroque style, with massive Doric columns. The interior has a richly ornamented Churrigueresque high altar and choir stalls that are truly works of art.

Santiago de Compostela

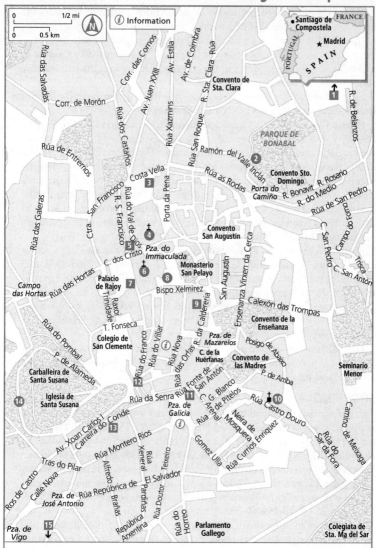

ATTRACTIONS ●
Casa de la Canónica **8**
Catedral **6**
Centro Gallego de Arte
    Contemporáneo **2**
Monasterio de San Martín
    Pinario **4**
Palacio de Gelmírez **6**
Paseo de la Herradura **14**

Plaza de la Quintana **8**
Plaza de las Platerías **8**
Santa María del Sar **10**

ACCOMMODATIONS ■
Casa Hotel as Artes **5**
Hesperia Compostela **11**
Hostal de los Reyes
    Católicos **7**

Hotel Entrecercas **12**
Hotel Real **11**
Hotel-Residencia Costa
    Vella **10**
Los Abetos Hotel **17**
Meliá Araguaney **5**
Pazo Cibran **15**

One of the most important squares in the old town is **Plaza de la Quintana,** to the left of the cathedral's Goldsmith's Doorway. This is a favorite square with students, who often perch on the flight of broad steps that connect the rear of the cathedral to the walls of a convent. The square is dominated by **Casa de la Canónica,** the former residence of the canon, which has wrought-iron window bars, lending it a rather severe appearance.

South of the square is the Renaissance-style **Plaza de las Platerías (Silver-smiths' Square),** which has an elaborate fountain.

Centro Gallego de Arte Contemporáneo, Rua Valle-Inclán s/n (© **98-154-66-29**), is the Galician Center of Contemporary Art, highlighting artworks from regional, national, and international artists. The center's changing exhibits display the works of contemporary artists, and it hosts retrospectives. Until the opening of this center, contemporary art had virtually no place in the city's agenda, which emphasized the ancient or the antique. Among the several exhibition rooms is a terrace for open-air exhibits, affording a panoramic view of the old quarter of Santiago. The admission-free museum is open Tuesday through Sunday from 11am to 8pm.

Farther afield, visit the Romanesque **Santa María del Sar,** on Calle Castron d'Ouro, .8km (½ mile) down Calle de Sar, which starts at the Patio de Madre. This collegiate church is one of the architectural gems of the Romanesque style in Galicia. Its walls and columns are on a 15° slant, thought to be attributable to either a fragile foundation or an architect's fancy. Visit the charming cloister with its slender columns. The church is open Monday through Saturday from 10am to 1pm and 4 to 7pm. Admission is free.

Cap off your day with a walk along **Paseo de la Herradura,** the gardens southwest of the old town, from where you have an all-encompassing view of the cathedral and the old city.

SHOPPING

The artfully naive blue-and-white porcelain that's a trademark of the town is available for sale at **Sargadelos,** Rua Nueva 16 (© **98-158-19-05**). A competitor that stocks similar ceramics, plus a wide range of other regional handicrafts, is **Amboa,** Rua Nueva 44 (© **98-158-33-59**). The best place in town to buy hammered silver, either in the form of jewelry or tableware, is **Fernando Mayer,** Plaza de las Platerías 2 (© **98-158-25-36**). You can find meticulously crafted lace, as well as textiles for the bathroom, dining room, and bedroom, at **Dosel,** Rua Nova 26 (© **98-156-60-78**).

A favorite of most tourists is *tarta Santiago,* a tart sold at virtually every pastry shop in the city. Also very popular is *queso de tetilla,* a local cheese shaped like breasts.

Many of the local wines, including assorted bottles of Ribeiro, Condado, and most famous of all, Albariño, are sold without fanfare in grocery stores throughout Galicia. But for a specialist in the subtleties of Galician and other Spanish wines, head for **Vinoteca Manxares de Galicia,** Rua do Franco 25 (© **98-157-72-27**).

WHERE TO STAY
EXPENSIVE
Hostal de los Reyes Católicos 🏆🏆🏆 This former 16th-century hospice, founded by Ferdinand and Isabella, is one of the most spectacular hotels in Europe. Next to the cathedral, it served as a resting place and hospital for pilgrims

The World's Oldest Hotel

The oldest hotel in the world has been giving travelers a place of rest for nearly 5 centuries. In 1499 the Catholic kings founded the Hospital Real (Royal Hospice) in Santiago de Compostela to serve as a respite for the hundreds of thousands of pilgrims who came to pay homage to the shrine of Saint James. Known today as the **Hostal de Los Reyes Católicos,** the same structure proudly stands as the world's most ancient hotel, and certainly one of the most luxurious.

During the Middle Ages, Santiago prevailed, together with Jerusalem and Rome, as one of the three holy cities of Christendom. The cult of Santiago (St. James) drew hordes of pilgrims trekking across northern Spain in search of the tomb of the saint. The route to Santiago proved long, arduous, and dangerous. Having made the pilgrimage themselves, the Catholic monarchs experienced firsthand the dearth of accommodations along the way—hence the decision by Ferdinand and Isabella to construct monasteries and hospitals to house and protect visitors, the best effort culminating in this prominent structure.

Construction on the Hospital Real began in the 15th century and continued through the 18th century. Set on Obradoiro Plaza, this grand edifice shares the square with the impressive cathedral of Santiago. In addition to its luxury rooms, this five-star hotel boasts a concert and exhibition room surrounded by various cloisters. The hotel doorway reflects the Plateresque style, and the windows display rich baroque detailing.

Architecturally, the old part of the city stopped developing in the baroque period, and, as a result, its buildings exude an aura of impressive grandeur—in fact, a sense of mysticism permeates Santiago. It is fitting, then, that one of Spain's great monumental cities should be home to one of the country's most luxurious, historically significant hotels.

visiting the tomb of Saint James. Even if you don't stay here, you should stop in and take a guided tour (see "The World's Oldest Hotel," above).

The hotel has four huge open-air courtyards, each with its own covered walk, gardens, and fountains. In addition, there are great halls, French grillwork, and a large collection of antiques. A Gothic chapel is the setting for weekly concerts. There's a full range of accommodations, everything from Franco's former bedchamber to small rooms. Many of the palatial rooms have ornate canopied beds draped in embroidered red velvet. Hand-carved chests, gilt mirrors, and oil paintings, along with private bathrooms, enhance the air of luxury. Bathrooms are quite sumptuous, with shower/tub combos and deluxe toiletries.

Plaza de Obradoido 1, 15705 Santiago de Compostela. **(C)** **98-158-22-00.** Fax 98-156-30-94. 136 units. 166€ double; from 331€ suite. AE, DC, MC, V. Parking 14€. Bus: 4, 21, 25, 26, 33, or 34. **Amenities:** 2 restaurants; bar; car rental; salon; room service; babysitting; laundry service; dry cleaning. *In room:* A/C, TV, minibar, hair dryer, safe.

Meliá Araguaney ★★ Located in Santiago's commercial and residential zone, about 8 blocks southwest of the cathedral, this is a comfortably streamlined hotel, newly renovated and boasting some of the most up-to-date dining, drinking, and conference facilities in town. The stylish, modern rooms range from small to midsize, each comfortably furnished with firm mattresses. All the tiled bathrooms are equipped with tub/shower combos. Locals cite the hotel as the city's most well-run modern hotel. It has one of the best and most efficient staffs in town, and people in the area on business often prefer this up-to-date choice.

Calle Alfredo Brañas 5, 15701 Santiago de Compostela. ✆ **98-159-59-00.** Fax 98-159-02-87. www. araguaney.com. 81 units. 166€ double; from 220€ suite. AE, DC, MC, V. Parking 11€. Bus: 4, 21, 25, 26, 33, or 34. **Amenities:** 2 restaurants; bar; pool; sauna; car rental; room service; babysitting; laundry service; dry cleaning. *In room:* A/C, TV, minibar, hair dryer, safe.

MODERATE

Hesperia Compostela ★ This hotel is conveniently located just a few short blocks from the cathedral, but it is also, unfortunately, close to the heavily trafficked city center. It has a grand granite facade, which belies the modern interior, and bedrooms filled with clean, angular, machine-made furniture. All the tiled bathrooms are equipped with tub/shower combos, and the housekeeping is excellent. Accommodations are generally roomy, although some units are quite small. The hotel was completely renovated in 1995.

Hórreo 1, 15702 Santiago de Compostela. ✆ **98-158-57-00.** Fax 98-158-52-90. www.hoteles-hesperia.es. 99 units. 60€–123€ double; 230€ suite. AE, DC, MC, V. Bus: 10. **Amenities:** Restaurant; bar; room service; laundry service; dry cleaning. *In room:* TV, minibar, hair dryer.

Los Abetos Hotel ★★ If you're seeking quaint charm from long ago, check into the Reyes Católicos parador. But if you want the best facilities in town and up-to-date comfort in a government-rated four-star hotel, make it Los Abetos. A favorite of business travelers, it works equally well for pilgrims to the old city. Surrounded by private gardens, the hotel also has the best fitness facilities, everything from the modern gym to a heated swimming pool. Fresh as tomorrow, bedrooms range from midsize to spacious, and each comes with a first-rate private bathroom with tub and shower.

San Lázaro, 15820 Santiago de Compostela. ✆ **98-155-70-26.** Fax 98-158-61-77. www.galinor.es/ mercurelosabetos/servicios-i.html. 148 units. 134€ double. Children under 10 free. AE, DC, MC, V. **Amenities:** Restaurant; bar; pool; tennis court; gym; sauna; library. *In room:* A/C, TV, minibar, hair dryer, safe.

INEXPENSIVE

Casa Hotel as Artes ★ *Finds* Lying in the vicinity of the cathedral, this hotel is a delight and a most inviting choice for those who can't afford the steep tariffs of Hostel de los Reyes Católicos. What makes the place so special is that each of its midsize and well-furnished rooms is named after a different international artist and decorated in the spirit of that artist. Rooms are decorated to honor Rodin, Dante, Vivaldi, Gaudí, Picasso, even Charlie Chaplin. A naked picture frames dancer, Isadora Duncan's room. The Picasso room has two reproductions of his paintings, including one from his so-called "blue period." The accommodations are decorated in an old Spanish style, with hardwood floors, wrought-iron double beds, and recessed windows with beveled shutters. All the units contain a small but tidily arranged private bathroom, each with shower, a few with tub as well.

Traversía de Dos Puertas 2, off Rúa San Francisco, 15707 Santiago de Compostela. ✆ **98-157-2950.** Fax 98-157-7823. www.asartes.com. 7 units. 52€–86€. AE, DC, MC, V. **Amenities:** Bar, sauna, laundry. *In room:* TV, hair dryer.

Hotel Entrecercas *(Value)*   This newly opened property not only offers some of the city's most affordable lodgings, but lies 30m (98 ft.) from the cathedral itself, so it's most central for exploring the medieval core on foot. This owner has sensitively restored this old building, retaining its ancient stonework and restoring exposed and time-blackened wooden beams. The bedrooms are simply but comfortably decorated, each with a little private bathroom with shower. In summer you should reserve as far in advance as possible.

Entrecercas 11, 15703 Santiago de Compostela. ⓒ **98-157-1151.** Fax 98-157-1112. 7 units. 57€–64€ double. Rates include breakfast. AE, DC, MC, V. **Amenities:** Cafeteria. *In room:* TV.

Hotel-Residencia Costa Vella   This well-run hotel lies on the street, Perta de la Peña, which means one of the seven doors leading into the medieval sector of Santiago. At one of the loftiest points in the city, this is a traditional glass-fronted building. The interior opens to reveal midsize bedrooms that have Galician styling in the use of carved wooden headboards and stone accents. Rooms manage to look both classical yet modern, with tidy bathrooms with both shower and tub. Breakfast is served with a view, and features such Galician delights as cheese with honey, almond cake, and homemade toasted bread.

Rúa Porta de Peña 17, 15704 Santiago de Compostela. ⓒ **98-156-9530.** Fax 98-156-9531. www.santiago hostelria.com. 14 units. 52€ double. MC, V. Closed Dec 23-Jan 8. **Amenities:** Cafeteria; room service; laundry/dry cleaning. *In room:* TV.

Hotel Real *★ (Finds)*   Only a few minutes walk from the cathedral, this small hotel is a charmer. A former house for university students, it's been successfully converted to receive guests at large. Its bedrooms are distributed across three floors, all of them enjoying natural light and a balcony overlooking the medieval city. The rooms are small but tastefully furnished and comfortable, each with a tidy, immaculate bathroom with tub and shower. Breakfast, the only meal offered, is served in a delightful little salon.

Caldereria 49, 15703 Santiago de Compostela. ⓒ **98-156-92-90.** Fax 98-156-92-91. www.hotelreal.com. 13 units. 60€–65€ double. Rates include breakfast. AE, MC, V. *In room:* TV.

Pazo Cibrán *★ (Finds)*   Sensitively restored, this is a farmhouse/manor that dates from the 1700s, lying 7km (4⅓ miles) to the south of Santiago, about 15 minutes by car if there's no traffic. You're welcomed by the hospitable proprietor, Mayka Iglesias, who offers six rooms in the main manor plus five more spacious accommodations in a converted stable. Bedrooms are beautifully and traditionally furnished, with handsome bathrooms with tubs or showers. Madam Iglesias has maintained her ancestral family living room, and it's filled with antiques and interesting objects, opening on a stunning garden where magnolias and camellias grow along with palm trees and grape vines. There's even a "bamboo walk." Nearby is the Restaurant Roberto in another converted house. Traditional Galician dishes with home-grown products are served here.

San Xulian a de Sales, 15885 Verda. ⓒ **98-151-1515.** Fax 98-1181-4766. www.pazocibran.com. 11 units. 60€–80€. AE, DC, MC,V. **Amenities:** Bar; babysitting; room service; laundry/dry cleaning. *In room:* No phone.

WHERE TO DINE

Alameda REGIONAL   Since 1954 a constant stream of diners, both foreign and local, has demonstrated the popularity of this government-rated "two-fork" restaurant, opposite the Parque de Alameda. There is a stylish cafeteria/snack bar on the ground floor, great for light meals and drinks; guests can sit at sidewalk tables in fair weather. The fare includes many Galician specialties, and the chef is noted for his paella. Start with the *caldo gallego* (Galician soup) and follow with another regional specialty, *lacón con grelos* (ham hock with greens). The *necoras* (spider crabs) are a real gourmet delight.

Porta Faxeira 15. ℂ **98-158-66-57.** Reservations recommended in summer. Main courses 11€–23€; fixed-price menu 18€. AE, DC, MC, V. Daily 1–4pm and 8pm–midnight.

Casa Manolo *Value* GALICIAN   Set in the large but cozy dining room of a brick-built house that's at least a century old, this family-run restaurant offers one of the best dining values in Santiago. There's only one option here: a two-course set-price menu whose components include different roasts and filets. Veal cutlets, either breaded in the "Milanese" style, or with cheese in the "Parmigiana" style, are enduringly popular, as are the pastas (especially cannelloni stuffed with a form of ricotta cheese). Filet steak served *a la plancha* (grilled) and pork chops are also good. Don't expect glamour, as that's not what this place is selling. Instead, you'll get generous portions of rib-sticking food that's more reasonably priced than virtually anywhere else.

Plaza Cerrantes s/n. ℂ **98-158-29-50.** Fixed-price menu 5.20€. MC, V. Daily 1–4:30pm; Mon–Sat 8–11:30pm.

Don Gaiferos ✦ GALICIAN   Acclaimed as the best restaurant in this historic city, this winning choice stands only 200m (656 ft.) from the cathedral and has been turning out a savory cuisine for 3 decades. The food is enjoyed as much by locals as by visitors. The decor is tasteful and inviting, and the location is right next to the Church of Santa María Salomé. The well-crafted cuisine, platter after platter, is made from first-rate ingredients. Tuck into the freshly caught *merluza* (hake), which is served with a delectable sauce. The scallops with Spanish rice are a delight, as are the giant prawns filled with smoked salmon. The zesty kettle of fish stew is the city's finest, and you can also order a well-flavored loin of beef or even steak tartare if you're not worried about "mad cow." To finish off, the chef makes some smooth dessert, including an utterly delightful cheesecake studded with bilberries or an almond tart, for which you'll want to pay homage to the pastry chef.

Rúa Nova 23. ℂ **98-158-3894.** Reservations required. Main courses 8€–18€. AE, DC, MC, V. Tues–Sat 1:30–3:45pm; daily 8:15–11:30pm.

Restaurante Vilas ✦ *Finds* SEAFOOD   Located on the outskirts of the old town on the road to Pontevedra, this reliable Spanish tavern, housed in a three-story town house, enjoys a devoted clientele, many from industry, politics, and the arts. Beyond the large bar near the entrance and display cases filled with fresh fish, you'll find the baronial stone-trimmed dining room. A wide variety of fish is available—fresh sardines, three different preparations of salmon, a *zarzuela* (seafood stew), and eels. Two kinds of paella are served, and non-fish dishes such as partridge and rabbit are also on the menu. The restaurant was founded in 1915 as a little eating house. Back then, it was on the outskirts of town, but it was enveloped by the city long ago. It stands on a street named after the illustrious female poet of Galicia. Today, the restaurant is run by the grandsons of the original founders.

Calle Rosalía de Castro 88. ℂ **98-159-21-70.** Reservations required. Main courses 12€–23€; fixed-price menu 27€. AE, DC, MC, V. Mon–Sat 1–5pm and 8pm–midnight.

Toñi Vicente ✦✦✦ GALICIAN/INTERNATIONAL   Set in the heart of town, on two floors of a building erected around 1950, this is the finest and most flamboyantly international restaurant in Santiago or for miles around. Within dining rooms accented with a neoclassical overlay, you can enjoy the celebrated cuisine of Toñi Vicente. Menu items change with the availability of the ingredients, but are likely to include such delectable dishes as a warm seafood salad with herbs, escalopes of veal with a confit of onions, turbot with chive sauce, unusual preparations of seasonal game dishes, and for dessert, a tart made with Galician pears.

Calle Rosalía de Castro 24. © 98-159-41-00. Reservations recommended. Main courses 17€–21€; fixed-price menu 48€. AE, DC, MC, V. Mon–Sat 1:30–4pm and 9pm–midnight. Closed first 2 weeks in Jan and Aug.

SANTIAGO AFTER DARK

There's much more to do in the religious centerpiece of Galicia after dark than just pray. There are an estimated 200 bars and *cafeterías* on the Rua do Franco and its neighbor, Rua da Raiña. The pavement along those streets on weekend evenings at around 11pm is mobbed. You can have a lot of fun ducking into any of them, but one that is particularly convivial is **Bar/Cafetería Dakar,** Rua do Franco 13 (© 98-157-81-92). Two highly appealing competitors are **Pub Borriquita de Belén,** Rua San Pelayo 22 (no phone), and its neighbor, **Bar Crechas,** Rua San Pelayo 28 (no phone), both of which appeal to barhoppers thanks to occasional live music that packs clients in anytime after 10pm. Know in advance that the de rigueur method for pursuing after-dark diversion in Santiago involves hitting a roster of bars and tapas joints before midnight, and dancing the night away beginning anytime after midnight.

Beiro, Rua da Raiña 3 (© 98-158-13-70), is one of the town's best wine bars with a marvelous selection of vintages throughout the country, especially those from Galicia itself. Slices of Serrano ham, savory sausages, and homemade country terrines round out the offerings along with one of the best selections of Galician cheese in town; try the breast-shaped *queso de tetilla,* a local favorite. You can also enjoy tapas at a little bar named **O 42,** Rua do Franco 42 (© 98-158-10-09), a friendly and inviting place that specializes in seafood. The octopus is especially good. Wash the tapas down with the house wine, an Albariño.

The most likely dance option in town, which begins after midnight and continues until 4 or 5am, is **Disco Casting Araguaney,** Rua Montero Ríos 25 (© 98-159-59-00).

3 Rías Altas ✯

In Norway they're called fiords; in Brittany, abers; in Scotland, lochs; and in Galicia, *rías.* These inlets have been cut into the Galician coastline by the turbulent Atlantic pounding against its shores. **Rías Altas** is a relatively modern name applied to all the estuaries on the northern Galician coast, from Ribadeo (the gateway to Galicia on the border with Asturias) to La Coruña (the big Atlantic seaport of northwest Spain). The part that begins at Ribadeo, part of Lugo province, is also called Marina Lucense. Four estuaries form the Artabro Gulf: La Coruña, Betanzoa, Ares, and Ferrol. All four converge on a single point, where the Marola crag rises.

ON THE ROAD FROM RIBADEO TO LA CORUÑA

From Ribadeo, take the corniche road west (N-634) until you reach the Ría de Foz. About 2.5km (1½ miles) south of the Foz-Barreiros highway, perched somewhat in isolation on a hill, stands the **Iglesia de San Martín de Mondoñeda,** part of a monastery that dates from 1112. Please keep in mind that while corniche roads are sinuous and panoramic, they are often located high above the road surface and have steep, usually rather dangerous, drop-offs on the other side.

The little town of **Foz** is a fishing village and a summer resort with beaches separated by a cliff. You might stop here for lunch.

From Foz, cut northwest along the coastal highway (C-642), going through **Burela,** another fishing village. You can make a slight detour south to **Sargadelos,** a ceramics center. You can purchase the famous Galician pottery here much more cheaply than elsewhere in Spain.

Back on the coastal road (C-642) at Burela, continue west approaching Ría de Viveiro and the historic village of **Viveiro.** Part of its medieval walls and an old gate, Puerta de Carlos V, have been preserved. The town has many old churches of interest, including the Gothic-style Iglesia San Francisco. Viveiro is a summer resort, attracting vacationers to its beach, the Playa Covas, and makes a good lunch stop.

The road continues northwest to **Vicedo,** passing such beaches as Xillo and Aerealong. Excellent vistas of the estuary greet you, and oxen can be seen plowing the cornfields.

Driving on, you'll notice the coastline becoming more saw-toothed. Eventually you reach **Ortigueira,** a major fishing village at the head of the *ría* (estuary) from which it takes its name. A Celtic folk festival is staged here at the end of August.

From here you can continue south along C-642 to **El Ferrol,** which used to be called El Caudillo, in honor of the late dictator Francisco Franco, who was born here and who used to spend part of his summers in this area. El Ferrol is one of the major shipbuilding centers of Spain, and since the 18th century it has been a center of the Spanish navy. It's a grimy town, but it lies on one of the region's most beautiful *rías*. Despite its parador, few tourists will want to linger at El Ferrol (also spelled O Ferrol).

From El Ferrol, C-642 continues south, passing through the small town of **Puentedeume** (also spelled Pontedeume), on the Rías Ares. Historically, it was the center of the counts of Andrade. The last remains of their 14th-century palace can be seen, along with the ruins of a 13th-century castle, rising to the east.

Shortly below Betanzos, head west along N-VI until you reach La Coruña. The entire trip from Ribadeo is roughly 242km (150 miles) and takes at least 4 hours.

WHERE TO DINE ALONG THE COAST

Nito SEAFOOD   Established in the early 1970s, this restaurant is in the center of Viveiro, only 90m (100 yd.) from the beach, with a sweeping view of the Atlantic. It starts serving dinner early for Spain (8:30pm) and maintains a nice balance between prices and quality of its ingredients, serving unpretentious but flavor-filled food. Shellfish, priced according to weight, is the specialty, but you can order grilled sea bream or perhaps a house-style beefsteak. Most diners begin their meal with a bowl of *caldo gallego*. A full range of wines is offered. Diners wanting to eat outside can sit on a garden-view terrace.

Playa de Area, Viveiro. ✆ **98-256-09-87.** Reservations recommended. Main courses 11€–20€; fixed-price menu 13€. AE, MC, V. Daily 1–4pm and 8:30pm–midnight.

EXPLORING THE RIAS ALTAS ON TWO WHEELS

Some of the best biking in Spain is found in the Rías Altas. Much of south and central Spain is too hot for biking, but here temperatures are generally cool, and an interesting vista unfolds at every turn. Depending on your time, stamina, and interest, the **tourist office** at Viveiro, Plaza Mayor 27 (© **98-223-13-61;** www.xunta.es), can give you a map and some suggested routes.

From Viveiro, the most scenic route is to the west, following along the C-642 to El Ferrol on the sea. A particularly dramatic stretch awaits if you head north along a secondary road when you come to the junction at the little town of Mera. Signs point north to another little town, Carino, opening onto views of Cabo Ortegal. To the east is a sheltered body of water, Ría de Santa María, and to the west the Atlantic Ocean. From Viveiro you can also go inland heading south along Route 640, following the signs to the hamlet of Oral. You can also take the coastal road east from Viveiro, signposted RIBADEO. Ribadeo is too built-up to interest most cyclists, but depending on your stamina, you can cycle to the little seaside villages of San Ciprian, Burella, and Foz.

FROM LA CORUÑA TO CAPE FISTERRA

This next section, the drive "to the end of the world," takes you from La Coruña to **Cabo Fisterra** ✦ (called Fisterra or Finisterre on most maps). It's a 145km (90-mile) trip that takes at least 3 hours. For the ancients, Cape Fisterra was the end of the world as they knew it.

This route takes you along **A Costa da Morte** (La Costa de la Muerte; **The Coast of Death**), so called because of the numerous shipwrecks that have occurred here.

Leaving La Coruña, take the coastal road west (Hwy. 552), heading first to the road junction of **Carballo,** a distance of 36km (22 miles). From this little town, many of the small coastal harbors are within an easy drive. **Malpica,** to the northwest, is the most interesting, with its own beach. An offshore seabird sanctuary exists here, and Malpica itself was a former whaling port. From Malpica, continue to the tiny village of **Corme** at Punta Roncudo. This sheltered fishing village draws summer beach fans, as there are many isolated sand dunes.

From Corme, continue along the winding roads to the whitewashed village of **Camariñas,** which stands on the *ría* of the same name. A road here leads all the way to the lighthouse at Cabo Vilán. Camariñas is known as a village of expert lace makers, and you'll see the work for sale at many places.

The road now leads to **Mugia** (shown on some maps as "Muxia"), below which stands the lighthouse at Cabo Touriñan. Continue driving south along clearly marked coastal roads that are sometimes perched precariously on cliff tops overlooking the sea. They will lead you to **Corcubión,** a village with a Romanesque church. From here, follow signs that lead you along a lonely southbound secondary road to the end of the line, **Cabo Fisterra,** for a panoramic view. The sunsets from here are among the most spectacular in the world. The Roman poet Horace said it best: "The brilliant skylight of the sun drags behind it the black night over the fruitful breasts of earth."

4 Rías Bajas ✦✦

After Cabo Fisterra, some of the most dramatic coastal scenery in Spain flanks coastal Highway 550, following the edge of one of the most tortuous shorelines in Europe. The four estuaries, collectively called the **Rías Bajas,** face the Atlantic from Cape Silleiro to Baiona to Point Louro in Muros. Two of these are in the province of Pontevedra (Ría de Pontevedra and Ría de Vigo); one is in the province of La Coruña (Ría de Muros y Noya); and one (Ría de Arousa) divides its shores between the two provinces. The 32km (20-mile) Vigo estuary is the longest, stretching from Ponte Sampasio to Baiona.

DRIVING FROM MUROS TO SANTA UXEA DE RIBEIRA

The seaside town of **Muros** has many old houses and a harbor, but **Noya** (also spelled Noia), to the southeast, is more impressive. If you don't have a car but would like to see at least one or two *ría* fishing villages, you can do so at either Noya or Muros: Both are on a bus route connecting them with Santiago de Compostela. Eleven buses per day leave from Santiago heading for Noya, and nine run to Muros. Some of the tiny villages and beaches are connected by bus routes.

If you do drive, the entire trip is only 76km (47 miles); at a leisurely pace it should take you 2 hours. Noya is known for its braided straw hats with black bands. It has a number of interesting, handsome old churches, including the 14th-century **Igrexa de Santa María** (with tombstones dating from the 10th c.) and the **Igrexa de San Francisco.** A lot of good beaches lie on the northern bank of the ría near Muros. Noya is your best bet for a lunch stop.

From Noya, the coast road (Hwy. 550) continues west to **Porto do Son.** You can take a detour to Cabo de Corrubedo, with its lighthouse, before continuing on to Santa Uxea de Ribeira at the southern tip. Ribeira is a fishing port and a canning center. At **Santa Uxea de Ribeira** you'll see Ría de Arousa, the largest and deepest of the inlets.

From Ribeira, continue east along the southern coastal road to **A Puebla de Caramiñal.** From here, take a marked route 10km (6 miles) inland into the mountains, to admire the most magnificent panorama in all of *rías* country— the **Mirador de la Curota** ★★★, at 498m (1,634 ft.). The four inlets of the Rías Bajas can, under the right conditions, be seen from the belvedere. In clear weather you can view Cape Fisterra.

Back on C-550, drive as far as Padrón, where, it is claimed, the legendary sea vessel arrived bringing Santiago (St. James) to Spain. Padrón was also the home of romantic poet Rosalía de Castro (1837–85), sometimes called the Emily Dickinson of Spain. Her house, the **Casa Museo de Rosalía de Castro,** Carretera de Herbrón (© **98-181-12-04**), is open to the public Tuesday through Saturday from 10am to 1:30pm and 4 to 8pm, and Sunday from 10am to 1:30pm. Admission is 1.40€. Padrón makes a good lunch stop.

From Padrón, follow the alleged trail of the body of St. James north along N-550 to Santiago de Compostela or take N-550 south to Pontevedra.

WHERE TO STAY & DINE

Ceboleiro II SEAFOOD   For about a century, this inn has provided food and accommodations to passersby. Set in the heart of Noya, it is owned and managed by three generations of the Fernández family. It offers hearty food from the sea, prepared in conservative but flavorful ways that usually correspond to the culinary traditions of Galicia and northern Portugal. The menu almost always includes several versions of hake, shellfish soup, several kinds of rice studded with fish or shellfish, pork and beef dishes, and, among other desserts, an apple tart. The establishment contains 13 simple but comfortable accommodations, each with private bathroom equipped with a tub/shower combination.

Galicia 15, Noya. © **98-182-44-97.** Main courses 10€–20€. Rooms 40€ double. AE, DC, MC, V. Daily 1–4pm and 9pm–midnight.

Chef Rivera (★) (Finds) GALICIAN/SPANISH   The name of the owner, to everyone in town, is simply El Chef. His cuisine is innovative but based on traditional continental recipes. His wife, Pierrette, attends to service in the dining room, which resembles an English pub with its dark, warm colors and leather upholstery. Try the shellfish soup or stew or the house-style monkfish. The restaurant is known for its *pimientos de Padrón,* which are tiny green peppers sautéed in olive oil. The trick is that about one in five of those peppers is very spicy. You might finish your meal with lemon mousse. The couple rents 20 simply furnished guest rooms equipped with neatly kept bathrooms containing shower stalls.

Enlace Parque 7, Padrón. (℃) **98-181-04-13.** Fax 98-181-14-54. Reservations recommended. Main courses 14€–22€; fixed-price menu 16€–22€. AE, DC, MC, V. Daily 1–4pm and 9pm–midnight. Closed Sun night in winter. Units 39€–45€ double.

5 Pontevedra (★)

58km (36 miles) S of Santiago de Compostela, 839km (521 miles) NW of Madrid

An aristocratic old Spanish town on the Lérez River and the capital of Pontevedra province, the city of **Pontevedra** still has vestiges of an ancient wall that once encircled the town. In medieval days, the town was called Pontis Veteris (Old Bridge).

Some of the best Galician seamen lived in Pontevedra in the Middle Ages. Sheltered at the end of the Pontevedra Ría, the city was a bustling port, and foreign merchants mingled with local traders, seamen, and fishers. It was the home of Pedro Sarmiento de Gamboa, the 16th-century navigator and cosmographer who wrote *Voyage to the Magellan Straits.* In the 18th century, the Lérez delta silted up and the busy commerce moved elsewhere, mainly to Vigo. Pontevedra entered a period of decline, which may account for its significant old section. Had it been a more prosperous town, the people might have torn down the ancient structures to rebuild.

The old *barrio,* a maze of colonnaded squares and cobbled alleyways, is between Calle Michelena and Calle del Arzobispo Malvar, stretching to Calle Cobián and the river. The old mansions are called *pazos,* and they speak of former marine glory, since it was the sea that provided the money to build them. Seek out such charming squares as Plaza de la Leña, Plaza de Mugártegui, and Plaza de Teucro.

ESSENTIALS
GETTING THERE   From Santiago de Compostela in the north, 16 **trains** per day make the 1-hour trip to Pontevedra at a cost of 4.10€ one-way. RENFE has an office on Calle Gondomar 3 (℃ **90-224-02-02**), where you can get information. The actual rail and bus stations are .8km (½ mile) from the town center on Alféreces Provisionales.

Pontevedra has good links to major Galician cities. From Vigo in the south, the **bus** traveling time is only half an hour if you take one of the 12 inland expresses leaving from Vigo daily. From Santiago de Compostela in the north, a bus leaves every hour during the day for Pontevedra (1 hr. away).

From Santiago de Compostela, head south along N-550 to reach Pontevedra.

VISITOR INFORMATION   The **tourist office** at General Gutiérrez Mellado 1 (℃ **98-685-08-14**) is open Monday through Friday from 9:30am to 2pm and 4:30 to 6:30pm, Saturday from 10am to 12:30pm.

A SPECIAL EVENT **A Rapa das Bestas (The Capture of the Beasts)** 🕊 is held every year in the beginning of July. In the hills of nearby San Lorenzo de Sabuceno, wild horses are rounded up and herded into a corral, in a ritual that evokes the Wild West. For information, contact the tourism office in Pontevedra (see above).

EXPLORING PONTEVEDRA

In the **old quarter** 🕊, the major attraction is the **Basílica de Santa María la Mayor** 🕊, Calle del Arzobispo Malvar, with its avocado-green patina, dating from the 16th century. This Plateresque church was constructed with funds provided by the mariners' guild. Its most remarkable feature is its west front, carved to resemble an altarpiece, with a depiction of the Crucifixion at the top.

The **Museo Provincial,** Pasantería 10 (© **98-685-14-55**), with a hodge-podge of everything from the Pontevedra attic, contains displays ranging from prehistoric artifacts to a still life by Zurbarán. Many of the exhibits are maritime-oriented, and there is a valuable collection of jewelry. Hours are Tuesday through Saturday from 10am to 1:30pm and 5 to 8:45pm, Sunday from 11am to 2pm. Admission is 1.20€, free for European Union citizens. The museum opens onto a major square in the old town, the Plaza de Leña (Square of Wood).

The **Iglesia de San Francisco,** Plaza de la Herrería, is another church of note. Its Gothic facade opens onto gardens. It was founded in the 14th century and contains a sculpture of Don Payo Gómez Charino, noted for his part in the 1248 Reconquest of Seville, when it was wrested from Muslim domination.

Directly south, the gardens lead to the 18th-century **Capilla de la Peregrina,** Plaza Peregrina, with a narrow half-moon facade connected to a rotunda and crowned by a pair of towers. It was constructed by followers of the cult of the Pilgrim Virgin, which was launched in Galicia sometime in the 17th century.

WHERE TO STAY
MODERATE

Parador de Pontevedra ★★ This parador is in the old quarter of Pontevedra, in a well-preserved 16th-century palace near the Basílica de Santa María la Mayor. Built on either 13th- or 14th-century foundations, this hotel became one of Spain's first paradors when it opened in 1955. The interior has been maintained very much as the old *pazo* (manor house) looked. It includes a quaint old kitchen, or *lar* ("heart"), typical of Galician country houses and furnished with characteristic items. Off the vestibule is a courtyard dominated by a large old stone staircase. Many of the attractively furnished accommodations—all with private bathrooms, including tub/shower combos—are large enough to include sitting areas. Many of the rooms overlook the walled-in formal garden.

Baron 19, 36002 Pontevedra. © **98-685-58-00**. Fax 98-685-21-95. www.parador.es. 47 units. 94€–109€ double. AE, DC, MC, V. **Amenities:** Restaurant; lounge; room service; babysitting; laundry service; dry cleaning. *In room:* A/C, TV, minibar, hair dryer, safe.

INEXPENSIVE

Hotel Rías Bajas On a busy street corner near Plaza de Galicia in the commercial center, this 1960s hotel is more comfortable than you might expect judging from the outside. The largest hotel in town, it is often used for community political meetings and press conferences. The lobby, in stone and wood paneling, has been designed to look like an English club. The midsize bedrooms are comfortable and well maintained, with private bathrooms equipped with tub/shower combos.

Daniel de la Sota 7, 36001 Pontevedra. © **98-685-51-00.** Fax 98-685-51-50. 100 units. 62€–85€ double; 80€–95€ suite. AE, DC, MC, V. Parking 6€. **Amenities:** Restaurant; bar; room service; laundry service; dry cleaning. *In room:* TV, minibar, safe.

Hotel Virgen del Camino   On a relatively quiet street off the highway C-531, at the edge of the suburbs, this balconied stucco hotel contains comfortable English-style sitting rooms. The midsize bedrooms have wall-to-wall carpeting and private bathrooms with tub/shower combos, plus central heating in winter. The best doubles contain separate salons and sitting rooms.

Virgen del Camino 55, 36001 Pontevedra. © **98-685-59-00.** Fax 98-685-09-00. 52 units. 53€–79€ double. AE, DC, MC, V. Parking 6€. **Amenities:** Restaurant; bar; room service; laundry service; dry cleaning. *In room:* TV, hair dryer.

WHERE TO DINE

Casa Román   GALICIAN   Known for the quality of its food, this long-established restaurant is on the street level of a brick apartment building in a leafy downtown development known as Campolongo, near Plaza de Galicia. To reach the dining room, you pass through a tavern. In addition to lobster (which you can see in the window), a wide array of well-prepared fish and shellfish dishes is served here, including sea bass, squid, sole, crab, and tuna.

Augusto García Sánchez 12. © **98-684-35-60.** Main courses 11€–19€; fixed-price menu 18€. AE, DC, MC, V. Daily 1:30–4pm; Mon–Sat 9pm–midnight. Closed Sun night Sept–Jan.

Casa Solla *Finds* GALICIAN   In business for nearly half a century, this is an old-time favorite that showcases the culinary imagination of its owner and chef, Pepe Solla. He calls his cuisine *comida de autur,* which means he creates his own recipes, although inspired by the Galician kitchen. His restaurant lies 2km (1¼ miles) from the center of town in the direction of the resort island of El Grove. Tables are placed out on a terrace with a stone wall. Whatever he selects to serve, including grilled loin of beef or the simple pork chop, Solla choses to imbue with his own taste, style, and flavor. He cooks both freshly caught Galician sole or a filet mignon in an albariño wine sauce, and both are a delight. One of his specialties is the very satisfying dish, green pepper stuffed with seafood. One of the most delightful finishes to a meal is the fresh figs of summer served with Cabrales cheese.

Avenida Sineiro 7, Km 2, San Salvador de Poio. © **98-6872-884.** Reservations recommended. Main courses 19€–25€. AE, DC, MC, V. Daily 1–4pm and 8pm–midnight. Closed Dec 20–Jan 5.

Doña Antonia *Finds* INTERNATIONAL   Without question, Pontevedra's best restaurant is Doña Antonia, under a stone arcade on one of the town's oldest streets, east of the Jardines Vincenti. You climb one flight to reach the dining room. In such a provincial town, it is surprising to come across a restaurant of such sophistication and refinement. Although a few readers have sometimes reported a disappointing meal, most diners are filled with joy at this discovery. There's a pristine freshness to the dishes prepared with fish just caught off the coast. The reward for all this culinary vigilance is a loyal clientele of contented food lovers. Menu items include baked suckling lamb, scaloppine with port, rolled filet of salmon, and kiwi sorbet.

Soportales de la Herrería 4 (2nd floor). © **98-684-72-74.** Reservations required. Main courses 11€–21€. MC, V. Mon–Sat 1:30–4pm and 9–11:30pm.

PONTEVEDRA AFTER DARK

The cool temperatures that descend over the hot, sultry plain surrounding Pontevedra seem to incite local residents into after-dark promenades through the old city. You'll find a random scattering of pubs and bars sprawling on either side of the streets that interconnect the Plaza Santa María la Mayor, in the northwestern quadrant of the town's historic core, with the very central Plaza de la Herrería. Part of the charm of the neighborhood involves stopping randomly at whatever pub or cafe appeals to you—each awakens from its slumber after around 8:30pm. By midnight on the weekends, rhythmic electronic music emanates from the town's most popular disco: **Disco Caravas,** Calle Cobian Rafinac 6 (no phone). Disco Caravas appeals to high-energy dance freaks in their early 20s. Don't even think of heading off to a Pontevedra disco before midnight, as it's likely to be locked until then (but the music keeps pumping until 4am). Expect entrance charges of around 4.20€, depending on the night of the week.

6 El Grove & La Toja ★

636km (395 miles) NW of Madrid, 32km (20 miles) W of Pontevedra, 73km (45 miles) S of Santiago de Compostela

A summer resort and fishing village with some 8km (5 miles) of beaches of varying quality, **El Grove** is on a peninsula west of Pontevedra. It juts out into the Ría de Arousa, a large inlet at the mouth of Ulla River. The village, sheltered from Atlantic gales because of its eastern position, has become more commercial than many visitors would like, but it is still renowned for its fine cuisine. A shellfish festival is held here every October.

La Toja (*A Toxa* in Galician), an island linked to El Grove by a bridge, is a famous spa and the most fashionable resort in Galicia, known for its sports and leisure activities. The casino and the golf course are both very popular. The island is covered with pine trees and surrounded by some of the finest scenery in Spain.

La Toja first became known for health-giving properties when, according to legend, the owner of a sick donkey left it on the island to die. The donkey recovered, and its cure was attributed to the waters of an island spring.

GETTING THERE

The **train** from Santiago de Compostela goes as far as Vilagarcía de Arousa; take the bus from there. For train schedules, call the station in Santiago de Compostela (© 90-224-02-02) for information.

From Pontevedra, **buses** heading for Ponte Vilagarcía de Arousa stop at La Toja. Call the transportation information number in Pontevedra (© 98-685-24-08) for details.

If you have a car, **drive** east from Pontevedra on the 550 coastal road via Sanxenxo. From Santiago de Compostela, expressway A-9 leads to Caldas de Reis, where you turn off onto the 550, heading west to the coast.

VISITOR INFORMATION The **tourist information office,** Plaza Do Corgo s/n (© 98-673-14-15), is open from July to October, Monday through Saturday from 9am to 1pm and 4 to 6pm.

WHERE TO STAY & DINE IN EL GROVE

Hotel Amandi This stylish and tasteful family-run hotel is a brisk 10-minute walk from the bridge that connects El Grove with La Toja. The midsize rooms are decorated with antique reproductions; most have tiny terraces with ornate cast-iron balustrades and sea views. All have neatly kept bathrooms most of which contain tub/shower combos. Breakfast is the only meal served.

Castelao 94, 36980 El Grove. (C) **98-673-19-42.** Fax 98-673-16-43. 30 units. 55€–85€ double. Rates include breakfast. MC, V. Parking 6€. Closed Jan. **Amenities:** Breakfast room; pool; laundry service. *In room:* TV.

La Pousada del Mar SEAFOOD   This warm, inviting place near the bridge leading to La Toja is the best dining spot outside those at the hotels. At times you can watch women digging for oysters in the river in front. The chef, naturally, specializes in fish, including a wide selection of shellfish. Among the specialties are a savory soup, outstanding shellfish paella, hake Galician style, and fresh grilled salmon. For dessert, try the *flan de la casa.*

Castelao 202. (C) **98-673-01-06.** Reservations required July–Aug. Main courses 10€–18€; fixed-price menu 18€. AE, DC, MC, V. Daily 1–4pm; Mon–Sat 8:30pm–midnight. Closed Dec 10–Feb 1.

WHERE TO STAY IN LA TOJA

Gran Hotel de La Toja ⭐⭐Enveloped by pine trees on well-landscaped grounds, this classic spa hotel is one of the finest in Galicia, government-rated five stars. It lies on a breeze-swept island off El Grove. Completely renovated, the resort is for both health and leisure. The bedrooms—try for one with a view—are both modern and functional, immaculately kept and containing some of the best bathrooms in the area, with both tub and shower. A year-round resort, the Gran has some of the best facilities and amenities in the area, ranging from a first-rate spa to a nine-hole golf course and even a casino. The food is worthy of the setting, a Galician cuisine with elaborate Continental dishes, the chefs specializing in fresh fish and shellfish harvested off the coast of northwest Spain. Try one of the abariño wines, which go with most dishes.

Isla de la Toja, 36991 Isla de la Toja, Pontevedra. (C) **98-673-0025.** Fax 98-6730-026. www.latojagrand hotel.com. 197 units. 150€–210€ double; 212€–300€ suite. AE, DC, MC, V. Free parking. **Amenities:** Restaurant; bar; 3 pools; 9-hole golf course; tennis court; health club; spa; fitness center; room service; laundry/dry cleaning; beach; casino; dance club. *In room:* TV, minibar, hair dryer, safe.

Hotel Louxo   Set on flatlands a few paces from the town's ornate casino is this modern white building, sheltered from the Atlantic winds. It offers clean, stylish, and modern accommodations. Most rooms are midsize, and each is equipped with a neatly kept bathroom equipped with a tub/shower combination. The many ground-floor public rooms have rows of comfortable seating areas and sweeping views over the nearby tidal flats.

36991 Isla de la A Toxa. (C) **98-673-02-00.** Fax 98-673-27-91. www.louxolatoja.com. 116 units. 78€–130€ double; 112€–174€ suite. Rates include breakfast. AE, DC, MC, V. Free parking. **Amenities:** Restaurant; bar; pool; fitness center; sauna; room service; babysitting; laundry service; dry cleaning. *In room:* A/C, TV, minibar, hair dryer, safe.

7 Túy (Túi) ⭐

29km (18 miles) S of Vigo, 48km (30 miles) S of Pontevedra

A frontier town first settled by the Romans, **Túy** is a short distance from Portugal, near the two-tiered road-and-rail bridge (over the Miño River) that links the two countries. The bridge was designed by Alexandre-Gustave Eiffel (he did a tower in Paris you may have heard of). If you're driving from Portugal's Valença do Minho, Túy is your introduction to Spain.

ESSENTIALS

GETTING THERE   **Trains** run daily for the 1½- to 2-hour trip from Vigo to Túy.

From Vigo, **buses** run south to Túy hourly, taking 1 hour.

If you're **driving** from Vigo, head south along the A-9 expressway until you see the turnoff for Túy.

VISITOR INFORMATION   The **tourist office,** at Rua Colón s/n, Edificio Sampaio (© **98-660-17-89**), is open Monday through Friday from 9am to 1pm and 4 to 6pm, Saturday from 10am to 2:30pm.

EXPLORING TUY

The winding streets of the old quarter lead to the **Catedral** 🐾, a national art treasure that dominates the *zona monumental.* The acropolis-like cathedral/fortress, built in 1170, wasn't used for religious purposes until the early 13th century. Its principal portal is exceptional. What is astounding about this cathedral is that later architects respected the original Romanesque and Gothic styles and didn't make changes in its design. If you have time, you may want to visit the Romanesque-style **Iglesia de San Bartolomé,** on the outskirts of town, and the **Iglesia de Santo Domingo,** a beautiful example of Gothic style (look for the bas-reliefs in the cloister). The latter church stands next to the Santo Domingo park. Walls built over Roman fortifications surround Túy.

WHERE TO STAY & DINE

Parador de Túy 🐾🐾   Advance reservations are essential if you want to stay in this elegant, fortress-style hacienda four streets north of the Miño River crossing. Built in 1968, the inn with its cantilevered roof was designed to blend in with the architectural spirit of the province, emphasizing local stone and natural woods. Brass chandeliers, paintings by well-known *gallegos,* and antiques combined with reproductions furnish the public rooms. In the main living room are a large inglenook fireplace, a tall banjo-shaped grandfather clock, hand-knotted rugs, 18th-century paintings, hand-hewn benches, and comfortable armchairs.

The midsize bedrooms are sober in style, but comfortable, and offer views across a colonnaded courtyard to the river and hills. They are furnished with Castilian-style pieces, and the tiled bathrooms are modern, with tub and shower combinations.

Av. de Portugal s/n, 36700 Túy. © **98-660-03-09.** Fax 98-660-21-63. www.parador.es. 30 units. 75€–95€ double; 100€–130€ suite. AE, DC, MC, V. Free parking. **Amenities:** Restaurant; lounge; pool; tennis courts; room service; babysitting; laundry service; dry cleaning. *In room:* TV, minibar, hair dryer, safe.

19

The Balearic Islands

The Balearic Islands *(Los Baleares),* an archipelago composed of the major islands of Majorca, Minorca, and Ibiza, plus the diminutive Formentera, Cabrera, and the uninhabited Dragonera, lie off the coast of Spain, between France and the coast of northern Africa. The islands have known many rulers and occupying forces—Carthaginians, Greeks, Romans, Vandals, and Moors. But despite a trove of Bronze Age megaliths and some fine Punic artifacts, the invaders who have left the largest imprint on Balearic culture are the hordes of sun-seeking vacationers who descend every year.

After the expulsion of the Moors by Jaume I in 1229, the islands flourished as the kingdom of Majorca. When they were integrated into the kingdom of Castile in the mid–14th century, they experienced a massive decline. The early 19th century provided a renaissance for the islands; artists such as George Sand and her lover, Chopin, and later the poet Robert Graves established the islands, especially Majorca and Ibiza, as a haven for musicians, writers, and artists (read Sand's book *A Winter in Majorca).* Gradually the artist colony attracted tourists of all dispositions.

Today, the Balearics are administrated by an autonomous government, *Govern Balear.* **Majorca,** the largest island, is the most commercial and tourist oriented. Many of its scenic expanses have given way to sprawling hotels and fast-food joints, although parts remain beautiful indeed. Freewheeling **Ibiza** attracts the international party crowd, as well as visitors who come to the island for its tamer offerings, such as white-sand beaches and sky-blue waters. The smallest of the major islands, **Minorca,** is also the most serene. It is less touristy than Majorca and Ibiza, and for that reason, it is now experiencing an antitourist tourist boom.

The government of the islands has finally awakened to the damage caused by overdevelopment of Majorca and Ibiza. Under new guidelines, some 35% of this island group is now safeguarded from exploitation by builders.

Very few visitors have time to explore all three islands, so you'll have to decide early which one is for you. Many vacationers include one of the Balearic Islands as an add-on to a visit to Barcelona or the Costa Brava, while others view them as destinations unto themselves.

1 Majorca ★★★

Majorca (*Mallorca* in Spanish) is the most popular of Spain's Mediterranean islands, drawing millions of visitors each year.

About 209km (130 miles) from Barcelona and 145km (90 miles) from Valencia, Majorca has a coastline 500km (310 miles) long. The beautiful island is an explorer's paradise in its exterior, although horribly overbuilt along certain

---

Tips **Not An Island for All Seasons**

July and August are high season for Majorca; don't even think of coming then without a reservation. It's possible to swim comfortably from June to October; after that it's too cold.

---

coastal regions. The north is mountainous; the fertile southern flatlands offer a landscape of olive and almond groves, occasionally interrupted by windmills.

The golden sands of Majorca are famous, with lovely beaches such as Ca'n Pastilla and El Arenal, but they tend to be overcrowded with sun worshippers on package tours. Tourist facilities line the shores of Cala Mayor and Sant Agustí; both have good beaches, including Playa Magaluf, the longest beach on the Calvía coast. Cala de San Vicente, 6.5km (4 miles) north of Pollença, is a beautiful beach bordered by a pine grove and towering cliffs. Sandy stretches of golden sand beaches lie between Cala Pi and Cala Murta in Formentor near the tip of the northern coast.

ISLAND ESSENTIALS

GETTING THERE   At certain times of the year the trip by boat or plane can be pleasant, but in August the routes to Palma must surely qualify as the major bottleneck in Europe. Don't travel without advance reservations, and be sure you have a return plane ticket if you come in August—otherwise you may not get off the island until September!

Iberia (✆ 97-178-99-73) flies to Palma's Aeroport Son San Joan (✆ 97-178-90-00) from Barcelona, Valencia, and Madrid. There are daily planes from Madrid and Valencia, and several daily flights from Barcelona in summer. **Spanair** (✆ 97-178-94-25) flies into Palma from Barcelona (up to 3 times a day during summer) and from Madrid, Bilbao, Minorca, Santiago de Compostela, Málaga, and Tenerife. **Air Europa** (✆ 97-117-81-00) flies to Palma from Barcelona a maximum of two times a day during peak season, and to a lesser extent, it flies to Palma from Madrid, Minorca, Ibiza, and Seville.

British and other European travelers should really consult a travel agent and look into the available package tours, which combine airfare and accommodations; they can save you a ton of money!

Countless charter flights also make the run. Bookings are very tight in August, and delays of at least 24 hours, sometimes more, are common. If you're flying—say, Iberia—on a transatlantic flight from New York to Madrid or Barcelona, you should have Majorca written into your ticket before your departure if you plan to visit the Balearics as part of your Spanish itinerary.

From the airport, bus no. 17 or 25 takes you to the Plaça Espanya in the center of Palma from 7am to 11:30pm daily; the cost is 2.05€. A metered cab costs 16€ for the 25-minute drive into the city center.

Transmediterránea, Estació Marítim in Palma (✆ 90-245-46-45 for schedules), operates two to five **ferries** a day from Barcelona, taking 8 hours and costing from 47€ for one-way passage. There are six ferries per week from Valencia, Monday through Saturday, taking 7 hours and costing 47€ one-way. In Barcelona, tickets can be booked at the Transmediterránea office at Estació Marítim (✆ 93-295-91-00), and in Valencia at the office at Terminal Transmediterraneo Muelle Deponiente (✆ 96-316-48-31). Any travel agent in Spain

The Balearic Islands

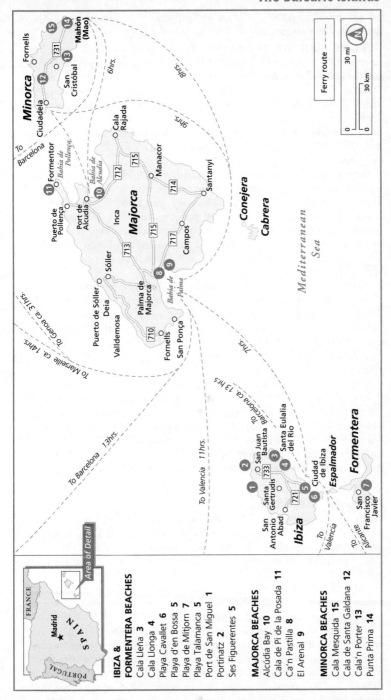

IBIZA & FORMENTERA BEACHES

Cala Lleña **3**
Cala Llonga **4**
Playa Cavallet **6**
Playa d'en Bossa **5**
Playa de Mitjorn **7**
Playa Talamanca **5**
Port de San Miguel **1**
Portinatz **2**
Ses Figuerentes **5**

MAJORCA BEACHES

Alcúdia Bay **10**
Cala de Pi de la Posada **11**
Ca'n Pastilla **8**
El Arenal **9**

MINORCA BEACHES

Cala Mesquida **15**
Cala de Santa Galdana **12**
Cala'n Porter **13**
Punta Prima **14**

can also book you a seat. Schedules and departure times (subject to change) should always be checked and double-checked.

GETTING AROUND   At the tourist office in Palma, you can pick up a **bus** schedule that explains island routes. Or call **Emprese Municipal de Transportes** (© 97-121-44-44). This company runs city buses from Estació Central D'Autobus, Plaça Espanya, the main terminal. The standard one-way fare is 1€ within Palma; at the station you can buy a booklet good for 10 rides, costing 7.50€.

The most popular destination routes on the island (Valldemossa, Deià, Sóller, and Port de Sóller) are offered by **Darbus,** Carrer Estada s/n (© 97-175-06-22) in Palma.

Ferrocarril de Sóller, Carrer Eusebio Estada 1 (© **97-175-20-51**), off Plaça Espanya, has **train** service, passing through majestic mountain scenery, to Sóller. Trains run from 8am to 7:15pm, and a one-way ticket costs 5€. A "tourist train" leaves daily at 10:50am and costs 7.40€ before reaching Sóller. The only thing special about this route is a 10-minute stop at Mirador del Pujol d'en Banya. The tourist train itself, however, is a worthy sightseeing trip. Privately owned, it was constructed by orange growers in the early 1900s and still uses the carriages of the Belle Epoque days.

Another train runs to Inca; it's often called "the leather express" because most passengers are on board to buy inexpensive leather goods in the Inca shops. This line is the **Servicios Ferroviarios de Mallorca,** and it, too, leaves from Plaça Espanya (© **97-175-22-45** for more information and schedules). The train ride is only 40 minutes, with 40 departures per day Monday through Saturday and 32 per day on Sunday. A one-way fare costs 1.80€. For a radio taxi, call © **97-176-45-45** or 97-140-14-14.

If you plan to stay in Palma, you don't need a car. The city is extremely traffic-clogged, and parking is scarce. If you'd like to take our driving tour (described later in this chapter), you can rent cars at such companies as the Spanish-owned **Atesa** at Passeig Marítim (© **97-145-66-02**), where rentals range from 44€ to 87€ per day. **Avis** at Passeig Marítim 16 (© **97-173-07-20**) is well stocked with cars; its rates range from 54€ to 168€ per day. Both Atesa and Avis maintain offices at the airport. Reservations should always be made in advance.

PALMA DE MAJORCA 🏛🏛

Palma, on the southern tip of the island, is the seat of the autonomous government of the Balearic Islands, as well as the center for most of Majorca's hotels, restaurants, and nightclubs. The Moors constructed Palma in the style of a Casbah, or walled city. Its roots are still visible, although obscured by the high-rise hotels that have cropped up.

Old Palma is typified by the area immediately surrounding the cathedral. Mazes of narrow alleys and cobblestoned streets echo the era when Palma was one of the chief ports in the Mediterranean.

Today Palma is a bustling city whose massive tourist industry has more than made up for its decline as a major seaport. It's estimated that nearly half the population of the island lives in Palma. Majorca attracts the largest number of visitors of any place in the Balearics. The islanders call Palma simply *Ciutat* ("City"), and it is the largest of the Balearic ports, its bay often clogged with yachts. Arrival by sea is the most impressive, with the skyline characterized by Bellver Castle and the bulk of the cathedral.

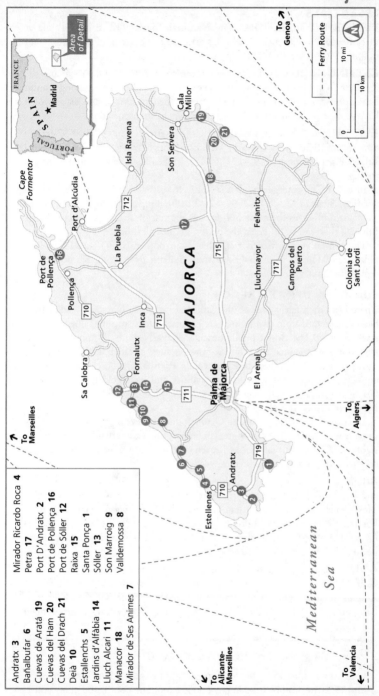

Majorca

ESSENTIALS

VISITOR INFORMATION   The **National Tourist Office** is in Palma at Plaça Reyna 2 (© **97-171-22-16**). It's open Monday through Friday from 9am to 8pm, Saturday from 10am to 2pm.

GETTING AROUND   In Palma, you can get around the Old Town and the Paseo on foot. Otherwise, you can make limited use of taxis for getting around Palma or use one of the buses that cut across the city. Out on the island, you'll have to depend mainly on buses or rented cars for transportation.

FAST FACTS   The **U.S. Consulate,** Calle Puerto Pi 8 (© **97-140-37-07**), is open from 10:30am to 1:30pm, Monday through Friday. The **British Consulate,** Plaça Mayor 3 (© **97-171-24-45**), is open from 9am to 3pm, Monday through Friday.

In case of an **emergency,** dial © **112.** If you fall ill, head to the **Centro Médico,** Av. Juan March 8 (© **97-121-22-00**), a private facility.

Majorca observes the same **holidays** as the rest of Spain but also celebrates June 29, the Feast of St. Peter, the patron saint of all fishers.

The central **post office** is at Carrer Paseo Bornet 10 (© **90-219-71-97**). Hours are Monday through Friday from 8:30am to 8:30pm, Saturday from 9:30am to 2pm.

FUN ON & OFF THE BEACH

There is a beach fairly close to the cathedral in Palma, but some readers have been discouraged from swimming here because of foul-smelling, albeit covered, sewers nearby. The closest public beach is **Playa Nova,** a 35-minute bus ride from downtown Palma. Some hotels, however, have private beaches. If you head east, you reach the excellent beaches of **Ca'n Pastilla.** The beaches at **El Arenal** are very well equipped with tourist facilities and have golden sands as well. Going to the southwest, you find good but often crowded beaches at **Cala Mayor** and **Sant Agustí.**

You can swim from late June to October; don't believe the promoters who try to sell you on mild Majorcan winters in January and February—it can get downright cold. Spring and fall can be heaven sent, and in summer the coastal areas are pleasantly cooled by sea breezes.

BIKING   The best places for biking on the island are C'an Picafort, Alcúdia, and Port de Pollença, all along the north coast, because they are relatively flat. Most roads have special bike lanes on the island, as it's a popular sport here. For rentals, go to **Belori Bike,** Edificio Pilari, Marbella 22, Playa de Palma (© **97-149-03-58**). Depending on their model, and how many gears they have, pedal bikes rent for around 10€ per day.

GOLF   Majorca is a golfer's dream. The best course is the Son Vida Club de Golf, Urbanización son Vida, about 13km (8 miles) east of Palma along the Andrade highway. This 18-hole course is shared by the guests of the island's two best hotels, Arabella Golf Hotel and the Son Vida. However, the course is open

---

⟮Tips⟯ **Where to Get Those Phone Cards**

Local newsstands and tobacco shops sell phone cards valued between 3€ and 15€. They can be used in any public telephone booth, and allow you to make both domestic and international calls.

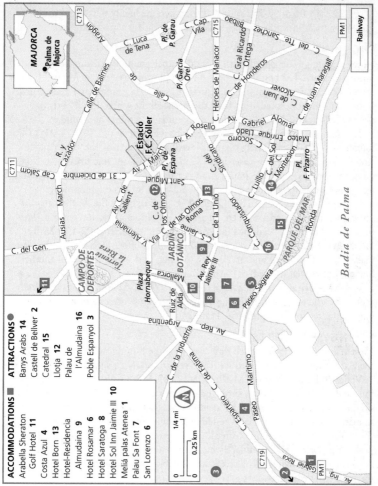

ACCOMMODATIONS ■

Arabella Sheraton
Golf Hotel **11**
Costa Azul **4**
Hotel Born **13**
Hotel-Residencia
Almudaina **9**
Hotel Rosamar **6**
Hotel Saratoga **8**
Hotel Sol Inn Jaimie III **10**
Meliá palas Atenea **1**
Palau Sa Font **7**
San Lorenzo **6**

ATTRACTIONS ●

Banys Arabs **14**
Castell de Bellver **2**
Catedral **15**
Llotja **12**
Palau de
l'Almudaina **16**
Poble Espanyol **3**

Railway

to all players who call for reservations (℘ **97-179-12-10**). Greens fees are 66€ for 18 holes.

HIKING   Because of the hilly terrain in Majorca, this sport is better pursued here than on Ibiza or Minorca. The mountains of the northwest, the Serra de Tramuntana, are best for exploring. The tourist office (see above) will provide you with a free booklet called *20 Hiking Excursions on the Island of Majorca.*

HORSEBACK RIDING   The best stables on the island are at **The Riding School of Majorca,** on the Palma-Sóller road. Call ℘ **97-161-31-57** to make arrangements and get directions from wherever you are on the island.

TENNIS   If your hotel doesn't have a court, head for the **Club de Tenis,** Carrer Sil s/n (℘ **97-169-22-61**).

WATERSPORTS   Most beaches have outfitters who will rent you Wind-surfers and dinghies. The best diving operation is **Planet Escuba,** Pont Adriano

(© **97-123-43-06** or 97-752-68-81). Divers here are highly skilled and will take you to the most intriguing sights underwater if you are a qualified diver.

SHOPPING

Stores in Palma offer handicrafts, elegant leather goods, Majorcan pearls, and fine needlework. The best shopping is on the following streets: San Miguel, Carrer Sindicato, Jaume II, Jaume III, Carrer Platería, Vía Roman, and Passeig des Borne, plus the streets radiating from the Borne all the way to Plaça Cort, where the city hall stands. Most shops close on Saturday afternoon and Sunday.

The famous **Casa Bonet,** Plaça Federico Chopin 2 (© **97-172-21-17**), founded in 1860, sells finely textured needlework. Each of the sheets, table-cloths, napkins, and pillowcases is made in Majorca from fine linen or cotton (also, for the less expensive items, from acrylic). Many are hand-embroidered, using ancient designs and floral motifs popularized by this establishment.

Loewe, Avinguda Jaume III 1 (© **97-171-52-75**), offers fine leather, elegant accessories for men and women, luggage, and chic apparel for women. For funkier leather items, head for **Pink,** Avinguda Jaume III 3 (© **97-172-23-33**). **Passy,** Avinguda Jaume III 6 (© **97-171-33-38**), offers high-quality, locally made shoes, handbags, and accessories for men and women. There's another branch, not as well stocked, at Carrer Tous y Ferrer 8 (© **97-171-73-38**).

Perlas Majorica, Avinguda Jaume III 11 (© **97-172-52-68**), is the authorized agency for the authentic Majorcan pearl. The pearl producers offer a decade-long guarantee for their products. Pearls come in varied sizes and settings.

SEEING THE SIGHTS

Most visitors don't spend much time exploring the historic sights in Palma, but there are a number of places to see if you've had too much sun.

Viajes Sidetours, Passeig Marítim 19 (© **97-128-39-00**), offers numerous full- and half-day excursions throughout Palma and the surrounding country-side. The full-day excursion to Valldemossa and Sóller takes visitors through the monastery where former island residents Chopin and his lover, George Sand, spent their scandalous winter. After leaving the monastery, the tour explores the peaks of the Sierra Mallorquina, then makes its way to the seaside town of Sóller. A visit to the Arabian gardens of Raixa or Alfàbia is included in the 32€ cost of the tour, on Wednesday only.

Another full-day tour of the mountainous western side of the island is conducted by train and boat, including a ride on one of Europe's oldest railways to the town of Sóller and the Monasterio de Lluch, as well as a boat ride between the port of Sóller and La Calobra. Daily tours cost 45€. The eastern coast of Majorca is explored in the Caves of Drach and Hams tour. A concert on the world's largest underground lake (Lake Martel), tours through the caves, a stop at an olive-wood works, and a visit to the Majorica Pearl Factory are all covered daily in the 33€ cost. Times of departure may vary.

Banys Arabs You can spend hours exploring the narrow streets of the medieval quarter (Barri Gòtic) east of the cathedral. Along the way, you may want to visit these Moorish baths that date from the 10th century. They are the only complete remaining Moorish-constructed buildings in Palma. One room contains a dome supported by 12 columns.

Carrer Serra 7. © **97-172-15-49.** Admission 1.50€. Daily 9am–6:30pm. Bus: 15.

Castell de Bellver ⭐ Erected in 1309, this hilltop round castle was once the summer palace of the kings of Majorca—during the short period when there were kings of Majorca. The castle, which was a fortress with a double moat, is well preserved and now houses the Museu Municipal, which is devoted to archaeological objects and old coins. It's really the view from here, however, that is the chief attraction. In fact, the name, Bellver, means beautiful view.

Between Palma and Son Armadams. ℂ 97-173-06-57. Admission 1.70€ adults, .85€ children, students, and seniors. Castle free on Sun. Daily 8am–8:30pm. Museum closed Sun. Bus: 3, 4, 21, or 22.

Catedral ✪✪ This Catalonian Gothic cathedral, called La Seu, stands in the old town overlooking the seaside. It was begun during the reign of Jaume II (1276–1311) and completed in 1601. Its central vault is 43m (144 ft.) high, and its columns rise 20m (65 ft.). There is a wrought-iron *baldachin* (canopy) by Gaudí over the main altar. The treasury contains supposed pieces of the True Cross and relics of San Sebastián, patron saint of Palma. Museum and cathedral hours often change; call ahead to make sure they're accepting visitors before you go.

Carrer Palau Almoyna. ℂ 97-172-31-30. Free admission to cathedral; museum and treasury 3.50€. Mon–Fri 10am–5:30pm; Sat 10am–2:30pm. Bus: 15.

Llotja ✪ This 15th-century Gothic structure is a leftover from the wealthy mercantile days of Majorca. La Lonja (its Spanish name) was, roughly, an exchange or guild. Exhibitions here are announced in local newspapers.

Passeig Sagrera. ℂ 97-171-17-05. Free admission. Tues–Sat 11am–2pm and 5–8pm; Sun 11am–2pm. Bus: 15.

Marineland Eighteen kilometers (11 miles) west of Palma, just off the coast road en route to Palma Nova, this attraction offers a variety of amusements—dolphin, sea lion, and parrot shows. There's a Polynesian pearl-diving demonstration and a small zoo. You'll find a cafeteria, picnic area, and children's playground, as well as beach facilities.

Costa d'en Blanes. ℂ 97-167-51-25. Admission 15€ adults, 10€ children 3–12, free for children under 3. Mon–Fri 9:30am–6pm; Sat–Sun 9:30am–6:30pm. Closed 4 weeks Nov–Dec. Direct bus, marked MARINELAND, from Palma rail station.

Museu d'Art Espanyol Contemporani, Fundació Juan March ✪ The Juan March Foundation's Museum of Spanish Contemporary Art reopened in 1997, with a series of newly acquired modern paintings. The works represent one of the most fertile periods of 20th-century art, with canvasses by Picasso, Miró, Dalí, and Juan Gris, as well as Antoni Tàpies, Carlos Saura, Miquel Barceló, Lluis Gordillo, Susana Solano, and Jordi Teixidor. A room devoted to temporary exhibits was added to the restored museum. One series, for example, featured 100 Picasso engravings from the 1930s. The oldest and best-known work in the museum is Picasso's *Head of a Woman,* from his cycle of paintings known as *Les Demoiselles d'Avignon.* These works form part of the collection that the Juan March Foundation began to amass in 1973.

Carrer Sant Miquel 11. ℂ 97-171-35-15. Admission 3€ adults, 1.50€ seniors and students. Mon–Fri 10am–6:30pm; Sat 10am–1:30pm.

Palau de l'Almudaina Long ago, Muslim rulers erected this splendid fortress surrounded by Moorish-style gardens and fountains opposite the cathedral. During the short-lived reign of the kings of Majorca, it was converted into a royal residence that evokes the Alcázar at Málaga. Now it houses a museum displaying antiques, arts, suits of armor, and Gobelin tapestries. Panoramic views of the harbor of Palma can be seen from here.

Carrer Palau Reial. © **97-121-41-34**. Admission 3.20€ adults, 2.30€ children; free on Wed. Mon–Fri 10am–5:45pm; Sat 10am–1:15pm. Closed holidays. Bus: 15.

Poble Espanyol ★ This is a touristy collection of buildings evoking Spain in miniature and is similar to the Poble Espanyol in Barcelona. Bullfights are held in its *corrida* on summer Sundays. There are mock representations of such famous structures as the Alhambra in Granada, the Torre de Oro in Seville, and El Greco's House in Toledo.

Carrer Pueblo Español s/n. © **97-173-70-75**. Admission 5€ adults, 4.50€ children. Apr–Nov daily 9am–6pm; Dec–Mar daily 9am–5pm. Bus: 5.

WHERE TO STAY

Majorca has a staggering number of hotels, but it's still not enough to hold the crowds in August. If you go in high season, reserve well in advance. Some of our hotel recommendations in Palma are in the El Terreno section, the heart of the local nightlife. Don't book into one of these hotels unless you like plenty of action, continuing until late at night. More conservative readers may find it unsavory. If you want peace and quiet, check our other suggestions.

Palma's suburbs, notably Cala Mayor, about 4km (2½ miles) from the center, and San Agustín, about 5km (3 miles) from town, continue to sprawl. In El Arenal, part of Playas de Palma, there is a huge concentration of hotels. The beaches at El Arenal are quite good but have a Coney Island atmosphere. We have a number of hotel recommendations in these suburbs for those who don't mind staying outside the city center.

Very Expensive

Arabella Sheraton Golf Hotel ★★★ Only Son Vida (see below) is more highly rated and more elegant, although the Arabella is more scenically located. In 1992, the German-based Arabella chain bought this hotel, as well as the Son Vida Hotel (which can be reached after a brisk 10-min. walk). The ecology of the area surrounding the complex has been fiercely protected; it's about 5km (3 miles) northwest of the center of Palma. Don't come here expecting raucous good times on the beach; the resort is elegant and rather staid. There's no health club and no shuttle to the beach; many visitors drive to the several nearby beaches. But it does boast one of the only hotel bullrings in Spain!

The complex is low-rise, intensely landscaped, and offers views over the lush green grounds (not of the sea) from many of its good-size rooms. Accommodations include white walls, dark-stained furnishings, wall-to-wall carpeting, bathrooms with tub/shower combos, and in all but the least expensive accommodations, a balcony or veranda.

Carrer de la Vinagrella, 07013 Palma de Majorca. © **97-179-99-99**. Fax 97-178-72-00. www.arabella sheraton.com. 93 units. 347€–362€ double; from 476€ suite. Rates include breakfast. AE, DC, MC, V. Parking free outside or 5€ in garage. Bus: 7. **Amenities:** 2 restaurants; bar; pool; golf course; tennis courts; fitness center; sauna; horseback riding; salon; room service; babysitting; laundry service; dry cleaning. *In room:* A/C, TV, minibar, hair dryer, safe.

Castillo Hotel Son Vida ★★★ Set in a 13th-century castle in the Son Vida hills, on a secluded hilltop several miles from Palma, this hotel commands the most panoramic views on the island. Many rooms are in a modern wing, a pleasing reproduction of a Spanish hacienda. Inside, the public rooms are swathed in sumptuous fabrics, Oriental rugs, and chandeliers. Guest rooms in the new building are not quite as distinctive as those in the castle. Many rooms have private balconies or terraces. Expect spacious rooms and closets, bathrooms with touches of marble, tub/shower combos, and deluxe toiletries.

Raixa 2, 07013 Palma de Majorca. © 800/223-6800 in the U.S., or 97-179-00-00. Fax 97-179-00-17. www. hotelsonvida.com. 169 units. 195€–340€ double; 665€–795€ suite. Rates include breakfast. AE, DC, MC, V. Free parking. Bus: 7. **Amenities:** 2 restaurants; bar; 2 pools; spa; sauna; whirlpool; Turkish bath; room service; massage; babysitting; laundry service; dry cleaning. *In room:* A/C, TV, kitchenette, minibar, coffeemaker, hair dryer, iron, safe.

Palacio Ca Sa Galesa ★★ *Finds*   Although not in the same league as the Arabella and Son Vida, this place is a delight and less expensive. For generations this 15th-century town house languished as a decaying apartment building facing the side of the cathedral. Beginning in 1993, an entrepreneurial couple from Cardiff, Wales, restored the place, salvaging the original marble floors and stained-glass windows, sheathing the walls of the public areas with silk, and adding modern amenities. Today, the setting is the most alluring in all of Palma, loaded with English and Spanish antiques and paintings. Most rooms overlook an enclosed courtyard draped with potted plants and climbing vines. The rooms are quite opulent, with antiques and Persian rugs. All rooms have neatly kept bathrooms with tub/shower combos. There's no restaurant, but a hearty buffet is served each morning (for an extra charge).

Miramar 8, 07001 Palma de Majorca. © **97-171-54-00.** Fax 97-172-15-79. www.palaciocasagalesa.com. 12 units. 198€–251€ double; 300€ suite. AE, MC, V. Parking 10€. **Amenities:** Lounge; sauna; whirlpool; room service; massage; babysitting; laundry service; dry cleaning. *In room:* A/C, TV, minibar, hair dryer, safe.

Expensive

Meliá Palas Atenea ★   A member of the Sol chain, this modern hotel offers extensive leisure facilities for vacationers, while still catering to business travelers. It overlooks the Bay of Palma, within walking distance of the town's major restaurants and shops. Spacious guest rooms have terraces, many overlooking the harbor or Bellver Castle. Furnishings are standardized, but the rooms are exceedingly comfortable, ranging from medium to spacious; all are fitted with excellently maintained tile bathrooms equipped with tub/shower combos. An entire floor is designed with business travelers' needs in mind.

Passeig Ingeniero Gabriel Roca 29, 07014 Palma de Majorca. © **97-128-14-00.** Fax 97-145-19-89. www. solmelia.com. 361 units. 190€ double; from 210€ suite. Rates include breakfast. AE, DC, MC, V. Parking 7€. Bus: 1. **Amenities:** 2 restaurants; cafe; bar; nightclub; 2 pools; sauna; whirlpool; salon; room service; massage; laundry service; dry cleaning; solarium. *In room:* A/C, TV, minibar, hair dryer, coffeemaker, safe.

Palau Sa Font ★ *Finds*   This is one of Majorca's most charming boutique hotels found in a 16th-century palace successfully converted into a hotel. The atmosphere is a bit funky unless you like jelly bean colors. Distressed iron and island stone add a more traditional note, however. Especially popular with English visitors, it's been called the hippest place to stay in the old town by some London tabloids. Lying a 15-minute walk from the cathedral, the place is imbued with lots of atmosphere. Designers transformed the bedrooms into a blend of modern with traditional, each with a shiny bathroom with tub or shower. Plump comforters, linen curtains, rustic iron furnishings, and plain walls lend style and grace. The breakfast is one of the reasons to stay here, featuring such delights as smoked salmon, Serrano ham, tortilla, and fresh fruits.

Carrer Apuntadores 38, Barrio Antiguo 07017, Palma de Majorca. © **97-171-22-77.** Fax 97-171-26-18. www.palausafont.com. 19 units. 140€–190€ double; 205€ junior suite. Rates include buffet breakfast. AE, MC, V. Closed Jan. **Amenities:** Breakfast lounge; bar; pool; babysitting; laundry service. *In room:* A/C, TV, minibar, hair dryer.

Moderate

Hotel-Residencia Almudaina   Located on the main commercial street in Palma, this simple hotel offers comfortable, clean, basic rooms. Although small, the units are well maintained and have neatly kept bathrooms, most with tub/shower combos. Because of its location, many of the rooms are quite loud; the quietest are in the rear. Some have terraces and glass doors letting in ample sunlight.

Avinguda Jaume III 9, 07012 Palma de Majorca. ℂ **97-172-73-40.** Fax 97-172-25-99. 77 units. 90€–99€ double. AE, DC, MC, V. Free parking. Bus: 13, 15, or 21. **Amenities:** Bar; room service; laundry service; dry cleaning. *In room:* A/C, TV, coffeemaker, hair dryer, safe.

Hotel Saratoga ✦   Under the arches of an arcade beside the old city's medieval moat stands the entrance to the Hotel Saratoga. Constructed in 1962 and renovated in 1992, the hotel features bright, well-furnished guest rooms, many with balconies or terraces with views of the bay and city of Palma. The mostly midsize rooms have well maintained, tiled bathrooms, mostly with tub/shower combos.

Passeig Majorca 6, 07012 Palma de Majorca. ℂ **97-172-72-40.** Fax 97-172-73-12. www.hotelsaratoga.es. 187 units. 134€–148€ double; 215€ suite. Rates include breakfast. AE, DC, MC, V. Parking 9€. Bus: 3, 7, or 15. **Amenities:** Restaurant; bar; 2 pools; fitness center; sauna; room service; babysitting; laundry service; dry cleaning. *In room:* A/C, TV, minibar, hair dryer, iron, safe.

San Lorenzo ✦✦   This antique hotel is set in the middle of the maze of winding streets that form the old city of Palma. The building is 18th century and the decor is a pleasant mixture of traditional Majorcan and modern. The rooms are airy, painted white, and have bathrooms that include tub/shower combos. All rooms have beamed ceilings and while some have only balconies, the more luxurious offer fireplaces and a private terrace. This hotel is perfect for relaxing after a day of sightseeing or shopping.

San Lorenzo 14, 07012 Palma de Majorca. ℂ **97-172-82-00.** Fax 97-171-19-01. www.hotelsanlorenzo.com. 6 units. 120€–210€ double; 210€ suite. AE, DC, MC, V. **Amenities:** Bar; pool; room service; babysitting; laundry service; dry cleaning. *In room:* A/C, TV, minibar, hair dryer, iron, safe.

Inexpensive

Costa Azul *Value*   Head here for a bargain—despite the reasonable rates, you'll get views of the yachts in the harbor. This place isn't glamorous, but it does offer good value. A short taxi ride will deposit you at night on the Plaça Gomila in El Terreno with its after-dark diversions. Barren, well-worn rooms are clean, but furnished in very modest style, each with a bathroom equipped with a tub/shower combo.

Passeig Marítim 7, 07014 Palma de Majorca. ℂ **97-173-19-40.** Fax 97-173-19-71. 126 units. 88€–111€ double. AE, DC, MC, V. Bus: 3 or 21. **Amenities:** Restaurant; bar; pool; sauna; room service; babysitting; laundry service; dry cleaning. *In room:* A/C, TV, safe.

Hotel Born ✦ *Value*   If you'd like to stay within the city of Palma itself, there is no better bargain than that found at this government-rated two-star hotel in the exact center. A 16th-century palace, once belonging to the Marquis of Ferrandell, was vastly altered and extended in the 18th century with a Majorcan courtyard. Today it's been converted into one of the small, cozy inns of the city, with all the modern amenities, although it still retains much of its original architecture such as Romanesque arches. Bedrooms for the most part are spacious and well equipped, with neatly tiled bathrooms with shower. Off Plaça Rei Juan Carlos, the hotel opens onto a tranquil side street. A mammoth palm shades the main courtyard.

Carrer Sant Jaume 3, 07012 Palma de Mallorca. ☎ **97-171-29-42.** Fax 97-171-86-18. www.mallorcaonline. com/hotel/bornu.htm. 30 units. 69€–114€ double; 114€ suite. Rates include breakfast. AE, DC, MC, V. **Amenities:** Bar; bike rentals. *In room:* A/C, TV.

Hotel Rosamar   Hotel Rosamar, right on the main road in the boomtown El Terreno district, is popular with Germans and Scandinavians. Fresh and clean small rooms have bathrooms with tub/shower combos and balconies overlooking a front patio surrounded by tall palm trees. The focus of the social life is the young, lively crowd that frequents the Rosamar.

Joan Miró 74, 07015 Palma de Majorca. ☎ **97-173-27-23.** Fax 97-128-38-28. www.rosamarpalma.com. 40 units. 42€–58€ double; 62€–70€ triple; 65€–72€ suite. Rates include breakfast. AE, MC, V. Closed Nov–Feb. Bus: 3, 4, 21, or 22. **Amenities:** Bar; lounge. *In room:* Ceiling fan.

At Illetas

This suburb of Palma lies immediately west of the center.

Hotel Bonsol ⭐ *(Kids*   Set across from a beach, about 6.5km (4 miles) west of Palma, this government-rated four-star hotel was built in 1953 and renovated last in 1997. It charges less than hotels with similar amenities, and the nearby beach makes it quite popular with vacationing families, who dine within the airy, somewhat spartan dining room. The core is a four-story, white-sided masonry tower, with some of the suites clustered into a simple collection of outlying villas. The hotel overlooks a garden, adjacent to the sea. The midsize rooms are larger than you might expect, efficient but comfortable and well suited to beachfront vacations.

Paseo de Illetas 30, 07181 Illetas. ☎ **97-140-21-11.** Fax 97-140-25-59. www.mallorcaonline.com/hotel/ bonsols.htm. 147 units. 77€ double; 135€ suite. Rates include breakfast. AE, DC, MC, V. Free parking. Closed Nov 20–Jan 2. **Amenities:** 2 restaurants; lounge; pool; 2 tennis courts; fitness center; sauna; room service; babysitting; laundry service; dry cleaning. *In room:* A/C, TV, minibar, hair dryer, safe.

Hotel Meliá de Mar ⭐⭐   Originally built in 1964, and renovated most recently in 1998, the Meliá de Mar is one of the most comfortable (albeit expensive) hotels in Palma. This seven-story hotel is close to the beach and sports a large garden. The marble-floored lobby and light, summery furniture offer a cool refuge from the hot sun and a calm, deliberately uneventful setting that's evocative of some of the spa hotels of central Europe. Rooms, mainly midsize, have many fine features, including original art, terra-cotta tiled balconies, marble or wrought-iron furnishings, excellent beds, and marble-clad bathrooms with deluxe toiletries, tub/shower combos, and dual basins.

Paseo Illetas 7, 07181 Calvia. ☎ **97-140-25-11.** Fax 97-140-58-52. www.solmelia.com. 144 units. 277€ double; from 527€ suite. AE, DC, MC, V. Free parking. **Amenities:** Restaurant; bar; pool; health spa; room service; massage; babysitting; laundry service; dry cleaning. *In room:* A/C, TV, minibar, coffeemaker, hair dryer, iron, safe.

At Portocolom

This hotel is on the eastern coast, reached by going east from Palma along C-717, then cutting north at the signposted directions.

Hotel Villa Hermosa/Restaurant Vista Hermosa ⭐⭐   This is one of the most creative government-rated five-star hotels on Majorca—a 1993 adaptation of a 19th-century farm. But it's not rustic; the building and outbuildings were recently reconstructed to take advantage of the soaring views available from the high-altitude hillside. Evocative of a severe, dignified monastery, this building is set on elaborate terraces cut into the rocky hillside. Rooms come in various shapes and sizes and each is exceedingly well furnished, with excellent beds and immaculately kept bathrooms with tub/shower combos.

Carretera Felanitx-Portocolom, Km 6, PM 401, 07200 Felanitx. (*C*) **97-182-49-60**. Fax 97-182-45-92. 15 units. 260€ double; 350€ suite. Rates include breakfast. AE, DC, MC, V. From Portocolom, follow signs to roads leading northeast to Felanitx. **Amenities:** Restaurant; lounge; 2 pools; health club; sauna; babysitting; laundry service. *In room:* A/C, TV, minibar, hair dryer, iron, safe.

At Santa María del Camí

Read's Hotel ★★ *Finds* Peacefully located in beautiful countryside, this hotel is only 18km (11 miles) from Palma on the way to Inca Alcudia. The 16th-century Majorcan villa is now run by a British family and is a favorite spot for well-heeled northern Europeans. The building has been carefully renovated and furnished with a combination of good-quality reproduction furniture as well as genuine antiques. An unspoiled view of the Tramuntana Mountains forms the backdrop to the hotel, which is surrounded by gardens. Beamed ceilings and wooden shutters add an authentically traditional touch to the rooms, which have all been recently refurbished and painted in a variety of subtle Mediterranean colors. They are decorated with prints of classical architecture and Turkish rugs on traditional stone floors. There are various categories of rooms; the four deluxe doubles and 10 suites have French doors opening onto terraces with stunning views. The beds are all extremely comfortable, and the bathrooms are well stocked and contain tub/shower combos. Four reception rooms include an extraordinary blue room with *trompe l'oeil* clouds painted on the walls and what was previously the olive pressing room, the *tafona*, in which the original fittings have been preserved.

Ca'n Moragues, 07320 Santa María. (*C*) **97-114-02-61**. Fax 97-114-07-62. www.readshotel.com. 23 units. 270€–445€ double; 445€ suite. Rates include breakfast. AE, DC, MC, V. Free parking. **Amenities:** Restaurant; bar; 2 pools; tennis court; health club; sauna; whirlpool; horseback riding; room service; babysitting; laundry service; dry cleaning. *In room:* A/C, TV, hair dryer, safe.

At Puigpunent

Gran Hotel Son Net ★★★ For those wanting a combination of total relaxation and luxury, this is the perfect destination. This 17th-century manor house is next to a nature reserve and nestles in a lush mountain valley 15km (9 miles) from Palma. It was converted from a private residence in 1998 by David Stein, a California tycoon and art collector. The result is one of Europe's best hotels. Apart from the glorious setting, the hotel boasts works by artists such as Hockney, Stella, and Christoph, and there's even a small Chagall on the walls. A classical Majorcan aristocratic sense of decoration has been followed faithfully, with white walls, stone floors, and dark wood beams and shutters. The rooms are spacious, the largest being 4151m (95 ft.) square, and all have satellite television. The most idyllic rooms are the corner units on the top floor with southern exposure. The bathrooms are fully equipped with necessities such as deep tubs and power showers and glamorous novelties such as antisteam mirrors. There are several reception rooms and an immense terrace with a seductive, curvaceous swimming pool of equally grandiose proportions. On Sunday, Mass is said in the hotel's private chapel.

Castillo Son Net, 07194 Puigpunent. (*C*) **97-114-70-00**. Fax 97-114-70-01. www.sonnet.es. 24 units. 275€–420€ double; from 550€ suite. AE, DC, MC, V. Free parking. **Amenities:** 2 restaurants; bar; pool; tennis court; health club; sauna; whirlpool; salon; room service; babysitting; laundry service; dry cleaning. *In room:* A/C, TV, minibar, hair dryer, safe.

At La Bonanova

This magnificently situated hotel is directly west of Palma and south of the sprawling grounds of Castell de Bellver, the round hilltop castle crowning Palma.

Valparaíso Palace ★★ Only minutes from the center of Palma and 2km (1¼ miles) from a good beach, this is a seven-story luxury property in business since 1976. The architecture is extremely modern and the entrance is set in the midst of landscaped gardens and an artificial lake. The lobby is impressive with its marble floors and pristine decor, and it's filled with an efficient and helpful staff. The rooms are spacious and handsomely furnished and have fully equipped bathrooms with tub/shower combos.

Calle Francisco Vidal Sureda 23, 07016 Palma de Majorca. ℰ **97-140-03-00.** Fax 97-140-59-04. www. fehm.es. 174 units. 200€–238€ double; from 278€–938€ suite. Rates include buffet breakfast. AE, DC, MC, V. Free parking. **Amenities:** 2 restaurants; 2 bars; 3 pools; tennis courts; minigolf; sauna; Turkish bath; salon; room service; massage; babysitting; laundry service; dry cleaning. *In room:* A/C, TV, minibar, hair dryer, safe.

At Palmanova

On the western coast, and west of Palma, this hotel enjoys a privileged position in Costa d'en Blanes. Count on a 10-minute drive from the center of Palma.

Hotel Punta Negra ★★ In an exclusive area, this two-story hotel is surrounded by two Mediterranean beaches and an array of golf courses. Elegant and posh, it's constructed in a classical Majorcan style with white walls, antique furnishings, carpeted floors, and panoramic views of either the sea or pine forests. The hotel is only 1.5km (1 mile) from the yachting port of Puerto Portals. Spacious and beautifully furnished rooms are equipped with elegant bathrooms containing tub/shower combos.

Carretera Andaitz, Km 12, Costa d'en Blanes, 07181 Majorca. ℰ **97-168-07-62.** Fax 97-168-39-19. www. hotelpuntanegra.com. 137 units. 108€–128€ double; 128€ suite. Rates include continental breakfast. AE, DC, MC, V. Free parking. **Amenities:** 2 restaurants; bar; 3 pools; 18-hole golf course; tennis courts; health club; sauna; salon; room service; babysitting; laundry service; dry cleaning; casino. *In room:* A/C, TV, minibar, hair dryer, iron, safe.

At Binissalem

Scott's Hotel ★★ *Finds* this is a handsomely restored 18th-century mansion lying in the little town of Binissalem in the center of Majorca. It's not for beach buffs, but if you have a car and want a retreat, you'll find this nugget lying 20km (12½ miles) from Palma and a 20-minute drive to a sandy beach. The beautifully furnished and rather elegant bedrooms come in a wide variety of sizes, singles ranging from two singles or two full suites, with units "in between" consisting of king-sized doubles, twins, queen-sized doubles, or junior suites. Each comes with a well-kept bathroom with tub or shower. This little jewel box could be one of your most satisfying stays on island. You feel more like you're living in a country manor house instead of a private home. The owners are helpful in recommending attractions, "secret beaches," restaurants, and island drives. One reader wrote us that Scott's is one of the most civilized and gracious inns on the island, "aggressively not touristy." Antiques, handmade beds, Persian rugs, and all that are just a backdrop for the grand tranquillity and wonderful hospitality found here.

Plaza de la Iglesia 12, 07350 Binissalem. ℰ **97-187-01-00.** Fax 97-187-02-67. www.scottshotel.com/eng/ index/html. 17 units. 175€–205€ double; 235€–330€ suite. AE, MC, V. **Amenities:** Nearby restaurant; pool; 2 sun terraces; laundry. *In room:* A/C, hair dryer, iron.

WHERE TO DINE

The most typical main dish of Majorca is *lomo,* or pork loin, and it appears as the specialty in any restaurant offering Majorcan cuisine. *Lomo con col* is a method of preparation where the loin is enveloped in cabbage leaves and served with a sauce made with tomatoes, grapes, pine nuts, and bay leaf.

A local sausage, *sabrosada,* is made with pure pork and red peppers. Paprika gives it its characteristic bright red color. *Sopas mallorquinas* can mean almost anything, but basically it is mixed greens in a soup flavored with olive oil and thickened with bread. When *garbanzos* (chickpeas) and meat are added, it becomes a meal in itself.

The best-known vegetable dish is *el tumbet,* a kind of cake with a layer of potato and another of lightly sautéed eggplant. Everything is covered with a tomato sauce and peppers, then boiled for a while. Eggplant, often served stuffed with meat or fish, is one of the island's vegetable mainstays. *Frito mallorquín* might include anything, but basically is a dish of fried onions and potatoes, mixed with red peppers, diced lamb liver, "lights" (lungs), and fennel. It's zesty, to say the least.

In the Balearic Islands, only Majorca produces wine, but this wine isn't exported. The red wine bottled around Felanitx and Binissalem adds Franja Roja and Viña Paumina to your wine list. Most of the wine, however, comes from Spain. *Café carajillo*—coffee with cognac—is a Spanish specialty particularly enjoyed by Majorcans.

Expensive

Koldo Royo ★★★ BASQUE   This is the premier place to enjoy savory Basque cuisine, and the island's finest restaurant next to Tristán (see below). If you're baffled by the unusual dishes on the menu, a staff member will assist you. This big-windowed establishment lies about three-fourths of a mile south of Palma's cathedral, adjacent to a marina and one of the island's most popular beaches. Menu items run the gamut of Basque seafood dishes, including baked hake, tripe, lamprey eel, and roasted pork. Meal after meal, Koldo Royo serves the best food in Palma.

Avinguda Gabriel Roca 3. ☎ **97-173-24-35**. Reservations required. Main courses 7€–22€; tasting menu 43€–50€. AE, DC, MC, V. Tues–Sat 1:30–3:30pm and 8–11pm.

La Lubina ★ SEAFOOD   La Lubina's location on the old pier is responsible for the freshest seafood in Palma. Begin with an aperitif in the tiled bar and then dine in the formal dining room or the more casual enclosed terrace. The menu consists mainly of seafood, and La Lubina is known for its unique preparation and presentation. *Caldereta* (lobster served in an almond broth) is an excellent choice. Try the traditional Majorcan fish *en papillote* (baked in paper and encrusted with salt) or the grilled swordfish.

Muelle Viejo s/n. ☎ **97-172-33-50**. Reservations recommended. Main courses 16€–19€. AE, DC, MC, V. Daily 1–4pm and 8pm–midnight. Bus: 1, 4, or 21.

Lonja del Pescado (Casa Eduardo) ★ SEAFOOD   Thriving since the 1930s, this no-frills restaurant serves the catch of the day, taken directly from the boat to the kitchen. Specialties include seafood paella and *zarzuela* (a fish stew). It's also possible to get fresh lobster. The rest of the menu consists of various types of fish, most prepared in the Majorcan style.

Muelle Viejo s/n. ☎ **97-172-11-82**. Reservations required. Main courses 8€–16€. AE, MC, V. Tues–Sat 1–3:30pm and 8–11pm. Bus: 1 or 4.

Mediterráneo 1930 ★ MEDITERRANEAN   Named after the Art Deco, 1930s-era styling that fills its interior, this is a well-managed, artfully hip restaurant adjacent to the Hotel Meliá Victoria. One of the top restaurants in Palma, with a sense of chic defined by its cosmopolitan owners Juan and Mary Martí, its beige and white decor is filled with verdant plants and Art Deco sculptures.

Finds **A Special Treat**

Dating from 1700, **Can Juan de S'aigo,** Carrer Sans 10 (☏ **97-171-07-59**), is the oldest ice-cream parlor on the island. Correspondingly elegant and old world, it serves its homemade ice creams (try the almond), pastries, cakes, *ensaimadas* (light-textured and airy specialty cakes of Palma), fine coffee, and several kinds of hot chocolate amid marble-top tables, beautiful tile floors, and an indoor garden with a fountain.

The menu relies heavily on seafood, with special emphasis on fish slowly baked in a salt crust, a process that adds a light-textured flakiness to even the most aromatic fish. Another specialty is beefsteak cooked on a hot stone that's carried directly to your table and then served with such sauces as béarnaise, pepper, or port.

Passeig Marítim 33. ☏ **97-173-03-77.** Reservations recommended. Main courses 12€–19€; fixed-price menu 17€. AE, MC, V. Daily 1–4pm and 8–11:30pm. Bus: 1.

Porto Pí ✿ MODERN MEDITERRANEAN   This restaurant, a favorite of King Juan Carlos, occupies an elegant 19th-century mansion above the yacht harbor at the west end of Palma. Contemporary paintings complement the decor, and there is an outdoor terrace. The food has a creative Mediterranean influence. Specialties change with the season but might include house-style fish *en papillote,* angelfish with shellfish sauce, and quail stuffed with foie gras cooked in a wine sauce. Game is a specialty in winter.

Joan Miró 174. ☏ **97-140-00-87.** Reservations required. Main courses 12€–25€. AE, DC, MC, V. Mon–Fri 1–3:30pm; daily 7:30–11:30pm. Bus: Palma-Illetas.

Tristán ✿✿✿ NOUVELLE CUISINE   Several miles southwest of Palma, Tristán overlooks the marina of Port Portals. This is the finest restaurant in the Balearics, winning a coveted two stars from Michelin, a designation previously unheard of in the archipelago. The sophisticated menu varies, depending on what's best in the market each day. Selections may include pigeon in rice paper, a medley of Mediterranean vegetables, or the catch of the day, usually prepared in Majorcan style. But this recitation doesn't prepare you for the exceptional burst of flavor you'll get when you sample the chef's creations.

Port Portals, Portals Nous. ☏ **97-167-55-47.** Reservations required. Main courses 19€–45€. AE, DC, MC, V. Daily 1–3:30pm and 8:30–11pm. Closed Jan 7–Feb 28. Bus: 22.

Moderate

Arrosería Catranca SEAFOOD   This sophisticated, bilingual restaurant has a setting overlooking the port. Arrosería Catranca (whose name translates as "Rice Restaurant Catranca") specializes in seafood (in many cases, mixed with rice) served in 16 different variations. The best way to appreciate its somewhat offbeat charm is beginning a meal with grilled baby sardines or a well-seasoned version of *buñuelos de bacalau* (minced and herb-laden cod formed into rounded patties). Either of these might be followed with a *parrillada*—an array of grilled fish and shellfish—or any of the above-mentioned rice casseroles. Two of the best of them include black rice with squid and squid ink, or a particularly succulent version with spider crabs, clams, and mussels. Other variations include vegetables, roasted goat, or hake with tomatoes and garlic.

Passeig Marítim 13. ☏ **97-173-74-47.** Reservations recommended. Main courses 9€–20€. AE, DC, MC, V. Tues–Sun 1–4pm; Tues–Sat 8pm–midnight. Bus: 1.

Caballito del Mar (Little Seahorse) SEAFOOD   Although there are several outdoor tables, many guests prefer to dine inside because of the lively spirit of this popular place along the seafront. The decor is vaguely nautical, and the activity is sometimes frenzied, but that's part of its charm. The food is well prepared from fresh ingredients; specialties include a Majorcan version of bouillabaisse, *zarzuela* (fish stew), assorted grilled fish (our favorite), oysters in season, red bream baked in salt, or sea bass with fennel. If you want something other than seafood, try the duck in orange sauce.

Passeig de Sagrera 5. ℭ **97-172-10-74**. Reservations recommended. Main courses 8€–26€. AE, DC, MC, V. Tues–Sun 1–4pm and 8pm–midnight. Bus: 5.

Inexpensive

Ca'an Carlos MAJORCAN   Set in two dining rooms of a much-renovated stone-sided house that's at least a century old, this restaurant is the domain of an entrepreneur (named Carlos) who accentuates his native Majorcan roots in his cooking. Well-prepared menu items include *sabrosada,* a soft pork sausage flavored with pepper and paprika; chicken or fish croquettes; stuffed squid; eggplant stuffed with pulverized shellfish; and a version of the Majorcan national dish, *cocida mallorquina,* a succulent stew.

Carrer de s'Aigua 5. ℭ **97-171-38-69**. Reservations recommended. Main courses 12€–21€. AE, MC, V. Mon–Sat 1–4pm and 8–11pm. Closed 3 weeks in Aug. Bus 3, 7, or 15.

Cellar Pagés MAJORCAN   The set menu here can include soup, noodles, or gazpacho; steak or fish; and dessert, bread, and wine. From the a la carte menu you can select the fish of the day, which most guests prefer grilled. Other dishes include the classic kidneys in sherry or a roast chicken. Admittedly, this isn't the best cooking on the island, but the price is right. The rustic setting is cramped and intimate, with original paintings on the white stucco walls. The location is 68m (75 yd.) west from the cathedral, a short walk from Plaça de la Reina.

Carrer Felipe Bauzá 2. ℭ **97-172-60-36**. Reservations recommended. Main courses 9€–15€; fixed-price menu 12€. AE, DC, MC, V. Mon–Sat 1–4pm and 8:30–11pm. Bus: 2, 3, 7, 8, or 15.

La Bóveda SPANISH   Set in the oldest part of Palma, a few steps from the cathedral, this rustic-looking restaurant maintains a busy tapas bar near the entrance, and no more than 14 tables set near the bar or in the basement. Menu items include a predictable list of Spanish staples, each well prepared, including roasted or fried veal, pork, chicken, and fish, served with fresh greens, potatoes, or rice. Any of the roster of tapas from the bar (fava beans with strips of ham, spinach *tortillas,* grilled or deep-fried calamari, and shrimp with garlic sauce) can be served while you're at your table, along with bottles of full-bodied red or more delicate white wines. A worthy and particularly refreshing dessert consists of freshly made sorbet, sometimes garnished with a shot of vodka or bourbon, depending on the flavor of the sorbet.

Calle Botería 3. ℭ **97-171-48-63**. Reservations recommended for a table in the restaurant, not necessary for the tapas bar. Main courses 7€–23€. AE, MC, V. Mon–Sat 1–4pm and 8:30pm–12:30am. Bus 7 or 13.

Mesón Can Pedro MAJORCAN   This restaurant has thrived since the early 1970s and is still going strong from a location in a hilltop suburb (Génova) overlooking Palma. A completely unpretentious local favorite, it has a bustling, animated atmosphere enhanced by odors wafting in from kitchens known for a succulent version of roasted baby lamb. Also worthwhile are T-bone steaks, roasted pork, spit-roasted chickens, spicy sausages, and different preparations of veal. One regional dish worth sampling is savory snails prepared with fennel and garlic and served with dollops of aioli.

Carrer Rector Vives 4 and 14, Génova. ☎ 97-140-24-79. Reservations recommended. Main courses 8€–16€. AE, DC, MC, V. Daily 1pm–1am. Bus: 4.

Sa Caseta ★ *Finds* MAJORCAN   For some of the best tasting regional cuisine, and to escape the heat of Palma, we like to head directly west of the city to the little satellite village of Gènova. Here in an *hacienda* you can enjoy a genuine and typical local cuisine served by a helpful staff in a series of attractive dining rooms. The chef obviously loves cod, and he cooks it superbly in at least 10 different preparations. If you're traveling with friends, you might want to order some of the best suckling pig or roast baby lamb in Majorca. Perhaps it's not quite as tantalizing as the versions served in Old Castile, but it's a rewarding dish especially when the weather is cool. On hotter days, you may prefer one of the local fish dishes, including (our favorite) monkfish in a shellfish sauce. For starter, paella is served with dried salt cod and vegetables, an unusual variation on this classic dish. *Sopas mallorquinas* (the island's famed vegetable soup) begins many a meal here. A series of homemade desserts, including ice cream, is a special feature.

Carrer Alférez Martínez Vaquer 1, Gènova. ☎ 97-140-42-81. Reservations recommended. Main courses 8€–16€; fixed-price menu 35€. DC, MC, V. Daily 1pm–midnight.

PALMA AFTER DARK

Palma is packed with bars and dance clubs. Sure, there are some fun hangouts along the island's northern tier, but for a rocking, laser- and strobe-lit club, you'll have to boogie in Palma.

Set directly on the beach, close to a dense concentration of hotels, **Tito's,** Passeig Marítim (☎ 97-173-00-17), charges a cover of 15€, including the first drink. A truly international crowd gathers to mingle on a terrace overlooking the Mediterranean. This club is the most popular, panoramic, and appealing disco on Majorca. If you only visit one nightclub during your time on the island, this should be it. Between June and September, it's open every night of the week from 11pm to at least 6am. The rest of the year, it's open only Thursday through Sunday, from 11pm to 6am.

Bar Barcelona, Carrer Apuntadores 5 (☎ 97-171-35-57), a popular jazz club, evokes its namesake city with its spiral staircase and atmospheric, subdued lighting. Despite its location, in the heart of Palma's busiest nightlife area, it attracts a predominately local crowd that comes to enjoy the live jazz every night from 11pm to 3am. There is no cover charge, and drinks are reasonably priced, making this one of Palma's best values for a night out. It's open every night till 4am.

B.C.M., Avinguda Olivera s/n, Magaluf (☎ 97-113-15-46), is the busiest, most lighthearted, and most cosmopolitan disco in Majorca. Boasting high-tech strobe lights and lasers, this sprawling, three-story venue offers a different sound system on each floor, giving you a wide variety of musical styles. If you're young, eager to mingle, and like to dance, this place is for you. The cover charge of 12€ includes your first drink and entitles you to party till 4am.

Come and enjoy a Caribbean cocktail with one of Palma's more charismatic bar owners, Pasqual, who just might invite you to dance a bit of salsa at **Bodeguida del Medio,** Paseo el Mar, Cala Ratjada (no phone). The music is Latin inspired and the crowd is a mix of locals and visitors from almost everywhere. Try their delicious "mojito" cocktail, more potent than it tastes. Inside is rustic in tone, outside is more intimate and romantic, with Chinese lanterns illuminating a garden that overlooks the sea.

ABACO, Carrer Sant Joan 1 (© **97-171-59-11**), just might be the most opulently decorated nightclub in Spain—a cross between a harem and a czarist Russian church. The bar is decorated with a trove of European decorative arts. The place is always packed, with many customers congregating in a beautiful courtyard, which has exotic caged birds, fountains, more sculpture than the eye can absorb, extravagant bouquets, and hundreds of flickering candles. All this exoticism is enhanced by the lushly romantic music (Ravel's *Boléro,* at our last visit) piped in through the sound system. Whether you view this as a bar, a museum, or a sociological survey, be sure to go. The bar is open daily from 9pm to 2:30am, from February to December only. Wandering around is free; however, drinks cost a whopping 10€ to 15€.

At the end of the Andraitz motorway, adjacent to the Cala Figuera turnoff, the **Casino de Majorca,** Urbanización Sol de Mallorca s/n, Costa del Calvía (© **97-113-00-00**), is the place to go in search of lady luck. The cover charge is 4€; dinner with no drinks, 55€; floor show without dinner but with two drinks, 40€. Children under 12 get discounts of 50%. If you bring your passport, you can indulge in American or French roulette, blackjack, or dice, or simply pull the lever on one of the many slot machines. A glittery cabaret show, styled in Monte Carlo fashion, is accessible through a separate entrance from the section of the casino devoted to gambling. It's presented every Tuesday through Saturday at 10:30pm. You might want to precede it with dinner, which is served beginning at 8pm, although we usually prefer to dine elsewhere on the island, then arrive in time for the 10:30 show. The casino's gambling facilities are open Monday through Thursday from 6pm to 4am (Sun until 3am), Friday and Saturday from 8pm to 5am.

Although Majorca is generally a pretty permissive place, it doesn't have the gay scene that Ibiza does. Still, one of Palma's most noteworthy gay bars is **Baccus,** Carrer Lluis Fábregas 1 (© **97-145-77-89**), catering to both gays and lesbians. It is open nightly from 9pm to at least 3am, and often later. There is no cover, and beers begin at 3.50€. If you feel like dancing, the largest and most popular disco in Palma is **Black Cat,** Avinguda Joan Miró 75 (no phone), which attracts a mixed crowd of young locals as well as visitors from Spain and the rest of the world. There are nightly shows at 3:30am. It is open daily from midnight to 6am but doesn't begin to get crowded until 2am. It is closed on Mondays during the winter. Admission is 7€.

EXPLORING MAJORCA BY CAR: THE WEST COAST

Mountainous Majorca has the most dramatic scenery in the Balearics. It's best appreciated if you have your own car and can explore easily on your own. Below, we'll outline a good daylong outing of about 142km (88 miles) that begins and ends in Palma.

Leave Palma heading west on C-719, passing through some of the most beautiful scenery of Majorca. Just a short distance from the sea rises the Sierra de Tramontana. The road passes the heavy tourist development of Palma Nova before coming to **Santa Ponça,** a town with a fishing harbor divided by a promontory. A fortified Gothic tower and a watchtower are evidence of the days when this little harbor suffered repeated raids and attacks. It was in a cove here that Jaume I's troops landed on September 12, 1229, to begin the reconquest of the island from the Muslims.

From Santa Ponça, continue along the highway, passing Paguera, Cala For-nells, and Camp de Mar, all beautiful spots with sandy coves. Between Camp de Mar and Port D'Andratx are corniche roads, a twisting journey to **Port D'An-dratx.** Summer vacationers mingle with fishers in this natural port, which is set against a backdrop of pines. Once the place was a haven for smugglers.

Leaving the port, continue northeast along C-719 to reach **Andratx,** 5km (3 miles) away. Because of frequent raids by Turkish pirates, this town moved inland. Lying 31km (19 miles) west of Palma, Andratx is one of the loveliest towns on the island, surrounded by fortifications and boasting a Gothic parish church and the mansion of Son Mas.

After leaving Andratx, take C-710 north, a winding road that runs parallel to the island's jagged northwestern coast. It's the highlight of the trip; most of the road is perched along the cliff edge and shaded by pine trees. It's hard to drive and pay attention to the scenery at the same time. Stop at the **Mirador Ricardo Roca** for a panoramic view of a series of coves. These coves can be reached only from the sea.

The road continues to **Estallenchs,** a town of steep slopes surrounded by pine groves, olive and almond trees, and fruit orchards (especially apricot). Estal-lenchs sits at the foot of the Galatzo mountain peak. Stop and explore some of its steep, winding streets on foot. From the town, you can walk to the Cala de Estallenchs cove, where a spring cascades down the high cliffs.

The road winds on to **Bañalbufar,** 8km (5 miles) from Estallenchs and about 26km (16 miles) west from Palma—one of the most scenic spots on the island. Set 100m (110 yd.) above sea level, it seems to perch directly over the sea. **Mirador de Ses Animes** ⋆, a belvedere constructed in the 17th century, offers a panoramic view of the coastline.

Many small excursions are possible from here. You might want to venture over to **Port d'es Canonge,** reached by a road branching out from the C-710 to the north of Bañalbufar. It has a beach, a simple restaurant, and some old fishers' houses. The same road takes you inland to **San Granja,** a mansion that was orig-inally constructed by the Cistercians as a monastery in the 13th century.

Back on C-710, continue to **Valldemossa,** the town where the composer Frédéric Chopin and the French writer George Sand spent their now-famous winter. After a visit to the **Cartuja** (Carthusian monastery), where they lived, you can wander at leisure through the steep streets of the old town. The cloister of **Ses Murteres** provides a romantic garden, and there is a pharmacy where Chopin, who was ill a lot during that winter, spent much time. The **Carthusian Church** is from the late 18th and early 19th centuries. Goya's father-in-law, Bayeu, painted the frescoes of the dome.

Beyond Valldemossa, the road runs along cliffs some 395m (1,300 ft.) high until they reach **San Marroig,** the former residence of Archduke Lluis Salvador (see "Valldemossa & Deià [Deyá]," below), which is actually within the town limits of Deià. He erected a small neoclassical temple on a slope overlooking the sea to give visitors a panoramic vista. Son Marroig, his former mansion, has been turned into a museum. From an arcaded balcony, you can enjoy a view of the famous pierced rock, the Foradada, rising out of the water.

By now you have reached **Deià,** where a series of small tile altars in the streets reproduces scenes from the Calvary. This was the home for many years of the English writer Robert Graves. He is buried at the **Campo Santo,** the cemetery, which you may want to visit for its panoramic view, if nothing else. Many other

---

Tips   Take the Train

If you're not driving, you can still reach Sóller aboard a turn-of-the-20th-century narrow-gauge railroad train from Palma. It's a spectacularly scenic 3-minute ride. You can catch the train at the Palma Terminal on Calle Eusebio Estada, near Plaça d'Espanya. It runs every hour on the hour from 8am to 8pm daily, and the fare is 4.80€ each way. Call ② **97-175-20-51** for information.

---

foreign painters, writers, and musicians have found inspiration in Deià. For living and dining, this is the choice spot on Majorca, a virtual Garden of Eden.

Continue north along the highway. You come first to **Lluch Alcari,** which Archduke Salvador considered one of the most beautiful spots on earth. Picasso retreated here for a short period in the 1950s. The settlement was once the victim of pirate raids, and you can see the ruins of several defense towers.

C-710 continues to **Sóller,** just 10km (6 miles) from Deià. The urban center has five 16th-century facades, an 18th-century convent, and a parish church of the 16th and 17th centuries. It lies on a broad basin where citrus and olive trees are abundant. Many painters, including Rusiñol, settled here and found inspiration.

Travel 5km (3 miles) north on C-711 to reach the coast and **Port de Sóller,** one of the best of the natural shelters along the island. It lies at the back of a bay that is almost round. A submarine base is here today, but it is also a harbor for pleasure craft. It has a lovely beach. The **Sanctuary of Santa Catalina** dominates one of the best views of the inlet.

Reached up a flight of stairs, **Restaurante Jaime,** Carrer Archiduque Lluis Salvador 24 (② **97-163-90-29**), attracts both foreign visitors and the family trade. This unpretentious, family-run restaurant, in business since 1964, makes a good lunch stop in high-priced Deià. Grilled meats and fresh fish are a specialty. Even if you don't want a full meal, consider stopping here for dessert, such as the almond cake with almond ice cream, before finishing your drive. Hours are Tuesday through Sunday from 1 to 4pm and 7:30 to 10:30pm.

After leaving the Sóller area, you face a choice. If you've run out of time, you can cut the tour in half here and head back along C-711 to Palma with two stops along the way. Your other option is to continue north, following the C-710 and local roads, to **Cape Formentor,** where even more spectacular scenery awaits you. Among the highlights of this coastal detour: **Fornalutx,** a lofty mountain village with steep cobbled streets, Moorish-tiled roofs, and groves of almond trees; the splendid, hair-raising road to the harbor village of **Sa Calobra,** plunging to the sea one minute, then climbing arduously past olive groves, oaks, and jagged boulders; and the 13th-century **Monasterio de Lluch,** some 45km (28 miles) north of Palma, which is home to the Black Virgin of Lluch, the island's patron saint. The well-known "boys' choir of white voices" sings there daily at noon and again at twilight.

Those not taking the coastal detour can head south along C-711 with a stop at **Jardins d'Alfàbia** (② **97-161-31-23**), Carretera Palma–Sóller, Km 17, a former Muslim residence. This estate is in the foothills of the sierra and includes both a palace and romantic gardens. The gardens are richly planted, and you can wander among pergolas, a pavilion, and ponds. Inside the palace you can see a good collection of Majorcan furniture and an Arabic coffered ceiling. The gardens are open from June to August, Monday through Friday from 9:30am to

6:30pm, Saturday from 9:30am to 1pm; from September to May, Monday through Friday from 9:30am to 5:30pm, Saturday from 9:30am to 1pm. Admission is 4.50€.

From Alfàbia, the highway becomes straight and Palma is just 18km (11 miles) away. But before reaching the capital, consider a final stop at **Raixa,** another charming place, built on the site of an old Muslim hamlet. It stands 1.5km (1 mile) outside the village of Buñola ("small vineyard"). The present building was once the estate of Cardinal Despuif and his family, who constructed it in the Italian style near the end of the 1700s. Ruins from Roman excavations are found on the grounds. Rusiñol came here, painting the place several times. It keeps the same hours as Jardins d'Alfàbia (see above).

After Raixa, the route leads directly to the northern outskirts of Palma.

VALLDEMOSSA & DEIA (DEYA)

Valldemossa is the site of the **Cartoixa Reial** *&*, Plaça de las Cartujas s/n (© **97-161-21-06**), where George Sand and the tubercular Frédéric Chopin wintered in 1838 and 1839. The monastery was founded in the 14th century, but the present buildings are from the 17th and 18th centuries. After monks abandoned the dwelling, the cells were rented to guests, which led to the appearance of Sand and Chopin, who managed to shock the conservative locals. They occupied cells 2 and 4. The only belongings left are a small painting and a French piano. The peasants burned most of it after the couple returned to the mainland, fearing they'd catch Chopin's tuberculosis. It may be visited Monday through Saturday from 9:30am to 6pm, Sunday from 10am to 1pm for 6€ adults, free for children under 10. Off season it shuts down an hour earlier.

It's also possible to visit the **Palau del Rei Sancho,** next door to the monastery, on the same ticket. This is a Moorish retreat built by one of the island kings. You'll be given a guided tour of the palace by a woman in Majorcan dress.

From Valldemossa, continue through the mountains following the signposts for 11km (6½ miles) to Deià. But before your approach to the village, consider a stopover at **San Marroig** (© **97-163-91-58**), at the Km 26 mark on the highway. Now a museum, this was once the estate of Archduke Lluis Salvador. Born in 1847, the archduke fled court life and found refuge here with his young bride in 1870. A tower on the estate is from the 1500s. Many of his personal furnishings and mementos, such as photographs and his ceramic collection, are still here. The estate is surrounded by lovely gardens, and there are many panoramic views on the property. It is open from April to October, Monday through Saturday from 9:30am to 2pm and 3 to 8pm (closing at 6pm in winter). Admission is 3€.

Set against a backdrop of olive-green mountains, **Deià (Deyá)** is peaceful and serene, with its stone houses and creeping bougainvillea. It has long had a special meaning for artists. Robert Graves, the English poet and novelist (*I, Claudius*

Moments **Just Ask a Painter Where the Sun Sets Best**

After walking through the old streets, you can stand on a rock overlooking the sea and watch the sun set over a field of silvery olive trees and orange and lemon groves. Then you'll know why painters come here to live on the slopes of a 1,200m (4,000-ft.) high mountain.

and *Claudius the God*), lived in Deià, and died here in 1985. He is buried in the local cemetery.

Valldemossa lacks basic services, including a tourist office. It is connected to a bus service from Palma, however. **Darbus** (℃ **97-175-06-22**) goes to Valldemossa five times daily for a one-way fare of 1.10€. Buses leave from Palma at the bar at Carrer Archiduque Lluis Salvador 1.

To reach Deià by public transportation from Palma, 27km (17 miles) away, just stay on the bus that stops in Valldemossa. If you're driving from Palma, take the Carretera Valldemossa–Deià to Valldemossa; from here, you can continue to Deià. Those with cars might want to consider one of the idyllic accommodations offered in this little Majorcan village, which has very few tourist facilities outside the hotels.

WHERE TO STAY

Deià offers some of the most tranquil and stunning retreats on Majorca—La Residencia and Es Molí—but it has a number of inexpensive little boarding houses as well.

Expensive

Hotel Es Molí ★★   One of the best-recommended and most spectacular hotels on Majorca originated in the 1880s as a severely dignified manor house in the rocky highlands above Deià, home of the landowners who controlled access to the town's freshwater springs. In 1966 the manor house was augmented with two annexes, transforming it into this luxurious four-star hotel. Rooms are beautifully furnished and impeccably maintained, often with access to a private veranda overlooking the gardens or the faraway village. All units have neatly kept bathrooms with tub/shower combos. Some hardy souls make it a point to hike for 30 minutes to the public beach at Deià Bay; others wait for the shuttle bus to take them to the hotel's private beach, 6km (4 miles) away.

Carretera Valldemossa s/n, 07179 Deià. ℃ **97-163-90-00**. Fax 97-163-93-33. www.esmoli.com. 87 units. 182€–242€ double; 367€–400€ suite. Rates include breakfast; half-board 17€ extra per person per day. AE, DC, MC, V. Free parking. Closed early Nov to late Apr. **Amenities:** Restaurant; bar; lounge; pool; tennis court; room service; babysitting; laundry service; dry cleaning. *In room:* A/C, TV, minibar, hair dryer, safe.

La Residencia ★★★   This is the most stylish, hip, elegant hotel on Majorca, a renowned hostelry that became even more famous in the early 1990s when it was acquired by British businessman and founder of Virgin Airlines Richard Branson. Since Branson took over, the hilltop property, affectionately called "La Res," has become a celebrity haven. Surely that's not Tom Hanks and Sting sunbathing in the buff around the pool at this star-caliber secluded haunt, which conceives of itself as "your revenge on everyday life." The ambience is luxurious but unpretentious at these two tawny, stone, 16th-century manor houses, surrounded by 5.3 hectares (13 acres) of rocky Mediterranean gardens. Guests have included everyone from Queen Sofía and the emperor of Japan to America's rock 'n' roll elite. Spacious rooms are outfitted with rustic antiques, terra-cotta floors, romantic-looking four-poster beds, and in some cases, beamed ceilings, all with luxurious appointments, including bathrooms with tub/shower combos. Open hearths, deep leather sofas, wrought-iron candelabra, and a supremely accommodating staff make this hotel internationally famous. Although it's technically defined as a four-star resort and a member of Relais & Châteaux, only the lack of certain luxuries prevents it from reaching government-rated five-star status.

San Canals s/n, 07179 Deià. © **97-163-90-11**. Fax 97-163-93-70. www.hotel-laresidencia.com. 63 units. 199€–375€ double; from 900€ suite. Rates include breakfast. AE, DC, MC, V. Free parking. **Amenities:** 2 restaurants; 3 bars; 3 pools; tennis court; fitness center; sauna; room service; babysitting; laundry service; dry cleaning. *In room:* A/C, TV, hair dryer, safe.

Inexpensive

Hotel Costa d'Or *Value*   This former villa, 1.5km (1 mile) north of Deià on the road to Sóller, offers the best possible view of the vine-covered hills and the rugged coast beyond. Surrounded by private gardens filled with fig trees, date palms, and orange groves, this old-fashioned hotel is furnished with odds-and-ends furniture, but it's clean and comfortable. Most rooms have good views, and all come with good beds and tidy, small bathrooms, most of which are equipped with tub/shower combos.

Lluch Alcari s/n, 07179 Deià. © **97-163-90-25**. Fax 97-163-93-47. 40 units. 84€–107€ double. Rates include breakfast. DC, MC, V. Closed Nov–Apr 1. **Amenities:** Restaurant; lounge; pool; laundry service; dry cleaning. *In room:* TV, safe.

WHERE TO DINE

Ca'n Costa MAJORCAN/INTERNATIONAL   This restaurant specializes in Majorcan cuisine but includes some international dishes to please the mostly foreign patronage. The owner has selected only the finest of wines from the island itself, which he has wisely combined with some good vintages from Rioja. The hearty regional fare includes roast pork loin with mushrooms from the fields and even thrush enveloped in cabbage. Try for a seat on the outdoor patio, with a panoramic vista of the coast.

Carretera Valldemossa–Deià s/n. © **97-161-22-63**. Reservations recommended. Main courses 9€–18€. AE, DC, MC, V. Wed–Mon 12:30–4pm and 7:30–11pm.

Ca'n Quet ✦ INTERNATIONAL   This restaurant, belonging to the Hotel Es Molí (see above), is one of the most sought-after dining spots on the island. Set on a series of terraces above a winding road leading out of town, the building is well scrubbed, modern, and stylish but with an undeniably romantic air. Cascades of pink geraniums ring its terraces, and if you wander along the sloping pathways you'll find groves of orange and lemon trees, roses, and a swimming pool ringed with neoclassical balustrades.

There is a spacious and sunny bar, an elegant indoor dining room with a blazing fire in winter, and alfresco dining on the upper terrace under an arbor. The food is well prepared and the portions generous. Meals can include a salad of marinated fish, terrine of fresh vegetables, fish crepes, shellfish stew, duck with sherry sauce, and an ever-changing selection of fresh fish.

Carretera Valldemossa–Sóller. © **97-163-91-96**. Reservations required. Main courses 18€–22€. AE, MC, V. Tues–Sun 1–4pm and 8–11pm. Closed Nov–Mar.

El Olivo ✦✦ INTERNATIONAL/MEDITERRANEAN   A 30- to 40-minute drive north of Palma, this is one of the island's most elegant and upscale restaurants, as shown by recent visits from Bruce Springsteen, the emperor of Japan, Sting, and the president, king, and queen of Spain. It's set within what was built several centuries ago as an olive press, a thick-walled outbuilding of La Residencia Hotel. Much of the illumination comes from theatrical-looking candelabra placed on every table, whose flickering light throws shadows against thick ceiling beams, antique accessories, and very formal table settings. The cuisine is modern and subtly flavored, and the chefs know how to take classic dishes and add inventive touches, making for an unexpected wake-up call for your taste buds. Menu items include a salad of red mullet with julienne of vegetables and vinaigrette, roasted rack of lamb with tomato and herb sauce, baked hake with a seafood risotto, and a dessert specialty of almond soufflé.

In La Residencia Hotel, San Canals. ℂ **97-163-93-92.** Reservations recommended. Main courses 30€–57€; set-price menu 75€. AE, DC, MC, V. Daily 1–3pm and 8–11pm.

INCA

About 27km (17 miles) north of Palma is Inca, the island's second-largest city and Majorca's market and agricultural center.

Thursday is market day for farming equipment and livestock, but visitors will be more interested in the variety of low-priced leather goods—shoes, purses, jackets, and coats—sold here. In general, stores in Inca selling these leather goods are open Monday through Friday from 9:30am to 7pm, Saturday from 9:30am to noon.

Modernization has deprived Inca of its original charm, but the parish church of Santa María la Mayor and the convent of San Jerónimo hold some interest, as does the original Son Fuster Inn, a reminder of an earlier, simpler era.

From Palma, **trains** (ℂ **97-150-00-59**) run Monday through Friday at the rate of 40 per day and 34 on Saturday and Sunday. Trip time is only 40 minutes. A round-trip ticket costs 3.25€.

Inca lies on C-713, the road leading to the Pollença–Formentor region.

WHERE TO DINE

Cellar Ca'n Amer ★ (Finds) MAJORCAN   If you can stay for lunch or dinner, we recommend this charming spot. In a building dating from 1850, you'll find the most authentic *cueva* (cave) dining on the island. A container of local wine, which everyone here seems to drink, is tapped from one of the dozens of casks that line the stone walls of the vaults. The interconnected dining rooms are furnished with wooden tables and rustic artifacts. A polite staff serves large portions of Majorcan specialties, including *lechona frit* (a mélange of minced pork offal fried and seasoned), bread and vegetable soup, Majorcan cod, thrush wrapped in cabbage leaves, and the chef's version of roast suckling pig with a bitter but tasty sauce. There is an array of fresh seafood and fish.

Carrer Pau 39. ℂ **97-150-12-61.** Main courses 25€–32€. AE, MC, V. Mon–Sat 1–4:30pm and 7pm– midnight.

PORT DE POLLENÇA/FORMENTOR

Beside a sheltered bay and between Cape Formentor to the north and Cape del Pinar to the south lies Port de Pollença, amid two hills: **Calvary** to the west and **Puig** to the east. From the town, the best views of the resort and the bay are from Calvary Chapel. The bay provides excellent water-skiing and sailing. The location is 65km (40 miles) north of Palma.

A series of low-rise hotels, private homes, restaurants, and snack bars lines the very attractive beach, which is somewhat narrow at its northwestern end but has some of the island's finest, whitest sand and warmest, clearest water. For several miles along the bay there is a pleasant pedestrian promenade. There is only one luxury hotel in the area, however, and that is out on the Formentor Peninsula.

Tons of fine white sand were imported to the beach at the southeastern end of Pollença Bay to create a broad ribbon of sunbathing space that stretches for several miles along the bay. Windsurfing, water-skiing, and scuba diving are among the watersports offered in the area.

Cabo de Formentor ★, "the devil's tail," can be reached from Port de Pollença via a spectacular road, twisting along to the lighthouse at the cape's end. Formentor is Majorca's fjord country—a dramatic landscape of mountains, pine trees, rock, and sea, plus some of the best beaches in Majorca. In Cape Formentor, you'll see *miradores,* or lookout windows, which provide panoramic views.

ESSENTIALS

GETTING THERE   Five **buses** a day leaving the Plaça Espanya in Palma pass through Inca and continue on to Port de Pollença. You can continue on from Deià (see above) along C-710, or from Inca on C-713, all the way to Pollença.

VISITOR INFORMATION   The **tourist information office** (✆ **97-189-26-15**), on Carretera de Artá, is open from May to October, Monday through Saturday from 9am to 7pm. It's closed off season. From November to March, another office can answer telephone queries (✆ **97-154-72-57**). Hours are Monday through Saturday from 9:30am to 8pm.

EXPLORING THE COAST

The plunging cliffs and rocky coves of Majorca's northwestern coast are a stunning prelude to Port de Pollença. The **Mirador de Colomer** provides an expansive view of the striking California-like coast that stretches from Punta de la Nau to Punta de la Troneta and includes El Colomer (Pigeon's Rock), named for the nests in its cave.

But it is the 20km (12½-mile) stretch of winding, at times vertiginous, road leading from Port de Pollença to the tip of the **Formentor Peninsula** that delivers the island's most intoxicating scenic views. Cliffs more than 197m (650 ft.) high and spectacular rock-rimmed coves embrace intense turquoise waters. About halfway along this road is the **Cala de Pi de la Posada,** where you will find a lovely bathing beach. Continuing on to the end you'll come to the lighthouse at **Cabo de Formentor.**

Wednesday is **market day** in Port de Pollença, so head for the town square (there's only 1) from 8am to 1pm and browse through the fresh produce, leather goods, embroidered tablecloths, ceramics, and more. Bargaining is part of the fun. Sunday is market day in the town of Pollença.

Alcúdia Bay is a long stretch of narrow, sandy beach with beautiful water backed by countless hotels, whose crowds rather overwhelm the area in peak season. The nightlife is more abundant and varied here than in Port de Pollença.

Between Port de Alcúdia and Ca'n Picafort is the **Parc Natural de S'Albufera,** Carretera Alcúdia–Artá, Km 27, 07458 C'an Picafort (no phone). A wetlands area of lagoons, dunes, and canals covering some 800 hectares (1,975 acres), it attracts bird-watchers and other nature enthusiasts. To date, more than 200 species of birds have been sighted here, among them herons, owls, ospreys, and warblers. The best times to visit are spring and fall, when migratory birds abound. Spring, too, offers a marvelous display of flora. The park is open daily (except Christmas) from October 1 to March 30 from 9am to 5pm, from April 1 to September 30 from 9am to 7pm. Visits are free, but you must get a permit at the reception center, where all motorized vehicles must be left. Binoculars are available for rent. The reception center has further information.

In the town of Pollença, about 6km (4 miles) from Port Pollença, is an 18th-century stairway leading up to an *ermita* (hermitage). Consisting of 365 stairs, it is known as the **Monte Calvario (Calvary),** but you can also reach the top by car via Carrer de las Cruces, which is lined with 3m (10-ft.) high concrete crosses.

Cala San Vicente, between Pollença and Port de Pollença, is a pleasant, small sandy cove with some notable surf. Several small hotels and restaurants provide the necessary amenities.

Various companies offer tours of Pollença Bay, and many provide glass-bottomed boats for viewing the varied aquatic creatures and plants. Many of these boats leave from Port de Pollença's Estació Marítim several times daily during the summer months, with less frequent departures in winter. Your hotel concierge or the marina can provide you with a schedule.

Part of the allure of a trip to the Balearics is boating in the Mediterranean; if you're in the market to rent either a small sailing craft or a glamorous yacht that comes with a full complement of staff and crew, Associación Provinciale d'Empresarios de Actividades Marítimas de Baleares, Muelle Viejo 6, in Palma (✆ **97-172-79-86**), can steer you in the right direction. Chances are they'll direct you to one of two well-respected maritime charter companies, both based in Palma. They are **Moorings Formentor,** Contramuelle 12 (✆ **97-121-42-31**), and **Alga Charter,** Contramuelle Mollet (✆ **97-171-64-28**). Both lease boats of different sizes by the day, week, or month.

If you want to go parasailing, head for **Deportes Náuticos,** Carrer Estornell 2, Sonferrer/Calvia (✆ **97-123-03-28**), which is about 15km (9 miles) southeast of Palma.

WHERE TO STAY
In Puerto Pollença

Hotel Illa d'Or ★   Originally built in 1929, and enlarged and improved several times since then, this four-story hotel sits at the relatively isolated northwestern edge of Pollença Bay—far from the heavily congested, touristed region around Palma. Decorated in a mixture of colonial Spanish and English reproductions, it offers a seafront terrace with a view of the mountains and airy, simply furnished rooms. Rooms are midsize to spacious, each with comfortable furnishings, including good beds and bathrooms with tub/shower combos. The beach is just a few steps away.

Passeig Colón 265, 07470 Port de Pollença. ✆ **97-186-51-00.** Fax 97-186-42-13. www.hoposa.es. 120 units. 111€–181€ double; 225€–376€ suite. Rates include breakfast. AE, DC, MC, V. Free parking. Closed Dec–Jan 9. **Amenities:** Restaurant; 2 bars; 2 pools; room service; fitness center; sauna; laundry service; dry cleaning. *In room:* A/C, TV, minibar, hair dryer, safe.

Hotel Miramar *Value*   This centrally located hotel is one of the grandly old-fashioned hostelries in town, in a desirable position across the coastal road from the beach. It has ornate front columns supporting a formal balustrade, tiled eaves, and several jardinieres. The lobby is furnished with antiques. Some rooms have private verandas overlooking the flower-filled courtyard in back. All the small to midsize rooms are comfortably furnished and well maintained, each with a firm bed and bathroom equipped with a tub/shower combo.

Passeig Anglada Camarasa 39, 07470 Port de Pollença. ✆ **97-186-64-00.** Fax 97-186-40-75. 84 units. 75€– 132€ double. Rates include breakfast. AE, DC, MC, V. Closed Nov–Mar. **Amenities:** Restaurant; lounge; room service; babysitting; laundry service; dry cleaning. *In room:* A/C, TV, hair dryer, safe.

Hotel Pollentia ★   This hotel is .8km (½ mile) from the commercial center of the resort, behind a screen of foliage. It's our favorite hotel in town because of its cool, airy spaciousness and the genial reception. The steps leading to the formal modern lobby are banked with dozens of terra-cotta pots overflowing with ivy and geraniums. The reception area has Majorcan glass chandeliers, and many of the well-furnished but small rooms have private terraces, and all have bathrooms with tub/shower combos. Guests have access to a private terrace overlooking the Mediterranean.

Passeig de Londres s/n, 07470 Port de Pollença. ℭ **97-186-52-00.** Fax 97-186-60-34. 70 units. 60€–70€ double. Rates include breakfast. AE, DC, MC, V. Closed Dec–Mar. **Amenities:** Bar; lounge; laundry service; dry cleaning. *In room:* A/C, hair dryer, safe.

WHERE TO DINE
In Port de Pollença

Stay Restaurant ☆ SPANISH/INTERNATIONAL   This restaurant offers a unique menu that changes about every 2 months, depending on what's available at the market. Main courses include fresh salmon filets in a white-wine sauce, roasted duck with a green peppercorn sauce, grilled filet of beef with a sauce of foie gras de *canard* (duckling) and port wine, and our favorite, *parrillada de mariscos,* a platter of assorted grilled fish and seafood. Finish your meal with a strudel of fresh figs, almonds, and raisins smothered in a hot vanilla sauce.

Muelle Nuevo, Estació Marítim s/n. ℭ **97-186-40-13.** Reservations recommended July–Aug. Main courses 12€–24€; fixed-price menu 26€. AE, MC, V. Daily noon–10:30pm.

In Pollença

Restaurant Clivia ☆ MALLORQUINA/SPANISH   This is the best and most appealing restaurant in Pollença, even attracting a clientele from other districts of Majorca. The restaurant is composed of two dining rooms and an outdoor patio in a century-old house in the heart of town. It has a scattering of antique furniture and a tactful, well-organized staff that produces a limited list of meats (veal, chicken, pork, and beef) and a more appealing roster of seafood prepared with skill and finesse. Specialties depend on the availability of fish such as cod, monkfish, dorado, eel, squid, and whitefish, either baked in a salt crust or prepared as part of a succulent *parrillada* (platter) of shellfish that's among the freshest anywhere. Begin with a spicy fish soup and accompany it with fresh vegetables, such as asparagus or spinach. The restaurant's name derives from the variety of bright red flowers *(las clivias)* that are planted profusely beside the patio and that bloom throughout the summer.

Avinguda Pollentia 4760. ℭ **97-153-46-16.** Reservations recommended. Main courses 12€–21€. AE, DC, MC, V. May–Oct Tues and Thurs–Sun 1–3pm and 7–11pm; Nov 1–14 and Dec 16–Apr daily 1–3pm and 7–11pm. Closed Nov 15–Dec 15.

MAJORCA'S EAST COAST: THE CAVA ROUTE

The east coast of Majorca is often called the *cava* route because of the caves that stud the coastline. Although there are scores, we'll include only the most important ones; other places mentioned are Manacor, where cultured Majorcan pearls are manufactured, and Petra, home of Fray Junípero Serra, founder of many California missions. In general, the east coast of Majorca does not have the dramatic scenery of the west coast but has worthy attractions in its own right.

Leave Palma on the freeway but turn onto Carretera C-715 in the direction of Manacor. About 56km (35 miles) east of Palma, you come to your first stop, Petra.

PETRA

Petra was founded by Jaume II over the ruins of a Roman settlement. This was the birthplace of Father Junípero Serra (1713–84), the Franciscan priest who founded the missions in California that eventually grew into San Diego, Monterey, and San Francisco. A statue commemorates him at the Capitol building in Washington, D.C., and you will also see a statue of Father Serra in this, his native village.

Museo Beato Junípero Serra, Carrer Barracar (© **97-156-11-49**), gives you an idea of how people lived on the island in the 18th century. The property was bought and fixed up by the San Francisco Rotary Club, which then presented it as a gift to the citizens of Petra in 1972. The museum, 457m (500 yd.) from the center of the village, is open every day of the year but doesn't keep regular hours. Visits are by appointment only. Admission is free, but donations are encouraged.

MANACOR

The C-715 continues east to Manacor, the town where the famous artificial pearls of Majorca are manufactured. The trade name for the pearls is "Perlas Majorica," so avoid such knock-offs as "Majorca." You can visit the factories where the pearls are made, and purchase some if you wish. Jewelry here may be 5% to 10% cheaper than at most retail outlets in Barcelona.

The largest outlet is **Perlas Majorica,** Pedro Riche s/n (© **97-155-09-00**), which offers organized tours. On the road to Palma at the edge of town, it is open Monday through Friday from 1pm to 7pm. On Saturday and Sunday, it is open from 9:45am to 1pm. Admission is free. They'll explain how the pearls are made (from fish scales that simulate the sheen of a real pearl). Some 300 artisans work here, shaping and polishing the pearls, and they're used to being inspected by foreign visitors while at work. Perlas Majorica carry a 10-year guarantee.

CUEVAS DEL DRACH ★★★

From Manacor, take the road southeast to the sea—about 12km (7½ miles)—and the town of **Porto Cristo,** 61km (38 miles) east of Palma. Go .8km (½ mile) south of town to **Cuevas del Drach (Caves of the Dragon;** © **97-182-07-53**), which contain an underground forest of stalactites and stalagmites as well as five subterranean lakes, where you can listen to a concert and later go boating a la Jules Verne. The roof appears to glitter with endless icicles. Martel Lake, 176m (581 ft.) long, is the largest underground lake in the world. E. A. Martel, a French speleologist who charted the then mysterious caves in 1896, described it better than anyone: "As far as the eye can see, marble cascades, organ pipes, lace draperies, pendants or brilliants, hang suspended from the walls and roof." From mid-march to October tours depart daily, every hour from 10am to 5pm (Nov–Mar 10:45am, noon, 2, and 3:30pm). Admission is 7.50€.

If you don't have a car, you can take one of the four daily buses that leave from the railroad station in Palma (inquire at the tourist bureau in Palma for times of departure). The buses pass through Manacor on the way to Porto Cristo.

CUEVAS DEL HAM

Discovered in 1906, these caves, whose name means "fish hooks," are .8km (½ mile) from Porto Cristo on the road to Manacor. **Cuevas del Ham** (© **97-182-09-88**) are far less impressive than the Cuevas del Drach and can be skipped if you're rushed. Tours depart every 10 minutes daily April through October from 10:30am to 5:30pm and November through March daily from 10am to 5pm, charging 9.50€ admission for adults, free for children under 12. These caves contain white stalactites and follow the course of an underground river. There is a link to the sea, so the water level inside the cave's pools rises and falls according to the tides.

CUEVAS DE ARTÁ ★★★

Near Platja de Canyamel (Playa de Cañamel on some maps), **Cuevas de Artá** (© **97-184-12-93**) lie on a stretch of land closing Canyamel Bay to the north. These caves are said to be the inspiration for the Jules Verne tale *Journey to the*

Center of the Earth, published in 1864. (Verne may have heard or read about the caves; it is not known if he ever actually visited them.) Formed by seawater erosion, the caves are about 32m (35 yd.) above sea level, and some of the rooms rise about 46m (150 ft.).

You enter an impressive vestibule and immediately see walls blackened by the torches used to light the caves for early tourists in the 1800s. There follows the *Reina de las Columnas* (Queen of the Columns), rising about 22m (72 ft.) tall, then a lower room whose Dante-esque appearance has led to it being called "inferno." It is followed by a field of stalagmites and stalactites, the "purgatory rooms," which eventually lead to the "theater" and "paradise."

The caves were once used by pirates, and centuries ago provided a haven for Spanish Moors fleeing the persecution of Jaume I. The stairs in the cave were built for Isabella II for her 1860 visit. In time, such luminaries as Sarah Bernhardt, Alexandre Dumas, and Victor Hugo arrived for the tour. Tours depart daily, every half-hour from 10am to 6pm May through June, daily from 10am to 7pm July through September, and daily from 10am to 5pm off season. Admission is 8€.

2 Ibiza *

Ibiza (ee-*bee*-thah) was once a virtually unknown and unvisited island; Majorca, its bigger neighbor, got all the business. But in the 1950s, Ibiza's art colony began to thrive, and in the 1960s it became the European resort most favored by the flower children. A New York art student once wrote, "Even those who come to Ibiza for the 'wrong' reason (to work!) eventually are seduced by the island's easy life. Little chores like picking up the mail from the post office stretch into daylong missions." Today, Ibiza is overrun by middle-class package-tour tourists, mainly from England, France, Germany, and Scandinavia, and it has become a major mecca for gay travelers, making it a wild combination of chic and middle-class.

At 585 sq. km (225 sq. miles), it is the third largest of the Balearic Islands. Physically, Ibiza has a jagged coastline, some fine beaches, whitewashed houses, secluded bays, cliffs, and a hilly terrain dotted with fig and olive trees. Warmer than Majorca, it's a better choice for a winter vacation, but it can be sweltering in July and August. Thousands of tourists descend on the island in summer, greatly taxing the island's limited water supply.

Ciudad de Ibiza boasts Playa Talamanca in the north and Ses Figueretes and Playa d'en Bossa in the south, two outstanding white sandy beaches. Las Salinas, in the south, near the old salt flats, offers excellent sands. Playa Cavallet and Aigües Blanques attract the nude sunbathers. Other good beaches include Cala Bassa, Port des Torrent, Cala Tarida, and Cala Conta—all within a short bus or boat ride from San Antonio de Portmany. The long sandy cove of Cala Llonga, south of Santa Eulalia del Río, and the white sandy beach of El Cana to the north, are sacred to Ibiza's sun worshipers. In Formentera, Playa de Mitjorn stretches 5km (3 miles) and is relatively uncrowded. Set against a backdrop of pines and dunes, the pure white sand of Es Pujols is the most popular of Ibiza's beaches and deservedly so.

Many travelers still arrive dreaming of soft drugs and hard sex. Both exist in great abundance, but there are dangers. It's common to pick up the local paper and read the list of the latest group of people deported because of *irresponsibilidad económica* (no money) or *conducta antisocial* (drunk and disorderly conduct).

Some young travelers, frankly, have forsaken Ibiza, taking a ferry 40 minutes away (and just 5km/3 miles as the crow flies) to the tiny island of Formentera, where they find less harassment (although anyone looking suspicious will be noticed out here too). Formentera is the most southern of the Balearic Islands, and because of limited accommodations, restaurants, and nightlife, it is most often visited on a day trip from Ibiza.

Eivissa is the local (Catalán) name for Ibiza. Catalán is the most common language of the island, but it is a dialectal variation—called *Eivissenc* or *Ibicenco*. The same language is spoken on Formentera.

ISLAND ESSENTIALS

GETTING THERE   Again, as with Palma, if you come in July and August, be sure you have a return ticket and a reservation. Stories of passengers who were stranded for days in Ibiza in midsummer are legend.

Iberia (© **97-180-93-35**) flies into **Es Codolar International Airport** (© **97-180-90-00**), 5.5km (3½ miles) from Ciudad de Ibiza. Four daily flights connect Ibiza with Palma de Majorca, and five flights a day arrive from Barcelona. It's possible to take one of two daily flights from Valencia or one of three from Madrid. With the exception of charter flights winging in from virtually everywhere, Iberia is the main carrier servicing Ibiza. Its only other competitor on this route is **Air Europa** (© **97-180-91-91** in Ibiza), which offers flights to Ibiza from Barcelona (a maximum of 2 flights a day), as well as from Madrid and Palma, at intervals much less frequent than those offered aboard Iberia. The price of flights to Ibiza varies considerably because of season, promotion, and availability.

Transmediterránea, Estación Marítim, Muelle Ibiza (© **97-131-50-50**), operates a **ferry service** from Barcelona at the rate of five per week Monday through Friday, costing 63€ for a one-way ticket. One boat per day departs from Valencia Monday through Friday, with a one-way ticket going for 45€. From Palma, there are three ferries per week, on Friday, Saturday, and Sunday; it costs 40€ one-way. Check with travel agents in Barcelona, Valencia, or Palma regarding ferry schedules. You can book tickets through any agent.

GETTING AROUND   If you land at Es Cordola airport outside Ciudad de Ibiza, you will find **bus** service for the 5.5km (3½-mile) ride into town. Sometimes taxis are shared. In Ciudad de Ibiza, buses leave for the airport from Avinguda Isidor Macabich 24 (by the ticket kiosk), every hour on the hour, daily from 7am to 10pm.

Once in Ibiza, you'll have to walk, but the city is compact and can be covered on foot. There are buses, however, leaving for the nearby beaches. The two main bus terminals are at Avinguda Isidor Macabich 20 and 42.

One of the most popular means of getting around the island, especially in the south, is by a moped or bicycle. Rental arrangements can be made through **Casa Valentín,** corner of Avinguda B.V. Ramón and Avinguda de la Paz s/n (© **97-131-08-22**). Mopeds cost from 25€ to 30€ per day.

If you'd like to rent a car, both Hertz and Avis have offices at the airport.

VISITOR INFORMATION   The **tourist information office** is at Antonio Riquer 2, in the port of Ciudad de Ibiza (© **97-130-19-00**). It is open Monday through Friday from 9:30am to 1:30pm and 5 to 7pm, Saturday from 10:30am to 1pm. There is another office at the airport (© **97-180-91-18**), which is open Monday through Saturday from 9am to 2pm and from 4 to 9pm, Sunday from 9am to 2pm.

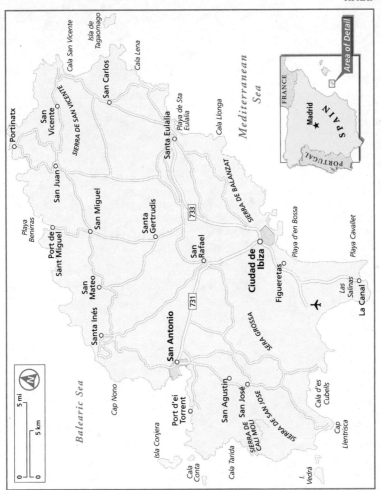

CIUDAD DE IBIZA

The island's capital, **Ciudad de Ibiza,** was founded by the Carthaginians 2,500 years ago. Today the town consists of a lively marina district around the harbor and an old town, **D'Alt Vila** ✈, with narrow cobblestoned streets and flat-roofed, whitewashed houses. The yacht-clogged marina and the district's main street, Vara de Rey, are constant spectacles—from old fishermen to the local Ibizan women swathed in black to the ubiquitous, scantily clad tourists. The marina district is fun to wander about with its art galleries, dance clubs, boutiques, bars, and restaurants.

Much of the medieval character of the old town has been preserved, in spite of massive development elsewhere. Many houses have Gothic styling and open onto spacious courtyards. These houses, some of which are 500 years old, are often festooned with geraniums and bougainvillea. The old quarter is entered through the Puerta de las Tablas, flanked by Roman statues.

Ciudad de Ibiza

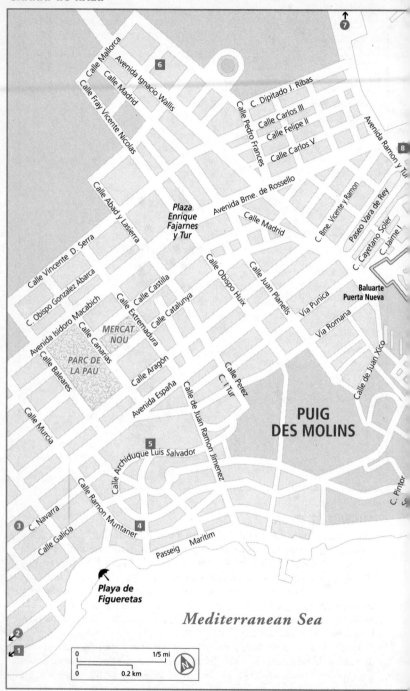

PUIG
DES MOLINS

Baluarte
Puerta Nueva

Plaza
Enrique
Fajarnes
y Tur

MERCAT
NOU

PARC DE
LA PAU

Playa de
Figueretas

Mediterranean Sea

Calle Mallorca
Avenida Ignacio Wallis
Calle Madrid
Calle Fray Vicente Nicolas
Calle Abad y Lasierra
Calle Vincente D. Serra
C. Obispo Gonzalez Abarca
Avenida Isidoro Macabich
Calle Canarias
Calle Baleares
Calle Murcia
Calle Navarra
Calle Galicia
Calle Ramon Muntaner
Calle Archiduque Luis Salvador
Calle Extremadura
Calle Castilla
Calle Catalunya
Calle Aragón
Avenida España
Calle de Juan Ramon Jimenez
C. I Tur
Calle Perez
Calle Obispo Huix
Calle Juan Planells
Via Punica
Via Romana
Calle de Juan Xico
C. Pintor
C. Dipitado J. Ribas
Calle Pedro Frances
Calle Carlos III
Calle Felipe II
Calle Carlos V
Avenida Bme. de Rossello
Calle Madrid
C. Bme. Vicente y Ramon
Paseo Vara de Rey
C. Cayetano Soler
C. Jaime I
Avenida Ramon y Tur
Passeig Maritim

0   1/5 mi
0   0.2 km

616

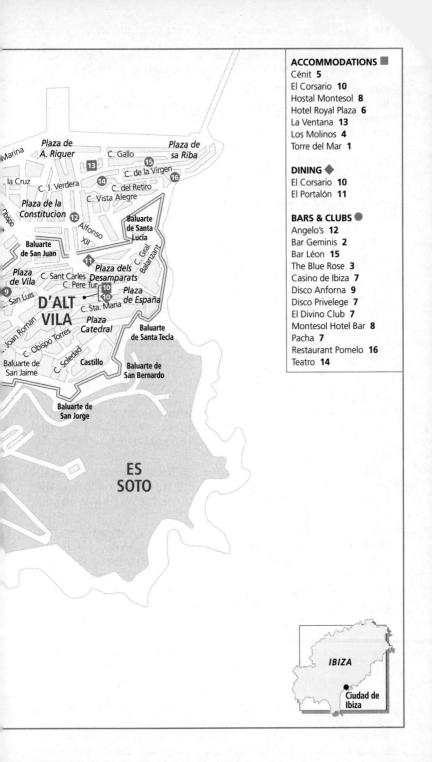

ACCOMMODATIONS ■
Cénit **5**
El Corsario **10**
Hostal Montesol **8**
Hotel Royal Plaza **6**
La Ventana **13**
Los Molinos **4**
Torre del Mar **1**

DINING ◆
El Corsario **10**
El Portalón **11**

BARS & CLUBS ●
Angelo's **12**
Bar Geminis **2**
Bar Léon **15**
The Blue Rose **3**
Casino de Ibiza **7**
Disco Anforna **9**
Disco Privelege **7**
El Divino Club **7**
Montesol Hotel Bar **8**
Pacha **7**
Restaurant Pomelo **16**
Teatro **14**

aça Desamparados, crowded with open-air restaurants and market stalls, lies at the top of the town. Traffic leaves town through the Portal Nou.

FUN ON & OFF THE BEACH

BEACHES　The most popular (and overcrowded) beaches are **Playa Talamanca** in the north and **Ses Figueretes** (also called Playa Figueretes) in the south. Don't be surprised to find a lot of nudity. The best beaches are connected by boats and buses. The remoter ones require a private car or private boat. Both Playa Talamanca and Ses Figueretes are near Ciudad de Ibiza, as is another popular beach, **Playa d'en Bossa** to the south.

To avoid the hordes near Ciudad de Ibiza, continue past Playa d'en Bossa until you reach **Las Salinas,** near the old salt flats farther south. Here beaches include **Playa Cavallet,** one of the officially designated nudist strands (though nudism doesn't always follow official designations laid down by Ibizan law).

The most horrendously overcrowded beach in Ibiza is **Playa San Antonio** at San Antonio de Portmany—if it got any worse, you'd have to stand up instead of lie down! However, a boat or bus will take you to several beaches southwest of the town, all far less congested. These include **Cala Bassa, Port des Torrent, Cala Tarida,** and **Cala Conta.**

Santa Eulalia del Río, site of the third major tourist development in Ibiza, has a less crowded beach, but it's also less impressive. If you stay in this east coast town, you can find a better beach at Cala Llonga in the south or at one of the beaches along the north, including **Playa d'es Caná** and **Cala Lleña.** These beaches are among the finest on Ibiza.

If you venture to the north coast, you'll discover more good beaches at the tourist developments of **Portinatz,** which is at the very northern tip, and at **Puerto de San Miguel,** north of the small town of San Miguel. The quickest way to reach San Miguel from Ciudad de Ibiza is to go inland via Santa Gertrudis, and then north. Along the way, you'll pass Río de Santa Eulalia, the only river in the Balearics.

HORSEBACK RIDING　This is a scenic, memorable experience. Two outfitters are **C'an Mayans,** in Santa Gertrudis (© **60-863-68-84**), and **Es Buig,** also in Santa Gertrudis (© **97-118-73-88**). The price is 13€ for a 1-hour ride, and an hour's class is 11€.

TENNIS　You'll find five public tennis courts at **Port San Miguel** (© **97-130-19-00**). Open during daylight hours, they're usually unsupervised. No appointments are necessary for access to these courts, but for information about their condition and whether there are players waiting to use them, contact the Hotel Hacienda (© **97-133-45-00**) directly.

SHOPPING

Fashion has been an important Ibiza industry since the late 1960s, when a nonconformist fashion philosophy took hold, combining elements of the traditional *pitiusa* (peasant dress) attire of the natives and the natural, free-flowing garments of the hippies who flocked here in the 1960s. In recent years Ibizan designs have become much more sophisticated and complex, but the individualistic spirit has not wavered.

At the corner of Conde Rosselón, master artisan Pedro Planells creates handsewn, original leather goods at **Pedro's,** Carrer Aníbal 8 (© **97-131-30-26**). Many items can be custom-made. Pedro creates stylish accessories and home furnishings in leather and silver. Well-heeled clients have included everyone from international celebrities to King Juan Carlos. Pedro's keeps conventional Spanish hours, but during the off season, hours and days vary.

Sandal Shop, Plaça de Vila 2 (© **97-130-54-75**), sells high-quality leather goods made by a cast of local artisans. One-of-a-kind accessories, including bejeweled belts and leather bags, are designed for individual clients. Custommade sandals can be created to suit personal fashion tastes.

A JOURNEY INTO IBIZA'S PAST

Although Ibiza is primarily a destination for sun and fun, there's a sightseeing attraction worth a special visit.

Museo Arqueològic de Ibiza y Formentera (Museum of Archaeology) ⭐

Located in Ibiza's old town, this museum in a former arsenal houses the world's most important collection of Punic remains. It contains pottery and other artifacts from prehistoric sites in Formentera and Ibiza, and Punic terra-cotta figurines and other items from the sanctuaries of Illa Plana (7th–5th c. B.C.) and Cuieram (4th–2nd c. B.C.). Also on display are vases, figurines, and other Carthaginian artifacts found in the island's burial grounds. Examples of Roman epigraphs, sculpture, and small glass bottles are included in the exhibit. Other displays include Moorish artifacts (10th–13th c. A.D.), various Christian wooden and stone sculptures, plus 14th- to 16th-century ceramics.

Plaça de Catedral 3. © 97-130-12-31. Admission 3€. Winter Tues–Sat 9am–3pm; Apr–Oct Tues–Sat 10am–2pm and 6–8pm, Sun 10am–2pm. Closed holidays.

WHERE TO STAY

The chances of finding space in peak summer months are dismal, more so than in any Mediterranean resort in Spain. At other overcrowded resorts, such as those on the Costa Brava and Costa del Sol, a visitor faced with the NO VACANCY sign can always press on or go inland to find a room for the night. But in Ibiza, because of infrequent transportation, a visitor without a reservation in July and August can land in a trap. You may end up sleeping on the beach on an air mattress (if the police let you; alternatively, there are camping areas), even though your pockets are bulging with euros.

The island is not always prepared for its hordes of international tourists. The hotels can't be built fast enough. Many of the hastily erected ones sprouting up in San Antonio de Portmany, Santa Eulalia del Río—even on the outskirts of Ciudad de Ibiza—are more frame than picture.

Individual bookings in most establishments range from the horrifically difficult to the impossible. In many cases hoteliers don't bother to answer requests for space in summer. Armed with a nice fat contract from a British tour group, they're not interested in the plight of the stranded pilgrim. So if you're set on going to Ibiza during the summer, *book through a package tour* to ensure an ironclad reservation. You'll probably find a better bargain, anyway. Try booking with **Viajes Urbis,** Gremio Carpinteros 11, 07009 Palma de Mayorca (© **97-143-00-01**), or **Viajes Ultramar Express,** Avinguda 16 de Julio 73, 07009 Palma de Mayorca (© **97-176-64-00**). In the less-busy months, using your credit card to reserve a room is enough to guarantee a hotel room upon your arrival.

In Town

In town, hotels are limited and often lack style and amenities, except for the following recommendations.

El Corsario ⭐ *Finds*   After your taxi deposits you near the church below, you'll have to walk the last 152m (500 ft.) up a hill to reach this hotel, within a labyrinth of cobblestone pedestrian walkways. The house was built in 1570, and it is rumored that its terraces were built by corsairs. The modest rooms are pleasant and clean, often containing antiques. Each of the small, tiled bathrooms is equipped with a tub/shower combo. Some overlook an enclosed garden of trailing bougainvillea and cultivated flowers. No parking is available.

Carrer Ponent 5, 07800 Ibiza. ☏ **97-130-12-48.** Fax 97-139-19-53. 15 units. 110€ double; 380€ suite. AE, DC, MC, V. **Amenities:** Restaurant; bar; room service; babysitting. *In room:* TV, minibar, hair dryer, safe.

Hostal Montesol   Completely renovated in 1997, this old favorite enjoys a new lease on life. Its proximity to the marina affords panoramic views of the sea, and the small rooms are clean and comfortable, though rather sterile. Nonetheless, this is a good bargain for Ibiza, especially if you plan to spend most of your time exploring the island and not in your room. Bathrooms are equipped with tub/shower combos. There is no restaurant; however, many bistros are outside your door.

Vara de Rey 2, 07800 Ibiza. ☏ **97-131-01-61.** Fax 97-131-06-02. 55 units. 60€–100€ double. MC, V. **Amenities:** Bar. *In room:* A/C, TV, safe.

Hotel Royal Plaza ☏☏   Located 3 blocks from the port, this six-story modern hotel offers in-town convenience plus a casual, resortlike atmosphere. For those who want to stay within Ciudad de Ibiza, this is the premier choice. The marble reception lobby exudes elegance. Well-appointed accommodations are mid-size and carpeted; most have private terraces. Beds are firm and the bathrooms are tidily organized, equipped with tub/shower combos. The rooftop pool offers a sunbathing platform, with commanding views of the port and town of Ibiza.

Carrer Pedro Francés 27–29, 07800 Ibiza. ☏ **800/528-1234** in the U.S., or 97-131-00-00. Fax 97-131-40-95. 117 units. 131€ double; 236€ suite. AE, DC, MC, V. **Amenities:** 2 restaurants; 3 bars; pool; fitness center; sauna; room service; babysitting; laundry. *In room:* A/C, TV, minibar, hair dryer, safe.

La Ventana ☏   This is a perfect name (the window) for what was once a castle and is now a hotel on the hillside of the old city, overlooking the Mediterranean. What is more, the hotel, peaceful as it is in itself, is one of the best places to get tickets for clubs featuring music. The present owners have succeeded in decorating the hotel very stylishly with a mixture of clever lighting, beautiful fittings, and various Asian objets d'art. The rooms are painted in wonderful, almost Indian colors, and have great beds with floating canopies of white net. All include bathrooms or shower stalls, and some even offer French doors opening onto balconies. The downside? Readers have complained about lack of water pressure in summer. There's a terrace on the roof with wide Moroccan-style sofas and an amazing view of the old city and the sea beyond.

Sa Carrossa 13, Dalt Vila, 07800 Ibiza. ☏ **97-139-08-57.** Fax 97-139-01-45. 14 units. Winter 85€–200€ double; high season 146€–360€ double. AE, MC, V. Free parking. **Amenities:** Restaurant; bar; room service; babysitting; laundry service; dry cleaning. *In room:* A/C, TV, minibar, hair dryer, safe.

In Playa de Ses Figueretes

On the edge of town, a number of modern beach hotels have been erected that are far superior to the ones in the city. With few exceptions, most are booked solidly in summer by tour groups.

Cénit   This is the bargain place to stay here. Circular in shape, the hotel looks like a quartered wedding cake. In the pueblo style, each floor has been staggered so as to provide a terrace for the rooms above. The small accommodations are routine but comfortable, and the beds are firm. All units contain bathrooms with shower stalls. The Cénit is perched on a hillside a short walk from the beach.

Carrer Archiduque Lluis Salvador, 07800 Ibiza. ℂ **97-130-14-04.** Fax 97-130-07-54. 63 units. 50€–69€ double. AE, DC, MC, V. Closed mid-Oct to Apr. **Amenities:** Dining room; lounge; pool. *In room:* TV.

Los Molinos ✮   This modern resort is a favorite with snowbirds from the north of Europe. Situated less than a mile from Ibiza town, it's the finest hotel in Ses Figueretes. Nestled between the water and a medieval village, Los Molinos offers resort life combined with proximity to town. The midsize accommodations, most with private terraces facing the sea, are comfortably furnished, with twin beds pushed together European style, and bathrooms equipped with tub/shower combos.

Ramón Muntaner 60, 07800 Ibiza. ℂ **97-130-22-50.** Fax 97-130-25-04. 154 units. 111€–179€ double; 250€ suite. AE, DC, MC, V. Free parking. **Amenities:** 2 restaurants; 2 bars; pool; fitness center; sauna; room service; babysitting; laundry service; dry cleaning. *In room:* A/C, TV, minibar, hair dryer, safe.

In Es Vivé

Torre del Mar ✮   This is the only new hotel in the area to compete with the standards and luxury of Royal Plaza. Lying 2km (1¼ miles) from the center of the city, opening onto a wide sandy beach, it's like a Florida resort hotel with absolutely no island character. But you don't come here for that, as it attracts beach lovers who like lots of facilities and much comfort. A government-rated, four-star hotel, and partially renovated in 1999, it's one of the best accessorized hotels on island, especially for those who are athletic. The beach, De'en Bossa, is its major attraction, as it is one of the largest on island. Bedrooms are a bit small for such a luxury hotel, but they are nicely furnished and comfortable, each with tiled bathroom with tub and shower. Rooms open onto views of the surrounding mountains or the sea.

Platja D'en Bossa, Es Vivé, 07819 Ibiza. ℂ **97-130-30-50.** Fax 97-130-40-60. www.hoteltorredelmar.com. 213 units. 200€–290€ double. AE, DC, MC, V. **Amenities:** Restaurant; 2 bars; 2 pools; solarium/gym; sauna; tennis court; Jacuzzi; *hamman* (bath); room service; babysitting; laundry service; dry cleaning; garden. *In room:* A/C, TV, minibar.

WHERE TO DINE

It's hard to find authentic Ibizan cuisine. The clientele and often the chefs are mainly from continental Europe, and the menu choices cater almost exclusively to their tastes.

Because of the lack of agriculture in some parts of the island, fish has always been the mainstay of the local Mediterranean diet. But budget travelers may be put off by the price of some of this fare. Once the cheapest item you could order on a menu, fish is now one of the most expensive. The fish is sautéed, baked, or broiled and might be blended into a rice dish called *arroz a la pescadora. Parrillada* and *zarzuela* are two stewlike dishes containing an assortment of fish.

As in Majorca, pork is important in the diet. Some islanders feed figs to these animals to sweeten their meat, which is turned into such pungent cooked sausages as *sabrosadas* or *longanizas.*

A local dish occasionally offered on some menus is a *sofrit pages,* a stew made with three kinds of meat and poultry—chicken, pork, and lamb—then cooked with pepper, cloves, cinnamon, and garlic. One of the best seafood plates is *borrida de rajada,* crayfish in an almond sauce.

The most famous dessert is *flaó,* a kind of cheesecake to which mint and anisette are added for flavoring. *Greixonera* is a spiced pudding, and *maccarrones de San Juan* is cinnamon- and lemon-flavored milk baked with cheese.

El Corsario ✮ INTERNATIONAL   Although we've reviewed its accommodations above, the dining room here, with its panoramic view, is so romantic it

---

Fun Fact **The True Spirits of Ibiza**

Wines are shipped over from the mainland; however, islanders make alcohol-based herbal concoctions. These include *rumaniseta*, made from rosemary, and *frigola*, golden in color and very sweet, with a strong aroma coming from wild thyme. A rather bitter aperitif known as *balo* comes from locally grown carob. For special occasions, islanders treasure *hierbas ibicencas*, made with numerous local herbs, including anise.

---

deserves special mention. This 400-year-old flower-draped villa is near the hilltop fortress. Your taxi deposits you about 152m (500 ft.) down the hill in a square fronting an old church, and you must climb the slippery cobblestones to reach it. There's a stand-up bar, two pleasant dining rooms with a handful of neatly laid tables, and a view of the harbor. Menu specialties include various pastas, two different preparations of lamb, and especially fresh fish brought up from the harbor. The cookery is home-style and well prepared, especially if you stick to the fish dishes.

Carrer Ponent 5. ℂ **97-130-12-48**. Reservations required. Main courses 16€–28€; tasting menu 86€. MC, V. Daily 7:30pm–midnight. Closed Nov–Apr.

El Portalón SPANISH/INTERNATIONAL   Before you hit the bars (go very late, as is the fashion), dine here in the old town. Alfresco courtyard dining is a lure, as is the handsome crowd. El Portalón attracts gay as well as straight couples, usually European. The food is a combination of Spanish, Catalán, and Mediterranean. It's expensive, but worth the extra euros.

Plaça dels Desamparats 1–2. ℂ **97-130-39-01**. Fax 97-130-08-52. Reservations recommended. Main courses 16€–20€. AE, DC, MC, V. Mon–Sat 12:30–4pm; daily 8pm–1am. Nov 1–Easter only open from 8pm–1am.

CIUDAD DE IBIZA AFTER DARK

In many ways, **El Divino Club,** Puerto Ibiza Nueva (ℂ **97-119-01-76**), is the most physically beautiful disco on Ibiza. Only open in summer, it prides itself on the supermodels, celebs, and trendies who have graced its premises with their presence. Wear the most hip outfit you packed. The club doesn't open its doors until 11:30pm; it remains open nightly until 6am, but only from June to September. The cover charge is 30€ and up; it tends to be more expensive in summer.

The crowd at the **Montesol** hotel bar, Vara de Rey 2 (ℂ **97-131-01-61**), a short walk from the harbor on the main street, is likely to include expatriates, newly arrived social climbers, and Spaniards along for the view. In many ways this is the greatest circus in town, made more pleasant by the well-prepared tapas and the generous drinks. If you enjoy people-watching, sit at one of the sidewalk tables. Montesol is open daily from 8am to midnight.

Despite its age (it's 1 of the oldest discos on Ibiza, with a nightlife pedigree extending back to the 1960s), **Pacha,** Av. 8 de Agosto s/n (ℂ **97-131-36-12**), a spacious split-level disco near the casino, is still hip. Made up of three separate bar areas and dance floors, and only open in the summer, it continues to attract the young and the not-so-young, the bored, the restless, and the merely jaded. In summer, overheated dancers can cool off in a swimming pool. The music, primarily droning disco and rap, evokes a pounding cadence of jackhammers. The cover is a painful 27€ to 42€.

Disco Privelege, Urbanización San Rafael (© **97-119-81-60**), is a sprawling nightclub built to entertain 5,000, many of whom seem to rush the dance floor simultaneously. Wander from room to room, stopping wherever you feel the urge, as the interior contains more bars, semi-secluded patios, and romantic trysting spots than most hotels. Dance music, however, will conspire to keep you on the floor dancing, dancing, dancing. The club is open from June to September, daily from midnight to 7:30am. The cover is 25€ to 30€, but could be as high as 42€ to 48€ for special events, in particular English Monday nights, when deejays are imported from London.

There's gambling by the sea in the modern **Casino de Ibiza,** Passeig Juan Carlos I (Passeig Marítim; © **97-131-33-12**). With the usual gaming tables and slot machines, it's open nightly from 9:30pm to 4am. There's a separate room for slot machines that operate daily from 6pm to 5am. The adjoining nightclub and dining hall offer live cabaret entertainment between May and October, with shows that feature a relatively tame assortment of magicians, comedians, and pretty women in feathers and spangles whose fancy stepping begins at 11pm. Casino entrance is 3€. Passport required for admission.

With the possible exception of Mykonos, few other islands in the Mediterranean cater to gay travelers as much as Ibiza. A stroll through the Ciudad Ibiza's old town reveals dozens of gay bars catering to international visitors; most are open from 9 or 10pm to 3am. Although many close and reopen with disconcerting frequency, some of the most deeply entrenched include **Disco Anfora,** Carrer San Carlos 7 (© **97-130-28-93**), an *haute-electronic* disco that blares away, to the dancing pleasure of a mostly gay clientele, between midnight and 6am every night in the summer. The cover charge of 12€ includes the first drink. More geared toward drinking and talking than dancing is **Bar Léon,** Calle de la Virgen 3 (no phone), and its almost equivalent counterpart, **Bar**

Finds **Letting It All Hang Out in the Goddess Temple**

Ibiza's newest, most controversial, and most appealing erotic club is **The Blue Rose,** Carrer Navarra 27, Figueretas (© **97-139-91-37**). There's a hefty cover of 30€, including your first drink. It occupies what was originally established in the 1960s as the island's first disco. In 1998, amid the same black-and-white floor tiles where flower children used to tune in, turn on, and dance, California-born entrepreneur Joy Borne installed an intensely theatrical, high-class strip joint that's become one of the most popular places on an island obsessed with after-dark diversions. Defined as an American-style "Goddess Temple," where none of the exotic *artistes* objects to getting an occasional bank note while she's on stage, the setting consists of a fireman's pole, equipment for some exhibitionistic acrobatics, and an area committed to exotic, tasteful nudity in a sexually provocative setting. Owned, operated, and for the most part staffed by women, drinks set you back from 7€ after the first. It is open every night from 11pm to 6am. Although most nights the club is filled with men watching women, Thursday nights feature male dancers performing for women from 11pm to 3am, and male dancers performing for gay patrons from 3am till closing. Most of the dancers come from northern Europe and, to a lesser extent, California.

Geminis, Figueretas (no phone). Other gay sites include **Angelo's,** Carrer Alfonso XII 11 (no phone), which serves drinks beginning around 9pm every evening, and **Teatro,** Calle de la Virgen 57 (no phone), which has an outdoor bar. And if you're hungry, there's a restaurant in Ciudad Ibiza's inner core, **Restaurant Pomelo,** Carrer de la Virgen 53 (© **97-131-31-22**), catering to an international clientele with a huge percentage of gay patronage. The restaurant is open from Easter to October, from 8pm to between 1 and 2am.

SAN ANTONIO DE PORTMANY

Known to the Romans as Portus Magnus and before that a Bronze Age settlement, this thriving town was discovered in the 1950s by foreigners and has remained popular ever since. Tourism here is "megamass." The town today goes by two names—San Antonio de Portmany for Spanish speakers or Sant Antoni de Portmany for Catalán speakers.

In summer you have as much chance of finding a room here as you would booking a reservation on the last flight to the moon if the earth were on fire. Virtually all the hotels have a direct pipeline to tour-group agencies in northern Europe, and the individual traveler probably won't get the time of day. If you're determined to stay in the area during peak travel season, your best bet is trying to arrange a package tour.

The resort, with a 14th-century parish church, is built on an attractive bay. Avoid the impossibly overcrowded narrow strip of sand at San Antonio itself. Take a ferry or bus to one of the major beaches, including Cala Gració, 1.5km (1 mile) to the north, set against a backdrop of pines, or Port des Torrent, 5km (3 miles) southwest. Cala Bassa in the south is also popular. San Antonio overlooks the Isla Conejera, an uninhabited rock island. With its hordes of visitors, San Antonio has an easygoing lifestyle, plus lots of mildly entertaining nightlife. Even if you're staying in Ibiza or Santa Eulalia, you may want to hop over for the day or evening.

When visiting hooligans have had too much cheap booze, San Antonio can get dangerous. In the earlier part of the evening, however, you may want to patronize one of the bars or open-air terraces around Avinguda Doctor Fleming.

ESSENTIALS

GETTING THERE **Buses** leave from Ciudad de Ibiza every 30 minutes.

VISITOR INFORMATION The **tourist information office** is at Passeig de Ses Fonts (© **97-134-33-63**). It's open Monday through Friday from 9:30am to 8:30pm, Saturday and Sunday from 9:30am to 1pm, from May to October. Off-season hours are Monday through Saturday from 9:30am to 1pm.

EXPLORING THE AREA

Throughout the day, boats leave from Passeig de Ses Fonts. They take you to **Cala Bassa,** a sandy beach on a thin strip, for 4.50€ one-way, or to **Cala Conta,** a slightly rocky beach, for 4.10€. If you negotiate, they will take you along the

---

Tips **Bottomless or Topless—It's Not for Prudes**

San Antonio is not for the conservative. It's not unusual to see bottomless women on the beach—and topless women in dance clubs. Note, however, that even though marijuana is common here, buying and selling it is strictly against the law.

Moments   Where Unearthly Forces Gather

Offshore at the popular southern beach of Cala d'Hort is the intriguing **Es Vedrá rock,** where, in times of hardship and hunger, the Ibicencos would go, at great personal risk, to gather seagull eggs for survival. A Carmelite priest once recorded mystical revelations and meetings with "unearthly beings surrounded by light" while meditating on the island. Gigantic circles of light, up to 50m (165 ft.) in diameter, have allegedly emerged from the sea here at times, discouraging fishers from working the area. It is said that a strong magnetic force emanating from Es Vedrá attracts such strange phenomena. Photographers and romantics, take note: After June 15 the sunrise here is especially dramatic, illuminating Es Vedrá while the surrounding hills remain in darkness.

coastline northwest to the far point of Portinatx. This is virtually the only way to see the coastline, since there isn't a road running along it, and most visitors agree it's the most beautiful coastline of Ibiza.

North of the waterfront, the chief attraction is **Sa Cova de Santa Agnès,** a national monument and an object of eerie devotion. This has been a place of sacred worship ever since a sailor prayed to Santa Agnès during a rough storm and was saved. The sailor, to show his gratitude, placed a figure of the saint in this dark hole. It's become a place of pilgrimage ever since, and it's open free on Monday and again on Saturday from 9am to noon.

If you have rented a car you can explore **Cueva de Ses Fontanelles,** north of Platja Calad Salada, where faintly colorful prehistoric paintings decorate the walls.

WHERE TO STAY

The prospect of finding a room here in July and August is bleak—some Brits reserve a year in advance. British package tourists virtually occupy the crescent beach and busy harbor all during the warm months. You stand a better chance of finding lodgings in Ciudad de Ibiza.

Arenal Hotel   This selection ranks among the top hotels in San Antonio de Portmany, offering value comparable to that of more expensively priced neighbors. During high season groups take over, but in October and from April to mid-May you can generally get a reservation if you write 2 weeks in advance. Off season all you need to do is arrive.

Located at the edge of town on its own private beach, the Arenal is a simple four-story establishment. The rooms are simple and attractive, furnished in contemporary style with comfortable beds, a bathroom with a tub/shower combo, and a balcony opening onto the sea or the little front garden lawn with palm trees.

Avinguda Doctor Fleming 16, 07820 San Antonio. © 97-134-01-12. Fax 97-134-25-65. 131 units. 65€–110€ double. Rates include breakfast. AE, DC, MC, V. Free parking. Closed Nov–Mar. **Amenities:** 2 restaurants; bar; pool; fitness center; sauna. In room: A/C, safe.

Hotel Tropical   Located away from the port area in a commercial section of town, this hotel has a private recreation area that's like a small public park, with dozens of reclining chairs and some billiard tables. The hotel was built in the early 1960s with a russet-and white-marbled lobby filled with armchairs. The Tropical is rated as one of the best hotels in the center, with comfortably furnished, modernized, but rather bland small to midsize rooms. Most tidy bathrooms come equipped with tub/shower combos.

Cervantes 28, 07820 San Antonio. ✆ **97-134-00-50.** Fax 97-134-40-69. 142 units. 53€–72€ double. Rates include breakfast. AE, DC, MC, V. Closed Nov–Mar. **Amenities:** 2 restaurants; 2 bars; 2 pools; fitness center; game room; babysitting; laundry service; dry cleaning. *In room:* A/C, minibar, hair dryer, safe.

Hotel Village ★ *Finds*   Located 24km (15 miles) west of Ibiza Town, this small, elegant hotel is one of our favorite refuges on the island. The midsize guest rooms, done in white marble, have terraces, most facing the sea, but several open onto the mountains. Each room is very comfortably furnished with adequate living space, plus tidy tiled bathrooms equipped with tub/shower combos. A walkway leads down the hill to a rocky beach, where guests can sunbathe.

Apartado 27, Urbanización Caló den Real (along the road to Cala Vadella), 07830 Sant Josep, Ibiza. ✆ **97-180-80-01.** Fax 97-180-80-27. www.hotelvillage.net. 20 units. 116€–273€ double; 273€ suite. Rates include breakfast. MC, V. Free parking. **Amenities:** Restaurant; bar; pool; tennis courts; health club; sauna; room service; babysitting; laundry service; dry cleaning. *In room:* A/C, TV, minibar, hair dryer, safe.

Les Jardins de Palerm   This intimate little hotel, outside the village of San José, is constructed in the style of a 17th-century hacienda. Patios and garden terraces scattered throughout the grounds are ideal locations for sunbathing, enjoying a lazy Ibiza afternoon, and getting away from the noise and bustle of the street. The small accommodations are rustic, with beamed ceilings, antiques, good beds, bathrooms with tub/shower combos, and ceiling fans. Each unit has its own terrace. Prices change every month—the lowest price quoted below is charged in the cool months of March, the highest for the hot month of August.

Apartado 62, 07080 San José, Ibiza. ✆ **97-180-03-18.** Fax 97-180-04-53. www.jardinsdepalerm.com. 9 units. 120€–154€ double; 198€ suite. Rates include breakfast. V. Closed Nov–Mar. **Amenities:** Restaurant; lounge; pool; babysitting; laundry service; dry cleaning. *In room:* A/C, TV, safe.

Pikes ★   Originally a *finca* (farm), this 600-year-old compound is now a luxurious playground for well-heeled travelers and celebrities from around the world. Touted for its "sophisticated informality," Pikes boasts spacious rooms with sensuous interiors, including king-size beds and bathrooms with showers and oversize bathtubs. The hotel offers activities and entertainment for its guests, ranging from flamenco shows to costume balls. Pikes provides a VIP card that allows entrance to most of the area's clubs and casinos.

Camino Sa-Vorera 1, Apartado 104, 07820 San Antonio, Ibiza. ✆ **97-134-22-22.** Fax 97-134-23-12. www. pikeshotel.com. 26 units. 135€–180€ double; 210€–720€ suite. AE, DC, MC, V. Children under 12 must be accompanied by a parent. **Amenities:** Restaurant; bar; pool; tennis court; health club; sauna; room service; babysitting; laundry service; dry cleaning. *In room:* A/C, TV, minibar, hair dryer, safe.

WHERE TO DINE

Many of Ibiza's restaurants are tucked away in quiet coves or in the countryside, so you really need a car to sample the full range of the island's culinary savoir-faire.

Cana Juana ★★ *Finds* MEDITERRANEAN   This 2½-century-old villa has been converted into the finest restaurant on Ibiza, thanks to the dedicated efforts of owner and chef Juana Biarnes and her husband, co-owner and maître d'hôtel Michel. Juana was a pioneering female reporter in Spain before retreating to Ibiza to perfect her cooking skills. Examples of what's available include filets of skate that are steamed and then grilled for added crispiness and served with strips of Jabugo ham and a confit of onions. Also appealing are such Catalán specialties as cod with spinach, raisins, and pine nuts; and an earthy but flavorful dish every Catalán remembers from his or her childhood, *butifarra* sausage served with white beans. Other examples include a confit of *canard* (duckling) in the French style; baked potatoes served with truffles; and roasted *dorada* (gilthead sea bream) served with vinegar, olive oil, garlic, and baby lettuce. The restaurant's cellars contain a sophisticated roster of Spanish and European wines, with a vintage to complement virtually anything.

Carretera Sant Josep, Km 10, 10km (6 miles) from Ciudad Ibiza, on road to Sant Josep. ℂ **97-180-01-58.** Reservations recommended. Main courses 16€–22€. AE, MC, V. June–Oct daily 8:15pm–midnight; Jan–May closed Sun night and Mon. Closed Nov–Dec.

Restaurante/Bar Rías Baixas GALICIAN   This rustic air-conditioned Iberian dining room, with its stucco arches, beamed ceiling, and open fireplace, is an apt setting for the Galician specialties served here. Seafood, flown in fresh every day from northern Spain, is the restaurant's specialty—mussels, Galician clams, crabmeat soup, *caldo gallego* (Galician broth), trout meunière, and Bilbao-style eels, each accompanied by a selection of Galician wine. Good-tasting beef, pork, and veal dishes are also available.

Carrer Cervantes Esquina, Carrer Progreso 14–16. ℂ **97-134-04-80.** Reservations recommended. Main courses 15€–22€. AE, DC, MC, V. Tues–Sun 1–4pm and 8pm–midnight. Closed Dec–Feb.

Sa Capella MEDITERRANEAN   This restaurant is set in a 600-year-old chapel with stone vaulting, rose windows, radiating alcoves, balconies, and chandeliers that can be lowered on pulleys from the overhead masonry. You pass beneath an arbor of magenta bougainvillea and are ushered to your table by a waiter dressed in red-and-white traditional Ibizan costume. Meals are flavorful and well versed in the culinary traditions of the Mediterranean. Examples include fresh broccoli as well as exotic mushrooms with strips of Serrano ham; John Dory cooked in a salt crust; roast suckling pig in the style of Segovia; shepherd's-style lamb chops served with potatoes and carrots; marinated mussels; roasted rabbit; and pepper steak. Dessert might consist of homemade cheesecake garnished with fresh raspberries. Partly because of its historic setting, partly because of its fine food, this dining choice has a deservedly devoted following.

Carretera de Santa Inés, Km 1.2. ℂ **97-134-00-57.** Reservations recommended. Main courses 16€–32€. DC, MC, V. Daily 8pm–midnight. Closed Nov–Mar.

THE NORTHERN COAST

The north remains largely untainted by the scourge of mass tourism, except for a handful of coves. Here you'll find some of the island's prettiest countryside, with fields of olive, almond, and carob trees and the occasional *finca* raising melons or grapes.

EXPLORING THE AREA

Off the road leading into Port de Sant Miquel (Puerto de San Miguel) is **Cova de Can Merca** (ℂ **97-133-47-76**), about 91m (300 ft.) from the Hotel Galeón (see below). There is a fine view of the bay from the hotel's snack bar. After a stunning descent down stairs clinging to the face of the cliff, you enter a cave that's more than 100,000 years old and forms its stalactites and stalagmites at the rate of about .6cm (¼ in.) per 100 years. A favored hiding place for smugglers and their goods in former days, today it's a beautifully orchestrated surrealistic experience—including a sound-and-light display—not unlike walking through a Dalí painting. Many of the limestone formations are delicate miniatures. The half-hour tour is conducted in several languages for groups of up to 70. From Holy Week to the end of October, tours are offered daily every half hour from 10:30am to 7:30pm. Admission is 5.50€ for adults and 3€ for children.

Tips **Escaping from the Hordes**

If you want to escape to a lovely beach that remains a stranger to hotel construction, head for **Playa Benirras** just north of Port de Sant Miquel. An unpaved but passable road leads out to this small, calm, pretty cove, where lounge chairs are available and pedal boats are for rent. There are snack bars and restaurants here.

At the island's northern tip is **Portinatx,** a pretty series of beaches and bays now marred by a string of souvenir shops and haphazardly built hotels. For a taste of its original, rugged beauty, go past all the construction to the jagged coast along the open sea.

Every Saturday year-round there is a **flea market** just beyond Sant Carles (San Carlos) on the road to Santa Eulalia (you'll know where it is by all the cars parked along the road). Open from about 10am until 8 or 9pm, it offers all kinds of clothing (both antique and new), accessories, crafts, and the usual odds and ends.

A beautiful drive leads from Sant Carles (San Carlos) along the coast to Cala Sant Vicent (San Vicente).

WHERE TO STAY

Hotel offerings are more limited in the north than in the traditional pockets of tourism in the south and west. Nevertheless, the island's finest hotel, the five-star Hacienda, is here, above Na Xamena Bay. Port de Sant Miquel, Cala Sant Vicent, and Portinatx—once tranquil, seaside havens—have become increasingly pockmarked with package-tour hotels.

Hotel Galeón   One of two hotels overlooking the little bay, this basic hotel offers simple, clean, comfortable, but small guest rooms, each equipped with a good bed and neatly kept bathrooms with shower stalls. Accommodations have terraces with views of the sea.

Puerto de San Miguel, 07815 San Miguel, Ibiza. © **97-133-45-34.** Fax 97-133-45-35. 189 units. 97€–113€ double. Rates include breakfast. AE, V. Free parking. Closed last week of Oct to May 1. **Amenities:** Restaurant; 3 bars; pool; tennis courts; exercise room; sauna. *In room:* A/C, TV, hair dryer, safe.

Hotel Hacienda ★★★   Located 23km (14 miles) northwest of Ciudad de Ibiza, this Moorish villa, set on a promontory overlooking Na Xamena Bay, is the top destination on Ibiza for well-heeled travelers and celebrities seeking leisure and sanctuary. Luxury, informality, privacy, and personal service—the Hacienda has it all. Public rooms are full of various cubbyholes, ideal for cozying up to a book or travel companion. Spacious guest rooms are decorated with four-poster beds, sumptuous carpets, and balconies overlooking the Mediterranean. Many rooms have marble bathrooms and private whirlpools; all are equipped with tub/shower combos.

Na Xamena, 07815 San Miguel, Ibiza. © **97-133-45-00.** Fax 97-133-46-06. www.ibiza-spotlight.com/ hacienda/index.html. 63 units. 187€–379€ double; 287€–890€ suite. AE, DC, MC, V. Closed Nov to mid-Apr. **Amenities:** 4 restaurants; bar; 2 pools; tennis courts; health club; sauna; bike rental; boat rental; room service; babysitting; laundry service; dry cleaning. *In room:* A/C, TV, minibar, hair dryer, safe.

SANTA EULALIA DEL RIO

Once patronized by expatriate artists from the capital, 14.5km (9 miles) to the south, Santa Eulalia del Río now attracts mostly middle-class northern Europeans.

Santa Eulalia is at the foot of the Puig de Missa, on the estuary of the only river in the Balearics. The principal monument in town is a fortress church standing on a hilltop, or *puig*. Dating from the 16th century, it has an ornate Gothic altar screen.

Santa Eulalia is relatively free of the sometimes plastic quality of San Antonio. Visitors often have a better chance of finding accommodations here than in the other two major towns.

ESSENTIALS

GETTING THERE   During the day, **buses** run between Ciudad de Ibiza and Santa Eulalia del Río every 30 minutes.

Seven **boats** a day run between Ciudad de Ibiza and Santa Eulalia del Río. The boats run on the hour, and the first leaves Ciudad de Ibiza at 10:30am and Santa Eulalia del Río at 9:30am. The boat ride takes 45 minutes and information can be obtained at ✆ **97-133-22-51.**

VISITOR INFORMATION   The **tourist information office,** at Carrer Mariano Riquer Wallis (✆ **97-133-07-28**), is open Monday through Friday, from 9:30am to 2pm, Saturday from 9am to 1pm. In summer the office is open daily from 10am to 2pm and 4 to 8pm, Saturday from 9am to 7pm.

EXPLORING THE AREA

You can reach the famous northern beaches from Santa Eulalia by bus or boat, departing from the harbor front near the boat basin. **Aigües Blanques** is one of the best beaches, just 10km (6 miles) north. (It's legal to go nude here.) It's reached by four buses a day. A long, sandy cove, **Cala Llonga,** is 5km (3 miles) south and is serviced by 10 buses a day. Cala Llonga fronts a bevy of package-tour hotels, so it's likely to be crowded. Boats depart Santa Eulalia for Cala Llonga every 30 minutes, from 9am to 6pm. **Es Caná** is a white-sand beach, 5km (3 miles) north of town; boats and buses leave every 30 minutes, from 8am to 9pm. Four buses a day depart for **Cala Llenya** and **Cala Nova.**

WHERE TO STAY

Hotel Catalonia Ses Estaques   A much-favored hotel in this resort, close to the seashore at the edge of town, Ses Estaques is open only in the good weather months. On the walk to the private beach you will find a beautiful garden filled with roses, palms, and ivy, and the swimming pool is edged with pines and a poolside snack bar. Inside, the hotel is filled with extra touches and hidden, charming corners. There's an aquarium in the spacious lobby, and a pleasant tropical restaurant on the beach a short walk away. Each of the comfortable terrazzo-floored rooms has a balcony with a view of the garden or the sea. The hotel was last renovated in 1998, with new mattresses and new plumbing added to the bathrooms, which contain tub/shower combos.

Ses Estaques s/n, 07840 Santa Eulalia del Río. ✆ **97-133-02-00.** Fax 97-133-04-86. www.hoteles-catalonia. es. 166 units. 108€–144€ double. Rates include breakfast. AE, DC, MC, V. Closed Nov–Apr. **Amenities:** 2 restaurants; 2 bars; pool; tennis court; minigolf; babysitting; laundry service; dry cleaning. *In room:* A/C, TV, minibar, hair dryer, safe.

Sol Élite S'Argamassa 🏖   Three kilometers (2 miles) outside Santa Eulalia del Río, near Roman ruins, the Hotel S'Argamassa is a well-run, family-oriented resort. The hotel is a short walk from the beach and maintains its own small pier. All the midsize guest rooms have terraces with sea views. Accommodations are comfortable; many have been recently renovated, and each comes with a bathroom equipped with a tub/shower combo. The hotel has no restaurant, but dining options are nearby.

Urbanización S'Argamassa, 07182 Santa Eulalia del Río. ℂ **97-133-00-51.** Fax 97-133-00-76. 230 units. 64€–191€ double. Half board 16€ supplement. AE, DC, MC, V. Closed Nov–Apr. **Amenities:** Bar; lounge; pool; tennis court; game room; fitness center; babysitting; laundry service; dry cleaning; bowling alley. *In room:* A/C, TV, minibar, hair dryer, safe.

WHERE TO DINE

Doña Margarita Puerto SPANISH/INTERNATIONAL   Although one of Santa Eulalia's most venerable restaurants moved into new premises in 1998, it managed to retain the loyalty of its local clientele and the managerial skill of its owner and resident Sr. Juan Torres Tur. A modern building with big windows that overlook the yachts bobbing at anchor in the nearby marina, it offers a solidly traditional menu that includes lots of very fresh fish that are painstakingly prepared. The fish is usually served with fresh salads, and finished off with succulent desserts that are fresh-made daily, including lemon mousse with raspberries. In between, you might enjoy mussels marinara, spicy fish soup, paella, salmon with green peppercorns, calves' kidneys with fried onions, a *parrillada* of prawns or a *zarzuela* of shellfish, and a changing roster of fresh fish and shellfish whose ingredients vary according to their availability in the marketplace.

Puerto Deportiva. ℂ **97-133-22-00.** Reservations recommended. Main courses 14€–28€. AE, DC, MC, V. Daily 12:30–4pm and 7:30pm–midnight. Closed Dec–Feb.

El Naranjo ⭐ CONTINENTAL   This chic nighttime rendezvous has altogether the most beautiful courtyard in town. Many refer to this place as "The Orange Tree," its name in English. The orange tree patio, with its flowering bougainvillea vines, has such appeal that many diners don't mind its out-of-the-way location (in town, several blocks from the water). If your table isn't ready when you arrive, enjoy an aperitif in the cozy bar. The menu items are beautifully prepared and served. One newspaper called the chef "an artist." Dishes include fresh fish and duckling in red-currant-and-pepper sauce. Begin with *las tres mousses* (3 mousses) as an appetizer, finishing with the lemon tart for dessert.

Carrer San José 31. ℂ **97-133-03-24.** Reservations required. Main courses 10€–18€. AE, MC, V. Tues–Sun 1–3:30pm and 7:30–11:30pm. Closed mid–Jan to Feb 1.

SANTA GERTRUDIS DE FRUITERA

Don't blink or you'll pass right through this hamlet in central Ibiza, lying inland and to the west of Santa Eulalia del Río (just visited). Yet visitors have found their way here, as the little handicrafts shops and galleries in the central square, Plaça de l'Església, testify. There is also a number of fine bars here if you'd like to escape inland from the beaches one day and see what an island village looks like. All of these bars serve a tasty snack called *bocadillo completo* (a roll of tomato, cheese, and Serrano ham).

The main reason for coming here is to stay at one of the island's most enchanting retreats, previewed below.

Cas Gasi ⭐ *Finds*   A cozy nest, this little inn lies in a valley in the heart of Ibiza, a 12-minute drive from Ciudad de Ibiza and its major beaches. If you shun beach hotels and want an authentic island experience, consider this 19th-century manorial hacienda in a rural setting of olive groves, almond trees, and gardens (they grow their own organic vegetables). Guests sit on porches and terraces in summer taking in the bucolic view, retreating in winter to the warm ambience of the living room with its roaring fireplace. The casa is like a country resort with its two swimming pools at different levels, each surrounded by garden terraces. Views from the property are of the 1,570m (5,150 ft.) Sa Talaiassa, the island's only mountain.

Under wooden beamed ceilings, the breezy and spacious bedrooms are immaculately kept and furnished, often with brass beds. Hand-painted wall tiles and handmade terra-cotta floor tiles add to the ambience. Bathrooms are cool, cozy, and up to date, with tub/shower combinations. Dinner can be served if requested in advance, and breakfast is offered on a terrace.

Cami Vell a Sant Mateau, Apdo. de Correos 117, 07814 Sta. Gertrudis, Ibiza. ✆ **97-119-77-00.** Fax 97-119-88-99. www.casgasi.com. 10 units. 180€–300€ double; 300€ suite. Rates include continental breakfast. MC, V. **Amenities:** Restaurant for guests; bar; 2 pools; laundry. *In room:* A/C, TV, minibar, hair dryer, safe.

3 Formentera ★

For years, Formentera was known as the "forgotten Balearic." The smallest of the archipelago, it's a 78 sq. km (30-sq.-mile), flat limestone plain. In the east it is flanked by La Mola, a peak rising 187m (615 ft.), and in the west it is protected by Berberia, at 96m (315 ft.).

The Romans called it Frumentaria (meaning "wheat granary"), when they oversaw it as a booming little agricultural center. But that was then. A shortage of water coupled with strong winds has allowed only meager vegetation to grow, notably some fig trees and fields of wild rosemary (which seem to be home to thousands of green lizards).

A few hearty goats live on the island, and, like Ibiza, Formentera has a salt industry. Its year-round population of 5,000 swells in summer, mostly with day-trippers from Ibiza. Limited hotels have kept development in check, and most visitors come over for the day to enjoy the beaches, where they often swim without bathing suits and sunbathe along the excellent stretches of sand. British and Germans form the majority of tourists that actually spend the night.

ISLAND ESSENTIALS

GETTING THERE   Formentera is serviced by up to 29 **boat** passages a day in summer and by about a dozen per day in winter. Boats depart from Ciudad de Ibiza, on Ibiza's southern coast, for La Savina (La Sabina), 3km (2 miles) north of the island's capital and largest settlement, Sant Francesc (San Francisco Javier). Depending on the design of the boat you select, passage across the 5km (3-mile) channel separating the islands takes between 35 minutes and 1 hour. For information on schedules, call ✆ **97-131-07-11,** although it's usually easier to ask employees at almost any hotel on the island, who are usually well versed in the hours of ferryboats to and from Ibiza.

GETTING AROUND   As ferryboats arrive at the quays of La Sabina, taxis line up at the pier. One-way passage to such points as Es Pujols and Playa de Mitjorn costs 7€ and 10€ to 11€, respectively, but it's always wise to negotiate

---

Tips **Hang 'em High But Carry Those Seasickness Pills**

On the ferry ride over from Ibiza, you pass **Isla Ahorcados (Hanged Men's Island),** where criminals from Ibiza were once strung up, and the more reassuring Isla Espalmador, with its sandy beaches. Carry some seasickness pills, as the ferry crossing can be turbulent.

or predetermine the fare before the journey begins. To call a taxi in Sant Francesc, dial ☏ **97-132-20-16;** in El Pujols, ☏ **97-132-80-16;** and in La Sabina, ☏ **97-132-20-02.** Regardless of when and where you call for a taxi, be prepared to wait.

Car rentals can be arranged through **Formotor** (☏ **97-132-22-42**), whose kiosk is at La Sabina, close to where you disembark from the ferryboats.

If you want to enjoy seeing Formentera by a bicycle or a motor scooter, they can be rented from **Moto-Rent** in La Sabina (☏ **97-132-27-52**) or in Pujols (☏ **97-132-26-74**). Motor scooters rent for 18€ a day, bicycles for around 5€ to 8€ a day.

VISITOR INFORMATION   The **tourist office** in Formentera, Edificio de Servicios de Puerto s/n, in Port de la Sabina (☏ **97-132-20-57**), is open Monday through Friday from 10am to 2pm and 5 to 7pm, Saturday from 10am to 2pm.

HITTING THE BEACH

Beaches, beaches, and more beaches—that's why visitors come here. You can see the ocean from any point on the island. Some say the island has the best beaches in the Mediterranean—an opinion not without merit. Formentera has been declared a "World Treasure" by UNESCO, one of four places so honored because of its special character as an ecological and wildlife preserve. This implies an indirect control by UNESCO of activities that could jeopardize the island's ecological well being.

Meanwhile, day-trippers from Ibiza have fun sampling its long, sedate beaches and solitary coves before returning to Ibiza's ebullience in the evening.

The island is ringed with beaches, so selecting the one you think will appeal to you is about the only problem you'll face—that and whether you should wear a bathing suit.

Playa de Mitjorn, on the southern coast, is 5km (3 miles) long; it has many uncrowded sections. This is the principal area for nude sunbathing. A few bars and hotels occupy the relatively undeveloped stretch of sand. You can make **Es Copinyars,** the name of one of the beachfronts, your stop for lunch, as it has a number of restaurants and snack bars.

At **Es Calo,** along the northern coast, west of El Pilar, there are some small boardinghouses, called *hostales.* From this point, you can see the lighthouse of La Mola, which was featured in Jules Verne's *Journey Round the Solar System,* and, if weather conditions are right, Majorca.

Sant Ferran serves the beach of **Es Pujols,** darling of the package-tour operators. This is the most crowded beach on Formentera, and you may want to avoid it. The beaches, however, are pure white sand, with a backdrop of dunes and pine trees. It's a place to go windsurfing and is the site of several tourist amenities. The beach is protected by the Punta Prima headland.

Westward, **Cala Sahona** is another popular tourist spot, lying near the lighthouse on Cabo Berberia. Often pleasure vessels anchor here on what is the most beautiful cove in Formentera.

WHERE TO STAY

Accommodations are scarce, so you must arrive with an ironclad reservation should you want to spend the night or a longer time.

Club La Mola   Located at Es Arenals, this is one of the best-equipped hotels on the island, and during the summer it is usually packed. Opening onto the longest beach on the island, La Mola is constructed in the style of a Spanish village. The good-size rooms are comfortable and well furnished, each with a firm bed and a tiled bathroom equipped with a tub/shower combo.

Apartado 23, 07871 Playa de Mitjorn, Formentera. ✆/fax **97-132-70-00**. www.rivhotel.es. 326 units. 50€–122€ double. Rates include breakfast. AE, MC, V. Closed Nov–Apr. **Amenities:** Restaurant; 2 bars; 2 pools; tennis courts; minigolf; health club; babysitting; laundry service; dry cleaning. *In room:* A/C, TV, minibar, hair dryer, safe.

Club Punta Prima ★★ Built in 1987 in a low-slung, two-story format hugging the coastline a short walk from the beach, this is the best and best-accessorized hotel on Formentera, with a loyal clientele from northern Europe, which tends to return year after year. The good-size rooms are comfortably furnished and well maintained, each with an excellent bed and bathroom equipped with a tub/shower combo. Great attention has been paid to the enhancement and preservation of the site's isolated natural beauty.

Punta Prima, 07871 Sant Ferran. ✆ **97-132-82-44**. Fax 97-132-81-28. www.puntaprima.es. 120 units. 52€–68€ double; 78€ suite. MC, V. Closed Nov–Apr. **Amenities:** Restaurant; lounge; pool; room service; laundry service; dry cleaning. *In room:* A/C, TV, hair dryer, safe.

Sa Volta This small hostal features good, clean, very modest rooms containing neatly kept bathrooms with shower stalls, and charges reasonable prices. It was totally renovated in 2000, with new beds added. It has no restaurant. However, you are in the midst of many cafes, restaurants, and nightlife possibilities because this is the tourist belt of Formentera. Reserve well in advance, as it's hard to get a room here.

Apartado 71, Sant Ferran, 07871 Es Pujols, Formentera. ✆ **97-132-81-25**. Fax 97-132-82-28. 25 units. 55€–115€ double. AE, DC, MC, V. **Amenities:** Restaurant; bar; pool; babysitting; laundry service; dry cleaning. *In room:* A/C, TV, minibar, hair dryer, safe.

WHERE TO DINE

Sa Palmera SPANISH/INTERNATIONAL Lying along the beach, Playa Es Pujols, this rustically decorated restaurant has been going strong ever since its opening in 1968. It is decorated with wood furniture inside, and on a chilly day you can enjoy that ambience, retreating outside when the weather is fair. The specialty is the fresh fish of the day, which can be grilled or else served in an herb-flavored green sauce. Another specialty is a *zarzuela* of mariscos, a seafood stew flavored with tomatoes, white wine, and fish broth. Paella is yet another choice dish, as is Argentine-styled barbecued beef. Beef loin is also served with onions, tomatoes, and peppers on a skewer as in a kabob.

Playa Es Pujols. ✆ **87-132-83-56**. Reservations not required. Main courses 6€–24€. MC, V. Mar–Oct noon–11pm. Closed Nov–Feb.

4 Minorca ★★

Minorca (also written "Menorca") is one of the most beautiful islands in the Mediterranean; miles of lovely beaches have made it a longtime favorite vacation spot for Europeans.

Barely 15km (9 miles) wide and less than 52km (32 miles) long, its principal city is Mahón (also called Maó; pop. 25,000), set on a rocky bluff overlooking the great port, which was fought over for centuries by the British, French, and Spanish.

After Majorca, it is the second largest of the Spanish Balearic Islands, but it has more beaches than Majorca, Ibiza, and Formentera combined—they range

---

Fun Fact *Taulas:* **Stonehenge Rocks of the Balearics**

In the south some 1,600 archaeological sites have been found, dating from prehistoric times. Of the mysterious monuments unearthed, the most spectacular are the *taulas,* Stonehenge-type structures made from two slabs of rock forming the letter T. Known only on Minorca, these megalithic structures are often more than 4m (12 ft.) high.

---

from miles-long silver or golden crescents of sand to rocky bays, or *calas,* reminiscent of Norwegian fjords. Our favorite is **Cala'n Porter,** 11km (7 miles) west of Mahón. Towering promontories guard the slender estuary where this spectacular beach is found. Another of Minorca's treasures, Cala de Santa Galdana, is 23km (14 miles) south of Ciudadela. Its gentle bay and excellent sandy beach afford the most scenic spot on the island. Illa d'en Colom, an island in the Mahón bay, is bordered with great beaches, but can be reached only by boat.

The beaches along 217km (135 miles) of pine-fringed coastline are the island's greatest attraction, although many are not connected by roads. Nude bathing is commonplace, even though the practice is officially illegal. Golf, tennis, and sailing are available at reasonable fees, and windsurfing is offered at all major beaches.

With about 60,000 permanent inhabitants, Minorca plays host to about half a million visitors a year. But it is not overrun with tourist developments and has none of the junky excess that has plagued Ibiza and Majorca for years.

Unlike those islands, Minorca is not utterly dependent on tourism; it has some industry, including leatherwork, costume jewelry making, dairy farming, and even gin manufacturing. Life here is quieter and more relaxed; it is not a place to go for glittering nightlife. Some clubs in Ibiza don't even open until 4 in the morning, but on Minorca nearly everybody, local and visitor alike, is in bed well before then.

In addition to trips to the beach, there are some fascinating things to do for those interested in history, archaeology, music, and art. Many artists live in Minorca, and exhibitions of their work are listed regularly in the local paper. The Catedral de Santa María in Mahón has one of the great pipe organs of Europe, and world-famous organists have appeared here, giving free concerts.

ISLAND ESSENTIALS

GETTING THERE   Minorca, lying off the eastern coast of Spain and northeast of Majorca, is reached by air, sea, or train. The most popular method of reaching Minorca, certainly the quickest, is to fly, but you can take a ferry from mainland Spain or from the other two major Balearic Islands, Ibiza and Majorca.

It is always good to arrive with everything arranged in advance—hotel rooms, car rentals, ferry or airplane tickets. In July and August, reservations are vital, because of the limited hotel and transportation facilities.

Minorca International Airport (© 97-115-70-00 for information) is 3km (2 miles) outside the capital city of Mahón. It receives dozens of charter flights, mainly from Germany, Italy, the Scandinavian countries, and Britain. However, both **Iberia** and **Aviaco** (© 97-136-90-15 for information on both airlines) operate regularly scheduled domestic flights from Barcelona, Palma de Majorca, and even Madrid.

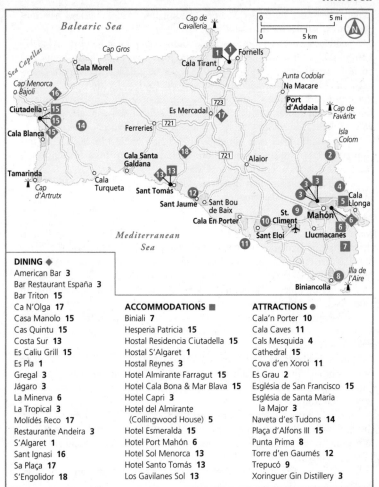

DINING ◆

American Bar **3**
Bar Restaurant España **3**
Bar Triton **15**
Ca N'Olga **17**
Casa Manolo **15**
Cas Quintu **15**
Costa Sur **13**
Es Caliu Grill **15**
Es Pla **1**
Gregal **3**
Jágaro **3**
La Minerva **6**
La Tropical **3**
Molídés Reco **17**
Restaurante Andeira **3**
S'Algaret **1**
Sant Ignasi **16**
Sa Plaça **17**
S'Engolidor **18**

ACCOMMODATIONS ■

Biniali **7**
Hesperia Patricia **15**
Hostal Residencia Ciutadella **15**
Hostal S'Algaret **1**
Hostal Reynes **3**
Hotel Almirante Farragut **15**
Hotel Cala Bona & Mar Blava **15**
Hotel Capri **3**
Hotel del Almirante
  (Collingwood House) **5**
Hotel Esmeralda **15**
Hotel Port Mahón **6**
Hotel Sol Menorca **13**
Hotel Santo Tomás **13**
Los Gavilanes Sol **13**

ATTRACTIONS ●

Cala'n Porter **10**
Cala Caves **11**
Cals Mesquida **4**
Cathedral **15**
Cova d'en Xoroi **11**
Es Grau **2**
Església de San Francisco **15**
Església de Santa Maria
  la Major **3**
Naveta d'es Tudons **14**
Plaça d'Alfons III **15**
Punta Prima **8**
Torre d'en Gaumés **12**
Trepucó **9**
Xoringuer Gin Distillery **3**

Regular **ferry service,** which operates frequently in the summer, connects Minorca with Barcelona, Palma de Majorca, and Ibiza. From Barcelona, the journey takes 9 hours aboard moderately luxurious lines. If you're on a real budget but still want a decent night's sleep, bunk in a four-person cabin, which is about the same price as a chair in the lounge. Meals can be purchased in a self-service restaurant onboard or else brought along.

The ferry service is operated by **Transmediterránea,** whose offices in Mahón are at Estació Marítim, along Moll (Andén) de Ponent (☎ **97-136-60-50**), open Monday through Friday from 8:30am to 1pm and 5 to 7pm. Saturday hours are from 6 to 9am, and Sunday from 2:30 to 5pm, but only to receive the ferry from Valencia. However, any travel agency in Barcelona or Palma, even Ibiza, can book you a ticket; you need not go directly to one of the company's offices.

GETTING AROUND **Transportes Menorca (TMSA),** Anselmo Clavé Junio Placa, Esplanada Mahón (☎ **97-136-04-75**), operates **bus** service around the island. The tourist office (see Mahón's "Visitor Information," below) has complete bus schedules for the island.

A good local car-rental company is **Morcams Gabermolar,** Ramirez 29 (✆ 97-136-44-05), with rentals beginning at 90€ for 3 days in the high season. The Spanish-owned **Atesa** (✆ 97-136-62-13) operates a desk at the airport, charging from 45€ for its cheaper models. **Avis** (✆ 97-136-15-76) operates out of the airport, asking from 50€ for its cheapest cars per day. Car-rental firms on the island will deliver a vehicle to the airport either upon your arrival or after you check into your hotel—but you must specify in advance.

To summon a local taxi, call ✆ 97-136-12-83 or 97-136-28-91. The taxi stop is at Plaça s'Esplanada in Mahón. Typical fare—say, from Mahón to the beaches at Cala'n Porter—is 12€ one-way.

To rent a bicycle, try **Just Bicicletas,** Carrer Infanta 19 (✆ 97-136-47-51), in Mahón. A 1-day bike rental costs 8€.

MAHON (MAO)

Mahón and neighboring Villacarlos still show traces of British occupation in their gorgeous Georgian architecture and Chippendale reproductions. There's also Golden Farm, the magnificent mansion north of the capital, overlooking Mahón harbor, where in October 1799 Admiral Lord Nelson enjoyed a brief rest and, according to local legend, hid out with his ladylove, Emma Hamilton. In truth, Nelson was here alone working on *Sketches of My Life.*

The largest city on the island, Mahón is an east-coast port. In the Minorcan language, it is called Maó. Mahón has allegedly lent its name to one of the world's most popular sauces, mayonnaise.

Mahón was built on the site of an old castle standing on a cliff overlooking one of Europe's finest natural harbors, some 5.5km (3½ miles) long. The castle and the town wall erected to dissuade pirates are long gone, except for the archway of San Roque.

The first Christian king from the mainland, Alfonso II, established a base in the harbor in 1287. It became known as **Isla del Rey (Island of the King).** When the British constructed a hospital here to tend to wounded soldiers, it was called "Bloody Island."

Since 1722, when the seat of government was moved here from Ciudadela, Mahón has been the capital of Minorca.

ESSENTIALS
GETTING THERE   From the airport (see above), you must take a taxi into Mahón, as there is no bus link. The approximate cost is 12€.

Mahón is the **bus** transport depot for the island, with departures from Calle José Anselmo Clave in the heart of town. The most popular run—seven buses per day in summer, four buses per day in winter—is to Ciudadela, but there are connections to other parts of the island. The tourist office (see "Visitor Information," below) distributes a list of schedules, and the list is published in the local newspaper, *Menorca Diario Insular.* Tickets are purchased once you're aboard. Make sure you carry some change.

VISITOR INFORMATION   The **tourist office,** Carrer Sa Rovellada de Talt 24 (✆ 97-136-37-90), is open Monday through Friday from 9am to 1:30pm and 5 to 7pm, Saturday from 9am to 1pm.

CITY LAYOUT   The heart of Mahón is the Plaça de la Constitució, with its Town Hall from the 18th century, constructed in an English Palladian style.

Plaça s'Esplanada, seat of the tourist office is actually the main square. Here on Sundays locals gather to enjoy ice cream, the best in the Balearics. In summer, a market is held on Tuesday and Saturday from 9am to 2pm. Island artisans from all over the island sell their wares at that time. The northern boundary of the city is formed by the **Puerto de Mahón,** which has many restaurants and shops along Muelle Comercial.

Mahón is not a beach town, but has some accommodations and is the center of the best shopping and nightclubs. The closest beaches for swimming are those at **Es Grau** and **Cala Mesquida.**

Villacarlos stretches east along the port, a virtual extension of the capital, and it doesn't have beaches either. Several good restaurants line the harbor leading toward Villacarlos. When the British founded this village, now a southeast suburb of Mahón, they called it Georgetown.

FUN ON & OFF THE BEACH

BEACHES   **Cala'n Porter,** 11km (7 miles) west of Mahón, is one of the most spectacular beaches on the island. It's a sandy beach at a narrow estuary inlet protected by high promontories. Thinly scattered houses perch upon a cliff. You can drop in on a bar here during the day. **La Cova d'en Xoroi,** ancient troglodyte habitations overlooking the sea from the upper part of the cliffs, can also be visited (see "Central & Southern Minorca," later in this chapter).

Going around the cliff face you'll discover more caves at **Cala Caves.** People still live in some of these caves and there are boat trips to see them from Cala'n Porter.

North of Mahón on the road to Fornells you'll encounter many beachside settlements. Close to Mahón and already being exploited is **Cala Mesquida,** one of the best beaches. To reach it, turn off the road to Cala Llonga and follow the signs to PLAYA.

The next fork in the road takes you to **Es Grau,** another fine beach. Along the way you see the salt marshes of S'Albufera, abundant in migrant birds. Reached by bus from Mahón, Es Grau, 8km (5 miles) north of Mahón, opens onto a sandy bay and gets very crowded in July and August. From Es Grau you can take a boat to **Illa d'en Colom,** an island in the bay with some good beaches. There are several bars at Es Grau for refueling.

South of Mahón is the little town of Sant Lluís and the large sandy beach to the east, **Punta Prima.** Patronized heavily by occupants of the local *urbanizaciones,* this beach is serviced by buses from Mahón, with six departures daily. The same buses will take you to an attractive necklace of beaches, the **Platges de Son Bou,** on the southern shore. Many tourist facilities are found here (see "Central & Southern Minorca," later in this chapter).

GOLF   The only course is **Urbanización Son Parc** (© 97-118-88-75), a traditional nine-hole course that recently added another nine holes.

HORSEBACK RIDING   For an equestrian tour of the island (subject to demand), call **Picadero Alaior** at © 60-832-35-66 in Alaior, which is 12km (7½ miles) from Mahón on the road to Sanbu. The outfit is in front of the bridge by the beach. Both beginner and advanced riders are accommodated, and an hour ride costs 16€.

WINDSURFING & SAILING   The best spots are at Fornells Bay, which is a mile wide and several miles long. **Windsurfing Fornells** (© 97-137-64-00) can supply you with gear.

SHOPPING

Es Portal, Sa Ravaleta 23 (© **97-136-30-36**), supplies Minorca's chic men and women with fashions from such high-priced and cutting-edge names as Moschino, Versace, Christian Lacroix, Dolce & Gabbana, and Armand Basi, as well as Spanish designers. Sophisticated accessories and shoes are available.

Looky Boutique, Carrer de Ses Moreres 43 (© **97-136-06-48**), is Minorca's outlet for chic, elegant leather accessories, which are produced in the company's factory in Ciudadela. The shop sells exquisite handbags, shoes, and leather clothing for men and women. Other locations include a shop in Fornells, at Passeig Marítim 23 (© **97-137-65-45**).

Patricia, Carrer de Ses Moreres 31 (© **97-136-91-78**), sells fine locally produced leather jackets, suits, skirts, and accessories. Other shops are at Camino Santandria/Ronda Baleares (© **97-138-50-56**).

SEEING THE SIGHTS

Most people don't take sightseeing too seriously in Mahón, as they are here mainly to enjoy the views of the port, to dine, or to shop. Even so, you may want to visit the **Esglesia de Santa María la Major,** Plaça Constitució. The church was founded in 1287 by the Christian conqueror Alfonso III, who wanted to celebrate the Reconquest. Over the years, the original Gothic structure has been much altered, and it was rebuilt in 1772. It has a celebrated organ with four keyboards and more than 3,000 pipes, constructed in 1810 by Johan Kyburz, a Swiss artisan. Admiral Collingwood brought it to Mahón during the Napoleonic wars. A music festival in July and August showcases the organ, whose melodic sounds can be heard even as you sit drinking in a nearby cafe.

The best way to see the changing aspect of Mahón's port involves taking an hour-long **catamaran tour.** Because part of the sailing craft's hull contains glass windows below the waterline, you'll get views of underwater life that would otherwise be possible only with a submarine. Tours begin year-round at 9:15am, then continue on the hour until 5:15pm. Departure time is not guaranteed, and the boat can leave up to 30 minutes later than scheduled. The cost is 9€ for adults, 5€ for children under 11. Tickets for this tour are available at **Xoriguer Gin Distillery.**

You can visit the **Xoriguer Gin Distillery** on the harbor front at Moll de Ponent 91 (© **97-136-21-97**). Here, giant copper vats simmer over wood-fed fires. Later, after watching the process by which the famed Minorcan gin is made, you can taste more than a dozen brews. The distillery and a store selling the products, including some potent liqueurs, is open Monday through Friday from 8am to 7pm, Saturday from 9am to 1pm.

SIDE TRIPS BACK IN TIME

From Mahón you can take excursions to some of the prehistoric relics in the area. One of these, marked off the Mahón-Villacarlos highway, is **Trepucó,** where you'll find both a 4m (13-ft.) *taula* (huge T-shaped stone structure) and a *talayot* (circular stone tower). The megalithic monuments stand on the road to Sant Lluís, only about a mile from Mahón. Of all the prehistoric remains on the island, this is the easiest to visit. It was excavated by Margaret Murray and a team from Cambridge University in the 1930s.

Another legacy of prehistoric people can be visited at Km 4 (a stone marker) off the Mahón-Ciudadela highway. The trail to **Talatí de Dalt** is marked. Your path will lead to this *taula* with subterranean caves.

Another impressive prehistoric monument is **Torre d'en Gaumés,** 15km (9 miles) from Mahón off the route to Son Bou (the path is signposted). You can take a bus from Mahón to Son Bou if you don't have a car. This megalithic settlement spreads over many acres, including both *taulas* and *talayots,* along with some ancient caves in which people once lived. The exact location is 3km (2 miles) south of Alayor off the road to Son Bou.

The restored **Naveta d'es Tudons** is accessible 5km (3 miles) east of Ciudadela, just to the south of the road to Mahón. This is the best-preserved and the most significant prehistoric collection of megalithic monuments on Minorca. Its *naveta* (a boat-shaped monument thought to be a dwelling or a burial chamber) is said to be among the oldest monuments constructed by humans in Europe. Archaeologists have found the remains of many bodies at this site, along with a collection of prehistoric artifacts, including pottery, decorative jewelry, and weapons—but they have now been removed to museums. The site is more easily visited if you're staying in Ciudadela.

WHERE TO STAY

Hostal Reynes   On a quiet, narrow street in the town center near the cathedral, this is a cozy, well-maintained, family-run, and very inexpensive hotel. Wide hallways lead to the simple but clean rooms on three floors of the building. Rooms are small but nicely maintained, each with a shared bathroom with a shower in the hall.

Carrer d'es Comerc 26, 07700 Mahón. ☎ 97-136-40-59. 28 units. 42€ double. No credit cards. **Amenities:** Dining room; lounge; laundry service; dry cleaning. *In room:* Safe, no phone.

Hotel Capri   If you don't stay at the more expensive and superior Hotel Port Mahón (see below), this comfortable, modern hotel, conveniently situated in the heart of Mahón, is the next best choice. Each of the simple rooms is comfortably but blandly furnished with conservative furniture, and each has a private balcony. It's well managed, with a sense of stewardship that derives from its long-term ownership and administration by a local family. Unlike many hotels on the island, this one is in the commercial core of Mahón and, as such, caters to business travelers from other parts of the Balearics and Europe and has more of a city-oriented outlook than hotels geared only to the resort trade. There's no pool, and the nearest beach is about 5km (3 miles) away.

Carrer Sant Esteve 8, 07703 Mahón. ☎ **97-136-14-00.** Fax 97-135-08-53. 75 units. 35€–72€ per person double. Rates include breakfast. AE, DC, MC, V. **Amenities:** Restaurant; bar; pool; fitness center; sauna; room service; babysitting; laundry service; dry cleaning. *In room:* A/C, TV, minibar, hair dryer, safe.

Hotel del Almirante (Collingwood House) ⭐ *(Finds)*   This is an offbeat choice. Originally built in the late 18th century for Admiral Collingwood, a close friend of Lord Nelson, this hotel later served as a convent, as the home of a German sculptor, and until the end of World War II, as the German embassy. Architecturally, it reflects a number of styles: Italianate, Georgian, and Minorcan.

In 1964, it was restored and enlarged into a hotel. The reception area, with its 18th-century staircase, is decorated with numerous oil paintings and, like the rest of the public rooms, successfully mixes antiques with British memorabilia. Guests are housed in the main building or in one of the more modern bungalow accommodations. The rooms are a mixed bag—you don't really know what you get until the maid opens the door. But all are clean and well kept, and many rooms have bathrooms with tub/shower combos and terraces overlooking the Bay of Mahón. The British love it here.

Carretera de Villacarlos s/n, 07700 Mahón. ✆ **97-136-27-00.** Fax 97-136-27-04. www.essa.net/hotel almirante. 40 units. 57€–87€ double. Rates include breakfast. DC, MC, V. Closed Nov–Apr. **Amenities:** Restaurant; bar; lounge; pool; tennis court; room service; laundry service; dry cleaning. *In room:* A/C, safe.

Hotel Port Mahón ⭐ Perched on a steep hillside above the harbor, this hotel looks like a large Georgian villa whose charms are largely of another era. It is, without question, the most traditional accommodation in Minorca, located in a residential neighborhood. It's one of the few large hotels that stays open year-round, and half of its rooms are usually reserved for tour groups. Some guests have been coming here since the 1950s, which indicates the age level of many of the patrons.

There is a sense of calm and unhurried comfort in the airy stone-floored public areas. The rooms overlook the harbor, the bougainvillea-filled garden, or the quiet street outside. Each has an ornate balcony with louvered shutters and potted flowers. All rooms are also equipped with simple luxuries such as immaculately kept bathrooms with tub/shower combos.

Avinguda Fort de L'Eau, 07701 Mahón. ✆ **97-136-26-00.** Fax 97-135-10-50. 80 units. 88€–172€ double; 148€–236€ suite. Rates include breakfast. AE, DC, MC, V. **Amenities:** Restaurant; 2 bars; lounge; pool; room service; laundry service; dry cleaning. *In room:* A/C, TV, minibar, hair dryer, safe.

A Nearby Place to Stay in Sant Lluís

Biniali ⭐ Biniali is one of the most charming hotels and restaurants in Minorca, about 1.6km (1 mile) south of Sant Lluis on the island's southwestern coastal road to Binibeca. The house, surrounded by English-style gardens, was originally the home of a prosperous Minorcan farmer in the 18th century. The comfortable midsize rooms are decorated with a scattering of antiques, seven with terraces and two with separate salons. All rooms come with firm beds and bathrooms equipped with tub/shower combos.

Tables and chairs are set out under an arcade overlooking the roses and geraniums in the garden. All in all, this is a retreat offering lots of peace, comfort, and quaintness within easy reach of Binibeca beach and the facilities and activities of Mahón.

Carretera S'Uestrà, Binibeca 50, 07710 Sant Lluis. ✆ **97-115-17-24.** Fax 97-115-03-52. www.hostal biniali.com. 9 units. 110€–130€ double. AE, DC, MC, V. Free parking. Closed late Oct to Easter. **Amenities:** Restaurant; lounge; bar; pool; room service; babysitting; laundry service; dry cleaning. *In room:* Hair dryer, safe.

WHERE TO DINE

Fish and seafood form most of the basis of the Minorcan diet. The sea harvest is abundant along the long coastline. The most elegant dish, *caldereta de langosta,* consists of pieces of lobster blended with onion, tomato, pepper, and garlic, and flavored with an herb liqueur. This is a favorite dish of King Juan Carlos when he visits Minorca.

Shellfish paella is also popular, as is *escupinas* ("warty Venus"), a local shellfish. *Tordos con col* (thrushes with cabbage) are served in autumn. A peasant dish, *pa amb oli,* often precedes a meal. This is bread flavored with salt and olive oil and rubbed with fresh tomato.

Wine is brought in from mainland Spain, but gin is made on the island, a legacy from the days of the British occupation. You can drink the gin by itself or mix it with lemon and ice. For the latter, ask the bartender for *palloza* (pronounced "pah-*yoh*-thah"). Gin mixed with soda or lemonade is called a *pomada.*

Expensive

La Minerva ⭐⭐ CATALAN This is the finest restaurant in Mahón. Lying on the port, it is cozy and traditional, specializing in fresh seafood such as clams, mussels, and lobster. Opposite Isla Pinto, it lies just east of the ferry terminal. Many nearby dining places offer lackluster, overpriced food, but this one is a winner. Imbued with a nautical decor, the restaurant feeds you well and lets you enjoy a view of the water and the coming and going of patrons in their tenders. The cuisine is prepared in the main building on the other side of the road, then rushed across by waiters long skilled in not getting run over by passing cars. To launch yourself, begin with an interesting variation on vichyssoise, this one velvety chilled with lobster bits. You might also enjoy the freshly made house special, a salad of prawns, avocado, black olives, radicchio, and hearts of palm. Some flavor-filled meat dishes appear on the menu and pork loin with fresh plums is especially tantalizing, as are Ping-Pong ball–size meatballs in an almond sauce. However, we prefer the seafood, including grouper baked with slices of garlic in an oil or vinegar sauce, served with an aromatic ratatouille. The most desirable and expensive main course is a *caldereta de langosta* (lobster), an enormous serving. An intriguing new offering is the tender ostrich steaks in a sweet sauce laced with sherry. For dessert, nothing can beat *borrachitos al gin de Menorca,* little cakes soaked in Menorcan gin and served with a strawberry coulis.

Moll del Llevant 87. ℂ **97-135-19-95.** Reservations required. Main courses 18€–30€. Daily 12:30–4pm and 7–11:30pm. AE, DC, MC, V.

Moderate

Jàgaro ★★ MEDITERRANEAN   The seafood menu here is Minorca's most eclectic and interesting. Begin with *ensalada templada con cigalitos y setas,* a mix of warm prawns and wild mushrooms served on a bed of lettuce, or Jàgaro's interpretation of gazpacho, flavored with shrimp and melon. The *mosaico de verduras,* a plate of grilled fresh vegetables, is an excellent choice. Main courses may include *carpaccio de mero* (grouper) served with a tangy green-mustard sauce, *caldereta de langosta* (lobster stew), or *ortigas* (sea anemones). Seafood offerings are extensive, although meat dishes, including duck *maigret* (breast) in orange sauce and foie gras with sweet-and-sour sauce, are very appealing. An extensive wine list ensures a vintage to accompany any meal. For dessert, try one of the homemade ice creams or sorbets.

Moll de Llevant 334. ℂ **97-136-23-90.** Reservations recommended. Main courses 9€–42€; *menú del día* 15€. AE, DC, MC, V. Daily noon–4pm and 7pm–midnight.

Restaurante Andeira ★ MINORCAN/MEDITERRANEAN   At this small, stylish restaurant in the center of Mahón, you'll feel as though you're dining in somebody's home. Even the small kitchen where the owner/chef works culinary wonders looks more like a domestic kitchen than a restaurant kitchen. There are about half a dozen tables indoors and another half a dozen spread around the rear patio in summer. A smattering of antique furnishings and Impressionistic artworks contribute to the coziness.

The menu is understandably limited, but of high quality and with great care taken in preparation. The market-fresh cuisine is largely *menorquín* with innovative variations. Based on a rigid allegiance to seasonal, high-quality, and very fresh ingredients, menu items change at least four times a year. Examples include Catalán-style blood sausage in puff pastry, served with a marmalade of onions and tomatoes; a soufflé of squid with almonds, prepared with squid ink; and veal trotters stuffed with Balearic herbs and served with a thyme-flavored honey sauce. For dessert try the homemade *pastel de nueces con chocolate* (walnut cake with chocolate).

Des Forn 61. ℂ **97-136-68-17**. Reservations recommended. Main courses 16€–22€; fixed-price lunch 15€. MC, V. Tues–Sat 1:30–3:30pm; Sept–July Mon–Sat 8:30–11:30pm; Aug daily 8:30–11:30pm. Closed Feb.

Inexpensive

American Bar MINORCAN/INTERNATIONAL   This is the traditional international meeting place in Mahón. Many come here for drinks on its pleasant terrace, but you can also order food, eating inside or alfresco. Menu items include traditional Catalán platters (soups, stews, grilled meats), as well as pastas, salads, and American-style burgers. Dessert might include locally made ice creams, many made with fresh fruit. No one will mind if you have a drink or two too many here; if you do, you certainly won't be alone.

Plaça Reial 8. ℂ **97-136-18-22**. Main courses 6€–15€. No credit cards. Mon–Sat 7am–10:30pm; Sun 6:30am–2pm.

Bar Restaurant España *Value* SPANISH   Originally established around 1938, this is one of the oldest continuously operating restaurants in Minorca, thanks to a solidly reliable clientele and well-prepared food served in generous portions at reasonable prices. Patrons include vacationing northern Europeans who tend to communicate with one another and the staff in English. Partly because of its cosmopolitan clientele, the menu is designed to appeal to a wide variety of palates. Examples include *cigales a la americana* (prawns in a spicy red sauce), shrimp with garlic, mussels marinara, baked fish (especially hake and cod), grilled veal and pork, and beefsteaks grilled and served with a decidedly Spanish flair.

Carrer Victori 48–50. ℂ **97-136-32-99**. Reservations recommended. Main courses 7€–18€; *menú del día* 7€. MC, V. Daily 1–3:30pm and 7:30pm–midnight. Closed Jan.

La Tropical SPANISH/MINORCAN/INTERNATIONAL   La Tropical is a three-in-one eatery. You can have snacks at the bar; and tapas, *bocadillos* (Spanish sandwiches) and *platos combinados* (combination plates) in the informal dining room; or full-fledged restaurant fare in the more formal dining area. The restaurant offers a good selection of Minorcan specialties, including a reasonably priced and savory fish-and-shellfish *caldereta* (stew). There is a daily market menu and an assorted selection of Spanish and international dishes.

Carrer Lluna 36. ℂ **97-136-05-56**. Main courses 10€–22€; *menú del día* 15€. MC, V. Daily 8am–midnight.

CIUDADELA (CIUTADELLA DE MENORCA) ⚘
44km (27 miles) W of Mahón

At the western end of the island, the town of Ciudadela has a typically Mediterranean air about it. Lining the narrow streets of the old city are noble mansions of the 17th and 18th centuries as well as numerous churches. It was the capital until 1722, when the British chose Mahón instead, largely because its harbor channel is more navigable than the one at Ciudadela. Subsequently, the British built the main island road to link the two cities.

Like Mahón, Ciudadela perches high above its harbor, which is smaller than Mahón's. The seat of Minorca's bishopric, Ciudadela pontificates while Mahón administrates.

Known as Medina Minurka under the Muslims, Ciudadela retains some Moorish traces despite the 1558 Turkish invasion and destruction of the city. An obelisk in memory of the city's futile defense against that invasion stands in the pigeon-filled Plaça d'es Born (Plaza del Born), the city's main square overlooking the port.

ESSENTIALS

GETTING THERE   From the airport, you must take a taxi to Ciudadela, as there is no bus link. The cost is approximately 40€ each way.

From Mahón six **buses** go back and forth every day. Departures are from Plaça s'Esplanada in Mahón.

VISITOR INFORMATION   The **tourist office,** located at Plaça Catedral 5 (*©* **97-138-26-93**), is open Monday through Friday from 9am to 1:30pm and 5 to 7pm, Saturday from 9am to 1pm.

EXPLORING CIUDADELA: THE BEACH & BEYOND

In Ciudadela, buses depart from Plaça d'Artrutx for most coastal destinations, including the best beaches. Of these, **Cala Santandria,** 3km (2 miles) to the south, is known for its white sands. This is a sheltered beach near a creek, and in the background are rock caves, which were inhabited in prehistoric times. The coves of **En Forcat, Blanes,** and **Brut** are near Ciudadela.

Cala de Santa Galdana, not reached by public transport, is the most stunning in the area, lying 23km (14 miles) south of Ciudadela. The bay here is tranquil and ringed with a beach of fine golden sand. Tall bare cliffs rise in the background, and the air is perfumed with the smell of pine trees. The road to this beach, unlike so many others on Minorca, is a good one.

The center of Ciudadela is **Plaça d'es Born,** site of tourist information. This was the center of life when the town was known to Jaume I. Back then Ciudadela was completely walled to protect itself from pirate incursions, which were a serious threat from the 13th century on. Much of the present look of this square, and of Ciudadela itself, is thanks to its demotion in 1722, when the capital was transferred to Mahón. For centuries that checked urban development in Ciudadela, and many buildings now stand that might have been torn down to make way for progress.

Plaça d'es Born looks over the port from the north. Once it was known as Plaza Generalísimo, honoring the dictator Franco. The square was built around the obelisk that remembers the hopeless struggle of the town against the invading Turks who entered the city in 1558 and caused much destruction. On the west side of the square is the Ayuntamiento (Town Hall).

To the southwest of the square stands **Esglesia de San Francisco.** This is a 14th-century Gothic building, with some excellent carved wood altars. The town once had a magnificent opera house, Casa Salort, but that cultural note sounds no more, as it's been turned into a somewhat seedy movie theater. Another once-splendid palace, Palacio de Torre-Saura, also opens onto the square. Still owner occupied, it was constructed in the 1800s.

The **cathedral,** Plaça Pío XII, was ordered built by the conquering Alfonso III on the site of the former mosque. It is Gothic in style and fortresslike in appearance. The facade of the church, in the neoclassical style, was added in 1813. The church suffered heavy damage in 1936, during the Spanish Civil War, but has since been restored.

Ciudadela is at its liveliest at the **port,** where you'll find an array of little shops, bars, restaurants, sailboats, along with some impressive yachts in summer. **Carrer Quadrado** is another street worth walking, as it is lined with shops and arcades.

The Moorish influence still lingers in a block of whitewashed houses in the **Voltes,** off the Plaça s'Esplanada. In Ciudadela the local people still meet at **Plaça d'Alfons III,** the square honoring their long-ago liberator.

WHERE TO STAY
Expensive

Hesperia Patricia ⊛   Built in 1988, this three-story building is in a centrally located position that business travelers find convenient and is Ciudadela's most respected, most luxurious hotel. Near the Plaça d'es Born, a half mile from the nearest beach (Playa de La Caleta), it has a polite hardworking staff well versed on the island's facilities and geography. The spacious rooms are comfortable, carpeted, outfitted pleasantly in pastels, and have large bathrooms, equipped with tub/shower combos.

Passeig Sant Nicolau 90, 07760 Ciudadela. ℂ **97-138-55-11.** Fax 97-148-11-20. www.hoteles-hesperia.es. 44 units. 85€–174€ double; from 97€–184€ junior suite. AE, DC, MC, V. Free parking on street. **Amenities:** Bar; pool; room service; laundry service; dry cleaning. *In room:* A/C, TV, minibar, hair dryer, safe.

Sant Ignasi ⊛⊛ *Finds*   For tranquillity seekers, this is a real discovery, as it lies outside of town surrounded by gardens and woodland of oak and palm trees. This was once the private hacienda address of a prestigious Menorcan family before its successful conversion to a hotel of elegance and charm. The location is within an easy drive of all the beaches on the northern and southwestern coast of the island. The staff can also direct you to such activities as horseback riding, watersports, and cycling.

The restored home has a lot of style and personality in its midsize bedrooms, each with a tub-and-shower combination. Each room on the ground floor, where the floors are two centuries old, have their own private garden. Units on the second landing open onto terraces with views of the countryside. For romantic escapists, there are rooms in the ancient loft of the house, with a lovely communal lounge and sloping wooden ceilings. Menorcan and English antiques, some from the 18th century, are placed alongside more modern pieces.

Carretera Cala Morell, Apdo. Correos 655, 07760 Ciutadella de Menorca. ℂ **97-138-55-75.** Fax 97-148-05-37. www.santignasi.com. 20 units. 97€–193€ double. MC, V. **Amenities:** Restaurant; bar; social club; 2 pools. *In room:* A/C, TV, minibar, hair dryer, safe.

Moderate

Hotel Almirante Farragut   Five kilometers (3 miles) outside Ciudadela, beside a small rock-lined inlet, this four-story building is one of the best hotels in the development of Los Delfines, a cluster of resort hotels initiated in the 1970s and 1980s. Public rooms are airy, large, sparsely furnished, and appropriate to the hotel's role as a warm-weather beach resort with an international clientele, often from England and Germany. Guest rooms are pleasant and standardized with bathrooms containing tub/shower combos and pleasant furnishings. Each has a balcony or terrace, usually overlooking either the rocky inlet or the open sea. Prices vary widely according to season, but lodgings that the hotel identifies as suites are nothing more than larger-than-usual double rooms.

The hotel, incidentally, was named for U.S. Admiral Farragut, a 19th-century U.S. naval officer whose grandparents lived in one of the nearby villages.

Urbanización Los Delfines, Cala'n Forcat, 07760 Ciudadela. ℂ **97-138-80-00.** Fax 97-138-81-07. 483 units. 50€–156€ double. Rates include breakfast. AE, MC, V. Closed Nov–Apr. **Amenities:** Restaurant; 2 bars; nightclub; 2 pools; tennis courts; minigolf; salon; babysitting; laundry service; dry cleaning. *In room:* A/C, TV, hair dryer, safe.

Hotel Esmeralda   This is a respectable government-rated three-star hotel, built in the 1960s and set near the entrance to the mouth of Ciudadela's harbor. It is within a 10-minute walk from the commercial heart of town, close to the better-accessorized Patricia Hotel, and rising three floors. The guest rooms are large but sparsely furnished, but bathrooms are big and bright with tub/shower combos and the beds are firm. In many cases, rooms have terraces and sea views. There's a beach within a 5-minute walk.

Pasaje de Sant Nicolau 171, 07760 Ciudadela. ⓒ **97-138-02-50**. Fax 97-138-02-58. www.mac-hotels.com. 158 units. 72€–88€ double. Rates include breakfast. MC, V. Free parking. Closed Nov–Apr. **Amenities:** 2 restaurants; bar; 2 pools; laundry service; dry cleaning. *In room:* A/C, TV, safe.

INEXPENSIVE

Hostal Residencia Ciutadella   Near Plaça d'Alfons III, on a quiet street just off the main shopping artery, this hotel offers comfortable, convenient, but small accommodations, each with a good bed and neatly kept bathroom with a shower stall. Tiled floors and floor-length windows provide an airy atmosphere. Furniture is covered in fresh, floral fabrics. *Beware:* This three-story hotel has no elevator.

Carrer Sant Eloi 10, 07760 Ciudadela. ⓒ/fax **97-138-34-62**. 17 units. 16€–65€ double; 52€–75€ triple. Rates include breakfast. AE, MC, V. **Amenities:** Restaurant; bar; babysitting; laundry/dry cleaning. *In room:* A/C, TV, safe.

Hotels Cala Bona & Mar Blava   These two hotels stand just a short walk from the town center, with views overlooking the little bay. Stairs lead down to a small beach, with a larger beach just 5 minutes away. Guest rooms are clean and comfortable with bathrooms containing showers; almost all have views facing the water. The rooms at the Mar Blava are smaller than those at the Cala Bona. The hotels share an outdoor terrace.

Avinguda del Mar 14–16, 07760 Ciudadela. ⓒ **97-138-00-16**. Fax 97-148-20-70. 44 units. 56€–72€ double. Rates include breakfast. No credit cards. Closed Nov–Mar. **Amenities:** Restaurant; bar; pool; room service; babysitting. *In room:* TV, hair dryer, safe.

A Nearby Place to Stay

Hotel Sol Menorca   This hotel gives the impression of a large, well-maintained hacienda, complete with lacy iron balconies and louvered shutters. Surrounded by lawns and flowering shrubs, it has a private beach, and a sweeping view of rocky islets. Many guests make their balconies an extension of their midsize rooms, reading, sitting, and talking within sight of the sea. Beds are firm and the tiled bathrooms come with tub/shower combos.

Playa Santo Tomás s/n, 07749 San Cristóbal. ⓒ **97-137-00-50**. Fax 97-137-03-48. 188 units. 65€–190€ double. Rates include half-board. AE, DC, MC, V. Closed late Oct to Apr 30. **Amenities:** Restaurant; bar; pool; fitness center; room service; laundry service; dry cleaning. *In room:* A/C, TV, minibar, hair dryer, safe.

WHERE TO DINE

The port of Ciudadela offers a wide selection of restaurants for all palates and prices. Beyond that, there are some commendable choices in and around town.

Bar Triton TAPAS   The best place for tapas in the port, Triton offers a wide range of snacks, including sausages, *tortillas* (Spanish omelets), meatballs, and a dozen or so seafood tapas, among them octopus, stuffed squid, and *escupiñas* (Minorcan clams). On the wall inside are photos and illustrations of the port before it was a haven for vacationers. As in those days, fishers still make up an important part of the clientele, and you'll often find the locals engaged in a friendly afternoon game of cards. For generations, this bar has made it a point to open every day at 4am, presumably in time to serve coffee, snacks, and in some cases, stiff drinks to fishermen headed out onto the nearby fishing banks. In recent years, however, it has also welcomed a *coterie* of fashionable night owls, who straggle in for a late-night (or early-morning) nightcap before tottering off to bed.

Muelle Ciutadella 55. ☎ **97-138-00-02.** Tapas and *platos combinados* 4€–30€. MC, V. Easter–Oct daily 4am–2am; Nov–Easter 4am–11:30pm.

Casa Manolo ★ SPANISH/MINORCAN   Located at the port, across from the spot where the larger yachts anchor, Casa Manolo is a favorite of the yachting crowd. You can dine indoors in a room carved out of stone, or alfresco on the intimate terrace. King Juan Carlos has been seen here enjoying the elegant atmosphere and outstanding cuisine. The menu consists mainly of fresh seafood and lobster dishes. The specialty of the house is *arroz de pescado caldoso,* a dish resembling paella, but with more of a focus on fish. The *caldereta de langosta,* a lobster-based bouillabaisse, is one of our favorites. The hardworking and affable owner, María Postores, supervises all aspects of your dining experience.

Marina 117. ☎ **97-138-00-03.** Reservations required in summer. Main courses 18€–35€; off-season fixed-price menu 25€. AE, DC, MC, V. Daily 1–4pm and 7:30–11:30pm. Closed Feb.

Cas Quintu SPANISH/MINORCAN   Thriving since the early 1960s from a position on an ornate square in the most historic core of town, Cas Quintu offers both indoor and outdoor tables that afford vantage points for observations of the passing crowd. You can order drinks and light food in the cafe daily from 9am to 2pm. This establishment's selection of tapas is among the best in town. Full meals are served outdoors or in one of a pair of rooms in back. Specialties include a zesty squid sautéed in butter, several different preparations of beefsteak, a perfect sole meunière, and a mixed grill of fish based on the catch of the day.

Cami De Bax 8. ☎ **97-138-10-02.** Main courses 10€–18€; fixed-price menu 11€–18€. AE, MC, V. Daily 1–4pm and 8pm–midnight.

Es Caliu Grill SPANISH   About 2.5km (1½ miles) south of Ciudadela, along the main road between Cala Santandria and Cala Blanca, Es Caliu is the place to come when you've had your fill of seafood. Specializing in grilled meats of the freshest quality, it offers lamb, veal, pork, rabbit, quail, and spit-roasted suckling pig. But beyond fine food, you get a special ambience. Above the bar hang hams and garlic braids, and off to the side are stacked wine barrels. The family-style tables and benches are made of cut and polished logs. The outdoor terrace is roofed and smothered with cascading flowers; indoors are two rustic dining areas, one with a fireplace.

Carretera Cala Blanca. ☎ **97-138-01-65.** Main courses 14€–20€. MC, V. May–Oct daily 1–4pm and 7pm–midnight; off season Fri 7pm–midnight, Sat–Sun 1–4pm and 7pm–midnight.

CIUDADELA AFTER DARK
Café El Molino, Camino de Mao 7 (☎ **97-138-00-00**), is one of our favorite bars, a hangout near the Avinguda de la Constitució. It has attracted virtually every drinker in town since it was established in 1905 within the circular premises of a windmill built in 1794. It provides a rustic but richly international contrast to the busy square it borders, and boasts the unusual distinction of having monumental walls and vaulted ceilings a lot older than those of the buildings surrounding it. The clientele includes visiting foreigners and local fishers, and the mood changes from that of an early morning cafe, whose opening is timed to coincide with the departure of fishing boats, to a late-night bar. This place is earthy, regional, and brusque, yet invaluable for an insight into old-time Minorca.

CENTRAL & SOUTHERN MINORCA
Topographically and climatically, this is the more tranquil part of the island. The beaches are more accessible, and the winds blow less—as a result, tourism has

taken a firmer foothold here than in the north. Santo Tomás, Cala Galdana, Platges de Son Bou, Cala Bosch, and Punta Prima are some of the focal points for travelers.

Es Mercadal, a town of several thousand inhabitants at the foot of Monte Toro, is an ensemble of white houses with grace notes of color. Among its claims to local fame are two types of almond confectionery—*carquinyols* (small, hard cookies) and *amargos* (a kind of macaroon). The place to get both is **Pastelería Villalonga Ca's Sucrer** (© **97-137-51-75**), Plaça Constitució 11, Es Mercadal (no phone), open Tuesday through Saturday from 9:30am to 1:30pm and 5 to 8:30pm, also open Sunday, from 11am to 2pm.

From Es Mercadal, you can take a road 4km (2½ miles) up to **Monte Toro,** the island's tallest mountain at 355m (1,170 ft.), crowned with a sanctuary that is a place of pilgrimage for Minorcans. The winding road leads to a panoramic view of the island's rolling green countryside dotted with *fincas* (farm estates), trim fields, and stands of trees. From this vantage point you can clearly see the contrast between the flatter southern part of the island and the hilly northern region. The hilltop sanctuary includes a small, simple church with an ornate gilded altar displaying the image (reportedly found nearby in 1290) of the Virgin Mare de Déu d'el Toro, the island's patron saint. In 1936 the church was destroyed, but the statue was saved from the flames and a new church built. The church is open daily from early morning to sunset; admission is free. In the courtyard of the sanctuary is a bronze monument to those Minorcans who left in the 18th century, while the island was still a British colony, to colonize Spanish settlements in North America. The large statue of Christ commemorates the dead in the Spanish Civil War. There is a snack bar with a pleasant terrace here.

Platges de Son Bou is a stunning beach scarred by two outsize hotels. Although still enchanting, the mile-long, narrow beach and clear, turquoise waters are now often crowded, even in the off season; in July and August they're best avoided. At the eastern end of the beach just beyond the two monster hotels are the ruins of a Paleo-Christian basilica, most probably dating from the 5th or 6th century. Visible in the cliffs beyond are cave dwellings, some of which appear quite prosperous, with painted facades and shades to keep out the noonday sun.

⸢Finds⸥ Where the Flintstones Boogie the Night Away

Just .8km (½ mile) to the east in Cala'n Porter is a unique nightspot. Embedded in a series of caves within a sheer cliff face rising from the sea, **La Cova d'en Xoroi** (© **97-137-72-36**) is a conglomeration of bars, terraces, intimate nooks and crannies, and a disco floor. For sheer drama, the setting is without equal. As you walk down the entrance stairway, all magnificently unfolds before you. Then you come to the dance floor overlooking the sea at the cliff's edge—there's no window, just a railing. Prehistoric vessels were found inside these caves, which according to legend, were once the refuge of a Moor called Xoroi, who had abducted a local maid and made his home here with her and their family. You can visit this unusual spot during the day as well, from 10:30am to 9pm. In the evening, from 11pm to 4am, La Cova d'en Xoroi transforms into a disco. Admission is 15€, including your first drink. Drinks cost from 5€.

WHERE TO STAY

Most of the hotels in this area cater almost exclusively to tour groups.

Hotel Santo Tomás ⭐   One of our favorite hotels on Minorca, Santo Tomás offers the best quality and comfort on the island; it's the only government-rated four-star hotel on the beach. Public areas are airy and spacious and accommodations are comfortable, with bathrooms equipped with tub/shower combos. Most rooms open onto a terrace that faces the sea. Various watersports can be arranged.

Playa Santo Tomás, 07749 Es Migjorn Gran. ℭ **97-137-00-25.** Fax 97-137-02-04. www.sethotels.com. 85 units. 95€–220€ double; 130€–275€ suite. Rates include half-board. AE, DC, MC, V. Closed Nov–Apr. **Amenities:** 2 restaurants; bar; 2 pools; minigolf; fitness center; sauna; room service; laundry service; dry cleaning. *In room:* A/C, TV, minibar, hair dryer.

Los Gavilanes Sol   A large resort hotel, Gavilanes Sol is fully equipped with swimming pools, discos, restaurants, and bars. It's atop a steep slope overlooking one of the most perfect beaches in the Mediterranean, surrounded by a grove of pines and palmettos. The original beauty of Cala Galdana has been substantially marred by construction, but you can enjoy the best end of its sandy, crescent-shaped beach and turquoise waters by staying here. Each of the sizable, functionally furnished rooms has a balcony, and all are equipped with a neatly kept bathroom with a tub/shower combo.

Many of the guests here are on group tours from England, so the sweeping lobby-level terraces take on a British flavor.

Urbanización Cala Galdana s/n, 07750 Ferreries. ℭ **97-115-45-45.** Fax 97-115-45-46. www.solmelia.com. 364 units. 80€–100€ double; 84€–122€ suite. Rates include breakfast. MC, V. Free parking. Closed Nov–Apr. **Amenities:** 2 restaurants; bar; fitness center; sauna; room service; babysitting; laundry service; dry cleaning. *In room:* A/C, TV, minibar, hair dryer, safe.

WHERE TO DINE

Some of the best dining in this area is offered in the inland villages rather than along the coast. **Es Mercadal,** in particular, has a few choice restaurants.

Ca N'Olga ⭐ MINORCAN/INTERNATIONAL   A stylish, sophisticated spot that attracts a similar clientele, Ca N'Olga is warm, winsome, and intimate. Occupying a typical white-stucco Minorcan house some 150 years old, this restaurant offers dining on a pretty outdoor patio or at a handful of indoor tables.

The eclectic menu changes frequently with the market offerings. It is likely to include quail with onion-and-sherry vinegar and osso buco. Some standard dishes that tend to appear regularly are *cap roig* (scorpionfish), *cabrito* (baby goat), some kind of fish terrine, and mussels au gratin. Among the homemade desserts you'll often find a velvety smooth fig ice cream and chestnut pudding.

Pont Na Macarrana, Es Mercadal. ℭ **97-137-54-59.** Reservations recommended on weekends. Main courses 13€–18€. AE, DC, MC, V. Mar–May and Oct–Nov Thurs–Sun 1–4pm and 8–11pm; June–Sept daily 7:45–11:30pm. Closed Dec–Feb.

Costa Sur INTERNATIONAL   The sophisticated aspirations of Costa Sur are hampered by its rather stark decor and well-meaning but untrained staff. The menu is equally divided between seafood and meat dishes, and the house rightly prides itself on its cheese soufflé, salmon crepes, pepper steak, and *suquet de rape* (monkfish stew). It serves a smattering of succulent pasta dishes.

Playa de Santo Tomás. ℭ **97-137-03-26.** Main courses 10€–18€. MC, V. Daily 7–11pm. Closed Nov–Apr.

Molí d'es Reco MINORCAN   Easily spotted by the 300-year-old windmill that inspired the name of this 1982 creation, Molí d'es Reco offers a pleasant outdoor patio but a rather plain indoor dining area. Overall, the place is a bit touristy, but it offers hearty Minorcan fare including stuffed eggplant, *oliaigua amb tomatecs* (a soup with tomato, onion, parsley, green pepper, and garlic), snails with spider crab, partridge with cabbage, and *calamares a la menorquina* (stuffed squid with an almond cream sauce).

Es Mercadal. ℂ **97-137-53-92.** Reservations recommended in summer. Main courses 8€–22€; *menú del día* 9€. AE, MC, V. Daily 1–4pm and 7–11pm.

Sa Plaça MINORCAN   Simple, unpretentious, and noted as a centerpiece of local gossip, this is a well-managed, family-run bistro and cafeteria rather than a full-fledged restaurant. In a simple and somewhat battered setting, you're free to order just coffee, a glass of wine, or any of 10 kinds of tapas and seek a refuge from the searing heat outside in a low-key environment that's thoroughly and completely Minorcan in its tastes, orientation, and self-definition.

Carrer d'Enmig (also Avinguda de la Constitució) 2, Es Mercadal. ℂ **97-137-50-48.** Main courses 8€–18€; fixed-price menu 10€. MC, V. Daily 1–4pm and 8–10:30pm.

S'Engolidor ⭑ *Finds* MINORCAN   In the village of Es Migjorn Gran (San Cristóbal), between Es Mercadal and Santo Tomás, is this cozy and relatively undiscovered restaurant. Except for a small sign on the door, it could be mistaken for any other house on this quiet side street. The building dates from 1740, with sections added throughout the years. The interior is simple: stark white walls accented with various works of art. The dining area consists of several small rooms, with only a few tables each. You can dine outdoors in one of the small patio areas; many overlook the owner's compact vegetable garden. The menu consists of various Minorcan specialties, including *olaigua,* eggplant stuffed with fish; rabbit and wild mushroom stew; and a particularly succulent version of roasted lamb. Owner José Luis maintains four simple rooms that, although clean and cozy, contain virtually no amenities other than a private bathroom and a sense of peace and quiet. A double room, with breakfast included, costs between 35€ and 44€ per night, and is available only between May and October.

Carrer Major 3, Es Migjorn Gran. ℂ **97-137-01-93.** Reservations recommended on weekends. Main courses 6€–15€. MC, V. May–Oct daily 8–11pm. Closed Dec–Apr.

FORNELLS & THE NORTHERN COAST

The road leading north from Es Mercadal to Fornells runs through some of the island's finer scenery. Mass-tourism hotels, so far, have not discovered this place, but there are several good dining choices. On the northern coast, the tiny town of Fornells snuggles around a bay filled with boats and windsurfers and lined with restaurants and a few shops. Built around four defense fortifications—the Talaia de la Mola (now destroyed), the Tower of Fornells at the harbor mouth, the fortress of the Island of Las Sargantanas (the Lizards) situated in the middle of the harbor, and the now-ruined Castle of San Jorge or San Antonio—Fornells today is a flourishing fishing village noted for its upscale restaurants featuring savory lobster *calderetas.*

West of Fornells is **Platja Binimella,** a beautiful beach (unofficially nudist) easily accessible by car. Its long, curving, sandy cove is peacefully set against undulating hills. A snack bar is the sole concession to civilization.

By far the most splendid panorama here is that from the promontory at **Cap de Cavalleria,** the northernmost tip of the island, marked by a lighthouse. Getting here requires some effort, however. At a bend in the road leading to Platja Binimella, a signpost indicates the turnoff to Cap de Cavalleria through a closed gate heading to a dirt road. The closed gate is typical of many of the roads leading to Minorca's undeveloped beaches. All the beaches in Spain, however, are public, so no one may impede access to them—although landowners might discourage visitors by making access difficult. The prevailing custom is simply to open the gate, go on through, and close it behind you. It is important that you close the gate because often they keep livestock confined to certain areas. As you follow the long dirt road (negotiable in a regular car or on a motorbike) out to Cap de Cavalleria, you come across several more sets of gates and travel through countryside that's somewhat reminiscent of the Scottish highlands, with cultivated fields and scattered grand *fincas,* or farmsteads. Shortly before the lighthouse is a parking area down to the left. You'll have to pick your way across the scrub and rocks for the views. The best one is from a circular tower in ruins up to the right of the lighthouse. Now brace yourself for a vista encompassing the whole of Minorca—a symphony of dramatic cliffs and jewel-blue water.

WHERE TO STAY

Hostal S'Algaret   This is for escapists only. It's really like an unpretentious inn. It's also a bit sleepy, so don't expect a lot in the way of hotel services. But adventurous do-it-yourself types often book the modest and very simply furnished guest rooms, which are clean and reasonably comfortable. Floors are tiled, the furnishings basic, but the spacious modern bathrooms with tub/shower combos are alluring. There are also sizable terraces opening onto views. If your expectations aren't high, you might go for this one. Few will complain, either, when the reasonable bill is presented.

Plaça S'Algaret 7, 07748 Fornells. © **97-137-65-52.** 21 units. 54€–76€ double. Rates include breakfast. AE, MC, V. Closed Nov–Mar. **Amenities:** Restaurant; lounge; pool; room service. *In room:* A/C, minibar, safe.

WHERE TO DINE

Fornells is noted for its fine seafood restaurants specializing in the Minorcan *calderetas.* King Juan Carlos has been known to sail in here when he wants to savor the seafood stew, and in peak summer season people call their favorite Fornells restaurant days in advance with their orders.

Es Pla 🐟 MINORCAN/SEAFOOD   If any restaurant in Minorca deserves a comparison to the grand Roman watering holes of *La Dolce Vita,* it would be this one, where King Juan Carlos and his family have come to dine several times. Stylish, airy, and elegant in a way that reflects the seagoing life of the island, Es Pla has thrived here since the 1960s, on a wood-floored porch that is only about 2m (6 ft.) above the swell of the surf. Large and informal, it has a long, stainless steel bar area and an indoor/outdoor design. Menu items include a roster of perfectly prepared fish, meat, and shellfish, but the acknowledged culinary winner— and the most frequently ordered dish—is paella with crayfish.

Pasage des Pla, Fornells. © **97-137-66-55.** Reservations recommended July–Aug. Main courses 8€–20€; *menú del día* 20€ Sept 20–June 20. AE, MC, V. Daily 1–3:30pm and 7pm–midnight.

S'Algaret SPANISH   Adjacent to the hostal of the same name (see above), S'Algaret is much frequented by locals and is one of the few economical alternatives for eating in Fornells (here, you eat rather than dine). The restaurant is sleepy, quiet, small in scale, and unpretentious. You can nibble on good-tasting tapas, sandwiches, a varied selection of *tortillas* (Spanish omelets), and a smattering of *platos combinados* (combination plates), the ingredients of which change daily.

Plaça S'Algaret 7, Fornells. © **97-137-64-46.** Tapas 2.50€–10€ per *ración* (serving); *menú del día* 15€; platters 9€–13€. AE, MC, V. Daily 1:30–3:30pm and 8–11pm.

Appendix A:
Spain in Depth

The once-accepted adage that "Europe ends at the Pyrenees" is no longer true. Today, the two countries forming the Iberian Peninsula at the southwestern end of the continent—Spain and Portugal—are totally integrated into Europe as members of the European Union (E.U.), with democratic governments and vibrant economies of their own. In fact, Spain has the second fastest-growing economy in the E.U.; new industries and an expanding infrastructure continue to alter its ancient landscape.

Political changes adopted after the 1975 death of Gen. Francisco Franco, Europe's remaining prewar dictator, contributed to a remarkable cultural renaissance. This rebirth has transformed Spain's two largest cities—Madrid, the capital, and Barcelona—into major artistic and intellectual centers. Amid some of the world's most innovative architecture and contemporary movements, art, literature, cinema, and fashion are constantly finding new and original expression; at night the cafes and bars hum with animated discussions on politics, the economy, and society. In every aspect of urban life, a visitor feels the Spanish people's reawakened self-confidence and pride in their newfound prosperity.

These developments contrast with Spain's unhappy experiences earlier this century, particularly during the devastating Civil War of 1936–39 and Franco's subsequent long iron-hand rule. During the Franco years, political and intellectual freedom was squelched, and Spain was snubbed by most of Europe.

Spain was previously, of course, a major world player. In the 16th century, it was the seat of a great empire; the Spanish monarchy dispatched fleets that conquered the New World, returning with its riches. Columbus sailed to America and Balboa to the Pacific Ocean; Cortés conquered Mexico for glory; and Pizarro brought Peru into the Spanish fold. The conquistadors too often revealed the dark side of the Spanish character, including brutality in the name of honor and glory, but they also represented a streak of boldness and daring.

It's difficult to visit this country without recalling its golden past: Those famous "castles in Spain" really do exist. Yet many Spaniards believe that Spain isn't merely a single country but a series of nations, united the way Yugoslavia used to be. Many groups, especially the Basques, the Cataláns, and the Gallegos in the northeast, are asserting their individuality in everything from culture to language. At least in the case of Basque separatists, that regional, "nationalistic" pride has taken violent turns. Castile and Andalusia, in the south, remain quintessentially Spanish. While linguistic and cultural differences are great, to the foreign visitor they are also subtle.

As the inheritors of a great and ancient civilization dating from before the Roman Empire, Spaniards inhabit a land that is not only culturally rich, but also geographically varied, with wooded sierra, arid plateaus, and sandy beaches. It is this exciting variety in landscape—as well as in art, architecture, music, and cuisine—that makes Spain one of the top countries in the world to visit.

1 Spain Today

As Spain moves on its journey into the millennium, tourism continues to boom and to dominate the economy—it remains a hot, hot industry with yearly arrivals in Spain bypassing the 45-million mark and closing in on 50 million.

The land is vibrant and fast-changing, an up-and-coming destination that is expected to propel Spain into a tourism position that ranks alongside such front-runners as France, the United States, and Italy.

Increasingly, North Americans are becoming part of the changing landscape. While many European visitors head for Spain's beach resorts, Americans occupy the number-one position in visits to three top Spanish cities: Madrid, Barcelona, and Seville.

No longer interested in the "lager lout" image its coastal resorts earned in the 1970s and 1980s by hosting so many cheap package tours from Britain, Spain has reached out to a more upscale visitor. Bargain Spain of the $5-a-day variety is now a distant memory, as prices have skyrocketed. The government is trying to lure visitors away from the overcrowded coasts (especially Majorca, the Costa del Sol, and the Costa Brava) and steer them to the country's less-traveled, but more historic, destinations. Government paradors and other improved tourist facilities, better restaurants, and spruced-up attractions have sent the message.

In 1999, Spain joined other European countries in adopting the euro as its national currency. Citizens began using the new coins and bank notes at the beginning of 2002. The peseta, which has been the Spanish monetary unit since 1868, disappeared completely on March 1, 2002.

Backers of the euro, mainly the Spanish government, have presented the new currency as the solution to many problems, including unemployment and deficits. Many economists in Spain remain skeptical and are watching the country's entry into the euro market with great caution.

Although unemployment, which remains high, continues to plague the government, progress has been made. The country's debt is some 70% of the gross domestic product. Inflation is about 2.5%, an all-time low in the post-Franco era. Consumer spending remains cautious, however, since most of the new jobs being created are on short-term contracts.

Spain continues to change as it moves deeper into the millennium. A drug culture and escalating crime—things virtually unheard of in Franco's day—are unfortunate signs of Spain's entry into the modern world. The most remarkable advance has been in the legal status of women, who now have access to contraception, abortion, and divorce. Sights once unimaginable are now taking place: an annual lesbian "kiss-in" at Madrid's Puerto del Sol, and women officiating as governors of men's prisons. Surprisingly, for a Catholic country, the birth rate continues to remain one of the lowest in the developed world, and the population is aging.

Spain's monarchy seems to be working. In 1975, when the king assumed the throne after the death of Franco, he was called "Juan Carlos the Brief," implying that his reign would be short. But almost overnight he distanced himself from Franco's dark legacy and became a hardworking and serious sovereign. He staved off a coup attempt in 1981, and he and the other Spanish royals remain popular. Juan Carlos even makes do on a meager $7 million salary—less than one-tenth of what England's Queen Elizabeth II is reputed to earn in a year.

The author John Hooper, in an updated version of his 1986 bestseller, *The New Spaniards,* remains optimistic about the future of Spain, in spite of its problems. He suggests Spaniards not forget that "to be true to themselves they may need to be different from others." Hooper believes that the new Spain will have arrived at adulthood "not on the day it ceases to be different from the rest of Europe, but on the day that it acknowledges that it is." Hooper was referring to the exotic, romantic, and varied faces of Spain that set it apart from other nations of Europe, ranging from flamenco to bullfighting and from its Moorish architecture to its pagan ceremonies. Nowhere—not even in Italy—are the festival and traditional, flamboyant dress more a part of annual life than in Spain, where religious processions are full of intense passion.

2 History 101

BARBARIAN INVASIONS, THE MOORISH KINGDOM & THE RECONQUEST Around 200 B.C. the Romans vanquished the Carthaginians and laid the foundations of the present Latin culture. Traces of Roman civilization can still be seen today. By the time of Julius Caesar, Spain (Hispania) was under Roman law and began a long period of peace and prosperity.

When Rome fell in the 5th century, Spain was overrun, first by the Vandals and then by the Visigoths from Eastern Europe. The chaotic rule of the Visigothic kings lasted about 300 years, but the barbarian invaders did adopt the language of their new country and tolerated Christianity as well.

In A.D. 711, Moorish warriors led by Tarik crossed over into Spain and conquered the disunited country. By 714, they controlled most of it, except for a few mountain regions around Asturias. For 8 centuries the Moors occupied their new land, which they called *al-Andalús*, or Andalusia, with Córdoba as the capital. A great intellectual center, Córdoba became the scientific capital of Europe; notable advances were made in agriculture, industry, literature, philosophy, and medicine. The Jews were welcomed by the Moors, often serving as administrators, ambassadors, and financial officers. But the Moors quarreled with one another, and soon the few Christian strongholds in the north began to advance south.

Dateline

- **11th century B.C.** Phoenicians settle Spain's coasts.
- **650 B.C.** Greeks colonize the east.
- **600 B.C.** Celts cross the Pyrenees and settle in Spain.
- **6th–3rd century B.C.** Carthaginians make Cartagena their colonial capital, driving out the Greeks.
- **218–201 B.C.** Second Punic War: Rome defeats Carthage.
- **2nd century B.C.–2nd century A.D.** Rome controls most of Iberia. Christianity spreads.
- **5th century** Vandals, then Visigoths, invade Spain.
- **8th century** Moors conquer most of Spain.
- **1214** More than half of Iberia is regained by Catholics.
- **1469** Ferdinand of Aragón marries Isabella of Castile.
- **1492** Catholic monarchs seize Granada, the last Moorish stronghold. Columbus lands in the New World.
- **1519** Cortés conquers Mexico. Charles I is crowned Holy Roman Emperor, as Charles V.
- **1556** Philip II inherits throne and launches the Counter-Reformation.
- **1588** England defeats Spanish Armada.
- **1700** Philip V becomes king. War of Spanish Succession follows.
- **1713** Treaty of Utrecht ends war. Spain's colonies reduced.
- **1759** Charles III ascends throne.
- **1808** Napoléon places brother Joseph on the Spanish throne.
- **1813** Wellington drives French out of Spain; the monarchy is restored.

continues

The Reconquest, the name given to the Christian efforts to rid the peninsula of the Moors, slowly reduced the size of the Muslim holdings, with Catholic monarchies forming in northern areas. The three powerful kingdoms of Aragón, Castile, and León were joined in 1469, when Ferdinand of Aragón married Isabella of Castile. Catholic kings, as they were called, launched the final attack on the Moors and completed the Reconquest in 1492 by capturing Granada.

That same year Columbus, the Genoese sailor, landed on the West Indies, laying the foundations for a far-flung empire that brought wealth and power to Spain during the 16th and 17th centuries.

The Spanish Inquisition, begun under Ferdinand and Isabella, sought to eradicate all heresy and secure the primacy of Catholicism. Non-Catholics, Jews, and Moors were mercilessly persecuted, and many were driven out of the country.

THE GOLDEN AGE & LATER DECLINE

Columbus's voyage to America and the conquistadors' subsequent exploration of that land ushered Spain into its golden age.

In the first half of the 16th century, Balboa discovered the Pacific Ocean, Cortés seized Mexico for Spain, Pizarro took Peru, and a Spanish ship (initially commanded by the Portuguese Magellan, who was killed during the voyage) circumnavigated the globe. The conquistadors took Catholicism to the New World and shipped cargoes of gold back to Spain. The Spanish Empire extended all the way to the Philippines. Charles V, grandson of Ferdinand and Isabella, was the most powerful prince in Europe—king of Spain and Naples, Holy Roman Emperor and lord of Germany, duke of Burgundy and the Netherlands, and ruler of the New World territories.

- **1876** Spain becomes a constitutional monarchy.
- **1898** Spanish-American War leads to Spain's loss of Puerto Rico, Cuba, and the Philippines.
- **1923** Primo de Rivera forms military directorate.
- **1930** Right-wing dictatorship ends; Primo de Rivera exiled.
- **1931** King Alfonso XIII abdicates; Second Republic is born.
- **1933–35** Falange party formed.
- **1936–39** Civil War between the governing Popular Front and the Nationalists led by Gen. Francisco Franco.
- **1939** Franco establishes dictatorship, which will last 36 years.
- **1941** Spain technically stays neutral in World War II, but Franco favors Germany.
- **1955** Spain joins the United Nations.
- **1969** Franco names Juan Carlos as his successor.
- **1975** Juan Carlos becomes king. Franco dies.
- **1978** New democratic constitution initiates reforms.
- **1981** Coup attempt by right-wing officers fails.
- **1982** Socialists gain power after 43 years of right-wing rule.
- **1986** Spain joins the European Community (now the European Union).
- **1992** Barcelona hosts the Summer Olympics; Seville hosts EXPO '92.
- **1996** A conservative party defeats Socialist party, ending 13-year rule. José María Aznar chosen prime minister.
- **1998** Two cultural milestones for Spain: the inauguration of the controversial Guggenheim Museum at Bilbao and the reopening of Madrid's opera house, Teatro Real.
- **1999** Spain falls under the euro umbrella.
- **2000** Economy goes on an upswing. Complete euro unity looms.
- **2001** Spain moves forward as an economic powerhouse in Latin America.
- **2002** Spain gives up its historic currency, the peseta, and adopts the euro as its national currency.

But much of Spain's wealth and human resources were wasted in religious and secular conflicts. First Jews, then Muslims, and finally Catholicized Moors were driven out—and with them much of the country's prosperity. When Philip II ascended the throne in 1556, Spain could indeed boast vast possessions: the New World colonies; Naples, Milan, Genoa, Sicily, and other portions of Italy; the Spanish Netherlands (modern Belgium and the Netherlands); and portions of Austria and Germany. But the seeds of decline had already been planted.

Philip, a fanatic Catholic, devoted his energies to subduing the Protestant revolt in the Netherlands and to becoming the standard-bearer for the Counter-Reformation. He tried to return England to Catholicism, first by marrying Mary I ("Bloody Mary") and later by wooing her half sister, Elizabeth I, who rebuffed him. When, in 1588, he resorted to sending the Armada, it was ignominiously defeated; and that defeat symbolized the decline of Spanish power.

In 1700, a Bourbon prince, Philip V, became king, and the country fell under the influence of France. Philip V's right to the throne was challenged by a Hapsburg archduke of Austria, thus giving rise to the War of the Spanish Succession. When it ended, Spain had lost Flanders, its Italian possessions, and Gibraltar (still held by the British today).

During the 18th century, Spain's direction changed with each sovereign. Charles III (1759–88) developed the country economically and culturally. Charles IV became embroiled in wars with France, and the weakness of the Spanish monarchy allowed Napoléon to place his brother Joseph Bonaparte on the throne in 1808.

THE 19TH & 20TH CENTURIES   Although Britain and France had joined forces to restore the Spanish monarchy, the European conflicts encouraged Spanish colonists to rebel. Ultimately, this led the United States to free the Philippines, Puerto Rico, and Cuba from Spain in 1898.

In 1876, Spain became a constitutional monarchy. But labor unrest, disputes with the Catholic Church, and war in Morocco combined to create political chaos. Conditions eventually became so bad that the Cortés, or parliament, was dissolved in 1923, and Gen. Miguel Primo de Rivera formed a military directorate. Early in 1930, Primo de Rivera resigned, but unrest continued.

On April 14, 1931, a revolution occurred, a republic was proclaimed, and King Alfonso XIII and his family were forced to flee. Initially, the liberal constitutionalists ruled, but soon they were pushed aside by the socialists and anarchists. These adopted a constitution separating church and state, secularizing education, and containing several other radical provisions (for example, agrarian reform and the expulsion of the Jesuits).

The extreme nature of these reforms fostered the growth of the conservative Falange party (*Falange española*, or Spanish Phalanx), modeled after Italy and Germany's fascist parties. By the 1936 elections, the country was divided equally between left and right, and political violence was common. On July 18, 1936, the army, supported by Mussolini and Hitler, tried to seize power, igniting the Spanish Civil War. Gen. Francisco Franco, coming from Morocco to Spain, led the Nationalist (rightist) forces in fighting that ravaged the country.

The popular front opposing Franco was forced to rely mainly on untrained volunteers, including a few heroic Americans called the "Lincoln brigade." For those who want an insight into the era, Ernest Hemingway's *For Whom the Bell Tolls* is a good read. It took time to turn untrained militias into an army fit to battle Franco's forces, and time was something the popular front didn't have.

The Spectacle of Death

For obvious reasons, many people consider bullfighting cruel and shock-ing, but as Ernest Hemingway pointed out in *Death in the Afternoon:* "The bullfight is not a sport in the Anglo-Saxon sense of the word; that is, it is not an equal contest or an attempt at an equal contest between a bull and a man. Rather it is a tragedy: the death of the bull, which is played, more or less well, by the bull and the man involved and in which there is danger for the man but certain death for the bull."

When the symbolic drama of the bullfight is acted out, some believe it reaches a higher plane, the realm of art. Some people argue that it is not a public exhibition of cruelty at all, but rather a highly skilled art form that requires the will to survive, courage, showmanship, and gallantry. Regardless of how you view it, the spectacle is an authentic Spanish experi-ence and reveals much about the character of the land and its people.

The *corrida* (bullfight) season lasts from early spring until around mid-October. Fights are held in a *plaza de toros* (bullring), including the oldest ring in remote Ronda and the big-time Plaza de Toros in Madrid. Sunday is *corrida* day in most major Spanish cities, although Madrid and Barcelona may also have fights on Thursday.

Tickets fall into three classifications, and prices are based on your exposure to the famed Spanish sun: *sol* (sun), the cheapest; *sombra* (shade), the most expensive; and *sol y sombra* (a mixture of sun and shade), the medium-price range.

The *corrida* begins with a parade. For many viewers, this may be the high point of the afternoon's festivities, as all the bullfighters are clad in their *trajes de luces,* or luminous suits.

Bullfights are divided into thirds. The first is the *tercio de capa* (cape), during which the matador tests the bull with various passes and gets

It was a war that would attract the attention of the world. By the summer of 1936, the USSR was sending rubles to aid the revolution by the republicans. Even Mexico sent war materiel to the popular front. Most—but not all—the volunteers were communists. Italy and Germany contributed war materiel to Franco's forces.

Madrid, controlled by the popular front, held out through a brutal siege that lasted for 28 months. Eventually, the government of the popular front moved to Valencia for greater safety in 1936.

But in the winter of 1936–37, Franco's forces slowly began to establish power, capturing the Basque capital of Bilbao and eventually Santander. The war shocked the world with its ruthlessness (World War II hadn't happened yet). Churches were burned, and mass executions occurred, especially memorable in the Basque town of Guernica, which became the subject of one of Picasso's most fabled paintings.

By October 1, 1936, Franco was clearly in charge of the leadership of nation-alist Spain, abolishing popular suffrage and regional autonomy—in effect, launching a totalitarian rule for Spain.

acquainted with him. The second portion, the *tercio de varas* (sticks), begins with the lance-carrying *picadores* on horseback, who weaken, or "punish," the bull by jabbing him in the shoulder area. The horses are sometimes gored, even though they wear protective padding, or the horse and rider might be tossed into the air by the now-infuriated bull. The *picadores* are followed by the *banderilleros,* whose job it is to puncture the bull with pairs of boldly colored darts.

In the final *tercio de muleta,* the action narrows down to the lone fighter and the bull. Gone are the fancy capes. Instead, the matador uses a small red cloth known as a *muleta,* which, to be effective, requires a bull with lowered head. (The *picadores* and *banderilleros* have worked to achieve this.) Using the *muleta* as a lure, the matador wraps the bull around himself in various passes, the most dangerous of which is the *natural;* here, the matador holds the *muleta* in his left hand, the sword in his right. Right-hand passes pose less of a threat, since the sword can be used to spread out the *muleta,* making a larger target for the bull. After a number of passes, the time comes for the kill, the moment of truth.

After the bull dies, the highest official at the ring may award the matador an ear from the dead bull, or perhaps both ears, or ears and tail. For a truly extraordinary performance, the hoof is sometimes added. Spectators cheer a superlative performance by waving white handkerchiefs, imploring the judge to award a prize. The bullfighter may be carried away as a hero, or if he has displeased the crowd, he may be jeered and chased out of the ring by an angry mob. At a major fight, usually six bulls are killed by three matadors in one afternoon.

The republicans were split by internal differences, and spy trials were commonplace. At the end of the first year of war, Franco held 35 of Spain's provincial capitals. In 1937, the republican forces were cut in two, and Madrid was left to fend for itself.

The last great offensive of the war began on December 28, 1938, with an attack by Franco's forces on Barcelona, which fell on January 26 after a campaign of 34 days. Republican forces fled toward France, as a succession of presidents occurred. On March 28 some 200,000 nationalist troops marched into Madrid, meeting no resistance. The war was over the next day when the rest of republican Spain surrendered. The war lasted 2 years and 254 days, costing some one million lives.

For memories and a sense of the Spanish Civil War, visitors can travel to El Valle de los Caídos (the Valley of the Fallen) outside El Escorial (see chapter 5).

Although Franco adopted a neutral position during World War II, his sympathies obviously lay with Germany and Italy. Spain, although a nonbelligerent, assisted the Axis powers. This action intensified the diplomatic isolation into which the country was forced after the war's end—in fact, it was excluded from the United Nations until 1955.

Before his death, General Franco selected as his successor Juan Carlos de Borbón y Borbón, son of the pretender to the Spanish throne. After the 1977 elections, a new constitution was approved by the electorate and the king; it guaranteed human and civil rights, as well as free enterprise, and canceled the status of the Roman Catholic Church as the church of Spain. It also granted limited autonomy to several regions, including Catalonia and the Basque provinces, both of which, however, are still clamoring for complete autonomy.

In 1981 a group of right-wing military officers seized the Cortés and called upon Juan Carlos to establish a Francoist state. The king, however, refused, and the conspirators were arrested. The fledgling democracy overcame its first test. Its second major accomplishment—under the Socialist administration of Prime Minister Felipe González, the country's first leftist government since 1939—was to gain Spain's entry into the European Community (now Union) in 1986.

The shocking news for 2000 was not political, but social. Spain came under increasing pressure to conform to short lunch breaks like those in the other E.U. countries. What? No 3-hour siesta? It was heresy. In spite of opposition, large companies began to cut lunch to 2 hours. Pro-siesta forces in Spain cited the American custom of "power naps" as reason to retain their beloved afternoon break.

So the siesta appears to be under serious attack, perhaps as a consequence of the Spanish economy's upswing, which created more new jobs than in any other country in the E.U. More and more families are moving to the suburbs, and more women are joining the workforce. A survey has revealed that only 25% of Spaniards still take the siesta.

On other fronts, Spain moved ahead as an economic powerhouse in Latin America. Only 20 years ago, Spain was a minor economic presence in Latin America. Today, it is second only to the United States. The long-held monopoly of the U.S. in the region is being challenged for the first time since the Spanish-American War of 1898. In the last tally, Spaniards in 1 year poured $20 billion worth of investment value into Latin America.

Although there were some rough transitional periods, and a lot of older citizens were bewildered, Spain officially abandoned its time-honored peseta and went under the euro umbrella in March 2002. During the transition period, as Spaniards struggled to adjust to the new currency, counterfeiters had a field day.

3 A Taste of Spain

Meals are an extremely important social activity in Spain, whether that means eating out late at night or having large family gatherings for lunch. Although Spain is faster paced than it once was, few Spaniards race through a meal on the way to an appointment.

The food in Spain is varied; the portions are immense, but the prices, by North American standards, are high. Whenever possible, try the regional specialties, particularly when you visit the Basque country or Galicia.

Many restaurants in Spain close on Sunday, so be sure to check ahead. Hotel dining rooms are generally open 7 days, and there's always something open in such big cities as Madrid and Barcelona or such well-touristed areas as the Costa del Sol. Generally, reservations are not necessary, except at popular, top-notch restaurants.

MEALS

BREAKFAST   In Spain the day starts with a continental breakfast of coffee, hot chocolate, or tea, with assorted rolls, butter, and jam. Spanish breakfast might also consist of *churros* (fried fingerlike doughnuts) and hot chocolate that is very sweet and thick. However, most Spaniards simply have coffee, usually strong, served with hot milk: either a *café con leche* (half coffee, half milk) or *cortado* (a shot of espresso "cut" with a dash of milk). If you find it too strong and bitter for your taste, you might ask for a more diluted *café americano*.

LUNCH   The most important meal of the day in Spain, lunch is comparable to the farm-style midday "dinner" in the United States. It usually includes three or four courses, beginning with a choice of soup or several dishes of hors d'oeuvres called *entremeses*. Often a fish or egg dish is served after this, then a meat course with vegetables. Wine is always part of the meal. Dessert is usually pastry, custard, or assorted fruit—followed by coffee. Lunch is served from 1 to 4pm, with "rush hour" at 2pm.

TAPAS   After the early evening stroll, many Spaniards head for their favorite *tascas,* bars where they drink wine and sample assorted tapas, or snacks, such as bits of fish, eggs in mayonnaise, or olives.

Because many Spaniards eat dinner very late, they often have an extremely light breakfast, certainly coffee and perhaps a pastry. However, by 11am they are often hungry and lunch might not be until 2pm or later, so many Spaniards have a late-morning snack, often at a cafeteria. Favorite items to order are a *tortilla* (Spanish omelet with potatoes) and even a beer. Many request a large tapa served with bread.

DINNER   Another extravaganza: A typical meal starts with a bowl of soup, followed by a second course, often a fish dish, and by another main course, usually veal, beef, or pork, accompanied by vegetables. Again, desserts tend to be fruit, custard, or pastries.

Naturally, if you had a heavy and late lunch and stopped off at a tapas bar or two before dinner, supper might be much lighter, perhaps some cold cuts, sausage, a bowl of soup, or even a Spanish omelet made with potatoes. Wine is always part of the meal. Afterward, you might have a demitasse and a fragrant Spanish brandy. The chic dining hour, even in one-donkey towns, is 10 or 10:30pm. (In well-touristed regions and hardworking Catalonia, you can usually dine at 8pm, but you still may find yourself alone in the restaurant.) In most middle-class establishments, people dine around 9:30pm.

THE CUISINE
SOUPS & APPETIZERS   Soups are usually served in big bowls. Cream soups, such as asparagus and potato, can be fine; sadly, however, they are too often made from powdered envelope soups such as Knorr and Liebig. Served year-round, chilled gazpacho, on the other hand, is tasty and particularly refreshing during the hot months. The combination is pleasant: olive oil, garlic, ground cucumbers, and raw tomatoes with a sprinkling of croutons. Spain also offers several varieties of fish soup—*sopa de pescado*—in all its provinces, and many of these are superb.

In the paradors (government-run hostelries) and top restaurants, as many as 15 tempting hors d'oeuvres are served. In lesser-known places, avoid these *entremeses,* which often consist of last year's sardines and shards of sausage left over from the Moorish conquest.

EGGS   These are served in countless ways. A Spanish omelet, a *tortilla española,* is made with potatoes and usually onions. A simple omelet is called a *tortilla francesa*. A *tortilla portuguesa* is similar to the American Spanish omelet.

FISH Spain's fish dishes tend to be outstanding and vary from province to province. One of the most common varieties is *merluza* (sweet white hake). *Langosta,* a variety of lobster, is seen everywhere—it's a treat but terribly expensive. The Portuguese in particular, but some Spaniards, too, go into raptures at the mention of *mejillones* (barnacles). Gourmets relish their seawater taste; others find them tasteless. *Rape* (pronounced "*rah*-peh") is the Spanish name for monkfish, a sweet, wide-boned ocean fish with a scalloplike texture. Also try a few dozen half-inch baby eels. They rely heavily on olive oil and garlic for their flavor, but they taste great. Squid cooked in its own ink is suggested only to those who want to go native. Charcoal-broiled sardines, however, are a culinary delight—a particular treat in the Basque provinces. Trout Navarre is one of the most popular fish dishes, usually stuffed with bacon or ham.

PAELLA You can't go to Spain without trying its celebrated paella. Flavored with saffron, paella is an aromatic rice dish usually topped with shellfish, chicken, sausage, peppers, and local spices. Served authentically, it comes steaming hot from the kitchen in a metal pan called a *paellera.* (Incidentally, what is known in the U.S. as Spanish rice isn't Spanish at all. If you ask an English-speaking waiter for Spanish rice, you'll be served paella.)

MEATS Don't expect Kansas City steak, but do try the spit-roasted suckling pig, so sweet and tender it can often be cut with a fork. The veal is also good, and the Spanish *lomo de cerdo,* loin of pork, is unmatched anywhere. Tender chicken is most often served in the major cities and towns today, and the Spanish are adept at spit-roasting it until it turns a delectable golden brown. However, in more remote spots of Spain, "free-range" chicken is often stringy and tough.

VEGETABLES & SALADS Through more sophisticated agricultural methods, Spain now grows more of its own vegetables, which are available year-round, unlike days of yore, when canned vegetables were used all too frequently. Both potatoes and rice are a staple of the Spanish diet, the latter a prime ingredient, of course, in the famous paella originating in Valencia. Salads don't usually get the attention they do in California, and are often made simply with just lettuce and tomatoes.

DESSERTS The Spanish do not emphasize dessert, often opting for fresh fruit. Flan, a home-cooked egg custard, appears on all menus—sometimes with a burnt-caramel sauce. Ice cream appears on nearly all menus as well. But the best bet is to ask for a basket of fruit, which you can wash at your table. Homemade pastries are usually moist and not too sweet. As a dining oddity—although it's not odd at all to Spaniards—many restaurants serve fresh orange juice for dessert.

OLIVE OIL & GARLIC Olive oil is used lavishly in Spain, the largest olive grower on the planet. You may not want it in all dishes. If you prefer your fish grilled in butter, the word is *mantequilla.* In some instances, you'll be charged extra for the butter. Garlic is also an integral part of the Spanish diet, and even if you love it, you may find Spaniards love it more than you do and use it in the oddest dishes.

WHAT TO DRINK

WATER   It is generally safe to drink water in all major cities and tourist resorts in Spain. If you're traveling in remote areas, play it safe and drink bottled water. One of the most popular noncarbonated bottled drinks in Spain is Solares. Nearly all restaurants and hotels have it. Bubbly water is *agua mineral con gas;* noncarbonated, *agua mineral sin gas.* Note that bottled water in some areas may cost as much as the regional wine.

SOFT DRINKS   In general, avoid the carbonated citrus drinks on sale everywhere. Most of them never saw an orange, much less a lemon. If you want a citrus drink, order old, reliable Schweppes. An excellent noncarbonated drink for the summer is called Tri-Naranjus, which comes in lemon and orange flavors. Your cheapest bet is a liter bottle of *gaseosa,* which comes in various flavors. In summer you should also try an *horchata.* Not to be confused with the Mexican beverage of the same name, the Spanish *horchata* is a sweet, milklike beverage made of tubers called *chufas.*

COFFEE   Even if you are a dedicated coffee drinker, you may find the *café con leche* (coffee with milk) a little too strong. We suggest *leche manchada,* a little bit of strong, freshly brewed coffee in a glass that's filled with lots of frothy hot milk.

MILK   In the largest cities you get bottled milk, but it loses a great deal of its flavor in the process of pasteurization. In all cases, avoid untreated milk and milk products. About the best brand of fresh milk is Lauki.

BEER   Although not native to Spain, beer *(cerveza)* is now drunk everywhere. Domestic brands include San Miguel, Mahou, Aguila, and Cruz Blanca.

WINE   Sherry *(vino de Jerez)* has been called "the wine with a hundred souls." Drink it before dinner (try the topaz-colored *finos,* a dry and very pale sherry) or whenever you drop into some old inn or bodega for refreshment; many of them have rows of kegs with spigots. *Manzanilla,* a golden-colored medium-dry sherry, is extremely popular. The sweet cream sherries (Harvey's Bristol Cream, for example) are favorite after-dinner wines (called *olorosos*). While the French may be disdainful of Spanish table wines, they can be truly noble, especially two leading varieties, Valdepeñas and Rioja, both from Castile. If you're not too exacting in your tastes, you can always ask for the *vino de la casa* (house wine) wherever you dine. The Ampurdán of Catalonia is heavy. From Andalusia comes the fruity Montilla. There are some good local sparkling wines *(cavas)* in Spain, such as Freixenet. One brand, Benjamín, comes in individual-size bottles.

Beginning in the 1990s, based partly on subsidies and incentives from the European Union, Spanish vintners have scrapped most of the country's obsolete winemaking equipment, hired new talent, and poured time and money into the improvement and promotion of wines from even high-altitude or arid regions not previously suitable for wine production. Thanks to irrigation, improved grape varieties, technological developments, and the expenditure of billions of pesetas, bodegas and vineyards are sprouting up throughout the country, opening their doors to visitors interested in how the stuff is grown, fermented, and bottled. These wines are now earning awards at wine competitions around the world for their quality and bouquet.

Interested in impressing a newfound Spanish friend over a wine list? Consider bypassing the usual array of Riojas, sherries, and sparkling Catalonian *cavas* in favor of, say, a Galician white from Rias Baixas, which some connoisseurs consider the perfect accompaniment for seafood. Among reds, make a beeline for vintages from the fastest-developing wine region of Europe, the arid, high-altitude district of Ribera del Duero, near Burgos, whose alkaline soil, cold nights, and sunny days have earned unexpected praise from winemakers (and encouraged massive investments) in the past 5 years.

For more information about these or any other of the 10 wine-producing regions of Spain (and the 39 officially recognized wine-producing *Denominaciones de Origen* scattered across those regions), contact **Wines from Spain,** c/o the Commercial Office of Spain, 405 Lexington Ave., 44th Floor, New York, NY 10174-0331 (© **212/661-4959**).

SANGRIA   The all-time favorite refreshing drink in Spain, sangria is a red-wine punch that combines wine with oranges, lemons, seltzer, and sugar. Be careful, however; many joints that do a big tourist trade produce a sickly sweet Kool-Aid version of sangria for unsuspecting visitors.

WHISKEY & BRANDY   Imported whiskeys are available at most Spanish bars but at a high price. If you're a drinker, switch to brandies and cognacs, where the Spanish reign supreme. Try Fundador, made by the Pedro Domecq family in Jerez de la Frontera. If you want a smooth cognac, ask for the "103" white label.

Appendix B:
Useful Terms & Phrases

Basic Vocabulary

Most Spaniards are very patient with foreigners who try to speak their language. Although you might encounter several regional languages and dialects in Spain, Castilian (*Castellano*, or simply *Español*) is understood everywhere. In Catalonia, they speak *Catalán* (the most widely spoken non-national language in Europe); in the Basque country, they speak *Euskera;* in Galicia, you'll hear *Gallego*. Still, a few words in Castilian will usually get your message across with no problem.

When traveling, it helps a lot to know a few basic phrases, so we've included a list of certain simple phrases in Castilian Spanish for expressing basic needs.

ENGLISH & CASTILIAN SPANISH PHRASES

English	Spanish	Pronunciation
Good day	**Buenos días**	*bweh*-nohs *dee*-ahs
How are you?	**¿Cómo está?**	*koh*-moh es-*tah*
Very well	**Muy bien**	mwee byehn
Thank you	**Gracias**	*grah*-syahs
You're welcome	**De nada**	deh *nah*-dah
Good bye	**Adiós**	ah-*dyohs*
Please	**Por favor**	pohr fah-*vohr*
Yes	**Sí**	see
No	**No**	noh
Excuse me	**Perdóneme**	pehr-*doh*-neh-meh
Give me	**Déme**	*deh*-meh
Where is . . . ?	**¿Dónde está . . . ?**	*dohn*-deh es-*tah*
the station	**la estación**	lah es-tah-*syohn*
a hotel	**un hotel**	oon oh-*tel*
a gas station	**una gasolinera**	*oo*-nah gah-so-lee-*neh*-rah
a restaurant	**un restaurante**	oon res-tow-*rahn*-teh
the toilet	**el baño**	el *bah*-nyoh
a good doctor	**un buen médico**	oon bwehn *meh*-dee-coh
the road to . . .	**el camino a/hacia**	el cah-*mee*-noh ah/*ah*-syah
To the right	**A la derecha**	ah lah deh-*reh*-chah
To the left	**A la izquierda**	ah lah ees-*kyehr*-dah
Straight ahead	**Derecho**	deh-*reh*-choh
I would like	**Quisiera**	kee-*syeh*-rah
I want	**Quiero**	*kyeh*-roh
to eat.	**comer**	ko-*mehr*
a room.	**una habitación**	*oo*-nah ah-bee-tah-*syohn*
Do you have?	**¿Tiene usted?**	tyeh-neh oo-*sted*
a book?	**un libro**	oon *lee*-broh
a dictionary?	**un diccionario**	oon deek-syoh-*na*-ryo
How much is it?	**¿Cuánto cuesta?**	*kwahn*-toh *kwehs*-tah

When?	¿Cuándo?	*kwahn*-doh
What?	¿Qué?	keh
There is (Is there . . . ?)	(¿)Hay (. . . ?)	aye
What is there?	¿Qué hay?	keh aye
Yesterday	Ayer	ah-*yehr*
Today	Hoy	oy
Tomorrow	Mañana	mah-*nyah*-nah
Good	Bueno	*bweh*-noh
Bad	Malo	*mah*-loh
Better (Best)	(Lo) Mejor	(loh) meh-*hor*
More	Más	mahs
Less	Menos	*meh*-nohs
No smoking	Se prohibe fumar	seh proh-*ee*-beh foo-*mahr*
Postcard	Tarjeta postal	tar-*heh*-tah pohs-*tahl*
Insect repellent	Repelente contra insectos	reh-peh-*lehn*-teh *cohn*-trah een-*sehk*-tohs

MORE USEFUL PHRASES

English	Spanish	Pronunciation
Do you speak English?	¿Habla usted inglés?	*ah*-blah oo-*sted* een-*glehs*
Is there anyone here who speaks English?	¿Hay alguien aquí que hable inglés?	eye *ahl*-gyehn ah-*kee* keh *ah*-bleh een-*glehs*
I speak a little Spanish.	Hablo un poco de español.	*ah*-bloh oon *poh*-koh deh es-pah-*nyol*
I don't understand Spanish very well.	No (lo) entiendo muy bien el español.	noh (loh) ehn-*tyehn*-doh mwee byehn el es-pah-*nyol*
The meal is good.	Me gusta la comida.	meh *goo*-stah lah koh-*mee*-dah
What time is it?	¿Qué hora es?	keh *oh*-rah es
May I see your menu?	¿Puedo ver el menú (la carta)?	*pweh*-do vehr el meh-*noo* (lah *car*-tah)
The check please.	La cuenta por favor.	lah *kwehn*-tah pohr fah-*vohr*
What do I owe you?	¿Cuánto le debo?	*kwahn*-toh leh *deh*-boh
What did you say?	¿Mande? (colloquial expression for American "Eh?")	*mahn*-deh
More formal:	¿Cómo?	*koh*-moh
I want (to see)	Quiero (ver)	*kyeh*-roh (vehr)
a room	un cuarto or una habitación	oon *kwahr*-toh, *oo*-nah ah-bee-tah-*syohn*
for two persons	para dos personas.	*pah*-rah dohs pehhr-*soh*-nas
with (without) bathroom.	con (sin) baño.	kohn (seen) *bah*-nyoh
We are staying here only . . .	Nos quedamos aquí solamente . . .	nohs keh-*dah*-mohs ah-*kee* soh-lah-*mehn*-teh
1 night.	una noche.	*oo*-nah *noh*-cheh
1 week.	una semana.	*oo*-nah seh-*mah*-nah
We are leaving	Partimos (Salimos)	pahr-*tee*-mohs (sah-*lee*-mohs)
tomorrow.	mañana.	mah-*nya*-nah

Do you accept traveler's checks?	¿Acepta usted cheques de viajero?	ah-*sehp*-tah oo-*sted cheh*-kehs deh byah-*heh*-roh
Is there a laundromat near here?	¿Hay una lavandería cerca de aquí?	eye *oo*-nah lah-*vahn*-deh-*ree*-ah *sehr*-kah deh ah-*kee*
Please send these clothes to the laundry.	Hágame el favor de mandar esta ropa a la lavandería.	*ah*-gah-meh el fah-*vohr* deh mahn-*dahr ehs*-tah *roh*-pah a lah lah-*vahn*-deh-*ree*-ah

NUMBERS

1	**uno** (*oo*-noh)	17	**diecisiete** (dyeh-see-*syeh*-teh)
2	**dos** (dohs)	18	**dieciocho** (dyeh-see-*oh*-choh)
3	**tres** (trehs)	19	**diecinueve** (dyeh-see-*nweh*-beh)
4	**cuatro** (*kwah*-troh)	20	**veinte** (*bayn*-teh)
5	**cinco** (*seen*-koh)	30	**treinta** (*trayn*-tah)
6	**seis** (says)	40	**cuarenta** (kwah-*rehn*-tah)
7	**siete** (*syeh*-teh)	50	**cincuenta** (seen-*kwehn*-tah)
8	**ocho** (*oh*-choh)	60	**sesenta** (seh-*sehn*-tah)
9	**nueve** (*nweh*-beh)	70	**setenta** (seh-*tehn*-tah)
10	**diez** (dyehs)	80	**ochenta** (oh-*chehn*-tah)
11	**once** (*ohn*-seh)	90	**noventa** (noh-*behn*-tah)
12	**doce** (*doh*-seh)	100	**cien** (*syehn*)
13	**trece** (*treh*-seh)	200	**doscientos** (doh-*syehn*-tohs)
14	**catorce** (kah-*tohr*-seh)	500	**quinientos** (kee-*nyehn*-tos)
15	**quince** (*keen*-seh)	1,000	**mil** (meel)
16	**dieciséis** (dyeh-see-*says*)		

TRANSPORTATION TERMS

English	Spanish	Pronunciation
Airport	**Aeropuerto**	ah-eh-roh-*pwehr*-toh
Flight	**Vuelo**	*bweh*-loh
Rental car agency	**Arrendadora de autos**	ah-rehn-da-*doh*-rah deh *ow*-tohs
Bus	**Autobús**	ow-toh-*boos*
Bus or truck	**Camión**	ka-*myohn*
Lane	**Carril**	kah-*reel*
Nonstop	**Directo**	dee-*reck*-toh
Baggage (claim area)	**Equipajes**	eh-key-*pah*-hehs
Intercity	**Foraneo**	foh-rah-*neh*-oh
Luggage storage area	**Guarda equipaje**	*gwahr*-dah eh-key-*pah*-heh
Arrival gates	**Llegadas**	yeh-*gah*-dahs
Originates at this station	**Local**	loh-*kahl*
Originates elsewhere	**De paso**	deh *pah*-soh
Stops if seats available	**Para si hay lugares**	*pah*-rah see aye loo-*gah*-rehs
First class	**Primera**	pree-*meh*-rah
Second class	**Segunda**	seh-*goon*-dah
Baggage claim area	**Recibo de equipajes**	reh-*see*-boh deh eh-key-*pah*-hehs
Waiting room	**Sala de espera**	*sah*-lah deh es-*peh*-rah
Toilets	**Sanitarios**	sah-nee-*tah*-ryos
Ticket window	**Taquilla**	tah-*key*-yah

Index

Great Trips Like Great Days Begin with a Plan

FranklinCovey and Frommer's Bring You *Frommer's Favorite Places* Planner

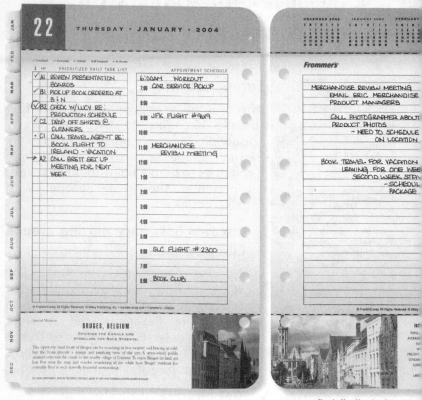

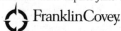

Classic Size Planning Pages $39.9

The planning experts at FranklinCovey have teamed up with the travel experts at Frommer's. The result is a full-year travel-themed planner filled with rich images and travel tips covering fifty-two of Frommer's Favorite Places.

- Each week will make you an expert about an intriguing corner of the world
- New facts and tips every day
- Beautiful, full-color photos of some of the most beautiful places on earth
- Proven planning tools from FranklinCovey for keeping track of tasks, appointments, notes, address/phone numbers, and more

Save 15%

when you purchase Frommer's Favorit Places travel-themed planner and a binder.

Order today before you next big trip.

www.franklincovey.com/frommers
Enter promo code 12252 at checkout for discount. Offer expires June 1, 2005.

◆ FranklinCovey.

Frommer's is a trademark of Arthur Frommer.

FROMMER'S® COMPLETE TRAVEL GUIDES

Alaska
Alaska Cruises & Ports of Call
Amsterdam
Argentina & Chile
Arizona
Atlanta
Australia
Austria
Bahamas
Barcelona, Madrid & Seville
Beijing
Belgium, Holland & Luxembourg
Bermuda
Boston
Brazil
British Columbia & the Canadian
 Rockies
Brussels & Bruges
Budapest & the Best of Hungary
California
Canada
Cancún, Cozumel & the Yucatán
Cape Cod, Nantucket & Martha's
 Vineyard
Caribbean
Caribbean Cruises & Ports of Call
Caribbean Ports of Call
Carolinas & Georgia
Chicago
China
Colorado
Costa Rica
Cuba
Denmark
Denver, Boulder & Colorado Springs
England
Europe
European Cruises & Ports of Call

Florida
France
Germany
Great Britain
Greece
Greek Islands
Hawaii
Hong Kong
Honolulu, Waikiki & Oahu
Ireland
Israel
Italy
Jamaica
Japan
Las Vegas
London
Los Angeles
Maryland & Delaware
Maui
Mexico
Montana & Wyoming
Montréal & Québec City
Munich & the Bavarian Alps
Nashville & Memphis
New England
New Mexico
New Orleans
New York City
New Zealand
Northern Italy
Norway
Nova Scotia, New Brunswick &
 Prince Edward Island
Oregon
Paris
Peru
Philadelphia & the Amish Country
Portugal

Prague & the Best of the Czech
 Republic
Provence & the Riviera
Puerto Rico
Rome
San Antonio & Austin
San Diego
San Francisco
Santa Fe, Taos & Albuquerque
Scandinavia
Scotland
Seattle & Portland
Shanghai
Sicily
Singapore & Malaysia
South Africa
South America
South Florida
South Pacific
Southeast Asia
Spain
Sweden
Switzerland
Texas
Thailand
Tokyo
Toronto
Tuscany & Umbria
USA
Utah
Vancouver & Victoria
Vermont, New Hampshire & Maine
Vienna & the Danube Valley
Virgin Islands
Virginia
Walt Disney World® & Orlando
Washington, D.C.
Washington State

FROMMER'S® DOLLAR-A-DAY GUIDES

Australia from $50 a Day
California from $70 a Day
England from $75 a Day
Europe from $70 a Day
Florida from $70 a Day
Hawaii from $80 a Day

Ireland from $60 a Day
Italy from $70 a Day
London from $85 a Day
New York from $90 a Day
Paris from $80 a Day

San Francisco from $70 a Day
Washington, D.C. from $80 a Day
Portable London from $85 a Day
Portable New York City from $90
 a Day

FROMMER'S® PORTABLE GUIDES

Acapulco, Ixtapa & Zihuatanejo
Amsterdam
Aruba
Australia's Great Barrier Reef
Bahamas
Berlin
Big Island of Hawaii
Boston
California Wine Country
Cancún
Cayman Islands
Charleston
Chicago
Disneyland®
Dublin
Florence

Frankfurt
Hong Kong
Houston
Las Vegas
Las Vegas for Non-Gamblers
London
Los Angeles
Los Cabos & Baja
Maine Coast
Maui
Miami
Nantucket & Martha's Vineyard
New Orleans
New York City
Paris
Phoenix & Scottsdale

Portland
Puerto Rico
Puerto Vallarta, Manzanillo &
 Guadalajara
Rio de Janeiro
San Diego
San Francisco
Savannah
Seattle
Sydney
Tampa & St. Petersburg
Vancouver
Venice
Virgin Islands
Washington, D.C.

FROMMER'S® NATIONAL PARK GUIDES

Banff & Jasper
Family Vacations in the National
 Parks

Grand Canyon
National Parks of the American West
Rocky Mountain

Yellowstone & Grand Teton
Yosemite & Sequoia/Kings Canyon
Zion & Bryce Canyon

FROMMER'S® MEMORABLE WALKS

Chicago
London

New York
Paris

San Francisco

FROMMER'S® WITH KIDS GUIDES

Chicago
Las Vegas
New York City

Ottawa
San Francisco
Toronto

Vancouver
Washington, D.C.

SUZY GERSHMAN'S BORN TO SHOP GUIDES

Born to Shop: France
Born to Shop: Hong Kong,
   Shanghai & Beijing

Born to Shop: Italy
Born to Shop: London

Born to Shop: New York
Born to Shop: Paris

FROMMER'S® IRREVERENT GUIDES

Amsterdam
Boston
Chicago
Las Vegas
London

Los Angeles
Manhattan
New Orleans
Paris
Rome

San Francisco
Seattle & Portland
Vancouver
Walt Disney World®
Washington, D.C.

FROMMER'S® BEST-LOVED DRIVING TOURS

Britain
California
Florida
France

Germany
Ireland
Italy
New England

Northern Italy
Scotland
Spain
Tuscany & Umbria

HANGING OUT™ GUIDES

Hanging Out in England
Hanging Out in Europe

Hanging Out in France
Hanging Out in Ireland

Hanging Out in Italy
Hanging Out in Spain

THE UNOFFICIAL GUIDES®

Bed & Breakfasts and Country
   Inns in:
   California
   Great Lakes States
   Mid-Atlantic
   New England
   Northwest
   Rockies
   Southeast
   Southwest
Best RV & Tent Campgrounds in:
   California & the West
   Florida & the Southeast
   Great Lakes States
   Mid-Atlantic
   Northeast
   Northwest & Central Plains

   Southwest & South Central
      Plains
      U.S.A.
   Beyond Disney
   Branson, Missouri
   California with Kids
   Central Italy
   Chicago
   Cruises
   Disneyland®
   Florida with Kids
   Golf Vacations in the Eastern U.S.
   Great Smoky & Blue Ridge Region
   Inside Disney
   Hawaii
   Las Vegas
   London
   Maui

Mexio's Best Beach Resorts
Mid-Atlantic with Kids
Mini Las Vegas
Mini-Mickey
New England & New York with
   Kids
New Orleans
New York City
Paris
San Francisco
Skiing & Snowboarding in the Wes
Southeast with Kids
Walt Disney World®
Walt Disney World® for
   Grown-ups
Walt Disney World® with Kids
Washington, D.C.
World's Best Diving Vacations

SPECIAL-INTEREST TITLES

Frommer's Adventure Guide to Australia &
   New Zealand
Frommer's Adventure Guide to Central America
Frommer's Adventure Guide to India & Pakistan
Frommer's Adventure Guide to South America
Frommer's Adventure Guide to Southeast Asia
Frommer's Adventure Guide to Southern Africa
Frommer's Britain's Best Bed & Breakfasts and
   Country Inns
Frommer's Caribbean Hideaways
Frommer's Exploring America by RV
Frommer's Fly Safe, Fly Smart

Frommer's France's Best Bed & Breakfasts and
   Country Inns
Frommer's Gay & Lesbian Europe
Frommer's Italy's Best Bed & Breakfasts and
   Country Inns
Frommer's Road Atlas Britain
Frommer's Road Atlas Europe
Frommer's Road Atlas France
The New York Times' Guide to Unforgettable
   Weekends
Places Rated Almanac
Retirement Places Rated
Rome Past & Present

Fly.
Sleep.
Save.

Now you can book your flights and
hotels together, so you can get even better deals
than if you booked them separately.

Travelocity

Visit www.travelocity.com
or call 1-888-TRAVELOCITY